Lecture Notes in Computer Science 9087

Commenced Publication in 1973
Founding and Former Series Editors:
Gerhard Goos, Juris Hartmanis, and Jan van Leeuwen

Editorial Board

David Hutchison
  Lancaster University, Lancaster, UK
Takeo Kanade
  Carnegie Mellon University, Pittsburgh, PA, USA
Josef Kittler
  University of Surrey, Guildford, UK
Jon M. Kleinberg
  Cornell University, Ithaca, NY, USA
Friedemann Mattern
  ETH Zürich, Zürich, Switzerland
John C. Mitchell
  Stanford University, Stanford, CA, USA
Moni Naor
  Weizmann Institute of Science, Rehovot, Israel
C. Pandu Rangan
  Indian Institute of Technology, Madras, India
Bernhard Steffen
  TU Dortmund University, Dortmund, Germany
Demetri Terzopoulos
  University of California, Los Angeles, CA, USA
Doug Tygar
  University of California, Berkeley, CA, USA
Gerhard Weikum
  Max Planck Institute for Informatics, Saarbrücken, Germany

More information about this series at http://www.springer.com/series/7412

Jean-François Aujol · Mila Nikolova
Nicolas Papadakis (Eds.)

Scale Space and Variational Methods in Computer Vision

5th International Conference, SSVM 2015
Lège-Cap Ferret, France, May 31 – June 4, 2015
Proceedings

Editors
Jean-François Aujol
University of Bordeaux
Talence
France

Nicolas Papadakis
CNRS
University of Bordeaux
Talence
France

Mila Nikolova
CNRS
ENS Cachan
Cachan
France

ISSN 0302-9743   ISSN 1611-3349   (electronic)
Lecture Notes in Computer Science
ISBN 978-3-319-18460-9   ISBN 978-3-319-18461-6   (eBook)
DOI 10.1007/978-3-319-18461-6

Library of Congress Control Number: 2015937535

LNCS Sublibrary: SL6 – Image Processing, Computer Vision, Pattern Recognition, and Graphics

Springer Cham Heidelberg New York Dordrecht London
© Springer International Publishing Switzerland 2015
This work is subject to copyright. All rights are reserved by the Publisher, whether the whole or part of the material is concerned, specifically the rights of translation, reprinting, reuse of illustrations, recitation, broadcasting, reproduction on microfilms or in any other physical way, and transmission or information storage and retrieval, electronic adaptation, computer software, or by similar or dissimilar methodology now known or hereafter developed.
The use of general descriptive names, registered names, trademarks, service marks, etc. in this publication does not imply, even in the absence of a specific statement, that such names are exempt from the relevant protective laws and regulations and therefore free for general use.
The publisher, the authors and the editors are safe to assume that the advice and information in this book are believed to be true and accurate at the date of publication. Neither the publisher nor the authors or the editors give a warranty, express or implied, with respect to the material contained herein or for any errors or omissions that may have been made.

Printed on acid-free paper

Springer International Publishing AG Switzerland is part of Springer Science+Business Media (www.springer.com)

Preface

The 5th International Conference on Scale Space and Variational Methods in Computer Vision (SSVM 2015, http://ssvm2015.math.u-bordeaux.fr/) was held in the picturesque village of Claouey at Lège-Cap Ferret in the Arcachon bay, France. Following the previous meeting, we kept the style of gathering people in a slightly remote and scenic place in order to encourage fruitful discussions during the day and in the evening. This conference, born in 2007 in Ischia, Italy, has become a major event in the communities with common research interests in scale space, variational, geometric, and level set methods and their numerous applications in computer vision and more generally in imaging science. SSVM 2015 was announced mid-May 2014 and it attracted the attention of an important international scientific audience of authors coming from more than 16 countries. We received 83 double-blind submissions. The papers underwent a peer-review process similar to that of high-level journals in the field: each paper was reviewed by at least three members of the Program Committee as well as by other referees. The reviews and the papers were then considered by the Conference Chairs. We recognize P. Arias Martinez, R. Duits, J. Rabin, G. Steidl, and J. Weickert for significant referee work on manuscripts submitted to the conference. Finally, 56 manuscripts were retained for SSVM 2015. Among them, 24 articles were selected for oral presentation and 32 for poster presentation. All these 12-page length original articles are contained in this book. A best student paper award was given during the conference.

Following the tradition of the previous SSVM conferences, we invited outstanding scientists to give keynote presentations. This year, we were happy to welcome the following invited keynote lectures:

- Gabriele Steidl (University of Kaiserslautern, Germany): "Second Order Non-Smooth Variational Models for Restoring Manifold-Valued Images";
- Alfred Hero (University of Michigan, USA): "Combinatorial Continuum Limits and Their Applications";
- Jean-Michel Morel (École Normale Supérieure de Cachan, France): "A Review of Image Denoising Methods";
- Marc Teboulle (Tel Aviv University, Israel): "Algorithms for High Dimensional Structured Optimization."

Also, we hosted the Editorial Board meeting of the Journal of Mathematical Imaging and Vision (JMIV) since many members were attending the conference, with the participation of Courtney Clark, Editor at Springer assisting with JMIV. Further, selected papers will be considered for a special issue of JMIV "Scale-Space and Variational Methods" thanks to the Editor-in-Chief, Joachim Weickert.

We would like to thank the authors for their contributions and the members of the Program Committee and the other referees for their time and valuable comments during the review process. We are grateful to the organizers of the previous editions of this conference for precious tips on how to organize the event: Fiorella Sgallari (SSVM

2007), Xue-Cheng Tai (SSVM 2009), Yana Katz (SSVM 2011), Arjan Kuijper (SSVM 2013) who gave us the most fresh information, as well as Joachim Weickert. Further, we would like to thank Karine Lecuona, Annie Nadeau, and Cathy Métivier (CNRS) for their enthusiastic help in financial management. Finally, we are lucky to acknowledge the generous support of Cluster of excellence CPU, Institut Universitaire de France, Centre National de la Recherche Scientifique (CNRS), and CNRS national network "Mathematics in Imaging sciences and Applications" (GDR MIA).

The manuscripts of all past SSVM editions were published by Springer in the series Lecture Notes in Computer Science as well: LNCS 4485 (Ischia, Italy 2007), LNCS 5567 (Voss, Norway 2009), LNCS 6667 (Ein Gedi, Israel 2011), and LNCS 7893 (Leibnitz, Austria 2013). It is interesting to observe the evolution of the topics covered by this conference. They naturally reflect the progress of mathematical and application-driven ideas in the field as well as the advent of powerful computers. This is expressed by the interest in more realistic mathematical models, the use of novel mathematical tools for modeling and for scientific computing, the advance in the processing of huge data volumes (e.g., in video and in 3D, among others). These new trends are well represented in this book.

May 2015

Jean-François Aujol
Mila Nikolova
Nicolas Papadakis

Organization

Conference Chairs

Jean-François Aujol   IUF, IMB – University of Bordeaux, France
Mila Nikolova   CNRS, CMLA – ENS Cachan, France
Nicolas Papadakis   CNRS, IMB – University of Bordeaux, France

Sponsoring Institutions

Centre National de la Recherche Scientifique (CNRS)
Cluster of Excellence for research CPU, University of Bordeaux
Institut Universitaire de France (IUF)
CNRS national network "Mathematics in Imaging sciences and Applications" (GDR MIA)

Scientific and Program Committee

Andrés Almansa	CNRS, LTCI, Télécom ParisTech, France
Luis Alvares	Universidad de Las Palmas de Gran Canaria, Spain
Pablo Arias Martínez	Universitat Pompeu Fabra, Spain
Jean-François Aujol	IUF, IMB – University of Bordeaux, France
Coloma Ballester	Universitat Pompeu Fabra, Spain
Marcelo Bertalmío	Universitat Pompeu Fabra, Spain
Laure Blanc-Féraud	CNRS, France
Kristian Bredies	University of Graz, Austria
Michael Breuß	Brandenburg University of Technology Cottbus, Germany
Thomas Brox	University of Freiburg, Germany
Andrés Bruhn	University of Stuttgart, Germany
Aurélie Bugeau	LaBRI, University of Bordeaux, France
Antonin Chambolle	CNRS, CMAP, Ecole Polytechnique, France
Raymond Chan	Chinese University of Hong Kong, Hong Kong
Laurent Cohen	CNRS, CEREMADE, Université Paris Dauphine, France
Thomas Corpetti	CNRS, France
Daniel Cremers	Technical University of Munich, Germany
Charles-Alban Deledalle	CNRS, IMB – University of Bordeaux, France
Agnès Desolneux	CNRS, CMLA, ENS Cachan, France
Charles Dossal	IMB, University of Bordeaux, France

Remco Duits	Eindhoven University of Technology, The Netherlands
Vincent Duval	Inria, France
Jalal Fadili	ENSICAEN, France
Michael Felsberg	Linköping University, Sweden
Luc Florack	Eindhoven University of Technology, The Netherlands
Guy Gilboa	Technion – Israel Institute of Technology, Israel
Yann Gousseau	Télécom ParisTech, France
Markus Grasmair	Catholic University Eichstätt-Ingolstadt, Germany
Lewis Griffin	University College London, UK
Moncef Hidane	INSA Centre Val de Loire, France
Atsushi Imiya	Chiba University, Japan
Sung Ha Kang	Georgia Institute of Technology, USA
Charles Kervrann	Inria, France
Ron Kimmel	Technion – Israel Institute of Technology, Israel
Nahum Kiryati	Tel Aviv University, Israel
Arjan Kuijper	IGD, Germany
Stefan Kunis	University of Osnabrück, Germany
Saïd Ladjal	LTCI, Télécom ParisTech, France
François Lauze	University of Copenhagen, Denmark
Carole Le Guyader	INSA Rouen, France
Antonio Leitao	Federal University of Santa Catarina, Brazil
Stacey Levine	Duquesne University, USA
Tony Lindeberg	KTH Royal Institute of Technology, Sweden
Dirk Lorenz	Technical University of Braunschweig, Germany
Simon Masnou	Institut Camille Jordan, Université Lyon 1, France
Etienne Mémin	Inria, France
Jan Modersitzki	University of Lübeck, Germany
Lionel Moisan	Université Paris Descartes, France
Mila Nikolova	CNRS, CMLA – ENS Cachan, France
Nicolas Papadakis	CNRS, IMB – University of Bordeaux, France
Gabriel Peyré	CNRS, CEREMADE, France
Thomas Pock	Graz University of Technology, Austria
Julien Rabin	ENSICAEN, France
Guy Rosman	Technion – Israel Institute of Technology, Israel
Martin Rumpf	University of Bonn, Germany
Chen Sagiv	SagivTech Ltd., Israel
Joseph Salmon	Télécom ParisTech, France
Otmar Scherzer	University of Vienna, Austria
Christoph Schnörr	University of Heidelberg, Germany
Carola-Bibiane Schönlieb	University of Cambridge, UK

Fiorella Sgallari   University of Bologna, Italy
Nir Sochen   Tel Aviv University, Israel
Jon Sporring   University of Copenhagen, Denmark
Kim Steenstrup Pedersen   University of Copenhagen, Denmark
Gabriele Steidl   University of Kaiserslautern, Germany
Vinh-Thong Ta   LaBRI, University of Bordeaux, France
Xue-Cheng Tai   University of Bergen, Norway
Bart ter Haar Romeny   Eindhoven University of Technology, The Netherlands
Joachim Weickert   Saarland University, Germany
Pierre Weiss   CNRS, ITAV-IMT, France
Gershon Wolansky   Technion – Israel Institute of Technology, Israel

Other Referees

Freddie Åström   Linköping University, Sweden
Laurent Hoeltgen   Saarland University, Germany
Sebastian Hoffmann   Saarland University, Germany
Reiner Lenz   Linköping University, Sweden
Solène Ozeré   INSA Rouen, France
Martin Schmidt   Saarland University, Germany
Christopher Schroers   Saarland University, Germany
Aaron Wetzler   Technion – Israel Institute of Technology, Israel
Xiaoming Yuan   Hong Kong Baptist University, Hong Kong

Organizing Chairs

Aurélie Bugeau   LaBRI – University of Bordeaux, France
Charles-Alban Deledalle   CNRS, IMB – University of Bordeaux, France
Charles Dossal   IMB – University of Bordeaux, France

Financial Management Staff

Karine Lecuona   CNRS, IMB – University of Bordeaux, France
Annie Nadeau   CNRS, Délégation Aquitaine, France
Cathy Métivier   CNRS, IMB – University of Bordeaux, France

Organizing Staff

Rémi Giraud   University of Bordeaux, IMB, LaBRI, France
Marc Nicodème   University of Bordeaux, IMB, IMS, France
Fabien Pierre   University of Bordeaux, IMB, LaBRI, France
Camille Sutour   University of Bordeaux, IMB, LaBRI, France

Contents

Scale Space and Partial Differential Equations Methods

Scale-Space Theory for Auditory Signals. 3
  Tony Lindeberg and Anders Friberg

Spectral Representations of One-Homogeneous Functionals. 16
  Martin Burger, Lina Eckardt, Guy Gilboa, and Michael Moeller

The Morphological Equivalents of Relativistic and Alpha-Scale-Spaces 28
  Martin Schmidt and Joachim Weickert

New Approximation of a Scale Space Kernel on SE(3) and Applications
in Neuroimaging. 40
  Jorg Portegies, Gonzalo Sanguinetti, Stephan Meesters, and Remco Duits

Partial Differential Equations of Bivariate Median Filters 53
  Martin Welk

Fundamentals of Non-Local Total Variation Spectral Theory. 66
  Jean-François Aujol, Guy Gilboa, and Nicolas Papadakis

Morphological Scale-Space Operators for Images Supported
on Point Clouds 78
  Jesús Angulo

Separable Time-Causal and Time-Recursive Spatio-Temporal
Receptive Fields. 90
  Tony Lindeberg

A Linear Scale-Space Theory for Continuous Nonlocal Evolutions. 103
  Giovanno Marcelo Cárdenas, Joachim Weickert, and Sarah Schäffer

Denoising, Restoration and Reconstruction

Bilevel Image Denoising Using Gaussianity Tests 117
  Jérôme Fehrenbach, Mila Nikolova, Gabriele Steidl, and Pierre Weiss

On Debiasing Restoration Algorithms: Applications to Total-Variation
and Nonlocal-Means 129
  Charles-Alban Deledalle, Nicolas Papadakis, and Joseph Salmon

Cartoon-Texture-Noise Decomposition with Transport Norms 142
  Christoph Brauer and Dirk Lorenz

Compressing Images with Diffusion- and Exemplar-Based Inpainting...... 154
Pascal Peter and Joachim Weickert

Some Nonlocal Filters Formulation Using Functional Rearrangements 166
Gonzalo Galiano and Julián Velasco

Total Variation Restoration of Images Corrupted by Poisson Noise
with Iterated Conditional Expectations 178
Rémy Abergel, Cécile Louchet, Lionel Moisan, and Tieyong Zeng

Regularization with Sparse Vector Fields: From Image Compression
to TV-type Reconstruction...................................... 191
Eva-Maria Brinkmann, Martin Burger, and Joana Grah

Solution-Driven Adaptive Total Variation Regularization 203
Frank Lenzen and Johannes Berger

Artifact-Free Variational MPEG Decompression...................... 216
Kristian Bredies and Martin Holler

Segmentation and Partitioning

Probabilistic Correlation Clustering and Image Partitioning
Using Perturbed Multicuts..................................... 231
*Jörg Hendrik Kappes, Paul Swoboda, Bogdan Savchynskyy,
Tamir Hazan, and Christoph Schnörr*

Optimizing the Relevance-Redundancy Tradeoff for Efficient Semantic
Segmentation.. 243
Caner Hazırbaş, Julia Diebold, and Daniel Cremers

Convex Color Image Segmentation with Optimal Transport Distances 256
Julien Rabin and Nicolas Papadakis

Piecewise Geodesics for Vessel Centerline Extraction and Boundary
Delineation with Application to Retina Segmentation 270
Da Chen and Laurent D. Cohen

Unsupervised Learning Using the Tensor Voting Graph 282
Shay Deutsch and Gérard Medioni

Interactive Multi-label Segmentation of RGB-D Images 294
*Julia Diebold, Nikolaus Demmel, Caner Hazırbaş, Michael Moeller,
and Daniel Cremers*

Fast Minimization of Region-Based Active Contours Using the Shape Hessian
of the Energy... 307
Günay Doğan

Flow, Motion and Registration

Sparse Aggregation Framework for Optical Flow Estimation 323
   Denis Fortun, Patrick Bouthemy, and Charles Kervrann

An Image Registration Framework for Sliding Motion with Piecewise
Smooth Deformations 335
   *Stefan Heldmann, Thomas Polzin, Alexander Derksen,
and Benjamin Berkels*

Nonlocal Joint Segmentation Registration Model 348
   Solène Ozeré and Carole Le Guyader

Deformable Image Registration with Automatic Non-Correspondence
Detection 360
   *Kanglin Chen, Alexander Derksen, Stefan Heldmann,
Marc Hallmann, and Benjamin Berkels*

Bézier Curves in the Space of Images 372
   *Alexander Effland, Martin Rumpf, Stefan Simon, Kirsten Stahn,
and Benedikt Wirth*

Computation and Visualization of Local Deformation for Multiphase Metallic
Materials by Infimal Convolution of TV-type Functionals 385
   *Frank Balle, Dietmar Eifler, Jan Henrik Fitschen, Sebastian Schuff,
and Gabriele Steidl*

Second Order Minimum Energy Filtering on SE_3 with Nonlinear Measurement
Equations 397
   *Johannes Berger, Andreas Neufeld, Florian Becker, Frank Lenzen,
and Christoph Schnörr*

Photography, Texture and Color Processing

Luminance-Hue Specification in the RGB Space 413
   Fabien Pierre, Jean-François Aujol, Aurélie Bugeau, and Vinh-Thong Ta

Variational Exposure Fusion with Optimal Local Contrast 425
   David Hafner and Joachim Weickert

A Variational Model for Color Assignment 437
   Jan Henrik Fitschen, Mila Nikolova, Fabien Pierre, and Gabriele Steidl

Duality Principle for Image Regularization and Perceptual Color
Correction Models 449
   Thomas Batard and Marcelo Bertalmío

PDE-Based Color Morphology Using Matrix Fields 461
    Ali Sharifi Boroujerdi, Michael Breuß, Bernhard Burgeth,
    and Andreas Kleefeld

Conditional Gaussian Models for Texture Synthesis 474
    Lara Raad, Agnès Desolneux, and Jean-Michel Morel

Multiscale Texture Orientation Analysis Using Spectral Total-Variation
Decomposition 486
    Dikla Horesh and Guy Gilboa

A L^1-TV Algorithm for Robust Perspective Photometric Stereo
with Spatially-Varying Lightings 498
    Yvain Quéau, François Lauze, and Jean-Denis Durou

Shape, Surface and 3D problems

Discrete Varifolds: A Unified Framework for Discrete Approximations
of Surfaces and Mean Curvature.................................. 513
    B. Buet, G.P. Leonardi, and S. Masnou

Robust Poisson Surface Reconstruction 525
    Virginia Estellers, Michael Scott, Kevin Tew, and Stefano Soatto

Variational Perspective Shape from Shading 538
    Yong Chul Ju, Andrés Bruhn, and Michael Breuß

Multiview Depth Parameterisation with Second Order Regularisation 551
    Christopher Schroers, David Hafner, and Joachim Weickert

Invertible Orientation Scores of 3D Images 563
    Michiel Janssen, Remco Duits, and Marcel Breeuwer

Edge-Preserving Integration of a Normal Field: Weighted Least-Squares,
TV and L^1 Approaches 576
    Yvain Quéau and Jean-Denis Durou

Reconstruction of Surfaces from Point Clouds Using a Lagrangian Surface
Evolution Model.. 589
    Patrik Daniel, Matej Medl'a, Karol Mikula, and Mariana Remešíková

Solving Minimal Surface Problems on Surfaces and Point Clouds 601
    Daniel Tenbrinck, François Lozes, and Abderrahim Elmoataz

Data-driven Sub-Riemannian Geodesics in SE(2) 613
    E.J. Bekkers, R. Duits, A. Mashtakov, and G.R. Sanguinetti

Optimization Theory and Methods in Imaging

A Sparse Algorithm for Dense Optimal Transport 629
   Bernhard Schmitzer

Activity Identification and Local Linear Convergence
of Douglas–Rachford/ADMM under Partial Smoothness 642
   Jingwei Liang, Jalal Fadili, Gabriel Peyré, and Russell Luke

Bilevel Optimization with Nonsmooth Lower Level Problems 654
   Peter Ochs, René Ranftl, Thomas Brox, and Thomas Pock

Convex Image Denoising via Non-Convex Regularization............. 666
   Alessandro Lanza, Serena Morigi, and Fiorella Sgallari

Infinite Dimensional Optimization Models and PDEs for Dejittering....... 678
   Guozhi Dong, Aniello Raffaele Patrone, Otmar Scherzer,
   and Ozan Öktem

Alternating Direction Method of Multiplier for Euler's Elastica-Based
Denoising 690
   Maryam Yashtini and Sung Ha Kang

Asymptotic Behaviour of Total Generalised Variation................. 702
   Konstantinos Papafitsoros and Tuomo Valkonen

Author Index 715

Scale Space and Partial Differential Equations Methods

Scale-Space Theory for Auditory Signals

Tony Lindeberg[1](✉) and Anders Friberg[2]

[1] Department of Computational Biology,
School of Computer Science and Communication,
KTH Royal Institute of Technology, Stockholm, Sweden
tony@csc.kth.se
[2] Department of Speech, Music and Hearing,
School of Computer Science and Communication,
KTH Royal Institute of Technology,
Stockholm, Sweden

Abstract. We show how the axiomatic structure of scale-space theory can be applied to the auditory domain and be used for deriving idealized models of auditory receptive fields via scale-space principles. For defining a time-frequency transformation of a purely temporal signal, it is shown that the scale-space framework allows for a new way of deriving the Gabor and Gammatone filters as well as a novel family of generalized Gammatone filters with additional degrees of freedom to obtain different trade-offs between the spectral selectivity and the temporal delay of time-causal window functions. Applied to the definition of a second layer of receptive fields from the spectrogram, it is shown that the scale-space framework leads to two canonical families of spectro-temporal receptive fields, using a combination of Gaussian filters over the logspectral domain with either Gaussian filters or a cascade of first-order integrators over the temporal domain. These spectro-temporal receptive fields can be either separable over the time-frequency domain or be adapted to local glissando transformations that represent variations in logarithmic frequencies over time. Such idealized models of auditory receptive fields respect auditory invariances, can be used for computing basic auditory features for audio processing and lead to predictions about auditory receptive fields with good qualitative similarity to biological receptive fields in the inferior colliculus (ICC) and the primary auditory cortex (A1).

1 Introduction

The information in sound is carried by variations in the air pressure over time, which for many sound sources can be modelled as a superposition of sine wave oscillations of different frequencies. To capture this information by auditory perception or signal processing, the sound signal has to be processed over some non-infinitesimal amount of time and in the case of a spectral analysis also over some range of frequencies. Such a region over time or over the spectro-temporal

---

Support from the Swedish Research Council contracts 2010-4766, 2012-4685 and 2014-4083, a KTH CSC Small Visionary Project and the EU project SkAT-VG FET-Open grant 618067 is gratefully acknowledged.

domain is referred to as a temporal or spectro-temporal *receptive field* (Aertsen and Johannesma [1]; Miller et al. [2]).

The subject of this article is to show how a principled theory for auditory receptive fields can be developed based on scale-space theory. Our aim is to express auditory operations that (i) are well localized over time and frequencies and (ii) allow for well-founded handling of temporal phenomena that occur at different temporal scales as well as (iii) receptive fields that operate over different ranges of frequencies in such a way that operations over different ranges of frequencies can be related in a well-defined manner.

When applied to the definition of a spectrogram, alternatively to the formulation of an idealized cochlea model, the scale-space approach can be used for deriving the Gabor (Gabor [3]; Wolfe et al. [4]) and Gamma-tone (Johannesma [5]; Patterson et al. [6]) approaches for computing local windowed Fourier transforms as specific cases of a complex-valued scale-space transform over different frequencies. In addition, the scale-space approach to defining spectrograms leads to a new family of *generalized Gamma-tone filters*, where the time constants of the individual first-order integrators coupled in cascade are not equal as for regular Gamma-tone filters but instead distributed logarithmically over temporal scales and allowing for different trade-offs in terms of *e.g.* the frequency selectivity of the spectrogram and the temporal delay of time-causal receptive fields.

When applied to a logarithmic transformation of the spectrogram, as motivated from the desire of handling sound signals of different strength (sound pressure) in an invariant manner and with a logarithmic transformation of the frequencies as motivated by the desire of enabling invariance properties under a frequency shift, such as transposing a musical piece by one octave, the theory also allows for the formulation of spectro-temporal receptive fields at higher levels in the auditory hierarchy in terms of spectro-temporal derivatives of spectro-temporal smoothing operations as obtained from scale-space theory.

Such second-layer receptive fields can be used for (i) *computing basic auditory features* such as onset detection, partial tone enhancement and formants, and (ii) generating *predictions of auditory receptive fields qualitatively similar to biological receptive fields* as measured by cell recordings in the inferior colliculus (ICC) and the primary auditory cortex (A1) (Miller et al. [2]; Qiu et al. [7]; Elhilali et al. [8]; Atencio and Schreiner [9]).

In this concise summary of the theory, we emphasize the scale-space aspects of auditory receptive fields. A more extensive treatment is given in [10].

2 Multi-Scale Spectrograms

To capture the frequency content in an auditory signal $f\colon \mathbb{R} \to \mathbb{R}$, the notion of spectrograms or locally windowed Fourier transforms constitutes a natural tool

$$S(t,\omega;\ \tau) = \int_{t'=-\infty}^{\infty} f(t')\, e^{-i\omega t'}\, w(t-t';\ \tau)\, dt'. \tag{1}$$

A basic question in this context concerns how to choose the window function. Would any choice of window function w do? Specifically, how long should the effective integration time τ be? *A priori* there may be no principled reason for preferring a particular duration of the temporal window function for the windowed Fourier transform over some other temporal duration. Specifically, different temporal durations may be appropriate for different auditory tasks, such as a preference for a short temporal duration for onset detection and a preference for a longer temporal duration to separate sounds with nearby frequencies.

If we apply a scale-space approach to this problem and associate a temporal window scale τ with any spectrogram, let us require that we should be able to relate spectrograms computed for different temporal window sizes between scales. If we assume a continuum of temporal window scales, then a *semi-group structure* $w(\cdot; \tau_2) = w(\cdot; \tau_2 - \tau_1) * w(\cdot; \tau_1)$ on the window functions implies a *cascade property* between the spectrograms

$$S(\cdot, \omega; \tau_2) = w(\cdot; \tau_2 - \tau_1) * S(\cdot, \omega; \tau_1). \tag{2}$$

If we instead assume a discrete set of temporal window scales, with each temporal window function $w(\cdot; n)$ at a coarser scale defined as the composition of a set of primitive temporal window functions $(\Delta w)(\cdot; k)$ such that $w(\cdot; n) = *_{k=1}^{n}(\Delta w)(\cdot; k)$, then we obtain a *Markov property* of the following type

$$S(\cdot, \omega; \tau_n) = (\Delta w)(\cdot; m \mapsto n) S(\cdot, \omega; \tau_m). \tag{3}$$

For pre-recorded sound signals we may in principle take the liberty of accessing the virtual future in relation to any time moment. For real-time audio processing or when modelling biological auditory perception there is on the other hand no way to access the future. For real-time audio models, the temporal window functions must therefore be *time-causal* such that $w(t; \tau) = 0$ for $t < 0$.

In the case of non-causal time and a continuum of temporal window scales, let us assume that the window functions in addition should guarantee non-creation of new structure in the sense of non-enhancement of local extrema in either of the real or purely imaginary channels. Then, it follows from general results in (Lindeberg [11], eq. (45)) that the temporal window function must be Gaussian

$$g(t; \tau) = \frac{1}{\sqrt{2\pi \Sigma_\tau}} e^{-(t-\delta_\tau)^2/2\tau} \tag{4}$$

with $\Sigma_\tau = \tau \Sigma_0$ and $\delta_\tau = \tau \delta_0$ where we without loss of generality can set $\Sigma_0 = 1$.

If we in the case of time-causal data and a discrete set of temporal window scales assume that the temporal window functions should guarantee non-creation of new structure in the sense of guaranteeing non-creation of new local extrema in either of the real or purely imaginary channels, then it follows from general results in (Lindeberg and Fagerström [12], eq. (8)) that the temporal window functions should be given by a cascade of truncated exponential functions

$$h_{composed}(t; \mu) = *_{k=1}^{K} h_{exp}(t; \mu_k) \tag{5}$$

where $\mu = (\mu_1, \ldots, \mu_k)$ and

$$h_{exp}(t; \mu_k) = \begin{cases} \frac{1}{\mu_k} e^{-t/\mu_k} & t \geq 0 \\ 0 & t < 0 \end{cases} \tag{6}$$

Thereby the convolution kernels in temporal scale spaces for a general time-varying signal are used as scale-dependent window functions for defining windowed Fourier transforms of different temporal extent. Specifically, this scale-space approach allows for the definition of windowed Fourier transforms for all temporal extents in such a way that a windowed Fourier transform at any coarse temporal scale can be related to a windowed Fourier transform at any finer temporal scale using the cascade property (2) or the Markov property (3) derived from the underlying scale-space kernels. Combined with the additional scale-space properties of non-creation of new structures with increasing scale, this guarantees well-founded theoretical properties between corresponding windowed Fourier transforms at different temporal scales.

Relations to Gabor functions. By rewriting the expressions (1) and (4) for the complex-valued spectrogram based on the Gaussian temporal scale space as

$$S_g(\omega, t;\ \tau) = e^{-i\omega t} \int_{t'=-\infty}^{\infty} g(t-t';\ \tau)\, e^{i\omega(t-t')} f(t')\, dt' \qquad (7)$$

it can be seen that up to a phase shift this multi-scale spectrogram can equivalently be interpreted as the convolution of the original auditory signal f by *Gabor functions* [3] of the form

$$G(t, \omega;\ \tau) = g(t;\ \tau)\, e^{i\omega t}. \qquad (8)$$

Such Gabor functions have been previously used for analyzing auditory signals by several authors, including Wolfe et al. [4] and Heckmann et al. [13].

Relations to Gammatone filters. In the special case when the time constants of the K truncated exponential filters that are coupled in cascade are all equal $\mu_k = \mu$, then the multi-scale spectrogram defined by (1) and (5) is given by [10]

$$S_h(t, \omega;\ \mu, K) = e^{-i\omega t} \int_{t'=-\infty}^{\infty} \frac{(t-t')^{K-1} e^{-(t-t')/\mu}}{\mu^K\, \Gamma(K)}\, e^{i\omega(t-t')} f(t')\, dt' \qquad (9)$$

and does up to a phase shift correspond to convolution of the input signal f by filters of the form

$$h_{cos}(t, \omega;\ \mu, K) = \frac{t^{K-1} e^{-t/\mu}}{\mu^K\, \Gamma(K)} \cos \omega t, \qquad (10)$$

$$h_{sin}(t, \omega;\ \mu, K) = \frac{t^{K-1} e^{-t/\mu}}{\mu^K\, \Gamma(K)} \sin \omega t. \qquad (11)$$

For comparison, the *Gammatone filter* with parameters a and b and frequency ϕ is defined according to $\gamma(t) = a\, t^{n-1} e^{-2\pi b t} \cos(2\pi \phi t + \alpha)$. By identifying the parameters $a = 1/(\mu^K \Gamma(K))$, $b = 1/(2\pi\mu)$ and $\omega = 2\pi\, \phi$, it follows that we can derive the Gammatone filter as a special case of applying a time-causal scale-space representation with discrete scale levels to the projections $f \cos \omega t$ and $f \sin \omega t$ of an auditory signal $f(t)$ onto a complex sine wave $e^{-i\omega t}$.

Gammatone filter banks are also commonly used in audio processing (Johannesma [5]; Patterson et al. [6]; Ngamkham et al. [14]).

Generalized Gammatone filters. By allowing for different time constants in the primitive truncated exponential filters, we obtain *generalized Gammatone filters*

$$h_{cos}(t, \omega; \mu) = h_{composed}(t; \mu) \cos \omega t \qquad (12)$$
$$h_{sin}(t, \omega; \mu) = h_{composed}(t; \mu) \sin \omega t \qquad (13)$$

with $h_{composed}$ according to (5) and $\mu = (\mu_1, \ldots, \mu_K)$. If we have the freedom of choosing the minimum temporal window scale τ_{min} freely, we can parameterize the intermediate temporal scale levels using a parameter $c > 1$ such that [16]

$$\tau_k = c^{2(k-K)} \tau_{max} \qquad (1 \leq k \leq K) \qquad (14)$$

which shares some qualitative similarities to the logarithmic transformation of the past used in the scale-time model proposed by Koenderink [15].

By the additive property of variances (which for a primitive truncated exponential filter (6) with time constant μ_k is given by μ_k^2) under convolution this implies that time constants of the individual first-order integrators will be [16]

$$\mu_1 = c^{1-K} \sqrt{\tau_{max}} \qquad (15)$$
$$\mu_k = \sqrt{\tau_k - \tau_{k-1}} = c^{k-K-1} \sqrt{c^2 - 1} \sqrt{\tau_{max}} \qquad (2 \leq k \leq K) \qquad (16)$$

By comparing graphs of the underlying temporal scale-space kernels [16], one finds that filters based on truncated exponentials with a logarithmic distribution of the intermediate temporal scales allow for a faster temporal response compared to the corresponding filters based on truncated exponentials with equal time constants. Thereby, these generalized Gammatone filters allow for additional degrees of freedom to obtain different trade-offs between the frequency selectivity and the temporal delay of time-causal window functions by varying the number of levels K and the distribution parameter c for a given τ_{max}.

Frequency-dependent window scale. To guarantee basic covariance properties of the spectrogram under a frequency shift $\omega \mapsto \alpha \omega$, it is natural to let the temporal window scale vary with the frequency ω in such a a way that the temporal window scale in units of $\sigma = \sqrt{\tau}$ is *proportional to the wavelength* $\lambda = 2\pi/\omega$

$$\tau = \left(\frac{2\pi n}{\omega}\right)^2 \qquad (17)$$

where n is a parameter. By such frequency dependent temporal window scale, the spectral selectivity in the spectrogram (the width of a spectral band) will be independent of the frequency ω. This is a prerequisite for the desirable property that a shift by one octave of a musical piece should imply that the corresponding spectrogram should appear similar while shifted by one octave, if the frequency axis of the spectrogram is parameterized on a logarithmic scale.

Additionally, to prevent the temporal window scale from being too short for high frequencies or too long at low frequencies, we also introduce soft lower and upper bounds on the temporal window scale. Thereby, self-similarity will only hold within a limited range of frequencies.

3 Second-Layer Receptive Fields over the Spectrogram

Given that a spectrogram has been computed by a first layer of auditory receptive fields, we define a *second layer of receptive fields* by operating on the spectrogram with 2-D spectro-temporal filters in a structurally similar way as visual receptive fields are applied to time-varying visual input (see overview in Lindeberg [17]).

3.1 Invariances by Logarithmic Transformations of the Spectrogram

Prior to the definition of receptive fields from the spectrogram, it is natural to allow for a self-similar *logarithmic transformation of the magnitude values*

$$S_{dB} = 20 \log_{10}\left(\frac{|S|}{S_0}\right). \tag{18}$$

Then, a multiplicative transformation of the sound pressure $f \mapsto a\,f$, corresponding to $|S| \mapsto a\,|S|$, or an inversely proportional reduction in the sound pressure of the signal from a single auditory point source as function of distance $f \mapsto f/R$, corresponding to $|S| \mapsto |S|/R$, are both transformed into a subtraction of the logarithmic magnitude by a constant.

If we operate on the logarithmically transformed spectrogram by a receptive field $\mathcal{A}_\Sigma$ that is based on a combination of a spectro-temporal smoothing operation $\mathcal{T}_\Sigma$ with logspectral and temporal scale parameters as determined by a spectro-temporal covariance matrix Σ, temporal and/or logspectral derivatives $\partial_t^\alpha \partial_\nu^\beta$ of orders α and β with at least one of $\alpha > 0$ or $\beta > 0$

$$\mathcal{A}_\Sigma\, S_{dB} = \partial_t^\alpha \partial_\nu^\beta \mathcal{T}_\Sigma\, S_{dB} \tag{19}$$

then the influence on the receptive field responses of the constants a and R

$$\mathcal{A}_\Sigma S_{dB} = \partial_t^\alpha \partial_\nu^\beta \mathcal{T}_\Sigma\, (S_{dB} + 20\log_{10} a - 20\log_{10} R) = \partial_t^\alpha \partial_\nu^\beta \mathcal{T}_\Sigma\, S_{dB} + 0 + 0 \tag{20}$$

will be eliminated if the constants a and R do not depend on time t or the logarithmic frequency ν, implying *invariance of the second-layer receptive field responses to variations in the sound pressure or the distance to a sound source*.

Since logarithmic frequencies constitute a natural metric for relating frequencies of sound and there is an approximately logarithmic distribution of frequencies both on the basilar membrane and in the auditory cortex, it is natural to express these derived receptive fields in terms of *logarithmic frequencies*

$$\nu = \nu_0 + C \log\left(\frac{\omega}{\omega_0}\right) \tag{21}$$

for some constants C and ω_0, where specifically $\nu_0 = 69$, $C = 12/\log 2$ and $\omega_0 = 2\pi \cdot 440$ correspond to the MIDI standard.

This logarithmic parameterization implies that a shift in frequency, caused by *e.g.* transposing a piece of music by one octave or varying the fundamental frequency in singing resulting in a multiplicative transformation of the harmonics (overtones), corresponds to a mere *translation* in logarithmic frequency.

Note, however, that some properties of voice or instruments, such as the formant structure in speech or physical resonances in instruments, are independent of the fundamental frequency and therefore not frequency invariant.

3.2 Structural Requirements on Second-Layer Receptive Fields

Given such a logarithmically transformed spectrogram, we define a family of *second-layer spectro-temporal receptive fields* $A(t, \omega; \Sigma)$ that are to operate on the transformed spectrogram $S_{dB}(t, \nu; \tau)$ and be parameterized by some multi-dimensional spectro-temporal scale parameter Σ comprising smoothing over time t and logarithmic frequencies ν, and obeying:

(i) *linearity* over the logarithmic spectrogram to ensure that (a) the multiplicative relations of the magnitude of the spectrogram that are mapped to linear relations by the logarithmic transformation (18) are preserved as linear relations over the receptive field responses and (b) the scale-space properties imposed to ensure non-creation of new structures in smoothed spectrograms as defined by spectro-temporal smoothing kernels do also transfer to spectro-temporal derivatives of these.

(ii) *shift-invariance* with respect to translations over time $t \mapsto t + \Delta t$ and logarithmic frequencies $\nu \mapsto \nu + \Delta \nu$ such that all temporal moments and all logarithmic frequencies are treated in a similar manner. Temporal shift invariance implies that an auditory stimulus should be perceived in a similar manner irrespective of when it occurs. Shift-invariance in the logarithmic frequency domain implies that, for example, a piece of music should be perceived in a similar manner if it is transposed by *e.g.* one octave.

(iii.a) For pre-recorded sound signals, for which we can take the freedom of accessing data from the virtual future in relation to any time moment, we impose a *continuous semi-group structure over spectro-temporal scales* on the second-layer receptive fields $T(\cdot, \cdot; \Sigma_2) = T(\cdot, \cdot; \Sigma_2 - \Sigma_1) T(\cdot, \cdot; \Sigma_1)$ corresponding to an additive structure over the multi-dimensional scale parameter Σ.

(iii.b) For time-causal signals, we require a *continuous semi-group structure over logspectral scales* s, $T(\cdot; s_2) = T(\cdot; s_2 - s_1) T(\cdot; s_1)$, and a *Markov property between adjacent temporal scales* τ, $T(\cdot; \tau_{k+1}) = (\Delta T)(\cdot; k) T(\cdot; \tau_k)$.

(iv.a) For the non-causal spectrogram (7) we require *non-enhancement of local extrema* in the sense that if for some scale Σ_0 the point (t_0, ν_0) is a local maximum (minimum) for the mapping $(t, \nu) \mapsto (A_\Sigma S_{dB})(t, \nu; \tau, \Sigma_0)$ then the value at this point must not increase (decrease) with increasing scale Σ.

(iv.b) For the time-causal spectrogram generated by (10)–(11) or (12)–(13) we require: (iv.b1) the smoothing operation over the logspectral domain to satisfy *non-enhancement of local extrema* in the sense that if at some logspectral scale s_0 a point ν_0 is a local maximum (minimum) of the mapping $\nu \mapsto (\mathcal{A}_\Sigma S_{dB})(\nu;\ \tau, s_0)$ obtained by disregarding the temporal variations, then the value at this point must not increase (decrease) with increasing logspectral scale s, and (iv.b2) the purely temporal smoothing operation to be a time-causal scale-space kernel guaranteeing *non-creation of new local extrema* under an increase of the temporal scale parameter τ.

(v) *glissando covariance* in the sense that if two local patches of two spectrograms are related by a local glissando transformation $S' = \mathcal{G}_v S$ of the form $\nu' = \nu + vt$ and corresponding to frequencies that vary smoothly over time, such as during singing or for instruments with continuous pitch control, then it should be possible to relate the local spectro-temporal receptive field responses such that $\mathcal{A}_{G_v(\Sigma)} \mathcal{G}_v S = \mathcal{G}_v \mathcal{A}_\Sigma S$ for some transformation $\Sigma' = G_v(\Sigma)$ of the spectro-temporal scale parameters Σ.

3.3 Idealized Models for Spectro-Temporal Receptive Fields

Given these structural requirements, it follows from derivations similar to those that are used for constraining visual receptive fields given structural requirements on a visual front-end (Lindeberg [17]) that the second layer of auditory receptive fields should be based on spectro-temporal receptive fields of the form

$$A(t, \nu;\ \Sigma) = \partial_t^\alpha \partial_\nu^\beta \left(g(\nu - vt;\ s)\, T(t;\ \tau) \right) \tag{22}$$

where

- ∂_t^α represents a *temporal derivative operator* of order α with respect to time t which could alternatively be replaced by a glissando-adapted temporal derivative of the form $\partial_{\bar{t}} = \partial_t + v\, \partial_\nu$,
- ∂_ν^β represents a *logspectral derivative operator* of order β with respect to logarithmic frequency ν,
- $T(t;\ \tau)$ represents a *temporal smoothing kernel* with temporal scale parameter τ, which should either be (i) a temporal Gaussian kernel $g(t;\ \tau)$ (4) or (ii) the equivalent kernel $h_{composed}(t;\ \mu)$ according to (5) and corresponding to a set of truncated exponential kernels coupled in cascade, and
- $g(\nu - vt;\ s)$ represents a Gaussian *spectral smoothing kernel* over logarithmic frequencies ν with logspectral scale parameter s and v representing a glissando parameter making it possible to adapt the receptive fields to variations in frequency $\nu' = \nu + vt$ over time and
- the spectro-temporal covariance matrix Σ in the left hand expression for spectro-temporal receptive fields comprises both the temporal scale parameter τ, the logspectral scale parameter s and the glissando parameter v.

Thereby, the spectro-temporal receptive fields (22) constitute a combination of a Gaussian scale-space concept over the logspectral dimension with purely temporal receptive fields obtained by either a non-causal Gaussian temporal scale space or a time-causal scale space obtained by coupling truncated exponential kernels/first-order integrators in cascade (see Figure 2, columns 2-3).

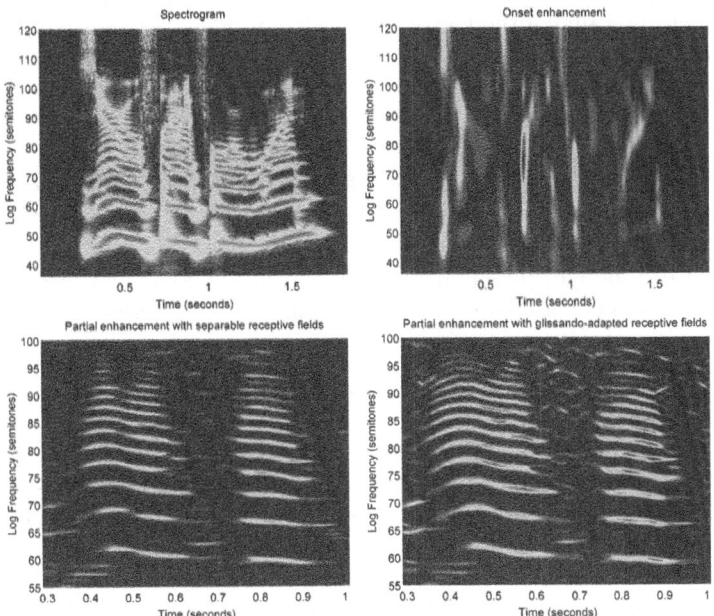

Fig. 1. (top left) Spectrogram of a male voice that reads "zero five four one" (from the TIDigits database) computed with generalized Gammatone functions. (top right) Onset enhancement by first-order temporal derivatives. (bottom left) Enhancement of partial tones by second-order logspectral derivatives using separable receptive fields. (bottom right) Enhancement of partial tones by the maximum of second-order logspectral derivatives over a filter bank of glissando-adapted receptive fields. Note the better ability of the glissando-adapted receptive fields to capture rapid frequency variations.

The proofs concerning spectro-temporal receptive fields are similar to those regarding spatio-temporal receptive fields over a 1+1-D spatio-temporal domain with the spatial dimension replaced by a logspectral dimension.

3.4 Auditory Features from Second-Layer Receptive Fields

In the following, we will show examples of auditory features that can be defined from a second layer of auditory receptive fields of this form:

Onset enhancement. Computation of first-order temporal derivatives $\mathcal{D}_t(t, \nu; \tau, s) = \sqrt{\tau}\, \partial_t T(t, \nu;\, \tau, s)$ where $\sqrt{\tau}$ is a scale normalization factor to approximate *scale-normalized derivatives* (Lindeberg [18]). To select receptive field responses that correspond to onsets only, we add the non-linear logical operation $D_t > 0$ such that $\mathcal{A}_{onset}\, S_{dB} = \mathcal{D}_t\, S_{dB}$ if $\mathcal{D}_t\, S_{dB} > 0$ and 0 otherwise (see Figure 1, top right).

Enhancement of partials. Computation of second-order logspectral derivatives $\mathcal{D}_{\nu\nu}(t, \nu;\, \tau, s) = s\, \partial_{\nu\nu} T(t, \nu;\, \tau, s)$ where the factor s is a scale normalization factor for scale-normalized derivatives in the Gaussian scale space (Lindeberg [18]).

Depending on the value of the logspectral scale parameter s, this operation may either enhance partial tones or formants. This operation is naturally combined with the (non-linear) logical operation $\mathcal{D}_{\nu\nu} < 0$ such that $\mathcal{A}_{band}\, S_{dB} = -\mathcal{D}_{\nu\nu}\, S_{dB}$ if $\mathcal{D}_{\nu\nu}\, S_{dB} < 0$ and 0 otherwise (see Figure 1, bottom left).

Enhancement of partials using filter bank of glissando-adapted receptive fields. To more accurately capture the harmonic components in sound for which the frequencies vary rapidly over time, we use a filter bank of receptive fields that are adapted to different glissando values v, which are combined by taking the maximum over all glissando-adapted filter responses (see Figure 1, bottom right).

4 Relations to Biological Receptive Fields

In the central nucleus of the inferior colliculus (ICC) of cats, Qiu et al. [7] report that about 60 % of the neurons can be described as separable in the time-frequency domain (see Figure 2, top row), whereas the remaining neurons are either obliquely oriented (see Figure 2, second row) or contain multiple excitatory/inhibitory subfields. This overall structure is nicely compatible with the treatment in Section 3.4, where the second-layer receptive fields are expressed in terms of spectro-temporal derivatives of either time-frequency separable spectro-temporal smoothing operations or corresponding glissando-adapted features as motivated by the structural requirements in Section 3.2.

Qualitatively similar shapes of receptive fields can be measured from neurons in the primary auditory cortex (see Figure 2, third row, as well as Miller et al. [2] regarding binaural receptive fields). Specifically, the use of multiple temporal and spectral scales as a main component in the model is in good agreement with biological receptive fields having different degrees of spectral tuning ranging from narrow to broad and different temporal extent (see Figure 2, rows 4-5).

5 Summary and Discussion

We have presented a theory for how idealized models of auditory receptive fields can be derived from structural constraints (scale-space axioms) on the first stages of auditory processing. The theory includes (i) the definition of multi-scale spectrograms at different temporal scales in such a way that a spectrogram at any coarser temporal scale can be related to a corresponding spectrogram at any finer temporal scale using theoretically well-defined scale-space operations, and additionally (ii) how a second layer of spectro-temporal receptive fields can be defined over a logarithmically transformed spectrogram in such a way that the resulting spectro-temporal receptive fields obey invariance or covariance properties under natural sound transformations including temporal shifts, variations in the sound pressure, the distance between the sound source and the observer, a shift in the frequencies of auditory stimuli or glissando transformations. Specifically, theoretical arguments have been presented showing how these idealized receptive fields are constrained to the presented forms from symmetry properties

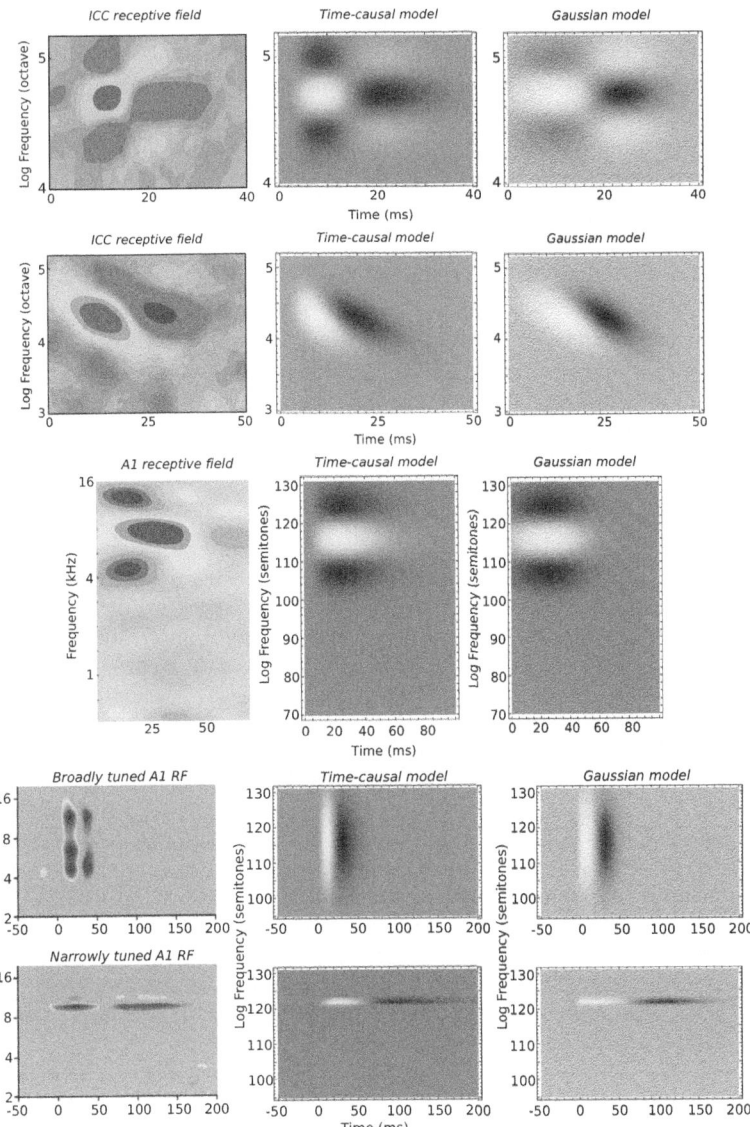

Fig. 2. (top row left) A separable monaural spectro-temporal receptive field in the central nucleus of the inferior colliculus (ICC) of cat as reported by Qiu et al. [7]. (second row left) A non-separable spectro-temporal receptive field in the central nucleus of the inferior colliculus (ICC) of cat as reported by Qiu et al. [7]. (third row left) A separable spectro-temporal receptive fields in the primary auditory cortex (A1) of ferret as reported by Elhilali et al. [8]. (fourth and bottom rows left) Spectro-temporal receptive fields of broadly and narrowly tuned neurons in the primary auditory cortex (A1) of cats as reported by Atencio and Schreiner [9]. (middle and right columns) Time-causal and non-causal receptive field models according to eq. (22). (Figures reprinted from [10] with permission.)

of the environment in combination with assumptions about the internal structure of auditory operations as motivated from requirements of handling different temporal and spectral scales in a theoretically well-founded manner.

We propose that this theory should be of wide general interest for the audio processing community by providing theoretically well-founded and provably invariant/covariant audio operations for processing sound signals and for computational modelling or measurements of receptive fields, auditory invariances, theoretical biology and psychophysics, by serving as a general theoretical foundation and understanding of how receptive fields in ICC and A1 support invariant visual processes at higher levels in the auditory hierarchy.

For spatial and spatio-temporal image data, scale-space theory has been been developed as a canonical model to handle image measurements that are subject to the variabilities of natural image transformations. This paper shows how the underlying ideas of scale-space theory can be transferred to the auditory domain

References

1. Aertsen, A.M.H.J., Johannesma, P.I.M.: The spectro-temporal receptive field: A functional characterization of auditory neurons. Biol. Cyb. **42**, 133–143 (1981)
2. Miller, L.M., Escabi, N.A., Read, H.L., Schreiner, C.: Spectrotemporal receptive fields in the lemniscal auditory thalamus and cortex. J. Neurophys. **87**, 516–527 (2001)
3. Gabor, D.: Theory of communication. J. of the IEE **93**, 429–457 (1946)
4. Wolfe, P.J., Godsill, S.J., Dorfler, M.: Multi-Gabor dictionaries for audio time-frequency analysis. In: Appl. of Signal Proc. to Audio and Acoustics, pp. 43–46 (2001)
5. Johannesma, P.I.M.: The pre-response stimulus ensemble of neurons in the cochlear nucleus. In: IPO Symposium on Hearing Theory, Eindhoven, pp. 58–69 (1972)
6. Patterson, R.D., Nimmo-Smith, I., Holdsworth, J., Rice, P.: An efficient auditory filterbank based on the gammatone function. In: A meeting of the IOC Speech Group on Auditory Modelling at RSRE, vol. 2, 7 (1987)
7. Qiu, A., Schreiner, C.E., Escabi, M.A.: Gabor analysis of auditory midbrain receptive fields: Spectro-temporal and binaural composition. J. of Neurophysiology **90**, 456–476 (2003)
8. Elhilali, M., Fritz, J., Chi, T.S., Shamma, S.: Auditory cortical receptive fields: Stable entities with plastic abilities. J. of Neuroscience **27**, 10372–10382 (2007)
9. Atencio, C.A., Schreiner, C.E.: Spectrotemporal processing in spectral tuning modules of cat primary auditory cortex. PLOS ONE **7**, e31537 (2012)
10. Lindeberg, T., Friberg, A.: Idealized computational models of auditory receptive fields. PLOS ONE, 10.1371/journal.pone.0119032 (2015) preprint arXiv:1404.2037
11. Lindeberg, T.: Generalized Gaussian scale-space axiomatics comprising linear scale-space, affine scale-space and spatio-temporal scale-space. J. of Mathematical Imaging and Vision **40**, 36–81 (2011)
12. Lindeberg, T., Fagerström, D.: Scale-space with causal time direction. In: Buxton, B., Cipolla, R. (eds.) ECCV 1996. LNCS, vol. 1064, pp. 229–240. Springer, Heidelberg (1996)
13. Heckmann, M., Domont, X., Joublin, F., Goerick, C.: A hierarchical framework for spectro-temporal feature extraction. Speech Communication **53**, 736–752 (2011)

14. Ngamkham, W., Sawigun, C., Hiseni, S., Serdijn, W.A.: Analog complex gammatone filter for cochlear implant channels. In: ISCAS, pp. 969–972 (2010)
15. Koenderink, J.J.: Scale-time. Biological Cybernetics **58**, 159–162 (1988)
16. Lindeberg, T.: Separable time-causal and time-recursive receptive fields. In: J.-F. Aujol et al. (eds.) SSVM 2015, LNCS 9087, pp. 90–102 (2015)
17. Lindeberg, T.: A computational theory of visual receptive fields. Biological Cybernetics **107**, 589–635 (2013)
18. Lindeberg, T.: Feature detection with automatic scale selection. Int. J. of Computer Vision **30**, 77–116 (1998)

Spectral Representations of One-Homogeneous Functionals

Martin Burger[1], Lina Eckardt[1], Guy Gilboa[2](✉), and Michael Moeller[3]

[1] Institute for Computational and Applied Mathematics,
University of Münster, Münster, Germany
[2] Electrical Engineering Department, Technion IIT, Haifa, Israel
guy.gilboa@ef.technion.ac.il
[3] Department of Mathematics, Technische Universität München, Munich, Germany

Abstract. This paper discusses a generalization of spectral representations related to convex one-homogeneous regularization functionals, e.g. total variation or ℓ^1-norms. Those functionals serve as a substitute for a Hilbert space structure (and the related norm) in classical linear spectral transforms, e.g. Fourier and wavelet analysis. We discuss three meaningful definitions of spectral representations by scale space and variational methods and prove that (nonlinear) eigenfunctions of the regularization functionals are indeed atoms in the spectral representation. Moreover, we verify further useful properties related to orthogonality of the decomposition and the Parseval identity.

The spectral transform is motivated by total variation and further developed to higher order variants. Moreover, we show that the approach can recover Fourier analysis as a special case using an appropriate ℓ^1-type functional and discuss a coupled sparsity example.

Keywords: Nonlinear spectral decomposition · Nonlinear eigenfunctions · Total variation · Convex regularization

1 Introduction

Eigenfunction analysis has been used extensively to solve numerous signal processing, computer vision and machine-learning problems such as segmentation [23], clustering [20] and subspace clustering [17], dimensionality reduction [5], and more. Recently, several attempts were made to generalize some of the properties of the linear setting to a nonlinear setting. Specifically, singular-value analysis of convex functionals (interpreted as "ground states") [8] and a spectral representation related to the total variation (TV) functional [16] were proposed.

We examine solutions of the following nonlinear eigenvalue problem:

$$\lambda u \in \partial J(u), \qquad (1)$$

where $J(u)$ is a convex functional and $\partial J(u)$ is its subgradient (precise definitions are given in Section 2). We refer to functions u admitting (1) as eigenfunctions with corresponding eigenvalue λ.

In [16] a generalization of eigenfunction analysis to the total-variation case was proposed in the following way. Let $u(t;x)$ be the TV-flow solution [1] or the gradient descent of the total variation energy $J_{TV}(u)$, with initial condition $f(x)$:

$$\partial_t u = -p, \qquad p \in \partial J_{TV}(u), \qquad u(t=0) = f(x), \qquad (2)$$

where

$$J_{TV}(u) = \sup_{\|\varphi\|_{L^\infty(\Omega)} \le 1} \int_\Omega u \operatorname{div} \varphi \, dx, \qquad (3)$$

with $\varphi \in C_0^\infty$. The TV spectral transform is defined by

$$\phi(t;x) := t\partial_{tt} u(t;x), \qquad (4)$$

where $\partial_{tt} u$ is the second time derivative of the solution $u(t;x)$ of the TV flow (2). For $f(x)$ admitting (1), with a corresponding eigenvalue λ, one obtains $\phi(t;x) = \delta(t - 1/\lambda) f(x)$, where δ denotes a Dirac delta distribution. When f is composed of separable eigenfunctions with eigenvalues λ_i one obtains through $\phi(t;x)$ a decomposition of the image into its eigenfunctions at $t = 1/\lambda_i$. In the general case, ϕ yields a continuum multiscale representation of the image, generalizing structure-texture decomposition methods like [3,18,21]. One can reconstruct the original image by:

$$f(x) = \int_0^\infty \phi(t;x) dt + \bar{f}, \qquad (5)$$

where $\bar{f} = \frac{1}{\Omega} \int_\Omega f(x) dx$. Given a transfer function $H(t) \in \mathbb{R}$, image filtering can be performed by:

$$f_H(x) := \int_0^\infty H(t) \phi(t;x) dt + \bar{f}. \qquad (6)$$

The spectrum $S(t)$ corresponds to the amplitude of each scale:

$$S(t) := \|\phi(t;x)\|_{L^1(\Omega)} = \int_\Omega |\phi(t;x)| dx. \qquad (7)$$

In Fig. 1 an example of spectral TV processing is shown. For example, an (ideal) high-pass filter is defined by $H(t) = 1$ for a range $t \in [0, t_c]$ and 0 otherwise, the filter response is calculated using Eq. (6). Similarly for band-pass and low-pass filters in different time domains (see precise definitions in [16]).

The analysis of eigenfunctions related to non-quadratic smoothing convex functionals has mainly focused on the TV functional. An extensive study was conducted in the past decade regarding the TV-flow, its properties like finite extinction time and some analytic solutions in the case of eigenfunctions, see [1,2,4,6,10,14,24]. In [7,19] eigenfunctions related to the total-generalized-variation (TGV) functional [9] are analyzed.

2 Spectral Representations

In the following we generalize the total variation spectral approach in [15,16] in two ways. First of all we now consider arbitrary one-homogeneous convex

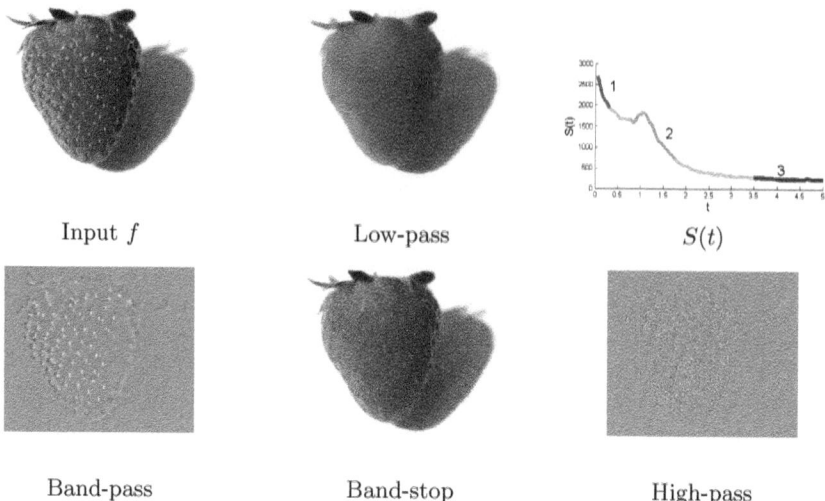

Fig. 1. Total-variation spectral filtering example. The input image (top left) is decomposed into its $\phi(t)$ components, the corresponding spectrum $S(t)$ is on the top right. Integration of the ϕ's over the t domains 1, 2 and 3 (top right) yields high-pass, band-pass and low-pass filters, respectively. The band-stop filter (bottom middle) is the complement integration domain of region 2.

functionals $J : \mathcal{X} \to \mathbb{R}^+ \cup \{\infty\}$ defined on Banach space $\mathcal{X}$ embedded into $L^2(\Omega)$. We assume that the properties of J are such that all differential equations and variational problems considered in the following are well-posed, which can be verified for standard examples such as total variation. Secondly we also consider alternative definitions of the spectral representation than the TV flow used in [15,16]. In particular we discuss the representations introduced by a standard variational approach and by the Bregman iterations respectively inverse scale space methods (cf. [11,12,22]). The latter has been investigated in the case of total variation in [13]. Finally we shall also discuss the issue of the spectral response.

We start with a given image $f \in L^2(\Omega)$ and consider three different versions of the spectral transform. The first one is the scale space from a gradient flow approach resembling the TV flow, the last one is obtained from the inverse scale space method. In between these methods there is the classical variational regularization. A potentially confusing issue is the fact that time in the inverse scale space method rather corresponds to an inverse of the time variable in the other models. For this sake we will make change of time variables in the end to ease comparison. Moreover, in addition to the spectral representation ϕ we introduce another one called ψ in the inverse time variable. Note that for small times ϕ measures changes in high frequencies and ψ measures changes in low frequencies. In analogy to classical signal processing we call ϕ *wavelength representation* and ψ *frequency representation*, respectively. Noticing that a change of variables $s = \frac{1}{t}$ yields

$$\int_0^\infty \phi(t) w(t) \, dt = \int_0^\infty \phi(\frac{1}{s}) w(\frac{1}{s}) \frac{1}{s^2} \, ds, \tag{8}$$

which motivates the consistency condition

$$\psi(s) = \phi(\frac{1}{s}) \frac{1}{s^2} \quad \text{respectively} \quad \phi(t) = \psi(\frac{1}{t}) \frac{1}{t^2}, \tag{9}$$

that ensures the desirable inverse time relation between frequency and wavelength representation, $\int_0^\infty \phi(t) w(t) \, dt = \int_0^\infty \psi(s) w(\frac{1}{s}) \, ds$.

For simplicity we assume $J(u) > 0$ for $u \in X \setminus \{0\}$, which is usually achieved by choosing X restricted in the right way (note that the null-space of a convex one-homogeneous functional is a linear subspace of X, [8]). E.g. in the case of total variation regularization we would consider the subspace of functions with vanishing mean value. The general case can be reconstructed by adding appropriate nullspace components. The detailed definitions of the spectral representations are given as follows:

Gradient Flow Representation: Let $u_{GF}(t)$ be the solution of

$$\partial_t u = -p_{GF}, \qquad p_{GF} \in \partial J(u) \tag{10}$$

for $t > 0$ with initial value $u(0) = f$. Then the corresponding wavelength spectral transform is defined by

$$\phi_{GF}(t) = t \partial_{tt} u_{GF}(t) = -t \partial_t p_{GF}(t). \tag{11}$$

We obtain the frequency representation as

$$\psi_{GF}(s) = \frac{1}{s^3} \partial_{tt} u_{GF}(\frac{1}{s}) = -\frac{1}{s^3} \partial_t p_{GF}(\frac{1}{s}) = \frac{1}{s} \partial_s q_{GF}(s), \tag{12}$$

where $q_{GF}(s) = p_{GF}(\frac{1}{s})$.

Variational Representation: Let $u_{VM}(t)$ be the minimizer of

$$\frac{1}{2} \|u - f\|_2^2 + tJ(u) \to \min_{u \in X}, \quad \text{i.e.} \quad u_{VM}(t) = f - t p_{VM}(t), \; p_{VM} \in \partial J(u_{VM}). \tag{13}$$

Then the corresponding high frequency spectral representation is defined by

$$\phi_{VM}(t) = t \partial_{tt} u_{VM}(t) = -\partial_t(t^2 \partial_t p_{VM}(t)). \tag{14}$$

The low frequency representation can be derived from the equivalent form of the variational problem

$$\frac{s}{2} \|v - f\|_2^2 + J(v) \to \min_{v \in X}, \tag{15}$$

with the relation $v_{VM}(s) = u_{VM}(\frac{1}{s})$, which yields

$$\psi_{VM}(s) = \frac{1}{s} \partial_{tt} u_{VM}(\frac{1}{s}) = s \partial_s(s^2 \partial_s v_{VM}(s)). \tag{16}$$

Inverse Scale Space Representation: Let $v_{IS}(s)$ be the solution of

$$\partial_s q_{IS} = f - v, \qquad q_{IS} \in \partial J(v) \tag{17}$$

for $s > 0$ with initial value $v(0) = 0$. Then the corresponding low frequency spectral representation is defined by

$$\psi_{IS}(s) = \partial_s v_{IS}(s) = -\partial_{ss} q_{IS}(s). \tag{18}$$

With $u_{IS}(t) = v_{IS}(\frac{1}{t})$ we obtain

$$\phi_{IS}(s) = -t^2 \partial_t u_{IS}(t). \tag{19}$$

Note that due to low regularity of J we expect ϕ_* to be a measure in time (here $*$ stands for either GF, VM, or IS). This is seen immediately from the canonical example of f being a (nonlinear) eigenfunction of J:

Theorem 1. *Let $f \in X$ satisfy (1) for some $\lambda > 0$ and $u = f$. Then, with the definitions made in (10) – (19) we have*

$$\phi_*(t) = f \delta_{\frac{1}{\lambda}}(t), \qquad \psi_*(s) = f \delta_\lambda(s) \qquad \text{for } * = GF, VM, IS. \tag{20}$$

Proof. It is straightforward to check that $u_{GF} = u_{VM} = (1 - \lambda t)_+ f$ and the a calculation of the second derivative in a distributional sense yields the corresponding ϕ. In a similar way one can check in the case of the inverse scale space method that $u_{IS}(s) = 0$ for $s < \lambda$ and $u_{IS}(s) = f$ for $s > \lambda$ is the solution (with piecewise linear p), see e.g. [8].

The above result confirms our intuition about the spectral decompositions, indeed the eigenfunctions give a pure spectrum and the position of certain wavelengths respectively frequencies in the spectral domain is proportional respectively inversely proportional to the eigenvalue.

As in (5) we can reconstruct the signal from the spectral response, noticing again that we have no nullspace components:

Theorem 2. *Let u_* be such that $u_*(0) = f$ and $u_*(t) \to 0$ sufficiently fast for $t \to \infty$, for $* =$ GF,VM,IS. Then*

$$f = \int_0^\infty \phi_*(t)\, dt = \int_0^\infty \psi_*(s)\, ds \qquad \text{for } * = GF, VM, IS. \tag{21}$$

Proof. Due to the consistency relation it suffices to verify the reconstruction formula only for ϕ or ψ. For the appropriate choice the result follows simply by integration by parts, noticing $u_*(t = 0) = f$ and all terms at infinity vanish due to the decay of u.

For the sake of brevity we shall restrict ourselves to the gradient flow case in the following arguments. An interesting property concerns the orthogonality of remaining signal and the spectral transform. In a classical Fourier series we have a decomposition into orthogonal components, so there is natural orthogonality between the spectral part at a certain frequency and the remaining signal at lower or higher frequency (the sum of orthogonal components with higher or lower indices). An analogous property holds for our spectral decomposition, i.e. we expect $u(t)$ to be orthogonal to $\phi(t)$. This can be seen from a formal computation of $\frac{d}{dt}(J(u(t)))$ in two ways. First of all we have

$$\frac{d}{dt}(J(u(t))) = \langle p(t), \partial_t u(t)\rangle = -\|p(t)\|^2.$$

On the other, since for one-homogeneous convex functionals $J(u(t)) = \langle p(t), u(t)\rangle$ holds, we find

$$\frac{d}{dt}(J(u(t))) = \frac{d}{dt}(\langle p(t), u(t)\rangle) = \langle \partial_t p(t), u(t)\rangle + \langle p(t), \partial_t u(t)\rangle = -\frac{1}{t}\langle \phi(t), u(t)\rangle - \|p(t)\|^2.$$

Hence, comparing the terms we obtain the orthogonality relation.

Finally let us discuss the spectral response S, which was defined before as the L^1-norm of ϕ in the TV case as mentioned above. This choice is somewhat arbitrary and in particular difficult to generalize to other functionals, so we need to derive a different version of the spectral response that can be expressed solely in terms of the functional J, the L^2-norm of f, and the method used to derive ϕ. Let us start with the gradient flow, for which it is natural to investigate the energy dissipation, i.e., we compute time derivatives of J. By the chain rule we (formally) find

$$\frac{d}{dt}J(u(t)) = \langle p(t), \partial_t u(t)\rangle = -\|p(t)\|^2.$$

Moreover, in the case of J differentiable, i.e. $p(t) = J'(u(t))$, we have

$$\frac{d^2}{dt^2}J(u(t)) = -2\langle \partial_t p(t), p(t)\rangle = -2\langle J''(u(t))\partial_t u(t), p(t)\rangle = 2\langle J''(u(t))p(t), p(t)\rangle,$$

which is a nonnegative quantity, since J is convex. For the nonsmooth case we might encounter even more interesting spectral responses this way, the nonexistence of a classical second derivative e.g. allows to have concentrated parts. This can be made precise again in the case of f being an eigenfunction for the eigenvalue λ, i.e., (1) holds for $u = f$. Then we know that $p(t) = \lambda f$ for $t < \frac{1}{\lambda}$ and $p(t) = 0$ for larger times. Computing $\|p(t)\|$ and its derivative we immediately find

$$\frac{d^2}{dt^2}J(u(t)) = \lambda^2\|f\|^2\delta_{\frac{1}{\lambda}}(t) = \frac{1}{t^2}\|f\|^2\delta_{\frac{1}{\lambda}}(t). \tag{22}$$

Since apparently $\|f\|$ is a suitable value for the magnitude, we define the spectral response as

$$S(t) = t\sqrt{\frac{d^2}{dt^2}J(u(t))} = \sqrt{\langle \phi(t), 2tp(t)\rangle}. \tag{23}$$

With this definition we have the following analogue of the Parseval identity, which follows again using integration by parts and sufficient decay of u and its derivatives:

$$\|f\|^2 = -\int_0^\infty \frac{d}{dt}\|u(t)\|^2 \, dt = 2\int_0^\infty \langle p(t), u(t)\rangle \, dt = 2\int_0^\infty J(u(t)) \, dt$$
$$= \int_0^\infty S(t)^2 \, dt, \tag{24}$$

which confirms that the spectral representation encodes the full norm of f.

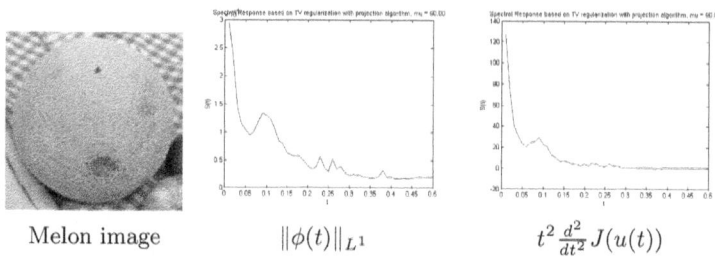

Melon image $\qquad \|\phi(t)\|_{L^1} \qquad t^2 \frac{d^2}{dt^2} J(u(t))$

Fig. 2. Spectral resonse for the total variation flow in an image of a melon (left). The original definition from [15] in the middle and the definition (23) on the right.

In computational experiments, the behaviour S as defined by (23) appears to be more suitable for the spectral decomposition, in particular there are the important maxima marking essential changes in the spectrum but less further oscillations. This is illustrated for total variation flow on an image already considered in [15] in Figure 2. We finally mentioned that a generalization of this definition to variational methods and in particular inverse scale space methods is a nontrivial task and beyond the scope of this paper.

3 Examples

In the following we discuss three interesting examples of one-homogeneous functionals beyond total variation, which all provide interesting spectral definitions in a different context.

3.1 Recovering Fourier Analysis

One particular example for a one-homogeneous regularization functional J which restores a very classical method is $J(u) = \|Vu\|_1$ for an orthonormal linear transform V, e.g. for V corresponding to frequency analyzing transforms like the Fourier or cosine transforms. A similar computation has previously been done by Xu and Osher in [25] in which they analyzed Bregman iteration as well as the inverse scale space flow for V corresponding to a wavelet transformation.

For the sake of simplicity let us consider the discrete problem. For any orthonormal V we obtain

$$\min_u \frac{1}{2}\|u - f\|_2^2 + t\|Vu\|_1, = \min_z \frac{1}{2}\|V^T z - f\|_2^2 + t\|z\|_1,$$
$$= \min_z \frac{1}{2}\|z - Vf\|_2^2 + t\|z\|_1,$$

where we have used the orthonormality of V along with the fact that the ℓ^2 norm is invariant with respect to multiplication with orthonormal matrices. Note that Vf becomes the frequency transform of the input data to which we apply ℓ^1 regularization. The above minimization problem in z admits a closed form solution known as soft-shrinkage, i.e.

$$z_{VM}(t) = \arg\min_z \frac{1}{2}\|z - Vf\|_2^2 + t\|z\|_1 = \mathrm{sign}(Vf)\,\max(|Vf| - t, 0), \quad (25)$$

and hence $u_{VM}(t) = V^T z_{VM}(t)$. The first time derivative of $z_{VM}(t)$ is

$$\partial_t (z_{VM}(t))_i = \begin{cases} 0 & \text{if } |(Vf)_i| < t, \\ -\mathrm{sign}((Vf)_i) & \text{else.} \end{cases} \quad (26)$$

Interestingly, we can see that this means that $\partial_t z_{VM}(t)$ is in its own negative subdifferential, i.e.

$$\partial_t z_{VM}(t) \in -\partial \|z_{VM}\|_1, \quad (27)$$

from which we can conclude that $z_{VM}(t) = z_{GF}(t)$ and $u_{VM}(t) = u_{GF}(t)$. The second time derivative of $z_*(t)$ (for $* \in \{VM, GF\}$) becomes

$$\partial_{tt} (z_*(t))_i = \mathrm{sign}((Vf)_i)\, \delta_{t=|(Vf)_i|}.$$

The wavelength transform function $\phi_*^z(t) = t\partial_{tt} z_*$ is therefore given as

$$(\phi_*^z(t))_i = \delta_{t=|(Vf)_i|}\, (Vf)_i.$$

As we can see the spectral transform ϕ_*^z simply reduces to the spectrum of the frequency coefficients Vf in this case. Moreover, the first possible definition of the spectrum,

$$S_*^z(t) = \|\phi_*^z(t)\|_1 = |\{i \mid |(Vf)_i| = t\}|\, t,$$

reduces to the sum over the absolute values of the frequencies that have magnitude t, when considered with respect to the z variable. With respect to the variable u we obtain $S_*^u(t) = t\|V^T e_{|(Vf)_i|=t}\|_1$, where $e_{|(Vf)_i|=t}$ denotes the vector with the ith entry being one if $|(Vf)_i| = t$ and zero else. Since for random DCT coefficients of f the vector $e_{|(Vf)_i|=t}$ is at most one-sparse with probability one, the peaks of the spectrum have magnitude $|(Vf)_i|\|v_i\|_1$ where v_i is the ith row of V. Since $\|v_i\|_1$ is not the same for all i and also does not have a specific interpretation, definition (23), i.e.

$$S(t) = t\sqrt{\frac{d^2}{dt^2} J(u(t))} = t\sqrt{\frac{d^2}{dt^2}\|Vu(t)\|_1} = t\sqrt{\frac{d^2}{dt^2}\|z(t)\|_1} \quad (28)$$

is preferable since it does not depend on the u or z representation. Since the first time derivative of $\|z(t)\|_1$ is just the number of nonzero entries of z, we obtain $S(t) = \sqrt{|\{i \mid |(Vf)_i| = t\}|}\, t$.

Finally, let us consider the third possible definition of a spectral definition, i.e. the inverse scale space flow. By following [25], we obtain

$$z_{IS}(s) = \begin{cases} 0 & \text{if } s|(Vf)_i| < 1, \\ -\text{sign}((Vf)_i) & \text{else.} \end{cases} \quad (29)$$

such that for $t = 1/s$ we obtain $z_{IS}(t) = z_{VM}(t) = z_{GF}(t)$ and all three definitions of wavelength and frequency representations coincide.

Figure 3 shows an example of the above setup using the discrete cosine transform (DCT) for V. As we can see, the low pass reconstructions are obtained as hard thresholdings of the coefficients, which is what we refer to as an ideal low pass filter.

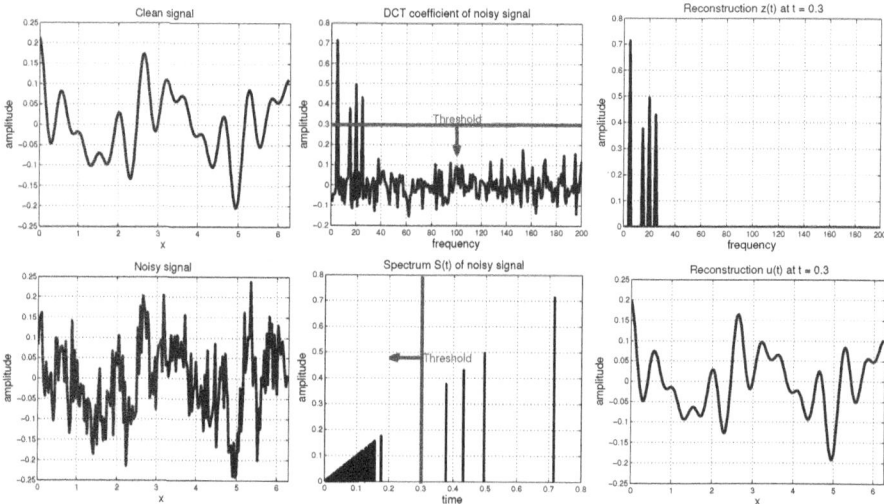

Fig. 3. Recovering classical spectral analysis: The upper left plot shows a clean signal suitable for classical spectral analysis, and below is its noisy version. The upper middle image shows the classical processing/denoising of such data. One determines the DCT coefficients and eliminates contributions of frequencies whose magnitude is below a certain threshold. The lower middle image shows the spectrum $S(t)$ we obtain with the proposed approach with $J(u) = \|Vu\|_1$ for all three variants of the spectral analysis. Due to the obvious separation of four of the peaks from the remaining ones, one could similarly choose to reconstruct the solution at time $t = 0.3$, which is equivalent to the threshold of 0.3 in the classical sense. The right plots show $z(0.3)$ and $u(0.3)$, i.e. the reconstruction of the ideal filter in the DCT and spatial domains.

3.2 Total Generalized Variation

Let us now look at a highly nonlinear variational approach and consider the second order total generalized variation (TGV) of [9], which – for sufficiently regular u – can be written as $J(u) = \min_{\nabla u = v + z} \beta \|v\|_1 + (1 - \beta) \|\nabla z\|_1$.

Figure 4 shows an analysis similar to the classical one of Figure 3, but now for the inverse TGV flow using $\beta = 0.05$. We provide the full movie showing the

$u(t)$ throughout an evolution of 1500 time steps in the supplementary material of this paper. As we can see, applying an ideal low pass filter leads to almost perfect reconstructions for signals consisting of piecewise linear parts and jumps.

This general behavior can be understood by considering eigenfunctions of the TGV. Examining our previous observations on the favorable properties of the spectral decomposition techniques on eigenfuctions as well as the observations in [8], eigenfunctions should reveal the types of signals the regularization 'likes' in the sense that they can be reconstructed easily. Recalling the TGV eigenfunction analysis in [7,19] one can observe that indeed the appearance of the eigenfunction coincides with our numerical observations in the spectral analysis: The original signal f is approximated by sequences of piecewise linear functions with discontinuities.

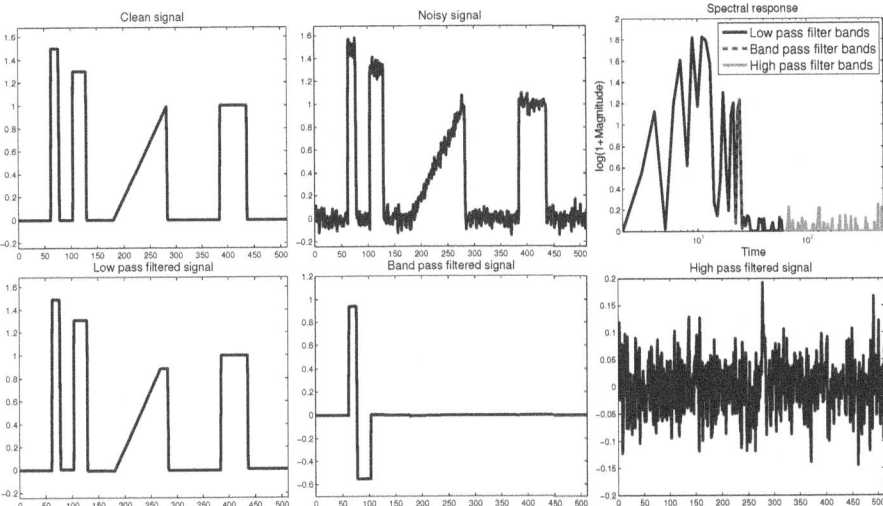

Fig. 4. Inverse scale space spectral analysis of a signal using TGV regularization. After we added noise to the clean signal (upper left) we obtain the noisy version shown in the upper middle. The spectrum we obtain using TGV analysis with $S(t) = \|\phi(t)\|_1$ is shown in the upper right in a semi logarithmic plot. By low pass, band pass or high pass filtering the spectral decomposition (marked blue, red and green in the spectrum) we obtain the lower left, middle, and right signals respectively. As we can see one can obtain nice reconstructions of the true signal by the low pass filtering. Certain frequencies (like the two peaks of the true signal) are contained in intermediate bands and can be isolated by band pass filtering. The high pass filter contains mostly noise.

3.3 Coupled Signal Analysis

As a third example, we'd like to mention that spectral decomposition could also serve as a tool for collaboratively analyzing input data. Just to point out possible applications, Figure 5 shows two examples: The left part corresponds to an analysis of 15 different input signals $f \in \mathbb{R}^{n \times 15}$ with the collaborative sparse regularization $J(u) = \|u\|_{\infty,1} = \sum_i \max_j |u_{i,j}|$. Similar to the DCT case, the problem decouples in one direction and yields ℓ^∞ regularized subproblems in each component. As we can see in the left part of figure 5, an ideal low-pass reconstruction yields exactly those peaks for which all input signals in f had non-zero entries.

Similar concepts could also be derived for collaborative jumps as shown in the right of 5, in which we used $J(u) = \|\nabla u\|_{\infty,1}$. As we can see, a strong low-pass filter leads to the best single joint jump approximation in our example.

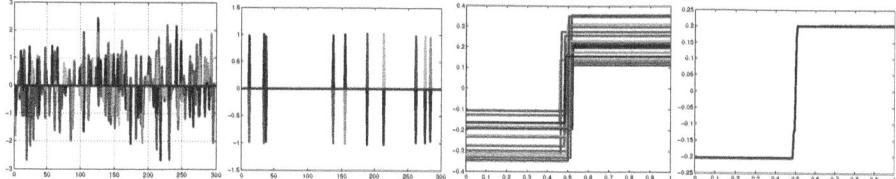

Fig. 5. Collaborative spectral analysis. Left: Fifteen different sparse input signals that have exactly ten peaks at common positions. Middle left: Ideal low pass filter in the $\|u\|_{\infty,1}$ sense – as we can see the location of the common nonzero peaks is recovered. Middle right: Fifteen input signals that all have a jump around the position 0.5. Right: Ideal low pass filter in the $\|\nabla u\|_{\infty,1}$ sense – all fifteen signals are approximated by one function which can be interpreted as the optimal single jump approximation of the input signals and hence naturally reflects the coarsest scale.

4 Conclusion

In this paper the theory of nonlinear spectral representation was generalized and extended in several ways. The framework of [16] was extended from the total variation functional to general one-homogeneous convex functionals. Analogue transform representations were formulated based on variational regularization and on inverse-scale-space [11] (in addition to the original gradient flow formulation). Moreover, an orthogonality of the decomposition is established and a new spectrum is suggested. Roughly, the spectrum measures the degree of activity of each scale. Here the spectrum is intrinsic to the functional space and can be viewed as a natural nonlinear extension of Parseval's identity. Three examples of smoothing one-homogeneous functionals, other than TV, illustrate possible benefits of this approach for enhanced image and signal representation.

Acknowledgments. MB acknowledges support by ERC via Grant EU FP 7 - ERC Consolidator Grant 615216 LifeInverse.

References

1. Andreu, F., Ballester, C., Caselles, V., Mazón, J.M.: Minimizing total variation flow. Differential and Integral Equations **14**(3), 321–360 (2001)
2. Andreu, F., Caselles, V., Díaz, J., Mazón, J.: Some qualitative properties for the total variation flow. Journal of Functional Analysis **188**(2), 516–547 (2002)

3. Aujol, J., Gilboa, G., Chan, T., Osher, S.: Structure-texture image decomposition - modeling, algorithms, and parameter selection. Int. J. Comp. Vision **67**, 111–136 (2006)
4. Bartels, S., Nochetto, R., Abner, J., Salgado, A.: Discrete total variation flows without regularization. arXiv preprint arXiv:1212.1137 (2012)
5. Belkin, M., Niyogi, P.: Laplacian eigenmaps for dimensionality reduction and data representation. Neural Computation **15**(6), 1373–1396 (2003)
6. Bellettini, G., Caselles, V., Novaga, M.: The total variation flow in R^N. Journal of Differential Equations **184**(2), 475–525 (2002)
7. Benning, M., Brune, C., Burger, M., Müller, J.: Higher-order tv methods: enhancement via bregman iteration. J. Sci. Comput. **54**, 269–310 (2013)
8. Benning, M., Burger, M.: Ground states and singular vectors of convex variational regularization methods. Meth. Appl. Analysis **20**(4), 295–334 (2013)
9. Bredies, K., Kunisch, K., Pock, T.: Total generalized variation. SIAM J. Imaging Sciences **3**(3), 492–526 (2010)
10. Burger, M., Frick, K., Osher, S., Scherzer, O.: Inverse total variation flow. Multiscale Modeling & Simulation **6**(2), 366–395 (2007)
11. Burger, M., Gilboa, G., Osher, S., Xu, J.: Nonlinear inverse scale space methods. Comm. in Math. Sci. **4**(1), 179–212 (2006)
12. Chan, T.F., Osher, S., Shen, J.: The digital TV filter and nonlinear denoising. IEEE Trans. Image Process. **10**(2), 231–241 (2001)
13. Eckardt, L.: Spektralzerlegung von Bildern mit TV-methoden, bachelor thesis, University of Münster (2014)
14. Giga, Y., Kohn, R.: Scale-invariant extinction time estimates for some singular diffusion equations. Hokkaido University Preprint Series in Mathematics (963) (2010)
15. Gilboa, G.: A spectral approach to total variation. In: Kuijper, A., Bredies, K., Pock, T., Bischof, H. (eds.) SSVM 2013. LNCS, vol. 7893, pp. 36–47. Springer, Heidelberg (2013)
16. Gilboa, G.: A total variation spectral framework for scale and texture analysis. SIAM J. Imaging Sciences **7**(4), 1937–1961 (2014)
17. Liu, G., Lin, Z., Yan, S., Sun, J., Yu, Y., Ma, Y.: Robust recovery of subspace structures by low-rank representation. IEEE Transactions on Pattern Analysis and Machine Intelligence **35**(1), 171–184 (2013)
18. Meyer, Y.: Oscillating patterns in image processing and in some nonlinear evolution equations (2001)
19. Müller, J.: Advanced image reconstruction and denoising: Bregmanized (higher order) total variation and application in pet, Ph.D. Thesis, Univ. Münster (2013)
20. Ng, A., Jordan, M., Weiss, Y.: On spectral clustering: Analysis and an algorithm. Advances in Neural Information Processing Systems **2**, 849–856 (2002)
21. Osher, S., Sole, A., Vese, L.: Image decomposition and restoration using total variation minimization and the H^{-1} norm. SIAM Multiscale Model. Simul. **1**, 349–370 (2003)
22. Rudin, L., Osher, S., Fatemi, E.: Nonlinear total variation based noise removal algorithms. Physica D **60**, 259–268 (1992)
23. Shi, J., Malik, J.: Normalized cuts and image segmentation. IEEE Transactions on Pattern Analysis and Machine Intelligence **22**(8), 888–905 (2000)
24. Steidl, G., Weickert, J., Brox, T., Mrzek, P., Welk, M.: On the equivalence of soft wavelet shrinkage, total variation diffusion, total variation regularization, and SIDEs. SIAM Journal on Numerical Analysis **42**(2), 686–713 (2004)
25. Xu, J., Osher, S.: Iterative regularization and nonlinear inverse scale space applied to wavelet-based denoising. IEEE Trans. Image Processing **16**(2), 534–544 (2007)

The Morphological Equivalents of Relativistic and Alpha-Scale-Spaces

Martin Schmidt$^{(\boxtimes)}$ and Joachim Weickert

Mathematical Image Analysis Group, Faculty of Mathematics and Computer Science,
Saarland University, Campus E1.7, 66041 Saarbrücken, Germany
{schmidt,weickert}@mia.uni-saarland.de

Abstract. The relations between linear system theory and mathematical morphology are mainly understood on a pure convolution/dilation level. A formal connection on the level of differential or pseudo-differential equations is still missing. In our paper we close this gap. We establish the sought relation by means of infinitesimal generators, exploring essential properties of the slope and a modified Cramér transform. As an application of our general theory, we derive the morphological counterparts of relativistic scale-spaces and of α-scale-spaces for $\alpha \in [\frac{1}{2}, \infty)$. Our findings are illustrated by experiments.

Keywords: Mathematical morphology · Alpha-scale-spaces · Relativistic scale-spaces · Cramér transform · Slope transform

1 Introduction

Linear system theory and mathematical morphology are two successful and widely-used concepts in signal and image processing. It is well-known that any shift-invariant linear system can be described as a convolution that can be elegantly computed as multiplication in the Fourier domain [14]. On the other hand, morphological systems are based on dilations with a concave structuring function, which comes down to additions in the slope domain [7,15]. First insights into the quasi-logarithmic connection between both worlds have been obtained by Burgeth and Weickert [5]: While linear system theory uses the classical algebra $(\mathbb{R}, \cdot, +)$, they showed that mathematical morphology is a system theory in the max-plus algebra $(\mathbb{R} \cup \{-\infty\}, +, \max)$. Moreover, they described this relation by means of the Cramér transform. So far, this formal connection is restricted to the level of convolutions on the linear system theory side and dilations on the morphological side.

Continuous-scale interpretations of both frameworks allow to describe linear and morphological systems in terms of partial differential equations (PDEs) or pseudo-differential equations. For example, Gaussian convolution comes down to a homogeneous diffusion equation, whose evolution in time creates the so-called Gaussian scale-space [11,12,21]. More recently, scale-spaces based on pseudo-differential operators have attracted attention, such as the Poisson scale-space [9], its embedding into the family of α-scale-spaces [8], and relativistic scale-spaces [4]. On the morphological side, continuous-scale versions of dilations are given by hyperbolic PDEs [2,19].

An interesting equivalence between Gaussian scale-space and morphological dilation with a quadratic structuring function has been discovered by van den Boomgaard [17]: While Gaussians are the only separable and rotationally invariant convolution kernels, quadratic functions are the only separable and rotationally invariant structuring functions. Other formal equivalences between the (pseudo-)differential operators governing linear shift-invariant scale-spaces and morphological scale-spaces are not known so far.

The goal of our paper is to address this problem. We establish a general theory that allows to transform a scale-scale evolution from one of these worlds to the other world. This framework extends the results of Burgeth and Weickert [5] to differential and pseudo-differential operators. In particular, it enables us to derive the morphological counterparts of α-scale-spaces for $\alpha \in [\frac{1}{2}, \infty)$, and of relativistic scale-spaces.

Organisation of the Paper. Sections 2 and 3 review relevant concepts for linear shift-invariant scale-spaces and morphological scale-spaces, respectively. These facts allow us to derive our general framework in Section 4. The fifth Section applies our theory to α-scale-spaces and relativistic scale-spaces. Experiments in Section 6 illustrate the behaviour of their morphological counterparts. Our paper is concluded with a summary in Section 7.

2 Convolution Scale-Spaces

Let us consider some bounded greyscale image $f : \mathbb{R}^2 \to \mathbb{R}$. A scale-space representation of f embeds this image into a family $u(.,t)$ of gradually smoother versions, where the scale parameter ("time") t determines the amount of smoothing or image simplification: $t = 0$ yields $u(.,0) = f$, and larger values for t correspond to simpler versions of f with less structure. Reasonable scale-spaces have to satisfy a number of architectural properties, simplification qualities, and invariances [1]. Typically their evolutions w.r.t. the scale-parameter t can be expressed in terms of differential or pseudo-differential equations. In our paper we focus on scale-space evolutions that are both linear and shift-invariant. More specifically, we consider the following processes:

- **Gaussian Scale-Space.** It computes smoothed versions $u(\boldsymbol{x},t)$ of $f(\boldsymbol{x})$ as solutions of the initial value problem

$$\partial_t u = \Delta u \quad \text{on } \mathbb{R}^2 \times (0,\infty), \qquad (1)$$
$$u(\boldsymbol{x},0) = f(\boldsymbol{x}) \quad \text{on } \mathbb{R}^2, \qquad (2)$$

where Δ denotes the spatial Laplace operator. It goes back to Iijima [11,20] and became popular in the western world by the work of Witkin [21], Koenderink [12], Lindeberg [13], and Florack [10] and many others.

- **α-Scale-Spaces.** They replace the homogeneous diffusion equation (1) by the pseudo-differential equation

$$\partial_t u = -(-\Delta)^\alpha u \tag{3}$$

with some parameter $\alpha \in (0, \infty)$. While these processes can already be found implicitly in Iijima's work [11], they became popular as scale-spaces due to a paper by Duits et al. [8]. Gaussian scale-space is recovered for $\alpha = 1$, while $\alpha = \frac{1}{2}$ gives the so-called Poisson scale-space [9]. If one renounces a maximum–minimum principle, one can also study scale-spaces for $\alpha > 1$, comprising e.g. the biharmonic scale-space for $\alpha = 2$ [6].

- **Relativistic Scale-Spaces.** Burgeth et al. [4] have advocated a generalisation of the Poisson scale-space by considering the evolution equation

$$\partial_t u = -\left(\sqrt{-\Delta + m^2} - m\right) u, \tag{4}$$

with $m \geq 0$.

Since all these processes are linear and shift-invariant, they can be expressed by convolutions with a suitable kernel k_t:

$$u(.,t) = k_t * f. \tag{5}$$

Thus, we can call such a linear, shift-invariant scale-space also a *convolution scale-space*. For some of the beforementioned convolution scale-spaces, however, the kernel does not have a closed form representation in the spatial domain. One exception is Gaussian scale-space, for which the kernel is given by the Gaussian

$$g_t(\boldsymbol{x}) = \frac{1}{4\pi t} \exp\left(-\frac{|\boldsymbol{x}|^2}{4t}\right). \tag{6}$$

For kernels that do not have a closed form representation in the spatial domain, it can be convenient to use a closed form description in the Fourier domain: We define the Fourier transform by

$$\hat{u}(\boldsymbol{\nu}) := \mathcal{F}[u](\boldsymbol{\nu}) := \int_{\mathbb{R}^2} u(\boldsymbol{x}) \, e^{-2\pi i \langle \boldsymbol{\nu}, \boldsymbol{x} \rangle} \, d\boldsymbol{x} \tag{7}$$

where $i^2 = -1$ and $\langle .,. \rangle$ denotes the Euclidean inner product. Then the Fourier transforms of the convolution kernels of the individual scale-spaces are summarised in Table 1.

Knowing such a kernel representation $\hat{k}_t(\boldsymbol{\nu})$ allows to compute the scale-space image $u(\boldsymbol{x},t)$ from its Fourier transform

$$\hat{u}(\boldsymbol{\nu},t) = \hat{k}_t(\boldsymbol{\nu}) \cdot \hat{f}(\boldsymbol{\nu}). \tag{8}$$

Table 1. Linear shift-invariant scale-spaces and the Fourier transform of their convolution kernels [3,4,8]

scale-space	Fourier transform of convolution kernel
Gaussian scale-space	$\hat{g}_t(\boldsymbol{\nu}) = \exp\left(-t\,|2\pi\boldsymbol{\nu}|^2\right)$
α-scale-spaces	$\hat{a}_{\alpha,t}(\boldsymbol{\nu}) = \exp\left(-t\,|2\pi\boldsymbol{\nu}|^{2\alpha}\right)$
relativistic scale-spaces	$\hat{r}_{m,t}(\boldsymbol{\nu}) = \exp\left(-t(\sqrt{|2\pi\boldsymbol{\nu}|^2 + m^2} - m)\right)$

3 Morphological Scale-Spaces

Mathematical morphology is based on the concepts of dilation and erosion. The dilation $\oplus$ resp. erosion $\ominus$ of an image f with some structuring function $s : \mathbb{R}^2 \to \mathbb{R} \cup \{-\infty\}$ is defined as

$$(f \oplus s)(\boldsymbol{x}) := \sup_{\boldsymbol{y} \in \mathbb{R}^2} \{f(\boldsymbol{y}) + s(\boldsymbol{x}-\boldsymbol{y})\}, \tag{9}$$

$$(f \ominus s)(\boldsymbol{x}) := \inf_{\boldsymbol{y} \in \mathbb{R}^2} \{f(\boldsymbol{y}) - s(\boldsymbol{y}-\boldsymbol{x})\}. \tag{10}$$

In the following, we only focus on dilation for our derivations.

In order to create scale-space, one performs a so-called *umbral scaling* of the structuring function $s(\boldsymbol{x})$, resulting in

$$s_t(\boldsymbol{x}) := t\, s\left(\frac{\boldsymbol{x}}{t}\right). \tag{11}$$

With $u(.,0) := f$, the (dilation) scale-space evolution $\{u(.,t) \mid t \geq 0\}$ of f is given by

$$u(.,t) = f \oplus s_t. \tag{12}$$

It is possible to derive PDE formulations for such scale-space evolutions, if one considers the *slope transform* of s [7,15]:

$$\mathcal{S}[s](\boldsymbol{w}) := \operatorname*{stat}_{\boldsymbol{x} \in \mathbb{R}^2} \{s(\boldsymbol{x}) - \langle \boldsymbol{w}, \boldsymbol{x}\rangle\}, \tag{13}$$

where the *stationary values* $\operatorname{stat}_{\boldsymbol{x}}\{h(\boldsymbol{x})\}$ denote the set of function values for which the gradient is zero:

$$\operatorname*{stat}_{\boldsymbol{x} \in \mathbb{R}^2} \{h(\boldsymbol{x})\} := \{h(\boldsymbol{x}) \mid \nabla h(\boldsymbol{x}) = \boldsymbol{0}\}. \tag{14}$$

With these definitions, Dorst and van den Boomgaard [18] have shown that $u(\boldsymbol{x},t)$ from (12) is the solution of

$$\partial_t u = \mathcal{S}[s](\nabla u) \quad \text{on } \mathbb{R}^2 \times (0,\infty), \tag{15}$$
$$u(\boldsymbol{x},0) = f(\boldsymbol{x}) \quad \text{on } \mathbb{R}^2. \tag{16}$$

For instance, choosing $s(\boldsymbol{x}) = -\frac{1}{4}|\boldsymbol{x}|^2$ as structuring function gives $\mathcal{S}[s](\boldsymbol{w}) = \boldsymbol{w}^2$. Thus, (15) becomes

$$\partial_t u = |\boldsymbol{\nabla} u|^2. \tag{17}$$

Van den Boomgaard has shown that quadratic structuring functions are the only structuring functions that are rotationally invariant and separable [17]. This has motivated him to regard (17) as the morphological equivalent of the Gaussian scale-space, since the latter one is the only scale-space with a rotationally invariant and separable convolution kernel.

If one uses as structuring function a flat disc

$$s(\boldsymbol{x}) = \begin{cases} 0 & (|\boldsymbol{x}| \leq 1), \\ -\infty & (\text{else}), \end{cases} \tag{18}$$

it has been shown in [2] that one arrives at

$$\partial_t u = |\boldsymbol{\nabla} u|. \tag{19}$$

So far, it was an open question if this equation has a corresponding convolution scale-space. We will answer this later on.

In our following discussion, we will also need the *inverse slope transform*. It is given by (see e.g. [7])

$$\mathcal{S}^{-1}[h](\boldsymbol{x}) = \underset{\boldsymbol{y} \in \mathbb{R}^2}{\operatorname{stat}} \{h(\boldsymbol{y}) + \langle \boldsymbol{x}, \boldsymbol{y} \rangle\}. \tag{20}$$

4 Morphological Equivalents of Convolution Scale-Spaces

In order to establish a connection between linear system theory and mathematical morphology, we follow [5]. However, instead of using the *Laplace transform*

$$\mathcal{L}[f](\boldsymbol{x}) = \int_{\mathbb{R}^2} f(\boldsymbol{x}) e^{\langle \boldsymbol{x}, \boldsymbol{y} \rangle} d\boldsymbol{y}, \tag{21}$$

we base our computations on the Fourier transform. This has the advantage that we do not require f to decay fast enough at infinity. We introduce a modified version of the Cramér transform which we call *Cramér-Fourier transform*:

$$\mathcal{C}_\mathcal{F}[f](\boldsymbol{x}) := \left(-\log(\mathcal{F}[f](\tfrac{\cdot}{2\pi}))\right)^*(\boldsymbol{x}). \tag{22}$$

Here, $\log \mathcal{F}[f]$ is assumed to be concave, and h^* denotes the *convex conjugate* of a function h:

$$h^*(\boldsymbol{x}^*) := \sup_{\boldsymbol{x} \in \mathbb{R}^2} \{\langle \boldsymbol{x}, \boldsymbol{x}^* \rangle - h(\boldsymbol{x})\}. \tag{23}$$

The key property of the Cramér transform is that it allows to convert a convolution in the usual algebra $(\mathbb{R}, \cdot, +)$ into a dilation in the max-plus algebra $(\mathbb{R} \cup \{-\infty\}, +, \max)$. This was proven by Burgeth and Weickert [5]. In the following lemma we prove the same result for the Cramér-Fourier transform.

Lemma 1. *For two functions f and g with concave logarithmic Fourier transform, it holds*

$$-\mathcal{C}_\mathcal{F}[f*g] = (-\mathcal{C}_\mathcal{F}[f]) \oplus (-\mathcal{C}_\mathcal{F}[g]). \tag{24}$$

Proof. Since convolution in the Fourier domain becomes multiplication, we have

$$\log \mathcal{F}[f*g] = \log(\mathcal{F}[f]\mathcal{F}[g]) = \log \mathcal{F}[f] + \log \mathcal{F}[g]. \tag{25}$$

Together with a well-known property of convex conjugation (see e.g [16]),

$$(f+g)^*(\boldsymbol{x}) = \inf_{\boldsymbol{y}\in\mathbb{R}^2}(f^*(\boldsymbol{y}) + g^*(\boldsymbol{x}-\boldsymbol{y})), \tag{26}$$

it follows that

$$-\mathcal{C}_\mathcal{F}[u*k_t](\boldsymbol{x}) = -\left(-\log(\mathcal{F}[u](\tfrac{\cdot}{2\pi})) - \log(\mathcal{F}[k_t](\tfrac{\cdot}{2\pi}))\right)^*(\boldsymbol{x}) \tag{27}$$

$$= -\inf_{\boldsymbol{y}\in\mathbb{R}^2}(\mathcal{C}_\mathcal{F}[u](\boldsymbol{y}) + \mathcal{C}_\mathcal{F}[k_t](\boldsymbol{x}-\boldsymbol{y})) \tag{28}$$

$$= \sup_{\boldsymbol{y}\in\mathbb{R}^2}(-\mathcal{C}_\mathcal{F}[u](\boldsymbol{y}) - \mathcal{C}_\mathcal{F}[k_t](\boldsymbol{x}-\boldsymbol{y})) \tag{29}$$

$$= (-\mathcal{C}_\mathcal{F}[u]) \oplus (-\mathcal{C}_\mathcal{F}[k_t])(\boldsymbol{x}). \tag{30}$$

□

In the following we say that a morphological scale-space is *equivalent* to a convolution scale-space, if they result from each other by exchanging the above two algebras. With these definitions and results we can state our main theorem.

Theorem 1. (Morphological Equivalents of Convolution Scale-Spaces). *The morphological equivalents of a convolution scale-space $u(t,\cdot) = f*k_t$ are solutions of*

$$\partial_t u = \overline{\log \mathcal{F}[k_1]}(\tfrac{1}{2\pi}\nabla u), \tag{31}$$

$$u(\cdot, 0) = f, \tag{32}$$

where the bar notation describes $\bar{h}(\boldsymbol{x}) := -h(-\boldsymbol{x})$.

Proof. As a first step we note that for some strictly convex function h we have

$$h^* = \mathcal{S}^{-1}[-h]. \tag{33}$$

This can be seen with the definition (20) of the inverse slope transform:

$$\mathcal{S}^{-1}[-h](\boldsymbol{x}) = \operatorname*{stat}_{\boldsymbol{y}\in\mathbb{R}^2}\{-h(\boldsymbol{y}) + \langle \boldsymbol{x},\boldsymbol{y}\rangle\} \tag{34}$$

$$= \sup_{\boldsymbol{y}\in\mathbb{R}^2}\{\langle \boldsymbol{x},\boldsymbol{y}\rangle - h(\boldsymbol{y})\} = h^*(\boldsymbol{x}), \tag{35}$$

since $\langle \boldsymbol{x},\boldsymbol{y}\rangle - h(\boldsymbol{y})$ is strictly concave in $\boldsymbol{y}$. Therefore, it has a unique stationary value which is a supremum. This proves (33).

With (24), it follows that $-\mathcal{C}_{\mathcal{F}}[k_t]$ creates a morphological scale-space as given in (15)–(16): We obtain

$$\begin{align}
\mathcal{S}[-\mathcal{C}_{\mathcal{F}}[k_1]] &= \overline{\mathcal{S}[\mathcal{C}_{\mathcal{F}}[k_1]]} && \text{(definition of } \mathcal{S}) & (36)\\
&= \overline{\mathcal{S}[(-\log \mathcal{F}[k_1](\tfrac{\cdot}{2\pi}))^*]} && \text{(definition (22))} & (37)\\
&= \overline{\mathcal{S}[\mathcal{S}^{-1}[\log \mathcal{F}[k_1](\tfrac{\cdot}{2\pi})]]} && \text{(equation (33))} & (38)\\
&= \overline{\log \mathcal{F}[k_1](\tfrac{\cdot}{2\pi})}. && & (39)
\end{align}$$

This implies the announced equations. □

It should be noted that Theorem 1 is also applicable in those cases where one does not have a closed form representation of the kernel k_t: It is sufficient to know a closed form representation of the Fourier transformed kernel $\hat{k}_t$.

5 Application to Specific Scale-Spaces

Now we are in a position to apply our theory to a number of convolution scale-spaces in order to derive their morphological counterparts.

5.1 Gaussian Scale-Space

Table 1 specifies the Fourier transform of the convolution kernel for Gaussian scale-space as

$$\mathcal{F}[g_t](\boldsymbol{\nu}) = \exp\left(-t|2\pi\boldsymbol{\nu}|^2\right). \tag{40}$$

Thus,

$$\mathcal{F}[g_t](\tfrac{1}{2\pi}\boldsymbol{x}) = \exp\left(-t|\boldsymbol{x}|^2\right) \tag{41}$$

and Theorem 1 gives the morphological evolution equation

$$\partial_t u = \overline{\log \mathcal{F}[g_1]}(\tfrac{1}{2\pi}\boldsymbol{\nabla} u) = |\boldsymbol{\nabla} u|^2. \tag{42}$$

As expected, this coincides with van den Boomgaard's result [17]. The corresponding structuring function is known to be

$$s_t(\boldsymbol{x}) = -\tfrac{1}{4t}|\boldsymbol{x}|^2. \tag{43}$$

5.2 α-Scale-Spaces

In the same way as above, one can show that the morphological equivalents for the α-scale-spaces are given by

$$\partial_t u = |\boldsymbol{\nabla} u|^{2\alpha}. \tag{44}$$

Interestingly, this proves that for $\alpha = \tfrac{1}{2}$, the convolution counterpart of the widely-used morphological scale-space

$$\partial_t u = |\boldsymbol{\nabla} u|, \tag{45}$$

which describe dilation with a flat disc of radius t, is given by the Poisson scale-space

$$\partial_t u = -\sqrt{-\Delta}\, u. \tag{46}$$

This is a scenario where the morphological process looks simpler and has been discovered nine years before its convolution pendant that involves a pseudo-differential operator [2,9].

It is also instructive to use our framework for deriving the structuring functions $s_{\alpha,t}$ for the family of morphological α-scale-spaces. Using (15) we know that the dilation α-scale-spaces have to satisfy

$$\mathcal{S}[s_{\alpha,1}](\boldsymbol{\nabla} u) = \partial_t u = |\boldsymbol{\nabla} u|^{2\alpha}. \tag{47}$$

Thus, we can compute s_α with the help of the inverse slope transform and some properties of the convex conjugate (see e.g. [16]):

$$s_{\alpha,t} = \mathcal{S}^{-1}\left[t|\boldsymbol{x}|^{2\alpha}\right] = -(t|\boldsymbol{x}|^{2\alpha})^* \tag{48}$$

where we have used $\mathcal{S}^{-1}[h] = -h^*$ for a strictly convex h. Since

$$\left(\tfrac{1}{2\alpha}|\boldsymbol{x}|^{2\alpha}\right)^* = \tfrac{2\alpha-1}{2\alpha}|\boldsymbol{x}|^{\frac{2\alpha}{2\alpha-1}}, \tag{49}$$

we get an explicit representation of the structuring function:

$$s_{\alpha,t}(\boldsymbol{x}) = -\left(2t\alpha\, \tfrac{1}{2\alpha}|\boldsymbol{x}|^{2\alpha}\right)^* = -t(2\alpha-1)\left|\frac{\boldsymbol{x}}{t 2\alpha}\right|^{\frac{2\alpha}{2\alpha-1}}. \tag{50}$$

Although this formula only holds for $\alpha > \tfrac{1}{2}$, where strictly concave of the structuring function is guaranteed, we can compute the pointwise limit

$$\lim_{\alpha \to \frac{1}{2}^+} s_{\alpha,t}(\boldsymbol{x}) = \begin{cases} 0 & |\boldsymbol{x}| \leq t, \\ -\infty & (\text{else}) \end{cases} \tag{51}$$

and obtain a flat disc of radius t.

5.3 Relativistic Scale-Spaces

From Table 1 we know that

$$\mathcal{F}[r_{m,t}](\boldsymbol{\nu}) = \exp\left(-t(\sqrt{|2\pi\boldsymbol{\nu}|^2 + m^2} - m)\right). \tag{52}$$

This gives

$$\overline{\log \mathcal{F}[r_{m,t}]}(\tfrac{1}{2\pi}\boldsymbol{x}) = t(\sqrt{|\boldsymbol{x}|^2 + m^2} - m), \tag{53}$$

and applying Theorem 1 yields the evolution equation of the morphological counterpart for the the relativistic space-spaces:

$$\partial_t u = \sqrt{|\boldsymbol{\nabla} u|^2 + m^2} - m. \tag{54}$$

The structuring function can be computed as before as the negative of the convex conjugate of (53):

$$s_{m,t}(\boldsymbol{x}) = -(t(\sqrt{|\boldsymbol{x}|^2 + m^2} - m))^* \tag{55}$$

$$= -\sup_{\boldsymbol{y} \in \mathbb{R}^2} \left(-t(\sqrt{|\boldsymbol{x}|^2 + m^2} - m) + \langle \boldsymbol{x}, \boldsymbol{y} \rangle \right). \tag{56}$$

With the solution for $\boldsymbol{y}$ given by

$$\boldsymbol{y} = \frac{\boldsymbol{x}\, m}{t^2 - |\boldsymbol{x}|^2} \tag{57}$$

for $|\boldsymbol{x}| \le t$, it follows that

$$s_{m,t}(\boldsymbol{x}) = \begin{cases} m\, t \left(\sqrt{1 - \left(\frac{|\boldsymbol{x}|}{t}\right)^2} - 1 \right) & |\boldsymbol{x}| \le t \\ -\infty & \text{(else)}. \end{cases} \tag{58}$$

For $m \to 0$ $s_{m,t}$ converges to a flat disc of radius t. This is expected from the results from the last section since the relativistic scale-spaces converge to the Poisson scale-space for $m \to 0$ and we identified the flat disc of radius t as the structuring function corresponding to the morphological Poisson scale-space. Table 2 summarises the results of this section.

Table 2. Equations for linear scale-spaces and their morphological equivalents

scale-space	linear (pseudo-)PDE	morphological PDE
Gaussian	$\partial_t u = \Delta u$	$\partial_t u = |\nabla u|^2$
Poisson	$\partial_t u = -\sqrt{-\Delta}\, u$	$\partial_t u = |\nabla u|$
α	$\partial_t u = -(-\Delta)^\alpha u$	$\partial_t u = |\nabla u|^{2\alpha}$
relativistic	$\partial_t u = -\left(\sqrt{-\Delta + m^2} - m\right) u$	$\partial_t u = \sqrt{|\nabla u|^2 + m^2} - m$

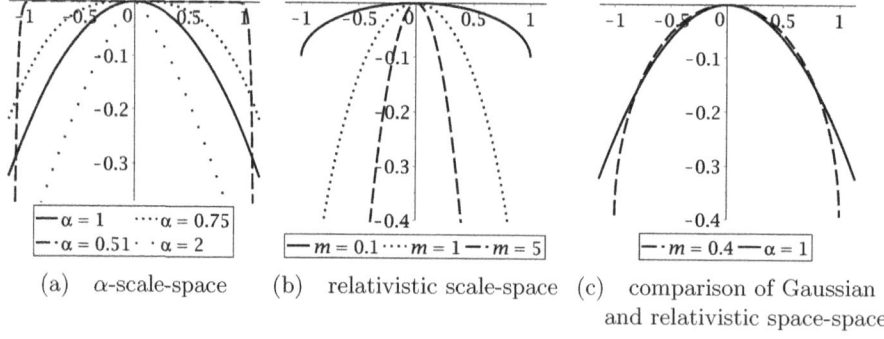

(a) α-scale-space   (b) relativistic scale-space   (c) comparison of Gaussian and relativistic space-space

Fig. 1. Structuring functions for morphological scale-spaces

6 Experiments

Figure 1 shows a comparison of the structuring functions for all discussed scale-spaces. In these examples, t was chosen to be 1 since umbral scaling can be used to obtain structuring functions for smaller or larger values of t.

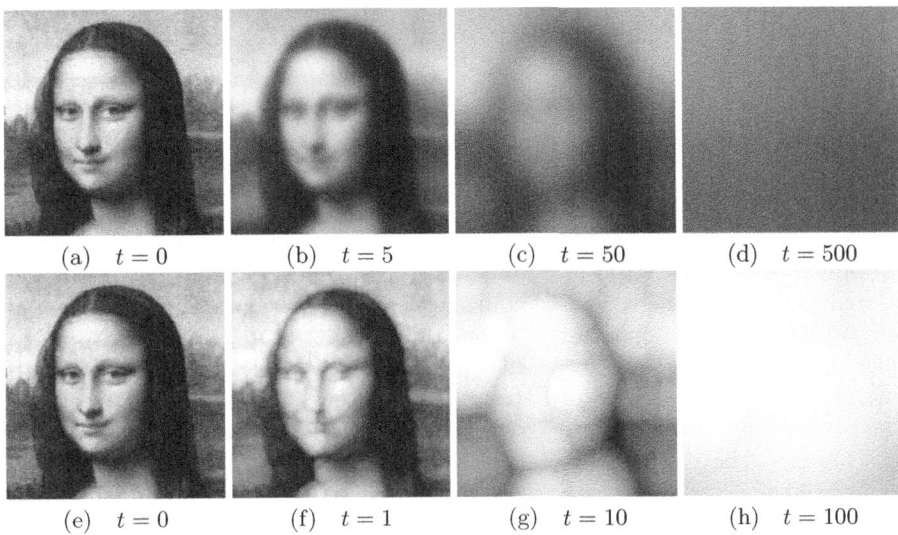

Fig. 2. Top: α-scale-space for $\alpha = 0.75$, Bottom: Morphological α-scale-space for $\alpha = 0.75$

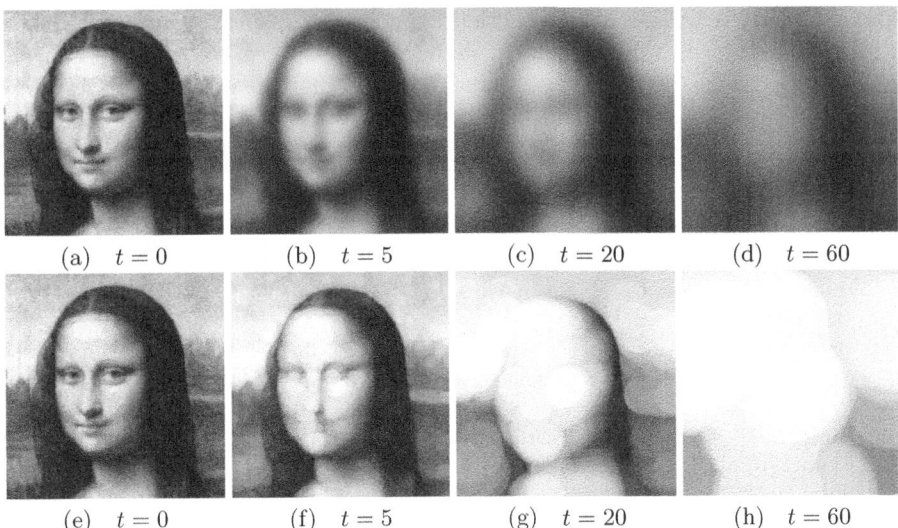

Fig. 3. Top: Relativistic scale-space for $m = 0.1$, Bottom: Morphological Relativistic scale-space for $m = 0.1$

To give a visual impression of the morphological counterpart of convolution scale-spaces, Figure 2 and 3 show evolutions of the Mona Lisa image. Whereas the convolution scale-spaces converge to the average greyvalue, their morphological counterparts converge to the brightest greyvalue. For Figure 3, the similarity to a disc-like structuring function is clearly visible for the morphological relativistic scale space with $m = 0.1$.

For the implementation we used a multiplication in the Fourier domain for the convolution scale-spaces. For the morphological scale-spaces, we solved for the maximum over the image domain in Equation (9).

7 Conclusions and Future Work

We have established a mathematical dictionary that allows to translate a convolution scale-space to a morphological scale-space and vice versa. In contrast to previous work on structural similarities between linear and morphological systems, we have achieved these equivalences in the terminology of differential or pseudo-differential operators. We have shown that there exist hitherto unexplored relations between known scale-spaces, such as the Poisson scale-space and morphology with a disc-shaped structuring element. Moreover, we have introduced new morphological scale-spaces that serve as nonlinear counterparts of α-scale-spaces beyond Poisson and Gaussian scale-space, and of relativistic scale-spaces. Their PDE formulations reveal striking structural similarities to their linear pendants.

There are numerous ways to extend these findings in interesting directions. Obviously, these new scale-spaces should be explored further in order to identify promising applications. On the other hand, it is also challenging to generalise this dictionary to other scale-spaces that are not covered within a classical convolution setting, for instance nonlinear diffusion scale-spaces. In this case, Fourier reasonings can no longer be used, and different mathematical techniques are required.

References

1. Alvarez, L., Guichard, F., Lions, P.-L., Morel, J.-M.: Axioms and fundamental equations in image processing. Archive for Rational Mechanics and Analysis **123**, 199–257 (1993)
2. Brockett, R.W., Maragos, P.: Evolution equations for continuous-scale morphology. In: Proc. IEEE International Conference on Acoustics, Speech and Signal Processing, vol. 3, pp. 125–128, San Francisco, CA (March 1992)
3. Burgeth, B., Didas, S., Weickert, J.: The Bessel Scale-Space. In: Fogh Olsen, O., Florack, L.M.J., Kuijper, A. (eds.) DSSCV 2005. LNCS, vol. 3753, pp. 84–95. Springer, Heidelberg (2005)
4. Burgeth, B., Didas, S., Weickert, J.: Relativistic scale-spaces. In: Kimmel, R., Sochen, N.A., Weickert, J. (eds.) Scale-Space 2005. LNCS, vol. 3459, pp. 1–12. Springer, Heidelberg (2005)

5. Burgeth, B., Weickert, J.: An explanation for the logarithmic connection between linear and morphological system theory. International Journal of Computer Vision **64**(2/3), 157–169 (2005)
6. Didas, S., Burgeth, B., Imiya, A., Weickert, J.: Regularity and scale-space properties of fractional high order linear filtering. In: Kimmel, R., Sochen, N.A., Weickert, J. (eds.) Scale-Space 2005. LNCS, vol. 3459, pp. 13–25. Springer, Heidelberg (2005)
7. Dorst, L., van den Boomgaard, R.: Morphological signal processing and the slope transform. Signal Processing **38**, 79–98 (1994)
8. Duits, R., Florack, L., de Graaf, J., ter Haar Romeny, B.: On the axioms of scale space theory. Journal of Mathematical Imaging and Vision **20**, 267–298 (2004)
9. Felsberg, M., Sommer, G.: Scale adaptive filtering derived from the laplace equation. In: Radig, B., Florczyk, S. (eds.) DAGM 2001. LNCS, vol. 2191, pp. 124–131. Springer, Heidelberg (2001)
10. Florack, L.: Image Structure. Computational Imaging and Vision, vol. 10. Kluwer, Dordrecht (1997)
11. Iijima, T.: Basic theory on normalization of pattern (in case of typical one-dimensional pattern). Bulletin of the Electrotechnical Laboratory **26**, 368–388 (1962). (In Japanese)
12. Koenderink, J.J.: The structure of images. Biological Cybernetics **50**, 363–370 (1984)
13. Lindeberg, T.: Scale-Space Theory in Computer Vision. Kluwer, Boston (1994)
14. Lyons, R.G.: Understanding Digital Signal Processing. Prentice Hall, Englewood Cliffs (2004)
15. Maragos, P.: Morphological systems: Slope transforms and max-min difference and differential equations. Signal Processing **38**(1), 57–77 (1994)
16. Rockafellar, R.T.: Convex Analysis. Princeton University Press, Princeton (1970)
17. van den Boomgaard, R.: The morphological equivalent of the Gauss convolution. Nieuw Archief Voor Wiskunde **10**(3), 219–236 (1992)
18. van den Boomgaard, R., Dorst, L.: The morphological equivalent of Gaussian scale-space. In: Sporring, J., Nielsen, M., Florack, L., Johansen, P. (eds.) Gaussian Scale-Space Theory. Computational Imaging and Vision, vol. 8, pp. 203–220. Kluwer, Dordrecht (1997)
19. van den Boomgaard, R., Smeulders, A.: The morphological structure of images: The differential equations of morphological scale-space. IEEE Transactions on Pattern Analysis and Machine Intelligence **16**, 1101–1113 (1994)
20. Weickert, J., Ishikawa, S., Imiya, A.: Linear scale-space has first been proposed in Japan. Journal of Mathematical Imaging and Vision **10**(3), 237–252 (1999)
21. Witkin, A.P.: Scale-space filtering. In: Proc. Eighth International Joint Conference on Artificial Intelligence, vol. 2, pp. 945–951, Karlsruhe, West Germany (August 1983)

New Approximation of a Scale Space Kernel on SE(3) and Applications in Neuroimaging

Jorg Portegies[1]([✉]), Gonzalo Sanguinetti[1], Stephan Meesters[1,2], and Remco Duits[1,3]

[1] Department of Mathematics and Computer Science,
Eindhoven University of Technology, Eindhoven, Netherlands
{j.m.portegies,g.r.sanguinetti,s.p.l.meesters,r.duits}@tue.nl
[2] Academic Center for Epileptology Kempenhaeghe and Maastricht UMC+, Heeze, Netherlands
[3] Department of Biomedical Engineering, Eindhoven University of Technology, Eindhoven, Netherlands

Abstract. We provide a new, analytic kernel for scale space filtering of dMRI data. The kernel is an approximation for the Green's function of a hypo-elliptic diffusion on the 3D rigid body motion group SE(3), for fiber enhancement in dMRI. The enhancements are described by linear scale space PDEs in the coupled space of positions and orientations embedded in SE(3). As initial condition for the evolution we use either a Fiber Orientation Distribution (FOD) or an Orientation Density Function (ODF). Explicit formulas for the exact kernel do not exist. Although approximations well-suited for fast implementation have been proposed in literature, they lack important symmetries of the exact kernel. We introduce techniques to include these symmetries in approximations based on the logarithm on SE(3), resulting in an improved kernel. Regarding neuroimaging applications, we apply our enhancement kernel (a) to improve dMRI tractography results and (b) to quantify coherence of obtained streamline bundles.

Keywords: Scale space on SE(3) · Contextual enhancement · Left-invariant diffusion · Group convolution · Tractography

1 Introduction

In dMRI it is assumed that axons grouped in bundles in human brain tissue restrict the Brownian motion of water molecules such that more diffusion occurs along the bundles [1]. By measuring the decay of signal due to diffusion in many directions it is possible to obtain information about the underlying microstructure of the brain tissue and further processing of this data provides clues about the anatomical brain connectivity. After a pre-processing procedure in which the raw data is corrected for e.g. distortions and motion artefacts, different models

---

The research leading to the results of this article has received funding from the European Research Council under the ECs 7th Framework Programme (FP7/2007 2014)/ERC grant agreement No. 335555.

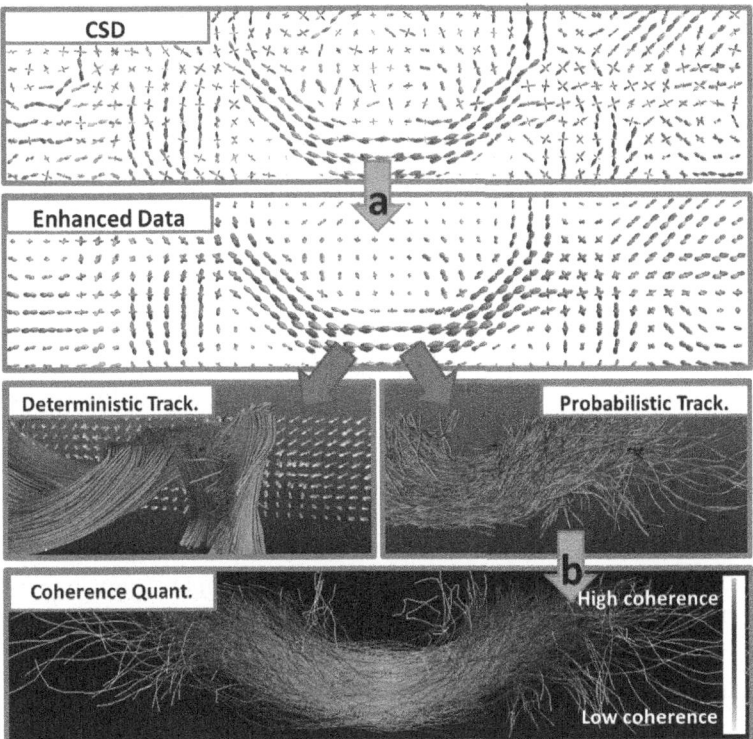

Fig. 1. The pipeline used in this paper for processing dMRI data. CSD provides an FOD, that can be enhanced by convolution with our proposed kernel as in Section 3**a**. We visualize the FOD U by a field of *glyphs*, where at each position **y** on a grid and each orientation **n** the radius is of the glyph is directly proportional to $U(\mathbf{y}, \mathbf{n})$. The color corresponds to direction of the orientation. Then, deterministic or probabilistic tractography produces fiber bundles, that often contain deviating fibers. They can be classified with our proposed coherence quantification, see Section 3**b**.

can be used for further processing of the data [2]. We construct from the data a fiber orientation distribution (FOD) function on positions and orientations, representing the probability density of finding a fiber in a certain position and orientation. For this we use Constrained Spherical Deconvolution (CSD) [3], but the methods in this paper can be combined with any model that outputs an FOD or an Orientation Density Function (ODF) of water molecules.

For regularization of dMRI data, various methods exist that include contextual information on position and/or orientation space [4–12]. In this paper we pursue the method of scale spaces on the group of positions and rotations $SE(3)$. For this we consider diffusions described by the Fokker-Planck equations of hypo-elliptic Brownian motion [6, Sect.4.2]. The effect of these evolutions on the FOD is that elongated structures are enhanced while crossings of bundles are preserved. No explicit formulas exist for the exact Green's function of the PDE, but approximations exist in literature [6]: one is the product of two SE(2)-kernels and one is based on the logarithmic modulus on $SE(3)$. However, two important invariance properties of the exact kernel are not automatically obeyed in these approximations, as pointed out in Section 2.3.

The first (and main) contribution of this paper is that we provide a new analytic kernel approximation for Brownian motion on $SE(3)$ that is, in contrast to previous analytic approximations, well-defined on the quotient. As such, it carries the appropriate symmetry. Furthermore, the novel, more precise approximation is still well-suited for fast kernel implementations [13].

The second contribution in this work is the application of the improved approximations in two different places (a) and (b) in the dMRI pipeline as in Fig. 1. We provide two clinically relevant experiments to illustrate this. We apply the enhancements to the FOD and show the advantages in the tractography result (a). Secondly, we use the enhancement kernel to construct a density on the space of positions and orientations, based on a set of fibers (b). From this we derive a measure for the coherence of fibers within a fiber bundle. The symmetry included in the new kernel leads to a reduction in computation time of the measure.

Section 2 covers the theory of the paper and compares previous and new approximation kernels. In Section 3 the applications (a) and (b) are presented.

2 Approximations of Scale Spaces on $SE(3)$

First we explain in Section 2.1 how the space of 3D positions and orientations, on which FODs are defined, can be embedded in the group of 3D rigid body motions $SE(3)$. This is followed by a brief introduction to scale spaces on $SE(3)$, see Section 2.2, together with a discussion of the two required invariances. In Section 2.3 we give two known kernel approximations and we propose an adaptation for the logarithmic approximation, such that the desired invariances are induced.

2.1 The Embedding of $\mathbb{R}^3 \rtimes S^2$ into $SE(3)$

Contextual enhancement of a function $U : \mathbb{R}^3 \times S^2 \to \mathbb{R}^+$, representing an FOD, means improving the alignment of elongated structures present in the FOD. Such alignment can only be done in a space where positions and orientations are coupled. Therefore we embed $\mathbb{R}^3 \times S^2$ in the group of 3D rigid body motions $SE(3)$, with group product $(\mathbf{x}, \mathbf{R})(\mathbf{x}', \mathbf{R}') = (\mathbf{x} + \mathbf{R}\mathbf{x}', \mathbf{R}\mathbf{R}')$, where $\mathbf{R}, \mathbf{R}' \in SO(3)$, the 3D rotation group, and $\mathbf{x}, \mathbf{x}' \in \mathbb{R}^3$. Square integrable functions U relate to a specific set of functions $\tilde{U} : SE(3) \to \mathbb{R}^+$ via

$$U \leftrightarrow \tilde{U} \Leftrightarrow \left\{ U(\mathbf{y}, \mathbf{n}) = \tilde{U}(\mathbf{y}, \mathbf{R_n}) \text{ and } \tilde{U}(\mathbf{y}, \mathbf{R}) = U(\mathbf{y}, \mathbf{R}\mathbf{e}_z) \right\}, \qquad (1)$$

where from now on, $\mathbf{R_n}$ denotes *any* rotation such that $\mathbf{R_n}\mathbf{e}_z = \mathbf{n}$, and where $\mathbf{e}_z = (0, 0, 1)^T$ denotes our reference axis. The functions $\tilde{U}$ carry a symmetry, as they are right-invariant w.r.t. right-action $\mathbf{R} \mapsto \mathbf{R}\mathbf{R}_{\mathbf{e}_z,\alpha}$, where from now on $\mathbf{R}_{\mathbf{a},\psi}$ denotes the counter-clockwise rotation around axis $\mathbf{a}$ by angle ψ. This implies we should consider left cosets on $SE(3)$, with equivalence relation

$$g := (\mathbf{y}, \mathbf{R}) \equiv g' := (\mathbf{y}', \mathbf{R}') \Leftrightarrow g^{-1}g' \in H \Leftrightarrow \mathbf{y} = \mathbf{y}' \text{ and } \mathbf{R}' = \mathbf{R}\mathbf{R}_{\mathbf{e}_z,\alpha}, \quad (2)$$

for some $\alpha \in [0, 2\pi)$, where from now on H denotes the subgroup of $SE(3)$ whose elements are equal to $h = (\mathbf{0}, R_{\mathbf{e}_z,\alpha})$. The total set of functions $\tilde{U}$, mentioned earlier, is given by:

$$\mathbb{L}_2^R(SE(3)) := \{\tilde{U} \in \mathbb{L}_2(SE(3)) \mid \tilde{U}(gh) = \tilde{U}(g) \text{ for all } g \in SE(3), h \in H\}.$$

From now on, we identify the function $U : \mathbb{R}^3 \times S^2 \to \mathbb{R}$ with a function on the group quotient $\mathbb{R}^3 \rtimes S^2 := SE(3)/H = SE(3)/(\{\mathbf{0}\} \times SO(2))$. Throughout the paper we use a tilde to distinguish functions on the group from functions on the quotient. Next, we present scale spaces for such functions $\tilde{U}$ and U.

2.2 Scale Spaces and Group Convolution on $\mathbb{R}^3 \rtimes S^2$ and $SE(3)$

We define the enhancement evolutions on $SE(3)$ in terms of the left-invariant vector fields. They can be considered as differential operators on locally defined smooth functions [14]. Left-invariant vector fields are obtained from a Lie-algebra basis for the tangent space $T_e(SE(3))$ at unity element $e = (0, I) \in SE(3)$, say $\{A_1, \ldots, A_6\}$. This is done with the pushforward $(L_g)_*$ of the left-multiplication $L_g q = gq$: $\mathcal{A}_g \tilde{U} = \mathcal{A}_e(\tilde{U} \circ L_g) = ((L_g)_* \mathcal{A}_e)(\tilde{U})$, for all smooth $\tilde{U} : SE(3) \to \mathbb{R}$. Explicit formulas for the vector fields $g \mapsto \mathcal{A}_i|_g$ can be obtained by

$$\mathcal{A}_j|_g \tilde{U} = \lim_{t \to 0} \frac{\tilde{U}(g\, e^{tA_j}) - \tilde{U}(g)}{t}, \quad j = 1, \ldots, 6, \quad (3)$$

where $T_e(SE(3)) \ni A \mapsto e^{tA} \in SE(3)$ denotes the exponential map yielding the 1-parameter subgroup $\{e^{tA} \mid t \in \mathbb{R}\}$. Note that $\mathcal{A}_i|_e = A_i$. We write $\{\mathcal{A}_i\}_{i=1}^6$, where $\{\mathcal{A}_1, \mathcal{A}_2, \mathcal{A}_3\}$ are spatial and $\{\mathcal{A}_4, \mathcal{A}_5, \mathcal{A}_6\}$ are rotation vector fields, for which we use the explicit expressions in two different Euler angle parametrizations as given in [6]. For geometric intuition, see Fig. 2. Now the (hypo-elliptic) diffusion process describing Brownian motion on $SE(3)$ [6], for $\tilde{U}$ on $SE(3)$ can be formulated as:

$$\begin{cases} \frac{\partial}{\partial t} \tilde{W}(\mathbf{y}, \mathbf{R}, t) = D_{33}(\mathcal{A}_3)^2 \tilde{W}(\mathbf{y}, \mathbf{R}, t) + D_{44}(\mathcal{A}_4^2 + \mathcal{A}_5^2)\tilde{W}(\mathbf{y}, \mathbf{R}, t), \\ \tilde{W}(\mathbf{y}, \mathbf{R}, 0) = \tilde{U}(\mathbf{y}, \mathbf{R}). \end{cases} \quad (4)$$

This yields a scale space representation $\tilde{W}$ of the function $\tilde{U}$ with scale parameter $t > 0$. Parameters $D_{33} > 0$ and $D_{44} > 0$ influence the amount of spatial and angular diffusion, respectively. Solutions for $\tilde{W}$ can be found via finite difference approximations of the PDE [15], or via convolution $\tilde{U}$ with a kernel. Fast kernel implementations exist [13] and are particularly suitable for our applications. The $SE(3)$-convolution with a probability kernel $\tilde{p}_t : SE(3) \to \mathbb{R}^+$ is given by

$$\tilde{W}(g, t) = (\tilde{p}_t *_{SE(3)} \tilde{U})(g) = \int_{SE(3)} \tilde{p}_t(q^{-1}g)\tilde{U}(q)\mathrm{d}q. \quad (5)$$

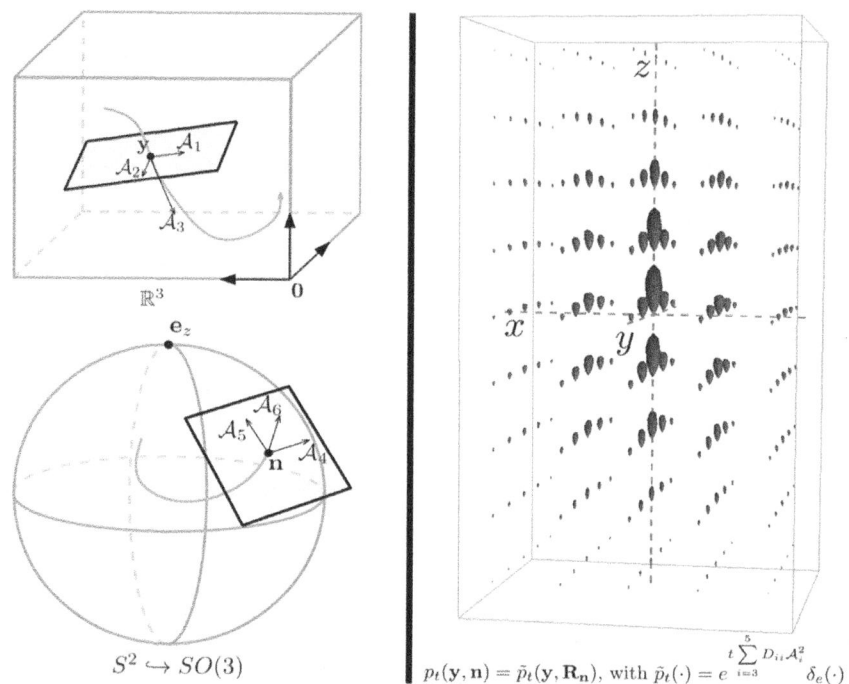

Fig. 2. *Left:* left-invariant vector fields $\{\mathcal{A}_i\}_{i=1}^{6}$ in $SE(3)$, restricted to $(\mathbf{y}, \mathbf{R_n})$. *Right:* glyph visualization of the impulse response p_t as the scale space kernel of (6), with $D_{33} = 1$, $D_{44} = D_{55} = 0.02$, $t = 2$.

where $dq = d\mathbf{x}dR$, representing the Haar measure, for all $q = (\mathbf{x}, R) \in SE(3)$. This evolution is well-defined also on $\mathbb{R}^3 \rtimes S^2$ and can be written as

$$\begin{cases} \frac{\partial}{\partial t} W(\mathbf{y}, \mathbf{n}, t) = D_{33}(\mathbf{n} \cdot \nabla)^2 W(\mathbf{y}, \mathbf{n}, t) + D_{44} \Delta_{LB} W(\mathbf{y}, \mathbf{n}, t), \\ W(\mathbf{y}, \mathbf{n}, 0) = U(\mathbf{y}, \mathbf{n}), \end{cases} \quad (6)$$

with Δ_{LB} the Laplace-Beltrami operator on S^2. Solutions of (6) are found by $\mathbb{R}^3 \rtimes S^2$-convolution with the exact solution kernel $p_t : \mathbb{R}^3 \rtimes S^2 \to \mathbb{R}^+$:

$$\begin{aligned} W(\mathbf{y}, \mathbf{n}, t) &= (p_t *_{\mathbb{R}^3 \rtimes S^2} U)(\mathbf{y}, \mathbf{n}) \\ &= \int_{S^2} \int_{\mathbb{R}^3} p_t(\mathbf{R}_{\mathbf{n}'}^T (\mathbf{y} - \mathbf{y}'), \mathbf{R}_{\mathbf{n}'}^T \mathbf{n}) \cdot U(\mathbf{y}', \mathbf{n}') d\mathbf{y}' d\sigma(\mathbf{n}'). \end{aligned} \quad (7)$$

The kernels $\tilde{p}_t$ and p_t should satisfy certain symmetries, as shown in the following definition, lemma and corollary.

Definition 1. *An operator $\tilde{\Phi} : \mathbb{L}_2^R(SE(3)) \to \mathbb{L}_2^R(SE(3))$ is called legal if*

$$\begin{cases} \mathcal{L}_g \circ \tilde{\Phi} = \tilde{\Phi} \circ \mathcal{L}_g & \forall g \in SE(3), \\ \tilde{\Phi} \circ \mathcal{R}_h = \tilde{\Phi} = \mathcal{R}_{h'} \circ \tilde{\Phi} & \forall h, h' \in H, \end{cases}$$

with $\mathcal{L}_g$ and $\mathcal{R}_h$ the left- and right-regular action on $SE(3)$ respectively, see [6].

Legal operators $\tilde{\Phi}$ induce well-posed operators Φ on $\mathbb{L}_2(\mathbb{R}^3 \rtimes S^2)$ via $\Phi(U)(\mathbf{y}, \mathbf{n}) = \tilde{\Phi}(\tilde{U})(\mathbf{y}, \mathbf{R_n})$. In particular, this holds for legal scale space operators.

Lemma 1. *Let $\tilde{\Phi} : \mathbb{L}_2^R(SE(3)) \to \mathbb{L}_2^R(SE(3))$ be linear and legal, and assume it maps $\mathbb{L}_2(SE(3))$ into $\mathbb{L}_\infty(SE(3))$. Then we have:*

1. *identity:* $(\tilde{\Phi}(\tilde{U}))(g) = \int_{SE(3)} \tilde{K}(g, q)\, \tilde{U}(q)\, \mathrm{d}q = (\check{\tilde{p}} *_{SE(3)} \tilde{U})(g)$, *with*
   $\tilde{K}(g,q) = \tilde{K}(e, (g^{-1}q)) =: \check{\tilde{p}}(q^{-1}g)$ *and with* $\tilde{p}(g) := \tilde{K}(g, e) = \check{\tilde{p}}(g^{-1})$.
2. *symmetry:* $\tilde{K}(gh, qh') = \tilde{K}(g, q)$ *for all* $h, h' \in H$ *and all* $g \in SE(3)$.
3. *preservation of correspondences:* $(U \leftrightarrow \tilde{U}) \Rightarrow \Phi(U) \leftrightarrow \tilde{\Phi}(\tilde{U})$ *with*

$$\begin{aligned}(\Phi(U))(\mathbf{y}, \mathbf{n}) &= \int_{\mathbb{R}^3 \times S^2} k(\mathbf{y}, \mathbf{n}, \mathbf{y}', \mathbf{n}') U(\mathbf{y}', \mathbf{n}') \mathrm{d}\mathbf{y}' \mathrm{d}\sigma(\mathbf{n}'), \quad \text{with} \\ k(\mathbf{y}, \mathbf{n}, \mathbf{y}', \mathbf{n}') &= \tfrac{1}{2\pi}\tilde{K}((\mathbf{y}, \mathbf{R_n}), (\mathbf{y}', \mathbf{R_{n'}})) \\ &= \tfrac{1}{2\pi}\tilde{p}((\mathbf{y}', \mathbf{R_{n'}'})^{-1}(\mathbf{y}, \mathbf{R_n})) = p(\mathbf{R_{n'}}^{-1}(\mathbf{y} - \mathbf{y}'), \mathbf{R_{n'}}^{-1}\mathbf{n}).\end{aligned} \quad (8)$$

Proof. By the Dunford-Pettis Theorem cf. [16], $\tilde{\Phi}$ is a kernel operator and $\|\tilde{\Phi}\|^2 = \sup_{q \in SE(3)} \int_{SE(3)} |\tilde{K}(g,q)|^2 \mathrm{d}q$, so we can write $(\tilde{\Phi}(\tilde{U}))(g) = \int_{SE(3)} \tilde{K}(g,q)\tilde{U}(q)\mathrm{d}q$.

1. Operator $\tilde{\Phi}$ is legal, so from the first identity in Definition 1 we have

$$\forall_{g' \in SE(3)} \forall_{\tilde{U} \in \mathbb{L}_2^R(SE(3))} : (\tilde{\Phi} \circ \mathcal{L}_g \circ \tilde{U})(g') = (\mathcal{L}_g \circ \tilde{\Phi} \circ \tilde{U})(g'). \quad (9)$$

This holds for all $\tilde{U}$ and by writing (9) in integral form, one can check that

$$\tilde{K}(g^{-1}g', q) = \tilde{K}(g', gq), \ \tilde{K}(e, g^{-1}q) = \tilde{K}(g, q), \ \text{for all } g, g', q \in SE(3). \quad (10)$$

2. The second identity in Definition 1, together with the unimodularity of the group $SE(3)$ gives $\tilde{K}(g, qh^{-1}) = \tilde{K}(g, q) = \tilde{K}(gh', q)$, so $\tilde{K}$ must be right-invariant under subgroup H with respect to both entries.

3. Suppose $U \leftrightarrow \tilde{U}$, then $\tilde{U}(\mathbf{y}', \mathbf{R_{n'}}) = U(\mathbf{y}', \mathbf{n}')$ and

$$\begin{aligned}(\tilde{\Phi}(\tilde{U}))(\mathbf{y}, \mathbf{R_n}) &= \int_{SE(3)} \tilde{K}(\mathbf{y}, \mathbf{R_n}, \mathbf{y}', \mathbf{R}') \tilde{U}(\mathbf{y}', \mathbf{R}') \mathrm{d}\mathbf{y}' \mathrm{d}\mathbf{R}' \\ &= 2\pi \int_{\mathbb{R}^3 \rtimes S^2} \tilde{K}(\mathbf{y}, \mathbf{R_n}, \mathbf{y}', \mathbf{R_{n'}}) \tilde{U}(\mathbf{y}', \mathbf{R_{n'}}) \mathrm{d}\mathbf{y}' \mathrm{d}\sigma(\mathbf{n}').\end{aligned} \quad (11)$$

Now $\tilde{p}(g) = \tilde{K}(g, e)$, $\check{\tilde{p}}(g) = \tilde{K}(e, g)$. Left-invariance then implies (8). □

Corollary 1. *The exact scale space kernels $\tilde{p}_t : SE(3) \to \mathbb{R}^+$ and $p_t : \mathbb{R}^3 \rtimes S^2 \to \mathbb{R}^+$ satisfy the following symmetries*

$$p_t(\mathbf{y}, \mathbf{n}) = p_t(\mathbf{R}_{\mathbf{e}_z, \alpha}\mathbf{y}, \mathbf{R}_{\mathbf{e}_z, \alpha}\mathbf{n}) \text{ and } \tilde{p}_t(h^{-1}g) = \tilde{p}_t(g) = \tilde{p}_t(gh') \quad (12)$$

for all $t > 0$, $\alpha > 0$, $(\mathbf{y}, \mathbf{n}) \in \mathbb{R}^3 \rtimes S^2$, $g \in SE(3)$, $h, h' \in H$. Moreover,

$$p_t(\mathbf{y}, \mathbf{n}) = p_t(-\mathbf{R}_\mathbf{n}^T \mathbf{y}, \mathbf{R}_\mathbf{n}^T \mathbf{e}_z) \text{ and } \tilde{p}_t(g) = \tilde{p}_t(g^{-1}). \quad (13)$$

Proof. The symmetry (12) is due to Lemma 1. The second symmetry (13) is due to reflectional invariance $(\mathcal{A}_3, \mathcal{A}_4, \mathcal{A}_5) \mapsto (-\mathcal{A}_3, -\mathcal{A}_4, -\mathcal{A}_5)$ in the diffusion (4) and reflection on the Lie algebra corresponds to inversion on the group. □

Remark 1. Note that (13) in terms of k would be: $k(\mathbf{y}, \mathbf{n}, \mathbf{0}, \mathbf{e}_z) = k(\mathbf{0}, \mathbf{e}_z, \mathbf{y}, \mathbf{n})$, by the relation $k(\mathbf{y}, \mathbf{n}, \mathbf{y}', \mathbf{n}') = p(\mathbf{R}_{\mathbf{n}'}^T(\mathbf{y} - \mathbf{y}'), \mathbf{R}_{\mathbf{n}'}^T \mathbf{n})$. This means that k defines a symmetric measure: evaluation in $(\mathbf{y}, \mathbf{n})$ of a kernel centered around the unity element $(\mathbf{0}, \mathbf{e}_z)$ should be equal to evaluation in the unity element of a kernel centered around $(\mathbf{y}, \mathbf{n})$.

Now the Gaussian kernel approximation, based on the logarithm on $SE(3)$ and the theory of coercive weighted operators on Lie groups [17], presented in earlier work [10, ch:8,thm.11] does not satisfy this symmetry. Next we will improve it by a new practical analytic approximation which does satisfy the property.

2.3 New vs. Previous Kernel Approximations

We first present two existing approximations for p_t and $\tilde{p}_t$, that do not automatically carry over the properties we have shown in the previous section. A possible approximation kernel for p_t is based on a direct product of two $SE(2)$-kernels, see [13, Eq.(10),Eq.(11)], to which we refer as $p_t^{prev,1}$. This approximation is easy to use since it is defined in terms of the Euler angles of the corresponding orientations. However, in Fig. 3 we show that the symmetries described before are not preserved by $p_t^{prev,1}$ and errors tend to be larger when D_{44} and t increase. Therefore we move to an approximation for the $SE(3)$-kernel $\tilde{p}_t$, for which we show that it can be adapted such that it has the important symmetries. We need the logarithm on $SE(3)$ for this approximation, so first consider an exponential curve in $SE(3)$, given by $\tilde{\gamma}(t) = g_0 \exp\left(t \sum_{i=1}^{6} c^i A_i\right)$. The logarithm $\log_{SE(3)} : SE(3) \to T_e(SE(3))$ is bijective, and it is given by

$$\log_{SE(3)}(g) = \log_{SE(3)}\left(\exp\left(\sum_{i=1}^{6} c^i(g) A_i\right)\right) = \sum_{i=1}^{6} c^i(g) A_i, \quad (14)$$

and we can relate to this the vector of coefficients $\mathbf{c}(g) = (\mathbf{c}^{(1)}(g), \mathbf{c}^{(2)}(g)) = (c^1(g), \cdots, c^6(g))^T$. We define matrix Ω as follows:

$$\Omega := \begin{pmatrix} 0 & -c^6 & c^5 \\ c^6 & 0 & -c^4 \\ -c^5 & c^4 & 0 \end{pmatrix}, \quad \mathbf{R} = e^{t\Omega}, \quad \mathbf{R} \in SO(3). \quad (15)$$

We can write $\mathbf{R}$ in terms of Euler angles, $\mathbf{R} = \mathbf{R}_{\mathbf{e}_z, \gamma} \mathbf{R}_{\mathbf{e}_y, \beta} \mathbf{R}_{\mathbf{e}_z, \alpha}$. Let the matrix $\Omega_{\gamma, \beta, \alpha}$ be such that $\exp(\Omega_{\gamma, \beta, \alpha}) = \mathbf{R}_{\mathbf{e}_z, \gamma} \mathbf{R}_{\mathbf{e}_y, \beta} \mathbf{R}_{\mathbf{e}_z, \alpha}$. The spatial coefficients $\mathbf{c}^{(1)} = \mathbf{c}^{(1)}_{\mathbf{x}, \gamma, \beta, \alpha}$ are given by the following equation:

$$\mathbf{c}^{(1)} = \left(I - \frac{1}{2}\Omega_{\gamma, \beta, \alpha} + q_{\gamma, \beta, \alpha}^{-2}\left(1 - \frac{q_{\gamma, \beta, \alpha}}{2} \cot\left(\frac{q_{\gamma, \beta, \alpha}}{2}\right)\right)(\Omega_{\gamma, \beta, \alpha})^2\right) \mathbf{x}, \quad (16)$$

where $q_{\gamma,\beta,\alpha}$ is the (Euclidean) norm of $\mathbf{c}^{(2)}$. Then another approximation for the kernel $\tilde{p}_t$ is given by [6]:

$$\tilde{p}_t^{log}(\mathbf{c}(g)) = \frac{1}{(4\pi t^2 D_{33} D_{44})^2} e^{-\frac{|\log_{SE(3)}(g)|^2_{D_{33},D_{44}}}{4t}}, \quad (17)$$

with the smoothed variant of the weighted modulus, [10, Eq.78,79], given by

$$|\log_{SE(3)}(\cdot)|_{D_{33},D_{44}} = \sqrt[4]{\frac{|c^1|^2 + |c^2|^2}{D_{33}D_{44}} + \frac{|c^6|^2}{D_{44}} + \left(\frac{(c^3)^2}{D_{33}} + \frac{|c^4|^2 + |c^5|^2}{D_{44}}\right)^2}. \quad (18)$$

Now the difficulty lies in the fact that the function U is defined on the quotient for elements $(\mathbf{y}, \mathbf{R_n})$, where the choice for α in the rotation matrix $\mathbf{R_n}$ (mapping $\mathbf{e}_z$ onto $\mathbf{n} \in S^2$) is not of importance. However, the logarithm is only well-defined on the group $SE(3)$, not on the quotient $\mathbb{R}^3 \rtimes S^2$, and explicitly depends on the choice of α. It is therefore not straightforward to use this approximation kernel such that the invariance properties in Corollary 1 are preserved. In view of Corollary 1, we need both left-invariance and right-invariance for $\tilde{p}_t(g)$ under the action of the subgroup H. As right-invariance is naturally included via $\tilde{p}_t(\mathbf{y}, R) = p_t(\mathbf{y}, R\mathbf{e}_z)$, left-invariance is equivalent to inversion invariance. In previous work the choice of $\alpha = 0$ is taken, giving rise to the approximation

$$p_t^{prev,2}(\mathbf{y}, \mathbf{n}(\beta, \gamma)) = \tilde{p}_t^{log}(\mathbf{c}(\mathbf{y}, \mathbf{R}_{\mathbf{e}_z, \gamma} \mathbf{R}_{\mathbf{e}_y, \beta})). \quad (19)$$

However, this section is not invariant under inversion, as is pointed out in Fig. 3. In contrast, we propose to take the section $\alpha = -\gamma$, which is invariant under inversion (since $(\mathbf{R}_{\mathbf{e}_z,\gamma}\mathbf{R}_{\mathbf{e}_y,\beta}\mathbf{R}_{\mathbf{e}_z,-\gamma})^{-1} = \mathbf{R}_{\mathbf{e}_z,\gamma}\mathbf{R}_{\mathbf{e}_y,-\beta}\mathbf{R}_{\mathbf{e}_z,-\gamma}$). Moreover, this choice for estimating the kernels in the group is natural, as it provides the weakest upper bound kernel since by direct computation one has $\alpha = -\gamma \Rightarrow c_6 = 0$. Finally, this choice indeed provides us the correct symmetry for the Gaussian approximation of $p_t(\mathbf{y}, \mathbf{n})$ as stated in the following theorem.

Theorem 1. *When the approximate kernel p_t^{new} on the quotient is related to the approximate kernel on the group $\tilde{p}_t^{log}$ by*

$$p_t^{new}(\mathbf{y}, \mathbf{n}(\beta, \gamma)) := \tilde{p}_t^{log}(\mathbf{c}(\mathbf{y}, \mathbf{R}_{\mathbf{e}_z,\gamma}\mathbf{R}_{\mathbf{e}_y,\beta}\mathbf{R}_{\mathbf{e}_z,-\gamma})), \quad (20)$$

i.e. we make the choice $\alpha = -\gamma$, we have the desired α-left-invariant property

$$p_t^{new}(\mathbf{y}, \mathbf{n}) = p_t^{new}(\mathbf{R}_{\mathbf{e}_z,\alpha'}\mathbf{y}, \mathbf{R}_{\mathbf{e}_z,\alpha'}\mathbf{n}), \qquad \alpha' \in [0, 2\pi]. \quad (21)$$

and the symmetry property

$$p_t^{new}(\mathbf{y}, \mathbf{n}) = p_t^{new}(-\mathbf{R}_\mathbf{n}^T\mathbf{y}, \mathbf{R}_\mathbf{n}^T\mathbf{e}_z) \quad (22)$$

Proof. We start by proving the α-invariance. Following definition (20) we have

$$p_t^{new}(\mathbf{R}_{\mathbf{e}_z,\alpha'}\mathbf{y}, \mathbf{R}_{\mathbf{e}_z,\alpha'}\mathbf{n}(\beta, \gamma)) = \tilde{p}_t^{log}(\mathbf{c}(\mathbf{R}_{\mathbf{e}_z,\alpha'}\mathbf{y}, \mathbf{R}_{\mathbf{e}_z,\gamma+\alpha'}\mathbf{R}_{\mathbf{e}_y,\beta}\mathbf{R}_{\mathbf{e}_z,-(\gamma+\alpha')}))$$

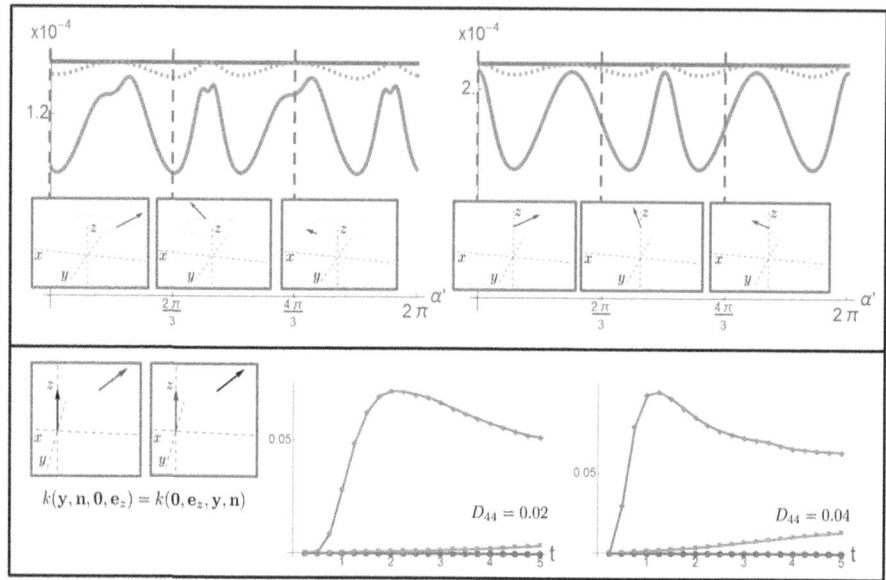

Fig. 3. *Top*: 2 positions and orientations, rotated around the z-axis. The graphs display $p_t(\mathbf{R}_{\mathbf{e}_z,\alpha'}\mathbf{y}, \mathbf{R}_{\mathbf{e}_z,\alpha'}\mathbf{n})$, for $p_t^{prev,1}$ in green, $p_t^{prev,2}$ in orange and p_t^{new} in blue. Parameters $D_{33} = 1, D_{44} = 0.02, t = 4$. *Bottom*: $k(\mathbf{y}, \mathbf{n}, \mathbf{0}, \mathbf{e}_z)$ should be equal to $k(\mathbf{0}, \mathbf{e}_z, \mathbf{y}, \mathbf{n})$, see Remark 1. The absolute sum of the difference of the two evaluations on a $5 \times 5 \times 5$ grid with at each point 42 uniformly distributed orientations is shown for $k^{prev,1}$, $k^{prev,2}$ and k^{new}, corresponding to $p_t^{prev,1}$, $p_t^{prev,2}$ and p_t^{new}, respectively, with coloring as above. Parameter $D_{33} = 1$ and t, D_{44} are as shown.

Recall that the matrix $\Omega_{\gamma,\beta,\alpha}$ is defined by $\mathbf{R}_{\gamma,\beta,\alpha} := \mathbf{R}_{\mathbf{e}_z,\gamma}\mathbf{R}_{\mathbf{e}_y,\beta}\mathbf{R}_{\mathbf{e}_z,\alpha} = e^{\Omega_{\gamma,\beta,\alpha}}$. Therefore in our case, where we choose $\alpha = -\gamma$, we find for all α':

$$\mathbf{R}_{\mathbf{e}_y,\beta} = \mathbf{R}_{\mathbf{e}_z,\gamma+\alpha'}^{-1} e^{\Omega_{\gamma+\alpha',\beta,-(\gamma+\alpha')}} \mathbf{R}_{\mathbf{e}_z,\gamma+\alpha'} = e^{\mathbf{R}_{\mathbf{e}_z,\gamma+\alpha'}^{-1}(\Omega_{\gamma+\alpha',\beta,-(\gamma+\alpha')})\mathbf{R}_{\mathbf{e}_z,\gamma+\alpha'}}$$
$$= e^{\mathbf{R}_{\mathbf{e}_z,\gamma}^{-1}\mathbf{R}_{\mathbf{e}_z,\alpha'}^{-1}(\Omega_{\gamma+\alpha',\beta,-(\gamma+\alpha')})\mathbf{R}_{\mathbf{e}_z,\alpha'}\mathbf{R}_{\mathbf{e}_z,\gamma}}$$

We see that $\mathbf{R}_{\mathbf{e}_z,\alpha'}(\Omega_{\gamma,\beta,-\gamma})\mathbf{R}_{\mathbf{e}_z,\alpha'}^{-1} = \Omega_{\gamma+\alpha',\beta,-(\gamma+\alpha')}$. From this we deduce:

$$\mathbf{c}^{(2)}_{\gamma+\alpha',\beta,-(\gamma+\alpha')} = \mathbf{R}_{\mathbf{e}_z,\alpha'}\mathbf{c}^{(2)}_{\gamma,\beta,-\gamma}, \text{ and } q_{\gamma+\alpha',\beta,-(\gamma+\alpha')} = q_{\gamma,\beta,-\gamma} =: q, \quad (23)$$

and together with (16) it gives $\mathbf{c}^{(1)}_{\mathbf{R}_{\mathbf{e}_z,\alpha'}\mathbf{x},\gamma+\alpha',\beta,-(\gamma+\alpha')} = \mathbf{R}_{\mathbf{e}_z,\alpha'}\mathbf{c}^{(1)}_{\mathbf{x},\gamma,\beta,-\gamma}$. Combining this with (23) gives

$$\mathbf{c}_{\mathbf{R}_{\mathbf{e}_z,\alpha'}\mathbf{x},\gamma+\alpha',\beta,-(\gamma+\alpha')} = Z_{\alpha'}^T \mathbf{c}_{\mathbf{x},\gamma,\beta,-\gamma}, \text{ with } Z_{\alpha'} = \begin{pmatrix} \mathbf{R}_{\mathbf{e}_z,\alpha'}^T & 0 \\ 0 & \mathbf{R}_{\mathbf{e}_z,\alpha'}^T \end{pmatrix} \quad (24)$$

It follows immediately that $c_1^2 + c_2^2, c_3, c_4^2 + c_5^2$ and c_6 are independent of α'. The proof for α-invariance is completed by stating that given $\alpha' \in [0, 2\pi]$:

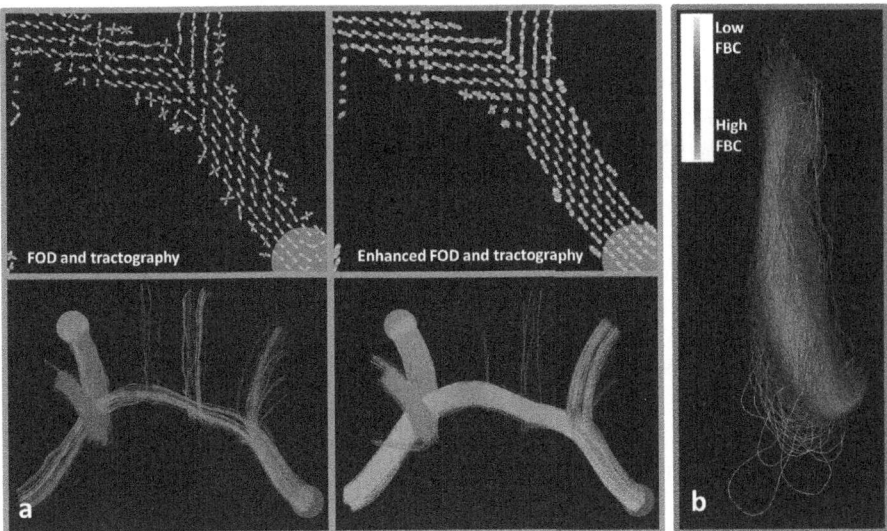

Fig. 4. *Blue frame:* Glyph field visualization, recall Fig. 1, of the FOD obtained with CSD from an artificial dataset (top left) can be improved significantly with enhancements (top right). Especially alignment on the boundary of the bundle is improved. This results in a more plausible tractography result (bottom). Here, $D_{33} = 1$, $D_{44} = 0.02$, $t = 4$. *Red frame:* example of the coherence quantification of a fiber bundle, the Optic Radiation.

$$p_t^{new}(\mathbf{R}_{\mathbf{e}_z,\alpha'}\mathbf{y}, \mathbf{R}_{\mathbf{e}_z,\alpha'}\mathbf{n}(\beta,\gamma)) = \tilde{p}_t^{log}(\log_{SE(3)}(\mathbf{R}_{\mathbf{e}_z,\alpha'}\mathbf{y}, \mathbf{R}_{\gamma+\alpha',\beta,-(\gamma+\alpha')})) =$$
$$\tilde{p}_t^{log}(Z_{\alpha'}^T \log_{SE(3)}(\mathbf{y}, \mathbf{R}_{\gamma,\beta,-\gamma})) = \tilde{p}_t^{log}(\log_{SE(3)}(\mathbf{y}, \mathbf{R}_{\gamma,\beta,-\gamma})) = p_t^{new}(\mathbf{y}, \mathbf{n}(\beta,\gamma)).$$

The symmetry property (22) directly follows from the fact that

$$g^{-1} = \exp_{SE(3)}\left(-\sum_{i=1}^{6} c^i A_i\right) = (\mathbf{y}, \mathbf{R})^{-1} = (-\mathbf{R}^{-1}\mathbf{y}, \mathbf{R}^{-1}),$$

the fact that our weighted modulus on $T_e(SE(3))$ is invariant under reflection $\mathbf{c} \mapsto (-\mathbf{c})$, and the fact that the section $\alpha = -\gamma$ is invariant under inversion. □

3 Neuroimaging Applications

The newly proposed enhancement kernel is used within the pipeline depicted in Fig. 1 for further processing of the dMRI data. There are two places where this is useful: for enhancement of the FOD obtained with e.g. CSD, and for quantifying the coherence of a fiber within a bundle.

a. Enhancing FODs: To illustrate the use of enhancement of FODs, we use the artifical IEEE ISBI 2013 Reconstruction Challenge dataset [18]. CSD is applied to a simulated dMRI signal, yielding an FOD as in Fig. 4. The tractography was done with MRtrix [19], with seed points randomly chosen in the bundle. Only the fibers that pass through the indicated spheres are shown. The alignment of glyphs improves due to the enhancements and this results in a better tracking: bundles are reconstructed fuller and less fibers take a wrong exit from the bundles.

b. Coherence quantification of tractographies: The result of a probabilistic tractography is typically less well-structured than in the deterministic case, recall Fig. 1. We employ our new approximation kernel p_t^{new} to construct an $\mathbb{R}^3 \rtimes S^2$ scale space representation of the set of fibers from a tractography. This density is locally low for a fiber that (partly) deviates in position or orientation from the other fibers in the bundle, as we explain next.

Suppose we have a set of N streamlines (fibers), the ith fiber having N_i points $\mathbf{y}_i^j \in \mathbb{R}^3$ and we set the orientation $\mathbf{n}_i^j = (\mathbf{y}_{i+1}^j - \mathbf{y}_i^j)/\|\mathbf{y}_{i+1}^j - \mathbf{y}_i^j\| \in S^2$. Next we use the set of streamline points $\left\{ (\mathbf{y}_i^j, \pm \mathbf{n}_i^j) \mid j = 1, \ldots N_i, \ i = 1, \ldots, N \right\}$ as follows in the initial condition of our scale space evolution (6):

$$U(\mathbf{y}, \mathbf{n}) = \frac{1}{N_{tot}} \sum_{\sigma=1}^{2} \sum_{i=1}^{N} \sum_{j=1}^{N_i} \delta_{(\mathbf{y}_i^j, (-1)^\sigma \mathbf{n}_i^j)}(\mathbf{y}, \mathbf{n}), \qquad (25)$$

with N_{tot} the total number of fiber points and $\delta_{(\mathbf{y}, \mathbf{n})}$ a δ-distribution in $\mathbb{R}^3 \rtimes S^2$, centered around $(\mathbf{y}, \mathbf{n})$. The solution is given by the convolution $W(\cdot, t) = (p_t^{new} *_{\mathbb{R}^3 \rtimes S^2} U)(\cdot)$. Intuitively, letting this sum of δ-distributions diffuse according to (6) results in a density indicating for each position and orientation how well it is aligned, in the coupled $\mathbb{R}^3 \rtimes S^2$-sense, with the fiber bundle.

In practice, we evaluate the convolution $(p_t^{new} *_{\mathbb{R}^3 \rtimes S^2} U)$ only in the fiber points, giving N_{tot}^2 kernel evaluations. However, this is reduced to $N_{tot}^2/2$ evaluations, since the order of arguments in k^{new} is irrelevant for every pair of fiber points, thanks to the included symmetry in the kernel. This implies a reduction of the computation time. Summation over one fiber then gives a value, which is the final measure for the fiber to bundle coherence (FBC). Fibers with low FBC can be removed from the tractography result and coherent fibers remain. A local FBC can be computed by summing over parts of the fibers instead of the entire fiber. Fig. 4 shows this local FBC for a tractography of the Optic Radiation, a brain white matter bundle connecting the Lateral Geniculate Nucleus and the visual cortex. It can be seen that where fibers deviate from the bundle, the FBC is lower and hence they could be excluded.

4 Conclusion

We have introduced a new approximation for the kernel of a linear scale space PDE (6) on $\mathbb{R}^3 \rtimes S^2$. This is done by the embedding of $\mathbb{R}^3 \rtimes S^2$ into $SE(3)$, on which the PDE coincides with the Fokker-Planck equation for a Brownian motion process. Due to this embedding, the kernel is subject to two constraints, recall Corollary 1. We have shown the application of the kernel in two dMRI neuroimaging applications. First, we have used the kernel implementation in combination with CSD to enhance fiber structures in dMRI and thereby improve tractography results. Secondly, the kernel was used to construct a measure for coherence of fibers in a fiber bundle. Thanks to the appropriate symmetries of the scale space kernels, this measure is based on symmetric distances on $\mathbb{R}^3 \rtimes S^2$ and a reduction of computation time is obtained. In future work we aim to quantify the improvement in tractography due to the enhancements, and we pursue the use of the FBC for better construction of the structural connectome [20].

References

1. Le Bihan, D., Breton, E., Lallemand, D., Grenier, P., Cabanis, E., Laval-Jeantet, M.: MR imaging of intravoxel incoherent motions: application to diffusion and perfusion in neurologic disorders. Radiology **161**, 401–407 (1986)
2. Descoteaux, M., Poupon, C.: Diffusion-weighted MRI. In: Comprehensive Biomedical Physics, pp. 81–97. Elsevier, Oxford (2014)
3. Tournier, J.D., Calamante, F., Connelly, A.: Robust determination of the fibre orientation distribution in diffusion MRI: Non-negativity constrained super-resolved spherical deconvolution. NeuroImage **35**, 1459–1472 (2007)
4. Tschumperlé, D., Deriche, R.: Orthonormal vector sets regularization with PDE's and applications. IJCV **50**, 237–252 (2002)
5. Burgeth, B., Didas, S., Weickert, J.: A general structure tensor concept and coherence-enhancing diffusion filtering for matrix fields. In: Visualization and Processing of Tensor Fields. Mathematics and Visualization, pp. 305–323 (2009)
6. Duits, R., Franken, E.: Left-invariant diffusions on the space of positions and orientations and their application to crossing-preserving smoothing of HARDI images. IJCV **92**, 231–264 (2011)
7. Reisert, M., Kiselev, V.G.: Fiber continuity: An anisotropic prior for ODF estimation. IEEE TMI **30**, 1274–1283 (2011)
8. Schultz, T.: Towards resolving fiber crossings with higher order tensor inpainting. In: New Developments in the Visualization and Processing of Tensor Fields, pp. 253–265. Springer (2012)
9. MomayyezSiahkal, P., Siddiqi, K.: 3D stochastic completion fields for mapping connectivity in diffusion MRI. IEEE PAMI **35**, 983–995 (2013)
10. Duits, R., Dela Haije, T.C.J., Creusen, E.J., Ghosh, A.: Morphological and linear scale spaces for fiber enhancement in DW-MRI. JMIV **46**, 326–368 (2013)
11. Becker, S., Tabelow, K., Mohammadi, S., Weiskopf, N., Polzehl, J.: Adaptive smoothing of multi-shell diffusion weighted magnetic resonance data by msPOAS. NeuroImage **95**, 90–105 (2014)
12. Batard, T., Sochen, N.: A class of generalized Laplacians on vector bundles devoted to multi-channel image processing. JMIV **48**, 517–543 (2014)
13. Rodrigues, P., Duits, R., ter Haar Romeny, B.M., Vilanova, A.: Accelerated diffusion operators for enhancing DW-MRI. In: Proc. of the 2nd EG Conference on VCBM, Eurographics Association, pp. 49–56 (2010)
14. Aubin, T.: A course in Differential Geometry, vol. 27. AMS, Providence (2001)
15. Creusen, E.J., Duits, R., Dela Haije, T.C.J.: Numerical schemes for linear and non-linear enhancement of DW-MRI. In: Bruckstein, A.M., ter Haar Romeny, B.M., Bronstein, A.M., Bronstein, M.M. (eds.) SSVM 2011. LNCS, vol. 6667, pp. 14–25. Springer, Heidelberg (2012)

16. Arendt, W., Bukhvalov, A.V.: Integral representations of resolvents and semigroups. Forum Mathematicum (6), 111–136 (1994)
17. Ter Elst, A., Robinson, D.W.: Weighted subcoercive operators on Lie groups. J. Funct. Anal. **157**, 88–163 (1998)
18. Daducci, A., Caruyer, E., Descoteaux, M., Thiran, J.P.: HARDI reconstruction challenge. IEEE ISBI (2013)
19. Tournier, J.D., Calamante, F., Connelly, A.: MRtrix: Diffusion tractography in crossing fiber regions. Int. J. Imag. Syst. Tech. **22**, 53–66 (2012)
20. Rodrigues, P., Prats-Galino, A., Gallardo-Pujol, D., Villoslada, P., Falcon, C., Prčkovska, V.: Evaluating structural connectomics in relation to different Q-space sampling techniques. In: Mori, K., Sakuma, I., Sato, Y., Barillot, C., Navab, N. (eds.) MICCAI 2013, Part I. LNCS, vol. 8149, pp. 671–678. Springer, Heidelberg (2013)

Partial Differential Equations of Bivariate Median Filters

Martin Welk[✉]

University for Health Sciences, Medical Informatics and Technology (UMIT),
Eduard-Wallnöfer-Zentrum 1, 6060 Hall/Tyrol, Austria
martin.welk@umit.at

Abstract. Multivariate median filters have been proposed as generalisations of the well-established median filter for grey-value images to multi-channel images. As multivariate median, most of the recent approaches use the L^1 median, i.e. the minimiser of an objective function that is the sum of distances to all input points. Many properties of univariate median filters generalise to such a filter. However, the famous result by Guichard and Morel about approximation of the mean curvature motion PDE by median filtering does not have a comparably simple counterpart for L^1 multivariate median filtering. We discuss the affine equivariant Oja median as an alternative to L^1 median filtering. We derive the PDE approximated by Oja median filtering in the bivariate case, and demonstrate its validity by a numerical experiment.

1 Introduction

Median filtering of signals and images goes back to the work of Tukey [17] and has since then been established in image processing as a simple and robust denoising method for grey-value images with favourable structure-preserving properties.

Like other local image filters, the median filter consists of a *selection step* that identifies for each pixel location those pixels which will enter the computation of the filtered value at that location, followed by an *aggregation step* that combines the intensities of these pixels into the filtered value. In the standard setting, the selection step uses a fixed-shape sliding window, which can be called *structuring element* following the naming convention from mathematical morphology. The aggregation step consists in taking the median of the selected intensities. The process can be iterated, giving rise to what is called *iterated median filter*.

The median filter, particularly in its iterated form, has been subject to intensive investigation over the decades. For example, [7] studied so-called *root signals*, non-trivial steady states that occur in the iterated median filter and depend subtly on the choice of the structuring element. Work by Guichard and Morel [9] has identified iterated median filtering as an explicit nonstandard discretisation of (mean) curvature motion [1], thus bridging the discrete filter concept with a partial differential equation (PDE).

Multivariate median filtering. Given the merit of median filtering in processing grey-value images one is interested in stating also a median filter for multi-channel images such as colour images, flow fields, tensor fields etc. As the switch from single- to multi-channel images does not affect the selection step mentioned above but solely the aggregation, it is clear that what is needed to accomplish this goal is the definition of a multivariate median. A starting point for such a definition is the following characterisation of the univariate median: The median of a finite set of real numbers is the real number that minimises the sum of distances to all numbers of the set. There happens to always exist a number within the given set for which this minimum is attained.

Early attempts to multi-channel median filtering, starting from [2] in 1990, defined therefore a vector-valued median (actually a medoid) that selects *from the set of input points* in $\mathrm{I\!R}^n$ the one that minimises the sum of distances to all other sample points.

More recent approaches, such as [12,16] for colour images or [22] for symmetric matrices, rely on the same minimisation but without the restriction to the given data points. The underlying multivariate median concept is known in the statistics literature as *spatial median* or L^1 *median*. It can be traced back to work by Hayford from 1902 [10] and Weber from 1909 [18], followed by [3,8,19] and many others.

However, this is not the only multivariate median concept in literature. For example, the *simplex median* established by Oja in 1983 [13] generalises the distances between points on the real line from the univariate median definition not into distances but into simplex volumes in higher dimensions. Thus, the simplex median of a finite set of points in $\mathrm{I\!R}^n$ is the point $p \in \mathrm{I\!R}^n$ that minimises the sum of simplex volumes $|[p, a_1, \ldots, a_n]|$ where a_i are distinct points of the input data set. An advantage of this concept that is relevant for many statistics applications is its affine equivariance, i.e. that it commutes with affine transformations of the data space. In contrast, the L^1 median only affords Euclidean equivariance. The Oja simplex median is not the only affine equivariant median concept; other concepts have been developed by modifying the L^1 median e.g. in [4,11,14], see also the survey in [5]. For further multivariate concepts see the review [15].

Multivariate median filters and PDE. While the above-mentioned relationship between univariate median filtering and the mean curvature motion PDE could be extended to relate also adaptive median filtering procedures [21] and further discrete filters [20] to well-understood PDEs of image processing, the picture changes when turning to multivariate median filtering. As demonstrated in [20], it is possible to derive some PDE for median filtering based on the spatial median as in [16]. However, this PDE involves complicated coefficient functions coming from elliptic integrals most of which cannot even be stated in closed form, see Section 3.1 of this paper.

Therefore the question arises whether other multivariate median concepts could be advantageous in multi-channel image processing. The present paper is intended as a first step in this direction.

Fig. 1. Median filtering of an image with two colour channels. **(a)** Test image, 512×512 pixels, reduced to a yellow–blue colour space. – **(b)** Filtered by one L^1 median filtering step with a disc-shaped structuring element of radius 5. – **(c)** Filtered by one Oja median filtering step with the same structuring element as in (b).

Our contribution. In this paper, we focus strictly on the bivariate case (e.g. two-channel images or 2D flow fields). We juxtapose the L^1 median and Oja median in the context of image filtering as well as in terms of basic geometric properties, and present PDEs approximated by both kinds of median filters. The novel PDE for Oja median filtering is validated by a numerical experiment.

Structure of the paper. In Section 2, we demonstrate bivariate median filtering by L^1 and Oja median on a simple two-channel colour image, and discuss basic geometric properties of both median concepts. Section 3 is dedicated to PDE approximation results that generalise Guichard and Morel's [9] result for univariate median filtering. For L^1 median filtering, the known result from [20] is rephrased more explicitly for the bivariate case. For Oja median filtering, a PDE is derived in Section 3.2 for the first time, which is the main result of this paper. This PDE is afterwards validated by a numerical experiment in Section 4. A summary and outlook in Section 5 conclude the paper.

2 Comparison of L^1 and Oja Median

Median filter demonstration. We start by demonstrating L^1 and Oja medians in the role of image filters. Since this paper focusses on the bivariate case, we can think e.g. of two-channel colour images or 2D flow fields as examples. While the latter are practically more relevant than the earlier, we prefer two-channel images here because the main focus of the present paper is theoretical, and two-channel images are visually easy to understand. To this end, a RGB colour image has been reduced to a yellow–blue colour space by averaging the red and green channels, see Figure 1(a). This image has been filtered by L^1 and Oja median filtering with identical parameters in Figure 1(b) and (c), respectively. The results of both filters look fairly similar. They display the same kind of structure simplification and smoothing contours as known from median filters.

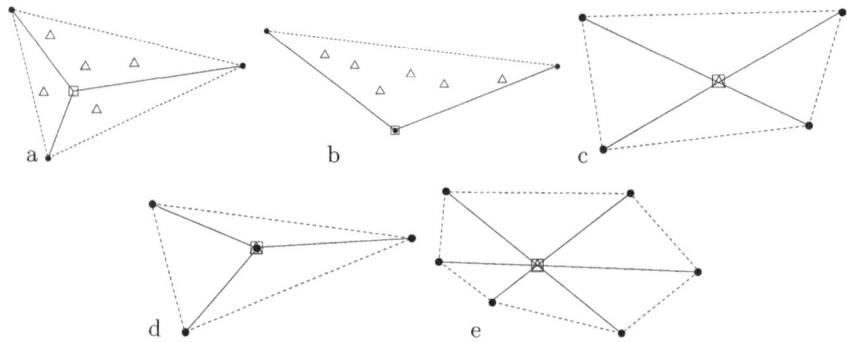

Fig. 2. Simple configurations of input data points (solid points) with their L^1 medians (squares) and Oja medians (triangles). **(a)** Three points forming a triangle with all interior angles less than 120 degrees: The L^1 median is the *Steiner point*; any point within the triangle is an Oja median. – **(b)** Three points forming a triangle with an obtuse angle of 120 degrees or more: The obtuse corner is the L^1 median; still, all points within the triangle are Oja medians. – **(c)** Four points forming a convex quadrangle: L^1 and Oja median coincide at the intersection of the diagonals. – **(d)** Four points whose convex hull is a triangle: L^1 and Oja median coincide at the data point that is not a corner of the convex hull. – **(e)** $2n$ points that form a convex $2n$-gon (hexagon shown as example) in which all diagonals between opposing points have a common intersection point: L^1 and Oja median coincide at this intersection point.

Geometric facts about L^1 and Oja median. To add some geometric intuition about the bivariate median filters under investigation, we consider small point sets in the plane and their medians. The following statements can easily be inferred from standard elementary geometry arguments such as the triangle inequality (for the L^1 median) and multiplicities of covering of the convex hull of input points by the triangles with input and median points as corners (for the 2D Oja median).

For two points, the L^1 median criterion is fulfilled equally for all points of their connecting line segment. The Oja median criterion is even fulfilled by all points of the straight line through these points since the Oja median definition degenerates for collinear sets of points. While this degeneracy can be mitigated by adding a continuity criterion, we do not further treat degenerate cases within the present paper.

For three points, the L^1 median depends on the sort of triangle they span. If all of its interior angles are smaller than 120 degrees, see Figure 2(a), the sum of distances to the corners is minimised by a unique point known as *Steiner point* or *Fermat-Torricelli point,* from which all sides of the triangle are seen under 120 degree angles. For a triangle with an obtuse corner of at least 120 degrees, this corner is the L^1 median, see Figure 2(b). The Oja median criterion is met in both cases by all points of the triangle. This is consistent with the affine equivariance of the Oja median that does not discriminate triangles by shape. It also shows how indeed simplices take the role of line segments from the univariate median definition – the three-point case of the bivariate Oja median is the analogue of the two-point case of the univariate median.

For four points, L^1 and Oja median always coincide: If the convex hull of the data points is a triangle, then the data point that is not a corner of the convex hull is the median, see Figure 2(d); if it is a convex quadrangle, then the intersection point of its diagonals is the median, see Figure 2(c).

The coincidence between L^1 and Oja median continues also in some configurations of more data points. A (non-generic) example is shown in Figure 2(e): A convex $2n$-gon in which all the diagonals that bisect the point set (i.e. those that span n sides) have a common intersection point, features this point as L^1 and Oja median.

We point out two observations that can be made from these simple configurations. Firstly, bivariate medians, unlike their univariate counterpart, cannot always be chosen from the input data set, but they happen to be input data points in some generic configurations. Only in cases when none of the input points lies sufficiently "in the middle" of the data, a new point is created. Secondly, despite their different definitions, also L^1 and Oja median coincide in some generic situations, or are not far apart from each other. This adds plausibility to why the image filtering results in Figure 1 are that similar.

3 PDE Limit Analysis

In this section, we study median filters in a space-continuous setting. As proven in [9], a univariate median filtering step of an image with disc-shaped structuring element of radius ϱ approximates for $\varrho \to 0$ a time step of size $\tau = \varrho^2/6$ of an explicit scheme for the mean curvature motion PDE. We will present PDEs that are approximated in the same sense by L^1 and Oja median filtering of bivariate images.

The formulation of a local image filter to a space-continuous setting is straightforward. The main modification is that the set of values that is returned by the selection step and is processed further in the aggregation step is now infinite and equipped with a density. This density is induced from the uniform distribution of function arguments in the structuring element in the image domain via the Jacobian of the image function.

3.1 L^1 Median

An analysis of the L^1 multivariate median filter for images $\boldsymbol{u} : \mathbb{R}^2 \supset \Omega \to \mathbb{R}^n$ has been given in [20]. Here, we break down the essential result to the bivariate case $n = 2$.

Proposition 1. *One step of L^1 median filtering of a bivariate image $\boldsymbol{u} : \mathbb{R}^2 \supset \Omega \to \mathbb{R}^2$, $(x,y) \mapsto (u,v)$, with a disc-shaped structuring element D_ϱ of radius ϱ approximates for $\varrho \to 0$ an explicit time step of size $\tau = \varrho^2/6$ of the PDE system*

$$\begin{pmatrix} u_t \\ v_t \end{pmatrix} = \boldsymbol{S}(\boldsymbol{\nabla} u, \boldsymbol{\nabla} v) \begin{pmatrix} u_{\eta\eta} \\ v_{\eta\eta} \end{pmatrix} + \boldsymbol{T}(\boldsymbol{\nabla} u, \boldsymbol{\nabla} v) \begin{pmatrix} u_{\xi\xi} \\ v_{\xi\xi} \end{pmatrix} \qquad (1)$$

with the coefficient matrices where $\boldsymbol{\eta}$ is the major, and $\boldsymbol{\xi}$ the minor eigenvector of the structure tensor $\boldsymbol{J} := \boldsymbol{J}(\nabla u, \nabla v) := \nabla u \nabla u^{\mathrm{T}} + \nabla v \nabla v^{\mathrm{T}}$. The coefficient matrices $\boldsymbol{S}(\nabla u, \nabla v)$, $\boldsymbol{T}(\nabla u, \nabla v)$ are given by

$$\boldsymbol{S}(\nabla u, \nabla v) := \boldsymbol{R} \operatorname{diag}\bigl(Q_1(|\partial_\eta u|/|\partial_\xi u|), Q_2(|\partial_\eta u|/|\partial_\xi u|)\bigr) \boldsymbol{R}^{\mathrm{T}}, \quad (2)$$

$$\boldsymbol{T}(\nabla u, \nabla v) := \boldsymbol{R} \operatorname{diag}\bigl(Q_2(|\partial_\xi u|/|\partial_\eta u|), Q_1(|\partial_\xi u|/|\partial_\eta u|)\bigr) \boldsymbol{R}^{\mathrm{T}}, \quad (3)$$

where $\boldsymbol{R} = (\mathrm{D}\boldsymbol{u}^{-1})^{\mathrm{T}} \boldsymbol{P} \operatorname{diag}(|\partial_\eta u|, |\partial_\xi u|)$ is a rotation matrix that depends on the Jacobian $\mathrm{D}\boldsymbol{u}$ of $\boldsymbol{u}$ and the eigenvector matrix $\boldsymbol{P} = (\boldsymbol{\eta} \mid \boldsymbol{\xi})$ of $\boldsymbol{J}$. The functions $Q_1, Q_2 : [0, \infty] \to \mathbb{R}$ are given by the quotients of elliptic integrals

$$Q_1(\lambda) = 3 \iint_{D_1(\boldsymbol{0})} \frac{s^2 t^2}{(s^2 + \lambda^2 t^2)^{3/2}} \, \mathrm{d}s \, \mathrm{d}t \Big/ \iint_{D_1(\boldsymbol{0})} \frac{s^2}{(s^2 + \lambda^2 t^2)^{3/2}} \, \mathrm{d}s \, \mathrm{d}t, \quad (4)$$

$$Q_2(\lambda) = 3 \iint_{D_1(\boldsymbol{0})} \frac{t^4}{(s^2 + \lambda^2 t^2)^{3/2}} \, \mathrm{d}s \, \mathrm{d}t \Big/ \iint_{D_1(\boldsymbol{0})} \frac{t^2}{(s^2 + \lambda^2 t^2)^{3/2}} \, \mathrm{d}s \, \mathrm{d}t \quad (5)$$

for $\lambda \in (0, \infty)$, together with the limits $Q_1(0) = Q_2(0) = 1$, $Q_1(\infty) = Q_2(\infty) = 0$.

The proof relies on the following statement which is proven in [20].

Lemma 1 (from [20]). *Let $\boldsymbol{u}$ be given as in Proposition 1. Assume that the Jacobian $\mathrm{D}\boldsymbol{u}$ at some location (x, y) is diagonal, i.e. $u_y = v_x = 0$, and $u_x \geq v_y \geq 0$. Then one step of L^1 median filtering with structuring element D_ϱ approximates for ϱ at (x, y) an explicit time step of size $\tau = \varrho^2/6$ of the PDE system*

$$\begin{aligned} u_t &= Q_1(u_x/v_y) u_{xx} + Q_2(v_y/u_x) u_{yy}, \\ v_t &= Q_2(u_x/v_y) v_{xx} + Q_1(v_y/u_x) v_{yy}, \end{aligned} \quad (6)$$

with the coefficient functions Q_1, Q_2 as stated in Proposition 1.

Proof (of Proposition 1). Consider an arbitrary fixed location (x^*, y^*). By applying rotations with $\boldsymbol{P}$ in the x-y plane and with $\boldsymbol{R}$ in the u-v plane, x, y can be aligned with the eigenvector directions $\boldsymbol{\eta}$ and $\boldsymbol{\xi}$, and u, v with the corresponding derivatives $\partial_\eta u$, $\partial_\xi u$. Then Lemma 1 can be applied. Reverting the rotations in the x-y and u-v planes, the PDE system (6) turns into the system (1)–(3) of the proposition. □

Remark 1. The derivation of the PDE (1) from a special case by Euclidean transform immediately implies its Euclidean equivariance.

Remark 2. The vectors $\boldsymbol{\eta}$ and $\boldsymbol{\xi}$ used in (1)–(3) are the directions of greatest and least change of the bivariate function $\boldsymbol{u}$, thus the closest analoga to gradient and level line directions of univariate images, see [6]. The use of these image-adaptive local coordinates characterises (1) as a curvature-based PDE remotely similar to the (mean) curvature motion PDE approximated by univariate median filtering.

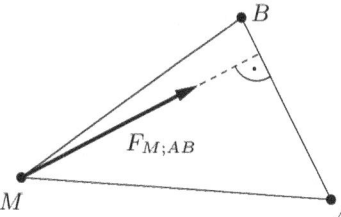

Fig. 3. Anti-gradient vector $F_{M;AB}$ for the area of a triangle MAB with variable point M

3.2 Oja's Simplex Median

Theorem 1. *Let a bivariate image $\boldsymbol{u} : \mathbb{R}^2 \supset \Omega \to \mathbb{R}^2$, $(x, y) \mapsto (u, v)$, be given. At any location where $\det D\boldsymbol{u} \ne 0$, one step of Oja median filtering of $\boldsymbol{u}$ with the structuring element D_ϱ approximates for $\varrho \to 0$ an explicit time step of size $\tau = \varrho^2/24$ of the PDE system*

$$\begin{pmatrix} u_t \\ v_t \end{pmatrix} = 2 \begin{pmatrix} u_{xx}+u_{yy} \\ v_{xx}+v_{yy} \end{pmatrix} - \boldsymbol{A}(\nabla u, \nabla v) \begin{pmatrix} u_{xx}-u_{yy} \\ v_{yy}-v_{xx} \end{pmatrix} + \boldsymbol{B}(\nabla u, \nabla v) \begin{pmatrix} u_{xy} \\ -v_{xy} \end{pmatrix} \quad (7)$$

with the coefficient matrices

$$\boldsymbol{A}(\nabla u, \nabla v) := \frac{1}{u_x v_y - u_y v_x} \begin{pmatrix} u_x v_y + u_y v_x & 2 u_x u_y \\ 2 v_x v_y & u_x v_y + u_y v_x \end{pmatrix}, \quad (8)$$

$$\boldsymbol{B}(\nabla u, \nabla v) := \frac{2}{u_x v_y - u_y v_x} \begin{pmatrix} u_x v_x - u_y v_y & u_x^2 - u_y^2 \\ v_x^2 - v_y^2 & u_x v_x - u_y v_y \end{pmatrix}. \quad (9)$$

Proof. We consider the median of the values $\boldsymbol{u}(x, y)$ within the Euclidean ϱ-neighbourhood of $(0, 0)$, and assume $\det D\boldsymbol{u}(0) \ne 0$. By the affine equivariance of Oja's simplex median, the u-v plane can be transformed in such a way that the Jacobian $D\boldsymbol{u}$ at $(x, y) = (0, 0)$ becomes equal to the unit matrix, i.e. $u_x = v_y = 1$, $u_y = v_x = 0$, and $u(0, 0) = v(0, 0) = 0$. Then the Taylor expansion of (u, v) up to second order around $(0, 0)$ reads as

$$\begin{pmatrix} u(x,y) \\ v(x,y) \end{pmatrix} = \begin{pmatrix} x \\ y \end{pmatrix} + \begin{pmatrix} \alpha x^2 + \beta xy + \gamma y^2 \\ \delta x^2 + \varepsilon xy + \zeta y^2 \end{pmatrix}, \quad (10)$$

where the coefficients are given by derivatives of u, v at $(x, y) = (0, 0)$ as

$$\alpha = \tfrac{1}{2} u_{xx}(0,0), \qquad \beta = u_{xy}(0,0), \qquad \gamma = \tfrac{1}{2} u_{yy}(0,0), \quad (11)$$
$$\delta = \tfrac{1}{2} v_{xx}(0,0), \qquad \varepsilon = v_{xy}(0,0), \qquad \zeta = \tfrac{1}{2} v_{yy}(0,0). \quad (12)$$

Restating the definition of Oja's simplex median for continuous data sets with density function $f(u, v)$, we seek the point $M := (u^*, v^*)$ which minimises the integral over all areas of triangles MAB with $A = (u_1, v_1)$ and $B = (u_2, v_2)$ with $(u_1, v_1) = (u(x_1, y_1), v(x_1, y_1))$, $(u_2, v_2) = (u(x_2, y_2), v(x_2, y_2))$, $(x_1, y_1), (x_2, y_2) \in D_\varrho(0, 0)$, weighted with the density $f(u_1, v_1) f(u_2, v_2)$.

For each triangle MAB, the negative gradient of its area as function of M is a force vector $F_{M;AB}$ perpendicular to AB with a length proportional to the length $|AB|$, see Figure 3. Assuming that MAB is positively oriented, this vector equals $\frac{1}{2}(y_2 - y_1, -x_2 + x_1)$.

Sorting the pairs (A, B) by the orientation angles φ of the lines AB, we see that the minimisation condition for the Oja median can be expressed as

$$\Phi(u^*, v^*) = \frac{1}{2} \int_0^{2\pi} \begin{pmatrix} \cos\varphi \\ \sin\varphi \end{pmatrix} F(u^*, v^*, \varphi) \, d\varphi = 0 \, . \tag{13}$$

Here, $F(\varphi)$ is essentially the resultant of all forces $F_{M;AB}$ for which the line AB intersects the ray from M in direction $(\cos\varphi, \sin\varphi)$ perpendicularly. Each force $F_{M;AB}$ is weighted with the combined density $f(A)f(B) = f(u_1, v_1)f(u_2, v_2)$.

Moreover, u^*, v^* will be of order $\mathcal{O}(\varrho)$ (in fact, even $\mathcal{O}(\varrho^2)$). Thus, (u^*, v^*) can be expressed up to higher order terms via linearisation as

$$\begin{pmatrix} u^* \\ v^* \end{pmatrix} = -(\mathrm{D}\Phi(0,0))^{-1} \Phi(0,0) \, . \tag{14}$$

We therefore turn now to derive an expression for $F(0, 0, \varphi)$. Considering first $\varphi = 0$, this means that all point pairs (A, B) in the u-v right half-plane with $u_1 = u_2$ contribute to $F(0, 0, 0)$, yielding

$$F(0,0,0) = \int_0^{+\infty} \int_{-\infty}^{+\infty} \int_v^{+\infty} f(u,v)f(u,w)(w-v)^2 \, dw \, dv \, du \, . \tag{15}$$

Note that the factor $(w - v)$ occurs squared in the integrand. One factor $(w - v)$ originates from the length of the triangle baseline AB. The second factor $(w - v)$ results from the fact that we have organised in (13), (15) an integration over point pairs (A, B) in the plane using a polar coordinate system similar to a Radon transform; $w - v$ arises as the Jacobian of the corresponding coordinate transform from Cartesian to Radon coordinates. The derivatives of $F(u^*, v^*, 0)$ with regard to the coordinates of M are

$$F_{u^*}(0,0,0) = -\int_{-\infty}^{+\infty} \int_v^{+\infty} f(0,v)f(0,w)(w-v)^2 \, dw \, dv \, , \tag{16}$$

$$F_{v^*}(0,0,0) = 0 \, . \tag{17}$$

Forces $F(0, 0, \varphi)$ and their derivatives for arbitrary angles φ can be obtained from (15), (16), (17) by rotating the u, v coordinates accordingly.

When considering a ϱ-neighbourhood of $(x, y) = (0, 0)$, the density $f(u, v)$ is zero outside of an $\mathcal{O}(\varrho)$-neighbourhood of $(0, 0)$, allowing to limit the indefinite integrals from (15) to the intervals $u \in [u^*, \bar{u}]$, $v \in [\underline{v}(u), \bar{v}(u)]$ and $w \in [v, \bar{v}(u)]$ such that

$$F(0,0,0) = \int_0^{\bar{u}} \int_{\underline{v}(u)}^{\bar{v}(u)} \int_v^{\bar{v}(u)} f(u,v)f(u,w)(w-v)^2 \, dw \, dv \, du \tag{18}$$

and similarly for (16).

To compute $F(0,0,0)$ and $F_{u^*}(0,0,0)$, we write them as functions of the coefficients of (10), i.e. $F(0,0,0) =: G(\alpha, \beta, \gamma, \delta, \varepsilon, \zeta)$ and $F_{u^*}(0,0,0) =: H(\alpha, \beta, \gamma, \delta, \varepsilon, \zeta)$.

We will linearise G and H around the point $(\alpha, \beta, \gamma, \delta, \varepsilon, \zeta) = \mathbf{0}$ that represents the linear function $(u(x,y), v(x,y)) = (x,y)$. To justify this linearisation, remember that we are interested in the limit $\varrho \to 0$, such that only the terms of lowest order in ϱ matter. Cross-effects between the different coefficients occur only in higher order terms. Denoting from now on by $\doteq$ equality up to higher order terms, we have therefore

$$G \doteq G^0 + G^0_\alpha \alpha + G^0_\beta \beta + G^0_\gamma \gamma + G^0_\delta \delta + G^0_\varepsilon \varepsilon + G^0_\zeta \zeta , \qquad (19)$$

$$H \doteq H^0 + H^0_\alpha \alpha + H^0_\beta \beta + H^0_\gamma \gamma + H^0_\delta \delta + H^0_\varepsilon \varepsilon + H^0_\zeta \zeta \qquad (20)$$

where G^0, G^0_α etc. are short for $G(\mathbf{0})$, $G_\alpha(\mathbf{0})$ etc.

To compute G^0 and H^0, we insert into (15) the bounds $\bar{u} = \varrho$, $\bar{v}(u) = \sqrt{\varrho^2 - u^2}$, $\underline{v}(u) = -\bar{v}(u)$. The density becomes constant within the region defined by $\bar{u}$, $\underline{v}(u)$ and $\bar{v}(u)$, with $f(u,v) = 1$. Thus (18) and (16) yield

$$G^0 = \tfrac{32}{45}\varrho^5 , \qquad\qquad H^0 = -\tfrac{4}{3}\varrho^4 . \qquad (21)$$

For G^0_α and H^0_α, one has to vary α to obtain the bounds $\bar{u} = \varrho + \alpha\varrho^2$, $\bar{v}(u) = \sqrt{\varrho^2 - u^2 - 2\alpha u^3}$, $\underline{v}(u) \doteq -\bar{v}(u)$ The density $f(u,v)$ within the so-given bounds is $1/\det(D\mathbf{u})$ at the location $(x(u,v), y(u,v))$ with $x = u - \alpha u^2 + \mathcal{O}(\varrho^3)$, $y = v$, i.e. $f(u,v) = 1 - 2\alpha u + \mathcal{O}(\varrho^2)$. Thus we have

$$G^0_\alpha \doteq \frac{d}{d\alpha} \int_0^{\bar{u}} \int_{\underline{v}(u)}^{\bar{v}(u)} \int_v^{\bar{v}(u)} (1 - 2\alpha u)^2 (w-v)^2 \, dw \, dv \, du \bigg|_{\alpha=0} = -\tfrac{4}{9}\varrho^6 , \qquad (22)$$

$$H^0_\alpha \doteq -\frac{d}{d\alpha} \int_{\underline{v}(0)}^{\bar{v}(0)} \int_v^{\bar{v}(0)} (w-v)^2 \, dw \, dv \bigg|_{\alpha=0} = 0 . \qquad (23)$$

Proceeding similarly for the other coefficients, we find

- for G^0_β, H^0_β: $\bar{u} = \varrho$, $\bar{v} \doteq \sqrt{\varrho^2 - u^2 + \beta^2 u^4} + \beta u^2$, $\underline{v} \doteq -\sqrt{\varrho^2 - u^2 + \beta^2 u^4} + \beta u^2$, $f(u,v) \doteq 1 - \beta v$;
- for G^0_γ, H^0_γ: $\bar{u} = \varrho$, $\bar{v} \doteq \sqrt{(\varrho^2 - u^2)(1 + 2\gamma u)}$, $\underline{v} \doteq -\bar{v}$, $f(u,v) = 1$;
- for G^0_δ, H^0_δ: $\bar{u} = \varrho$, $\bar{v} \doteq \sqrt{\varrho^2 - u^2 + \delta^2 u^4} + \delta u^2$, $\underline{v} \doteq -\sqrt{\varrho^2 - u^2 + \delta^2 u^4} + \delta u^2$, $f(u,v) = 1$;
- for G^0_ε, H^0_ε: $\bar{u} = \varrho$, $\bar{v} \doteq \sqrt{(\varrho^2 - u^2)(1 + 2\varepsilon u)}$, $\underline{v} \doteq -\bar{v}$, $f(u,v) \doteq 1 - \varepsilon u$;
- for G^0_ζ, H^0_ζ: $\bar{u} = \varrho$, $\bar{v} \doteq \sqrt{\varrho^2 - u^2} + \zeta(\varrho^2 - u^2)$, $\underline{v} \doteq -\sqrt{\varrho^2 - u^2} + \zeta(\varrho^2 - u^2)$, $f(u,v) \doteq 1 - 2\zeta v$.

From these it follows that

$$G^0_\gamma = \tfrac{8}{9}\varrho^6 , \quad G^0_\varepsilon = \tfrac{4}{9}\varrho^6 , \quad G^0_\beta = G^0_\delta = G^0_\zeta = H^0_\beta = H^0_\gamma = H^0_\delta = H^0_\varepsilon = H^0_\zeta = 0 . \qquad (24)$$

Inserting (21), (22), (23), (24) into (19) and (20), we have

$$F(0,0,0) = \tfrac{32}{45}\varrho^5 + \tfrac{4}{9}\varrho^6(-\alpha + 2\gamma + \varepsilon), \qquad F_{u^*}(0,0,0) = \tfrac{4}{3}\varrho^4, \tag{25}$$

and by orthogonal transform in the u-v plane

$$\begin{aligned}F(0,0,\varphi) = \tfrac{32}{45}\varrho^5 + \tfrac{4}{9}\varrho^6 \Big(&-(\alpha\cos\varphi + \delta\sin\varphi)\cos^2\varphi \\
&- 2(\beta\cos\varphi + \varepsilon\sin\varphi)\cos\varphi\sin\varphi - (\gamma\cos\varphi + \zeta\sin\varphi)\sin^2\varphi \\
&+ 2(\alpha\cos\varphi + \delta\sin\varphi)\sin^2\varphi - 4(\beta\cos\varphi + \varepsilon\sin\varphi)\cos\varphi\sin\varphi \\
&+ 2(\gamma\cos\varphi + \zeta\sin\varphi)\cos^2\varphi - 2(-\alpha\sin\varphi + \delta\cos\varphi)\cos\varphi\sin\varphi \\
&+ (-\beta\sin\varphi + \varepsilon\cos\varphi)(\cos^2\varphi - \sin^2\varphi) \\
&+ 2(-\gamma\sin\varphi + \zeta\cos\varphi)\cos\varphi\sin\varphi\Big), \end{aligned} \tag{26}$$

$$F_{u^*}(0,0,\varphi) = \tfrac{4}{3}\varrho^4\cos\varphi, \qquad F_{v^*}(0,0,\varphi) = \tfrac{4}{3}\varrho^4\sin\varphi. \tag{27}$$

Integration (13) then yields

$$\Phi(0,0) = \frac{\pi}{18}\varrho^6\begin{pmatrix}\alpha + 3\gamma - \varepsilon \\ -\beta + 3\delta - \zeta\end{pmatrix}, \qquad D\Phi(0,0) = -\frac{2}{3}\pi\varrho^4\begin{pmatrix}1 & 0 \\ 0 & 1\end{pmatrix} \tag{28}$$

and via (14) eventually

$$\begin{pmatrix}u^* \\ v^*\end{pmatrix} = \frac{\varrho^2}{12}\begin{pmatrix}\alpha + 3\gamma - \varepsilon \\ -\beta + 3\delta + \zeta\end{pmatrix}. \tag{29}$$

Inserting (11), (12) into (29), we see that for $D\boldsymbol{u} = \operatorname{diag}(1,1)$ the Oja median filtering step approximates an explicit time step of size $\tau = \varrho^2/24$ of the PDE system

$$u_t = u_{xx} + 3u_{yy} - 2v_{xy}, \qquad v_t = 3v_{xx} + v_{yy} - 2u_{xy}. \tag{30}$$

Transfer to the general case with arbitrary $D\boldsymbol{u}$ is accomplished by an affine transformation in the u-v coordinates. This yields the PDE system from equations (7)–(9) of the theorem. □

Remark 3. The derivation of the PDE of Theorem 1 by affine transformation immediately implies its affine equivariance.

Remark 4. The equations (7)–(9) are degenerate at locations where $\det D\boldsymbol{u} = 0$. This corresponds to the degeneracy of the Oja median itself for collinear input data. Future work will be concerned with this non-generic case.

Remark 5. The eigenvector directions $\boldsymbol{\eta}$ and $\boldsymbol{\xi}$ of the structure tensor do not appear in a natural way in the presentation of (7). This is plausible because these eigenvectors are strongly related with a Euclidean geometry concept of the u-v plane, and are thereby inappropriate for an affine equivariant process like Oja median filtering.

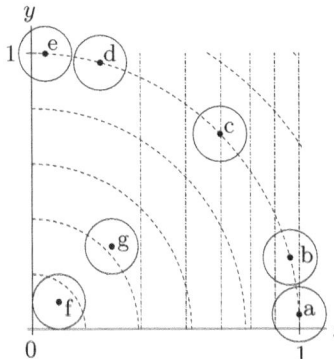

Fig. 4. Example function $(u, v) = (x^2, \sqrt{x^2 + y^2})$ used to demonstrate PDE approximation of Oja median filtering. Dot-dashed lines are level lines $u = \text{const}$, dashed lines are level lines $v = \text{const}$. Points a–g are the sample locations for which numerical results are given in Table 1, surrounded by their structuring elements as solid circles.

4 Experimental Demonstration of Oja Median Filtering

To demonstrate the validity of the PDE approximation result stated in Theorem 1, we consider a simple bivariate example function given by

$$u(x,y) = x^2, \qquad v(x,y) = \sqrt{x^2 + y^2}. \tag{31}$$

Level sets of u and v for this function in the range $[0,1] \times [0,1]$ are depicted in Figure 4. In this figure, also seven test locations a–g are depicted for which Table 1 contains analytically computed time steps $(\tau u_t, \tau v_t)$ of the PDE (7) and results of numerical approximations of the Oja median on a discrete grid within a structuring element of radius $\varrho = 0.1$. For the Oja median computation, we first normalise the input data set by a principal axis transform to zero mean and isotropic unit standard deviation, and apply then a gradient descent method with adaptive step size control, after which the normalising transform is reverted.

The results for locations b, c, d and g in Table 1 confirm that in the generic setting where $\det \mathbf{D}\boldsymbol{u}$ is sufficiently far away from zero, the PDE time step and the median update $(u^* - u, v^* - v)$ computed on the discrete grid match each other well. The observed relative errors in the range of $\leq 3\%$ (based on the Euclidean norm of $(\tau u_t, \tau v_t)$) are reasonable given the structuring element radius $\varrho = 0.1$ and the grid resolution.

Larger discrepancies are observed for locations a, e, and f which are closer to the coordinate axes. Note that on the x axis, $\mathbf{D}\boldsymbol{u}$ becomes singular due to coinciding gradient directions for u and v, while on the y axis it does so due to the vanishing of $\boldsymbol{\nabla} u$. These discrepancies indicate numerical problems of the median computation rather than inaccuracy of the PDE, pointing to the need for algorithmic improvements in the Oja median computation.

5 Summary and Outlook

In this paper, we have analysed the Oja median filter in the bivariate case and shown that it asymptotically approximates for vanishing structuring element size

Table 1. Comparison of analytically computed time steps $(\tau u_t, \tau v_t)$ of the PDE (7)–(9), with numerical computation of the Oja median (u^*, v^*) for the function $(u, v) = (x^2, \sqrt{x^2 + y^2})$. To compute (u^*, v^*), the structuring element of radius $\varrho = 0.1$ was sampled using a grid with spatial mesh size $h = 0.001$, generating about 31,000 data points. The time step size for (7) was chosen as $\tau = \varrho^2/24 = 0.4167$.

	Location		Function value		PDE time step		Discrete Oja median	
	x_0	y_0	u	v	τu_t	τv_t	$u^* - u$	$v^* - v$
a)	0.9986	0.0523	0.9973	1.0000	0.002 495	0.000 417	0.001 896	0.000 538
b)	0.9659	0.2588	0.9330	1.0000	0.002 388	0.000 417	0.002 355	0.000 417
c)	0.7071	0.7071	0.5000	1.0000	0.001 667	0.000 417	0.001 650	0.000 404
d)	0.2588	0.9659	0.0670	1.0000	0.000 945	0.000 417	0.000 943	0.000 407
e)	0.0523	0.9986	0.0027	1.0000	0.000 838	0.000 417	0.000 920	0.000 448
f)	0.1000	0.1000	0.0100	0.1414	0.001 667	0.002 946	0.001 587	0.003 668
g)	0.3000	0.3000	0.0900	0.4243	0.001 667	0.000 982	0.001 654	0.001 009

a second-order PDE which is more favourable than that approximated by the more popular L^1 median filter. This gives a strong motivation to deeper investigate the applicability of Oja median filtering in multi-channel image processing.

The proof of Theorem 1 will be presented in more detail in forthcoming work, where also the degenerate case $\det D\boldsymbol{u}$ will be given broader attention. It will be of high interest to extend our results from the bivariate to the general multivariate case. Moreover, analysis of further multivariate median filters proposed in the statistical literature, as mentioned in the introduction, is another goal of ongoing research.

Finally, a straightforward computation of the Oja median filter has higher complexity than that of the L^1 median filter (due to the point pairs to be iterated over instead of points). Further development of efficient algorithms will therefore be important in order to establish Oja median filtering as a practical image filter.

References

1. Alvarez, L., Lions, P.-L., Morel, J.-M.: Image selective smoothing and edge detection by nonlinear diffusion. II. SIAM Journal on Numerical Analysis **29**, 845–866 (1992)
2. Astola, J., Haavisto, P., Neuvo, Y.: Vector median filters. Proceedings of the IEEE **78**(4), 678–689 (1990)
3. Austin, T.L.: An approximation to the point of minimum aggregate distance. Metron **19**, 10–21 (1959)
4. Chakraborty, B., Chaudhuri, P.: On a transformation and re-transformation technique for constructing an affine equivariant multivariate median. Proceedings of the AMS **124**(6), 2539–2547 (1996)
5. Chakraborty, B., Chaudhuri, P.: A note on the robustness of multivariate medians. Statistics and Probability Letters **45**, 269–276 (1999)
6. Chung, D.H., Sapiro, G.: On the level lines and geometry of vector-valued images. IEEE Signal Processing Letters **7**(9), 241–243 (2000)

7. Eckhardt, U.: Root images of median filters. Journal of Mathematical Imaging and Vision **19**, 63–70 (2003)
8. Gini, C., Galvani, L.: Di talune estensioni dei concetti di media ai caratteri qualitativi. Metron **8**, 3–209 (1929)
9. Guichard, F., Morel, J.-M.: Partial differential equations and image iterative filtering. In: Duff, I.S., Watson, G.A. (eds.) The State of the Art in Numerical Analysis. IMA Conference Series (New Series), vol. 63, pp. 525–562. Clarendon Press, Oxford (1997)
10. Hayford, J.F.: What is the center of an area, or the center of a population? Journal of the American Statistical Association **8**(58), 47–58 (1902)
11. Hettmansperger, T.P., Randles, R.H.: A practical affine equivariant multivariate median. Biometrika **89**(4), 851–860 (2002)
12. Kleefeld, A., Breuß, M., Welk, M., Burgeth, B.: Adaptive filters for color images: median filtering and its extensions. In: Trémeau, A., Schettini, R., Tominaga, S. (eds.) CCIW 2015. LNCS, vol. 9016, pp. 149–158. Springer, Heidelberg (2015)
13. Oja, H.: Descriptive statistics for multivariate distributions. Statistics and Probability Letters **1**, 327–332 (1983)
14. Rao, C.R.: Methodology based on the l_1-norm in statistical inference. Sankhyā A **50**, 289–313 (1988)
15. Small, C.G.: A survey of multidimensional medians. International Statistical Review **58**(3), 263–277 (1990)
16. Spence, C., Fancourt, C.: An iterative method for vector median filtering. In: Proc. 2007 IEEE International Conference on Image Processing, vol. 5, pp. 265–268 (2007)
17. Tukey, J.W.: Exploratory Data Analysis. Addison-Wesley, Menlo Park (1971)
18. Weber, A.: Über den Standort der Industrien. Mohr, Tübingen (1909)
19. Weiszfeld, E.: Sur le point pour lequel la somme des distances de n points donnés est minimum. Tôhoku Mathematics Journal **43**, 355–386 (1937)
20. Welk, M., Breuß, M.: Morphological amoebas and partial differential equations. In: Hawkes, P.W. (ed.) Advances in Imaging and Electron Physics, vol. 185, pp. 139–212. Elsevier Academic Press (2014)
21. Welk, M., Breuß, M., Vogel, O.: Morphological amoebas are self-snakes. Journal of Mathematical Imaging and Vision **39**, 87–99 (2011)
22. Welk, M., Feddern, C., Burgeth, B., Weickert, J.: Median filtering of tensor-valued images. In: Michaelis, B., Krell, G. (eds.) DAGM 2003. LNCS, vol. 2781, pp. 17–24. Springer, Heidelberg (2003)

Fundamentals of Non-Local Total Variation Spectral Theory

Jean-François Aujol[1,2], Guy Gilboa[3](✉), and Nicolas Papadakis[1,2]

[1] University of Bordeaux, IMB, UMR 5251, 33400 Talence, France
[2] CNRS, IMB, UMR 5251, 33400 Talence, France
[3] Electrical Engineering Department, Technion - IIT, Haifa, Israel
guy.gilboa@ee.technion.ac.il

Abstract. Eigenvalue analysis based on linear operators has been extensively used in signal and image processing to solve a variety of problems such as segmentation, dimensionality reduction and more. Recently, non-linear spectral approaches, based on the total variation functional have been proposed. In this context, functions for which the nonlinear eigenvalue problem $\lambda u \in \partial J(u)$ admits solutions, are studied. When u is the characteristic function of a set A, then it is called a calibrable set. If $\lambda > 0$ is a solution of the above problem, then $1/\lambda$ can be interpreted as the scale of A. However, this notion of scale remains local, and it may not be adapted for non-local features. For this we introduce in this paper the definition of non-local scale related to the non-local total variation functional. In particular, we investigate sets that evolve with constant speed under the non-local total variation flow. We prove that non-local calibrable sets have this property. We propose an onion peel construction to build such sets. We eventually confirm our mathematical analysis with some simple numerical experiments.

Keywords: Non-local · Total variation · Calibrable sets · Scale · Non-linear eigenvalue problem

1 Introduction

Since the seminal work by Rudin et al in [19], total variation is established as a main tool in mathematical image processing. It has been used for many applications such as denoising, deblurring, inpainting (see e.g. [3] and references herein). In a series of papers, V. Caselles and his co-authors have computed explicit solutions of the total variation flow problem [1,2,9]:

$$\begin{cases} u(x,0) = f(x), \\ \frac{\partial u}{\partial t} = \mathrm{div}\left(\frac{\nabla u}{|\nabla u|}\right). \end{cases} \quad (1)$$

In particular, it is shown that if $f = \chi_A$ with A a non empty closed convex set, such that the absolute value of its curvature is smaller than $\lambda_A = \frac{\mathrm{Per}(A)}{|A|}$ (with $\mathrm{Per}(A)$ the perimeter of A and $|A|$ its area), then the solution of (1) is given by

$u(t) = (1 - t\lambda_A)^+ \chi_A$. More generally, calibrable sets evolve with constant speed under the total variation flow. Notice that the notion of calibrable sets was also a key ingredient to build explicit solutions of the $TV - L^1$ problem [10,11]. The quantity $\lambda_A = \frac{\text{Per}(A)}{|A|}$, known as the Cheeger constant, can be seen as the inverse of a scale, and this has been used in works such as [7,15,20,21].

A calibrable set A is such that the following nonlinear eigenvalue problem has a solution (with $u = \chi_A$):

$$p(u) = \lambda u, \ p(u) \in \partial J(u), \qquad (2)$$

where $J(u)$ is the total variation functional and $\partial J(u)$ is its subgradient.

In [13] a generalization of eigenfunction analysis to the nonlinear case was proposed in the following way. Define

$$\phi(t; x) := u_{tt}(t; x)t, \qquad (3)$$

where u_{tt} is the second time derivative of the solution $u(t; x)$ of the TV-flow (1). For $f(x)$ admitting (2), with a corresponding eigenvalue λ, one obtains $\phi(t; x) = \delta(t - 1/\lambda)f(x)$. When f is composed of separable eigenfunctions with eigenvalues λ_i one obtains through $\phi(t; x)$ a decomposition of the image into its eigenfunctions at $t = 1/\lambda_i$. In the general case, ϕ yields a continuum multi-scale representation of the image, generalizing structure-texture decomposition methods like [4,5,17]. One can reconstruct the original image by:

$$f(x) = \int_0^\infty \phi(t; x)dt + \bar{f}, \qquad (4)$$

where $\bar{f} = \frac{1}{|\Omega|} \int_\Omega f(x)dx$. Given a transfer function $H(t) \in \mathbb{R}$, image filtering can be performed by:

$$f_H(x) := \int_0^\infty H(t)\phi(t; x)dt + \bar{f}.$$

The spectrum $S(t)$ corresponds to the amplitude of each scale:

$$S(t) := \|\phi(t; x)\|_{L^1(\Omega)} = \int_\Omega |\phi(t; x)| dx. \qquad (5)$$

The goal of this paper is to extend this notion of scale to a non-local setting. Non-local approaches have become very popular in the last past years since the seminal work by Buades et al [8]. A non-local version of the total variation based on graphs was introduced in [14]. See recent related studies analyzing non-local and double-integral functionals in [6,18]. Here we intend to propose a non-local notion of scale, and to this end we will introduce a notion of non-local disks and more generally of non-local calibrable sets.

The plan of the paper in the following. In section 2, we recall the non-local setting introduced in [14], and how it connects to the classical local setting. In section 3, we consider the graph point of view of [12,22] to define all the non-local notions we need, and in particular a non-local scale. In section 4, we propose a construction of non-local disks based on an onion peel analysis. We eventually show some numerical results to illustrate our analysis in Section 5.

2 Background and Definitions of Non-Local Operators

We first recall the basic non-local operators. We give the definitions in the continuous setting in order to make clear connections with respect to the classical local variational approaches.

2.1 Non-Local Operators

Given a bounded domain $\Omega \subset \mathbb{R}^2$ we have non-negative weights $w(x,y) \geq 0$ between any two points $x, y \in \Omega$. These weights correspond to affinities between the points. For simplicity, we assume that the weights are symmetric, that is $w(x,y) = w(y,x)$, the extension to non symmetric weights being straightforward. In this context we have two types of functions: scalar functions and vector functions. Scalars are the standard functions $u : \Omega \to \mathbb{R}$, whereas vectors, denoted $\boldsymbol{v}(x)$, or $v(x,y)$, have the following mapping $v : \Omega \times \Omega \to \mathbb{R}$. For example, a non-local gradient maps a scalar to a vector function.

The inner product of two vectors $\boldsymbol{v}_1(x)$ and $\boldsymbol{v}_2(x)$ is defined as:

$$\langle \boldsymbol{v}_1, \boldsymbol{v}_2 \rangle_\Omega := \int_\Omega v_1(x,y) v_2(x,y) dy. \tag{6}$$

We can now define the main non-local operators. The non-local gradient $\nabla_w u(x) : \Omega \to \Omega \times \Omega$ is defined as:

$$(\nabla_w u)(x,y) := (u(y) - u(x))\sqrt{w(x,y)}, \quad x, y \in \Omega. \tag{7}$$

The non-local divergence $\operatorname{div}_w \boldsymbol{v}(x) : \Omega \times \Omega \to \Omega$ is:

$$(\operatorname{div}_w \boldsymbol{v})(x) := \int_\Omega (v(x,y) - v(y,x))\sqrt{w(x,y)} dy. \tag{8}$$

Some basic properties, similar to the standard local operators, can be shown, as for example the gradient and divergence adjoint relation:

$$\langle \nabla_w u, \boldsymbol{v} \rangle = \langle u, -\operatorname{div}_w \boldsymbol{v} \rangle. \tag{9}$$

2.2 Non-Local Total-Variation

The difference-based functional we consider is

$$J(u) = \int_{\Omega \times \Omega} \psi((u(y) - u(x))^2 w(x,y)) dy dx, \tag{10}$$

and its variation with respect to u reads

$$\partial_u J(u) = -4 \int_\Omega (u(y) - u(x)) w(x,y) \psi'((u(y) - u(x))^2 w(x,y)) dy. \tag{11}$$

Taking $\psi(s) = \sqrt{s}/2$ we define the non-local total-variation as:

$$J_{NL-TV}(u) = \frac{1}{2} \int_{\Omega \times \Omega} |u(x) - u(y)| \sqrt{w(x,y)} dy dx \tag{12}$$

The above functional corresponds in the local two dimensional case to the anisotropic TV:
$$J_{TV}(u) = \int_\Omega (|u_{x_1}| + |u_{x_2}|) dx.$$

Although all the results of the paper remain true in the isotropic case, we have decided to present in this work only the anisotropic setting. Following the clocal TV-flow [16], we are investigating the non-local total variation flow (NL-TV-flow):

$$\begin{cases} -\frac{\partial u}{\partial t} \in \partial_u J_{NL-TV}(u) \\ u(0,x) = f(x) \end{cases} \qquad (13)$$

Now that we have recalled the non-local notions we are interested in, we turn in the next section to a graph setting which will prove more adapted to the non-local framework.

3 A Graph Point of View

As soon as we consider a discrete image, the connections between pixels can be explained with a graph representation. We will place ourselves in this setting from now on.

3.1 Definitions

We consider a graph $\mathcal{G}$ (which corresponds to the bounded domain Ω considered in the previous section). It is composed of $|\mathcal{G}|$ points $x \in \mathcal{G}$ and characterized by the adjacency matrix $w(x,y) : \mathcal{G} \times \mathcal{G} \to \in [0;1]^{|\mathcal{G}|}$. We assume that this matrix is symmetric. Notice that this adjacency matrix corresponds to the non negative weights $w(x,y)$ introduced in the previous section. We have decided to use the same notation for the sake of clarity.

Definition 1 (Boundary of a set). *The intern boundary of a set A is defined as:*
$$\partial A = \{x \in A,\ s.t\ \exists y \in \mathcal{G} \backslash A,\ with\ w(x,y) > 0\}.$$

The extern boundary of a set A is defined as:
$$\partial A^+ = \{x \in \mathcal{G} \backslash A,\ s.t\ \exists y \in A,\ with\ w(x,y) > 0\}.$$

Let χ_A be a characteristic function of $A \subset \mathcal{G}$. We remind the reader that $\chi_A(x) = 1$ if $x \in A$ and 0 otherwise.

Definition 2 (Perimeter of a set).
The perimeter of a set A is defined as:
$$Per_w(A) = J_{NL-TV}(\chi_A) = \frac{1}{2} \sum_{\mathcal{G} \times \mathcal{G}} |\chi_A(x) - \chi_A(y)| \sqrt{w(x,y)} \qquad (14)$$

Definition 3 (Normal of a set). *The normal of a set A is defined on its boundary $x \in \partial A$ as, for $y \in \partial A^+$: $\nu_A(x,y) = -sgn(\nabla_w \chi_A(x,y)) = \chi_{w(x,y)>0}$. The minus is a convention. Observe that $Per_w(A) = -\langle \nu_A^a, \nabla_w \chi_A \rangle_{\mathcal{G} \times \mathcal{G}}$.*

Definition 4 (Curvature of a set). *The curvature of a set $A \subset \mathcal{G}$ is*

$$\kappa_w(\chi_A)(x) = \operatorname{div}_w(-sgn(\nabla_w \chi_A(x,y))) \tag{15}$$

We assume that the domain $\mathcal{G}$, the set A and its complement $\mathcal{G} \backslash A$ are all connected sets.

3.2 Sets With Constant Curvature

Now that we have introduced the necessary material, we can characterize the sets with constant curvatures. Notice that in the classical local setting, these sets are just balls (whose shape depends on the considered norm). As we will see in the following, we get a necessary and sufficient condition to characterize sets with constant curvature. Sets with constant curvature will be key ingredients to introduce non-local calibrable sets.

Proposition 1. *A necessary and sufficient condition for $\kappa_w(\chi_A)(x)|_{x \in \partial A} = K \in \mathbb{R}$ is:*

$$\sum_{y \in \partial A^+} \sqrt{w(x,y)} = a^+ \in \mathbb{R}^+, \forall x \in \partial A.$$

The curvature value at the boundary ∂A is $K = 2a^+$.

Proof. We can use the definition (15) of the mean curvature for χ_A, the characteristic function of $A \subset \mathcal{G}$. For $x \in \partial A$, as $w(x,y) = 0$, $\forall y \in \mathcal{G} \backslash (A \cup \partial A^+)$ we get:

$$\kappa_w(\chi_A)(x) = -\sum_{y \in \mathcal{G}} \left(sgn\left((\chi_A(y) - \chi_A(x))w_{xy}\right) - sgn\left((\chi_A(x) - \chi_A(y))w_{xy}\right) \right) w_{xy}$$

$$= -\sum_{y \in A \cup \partial A^+} \left(sgn\left((\chi_A(y) - 1)w_{xy}\right) - sgn\left((1 - \chi_A(y))w_{xy}\right) \right) w_{xy}$$

$$= -\sum_{y \in A} \left(sgn(0) - sgn(0) \right) w_{xy} \, dy + \sum_{\partial A^+} \left(sgn(-w_{xy}) - sgn(w_{xy}) \right) w_{xy}$$

$$= 2 \sum_{y \in \partial A^+} w_{xy},$$

since $w_{xy} = \sqrt{w(x,y)} \geq 0$. A necessary and sufficient condition for $\kappa_w(\chi_A)(x)|_{x \in \partial A} = 2a^+ \in \mathbb{R}^+$ is then

$$\sum_{y \in \partial A^+} \sqrt{w(x,y)} = a^+ \in \mathbb{R}^+, \forall x \in \partial A.$$

In the same way, we get:

$$\kappa_w(\chi_A)(x) = \begin{cases} 2a^+ & if\ x \in \partial A \\ 0 & if\ x \in A\setminus\partial A \\ -2a^- & if\ x \in \partial A^+ \\ 0 & if\ x \in \mathcal{G}\setminus(A \cup \partial A^+), \end{cases} \quad (16)$$

under the assumption $\sum_{y \in \partial A} \sqrt{w(x,y)} = a^- \in \mathbb{R}^+, \forall x \in \partial A^+$.

From the last proposition, the curvature is constant iff:

- for $x \in \partial A$, $\sum_{y \in \partial A^+} \sqrt{w(x,y)} = a^+ > 0$
- for $x \in \partial A^+$, $\sum_{y \in \partial A} \sqrt{w(x,y)} = a^- > 0$

A set with constant curvature in its intern and extern boundaries is then characterized with the parameters (a^+, a^-).

Proposition 2 (Sets with constant curvature). *When the intern and extern curvatures of a set A are constants with parameters (a^+, a^-), the perimeter reads:*

$$Per_w(A) = \frac{1}{2}(|\partial A|a^+ + |\partial A^+|a^-) = |\partial A|a^+.$$

Proof. We have:

$$Per_w(A) = \frac{1}{2}\sum_{\mathcal{G}\times\mathcal{G}} |\chi_A(x) - \chi_A(y)|\sqrt{w(x,y)}$$

$$= \frac{1}{2}\sum_{x\in\partial A,\, y\in\mathcal{G}} |\chi_A(x) - \chi_A(y)|\sqrt{w(x,y)} + \frac{1}{2}\sum_{x\in\partial A^+,\, y\in\mathcal{G}} |\chi_A(x) - \chi_A(y)|\sqrt{w(x,y)}$$

$$= \frac{1}{2}(|\partial A|a^+ + |\partial A^+|a^-)$$

and as w is symmetric, we have that the total weights a^+ going from ∂A to ∂A^+ is the same than the weights a^- going from ∂A^+ to ∂A: $|\partial A|a^+ = \sum_{x\in\partial A,\, y\in\mathcal{G}} |\chi_A(x) - \chi_A(y)|\sqrt{w(x,y)} = \sum_{x\in\partial A^+,\, y\in\mathcal{G}} |\chi_A(x) - \chi_A(y)|\sqrt{w(x,y)} = |\partial A^+|a^-$.

3.3 Subdifferential of J_{NL-TV}

Another ingredient needed to introduce non-local calibrable sets is the subdifferential of non-local TV. As recalled in [22], the subdifferential of $NL - TV$ is characterized by:

$$\partial J_{NL-TV}(u) = \{\mathrm{div}_w(z)\ /\ \max|z| \leq 1 \text{ and } \langle \mathrm{div}_w z, u\rangle_\mathcal{G} = J_{NL-TV}(u)\} \quad (17)$$

Denoting $z = -sign(\nabla_w u)$, with $sign(0) \in [-1,1]$, the subdifferential of J_{NL-TV} is:

$$\partial J_{NL-TV}(u) = \mathrm{div}_w(z). \quad (18)$$

From Definition 3, it can be noticed that

$$\partial J_{NL-TV}(\chi_A) = \mathrm{div}_w(\nu_A). \quad (19)$$

3.4 Non-Local Calibrable Sets

We have all the required material to define non-local calibrable sets. As we will see later, such sets evolve with constant speed with the non-local total variation flow.

Definition 5 (Non-local calibrable set). A is a non-local calibrable set iff there exists $\lambda_A > 0$ and $\operatorname{div}_w(z) \in \partial J_{NL-TV}(\chi_A)$ such that $(\operatorname{div}_w z)(x) = \lambda_A \chi_A(x) + c$, $\forall x \in A$, $c \in \mathbb{R}$. Such z is called a calibration of the set A.

Remark 1. Notice that contrary to the continuous local case (see e.g. [1]), there are no boundary conditions such as Neuman boundary conditions. We have these boundary conditions for free here since the non-local divergence operator was defined as the opposite of the adjoint of the non-local gradient operator. Moreover, as noted in [22], the value of the divergence outside A is irrelevant, so that we just focus on finding a flow with constant divergence inside A.

Proposition 3. *If z is a calibration of a non-local set A, then*

$$(\operatorname{div}_w z)(x) = \frac{\operatorname{Per}_w(A)}{|A|} \chi_A \qquad (20)$$

and thus $\lambda_A = \frac{\operatorname{Per}_w(A)}{|A|}$. Moreover, $z(x,y) = \nu_A(x,y)$ for $x \in \partial A$, $y \in \partial A^+$.

Proof. From Definition 5, we can observe that $\langle \operatorname{div}_w z, \chi_A \rangle_{\mathcal{G}} = \lambda_A |A|$. Hence, as $z \in \partial J_{NL-TV}(\chi_A)$, relation (17) gives $\langle \operatorname{div}_w z, \chi_A \rangle_{\mathcal{G}} = J_{NL-TV}(\chi_A) = \operatorname{Per}_w(A)$ so that $\lambda_A = \frac{\operatorname{Per}_w(A)}{|A|}$.

Moreover, from Definition 3, we have that $\operatorname{Per}_w(A) = -\langle \nu_A, \nabla_w \chi_A \rangle$. Since $\langle \operatorname{div}_w z, \chi_A \rangle_{\mathcal{G}} = -\langle z, \nabla_w \chi_A \rangle_{\mathcal{G} \times \mathcal{G}}$, we deduce that $z(x,y) = \nu_A(x,y)$ for $x \in \partial A$, $y \in \partial A^+$.

3.5 Non-Local TV Flow

For a set $A \in \mathcal{G}$, the non-local TV flow evolution equation is Eq. (13) with $u(t=0) = \chi_A$.

Proposition 4. *If A is a non-local calibrable set, then $u(t) = (1 - t\lambda_A)^+ \chi_A$ is a solution of Problem (13), with $\lambda_A = \frac{\operatorname{Per}_w(A)}{|A|}$.*

We remind the reader that $(1 - t\lambda_A)^+ = \max(0, 1 - t\lambda_A)$. This result shows that a non-local calibrable set evolves with constant speed with the non-local total variation flow. We know that such sets exist (and the onion peel story of section 4 is a way to build such sets).

Proof. With the above results, if A is a non-local calibrable set, then we can build a flow z such that $||z||_\infty \le 1$, $z = \nu_A$ on $\partial A \cup \partial A^+$ and $(\operatorname{div}_w z)(x) = \lambda_A$ for $x \in A$. We therefore have $\langle \operatorname{div}_w z, \chi_A \rangle_{\mathcal{G}} = \lambda_A |A| = \operatorname{Per}_w(A) = J_{NL-TV}(\chi_A)$. From the definition (17) of the NL-TV functional, we also have $J_{NL-TV}(u) = \sup_{||z||_\infty \le 1} \int_{\Omega \times \Omega} (\operatorname{div}_w z) u$.

We can see that the z we built is such that $\operatorname{div}_w z$ belongs to the subdifferential of J_{NL-TV} so that $(\operatorname{div}_w z)(x) = \lambda_A$ for $x \in A$. Hence, by defining $u(t) = (1 - t\lambda_A)^+ \chi_A$, we have for $t > 0$ that $\partial_t u = -\lambda_A \chi_A$ so that $-\partial_t u \in J_{NL-TV}(u)$ and u is a solution of problem (13).

3.6 Non-Local Scale

From the previous proposition, it makes sense to define the non-local scale in the following way:

Definition 6 (Non-local scale). *The non-local scale of a point in an image is defined as the inverse of its average speed of decrease under the non-local total variation flow.*

Remark 2. In the case when a point x belongs to a non-local disk A, then its speed of decrease under the non-local total variation flow is the one of A, that is $\lambda_A = \frac{\operatorname{Per}_w(A)}{|A|}$. Hence the scale of x is $\frac{1}{\lambda_A}$. This generalizes the local case, where λ_A is the Cheeger constant of A [2,11].

4 The Onion Peel Decomposition

The purpose of this section is to show a way to build non trivial non-local calibrable sets. In the following, we denote as $\{B_r\}_{r=1}^R$ a partition of A ($\cup_{r=1}^R B_r = A$ and $B_r \cap B_{r'} = \emptyset$, for $r \neq r'$) and define $A_r = \cup_{i=1}^r B_i$. The idea developed here is inspired from the local discrete case: if we remove the boundary of a calibrable set, the resulting set is also calibrable.

Definition 7 (Onion peel partition). *Let A be a connected set. We say that A can be partitioned into onion peels if there exists a partition that checks:*

(i) $\partial A_r = B_r$, $\forall r = 1 \cdots R$.
(ii) $\partial A_r^+ = B_{r+1}$, $\forall r = 1 \cdots R-1$.

We then have $\partial A = B_R$ since $A = A_R$.

Definition 8 (Non-local Disk). *A is a non-local disk iff A is a non-local calibrable set with constant curvature on ∂A.*

Proposition 5 (Calibrable onion peel). *If (i) A can be partitioned into an onion peel $\{B_r\}_{r=0}^R$, (ii) $A_r = \cup_{i=0}^r B_i$ has a constant curvature (a_r^+, a_r^-) and (iii) $A = A_R = \operatorname{argmin}_r \operatorname{Per}_w(A_r)/|A_r|$, then A is a non-local disk, and its non-local scale is $\frac{|A|}{\operatorname{Per}_w(A)}$.*

Proof. We build a calibration z for an onion peel. By definition of the onion peel, we first recall that for $x \in B_r$, $w(x,y) = w(y,x) > 0$ iff $y \in B_{r-1}$ or $y \in B_r$ or $y \in B_{r+1}$. From proposition 2, we can observe that $a_r^+|B_r| = a_r^-|B_{r+1}|$ and $\operatorname{Per}_w(A_r) = \frac{1}{2}(|\partial A_r|a_r^+ + |\partial A_r^+|a_r^-) = |\partial A_r|a_r^+$. We recall that a_r^- denotes the constant curvature value of points ∂A_r^+ with respect to the set A_r.

We define $K_0 = 0$, $a_0^- = 0$, initialize $z = 0$ and consider a value $\alpha > 0$. Then for $r = 1 \cdots R$ we can do the following recursive construction: $\forall x \in B_r$, find the $y \in B_{r+1}$ such that $w(x,y) > 0$ and set $z(x,y) = K_r = \frac{a_{r-1}^- K_{r-1} + \alpha}{a_r^+}$. We then have $z(x,y) = K_r > 0$ for $x \in B_r$, $y \in B_{r+1}$ and $w(x,y) > 0$ and $z = 0$ otherwise. With such a construction, we have that, for $x \in B_r$, $0 \leq r \leq R$:

$$(\text{div}_w z)(x) = \sum_y (z(x,y) - z(y,x))\sqrt{w(x,y)}$$

$$= \sum_{y \in B_{r+1}} z(x,y)\sqrt{w(x,y)} - \sum_{y \in B_{r-1}} z(y,x)\sqrt{w(x,y)}$$

$$= K_r \sum_{y \in B_{r+1}} \sqrt{w(x,y)} dy - K_{r-1} \sum_{y \in B_{r-1}} \sqrt{w(x,y)} dy$$

$$= \frac{a_{r-1}^- K_{r-1} + \alpha}{a_r^+} a_r^+ - K_{r-1} a_{r-1}^-$$

$$= \alpha,$$

For $x \in A$, we have that $\|z(x)\|_\infty \leq \max_r K_r = K^*$. We then obtain that $\|z(x)/K^*\|_\infty \leq 1$ and $(\text{div}_w z/K^*)(x) = \alpha/K^*$, for $x \in A$.

Next, with our assumption on the constant curvature of the onion peel partition (see Definitions 7 and 5), we know that: $a_r^+|B_r| = a_r^-|B_{r+1}|$: the total weights a_r^+ going from B_r to B_{r+1} is the same as the weights a_r^- going from B_{r+1} to B_r. Since $K_1 = \alpha/a_1^+$, we have that

$$K_2 = \frac{a_1^- K_1 + \alpha}{a_1^+} = \frac{a_1^- \alpha/a_1^+ + \alpha}{a_2^+} = \frac{\alpha}{a_2^+}\left(1 + \frac{|B_1|}{|B_2|}\right) = \frac{\alpha(|B_1| + |B_2|)}{a_2^+|B_2|}$$

We can prove by induction that for $r = 1 \cdots R$:

$$K_r = \frac{\alpha \sum_{i=0}^r |B_i|}{a_r^+ |B_r|} = \frac{\alpha|A_r|}{a_r^+|\partial A_r|} = \frac{\alpha|A_r|}{\text{Per}_w(A_r)}$$

Hence, $K^* = \max_r K_r = \alpha/\lambda_A$ where

$$\lambda_A = \min_{A_r \subset A} \frac{\text{Per}_w(A_r)}{|A_r|}.$$

We then have that, for $x \in A$, $(\text{div}_w z/K^*)(x) = \alpha/K^* = \lambda_A$. Hence: $\langle \text{div}_w z, \chi_A \rangle = \lambda_A|A|$. If $A = A_R = \text{argmin}_r \text{Per}_w(A_r)/|A_r|$, then $K^* = K_R$. We thus obtain that $\|z(x,y)/K^*\| = 1$ for $x \in \partial A$, $y \in \partial A^+$ and $w(x,y) > 0$ so that the flow corresponds to the normal of the set at these points: $z(x,y) = \nu_A(x,y)$ (see Definition 3) and A is a non-local disk from definition 8. In this case, it also means that $\langle \text{div}_w z, \chi_A \rangle = \lambda_A|A| = \text{Per}_w(A)$.

Remark 3. Notice that since $K_r = \frac{a_{r-1}^- K_{r-1} + \alpha}{a_r^+}$, then a sufficient condition to have a disk through $K^* = K_R$ is $a_{r-1}^- \geq a_r^+$, which means that for each $x \in B_r$ the total weights of its links with B_{r-1} is larger than with B_{r+1}. With respect to the aniotropic local case and a 4-neighborhood system with weights $w(x,y) \in \{0;1\}$, such property is trivially checked since $a_r^+ = a_r^- = 2$.

5 Numerical Experiments

In this section, we show some simple numerical experiments which confirm the theoretical results presented in the previous sections. We consider synthetic images representing the characteristic function of some objects and build two graphs. First, we consider a local graph corresponding to a 4 neighborhood system to compute the anisotropic TV flow. The local adjacency matrix thus reads $w^L(x,y) = 1$ if x and y are neighbors in the image domain and 0 otherwise. Then, a full non-local graph is built from self-similarities between patches centered on every pixels of a considered image f. The adjacency matrix is in this case defined as: $w^{NL}(x,y) = exp(-||P_x^f - P_y^f||^2)$, where P_x^f denotes the image patch centered on pixel x. This corresponds to a non-local mean graph construction for the image f. The non-local TV flow (13) is then applied to the synthetic images for the two graph settings giving us two sequences $u^L(t,x)$ and $u^{NL}(t,x)$. We then compute the NL-TV spectral transform $\phi(t,x)$ and spectrum $S(t)$ as in Eqs. (3) and (5), respectively, with $u(t,x)$ the NL-TV flow solution of (13). High amplitudes in $S(t)$ indicate the dominant scales contained in the image. Notice that the non-local TV flow, derived from the the local graph with weights w^L, is in fact the classical TV flow. In our illustrations, we considered two objects of different scales for each tested image. As illustrated in Fig. 1, in the local setting, each object has a different scale, since two main peaks appear in $S^L(t)$. On the other hand, with the non-local weights, the two objects are considered as a single one as $S^{NL}(t)$ only contains one peak.

In the first row of Fig. 1, the objects are squares so that they correspond to a disk for the local anisotropic TV flow. As the local anisotropic Cheeger constants of the two squares are 8/3 and 4/3, we see from proposition 4 that the objects vanish with the TV flow for $t = 3/8$ and $t = 3/4$, which correspond to the positions of the two peaks of $S^L(t)$. With the non-local graph represented by w^{NL}, the non-local scale of the union of the two squares can thus be deduced from $S^{NL}(t)$ where the most important peak is at time $t = 0.015$. As the non-local curvature of the shape is not constant, we nevertheless observe a spread peak and the union of the two squares is just a raw approximation of a non-local calibrable set for the graph w^{NL}.

In the second row, the example is composed of non-rectangular shapes, the objects are not calibrable sets anymore for the local graph w^L. This is exhibited by the spread peaks of $S^L(t)$. It is difficult to assess the presence of two objects with the local framework since $S^L(t)$ contains 4 peaks. With the full non-local graph, one peak is recovered and its non-local scale is almost the same as in the square example. The non-local curvature is here almost constant so that we recover a main peak. This shows that these objects approach non-local calibrable sets for the graph w^{NL}.

These results give an interesting point of view of the non-local means behaviour. When constructing a graph with respect to the similarities contained in an image and applying the NL-TV flow to this image, one can expect that groups of similar patterns will have a constant speed of decrease.

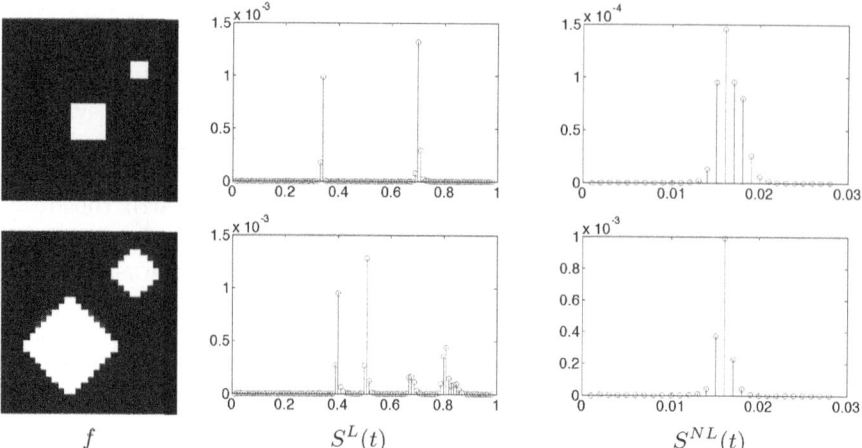

Fig. 1. Examples of scale computation. First column: images f; second column: local scale $S^L(t)$; third column: non-local scale $S^{NL}(t)$. The non-local scale gives indeed the same scale to the two shapes, whereas the local version give two different scales and even badly characterize the 2 objects for the second row.

6 Conclusion

The paper formulates a platform for spectral analysis related to the non-local total variation functional. Non-local calibrable sets, which are nonlinear eigenfunctions in the sense of (2), or atoms of the functional, are defined. A constructive way to build a subset of them is given. New structures such as non-local disks are examined through this framework, extending the standard geometrical concepts. The framework is a first step toward a better analysis and design of non-local, image-driven and patch-based algorithms, which have shown to yield state-of-the-art results in image processing and computer vision in recent years.

Acknowledgments. This study has been carried out with financial support from the French State, managed by the French National Research Agency (ANR) in the frame of the Investments for the future Programme IdEx Bordeaux (ANR-10-IDEX-03-02). J-F. Aujol acknowledges the support of Institut Universitaire de France. G. Gilboa acknowledges the support of the Mallat Family Fund.

References

1. Andreu, F., Ballester, C., Caselles, V., Mazon, J.M.: Minimizing total variation flow. Differential and Integral Equations **14**(3), 321–360 (2001)
2. Andreu-Vaillo, F., Caselles, V., Mazon, J.M.: Parabolic quasilinear equations minimizing linear growth functionals. Progress in Mathematics, vol. 223. Birkhauser (2002)
3. Aubert, G., Kornprobst, P.: Mathematical Problems in Image Processing. Applied Mathematical Sciences, vol. 147. Springer (2002)

4. Aujol, J.-F., Gilboa, G., Chan, T., Osher, S.: Structure-texture image decomposition - modeling, algorithms, and parameter selection. International Journal of Computer Vision **67**(1), 111–136 (2006)
5. Aujol, J.F., Aubert, G., Blanc-Féraud, L., Chambolle, A.: Image decomposition into a bounded variation component and an oscillating component. Journal of Mathematical Imaging and Vision **22**(1), 71–88 (2005)
6. Boulanger, J., Elbau, P., Pontow, C., Scherzer, O.: Non-local functionals for imaging. In: Fixed-Point Algorithms for Inverse Problems in Science and Engineering, pp. 131–154. Springer (2011)
7. Brox, T., Weickert, J.: A tv flow based local scale measure for texture discrimination. In: Pajdla, T., Matas, J.G. (eds.) ECCV 2004. LNCS, vol. 3022, pp. 578–590. Springer, Heidelberg (2004)
8. Buades, A., Coll, B., Morel, J.M.: A review of image denoising algorithms, with a new one. Multiscale Modeling and Simulation (SIAM Interdisciplinary Journal) **4**, 490–530 (2005)
9. Caselles, V., Chambolle, A., Moll, S., Novaga, M.: A characterization of convex calibrable sets in $\mathbb{R}^n$ with respect to anisotropic norms. Annales de l'Institut Henri Poincaré **25**, 803–832 (2008)
10. Chan, T.F., Esedoglu, S.: Aspects of total variation regularized L^1 function approximation. SIAM Journal on Applied Mathematics **65**(5), 1817–1837 (2005)
11. Duval, V., Aujol, J.-F., Gousseau, Y.: The tvl1 model: a geometric point of view. SIAM Journal on Multiscale Modeling and Simulation **8**(1), 154–189 (2009)
12. Elmoataz, A., Lezoray, O., Bougleux, S.: Nonlocal discrete regularization on weighted graphs: A framework for image and manifold processing. IEEE Transactions on Image Processing **17**(7), 1047–1060 (2008)
13. Gilboa, G.: A total variation spectral framework for scale and texture analysis. SIAM Journal on Imaging Sciences **7**(4), 1937–1961 (2014)
14. Gilboa, G., Osher, S.: Nonlocal operators with applications to image processing. SIAM Multiscale Modeling and Simulation **7**(3), 1005–1028 (2008)
15. Luo, B., Aujol, J.-F., Gousseau, Y.: Local scale measure from the topographic map and application to remote sensing images. SIAM Journal on Multiscale Modeling and Simulation (in press 2009)
16. Moll, J.S.: The anisotropic total variation flow. Mathematische Annalen **332**, 177–218 (2005)
17. Osher, S.J., Sole, A., Vese, L.A.: Image decomposition and restoration using total variation minimization and the H^{-1} norm. Multiscale Modeling and Simulation: A SIAM Interdisciplinary Journal **1**(3), 349–370 (2003)
18. Pontow, C., Scherzer, O.: Analytical Evaluations of Double Integral Expressions Related to Total Variation. Springer (2012)
19. Rudin, L., Osher, S., Fatemi, E.: Nonlinear total variation based noise removal algorithms. Physica D **60**, 259–268 (1992)
20. Strong, D., Aujol, J.-F., Chan, T.F.: Scale recognition, regularization parameter selection, and Meyer's G norm in total variation regularization. SIAM Journal on Multiscale Modeling and Simulation **5**(1), 273–303 (2006)
21. Strong, D., Chan, T.: Edge-preserving and scale-dependent properties of total variation regularization. Inverse Problems **19**(6), 165–187 (2003)
22. van Gennip, Y., Guillen, N., Osting, B., Bertozzi, A.L.: Mean curvature, threshold dynamics, and phase field theory on finite graphs. Milan Journal of Mathematics **82**(1), 3–65 (2014)

Morphological Scale-Space Operators for Images Supported on Point Clouds

Jesús Angulo[✉]

CMM-Centre de Morphologie Mathématique, MINES ParisTech,
PSL-Research University, Paris, France
jesus.angulo@mines-paristech.fr

Abstract. The aim of this paper is to develop the theory, and to propose an algorithm, for morphological processing of images painted on point clouds, viewed as a length metric measure space (X, d, μ). In order to extend morphological operators to process point cloud supported images, one needs to define dilation and erosion as semigroup operators on (X, d). That corresponds to a supremal convolution (and infimal convolution) using admissible structuring function on (X, d). From a more theoretical perspective, we introduce the notion of abstract structuring functions formulated on length metric Maslov idempotent measurable spaces, which is the appropriate setting for (X, d). In practice, computation of Maslov structuring function is approached by a random walks framework to estimate heat kernel on (X, d, μ), followed by the logarithmic trick.

Keywords: Mathematical morphology · Point clouds image · Metric measure space · Idempotent measure · Hamilton-Jacobi semigroup

1 Introduction

With the development of 3D scanning technology it is now easy to generate 3D models from real objects, together with standard images painted on them. These discrete objects can be represented either by surfaces (typically as polygonal meshes) or by scattered point clouds. In this paper we focus exclusively on a point cloud representation. A typical case of such generalized 3D images are the point clouds obtained from range cameras, like the Kinect camera. Indeed, this is the case-study which will be used in the paper to illustrate our methods.

Let us formalize the notion of point cloud and of image on it. A point cloud (X, d) is a finite set of points $X = \{x_i\}_{i=1}^{N}$ equipped with a distance function d, which corresponds typically to the Euclidean distance in the ambient space where X is endowed. This set of points has been irregularly sampled from a metric space; typically $X \subset \mathbb{R}^d$ (for instance the 3D space) but X can be also a sampled manifold with possible complex topological/geometric structure. We assume unknown inner product and geodesic structure of the underlying manifold. It is also important to note that (X, d) is neither a graph nor a discretized surface with triangulations. Thus there is a lack of natural connectivity

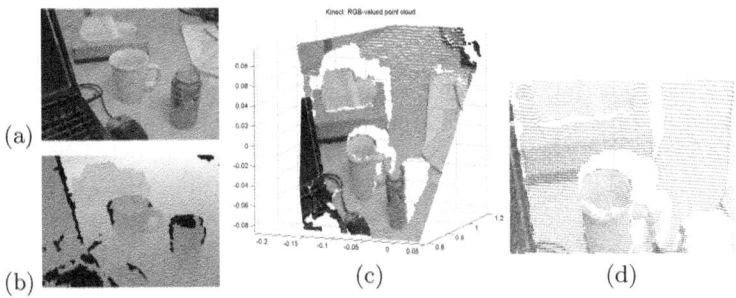

Fig. 1. Example of RGB-valued point cloud from a Kinect image: (a) $f_{\text{color}}(x)$, (b) $f_{\text{depth}}(x)$, (c) $f(x_i)$, (d) zoom-in of (c)

(or neighborhood relationship) between the points. A real-valued point cloud (X, d, f), or image f supported on a point cloud (X, d), is the function f which maps each point of X to a valuation space, typically the extended real line for gray-scale images, i.e., $f : \{x_i\}_{i=1}^{N} \longrightarrow \bar{\mathbb{R}}$. Fig. 1 depicts an example of RGB-valued point cloud obtained from a Kinect image, based on the 3D reconstruction of the scene according to the $f_{\text{depth}}(x)$ image.

Point clouds processing is an active research area which have been approached using geodesic distance methods [19], laplace operator [6] or diffusion PDEs [14]. Connection between heat method on manifolds and shortest geodesic distance via the Varadhan's formula has been used in [9], which integrates the heat flow. Morphological operators have been also considered for point cloud processing [8]. However, here we are interested on processing images painted on point clouds, without modifying the point cloud itself. The problem of smoothing images painted on surfaces using the short-time Beltrami kernel was considered for instance in [23].

In this context, the aim of this paper is to develop the theory and to propose an algorithm for morphological processing of such generalized manifold images.

Mathematical morphology is a nonlinear image processing methodology based on two basic operators, dilation and erosion, which correspond respectively to the convolution in the max-plus algebra and its dual. More precisely, in Euclidean (translation invariant) mathematical morphology the pair of adjoint and dual operators, dilation (sup-convolution) $(f \oplus b)(x)$ and erosion (inf-convolution) $(f \ominus b)(x)$ of an image $f : E \subset \mathbb{R}^n \to \bar{\mathbb{R}} = \mathbb{R} \cup \{-\infty, +\infty\}$, are given by [12,21]:

$$\begin{cases} \delta_b(f)(x) = (f \oplus b)(x) = \sup_{y \in E} \{f(y) + b(y - x)\}, \\ \varepsilon_b(f)(x) = (f \ominus b)(x) = \inf_{y \in E} \{f(y) - b(y + x)\}, \end{cases}$$

where $b : \mathbb{R}^n \to \bar{\mathbb{R}}$ is the structuring function which determines the effect of the operator. The structuring function plays a similar role to the kernel in classical convolution filtering. The structuring function is typically a parametric family $b_t(x)$, where $t > 0$ is the scale parameter. In particular, the canonic structuring function is the parabolic shape (i.e., square of the Euclidean distance): $b_t(x) = -\frac{\|x\|^2}{2t}$, such that the corresponding dilation and erosion are equivalent to the viscosity solution of the standard Hamilton-Jacobi PDE [17]: $u_t(t,x) \mp \|u_x(t,x)\|^2 = 0$, $(t,x) \in (0,+\infty) \times E$; $u(0,x) = f(x)$, $x \in E$. Theory of morphological filtering is based on opening and closing operators, obtained respectively by composition product of erosion-dilation and dilation-erosion. Opening (resp. closing) is increasing, idempotent and anti-extensive (resp. extensive). Evolved filters are obtained by composition of openings and closings [12, 21]. Morphological operators are classically defined for images supported on Euclidean spaces. A recent work has introduced mathematical morphology for real valued images whose support space is a Riemannian manifold [5].

In order to extend morphological operators to process point cloud supported images, one needs to define dilation and erosion as semigroup operators in framework adapted to point clouds (X,d). That corresponds to a supremal convolution (and infimal convolution) using admissible structuring function on (X,d). These operators are formulated in Section 3. In a more theoretical perspective, we start in Section 2 by introducing the notion of abstract structuring functions formulated on length metric Maslov idempotent measurable spaces, which is the appropriate setting for (X,d). In practice, computation of Maslov structuring function will be approached by a random walk framework to estimate heat kernel on a metric measure space (X,d,μ), followed by the logarithmic trick, as shown in Section 4. Some preliminary examples of morphological processing RGB-valued point cloud images are also given in Section 4.

2 From Abstract Heat Semigroups to Maslov Structuring Functions

Before introducing the morphological framework, let us review the theory of abstract heat kernels on a metric measure space, which is based on recent works by Grigor'yan and co-workers [10, 11].

2.1 Heat Kernel on Metric Measure Spaces

Let (M,d,μ) be a locally compact, separable metric space, endowed with a Radon measure μ. Then a family $\{p_t\}_{t\geq 0}$ of measurable functions $p_t(x,y)$ on $M \times M$ is called a heat kernel is the following conditions are almost surely satisfied $\forall x,y \in M$ and $t,s > 0$: i) Positivity: $p_t(x,y) \geq 0$; ii) Total mass inequality: $\int_M p_t(x,y)d\mu(y) \leq 1$, iii) Symmetry: $p_t(x,y) = p_t(y,x)$, iv) Semigroup property $p_{s+t}(x,y) = \int_M p_s(x,z)p_t(z,y)d\mu(z)$, v) Approximation to identity: For any $f \in L^2(M,\mu)$ $\int_M p_t(x,y)f(y)d\mu(y) \xrightarrow{L^2} f(x)$ as $t \to 0^+$. In addition, the heat kernel is called stochastically complete (conservative) when $\int_M p_t(x,y)d\mu(y) = 1$.

Given a measurable function f on M, any heat kernel gives rise to the family of operators $\{P_t\}_{t\geq 0}$, called the heat semigroup, where $P_0 = \text{id}$ and P_t for $t>0$ is defined by

$$P_t f(x) = \int_M p_t(x,y)f(y)d\mu(y). \tag{1}$$

such that $\{P_t\}_{t\geq 0}$ is continuous, symmetric and a Markovian semigroup $P_t P_s = P_{s+t}$.

Heat kernels and heat semigroups arise naturally from Markov processes. Let $(\{X_t\}_{t\geq 0}; \{\mathbb{P}_x\}_{x\in \mathcal{M}})$ be a Markov process on $\mathcal{M}$, that is reversible with respect to measure μ. Assume that it has the transition density $p_t(x,y)$, i.e., a function such that $\forall x \in \mathcal{M}$, $t > 0$, and all Borel sets $A \subset \mathcal{M}$, one has $\mathbb{P}_x(X_t \in A) = \int_\mathcal{M} p_t(x,y) d\mu(y)$.

If $\mathcal{M}$ is a smooth connected compact Riemannian manifold such that $\triangle_\mu$ is the Laplace-Beltrami operator on $\mathcal{M}$, where μ is the Riemannian measure, it is well known that starting from the heat equation $\frac{\partial u}{\partial t} = \triangle_\mu u$, we have that, for any $y \in \mathcal{M}$, the function $(t,x) \mapsto p_t(x,y)$ is the smallest positive fundamental solution of the heat equation with a source at y, i.e., if $u(x,0) = u_0(x)$, then $u(x,t) = \int_\mathcal{M} p_t(x,y) u_0(y) d\mu(y)$. In addition, let $\{\varphi_k\}_{k=0}^{+\infty}$ be an orthonormal basis of eigenfunctions of Laplace-Beltrami operator $-\triangle_\mu$, with eigenvalues $0 = \lambda_0 < \lambda_1 \leq \lambda_2 \leq \cdots$, then the heat kernel is determined by $p_t(x,y) = \sum_{k=0}^{+\infty} e^{-\lambda_k t} \varphi_k(x) \varphi_k(y)$.

As mentioned in the introduction, all these different viewpoints on heat kernel theory have been considered in the image processing state-of-the-art dealing with meshes and point clouds.

The explicit expression of the heat kernel in the Euclidean space $(\mathcal{M}, d, \mu) = \mathbb{R}^n$ is just the Gaussian kernel. In the case of a Riemannian manifold $(\mathcal{M}, \mu)$, only estimates are available, which typically depends on the geodesic distance in $\mathcal{M}$, see [10,11]. Similarly, in the case of a metric measure space $(\mathcal{M}, d, \mu)$, the sub-Gaussian estimate has the following form (assuming a walk dimension equals to 2) [10,11]:

$$p_t(x,y) \asymp \frac{C}{V(x, t^{1/2})} \exp\left(-c \frac{d^2(x,y)}{t}\right) \quad (2)$$

where $d(x,y)$ is a metric, $V(x,r)$ is the volume function of a metric ball on the space and C and c are positive constants.

2.2 Structuring Functions on Length Metric Maslov Measure Spaces

We need the counterpart of this abstract theory in the context max-plus mathematics (also known as idempotent analysis [15,18]). More precisely, the max-plus equivalent of the heat kernel will be here named structuring functions on a length metric Maslov measure space.

Length metric Maslov measure space. Theoretical foundations of Maslov idempotent measure theory [1,20] are based on replacing in the structural axioms of probability theory the role of the classical semiring $S_{(+, \times)} = (\mathbb{R}_+, +, \times, 0, 1, \leq)$ of positive real numbers by the idempotent semiring:

$S_{(\max, +)} = (\bar{\mathbb{R}}, \max, +, -\infty, 0, \leq)$. In this context, a change of the measure involves a consistent counterpart to the standard probability theory.

Let (X, d) be a (Hausdorff topological) metric space and let $\mathfrak{m}$ be a Maslov idempotent measure on X, i.e., mapping from X in the max-plus semiring such that for every function $f: X \to \bar{\mathbb{R}}$, we have $A \subset X$,

$$\mathfrak{m}_f(A) = \sup_{x \in A} f(x).$$

In addition, we should assume that (X, d) is a length space. We remind that a length space is a metric space such that for any pair of points, their distance is the length of the shortest path between the two points. The triple $(X, d, \mathfrak{m})$ is called a length metric Maslov measure space.

Maslov structuring function. A family $\{\mathfrak{b}_t\}_{t>0}$ of Maslov idempotent measurable functions $\mathfrak{b}_t : X \times X \to \bar{\mathbb{R}}$ is called for us a Maslov structuring function in $(X, d, \mathfrak{m})$ if the following conditions are satisfied $\forall x, y \in X$ and all $t, s > 0$

- Nonpositivity and total mass inequality:

$$\mathfrak{m}\left(\mathfrak{b}_t(x, \cdot)\right) = \sup_{y \in X} \mathfrak{b}_t(x, y) \leq 0 \Leftrightarrow \mathfrak{b}_t(x, y) \leq 0.$$

- Completeness (or conservative):

$$\mathfrak{m}\left(\mathfrak{b}_t(x, x)\right) = 0 \Leftrightarrow \mathfrak{b}_t(x, x) = 0.$$

- Symmetry: $\mathfrak{b}_t(x, y) = \mathfrak{b}_t(y, x)$.
- Semi-group property:

$$\mathfrak{b}_{t+s}(x, y) = \sup_{z \in X} \{\mathfrak{b}_t(x, z) + \mathfrak{b}_s(z, y)\}.$$

- Approximation to identity:

$$\sup_{y \in X} \{f(y) + \mathfrak{b}_t(x, y)\} \longrightarrow f(x) \text{ as } t \to 0^+.$$

Logarithmic trick: from heat kernel to Maslov structuring function. Our approach is based on the so-called logarithmic connection between linear and morphological system theory [7]. The theory of this connection between the usual convolution and the convolution in max-plus mathematics is based on the Cramer transform [1], which is defined as the Legendre transform of the logarithm of the Laplace transform. In the particular case of a canonic Gaussian kernel of type: $1/\sqrt{2\pi\sigma^2}e^{-x^2/(2\sigma^2)}$, it is well known that the Laplace transform is $e^{(\sigma^2 s^2)/2}$ and the final Cramer transform is $-x^2/(2\sigma^2)$. In summary the Cramer transform of the Gaussian kernel is equal to quadratic structuring function.

Similarly, we can easily show that, up to a normalizing constant, the logarithm of the heat kernel $p_t(x, y)$ in a metric measure space (X, d, μ) is a Maslov structuring function $\mathfrak{b}_t(x, y)$ in the counterpart idempotent metric measure space. Let us consider for instance the case of the sub-Gaussian estimate of the heat kernel (2). First, a normalization version $\tilde{p}_t(x,y)$ is required such that $\tilde{p}_t(x,x) = 1$, i.e., $\tilde{p}_t(x,y) = V(x,t^{1/2})/Cp_t(x,y)$. Then, the corresponding Maslov structuring function is defined as

$$\mathfrak{b}_t(x,y) = \log \tilde{p}_t(x,y) \asymp -c\frac{d^2(x,y)}{t}, \tag{3}$$

and, without loss of generality, we fix $c = 1/2$. The nonpositivity, total mass inequality, completeness, symmetric and approximation to the identity are obvious. In order to prove the semigroup property, we need to assume that $d(x,y)$ is a metric distance in a length space such that [16]

$$\mathfrak{b}_{t+s}(x,y) = \sup_{z \in X}\{\mathfrak{b}_t(x,z) + \mathfrak{b}_s(z,y)\} = \sup_{z \in X}\left\{-\frac{d^2(x,z)}{2t} - \frac{d^2(z,y)}{2s}\right\}$$
$$= -\inf_{z \in X}\left\{\frac{d^2(x,z)}{2t} + \frac{d^2(z,y)}{2s}\right\} = -\frac{d^2(x,y)}{2(t+s)}.$$

The last equality in length spaces comes from $d^2(x,y)/(2(t+s)) \leq \inf_{z \in Z}[d^2(x,z)/(2t) + d^2(z,y)/(2t)]$ (by triangle inequality) by choosing a minimal geodesic between x and y, and a point z on this geodesic with $d(x,z) = t/(t+s)d(x,y)$.

3 Morphological Scale-Space Operators on Metric Maslov-Measurable Space

Let us consider a metric Maslov-measurable space $(X, d, \mathfrak{m})$ and a given function $f: X \to \overline{\mathbb{R}}$. Once an admissible structuring function $\{\mathfrak{b}_t\}_{t>0}$ has been defined, the max-plus semigroups $D_t f(x)$ and $E_t f(x)$ are given by

$$D_t f(x) = \sup_{y \in X}\{f(y) + \mathfrak{b}_t(x,y)\}, \tag{4}$$

$$E_t f(x) = \inf_{y \in X}\{f(y) - \mathfrak{b}_t(y,x)\}. \tag{5}$$

which, in the context of mathematical morphology, correspond respectively to the multi-scale dilation $\delta_{\mathfrak{b}_t}(f)(x) = D_t f(x)$ and erosion $\varepsilon_{\mathfrak{b}_t}(f)(x) = E_t f(x)$ of function f by structuring function $\mathfrak{b}_t$. By the way, we note that by the symmetry, one has $\mathfrak{b}_t(x,y) = \mathfrak{b}_t(y,x)$. In max-plus mathematics on Hilbert spaces, dilation and erosion are known as the Hopf-Lax-Oleinik semigroups. By considering for instance the sub-gaussian estimate as Maslov structuring function (3), the obtained semigroups in $(X, d, \mathfrak{m})$: $D_t f(x) = \sup_{y \in X}\left\{f(y) - \frac{d^2(x,y)}{2t}\right\}$ and $E_t f(x) = \inf_{y \in X}\left\{f(y) + \frac{d^2(x,y)}{2t}\right\}$, are equal to the so-called Hamilton-Jacobi semigroup on length spaces, introduced by Lott and Villani in [16] and extendedly considered more recently by Ambrosio et al. in [3] for the study of Ricci curvature bounds in metric spaces.

3.1 Properties of Semigroups $\delta_{\mathfrak{b}_t}$ and $\varepsilon_{\mathfrak{b}_t}$

The following properties can be easily proved using the properties of a Maslov structuring function.

1. (Adjunction) For any two real-valued functions f and g on $(X, d, \mathfrak{m})$, the pair $(\varepsilon_{\mathfrak{b}_t}, \delta_{\mathfrak{b}_t})$ forms an adjunction, i.e., $\forall x \in X$
$$\delta_{\mathfrak{b}_t}(f)(x) \leq g(x) \Leftrightarrow f(x) \leq \varepsilon_{\mathfrak{b}_t}(g)(x).$$
2. (Duality by involution) For any function $f(x)$ and $\forall x \in X$, one has $\delta_{\mathfrak{b}_t}(f)(x) = -\varepsilon_{\mathfrak{b}_t}(-f)(x)$.
3. (Increaseness) If $f(x) \leq g(x)$, $\forall x \in X$, then $\delta_{\mathfrak{b}_t}(f)(x) \leq \delta_{\mathfrak{b}_t}(g)(x)$ and $\varepsilon_{\mathfrak{b}_t}(f)(x) \leq \varepsilon_{\mathfrak{b}_t}(g)(x)$, $\forall x \in X$ and $\forall t > 0$.
4. (Extensivity and anti-extensivity) $\delta_{\mathfrak{b}_t}(f)(x) \geq f(x)$ and $\varepsilon_{\mathfrak{b}_t}(f)(x) \leq f(x)$, $\forall x \in X$ and $\forall t > 0$.
5. (Ordering property) If $0 < s < t$ then $\varepsilon_{\mathfrak{b}_t}(f)(x) \leq \varepsilon_{\mathfrak{b}_s}(f)(x) \leq f(x) \leq \delta_{\mathfrak{b}_s}(f)(x) \leq \delta_{\mathfrak{b}_t}(f)(x)$, $\forall x \in X$.
6. (Scale-space) For any function f and $\forall x \in X$, and for all pair of scales $s > 0$ and $t > 0$, we have the Maslovian semigroup:
$$\delta_{\mathfrak{b}_t}\left(\delta_{\mathfrak{b}_s}(f)\right)(x) = \delta_{\mathfrak{b}_{s+t}}(f)(x),$$
$$\varepsilon_{\mathfrak{b}_t}\left(\varepsilon_{\mathfrak{b}_s}(f)\right)(x) = \varepsilon_{\mathfrak{b}_{s+t}}(f)(x).$$

In addition, the semigroups operators $\delta_{\mathfrak{b}_t}(f)$ and $\varepsilon_{\mathfrak{b}_t}(f)$ are continuous in t.

We note that these properties are a natural generalization of some well known properties of morphological scale-spaces [13, 17].

3.2 Multi-Scale Openings and Closings and Other Derived Operators

From these two basic well formalized operators, all the morphological filtering theory is generalized to images on $(X, d, \mathfrak{m})$. In particular, as a consequence of the classic theory of morphological operators [12, 21], the composition products of the adjoint operators $(\varepsilon_{\mathfrak{b}_t}, \delta_{\mathfrak{b}_t})$ lead to the multi-scale opening and closing:

$$\gamma_{\mathfrak{b}_t}(f)(x) = \delta_{\mathfrak{b}_t} \circ \varepsilon_{\mathfrak{b}_t}(f)(x) = \sup_{z \in X} \inf_{y \in X} \{f(y) - \mathfrak{b}_t(y, z) + \mathfrak{b}_t(z, x)\},$$

$$\varphi_{\mathfrak{b}_t}(f)(x) = \varepsilon_{\mathfrak{b}_t} \circ \delta_{\mathfrak{b}_t}(f)(x) = \inf_{z \in X} \sup_{y \in X} \{f(y) + \mathfrak{b}_t(z, y) - \mathfrak{b}_t(x, z)\}.$$

Having the opening and closing, all the other morphological filters defined by composition of them are easily obtained, such as the alternate sequential filters. It is also possible to extend the geodesic dilation [12], denoted by $\delta_{\mathfrak{b}_t}^{geo}(m; f)$, of a marker function m constrained by the reference function f, defined as $\delta_{\mathfrak{b}_t}^{geo}(m; f)(x) = \delta_{\mathfrak{b}_t}(m)(x) \wedge f(x)$ and t being a small scale. The iteration of this operator until converge is called geodesic reconstruction [12]. This is an extremely useful operator which, based for instance on an opening $m = \gamma_{\mathfrak{b}_t}(f)$ as marker, removes the bright objects and leaving intact the contours of dark structures.

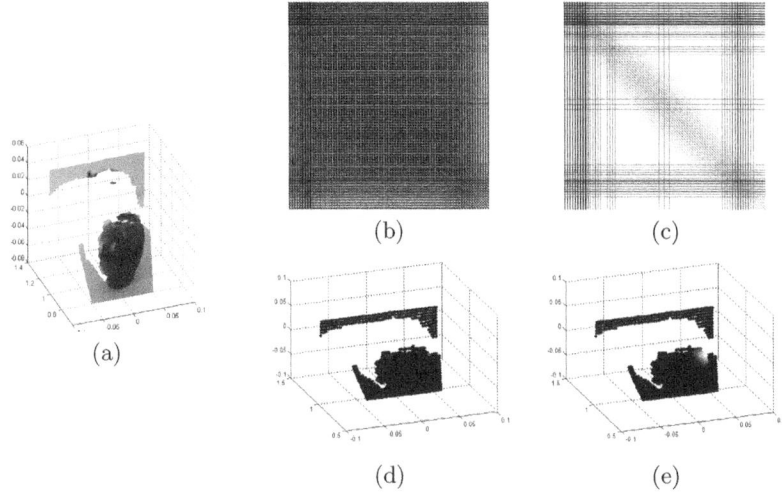

Fig. 2. Heat kernel at a given point: (a) RGB-valued point cloud $f(x_i)$ of N points; (b) matrix of all-pairs of Euclidean distances $d^{Euclid}(x_i, x_j)$, $1 \leq i \leq N$, $1 \leq j \leq N$; (c) matrix of all-pairs of heat distances $d_T^{Heat}(x_i, x_j)$, $1 \leq i \leq N$, $1 \leq j \leq N$; (d) in red, a given point x_k, (e) heat kernel $p_t(x_k, x_i)$ at this point x_k

4 Application to Processing Images Supported on Point Clouds

4.1 Computing Maslov Structuring Functions on Point Clouds

According to the theory discussed above, to compute a Maslov structuring function on a point cloud is equivalent to compute the heat kernel followed by the logarithmic trick. In the case of point clouds, like those of the Kinect camera, the initial ambient space embedding (X, d^{Euclid}) is not straightforwardly useful for image processing since the intrinsic geometry of the 3D objects is not taken into account by $d^{Euclid}(x, y)$. Local geometry of the underlaying sampled manifold could be approximated by means of manifold learning techniques (e.g., ISOMAP). That is basically computation of geodesic distances which are then plugged into the heat kernel. Another possibility involves to transform the point cloud into a triangular mesh surface. Heat kernel can be obtained by numerical computation of eigenfunctions of Laplace-Beltrami operator.

We consider here an alternative approach based on random walk paradigm, which does not need a mesh nor an explicit graph. Hence, heat diffusion can be modeled as a large collection of hot particles taking random walks on space X starting at $x_i \in X$: any particle that reaches a distance point y after a small time has had little time to deviate from the shortest possible path. Probabilities of random walks of length p can be computed by looking at the power p of the transition probability matrix of the stationary Markov chain. A similar approach was used in [4], to formulate the notion of stochastic morphological filtering on Euclidean images.

In practice, the algorithm is based on the following steps.

1. *Euclidean distance matrix.* Given a point cloud (X, d^{Euclid}), compute the matrix of all Euclidean distances between pairs of points of X: $D(i,j) = d^{Euclid}(x_i, x_j), \forall x_i, x_j \in X$. This matrix can be made sparse by hard thresholding at ϵ (this is equivalent to so-called ϵ-graph).
2. *From Euclidean distance matrix to stochastic matrix.* Transform distances of each point i to the others (column i of matrix D) into transition probabilities using Boltzmann-Gibbs distribution depending on temperature T: $P_T(i,j) = Z_i^{-1} e^{-D(i,j)^2/T}$, $Z_i = \sum_j e^{-D(i,j)^2/T}$.
3. *Probability of going from point i to j after p steps:* Compute power to p of stochastic matrix P_T. Each i column of the corresponding matrix can be interpreted as the approximation to the heat kernel at point i, $k_T^{Heat}(x_i, x_j)$, on the underlying manifold when $p \to +\infty$.
4. *Maslov structuring function.* Compute the scaled logarithm of the heat kernel: $\mathfrak{b}_t(x_i, x_j) = \frac{\log(k_T^{Heat}(x_i, x_j))}{2t}$.

Fig. 2 illustrates the approach for a RGB-valued point cloud image $f(x_i)$ of N points. Including the shape of the heat kernel at a given point. Structure of the matrix of Euclidean distances with the respect to that of the "heat distances", obtained as $d_T^{Heat}(x_i, x_j) = \sqrt{-2T \log k_T^{Heat}(x_i, x_j)}$, are compared too. We note that this distance can be considered as an approximation based on the well-known Varadhan's formula which link the short time heat kernel to the geodesic distance, i.e.,

$$d^{Geodesic}(x,y) = \lim_{t \to 0} \sqrt{-2t \log p_t(x,y)}.$$

4.2 Examples of Morphological Processing

Figure 3 depicts some examples of morphological processing of a RGB-valued point cloud $f(x_i)$, using the multi-scale structuring functions $\mathfrak{b}_t(x_i, x_j)$ obtained by the random walk paradigm. We first note that each color component is processed separately; but using the same structuring function for the three components. The effects of morphological operators are as expected: erosion $\varepsilon_{\mathfrak{b}_t}(f)(x_i)$ in Fig. 3(b) to (f), (resp. dilation $\delta_{\mathfrak{b}_t}(f)(x_i)$ in (g)) enlarges dark structures and reduces bright ones (resp. enlarges bright zones and reduces dark areas). Opening $\gamma_{\mathfrak{b}_t}(f)(x_i)$, in (h) removes bright structures at the corresponding scale t, without modifying the dark ones. The difference between the original image $f(x_i)$ and the opening, given in (i), shows the removed bright zones.

Considering for instance the erosion $\varepsilon_{\mathfrak{b}_t}(f)(x_i)$ at a given scale $t = 1$, it is compared, on the one hand, the effect of the temperature parameter T. As usual in such probabilistic framework, for very low temperatures, e.g. $T = 0.05$ as in (b), the estimated heat kernel is too tightly adjusted to the local shape of the point cloud. On the contrary, with high temperatures, e.g. $T = 0.4$ in (c), the

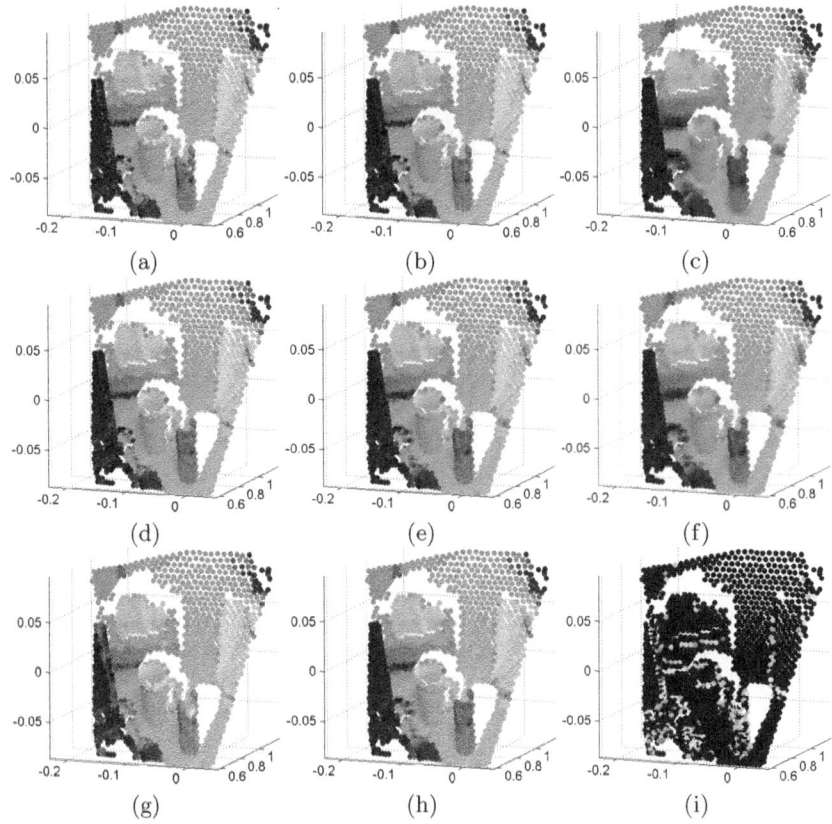

Fig. 3. Morphological processing a RGB-valued point cloud: (a) original image $f(x_i)$. Erosion $\varepsilon_{b_t}(f)(x_i)$ with (b) $t = 1$, $T = 0.05$, (c) $t = 1$, $T = 0.4$, (d) $t = 0.5$, $T = 0.1$, (e) $t = 1$, $T = 0.1$, (f) $t = 2$, $T = 0.1$. (g) Dilation $\delta_{b_t}(f)(x_i)$ with $t = 1$, $T = 0.1$. (h) opening $\gamma_{b_t}(f)(x_i)$ and (i) top-hat transform $f(x_i) - \gamma_{b_t}(f)(x_i)$ with $t = 1$, $T = 0.1$.

geometry of the point cloud is not captured by the heat kernel. For the current example, $T = 0.1$ seems an appropriate choice. Then, by fixing $T = 0.1$, we observe that by modifying the scale, $t = 0.5$ (d), $t = 1$ (e) and $t = 2$ (f), a scale-space representation is obtained.

Other examples of morphological transforms on the same image are included in Fig. 4. See legend of the figure for details.

5 Perspectives

We have formulated the abstract theory of morphological semi-groups on length metric Maslov-measurable spaces. These operators can be used for processing images on valued point clouds by heat kernel embedding. Typical applications are: geometric object extraction, non-linear scale-space representation and decomposition, regularization, etc.

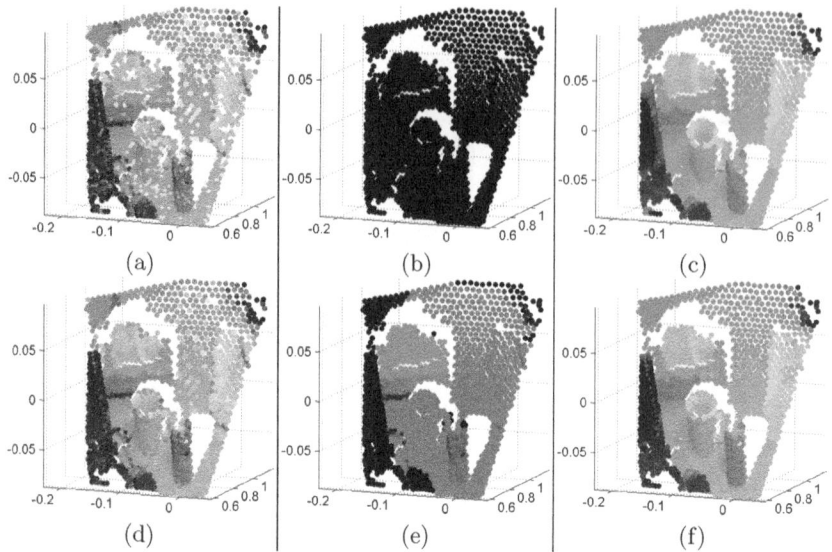

Fig. 4. Morphological processing a RGB-valued point cloud (original image in 3(a)). Corrupted image $\tilde{f}(x_i)$ by white impulse noise in (a) and restored image by opening $\gamma_{b_t}(\tilde{f})(x_i)$ in (d). In (e), geodesic reconstruction using a single-pixel marker (blue point in (b)): we note that all brighter objects than the marker zones are removed. Closing $\varphi_{b_t}(f)(x_i)$ in (e), which removes dark areas, and corresponding dual geodesic reconstruction which perfectly restores contour of bright objets.

Our estimation of the heat kernel, based on random walks, is not very precise. A better approximation of underlying geodesic distances can be obtained by a local tangent space approximation and local mesh construction, by introducing the measure of Voronoi volumes, etc. However for the purpose of computing the Maslov structuring function on the point cloud, the random walk estimation can be considered as satisfactory.

In metric measure spaces, the heat kernel can be also approximated using Laplace-Beltrami eigenfunctions. For the need of morphological operators, the equivalent paradigm involves harmonic functions in max-plus algebra and eigenfunctions of Hopf-Lax-Oleinik semigroups. The theory is known in the Euclidean case (also some results in graph optimization) [2, 22]. This point will be explored in ongoing research.

References

1. Akian, M.: Densities of idempotent measures and large deviations. Trans. of the American Mathematical Society **351**(11), 4515–4543 (1999)
2. Akian, M., Gaubert, S., Walsh, C.: The Max-Plus Martin boundary. Documenta Mathematica **14**, 195–240 (2009)

3. Ambrosio, L., Gigli, N., Savaré, G.: Calculus and heat flow in metric measure spaces and applications to spaces with Ricci bounds from below. Inventiones Mathematicae **195**(2), 289–391 (2014)
4. Angulo, J., Velasco-Forero, S.: Stochastic morphological filtering and bellman-maslov chains. In: Hendriks, C.L.L., Borgefors, G., Strand, R. (eds.) ISMM 2013. LNCS, vol. 7883, pp. 171–182. Springer, Heidelberg (2013)
5. Angulo, J., Velasco-Forero, S.: Riemannian Mathematical Morphology. Pattern Recognition Letters **47**, 93–101 (2014)
6. Belkin, M., Sun, J., Wang, Y.: Constructing laplace operator from point clouds in R^d. In: Proc. of ACM Symp. on Discrete Algorithms, pp. 1031–1040 (2009)
7. Burgeth, B., Weickert, J.: An Explanation for the Logarithmic Connection between Linear and Morphological System Theory. International Journal of Computer Vision **64**(2–3), 157–169 (2005)
8. Calderon, S., Boubekeur, T.: Point Morphology. ACM Transactions on Graphics (Proc. SIGGRAPH 2014) (2014)
9. Crane, K., Weischedel, C., Wardetzky, M.: Geodesics in Heat: A New Approach to Computing Distance Based on Heat Flow. ACM Trans. Graph. **32**(5) (2013)
10. Grigor'yan, A.: Heat Kernel and Analysis on Manifolds. American Mathematical Society (2012)
11. Grigor'yan, A., Hu, J., Lau, K.-S.: Heat kernels on metric measure spaces. In: Geometry and Analysis on Fractals. Springer Proceedings in Mathematics & Statistics, vol. 88, pp. 147–208 (2014)
12. Heijmans, H.J.A.M.: Morphological image operators. Academic Press, Boston (1994)
13. Jackway, P.T., Deriche, M.: Scale-Space Properties of the Multiscale Morphological Dilation-Erosion. IEEE Trans. Pattern Anal. Mach. Intell. **18**(1), 38–51 (1996)
14. Liang, J., Zhao, H.: Methods and Algorithms for Scientific Computing Solving Partial Differential Equations on Point Clouds. SIAM J. Sci. Comput. **35**(3), A1461–A1486 (2013)
15. Litvinov, G.L., Maslov, V.P., Shpiz, G.B.: Idempotent Functional Analysis: An Algebraic Approach. Mathematical Notes **69**(5–6), 696–729 (2001)
16. Lott, J., Villani, C.: Hamilton-Jacobi semigroup on length spaces and applications. Journal de Math. Pures et Appliquées **88**, 219–229 (2007)
17. Maragos, P.: Differential morphology and image processing. IEEE Transactions on Image Processing **5**(1), 922–937 (1996)
18. Maslov, V.: Méthodes opératorielles. Editions Mir (1987)
19. Mémoli, F., Sapiro, G.: A theoretical and computational framework for isometry invariant recognition of point cloud data. Foundations of Computational Mathematics **5**(3), 313–347 (2005)
20. Del Moral, P.: Maslov optimization theory: optimality versus randomness. In: Kolokoltsov, V.N., Maslov, V.P. (eds.) Idempotency Analysis and its Applications. Kluwer Publishers (1997)
21. Serra, J.: Image Analysis and Mathematical Morphology. Theoretical Advances, vol. II. Academic Press, London (1988)
22. Sobolevskii, A.N.: Aubry-Mather theory and idempotent eigenfunctions of Bellman operator. Commun. Contemp. Math. **1**, 517–533 (1999)
23. Spira, A., Kimmel, R., Sochen, N.: A short-time Beltrami kernel for smoothing images and manifolds. IEEE Trans. on Image Processing **16**(6), 1628–1636 (2007)

Separable Time-Causal and Time-Recursive Spatio-Temporal Receptive Fields

Tony Lindeberg[✉]

Department of Computational Biology, School of Computer Science
and Communication, KTH Royal Institute of Technology, Stockholm, Sweden
tony@csc.kth.se

Abstract. We present an improved model and theory for time-causal and time-recursive spatio-temporal receptive fields, obtained by a combination of Gaussian receptive fields over the spatial domain and first-order integrators or equivalently truncated exponential filters coupled in cascade over the temporal domain. Compared to previous spatio-temporal scale-space formulations in terms of non-enhancement of local extrema or scale invariance, these receptive fields are based on different scale-space axiomatics over time by ensuring non-creation of new local extrema or zero-crossings with increasing temporal scale. Specifically, extensions are presented about parameterizing the intermediate temporal scale levels, analysing the resulting temporal dynamics and transferring the theory to a discrete implementation in terms of recursive filters over time.

1 Introduction

Spatio-temporal receptive fields constitute an essential concept in biological vision (Hubel and Wiesel [1]; DeAngelis et al. [2,3]) and for expressing computer vision methods on video data (Adelson and Bergen [4]; Zelnik-Manor and Irani [5]; Laptev and Lindeberg [6]; Jhuang et al. [7]; Shabani et al. [8]).

For off-line processing of pre-recorded video, non-causal Gaussian or Gabor-based spatio-temporal receptive fields may in some cases be sufficient. When operating on video data in a real-time setting or when modelling biological vision computationally, one does however need to take into explicit account the fact that the future cannot be accessed and that the underlying spatio-temporal receptive fields must be *time-causal*. For computational efficiency and for keeping down memory requirements, it is also desirable that the computations should be *time-recursive*, so that it is sufficient to keep a limited memory of the past that can be recursively updated over time.

The subject of this article is to present an improved scale-space model for spatio-temporal receptive fields based on time-causal temporal scale-space kernels in terms of first-order integrators coupled in cascade, which can also be transferred to a discrete implementation in terms of recursive filters. The model

---

Support from the Swedish Research Council contracts 2010-4766 and 2014-4083 is gratefully acknowledged.

builds on previous work by (Fleet and Langley [9]; Lindeberg and Fagerström [10]; Lindeberg [11,12]) which is here complemented by a better design for the degrees of freedom in the choice of time constants for intermediate temporal scale levels, an analysis of the resulting temporal response dynamics and details for discrete implementation in a spatio-temporal visual front-end.

2 Spatio-Temporal Receptive Fields

The theoretical structure that we start from is a general result from axiomatic derivations of a spatio-temporal scale-space based on assumptions of non-enhancement of local extrema and the existence of a continuous temporal scale parameter, which states that the spatio-temporal receptive fields should be based on spatio-temporal smoothing kernels of the form (see overviews in Lindeberg [11,12]):

$$T(x_1, x_2, t;\; s, \tau, v, \Sigma) = g(x_1 - v_1 t, x_2 - v_2 t;\; s, \Sigma)\, h(t;\; \tau) \qquad (1)$$

where

- $x = (x_1, x_2)^T$ denotes the image coordinates,
- t denotes time,
- s denotes the spatial scale,
- τ denotes the temporal scale,
- $v = (v_1, v_2)^T$ denotes a local image velocity,
- Σ denotes a spatial covariance matrix determining the spatial shape of an affine Gaussian kernel $g(x;\; s, \Sigma) = \frac{1}{2\pi s \sqrt{\det \Sigma}} e^{-x^T \Sigma^{-1} x / 2s}$,
- $g(x_1 - v_1 t, x_2 - v_2 t;\; s, \Sigma)$ denotes a spatial affine Gaussian kernel that moves with image velocity $v = (v_1, v_2)$ in space-time and
- $h(t;\; \tau)$ is a temporal smoothing kernel over time.

For simplicity, we shall here restrict the family of affine Gaussian kernels over the spatial domain to rotationally symmetric Gaussians of different size s, by setting the covariance matrix Σ to a unit matrix. We shall mainly restrict ourselves to space-time separable receptive fields by setting the image velocity v to zero.

A conceptual difference that we shall pursue is by relaxing the requirement of a continuous temporal scale parameter in the above axiomatic derivations by a discrete temporal scale parameter. We shall also replace the previous axiom about non-creation of new image structures with increasing scale in terms of non-enhancement of local extrema (which requires a continuous scale parameter) by the requirement that the temporal smoothing process, when seen as an operation along a one-dimensional temporal axis only, must not increase the number of local extrema or zero-crossings in the signal. Then, another family of time-causal scale-space kernels becomes permissible and uniquely determined, in terms of first-order integrators or truncated exponential filters coupled in cascade.

The main topics of this paper are to handle the remaining degrees of freedom resulting from this construction about: (i) choosing and parameterizing the distribution of temporal scale levels, (ii) analysing the resulting temporal dynamics and (iii) describing how this model can be transferred to a discrete implementation while retaining discrete scale-space properties.

3 Time-Causal Temporal Scale-Space

When constructing a system for real-time processing of sensory data, a fundamental constraint on the temporal smoothing kernels is that they have to be *time-causal*. The ad hoc solution of using a truncated symmetric filter of finite temporal extent in combination with a temporal delay is not appropriate in a time-critical context. Because of computational and memory efficiency, the computations should furthermore be based on a compact temporal buffer that contains sufficient information for representing sensory information at multiple temporal scales and computing features therefrom. Corresponding requirements are necessary in computational modelling of biological perception.

Time-causal scale-space kernels for pure temporal domain. Given the requirement on temporal scale-space kernels by non-creation of local extrema over a pure temporal domain, *truncated exponential kernels*

$$h_{exp}(t;\ \mu_k) = \begin{cases} \frac{1}{\mu_k} e^{-t/\mu_k} & t \geq 0 \\ 0 & t < 0 \end{cases} \qquad (2)$$

can be shown to constitute the only class of time-causal scale-space kernels over a continuous temporal domain in this sense (Lindeberg [13]; Lindeberg and Fagerström [10]). The Laplace transform of such a kernel is given by

$$H_{exp}(q;\ \mu_k) = \int_{t=-\infty}^{\infty} h_{exp}(t;\ \mu_k)\, e^{-qt}\, dt = \frac{1}{1 + \mu_k q} \qquad (3)$$

and coupling K such kernels in cascade leads to a composed filter

$$h_{composed}(t;\ \mu) = *_{k=1}^{K} h_{exp}(t;\ \mu_k) \qquad (4)$$

having a Laplace transform of the form

$$H_{composed}(q;\ \mu) = \int_{t=-\infty}^{\infty} (*_{k=1}^{K} h_{exp}(t;\ \mu_k))\, e^{-qt}\, dt = \prod_{k=1}^{K} \frac{1}{1 + \mu_k q}. \qquad (5)$$

The composed filter has temporal mean and variance

$$m_K = \sum_{k=1}^{K} \mu_k \qquad \tau_K = \sum_{k=1}^{K} \mu_k^2. \qquad (6)$$

In terms of physical models, repeated convolution with such kernels corresponds to coupling a series of *first-order integrators* with time constants μ_k in cascade

$$\partial_t L(t;\ \tau_k) = \frac{1}{\mu_k} \left(L(t;\ \tau_{k-1}) - L(t;\ \tau_k) \right) \qquad (7)$$

with $L(t;\ 0) = f(t)$. These temporal smoothing kernels satisfy scale-space properties in the sense that the number of local extrema or the number of zero-crossings in the temporal signal are guaranteed to not increase with the temporal scale. In this respect, these kernels have a desirable and well-founded smoothing property that can be used for defining multi-scale observations over time. A constraint on this type of temporal scale-space representation, however, is that the *scale levels are required to be discrete* and that the scale-space representation does hence not admit a continuous scale parameter. Computationally, however, the scale-space representation based on truncated exponential kernels can be highly efficient and admits for direct implementation in terms of hardware (or wetware) that emulates first-order integration over time, and where the temporal scale levels together also serve as a sufficient time-recursive memory of the past.

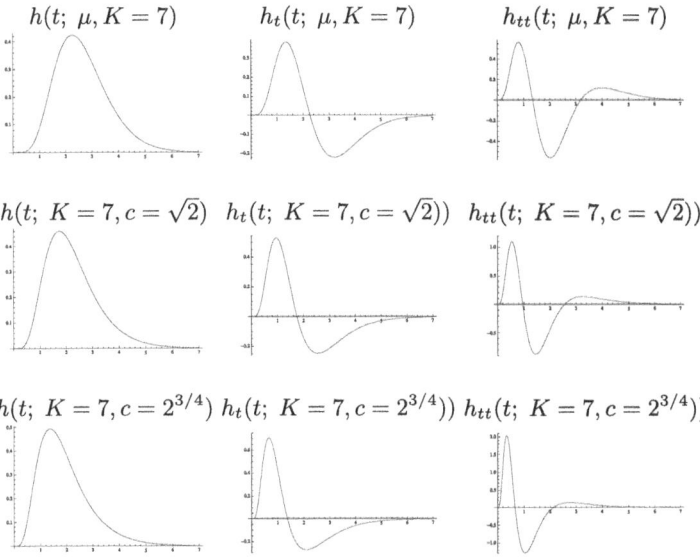

Fig. 1. Equivalent kernels with temporal variance $\tau = 1$ corresponding to the composition of K *truncated exponential kernels* in cascade and their first- and second-order derivatives. (top row) Equal time constants μ. (middle row) Logarithmic distribution of the scale levels for $c = \sqrt{2}$. (bottom row) Logarithmic distribution for $c = 2^{3/4}$.

When implementing this temporal scale-space concept, a set of intermediate scale levels τ_k has to be distributed between some minimum and maximum scale levels $\tau_{min} = \tau_1$ and $\tau_{max} = \tau_K$. Assuming that a total number of K scale levels is to be used, it is natural to distribute the temporal scale levels according to a geometric series, corresponding to a uniform distribution in units of effective temporal scale $\tau_{eff} = \log \tau$. Using such a logarithmic distribution of the temporal scale levels, the different levels in the temporal scale-space representation at increasing temporal scales will serve as a logarithmic memory of the past, with qualitative similarity to the mapping of the past onto a logarithmic time axis in the scale-time model by Koenderink [14]. If we have the freedom of choosing

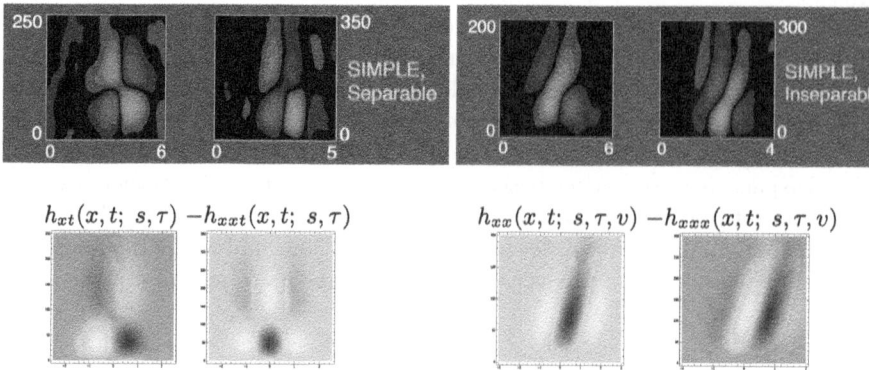

Fig. 2. Computational modelling of simple cells in V1 as reported by DeAngelis et al. [2] using spatio-temporal receptive fields of the form $T(x, t;\ s, \tau, v) = \partial_{x^\alpha} \partial_{t^\beta} g(x - vt;\ s) h(t;\ \tau)$ according to equation (1) with the temporal smoothing function $h(t;\ \tau)$ modelled as a cascade of first-order integrators/truncated exponential kernels of the form (4) and using a logarithmic distribution of the intermediate scale levels of the form (8). (left column) Separable receptive fields corresponding to mixed derivatives of first- or second-order derivatives over space with first-order derivatives over time. (right column) Inseparable velocity-adapted receptive fields corresponding to second- or third-order derivatives over space. Parameter values: (a) h_{xt}: $\sigma_x = 0.6$ degrees, $\sigma_t = 60$ ms. (b) h_{xxt}: $\sigma_x = 0.6$ degrees, $\sigma_t = 80$ ms. (c) h_{xx}: $\sigma_x = 0.7$ degrees, $\sigma_t = 50$ ms, $v = 0.007$ degrees/ms. (d) h_{xxx}: $\sigma_x = 0.5$ degrees, $\sigma_t = 80$ ms, $v = 0.004$ degrees/ms.

τ_{min} freely, a natural way of parameterizing these temporal scale levels using a distribution parameter $c > 1$

$$\tau_k = c^{2(k-K)} \tau_{max} \qquad (1 \leq k \leq K) \qquad (8)$$

which by equation (6) implies that time constants of the individual first-order integrators will be given by

$$\mu_1 = c^{1-K} \sqrt{\tau_{max}} \qquad (9)$$

$$\mu_k = \sqrt{\tau_k - \tau_{k-1}} = c^{k-K-1} \sqrt{c^2 - 1} \sqrt{\tau_{max}} \qquad (2 \leq k \leq K) \qquad (10)$$

If the temporal signal is on the other hand given at some minimum temporal scale level τ_{min}, we can instead determine $c = \left(\frac{\tau_{max}}{\tau_{min}}\right)^{\frac{1}{2(K-1)}}$ in (8) such that $\tau_1 = \tau_{min}$ and add $K-1$ temporal scales with μ_k according to (10). Alternatively, if one chooses a uniform distribution of the intermediate temporal scale levels

$$\tau_k = \frac{k}{K} \tau_{max} \qquad (11)$$

then the time constants are given by $\mu_k = \sqrt{\frac{\tau_{max}}{K}}$.

Figure 1 shows graphs of such kernels that correspond to the same value of the composed variance, using either a uniform distribution or a logarithmic distribution of the intermediate scale levels. Generally, these kernels are highly asymmetric for small values of K, whereas they become gradually more symmetric as K increases. The degree of continuity at the origin and the smoothness of transition phenomena increase with K such that coupling of $K \geq 2$ kernels in cascade implies a C^{K-2}-continuity of the temporal scale-space kernel. Specifically, the kernels based on a logarithmic distribution of the intermediate scale levels allow for faster temporal dynamics compared to the kernels based on a uniform distribution of the intermediate scale levels.

Figure 2 shows the result of modelling the spatio-temporal receptive fields of simple cells in V1 in this way, using the general idealized model of spatio-temporal receptive fields in equation (1) in combination with a temporal smoothing kernel obtained by coupling a set of first-order integrators/truncated exponential kernels in cascade. This result complements the general theoretical model for visual receptive fields in [12] with explicit modelling results and a theory for choosing and parameterizing the intermediate discrete temporal scale levels.

4 Temporal Dynamics of the Time-Causal Kernels

For the time-causal filters obtained by coupling truncated exponential kernels in cascade, there will be an inevitable temporal delay depending on the time constants μ_k of the individual filters. A straightforward way of estimating this delay is by using the additive property of mean values under convolution $m_K = \sum_{k=1}^{K} \mu_k$ according to (6). In the special case when all the time constants are equal $\mu_k = \sqrt{\tau/K}$, this measure is given by

$$m_{uni} = \sqrt{K\tau} \qquad (12)$$

showing that the temporal delay increases if the temporal smoothing operation is divided into a larger number of smaller individual smoothing steps.

In the special case when the intermediate temporal scale levels are instead distributed logarithmically according to (8), with the individual time constants given by (9) and (10), this measure for the temporal delay is given by

$$m_{log} = \frac{c^{-K}\left(c^2 - \left(\sqrt{c^2-1}+1\right)c + \sqrt{c^2-1}\,c^K\right)}{c-1}\sqrt{\tau} \qquad (13)$$

with the limit value $m_{log-limit} = \lim_{K \to \infty} m_{log} = \frac{\sqrt{c^2-1}}{c-1}\sqrt{\tau}$ when the number of filters tends to infinity.

By comparing equations (12) and (13) including the limit value of the latter, we can specifically note that with increasing number of intermediate temporal scale levels, a logarithmic distribution of the intermediate scales implies shorter temporal delays than a uniform distribution of the intermediate scales.

Table 1 shows numerical values of these measures for different values of K and c. As can be seen, the logarithmic distribution of the intermediate scales allows for significantly faster temporal dynamics than a uniform distribution.

Table 1. Numerical values of the *temporal delay in terms of the temporal mean* $m = \sum_{k=1}^{K} \mu_k$ in units of $\sigma = \sqrt{\tau}$ for time-causal kernels obtained by coupling K truncated exponential kernels in cascade in the cases of a uniform distribution of the intermediate temporal scale levels $\tau_k = k\tau/K$ or a logarithmic distribution $\tau_k = c^{2(k-K)}\tau$ with $c > 1$

	Temporal mean values of time-causal kernels			
K	m_{uni}	$m_{log}\ (c=\sqrt{2})$	$m_{log}\ (c=2^{3/4})$	$m_{log}\ (c=2)$
2	1.414	1.414	1.399	1.366
3	1.732	1.707	1.636	1.549
4	2.000	1.914	1.777	1.641
5	2.236	2.061	1.860	1.686
6	2.449	2.164	1.910	1.709
7	2.646	2.237	1.940	1.721
8	2.828	2.289	1.957	1.732

Table 2. Numerical values for the *temporal delay of the local maximum* in units of $\sigma = \sqrt{\tau}$ for time-causal kernels obtained by coupling K truncated exponential kernels in cascade in the cases of a uniform distribution of the intermediate temporal scale levels $\tau_k = k\tau/K$ or a logarithmic distribution $\tau_k = c^{2(k-K)}\tau$ with $c > 1$

	Temporal delays from the maxima of time-causal kernels			
K	$t_{max,uni}$	$t_{max,log}\ (c=\sqrt{2})$	$t_{max,log}\ (c=2^{3/4})$	$t_{max,log}\ (c=2)$
2	0.707	0.707	0.688	0.640
3	1.154	1.122	1.027	0.909
4	1.500	1.385	1.199	1.014
5	1.789	1.556	1.289	1.060
6	2.041	1.669	1.340	1.083
7	2.268	1.745	1.370	1.095
8	2.475	1.797	1.388	1.100

Additional temporal characteristics. Because of the asymmetric tails of the time-causal temporal smoothing kernels, temporal delay estimation by the mean value may however lead to substantial overestimates compared to *e.g.* the position of the local maximum. To provide more precise characteristics in the case of a uniform distribution of the intermediate temporal scale levels, for which a compact closed form expression is available for the composed kernel

$$h_{composed}(t;\ \mu, K) = \frac{t^{K-1}\,e^{-t/\mu}}{\mu^K\,\Gamma(K)} \tag{14}$$

let us differentiate this function $\partial_t\left(h_{composed}(t;\ \mu, K)\right) = \frac{e^{-\frac{t}{\mu}}((K-1)\mu - t)\left(\frac{t}{\mu}\right)^{K+1}}{t^3\,\Gamma(K)}$ and solve for the positions of the local maximum

$$t_{max,uni} = (K-1)\mu = \frac{(K-1)}{\sqrt{K}}\sqrt{\tau}. \tag{15}$$

Table 2 shows numerical values for the position of the local maximum for both types of time-causal kernels. As can be seen from the data, the temporal response properties are significantly faster for a logarithmic distribution of the intermediate scale levels compared to a uniform distribution and the difference increases rapidly with K. These temporal delay estimates are also significantly shorter than the temporal mean values, in particular for the logarithmic distribution.

If we consider a temporal event that occurs as a step function over time (*e.g.* a new object appearing in the field of view) and if the time of this event is estimated from the local maximum over time in the first-order temporal derivative response, then the temporal variation in the response over time will be given by the shape of the temporal smoothing kernel. The local maximum over time will occur at a time delay equal to the time at which the temporal kernel has its maximum over time. Thus, the position of the maximum over time of the temporal smoothing kernel is highly relevant for quantifying the temporal response dynamics.

5 Computational Implementation

The computational model for spatio-temporal receptive fields presented here is based on spatio-temporal image data that are assumed to be continuous over time. When implementing this model on sampled video data, the continuous theory must be transferred to discrete space and discrete time.

In this section we describe how the temporal and spatio-temporal receptive fields can be implemented in terms of corresponding discrete scale-space kernels that possess scale-space properties over discrete spatio-temporal domains.

5.1 Discrete Temporal Scale-Space Kernels Based on Recursive Filters

Given video data that has been sampled by some temporal frame rate r, the temporal scale σ_t in the continuous model in units of seconds is first transformed to a variance τ relative to a unit time sampling

$$\tau = r^2 \sigma_t^2 \tag{16}$$

where r may typically be either 25 Hz or 50 Hz. Then, a discrete set of intermediate temporal scale levels τ_k is defined by (8) or (11) with the difference between successive scale levels according to $\Delta\tau_k = \tau_k - \tau_{k-1}$ (with $\tau_0 = 0$).

For implementing the temporal smoothing operation between two such adjacent scale levels (with the lower level in each pair of adjacent scales referred to as f_{in} and the upper level as f_{out}), we make use of a *first-order recursive filter*

$$f_{out}(t) - f_{out}(t-1) = \frac{1}{1+\mu_k} \left(f_{in}(t) - f_{out}(t-1) \right) \tag{17}$$

with generating function

$$H_{geom}(z) = \frac{1}{1 - \mu_k(z-1)} \tag{18}$$

which is a time-causal kernel and satisfies discrete scale-space properties of guaranteeing that the number of local extrema or zero-crossings in the signal will not increase with increasing scale (Lindeberg [13]; Lindeberg and Fagerström [10]). Each such filter has temporal mean value $m_k = \mu_k$ and temporal variance $\Delta \tau_k = \mu_k^2 + \mu_k$, and we compute μ_k from $\Delta \tau_k$ according to

$$\mu_k = \frac{\sqrt{1 + 4\Delta \tau_k} - 1}{2}. \tag{19}$$

By the additive property of variances under convolution, the discrete variances of the discrete temporal scale-space kernels will perfectly match those of the continuous model, whereas the mean values and the temporal delays may differ somewhat. If the temporal scale τ_k is large relative to the temporal sampling density, the discrete model should be a good approximation in this respect.

By the time-recursive formulation of this temporal scale-space concept, the computations can be performed based on a compact temporal buffer over time, which contains the temporal scale-space representations at temporal scales τ_k and with no need for storing any additional temporal buffer of what has occurred in the past to perform the corresponding temporal operations.

5.2 Discrete Implementation of Spatial Gaussian Smoothing

To implement the spatial Gaussian operation on discrete sampled data, we do first transform a spatial scale parameter σ_x in units of *e.g.* degrees of visual angle to a spatial variance s relative to a unit sampling density according to

$$s = p^2 \sigma_x^2 \tag{20}$$

where p is the number of pixels per spatial unit *e.g.* in terms of degrees of visual angle at the image center. Then, we convolve the image data with the separable two-dimensional *discrete analogue of the Gaussian kernel* (Lindeberg [13])

$$T(n_1, n_2;\, s) = e^{-2s} I_{n_1}(s)\, I_{n_2}(s) \tag{21}$$

where I_n denotes the modified Bessel functions of integer order and which corresponds to the solution of the semi-discrete diffusion equation

$$\partial_s L(n_1, n_2;\, s) = \frac{1}{2}(\nabla_\times^2 L)(n_1, n_2;\, s) \tag{22}$$

where $\nabla_\times^2$ denotes the five-point discrete Laplacian operator defined by $(\nabla_\times^2 f)(n_1, n_2) = f(n_1 - 1, n_2) + f(n_1 + 1, n_2) + f(n_1, n_2 - 1) + f(n_1, n_2 + 1) - 4f(n_1, n_2)$. These kernels constitute the natural way to define a scale-space concept for discrete signals corresponding to the Gaussian scale-space over a symmetric domain in the sense of guaranteeing non-enhancement of local extrema, while also ensuring a semi-group property $T(\cdot, \cdot;\, s_1) * T(\cdot, \cdot;\, s_2) = T(\cdot, \cdot;\, s_1 + s_2)$ over the discrete domain which implies that representations at coarser scales can be computed from representations at finer scales using a cascade property.

This operation can be implemented either by explicit spatial convolution with spatially truncated kernels $\sum_{n_1=-N}^{N}\sum_{n_2=-N}^{N} T(n_1, n_2; s) > 1 - \varepsilon$ for small ε of the order 10^{-8} to 10^{-6} with mirroring at the image boundaries (adiabatic boundary conditions) or using the closed-form expression of the Fourier transform $\varphi(\theta_1, \theta_2) = \sum_{n_1=-\infty}^{\infty}\sum_{n_1=-\infty}^{\infty} T(n_1, n_2; s)\, e^{-i(n_1\theta_1 + n_2\theta_2)} = e^{-2t(\sin^2(\frac{\theta_1}{2}) + \sin^2(\frac{\theta_2}{2}))}$.

5.3 Discrete Implementation of Spatio-Temporal Receptive Fields

For separable spatio-temporal receptive fields, we implement the spatio-temporal smoothing operation by separable combination of the spatial and temporal scale-space concepts in sections 5.1 and 5.2. From this representation, spatio-temporal derivative approximations are then computed from *difference operators*

$$\delta_t = (-1, +1) \qquad \delta_{tt} = (1, -2, 1) \qquad (23)$$

$$\delta_x = (-\frac{1}{2}, 0, +\frac{1}{2}) \qquad \delta_{xx} = (1, -2, 1) \qquad (24)$$

expressed over the appropriate dimension. From the general theory in (Lindeberg [15]) it follows that the scale-space properties for the original zero-order signal will be transferred to such derivative approximations, thereby implying theoretically well-founded implementation of discrete derivative approximations.

For non-separable spatio-temporal receptive fields corresponding to a non-zero image velocity $v = (v_1, v_2)^T$, we implement the spatio-temporal smoothing operation by first warping the video data $(x'_1, x'_2)^T = (x_1 - v_1 t, x_2 - v_2 t)^T$ using spline interpolation. Then, we apply separable spatio-temporal smoothing in the transformed domain and unwarp the result back to the original domain. Over a continuous domain, such an operation is equivalent to convolution with corresponding velocity-adapted spatio-temporal receptive fields, while being significantly faster in a discrete implementation than corresponding explicit convolution with non-separable receptive fields over three dimensions.

In addition to a transfer of the scale-space properties from the continuous model to the discrete implementation, all the components in this discretization, the discrete Gaussian kernel, the time-recursive filters and the discrete derivative approximations, can be seen as mathematical approximations of the corresponding continuous counterparts. Thereby, the behaviour of the discrete implementation will approach the corresponding continuous model.

6 Summary and Discussion

We have presented an improved computational model for spatio-temporal receptive fields based on time-causal and time-recursive spatio-temporal scale-space representation defined from a set of first-order integrators or truncated exponential filters coupled in cascade over the temporal domain in combination with a Gaussian scale-space concept over the spatial domain. This model can be efficiently implemented in terms of recursive filters and we have shown how the continuous model can be transferred to a discrete implementation while retaining discrete scale-space properties. Specifically, we have analysed how remaining design parameters within the theory, in terms of the number of first-order integrators coupled in cascade and a distribution parameter of a logarithmic distribution, affect the temporal response dynamics in terms of temporal delays.

Compared to other spatial and temporal scale-space representations based on continuous scale parameters, a conceptual difference with the temporal scale-space representation underlying the proposed spatio-temporal receptive fields, is that the temporal scale levels have to be discrete. Thereby, we sacrifice scale invariance as resulting from Gaussian scale-space concepts based on causality or non-enhancement of local extrema (Koenderink [16]; Lindeberg [11]) or used as a scale-space axiom in certain axiomatic scale-space formulations (Iijima [17]; Florack et al. [18]; Pauwels et al. [19]; Weickert et al. [20]; Duits et al. [21]; Fagerström [22]); see also Koenderink and van Doorn [23], Florack et al. [24] and Tschirsich and Kuijper [25] for other scale-space approaches closely related to this work. For a vision system intended to operate in real time using no other explicit storage of visual data from the past than a compact time-recursive buffer of spatio-temporal scale-space at different temporal scales, the loss of a continuous temporal scale parameter may however be less of a practical constraint, since one would anyway have to discretize the temporal scale levels in advance to be able to register the image data to perform any computations at all.

In the special case when all the time constants of the first-order integrators are equal, the resulting temporal smoothing kernels in the continuous model (14) correspond to Laguerre functions, which have been previously used for modelling the temporal response properties of neurons in the visual system (den Brinker and Roufs [26]) and for computing spatio-temporal image features in computer vision (Rivero-Moreno and Bres [27]; Berg et al. [28]). Regarding the corresponding discrete model with all time constants equal, the corresponding discrete temporal smoothing kernels approach Poisson kernels when the number of temporal smoothing steps increases while keeping the variance of the composed kernel fixed (Lindeberg and Fagerström [10]). Such Poisson kernels have also been used for modelling biological vision (Fourtes and Hodgkin [29]). Compared to the special case with all time constants equal, a logarithmic distribution of the intermediate temporal scale levels (8) does on the other hand allow for larger flexibility in the trade-off between temporal smoothing and temporal response characteristics, specifically enabling faster temporal responses (shorter temporal delays) and higher computational efficiency when computing multiple temporal or spatio-temporal receptive field responses involving coarser temporal scales.

References

1. Hubel, D.H., Wiesel, T.N.: Brain and Visual Perception: The Story of a 25-Year Collaboration. Oxford University Press (2005)
2. DeAngelis, G.C., Ohzawa, I., Freeman, R.D.: Receptive field dynamics in the central visual pathways. Trends in Neuroscience **18**, 451–457 (1995)

3. DeAngelis, G.C., Anzai, A.: A modern view of the classical receptive field: linear and non-linear spatio-temporal processing by V1 neurons. In: Chalupa, L.M., Werner, J.S., (eds.) The Visual Neurosciences, vol. 1, pp. 704–719. MIT Press (2004)
4. Adelson, E., Bergen, J.: Spatiotemporal energy models for the perception of motion. J. Optical Society of America **A 2**, 284–299 (1985)
5. Zelnik-Manor, L., Irani, M.: Event-based analysis of video. In: Proc. Computer Vision and Pattern Recognition, Kauai Marriott, Hawaii, pp. II:123–II:130 (2001)
6. Laptev, I., Lindeberg, T.: Local descriptors for spatio-temporal recognition. In: MacLean, W.J. (ed.) SCVMA 2004. LNCS, vol. 3667, pp. 91–103. Springer, Heidelberg (2006)
7. Jhuang, H., Serre, T., Wolf, L., Poggio, T.: A biologically inspired system for action recognition. In: Int. Conf. on Computer Vision, pp. 1–8 (2007)
8. Shabani, A.H., Clausi, D.A., Zelek, J.S.: Improved spatio-temporal salient feature detection for action recognition. In: British Machine Vision Conf., pp. 1–12 (2011)
9. Fleet, D.J., Langley, K.: Recursive filters for optical flow. IEEE Trans. Pattern Analysis and Machine Intell. **17**, 61–67 (1995)
10. Lindeberg, T., Fagerström, D.: Scale-space with causal time direction. In: Buxton, B.F., Cipolla, R. (eds.) ECCV 1996. LNCS, vol. 1064, pp. 229–240. Springer, Heidelberg (1996)
11. Lindeberg, T.: Generalized Gaussian scale-space axiomatics comprising linear scale-space, affine scale-space and spatio-temporal scale-space. J. of Mathematical Imaging and Vision **40**, 36–81 (2011)
12. Lindeberg, T.: A computational theory of visual receptive fields. Biological Cybernetics **107**, 589–635 (2013)
13. Lindeberg, T.: Scale-space for discrete signals. IEEE Trans. Pattern Analysis and Machine Intell. **12**, 234–254 (1990)
14. Koenderink, J.J.: Scale-time. Biological Cybernetics **58**, 159–162 (1988)
15. Lindeberg, T.: Discrete derivative approximations with scale-space properties: A basis for low-level feature extraction. J. Math. Imaging Vision **3**, 349–376 (1993)
16. Koenderink, J.J.: The structure of images. Biol. Cyb. **50**, 363–370 (1984)
17. Iijima, T.: Observation theory of two-dimensional visual patterns. Papers of Technical Group on Automata and Automatic Control, IECE, Japan (1962)
18. Florack, L.M.J., ter Haar Romeny, B.M., Koenderink, J.J., Viergever, M.A.: Scale and the differential structure of images. Image Vision Comp. **10**, 376–388 (1992)
19. Pauwels, E.J., Fiddelaers, P., Moons, T., van Gool, L.J.: An extended class of scale-invariant and recursive scale-space filters. IEEE Trans. Pattern Analysis and Machine Intell. **17**, 691–701 (1995)
20. Weickert, J., Ishikawa, S., Imiya, A.: On the history of Gaussian scale-space axiomatics. In: Gaussian Scale-Space Theory, pp. 45–59. Springer (1997)
21. Duits, R., Florack, L., de Graaf, J., ter Haar Romeny, B.: On the axioms of scale space theory. J. of Mathematical Imaging and Vision **22**, 267–298 (2004)
22. Fagerström, D.: Spatio-temporal scale-spaces. In: Sgallari, F., Murli, A., Paragios, N. (eds.) SSVM 2007. LNCS, vol. 4485, pp. 326–337. Springer, Heidelberg (2007)
23. Koenderink, J.J., van Doorn, A.J.: Receptive field families. Biological Cybernetics **63**, 291–298 (1990)
24. Florack, L.M.J., ter Haar Romeny, B.M., Koenderink, J.J., Viergever, M.A.: Families of tuned scale-space kernels. In: Sandini, G. (ed.) ECCV 1992. LNCS, vol. 588, pp. 19–23. Springer, Heidelberg (1992)
25. Tschirsich, M., Kuijper, M.: Notes on discrete Gaussian scale space. J. of Mathematical Imaging and Vision **51**, 106–123 (2015)

26. den Brinker, A.C., Roufs, J.A.J.: Evidence for a generalized Laguerre transform of temporal events by the visual system. Biological Cybernetics **67**, 395–402 (1992)
27. Rivero-Moreno, C.J., Bres, S.: Spatio-temporal primitive extraction using Hermite and Laguerre filters for early vision video indexing. In: Campilho, A.C., Kamel, M.S. (eds.) ICIAR 2004. LNCS, vol. 3211, pp. 825–832. Springer, Heidelberg (2004)
28. van der Berg, E.S., Reyneke, P.V., de Ridder, C.: Rotational image correlation in the Gauss-Laguerre domain. In: SPIE, vol. 9257, pp. 92570F-1–92570F-17 (2014)
29. Fourtes, M.G.F., Hodgkin, A.L.: Changes in the time scale and sensitivity in the omatadia of limulus. Journal of Physiology **172**, 239–263 (1964)

A Linear Scale-Space Theory for Continuous Nonlocal Evolutions

Giovanno Marcelo Cárdenas[(✉)], Joachim Weickert, and Sarah Schäffer

Mathematical Image Analysis Group, Faculty of Mathematics and Computer Science,
Saarland University, Campus E1.7, 66041 Saarbrücken, Germany
{cardenas,weickert,schaeffer}@mia.uni-saarland.de

Abstract. Most scale-space evolutions are described in terms of partial differential equations. In recent years, however, nonlocal processes have become an important research topic in image analysis. The goal of our paper is to establish well-posedness and scale-space properties for a class of nonlocal evolutions. They are given by linear integro-differential equations with measures. In analogy to Weickert's diffusion theory (1998), we prove existence and uniqueness, preservation of the average grey value, a maximum–minimum principle, image simplification properties in terms of Lyapunov functionals, and we establish convergence to a constant steady state. We show that our nonlocal scale-space theory covers nonlocal variants of linear diffusion. Moreover, by choosing specific discrete measures, the classical semidiscrete diffusion framework is identified as a special case of our continuous theory. Last but not least, we introduce two modifications of bilateral filtering. In contrast to previous bilateral filters, our variants create nonlocal scale-spaces that preserve the average grey value and that can be highly robust under noise. While these filters are linear, they can achieve a similar performance as nonlinear and even anisotropic diffusion equations.

Keywords: Nonlocal processes · Scale-space · Diffusion · Integro-differential equations · Well-posedness · Bilateral filtering

1 Introduction

Starting with Iijima's pioneering work in 1962 [1] and its western counterparts by Witkin [2] and Koenderink [3] two decades later, the scale-space concept has become an integral part of many image processing and computer vision methods. For example, it is the backbone of the widely used SIFT detector for feature matching [4].

Scale-spaces embed an original image f into a family $\{T_t f \,|\, t \geq 0\}$ such that $T_0 f = f$ and larger values of t correspond to simpler representations of f. Numerous attempts have been made to formalise this idea and supplement it with additional assumptions in order to restrict the scale-space evolution to a specific class of processes, or even single out a unique scale-space in an axiomatic way. Such evolutions include linear processes such as Gaussian scale-space [1–3,5–7], the Poisson scale-space [8] and its generalisation to α-scale-spaces [9]. Typical representatives of nonlinear scale-spaces are given by nonlinear diffusion scale-spaces [10], the morphological equivalent of Gaussian scale-space [11], and curvature-driven evolutions such as the affine morphological scale-space [12]. Moreover, also spatio-temporal scale-spaces have been considered [13,14], and regularisation methods have been identified as scale-spaces [15].

Many of these processes exhibit a local behaviour and can be described in terms of partial differential equations (PDEs) or pseudodifferential equations. More recently, however, nonlocal processes have become very popular in research. For instance, bilateral filters [16,17] and patch-based methods [18,19] are widely-used in image processing applications, and classical PDEs and variational methods have been generalised to nonlocal evolutions [20]. However, less is known about scale-space theory for nonlocal processes. Related work can be found in [25], where the authors develop nonlocal morphological scale-spaces as an extension of [12].

The goal of our paper is to address this issue from the point of view of diffusion processes. By restricting ourselves to a class of nonlocal evolutions that are given by linear integro-differential equations, we establish well-posedness and scale-space results that are in analogy to the diffusion framework by Weickert [10]. This includes existence and uniqueness, preservation of the average grey value, an extremum principle, a large class of Lyapunov functionals, and convergence to a flat steady state. We show that our framework covers nonlocal generalisations of Gaussian scale-space as well as space-discrete diffusion scale-spaces. Moreover, we introduce two modifications of bilateral filtering that are in accordance with our theory and can be much more robust under noise.

Our paper is organised as follows. In Section 2 we derive theoretical results on well-posedness and scale-space properties. The third section discusses examples and presents experiments. Our paper is concluded with a summary in Section 4.

2 Theoretical Results

Let us begin by giving a precise formulation of the problem we are concerned with. For this matter let $\Omega \subset \mathbb{R}^N$ be a bounded N-dimensional image domain, and let μ be a locally finite Borel measure in $\mathbb{R}^N$. We consider the following linear evolution process:

$$\partial_t u(\mathbf{x}, t) = \int_\Omega K(\mathbf{x}, \mathbf{y}) \left(u(\mathbf{y}, t) - u(\mathbf{x}, t) \right) d\mu(\mathbf{y}) \quad \text{in} \quad \bar{\Omega} \times [0, t_0], \qquad (1)$$

$$u(\mathbf{x}, 0) = f(\mathbf{x}) \quad \text{in} \quad \bar{\Omega}, \qquad (2)$$

with the subsequent assumptions:

(NL1) Regularity: $K \in C(\bar{\Omega} \times \bar{\Omega})$ and $f \in C(\bar{\Omega})$.
(NL2) Symmetry: $K(\mathbf{x}, \mathbf{y}) = K(\mathbf{y}, \mathbf{x})$ in $\bar{\Omega} \times \bar{\Omega}$.
(NL3) Nonnegativity: $K(\mathbf{x}, \mathbf{y}) \geq 0$ in $\bar{\Omega} \times \bar{\Omega}$.

(NL4) Irreducibility: There exists a finite family of μ-measurable sets $\mathcal{F} := \{B_i \subset \Omega : 1 \leq i \leq p\}$, such that:
  (i) There exists a constant $c > 0$ such that $K(\mathbf{x},\mathbf{y}) \geq c$ whenever $B \in \mathcal{F}$ and $\mathbf{x}, \mathbf{y} \in B$.
  (ii) $\Omega = \bigcup_{i=1}^{p} B_i$ and $\mu(B_i \cap B_{i+1}) > 0$ for $1 \leq i \leq p-1$.

We will see that not all of these assumptions will be necessary for our results: (NL1) is needed for establishing well-posedness, the proof of a maximum–minimum principle involves (NL1) together with (NL3), while preservation of the average grey value uses (NL1) and (NL2). The existence of Lyapunov functionals and the convergence to a constant steady state require (NL1)–(NL4).

2.1 Well-Posedness

Let us first define a solution concept for (1)–(2).

Definition 1. We say that $u \in C(\bar{\Omega} \times [0, t_0])$ is a *solution* of problem (1)–(2) if

$$u(\mathbf{x}, t) = f(\mathbf{x}) + \int_0^t \int_\Omega K(\mathbf{x}, \mathbf{y})(u(\mathbf{y}, s) - u(\mathbf{x}, s)) \, d\mu(\mathbf{y}) \, ds, \qquad 0 \leq t \leq t_0. \quad (3)$$

This definition allows us to prove the following result.

Proposition 1 (Existence and Uniqueness). *There exists a solution of (1)–(2), and this solution is unique.*

Proof. The proof is similar to the one given in [21], where the authors considered this type of processes with a special function $K(\mathbf{x}, \mathbf{y}) = J(\mathbf{x} - \mathbf{y})$, for some continuous radial and symmetric function J and with μ being equal to the Lebesgue measure. The fixed point arguments in [21] also work under the conditions of our more general framework. In our case, we consider the operator given by the r.h.s. of (3) defined on the space $C(\bar{\Omega} \times [0, t_0])$. □

Remark 1. We will interpret $\partial_t u$ as the right and left derivative when $t = 0$ and $t = t_0$, respectively. In this case, the unique solution u in the sense of Definition 1 satisfies (1)–(2). In fact, it is not hard to verify that the expression $\int_\Omega K(\mathbf{x},\mathbf{y})(u(\mathbf{y},s) - u(\mathbf{x},s)) \, d\mu(\mathbf{y})$ is continuous with respect to the variable s. Thus, (3) and the fundamental theorem of integral calculus imply that $\partial_t u$ exists and that (1)–(2) hold.

2.2 Scale-Space Properties

Now that we have established the existence of a unique solution, we are in a position to prove a number of scale-space results that are in analogy to the ones for anisotropic diffusion [10].

Proposition 2 (Preservation of the Average Grey Value). The solution of (1)–(2) preserves the average grey value:

$$\frac{1}{\mu(\Omega)} \int_\Omega u(\mathbf{x}, t)\, d\mu(\mathbf{x}) = \frac{1}{\mu(\Omega)} \int_\Omega f(\mathbf{x})\, d\mu(\mathbf{x}) \qquad \text{for } 0 \le t \le t_0. \tag{4}$$

Proof. Integrating (3) over Ω with respect to μ and applying the Tonelli-Fubini theorem together with (NL2), we obtain

$$\int_\Omega (u(\mathbf{x},t) - f(\mathbf{x}))\, d\mu(\mathbf{x}) = \int_0^t \int_\Omega \int_\Omega K(\mathbf{x},\mathbf{y})(u(\mathbf{y},s) - u(\mathbf{x},s))\, d\mu(\mathbf{y})\, d\mu(\mathbf{x})\, ds$$
$$= -\int_0^t \int_\Omega \int_\Omega K(\mathbf{x},\mathbf{y})(u(\mathbf{y},s) - u(\mathbf{x},s))\, d\mu(\mathbf{y})\, d\mu(\mathbf{x})\, ds. \tag{5}$$

This implies the result. □

Proposition 3 (Preservation of Nonnegativity). If u is a solution of (1)–(2) with $f(\mathbf{x}) \ge 0$, then

$$\min_{(\mathbf{x},t) \in \bar\Omega \times [0,t_0]} u(\mathbf{x}, t) \ge 0. \tag{6}$$

Proof. Assume that $f(\mathbf{x}) \ge 0$ and that $\min_{(\mathbf{x},t) \in \bar\Omega \times [0,t_0]} u(\mathbf{x},t) < 0$. Then there exists an $\epsilon > 0$ such that the function $v := u + t\epsilon$ has a strictly negative minimum in some point $(\mathbf{x_m}, t_m) \in \bar\Omega \times]0, t_0]$. However,

$$0 = \partial_t v(\mathbf{x_m}, t_m) = \epsilon + \int_\Omega K(\mathbf{x_m}, \mathbf{y})(u(\mathbf{y}, t_m) - u(\mathbf{x_m}, t_m))\, d\mu(\mathbf{y}) > 0. \tag{7}$$

This is a contradiction. □

From this last proposition we get the following maximum–minimum principle.

Proposition 4 (Maximum–Minimum Principle). If u is a solution of (1)–(2), then

$$\min_{\mathbf{z} \in \bar\Omega} f(\mathbf{z}) \le u(\mathbf{x}, t) \le \max_{\mathbf{z} \in \bar\Omega} f(\mathbf{z}) \qquad \forall\, (\mathbf{x}, t) \in \bar\Omega \times [0, t_0]. \tag{8}$$

Proof. To prove the first inequality, we apply Proposition 3 to problem (1)–(2) with f replaced by $v_0 := f - \min_{\mathbf{x} \in \bar\Omega} f$. In fact, $v_0 \ge 0$, and it follows that the solution v of this problem should satisfy $v \ge 0$. However, from the linearity of (1)–(2), we also know that $v = u - \min_{\mathbf{x} \in \bar\Omega} f$, which gives the result. The second inequality can be proven in a similar way, applying Proposition 3 to problem (1)–(2) with f replaced by $\max_{\mathbf{x} \in \bar\Omega}(f) - f$. □

Our next goal is to analyse the behaviour of the solution of (1)–(2) as $t_0 \to \infty$. We will need the following lemma.

Lemma 1. Let $r : \mathbb{R} \to \mathbb{R}$ be a convex C^2 function. If u is a solution of (1)–(2), then $\frac{d}{dt} \int_\Omega r(u(\mathbf{x},t)) \, d\mu(\mathbf{x})$ exists for $t \in [0, t_0]$ (here we mean the right and left derivative for $t = 0$ and $t = t_0$, respectively). Moreover, this expression is equal to $\int_\Omega r'(u(\mathbf{x},t)) \, \partial_t u(\mathbf{x},t) \, d\mu(\mathbf{x})$.

Proof. Let $t \in [0, t_0]$ and define $F_h(\mathbf{x}) := \frac{1}{h} \left(r(u(\mathbf{x}, t+h)) - r(u(\mathbf{x},t)) \right)$, for $t, t + h \in [0, t_0]$. Then, since $r \in C^2$, we obtain from Remark 1 that $\partial_t r(u(\mathbf{x},t))$ exists for every $(\mathbf{x}, t) \in \bar{\Omega} \times [0, t_0]$ and is equal to $r'(u(\mathbf{x},t)) \partial_t u(\mathbf{x}, t) = \lim_{h \to 0} F_h(\mathbf{x})$. On the other hand, since $u \in C(\bar{\Omega} \times [0, t_0])$, we also know that

$$|F_h(\mathbf{x})| = |r'(u(\mathbf{x}, t_x))| \tag{9}$$

for some $t_x \in [0, t_0]$ such that $|t_x - t| < h$. Thus, we may bound $F_h(\mathbf{x})$ with a constant $M > 0$ which is independent of x and h. This allows us to apply Lebesgue's convergence theorem to obtain that

$$\lim_{h \to 0} \int_\Omega F_h(\mathbf{x}) \, d\mu(x) = \int_\Omega \lim_{h \to 0} F_h(\mathbf{x}) \, d\mu(\mathbf{x}), \tag{10}$$

as wanted. □

In what follows we will denote the constant function that is equal to the average grey value of f by

$$\tilde{u}(\mathbf{x}) := \frac{1}{\mu(\Omega)} \int_\Omega f(\mathbf{z}) \, d\mu(\mathbf{z}) \quad \forall \, \mathbf{x} \in \bar{\Omega}. \tag{11}$$

With this notation we can state the following result.

Proposition 5 (Lyapunov Functionals). Let u be the solution of (1)–(2). For any convex C^2 function $r : \mathbb{R} \to \mathbb{R}$, the expression

$$V(t) = \Phi(u(.,t)) := \int_\Omega r(u(\mathbf{x},t)) \, d\mu(\mathbf{x}) \tag{12}$$

is a Lyapunov functional, i.e.

(i) $\Phi(u(.,t)) \geq \Phi(\tilde{u})$ for all $t \geq 0$.
(ii) $V \in C^1[0, \infty[$ and $V'(t) \leq 0$ for all $t \geq 0$.

Moreover, if $r'' > 0$, then $V(t)$ is even a strict Lyapunov functional, i.e.

(iii) For all $t \geq 0$ we have that $\Phi(u(.,t)) = \Phi(\tilde{u})$, if and only if $u(.,t) = \tilde{u}$ μ-a.e. in Ω.
(iv) If $t \geq 0$, then $V'(t) = 0$, if and only if $u(t) = \tilde{u}$ μ-a.e. in Ω.
(v) $V(0) = V(T)$ for $T > 0$, if and only if $\forall t \in [0, T] : u(\mathbf{x}, t) = \tilde{u}$ μ-a.e. in Ω.

Proof.

(i) From Jensen's inequality and the preservation of the average grey value we obtain that

$$\Phi(u(.,t)) = \int_\Omega r(u(\mathbf{z},t))\,d\mu(\mathbf{z}) \geq \int_\Omega r\left(\int_\Omega \frac{u(\mathbf{z},t)}{\mu(\Omega)}\,d\mu(\mathbf{z})\right) d\mu(\mathbf{y}) = \Phi(\tilde u).\tag{13}$$

(ii) From Lemma 1 we know that

$$V'(t) = \int_\Omega r'(u(\mathbf{x},t))\frac{d}{dt}u(\mathbf{x},t)\,d\mu(\mathbf{x}).\tag{14}$$

Then, from (1)–(2) we obtain that

$$2V'(t) = 2\int_\Omega \int_\Omega K(\mathbf{y},\mathbf{x})\,r'(u(\mathbf{x},t))(u(\mathbf{y},t)-u(\mathbf{x},t))\,d\mu(\mathbf{y})\,d\mu(\mathbf{x})$$
$$= \int_\Omega \int_\Omega K(\mathbf{y},\mathbf{x})(r'(u(\mathbf{x},t))-r'(u(\mathbf{y},t)))\cdot$$
$$\cdot (u(\mathbf{y},t)-u(\mathbf{x},t))\,d\mu(\mathbf{y})\,d\mu(\mathbf{x})\tag{15}$$

where we used (NL2) for the second equality. Since r is convex we know that r' is nondecreasing. Therefore, the quantity $(r'(u(\mathbf{x},t))-r'(u(\mathbf{y},t))) \cdot (u(\mathbf{y},t)-u(\mathbf{x},t))$ is allways nonpositive and it follows from the nonnegativity of K (NL3) that $V'(t)\leq 0$. Continuity of $V(t)$ and $V'(t)$ follows from the uniform continuity of u in $\bar\Omega\times[0,t_0]$ and (15).

(iii) If we assume that r is strictly convex, then we obtain from the strict Jensen's inequality that $\Phi(u(.,t)) = \Phi(\tilde u)$ if and only if $u(\mathbf{x},t) = C$ μ-a.e. for some constant C. However, from the preservation of the average grey value (Proposition 2) we conclude that the only possibility is $C = \tilde u$, as wanted.

(iv) From (15) and the irreducibility condition (NL4) we obtain that u is μ-a.e. equal to a constant. However, this constant can only be $\tilde u$ because of the preservation of the average grey value. This proves the result.

(v) We use the fact that V is nonincreasing together with (iv). □

As explained in [10], Lyapunov functionals guarantee that a scale-space acts image simplifying in many ways. By choosing specific strictly convex functions for r, it follows that the scale-space evolution reduces all L^p norms for $p \geq 2$, all even central moments, and it increases the entropy of the image. Last but not least, Lyapunov functionals are also useful for proving the following convergence result.

Proposition 6 (Convergence). Let u be a solution of (1)–(2). Then

$$\lim_{t\to\infty} ||u(t)-\tilde u||_{L^2(\Omega,\mu)} = 0.\tag{16}$$

Proof. Let $v = u - \tilde{u}$ be the solution of (1)–(2) when f is replaced by $f - \tilde{u}$. If we consider the Lyapunov functional of Proposition 5 for the solution v, with the particular choice $r(x) = x^2$ in the definition (12) of V, we get that

$$\lim_{t\to\infty} ||u(.,t) - \tilde{u}||_{L^2(\Omega,\mu)} = \ell, \tag{17}$$

for some finite value $\ell \geq 0$, as a consequence of (i) and (ii) of Proposition 5. Moreover, we know that

$$\int_0^\infty |V'(t)|dt \leq V(0) - \lim_{t\to\infty} V(t) < \infty. \tag{18}$$

This implies that there exists a sequence t_i such that $\lim_{i\to\infty} t_i = \infty$ and $\lim_{i\to\infty} V'(t_i) = 0$, or equivalently,

$$\lim_{i\to\infty} \int_\Omega \int_\Omega K(\mathbf{y},\mathbf{x})(u(\mathbf{y},t_i) - u(\mathbf{x},t_i))^2 \, d\mu(\mathbf{y}) \, d\mu(\mathbf{x}) = 0. \tag{19}$$

Now, for every B in the family $\mathcal{F}$ of condition (NL4) we may apply the Cauchy-Schwartz inequality to obtain

$$\int_B \left| u(\mathbf{x},t) - \frac{1}{\mu(B)} \int_B u(\mathbf{y},t) \, d\mu(\mathbf{y}) \right|^2 d\mu(\mathbf{x})$$

$$\leq \frac{1}{\mu(B)} \int_B \int_B |u(\mathbf{y},t) - u(\mathbf{x},t)|^2 \, d\mu(\mathbf{x}) \, d\mu(\mathbf{y})$$

$$\leq \frac{1}{\mu(B)} \int_B \int_B \frac{K(\mathbf{x},\mathbf{y})}{c} |u(\mathbf{y},t) - u(\mathbf{x},t)|^2 \, d\mu(\mathbf{x}) \, d\mu(\mathbf{y}), \tag{20}$$

where $c > 0$ is the lower bound for K in condition (NL4). Let us denote by $h_k(t)$ the constant function defined on each $B_k \in \mathcal{F}$ of condition (NL4) that is equal to $\frac{1}{\mu(B_k)} \int_{B_k} u(\mathbf{x},t) d\mu(x)$ for $1 \leq k \leq p$. The last inequality and (19) imply that

$$||u(.,t_i) - h_k(t_i)||_{L^2(B_k,\mu)} \to 0. \tag{21}$$

Moreover, from (17) we know that $u(.,t_i)$ is bounded in $L^2(\Omega,\mu)$. Therefore, also $h_k(t_i)$ is bounded. We may choose a subsequence of t_i which we continue to denote the same way, such that $\lim_{i\to\infty} h_k(t_i)$ exists and is finite for $1 \leq k \leq p$. Furthermore, the quantity $\gamma := \min \{\mu(B_k \cap B_{k+1}) : 1 \leq k \leq p-1\}$ is positive because of (NL4). Therefore, we obtain that

$$\gamma |h_k(t) - h_{k+1}(t)|^2 \leq |h_k(t) - h_{k+1}(t)|^2 \int_{B_k \cap B_{k+1}} d\mu(\mathbf{x})$$

$$= ||h_k(t) - h_{k+1}(t)||_{L^2(B_k \cap B_{k+1},\mu)}$$

$$\leq ||u(.,t) - h_k(t)||_{L^2(B_k,\mu)} + ||u(.,t) - h_{k+1}(t)||_{L^2(B_{k+1},\mu)} \tag{22}$$

for $0 \leq k \leq p-1$. These inequalities, together with (NL4) and (21), allow us to conclude that all $h_k(t_i)$ converge to the same constant. Hence, it follows that u converges in $L^2(\Omega,\mu)$ to a constant. This implies that the value ℓ in (17) has to be 0 as wanted. □

3 Examples

3.1 Continuous Setting with Shift-Invariant Kernels

Let us consider the specific problem

$$\partial_t u(\mathbf{x}, t) = \int_\Omega J(\mathbf{x} - \mathbf{y}) \left(u(\mathbf{y}, t) - u(\mathbf{x}, t) \right) d\mathbf{y}, \quad \text{in }]0, t_0] \times \Omega, \quad (23)$$

$$u(\mathbf{x}, 0) = f(\mathbf{x}) \quad \text{in } \Omega, \quad (24)$$

with $f \in L^1(\Omega)$ and some nonnegative radial function $J \in C(\mathbb{R}^N, \mathbb{R})$ such that $J(0) > 0$ and $\int_{\mathbb{R}^N} J(\mathbf{x}) \, d\mathbf{x} = 1$. Notice that since we restrict ourselves to continuous initial data, i.e. $f \in C(\bar{\Omega})$, it is not difficult to check that (23) satisfies all conditions (NL1)–(NL4). Thus, we may apply the results of the previous section, for μ equal to the Lebesgue measure of $\mathbb{R}^N$.

Interestingly, this process was studied also in [21]. The authors proved that the family of solutions u_ϵ of (23) with J replaced by an appropriate rescaled version J_ϵ, approximates the solution of the usual Neumann problem for homogeneous diffusion. More precisely, if v is a solution of

$$\partial_t u = \Delta u \quad \text{in }]0, t_0] \times \Omega, \quad (25)$$

$$\frac{du}{d\nu} = 0 \quad \text{on } \partial\Omega, \quad (26)$$

$$u(\mathbf{x}, 0) = f(\mathbf{x}) \quad \text{in } \Omega, \quad (27)$$

where ν denotes the outer normal vector to $\partial\Omega$, then

$$\lim_{\epsilon \to 0} \|u_\epsilon - v\|_{L^\infty(\Omega \times [0, t_0])} = 0. \quad (28)$$

For this reason, the nonlocal problem (23) solves a diffusion problem. In other words, observe that using any kernel J as specified above will always lead us to Gaussian scale-space. This statement has its stochastic counterpart in the central limit theorem, which tells us that an iterated application of a smoothing kernel converges to a Gaussian. This motivates us to consider more general filters below, where the kernel can be a space-variant function of the initial image f.

3.2 Discrete Setting

Now we discuss the case when the measure μ is a discrete measure concentrated on a finite subset of Ω. We will focus on the one-dimensional case since the extension to higher dimension is straightforward.

Let $\Omega =]0, 1[$ and let $h = \frac{1}{M}$ for some fixed integer $M > 1$. Moreover, we define μ as the restriction to Ω of the discrete measure that is concentrated on the set $\mathcal{Z}_h := \{h(z - \frac{1}{2}) \, ; \, z \in \mathbb{Z}\}$. In what follows we set $k_{i,j} := K((i - \frac{1}{2})h, (j - \frac{1}{2})h)$

and $u_i(t) := u((i-\frac{1}{2})h, t)$ for $1 \leq i, j \leq M$. With these choices, the problem (1)–(2) becomes

$$\frac{d}{dt} u_i = \sum_{j=1}^{M} k_{i,j}(u_j - u_i) \qquad (1 \leq i \leq M), \qquad (29)$$

$$u_i(0) = f_i \qquad (1 \leq i \leq M). \qquad (30)$$

This is a semidiscrete evolution process for the vector $\mathbf{u} := (u_1, u_2, ..., u_M)^\top$. Conditions (NL1)-(NL4) imply that the matrix $\mathbf{K} = (k_{i,j})_{i,j=1}^M$ is symmetric, nonnegative, and irreducible. Notice that (29) can be written as

$$\frac{d}{dt} \mathbf{u}(t) = \mathbf{A}\mathbf{u}(t), \qquad (31)$$

$$\mathbf{u}(0) = \mathbf{f}, \qquad (32)$$

where $\mathbf{f} = (f_1, f_2, ..., f_M)^\top$ and $\mathbf{A} = (a_{i,j})_{i,j=1}^M$ is the matrix with entries

$$a_{i,j} = \begin{cases} k_{i,j} & (i \neq j), \\ -\sum_{n \neq i} k_{i,n} & (i = j). \end{cases} \qquad (33)$$

This process satisfies all the properties of the semidiscrete framework for anisotropic diffusion considered in [10]. In fact, since $\mathbf{K}$ is a matrix, the corresponding linear operator is Lipschitz-continuous. Moreover, $\mathbf{K}$ is symmetric, has nonnegative entries, and is irreducible. Thus, it follows that $\mathbf{A}$ is Lipschitz-continuous, symmetric, has nonegative off-diagonal entries, and is irreducible. Moreover, (33) implies that $\mathbf{A}$ has zero row sums. These are the conditions required in [10].

Remarks 2.

(a) Note that the fact that in the linear case, the semidiscrete diffusion framework is covered by our nonlocal continuous framework is a benefit of our formulation in terms of measures.
(b) This also shows that Weickert's semidiscrete diffusion theory is more general than his continuous one, which requires local processes in terms of PDEs.
(c) Extensions to higher dimensions can be obtained by choosing $\Omega \subset \mathbb{R}^N$ and the measure $\mu_n := \mu \times \mu \times .... \times \mu$, where the product is taken n times, and μ is a discrete measure concentrated on $\mathcal{Z}_h := \{h(z - \frac{1}{2}) \,;\, z \in \mathbb{Z}\}$ as above.

3.3 A Scale-Space Variant of Bilateral Filtering

Bilateral filtering goes back to Aurich and Weule [16] and became popular by a paper of Tomasi and Manduchi [17]. In a continuous notation, it filters a greyscale image $f : \Omega \to \mathbb{R}$ by means of spatial and tonal averaging with Gaussian weights:

$$u(\mathbf{x}) = \frac{\int_\Omega g_\lambda(|f(\mathbf{y}) - f(\mathbf{x})|) \, g_\rho(|\mathbf{y} - \mathbf{x}|) \, f(\mathbf{y}) \, d\mathbf{y}}{\int_\Omega g_\lambda(|f(\mathbf{y}) - f(\mathbf{x})|) \, g_\rho(|\mathbf{y} - \mathbf{x}|) \, d\mathbf{y}}, \qquad (34)$$

Fig. 1. Bilateral scale-space evolution (35) of a test image (256 × 256 pixels, $\rho = 5$, $\lambda = 10$). **From left to right:** $t = 0$, 500, 10000, and 200000.

where $g_\rho(s) := \exp(-s^2/(2\rho^2))$. While bilateral filtering is a nonlocal process, it does not preserve the average grey value. Moreover, it is typically applied in a noniterative way.

We propose the following modification that leads to an evolution equation:

$$\partial_t u(\mathbf{x},t) = \frac{1}{c}\int_\Omega g_\lambda(|f(\mathbf{y})-f(\mathbf{x})|)\, g_\rho(|\mathbf{y}-\mathbf{x}|)\, (u(\mathbf{y},t) - u(\mathbf{x},t))\, d\mathbf{y}, \qquad (35)$$

where $c := \int_\Omega g_\rho(\mathbf{y})\, d\mathbf{y}$ performs a normalisation of the spatial weighting. In our terminology, this is a nonlocal linear scale-space with the specific kernel $K(\mathbf{x},\mathbf{y}) = \frac{1}{c} g_\lambda(|f(\mathbf{y}) - f(\mathbf{x})|)\, g_\rho(|\mathbf{y}-\mathbf{x}|)$ and the Lebesgue measure μ. It is straightforward to check that it satisfies the requirements (NL1)–(NL4) of our theory. This implies e.g. that it preserves the average grey value.

Figure 1 illustrates such a scale-space evolution. It has been obtained with an explicit finite difference scheme. As predicted by the theory, we observe that the image is gradually simplified. For $t \to \infty$, it converges to a flat steady state with the same average grey value as the initial image. It is remarkable how well the localisation of edges is preserved.

3.4 Robustified Bilateral Scale-Space

While our bilateral integro-differential equation (35) gives an interesting scale-space evolution, its performance under noise is less favourable. The reason is easy to understand: Noise creates large values for $|f(\mathbf{y}) - f(\mathbf{x})|$, such that the corresponding tonal weight $g_\lambda(|f(\mathbf{y})-f(\mathbf{x})|)$ becomes very small. As a result, noisy structures are rewarded by a longer lifetime in scale-space. Similar problems are also well-known for the Perona–Malik diffusion filter [22]. Therefore, we can also use a similar strategy to overcome this problem: Following Catté et al. [23], we replace the image f in the argument of the tonal weight g_λ by a Gaussian-smoothed variant f_σ, where σ denotes the standard deviation of the Gaussian. Hence, our robustified bilateral evolution is given by

$$\partial_t u(\mathbf{x},t) = \frac{1}{c}\int_\Omega g_\lambda(|f_\sigma(\mathbf{y})-f_\sigma(\mathbf{x})|)\, g_\rho(|\mathbf{y}-\mathbf{x}|)\, (u(\mathbf{y},t) - u(\mathbf{x},t))\, d\mathbf{y}. \qquad (36)$$

Its behaviour is illustrated in Fig. 2. We observe that this process is well-suited for removing even a large amount of noise, while keeping the semantically

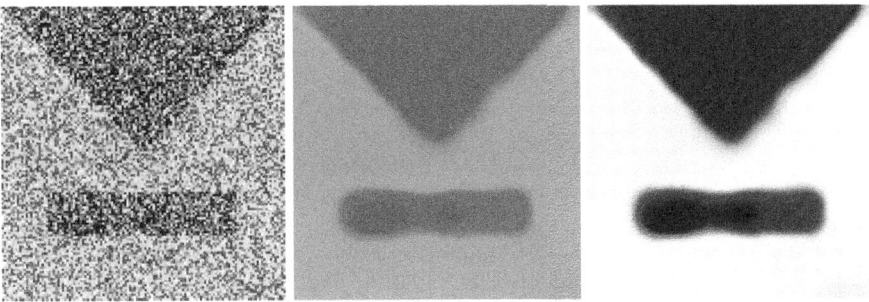

Fig. 2. (a) Left: Noisy test image, 128×128 pixels. **(b) Middle:** After processing with the robustified bilateral process (36) with $\sigma = 2$, $\rho = 5$, $\lambda = 1.4$, and $t = 500$. **(c) Right:** After rescaling the filtered result from (b) to the greyscale interval $[0, 255]$.

important edge structures. Its performance is comparable to the edge-enhancing anisotropic nonlinear diffusion filter from [24]. However, this is achieved with a linear process, that does not require to struggle with the numerical challenges of implementing anisotropic filters with a diffusion tensor.

4 Conclusions

In our paper we have established a nonlocal scale-space theory. To this end, we have studied a general type of linear nonlocal problems and have proven scale-space properties. We have shown that some existing diffusion methods can be interpreted within this general formulation. More importantly we have also introduced two modifications of bilateral filtering that satisfy our nonlocal scale-space requirements and can be highly robust under noise.

In our future work we intend to generalise our theory from the linear to the nonlinear setting, such that its applicability is further broadened.

References

1. Iijima, T.: Basic Theory on Normalization of Pattern (in Case of Typical One-Dimensional Pattern). Bulletin of the Electrotechnical Laboratory **26**, 368–388 (1962) (in Japanese)
2. Witkin, A.P.: Scale-space filtering. In: Proc. Eighth International Joint Conference on Artificial Intelligence, vol. 2, Karlsruhe, West Germany, pp. 945–951 (August 1983)
3. Koenderink, J.J.: The Structure of Images. Biological Cybernetics **50**, 363–370 (1984)
4. Lowe, D.L.: Distinctive Image Features From Scale-Invariant Keypoints. International Journal of Computer Vision **60**(2), 91–110 (2004)
5. Lindeberg, T.: Scale-Space Theory in Computer Vision. Kluwer, Boston (1994)
6. Florack, L.: Image Structure. Computational Imaging and Vision, vol. 10. Kluwer, Dordrecht (1997)

7. Weickert, J., Ishikawa, S., Imiya, A.: Linear Scale-Space has First been Proposed in Japan. Journal of Mathematical Imaging and Vision **10**(3), 237–252 (1999)
8. Felsberg, M., Sommer, G.: Scale-adaptive filtering derived From the laplace equation. In: Radig, B., Florczyk, S. (eds.) DAGM 2001. LNCS, vol. 2191, pp. 124–131. Springer, Heidelber (2001)
9. Duits, R., Florack, L., de Graaf, J., ter Haar Romeny, B.: On the Axioms of Scale Space Theory. Journal of Mathematical Imaging and Vision **20**, 267–298 (2004)
10. Weickert, J.: Anisotropic Diffusion in Image Processing. Teubner, Stuttgart (1998)
11. van den Boomgaard, R.: The Morphological Equivalent of the Gauss Convolution. Nieuw Archief Voor Wiskunde **10**(3), 219–236 (1992)
12. Alvarez, L., Guichard, F., Lions, P.L., Morel, J.M.: Axioms and Fundamental Equations in Image Processing. Archive for Rational Mechanics and Analysis **123**, 199–257 (1993)
13. Guichard, F.: A Morphological, Affine, and Galilean Invariant Scale-Space for movies. IEEE Transactions on Image Processing **7**(3), 444–456 (1998)
14. Lindeberg, T.: Generalized Gaussian Scale-Space Axiomatics Comprising Linear Scale-Space, Affine Scale-Space and Spatio-Temporal Scale-Space. Journal of Mathematical Imaging and Vision **40**, 36–81 (2011)
15. Scherzer, O., Weickert, J.: Relations Between Regularization and Diffusion Filtering. Journal of Mathematical Imaging and Vision **12**(1), 43–63 (2000)
16. Aurich, V., Weule, J.: Non-linear gaussian filters performing edge preserving diffusion. In: Sagerer, G., Posch, S., Kummert, F. (eds.): Mustererkennung 1995, pp. 538–545. Springer, Berlin (1995)
17. Tomasi, C., Manduchi, R.: Bilateral filtering for gray and color images. In: Proc. Sixth International Conference on Computer Vision, pp. 839–846. Narosa Publishing House, Bombay (1998)
18. Buades, A., Coll, B., Morel, J.M.: A Review of Image Denoising Algorithms, with a New One. Multiscale Modeling and Simulation **4**(2), 490–530 (2005)
19. Dabov, K., Foi, A., Katkovnik, V., Egiazarian, K.: Image Denoising by Sparse 3D Transform-Domain Collaborative Filtering. IEEE Transactions on Image Processing **16**(8), 2080–2095 (2007)
20. Gilboa, G., Osher, S.: Nonlocal Operators with Applications to Image Processing. Multiscale Modeling and Simulation **7**, 1005–1028 (2008)
21. Andreu-Vaillo, F., Mazón, J.M., Rossi, J.D.: Nonlocal Diffusion Problems. American Mathematical Society, Providence (2010)
22. Perona, P., Malik, J.: Scale-Space and Edge Detection using Anisotropic diffusion. IEEE Transactions on Pattern Analysis and Machine Intelligence **12**, 629–639 (1990)
23. Catté, F., Lions, P.L., Morel, J.M., Coll, T.: Image Selective Smoothing and Edge Detection by Nonlinear Diffusion. SIAM Journal on Numerical Analysis 32, 1895–1909 (1992)
24. Weickert, J.: Theoretical Foundations of Anisotropic Diffusion in Image Processing. Computing Supplement **11**, 221–236 (1996)
25. Ballester, C., Calderero, F., Caselles, V., Facciolo, G.: Multiscale Analysis of Similarities between Images on Riemannian Manifolds. Multiscale Modeling and Simulation **12**(2), 616–649 (2014)

Denoising, Restoration
and Reconstruction

Bilevel Image Denoising Using Gaussianity Tests

Jérôme Fehrenbach[1], Mila Nikolova[2], Gabriele Steidl[3], and Pierre Weiss[4](✉)

[1] CNRS, IMT (UMR5219) and ITAV (USR 3505), Université de Toulouse,
Toulouse, France
jerome.fehrenbach@math.univ-toulouse.fr
[2] CNRS, CMLA, ENS Cachan, Cachan, France
nikolova@cmla.ens-cachan.fr
[3] University of Kaiserslautern, Kaiserslautern, Germany
steidl@mathematik.uni-kl.de
[4] CNRS, IMT (UMR5219) and ITAV (USR 3505), Université de Toulouse,
Toulouse, France
pierre.armand.weiss@gmail.com

Abstract. We propose a new methodology based on bilevel programming to remove additive white Gaussian noise from images. The lower-level problem consists of a parameterized variational model to denoise images. The parameters are optimized in order to minimize a specific cost function that measures the residual Gaussianity. This model is justified using a statistical analysis. We propose an original numerical method based on the Gauss-Newton algorithm to minimize the outer cost function. We finally perform a few experiments that show the well-foundedness of the approach. We observe a significant improvement compared to standard TV-ℓ^2 algorithms and show that the method automatically adapts to the signal regularity.

Keywords: Bilevel programming · Image denoising · Gaussianity tests · Convex optimization

1 Introduction

In this paper, we consider the following simple image formation model:

$$u_b = u_c + b \tag{1}$$

where $u_c \in \mathbb{R}^n$ denotes a clean image, $b \in \mathbb{R}^n$ is a white Gaussian noise of variance σ^2 and $u_b \in \mathbb{R}^n$ is the noisy image. Our aim is to denoise u_b, i.e. to retrieve an approximation of u_c knowing u_b.

1.1 Variational Denoising

The standard way to achieve image restoration using variational methods consists in solving an optimization problem of the form

$$\text{Find } u^*(\alpha) = \arg\min_{u \in \mathbb{R}^n} \alpha R(u) + \frac{1}{2\sigma^2}\|u - u_b\|_2^2, \tag{2}$$

where α is a regularization parameter and $R : \mathbb{R}^n \to \mathbb{R} \cup \{+\infty\}$ is a regularizing term such as total variation (TV) [11] or alternative priors. This approach can be justified using a Bayesian point of view, assuming that images are random vectors with a density $\mathbb{P}(u) \propto \exp\left(-\alpha R(u)\right)$ and using the fact that b is a white Gaussian noise. This reasoning is widespread in the imaging community since the seminal paper [4]. Despite its success in applications, it suffers from serious drawbacks. First, it is now well known that Bayesian estimators strongly deviate from the data and noise models [1,10]. Second, one needs to design a probability density function that describes the set of natural images. This task is extremely hard and simple models (e.g. based on total variation) are very unlikely to correctly describe the density of natural images. This problem is studied and discussed thoroughly in [9]. As a consequence, denoising models such as (2) are only partially satisfactory and the residuals $b^*(\alpha) = u_b - u^*(\alpha)$ obtained by solving (2) are usually non-white. This is illustrated in Figure 1.

Fig. 1. An example of TV-ℓ^2 denoising. Top-left: original image. Top-mid: noisy image. Top-right: denoising result. Bottom-mid: noise. Bottom-right: retrieved residual $u^*(\alpha) - u_b$. The residual contains a lot of structure, showing the limits of this approach.

In this work, we depart from the standard setting (2). Our starting observation is that in many applications, one has a quite good knowledge of the noise properties and only a very rough idea of the image contents. The data and regularization terms should thus play modified roles: the regularization should be adaptive to the image contents while the data term should measure Gaussianity in a more efficient way than the standard ℓ^2-norm. This idea is not new and led to state-of-the-art results in wavelet thresholding based methods [7].

1.2 The Proposed Framework

Instead of fixing the regularization term, we propose to use a parametric restoration model and to optimize the parameters with a bilevel programming approach, in order to make the residual "look" Gaussian. This idea is close in spirit to the recent work [5] and very different from the simple model (2), where the regularization term R is fixed and the Gaussianity measure is just the ℓ^2-norm.

We propose using a parameterized model of type:

$$u^*(\alpha) = \arg\min_{u \in \mathbb{R}^n} \sum_{i=1}^{p} \alpha_i \phi_i(R_i u) + \frac{1}{2\sigma^2}\|u - u_b\|_2^2, \qquad (3)$$

where

- $\alpha = (\alpha_i)_{i=1}^{p}$ is a non negative vector of regularization parameters,
- $\phi_i : \mathbb{R}^{m_i} \to \mathbb{R}$, $i \in \{1, \ldots, p\}$ are C^2 symmetric functions (typically smoothed l^1-norms),
- $R_i \in \mathbb{R}^{m_i \times n}$ are known analysis-based operators.

Model (3) thus encompasses total variation like regularization. It is however more flexible since the vector of parameters α can be chosen differently depending on the image contents. Since the residual $b^*(\alpha) = u_b - u^*(\alpha)$ plays an important role in this paper, we use the change of variable $b = u_b - u$ and denote

$$J_\alpha(b) := \sum_{i=1}^{p} \alpha_i \phi_i(R_i(u_b - b)) + \frac{1}{2}\|b\|_2^2.$$

Let $G : \mathbb{R}^n \to \mathbb{R}$ denote a C^1 function that measures noise Gaussianity. The proposed denoising model consists in finding $\alpha^* \in \mathbb{R}_+^p$ and $b^*(\alpha^*) \in \mathbb{R}^n$ solutions of the following bi-level programming problem:

$$\begin{cases} \min_{\alpha \geq 0} g(\alpha) := G(b^*(\alpha)) \\ \text{with } b^*(\alpha) = \arg\min_{b \in \mathbb{R}^n} J_\alpha(b). \end{cases} \qquad (4)$$

The lower-level problem $\min_{b \in \mathbb{R}^n} J_\alpha(b)$ corresponds to a denoising step with a fixed regularization vector, while the upper-level problem corresponds to a parameter optimization.

1.3 Contributions of the Paper

The first contribution of this paper is the variational formulation (4) with a new cost function $g(\alpha)$ (derived in Section 2). This function is motivated by a statistical analysis of white Gaussian noise properties. The bilevel problem (4) shares a connection with [5] and was actually motivated by this paper. In [5], the authors propose to *learn* the parameters using an image database, while our method simply uses the noisy image, making the parameter estimation self-contained.

Moreover, the proposed methodology makes our algorithm *auto-adaptive* to the image contents, meaning that the denoising model adapts to the type of image to denoise.

The second contribution of this paper is the design of an optimization method based on Gauss-Newton's algorithm in Section 3. The preliminary numerical experiments we performed suggest that it is very efficient, while being simpler to implement than the semi-smooth Newton based method proposed in [5].

Finally, we present preliminary denoising experiments in Section 4, showing the well-foundedness of the proposed approach.

2 Measuring Residual Gaussianity

In this section, we propose a function g that measures the residuals Gaussianity and whiteness and allows identifying the vector $\alpha \in \mathbb{R}^p$.

2.1 The Case $p = 1$

In this paper, we assume that the discrete image domain Ω satisfies $|\Omega| = n$. To expose our ideas, let us begin with the simple case where only one regularizer is used, i.e. $p = 1$. A basic idea to select the regularization parameter is to find α such that $\|b^*(\alpha)\|_2^2 \simeq \sigma^2 n$, since $\mathbb{E}(\|b\|_2^2) = \sigma^2 n$. One could thus set $g(\alpha) = \frac{1}{2}\left(\|b^*(\alpha)\|_2^2 - \sigma^2 n\right)^2$. This idea is similar to Morozov's discrepancy principle [8].

This simple method is however unlikely to provide satisfactory results with more than 1 regularizer (i.e. $p > 1$), since many vectors $\alpha \in \mathbb{R}_+^p$ may lead to $\|b^*(\alpha)\|_2^2 = \sigma^2 n$. Said differently, the function g here does not allow identifying a unique α since there are two many degrees of freedom in the model. Moreover, the accurate knowledge of the noise distribution b is boiled down to a simple scalar corresponding to the mean of the ℓ^2-norm. Our aim below is therefore to construct measures of Gaussianity allowing to identify the parameters and to better characterize the noise distribution.

2.2 The Case $p > 1$

The idea proposed in the case of a single parameter can be generalized by defining a set of q Euclidean semi-norms $(\|\cdot\|_{M_i}^2)_{i=1}^q$. These semi-norms are defined by

$$\|x\|_{M_i}^2 := \|M_i x\|_2^2,$$

where $M_i \in \mathbb{R}^{m_i \times n}$. Let $b \sim \mathcal{N}(0, \sigma^2 \mathrm{Id})$ be white Gaussian noise with $\mu_i = \mathbb{E}(\|b\|_{M_i}^2)$ and $v_i = \mathrm{Var}(\|b\|_{M_i}^2)$. A natural idea to extend the principle presented in Subsection 2.1 consists in setting

$$g(\alpha) := \frac{1}{2} \sum_{i=1}^{q} \frac{(\|b^*(\alpha)\|_{M_i}^2 - \mu_i)^2}{v_i}. \tag{5}$$

This choice can be justified using a maximum likelihood approach. In cases where n is large enough and where the singular values of M_i are sufficiently spread out, the distribution of $\|b\|_{M_i}^2$ is well approximated by a normal distribution $\mathcal{N}(\mu_i, v_i)$. The probability density function of $\|b\|_{M_i}^2$ approximately satisfies

$$f_{M_i}(b) \propto \exp\left(-\frac{(\|b\|_{M_i}^2 - \mu_i)^2}{2v_i}\right).$$

The random variables $(\|b\|_{M_i}^2)_{i=1}^q$ are not independent in general. However, if the matrices M_i are chosen in such a way that they measure different noise properties (e.g. different frequencies components), the likelihood of the random vector $(\|b\|_{M_i}^2)_{i=1}^q$ is approximately equal to

$$f(b) \propto \prod_{i=1}^q f_{M_i}(b). \tag{6}$$

Using a maximum likelihood approach to set the parameter α leads to minimizing $-\log(f(b^*(\alpha)))$, i.e. to set g as in equation (5).

2.3 The Choice of M_i

In this paper, we propose to analyse residuals using Fourier decompositions: we construct a partition $\Omega = \cup_{i=1}^q \Omega_i$ of the discrete Fourier domain and set $M_i = F\mathrm{diag}(1_{\Omega_i})F^*$, where F denotes the discrete Fourier transform and 1_{Ω_i} denotes a vector equal to 1 on Ω_i and 0 elsewhere. In other words the matrices M_i correspond to discrete convolutions with filters $\varphi_i = F 1_{\Omega_i}$. For this specific choice, it is quite easy to show that

$$\mu_i = n\sigma^2 \|\varphi_i\|^2$$

and that

$$v_i = n\sigma^4 \|\varphi_i\|^4.$$

Moreover, the random variables $\|b\|_{M_i}^2$ are independent. Therefore, the likelihood (6) is a good approximation of the random vector $(\|b\|_{M_i}^2)_{i=1}^q$ as soon as the cardinals $|\Omega_i|$ are sufficiently large, due to the central limit theorem.

The rationale behind a partition of the Fourier domain is that residuals containing image structures usually exhibit anormal structured spectra. This phenomenon is illustrated in Figure 2. The Fourier transform of white Gaussian noise is still white Gaussian noise. Therefore, if the residual was "correct", its Fourier transforms should "look" white. The spectrum of a residual obtained using a TV-ℓ^2 minimization (Figure 2, middle) is clearly not white. In particular, the modulus of its Fourier transform is too low in the center of the frequency domain. On the contrary, it is too large on directions orthogonal to the main components of the image: the vertical stripes and the diagonal elements of Lena's hat.

In this paper, we propose to define the sets Ω_i similarly to frequency tilings of curvelet or shearlet transforms [2,6]. This is illustrated in Figure 2, right. Each set Ω_i corresponds to the union of a trapezoid and its symmetric with respect to the origin. Its size and angular resolution increases in a dyadic way with the frequencies.

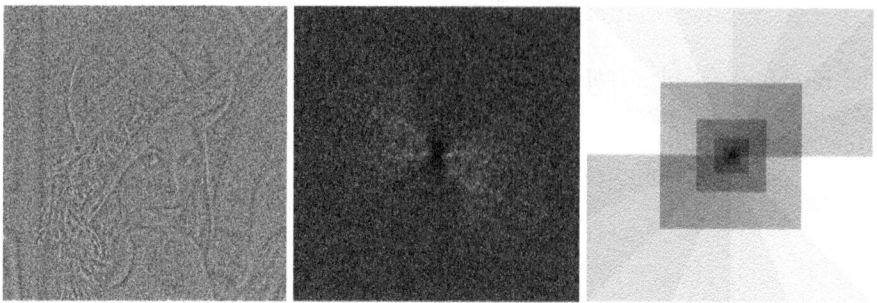

Fig. 2. Analysis of residuals in the Fourier domain. Left: residual of a TV-ℓ^2 minimization. Middle: discrete Fourier transform modulus of the residual. This modulus should be an i.i.d. sequence with constant mean. It exhibits a lot of structure, especially in the low frequencies. Right: frequency tiling proposed to analyse the spectrum.

In order to assess whether a residual is likely to correspond to white Gaussian noise, we will make use of the standard score (or z-score) defined by

$$z_i = \frac{\|b\|_{M_i}^2 - \mu_i}{\sqrt{v_i}}.$$

This score measures the (signed) number of standard deviations $\|b\|_{M_i}^2$ is above the mean. For sufficiently large n (which is typical for contemporary pictures), $\|b\|_{M_i}^2$ can be assimilated to a Gaussian random variable and therefore $\mathbb{P}(|z_i| \geq k) \simeq 1 - \mathrm{erf}\left(\frac{k}{\sqrt{2}}\right)$. The values are displayed in Table 1. As can be seen in this table, it is extremely unlikely that $|z_i|$ be larger than 3. Using the frequency tiling proposed in Figure 2, composed of 45 tiles, we get a maximum z-score $\max_{i \in \{1,\cdots,q\}} |z_i| = 30.3$ and a mean z-score of 6.0. By looking at Table 1, it is clear that such a residual is *extremely* unlikely to correspond to white Gaussian noise.

Table 1. Probability that a standard normally distributed random variable deviates from its mean more than k times its standard deviation

k	0	1	2	3	4	5	6	7
$P(|z_i| \geq k)$	1	$3.2 \cdot 10^{-1}$	$4.6 \cdot 10^{-2}$	$2.7 \cdot 10^{-3}$	$6.3 \cdot 10^{-5}$	$5.7 \cdot 10^{-7}$	$2.0 \cdot 10^{-9}$	$2.6 \cdot 10^{-12}$

3 A Bilevel Programming Approach Based on a Gauss-Newton Algorithm

In this section, we describe a numerical method based on the Gauss-Newton algorithm to solve problem (4) with

$$g(\alpha) = \sum_{i=1}^{q} \frac{\left(\|\varphi_i \star b^*(\alpha)\|^2 - \mu_i\right)^2}{2v_i}.$$

The solution of bilevel programs of type (4) is a well studied problem with many different solution algorithms, see, e.g., the monograph [3]. Bilevel problems are usually NP-hard so that only local minima can be expected. Similarly to standard optimization, there exists multiple algorithms which should be chosen depending on the context (problem dimension, lower and upper-level problem regularity, convexity,...). In this paper, we suggest using the following combination:

- Handle the positivity constraint $\alpha_i \geq 0$ by writing $\alpha = \exp(\beta)$, allowing to have an unconstrained minimization problem with parameter β.
- Use the implicit function theorem to estimate the Jacobian $\mathrm{Jac}_{b^*}(\alpha)$ (i.e. the first order variations of b^* w.r.t. α).
- Use this information to design a Gauss-Newton algorithm.

The advantage of the Gauss-Newton algorithm is that it usually converges much faster than gradient descent methods since the metric adapts to the local function curvatures. It is also much simpler to use than the semi-smooth approach suggested in [5] while still showing a very good performance.

The change of variable $\alpha = \exp(\beta)$ ensures that $\alpha > 0$ without bringing any extra difficulty in the design of the numerical algorithm since the chain rule allows a straightforward modification. More precisely we aim at minimizing

$$h(\beta) = g(\exp(\beta)),$$

and we use the following identity:

$$Dh(\beta) = Dg(\exp(\beta))\Sigma,$$

where Σ is the diagonal matrix with entries $\exp(\beta_i)$. Next, remark that function h can be rewritten as

$$h(\beta) = \frac{1}{2}\|f(\beta)\|_2^2 = \frac{1}{2}\|F(b^*(\exp(\beta)))\|_2^2 \tag{7}$$

with

$$F(b) := \begin{pmatrix} F_1(b) \\ \vdots \\ F_q(b) \end{pmatrix}, \quad f(\beta) := \begin{pmatrix} f_1(\exp(\beta)) \\ \vdots \\ f_q(\exp(\beta)) \end{pmatrix},$$

$$f_i(\alpha) := F_i(b^*(\alpha)) \quad \text{and} \quad F_i(b) := \frac{\|\varphi_i \star b\|_2^2 - \mu_i}{\sqrt{2}v_i}. \tag{8}$$

Then the k-th iteration of the Gauss-Newton algorithm adapted to functions of type (7) reads as follows:

1. Set
$$d^k = \arg\min_{d \in \mathbb{R}^p} \|f(\beta^k) + \mathrm{Jac}_f(\beta^k)d\|_2^2 \tag{9}$$

2. Set
$$\beta^{k+1} = \beta^k + d^k \tag{10}$$

The descent direction d^k computed in (9) satisfies
$$\mathrm{Jac}_f(\beta^k)^T \mathrm{Jac}_f(\beta^k) d^k = -\mathrm{Jac}_f(\beta^k)^T f(\beta^k).$$

The lower-level problem in (4) is solved using an accelerated proximal gradient descent algorithm on the dual of (3), see, e.g., [12]. We do not detail further this algorithm for lack of space.

4 Numerical Results

4.1 A Test Example

To begin with, we perform a simple denoising experiment to validate the overall principle and the numerical algorithm. We consider the following simple denoising model:
$$\min_{u \in \mathbb{R}^n} \alpha_1 \phi(\partial_x u) + \alpha_2 \phi(\partial_y u) + \frac{1}{2}\|u - u_b\|_2^2, \tag{11}$$
where $\phi(x) := \sqrt{x^2 + \epsilon^2}$ is an approximation of the ℓ^1-norm, ∂_x and ∂_y are first order difference operators in the x and y directions, respectively. We use the smooth 64×64 images which are constant along the x or y axes in Figure 3. The algorithm is initialized with $\alpha = (1,1)$. After 20 iterations of our Gauss-Newton algorithm, the regularization parameters become $\alpha = (186.3, 0.03)$ for the image constant in the x-direction and $\alpha = (0.03, 155.11)$ for the image constant in the y-direction. This choice basically corresponds to a very strong regularization in the direction of the level lines of the image: the method is capable of automatically detecting the smoothness directions.

We compare the output of our algorithm with a TV-ℓ^2 model, where the regularization coefficient is chosen in order to maximize the mean square error (hence the choice of this optimal coefficient requires the knowledge of the ground truth image).

Compared to the TV-ℓ^2 model, the denoising results are significantly better. In particular, no structure can be found in the residual of the proposed method, while a lot of structure is apparent in the residual of the TV-ℓ^2 model. The maximum z-score is 88.2 for the TV-ℓ^2 algorithm and 1.8 for the bilevel approach.

Regarding the numerical behavior, even though we performed 20 iterations, a satisfactory and stable solution is found after just 6 iterations of our Gauss-Newton algorithm. The cost function with respect to the iteration number is displayed in Figure 4.

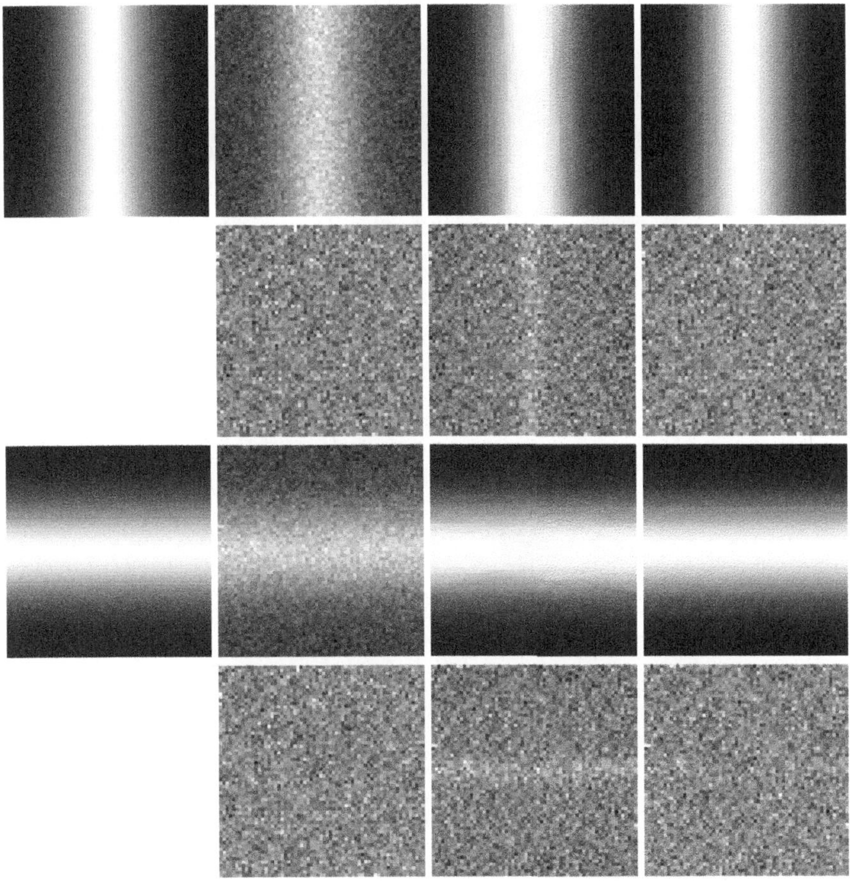

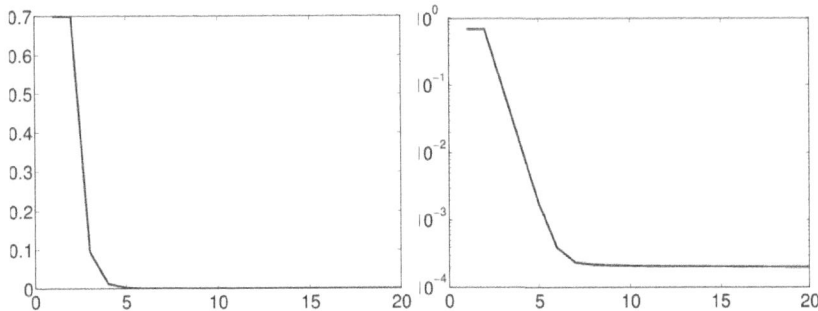

Fig. 3. Denoising results for a toy example. First and third rows, from left to right: original image, noisy image (PSNR=14.7dB), denoised with TV (PSNR=27.9dB), denoised with the bilevel approach (PSNR=34.9dB). Second and fourth rows: residuals associated to the top images.

Fig. 4. Function $g(\alpha_k)$ with respect to k. Left: standard scale. Right: log_{10} scale. The cost function reaches a plateau after 6 iterations.

Fig. 5. Denoising results for a true example. First row, from left to right: original image, noisy image (SNR=15.4dB), denoised with TV and a regularization parameter maximizing the SNR (SNR=23.1dB, worst z-score: 69.9), denoised with the bilevel approach (SNR=24.5dB, worst z-score: 7.7). Second row: residuals associated to the top images. (same scale for the gray-level).

4.2 A Real-World Denoising Experiment

We now turn to a real denoising example of Lena. Similarly to [5], the transforms R_i are set as convolution products with the 25 elements of the discrete cosine transform basis on 5×5 windows. The number of elements of the Fourier domain partition is 50. The results are presented in Figure 5. The bilevel denoising result is significantly better (1.5dB) than the standard TV result. The z-test indicates that the TV residual is extremely unlikely to correspond to white Gaussian noise. It also indicates that the bilevel residual is unlikely. This result suggests that much better denoising results could be expected by considering different parameterized denoising models.

5 Conclusion and Outlook

In this work, we explored the use of bilevel programming to choose an optimal parameterized denoising model by measuring the Gaussianity of the residuals. The results are encouraging and provide significantly better results than standard variational models. They are probably not comparable to state-of-the-art methods based on nonlocal means or BM3D for instance both in terms of restoratin quality and computing times.

We still believe that this approach has a great potential in applications since i) the method can be adapted to arbitrary inverse problems and ii) the method is capable of automatically finding the class of regularity of the considered signals. This is a very nice feature that is absent in most current approaches.

Finally, let us mention that the considered parameterized denoising models can probably be improved significantly by considering not only adapting to the global regularity of signals, but also to the local regularity. To achieve this, the operators R_i should be localized in space. We plan to investigate this issue in our forthcoming work.

Acknowledgments. This research was partially supported by the FMJH Program Gaspard Monge in optimization and operation research (MAORI project), and by the assistance to this program from EDF.

References

1. Baus, F., Nikolova, M., Steidl, G.: Smooth objectives composed of asymptotically affine data-fidelity and regularization: Bounds for the minimizers and parameter choice. Journal of Mathematical Imaging and Vision **48**(2), 295–307 (2013)
2. Candes, E., Demanet, L., Donoho, D., Ying, L.: Fast discrete curvelet transforms. Multiscale Modeling & Simulation **5**(3), 861–899 (2006)
3. Dempe, S.: Foundations of Bilevel Programming. Springer (2002)
4. Geman, S., Geman, D.: Stochastic relaxation, gibbs distributions, and the bayesian restoration of images. IEEE Transactions on Pattern Analysis and Machine Intelligence **6**, 721–741 (1984)

5. Kunisch, K., Pock, T.: A bilevel optimization approach for parameter learning in variational models. SIAM Journal on Imaging Sciences **6**(2), 938–983 (2013)
6. Labate, D., Lim, W.-Q., Kutyniok, G., Weiss, G.: Sparse multidimensional representation using shearlets. In: Papadakis, M., Laine, A.F., Unser, M.A. (eds.) Proceedings of Wavelets XI. Proc. SPIE, vol, 5914, San Diego (2005)
7. Luisier, F., Blu, T., Unser, M.: A new SURE approach to image denoising: Interscale orthonormal wavelet thresholding. IEEE Transactions on Image Processing **16**(3), 593–606 (2007)
8. Morozov, V.A., Stessin, M.: Regularization Methods for Ill-posed Problems. CRC Press Boca Raton, FL (1993)
9. Mumford, D., Desolneux, A., et al.: Pattern theory: The Stochastic Analysis of Real-world Signals (2010)
10. Nikolova, M.: Model distortions in Bayesian MAP reconstruction. Inverse Problems and Imaging **1**(2), 399 (2007)
11. Rudin, L.I, Osher, S., Fatemi, E.: Nonlinear total variation based noise removal algorithms. Physica D: Nonlinear Phenomena **60**(1), 259–268 (1992)
12. Weiss, P., Blanc-Féraud, L., Aubert, G.: Efficient schemes for total variation minimization under constraints in image processing. SIAM Journal on Scientific Computing **31**(3), 2047–2080 (2009)

On Debiasing Restoration Algorithms: Applications to Total-Variation and Nonlocal-Means

Charles-Alban Deledalle[1,2](✉), Nicolas Papadakis[1,2], and Joseph Salmon[3]

[1] IMB, University of Bordeaux, UMR 5251, 33400 Talence, France
{charles-alban.deledalle,nicolas.papadakis}@math.u-bordeaux.fr
[2] CNRS, IMB, University of Bordeaux, UMR 5251, 33400 Talence, France
[3] CNRS LTCI, Institut Mines-Télécom, Télécom ParisTech, Paris, France
joseph.salmon@telecom-paristech.fr

Abstract. Bias in image restoration algorithms can hamper further analysis, typically when the intensities have a physical meaning of interest, e.g., in medical imaging. We propose to suppress a part of the bias – *the method bias* – while leaving unchanged the other unavoidable part – *the model bias*. Our debiasing technique can be used for any locally affine estimator including ℓ_1 regularization, anisotropic total-variation and some nonlocal filters.

1 Introduction

Restoration of an image of interest from its single noisy degraded observation necessarily requires imposing some regularity or *prior* on the solution. Being often only crude approximations of the true underlying signal of interest, such techniques always introduce a bias towards the *prior*. However, in general, this is not the only source of bias. In many cases, even though the model was perfectly accurate, the method would remain biased. This part of the bias often emerges from technical reasons, e.g., when approaching an NP-hard problem by an easier one (typically, using the ℓ_1 convex relaxation of an ℓ_0 pseudo-norm).

It is well known that reducing bias is not always favorable in terms of mean square error because of the so-called bias-variance trade-off. It is important to highlight that a debiasing procedure is expected to re-inject part of the variance, therefore increasing the residual noise. Hence, the mean square error is not always expected to be improved by such techniques. Debiasing is nevertheless essential in applications where the image intensities have a physical sense and critical decisions are taken from their values. For instance, the authors of [7] suggest using image restoration techniques to estimate a temperature map within a tumor tissue for real time automatic surgical intervention. In such applications, it is so crucial that the estimated temperature is not biased. A remaining residual noise is indeed favorable compared to an uncontrolled bias.

We introduce a debiasing technique that suppresses the extra bias – *the method bias* – emerging from the choice of the method and leave unchanged the bias that is due to the unavoidable choice of the model – *the model bias*. To that end, we rely on the notion of model subspace essential to carefully define different notions of bias. This leads to a mathematical definition of debiasing for any locally affine estimators that respect some mild assumptions.

Interestingly, our debiasing definition for the ℓ_1 synthesis (also known as LASSO [20] or Basis Pursuit [5]) recovers a well known debiasing scheme called refitting that goes back to the "Hybrid LASSO" [9] (see [15] for more details).

For the ℓ_1 analysis [10], including the ℓ_1 synthesis but also the anisotropic total-variation [18], we show that debiasing can be performed with the same complexity as the primal-dual algorithm of [4] producing the biased estimate.

In other cases, e.g., for an affine version of the popular nonlocal-means [2], we introduce an iterative scheme that requires only a few run of an algorithm of the same complexity as the original one producing the biased estimate.

2 Background

We consider observing $f = f_0 + w \in \mathbb{R}^P$ a corrupted linear observation of an unknown signal $u_0 \in \mathbb{R}^N$ such that $f_0 = \Phi u_0$ where $\Phi \in \mathbb{R}^{N \times P}$ is a linear operator and w is a random vector modeling the noise fluctuations. We assume that $\mathbb{E}[w] = 0$ where $\mathbb{E}$ is the expectation operator. The linear operator Φ is a degrading operator typically with $P \leqslant N$ and with a non-empty kernel encoding some information loss such that the problem becomes ill-posed.

We focus on estimating the unknown signal u_0. Due to the ill-posedness of the observation model, we consider variational approaches that attempt to recover u_0 from the single observation f as a solution of the optimization problem

$$u_f^\star \in \underset{u \in \mathbb{R}^N}{\mathrm{argmin}}\, E(u, f) \,. \qquad (1)$$

where $E : \mathbb{R}^N \times \mathbb{R}^P \to \mathbb{R}$ is assumed to have at least one minimum. The objective E is typically chosen to promote some structure, e.g., smoothness, piece-wise constantness, sparsity, etc., that is captured by the so-called *model subspace* $\mathcal{M}_f^\star$. Providing $u_f^\star$ is uniquely defined and differentiable at f, we define $\mathcal{M}_f^\star \subseteq \mathbb{R}^N$ as the tangent affine subspace at f of the mapping $f \mapsto u_f^\star$, i.e.,

$$\mathcal{M}_f^\star = u_f^\star + \mathrm{Im}[J_f^\star] = \{u \in \mathbb{R}^N\, ;\, \exists z \in \mathbb{R}^P, u = u_f^\star + J_f^\star z\} \quad \text{with} \quad J_f^\star = \left.\frac{\partial u_f^\star}{\partial f}\right|_f \qquad (2)$$

where $J_f^\star$ is the Jacobian operator at f of the mapping $f \mapsto u_f^\star$ (see [23] for an alternative but related definition of model subspace). When $u_f^\star \in \mathrm{Im}[J_f^\star]$, the model subspace restricts to the linear vector subspace $\mathcal{M}_f^\star = \mathrm{Im}[J_f^\star]$. In the rest of the paper, $u_f^\star$ is assumed to be differentiable at f_0 and for almost all f.

Example 1. *The least square estimator constrained to the affine subspace $C = b + \mathrm{Im}[A]$, $b \in \mathbb{R}^N$ and $A \in \mathbb{R}^{N \times Q}$, is a particular instance of (1) where*

$$E(u, f) = \|\Phi u - f\|^2 + \iota_C(u) \qquad (3)$$

and for any set C, ι_C is its indicator function: $\iota_C(u) = 0$ if $u \in C$, $+\infty$ otherwise. The solution of minimum Euclidean norm is unique and given by

$$u_f^\star = b + A(\Phi A)^+ (f - \Phi b) \qquad (4)$$

where for a matrix M, M^+ is its Moore-Penrose pseudo-inverse. The affine constrained least square restricts the solution $u_f^\star$ to the affine model subspace $\mathcal{M}_f^\star = b + \mathrm{Im}[A(\Phi A)^t]$ (as $\mathrm{Im}[M^+] = \mathrm{Im}[M^t]$). Taking $C = \mathbb{R}^N$ with for instance $Q = N$, $A = \mathrm{Id}$ and $b = 0$, leads to an unconstrained solution $u_f^\star = \Phi^+ f$ whose model subspace is $\mathcal{M}_f^\star = \mathrm{Im}[\Phi^t]$ reducing to $\mathbb{R}^N$ when Φ has full column rank.

Example 2. *The Tikhonov regularization (or Ridge regression) [14, 21] is another instance of (1) where, for some parameter $\lambda > 0$ and matrix $\Gamma \in \mathbb{R}^{L \times N}$,*

$$E(u, f) = \frac{1}{2} \|\Phi u - f\|^2 + \frac{\lambda}{2} \|\Gamma u\|^2 . \qquad (5)$$

Provided $\mathrm{Ker}\,\Phi \cap \mathrm{Ker}\,\Gamma = \{0\}$, $u_f^\star$ is uniquely defined as $u_f^\star = (\Phi^t \Phi + \lambda \Gamma^t \Gamma)^{-1} \Phi^t f$ which has a linear model subspace given by $\mathcal{M}_f^\star = \mathrm{Im}[\Phi^t]$.

Example 3. *The hard thresholding [8], used when $\Phi = \mathrm{Id}$ and f_0 is supposed to be sparse, is a solution of (1) where, for some parameter $\lambda > 0$,*

$$E(u, f) = \frac{1}{2} \|u - f\|^2 + \frac{\lambda^2}{2} \|u\|_0 , \qquad (6)$$

where $\|u\|_0 = \#\{i \in [P] ;\ u_i \neq 0\}$ counts the number of non-zero entries of u and $[P] = \{1, \ldots, P\}$. The hard thresholding operation writes

$$(u_f^\star)_{\mathcal{I}_f} = f_{\mathcal{I}_f} \quad \text{and} \quad (u_f^\star)_{\mathcal{I}_f^c} = 0 \qquad (7)$$

where $\mathcal{I}_f = \{i \in [P] ;\ |f_i| > \lambda\}$ is the support of $u_f^\star$, $\mathcal{I}_f^c$ is the complement of $\mathcal{I}_f$ on $[P]$, and for any vector v, $v_{\mathcal{I}_f}$ is the sub-vector whose elements are indexed by $\mathcal{I}_f$. As $u_f^\star$ is piece-wise differentiable, its model subspace is only defined for almost all f as $\mathcal{M}_f^\star = \{u \in \mathbb{R}^N ;\ u_{\mathcal{I}_f^c} = 0\} = \mathrm{Im}[\mathrm{Id}_{\mathcal{I}_f}]$, where for any matrix M, $M_{\mathcal{I}_f}$ is the sub-matrix whose columns are indexed by $\mathcal{I}_f$. Note that $\mathrm{Id}_{\mathcal{I}_f} \in \mathbb{R}^{N \times \#\mathcal{I}_f}$.

Example 4. *The soft thresholding [8], used when $\Phi = \mathrm{Id}$ and f_0 is supposed to be sparse, is another particular solution of (1) where*

$$E(u, f) = \frac{1}{2} \|u - f\|^2 + \lambda \|u\|_1 , \qquad (8)$$

with $\|u\|_1 = \sum_i |u_i|$ the ℓ_1 norm of u. The soft thresholding operation writes

$$(u_f^\star)_{\mathcal{I}_f} = f_{\mathcal{I}_f} - \lambda \,\mathrm{sign}(f_{\mathcal{I}_f}) \quad \text{and} \quad (u_f^\star)_{\mathcal{I}_f^c} = 0 , \qquad (9)$$

where $\mathcal{I}_f$ is defined as above, and, as for the hard thresholding: $\mathcal{M}_f^\star = \mathrm{Im}[\mathrm{Id}_{\mathcal{I}_f}]$.

3 Bias of Reconstruction Algorithms

Due to the ill-posedness of our observation model and without any assumptions on u_0, one cannot ensure the noise variance to be reduced while keeping the solution $u_f^\star$ unbiased. Recall that the statistical bias is defined as the difference

$$\text{Statistical bias} = \mathbb{E}[u_f^\star] - u_0 \,. \tag{10}$$

An estimator is said unbiased when its statistical bias vanishes. Unfortunately the statistical bias is difficult to manipulate when $f \mapsto u_f^\star$ is non linear. We therefore restrict to a definition of bias at $f_0 = \Phi u_0$ as the error $u_{f_0}^\star - u_0$. Note that when $f \mapsto u_f^\star$ is affine, both definitions match (the expectation being linear). Most methods are biased since, without assumptions, u_0 cannot be guaranteed to be in complete accordance with the model subspace, i.e., $u_0 \notin \mathcal{M}_{f_0}^\star$. It is then important to distinguish techniques that are only biased due to a problem of modeling to the ones that are biased due to the method. We then define the model bias and the method bias as the quantities

$$u_{f_0}^\star - u_0 = \underbrace{u_{f_0}^\star - \Pi_{\mathcal{M}_{f_0}^\star}(u_0)}_{\text{Method bias}} - \underbrace{\Pi_{(\mathcal{M}_{f_0}^\star)^\perp}(u_0)}_{\text{Model bias}} \,, \tag{11}$$

where for any set S, Π_S denotes the orthogonal projection on S and $S^\perp$ denotes its orthogonal set. We now define a methodically unbiased estimator as follows.

Definition 1. *An estimator $u_f^\star$ is <u>methodically unbiased</u> if*

$$\forall u_0 \in \mathbb{R}^N, \quad u_{f_0}^\star = \Pi_{\mathcal{M}_{f_0}^\star}(u_0)$$

We also define the weaker concept of weakly unbiased estimator as follows.

Definition 2. *An estimator $u_f^\star$ is <u>weakly unbiased</u> if*

$$\forall u_0 \in \mathcal{M}_{f_0}^\star, \quad u_{f_0}^\star = u_0.$$

The quantity $u_{f_0}^\star - u_0$ for $u_0 \in \mathcal{M}_{f_0}^\star$ is called the weak bias of $u_f^\star$ at u_0.

Remark that a methodically unbiased estimator is also weakly unbiased.

Examples. The unconstrained least-square estimator is methodically unbiased since $u_{f_0}^\star = \Phi^+ f_0 = \Phi^+ \Phi u_0 = \Pi_{\text{Im}[\Phi^t]}(u_0) = \Pi_{\mathcal{M}_{f_0}^\star}(u_0)$. Moreover, being linear, it becomes statistically unbiased whenever Φ has full column rank since $\Phi^+\Phi = \text{Id}$. However the constrained least-square estimator is only weakly unbiased: its methodical bias only vanishes when $u_0 \in \mathcal{M}_{f_0}^\star$, i.e., when there exists $t_0 \in \mathbb{R}^Q$ such that $u_0 = b + A(\Phi A)^t t_0$. The hard thresholding is also methodically unbiased remarking that $u_{f_0}^\star$ is the orthogonal projection on $\mathcal{M}_{f_0}^\star = \text{Im}[\text{Id}_{\mathcal{I}_{f_0}}]$. Unlike the unconstrained least-square estimator, Tikhonov regularization has a non zero weak bias. The soft thresholding is also known to be biased [11] and its weak bias is given by $-\lambda \text{Id}_{\mathcal{I}_{f_0}} \text{sign}(f_0)_{\mathcal{I}_{f_0}}$. Often, estimators are said to be unbiased when they are actually only weakly unbiased.

4 Definitions of Debiasing

Given an estimate $u_f^\star$ of u_0, we define a debiasing of $u_f^\star$ as follows.

Definition 3. *An estimator $\tilde{u}_f^\star$ of u_0 is a <u>weak debiasing</u> of $u_f^\star$ if it is weakly unbiased and $\tilde{\mathcal{M}}_f^\star = \mathcal{M}_f^\star$ for almost all f, with $\tilde{\mathcal{M}}_f^\star$ the model subspace of $\tilde{u}_f^\star$ at f. Moreover, it is a <u>methodical debiasing</u> if it is also methodically unbiased.*

Examples. The unconstrained least square estimator is a methodical debiasing of the Tikhonov regularization, since it is a methodically unbiased estimator of u_0 and they share the same model subspace. The hard thresholding is a methodical debiasing of the soft thresholding, for the same reasons.

A good candidate for debiasing $u_f^\star$ is the constraint least squares on $\mathcal{M}_f^\star$:

$$\tilde{u}_f^\star = u_f^\star + U_f^\star(\Phi U_f^\star)^+(f - \Phi u_f^\star) \in \operatorname*{argmin}_{u \in \mathcal{M}_f^\star} \|\Phi u - f\|^2 \qquad (12)$$

where $U_f^\star \in \mathbb{R}^{N \times n}$ with $n = \mathrm{rank}[J_f^\star]$ is a matrix whose columns form a basis of $\mathrm{Im}[J_f^\star]$. Let $V_f^\star \in \mathbb{R}^{n \times P}$ be a matrix such that $J_f^\star = U_f^\star V_f^\star$. The following theorem shows that under mild assumptions this choice corresponds to a debiasing of $u_f^\star$.

Theorem 1. *Assume that $f \mapsto u_f^\star$ is locally affine for almost all f and that Φ is invertible on $\mathcal{M}_f^\star$. Then $\tilde{u}_f^\star$ defined in Eq. (12) is a weak debiasing of $u_f^\star$.*

Proof. Since $f \mapsto u_f^\star$ is locally affine, $f \mapsto U_f^\star$ can be chosen locally constant. Deriving (12) for almost all f leads to the Jacobian $\tilde{J}_f^\star$ of $\tilde{u}_f^\star$ given by

$$\tilde{J}_f^\star = \frac{\partial \tilde{u}_f^\star}{\partial f} = \frac{\partial u_f^\star}{\partial f} + U_f^\star(\Phi U_f^\star)^+ \left(\frac{\partial f}{\partial f} - \Phi \frac{\partial u_f^\star}{\partial f}\right) = J_f^\star + U_f^\star(\Phi U_f^\star)^+(\mathrm{Id} - \Phi J_f^\star)$$
$$= U_f^\star V_f^\star + U_f^\star(\Phi U_f^\star)^+(\mathrm{Id} - \Phi U_f^\star V_f^\star) = U_f^\star(\Phi U_f^\star)^+ , \qquad (13)$$

since $\Phi U_f^\star$ has full column rank due to the assumption that Φ is invertible on $\mathcal{M}_f^\star$. It follows that

$$\tilde{\mathcal{M}}_f^\star = \tilde{u}_f^\star + \mathrm{Im}[\tilde{J}_f^\star] = u_f^\star + U_f^\star(\Phi U_f^\star)^+(f - \Phi u_f^\star) + \mathrm{Im}[U_f^\star(\Phi U_f^\star)^+] \qquad (14)$$
$$= u_f^\star + \mathrm{Im}[U_f^\star(\Phi U_f^\star)^+] = u_f^\star + \mathrm{Im}[U_f^\star] = \mathcal{M}_f^\star , \qquad (15)$$

since $\Phi U_f^\star$ has full column rank. Moreover, for any $u_0 \in \mathcal{M}_{f_0}^\star$, the equation $\Phi u = f_0$ has a unique solution $u = u_0$ in $\mathcal{M}_{f_0}^\star$ since Φ is invertible on $\mathcal{M}_{f_0}^\star$. Hence, $\tilde{u}_{f_0}^\star = u_0$ is the unique solution of (12), which concludes the proof. □

The next proposition shows that the condition "Φ invertible on $\mathcal{M}_f^\star$" can be dropped when looking at $u_f^\star$ and $\tilde{u}_f^\star$ through Φ. The debiasing becomes furthermore methodical.

Proposition 1. *Assume $f \mapsto u_f^\star$ is locally affine for almost all f. Taking $\tilde{u}_f^\star$ defined in Eq. (12), then the predictor $\Phi \tilde{u}_f^\star$ of $f_0 = \Phi u_0$ is equal to $\Pi_{\Phi \mathcal{M}_f^\star}(f)$ and is a methodical debiasing of $\Phi u_f^\star$.*

Proof. Since $\Phi U_f^\star (\Phi U_f^\star)^+ = \Pi_{\mathrm{Im}[\Phi U_f^\star]}$, we have $\Phi \tilde{u}_f^\star = \Pi_{\Phi \mathcal{M}_f^\star}(f)$. As the orthogonal projector on its own model space, it is methodically unbiased. Moreover $\mathrm{Im}[\Pi_{\mathrm{Im}[\Phi U_f^\star]}] = \mathrm{Im}[\Phi U_f^\star]$, hence $\Phi \tilde{u}_f^\star$ and $\Phi u_f^\star$ share the same model subspace. □

Remark 1. *As an immediate consequence, the debiasing of any locally affine denoising algorithm is a methodical debiasing, since $\Phi \tilde{u}_f^\star = \tilde{u}_f^\star$.*

We focus in the next sections on the debiasing of estimators without explicit expression for $\mathcal{M}_f^\star$, meaning that Eq. (12) cannot be used directly. We first introduce an algorithm for the case of ℓ_1 analysis relying on the computation of the directional derivative $J_f^\star f$. We propose next a general approach, applied to an affine nonlocal estimator, that requires $J_f^\star \delta$ for randomized directions δ.

5 Debiasing the ℓ_1 Analysis Minimization

From now on, the dependency of all quantities with respect to the observation f will be dropped for the sake of simplicity. Given a linear operator $\Gamma \in \mathbb{R}^{L \times N}$, the ℓ_1 analysis minimization reads, for $\lambda > 0$, as

$$E(u,f) = \frac{1}{2}\|\Phi u - f\|^2 + \lambda \|\Gamma u\|_1 . \qquad (16)$$

Provided $\mathrm{Ker}\,\Phi \cap \mathrm{Ker}\,\Gamma = \{0\}$, there exists a solution given implicitly, see [22], as

$$u^\star = U(\Phi U)^+ f - \lambda U(U^t \Phi^t \Phi U)^{-1} U^t (\Gamma^t)_\mathcal{I} s_\mathcal{I} \qquad (17)$$

for almost all f and where $\mathcal{I} = \{i\,;\,(\Gamma u^\star)_i \neq 0\} \subseteq [L] = \{1,\ldots,L\}$ is called the co-support of the solution, $s = \mathrm{sign}(\Gamma u^\star)$, $U = U_f^\star$ is a matrix whose columns form a basis of $\mathrm{Ker}[\mathrm{Id}_{\mathcal{I}^c}^t \Gamma]$ and ΦU has full column rank. Note that $s_\mathcal{I}$ and U are locally constant almost everywhere since the co-support is stable with respect to small perturbations [22]. It then follows that the model subspace is implicitly defined as $\mathcal{M}^\star = \mathrm{Im}[U] = \mathrm{Ker}[\mathrm{Id}_{\mathcal{I}^c}^t \Gamma]$, and so, the ℓ_1 analysis minimization suffers from a weak bias equal to $-\lambda U(U^t \Phi^t \Phi U)^{-1} U^t (\Gamma^t)_\mathcal{I} s_\mathcal{I}$. Given that $u^\star \in \mathrm{Im}[U]$ and it is locally affine, its weak debiased solution is defined for almost all f as

$$\tilde{u}^\star = U(\Phi U)^+ f . \qquad (18)$$

The ℓ_1 *synthesis* [8,20] consists in taking $\Gamma = \mathrm{Id}$, hence $U = \mathrm{Id}_\mathcal{I}$, so (17) becomes

$$u_\mathcal{I}^\star = (\Phi_\mathcal{I})^+ f - \lambda((\Phi_\mathcal{I})^t \Phi_\mathcal{I})^{-1} s_\mathcal{I} \quad \text{and} \quad u_{(\mathcal{I})^c}^\star = 0 . \qquad (19)$$

Its model subspace is implicitly defined as $\mathcal{M}^\star = \mathrm{Im}[\mathrm{Id}_\mathcal{I}]$, its weak bias is $-\lambda \mathrm{Id}_\mathcal{I}((\Phi_\mathcal{I})^t \Phi_\mathcal{I})^{-1} s_\mathcal{I}$ and its weak debiasing is $\tilde{u}^\star = \mathrm{Id}_\mathcal{I}(\Phi_\mathcal{I})^+ f$. Subsequently, taking $\Phi = \mathrm{Id}$ leads to the soft-thresholding presented earlier.

The *anisotropic Total-Variation (TV)* [18] is a particular instance of (16) where $u_0 \in \mathbb{R}^N$ can be identified to a d-dimensional discrete signal, for which $\Gamma \in \mathbb{R}^{L \times N}$, with $L = dN$, is the concatenation of the discrete gradient operators in each canonical directions. In this case $\mathcal{I}$ is the set of indexes where the solution has discontinuities (non-null gradients) and $\mathcal{M}^\star$ is the space of piece-wise constant signals sharing the same discontinuities as the solution. Its weak bias reveals a loss of contrast: a shift of intensity on each piece depending on its surrounding and the ratio between its perimeter and its area, as shown, e.g., in [19]. Note that the so-called *staircasing* effect of TV regularization is encoded in our framework as a model bias, and is therefore not reduced by our debiasing technique. Strategies devoted to the reduction of this effect have been studied in, e.g., [16].

Since in general $u^\star$ has no explicit solutions, it is usually estimated thanks to an iterative algorithm that can be expressed as a sequence u^k converging to $u^\star$. The question we address is how to compute $\tilde{u}^\star$ in practice, i.e., to evaluate Eq. (18), or more precisely, how to jointly build a sequence $\tilde{u}^k$ converging to $\tilde{u}^\star$.

We propose a technique that relies on the observation that, given (17), for almost all f, the Jacobian $J^\star$ of $u^\star$ at f applied to f, leads to Eq. (18), i.e.,

$$J^\star[f] = U(\Phi U)^+ f = \tilde{u}^\star \qquad (20)$$

since U and $s_\mathcal{I}$ are locally constant [22]. We so define a sequence $\tilde{u}^k$ which is, up to a slight modification, the closed-form derivation of the primal-dual sequence u^k of [4]. Most importantly, we provide a proof of its convergence towards $\tilde{u}^\star$.

Note that other debiasing techniques could be employed for the ℓ_1 analysis, e.g., using iterative hard-thresholding [1,13], refitting techniques [9,15], post-refinement techniques based an Bregman divergences and nonlinear inverse scale spaces [3,17,24] or with ideal spectral filtering in the analysis sense [12].

5.1 Primal-Dual Algorithm

Before stating our main result, let us recall some of the properties of primal-dual techniques. Dualizing the ℓ_1 analysis norm $u \mapsto \lambda \|\Gamma u\|_1$, the primal problem can be reformulated as the following saddle-point problem

$$z^\star = \underset{z \in \mathbb{R}^L}{\operatorname{argmax}} \min_{u \in \mathbb{R}^N} \frac{1}{2}\|\Phi u - f\|^2 + \langle \Gamma u, z \rangle - \iota_{B_\lambda}(z) \qquad (21)$$

where $z^\star \in \mathbb{R}^L$ is the dual variable, and $B_\lambda = \{z \ ; \ \|z\|_\infty \leqslant \lambda\}$ is the ℓ_∞ ball.

First order primal-dual optimization. Taking $\sigma\tau < \frac{1}{\|\Gamma\|_2^2}$, $\theta \in [0,1]$ and initializing (for instance,) $u^0 = v^0 = 0 \in \mathbb{R}^N$, $z^0 = 0 \in \mathbb{R}^L$, the primal-dual algorithm of [4] applied to problem (21) reads

$$\begin{cases} z^{k+1} = \Pi_{B_\lambda}(z^k + \sigma \Gamma v^k), \\ u^{k+1} = (\mathrm{Id} + \tau \Phi^t \Phi)^{-1}\left(u^k + \tau(\Phi^t f - \Gamma^t(z^{k+1}))\right), \\ v^{k+1} = u^{k+1} + \theta(u^{k+1} - u^k), \end{cases} \qquad (22)$$

where the projection of z over B_λ is done component-wise as

$$\Pi_{B_\lambda}(z)_i = \begin{cases} z_i & \text{if } |z_i| \leqslant \lambda, \\ \lambda \operatorname{sign}(z_i) & \text{otherwise.} \end{cases} \qquad (23)$$

The primal-dual sequence u^k converges to a solution $u^\star$ of (16) [4]. We assumed here that $u^\star$ verifies (17) with ΦU full-column rank. This could be enforced as shown in [22], but it did not seem to be necessary in our experiments.

5.2 Debiasing Algorithm

As pointed out earlier, the debiasing of $u^\star$ consists in applying the Jacobian matrix $J^\star$ at f to f itself. This idea leads to the proposed debiasing algorithm that constructs a sequence of debiased iterates from the original biased primal-dual sequence with initialization $\tilde{u}^0 = \tilde{v}^0 = 0 \in \mathbb{R}^N$, $\tilde{z}^0 = 0 \in \mathbb{R}^L$ as follows

$$\begin{cases} \tilde{z}^{k+1} = \Pi_{z^k + \sigma \Gamma v^k}(\tilde{z}^k + \sigma \Gamma \tilde{v}^k), \\ \tilde{u}^{k+1} = (\mathrm{Id} + \tau \Phi^t \Phi)^{-1}\left(\tilde{u}^k + \tau(\Phi^t f - \Gamma^t \tilde{z}^{k+1})\right), \\ \tilde{v}^{k+1} = \tilde{u}^{k+1} + \theta(\tilde{u}^{k+1} - \tilde{u}^k), \end{cases} \quad (24)$$

where $\Pi_{z^k + \sigma \Gamma v^k}(\tilde{z}_i) = \begin{cases} \tilde{z}_i & \text{if } |z^k + \sigma \Gamma v^k|_i \leqslant \lambda + \beta, \\ 0 & \text{otherwise.} \end{cases}$

with $\beta \geqslant 0$. Note that when $\beta = 0$, deriving z^k, u^k and v^k for almost all f at f in the direction f using the chain rule leads to the sequences $\tilde{z}^k$, $\tilde{u}^k$ and $\tilde{v}^k$ respectively (see also [6]). However, as shown in Theorem 2, it is important to choose $\beta > 0$ to guarantee the convergence of the sequence[1].

Theorem 2. *Let $\alpha > 0$ be the minimum non zero value[2] of $|\Gamma u^\star|_i$ for all $i \in [L]$. Choose β such that $\alpha \sigma > \beta > 0$. The sequence $\tilde{u}^k$ defined in (24) converges to the debiasing $\tilde{u}^\star$ of $u^\star$.*

Before turning to the proof of this theorem, let us introduce a first lemma.

Lemma 1. *The debiasing $\tilde{u}^\star$ of $u^\star$ is the solution of the saddle-point problem*

$$\min_{\tilde{u} \in \mathbb{R}^N} \max_{\tilde{z} \in \mathbb{R}^L} \|\Phi \tilde{u} - f\|^2 + \langle \Gamma \tilde{u}, \tilde{z} \rangle - \iota_{F_\mathcal{I}}(\tilde{z}), \quad (25)$$

where $\iota_{F_\mathcal{I}}$ is the indicator function of the convex set $F_\mathcal{I} = \{p \in \mathbb{R}^L \;;\; p_\mathcal{I} = 0\}$.

Proof. As ΦU has full column rank, the debiased solution is the unique solution of the constrained least square estimation problem

$$\tilde{u}^\star = U(\Phi U)^+ f = \underset{\tilde{u} \in \mathcal{U}^\star}{\mathrm{argmin}} \, \|\Phi \tilde{u} - f\|^2 \, . \quad (26)$$

Remark that $\tilde{u} \in \mathcal{U}^\star = \mathrm{Ker}[\mathrm{Id}^t_{\mathcal{I}^c}\Gamma] \Leftrightarrow (\Gamma \tilde{u})_{\mathcal{I}^c} = 0 \Leftrightarrow \iota_{F_{\mathcal{I}^c}}(\Gamma \tilde{u}) = 0$, where $F_{\mathcal{I}^c} = \{p \in \mathbb{R}^L \;;\; p_{\mathcal{I}^c} = 0\}$.

Using Fenchel transform, $\iota_{F_{\mathcal{I}^c}}(\Gamma \tilde{u}) = \max_{\tilde{z}} \langle \Gamma \tilde{u}, \tilde{z} \rangle - \iota^*_{F_{\mathcal{I}^c}}(\tilde{z})$, where $\iota^*_{F_{\mathcal{I}^c}}$ is the convex conjugate of $\iota_{F_{\mathcal{I}^c}}$. Observing that $\iota_{F_\mathcal{I}} = \iota^*_{F_{\mathcal{I}^c}}$ concludes the proof. $\square$

Given Lemma 1, replacing $\Pi_{z^k + \sigma \Gamma v^k}$ in (24) by the projection onto $F_\mathcal{I}$, i.e.,

$$\Pi_{F_\mathcal{I}}(\tilde{z})_{\mathcal{I}^c} = \tilde{z}_{\mathcal{I}^c} \quad \text{and} \quad \Pi_{F_\mathcal{I}}(\tilde{z})_\mathcal{I} = 0 \, , \quad (27)$$

leads to the primal-dual algorithm of [4] applied to problem (25) which converges to the debiased estimator $\tilde{u}^\star$. It remains to prove that the projection $\Pi_{z^k + \sigma \Gamma v^k}$ defined in (24) converges to $\Pi_{F_\mathcal{I}}$ in finite time.

---

[1] In practice, β can be chosen as the smallest positive floating number.
[2] If $|\Gamma u^\star|_i = 0$ for all $i \in [L]$, the result remains true for any $\alpha > 0$.

Proof (Theorem 2). First consider $i \in \mathcal{I}$, i.e., $|\Gamma u^\star|_i > 0$. By assumption on α, $|\Gamma u^\star|_i \geq \alpha > 0$. Necessary $z_i^\star = \lambda \operatorname{sign}(\Gamma u^\star)_i$ in order to maximize (21). Hence, $|z^\star + \sigma \Gamma u^\star|_i \geq \lambda + \sigma\alpha$. Using the triangle inequality shows that

$$\lambda + \sigma\alpha \leq |z^\star + \sigma \Gamma u^\star|_i \leq |z^\star - z^k|_i + \sigma|\Gamma u^\star - \Gamma v^k|_i + |z^k + \sigma \Gamma v^k|_i \ . \quad (28)$$

Choose $\varepsilon > 0$ sufficiently small such that $\sigma\alpha - \varepsilon(1+\sigma) > \beta$. From the convergence of the primal-dual algorithm of [4], the sequence (z^k, u^k, v^k) converges to $(z^\star, u^\star, u^\star)$. Therefore, for k large enough, $|z^\star - z^k|_i < \varepsilon$, $|\Gamma u^\star - \Gamma v^k|_i < \varepsilon$, and

$$|z^k + \sigma \Gamma v^k|_i \geq \lambda + \sigma\alpha - \varepsilon(1+\sigma) > \lambda + \beta \ . \quad (29)$$

Next consider $i \in \mathcal{I}^c$, i.e., $|\Gamma u^\star|_i = 0$, where by definition $|z^\star|_i \leq \lambda$. Using again the triangle inequality shows that

$$|z^k + \sigma \Gamma v^k|_i \leq |z^k - z^\star|_i + \sigma|\Gamma v^k - \Gamma u^\star|_i + |z^\star|_i \ . \quad (30)$$

Choose $\varepsilon > 0$ sufficiently small such that $\varepsilon(1+\sigma) < \beta$. As $(z^k, u^k, v^k) \to (z^\star, u^\star, u^\star)$, for k large enough, $|z^k - z^\star|_i < \varepsilon$, $|\Gamma v^k - \Gamma u^\star|_i < \varepsilon$, and

$$|z^k + \sigma \Gamma v^k|_i < \lambda + \varepsilon(1+\sigma) \leq \lambda + \beta \ . \quad (31)$$

It follows that for k sufficiently large $|z^k + \sigma \Gamma v^k|_i \leq \lambda + \beta$ if and only if $i \in \mathcal{I}^c$, and hence $\Pi_{z^k + \sigma K v^k}(\tilde{z}) = \Pi_{F_\mathcal{I}}(\tilde{z})$. As a result, all subsequent iterations of (24) will solve (25), and hence from Lemma 1 this concludes the proof of the theorem. □

6 Debiasing Other Affine Estimators

In most cases, $U^\star$ cannot be computed in reasonable memory load and/or time, such that Eq. (12) cannot be used directly. However, the directional derivative, i.e., the application of $J^\star$ to a direction δ, can in general be obtained with an algorithm of the same complexity as the one providing $u^\star$. If one can compute the directional derivatives for any direction, a general iterative algorithm for the computation of $\tilde{u}^\star$ can be derived as given in Algorithm 1.

The proposed technique relies on the fact that given $n = \dim(\mathcal{M}^\star)$ uniformly random directions $\delta_1, \ldots, \delta_n$ on the unit sphere of $\mathbb{R}^P$, $J^\star \delta_1, \ldots, J^\star \delta_n$ forms a basis of $\operatorname{Im}[J^\star]$ almost surely. Given this basis, the debiased solution can so be retrieved from (12). Unfortunately, computing the image of the usually large number n of random directions can be computationally prohibitive.

The idea is to approach the debiased solution by retrieving only a low dimensional subspace of $\mathcal{M}^\star$ leading to a small approximation error. Our greedy heuristic is to chose random perturbations around the current residual (the strength of the perturbation being controlled by a parameter ε). As soon as $\varepsilon > 0$, the algorithm converges in n iterations as explained above. But, by focusing in directions guided by the current residual, the algorithm refines in priority the directions for which the current debiasing gets significantly away from the data f, i.e., directions that encodes potential remaining bias. Hence, the debiasing can be very effective even though a small number of such directions has been explored. We notice in our experiments that with a small value of ε, this strategy leads indeed to a satisfying debiasing, close to convergence, reached in a few iterations.

Algorithm 1. General debiasing pseudo-algorithm for the computation of $\tilde{u}^*$.

Inputs: $f \in \mathbb{R}^P$, $u^* \in \mathbb{R}^N$, $\delta \in \mathbb{R}^P \to J^*\delta \in \mathbb{R}^N$, $\varepsilon > 0$.
Outputs: $\tilde{u}^* \in \mathbb{R}^N$ and $U \in \mathbb{R}^{N \times n'}$ with $n' \leqslant n$ an orthonormal family of $\mathrm{Im}[J^*]$

Initialize $\quad U \leftarrow [\,]$
repeat until $\tilde{u}^*$ reaches convergence
$\quad$ Generate $\quad \delta \leftarrow \eta/\|\eta\|, \eta \sim \mathcal{N}_P(0, \mathrm{Id})$ $\qquad$ (perturbation ensuring convergence)
$\quad$ Compute $\quad u' \leftarrow J^*(f - \Phi\tilde{u}^* + \varepsilon\delta)$ $\qquad$ (perturbed image of the current residual)
$\quad$ Compute $\quad e \leftarrow u' - U(U^t u')$ $\qquad$ (projection on the orthogonal of the current $\mathcal{M}^*$)
$\quad$ Update $\quad U \leftarrow [U\ e/\|e\|]$
$\quad$ Update $\quad \tilde{u}^* \leftarrow u^* + U((\Phi U)^+(f - \Phi u^*))$

The nonlocal-means example. The block-wise nonlocal-means proposed in [2] can be rewritten as an instance of the minimization problem (1) with

$$E(u,f) = \frac{1}{2}\sum_{i,j} w_{i,j}\|\mathcal{P}_i u - \mathcal{P}_j f\|^2 \quad \text{with} \quad w_{i,j} = \varphi\left(\frac{\|\mathcal{P}_i f - \mathcal{P}_j f\|^2}{2\sigma^2}\right) \qquad (32)$$

where $i \in [n_1] \times [n_2]$ spans the whole image domain, $j - i \in [-s, s] \times [-s, s]$ spans a limited search window domain and σ^2 is the noise variance. We denote by $\mathcal{P}_i$ the linear operator extracting the patch at pixel i of size $(2p+1) \times (2p+1)$. Note that we assume periodical conditions such that all quantities remain inside the image domain. The kernel $\varphi : \mathbb{R}^+ \to [0,1]$ is a decreasing function which is typically a decay exponential function. Taking φ piece-wise constant[3], leads to computing u^* and its Jacobian at f applied to δ for almost all f as follow

$$u_i^* = \frac{\sum_j \bar{w}_{i,j} f_j}{\sum_j \bar{w}_{i,j}} \quad \text{and} \quad (J^*\delta)_i = \frac{\sum_j \bar{w}_{i,j}\delta_j}{\sum_j \bar{w}_{i,j}} \quad \text{with} \quad \bar{w}_{i,j} = \sum_k w_{i-k,j-k} \qquad (33)$$

where $k \in [-p,p] \times [-p,p]$ spans the patch domain. Note that the values of w and $\bar{w}$ can be obtained by discrete convolutions leading to an algorithm with complexity in $O(Ns^2)$, independent of the half patch size p.

With such a choice of φ, the block-wise nonlocal filter becomes a piece-wise affine mapping of f and hence Algorithm 1 applies.

7 Numerical Experiments and Results

Figure 1 gives an illustration of TV used for denoising a 1D piece-wise constant signal in $[0, 192]$ and damaged by additive white Gaussian noise (AWGN) with a standard deviation $\sigma = 10$. Even though TV has perfectly retrieved the support of ∇u_0 with one more extra jump, the intensities of some regions are biased. Our debiasing is as expected unbiased for every region.

Figure 2 gives an illustration of our debiasing of 2D anisotropic TV used for the restoration of an *8bits* approximately piece-wise constant image damaged by AWGN with $\sigma = 20$. The observation operator Φ is a Gaussian convolution kernel

---

[3] For instance, by quantification on a subset of predefined values in $[0, 1]$.

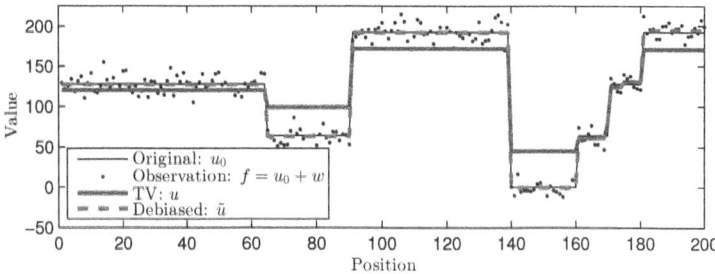

Fig. 1. Solutions of 1D-TV and our debiasing on a piece-wise constant signal

Fig. 2. (left) Blurry image $f = \Phi u_0 + w$, (center) TV $u^\star$, (right) debiased $\tilde{u}^\star$

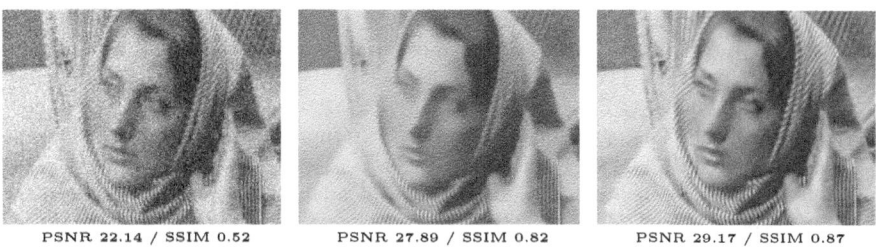

Fig. 3. (left) Noisy image $f = u_0 + w$, (center) nonlocal-means $u^\star$, (right) debiased $\tilde{u}^\star$

of bandwidth 2px. TV introduced a significant loss of contrast, typically for the thin contours of the drawing, which are re-enhanced by our debiased result.

Figure 3 gives an illustration of our iterative debiasing for the block-wise nonlocal-means algorithm used in a denoising problem for an $8bits$ image enjoying many repetitive patterns and damaged by AWGN with $\sigma = 20$. Convergence has been considered as reached after 4 iterations only. Our debiasing provides favorable results with many enhanced details compared to the biased result.

8 Conclusion

We have introduced in this paper a mathematical definition of debiasing which has led to an effective debiasing technique that can remove the method bias that does not arise from the unavoidable choice of the model. This debiasing technique simply consists in applying a least-square estimation constrained to the model subspace chosen implicitly by the original biased algorithm. Numerical experiments have demonstrated the efficiency of our technique in retrieving the correct intensities while respecting the structure of the original model subspace. Our technique is nevertheless limited to locally affine estimators. Isotropic total variation, structured sparsity or nonlocal-means with smooth kernels are not yet handled by our debiasing technique, and left for future work.

References

1. Blumensath, T., Davies, M.E.: Iterative thresholding for sparse approximations. J. Fourier Anal. Appl. **14**(5–6), 629–654 (2008)
2. Buades, A., Coll, B., Morel, J.-M.: A review of image denoising algorithms, with a new one. SIAM J. Multiscale Model. Simul. **4**(2), 490–530 (2005)
3. Burger, M., Gilboa, G., Osher, S., Xu, J., et al.: Nonlinear inverse scale space methods. Communications in Mathematical Sciences **4**(1), 179–212 (2006)
4. Chambolle, A., Pock, T.: A first-order primal-dual algorithm for convex problems with applications to imaging. J. Math. Imaging Vis. **40**, 120–145 (2011)
5. Chen, S.S., Donoho, D.L., Saunders, M.A.: Atomic decomposition by basis pursuit. SIAM J. Sci. Comput. **20**(1), 33–61 (1998)
6. Deledalle, C.-A., Vaiter, S., Peyré, G., Fadili, J.M.: Stein unbiased gradient estimator of the risk (SUGAR) for multiple parameter selection. SIAM J. Imaging Sciences **7**(4), 2448–2487 (2014)
7. Denis De Senneville, B., Roujol, S., Hey, S., Moonen, C., Ries, M.: Extended Kalman filtering for continuous volumetric MR-temperature imaging. IEEE Trans. Med. Imaging **32**(4), 711–718 (2013)
8. Donoho, D.L., Johnstone, J.M.: Ideal spatial adaptation by wavelet shrinkage. Biometrika **81**(3), 425–455 (1994)
9. Efron, B., Hastie, T., Johnstone, I., Tibshirani, R.: Least angle regression. Ann. Statist. **32**(2), 407–499 (2004)
10. Elad, M., Milanfar, P., Rubinstein, R.: Analysis versus synthesis in signal priors. Inverse Problems **23**(3), 947 (2007)
11. Fan, J., Li, R.: Variable selection via nonconcave penalized likelihood and its oracle properties. J. Am. Statist. Assoc. **96**(456), 1348–1360 (2001)
12. Gilboa, G.: A total variation spectral framework for scale and texture analysis. SIAM J. Imaging Sciences **7**(4), 1937–1961 (2014)
13. Herrity, K.K, Gilbert, A.C., Tropp, J.A.: Sparse approximation via iterative thresholding. In: ICASSP, vol. 3, pp. III-III. IEEE (2006)
14. Hoerl, A.E., Kennard, R.W.: Ridge regression: Biased estimation for nonorthogonal problems. Technometrics **12**(1), 55–67 (1970)
15. Lederer. J.: Trust, but verify: benefits and pitfalls of least-squares refitting in high dimensions (2013). arXiv preprint arXiv:1306.0113
16. Louchet, C., Moisan, L.: Total variation as a local filter. SIAM Journal on Imaging Sciences **4**(2), 651–694 (2011)

17. Osher, S., Burger, M., Goldfarb, D., Xu, J., Yin, W.: An iterative regularization method for total variation-based image restoration. SIAM J. Multiscale Model. Simul. **4**(2), 460–489 (2005)
18. Rudin, L.I., Osher, S., Fatemi, E.: Nonlinear total variation based noise removal algorithms. Physica D: Nonlinear Phenomena **60**(1), 259–268 (1992)
19. Strong, D., Chan, T.: Edge-preserving and scale-dependent properties of total variation regularization. Inverse problems **19**(6), S165 (2003)
20. Tibshirani, R.: Regression shrinkage and selection via the lasso. J. Roy. Statist. Soc. Ser. B, 267–288 (1996)
21. Tikhonov, A.N.: On the stability of inverse problems. Dokl. Akad. Nauk SSSR **39**, 176–179 (1943)
22. Vaiter, S., Deledalle, C.-A., Peyré, G., Dossal, C., Fadili, J.: Local behavior of sparse analysis regularization: Applications to risk estimation. Appl. Comput. Harmon. Anal. **35**(3), 433–451 (2013)
23. Vaiter, S., Golbabaee, M., Fadili, M., Peyré, G.: Model selection with low complexity priors (2014). arXiv preprint arXiv:1307.2342
24. Xu, J., Osher, S.: Iterative regularization and nonlinear inverse scale space applied to wavelet-based denoising. IEEE Trans. Image Proc. **16**(2), 534–544 (2007)

Cartoon-Texture-Noise Decomposition with Transport Norms

Christoph Brauer(✉) and Dirk Lorenz

Institut für Analysis und Algebra, TU Braunschweig, Braunschweig, Germany
{ch.brauer,d.lorenz}@tu-braunschweig.de

Abstract. We investigate the problem of decomposing an image into three parts, namely a cartoon part, a texture part and a noise part. We argue that norms originating in the theory of optimal transport should have the ability to distinguish certain noise types from textures. Hence, we present a brief introduction to optimal transport metrics and show their relation to previously proposed texture norms. We propose different variational models and investigate their performance.

Keywords: Image decomposition · Texture · Optimal transport · Oscillating patterns

1 Introduction

An ubiquitous topic in image processing is the reconstruction and interpretation of a genuine image $u^\dagger$ from an observed image u^0. The original image $u^\dagger$ may be regarded as a superposition of certain structural elements. The separation of these different structures, and also the separation of the genuine image $u^\dagger$ from possible *noise* is known as *image decomposition*. In this work we investigate the problem of decomposing an image into three parts, namely a *cartoon* part, a *texture* part and a noise part. While decomposition into either cartoon and texture or cartoon and noise is done frequently, the separation of cartoon, noise and texture is a challenging task.

We use the common setting, where $\Omega \subset \mathbb{R}^2$ is the image domain and an image u is a function $u : \Omega \to \mathbb{R}$. Cartoon parts typically denote smooth regions which are separated by discontinuities referred to as edges. One may think of uniformly coloured objects in an image which are separated from other objects by their natural boundaries or themselves subdivided by sharp changes of illumination. On the other hand, textures can be understood as fine structures obeying characteristic patterns. Examples for textures are oscillating patterns and ornamental elements. In case of an observed image u^0, another common element is noise which can be seen as a random perturbation of the original image without spatial structure.

The main goal of this paper is the decomposition of an obeserved image u^0 into a cartoon component u, a texture component v and a noise component w. Since Rudin, Osher and Fatemi [1] proposed the now called ROF model for total variation (TV) denoising $\min_{u \in BV(\Omega)} \alpha TV(u) + \frac{\beta}{2} \|u^0 - u\|_{L^2}^2$, it is well understood that the solution u^* tends to be piecewise constant, may contain discontinuities along edges and that this model is able to extract a cartoon like image. Therein, $BV(\Omega)$ is the space of functions of bounded total variation, $TV(u)$ is the total variation of u and $\alpha, \beta > 0$ are regularization parameters. However, as Meyer [2] outlines, this model may be inappropriate in case u^0 contains textures as sufficiently small values of β cause the absence of textures in u^*. In other words, the residual part $v = u^0 - u^*$ contains both noise and texture. To capture the oscillating feature of texture better, Meyer [2] proposed the problem

$$\min_{(u,v) \in BV(\Omega) \times G(\Omega)} \alpha TV(u) + \beta \|v\|_G \quad \text{s.t. } u + v = u^0, \tag{1}$$

where $G(\Omega) = \{v \in L^2(\Omega) \mid \exists g \in L^\infty(\Omega, \mathbb{R}^2) : \operatorname{div} g = v\}$ and

$$\|v\|_G = \inf \{\||g|\|_{L^\infty} \mid \operatorname{div} g = v\}. \tag{2}$$

Meyer [2] showed that $G(\Omega)$ contains functions representing textures and that the related norm $\|\cdot\|_G$ is suitable to regularize textured images. Vese and Osher [3] proposed to solve the related problem

$$\min_{(u,g) \in BV(\Omega) \times L^p(\Omega, \mathbb{R}^2)} \alpha TV(u) + \frac{\beta}{p} \||g|\|_{L^p}^p + \frac{\gamma}{2} \|u^0 - u - \operatorname{div} g\|_{L^2}^2, \tag{3}$$

where $\gamma > 0$ is an additional regularization parameter. For $p \to \infty$ and $\gamma \to \infty$, (3) approximates (1). This becomes clear as we may substitute $v = \operatorname{div} g$. Osher, Solé and Vese [4] considered the special case where $p = 2$ in (3) and exploited the relation

$$\inf_{g \in L^2(\Omega) \cap \{\operatorname{div} g = v\}} \||g|\|_{L^2} = \|v\|_{H^{-1}}.$$

Further, after an appropriate definition of the inverse Laplace operator Δ^{-1} (see [4]), one can write $\|v\|_{H^{-1}}^2 = \|\nabla \Delta^{-1} v\|_{L^2}^2$. Thereupon, Osher, Solé and Vese [4] proposed the problem

$$\min_{u \in BV(\Omega)} \alpha TV(u) + \frac{\beta}{2} \|u^0 - u\|_{H^{-1}}^2, \tag{4}$$

which is a simplified version of (3) in the sense that (3) leads to a decomposition of u^0 into u, $v := \operatorname{div} g$ and $w := u^0 - u - v$ while (4) leads to a decomposition into u and $v := u^0 - u$.

Although Vese and Osher had a different motivation, the problem (3) may be seen as a model to decompose u^0 into cartoon u, texture $v = \operatorname{div} g$ and noise $w = u^0 - u - v$. In this paper we will investigate this decomposition problem closer. We will do so by exploiting recent advances in non-smooth large-scale optimization algorithms [5,6] which makes problems of the form (3), (4) and also (1) practically solvable. Moreover, inspired by [7] we illustrate the relations of the proposed models for cartoon-texture-noise decomposition to the theory of optimal transport. This connection provides some deeper understanding of the decomposition problem and shows why Meyer's G-norm can indeed capture texture, but still does not discriminate Gaussian noise from texture.

The outline of the paper is as follows. In Section 2 we state the problem of decomposing an image into cartoon, texture and noise, in Section 3 we introduce metrics and norms related to optimal transport and use them to derive different models for cartoon-texture-noise decomposition in Section 4. Section 5 presents numerical results.

2 Problem Statement

The general idea of variational image decomposition into two components is that one considers all decompositions $u^0 = u + w$ and minimizes a certain objective functional $\Phi(u,w) = F_u(u) + F_w(w)$ with respect to these decompositions. This objective should be designed such that the functional F_u honors a good fit to the respective u-components in that it delivers small values $F_u(u)$ if u has the desired characteristics, and similarly for F_w. For the ROF model that decomposes into cartoon u and noise w, the functionals are $F_u(u) = \mathrm{TV}(u)$ and $F_w(w) = \frac{\beta}{2}\|w\|_{L^2}^2$. The TV-seminorm favors piecewise constant functions while the L^2-norm is well suited for Gaussian noise (as can be seen from a Bayesian motivation [8]). If the noise in the image follows a different characteristic, the decomposition into cartoon and noise is improved by an adapted functional F_w. For impulsive noise, i.e. noise consisting of sparse outliers, the functional $F_w(w) = \|w\|_{L^1}$ is well suited [9,10] while for quantization noise or uniformly distributed noise, the L^∞-norm is appropriate [11].

To decompose an image into more than two components, one can follow the same approach. To be concrete, we focus on the decomposition of an image u^0 into cartoon u, texture v and noise w, i.e. $u^0 = u + v + w$. This can be realized by minimizing the sum $F_u(u) + F_v(v) + F_w(w)$ of appropriate functionals F_u, F_v and F_w over all decompositions.

The success of a decomposition model hinges on the ability to identify discriminating features of the sought-after components that in turn can be expressed effectively in objective functionals. As explained above, for piecewise constant images, the TV-seminorm is a good choice while for piecewise affine images, the total generalized variation TGV [12] works well. Objective functionals for noise components are usually of the form $F_w(w) = \int_\Omega \phi(w(x))\mathrm{d}x$ for some function $\phi : \mathbb{R} \to [0,\infty[$. This is motivated by the assumption that the noise in different points is independent and identically distributed. Regarding the typical characteristics of texture, Meyer elaborated in [2] that local oscillations are a discriminating feature and he proposed the G-norm, which is in some sense dual to the BV-norm. As the space BV is closely related to the Sobolev space $W^{1,1}$, the G norm is closely related to the dual norm of the $W^{1,1}$-norm.

Regarding the decomposition into texture and noise one notes that some noise types, e.g. Gaussian noise, also inherit local oscillation. Although noise is not oscillating in the strict sense, local averages of Gaussian noise are usually fairly small. As we will see below, it can be observed in experiments, that the separation of texture and Gaussian noise is inherently difficult due to the similar characteristics.

Hence, we focus on different noise which may be more different from texture, namely impulsive noise. Impulsive noise consists of sparse outliers and thus, does not necessarily provide local oscillations, especially if the outliers are well spaced. This motivates the following discrimination for impulsive noise and texture:

- Impulsive noise is sparse in the sense that it consists, in the continuous case, of a superposition of Dirac peaks. Hence, it is a quantity in measure space, namely a signed measure, with finite variation norm $\|\cdot\|_{\mathfrak{M}}$ and usually zero mean, i.e. the total positive mass is equal to the total negative mass. The position of the Dirac peaks is uniformly distributed (note that other distributions are possible but we focus on this assumption in the this paper for simplicity).
- Texture is related to functions that are oscillating in the sense that local averages of the functions are small, i.e. the integral of the function in every neighborhood is close to zero. In other words, not only the total positive mass is equal to the total negative mass, but this property is also true locally.

To translate this discrimination into a functional suited for a variational setting, we make the following observation: For both texture and impulsive noise one can "move the positive mass and the negative mass around to cancel each other out". However, for texture one usually needs to move the mass just a little, while for impulsive noise that is fairly sparse one has to move the mass over larger distances. Hence, the functionals F_v for the texture part and F_w for the noise part should be such that F_v is small if the positive and negative mass in the texture v can be moved around to cancel each other easily, while F_w can be of the type as described above.

This "moving of mass" can be captured and measured by so called transport metrics which we discuss in the next section.

3 Transport Metrics and Norms

The problem of optimal transport of mass goes back as far as to the 18th century when Gaspard Monge asked the question "How to optimally transport some pile of excavation to create a specified dam somewhere else?" [13]. Important progress has been made in the 40s of the 20th century when Kantorovich formulated the problem in the context of measures [14].

3.1 Wasserstein Metrics

In the Kantorovich form, the optimal transport problem reads as follows: Consider $\Omega \subset \mathbb{R}^n$ and two measures μ and ν on Ω with equal mass, i.e. $\int_\Omega \mathrm{d}\mu = \int_\Omega \mathrm{d}\nu$. Also consider a non-negative function $c : \Omega \times \Omega \to \mathbb{R}$ such that $c(x,y)$ is the cost to transport a unit amount of mass from x to y. Then the minimal cost to transport μ to ν is

$$\inf\{\int_{\Omega\times\Omega} c(x,y)\mathrm{d}\gamma(x,y) \; : \; \mathrm{proj}_1\gamma = \mu, \; \mathrm{proj}_2\gamma = \nu\}$$

where the infimum is taken over all measures γ on $\Omega\times\Omega$ such that its projections (i.e. its marginals) on the first and second component yield μ and ν, respectively. In the case that the cost function c is of the form $c(x,y) = d(x,y)^p$ for some metric d and $p \geq 1$ this minimization problem gives rise to a metric

$$W_p(\mu,\nu) = \inf\{\int_{\Omega\times\Omega} d(x,y)^p \mathrm{d}\gamma(x,y) \; : \; \mathrm{proj}_1\gamma = \mu, \; \mathrm{proj}_2\gamma = \nu\}^{1/p}$$

on the space of probability measures, and these metrics are called "Wasserstein metrics" with reference to [15] although the metric properties have already been investigated by Kantorovich and Rubinstein in [16].

3.2 Kantorovich-Rubinstein Norms

Using the transport metric in the case of image processing, where Ω is usually a two-dimensional region discretized to at least several hundred thousand pixels, faces some problems, the most severe one being that the minimization variable γ is defined on the four dimensional region $\Omega \times \Omega$, discretized by several *billion* pixels. In the particular case of $p = 1$ one can circumvent this problem using the celebrated Kantorovich-Rubinstein duality that states that

$$W_1(\mu,\nu) = \sup\{\int_\Omega f\mathrm{d}(\mu-\nu) \; : \; \mathrm{Lip}(f) \leq 1\} \quad (5)$$

where the supremum is taken over all functions f with Lipschitz constant smaller than 1. Note that for this distance to be finite it is needed that $\int_\Omega \mathrm{d}\mu = \int_\Omega \mathrm{d}\nu$ since otherwise addition of constants to f make the integral in the supremum arbitrarily large. This shows that W_1 can be seen as a metric on the space of measures with equal total mass, and note that it only depends on the difference of the arguments. In [7] the variant

$$\|\mu-\nu\|_{\mathrm{KR},\beta,\gamma} = \sup\{\int_\Omega f\mathrm{d}(\mu-\nu) \; : \; |f| \leq \gamma, \; \mathrm{Lip}(f) \leq \beta\} \quad (6)$$

has been proposed which is then a *norm* on the space of signed measures and can be used to measure the distance between two measures with different total mass. The additional constraint on the boundedness of the function f allows for a different total mass and the introduction of the parameters $\beta, \gamma \geq 0$ allows to scale the penalty on "mass missmatch" and "transport cost".

By formulating the Lipschitz constraint $\mathrm{Lip}(f) \leq \beta$ with the help of the weak gradient as $\|\|\nabla f\|\|_{L^\infty} \leq \beta$ and employing Fenchel-Rockafellar duality one obtains another formulation of the norm (cf. [7, Thm.3.4])

$$\min_{\nu\in W^{1,1}(\Omega;\mathrm{div})} \gamma\|\mu - \mathrm{div}\,\nu\|_{L^1} + \beta\|\|\nu\|\|_{L^1}$$

where the minimum is taken over the space $W^{1,1}(\Omega;\mathrm{div})$ of L^1 vector fields such that their divergence is also in L^1. The minimizer ν balances the *transport cost* $\|\nu\|_{L^1}$ and the *mass missmatch* $\|\mu - \mathrm{div}\,\nu\|_{L^1}$. In the context of texture separation, the transport cost refers to the cost that is used to transport gray values to cancel each other out and this cost is suited to capture the texture part of the image. The mass missmatch part captures the part of the image that is not moved to cancel each other out by transport and is suited to capture the noise. Since the noise is measured in the L^1-norm, this model is best suited for impulsive noise. Obviously one can vary this model to capture different types of noise by replacing the L^1-norm by other functionals such as the L^2-norm or the Kullback-Leibler divergence but then the direct link to optimal transport metrics is lost. We will not pursue such generalizations in this paper.

3.3 The G-Norm as Transport Norm

The G-norm from (2) and the decomposition method (1) related to it has a natural interpretation as a transport metric: The constraint $\mathrm{div}\,g = v$ shows that the vector field g is a field along which the "positive mass" v^+ is transported to the "negative mass" v^- and the G-norm chooses the vector field that does so with the smallest supremum norm of g. By duality, we can write

$$\|u^0 - u\|_G = \sup\{\int f(u^0 - u) \ : \ \||\nabla f|\|_{L^1} \leq 1\}$$

which resembles the form (5) of the W^1-metric. This new representation of the G norm makes it clear that $\|u^0 - u\|_G$ is infinite if the mass of u^0 and u does not coincide and also motivates the following generalization in spirit of (6)

$$\|u^0 - u\|_{G',\beta,\gamma} = \sup\{\int f(u^0 - u) \ : \ \|f\| \leq \gamma, \ \||\nabla f|\|_{L^1} \leq \beta\}$$

with some, for now, unspecified norm $\|\cdot\|$. The parameter γ allows for a mass missmatch in the transport and hence, unequal mass for u and u^0. Here we propose to use the L^∞-norm of f to allow for mass missmatch (which is similar to the KR-norm (6)). Formally dualizing the minimization problem for the G'-norm we arrive at

$$\|u^0 - u\|_{G',\beta,\gamma} = \inf_g \gamma \|u^0 - u - \mathrm{div}\,g\|_{L^1} + \beta \||g|\|_{L^\infty} . \qquad (7)$$

This norm is a mixture of Meyer's G-norm and the KR-norm and we will use it for noise-texture-separation in Section 4.3. Note that the G'-norm is closely related to the Vese-Osher model (3) (with $p = \infty$) from [3]. The new interpretation as a transport norm allows to explain its usefulness for texture-noise discrimination.

4 Modeling and Algorithms

Using the notation of Section 2, we propose the model

$$\min_{u,v} \ \alpha F_u(u) + \beta F_v(v) + \gamma F_w(u^0 - u - v) \qquad (8)$$

which yields a decomposition of the genuine image u^0 into a cartoon component u, a texture component v and a noise component $w = u^0 - u - v$. In this context, we will throughout use $F_u(u) = \mathrm{TV}(u)$.

For the solution of the respective optimization problems, we use the inertial forward-backward algorithm developed in [6] which is particularly applicable to problems of the form

$$\min_{u,v} \max_{\psi,\phi} \; G(u,v) + Q(u,v) + \left\langle K\begin{pmatrix}u\\v\end{pmatrix}, \begin{pmatrix}\phi\\\psi\end{pmatrix} \right\rangle - F^*(\phi,\psi) - P^*(\phi,\psi) \qquad (9)$$

with convex G, Q, F^* and P^* and a linear and bounded operator K. In addition, Q and P^* are required to be differentiable with Lipschitz gradient. Writing $x = (u,v)$ and $y = (\phi,\psi)$, one iteration of the proposed algorithm consists of

$$\begin{cases} \bar{x}^k = x^k + \theta(x^k - x^{k-1}), & \bar{y}^k = y^k + \theta(y^k - y^{k-1}) \\ x^{k+1} = \mathrm{prox}_{\tau G}(\bar{x}^k - \tau[\nabla Q(\bar{x}^k) + K^*\bar{y}^k]) \\ y^{k+1} = \mathrm{prox}_{\sigma F^*}(\bar{y}^k - \sigma[\nabla P^*(\bar{y}^k) - K(2x^{k+1} - \bar{x}^k)]) \end{cases}, \qquad (10)$$

where θ is an extrapolation factor and τ, σ are step size parameters. For choice rules for θ, τ and σ that guarante convergence (depending on $\|K\|$ and on the Lipschitz constants of ∇Q and ∇P^*) see [6]. In the following we always abbreviate the extrapolation steps because the these steps do not depend on the function to be minimized.

From now on, we work with discrete quantities, i.e. we assume $\Omega = \mathbb{R}^{N \times M}$ and use the respective discrete norms and operators on this space. In the following, always $u, v, \psi, f \in \mathbb{R}^{N \times M}$ and $\phi, g \in \mathbb{R}^{N \times M \times 2}$.

4.1 TV-H^{-1}-L^2

We consider the problem

$$\min_{u,v} \; \alpha \mathrm{TV}(u) + \frac{\beta}{2}\|v\|^2_{H^{-1}} + \frac{\gamma}{2}\|u^0 - u - v\|^2_2 \qquad (11)$$

which corresponds to the case $p = 2$ in (3). Using the characterization of $\|v\|^2_{H^{-1}}$ from Section 1 and $\nabla^* = -\mathrm{div}$, we obtain $\frac{\beta}{2}\|v\|^2_{H^{-1}} = -\frac{\beta}{2}\langle \Delta^{-1}v, v\rangle$. The associated Fenchel conjugate is given by $\left(\frac{\beta}{2}\|\cdot\|^2_{H^{-1}}\right)^*(\psi) = -\frac{1}{2\beta}\langle \Delta\psi, \psi\rangle$. Dual representations of $\alpha \mathrm{TV}(u)$ and $\frac{\beta}{2}\|v\|^2_{H^{-1}}$ allow us now to restate problem (11) in terms of the convex-concave saddle-point problem

$$\min_{u,v} \max_{\psi,\phi} \; -\langle \nabla u, \phi\rangle - I_{\|\|\cdot\|\|_\infty \leq \alpha}(\phi) + \langle v,\psi\rangle + \frac{1}{2\beta}\langle \Delta\psi,\psi\rangle + \frac{\gamma}{2}\|u^0 - u - v\|^2_2. \qquad (12)$$

Notice, that $F^*(\phi,\psi) = I_{\|\|\cdot\|\|_\infty \leq \alpha}(\phi)$ is convex, $P^*(\phi,\psi) = -\frac{1}{2\beta}\langle \Delta\psi,\psi\rangle$ is convex and differentiable with Lipschitz gradient $\nabla P^*(\phi,\psi) = [0, -\frac{1}{\beta}\Delta\psi]^T$, $Q(u,v) = \frac{\gamma}{2}\|u^0 - u - v\|^2_2$ is convex and differentiable with Lipschitz gradient

$$\nabla Q(u,v) = \gamma \begin{bmatrix} u + v - u^0 \\ u + v - u^0 \end{bmatrix}$$

and the operator $K = \begin{bmatrix} -\nabla & 0 \\ 0 & \mathrm{Id} \end{bmatrix}$ is linear and bounded. Thus, with $G(u,v) = 0$, problem (12) has exactly the form (9). Since $G(u,v) = 0$, we have $\mathrm{prox}_{\tau G} = \mathrm{Id}$. Moreover,
$$\mathrm{prox}_{\sigma F^*}(\phi, \psi) = [\mathrm{proj}_{\|\|\cdot\|\|_\infty \leq \alpha}(\phi), \psi]^T.$$
Also note that $K^* = \begin{bmatrix} \mathrm{div} & 0 \\ 0 & \mathrm{Id} \end{bmatrix}$. All in all, we obtain the iteration

$$\begin{cases} \text{extrapolate } \overline{u}^k, \overline{v}^k, \overline{\phi}^k, \overline{\psi}^k \\ u^{k+1} = \overline{u}^k - \tau(\gamma[\overline{u}^k + \overline{v}^k - u^0] + \mathrm{div}\,\overline{\phi}^k) \\ v^{k+1} = \overline{v}^k - \tau(\gamma[\overline{u}^k + \overline{v}^k - u^0] + \overline{\psi}^k) \\ \phi^{k+1} = \mathrm{proj}_{\|\|\cdot\|\|_\infty \leq \alpha}(\overline{\phi}^k - \sigma\nabla[2u^{k+1} - \overline{u}^k]) \\ \psi^{k+1} = \overline{\psi}^k - \sigma(-\frac{1}{\beta}\Delta\overline{\psi}^k - [2v^{k+1} - \overline{v}^k]) \end{cases} \quad (13)$$

4.2 TV-H^{-1}-L^1

Next, we consider the problem

$$\min_{u,v} \alpha \mathrm{TV}(u) + \tfrac{\beta}{2}\|v\|_{H^{-1}}^2 + \gamma \|u^0 - u - v\|_1. \quad (14)$$

In comparison with (11), we replaced the differentiable L^2-norm data fidelity term by a non-differentiable L^1-norm data fidelity term. Thus, in terms of (9), we choose $G(u,v) = \gamma \|u^0 - u - v\|_1$ and $Q(u,v) = 0$. Hence, also $\nabla Q = 0$. In order to perform the associated iteration, we are in need of the mapping $\mathrm{prox}_{\tau G}$ which is subject of the following Lemma.

Lemma 1. *Let $r = u^0 - u - v$ and $s = \min(1, \max(-1, \frac{r}{2\tau\gamma}))$. Then, it holds*
$$\mathrm{prox}_{\tau G}(u,v) = [u + \tau\gamma s, v + \tau\gamma s]^T.$$

Proof. The proximal mapping can be calculated using
$$\mathrm{prox}_{\tau G}(u,v) = \arg\min_{\tilde{u},\tilde{v}} \tfrac{1}{2}\left\|\begin{pmatrix}u\\v\end{pmatrix} - \begin{pmatrix}\tilde{u}\\\tilde{v}\end{pmatrix}\right\|_2^2 + \tau\gamma \|u^0 - \tilde{u} - \tilde{v}\|_1.$$

A point $(\tilde{u}, \tilde{v})$ is the unique minimizer of this problem if and only if $\tilde{u} = u + \tau\gamma s$ and $\tilde{v} = v + \tau\gamma s$ for some $s \in \mathrm{Sign}(u^0 - \tilde{u} - \tilde{v})$. With r and s as proposed, we have $s \in \mathrm{Sign}(u^0 - [u + \tau\gamma s] - [v + \tau\gamma s])$ and that completes the proof. □

With the help of Lemma 1, we are now able to evaluate the iteration

$$\begin{cases} \text{extrapolate } \overline{u}^k, \overline{v}^k, \overline{\phi}^k, \overline{\psi}^k \\ (u^{k+1}, v^{k+1}) = \mathrm{prox}_{\tau G}(\overline{u}^k - \tau\,\mathrm{div}\,\overline{\phi}^k, \overline{v}^k - \tau\overline{\psi}^k) \\ \phi^{k+1} = \mathrm{proj}_{\|\|\cdot\|\|_\infty \leq \alpha}(\overline{\phi}^k - \sigma\nabla[2u^{k+1} - \overline{u}^k]) \\ \psi^{k+1} = \overline{\psi}^k - \sigma(-\frac{1}{\beta}\Delta\overline{\psi}^k - [2v^{k+1} - \overline{v}^k]). \end{cases}$$

4.3 TV-L^∞-L^1

Last, we consider the problem

$$\min_g \alpha \mathrm{TV}(u) + \|u^0 - u\|_{G',\beta,\gamma} \qquad (15)$$
$$= \min_{u,g} \alpha \mathrm{TV}(u) + \beta \||g\|\|_\infty + \gamma \|u^0 - u - \mathrm{div}\, g\|_1$$

where we use the G'-norm from (7). In terms of our notation and with an appropriate definition of div^{-1}, we can interpret $F_v(v) = \||\mathrm{div}^{-1} v\|\|_\infty$ and $F_w(w) = \|w\|_1$. We model $G(u,g) = \beta \||g\|\|_\infty$, $Q(u,g) = 0$, $F^*(\phi, f) = I_{\||\cdot\|\|_\infty \leq \alpha}(\phi) + I_{\|\cdot\|_\infty \leq \gamma}(f) + \langle u^0, f\rangle$, $P^*(\phi, f) = 0$,

$$K = \begin{bmatrix} -\nabla & 0 \\ \mathrm{Id} & \mathrm{div} \end{bmatrix} \quad \text{and} \quad K^* = \begin{bmatrix} \mathrm{div} & \mathrm{Id} \\ 0 & -\nabla \end{bmatrix},$$

respectively, to make the framework (9) applicable. Thus, we obtain the iteration

$$\begin{cases} \text{extrapolate } \bar{u}^k, \bar{g}^k, \bar{\phi}^k, \bar{f}^k \\ u^{k+1} = \bar{u}^k - \tau(\mathrm{div}\, \bar{\phi}^k + \bar{f}^k) \\ g^{k+1} = \mathrm{prox}_{\tau\beta\||\cdot\|\|_\infty}(\bar{g}^k + \tau\nabla \bar{f}^k) \\ \phi^{k+1} = \mathrm{proj}_{\||\cdot\|\|_\infty \leq \alpha}(\bar{\phi}^k - \sigma\nabla[2u^{k+1} - \bar{u}^k]) \\ f^{k+1} = \mathrm{proj}_{\|\cdot\|_\infty \leq \gamma}(\bar{f}^k + \sigma[(2u^{k+1} - \bar{u}^k) + \mathrm{div}(2g^{k+1} - \bar{g}^k)] - \sigma u^0). \end{cases}$$

5 Results

In this section we present results on cartoon-texture-noise decomposition by means of the three methods proposed in Section 4. We used the well known Barbara image since it contains nice textured parts. We considered the images with gray values in the interval $[0, 1]$. To show the texture and noise parts we

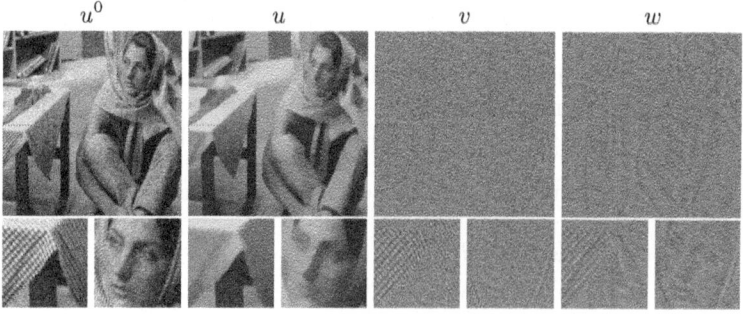

Fig. 1. Cartoon-texture decomposition with TV-H^{-1}-L^2. Top left: original image with additive Gaussian noise: $\alpha = 0.15$, $\beta = 0.5$, $\gamma = 1$.

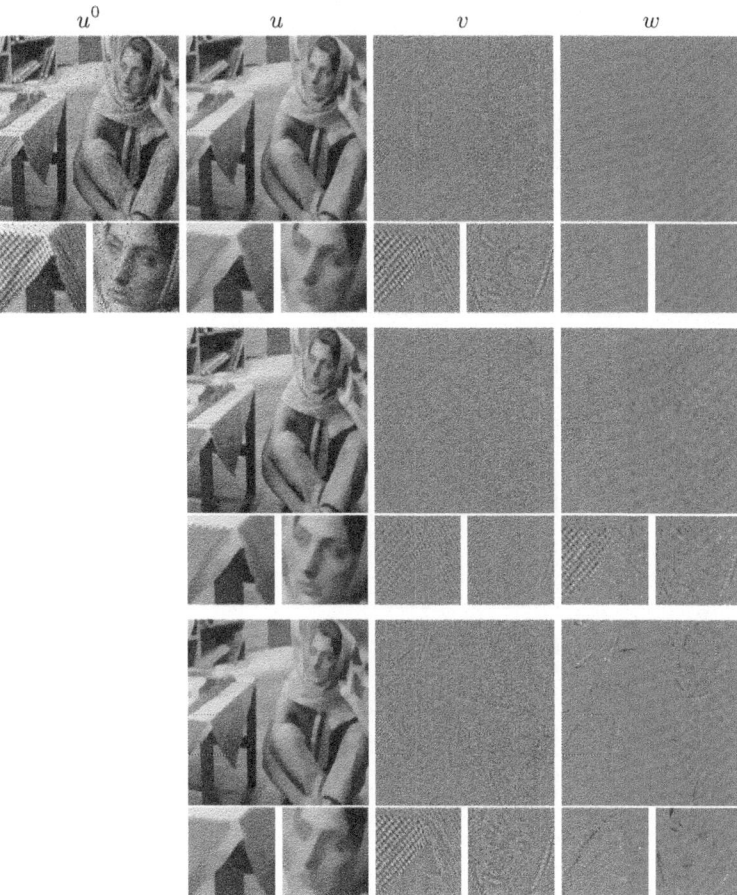

Fig. 2. Cartoon-texture decomposition with TV-H^{-1}-L^1. Top left: original image with impulsive noise, top row: $\alpha = 1.5$, $\beta = 3$, $\gamma = 1$, middle row: $\alpha = 1.5$, $\beta = 15$, $\gamma = 1$, bottom row: $\alpha = 3$, $\beta = 3$, $\gamma = 1$.

added an offset of 0.5 to these images to make the oscillations around zero visible and comparable. However, for the impulsive noise in Figures 2 and 3 this introduces a slight cut-off, since the noise has largest and smallest values of magnitude about 0.6.

For the TV-H^{-1}-L^2 method we added a small amount of Gaussian noise and applied the algorithm from Section 4.1 and tuned parameters α, β and γ by hand to obtain an optimal separation. Figure 1 shows the result which is not encouraging since there is a severe mixture of noise and structure in the noise part w. This can be explained as follows: The TV term produces a cartoon like approximation u and the remaining part, containing texture and noise, is separated by the two other penalty terms. By means of the Fourier transform we can express the noise penalty simply as $F_w(w) = \frac{\gamma}{2}\int |\hat{w}(\omega)|^2 d\omega$ while the penalty

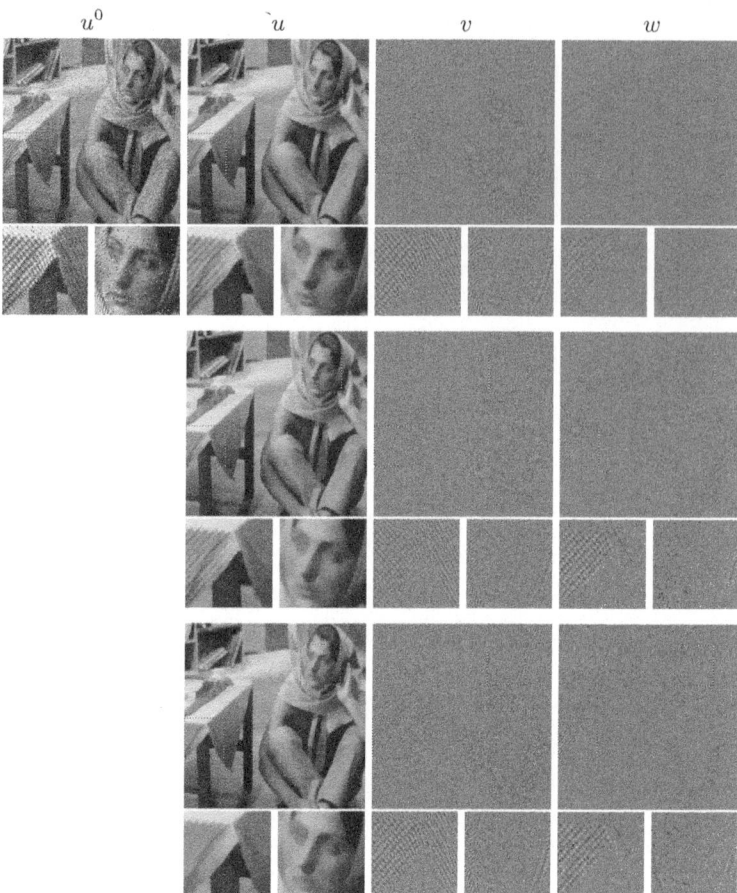

Fig. 3. Cartoon-texture decomposition with TV-L^∞-L^1. Top left: original image with impulsive noise, top row: $\alpha = 0.002$, $\beta = 10$, $\gamma = 0.001$, middle row: $\alpha = 0.0023$, $\beta = 50$, $\gamma = 0.001$, bottom row: $\alpha = 0.003$, $\beta = 10$, $\gamma = 0.001$.

for the texture is $F_v(v) = \frac{\beta}{2} \int \frac{|\hat{v}(\omega)|^2}{|\omega|^2} d\omega$. Roughly speaking, this gives a linear decomposition of $u^0 - u$ while the noise part w captures the low-frequency part and the texture part v captures the high-frequency contributions. This explains the poor decomposition obtained in Figure 1.

For the method TV-H^{-1}-L^1 we added impulsive noise (with a strength of 3%) and again tuned parameters by hand. As Figure 2 shows, this leads to a much better, but still not perfect, separation of noise and texture. By varying the parameters, one can shift parts of the non-cartoon image from the texture to the noise component. However, it can be seen that different textures behave differently: The checkered blanket appears in the noise part before the stripes of the clothes do.

For the method TV-L^∞-L^1 we also used impulsive noise of the same strength as in the previous example. One sees that one gets more of the noise into the noise part while also some of the texture starts to appear in the noise component well before the texture part is noise free. But the texture parts that appear in the noise component are precisely the ones for which a mass-transport to cancel out the oscillation is fairly expensive and treating these parts as sparse outliers is cheaper.

References

1. Rudin, L.I., Osher, S., Fatemi, E.: Nonlinear total variation based noise removal algorithms. Physica D **60**, 259–268 (1992)
2. Meyer, Y.: Oscillating Patterns in Image Processing and Nonlinear Evolution Equations, vol. 22(University Lecture Series). AMS (2001)
3. Vese, L.A., Osher, S.J.: Modeling textures with total variation minimization and oscillating patterns in image processing. Journal of Scientific Computing **19**(1–3), December 2003
4. Osher, S., Solé, A., Vese, L.: Image decomposition and restoration using total variation minimization and the H^{-1} norm. SIAM Multiscale Modeling and Simulation **1**(3), 349–370 (2003)
5. Chambolle, A., Pock, T.: A first-order primal-dual algorithm for convex problems with applications to imaging. Journal of Mathematical Imaging and Vision **40**, 120–145 (2011)
6. Lorenz, D., Pock, T.: An inertial forward-backward algorithm for monotone inclusions. Journal of Mathematical Imaging and Vision (2014)
7. Lellmann, J., Lorenz, D.A., Schönlieb, C.B., Valkonen, T.: Imaging with Kantorovich-Rubinstein discrepancy. SIAM Journal on Imaging Sciences, July 2014 (to appear). arXiv
8. Kaipio, J., Somersalo, E.: Statistical and computational inverse problems. Springer-Verlag, New York (2005)
9. Chan, T.F., Esedoglu, S.: Aspects of total variation regularized L^1 function approximation. SIAM Journal on Applied Mathematics **65**(5), 1817–1837 (2005)
10. Clason, C., Jin, B., Kunisch, K.: A semismooth Newton method for L^1 data fitting with automatic choice of regularization parameters and noise calibration. SIAM Journal on Imaging Sciences **3**(2), 199–231 (2010)
11. Clason, C.: L^∞ fitting for inverse problems with uniform noise. Inverse Problems **28**(10), 104007 (2012)
12. Bredies, K., Kunisch, K., Pock, T.: Total generalized variation. SIAM Journal on Imaging Sciences **3**(3), 492–526 (2010)
13. Monge, G.: Mémoire sur la théorie des déblais et des remblais. De l'Imprimerie Royale (1781)
14. Kantorovič, L.V.: On the translocation of masses. C. R. (Doklady) Acad. Sci. URSS (N.S.) **37**, 199–201 (1942)
15. Vasershtein, L.N.: Markov processes over denumerable products of spaces describing large system of automata. Problemy Peredači Informacii **5**(3), 64–72 (1969)
16. Kantorovič, L.V., Rubinšteĭn, G.Š.: On a functional space and certain extremum problems. Doklady Akademii Nauk SSSR **115**, 1058–1061 (1957)

Compressing Images with Diffusion- and Exemplar-Based Inpainting

Pascal Peter[(✉)] and Joachim Weickert

Mathematical Image Analysis Group, Faculty of Mathematics and Computer Science,
Saarland University, Campus E1.7, 66041 Saarbrücken, Germany
{peter,weickert}@mia.uni-saarland.de

Abstract. Diffusion-based image compression methods can surpass state-of-the-art transform coders like JPEG 2000 for cartoon-like images. However, they are not well-suited for highly textured image content. Recently, advances in exemplar-based inpainting have made it possible to reconstruct images with non-local methods from sparse known data. In our work we compare the performance of such exemplar-based and diffusion-based inpainting algorithms, dependent on the type of image content. We use our insights to construct a hybrid compression codec that combines the strengths of both approaches. Experiments demonstrate that our novel method offers significant advantages over state-of-the-art diffusion-based methods on textured image data and can compete with transform coders.

Keywords: Exemplar-based inpainting · Diffusion-based inpainting · Image compression · Texture

1 Introduction

From the initial compression approach with diffusion proposed by Galić et al. [9], a whole class of diffusion-based codecs has evolved during the last years. The R-EED codec by Schmaltz et al. [23] has demonstrated that diffusion coders can beat JPEG [18] and JPEG 2000 [25] on greyscale images. Peter and Weickert have shown in [20] that this is also possible on colour data.

The key element to the success of these methods is the ability of edge-enhancing anisotropic diffusion (EED) [26] to reconstruct images from sparse pixel data. Unfortunately, EED is not well-suited for reproducing fine-scale textures from small amounts of data. This implies that the performance of diffusion-based algorithms degrades with increasing amount of texture content in the original images. In such cases, transform-based coders still provide superior results.

In 1999, Efros and Leung [7] pioneered exemplar-based inpainting for the purpose of extending images and filling in missing or corrupted image parts. More recently, Facciolo et al. [8] have proposed exemplar-based inpainting methods that are suited for sparse known data. In our work we explore the potential of this sparse exemplar-based inpainting for image compression.

Our Contribution. We assess the suitability of exemplar-based inpainting for image compression and compare it to diffusion-based inpainting. Following the results of this analysis, we construct a novel compression codec that combines the strengths of both approaches while minimising the effect of their drawbacks. In our experiments on well-known test images we demonstrate that this hybrid inpainting approach can beat established diffusion-based methods and is competitive to transform codecs also for images with rich texture.

Related Work. Regarding diffusion-based compression, we rely on the anisotropic approach by Schmalz et al. [22,23]. While our novel codec is the only diffusion-based method that deals specifically with textured images, there are PDE-based coders dedicated to other classes of data such as cartoon images [16], 3-D data [19], or depth maps [10,12,13].

The exemplar-based inpainting on sparse images by Facciolo et al. [8] that we use in our paper is related to a long line of classic patch-based approaches, starting with texture synthesis methods like the influental work of Efros and Leung [7]. Since a full review of the field is beyond the scope of our paper, we focus on selected publications that are related to our own work and refer to Arias et al. [2] for an in-depth review.

During the last decade, the concept of combining structure adaptive inpainting with exemplar-based ideas has been explored in several different directions. The approach of Bertalmío et al. [3] comes closest to our method since it also employs an explicit decomposition into a cartoon and a texture image. The cartoon reconstruction relies on an inpainting process that propagates information along isophotes. Patch-based inpainting restores missing parts of the texture image. However, in contrast to our paper, their decomposition is additive. This doubles the amount of original data, which is disadvantageous for compression.

Many patch-based approaches incorporate the image structure as additional guidance information. Sun et al. [24] perform patch-based texture reconstruction along manually specified curves, while Criminisi et al. [6] prioritise the reconstruction of missing image points in such a way that existing image structures are continued. In the work of Cao et al. [4], level lines extracted from a simplified version of the image are the guidance feature for exemplar-based inpainting. A different approach is pursued by Arias et al. [2] who include gradient information in a variational model for exemplar-based inpainting.

All aforementioned publications focus on image inpainting. In regards to actual compression, there are two related approaches that modify existing transform-based coders with exemplar-based inpainting. Rane et al. [21] propose a scheme that removes selected JPEG blocks and reconstructs them either with the method of Efros and Leung [7] or structure inpainting. The method of Liu et al. [14] focuses on removing visual redundancy in transform coders like H.264 or JPEG without minimising the pixel-wise error. To this end, the image is decomposed into edge-regions that are reconstructed with a combination of structure propagation and exemplar-based inpainting and texture regions that are synthesised with purely patch-based methods. Moreover, there are distantly related methods from the area of compressed sensing. These dictionary approaches (e.g. [1,11]) use databases of image prototypes or patches for reconstruction instead of relying on partially known data like the exemplar-based methods. Aharon et al. [1] also explicitly propose compression as one application of their approach.

Organisation of the Paper. First we explain the concepts of the two inpainting techniques that we combine in our paper: Section 2 covers diffusion-based inpainting, while exemplar-based inpainting is reviewed in Section 3. In Section 4 we assess the strengths and weaknesses of both approaches with respect to image compression. From these conclusions we motivate a novel hybrid compression scheme in Section 5 and analyse its performance in Section 6. We conclude our paper with a summary and outlook on future work in Section 7.

2 Diffusion-Based Inpainting

Let us consider an image $f : \Omega \to \mathbb{R}$ that maps a rectangular image domain Ω to the corresponding grey values. In image compression, diffusion-based inpainting is used to reconstruct an image from a small amount of known data. Known data is only provided on the subset $K \subset \Omega$, the so-called *inpainting mask*.

The role of the diffusion process is to propagate the known information to the *inpainting domain* $\Omega \setminus K$. Thereby, the missing parts are filled in. This process of data propagation follows the partial differential equation (PDE)

$$\partial_t u = \text{div}(\boldsymbol{D}\boldsymbol{\nabla} u) \quad \text{on } \Omega \setminus K, \tag{1}$$

with reflecting boundary conditions on $\partial \Omega$. Note that the known data on K imposes Dirichlet boundary conditions on the PDE. This implies that the diffusion process converges to a nontrivial steady-state for $t \to \infty$ which yields the reconstruction of the image. Experiments show that the reconstruction does not depend on the initialisation in the inpainting domain $\Omega \setminus K$.

The most important part of the diffusion equation (1) is the diffusion tensor $\boldsymbol{D} \in \mathbb{R}^{2 \times 2}$. It guides the diffusion process in terms of its eigenvalues λ_1 and λ_2 that specify the amount of diffusion in the direction of the corresponding eigenvectors $\boldsymbol{v}_1$ and $\boldsymbol{v}_2$. Thus, the choice of $\boldsymbol{D}$ is essential for the quality of the reconstruction.

For the task of image compression, Schmaltz et al. [22] have shown that edge-enhancing anisotropic diffusion (EED) [26] is particularly well-suited. EED uses an anisotropic, structure-adaptive diffusion tensor of the form

$$\boldsymbol{D} := \lambda_1(\boldsymbol{\nabla} u_\sigma) \boldsymbol{v}_1 \boldsymbol{v}_1^\top + \lambda_2 \boldsymbol{v}_2 \boldsymbol{v}_2^\top, \tag{2}$$

$$\boldsymbol{v}_1 \parallel \boldsymbol{\nabla} u_\sigma, \quad \lambda_1(\boldsymbol{\nabla} u_\sigma) := g(|\boldsymbol{\nabla} u_\sigma|^2), \tag{3}$$

$$\boldsymbol{v}_2 \perp \boldsymbol{\nabla} u_\sigma, \quad \lambda_2 := 1, \tag{4}$$

where $u_\sigma := K_\sigma * u$ denotes a convolution of the evolving image u with a Gaussian K_σ of standard deviation σ. The tensor design in Eq. (2) implies that diffusion *across* edges is inhibited by the Charbonnier diffusivity [5]

$$g(s^2) := \frac{1}{\sqrt{1 + s^2/\lambda^2}} \tag{5}$$

with some contrast parameter $\lambda > 0$. Full diffusion *along* edges is achieved with a constant second eigenvalue $\lambda_2 := 1$. Optimising both the positions of the known data, i.e. the inpainting mask K, as well as the contrast parameter λ can improve the reconstruction quality.

Experiments in [22] show that the Gaussian convolution with K_σ in Eq. (2) plays an important role for the application of EED in image compression. It propagates structural information into the neighbourhood of each pixel and thereby allows reconstruction of edges from a very sparse inpainting mask. In EED-based compression codecs, the set K therefore usually contains scattered, isolated known pixels.

3 Exemplar-Based Inpainting

The so-called *non-local inpainting* (NLI) approach of Facciolo et al. [8] follows the core idea of all patch-based methods: Missing information is filled in by exchanging information between image patches. However, in contrast to other algorithms from the field, it allows inpainting from sparse data. Therefore, we can compare it to the inpainting capabilities of EED from Section 2. For the sake of comprehensibility, we only discuss a special case of the flexible NLI framework: We have chosen algorithm AB with patch-wise non-local means from [8] for the specific task at hand.

Let us consider the same inpainting problem as in the previous section, namely finding a reconstruction u of the missing data on $\Omega \setminus K$ from the sparse known data on $K \subset \Omega$. In essence, NLI reconstructs u by minimising a patch similarity function V between pairs of image patches. It forces unknown pixel values in one patch to be similar to known values in the other patch. To this end, consider two disk-shaped patches centred in image points x and x', respectively. The similarity function V is defined as the weighted squared difference

$$V(x, x') = \int_D g(x, x', y)\Big(u(x + y) - u(x' + y)\Big)^2 dy. \qquad (6)$$

Here, D is a disk around the origin, and y a coordinate relative to the respective patch centre. A common practice in patch-based methods is to rescale the individual pixel differences $u(x + y) - u(x' + y)$ with Gaussian weights that reflect descending importance with the distance to the patch centres. However, in NLI, the weights g additionally account for the fact that, given a sparse inpainting mask, both patches can contain similar amounts of known data. Thus, a mutual exchange of information can be beneficial. The weights are defined as

$$g(x, x', y) = \frac{K_\sigma(y)}{\rho(x, x')}(\chi_K(x + y) + \chi_K(x' + y)), \qquad (7)$$

where $\rho(x, x')$ is a normalisation term that ensures $\int_D g(x, x', y) dy = 1$ and K_σ is a Gaussian with standard deviation σ. The characteristic function χ_K of the set of known data indicates where similarities between patches should be enforced.

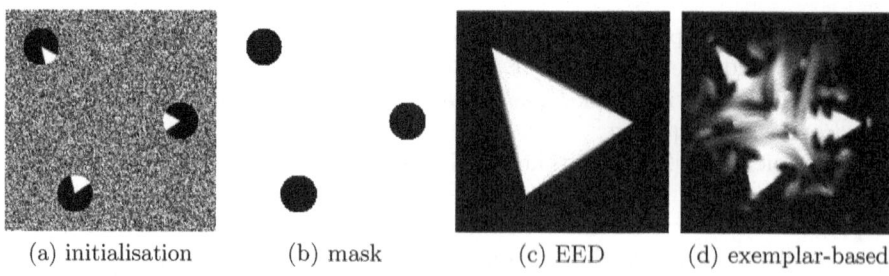

(a) initialisation (b) mask (c) EED (d) exemplar-based

Fig. 1. Experiment: Structure Propagation Known data is only given at black locations in the mask. EED ($\lambda = 0.01$, $\sigma = 4$) continues the edge structures into the inpainting domain and reconstructs an almost perfect triangle. The exemplar-based method ($h = 100$) propagates structure only locally and creates copies of structure.

Let $\boldsymbol{x}_1 := \boldsymbol{x} + \boldsymbol{y}$ denote an image point from the first patch and $\boldsymbol{x}_2 := \boldsymbol{x}' + \boldsymbol{y}$ the corresponding point in the second patch. If both points are unknown, i.e. not contained in K, g becomes 0 and thus, no information exchange takes place. If at least one of the two points $\boldsymbol{x}_1$ and $\boldsymbol{x}_2$ is known, we have $g > 0$ and thus V enforces similarity between those two pixels.

The second important ingredient of NLI is the decision, for which pairs of patches the similarity function V should be minimised. To this end, Facciolo et al. introduce a patch similarity weight function w and minimise the energy

$$E(u, w) = \frac{1}{h} \int_\Omega \int_K w(\boldsymbol{x}, \boldsymbol{x}') V(\boldsymbol{x}, \boldsymbol{x}') \, d\boldsymbol{x} \, d\boldsymbol{x}' - \int_\Omega H(\boldsymbol{x}, w) \, d\boldsymbol{x}, \quad (8)$$

$$\text{s.t.} \int_K w(\boldsymbol{x}, \boldsymbol{x}') \, d\boldsymbol{x}' = 1. \quad (9)$$

Optimal weights w minimise the weighted total patch error according to V while maximising the entropy

$$H(\boldsymbol{x}, w) = -\int_K w(\boldsymbol{x}, \boldsymbol{x}') \log w(\boldsymbol{x}, \boldsymbol{x}') \, d\boldsymbol{x}'. \quad (10)$$

For a given u, the patch similarity weights w impose a Gaussian-like weighting of the patch differences $V(\boldsymbol{x}, \boldsymbol{x}')$:

$$w(\boldsymbol{x}, \boldsymbol{x}') = \exp\left(-\frac{1}{h} V(\boldsymbol{x}, \boldsymbol{x}')\right). \quad (11)$$

Thus, the parameter $h \in \mathbb{R}$ from Eq. (8) steers the standard deviation of the Gaussian weights w. In practice, the reconstruction u is found by alternating minimisation of u and w.

4 Strengths and Weaknesses of the Inpainting Techniques

In the following sections we assess the advantages and drawbacks of diffusion and exemplar-based inpainting in the context of image compression. To this end, we

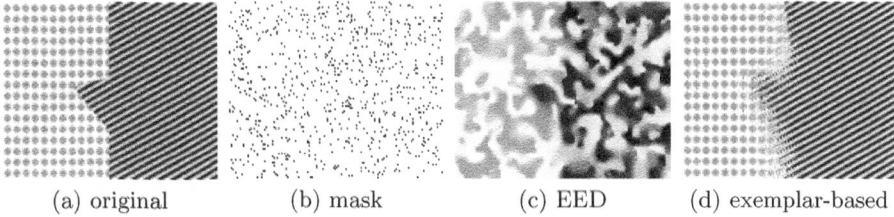

(a) original (b) mask (c) EED (d) exemplar-based

Fig. 2. Experiment: Texture. Known data from the original image is only given at black locations in the mask. EED with $\sigma = 0.8$ and $\lambda = 0.9$ completely fails to reconstruct the texture and creates a coarser pattern instead. Exemplar-based inpainting ($h = 150$) reconstructs regular texture very well, but has problems at the interface between textures.

demonstrate specific properties with simple synthetic examples and discuss their implications for practical purposes.

Let us first consider the capabilities of both algorithms in respect to structure propagation. To this end, we consider a variation of the well-known Kanizsa triangle that was used in [22] to demonstrate the capabilities of EED. For a human observer, the known data in Fig. 1(a) suggests that three corners of a triangle are given here, since human perception tends to continue sharp edges.

EED is able to preserve sharp edges and propagates image structure due to the locally adaptive diffusion tensor. Therefore, with adequate parameter choices, it is possible to match the expected reconstruction very well (see Fig. 1(c)). In contrast, exemplar-based inpainting continues structures only in close vicinity to the known data (Fig. 1(d)). In regions of the inpainting domain where known data is far away, structures are copied and multiplied.

For image compression, this behaviour implies that EED is well-suited to reconstruct coarse-scale image features from sparse known data, if they consist of mostly homogeneous areas that are separated by high contrast edges. Exemplar-based inpainting, however, tends to create visually distracting artefacts in such a setting. The reconstructions of the test image *barbara* in Fig. 3(a) and (b) illustrate the practical effects well. For example in the face region, exemplar-based inpainting repeats vertical structures of the hood in the cheeks, while EED produces a much more convincing reconstruction. Similar effects can be observed throughout the whole image.

In a second synthetic experiment we consider the reconstruction of textured areas. Fig. 2 displays the test image *interface* from [8], a representative for another extreme type of image content, namely repetitive texture. Here, EED completely fails to reconstruct the texture in a satisfying way. If an isolated region like e.g. a grey dot in the left hand side of the image is not represented by several known pixels that encode both its grey value and its shape, EED has no chance to recreate it. In contrast, exemplar-based inpainting benefits from its tendency to copy structure and create regular patterns. Its reconstruction in Fig. 2(d) is fairly close to the original, except for the sharp boundary between both repetitive patterns.

Fig. 3. Reconstruction of the image *barbara* with EED (a) and NLI (b) from the same known data. The reconstructions correspond to intermediate results from steps 1 and 2 of the hybrid algorithm for a compression rate of $\approx 18:1$. The block decomposition (c) with $b = 48$ indicates where EED (black) and NLI (white) yield better results.

In practical compression applications, EED struggles with repetitive small-scale structure even when a lot of known data is given (e.g. Barbara's trousers in Fig. 3(a)). Therefore, compression algorithms that purely use EED for reconstruction have to store textures almost verbatim to achieve a good reconstruction. NLI produces a visually much more pleasing texture inpainting (see Fig. 3(b)) that is also close to the ground truth in regard to quantitative error measures. Therefore, a sparse inpainting mask in combination with NLI inpainting can potentially be used for compression.

5 A Hybrid Compression Algorithm for Textured Images

Block Decomposition. The core idea of our hybrid algorithm is to combine the strengths of diffusion- and exemplar-based inpainting by decomposing the image into EED and NLI blocks. From a common set of known data, EED blocks are reconstructed with diffusion inpainting and NLI blocks with exemplar-based inpainting. Shared known data for both methods offers two distinct advantages: *storage efficiency* and *direct decomposition*. Since the inpainting mask is only stored once, the only overhead generated by employing two different inpainting methods is the block decomposition and the respective model parameters. In addition, no a priori method for texture/cartoon decomposition is needed. Blocks can be directly classified as EED and NLI blocks by comparing the corresponding reconstructions to the original file, which is (in contrast to the inpainting case) available during compression.

Point Selection and Storage. In the previous sections we have only discussed diffusion and patch-based ideas in an inpainting context, where the inpainting mask $K \subset \Omega$ is already known. For compression, in addition to the right reconstruction method, also a good inpainting mask must be chosen and stored efficiently.

To this end, we employ a rectangular subdivision technique that proves to be successful in the R-EED codec [22,23]. It limits the choice of the known data positions K to a rectangular adaptive grid that can be represented by a binary decision tree. We iteratively refine this grid by adding known pixels in image regions, where the local reconstruction error with EED inpainting exceeds a given threshold. This strategy yields a mask that is optimised for a good diffusion-based reconstruction and efficient storage in form of a binary tree. As soon as the mask is known, we apply a so-called brightness optimisation step: Introducing errors to the small amount of known pixel values can improve the reconstruction quality in the large inpainting domain $\Omega \setminus K$. For more details, we refer to [22]. The optimised grey values are finally quantised and stored with the entropy coder PAQ [15].

Our goal to create a hybrid algorithm requires some modifications to this point selection strategy. Since the subdivision grid adapts to the reconstruction abilities of EED, the point density in an R-EED inpainting mask is low in homogeneous regions, medium near coarse scale edges and very high in textured areas. Since our goal is to reconstruct homogeneous areas and sharp edges with EED and textures with exemplar-based inpainting, this point distribution is not ideal. In particular, textured areas are over-represented in the inpainting mask at the cost of more coarsely quantised grey values. Therefore, we limit the depth N of the binary tree and by that also the minimum grid size of the adaptive inpainting mask.

Avoiding Block Artefacts. For compression algorithms that use block decomposition steps, there is always the danger of visually very distracting discontinuities at block boundaries. In order to keep such effects to a minimum and simultaneously improve the overall reconstruction quality, we propose a modified diffusion-reconstruction in the decompression step. In addition to the known data on K, we also consider the reconstructed NLI blocks as Dirichlet boundary data for the final EED reconstruction. This ensures smoother transitions between NLI and EED blocks and can even improve the EED block reconstructions due to the good approximation of additional known data.

Compression Algorithm. The complete compression pipeline for our hybrid scheme consists of five steps.

1. **Depth-Limited Subdivision**: Perform rectangular subdivision with a maximum tree depth N to avoid oversampling in highly textured areas. Create a preliminary diffusion reconstruction of the whole image with EED.
2. **Exemplar-Based Inpainting**: Reconstruct the image with NLI and the inpainting mask acquired in the previous step. In order to provide a good prior for structure propagation in non-texture areas to the exemplar-based method, we initialise the inpainting domain $\Omega \setminus K$ with the diffusion reconstruction from Step 1.
3. **Block Decomposition**: Compute a block decomposition: If the mean square error (MSE) of the diffusion reconstruction is lower than the MSE of the exemplar-based inpainting in a given block, consider it to be an EED block,

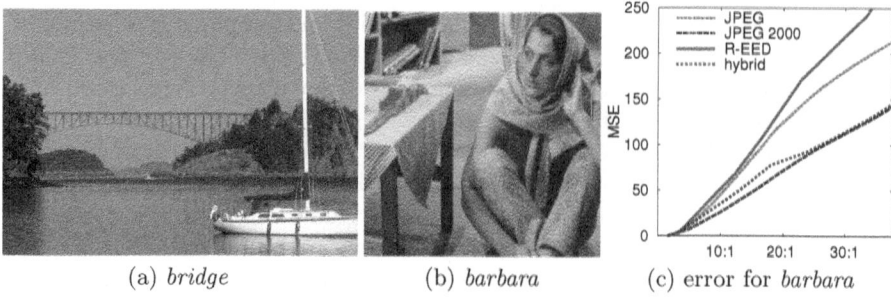

Fig. 4. (a)+(b) Original images *bridge* (No. 22090 in the Berkeley database [17]) and *barbara*. (c) Error comparison of *barbara* at different compression rates.

otherwise mark it as an NLI block. Optimising the number b of blocks in x- and y-direction can improve the overall compression quality.

4. **Encoding**: Store the known data in a modified R-EED file format (see [22]) with the number of blocks in the file header. Encode the block decomposition row-wise as a sequence of binary flags for each block (1: EED block, 0: texture block). Here, the context mixing method PAQ [15] yields the best results by encoding the binary tree, block decomposition and grey values jointly.

Decompression Algorithm. Decompression comes down to three straightforward inpainting steps, since the compressed file provides all parameters, known data and the cartoon/texture-decomposition.

1. **Diffusion-Based Reconstruction**: Extract the inpainting mask and R-EED parameters from the compressed file and reconstruct all missing data on $\Omega \setminus K$ with EED inpainting.
2. **Exemplar-Based Reconstruction**: Initialise $\Omega \setminus K$ with the result from step 1 and perform an NLI reconstruction of the inpainting domain.
3. **Final Inpainting**: Reconstruct the EED blocks with EED inpainting. Use the data of the inpainting mask Ω as well as the reconstructed NLI blocks as known data to improve the final reconstruction.

6 Experiments

In the following we evaluate the performance of our hybrid approach in comparison to the R-EED codec and the transform-based coders JPEG and JPEG 2000. For the first step in our hybrid algorithm and the results of R-EED we use the same reference implementation with PAQ for entropy coding. We optimise all model parameters as described in [23]. In our R-EED experiments, we allow larger tree depths N than in the depth-restricted hybrid step wherever this improves the result. For the implementation of NLI in our hybrid scheme we use the publicly available reference implementation of Facciolo et al. [8]. In particular, we apply the fast approximation to the variational NLI scheme AB

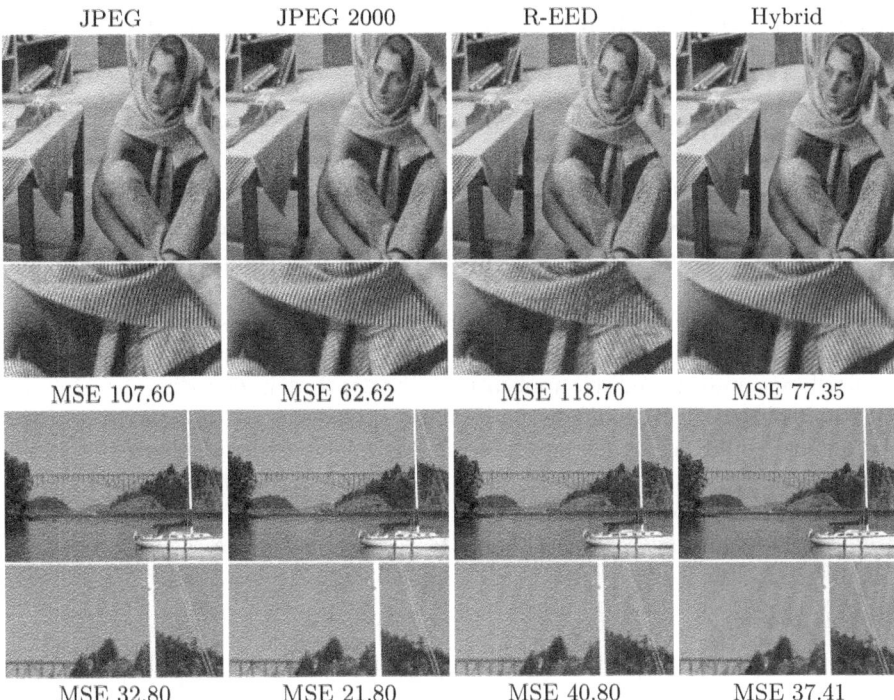

Fig. 5. Top rows: Results for *barbara* with ratio ≈ 18 : 1. The hybrid algorithm uses the upper tree limit $N = 16$, block parameter $b = 48$ and the NLI parameter $h = 100$.
Bottom rows: Results for *bridge* with ratio ≈ 19 : 1. The hybrid algorithm uses the upper tree limit $N = 16$, the block size $b = 62$ and the NLI parameter $h = 25$.

that is referred to as algorithm O in [8]. All JPEG and JPEG 2000 images were created with the converter from ImageMagick 6.8.3-6 2013-03-04 Q16.

The results on the test image *barbara* in Fig. 4(c) and Fig. 5 demonstrate that on images with significant amounts of regular texture content, the hybrid scheme offers a significant quality gain over R-EED. R-EED stores some of the texture almost completely as known data (e.g. in the trouser region) and fails to reconstruct other parts completely (e.g. parts of the hood and tablecloth). Depending on the compression rate, the hybrid algorithm improves the mean square error (MSE) by more then 50% and is visually much more compelling. It also surpasses JPEG quantitatively by a large margin and does not suffer from similarly obvious artefacts. For compression rates larger than 25:1, the hybrid algorithm is quantitatively on par with JPEG 2000. While is not able to beat JPEG 2000, yet, it is the first time that a diffusion-based algorithm achieves comparable results on images with such a high amount of texture.

On images with irregular texture, e.g. *bridge* from Fig. 4(a), the quality gain of the hybrid algorithm over R-EED is less significant, but can still reach around 10% depending on the compression rate. While the image quality is quantitatively worse than JPEG, it is subjectively better due to the absence of block artefacts, especially in zoom-ins.

7 Conclusion

With the first combination of diffusion-based and exemplar-based inpainting from sparse data, textured images can be compressed efficiently. Our hybrid algorithm uses the full spectrum of inpainting ideas for compression while keeping the resulting overhead small. This is an important step towards closing the gap between the widely accepted general purpose encoders JPEG and JPEG 2000 and diffusion-based methods that have thus far shown their advantages primarily in more specialised applications like depth-map encoding.

For future work it would be particularly interesting to investigate how far the quality could be further improved if exemplar-based inpainting is treated equally with EED instead of using it as a post processing step. In particular, a lot of additional potential lies in optimising the choice of known data for a good trade-off between quality in EED and NLI reconstructions instead.

References

1. Aharon, M., Elad, M., Bruckstein, A.: K-SVD: An algorithm for designing overcomplete dictionaries for sparse representation. IEEE Transactions on Signal Processing **54**(11), 4311–4322 (2006)
2. Arias, P., Facciolo, G., Caselles, V., Sapiro, G.: A variational framework for exemplar-based image inpainting. International Journal of Computer Vision **93**(3), 319–347 (2011)
3. Bertalmio, M., Vese, L., Sapiro, G., Osher, S.: Simultaneous structure and texture image inpainting. IEEE Transactions on Image Processing **12**(8), 882–889 (2003)
4. Cao, F., Gousseau, Y., Masnou, S., Pérez, P.: Geometrically guided exemplar-based inpainting. SIAM Journal on Imaging Sciences **4**(4), 1143–1179 (2011)
5. Charbonnier, P., Blanc-Féraud, L., Aubert, G., Barlaud, M.: Deterministic edge-preserving regularization in computed imaging. IEEE Transactions on Image Processing **6**(2), 298–311 (1997)
6. Criminisi, A., Pérez, P., Toyama, K.: Region filling and object removal by exemplar-based image inpainting. IEEE Transactions on Image Processing **13**(9), 1200–1212 (2004)
7. Efros, A.A., Leung, T.K.: Texture synthesis by non-parametric sampling. In: Proc. Seventh IEEE International Conference on Computer Vision, Corfu, vol. 2, pp. 1033–1038, September 1999
8. Facciolo, G., Arias, P., Caselles, V., Sapiro, G.: Exemplar-based interpolation of sparsely sampled images. In: Cremers, D., Boykov, Y., Blake, A., Schmidt, F.R. (eds.) EMMCVPR 2009. LNCS, vol. 5681, pp. 331–344. Springer, Heidelberg (2009)
9. Galić, I., Weickert, J., Welk, M., Bruhn, A., Belyaev, A., Seidel, H.-P.: Towards PDE-based image compression. In: Paragios, N., Faugeras, O., Chan, T., Schnörr, C. (eds.) VLSM 2005. LNCS, vol. 3752, pp. 37–48. Springer, Heidelberg (2005)
10. Gautier, J., Meur, O.L., Guillemot, C.: Efficient depth map compression based on lossless edge coding and diffusion. In: Proc. 29th Picture Coding Symposium, Krakow, Poland, pp. 81–84, May 2012

11. Hays, J., Efros, A.A.: Scene completion using millions of photographs. ACM Transactions on Graphics **26**(3), 4 (2007)
12. Hoffmann, S., Mainberger, M., Weickert, J., Puhl, M.: Compression of depth maps with segment-based homogeneous diffusion. In: Kuijper, A., Bredies, K., Pock, T., Bischof, H. (eds.) SSVM 2013. LNCS, vol. 7893, pp. 319–330. Springer, Heidelberg (2013)
13. Li, Y., Sjostrom, M., Jennehag, U., Olsson, R.: A scalable coding approach for high quality depth image compression. In: 3DTV-Conference: The True Vision - Capture, Transmission and Display of 3D Video, Zurich, Switzerland, pp. 1–4, October 2012
14. Liu, D., Sun, X., Wu, F., Li, S., Zhang, Y.Q.: Image compression with edge-based inpainting. IEEE Transactions on Circuits, Systems and Video Technology **17**(10), 1273–1286 (2007)
15. Mahoney, M.: Adaptive weighing of context models for lossless data compression. Tech. Rep. CS-2005-16, Florida Institute of Technology, Melbourne, Florida, December 2005
16. Mainberger, M., Bruhn, A., Weickert, J., Forchhammer, S.: Edge-based compression of cartoon-like images with homogeneous diffusion. Pattern Recognition **44**(9), 1859–1873 (2011)
17. Martin, D., Fowlkes, C., Tal, D., Malik, J.: A database of human segmented natural images and its application to evaluating segmentation algorithms and measuring ecological statistics. In: Proc. Eigth International Conference on Computer Vision, Vancouver, Canada, pp. 416–423, July 2001
18. Pennebaker, W.B., Mitchell, J.L.: JPEG: Still Image Data Compression Standard. Springer, New York (1992)
19. Peter, P.: Three-dimensional data compression with anisotropic diffusion. In: Weickert, J., Hein, M., Schiele, B. (eds.) GCPR 2013. LNCS, vol. 8142, pp. 231–236. Springer, Heidelberg (2013)
20. Peter, P., Weickert, J.: Colour image compression with anisotropic diffusion. In: Proc. 21st IEEE International Conference on Image Processing, Paris, France, October 2014 (in press)
21. Rane, S.D., Sapiro, G., Bertalmio, M.: Structure and texture fillingin of missing image blocks in wireless transmission and compression applications. IEEE Transactions on Image Processing **12**(3), 296–302 (2003)
22. Schmaltz, C., Peter, P., Mainberger, M., Ebel, F., Weickert, J., Bruhn, A.: Understanding, optimising, and extending data compression with anisotropic diffusion. International Journal of Computer Vision **108**(3), 222–240 (2014)
23. Schmaltz, C., Weickert, J., Bruhn, A.: Beating the quality of JPEG 2000 with anisotropic diffusion. In: Denzler, J., Notni, G., Süße, H. (eds.) Pattern Recognition. LNCS, vol. 5748, pp. 452–461. Springer, Heidelberg (2009)
24. Sun, J., Yuan, L., Jia, J., Shum, H.Y.: Image completion with structure propagation. ACM Transactions on Graphics **24**(3), 861–868 (2005)
25. Taubman, D.S., Marcellin, M.W. (eds.): JPEG 2000: Image Compression Fundamentals, Standards and Practice. Kluwer, Boston (2002)
26. Weickert, J.: Theoretical foundations of anisotropic diffusion in image processing. Computing Supplement, vol. 11, pp. 221–236 (1996)

Some Nonlocal Filters Formulation Using Functional Rearrangements

Gonzalo Galiano[✉] and Julián Velasco

Department of Mathematics, Universidad de Oviedo, Oviedo, Spain
{galiano,juliano}@uniovi.es

Abstract. We present an exact reformulation of a broad class of nonlocal filters, among which the bilateral filters, in terms of two functional rearrangements: the decreasing and the relative rearrangements.

Independently of the *image* spatial dimension, these filters are expressed as integral operators defined in a one-dimensional space, corresponding to the level sets measures.

We provide some insight into the properties of this new formulation and show some numerical demonstrations to illustrate them.

Keywords: Neighborhood filter · Bilateral filter · Decreasing rearrangement · Relative rearrangement · Denoising · Segmentation

1 Introduction

Let $\Omega \subset \mathbb{R}^d$ be an open and bounded set, $u \in L^\infty(\Omega)$ be an intensity image, and consider the family of filters, for h and ρ positive constants,

$$F u(\mathbf{x}) = \frac{1}{C(\mathbf{x})} \int_\Omega \mathcal{K}_h(u(\mathbf{x}) - u(\mathbf{y})) w_\rho(|\mathbf{x} - \mathbf{y}|) u(\mathbf{y}) d\mathbf{y},$$

where $C(\mathbf{x}) = \int_\Omega \mathcal{K}_h(u(\mathbf{x}) - u(\mathbf{y})) w_\rho(|\mathbf{x} - \mathbf{y}|) d\mathbf{y}$ is a normalization factor.

Functions $\mathcal{K}_h(\xi) = \mathcal{K}(\xi/h)$ and w_ρ are the *range* kernel and the *spatial* kernel of the filter, respectively, making reference to their type of interaction with the image domain. A usual choice for $\mathcal{K}$ is the Gaussian $\mathcal{K}(\xi) = \exp(-\xi^2)$, while different choices of w_ρ give rise to several well known nonlocal filters, e.g.,

- The Neighborhood filter, see [7], for $w_\rho \equiv 1$.
- The Yaroslavsky filter [40], for $w_\rho(|\mathbf{x} - \mathbf{y}|) \equiv \chi_{B_\rho(\mathbf{x})}(\mathbf{y})$, the characteristic function of a ball centered at $\mathbf{x}$ of radios ρ.
- The SUSAN [34] or Bilateral filters [36], for $w_\rho(s) = \exp(-(s/\rho)^2)$.

Other related filters which can be easily included in our discussion are the joint or cross bilateral filters, see [13,27].

Nonlocal filters have been introduced in the last decades as alternatives to local methods such as those expressed in terms of nonlinear diffusion partial

---

The authors are partially supported by the Spanish DGI Project MTM2013-43671-P.

© Springer International Publishing Switzerland 2015
J.-F. Aujol et al. (Eds.): SSVM 2015, LNCS 9087, pp. 166–177, 2015.
DOI: 10.1007/978-3-319-18461-6_14

differential equations (PDE), among which the pioneering approaches of Perona and Malik [26], Álvarez, Lions and Morel [2] and Rudin, Osher and Fatemi [32] are fundamental. We refer the reader to [9] for a review of these methods.

Nonlocal filters have been mathematically analyzed from different points of view. For instance, Barash [4], Elad [14], Barash et al. [5], and Buades et al. [8] investigate the asymptotic relationship between the Yaroslavsky filter and the Perona-Malik equation. Gilboa et al. [20] study certain applications of nonlocal operators to image processing. In [28], Peyré establishes a relationship between nonlocal filtering schemes and thresholding in adapted orthogonal basis. In a more recent paper, Singer et al. [33] interpret the Neighborhood filter as a stochastic diffusion process, explaining in this way the attenuation of high frequencies in the processed images.

From the computational point of view, until the reformulation given by Porikli [29], their actual implementation was of limited use due to the high computational demand of the direct space-range discretization. Only window-sliding optimization, like that introduced by Weiss [37] to avoid redundant kernel calculations, or filter approximations, like the one introduced by Paris and Durand [25], were of computational use. In [25], the space and range domains are merged into a single domain where the bilateral filter may be expressed as a linear convolution, followed by two simple nonlinearities. This allowed the authors to derive simple down-sampling criteria which were the key for filtering acceleration.

However, in [29], the author introduced a new *exact* discrete formulation of the bilateral filter for spatial box kernel (Yarsolavsky filter) using the local histograms of the image, $h_\mathbf{x} = h|_{B_\rho(\mathbf{x})}$, where $B_\rho(\mathbf{x})$ is the box of radious ρ centered at pixel $\mathbf{x}$, arriving to the formula

$$F u(\mathbf{x}) = \frac{1}{C(\mathbf{x})} \sum_{i=1}^{n} q_i h_\mathbf{x}(q_i) \mathcal{K}_h(u(\mathbf{x}) - q_i), \quad (1)$$

where the range of summation is over the quantized values of the image, $q_1, \ldots, q_n$, instead of over the pixel spatial range. In addition, a zig-zag pixel scanning technique was used so that the local histogram is actualized only in the borders of the spatial kernel box.

Formula (1) is an exact formulation of the box filter where all the terms but the local histogram may be computed separately in constant time, and it is therefore referred to as a *constant time $O(1)$ method*.

Unfortunately, the use of local histograms is only valid for constant-wise spatial kernels, and subsequent applications of the new formulation to general spatial kernels is, with the exception of polynomial and trigonometric polynomial kernels, only approximated. Thus, in [29] polynomial approximation was used to deal with the usual spatial Gaussian kernel. This idea was improved in [11] by using trigonometric expansions.

In [38], Yang et al. introduced a new $O(1)$ method capable of handling arbitrary spatial and range kernels, as an extension of the ideas of Durand et al [12]. They use the so-called Principle Bilateral Filtered Image Component J_k, given by, for $u(\mathbf{x}) = q_k$, and for some neighborhood of $\mathbf{x}$, $N(\mathbf{x})$,

$$J_{q_k}(\mathbf{x}) = \frac{\sum_{\mathbf{y} \in N(\mathbf{x})} \mathcal{K}(q_k - u(\mathbf{y})) w_\rho(|\mathbf{x} - \mathbf{y}|) u(\mathbf{y})}{\sum_{\mathbf{y} \in N(\mathbf{x})} \mathcal{K}(q_k - u(\mathbf{y})) w_\rho(|\mathbf{x} - \mathbf{y}|)}. \tag{2}$$

Then, the bilateral filter may be expressed as $F u(\mathbf{x}) = J_{u(\mathbf{x})}(\mathbf{x})$. In practice, only a subset of the range values is considered, and the final filtered image is produced by linear interpolation. In this situation this filter is an approximation to the bilateral filter. The same authors have recently extended and optimized [39] the method of Paris et al. [25] by solving cost volume aggregation problems. Other approaches may be found in [1, 22, 31].

2 Nonlocal Filters in Terms of Functional Rearrangements

Apart from the pure mathematical interest, the reformulation of nonlocal filters in terms of functional rearrangements is useful for computational purposes, specially when the spatial kernel, w, is homogeneous, that is $w_\rho \equiv 1$. In this case, it may be proven [18] that the level sets of u are invariant through the filter, i.e. $u(\mathbf{x}) = u(\mathbf{y})$ implies $F(u)(\mathbf{x}) = F(u)(\mathbf{y})$, and thus, it is sufficient to compute the filter only for each (quantized) level set, instead of for each pixel, meaning a huge gain of computational effort.

For non-homogeneous kernels the advantages of the filter rearranged version are kernel-dependent, and in any case, the gain is never comparable to that of homogeneous kernels. The main reason is that the non-homogeneity of the spatial kernel breaks, in general, the invariance of level sets.

In the following lines, for a smoother introduction of the bilateral filter rearranged version, we provide a formal derivation deduced from the coarea formula. However, notice that the resulting formula is valid in a more general setting, see [19, Theorem 1]. In particular, the condition $\nabla u(\mathbf{y}) \neq 0$ used below is seen to be not necessary.

For this task, we recall the notion of *decreasing rearrangement*, $u_* : [0, |\Omega|] \to \mathbb{R}$, of a function $u : \Omega \subset \mathbb{R}^d \to \mathbb{R}$, which is defined [21, 23] as the (generalized) inverse of the *distribution function of u*, given by $m_u(q) = |\{\mathbf{x} \in \Omega : u(\mathbf{x}) > q\}|$, for $q \in \mathbb{R}$, where $|\cdot|$ denotes the Lebesgue measure.

Under suitable regularity assumptions, the coarea formula states

$$\int_\Omega g(\mathbf{y}) |\nabla u(\mathbf{y})| d\mathbf{y} = \int_{-\infty}^\infty \int_{u=t} g(\mathbf{y}) d\Gamma(\mathbf{y}) dt,$$

where we used the notation $u = t$ to denote the set $\{\mathbf{x} \in \Omega : u(\mathbf{x}) = t\}$. Taking $g(\mathbf{y}) = \mathcal{K}_h(u(\mathbf{x}) - u(\mathbf{y})) w_\rho(|\mathbf{x} - \mathbf{y}|) u(\mathbf{y}) / |\nabla u(\mathbf{y})|$, and using $u(\mathbf{x}) \in [0, Q]$ for all $\mathbf{x} \in \Omega$ we get, for the numerator of the filter F,

$$I(\mathbf{x}) := \int_\Omega \mathcal{K}_h(u(\mathbf{x}) - u(\mathbf{y})) w_\rho(|\mathbf{x} - \mathbf{y}|) u(\mathbf{y}) d\mathbf{y}$$
$$= \int_0^Q \mathcal{K}_h(u(\mathbf{x}) - t) t \int_{u=t} \frac{w_\rho(|\mathbf{x} - \mathbf{y}|)}{|\nabla u(\mathbf{y})|} d\Gamma(\mathbf{y}) dt.$$

Assuming that the decreasing rearrangement of u, u_*, is in fact strictly decreasing and introducing the change of variable $t = u_*(s)$ we find

$$I(\mathbf{x}) = -\int_0^{|\Omega|} \mathcal{K}_h(u(\mathbf{x}) - u_*(s))u_*(s) \frac{du_*(s)}{ds} \int_{u=u_*(s)} \frac{w_\rho(|\mathbf{x}-\mathbf{y}|)}{|\nabla u(\mathbf{y})|} d\Gamma(\mathbf{y}) ds$$

$$= \int_0^{|\Omega|} \mathcal{K}_h(u(\mathbf{x}) - u_*(s))u_*(s) w_\rho(|\mathbf{x}-\cdot|)_{*u}(s) ds.$$

Here, the notation v_{*u} stands for the *relative rearrangement of v with respect to u* [30] which, under regularity conditions, may be expressed as

$$v_{*u}(s) = \frac{\int_{u=u_*(s)} \frac{v(\mathbf{y})}{|\nabla u(\mathbf{y})|} d\Gamma(\mathbf{y})}{\int_{u=u_*(s)} \frac{1}{|\nabla u(\mathbf{y})|} d\Gamma(\mathbf{y})}. \tag{3}$$

Transforming the denominator of the filter, $C(\mathbf{x})$, in a similar way we get

$$\mathrm{F}\,u(\mathbf{x}) = \frac{\int_0^{|\Omega|} \mathcal{K}_h(u(\mathbf{x}) - u_*(s)) w_\rho(|\mathbf{x}-\cdot|)_{*u}(s) u_*(s) ds}{\int_0^{|\Omega|} \mathcal{K}_h(u(\mathbf{x}) - u_*(s)) w_\rho(|\mathbf{x}-\cdot|)_{*u}(s) ds}. \tag{4}$$

Remark 1. The relative rearrangement is defined in its full generality as the weak-$L^p(\Omega_*)$ directional derivative

$$v_{*u} = \lim_{t \to 0} \frac{(u+tv)_* - u*}{t}. \tag{5}$$

Under the additional assumptions $u \in W^{1,1}(\Omega)$ (that is, $u \in L^1(\Omega)$ and $\nabla u \in L^1(\Omega)^d$), and $|\{\mathbf{y} \in \Omega : \nabla u(\mathbf{y}) = 0\}| = 0$, i.e. the non-existence of flat regions of u, the identity is well defined and coincides with (5). In this case, the relative rearrangement represents an averaging procedure of the values of v on the level sets of u labeled by the superlevel sets measures, s. When formula (3) does not apply (flat regions of u) we may resort to (5) to interpret the relative rearrangement as the decreasing rearrangement of v restricted to flat regions.

Example: Rearrangement of Constant-Wise Functions. Consider the constant-wise functions $u, v : [0, 13] \to \mathbb{R}$ given in Fig. 1 (a). Writing $\max(u) = 5 = q_1 > \ldots > q_6 = 0 = \min(u)$, we may express u as $u(x) = \sum_{i=1}^6 q_i \chi_{E_i}(x)$, where E_i are the level sets of u, $E_1 = (10, 11]$, $E_2 = (8, 10]$, etc. Then, the decreasing rearrangement of u is constant-wise too, and given by

$$u_*(s) = \sum_{i=1}^n q_i \chi_{I_i}(s),$$

with $I_i = [a_{i-1}, a_i)$ for $i = 1, \ldots, 6$, and with $a_0 = 0$, $a_1 = |E_1| = 1$, $a_2 = |E_1| + |E_2| = 3, \ldots, a_6 = \sum_{i=1}^6 |E_i| = |\Omega| = 13$. The corresponding plot is shown in Fig. 1 (b).

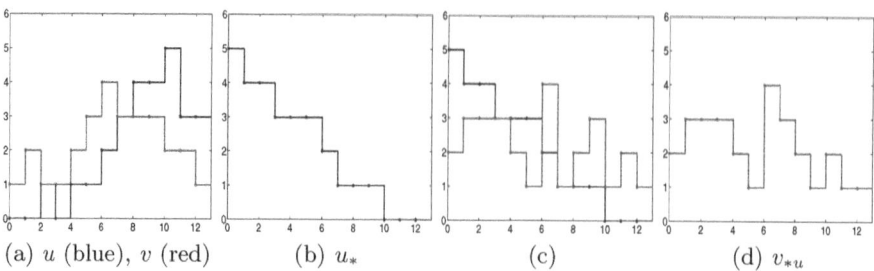

(a) u (blue), v (red) (b) u_* (c) (d) v_{*u}

Fig. 1. Example of construction of the relative rearrangement. (c) shows u_* (blue) and v transported as by the displacement of u level sets (red). (d) shows the decreasing rearrangement of v restricted to the level sets of u, that is v_{*u}.

In Fig. 1 (c) we show the graphs $\{E_i, v(E_i)\}_{i=1}^{6}$ transported as it was done in the step before to construct u_*. For instance, the highest level set of u, $E_1 = (10, 11]$, was transported to $[0, 1]$; $E_2 = (8, 10]$ to $(1, 3]$, etc. Thus $\{E_1, v(E_1)\} = \{(10, 11], \{2\}\}$ is transported to $\{[0, 1], \{2\}\}$; $\{E_2, v(E_2)\} = \{(8, 10], \{3\}\}$ is transported to $\{[1, 3], \{3\}\}$, etc.

Finally, to obtain the decreasing rearrangement of v with respect to u, v_{*u}, we rearrange decreasingly the restriction of v to E_i, as shown in Fig. 1 (d).

2.1 Discrete Setting

To gain some insight into formula (4), let us consider a constant-wise interpolation of a given image, u, quantized in n levels labeled by q_i, with $\max(u) = q_1 > \ldots > q_n = 0$. That is $u(\mathbf{x}) = \sum_{i=1}^{n} q_i \chi_{E_i}(\mathbf{x})$, where E_i are the level sets of u,

$$E_i = \{\mathbf{x} \in \Omega : u(\mathbf{x}) = q_i\}, \quad i = 1, \ldots, n.$$

Similarly, let w_ρ be a constant-wise interpolation of the spatial kernel quantized in m levels, r_j, with $\max(w_\rho) = r_1 > \ldots > r_m = \min(w_\rho) \geq 0$. For each $\mathbf{x} \in \Omega$, consider the partition of E_i given by $F_j^i(\mathbf{x}) = \{\mathbf{y} \in E_i : w_\rho(|\mathbf{x} - \mathbf{y}|) = r_j\}$. Then, it may be shown [19] that for each $\mathbf{x} \in E_k$, $k = 1, \ldots, n$,

$$F u(\mathbf{x}) \equiv F_* u(\mathbf{x}) = \frac{\sum_{i=1}^{n} \mathcal{K}_h(q_k - q_i) W_{im}(\mathbf{x}) q_i}{\sum_{i=1}^{n} \mathcal{K}_h(q_k - q_i) W_{im}(\mathbf{x})}, \quad (6)$$

where $W_{im}(\mathbf{x}) = \sum_{j=1}^{m} r_j |F_j^i(\mathbf{x})|$. Here, $|F_j^i(\mathbf{x})|$ is the number of pixels in the q_i-level set of u that belongs to the r_j-level set of w_ρ. We refer to $F_* u(\mathbf{x})$ as to the *rearranged version* of $Fu(\mathbf{x})$.

2.2 Examples

The main difficulty for the computation of formula (6) is the determination of the measures of $F_j^i(\mathbf{x})$ which, in general, must be computed for each $\mathbf{x} \in \Omega$.

The Neighborhood filter. In this case, $w_\rho \equiv 1$, and therefore $m = 1$ and $F_1^i(\mathbf{x}) = E_i$ is independent of $\mathbf{x}$ for all $i = 1, \ldots, n$. Thus, formula (6) is computed only on the level sets of u, that is, for all $\mathbf{x} \in E_k$

$$F_* u(\mathbf{x}) = \frac{\sum_{i=1}^n \mathcal{K}_h(q_k - q_i)|E_i|q_i}{\sum_{i=1}^n \mathcal{K}_h(q_k - q_i)|E_i|}. \tag{7}$$

The Yaroslavsky or box filter. In this case, $w_\rho(|\mathbf{x}-\mathbf{y}|) = \chi_{B_\rho(\mathbf{x})}(\mathbf{y})$, and therefore there are only two levels $r_1 = 1$, $r_2 = 0$ of w_ρ corresponding to the sets $F_1^i(\mathbf{x}) = E_i \cap B_\rho(\mathbf{x})$ and $F_2^i(\mathbf{x}) = E_i \cap B_\rho(\mathbf{x})^c$. Thus, formula (6) reduces to: for each $\mathbf{x} \in E_k$, $k = 1, \ldots, n$

$$F_* u(\mathbf{x}) = \frac{\sum_{i=1}^n \mathcal{K}_h(q_k - q_i)|F_1^i(\mathbf{x})|q_i}{\sum_{i=1}^n \mathcal{K}_h(q_k - q_i)|F_1^i(\mathbf{x})|},$$

where $|F_1^i(\mathbf{x})|$ denotes the number of pixel of the i-level set of u which belong to the box $B_\rho(\mathbf{x})$.

The general bilateral filter. In this case, the full formula (6) must be used. The spatial kernel is a smooth varying function, e.g. a Gaussian, and therefore there is a continuous range of levels of w_ρ. For computational purposes the range of w_ρ is quantized to some finite number of levels, determined by the size of ρ and the machine ϵ.

The bilateral filter may be accelerated by manipulating the quantization levels of the image, and/or of the spatial range. As shown in [38] for the Yaroslavsky filter, the reduction of the image quantization levels leads to poor denoising results. However, we checked that a similar restriction applied to the spatial kernel reduces the execution time while conserving good denoising quality.

Finally, observe that in all these rearranged versions the range kernel $\mathcal{K}_h(u(\mathbf{x}) - u(\mathbf{y}))$ is transformed into $\mathcal{K}_h(q_k - q)$ which, for coding, may be computed and stored outside the main loop running over all the pixels.

2.3 The Special Case of the Neighborhood Filter

The Neighborhood filter, that is the bilateral filter for a homogeneous spatial kernel $w_\rho \equiv 1$, is a special case from the rearranged version point of view. Formula (7) shows that in this case all the pixels of a given level set, E_i, are jointly filtered to the same value, producing a huge gain in execution time.

Moreover, the usual iterative scheme under which this filter is employed

$$u_{j+1}(\mathbf{x}) = \frac{1}{C_j(\mathbf{x})} \int_\Omega \mathcal{K}_h(u_j(\mathbf{x}) - u_j(\mathbf{y})) u_j(\mathbf{y}) d\mathbf{y},$$

with $C_j(\mathbf{x}) = \int_\Omega \mathcal{K}_h(u_j(\mathbf{x}) - u_j(\mathbf{y})) d\mathbf{y}$, also satisifes this level sets invariant structure property [17,18], from where the following recurrent formula is deduced: For $u_0 = u$ (initial image) and for all $\mathbf{x} \in E_k^j \{\mathbf{x} \in \Omega : u_n(\mathbf{x}) = q_k\}$, $j = 0, 1, \ldots$,

$$u_{j+1}(\mathbf{x}) = \frac{\sum_{i=1}^n \mathcal{K}_h(q_k - q_i)|E_i^j|q_i}{\sum_{i=1}^n \mathcal{K}_h(q_k - q_i)|E_i^j|}.$$

As shown in [18], a notable property of this recurrent formula is the formation of large gradients around inflexion points of u_*, like in some type of shock filters [3]. Using the connection between the image histogram, $h_u(q)$ and the distribution function, $m_u(q)$, given by $m_u(q) = \int_q^{\max u} h(s)ds$, we see that critical points of the histogram coincides with inflexion points of the distribution function and, hence, of the decreasing rearrangement, u_*. Since histogram critical points detection is the base for some intensity based segmentation algorithms [10,24], the iterated Neighborhood filter may be used as an *automatic* segmentation algorithm, in which the only tunning parameter is the window size, h. We provide some examples in the next section.

3 Experiments

3.1 Denoising

We conducted an experiment on standard natural images to check the performance of the discrete formula (6) in comparison to the *brute force* pixel based implementation of the bilateral filter, and to a well known state of the art denoising algorithm introduced by Yang et al. [38], see formula (2).

Both formula (6) and Yang's et al. algorithm are exact representations of the bilateral filter when the maximum number of spatial kernel quantization levels or the whole image range, respectively, are considered. Therefore, in this case, the only source of disagreement is caused by rounding error.

Thus, we experimented with smaller values of these parameters for the sake of execution time saving. We chose twenty values for the discretization of the bilateral spatial kernel (Gaussian) in the rearranged formula (6), and eight values for Yang's et al. algorithm, like in [38].

The first aim of our experiment was to investigate the quality of the algoruthms approximation, in terms of the peak signal to noise ratio (PSNR), to the ground truth, and to the exact pixel-based bilateral filter. The second, was the comparison of execution times as delivered straightly from the available codes. Notice that execution time depends on code optimization and therefore a rigorous study of this aspect requires some kind of code normalization which was out of the scope of our study.

We used three intensity images of different sizes corrupted with an additive Gaussian white noise of SNR = 10, according to the noise measure SNR = $\sigma(u)/\sigma(\nu)$, where σ is the empirical standard deviation, u is the original image, and ν is the noise. The images, available at the data base of the Signal and Image Processing Institute, University of Southern California, are *Clock* (256 × 256), *Boat* (512 × 512), and *Airport* (1024 × 1024).

We considered different spatial window sizes determined by ρ, with $\rho = 4, 8, 16, 32$. The range size of the filter was taken as $h = \rho$ which, according to [8], is the regime in which the corresponding iterative filter behaves asymptotically as a Perona-Malik type filter. The shape of the range filter is a Gaussian.

The discretization of the pixel-based and the rearranged version of both filters was implemented in non-optimized C++ codes by the authors, while for Yang's

Table 1. Denoising experiment. From left to right. GT block: PSNR between the ground truth image and the pixel-based Bilateral filter (BPB), its rearranged version for 20 levels (BRR), Yang's algorithm with 8 interpolation elements (Y8), and the Yaroslavsky filter in its rearranged version (YRR). BPB block: PSNR between the BPB and the other algorithms. ET block: Execution times of BPB, BRR, Y8, and YRR. ETBPB block: Ratio between execution time of the algorithm and execution time of BPB.

	GT				BPB			ET				ETBPB		
						Clock (256 × 256)								
h	BPB	BRR	Y8	YRR	BRR	Y8	YRR	BPB	BRR	Y8	YRR	BRR	Y8	YRR
4	3.62	3.62	-1.24	3.64	42.6	1.17	29.7	0.56	0.17	0.02	0.02	3.29	28	28
8	4.08	4.08	3.89	4.03	43.1	21.3	27.2	2.06	0.25	0.02	0.02	8.24	103	103
16	4.4	4.4	4.1	4.31	41.5	20.3	21.1	7.98	0.62	0.02	0.03	12.9	399	266
32	4.31	4.31	4.04	3.55	38.4	16	12.4	31.41	1.8	0.02	0.06	17.4	1570	524
						Boat (512 × 512)								
4	10.6	10.6	4.36	10.6	42.7	5.26	29.4	2.19	0.68	0.1	0.06	3.22	21.9	36.5
8	11	11	10.5	10.7	42.1	20.6	26	8.33	1.12	0.06	0.08	7.44	138.8	104
16	9.23	9.23	8.8	8.69	40.7	18.3	20.3	32.64	2.44	0.06	0.14	13.4	544	233
32	4.83	4.83	4.22	3.95	38.4	15.8	14.2	132.1	7.27	0.06	0.22	18.2	2201	600
						Airport (1024 × 1024)								
4	3.83	3.83	3.15	3.83	42.6	11	29.4	8.76	2.78	0.24	0.23	3.15	36.5	38.1
8	3.89	3.89	3.85	3.87	42.2	21.7	26.7	33.37	4.29	0.22	0.3	7.78	151.7	111
16	3.6	3.59	3.59	3.59	41.1	17	21.7	132.8	9.36	0.22	0.58	14.2	603.8	229
32	2.45	2.44	2.35	2.38	38.7	11.5	15.5	529.5	28.1	0.2	0.92	18.8	2648	576

Table 2. Segmentation experiment. Comparison among several algorithms.

	Dice coefficient			
	Freesurfer	FSL	SPM	NF
white	0.9490	0.9435	0.9468	0.9563
grey	0.8509	0.8599	0.8835	0.8797

algorithm available code[1] was employed. Time execution was measured by means of function clock.

In Table 1 we show the measures resulting from our experiments. We see that all the algorithms give similar results when compared to the ground truth. Thus, if this were the choice criterium, the faster, that is $Y8$, should be considered.

However, when compared to the exact bilateral filter (BPB), the PSNR's are quite different. The rearranged bilateral filter with twenty spatial kernel levels (BRR20) has always values of PSNR around 40dB, which makes it indistinguishable from the exact filtered image. The Yaroslavsky filter (YRR) lowers this figure to about 20dB. Yang's et al. with eight range values (Y8) gives always poorer results. In fact, the use of Yang's algorithm with the maximum number

---

[1] C++ code in http://www.cs.cityu.edu.hk/~qiyang/

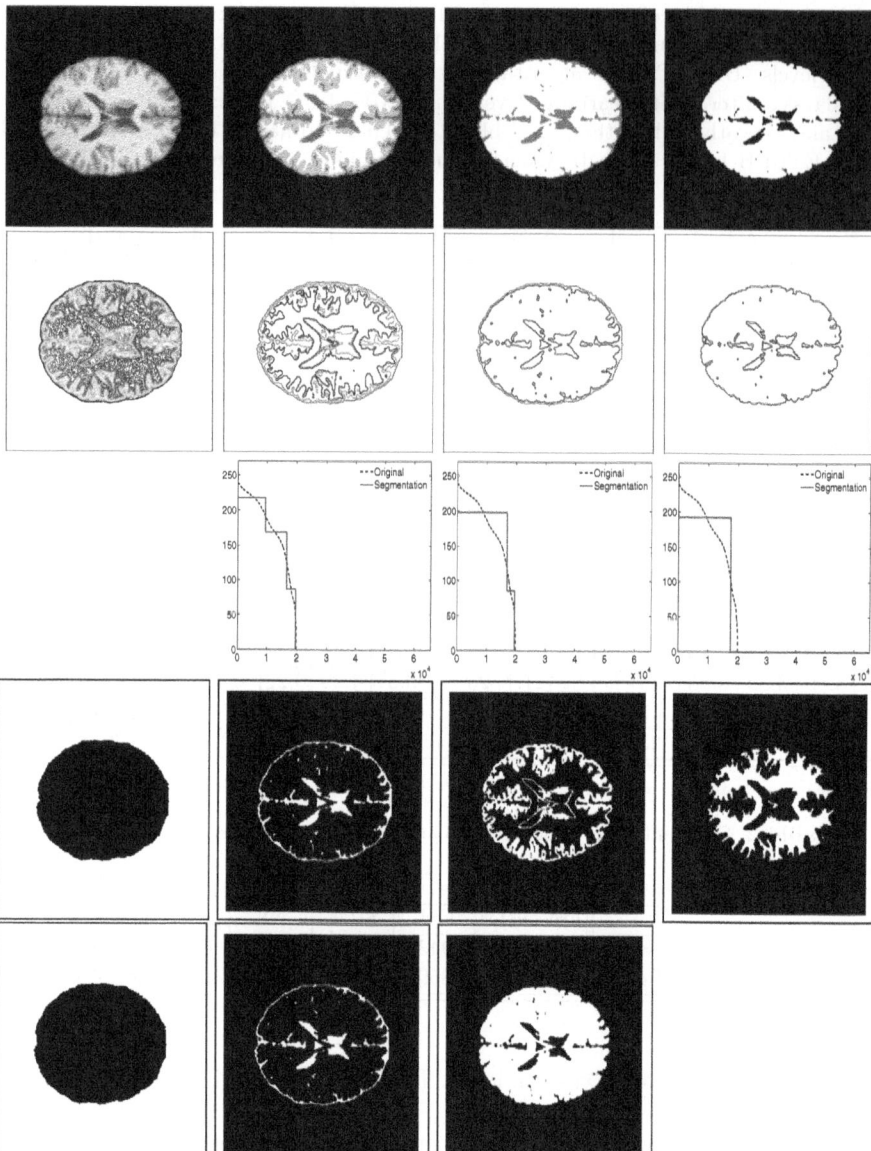

Fig. 2. Segmentation experiment. Results of applying the Neighborhood filter (NF) with several values of the window size h. Rows 1-3: Image, level curves and decreasing rearrangement both of the original image and of the final result, showing the number of segmented regions (flat regions). Columns for rows 1-3: Results of applying the NF with $h = 17$, $h = 20$, and $h = 50$, respectively. Rows 4-5: Masks of the segmented regions. Row 4: $h = 17$. The NF produces four regions, corresponding to background, dura-mater and ventricles, grey matter and white matter. Row 5: $h = 20$. The NF produces three regions, corresponding to background, duramatter and ventricles, grey plus white matter.

of levels (not shown in the table), although *should* give exact results, it does not, revealing other sources of error beyond rounding errors.

In Table 1 we also collect the execution times obtained in this experiment. Only for the smaller image sizes and h−values Y8 has a competitor in YRR. BRR20 gives execution times considerably higher than the other algorithms, for our non-optimized codes.

3.2 Segmentation with the Neighborhood Filter

To demonstrate the capability of the Neighborhood filter as a segmentation algorithm, we applied it to MRI brain segmentation. We used a phantom brain from the Simulated Brain Database [6] with a 9% of additive Riccian noise and compared the result to the grey-white matter segmentation performed with some standard packages: Freesurfer [15], FSL [16] and SPM8 [35].

In Fig. 2, rows 1 to 3, we show an axial slice of the volume (initial image) and the corresponding segmentation in four, three and two regions reached by setting $h = 17, 20, 50$, respectively. The contour lines and the decreasing rearrangement of the original image, u, and the final filtered image are shown too. In rows 4 to 5, we show the masks of the segmented regions corresponding to $h = 17, 20$.

To check the Neighborhood filter segmentation performance, the Dice coincidence coefficient is computed for all the algorithms, see Table 2, showing a good performance of the Neighborhood filter in relation to the more sophisticated algorithms implemented in the mentioned packages. Notice that the Dice coefficient is one for a perfect match to the ground truth, and zero on the contrary.

Although we have shown the results for one slice, the Neighborhood filter is applied directly to the whole volume, meaning that the dimension reduction is from a three dimensional space (the space of voxels) to a one dimensional space (the space of level sets measures). Thus, the time execution of the NF is several orders of magnitude lower than the others (a standard volume takes few seconds in a standard laptop). However, this is no more than a toy example, from where general conclusions can not be inferred.

4 Summary

In this paper we used functional rearrangements to express bilateral type filters in terms of integral operators in the one-dimensional space $[0, |\Omega|]$.

In the case in which the spatial kernel, w_ρ, is homogeneous (e.g. the Neighborhood filter), the level set structure of the image is left invariant through the filtering process, allowing to compute the filter jointly for all the pixels in each level set, instead of pixel-wise. This can be done also for the associated iterative scheme, which is seen to be related to intensity-based histogram-related image segmentation.

If the spatial kernel is not homogeneous the invariance of the $u-$level sets through the filter is, in general, broken. Despite this fact, there still remains an important property of the rearranged version: the range kernel $\mathcal{K}_h(u(\mathbf{x}) - u(\mathbf{y}))$ is transformed into a pixel-independent kernel $\mathcal{K}(q_k - q_i)$, implying a large gain in computational effort, as already observed for particular cases in [29].

References

1. Adams, A., Baek, J., Davis, M.A.: Fast high-dimensional filtering using the permutohedral lattice. Computer Graphics Forum **29**(2), 753–762 (2010)
2. Álvarez, L., Lions, P.L., Morel, J.M.: Image selective smoothing and edge detection by nonlinear diffusion. ii. Siam J Numer Anal **29**(3), 845–866 (1992)
3. Álvarez, L., Mazorra, L.: Signal and image restoration using shock filters and anisotropic diffusion. Siam J Numer Anal **31**(2), 590–605 (1994)
4. Barash, D.: Fundamental relationship between bilateral filtering, adaptive smoothing, and the nonlinear diffusion equation. IEEE T Pattern Anal **24**(6), 844–847 (2002)
5. Barash, D., Comaniciu, D.: A common framework for nonlinear diffusion, adaptive smoothing, bilateral filtering and mean shift. Image Vision Comput **22**(1), 73–81 (2004)
6. Brainweb. http://brainweb.bic.mni.mcgill.ca/brainweb,Vol.t1_icbm_normal_1mm_ pn9_rf20_resampled_brain.nii.gz
7. Buades, A., Coll, B., Morel, J.M.: A review of image denoising algorithms, with a new one. Multiscale Model Sim **4**(2), 490–530 (2005)
8. Buades, A., Coll, B., Morel, J.M.: Neighborhood filters and pde's. Numer Math **105**(1), 1–34 (2006)
9. Buades, A., Coll, B., Morel, J.M.: Image denoising methods. a new nonlocal principle. Siam Rev **52**(1), 113–147 (2010)
10. Chang, C.I., Du, Y., Wang, J., Guo, S.M., Thouin, P.: Survey and comparative analysis of entropy and relative entropy thresholding techniques. In: IEE Proceedings-Vision, Image and Signal Processing, vol. 153, pp. 837–850. IET (2006)
11. Chaudhury, K.N., Sage, D., Unser, M.: Fast O(1) bilateral filtering using trigonometric range kernels. TIP 2011 (2011)
12. Durand, F., Dorsey, J.: Fast bilateral filtering for the display of high-dynamic-range images. ACM Siggraph **21**, 257–266 (2002)
13. Eisemann, E., Durand, F.: Flash photography enhancement via intrinsic relighting. Siggraph **23**(3), 673–678 (2004)
14. Elad, M.: On the origin of the bilateral filter and ways to improve it. IEEE T Image Process **11**(10), 1141–1151 (2002)
15. Freesurfer. http://freesurfer.net
16. FMRIB Software Library. http://fsl.fmrib.ox.ac.uk/fsl/fslwiki
17. Galiano, G., Velasco, J.: On a non-local spectrogram for denoising one-dimensional signals. Appl Math Comput **244**, 859–869 (2014)
18. Galiano, G., Velasco, J.: Neighborhood filters and the decreasing rearrangement. J Math Imaging Vision (2014). doi:10.1007/s10851-014-0522-3
19. Galiano, G., Velasco, J.: On a fast bilateral filtering formulation using functional rearrangements. arXiv:1406.7128v1 (2015) (submitted)
20. Gilboa, G., Osher, S.: Nonlocal operators with applications to image processing. Multiscale Model Sim **7**(3), 1005–1028 (2008)

21. Hardy, G.H., Littlewood, J.E., Polya, G.: Inequalities. Cambridge, U.P. (1964)
22. Kass, M., Solomon, J.: Smoothed local histogram filters. ACM TOG **29**(4), 100:1–100:10 (2010)
23. Lieb, E.H., Loss, M.: Analysis, vol. 4. American Mathematical Soc. (2001)
24. Nath, S., Agarwal, S., Kazmi, Q.A.: Image histogram segmentation by multi-level thresholding using hill climbing algorithm. Int J Comput Appl **35**(1) (2011)
25. Paris, S., Durand, F.: A fast approximation of the bilateral filter using a signal processing approach. In: Leonardis, A., Bischof, H., Pinz, A. (eds.) ECCV 2006. LNCS, vol. 3954, pp. 568–580. Springer, Heidelberg (2006)
26. Perona, P., Malik, J.: Scale-space and edge detection using anisotropic diffusion. IEEE T Pattern Anal **12**(7), 629–639 (1990)
27. Petschnigg, G., Agrawala, M., Hoppe, H., Szeliski, R., Cohen, M., Toyama, K.: Digital photography with flash and no-flash image pairs. ACM Siggraph **23**(3), 664–672 (2004)
28. Peyré, G.: Image processing with nonlocal spectral bases. Multiscale Model Sim **7**(2), 703–730 (2008)
29. Porikli, F.: Constant time O(1) bilateral filtering. CVPR 2008 (2008)
30. Rakotoson, J.M.: Réarrangement Relatif: Un instrument d'estimations dans les problĕmes aux limites, vol 64. Springer (2008)
31. Ram, I., Elad, M., Cohen, I.: Image processing using smooth ordering of its patches. IEEE T Image Process **22**(7), 2764–2774 (2013)
32. Rudin, L.I., Osher, S., Fatemi, E.: Nonlinear total variation based noise removal algorithms. Physica D **60**(1), 259–268 (1992)
33. Singer, A., Shkolnisky, Y., Nadler, B.: Diffusion interpretation of nonlocal neighborhood filters for signal denoising. SIAM J Imaging Sci **2**(1), 118–139 (2009)
34. Smith, S.M., Brady, J.M.: Susan. a new approach to low level image processing. Int J Comput Vision **23**(1), 45–78 (1997)
35. Statistical Parametric Mapping (SPM). http://www.fil.ion.ucl.ac.uk/spm
36. Tomasi, C., Manduchi, R.: Bilateral filtering for gray and color images. In: Sixth International Conference on Computer Vision, pp. 839–846. IEEE (1998)
37. Weiss, B.: Fast median and bilateral filtering. ACM Siggraph **25**, 519–526 (2006)
38. Yang, Q., Tan, K.H., Ahuja, N.: Real-time O(1) bilateral filtering. CVPR 2009 (2009)
39. Yang, Q., Ahuja, N., Tan, K.H.: Constant time median and bilateral filtering. Int J Comput Vis (2014). doi:10.1007/s11263-014-0764-y
40. Yaroslavsky, L.P.: Digital picture processing. An introduction. Springer Verlag, Heidelberg (1985)

Total Variation Restoration of Images Corrupted by Poisson Noise with Iterated Conditional Expectations

Rémy Abergel[1], Cécile Louchet[2], Lionel Moisan[1(✉)], and Tieyong Zeng[3]

[1] MAP5 (CNRS UMR 8145), Université Paris Descartes, Paris, France
lionel.moisan@parisdescartes.fr
[2] MAPMO (CNRS UMR 6628), Université d'Orléans, Paris, France
[3] Department of Mathematics, Hong Kong Baptist University,
Kowloon Tong, Hong Kong

Abstract. Interpreting the celebrated Rudin-Osher-Fatemi (ROF) model in a Bayesian framework has led to interesting new variants for Total Variation image denoising in the last decade. The Posterior Mean variant avoids the so-called staircasing artifact of the ROF model but is computationally very expensive. Another recent variant, called TV-ICE (for Iterated Conditional Expectation), delivers very similar images but uses a much faster fixed-point algorithm. In the present work, we consider the TV-ICE approach in the case of a Poisson noise model. We derive an explicit form of the recursion operator, and show linear convergence of the algorithm, as well as the absence of staircasing effect. We also provide a numerical algorithm that carefully handles precision and numerical overflow issues, and show experiments that illustrate the interest of this Poisson TV-ICE variant.

Keywords: Poisson noise removal · Image denoising · Total variation · Posterior mean · Marginal conditional mean · Staircasing effect · Fixed-point algorithm · Incomplete gamma function

1 Introduction

Since the seminal paper of Rudin, Osher and Fatemi [1], total variation (TV) regularization has been used in numerous image processing applications (see, e.g., [2] and references therein). Reasons for this popularity are multiple. First, TV regularization allows discontinuities (contrary to the L^2 norm of the gradient), which is essential in the world of natural images, dominated by occlusions. Second, its continuous counterpart is part of a fruitful mathematical theory (the space of functions with bounded variation) which results in strong possibilities of theoretical interpretations [3]. Third, in the last decade several very efficient algorithms have been designed to handle the non-smooth convex optimization problems occurring with TV regularization (e.g., [4,5]). In terms of pure denoising performances, TV denoising is less efficient than modern patch-based approaches like NL-means [6] or BM3D [7] for example, but remains useful as the simplest possible framework for the study of TV regularization. Understanding the strengths and weaknesses of TV denoising (and variants) certainly helps a lot apprehending more complex inverse problems involving TV regularization.

One weakness of TV regularization is the so-called staircasing effect: where one would have expected a smoothly varying image, the L^1 norm promotes a sparse gradient that results in piecewise constant zones with artificial boundaries. This undesirable effect can be avoided by using a smoother functional, but at the expense of loosing the nice theoretical properties of TV. Other solutions have been proposed that keep the true definition of TV but change the minimization framework. Indeed, when considering the TV as the Gibbs energy of an image prior in a Bayesian framework, the ROF model can be reinterpreted as finding the image that maximizes the associated posterior density. Replacing this maximum a posteriori (MAP) estimate with the posterior mean leads to a variant of the ROF model, called TV-LSE, that delivers images without staircasing artifacts [8,9]. More recently, a new variant called TV-ICE [10] was proposed to overcome the slow convergence rate of the TV-LSE Monte-Carlo algorithm. It is based on the repeated estimation of conditional marginal posterior means, which boils down to iterating an explicit local operator. In practice, TV-ICE delivers images very similar to TV-LSE results, but at a much smaller computational expense.

In the present work, we propose to adapt to the case of Poisson noise this TV-ICE method, derived in [10] in the case of Gaussian noise. Contrary to most noise sources (electronic noise, dark current, thermal noise) whose effects can be reduced by the improvement of captors, Poisson noise is inherent to the quantum nature of light and thus unavoidable for images acquired in low-light conditions, which is very common in astronomy or in microscopy for example. Even if image restoration models are generally first designed in the simpler case of a white Gaussian additive noise, they need to be adapted to the specific case of Poisson noise. Due to the importance and the inevitability of Poisson noise, this adaptation is almost systematic, as shows for example the case of TV-based image deblurring [11] or NL-means denoising [12].

In the case of the TV prior, the posterior distribution obtained with Poisson noise strongly differs from the Gaussian case, but the conditional marginal posterior means can be explicitly computed using the incomplete Gamma function. In Section 2, we show that the associated iterative algorithm converges linearly and that no staircasing occurs, thanks in particular to the log-concavity of the Poisson distribution. We then give the explicit form of the recursion operator defining our Poisson-TV-ICE model (Section 3) and discuss numerical issues, in particular the handling of machine over/under-flow and the efficient computation of the (slightly generalized) incomplete Gamma function. We then numerically check the theoretical properties of the method (convergence rate, absence of staircasing) in Section 4, and compare the obtained results with the Poisson noise variant of the ROF model, before we conclude in Section 5.

2 The Poisson TV-ICE Model

2.1 Definition

Let $u : \Omega \to \mathbb{R}_+$ be an (unobserved) intensity image defined on a discrete domain Ω (a rectangular subset of $\mathbb{Z}^2$). A photon-count observation of the ideal image u is a random image v following the Poisson probability density function (p.d.f.)

$$p(v|u) = \prod_{x \in \Omega} \frac{u(x)^{v(x)}}{v(x)!} e^{-u(x)} \propto \exp\left(-\langle u - v \log u, \mathbb{1}_\Omega \rangle\right), \qquad (1)$$

where $\mathbb{1}_\Omega$ denotes the constant image equal to 1 on Ω and $\langle \cdot, \cdot \rangle$ is the usual inner product on $\mathbb{R}^\Omega$. The notation $\propto$ here indicates an equality up to a global multiplicative constant (which depends on v). Note that we have to take the convention that $v(x) \log u(x) = 0$ as soon as $v(x) = 0$ in (1). The discrete anisotropic TV of u is

$$\mathrm{TV}(u) = \frac{1}{2} \sum_{x \in \Omega} \sum_{y \in \mathcal{N}_x} |u(y) - u(x)|, \qquad (2)$$

where $\mathcal{N}_x$ denotes the 4-neighborhood of a pixel x with a mirror boundary condition. Using the improper TV prior $p(u) \propto e^{-\lambda \mathrm{TV}(u)}$ (where λ is a positive regularization parameter) and Equation (1), we get thanks to the Bayes rule the posterior density

$$\pi(u) = p(u|v) = \frac{p(v|u)p(u)}{\int_{\mathbb{R}_+^\Omega} p(v|w)p(w)dw} = \frac{e^{-\langle u - v \log u, \mathbb{1}_\Omega \rangle - \lambda \mathrm{TV}(u)}}{\int_{\mathbb{R}_+^\Omega} e^{-\langle w - v \log w, \mathbb{1}_\Omega \rangle - \lambda \mathrm{TV}(w)}dw}. \qquad (3)$$

The equivalent of the classical ROF model [1] in the case of a Poisson noise model corresponds to the unique maximizer $\hat{u}_{\mathrm{MAP}}$ of π, or equivalently the minimizer of the convex energy $E(u) = \langle u - v \log u, \mathbb{1}_\Omega \rangle + \lambda TV(u)$. It can be efficiently computed using the primal-dual algorithm recently proposed in [5]. As mentioned in Introduction, a main drawback of this approach is that $\hat{u}_{\mathrm{MAP}}$ generally suffers from the staircasing effect, which results in the appearance of flat regions separated by artificial boundaries.

In the case of a Gaussian noise model (when $\pi(u) \propto e^{-\|u-v\|^2/(2\sigma^2) - \lambda \mathrm{TV}(u)}$), this can be avoided by considering, instead of $\hat{u}_{\mathrm{MAP}}$, the posterior mean

$$\hat{u}_{\mathrm{LSE}} = \mathbb{E}_{u \sim \pi}(u) = \int_{\mathbb{R}^\Omega} u \, \pi(u) du, \qquad (4)$$

which is the image that reaches the Least Square Error under π (see [8,9]). The numerical computation of $\hat{u}_{\mathrm{LSE}}$ proposed in [8] is based on a Markov Chain Monte Carlo Metropolis-Hastings algorithm, which exhibits a slow convergence rate ($\mathcal{O}(n^{-1/2})$ for n iterations). To overcome this computational limitation, the same authors proposed in [10] a new variant based on the iteration of conditional marginal posterior means. More precisely, the estimate $\hat{u}_{\text{ICE}}$ is defined as the limit (for an appropriate initialization) of the iterative scheme

$$u^{n+1}(x) = \mathbb{E}_{u \sim \pi}\left(u(x) \mid u(x^c) = u^n(x^c)\right) = \int_{\mathbb{R}} u^n(x)\,\pi(u^n)du^n(x), \quad (5)$$

where $u(x^c)$ denotes the restriction of u to $\Omega \setminus \{x\}$. In the case of the Poisson noise model (3), we obtain the following

Definition 1 (Poisson TV-ICE). *The Poisson TV-ICE recursion is*

$$\forall n \in \mathbb{N},\ \forall x \in \Omega, \quad u^{n+1}(x) = \frac{\int_{\mathbb{R}_+} s^{v(x)+1} e^{-\left(s + \lambda \sum_{y \in \mathcal{N}_x} |u^n(y) - s|\right)} ds}{\int_{\mathbb{R}_+} s^{v(x)} e^{-\left(s + \lambda \sum_{y \in \mathcal{N}_x} |u^n(y) - s|\right)} ds}. \quad (6)$$

2.2 Convergence

Theorem 1. *Given an image $v \in \mathbb{R}^{\Omega}$, the sequence of images $(u^n)_{n \geq 0}$ defined by $u^0 = 0$ and the recursion (6) converges linearly to an image $\hat{u}_{\text{ICE}}$.*

In the following, we denote by $P_p(s)$ the pointwise Poisson noise p.d.f. with parameter p, that is, $P_p(s) = s^p e^{-s} \mathbf{1}_{\mathbb{R}_+}(s)/p!$. If $a = (a_i)_{1 \leq i \leq 4}$, we write

$$f_p(a) = \frac{\int s\, P_p(s)\, e^{-\lambda \sum_{i=1}^{4} |s - a_i|}\, ds}{\int P_p(s)\, e^{-\lambda \sum_{i=1}^{4} |s - a_i|}\, ds} = \frac{\int_0^{+\infty} s^{p+1} e^{-s}\, e^{-\lambda \sum_{i=1}^{4} |s - a_i|}\, ds}{\int_0^{+\infty} s^p e^{-s}\, e^{-\lambda \sum_{i=1}^{4} |s - a_i|}\, ds} \quad (7)$$

and $\quad F : u \mapsto \left(x \mapsto f_{v(x)}(u(\mathcal{N}_x))\right), \quad (8)$

so that the recursion (6) can be simply rewritten $u^{n+1} = F(u^n)$.

To prove Theorem 1, we need some intermediate Lemmas.

Lemma 1. *[13] Assume that X, a random variable defined on $\mathbb{R}^{\Omega}$, has a finite second order moment. Then the inequality*

$$\text{cov}(X, g(X)) \geq 0$$

holds for every nondecreasing function $g : \mathbb{R}^{\Omega} \to \mathbb{R}$ for which $g(X)$ has a finite second order moment. If, moreover, X is not deterministic and g is strictly increasing, then $\text{cov}(X, g(X)) > 0$.

Proof. One has

$$\text{cov}(X, g(X)) = \mathbb{E}[(X - \mathbb{E}[X])(g(X) - \mathbb{E}[g(X)])]$$
$$= \mathbb{E}[(X - \mathbb{E}[X])(g(X) - g(\mathbb{E}[X]))]$$

The assertion follows because g is increasing. If X is not deterministic, then there exists a Borel set A such that $P(X \in A) > 0$ with $\mathbb{E}[X] \notin A$. Hence the covariance is a sum of nonnegative terms, some of which (those for $X \in A$) are positive. Finally $\text{cov}(X, g(X))$ is positive.

Lemma 2. F is monotone: for all images u_0 and u_1,
$$u_0 \leq u_1 \Rightarrow F(u_0) \leq F(u_1).$$

Proof. Using Lebesgue dominated convergence theorem, one can prove the differentiability of f_p with respect to each a_i and obtain

$$\frac{\partial f_p}{\partial a_i}(a) = \frac{\int \lambda \operatorname{sign}(s - a_i)\, s\, P_p(s)\, e^{-\lambda \sum_{j=1}^4 |s - a_j|}\, ds}{\int P_p(s)\, e^{-\lambda \sum_{j=1}^4 |s - a_j|}\, ds}$$

$$- \frac{\int s\, P_p(s)\, e^{-\lambda \sum_{j=1}^4 |s - a_j|}\, ds}{\int P_p(s)\, e^{-\lambda \sum_{j=1}^4 |s - a_j|}\, ds} \cdot \frac{\int \lambda \operatorname{sign}(s - a_i)\, P_p(s)\, e^{-\lambda \sum_{j=1}^4 |s - a_j|}\, ds}{\int P_p(s)\, e^{-\lambda \sum_{j=1}^4 |s - a_j|}\, ds}.$$

Hence $\frac{\partial f_p}{\partial a_i}(a)$ can be seen as the covariance of S and $\lambda \operatorname{sign}(S - a_i)$, where S is a random variable with p.d.f. $s \mapsto \frac{1}{Z} P_p(s)\, e^{-\lambda \sum_{j=1}^4 |s - a_j|}$, which has a finite second order moment. Using Lemma 1, the quantity $\frac{\partial f_p}{\partial a_i}(a)$, as the covariance of S with a nondecreasing function of S, is nonnegative. Now if $u_0 \leq u_1$, then as f_p is $\mathcal{C}^1$ we can write

$$(F(u_1) - F(u_0))(x) = \int_0^1 \nabla f_{v(x)}(u_t(\mathcal{N}_x)) \cdot (u_1(\mathcal{N}_x) - u_0(\mathcal{N}_x))\, dt,$$

where $u_t(\mathcal{N}_x) = (1 - t)u_0(\mathcal{N}_x) + t u_1(\mathcal{N}_x)$. As $\frac{\partial f_{v(x)}}{\partial u(y)}$ and $u_1(y) - u_0(y)$ are both nonnegative, so is $(F(u_1) - F(u_0))(x)$ as the integral of a nonnegative function.

Lemma 3. F is strictly nonexpansive for the ℓ^∞ norm: for any images $u \neq u'$,
$$\|F(u') - F(u)\|_\infty < \|u' - u\|_\infty.$$

Proof. For fixed values of p and $a = (a_i)_{1 \leq i \leq 4}$, let us define the real mapping

$$g : c \mapsto f_p(a + c) - c,$$

where $a + c$ is a shorthand for $(a_i + c)_{1 \leq i \leq 4}$. We first prove that the strict decrease of g on $\mathbb{R}$ for all p and a implies the strict nonexpansiveness of F. We must prove that $F(u') < F(u) + c$ and that $F(u') > F(u) - c$ for $c = \|u' - u\|_\infty$. As $u' \leq u + c$ and as F is monotone, we have $F(u') \leq F(u + c)$. It remains to prove that $F(u + c) < F(u) + c$, i.e. that

$$\forall p \in \mathbb{N},\ \forall a \in \mathbb{R}^4,\ \forall c > 0,\quad f_p(a + c) < f_p(a) + c,$$

which is true as soon as g is strictly decreasing on $\mathbb{R}_+$. For the other inequality, we have $F(u') \geq F(u - c)$, so that it remains to prove that $F(u - c) > F(u) - c$, i.e. that

$$\forall p \in \mathbb{N},\ \forall a \in \mathbb{R}^4,\ \forall c > 0,\quad f_p(a - c) > f_p(a) - c,$$

which is true as soon as g is strictly decreasing on $\mathbb{R}_-$.

Second, we prove that g is strictly decreasing. One can prove that

$$g'(c) = \operatorname{cov}\left(S, \frac{P_p'(S + c)}{P_p(S + c)}\right) = \operatorname{cov}(S, (\log P_p)'(S + c)),$$

where S follows a distribution with p.d.f. $s \mapsto \frac{1}{Z} P_p(s+c) e^{-\lambda \sum_{i=1}^{4} |s-a_i|} ds$. Now, P_p is positive and differentiable and $(\log P_p)'(s) = p/s - 1$ so for all c, the mapping $s \mapsto (\log P_p)'(s+c)$ is strictly decreasing on $(-c, \infty)$. Again thanks to Lemma 1, as the distribution on S is not deterministic, we get that $g'(c)$ is negative. Hence g is strictly decreasing and the proof is complete.

Lemma 4. *There exists a subset K of $\mathbb{R}^{\Omega}$ containing 0 such that $F(K) \subset K$.*

Proof (abridged). We set $G(p,c) = f_p(c \mathbb{1}_\mathcal{N}) - c$ and proceed in 4 steps:

1) For every $p \in \mathbb{N}$, the function $c \mapsto G(p, c)$ is continuous and decreasing. Indeed, $G(p, c)$ is exactly $g(c)$, defined in the proof of Lemma 3, with $a = 0$. So it is differentiable and decreasing.

2) For each $p \in \mathbb{N}$, the limit of $G(p, c)$, when c goes to $+\infty$, is negative (proof not given here).

3) We deduce from 1) and 2) that

$$\forall p \in \mathbb{N}, \exists \mathbf{c}(p) \in \mathbb{R}, \quad c \geq \mathbf{c}(p) \Rightarrow G(p, c) \leq 0.$$

4) With the latter definition for $p \mapsto \mathbf{c}(p)$, we define $c = \max_{x \in \Omega} \mathbf{c}(v(x))$ and $K = [0, c]^{\Omega}$. If $u \in K$, then $u \leq c$, and as F is monotone, $F(u) \leq F(c \mathbb{1}_\Omega)$. Now, as $c \geq \mathbf{c}(v(x))$, by definition of $\mathbf{c}$, $f_{v(x)}(c) \leq c$ holds for each $x \in \Omega$, which exactly means that $F(u) \leq F(c \mathbb{1}_\Omega) \leq c$. Secondly, as $F(u)(x)$ is a ratio of nonnegative quantities, it is nonnegative and $F(u) \geq 0$. In conclusion, $F(u) \in K$.

Proof (of Theorem 1). Since the map F is strictly non-expansive (Lemma 3) and continuous on the compact set K, there exists a real number $\alpha \in (0, 1)$ such that $\|F(w_1) - F(w_2)\|_\infty \leq \alpha \|w_1 - w_2\|_\infty$ for all images $w_1, w_2 \in K$. Moreover, K is stable by F (Lemma 4), so the Banach fixed-point theorem applies and the sequence (u^n) defined in Theorem 1 converges to a fixed point of F, which is unique. The convergence is linear as $\|u^{n+1} - \hat{u}_{\text{ICE}}\|_\infty \leq \alpha \|u^n - \hat{u}_{\text{ICE}}\|_\infty$, or in other terms, $\|u^n - \hat{u}_{\text{ICE}}\|_\infty = \mathcal{O}(\alpha^n)$ as $n \to \infty$.

2.3 No Staircasing for Poisson TV-ICE

We here prove that Poisson TV-ICE cannot produce large constant regions that were not at least partially present in the initial data.

Theorem 2. *Let $v : \Omega \to \mathbb{N}$ be a noisy image, and $\hat{u}_{\text{ICE}}$ its denoised version. Let x and y be two pixels in Ω. Then if $\hat{u}_{\text{ICE}}$ is constant on $\mathcal{N}_x \cup \mathcal{N}_y \cup \{x, y\}$, necessarily $v(x) = v(y)$.*

To establish the proof, we need the following

Lemma 5. *For any constant c, the mapping $p \mapsto f_p(c \mathbb{1}_\mathcal{N})$ is strictly increasing.*

Proof. The mapping $p \mapsto f_p(c \mathbb{1}_\mathcal{N})$ can be naturally extended to real positive values of p using the right-hand part of Equation (7). Using the dominated convergence theorem, we can assess the differentiability of $p \mapsto f_p(c\mathbb{1}_\mathcal{N})$ and obtain

$$\frac{\partial f_p}{\partial p}(c\mathbb{1}_\mathcal{N}) = \mathrm{cov}(S, \log S),$$

where S is a random variable with p.d.f. $s \mapsto \frac{1}{Z}P_p(s)e^{-4\lambda|s-c|}$. But as the log function is strictly increasing, using Lemma 1, we have that $\frac{\partial f_p}{\partial p}(c\mathbb{1}_\mathcal{N})$ is positive. Considering only integer values of p, we obtain the desired result.

Proof (of Theorem 2). Assume that $\hat{u}_{\mathrm{ICE}}$ has value $c \in \mathbb{R}$ for every pixel in $\mathcal{N}_x \cup \mathcal{N}_y \cup \{x, y\}$. Then taking the limit in (6) tells us that $c = \hat{u}_{\mathrm{ICE}}(x) = f_{v(x)}(\hat{u}_{\mathrm{ICE}}(\mathcal{N}_x)) = f_{v(x)}(c\mathbb{1}_\mathcal{N})$, and similarly $c = \hat{u}_{\mathrm{ICE}}(y) = f_{v(y)}(c\mathbb{1}_\mathcal{N})$. But using Lemma 5, $p \mapsto f_p(c\mathbb{1}_\mathcal{N})$ is strictly increasing, so there exists at most one value p such that $f_p(c\mathbb{1}_\mathcal{N}) = c$. We conclude that necessarily $v(x) = p = v(y)$, which finishes the proof.

3 Numerical Computation of Poisson TV-ICE

3.1 Explicit form of the Poisson TV-ICE Recursion Operator

Proposition 1. *The Poisson TV-ICE recursion $u^{n+1}(x) = f_{v(x)}(u^n(\mathcal{N}_x))$ can be written*

$$u^{n+1}(x) = \frac{\sum_{1 \leq k \leq 5} c_k I_{a_{k-1}, a_k}^{\mu_k, v(x)+1}}{\sum_{1 \leq k \leq 5} c_k I_{a_{k-1}, a_k}^{\mu_k, v(x)}}, \quad (9)$$

where a_1, a_2, a_3, a_4 are the values of $u^n(\mathcal{N}_x)$ sorted in nondecreasing order (that is, $0 = a_0 \leq a_1 \leq a_2 \leq a_3 \leq a_4 \leq a_5 = +\infty$),

$$\forall k \in \{1, \ldots, 5\}, \quad \mu_k = 1 - (6 - 2k)\lambda, \quad \log c_k = \lambda \left(\sum_{j=1}^{k-1} a_j - \sum_{j=k}^{4} a_j \right), \quad (10)$$

$$\text{and} \quad I_{x,y}^{\mu,p} = \int_x^y s^p e^{-\mu s} ds. \quad (11)$$

Proof. This result is directly obtained after breaking the integration domain in Equation (6) so as to get rid of all absolute values.

3.2 Numerical Issues

To compute the integral (11), we introduce the following generalized lower (γ_μ) and upper (Γ_μ) incomplete gamma functions,

$$\gamma_\mu(p, x) = \int_0^x s^{p-1} e^{-\mu s} ds, \quad \Gamma_\mu(p, x) = \int_x^{+\infty} s^{p-1} e^{-\mu s} ds, \quad (12)$$

$$\text{so that} \quad I_{x,y}^{\mu,p} = \gamma_\mu(p+1, y) - \gamma_\mu(p+1, x) \quad (13)$$

and, for $\mu > 0$,

$$I_{x,y}^{\mu,p} = \Gamma_\mu(p+1, y) - \Gamma_\mu(p+1, x) = \frac{p!}{\mu^{p+1}} - \gamma_\mu(p+1, x) - \Gamma_\mu(p+1, y). \quad (14)$$

Note that when $\mu > 0$, the change of variable $t = \mu s$ would lead us back to the standard definition of incomplete gamma functions (corresponding to $\mu = 1$), but this is not the case when $\mu < 0$.

The effective computation of (9) with one of the formulas given in (13)-(14) raises several numerical issues:

1. For some values of the parameters, the numerator and the denominator cannot be represented in the computer floating point arithmetic (for example because they both exceed $1.9 \cdot 10^{308}$, the largest double precision number), although their ratio can be represented. To solve that issue, we represent each integral $I_{x,y}^{\mu,p}$ involved in (9) under the form $\rho \cdot e^\sigma$, where ρ and σ are floating point (double precision) numbers.
2. The possibility to compute efficiently $\gamma_\mu(p, x)$ and $\Gamma_\mu(p, x)$ depends on the parameters μ, p, x. We divided the plane $(\mu x, p)$ so as to compute $\gamma_\mu(p, x)$ or $\Gamma_\mu(p, x)$ efficiently for each parameter set μ, p, x.
3. When the difference $A - B$ is computed numerically, the result can be very inaccurate if A and B are close to each other, which may happen for the differences given in Equations (13)-(14). When x and y are very close to each other, the integral (11) is very well approximated by the rectangle numerical integration formula (with one term); we found a good criterion to decide when this approximation should be used.

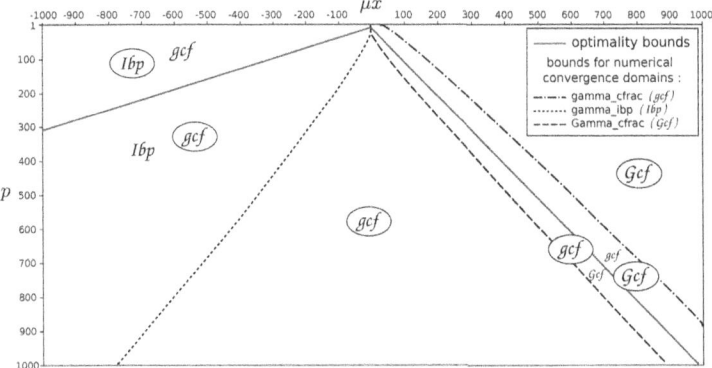

Fig. 1. Partition of the domain $(\mu x, p)$ for the evaluation of the generalized incomplete gamma function. The rectangular domain of the plane $(\mu x, p)$ above is cut into three regions delimited by the red curves (their equations appear in Algorithm 1). On each region, one of the three selected algorithm (circled) is used to compute numerically either $\gamma_\mu(p, x)$ or $\Gamma_\mu(p, x)$: the continued fraction for γ_μ (gcf), the recursive integration by parts for γ_μ (Ibp), or the continued fraction for Γ_μ (Gcf). Names without circles and dotted/dashed lines correspond to regions where another of the 3 algorithms could be used too.

Algorithm 1. Numerical estimation of $I_{x,y}^{\mu,p}$

inputs: three numbers $\mu \in \mathbb{R}$, $x \in \mathbb{R}_+$, $y \in \mathbb{R}_+ \cup \{+\infty\}$ such as $x \leq y$, and an integer $p \geq 0$. The value $y = +\infty$ is allowed only when $\mu > 0$.
outputs: ρ and σ such that $\rho \cdot e^\sigma$ is an accurate estimate of $I_{x,y}^{\mu,p}$.

if $x = y$ up to machine precision **then** $(\rho, \sigma) \leftarrow (0, -\infty)$
else if $0 < \frac{y-x}{y} \leq 10^{-9}$ **then** $(\rho, \sigma) \leftarrow \left(\frac{y-x}{y}, -\mu y + (p+1) \cdot \log y\right)$
else if $\mu \leq 0$ **then**
    if $\mu = 0$ or $p \geq -0.33\mu x + 8$ **then** $(\rho_x, \sigma_x) \leftarrow \gamma_\mu^{\text{cfrac}}(p+1, x)$
    else $(\rho_x, \sigma_x) \leftarrow \gamma_\mu^{\text{ibp}}(p+1, x)$ **end**
    if $\mu = 0$ or $p \geq -0.33\mu y + 8$ **then** $(\rho_y, \sigma_y) \leftarrow \gamma_\mu^{\text{cfrac}}(p+1, y)$
    else $(\rho_y, \sigma_y) \leftarrow \gamma_\mu^{\text{ibp}}(p+1, y)$ **end**
    $(\rho, \sigma) \leftarrow \left(\rho_y - \rho_x e^{\sigma_x - \sigma_y}, \sigma_y\right)$
else
    if $p \geq \mu y$ **then**
        $(\rho_x, \sigma_x) \leftarrow \gamma_\mu^{\text{cfrac}}(p+1, x)$; $(\rho_y, \sigma_y) \leftarrow \gamma_\mu^{\text{cfrac}}(p+1, y)$
        $(\rho, \sigma) \leftarrow \left(\rho_y - \rho_x e^{\sigma_x - \sigma_y}, \sigma_y\right)$
    else if $p < \mu x$ **then**
        $(\rho_x, \sigma_x) \leftarrow \Gamma_\mu^{\text{cfrac}}(p+1, x)$; $(\rho_y, \sigma_y) \leftarrow \Gamma_\mu^{\text{cfrac}}(p+1, y)$
        $(\rho, \sigma) \leftarrow \left(\rho_x - \rho_y e^{\sigma_y - \sigma_x}, \sigma_x\right)$
    else
        $(\rho_x, \sigma_x) \leftarrow \gamma_\mu^{\text{cfrac}}(p+1, x)$; $(\rho_y, \sigma_y) \leftarrow \Gamma_\mu^{\text{cfrac}}(p+1, y)$
        $(\rho, \sigma) \leftarrow \left(1 - \rho_x e^{\sigma_x - \sigma} - \rho_y e^{\sigma_y - \sigma}, \log p! - (p+1) \log \mu\right)$
    end
end

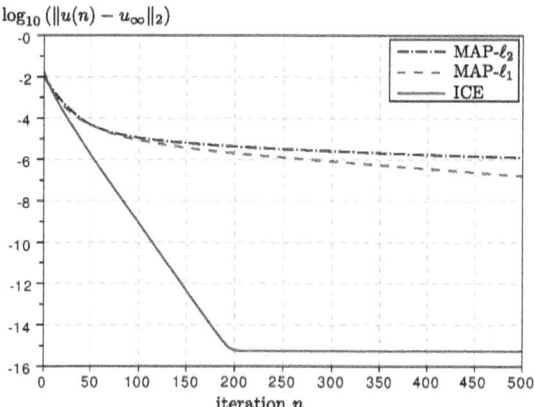

Fig. 2. Convergence rates for TV-MAP and TV-ICE. We display in logarithmic scale the convergence rates obtained for the proposed implementation of the Poisson TV-ICE algorithm (green plain curve), and for the Chambolle-Pock [5] implementation of the Poisson TV-MAP (with anisotropic and isotropic TV) algorithms (red/blue dashed curves). As expected, Poisson TV-ICE achieves a linear convergence rate.

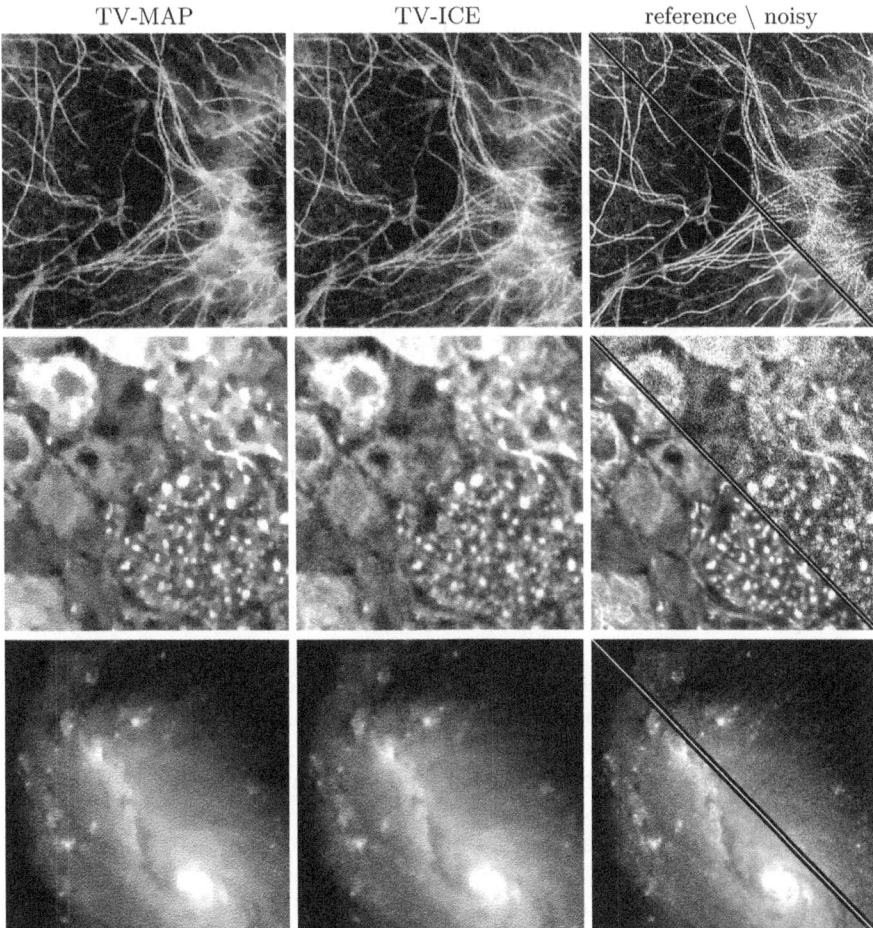

Fig. 3. Comparison of Poisson TV-MAP and Poisson TV-ICE. Three images (first row: actin filaments and microtubules in interphase cells, second row: mouse dorsal root ganglion, third row: NGC 1672 spiral galaxy) were corrupted with Poisson noise, then denoised with the Poisson TV-MAP algorithm (left column) and the proposed Poisson TV-ICE method (middle column). For each algorithm, we selected the value of the λ parameter that achieved the smallest Csiszar I-divergence [20] (a measure of distance adapted to the case of Poisson noise) between the reference image u_{ref} (bottom-left part of the images in the right column) and the denoised image $\hat{u}$, which is defined by I-div$(u_{\text{ref}}, \hat{u}) = \langle u_{\text{ref}} \log(u_{\text{ref}}/\hat{u}) - (u_{\text{ref}} - \hat{u}), \mathbb{1}_\Omega \rangle$. One can clearly see that TV-MAP results exhibit staircasing effects and an associated loss of details in the corresponding flat regions; on the contrary, the TV-ICE images are more natural and more faithful to the fine details of the reference, especially in the regions where TV-MAP produces staircasing. Note that in order to increase the readability of the figure, the dynamic of the images has been linearly amplified, causing some (limited) saturation in dark and white areas. Image sources: cellimagelibrary.org and wikimedia.org.

We reviewed the literature to find the available methods for the computation of $\gamma_\mu(p,x)$ and $\Gamma_\mu(p,x)$, and found that for the explored domain $|\mu x| \leq 1000$, $1 \leq p \leq 1000$ (and even far beyond in fact), the selection of the three following algorithms was satisfactory :

1. A continued fraction [14–17] for the computation of $\gamma_\mu^{\text{cfrac}}(p+1,x) = \rho e^\sigma$ with $\rho = \frac{\alpha_1}{\beta_1+} \frac{\alpha_2}{\beta_2+} \frac{\alpha_3}{\beta_3+} \cdots$ and $\alpha_1 = 1$, $\alpha_{2n} = -(p+n) \cdot \mu x$, $\alpha_{2n+1} = n \cdot \mu x$, $\beta_n = p + n$ for $n \geq 1$, valid for any μ.
2. An simple recursive integration by parts formula, only valid when $\mu < 0$, yielding $\gamma_\mu^{\text{ibp}}(p+1,x) = \rho e^\sigma$ with $\rho = \frac{1}{\mu x}\left(p! \frac{e^{\mu x}}{(\mu x)^p} - \sum_{0 \leq k \leq p} \frac{p!(\mu x)^{-k}}{(p-k)!}\right)$.
3. A continued fraction [18,19] for the computation of $\Gamma_\mu^{\text{cfrac}}(p+1,x) = \rho e^\sigma$ with $\rho = \frac{\alpha_1}{\beta_1+} \frac{\alpha_2}{\beta_2+} \frac{\alpha_3}{\beta_3+} \cdots$, $\beta_n = \mu x + 2n - 2 - p$ $(n \geq 1)$, $\alpha_1 = 1$ and $\alpha_n = -(n-1) \cdot (n-p-2)$ $(n > 1)$, valid for any $\mu > 0$.

In all cases, $\sigma = -\mu x + (p+1)\log x$. Fig. 1 shows the partition of the plane $(\mu x, p)$ we found as nearly optimal (in terms of computation time) to choose between these 3 algorithms. The resulting procedure used to compute $I_{x,y}^{\mu,p}$ is given in Algorithm 1.

4 Experiments

We first checked the convergence of the proposed Poisson TV-ICE algorithm obtained by iterating the recursion (9) using Algorithm 1 and the initialization $u^0 = 0$. As can be seen in Fig. 2, numerical convergence is attained for Poisson TV-ICE after a few hundred iterations, and the convergence rate is linear as expected.

We then chose 3 images taken from areas concerned with Poisson noise (2 from microscopy, 1 from astronomy), and simulated a low-light observation (that is, a Poisson noise process) for each of them. Then, we restored the noisy images with both the Poisson TV-MAP and the proposed Poisson TV-ICE methods (see Fig. 3). As predicted by the theory, TV-ICE results do not exhibit staircasing effects, contrary to TV-MAP images which provide less details, in particular in the areas where the staircasing artifact causes an important loss of contrast (see, e.g., the bottom-right part of the images of the first row of Fig. 3). This visual effect was confirmed by the systematically smaller I-divergence values obtained with TV-ICE.

5 Conclusion

We proposed a variant of the recent TV-ICE denoising method adapted to the special case of Poisson noise. The absence of staircasing and the better-quality restored images attested by experiments make Poisson TV-ICE a good alternative to Poisson TV-MAP, and suggests that it could be interesting to derive Poisson TV-ICE variants for more complex inverse problems involving TV terms.

The linear convergence rate of the method is appealing but is not sufficient to compensate for the heavy computations required by the form of the recursion operator (several evaluations of the exponential and logarithm functions are required for each pixel). In our current (non-optimized) implementation, one iteration of TV-ICE is approximately 100 times slower than one iteration of TV-MAP. However, further work could focus on the fast approximation of TV-ICE, and the precise implementation we here proposed would be useful in that context to check the quality of the approximation.

As in the Gaussian case, the generalization of the proposed algorithm to three-dimensional images (or more), or to larger neighborhood systems, is straightforward. However, the comparison with the Poisson TV-LSE variant is, both from a theoretical or practical point of view, still open.

Acknowledgments. This work has been partially supported by NSFC 11271049, RGC 211911, 12302714 and RFGs of HKBU.

References

1. Rudin, L.I., Osher, S., Fatemi, E.: Nonlinear total variation based noise removal algorithms. Physica D **60**(1), 259–268 (1992)
2. Caselles, V., Chambolle, A., Novaga, M.: Total variation in imaging. In: Handbook of Mathematical Methods in Imaging, pp. 1016–1057. Springer, New York (2011)
3. Chambolle, A., Caselles, V., Cremers, D., Novaga, M., Pock, T.: An introduction to total variation for image analysis. Theoretical foundations and numerical methods for sparse recovery **9**, 263–340 (2010)
4. Darbon, J., Sigelle, M.: Image restoration with discrete constrained total variation part I: Fast and exact optimization. J. Math. Imag. Vis. **26**(3), 261–276 (2007)
5. Chambolle, A., Pock, T.: A first-order primal-dual algorithm for convex problems with applications to imaging. J. Math. Imag. Vis. **40**(1), 120–145 (2011)
6. Buades, A., Coll, B., Morel, J.-M.: A review of image denoising algorithms, with a new one. Multiscale Model. Simul. **4**(2), 490–530 (2005)
7. Dabov, K., Foi, A., Katkovnik, V., Egiazarian, K.: Image denoising by sparse 3-D transform-domain collaborative filtering. IEEE Trans. Image Processing **16**(8), 2080–2095 (2007)
8. Louchet, C., Moisan, L.: Total variation denoising using posterior expectation. In: Proc, European Signal Processing Conf (2008)
9. Louchet, C., Moisan, L.: Posterior Expectation of the Total Variation model: Properties and Experiments. SIAM J. Imaging Sci. **6**(4), 2640–2684 (2013)
10. Louchet, C., Moisan, L.: Total variation denoising using iterated conditional expectation. In: Proc, European Signal Processing Conf (2014)
11. Setzer, S., Steidl, G., Teuber, T.: Deblurring Poissonian images by split Bregman techniques. J. Vis. Comm. Image Representation **21**(3), 193–199 (2010)
12. Deledalle, C., Tupin, F., Denis, L.: Poisson NL means: Unsupervised non local means for poisson noise. In: Proc. Int. Conf. Imag. Processing, pp. 801–804 (2010)
13. Schmidt, K.D.: On the covariance of monotone functions of a random variable. Unpublished note, University of Dresden (2003)
14. Olver, F.W.J., Lozier, D.W., Boisvert, R.F., Clark, C.W. (eds.): NIST Handbook of Mathematical Functions. Cambridge University Press, New York (2010)

15. NIST Digital Library of Mathematical Functions (2014). http://dlmf.nist.gov/ (release 1.0.9 of August 29, 2014)
16. Cuyt, A., Petersen, V.B., Verdonk, B., Waadeland, H., Jones, W.B.: Handbook of continued fractions for special functions. Springer, New York (2008)
17. Jones, W.B., Thron, W.J.: Continued Fractions: Analytic Theory and Applications. Encyclopedia of Mathematics and its Applications, vol. 11. Addison-Wesley Publishing Co., Reading, MA (1980)
18. Numerical recipes: The art of scientific computing, 2nd edn. Cambridge University (2007)
19. Abramowitz, M., Stegun, I.A.: Handbook of mathematical functions: with formulas, graphs, and mathematical tables. Courier Dover Publications no. 55 (1972)
20. Csiszar, I.: Why least squares and maximum entropy? An axiomatic approach to inference for linear inverse problems. Ann. Stat. **19**, 2032–2066 (1991)

Regularization with Sparse Vector Fields: From Image Compression to TV-Type Reconstruction

Eva-Maria Brinkmann[1], Martin Burger[1(✉)], and Joana Grah[1,2]

[1] Institute for Computational and Applied Mathematics, Westfälische Wilhelms-Universität Münster, Einsteinstr. 62, 48149 Münster, Germany
{e.brinkmann,martin.burger}@wwu.de, jg704@cam.ac.uk
[2] Department of Applied Mathematics and Theoretical Physics, University of Cambridge, Centre for Mathematical Sciences, Wilberforce Road, Cambridge CB3 0WA, UK

Abstract. This paper introduces a novel variational approach for image compression motivated by recent PDE-based approaches combining edge detection and Laplacian inpainting. The essential feature is to encode the image via a sparse vector field, ideally concentrating on a set of measure zero. An equivalent reformulation of the compression approach leads to a variational model resembling the ROF-model for image denoising, hence we further study the properties of the effective regularization functional introduced by the novel approach and discuss similarities to TV and TGV functionals. Moreover, we computationally investigate the behaviour of the model with sparse vector fields for compression in particular for high resolution images and give an outlook towards denoising.

Keywords: Image compression · Denoising · Reconstruction · Diffusion inpainting · Sparsity · Total variation

1 Introduction

Image compression is a topic of interest since the beginning of digital imaging, remaining relevant continuously due to the ongoing improvement in image resolution. While standard approaches are based on orthogonal bases and frames like cosine transforms or wavelets, an alternative route based on ideas from partial differential equations has emerged recently (cf. [13,14]). In the latter case particular attention is paid to compressions from which cartoons can be reconstructed accurately avoiding the artefacts of the above mentioned standard approaches by a direct treatment of edges. Roughly speaking, their idea is to detect edges and store the image value in pixels on both sides of an edge. The remaining parts of the image are completed by harmonic inpainting. An alternative interpretation of the two-sided pixel values, worked out more clearly in the osmosis setting of [20], is that a vector field v corresponding to the normal derivatives of the image

at the edge location is stored. The inpainting of the image u then corresponds to a solution of
$$\Delta u = \nabla \cdot v \quad \text{in } \Omega, \tag{1}$$
where Ω is the image domain into which v is extended by zero off the edges.

In this paper we start from reinterpretation of the PDE-based compression in terms of sparsity, which directly translates into a variational framework. The key observation is that with the edge detection and zero extension of v one essentially looks for a sparse vector field that leads to a certain precision in the reconstruction via (1). In the spirit of the predominant sparsity regularization of imaging problems we study a direct variational approach: we minimize an L^1-type norm of the vector field subject to the constraint that u reconstructed via (1) approximates a given image f up to a certain tolerance, i.e.
$$\|v\|_1 \to \min_{u,v} \quad \text{subject to} \quad \Delta u = \nabla \cdot v, \quad \|u - f\|_2 \leq \epsilon. \tag{2}$$

As we shall discuss below a more rigorous statement of the problem takes into account that v needs to be interpreted as a vectorial Radon measure on Ω (similar to gradients of BV-functions) in a continuum setting. The properties of a limiting continuum model appear to be of particular advantage for the compression issues, since one expects to concentrate the measure v on a set of Lebesgue measure zero. This means that for a suitable discrete approximation of the model the number of pixels we need to store the vector field in divided by the total number of pixels tends to zero. A direct consequence is an increase in the compression rates as image resolution increases, a highly desirable property.

Apart from compression we shall investigate models like the above one as a regularization for more general imaging problems. The relation to denoising models can readily be seen when the above constraint of approximating f is incorporated via a Lagrange functional. Indeed, there exists a Lagrange parameter $\lambda > 0$ such that (2) is equivalent to
$$\frac{\lambda}{2}\|u - f\|_2^2 + \|v\|_1 \to \min_{u,v} \quad \text{subject to} \quad \Delta u = \nabla \cdot v. \tag{3}$$

Hence, we may also interpret the norm of v as an implicit regularization of v and simply replace the first term by an arbitrary data term to treat other imaging problems. This is more apparent when we replace the constraint by a natural special solution $v = \nabla u$. In this case (3) is just the ROF-model for denoising (cf. [18]) and indeed an equivalence relation holds in spatial dimension one. In higher spatial dimensions it becomes apparent that a key role is played by the curl $\nabla \times v$. If the curl of v vanishes, v simply becomes a gradient vector field and hence we again recover the ROF-model. This motivates to study further generalizations of the model also penalizing $\nabla \times v$. With the interpretation that v is related to the gradient of u, the additional term becomes a higher order regularization effectively. Functionals of this type are currently studied in particular to reduce staircasing artefacts in total variation regularization (cf. [2,4,9]), and indeed we shall be able to draw very close analogies to the recently very popular TGV-approach (cf. [4]). The reduction of staircasing is confirmed by computational experiments. However, in the denoising case we shall see that the divergence part alone does not suffice for appropriate smoothing.

The remainder of the paper is organized as follows: In Section 2 we discuss the model and its variants. Then, we proceed to a discussion of some theoretical properties in Section 3, which provide some insights into the sparse vector field model. Section 4 introduces a numerical solution based on primal-dual optimization methods, which is used for some experimental studies in Section 5. Finally, we provide a conclusion and directions for future research.

2 Variational Model and Regularization Functionals

In order to obtain an appropriate formulation of (3) we proceed as in [5] and interpret v as a d-dimensional Radon measure on $\Omega \subset \mathbb{R}^d$. The regularization functional is then

$$\|v\|_{\mathcal{M}(\Omega)} = \sup_{\varphi \in C(\Omega)^d, \|\varphi\|_\infty \leq 1} \int_\Omega \varphi \cdot dv, \qquad (4)$$

where (1) is to be understood in a weak form as well. Hence, (3) is rewritten as

$$\frac{\lambda}{2}\|u - f\|_2^2 + \|v\|_{\mathcal{M}(\Omega)} \to \min_{u \in L^2(\Omega), v \in \mathcal{M}(\Omega)^d} \quad \text{subject to} \quad \Delta u = \nabla \cdot v. \qquad (5)$$

The model can be formulated as in recent approaches for denoising by defining $w = \nabla u - v$ (in the sense of distributions). With χ_0 being the characteristic function of the set $\{0\}$ we obtain

$$\frac{\lambda}{2}\|u - f\|_2^2 + \|\nabla u - w\|_{\mathcal{M}(\Omega)} + \chi_0(\nabla \cdot w) \to \min_{u \in L^2(\Omega), w \in \mathcal{D}'(\Omega)^d}. \qquad (6)$$

One observes that the regularization functional is now an infimal convolution of total variation and a functional of ∇w. The same structure is apparent in the recently popularized TGV-model (cf. [4]), which in the analogous setting reads

$$\frac{\lambda}{2}\|u - f\|_2^2 + \|\nabla u - w\|_{\mathcal{M}(\Omega)} + \|\nabla w\|_{\mathcal{M}(\Omega)} \to \min_{u \in L^2(\Omega), w \in \mathcal{M}(\Omega)^d}. \qquad (7)$$

A major difference of the TGV approach to our new model is the fact that in our case only the divergence of v respectively w is penalized, which might be too weak to achieve suitable regularization properties. This can obviously be realized if we add additional regularization terms depending on $\nabla \times v$, which is natural since a divergence-free vector field is constant if and only if its curl vanishes. Note that $\nabla \times \nabla u = 0$, hence $\nabla \times v = -\nabla \times w$, i.e. we can formulate regularization either on v or on w. The most general formulation is given by

$$\frac{\lambda}{2}\|u - f\|_2^2 + \|\nabla u - w\|_{\mathcal{M}(\Omega)} + F(\nabla \cdot w) + G(\nabla \times w) \to \min_{u \in L^2(\Omega), w \in \mathcal{D}'(\Omega)^d}, \qquad (8)$$

with convex functionals F and G, which however exceeds the scope of this paper and is left as subject of future research.

We finally recast the above results in terms of the regularization they induce on u. In this respect we also discuss the boundary conditions in (1), respectively its weak formulation. Natural boundary conditions are no-flux conditions ($\nabla u - v) \cdot n = 0$ on $\partial\Omega$, which means the used weak formulation of (1) is

$$\int_\Omega \Delta\varphi\, u\, dx + \int_\Omega \nabla\varphi \cdot dv(x) = 0 \quad \forall \varphi \in C^2(\Omega), \nabla\varphi \cdot n = 0 \text{ on } \partial\Omega. \quad (9)$$

Hence, we can define the regularization functional $R : L^1(\Omega) \to [0, \infty]$

$$R(u) := \inf_{v \text{ satisfying } (9)} \|v\|_{\mathcal{M}(\Omega)}. \quad (10)$$

Once we have defined the regularization terms it is straight-forward to extend the variational model to other imaging tasks, e.g. by just changing the data fidelity. Moreover, we can consider Bregman iterations (cf. [16])

$$u^{k+1} \in \arg\min_u \left(\frac{\lambda}{2}\|u - f\|_2^2 + R(u) - \langle p^k, u \rangle \right), \quad p^k \in R(u^k), \quad (11)$$

as well as other scale space methods such as the gradient flow (cf. [1]) $\partial_t u \in -\partial R(u)$ and the inverse scale space method (cf. [6]).

3 Properties of Regularization by Sparse Vector Fields

In the following we further discuss some properties of the regularization functional R defined via (10). To avoid obvious technicalities with constants, we restrict ourselves to the space

$$L^1_\diamond(\Omega) = \{\, u \in L^1(\Omega) \mid \int_\Omega u\, dx = 0 \,\} \quad (12)$$

if Ω is a bounded domain.

We start with some topological properties induced by R:

Theorem 1. *Let Ω be a sufficiently regular domain. Then there exists a constant $c > 0$ such that*

$$\|u\|_{L^1(\Omega)} \leq c R(u) \quad (13)$$

for all $u \in L^1_\diamond(\Omega)$. Moreover, $\mathrm{dom}(R)$ is a subspace of $L^1(\Omega)$ and R is a norm on $\mathrm{dom}(R) \cap L^1_\diamond(\Omega)$. Finally,

$$R(u) \leq TV(u) \quad \forall\, u \in BV(\Omega). \quad (14)$$

Proof. We have

$$\|u\|_{L^1(\Omega)} = \sup_{\phi \in L^\infty(\Omega), \|\phi\|_\infty \leq 1} \int_\Omega u(x)\phi(x)\, dx. \quad (15)$$

For $\phi \in L^\infty(\Omega)$ we define w as the weak solution of the Poisson equation $-\Delta w = \phi$ with homogeneous Neumann boundary conditions and mean value zero. Thus, using the weak formulations we have

$$\int_\Omega u(x)\phi(x)\,dx = \int_\Omega \nabla w(x) \cdot dv(x). \tag{16}$$

Regularity of solutions of the Poisson equation yields continuity of w and the existence of a constant c such that $\|\nabla w\|_\infty \leq c\|\phi\|_\infty = c$, for all $\phi \in L^\infty(\Omega)$. Hence,

$$\sup_{\phi \in L^\infty(\Omega), \|\phi\|_\infty \leq 1} \int_\Omega u(x)\phi(x)\,dx \leq c\|v\|_{\mathcal{M}(\Omega)}, \tag{17}$$

which yields the estimate of the L^1-norm.

The one-homogeneity and triangle inequality follow in a straight-forward way from the definition, consequently R is a norm on a subspace of $L^1_\diamond(\Omega)$. Estimate (14) is obtained since $v = \nabla u$ satisfies (9), hence the infimum over all admissible v is less or equal to the total variation.

A next step towards the understanding of properties of R is an investigation of its subdifferential, with subsequent consequences for optimality conditions of (5). For brevity we use a formal approach based on Lagrange multipliers. We have $p \in \partial R(u)$ if and only if $p = \partial_u L(u, v, q)$, for solutions (v, q) of the saddle-point problem

$$\inf_v \sup_q L(u, v, q) \tag{18}$$

for given u and the Lagrangian is defined as

$$L(u, v, q) = \|v\|_{\mathcal{M}(\Omega)} + \int_\Omega \Delta q\, u\, dx + \int_\Omega \nabla q \cdot dv(x). \tag{19}$$

Thus, we find $p = \Delta q$ and the optimality conditions for the saddle point problem yield (9) and $-\nabla q \in \partial \|v\|_{\mathcal{M}(\Omega)}$.

It is instructive to compare the subgradients of R with those of TV. Indeed with similar reasoning one can show that $p \in \partial TV(u)$ if $p = -\nabla \cdot g$ for a vector field $g \in \partial \|v\|_{\mathcal{M}(\Omega)}$ and $v = \nabla u$. This means that if we can write $g = -\nabla q$ we also obtain $p \in \partial R(u)$. In particular this opens the door towards a simple verification whether solutions of the ROF-model are also solutions of the sparse vector field model (5). One simply has to inspect the subgradient in the optimality condition and check whether the associated vector field g can be written as a gradient. We will exemplify this in the case of the most well-known example for the ROF model, the reconstruction of the indicator function of a ball on $\Omega = \mathbb{R}^d$ (cf. [15]). This function is an eigenfunction of TV, i.e. there exists λ (depending on the radius R of the ball) such that

$$\lambda u = \nabla \cdot g \in \partial TV(u). \tag{20}$$

It is easy to see that $g = \nabla F(b)$, where b is the signed distance function of the ball (cf. [10]) and F satisfies

$$F'(z) = \begin{cases} 1 & \text{if } z \leq 0 \\ \frac{R}{z+R} & \text{if } z > 0. \end{cases} \qquad (21)$$

Hence, we have $g = -\nabla q$ for $q = -F(b)$, which implies that $\lambda u \in \partial R(u)$, with the same value. The results in [3] imply that the variational model (5) reconstructs data f being the indicator function of a ball in the form $u = cf$, with $c < 1$ depending on λ and α. Moreover, the Bregman iteration and inverse scale space methods reconstruct f exactly after a finite number of iterations.

Finally we return to the original idea of compressing an image by encoding a sparse vector field. For this sake it is desirable that v has support on a set of small (or even zero) Lebesgue measure. Thinking about the continuum case as a limit of discrete pixel images, the asymptotic property of zero Lebesgue measure means that the image (in 2D) can be encoded by a number of values proportional to the square root of the number of pixels. Consequently the compression rate of such a PDE-based approach should improve with higher image resolution, which is highly relevant given the current trend of screen and camera resolution. We already see from the example of the indicator function of a ball above that we can expect the method to encode a piecewise constant image by vector fields concentrated on the edge sets. For more complicated images the vector field potentially needs to have a larger support to obtain a suitable reconstruction, since away from the support of v the function u is just harmonic. A better understanding of the compression properties would need a characterization of the structure of minimizers, similar to [7,19]. While the one-dimensional case is equivalent to total variation regularization and hence always yields v concentrated on a set of zero Lebesgue measure (cf. [17]), the multi-dimensional case is less clear and left as an interesting topic of future research. Further studies on the compression properties will be carried out below by computational experiments.

4 Numerical Solution via Primal-Dual Methods

In order to solve our minimization problem (5) numerically, we at first need to discretize it. Thereto we will adopt the notation of the continuous functions u, v, f and the operators ∇, $\nabla\cdot$ and Δ, but from now on, we are thereby referring to their discretized versions, which we shall comment on in the following. For simplification, we assume the normalized images to be quadratic, i.e. $f, u \in [0,1]^{N \times N}$. The pixel grid can be written as $\{(ih, jh): 1 \leq i, j \leq N\}$, where h denotes the spacing size. We use forward finite differences with Neumann boundary conditions for the discretization of the gradient of u and in order to preserve the adjoint structure the divergence is discretized with backward finite differences. Moreover, in this discrete setting the d-dimensional Radon measure on $\Omega \subset \mathbb{R}^d$ becomes the discrete L1-norm. Considering v as being related to the gradient of u, the regularization term in problem (5) can be interpreted as the discrete total variation norm. We decided to use its isotropic version given by

$$\|\nabla u\|_1 = \sum_{i,j} |(\nabla u)_{i,j}| = \sum_{i,j} \sqrt{((\nabla u)^1_{i,j})^2 + ((\nabla u)^2_{i,j})^2}. \qquad (22)$$

Consequently, the minimization problem (5) reads:

$$\frac{\lambda}{2}\|u - f\|_2^2 + \|v\|_1 \to \min_{u,v} \quad \text{subject to} \quad \Delta u = \nabla \cdot v \qquad (23)$$

or equivalently:

$$\frac{\lambda}{2}\|u - f\|_2^2 + \|v\|_1 + \chi_0(\Delta u - \nabla \cdot v) \to \min_{u,v}, \qquad (24)$$

where χ_0 is again the characteristic function of the set $\{0\}$. Defining

$$x := (u,v)^T, \ G(x) := \frac{\lambda}{2}\|u - f\|_2^2 + \|v\|_1, \ F(Kx) := \chi_0(\Delta u - \nabla \cdot v), \quad (25)$$

one can easily see that we can calculate a solution of the above problem (24) by applying a version of the recently very popular primal-dual algorithms (cf. [8,11]) designed for efficiently solving general minimization problems of the form

$$F(Kx) + G(x) \to \min_x, \qquad (26)$$

where F and G are proper convex lower-semicontinuous functionals.

We decided to use the first-order primal-dual algorithm as proposed by Chambolle and Pock (cf. [8]) given by Algorithm 1.

Algorithm 1 Primal-Dual Algorithm by Chambolle and Pock

Input: $\tau, \sigma > 0$, $\theta \in [0,1]$
Initialization: x^0, y^0, $\bar{x}^0 = x^0$
  for $n \geq 0$ **do**
   $y^{n+1} = (I + \sigma \partial F^*)^{-1} (y^n + \sigma K \bar{x}^n)$
   $x^{n+1} = (I + \tau \partial G)^{-1} (x^n - \tau K^* y^{n+1})$
   $\bar{x}^{n+1} = x^{n+1} + \theta (x^{n+1} - x^n)$
  end for

Adopting their notation we can now derive the updates concerning our minimization problem (24). Thereto we at first calculate the dual functional $F^*(y) = \sup_x\{\langle y, x \rangle - F(x)\}$. Since in our case F is the characteristic function of the set $\{0\}$, it is straightforward to see that F^* equals zero and hence the dual variable y is given by $y^{n+1} = y^n + \sigma K \bar{x}^n$. Next we consider the update for the primal variable x. As the subdifferentials of G with respect to u and v are independent of v and u, respectively, we can update each component of x separately.

Using the norm of the sum of the primal and dual residual given by (cf. [12])
$$\|P^{n+1}\|^2 + \|D^{n+1}\|^2, \qquad (27)$$
where
$$P^{n+1} = \frac{x^n - x^{n+1}}{\tau} - K^*(y^n - y^{n+1}), \quad D^{n+1} = \frac{y^n - y^{n+1}}{\sigma} - K(x^n - x^{n+1}), \quad (28)$$
as a stopping criterion the implementation of our minimization problem (24) can be summarized by Algorithm 2, where the two-dimensional isotropic shrinkage operator is defined by:
$$shrinkage(z, \gamma) = \max(\|z\|_1 - \gamma)\frac{z}{\|z\|_1}. \qquad (29)$$

Algorithm 2 Primal-Dual Algorithm for Minimization of (24)

Input: image f, $\lambda > 0$, $\tau, \sigma > 0$, $\theta \in [0,1]$, max no of iterations, $\epsilon > 0$
Initialization: u^0, v^0, y^0, $\bar{u}^0 = u^0$, $\bar{v}^0 = v^0$
    while primal-dual residual $> \epsilon$ **and** $n <$ max no of iterations **do**
        $y^{n+1} = (I + \sigma \partial F^*)^{-1} (y^n + \sigma \nabla \cdot (\nabla \bar{u}^n - \bar{v}^n)) = y^n + \sigma \nabla \cdot (\nabla \bar{u}^n - \bar{v}^n)$
        $u^{n+1} = (I + \tau \partial_u G)^{-1} (u^n - \tau \Delta y^{n+1}) = \frac{1}{1+\lambda\tau}(\lambda\tau f + u^n - \tau \Delta y^{n+1})$
        $v^{n+1} = (I + \tau \partial_d G)^{-1} (v^n - \tau \nabla y^{n+1}) = $ shrinkage$(v^n - \tau \nabla y^{n+1}, \tau)$
        $\bar{u}^{n+1} = u^{n+1} + \theta(u^{n+1} - u^n)$
        $\bar{v}^{n+1} = v^{n+1} + \theta(v^{n+1} - v^n)$
    end while

As already mentioned in Section 2 the model discussed so far can be further extended by considering for example Bregman iterations as proposed by Osher and coworkers [16]. To incorporate this iterative regularization method in our algorithm, we use their "adding-back-the-noise" formulation such that the update for u in the previously introduced routine is replaced by
$$u^{n+1} = \frac{1}{1+\lambda\tau}(\lambda\tau f + h^k + u^n - \tau \Delta y^{n+1}). \qquad (30)$$
Besides, the existing implementation is extended by an outer loop over a given number of Bregman iterations in which h is updated by $h^{k+1} = h^k + f - u$ after each complete cycle of the inner loop.

5 Computational Results

In the following we present some results for the cases of image compression and denoising discussed above. As an example we chose the frequently used image "Trui" (257×257 pixels), making the approach comparable to previous results such as [13]. However, since the size of this image does not correspond to modern HD resolutions, we also created two similar images with sizes of 1024×1024 and 4800×4800 pixels, respectively.

5.1 Image Compression

We start by discussing the compression of the cartoon part of an image, which is illustrated in Figure 1 for the Trui test image. We plot the relative error vs. the non-zero gradient ratio, which means the number of pixels with non-zero v divided by the total number of pixels. On the left we show a comparison of the sparse vector field (SVF) model with the classical ROF model, which demonstrates the improved compression properties. On the right we plot the results for the variational SVF model compared to the Bregman iteration, which illustrates that no significant improvement can be obtained with respect to compression by the latter.

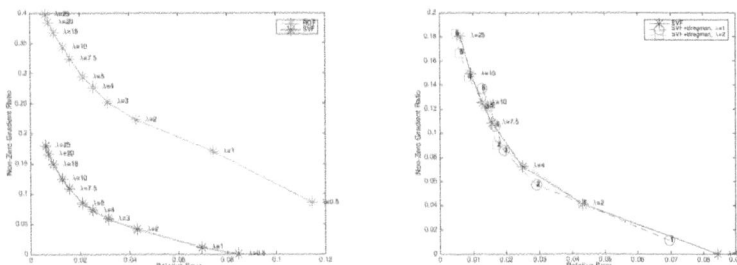

Fig. 1. Comparison of the non-zero gradient ratio for different parameter values

In Figure 2 we display the results of the compression and the corresponding vector fields for $\lambda = 10$. One observes that the support of v corresponds well to an edge indicator, confirming the relation to the approach in [13]. The reconstructed image seems to preserve the main edges well, but does not have the strict piecewise constant behaviour as total variation regularization, which seems attractive for further reconstruction tasks. We also investigate the behaviour for higher

Fig. 2. From left to right: Original image, vector field v in x- and y-direction, norm of v, and the corresponding reconstruction for $\lambda = 10$

resolution. In order to mimic increasing resolution we simply downscale the test images to r times the number of original pixels, $r \in (0, 1]$. We then perform compression at fixed error tolerance (corresponding to constant λ when appropriately scaled) for the images of different size and finally plot the non-zero gradient ratio

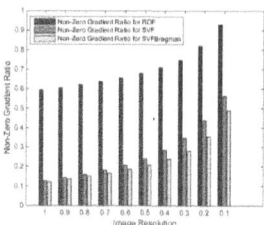  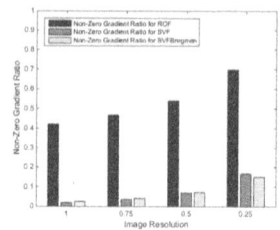

Fig. 3. Comparison of the Non-Zero Gradient Ratios of the SVF ($\lambda = 10$), the SVF-Bregman ($\lambda = 1$ and 5 Bregman Iterations) and the ROF ($\lambda = 10$) algorithms for the Trui test image (left) and an additional test image of size 1024x1024 pixels (right). The latter test image is displayed in the middle.

vs. r in Figure 3. Our expectation that due to continuum limit and the potential convergence towards a concentrated measure the ratio decreases with increasing resolution is well-confirmed for the Trui image as well as for a similar image at higher resolution.

Finally we display the result of the SVF model on a high definition image and compare it to a jpg image with the same compression rate in Figure 4. Indeed we achieve an improved PSNR with the SVF model. We also mention that several further compression steps on v can be carried out in an analogous way to [13], which will lead to highly improved rates, but is beyond the scope of this paper.

 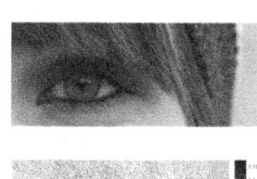 

Fig. 4. From left to right: Original image with a resolution of 16.1068 bits per pixel, our reconstruction at a compression of 1.1892 bits per pixel ($\lambda = 10$) with a PSNR value of *34.0767 dB* and the jpg image at the same compression rate with a PSNR value of 33.3214 dB, corresponding difference images to original one in bottom row.

5.2 Denoising

We finally give an outlook towards other tasks such as denoising with sparse vector fields. For this sake we compare our results to the classical ROF model and choose in both cases λ such that the PSNR to the original image is maximized. We illustrate the result in Figure 5, which appears to be representative for all our tests. One observes that the reduced staircasing in the SVF model compared to

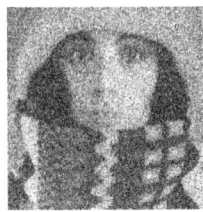

Fig. 5. Noisy image (Gaussian noise, variance 0.05, left), ROF denoising result ($\lambda = 5$, middle left), SVF denoising result ($\lambda = 4$, middle right), norm of vector field v in SVF model (right).

the ROF model is less visible, which is due to point like artefacts that were not present without noise. This results in a lower PSNR than for the ROF model, which is consistent for all our tests. The reason for the artefacts is that v is too sparse in this case and does not encode the contours anymore (see Figure 5).

6 Conclusion

We have introduced the SVF model for image compression motivated by diffusion inpainting and found several interesting connections to TV-type regularization methods. The SVF approach leads to significantly sparser vector fields than the gradients of total variation, which appears useful for compression. Besides, it seems not to suffer from staircasing artefacts, which is attractive for other reconstruction tasks. However, the denoising performance of the SVF model is not convincing, since it creates point artefacts at reasonable choice of the regularization parameter. This is probably due to the fact that the norm induced by the corresponding regularization is too weak (there is an upper but no lower bound in terms of TV). For future improvement it seems natural to consider regularization on the curl of the vector field as well, such that v becomes again concentrated on contours rather than scattered points. In particular we suggest to study the more general problem

$$\frac{\lambda}{2}\|u - f\|_2^2 + \|\nabla u - w\|_1 + \beta\|\nabla \times w\|_1 + \gamma\|\nabla \cdot w\|_1 \to \min_{u,w} \qquad (31)$$

for positive β and γ where again $w = \nabla u - v$ (see (8)). Due to the exact penalization properties of one-norms we expect that the ROF model corresponds to the case of β and γ sufficiently large, while the SVF model in this paper is $\beta = 0$ and γ sufficiently large.

Acknowledgments. This work has been supported by ERC via Grant EU FP 7 - ERC Consolidator Grant 615216 LifeInverse. MB acknowledges support by the German Science Foundation DFG via EXC 1003 Cells in Motion Cluster of Excellence, Münster. JG acknowledges support by the Cambridge Biomedical Research Centre. The authors thank Tim Löpmeier (Münster) and Johannes Hjorth (Cambridge) for the acquisition of HD photographs used as test data.

References

1. Andreu, F., Ballester, C., Caselles, V., Mazon, J.M.: Minimizing total variation flow. Differential and integral equations **14**, 321–360 (2001)
2. Benning, M., Brune, C., Burger, M., Müller, J.: Higher-order TV methods: Enhancement via Bregman iteration. J Sci Comput **54**, 269–310 (2013)
3. Benning, M., Burger, M.: Ground states and singular vectors of convex variational regularization methods. Methods and Applications of Analysis **20**, 295–334 (2013)
4. Bredies, K., Kunisch, K., Pock, T.: Total generalized variation. SIAM J. Imaging Sci. **3**, 492–526 (2010)
5. Bredies, K., Pikkarainen, H.K.: Inverse problems in spaces of measures. ESAIM: Control, Optimisation and Calculus of Variations **19**, 190–218 (2013)
6. Burger, M., Gilboa, G., Osher, S., Xu, J.: Nonlinear inverse scale space methods. Communications in Mathematical Sciences **4**, 179–212 (2006)
7. Chambolle, A., Caselles, V., Cremers, D., Novaga, M., Pock, T.: An introduction to total variation for image analysis. In: Fornasier, M. (ed.) Theoretical Foundations and Numerical Methods for Sparse Recovery, pp. 263–340. DeGruyter, Berlin (2010)
8. Chambolle, A., Pock, T.: A first-order primal-dual algorithm for convex problems with applications to imaging. J. Math. Imaging Vis. **40**, 120–145 (2011)
9. Chan, T., Marquina, A., Mulet, P.: High-order total variation-based image restoration. SIAM Journal on Scientific Computing **22**, 503–516 (2000)
10. Delfour, M.C., Zolesio, J.-P.: Shapes and geometries: metrics, analysis, differential calculus, and optimization. SIAM, Philadelphia (2011)
11. Esser, E., Zhang, X., Chan, T.: A general framework for a class of first order primal-dual algorithms for convex optimization in imaging science. SIAM J. Imaging Sci. **3**(4), 1015–1046 (2010)
12. Goldstein, T., Esser, E., Baraniuk, R.: Adaptive Primal-Dual Hybrid Gradient-Methods for Saddle-Point Problems. arXiv Preprint arxiv:1305.0546v1 (2013)
13. Mainberger, M., Bruhn, A., Weickert, J., Forchhammer, S.: Edge-based compression of cartoon-like images with homogeneous diffusion. Pattern Recognition **44**(9), 1859–1873 (2011)
14. Mainberger, M., Weickert, J.: Edge-based image compression with homogeneous diffusion. In: Jiang, X., Petkov, N. (eds.) CAIP 2009. LNCS, vol. 5702, pp. 476–483. Springer, Heidelberg (2009)
15. Meyer, Y.: Oscillating Patterns in Image Processing and Nonlinear Evolution Equations. AMS, Providence (2001)
16. Osher, S., Burger, M., Goldfarb, D., Xu, J., Yin, W.: An Iterative Regularization Method for Total Variation-Based Image Restoration. Multiscale Model. Simul. **4**, 460–489 (2005)
17. Ring, W.: Structural properties of solutions to total variation regularization problems. ESAIM: Math. Modelling Numer. Analysis **34**, 799–810 (2000)
18. Rudin, L.I., Osher, S., Fatemi, E.: Nonlinear total variation based noise removal algorithms. Physica D **60**, 259–268 (1992)
19. Valkonen, T.: The jump set under geometric regularisation. Part 1: Basic technique and first-order denoising. arXiv preprint arXiv:1407.1531 (2014)
20. Weickert, J., Hagenburg, K., Breuß, M., Vogel, O.: Linear osmosis models for visual computing. In: Heyden, A., Kahl, F., Olsson, C., Oskarsson, M., Tai, X.-C. (eds.) EMMCVPR 2013. LNCS, vol. 8081, pp. 26–39. Springer, Heidelberg (2013)

Solution-Driven Adaptive Total Variation Regularization

Frank Lenzen[✉] and Johannes Berger

HCI and IPA, University of Heidelberg, Heidelberg, Germany
{frank.lenzen,johannes.berger}@iwr.uni-heidelberg.de

Abstract. We consider solution-driven adaptive variants of Total Variation, in which the adaptivity is introduced as a fixed point problem. We provide existence theory for such fixed points in the continuous domain. For the applications of image denoising, deblurring and inpainting, we provide experiments which demonstrate that our approach in most cases outperforms state-of-the-art regularization approaches.

Keywords: Regularization · Inverse problems · Adaptive total variation · Solution-driven adaptivity · Fixed point problems · Image restoration

1 Introduction

In recent years, several adaptive variants of Total Variation (TV) for the task of image restoration have been proposed, see e.g. [3,7,8,11–13,16,20]. When adaptivity is introduced, there are several alternatives how to provide the information which is required to steer the adaptivity. The standard approach is to use the (pre-smoothed) input data to estimate prominent image structures (referred to as *data-driven adaptivity* in the following). Another way is to let the adaptivity depend directly on the solution (*solution-driven adaptivity*). In this paper we follow an approach which we have proposed in [14]: The adaptivity is defined based on an arbitrary input image v. Fixing v yields a convex optimization problem with uniquely determined minimizer u. One then seeks for a fixed point of the mapping from v to u, which makes the adaptivity solution-driven.

In [15,16] we have shown that in the **discrete** setting under sufficient conditions a fixed point of this approach exists. Uniqueness can also be obtained with more restrictive assumptions.

In the work presented here, we consider the **continuous** setting of this ansatz, for which we provide existence results for a class of adaptive TV regularizers. Such theory has not been provided in literature so far. As exemplary applications we consider image denoising, non-blind deblurring and inpainting. Our approach, however, is applicable as regularization method for any inverse problem under the conditions retrieved in this paper.

2 Motivation

We start with the classical ROF functional [17] for denoising images, in which the data to be denoised are represented as a function $f \in L^2(\Omega)$ for some open bounded domain $\Omega \subset \mathbb{R}^d$ with Lipschitz boundary. The denoised image is represented by a function u lying in $L^2(\Omega) \cap BV(\Omega)$, where $BV(\Omega)$ is the space of functions of bounded variation [18]. Function u is obtained as minimizer of the strictly convex functional

$$\mathcal{F}(u;f) := \mathcal{S}(u;f) + \alpha \operatorname{TV}(u), \qquad (1)$$

where $\mathcal{S}(u;f) := \frac{1}{2}\|u-f\|^2_{L^2(\Omega)}$ is the data term, $TV(u) := \sup\{\int_\Omega \operatorname{div} \varphi\, u\, d\mathcal{L} \mid \varphi \in C_c^1(\Omega, \mathbb{R}^d), \|\varphi(x)\|_2 \leq 1\}$ is the total-variation semi-norm and $\alpha > 0$ is the regularization strength. We generalize this approach by replacing $\alpha\operatorname{TV}(u)$ by an regularization term $\mathcal{R}_v(u)$, i.e. $\mathcal{F}_v(u;f) := \frac{1}{2}\|u-f\|^2_{L^2} + \mathcal{R}_v(u)$, where v is a function steering the regularization. We assume an $\mathcal{R}_v(u)$ of the form

$$\mathcal{R}_v(u) := \sup\{\int_\Omega u(x)\operatorname{div}(A(x,v)\varphi(x))\, d\mathcal{L} \mid \varphi \in \mathcal{D}\}, \qquad (2)$$

where $\mathcal{D} := \{C_c^1(\Omega, \mathbb{R}^d), \|\varphi(x)\|_2 \leq 1\}$ and $A(x,v)$ is continuously differentiable w.r.t. x and maps to the space of symmetric matrices.

Example 1. Let $v \in C^1(\Omega, \mathbb{R})$. We consider an adaptive TV regularization, where the regularization strength α is reduced at locations, where the gradient of v is high. To this end, we set $A(x,v) = \alpha(x,v)\operatorname{Id}$ with $\alpha(x,v) = \widetilde{\max}(\alpha_0(1-\kappa\|\nabla v(x)\|_2), \varepsilon_0)$, where $\widetilde{\max}$ is a smoothed version of the max operator and $\varepsilon_0, \alpha_0 > 0$ and $\kappa \geq 0$. ⋄

Let us assume that the functional $\mathcal{F}_v(u;f)$ attains a unique minimizer $\bar{u}$. We introduce the short notation $\bar{u} := T(v;f) := \arg\min_u \mathcal{F}_v(u;f)$.

In the following, we assume that v is also an image. A special case would be to set $v = f$ (or a pre-smoothed version of f to be robust against noise). We refer to such an approach as *data-driven* adaptivity. Here, we follow a different approach by searching for a fixed point u^* of the mapping $v \to T(v;f)$. For such a fixed point $u^* = \bar{u} = v$, the regularization term becomes $\mathcal{R}_{u^*}(u)$, i.e. the adaptivity is determined by the solution u^* itself. For our example, this means that the adaptivity is reduced at edges of u^*. We refer to this approach as a *solution-driven* adaptivity. It has to be noted that this approach is in general not equivalent to solving the non-convex problem $\arg\min_u \mathcal{F}_u(u;f)$.

Two open issues remain, which are the *well-posedness* of the problem $\bar{u} = \arg\min \mathcal{F}_v(u;f)$ (and operator $T(v;f)$), and the *existence of a fixed point* $u^* = \bar{u} = v$ of T. We address both issues in the next section.

3 Theory

In the following, for the simplicity of notation, we omit the dependency of data term $\mathcal{S}$, functional $\mathcal{F}$ and operator T on the input data f. Moreover, we omit the argument x of functions, if it is clear from the context. We generalize the variational problem by considering a larger class of data terms $\mathcal{S}(u)$. The presentation of our approach concentrates on the two-dimensional case $\Omega \subset \mathbb{R}^2$. The generalization to a d-dimensional domain is straightforward.

First, we generalize the approach from last section to general inverse problems by considering arbitrary data terms $\mathcal{S}(u)$ with certain conditions stated below and additional constraints $u \in \mathcal{C}$, where $\mathcal{C} \subset BV(\Omega)$ is convex and weakly closed in $L^2(\Omega)$. Second, we state operator T more precisely:

$$T : L^2(\Omega) \to BV(\Omega) \cap L^2(\Omega) \quad T(v) := \arg\min_{u \in \mathcal{C}} \mathcal{F}_v(u). \qquad (3)$$

3.1 Well-Posedness of Operator T

Remark 1. Recall that $\Omega \subset \mathbb{R}^d$ is open bounded with Lipschitz boundary. In the case $d = 2$, on which we focus here, the embedding from $BV(\Omega)$ to $L^2(\Omega)$ is continuous [18, Thm 9.78]. Thus $\mathcal{F}_v(u)$ is well-defined on $BV(\Omega)$. In the case $d > 2$ we have to restrict the optimization of $\mathcal{F}_v(u)$ to the space $L^2(\Omega) \cap BV(\Omega)$.

Assumption 1.

(i) $\mathcal{S} : L^2(\Omega) \to \mathbb{R}$ *is strictly convex and lower semi-continuous w.r.t. the weak convergence in* $L^2(\Omega)$.
(ii) *There exist constants* $c_1, c_2 > 0$ *such that* $\|u\|_{L^2} \leq c_1 \mathcal{S}(u) + c_2$ *for any* $u \in \mathcal{C}$.
(iii) *Let* $\lambda_i(x,v)$, $i = 1, 2$, *be the eigenvalues of* $A(x,v)$. *We assume that there exist* $C_{min}, C_{max} > 0$ *such that* $C_{min} \leq \lambda_i(x,v) \leq C_{max}$, $i = 1, 2$.

Proposition 1. *For* $v \in L^2(\Omega)$, $\mathcal{F}_v(\cdot)$ *has a unique minimizer* $\overline{u} \in \mathcal{C} \subset BV(\Omega)$. *Moreover, there exists an* $R_{max} \geq 0$ *independent from* v, *such that* $\|\overline{u}\|_{BV} \leq R_{max}$. *Thus* $T(v) : L^2(\Omega) \to U := \{u \in \mathcal{C} \mid \|u\|_{BV} \leq R_{max},\}$, *is well defined.*

Remark 2 (Sketch of the proof of Prop. 1). The proof follows the standard proof for convex minimization problems. Starting with a minimizing sequence, one first shows that the sequence is bounded in $BV(\Omega)$: Using Ass. 1(iii), one can prove that $C_{min} TV(u) \leq \mathcal{R}(u, v)$. Together with Ass. 1(ii) boundedness of the sequence follows. We therefore can find a subsequence weakly* converging to some $\overline{u} \in BV(\Omega)$, also converging weakly in $L^2(\Omega)$. Analogously to the proof of Thm. 1 in [9, Sect. 5.2.1], we can show that $\mathcal{R}_v(u)$ is weakly* lower semi-continuous. This requires the upper bound C_{max} from Ass. 1(iii). Together with Ass. 1(i) we have that $\mathcal{F}_v(u)$ is weakly* lower semi-continuous, and thus $\overline{u}$ is a minimizer. From the strict convexity of $\mathcal{F}_v(u)$ it follows that $\overline{u}$ is unique.

3.2 Existence of a Fixed Point

Assumption 2. $A(x,v)$ *is continuously differentiable w.r.t.* x *and Lipschitz-continuous with constant w.r.t.* v. *Moreover, for any* $u \in C^\infty(\Omega)$ *and* $v \in L^1(\Omega)$

there exists a function $a(x, u, v)$ continuous in x such that

$$\sup_{\varphi \in \mathcal{D}} \int_\Omega \varphi(x)^\top A(x, v) \nabla u(x) \, d\mathcal{L} = \int_\Omega a(x, u, v) \|\nabla u(x)\|_2 \, d\mathcal{L}, \qquad (4)$$

where $a(x, u, v)$ is Lipschitz-continuous w.r.t. v: there exists a constant $C_l > 0$ independent from u and v such that

$$\|a(x, u, v_1) - a(x, u, v_2)\|_{L^\infty} \le C_l \|v_1 - v_2\|_{L^1}. \qquad (5)$$

Theorem 1. *Let Ass. 1 and 2 be satisfied. Then, there exists a fixed point u^* of $T(v)$, i.e. u^* minimizes $\mathcal{F}_{u^*}(u)$.*

The proof of Thm.1 requires the following definition and proposition.

Definition 1. *We consider the weak topology in $L^2(\Omega)$ (cf. [2]). We call $\mathcal{F}: L^2(\Omega) \to L^2(\Omega)$ weakly upper semi-continuous if for any weakly closed subset B of $\mathrm{im}(\mathcal{F})$ the set $\mathcal{F}^{-1}(B)$ is weakly closed.*

Proposition 2. *The mapping $v \mapsto T(v)$ from $\mathcal{C}$ to $U \subset \mathcal{C} \subset L^2(\Omega)$ is weakly upper semi-continuous w.r.t. the weak topology in $L^2(\Omega)$.*

The proof of Prop. 2 will be given below. First we state two required lemmas, the proofs of which are provided in the appendix.

Lemma 1. *Let U be a bounded subset of $BV(\Omega)$ and let $v^k \to v$ in $L^1(\Omega)$. Then, we have $\mathcal{R}_{v^k}(u) \to \mathcal{R}_v(u)$ and $\mathcal{F}_{v^k}(u) \to \mathcal{F}_v(u)$ uniformly for every $u \in U$.*

Lemma 2. *For $v^k \to v^0$ in $L^1(\Omega)$ and $u^k := T(v^k) := \arg\min_u \mathcal{F}_{v^k}(u)$:*

$$\liminf_{k \to \infty} \mathcal{F}_{v^0}(u^k) \le \limsup_{k \to \infty} \mathcal{F}_{v^k}(u^k). \qquad (6)$$

Proof (Proof of Proposition 2). Let B be a weakly closed subset of U (recall that $\mathrm{im}(T) \subset U$). Let $(v^k)_k$ be a sequence in $T^{-1}(B) \subset V$ weakly converging in $L^2(\Omega)$ to some $v^0 \in V$, i.e. there exists a sequence $(u^k)_k \in B$ such that $u^k = T(v^k)$, and $v^k \stackrel{L^2}{\rightharpoonup} v^0$. Let $u^0 := T(v^0)$. Since U is weakly* pre-compact in $BV(\Omega)$ and weakly in $L^2(\Omega)$, there exists a subsequence also denoted by $(u^k)_k$, such that $u^k \stackrel{*}{\rightharpoonup} u$ for some $u \in BV_\Omega$ and $u^k \stackrel{L^2}{\rightharpoonup} u$. Since B is weakly closed in $L^2(\Omega)$, we find $u \in B$. Next, we show that $u = u^0$, i.e. u is the unique minimizer of $\mathcal{F}_{v^0}(\cdot)$. Since the embedding from $L^2(\Omega)$ to $L^1(\Omega)$ is compact, we can find a subsequence $(v^{k'})_{k'}$, of $(v^k)_k$, which converges to v strongly in $L^1(\Omega)$. Using the weakly* lower semi-continuity of $\mathcal{F}_{v^0}$ (cf. Rem. 2) together with Lem. 2 we find

$$\begin{aligned} 0 \le \mathcal{F}_{v^0}(u) - \mathcal{F}_{v^0}(u^0) &\le \liminf_{k' \to \infty} \mathcal{F}_{v^0}(u^{k'}) - \mathcal{F}_{v^0}(u^0) \\ &\le \limsup_{k' \to \infty} \mathcal{F}_{v^{k'}}(u^{k'}) - \mathcal{F}_{v^0}(u^0). \end{aligned} \qquad (7)$$

Recall that $u^{k'}$ is the minimizer of $\mathcal{F}_{v^{k'}}(\cdot)$ for all $k' \geq 0$, which induces $\mathcal{F}_{v^{k'}}(u^{k'}) \leq \mathcal{F}_{v^{k'}}(u^0)$. Using this fact, we obtain from (7) that

$$0 \leq \mathcal{F}_{v^0}(u) - \mathcal{F}_{v^0}(u^0) \leq \limsup_{k' \to \infty} \mathcal{F}_{v^{k'}}(u^0) - \mathcal{F}_{v^0}(u^0). \qquad (8)$$

Lemma 1 guarantees that the r.h.s. of (8) tends to zero, thus $\mathcal{F}_{v^0}(u) = \mathcal{F}_{v^0}(u^0)$. On the other hand, u^0 by definition is the unique minimizer of $\mathcal{F}_{v^0}(\cdot)$, from which $u = u^0$ follows. Since $u \in B$ and $u = u^0 = T(v^0)$, we have shown that $v^0 \in T^{-1}(B)$ and thus $T^{-1}(B)$ is weakly closed. □

Proof (Proof of Thm. 1). The claim follows from Theorem 2.3. in [1], since $\mathcal{C}$ is convex and closed in $L^2(\Omega)$ and $v \to T(v)$ is weakly compact in $L^2(\Omega)$ (it maps to the pre-compact set U, thus $T(B)$ is pre-compact for any $B \subset \mathcal{C}$) and weakly upper semi-continuous in $L^2(\Omega)$ (Prop. 2). □

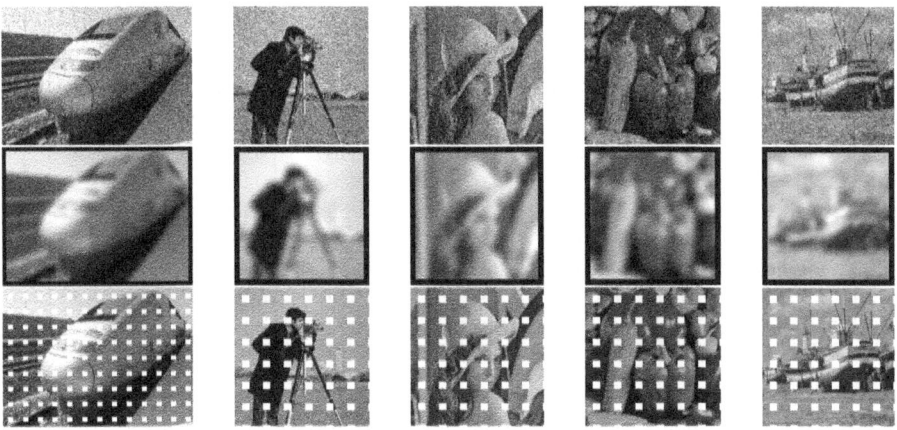

Fig. 1. Test images used for evaluation. Top row – denoising: with additive Gaussian noise (zero mean, standard deviation 0.1). Middle row – deblurring: blurred images with Gaussian noise (zero mean, standard deviation 0.01). Bottom row – inpainting: white regions mark the regions to be inpainted.

4 Image Restortation

Data terms We consider the applications of denoising, non-blind deblurring and inpatining. In the case of denoising, we utilize the standard L^2 data term, which is strictly convex. In the case of deblurring, we assume a kernel K with bounded support, such that $u \in L^2(\Omega)$ leads to data $f(x) := (K * u)(x)$ in $L^2(\Omega_0)$, $\Omega_0 \subset \Omega$. We set $\mathcal{S}(u) := \frac{1}{2}\|K * u - f\|_{L^2(\Omega_0)}$. By an additional regularization of the data term, i.e. by adding $\varepsilon\|u\|^2_{L^2(\Omega)}$ with small $\varepsilon > 0$, we assert strict convexity of $\mathcal{F}(u)$. For inpainting, we consider the domain $\Omega_0 \subset \Omega$ on which the data f are known and set $\mathcal{C} := \{u \in BV(\Omega) \mid u = f \text{ a.e. on } \Omega_0\}$. Moreover, to obtain a strictly convex problem we choose $\mathcal{S}(u) = \varepsilon\|u\|^2_{L^2(\Omega \setminus \overline{\Omega_0})}$. In all three applications Ass 1(i) and (ii) are satisfied.

Table 1. Similarity [21] to ground truth for the different applications, methods and test images. (dd=data-driven, sd= solution-driven, numbers in brackets are the iterations of the outer loop.) Except for the application of denoising, our approaches in most cases provide the best results compared to the other methods.

	Method	Train	Cameraman	Lena	Peppers	Boat
Denoising	std. TV [17]	0.789	0.808	0.793	0.794	0.718
	TGV [4]	0.791	0.814	0.798	0.810	0.723
	BM3D [6]	**0.840**	**0.856**	**0.845**	**0.834**	**0.762**
	adapt. TV (dd)	0.789	0.813	0.793	0.794	0.718
	adapt. TV (sd)	0.790 (4)	0.822 (4)	0.793 (3)	0.794 (4)	0.718 (4)
	anisotr. TV(dd)	0.793	0.808	0.796	0.794	0.718
	anisotr. TV(sd)	0.803 (4)	0.820 (4)	0.819 (4)	0.798 (4)	0.723 (4)
Deblurring	std. TV	0.774	0.766	0.760	0.795	0.644
	TGV	0.775	0.747	0.749	0.799	0.691
	Schmidt [19]	0.571	0.612	0.697	0.682	0.705
	adapt. TV(dd)	0.774	0.757	0.762	0.794	0.631
	adapt. TV(sd)	0.813 (3)	0.829 (4)	0.808 (2)	0.811 (2)	0.715 (4)
	anisotr. TV(dd)	0.774	0.783	0.762	0.797	0.660
	anisotr. TV(sd)	**0.839** (4)	**0.841** (4)	**0.848** (4)	**0.864** (4)	**0.776** (4)
Inpainting	std. TV	0.930	0.945	0.940	0.951	0.933
	TGV	0.958	0.958	0.958	0.963	0.954
	Garcia [10]	0.957	0.966	0.966	**0.969**	**0.961**
	adapt. TV(dd)	0.938	0.945	0.940	0.951	0.933
	adapt. TV(sd)	0.972 (4)	0.969 (4)	0.957 (4)	0.964 (4)	0.950 (4)
	anisotr. TV(dd)	0.947	0.946	0.942	0.952	0.936
	anisotr. TV(sd)	**0.976** (4)	**0.973** (4)	**0.971** (4)	0.968 (4)	0.958 (4)

Adaptivity We consider two examples of adaptive TV regularization. In both, we steer the adaptivity by choosing appropriate functions $A(x, v)$.

First, we revisit Example 1, where we locally adapt the regularization strength. Assuming that v lies in $BV(\Omega)$, since it is expected to be the fixed point of operator T, we face the problem that the gradient of v cannot be interpreted as a function on Ω. To circumvent this problem, we introduce a pre-smoothing of v as follows: Let $K_\sigma(x)$ be a Gaussian kernel with variance σ^2. We define $v_\sigma := K_\sigma * v$, where $*$ is the convolution operator. We choose suitable boundary conditions to accommodate to the fact that v is only defined on Ω. We then set

$$A(x,v) := \alpha(x, v_\sigma)\,\text{Id}, \text{ with } \alpha(x, v_\sigma) := \widetilde{\max}(\alpha_0(1 - \kappa\|\nabla v_\sigma\|_2), \varepsilon_0), \quad (9)$$

where $\widetilde{\max}$ is a smoothed version of the max-operator and $\alpha_0, \varepsilon_0 > 0$, $\kappa \geq 0$.

We refer to this example as solution-driven *adaptive* TV regularization. Note that $\alpha(x) \in [\varepsilon_0, \alpha_0]$, such that Assumption 1(iii) is satisfied. The following lemma shows, that Assumption 2 also holds.

Lemma 3. *Let $A(x, v)$ be defined as in (9). Then, Assumption 2 is satisfied with $a(x, u, v) = \alpha(x, v_\sigma)$.*

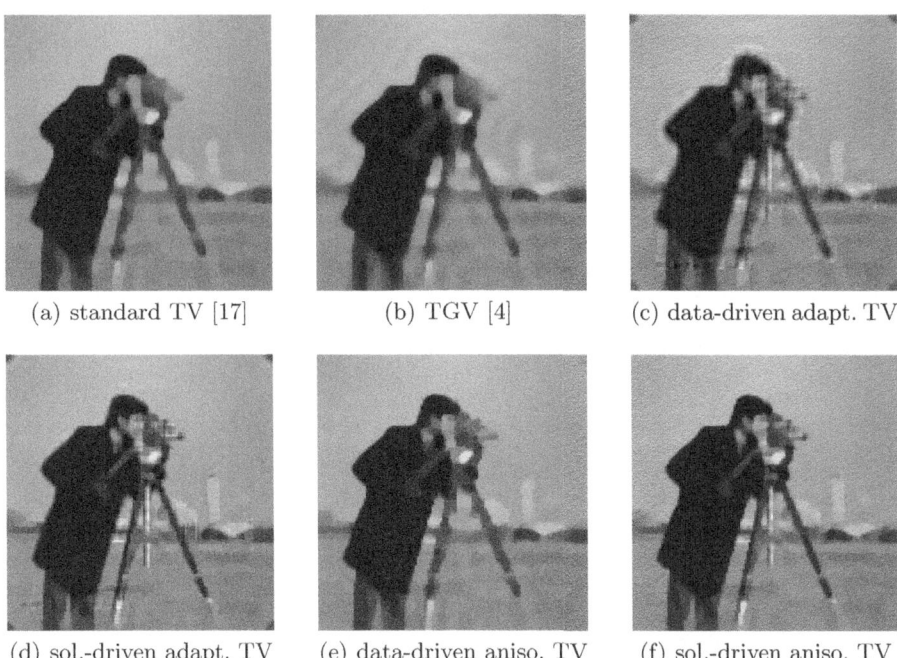

Fig. 2. Deblurring: best performing methods on the cameraman image. The solution-driven variants outperform the data-driven variants. Solution-driven *anisotropic* TV gives the best result.

Proof. For $u \in C^\infty(\Omega)$ we have

$$\sup_{\varphi \in \mathcal{D}} \int_\Omega \varphi^\top A(v) \nabla u \, d\mathcal{L} = \sup_{\varphi \in \mathcal{D}} \int_\Omega \varphi^\top \alpha(x,v) \nabla u(x) \, d\mathcal{L} \leq \int_\Omega \alpha(x,v) \|\nabla u(x)\|_2 \, d\mathcal{L}. \tag{10}$$

We show equality in (10). Let $\varphi(x) := \nabla u(x)/\|\nabla u(x)\|_2$ if $\nabla u(x) \neq 0$ and $\varphi(x) := 0$ otherwise. Then $\|\nabla u\|_2 = \varphi^\top \nabla u$. Let $\varphi_\varepsilon \in C_c^\infty(\Omega, \mathbb{R}^2) \to \varphi$ in $L^2(\Omega; \mathbb{R}^2)$ and

$$\int_\Omega \left| \varphi_\varepsilon^\top \alpha(x,v) \nabla u - \alpha(x,v) \|\nabla u\|_2 \right| \, d\mathcal{L} \leq \|\alpha(x,v)\|_{L^\infty} \|\varphi_\varepsilon - \varphi\|_{L^2} \|\nabla u\|_{L^2} \to 0. \tag{11}$$

The Lipschitz continuity of $v \to \alpha(x,v)$ follows form the continuous differentiability of α w.r.t. v_σ together with $\|\nabla(v_1)_\sigma - \nabla(v_2)_\sigma\|_{L^\infty} \leq C\|v_1 - v_2\|_{L^1}$ as a property of convolutions. □

Our second example is a solution-driven *anisotropic* TV variant:

$$A(x,v) := \alpha(x) r(x) r(x)^\top + \beta(x) (r^\perp(x))(r^\perp(x))^\top \tag{12}$$

for some vector field $r(x) : \Omega \to \mathbb{R}^2$ and scalar functions $\alpha(x), \beta(x) : \Omega \to \mathbb{R}_+$. To determine $r(x)$ we consider the structure tensor $J_\rho(v_\sigma) := (\nabla v_\sigma \nabla v_\sigma^\top)_\rho$, where

Fig. 3. Inpainting: best performing methods on the cameraman image. The solution-driven variants outperform the data-driven variants. Solution-driven *anisotropic* TV gives the best result.

$(M)_\rho$ denotes the elementwise convolution of matrix M with kernel K_ρ. Let $\mu_1(x) \geq \mu_2(x) \geq 0$ be the eigenvalues of $J_\rho(v_\sigma)(x)$. We choose $r(x)$ as the normalized eigenvector to eigenvalue $\mu_1(x)$. $\alpha(x)$ and $\beta(x)$ are chosen as

$$\alpha(x) = g(\mu_1(x) - \mu_2(x))\alpha_0 + (1 - g(\mu_1(x) - \mu_2(x)))\beta_0, \qquad \beta(x) = \beta_0,$$

with $g(s) = \min(c \cdot s, 1)$, $c > 0$. For $c_{min} := \min\{\alpha_0, \beta_0\}$, $C_{max} := \max\{\alpha_0, \beta_0\}$ we have $0 < c_{min} \leq \alpha(x), \beta(x) \leq C_{max} < \infty$, so that Ass. 1(iii) follows. Due to space constraints we omit the proof that Assumption 2 is satisfied.

5 Experiments

Numerically, we solve the problem of finding a fixed point of T by two nested iterations. In the outer iteration, function v is updated; in the inner iteration we solve the discretized convex problem $\arg\min_u \mathcal{F}_v(u)$ with a primal-dual method [5].

We consider three different applications: denoising, non-blind deblurring and inpainting. As test images, we consider the five images depicted in Fig. 1. (*Train* image by courtesy of Kristian Bredies.) All ground truth images are scaled to the range $[0, 1]$. We compare our method to regularization with standard TV,

Total Generalized Variation (TGV) [4] and the data-driven variants (i.e. using $T(f)$, where f are the input data) of our approach. Moreover, we compare with BM3D [6] for denoising, the method by Schmidt [19] for deblurring and to Garcia's method [10] for inpainting. For comparison, we utilize the similarity measure from [21] applied to result and ground truth. To find the optimal parameters for each method w.r.t this measure we applied a hierarchical grid search. The similarity measures for each application and each method are listed in Table 3.2. For the task of denoising, we observe that we cannot cope with the BM3D method, but obtain better results than the other regularization approaches. Concerning deblurring and inpainting, we obtain in most cases the best results compared to the other methods. For deblurring and inpainting, the results of the best performing methods on the cameraman image are depicted in Figs. 2 and 3. (The other results are omitted due to space constraints.)

6 Conclusion

We have considered solution-driven adaptive variants of Total Variation. In our ansatz the adaptivity leads to a fixed point problem, for which we provided existence theory. Our experiments demonstrated for the applications of image denoising, deblurring and inpainting, that our approach in most cases outperforms state-of-the-art *regularization* approaches. In future work we will study the issue of uniqueness of fixed points in the continuous setting.

Appendix

The following lemma is required in the proof of Lemma 1.

Lemma 4. *For any $u \in BV(\Omega)$ there exists $(u^k)_k \in C^\infty(\Omega)$ such that $u^k \xrightarrow{L^1} u$, $TV(u^k) \to TV(u)$ and $\mathcal{R}_{v_i}(u^k) \to \mathcal{R}_{v_i}(u)$ simultaneously for a finite set of $\{v_i\}_i$.*

Proof. For fixed v the proof follows the proof of [9, Thm. 2,Sect. 5.2], with some modifications. Recall $\mathcal{D} = \{C_c^1(\Omega, \mathbb{R}^2), \|\varphi(x)\|_2 \leq 1\}$. Let $\varepsilon > 0$ be fixed. For a $m \in \mathbb{N}, m > 0$ and $k \in \mathbb{N}$ we define open sets $\Omega_k := \{x \in \Omega \mid \text{dist}(x, \partial\Omega) > \frac{1}{m+k}\}$ and choose m large enough to guarantee

$$TV(u)(\Omega \setminus \Omega_1) < \varepsilon, \tag{13}$$

where $TV(u)(B)$ is the variation measure of u evaluated on the set B. Set $\Omega_0 := \emptyset$ and define $V_k := \Omega_{k+1} \setminus \overline{\Omega}_{k-1}$. Please note that each $x \in \Omega$ is contained in at most three sets V_k. Moreover, let $\{\zeta_k\}_{k=1}^\infty$ be a sequence of smooth functions with $\zeta_k \in C_c^\infty(V_k)$, $0 \leq \zeta_k \leq 1$ and $\sum_{k=1}^\infty \zeta_k = 1$ on Ω. Let η be a mollifier as in [9, Sect. 4.2.1]). For each k, select $\varepsilon_k > 0$ small enough such that for $\eta_{\varepsilon_k} := \frac{1}{\varepsilon_k^2}\eta(\frac{x}{\varepsilon_k})$

$$\begin{aligned}\text{supp}(\eta_{\varepsilon_k} * (u\zeta_k)) \subset V_k, \quad &\int_\Omega |\eta_{\varepsilon_k} * (u\zeta_k) - u\zeta_k|\, d\mathcal{L} < \frac{\varepsilon}{2^k},\\ &\int_\Omega \|\eta_{\varepsilon_k} * (u\nabla\zeta_k) - u\nabla\zeta_k\|_2\, d\mathcal{L} < \frac{\varepsilon}{2^k}.\end{aligned} \tag{14}$$

Define $u_\varepsilon := \sum_{k=1}^\infty \eta_{\varepsilon_k} * (u\zeta_k)$. In this sum there are only finitely many terms, which are non-zero on a neighborhood of each $x \in \Omega$. Thus, $u_\varepsilon \in C^\infty(\Omega)$. Since also $u = \sum_{k=1}^\infty u\zeta_k$, we find from (14) that

$$\|u_\varepsilon - u\|_{L^1(\Omega)} \le \sum_{k=1}^\infty \int_\Omega |\eta_{\varepsilon_k} * (u\zeta_k) - u\zeta_k| \, d\mathcal{L} < \varepsilon. \tag{15}$$

Thus, $u_\varepsilon \to u$ in $L^1(\Omega)$. Moreover, for $\varphi \in \mathcal{D}$, we have

$$\int_\Omega u_\varepsilon \operatorname{div} \varphi \, d\mathcal{L} = \int_\Omega u \left(\sum_k \zeta_k \operatorname{div}(\eta_{\varepsilon_k} * \varphi) \right) d\mathcal{L} \le 3 \operatorname{TV}(u), \tag{16}$$

where we used that for every $x \in \Omega$ there exist at most three $\zeta_k(x) > 0$. Taking the supremum over all such φ we find $\operatorname{TV}(u_\varepsilon) \le 3 \operatorname{TV}(u) < \infty$. Thus $u_\varepsilon \overset{*}{\rightharpoonup} u$. Then, due to the weak* lower semi-continuity of $\mathcal{R}_v(u)$ (cf. Rem. 2) we have

$$\mathcal{R}_v(u) \le \liminf_{\varepsilon \to 0} \mathcal{R}_v(u_\varepsilon). \tag{17}$$

For any $\varphi \in \mathcal{D}$

$$\int_\Omega u_\varepsilon \operatorname{div}(A(v)\varphi) \, d\mathcal{L} = \sum_{k=1}^\infty \int_\Omega (\eta_{\varepsilon_k} * (u\zeta_k)) \operatorname{div}(A(v)\varphi) \, d\mathcal{L}$$

$$= \sum_{k=1}^\infty \int_\Omega u\zeta_k \operatorname{div}(\eta_{\varepsilon_k} * (A(v)\varphi)) \, d\mathcal{L}$$

$$= \underbrace{\sum_{k=1}^\infty \int_\Omega u \operatorname{div}(\zeta_k(\eta_{\varepsilon_k} * (A(v)\varphi))) \, d\mathcal{L}}_{:=I_1^\varepsilon} - \underbrace{\sum_{k=1}^\infty \int_\Omega \varphi^\top A(v)(\eta_{\varepsilon_k} * (u\nabla\zeta_k) - u\nabla\zeta_k) \, d\mathcal{L}}_{=:I_2^\varepsilon},$$
$$\tag{18}$$

where we used the fact $\sum_{k=1}^\infty \nabla \zeta_k = 0$ on Ω. Since $\|A(x,v)\varphi(x)\|_2 \le C_{max}$, we find that $\|\zeta_k(x)(\eta_{\varepsilon_k} * (A(v)\varphi))(x)\|_2 \le C_{max}$. Thus, we can bound I_1^ε by

$$|I_1^\varepsilon| = \left| \int_\Omega u \operatorname{div}(\zeta_1(\eta_{\varepsilon_1} * (A(v)\varphi))) \, d\mathcal{L} + \sum_{k=2}^\infty \int_\Omega u \operatorname{div}(\zeta_k(\eta_{\varepsilon_k} * (A(v)\varphi))) \, d\mathcal{L} \right|$$

$$\le \mathcal{R}_v(u) + C_\eta L(v)\varepsilon + \sum_{k=2}^\infty C_{max} \operatorname{TV}(u)(V_k), \tag{19}$$

where $L(v)$ is the Lipschitz-constant of $x \to A(x,v)$ and where we use that

$$\|\eta_{\varepsilon_k} * (A(v)\varphi) - A(v)(\eta_{\varepsilon_k} * \varphi)\| \le C_\eta L(v) \|\varphi\|_{L^\infty} \varepsilon \tag{20}$$

(which follows from standard calculus) with $C_\eta > 0$ only depending on η.

Since each point in Ω belongs to at most three sets V_k, together with $V_k \subset \Omega \setminus \Omega_1$ and (13), (19) can be bounded by

$$|I_1^\varepsilon| \le \mathcal{R}_v(u) + C_\eta L(v)\varepsilon + 3C_{max} \operatorname{TV}(u)(V_k) < \mathcal{R}_v(u) + (3C_{max} + C_\eta L(v))\varepsilon. \tag{21}$$

Since $\|A(x,v)\varphi(x)\|_2 \leq C_{max}$ we obtain from (14) that

$$|I_2^\varepsilon| = |\sum_{k=1}^\infty \int_\Omega \varphi^\top A(v)(\eta_{\varepsilon_k} * (u\nabla \zeta_k) - u\nabla \zeta_k)\,d\mathcal{L}| \leq C_{max} \sum_{k=1}^\infty \frac{\varepsilon}{2^k} = C_{max}\varepsilon. \quad (22)$$

Combining (18), (21) and (22), we find

$$\int_\Omega u_\varepsilon \operatorname{div}(A(v)\varphi)\,d\mathcal{L} < \mathcal{R}_v(u) + (4C_{max} + C_\eta L(v))\varepsilon. \quad (23)$$

Taking in (23) the supremum over all $\varphi \in \mathcal{D}$, we obtain $\mathcal{R}_v(u_\varepsilon) < \mathcal{R}_v(u) + (4C_{max} + C_\eta L(v))\varepsilon$. Together with (17) we have

$$|\mathcal{R}_v(u_\varepsilon) - \mathcal{R}_v(u)| < (4C_{max} + C_\eta L(v))\varepsilon \quad (24)$$

for ε small enough. Since the choice of $\Omega_k, V_k, \varepsilon_k, \zeta_k$ and η_{ε_k} was independent from v, we get a simultaneous convergence for a finite set of v_{ii}. Moreover, as we can express $\mathrm{TV}(u)$ as $\mathcal{R}_v(u)$ with $A(v) = \mathrm{Id}$, (24) provides also $|\mathrm{TV}(u_\varepsilon) - \mathrm{TV}(u)| < (4C_{max} + C_\eta)\varepsilon$. □

Proof (of Lemma 1). We show that for arbitrary $u, v_1, v_2 \in BV(\Omega)$

$$|\mathcal{R}_{v_1}(u) - \mathcal{R}_{v_2}(u)| \leq C_l\,R_{max}\,\|v_1 - v_2\|_{L^1}, \quad (25)$$

from which the claim for $\mathcal{R}_v(u)$ follows. Consider first a fixed $u \in C^\infty(\Omega)$. Then, by Assumption 2

$$|\mathcal{R}_{v_1}(u) - \mathcal{R}_{v_2}(u)| = \int_\Omega |a(x, u, v_1) - a(x, u, v_2)|\,\|\nabla u(x)\|_2\,d\mathcal{L} \quad (26)$$
$$\leq \|a(x, u, v_1) - a(x, u, v_2)\|_{L^\infty}\,\mathrm{TV}(u) \leq C_l\|v_1 - v_2\|_{L^1}\,\mathrm{TV}(u).$$

Now, let $u \in U$ be arbitrary. Using Lemma 4 we can find for any $\varepsilon > 0$ a function $\tilde{u} \in C^\infty(\Omega)$ such that

$$|\mathcal{R}_{v_i}(u) - \mathcal{R}_{v_i}(\tilde{u})| \leq \varepsilon \text{ for } i = 1, 2, \quad |\mathrm{TV}(u) - \mathrm{TV}(\tilde{u})| \leq \varepsilon. \quad (27)$$

Then,

$$|\mathcal{R}_{v_1}(u) - \mathcal{R}_{v_2}(u)| \overset{(27)}{\leq} |\mathcal{R}_{v_1}(\tilde{u}) - \mathcal{R}_{v_2}(\tilde{u})| + 2\varepsilon \overset{(26)}{\leq} C_l\|v_1 - v_2\|_{L^1}\,\mathrm{TV}(\tilde{u}) + 2\varepsilon$$
$$\overset{(27)}{\leq} C_l\|v_1 - v_2\|_{L^1}(\mathrm{TV}(u) + \varepsilon) + 2\varepsilon \overset{u \in U}{\leq} C_l\|v_1 - v_2\|_{L^1}(R_{max} + \varepsilon) + 2\varepsilon.$$

Since we can find $\tilde{u}$ such that ε becomes arbitrary small, (25) follows for fixed u. Since the r.h.s. of (25) does not depend on u, we achieve an uniform convergence of $\mathcal{R}_{v^k}(\cdot) \to \mathcal{R}_v(\cdot)$ on U for $v^k \to v$ in $L^1(\Omega)$. Since $\mathcal{R}_v(u)$ and $\mathcal{F}_v(u)$ differ by $\mathcal{S}(u)$ not depending on v, the uniform convergence $\mathcal{F}_{v^k}(\cdot) \to \mathcal{F}_v(\cdot)$ follows. □

Proof (of Lemma 2). Let $v^k \to v^0$ in $L^1(\Omega)$. For the sequence $u^k := T(v^k)$, let $\liminf_{k \to \infty} \mathcal{F}_{v_0}(u^k) := c$. For any $\varepsilon > 0$ Lemma 1 guarantees the existence of a $K > 0$ such that $|\mathcal{F}_{v^k}(u) - \mathcal{F}_{v^0}(u)| \leq \frac{\varepsilon}{2}$ for all $u \in U$ and all $k \geq K$. Moreover, we can find a $k' \geq K$ such that $|\mathcal{F}_{v^0}(u^{k'}) - c| \leq \frac{\varepsilon}{2}$. From both together, we find

$$|\mathcal{F}_{v^{k'}}(u^{k'}) - c| \leq |\mathcal{F}_{v^{k'}}(u^{k'}) - \mathcal{F}_{v^0}(u^{k'})| + |\mathcal{F}_{v^0}(u^{k'}) - c| \leq \varepsilon. \quad (28)$$

In other words, there exists a sequence $k' \to \infty$, such that $\mathcal{F}_{v^{k'}}(u^{k'}) \to c$ and thus $\liminf_{k \to \infty} \mathcal{F}_{v^0}(u^k) = c \leq \limsup_{k \to \infty} \mathcal{F}_{v^k}(u^k)$. □

References

1. Agarwal, R., O'Regan, D.: Fixed-point theory for weakly sequentially upper-semicontinuous maps with applications to differential inclusions. Nonlinear Oscillations **5**(3) (2002)
2. Alt, H.W.: Linear functional analysis. An application oriented introduction. Springer (2006)
3. Berkels, B., Burger, M., Droske, M., Nemitz, O., Rumpf, M.: Cartoon extraction based on anisotropic image classification. In: VMV (2006)
4. Bredies, K., Kunisch, K., Pock, T.: Total Generalized Variation. SIAM J. Imaging Sciences **3**(3), 492–526 (2010)
5. Chambolle, A., Pock, T.: A first-order primal-dual algorithm for convex problems with applications to imaging. Journal of Mathematical Imaging and Vision **40**(1), 120–145 (2011)
6. Dabov, K., Foi, A., Katkovnik, V., Egiazarian, K., et al.: BM3D image denoising with shape-adaptive principal component analysis. In: SPARS (2009)
7. Dong, Y., Hintermüller, M., Rincon-Camacho, M.M.: Automated regularization parameter selection in multi-scale total variation models for image restoration. Journal of Mathematical Imaging and Vision **40**(1), 82–104 (2011)
8. Estellers, V., Soato, S., Bresson, X.: Adaptive regularization with the structure tensor. Technical report, UCLA VisionLab (2014)
9. Evans, L.C., Gariepy, R.F.: Measure theory and fine properties of functions, vol. 5. CRC Press (1992)
10. Garcia, D.: Robust smoothing of gridded data in one and higher dimensions with missing values. Computational statistics & data analysis **54**(4), 1167–1178 (2010)
11. Grasmair, M.: Locally adaptive total variation regularization. In: Tai, X.-C., Mørken, K., Lysaker, M., Lie, K.-A. (eds.) SVM 2009. LNCS 5567, vol. 5567, pp. 331–342. Springer, Heidelberg (2009)
12. Grasmair, M., Lenzen, F.: Anisotropic total variation filtering. Applied Mathematics & Optimization **62**, 323–339 (2010)
13. Lefkimmiatis, S., Roussos, A., Unser, M., Maragos, P.: Convex generalizations of total variation based on the structure tensor with applications to inverse problems. In: Pack, T. (ed.) SSVM 2013. LNCS, vol. 7893, pp. 48–60. Springer, Heidelberg (2013)
14. Lenzen, F., Becker, F., Lellmann, J., Petra, S., Schnörr, C.: Variational Image Denoising with Adaptive Constraint Sets. In: Bruckstein, A.M., ter Haar Romeny, B.M., Bronstein, A.M., Bronstein, M.M. (eds.) SSVM 2011. LNCS, vol. 6667, pp. 206–217. Springer, Heidelberg (2012)

15. Lenzen, F., Becker, F., Lellmann, J., Petra, S., Schnörr, C.: A class of Quasi-Variational Inequalities for adaptive image denoising and decomposition. Computational Optimization and Applications **54**(2), 371–398 (2013)
16. Lenzen, F., Lellmann, J., Becker, F., Schnörr, C.: Solving Quasi-Variational Inequalities for image restoration with adaptive constraint sets. SIAM Journal on Imaging Sciences (SIIMS) **7**, 2139–2174 (2014)
17. Rudin, L., Osher, S., Fatemi, E.: Nonlinear total variation based noise removal algorithms. Physica D **60**, 259–268 (1992)
18. Scherzer, O., Grasmair, M., Grossauer, H., Haltmeier, M., Lenzen, F.: Variational methods in imaging, vol. 167 of Applied Mathematical Sciences. Springer (2009)
19. Schmidt, U., Schelten, K., Roth, S.: Bayesian deblurring with integrated noise estimation. In: CVPR (2011)
20. Steidl, G., Teuber, T.: Anisotropic smoothing using double orientations. In: Tai, X.-C., Mørken, K., Lysaker, M., Lie, K.-A. (eds.) SVM 2009. LNCS 5567, vol. 5567, pp. 477–489. Springer, Heidelberg (2009)
21. Wang, Z., Bovik, A., Sheikh, H., Simoncelli, E.: Image quality assessment: from error visibility to structural similarity. IEEE Transactions on Image Processing **13**(4), 600–612 (2004)

Artifact-Free Variational MPEG Decompression

Kristian Bredies and Martin Holler(✉)

Institute for Mathematics and Scientific Computing,
University of Graz, Graz, Austria
{kristian.bredies,martin.holler}@uni-graz.at

Abstract. We propose a variational method for artifact-free video decompression that is capable of processing *any* MPEG-2 encoded movie. The method extracts, from a given MPEG-2 file, a set of admissible image sequences and minimizes an artifact-penalizing spatio-temporal regularization functional over this set, giving an optimal decompressed image sequence. For regularization, we use the *infimal convolution* of spatio-temporal *Total Generalized Variation* functionals (ICTGV). Numerical experiments on MPEG encoded files show that our approach significantly increases image quality compared to standard decompression.

Keywords: MPEG decompression · Image sequence regularization · Total generalized variation · Infimal convolution type functionals

1 Introduction

The MPEG (Motion Picture Experts Groups) video compression standard is one of the most well-known and widely-used methods to compress and store digital video data. The underlying concepts of MPEG compression, namely motion compensation and Block Discrete Cosine Transform (BDCT) encoding, are at the heart of almost any modern video compression method. Currently, several versions of MPEG are available of which MPEG-2 and MPEG-4 are the most popular, with MPEG-2 being used for DVD videos and HDTV broadcasting. MPEG achieves high compression rates such that the storage and transmission of the huge amount of data usually required by videos becomes feasible. However, the high compression comes with the cost of loss of data due to quantization (rounding) of BDCT coefficients which is responsible for disturbing artifacts in the decompressed movie.

In this work, we propose a variational method for improved MPEG decompression which is able to reduce compression-induced artifacts. By utilizing the information provided by the compressed MPEG file, our approach relies on the extraction of quantization intervals associated with the compressed data. These intervals must contain the "original data", i.e., the data prior to compression, and are used to describe the convex set D of all possible reconstructions. We then variationally decompress the video by minimizing a spatio-temporal regularization functional $\mathcal{R}$ subject to the data being contained in D. As the decoding process, i.e., the mapping which takes the stored coefficients to the spatio-temporal video data, constitutes a linear operator A, the variational problem can be phrased as

$$\min_{d \in D} \mathcal{R}(Ad). \tag{1}$$

This allows, to the best knowledge of the authors for the first time, to apply the very successful concept of variational regularization to genuine MPEG compressed data and, depending on the regularization functional $\mathcal{R}$, has the potential for a strong quality improvement for any MPEG compressed movie.

Our method conceptually works for all versions of MPEG compression, but is implemented for MPEG-2 compressed video data, as this version is still one of the standard encoding formats and can be seen as a realistic but still tractable blueprint for most video compression methods. For regularization, we use the *Infimal Convolution of Total Generalized Variation* (ICTGV) functionals as introduced in [8], but also compare to spatio-temporal *Total Generalized Variation* (TGV) regularization [5] as this turned out to be successful in artifact-reduced JPEG still image decompression which shares the concept of BDCT coding with MPEG, see [2,3] and [15] for an early work on variational JPEG decompression.

For the numerical solution of (1) we use the primal dual algorithm of [6] and provide an implementation that covers all orders of spatio-temporal TGV regularization and infimal convolutions thereof. Our numerical experiments confirm that, using ICTGV regularization, we are able to significantly reduce compression artifacts in MPEG compressed videos and obtain a good reconstruction quality even at relatively high compression rates.

As already mentioned, we are not aware of any other work on variational MPEG decompression. In contrast to that, there are many filter based post-processing techniques for MPEG compressed video available and we refer to [9] for an overview. The field of image sequence regularization is also not yet as well investigated as its still image counterpart. For recent approaches in the direction of spatio-temporal regularization we refer to [8,12]. In [12] the authors aim at reconstructing video which has been compressed using a particular video compressive sensing method and employ the total variation applied to the difference between adjacent frames as temporal regularization. In [8] the ICTGV functional, which is also used in the present work, is introduced in an analytical setting and employed for spatio-temporal regularization of MJPEG compressed grayscale video data, i.e., data were each frame undergoes simple JPEG encoding.

2 A Variational Model for MPEG Decompression

The key observation for improving MPEG decompression within a variational framework is that the decoding of MPEG compressed video data can be seen as a linear operator mapping block cosine data to image space, and that bounds for the block cosine data can be derived from the compressed file. Hence the problem of artifact-free MPEG decompression can be cast in the form (1).

A short overview on MPEG-2 compression. The MPEG standard builds on the JPEG still image standard for which a short overview is given first. For JPEG encoding, the image first undergoes a discrete blockwise cosine transformation (BDCT) on blocks of size 8×8 pixels. This yields a representation of each block as a linear combination in terms of frequencies. Based on the assumption that higher frequencies are less important for the perceived image quality, the cosine coefficients are then quantized according to a predefined quantization table (which is stored in the JPEG file) and rounded to integer. For color images, the JPEG standard encodes each channel of the image in YCbCr color space separately. Additionally, the chroma components, i.e., the Cb and Cr channel, may be subsampled (by a factor of 2 either in horizontal or both directions) accounting for the fact that the human visual system is less sensitive to spatial color variations.

For movies, MPEG compression now essentially incorporates additional prediction of neighboring frames by motion estimation and possible additive correction by BDCT data. Like JPEG, it codes 3 channels in YCbCr color space, allowing for different types of subsampling. The MPEG standard realizes three different types of frames, the I (intra), P (forward prediction) and B (bidirectional prediction) frames, respectively. An I frame codes the whole spatial image data independently from other frames in terms of quantized block DCT coefficients, similarly to the JPEG standard. For these frames, the quantization intervals for the BDCT data can be obtained from the MPEG file. Unlike I frames, a P frame refers to the spatial data of the previously decoded I or P frame. Such a frame is reconstructed macroblockwise (i.e. in blocks of size 16×16) by either decoding 8×8 quantized BDCT data for this macroblock or copying data from the previous I or P frame (motion compensation). For the latter, the position of the source block is determined by *motion vectors* which are coded in the MPEG file. Additionally, the outcome is possibly corrected by adding some BDCT-coded residual data whose quantization intervals can also be obtained. Finally, B frames may appear between two I or P frames and allow, in addition to P frames, to choose, for each macroblock, whether data should be copied from the previous or next I or P frame, or whether the data from both surrounding I or P frames should be averaged. Again, the corresponding motion vectors are obtained from the file.

Finally, in the MPEG data stream the coded frames are arranged in *groups of pictures* (GOPs) which usually contain exactly one I frame and some subsequent P or B frames. A typical GOP spans 12–15 frames and its structure could look like IBBPBBP...BBP, but also BBIBBP...BBP is possible. Consequently, one can consider each GOP as essentially independent and for the variational MPEG decompression, it suffices to optimize over one or two GOPs and not over the whole video.

Modelling related aspects. An MPEG compressed file provides, for each macroblock of each frame, BDCT data and/or motion vectors. Each macroblock is decoded by performing some of the following basic operations:

- Copying/Averaging of motion compensated macroblock data from other frames.
- Copying/Addition of inverse BDCT transformed 8×8 data blocks.

This gives a linear decompression operator which maps BDCT coefficients to the decoded image sequence. Standard decompression can be interpreted as applying this operator to the integer coefficients given by the file. In our model we allow the BDCT coefficients, as these result from rounding, being contained in the intervals

$$J_i = [d_i^0 - 1/2, d_i^0 + 1/2] = [d_i^l, d_i^r], \qquad (2)$$

where $d_i^0 \in \mathbb{Z}$ is the ith quantized BDCT coefficient and d_i^l, d_i^r abbreviate the interval bounds. With that, the set of possible source coefficients is then given by

$$D = \{(d_i)_i \,|\, d_i \in J_i\}. \qquad (3)$$

The above-mentioned decompression operator, denoted by A, maps any element $d \in D$ to an image sequence (with possibly subsampled color components). To compensate for the color subsampling, we also introduce an upsampling operator $\hat{S}$ that performs pixel repetition. The missing color detail information is modelled by $\hat{s}$, which is required to be in the kernel of the color subsampling operator S. MPEG decompression then amounts to finding an image sequence $\hat{u}$ satisfying

$$\hat{u} = \hat{s} + \hat{S}A\hat{d} \qquad (4)$$

with $\hat{s} \in \ker(S)$ and $\hat{d} \in D$ unknown.

Before this is incorporated in an optimization problem, we discuss two additional aspects concerning the data intervals $(J_i)_i$. First, as the BDCT coefficients of a single block are potentially used to construct image data for multiple frames, optimization over D would not take into account block matching errors, e.g., the same block might be copied to several positions at different frames. To compensate for that, we decouple the blocks by introducing new BDCT coefficients with the same data bounds each time a set of coefficients influences different blocks. Second, as the residual BDCT data of a macroblock in which motion compensation is performed is typically highly quantized, the resulting error intervals for the dequantized residual data are large, even though often only the DC coefficient is coded. We compensate for that by setting all error intervals describing residual data to be point intervals containing the center point. As this is just done for residual data, each block coefficient has still at least one degree of freedom that results from reproducing the data of other blocks.

The optimization problem. Now suppose that the space of discrete full resolution color movies is given by $U = \mathbb{R}^{n \times m \times T \times 3}$, where n, m are the horizontal and vertical number of pixels and T is the number of image frames. Recall that, as the I frames are encoded independent of the other frames, we can typically process one or two GOPs separately and hence T is not too large. Further define the space of coefficient data as $Z = \mathbb{R}^N$. The data set D is then given as

$$D = \{d \in Z \,|\, d_i \in J_i \text{ for all } i = 1, \ldots, N\}, \qquad (5)$$

with $(J_i)_i$ as described above. With $\mathcal{R}$ a convex regularizer, artifact-free MPEG decompression can then be phrased as solving

$$\min_{s \in U, d \in Z} \mathcal{R}(s + \hat{S}Ad) + \mathcal{I}_D(d) + \mathcal{I}_{\ker(S)}(s) \tag{6}$$

where $\mathcal{I}_L$ denotes the convex indicator function of a given set L. $\mathcal{R}$ needs to be a suitable spatio-temporal regularization functional. Motivated by the results of [8], we use the *Infimal Convolution of Total Generalized Variation* type functionals as regularization. For comparison, we also employ spatio-temporal *Total Generalized Variation* (TGV) regularization. Before providing a definition of these functionals in the finite dimensional setting, we consider well posedness of the minimization problem (6) given in a general form.

In the infinite dimensional setting, all the above-mentioned functionals are lower semi-continuous semi-norms that are invariant on a finite dimensional space and coercive on its orthogonal complement (see [4,8]). These results transfer to the finite dimensional setting, where any semi-norm is continuous, invariant on its (linear) kernel and coercive on the complement of its kernel. This allows the following general existence result, from which existence of a solution to (6) with $\mathcal{R}$ being any semi-norm will immediately follow.

Proposition 1. *Let V be a finite dimensional vector space, $\mathcal{C} = \{v \in V \mid Mv \leq b\}$ be a convex polyhedron with $M : V \to R^m$ linear, $m \in \mathbb{N}$, $b \in \mathbb{R}^m$, and $\mathcal{H}$ a semi-norm on V. Then there exists a solution to*

$$\min_{v \in \mathcal{C}} \mathcal{H}(v) \tag{7}$$

Proof. Denote by $P : V \to \ker(\mathcal{H})^\perp$ the linear projection to the orthogonal complement of the kernel of $\mathcal{H}$. Then, since $\mathcal{C}$ is a polyhedron, the set $P(\mathcal{C})$ is again a polyhedron, in particular closed. This can be deduced from linearity of P and the fact that, by the Minkowski-Weyl theorem (see [13, Corollary 7.1b]), any polyhedron can equivalently be written as the sum of the convex hull of finitely many vectors and a finitely generated convex cone.

As $\mathcal{H}$ is coercive and continuous on the closed set $P(\mathcal{C})$, it admits a minimizer $v_{P(\mathcal{C})}$ over this set. Denoting $v^* \in \mathcal{C}$ such that $P(v^*) = v_{P(\mathcal{C})}$, it follows that v^* is a solution to (7). Indeed, for any $v \in \mathcal{C}$ we have

$$\mathcal{H}(v) = \mathcal{H}(P(v)) \geq \mathcal{H}(v_{P(\mathcal{C})}) = \mathcal{H}(v^*)$$

and hence the proof is complete.

Now as for the MPEG decompression case all data intervals $(J_i)_i$ are closed, the set $\mathcal{C} := \ker(S) \times D \subset U \times Z$ can be written as convex polyhedron. Choosing $\mathcal{R}$ to be any semi-norm, existence of a solution to (6) then follows from the above proposition with $\mathcal{H}(s,d) = \mathcal{R}(s + \hat{S}Ad)$. In particular (6) is well-posed when choosing either of the regularizers described on the following.

Spatio-temporal second order Total Generalized Variation. The Total Generalized Variation functional was introduced in [5] in the still image context as convex regularizer that is aware of higher order smoothness and hence avoids first order staircasing artifacts that result from TV regularization. As flickering artifacts that have been observed with spatio-temporal TV regularization [1] might be interpreted as temporal staircasing, there is hope that TGV regularization is superior also in the spatio-temporal context.

For $u = (u_{i,j,t}) \in U$ we define the forward finite difference operator

$$(\delta_1^+ u)_{i,j,t} = \begin{cases} u_{i+1,j,t} - u_{i,j,t} & \text{if } i = 0, \ldots, n-2 \\ 0 & \text{else} \end{cases} \quad (8)$$

and δ_2^+, δ_3^+ similarly. Note that $(\delta_1^+ u)_{i,j,t} \in \mathbb{R}^3$ as u has three color components. For $\lambda > 0$, a weighted spatio-temporal gradient $\nabla_\lambda : U \to U^3$ is given as

$$\nabla_\lambda u = (\delta_1^+ u, \delta_2^+ u, \lambda \delta_3^+ u). \quad (9)$$

The weight λ is introduced to fix the ratio between the temporal and spatial step-size for the finite difference operands which is not given a-priori. We further define the backward finite difference operator

$$(\delta_1^- u)_{i,j,t} = \begin{cases} u_{i,j,t} - u_{i-1,j,t} & \text{if } i = 1, \ldots, n-1 \\ 0 & \text{else} \end{cases} \quad (10)$$

and δ_2^-, δ_3^- similarly. The symmetrized gradient $\mathcal{E}_\lambda$ with temporal weighting is then defined for a vector field $v = (v^1, v^2, v^3) \in U^3$ as

$$\mathcal{E}_\lambda v = \frac{1}{2}(\nabla_{2,\lambda} v + (\nabla_{2,\lambda} v)^T), \quad \nabla_{2,\lambda} u = \begin{pmatrix} \delta_1^- v_1 & \delta_2^- v_1 & \lambda \delta_3^- v_1 \\ \delta_1^- v_2 & \delta_2^- v_2 & \lambda \delta_3^- v_2 \\ \delta_1^- v_3 & \delta_2^- v_3 & \lambda \delta_3^- v_3 \end{pmatrix}. \quad (11)$$

The second order TGV functional (see [4,5]) can now be defined as

$$\mathrm{TGV}^2_{\lambda,\alpha}(u) = \min_v \alpha_1 \|\nabla_\lambda u - v\|_1 + \alpha_0 \|\mathcal{E}_\lambda v\|_1 \quad (12)$$

where, abusing notation, $\|\cdot\|_1$ denotes discrete L^1 norms using the Frobenius norm on the matrix and tensor components, respectively. Notice that in practice the symmetrized parts of $\mathcal{E}v$ are stored only once and the Frobenius norm is adapted accordingly.

Infimal Convolution of second order Total Generalized Variation. The weighting of the temporal derivative by λ is an additional degree of freedom that appears in spatio-temporal regularization and balances spatial versus temporal regularity. It has been observed in [8] that this degree of freedom can be exploited to further improve reconstruction quality by optimally balancing between two choices of λ. This balancing might for instance be realized by the infimal convolution of two second order total generalized variation functionals (ICTGV), which is given, for $\lambda_1, \lambda_2, \beta > 0$, as

$$\mathrm{ICTGV}^2_{\lambda,\beta,\alpha}(u) = \min_v \mathrm{TGV}^2_{\lambda_1,\alpha}(u-v) + \beta \, \mathrm{TGV}^2_{\lambda_2,\alpha}(v). \quad (13)$$

The rationale behind this balancing is that one aims at an additive decomposition of the image sequence into two parts for which either strong or weak temporal regularization is favourable, in particular regularizing almost static background strongly and moving objects weakly in time.

3 Numerical Solution

In order to solve the minimization problem (6) numerically, we use the primal-dual algorithm of [6]. As we are interested in testing different spatio-temporal regularization approaches, we formulate the resulting framework in a way that covers all orders of spatio-temporal TGV regularization and infimal convolutions thereof.

For motivational purposes, consider for instance a saddle-point reformulation for minimizing the second order TGV functional plus a data fidelity $\mathcal{D}$, which is given formally as

$$\min_{(u,v)\in X} \|K(u,v)\|_{1,\gamma} + \mathcal{D}(u) = \min_{(u,v)\in X} \sup_{\substack{w\in Y \\ \|w\|_{\infty,\gamma}\leq 1}} (K(u,v),w) + \mathcal{D}(u) \qquad (14)$$

with

$$K = \begin{pmatrix} \nabla_\lambda & -I \\ 0 & \mathcal{E}_\lambda \end{pmatrix} : X \to Y \qquad (15)$$

a linear operator and $\|\cdot\|_{1,\gamma}$ a weighted sum of ℓ^1 norms. Here, the primal and dual variables are given as $(u,v) \in X = U \times U^3$ and $w \in Y = U^3 \times U^9$, respectively, with u containing image data and v balancing between different orders of differentiation. Keeping this in mind, we now consider the numerical solution of (6) in a slightly more general form. For $L_X, L_Y \in \mathbb{N}\cup\{0\}, l_k^X, l_k^Y \in \mathbb{N}$, we define the spaces of primal and dual variables X and Y as

$$X = \underset{k=0}{\overset{L_X}{\times}} U^{l_k^X} \quad \text{and} \quad Y = \underset{k=0}{\overset{L_Y}{\times}} U^{l_k^Y} \qquad (16)$$

with $l_0^X = 1$ and the norms $\|\cdot\|_X, \|\cdot\|_Y, \|\cdot\|_Z$ on X, Y, Z being the standard inner product norms. Further we define the norm $\|\cdot\|_{1,\gamma}$ on Y as

$$\|w\|_{1,\gamma} = \sum_{k=0}^{L_Y} \gamma_k \|w_k\|_1 \qquad (17)$$

where, abusing notation, the norms $\|\cdot\|_1$ on $U^{l_k^Y}$ are given as $\|r\|_1 = \sum_{i,j,t}|r_{i,j,t}|$, with $|r_{i,j,t}|$ the Frobenius norm of $r_{i,j,t} \in \mathbb{R}^{3\times l_k^Y}$.

Letting $K : X \to Y$ be a linear operator, the minimization problem (6) with any order of TGV regularization and infimal convolutions thereof can be written as

$$\min_{\substack{(s,v)\in X, \\ d\in Z}} \|K(s+\hat{S}Ad, v)\|_\gamma + \mathcal{I}_D(d) + \mathcal{I}_{\ker(S)}(s). \qquad (18)$$

A particular instance of this setting is for example obtained with

$$L_X = L_Y = 0, \ K = \nabla_\lambda, \ \gamma_0 = 1 \tag{19}$$

and corresponds to spatio-temporal TV regularization (which we do not consider in this paper). The case

$$L_X = L_Y = 1, \ K = \begin{pmatrix} \nabla_\lambda & -I \\ 0 & \mathcal{E}_\lambda \end{pmatrix}, \ \gamma_i = \alpha_{1-i} \tag{20}$$

corresponds to second order TGV regularization. ICTGV regularization can be obtained by setting

$$L_X = L_Y = 3, \ K = \begin{pmatrix} \nabla_{\lambda_1} & \nabla_{\lambda_1} & -I & 0 \\ 0 & 0 & \mathcal{E}_{\lambda_1} & 0 \\ 0 & \nabla_{\lambda_2} & 0 & -I \\ 0 & 0 & 0 & \mathcal{E}_{\lambda_2} \end{pmatrix}, \ \gamma_i = \alpha_{1-i}, \gamma_{i+2} = \beta\alpha_{1-i} \text{ for } i=1,2. \tag{21}$$

In order to find an optimal solution of (18) we apply the primal dual algorithm of [6] to the equivalent saddle point problem

$$\min_{\substack{(s,v)\in X,\\ d\in Z}} \max_{w\in Y} (K(s+\hat{S}Ad,v),w) - \mathcal{I}_{\{\|r\|_{\infty,\gamma}\leq 1\}}(w) + \mathcal{I}_D(d) + \mathcal{I}_{\ker(S)}(s) \tag{22}$$

where $\{\|r\|_{\infty,\gamma} \leq 1\} = \{r \in Y \mid \max_{i,j,t} |(r_k)_{i,j,t}| \leq \gamma_k \text{ for all } k\}$. Note that, as the regularization functional is continuous, it follows by standard arguments from convex analysis [7, Theorem III.4.1] that the saddle-point problem is indeed equivalent, in particular possesses a solution and the primal solution $((s,v),d)$ of the saddle-point problem is a solution to the original problem.

A first version of the primal-dual algorithm for MPEG decompression can now be written as Algorithm 1. There, the operator $\text{prox}_\gamma(w)$ is a projection on the set $\{\|r\|_{\infty,\gamma} \leq 1\}$ which can be calculated explicitly and pointwise. The operator $\text{proj}_D(d)$ can also be calculated explicitly and pointwise as the projection on the set $\{d \in Z \mid d_i \in J_i, \ i=1,\ldots,N\}$.

In order to ensure convergence of the algorithm we apply an adaptive step-size choice that has been proposed in [8]: With $\eta > 0$ used to fix a ratio between the primal and dual step-size σ and τ, we update the step-size parameters σ, τ at the end of each iteration as

$$\sigma = \mathcal{S}(\sigma\tau,\mathfrak{n})\eta, \quad \tau = \mathcal{S}(\sigma\tau,\mathfrak{n})/\eta \tag{23}$$

with $\mathfrak{n} = \|(s_+ - s, v_+ - v, d_+ - d)\|^2_{X\times Z}/\|K(s_+ - s + \hat{S}A(d_+ - d), v_+ - v)\|^2_Y$ (see the algorithm description). The function $\mathcal{S}(\cdot,\cdot)$ is chosen such that a reduction of the step-sizes σ and τ occurs finitely many – say k_0 – times, and ensures that after these reductions $\sigma\tau L^2_{k_0} < 1$ with $L_{k_0} = \sup_{k>k_0}\{\sqrt{1/\mathfrak{n}_k}\}$ and $\mathfrak{n}_k$ being the above quotient for the kth iterates. As can be seen by checking the convergence proof of [6], this is sufficient to ensure convergence of the proposed algorithm.

Algorithm 1. Regularized MPEG decompression

1: **function** MPEG-REC(FILE)
2:     $D \leftarrow$ Decoding of FILE
3:     $d, d_+ \leftarrow$ Center point(D), $s, s_+ \leftarrow 0$, $v, v_+ \leftarrow 0$, $w \leftarrow 0$, $\sigma, \tau > 0$
4:     **repeat**
5:         $w \leftarrow \mathrm{prox}_\gamma \big(w + \sigma K(s_+ + \hat{S}Ad_+, v_+)\big)$
6:         $(s_+, v_+) \leftarrow K^*(w)$
7:         $d_+ \leftarrow d - \tau A^* \hat{S}^*(s_+)$
8:         $(s_+, v_+) \leftarrow (s, v) - \tau(s_+, v_+)$
9:         $s_+ \leftarrow s_+ - \hat{S}S(s)$
10:        $d_+ \leftarrow \mathrm{proj}_D(d_+)$
11:        $((s, v, d), (s_+, v_+, d_+)) \leftarrow ((s_+, v_+, d_+), (2s_+ - s, 2v_+ - v, 2d_+ - d))$
12:     **until** Stopping criterion fulfilled
13:     **return** $(s + \hat{S}Ad)$
14: **end function**

At last, we define a suitable stopping criterion for Algorithm 1 that ensures optimality. For that purpose, we use a modified primal dual gap. By Fenchel-Rockafellar duality, a solution $(\hat{s}, \hat{v}, \hat{d}, \hat{w})$ of the saddle-point problem (22) must satisfy

$$0 = \|K(\hat{s} + \hat{S}A\hat{d}, \hat{v})\|_\gamma + \mathcal{I}_D(\hat{d}) + \mathcal{I}_{\ker(S)}(\hat{s}) + \mathcal{I}_{\{\|w\|_{\infty,\gamma} \leq 1\}}(\hat{w}) + G^*(\hat{r}_1, \hat{r}_2, A^*\hat{S}^*\hat{r}_1) \quad (24)$$

with $(\hat{r}_1, \hat{r}_2) = -K^*\hat{w}$ and G^* the convex-conjugate of $(s, v, d) \mapsto \mathcal{I}_D(d) + \mathcal{I}_{\ker(S)}(s)$. An easy calculation shows that G^* can be given explicitly as

$$G^*(s, v, d) = \left(\sum_{i=1}^N \frac{d_i^l + d_i^r}{2}d_i + \frac{d_i^r - d_i^l}{2}|d_i|\right) + \mathcal{I}_{\ker(I - \hat{S}S)}(s) + \mathcal{I}_{\{0\}}(v). \quad (25)$$

Replacing the equality constraints by an ℓ^1-type penalty results in the following normalized approximate primal-dual gap as stopping criterion

$$\mathcal{G}(s, v, d, w) = \frac{1}{nmT}\left|\|K(s + \hat{S}Ad, v)\|_\gamma + \tilde{G}^*(r_1, r_2, A^*\hat{S}^*r_1)\right| \quad (26)$$

where again $(r_1, r_2) = -K^*w$ and

$$\tilde{G}^*(s, v, d) = \left(\sum_{i=1}^N \frac{d_i^l + d_i^r}{2}d_i + \frac{d_i^r - d_i^l}{2}|d_i|\right) + \left(\sum_{i,j,t} |(s - \hat{S}Ss)_{i,j,t}| + |v_{i,j,t}|\right). \quad (27)$$

Straightforward evaluation of the step-size rule and the approximate primal-dual gap would result in two additional evaluations of K and A and one additional evaluation of K^* and A^* in each iteration step. As these operations are computationally expensive, we use an equivalent formulation of the primal-dual algorithm, see Algorithm 2. It includes the step-size adaptation and approximate primal-dual gap computation without additional evaluations of K, K^*, A, A^* at the cost of slightly more memory requirement.

Algorithm 2. Regularized MPEG decompression (+ step-size and error control)

1: **function** MPEG-REC(FILE)
2:     $D \leftarrow$ Decoding of FILE
3:     $d_+, d \leftarrow$ Center point(D), $s_+, s \leftarrow 0$, $v_+, v \leftarrow 0$, $w \leftarrow 0$
4:     $x_+, x \leftarrow K(s + \hat{S}Ad, v)$, $\epsilon, \eta > 0$, $\sigma \leftarrow \eta$, $\tau \leftarrow 1/\eta$
5:     **repeat**
6:         $w \leftarrow \text{prox}_\gamma(w + \sigma(2x_+ - x))$
7:         $(s, v) \leftarrow -K^*(w)$
8:         $d \leftarrow A^*\hat{S}^*s$
9:         $\mathcal{G} \leftarrow \tilde{G}^*(s, v, d)$
10:        $(s, v, d) \leftarrow (s_+, v_+, d_+) + \tau(s, v, d)$
11:        $(s, d) \leftarrow (s - \hat{S}\hat{S}s, \text{proj}_D(d))$
12:        $n_1 \leftarrow \|(s, v, d) - (s_+, v_+, d_+)\|^2_{X \times Z}$
13:        $x \leftarrow K(s + SAd, v)$
14:        $n_2 \leftarrow \|x - x_+\|^2_Y$
15:        $(\sigma, \tau) \leftarrow (S_\eta(\sigma\tau, n_1/n_2)\eta, S_\eta(\sigma\tau, n_1/n_2)/\eta)$
16:        $\mathcal{G} \leftarrow (\mathcal{G} + \|x\|_\gamma)/(nmT)$
17:        $((s_+, v_+, d_+, x_+), x) \leftarrow ((s, v, d, x), x_+)$
18:     **until** $\mathcal{G} < \epsilon$
19:     **return** $(s_+ + \hat{S}Ad_+)$
20: **end function**

4 Numerical Experiments

We carry out numerical experiments on two test videos that have been compressed using a standard MPEG-2 compression software. For regularization, we use spatio-temporal TGV and ICTGV regularization as in (12) and (13), respectively. The TGV^2_α functional was defined using a time-weight of $\lambda = 0.5$ and parameters $\alpha_0 = 3$, $\alpha_1 = 1$. The parameters for the ICTGV functional were fixed empirically as $\lambda_1 = \beta = \lambda$, $\lambda_2 = 1/\lambda$, $\lambda = 0.2$ and α as before, which implies a weighting of the spatial and temporal derivative by 1 and 0.2 for the first term and by 0.2 and 1.0 for the second one, respectively. To ensure optimality, we require the approximate primal-dual gap as defined in (26) to be below 0.2.

For the first experiment, we consider the *Juggler* image sequence obtained from [11]. The compressed MPEG file consists of one GOP of 8 frames and requires 0.38 bits per pixel (bpp), which means a compression ratio of 62. The GOP consists of one initial I frame and seven P frames. Figure 1 shows the standard decompressed version of this image sequence together with a second order TGV and ICTGV regularized version. As one can observe, both regularizations are able to significantly reduce compression artifacts. The ICTGV based reconstruction shows more details for example in the slowly moving face of the juggler, which can be recovered due to the strong temporal regularization of the second component of the functional. We also observe that, in particular in

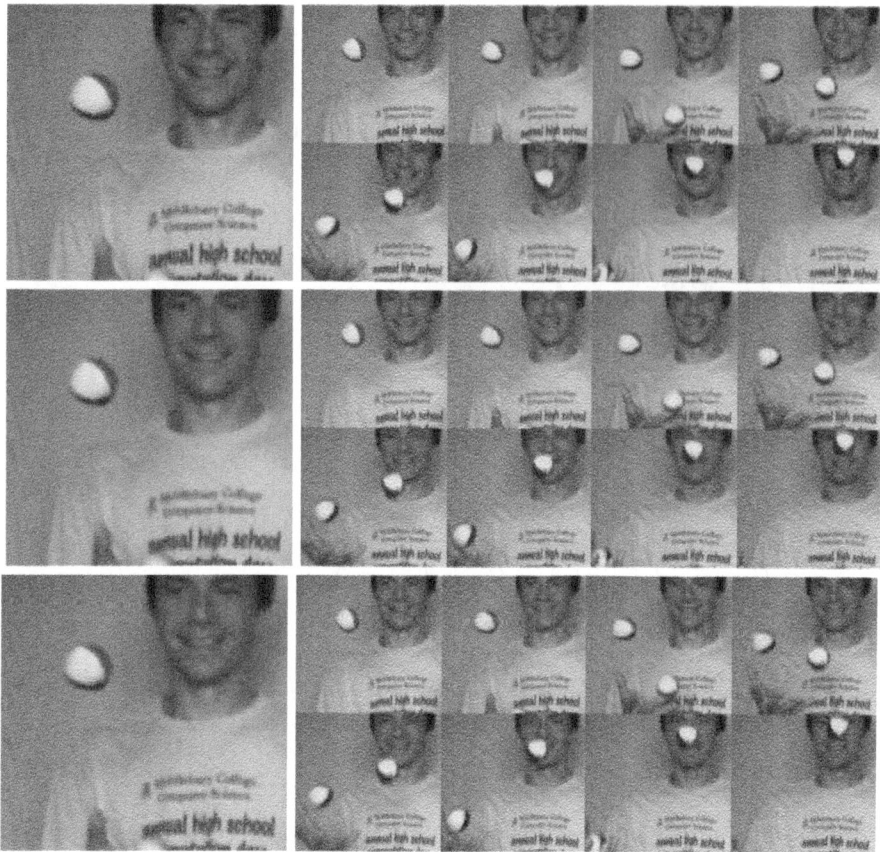

Fig. 1. From top to bottom: Standard, TGV-based and ICTGV-based decompression of the *Juggler* video. On the left, the second frame (P-frame) is shown in detail while on the right all 8 frames are depicted.

the later frames, some compression artifacts are still visible. This is due to the fact that the data intervals for the residual BDCT data of motion-compensated macroblocks have been reduced to point intervals. Improving on this will be subject of future research. To allow a more detailed evaluation, we have made results for different compression rates available online at [10].

For a second test, we use the *Tempete* image sequence obtained from [14]. The compressed MPEG file consists of 32 frames and requires 0.98 bpp, which implies a compression ratio of 24. The GOP size was set to 9 and the frame structure of each GOP is given as IBPBPBPBP. The image sequence shows a slow zoom-out of a landscape with quickly moving leaves in the foreground, in particular there

Fig. 2. Left: Standard decompression of frame four (B-frame) of the *Tempete* video with a close up. Right: The same frame of the ICTGV based decompression.

is, in contrast to the juggler sequence, no constant background region. Figure 2 show the result of standard decompression and ICTGV based decompression for the fourth frame, which is a B-frame. We can observe in the top images that the ICTGV based reconstruction still shows a high level of detail while, as can be seen in the close ups, compression artifacts are significantly reduced.

References

1. Aubert, G., Kornprobst, P.: Mathematical Problems in Image Processing. Springer (2006)
2. Bredies, K., Holler, M.: A total variation-based JPEG decompression model. SIAM J. Imag. Sci. **5**(1), 366–393 (2012)
3. Bredies, K., Holler, M.: Artifact-free decompression and zooming of JPEG compressed images with total generalized variation. In: Csurka, G., Kraus, M., Laramee, R.S., Richard, P., Braz, J. (eds.) VISIGRAPP 2012. CCIS, vol. 359, pp. 242–258. Springer, Heidelberg (2013)
4. Bredies, K., Holler, M.: Regularization of linear inverse problems with total generalized variation. J. Inverse Ill-Posed Probl. (2014). doi:10.1515/jip-2013-0068
5. Bredies, K., Kunisch, K., Pock, T.: Total generalized variation. SIAM J. Imag. Sci. **3**(3), 492–526 (2010)
6. Chambolle, A., Pock, T.: A first-order primal-dual algorithm for convex problems with applications to imaging. J. Math. Imaging Vision **40**, 120–145 (2011)
7. Ekeland, I., Témam, R.: Convex Analysis and Variational Problems. SIAM (1999)
8. Holler, M., Kunisch, K.: On infimal convolution of TV-type functionals and applications to video and image reconstruction. SIAM J. Imag. Sci. **7**(4), 2258–2300 (2014)

9. Kocovski, B., Kartalov, T., Ivanovski, Z., Panovski, L.: An adaptive deblocking algorithm for low bit-rate video. In: 3rd International Symposium on ISCCSP 2008, pp. 888–893, March 2008
10. Webpage of Martin Holler. http://www.uni-graz.at/~hollerm/research.html
11. Middlebury optical flow dataset. http://vision.middlebury.edu/flow/
12. Schaeffer, H., Yang, Y., Osher, S.: Space-time regularization for video decompression (2014). Preprint
13. Schrijver, A.: Theory of Linear and Integer Programming. John Wiley & Sons (1986)
14. Arizona State University. Video trace library. http://trace.eas.asu.edu/
15. Zhong, S.: Image coding with optimal reconstruction. International Conference on Image Processing **1**, 161–164 (1997)

Segmentation and Partitioning

Probabilistic Correlation Clustering and Image Partitioning Using Perturbed Multicuts

Jörg Hendrik Kappes[1](✉), Paul Swoboda[2], Bogdan Savchynskyy[1],
Tamir Hazan[3], and Christoph Schnörr[1,2]

[1] Heidelberg Collaboratory for Image Processing,
Heidelberg University, Heidelberg, Germany
kappes@math.uni-heidelberg.de
[2] Image and Pattern Analysis Group, Heidelberg University, Heidelberg, Germany
[3] Department of Computer Science, University of Haifa, Haifa, Israel

Abstract. We exploit recent progress on globally optimal MAP inference by integer programming and perturbation-based approximations of the log-partition function. This enables to locally represent uncertainty of image partitions by approximate marginal distributions in a mathematically substantiated way, and to rectify local data term cues so as to close contours and to obtain valid partitions. Our approach works for any graphically represented problem instance of correlation clustering, which is demonstrated by an additional social network example.

Keywords: Correlation clustering · Multicut · Perturb and MAP

1 Introduction

Clustering, image partitioning and related NP-hard decision problems abound in the fields image analysis, computer vision, machine learning and data mining, and much research has been done on alleviating the combinatorial difficulty of such inference problems using various forms of relaxations. A recent assessment of the state-of-the-art using discrete graphical models has been provided by [13]. A subset of specific problem instances considered there (Potts-like functional minimisation) are closely related to continuous formulations investigated, e.g., by [7,17].

From the viewpoint of statistics and Bayesian inference, such *Maximum-A-Posteriori (MAP)* point estimates have been always criticised as falling short of the scope of probabilistic inference, that is to provide – along with the MAP estimate – "error bars" that enable to assess sensitivities and uncertainties for further data analysis. Approaches to this more general objective are less uniquely defined than the MAP problem. For example, a variety of approaches have been suggested from the viewpoint of clustering (see more comments and references below) which, on the other hand, differ from the variational marginalisation problem in connection with discrete graphical models [25]. From the computational viewpoint, these more general problems are not less involved than the corresponding MAP(-like) combinatorial inference problems.

In this paper, we consider the general multicut problem [8], also known as correlation clustering in other fields [5], which includes the image partitioning problem as special case. Our work is based on

(i) recent progress [10,19] on the probabilistic analysis of perturbed MAP problems applied to our setting in order to establish a sound link to basic variational approximations of inference problems [25],
(ii) recent progress on *exact* solvers of the multicut problem [15,16], which is required in connection with (i).

Figure 1 provides a first illustration of our approach. Our general problem formulation enables to address not only the image partitioning problem. We demonstrate this in the experimental section by applying correlation clustering to a problem instance from machine learning that involves network data on a general graph.

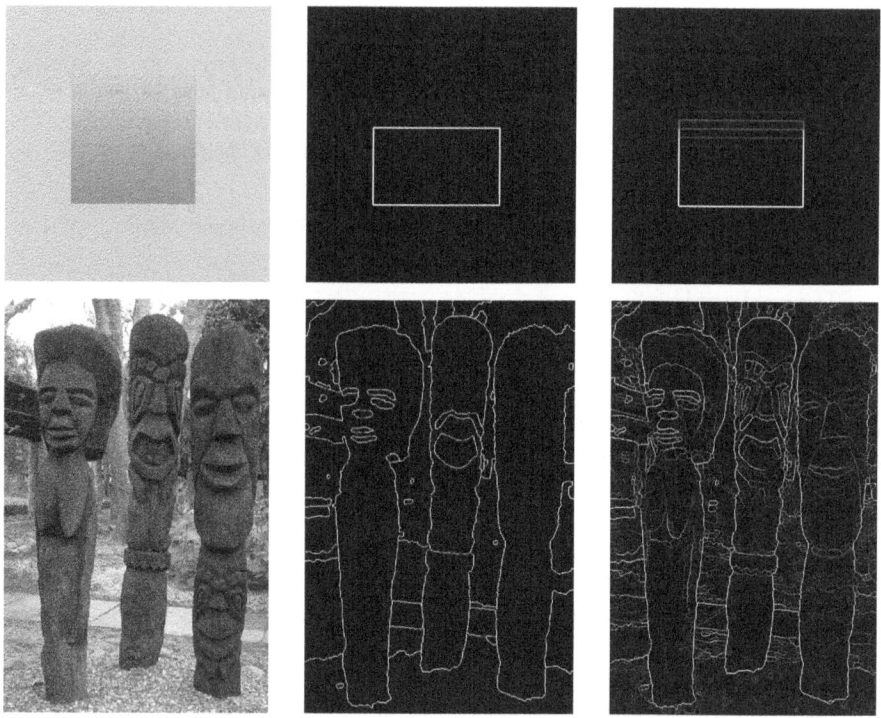

Fig. 1. Two examples demonstrating our approach. **Left column:** images subject to unsupervised partitioning. **Center column:** globally optimal partitions. **Right column:** probabilistic inference provided along with the partition. The color order: white → yellow → red → black, together with decreasing brightness, indicate uncertainty, cf.Fig. 2. We point out that *all local* information provided by our approach is intrinsically *non-locally* inferred and relates to partitions, that is to *closed* contours.

Related Work. The susceptibility of clustering to noise is well known. This concerns, in particular, clustering approaches to image partitioning that typically employ spectral relaxation [12,22,23]. Measures proposed in the literature [24] to quantitatively assess confidence in terms of stability, employ data perturbations and various forms of cluster averaging. While this is intuitively plausible, a theoretically more convincing substantiation seems to be lacking, however.

In [11], a deterministic annealing approach to the unsupervised graph partitioning problem (called pairwise clustering) was proposed by adding an entropy term weighted by an artificial temperature parameter. Unlike the simpler continuation method of Blake and Zisserman [6], this way of smoothing the combinatorial partitioning problem resembles the variational transition from marginalisation to MAP estimation, by applying the log-exponential function to the latter objective [25]. As in [6], however, the primary objective of [11] is to compute a single "good" local optimum by solving a sequence of increasingly non-convex problems parametrised by an artificial temperature parameter, rather than sampling various "ground states" (close to zero-temperature solutions) in order to assess stability, and to explicitly compute alternatives to the single MAP solution. The latter has been achieved in [18] using a non-parametric Bayesian framework. Due to the complexity of model evaluation, however, authors have to resort to MCMC sampling.

Concerning continuous problem formulations, a remarkable approach to assess "error bars" of variational segmentations has been suggested by [20]. Here, the starting point is the "smoothed" version of the Mumford-Shah functional in terms of the relaxation of Ambrosio and Tortorelli [2] that is known to Γ-converge to the Mumford-Shah functional in the limit of corresponding parameter values. Authors of [20] apply a particular perturbation ("polynomial chaos") that enables to locally infer confidence of the segmentation result. Although being similar in scope to our approach, this approach is quite different. An obvious drawback results from the fact that minima of the Ambrosio-Tortorelli functional do not enforce partitions, i.e. may involve contours that are not closed.

Finally, we mention recent work [21] that addresses the same problem using – again – a quite different approach: "stochastic" in [21] just refers to the relaxation of binary indicator vectors to the probability simplex, and this relaxation is solved by a *local* minimisation method. Our approach, on the other hand, is based on random perturbations of *exact* solutions of the correlation clustering problem. This yields a truly probabilistic interpretation in terms of the induced approximation of the log-partition function, whose derivatives generate the expected values of the variables of interest.

Organization. Sec. 2 defines the combinatorial correlation clustering problem and introduces multicuts. The variational formulation for probabilistic inference is presented in Sec. 3, followed by the perturbation approach in Sec. 4. A range of experiments demonstrate the approach in Sec. 5. Since alternative approaches rely on quite different methods, as explained above, a re-implementation is beyond the scope of this paper. We therefore restrict our comparison to the evaluation of *local* potentials that we consider as an efficient alternative. This comparison reveals that contrary to this local method, our perturbation approach effectively enforces *global* topological constraints so as to sample from most likely partitions.

Basic Notation. We set $[n] := \{1, 2, \ldots, n\}$, $n \in \mathbb{N}$ and use the indicator function $\mathbb{I}(p) = 1$ if the predicate p is true, and $\mathbb{I}(p) = 0$ otherwise. $|S|$ denotes the cardinality of a finite set S. $\langle x, y \rangle = \sum_{i \in [n]} x_i y_i$ denotes the Euclidean inner product of vectors $x, y \in \mathbb{R}^n$. $\mathbb{E}[X]$ denotes the expected value of a random variable X. $\Pr[\Omega]$ denotes the probability of an event Ω.

2 Correlation Clustering and Multicuts

The correlation clustering problem is defined in terms of partitions of an undirected weighted graph

$$G = (V, E, w), \quad V = [n], \quad E \subseteq V \times V, \tag{1a}$$
$$w \colon E \to \mathbb{R}, \quad e \mapsto w_e := w(e) \tag{1b}$$

with signed edge-weight function w. A positive weight $w_e > 0$, $e \in E$ indicates that two adjacent nodes should be merged, whereas a negative weight indicates that these nodes should be separated into distinct clusters S_i, S_j.

We formally define valid partitions and interchangeably call them segmentations or clusterings.

Definition 1 (partition, segmentation, clustering). *A set of subsets* $\{S_1, \ldots, S_k\}$, *called* shores, components or clusters, *is a* (valid) partition *of a graph* $G = (V, E, w)$ *iff* [(**a**)] *1.* $S_i \subseteq V$, $i \in [k]$, *2.* $S_i \neq \emptyset$, $i \in [k]$, *3. the induced subgraphs* $G_i := (S_i, (S_i \times S_i) \cap E)$ *are connected, 4.* $\bigcup_{i \in [k]} S_i = V$, *5.* $S_i \cap S_j = \emptyset$, $i, j \in [k]$, $i \neq j$. *The set of all valid partitions of G is denoted by* $\mathcal{S}(G)$.

The number $|\mathcal{S}(G)|$ of all possible partitions is upper-bounded by the Bell number [1] that grows very quickly with $|V|$.

The *correlation clustering* or *minimal cost multicut problem* is to find a partition that minimizes the cost of intra cluster edges as defined by the weight function w. This problem can be formulated as a minimization problem of a Potts model

$$\arg\min\nolimits_{x \in V^{|V|}} \sum_{ij \in E} w_{ij} \mathbb{I}(x_i \neq x_j). \tag{2}$$

Because any node can form its own cluster, $|V|$ labels are needed to represent all possible assignments in terms of variables x_i, $i \in V$.

A major drawback of this formulation is the huge inflated space representing the assignments. Furthermore, due to the lack of an external field (unary terms), any permutation of an optimal assignment results in another optimal labeling. As a consequence, the standard relaxation in terms of the so-called local polytope [25] becomes too weak.

In order to overcome these problems, we adopt an alternative representation of partitions based on the set of *inter* cluster edges [8]. We call the edge set

$$\delta(S_1,\ldots,S_k) := \{uv \in E \colon u \in S_i,\, v \in S_j,\, i \neq j,\, i,j \in [k]\} \qquad (3)$$

a *multicut*. To obtain a polyhedral representation of multicuts, we define *indicator vectors* $\chi(E') \in \{0,1\}^{|E|}$ for each subset $E' \subseteq E$ by

$$\chi_e(E') := \begin{cases} 1, & \text{if } e \in E', \\ 0, & \text{if } e \in E \setminus E'. \end{cases}$$

The *multicut polytope* $\mathcal{MC}(G)$ then is given by the convex hull

$$\mathcal{MC}(G) := \operatorname{conv}\{\chi(\delta(S)) \colon S \in \mathcal{S}(G)\}. \qquad (4)$$

The vertices of this polytope are the indicator functions of valid partitions and denoted by

$$\mathcal{Y}(G) := \{\chi(\delta(S)) \colon S \in \mathcal{S}(G)\}. \qquad (5)$$

The *correlation clustering problem* then amounts to find a partition $S \in \mathcal{S}(G)$ that minimizes the sum of the weights of edges cut by the partition

$$\arg\min_{S \in \mathcal{S}(G)} \sum_{e \in E} w_e \cdot \chi_e(\delta(S)) = \arg\min_{y \in \mathcal{MC}(G)} \sum_{e \in E} w_e \cdot y_e. \qquad (6)$$

Although problem (6) is a linear program, solving it is NP-hard, because a representation of the multicut polytope $\mathcal{MC}(G)$ by half-spaces is of exponential size and moreover, unless $P = NP$, it is not separable in polynomial time. However, one can develop efficient separation procedures for an outer relaxation of the multicut polytope which involves all facet-defining cycle inequalities. Together with integrality constraints, this guarantees globally optimal solutions of problem (6) and performs best on benchmark datasets [13,14].

3 Probabilistic Correlation Clustering

A major limitation of solutions to the correlation clustering problem is that the most likely segmentations are returned without any measurement of the corresponding uncertainty. To overcome this, one would like to compute the marginal probability that an edge is an inter-cluster edge or, in other words, that an edge is cut.

The most direct approach to accomplish this is to associate a Gibbs distribution with the Potts model in (2)

$$p(x|w,\beta) = \exp\Big(-\beta \sum_{ij \in E} w_{ij}\mathbb{I}(x_i \neq x_j) - \log\big(Z_x(w,\beta)\big)\Big), \qquad (7a)$$

$$Z_x(w,\beta) = \sum_{x \in \mathcal{X}} \exp\Big(-\beta \sum_{ij \in E} w_{ij}\mathbb{I}(x_i \neq x_j)\Big), \qquad (7b)$$

where $\mathcal{X}$ denotes the feasible set of (2)

$$\mathcal{X} := \mathcal{X}_1 \times \ldots \times \mathcal{X}_{|V|} := V^{|V|}, \qquad \mathcal{X}_i = V, \ i \in V. \tag{8}$$

Parameter β is a free parameter (in physics: "inverse temperature") and $Z(w, \beta)$ the partition function. Performing the reformulation

$$-\beta \sum_{ij \in E} w_{ij} \mathbb{I}(x_i \neq x_j) = \sum_{ij \in E} \sum_{\substack{x'_i \in \mathcal{X}_i \\ x'_j \in \mathcal{X}_j}} \underbrace{-\beta\, w_{ij}\, \mathbb{I}(x'_i \neq x'_j)}_{:=\theta_{ij;x'_i,x'_j}} \cdot \underbrace{\mathbb{I}(x_i = x'_i \vee x_j = x'_j)}_{:=\phi_{ij;x'_i,x'_j}(x)}, \tag{9}$$

we recognise the distribution as a member of the exponential family with model parameter θ and sufficient statistics $\phi(x)$:

$$p(x|\theta) = \exp\left(\langle \theta, \phi(x) \rangle - \log\left(Z_x(\theta)\right)\right), \tag{10a}$$

$$Z_x(\theta) = \sum_{x \in \mathcal{X}} \exp\left(\langle \theta, \phi(x) \rangle\right). \tag{10b}$$

Note that the dimension $d = |V| \cdot |V| \cdot |E|$ of the vectors θ, ϕ is large. Therefore, while (10) in principle provides the "correct" basis for assessing uncertainty in terms of marginal distributions $p(x_i, x_j|\theta)$, $ij \in E$, this is infeasible computationally due to the huge space X and the aforementioned permutation invariance.

To overcome this problem, we resort to the problem formulation (6) in terms of multicuts, define the model parameter vector θ and the sufficient statistics $\phi(y)$ by

$$\theta = -\beta w, \qquad \phi(y) = y, \tag{11}$$

to obtain the distribution

$$p(y|\theta) = \exp\left(\langle \theta, y \rangle - \log\left(Z(\theta)\right)\right), \tag{12a}$$

$$Z(\theta) = \sum_{y \in \mathcal{Y}(G)} \exp\left(\langle \theta, y \rangle\right). \tag{12b}$$

Note that the dimension $d = |E|$ of the vectors w, y is considerably smaller than in problem (10).

Applying basic results that hold for distributions of the exponential family [25], the following holds regarding (12). For the random vector $Y = (Y_e)_{e \in E}$ taking values in $\mathcal{Y}(G)$, the marginal distributions, also called *mean parameters* in a more general context, are defined by

$$\mu_e := \mathbb{E}[\phi_e(Y)] = \sum_{y \in \mathcal{Y}(G)} \phi_e(y) p(y|\theta), \qquad \forall e \in E. \tag{13}$$

Likewise, the entire vector $\mu \in \mathbb{R}^{|E|}$ results as convex combination of the vectors $\phi(y)$, $y \in \mathcal{Y}(G)$. The closure of the convex hull of all such vectors corresponds to the (closure) of vectors μ that can be generated by valid distributions. This results in the representation of the multicut polytope (4)

$$\mathcal{MC}(G) = \text{conv}\{\phi(y) \colon y \in \mathcal{Y}(G)\} \tag{14a}$$

$$= \Big\{ \mu \in \mathbb{R}^{|E|} \colon \mu = \sum_{y \in \mathcal{Y}(G)} p(y)\phi(y) \text{ for some } p(y) \geq 0, \sum_{y \in \mathcal{Y}(G)} p(y) = 1 \Big\}. \tag{14b}$$

Furthermore, the log-partition function generates the mean parameters through

$$\mu = \nabla_\theta \log Z(\theta), \tag{15}$$

which a short computation using (12) shows. Due to this relation, approximate probabilistic inference rests upon approximations of the log-partition function. In connection with discrete models, the Bethe-Kikuchi approximation and the local polytope relaxation provide basic examples for the marginal polytope [25].

In connection with the multicut polytope (14), however, we are not aware of an established outer relaxation and approximation of the log-partition function that is both tight enough and of manageable polynomial size. It is this fact that makes our approach presented in the subsequent section an attractive alternative, because it rests upon progress on solving several times problem (6) instead, together with perturbing the objective function.

4 Perturbation and MAP for Correlation Clustering

Recently, Hazan and Jaakkola [10] showed the connection between extreme value statistics and the partition function, based on the pioneering work of Gumbel [9]. In particular they provided a framework for approximating and bounding the partition function using MAP-inference with randomly perturbed models.

Analytic expressions for the statistics of a random MAP perturbation can be derived for general discrete sets, whenever independent and identically distributed random perturbations are applied to every assignment.

Theorem 1 ([9]). *Given a discrete Gibbs distribution $p(x) = 1/Z(\theta) \exp(\theta(x))$ with $x \in \mathcal{X}$ and $\theta \colon \mathcal{X} \to \mathbb{R} \cup \{-\infty\}$, let Γ be a vector of i.i.d. random variables Γ_x indexed by $x \in \mathcal{X}$, each following the Gumbel distribution whose cumulative distribution function is $F(t) = \exp\big(-\exp(-(t+c))\big)$ (here c is the Euler-Mascheroni constant). Then*

$$\Pr\big[\hat{x} = \arg\max_{x \in \mathcal{X}} \{\theta(x) + \Gamma_x\}\big] = 1/Z(\theta) \cdot \exp\big(\theta(\hat{x})\big), \tag{16a}$$

$$\mathbb{E}\big[\max_{x \in \mathcal{X}} \{\theta(x) + \Gamma_x\}\big] = \log Z. \tag{16b}$$

For our problem at hand the set $\mathcal{X} = \mathcal{Y}(G)$ is complex and thus Thm. 1 not directly applicable. Hazan and Jaakkola [10] develop computationally feasible approximations and bounds of the partition function based on *low*-dimensional random MAP perturbations.

Theorem 2 ([10]). *Given a discrete Gibbs distribution $p(x) = 1/Z(\theta) \exp(\theta(x))$ with $x \in \mathcal{X} = [L]^n$, $n = |V|$ and $\theta : \mathcal{X} \to \mathbb{R} \cup \{-\infty\}$. Let Γ' be a collection of i.i.d. random variables $\{\Gamma'_{i;x_i}\}$ indexed by $i \in V = [n]$ and $x_i \in X_i = [L]$, $i \in V$, each following the Gumbel distribution whose cumulative distribution function is $F(t) = \exp(-\exp(-(t+c)))$ (here c is the Euler-Mascheroni constant). Then*

$$\log Z(\theta) = \mathbb{E}_{\Gamma'_{1;x_1}} \left[\max_{x_1 \in \mathcal{X}_1} \cdots \mathbb{E}_{\Gamma'_{N;x_n}} \left[\max_{x_n \in \mathcal{X}_n} \theta(x) + \sum_{i \in V} \Gamma'_{i;x_i} \right] \cdots \right]. \quad (17)$$

Note that the random vector Γ' includes only nL random variables. Appying Jensen's inequality, we arrive at a computationally feasible upper bound of the log partition function,

$$\log Z(\theta) \leq \mathbb{E}_{\Gamma'} \left[\max_{x \in X} \theta(x) + \sum_{i \in V} \Gamma'_{i;x_i} \right]. \quad (18)$$

In the case of graph partitioning, we specifically have

$$\theta(y) = \begin{cases} \langle \theta, y \rangle & \text{if } y \in \mathcal{Y}(G) \\ -\infty & \text{else} \end{cases}, \quad y \in \{0,1\}^{|E|} \quad (19)$$

with $\theta = -\beta w$ due to (11) which after insertion into Eq. (18) yields

$$\log Z(\theta) \leq \mathbb{E}_{\Gamma'} \left[\max_{y \in \mathcal{Y}(G)} \langle \theta, y \rangle + \sum_{e \in E} \Gamma'_{e;y_e} \right] =: \tilde{A}(\theta). \quad (20)$$

Our final step towards estimating the marginals (13) consists in replacing the log-partition function in (15) by the approximation (20) and computing estimates for the mean parameters

$$\mu \approx \tilde{\mu} := \nabla_\theta \tilde{A}(\theta) := \mathbb{E}_{\Gamma'} \left[\arg\max_{y \in \mathcal{Y}(G)} \left\{ \langle \theta, y \rangle + \sum_{e \in E} \Gamma'_{e;y_e} \right\} \right] \quad (21a)$$

$$\approx \frac{1}{M} \sum_{k=1}^{M} \arg\max_{y \in \mathcal{Y}(G)} \left\{ \langle \theta, y \rangle + \sum_{e \in E} \gamma'^{(n)}_{e;y_e} \right\}, \quad \gamma'^{(n)}_{e;y_e} \sim \Gamma'_{e;y_e}. \quad (21b)$$

Note that the expression in the brackets [...] is a subgradient of the corresponding objective function. Thus, in words, we *define* our mean parameter estimate as empirical average of specific subgradients of the randomly perturbed MAP objective function.

5 Experiments

5.1 Setup

For the empirical evaluation of our approach we consider standard benchmark datasets for correlation clustering [14]. As solver for the correlation clustering problems we use the cutting-plane solver suggested by Kappes et al. [16], which can solve these problems to global optimality. We use the publicly available implementation of OpenGM2 [3].

For each instance we compare the globally optimal solution (mode)

$$\mu^* = \arg\max_{y \in \mathcal{Y}(G)} \sum_e w_e \cdot y_e \qquad (22)$$

and the *local* boundary probabilities $\bar{\mu}$ given as softmax-function of the edge-weight

$$\bar{\mu}_e = \Pr_\beta^{\text{local}}(y_e = 1) := \frac{\exp(-\beta \cdot w_e)}{\exp(-\beta \cdot w_e) + 1} \qquad (23)$$

with our estimates (21) for the boundary marginals based on the global model

$$\tilde{\mu}_e \stackrel{\text{Eq.(21)}}{\approx} \Pr_\beta(y_e = 1) := \sum_{y' \in \mathcal{Y}(G), y'_e = y_e} \frac{1}{Z(w,\beta)} \exp\left(-\beta \cdot \sum_e w_e \cdot y'_e\right) \qquad (24)$$

for the same β as in eq. 23 and $M = 100$ samples for eq. 21. While μ^* and $\tilde{\mu}$ are by definition contained in the multicut polytope $\mathcal{MC}(G)$ and hence valid mean parameters, for $\bar{\mu}$ this is not necessarily the case, as the experiments will clearly show. For visualization we use the color map shown in Fig. 2.

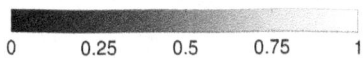

Fig. 2. Color coding used for visualization of boundary probabilities

5.2 Evaluation and Discussion

Synthetic Example. We considered the image shown in Fig. 3(a). Local boundary detection was simply estimated by gray-value difference, i.e.

$$w_{ij} = |I(i) - I(j)| - 0.1. \qquad \forall ij \in E.$$

As shown in Fig. 3(c) this gives a strong boundary prediction in the lower part, but obviously no response in the upper part of the image. Applying correlation clustering to find the most likely clustering returns the partition shown in Fig. 3(b). However, this gives no information on the uncertainty of the solution. Fig. 3(d) shows our estimated mean parameters. These not only encode uncertainty but also enforce the boundary probability to be topologically consistent in terms of a convex combination of *valid* partitions.

Image Segmentation. For real world examples we use the public available benchmark model of Andres et al. [4,14]. This model is based on super pixels and local boundary probabilities are learned by a random forest. Fig. 4 shows as example one of the 100 instances. Contrary to the mode (Fig. 4(b)), the

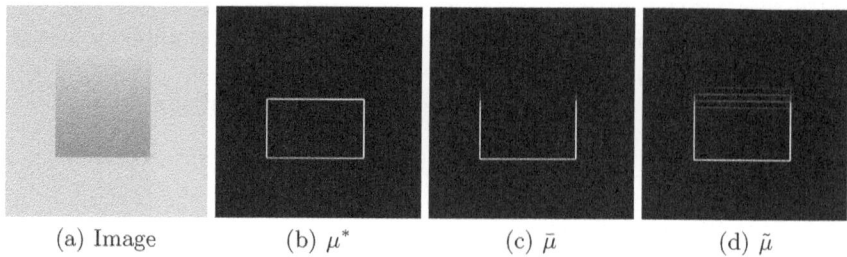

(a) Image (b) μ^* (c) $\bar{\mu}$ (d) $\tilde{\mu}$

Fig. 3. The optimal clustering (b) encodes no uncertainty, the local probability (c) is topological not consistent. Our estimate (d) encodes uncertainty and is topological consistent.

boundary marginals (Fig. 4(d)) describe the uncertainty of the boundary and alternative contours. In contrast to the local boundary probability learned by a random forest, shown in Fig. 4(c), our marginal contours are closed and have no dangling contour-parts. This leads to a better boundary of the brown tree and removes or closes local artefacts in the koalas head. Note that Fig. 4(c) cannot be described as a convex combinations of valid clusterings.

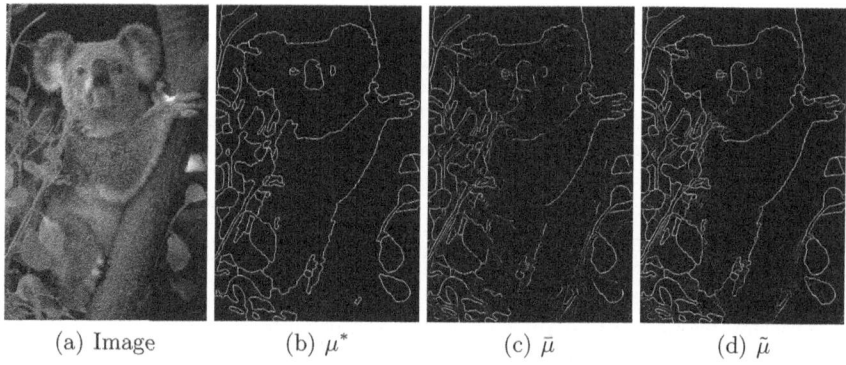

(a) Image (b) μ^* (c) $\bar{\mu}$ (d) $\tilde{\mu}$

Fig. 4. The proposed global boundary probability (d) can only guarantee topological consistency and reflect uncertainty. This leads to a better boundary probabilities of the brown tree and removes or closes local artefacts in the koalas head compared to (c). The optimal partitioning (b) and the local boundary probabilities (c) can handle only either aspect and, in the latter case, signal *invalid* partitions.

Social Networks. As an example for data mining and to demonstrate the generality of our approach, we consider the karate network [13]. Nodes in the graph correspond to members of the karate club and edges indicate friendship of members. The task is to cluster the graph such that the modularity is maximized, which can be reformulated into a correlation clustering problem over a fully connected graph with the same nodes. Because edge weights are not probabilistically motivated for this model, the local boundary probabilities are poor (Fig. 5(c)).

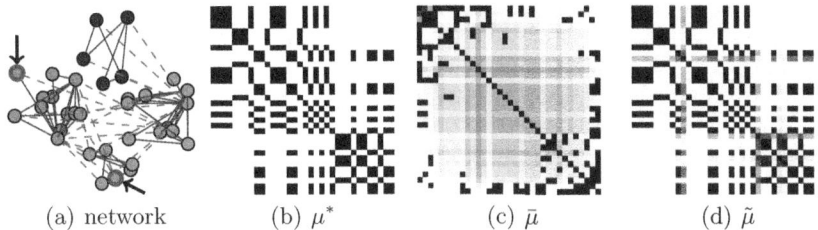

(a) network (b) μ^* (c) $\bar{\mu}$ (d) $\tilde{\mu}$

Fig. 5. The clustering of members of a karate club is a example for correlation clustering in social networks. Figure **(a)** and **(b)** show the clustering that maximizes the modularity. Nodes marked with a red boundary in **(a)** are nodes with an uncertain assignment. The uncertainty is measured by the marginal probabilities **(d)**. Pseudo probabilities calculated by local weights only, shown in **(c)**, do not reveal this detailed information. Our result **(d)** enables to conclude that for the network graph **(a)** the modularity would not change much if the two nodes with uncertain assignment would be moved to the orange and brown cluster, respectively.

Global inference helps to detect the two members (nodes) for which the assignment to the cluster is uncertain (Fig. 5(d)). Fig. 5(a) shows the clustering that maximizes the modularity. Our result enables the conclusion that the two uncertain nodes (marked with red boundary and arrows) can be moved to another cluster without much worsening the modularity.

6 Conclusion

We presented a probabilistic approach to correlation clustering and showed how perturbed MAP estimates can be used to efficiently calculate globally consistent approximations to marginal distributions. Regarding image partitioning, by enforcing this marginal consistency, we are able to close open contour parts caused by imperfect local detection and thus reduce local artefacts by topological priors. In future work we would like to speed up our method by making use of warm start techniques, to reduce the computation time from a few minutes to seconds.

Acknowledgments. We thank Johannes Berger for inspiring discussions. This work has been supported by the German Research Foundation (DFG) within the program Spatio/Temporal Graphical Models and Applications in Image Analysis", grant GRK 1653.

References

1. Aigner, M.: Combinatorial Theory. Springer (1997)
2. Ambrosio, L., Tortorelli, V.: Approximation of Functionals Depending on Jumps by Elliptic Functionals via γ-Convergence. Comm. Pure Appl. Math. **43**(8), 999–1036 (1990)
3. Andres, B., Beier, T., Kappes, J.H.: OpenGM: A C++ library for Discrete Graphical Models. CoRR, abs/1206.0111 (2012)

4. Andres, B., Kappes, J.H., Beier, T., Köthe, U., Hamprecht, F.A.: Probabilistic image segmentation with closedness constraints. In: ICCV, pp. 2611–2618. IEEE (2011)
5. Bansal, N., Blum, A., Chawla, S.: Correlation clustering. Machine Learning **56**(1–3), 89–113 (2004)
6. Blake, A., Zisserman, A.: Visual Reconstruction. MIT Press (1987)
7. Chambolle, A., Cremers, D., Pock, T.: A Convex Approach to Minimal Partitions. SIAM J. Imag. Sci. **5**(4), 1113–1158 (2012)
8. Chopra, S., Rao, M.: The partition problem. Mathematical Programming **59**(1–3), 87–115 (1993)
9. Gumbel, E.: Statistical theory of extreme values and some practical applications: a series of lectures. Applied mathematics series. U. S. Govt. Print. Office (1954)
10. Hazan, T., Jaakkola, T.: On the partition function and random maximum a-posteriori perturbations. In: ICML. icml.cc / Omnipress (2012)
11. Hofman, T., Buhmann, J.: Pairwise Data Clustering by Deterministic Annealing. IEEE Trans. Patt. Anal. Mach. Intell. **19**(1), 1–14 (1997)
12. Kannan, R., Vempala, S., Vetta, A.: On clusterings: good, bad and spectral. J. ACM **51**(3), 497–515 (2004)
13. Kappes, J., Andres, B., Hamprecht, F., Schnörr, C., Nowozin, S., Batra, D., Kim, S., Kausler, B., Kröger, T., Lellmann, J., Komodakis, N., Savchynskyy, B., Rother, C.: A Comparative Study of Modern Inference Techniques for Structured Discrete Energy Minimization Problems (2014). http://arxiv.org/abs/1404.0533
14. Kappes, J.H., Andres, B., Hamprecht, F.A., Schnörr, C., Nowozin, S., Batra, D., Kim, S., Kausler, B.X., Lellmann, J., Komodakis, N., Rother, C.: A comparative study of modern inference techniques for discrete energy minimization problems. In: CVPR (2013)
15. Kappes, J.H., Speth, M., Andres, B., Reinelt, G., Schn, C.: Globally optimal image partitioning by multicuts. In: Boykov, Y., Kahl, F., Lempitsky, V., Schmidt, F.R. (eds.) EMMCVPR 2011. LNCS, vol. 6819, pp. 31–44. Springer, Heidelberg (2011)
16. Kappes, J.H., Speth, M., Reinelt, G., Schnörr, C.: Higher-order segmentation via multicuts. CoRR, abs/1305.6387 (2013)
17. Lellmann, J., Schnörr, C.: Continuous Multiclass Labeling Approaches and Algorithms. SIAM J. Imaging Science **4**(4), 1049–1096 (2011)
18. Orbanz, P., Buhmann, J.: Nonparametric Bayesian Image Segmentation. Int. J. Comp. Vision **77**(1–3), 25–45 (2008)
19. Papandreou, G., Yuille, A.: Perturb-and-MAP random fields: using discrete optimization to learn and sample from energy models. In: Proc. ICCV (2011)
20. Pätz, T., Kirby, R., Preusser, T.: Ambrosio-Tortorelli Segmentation of Stochastic Images: Model Extensions, Theoretical Investigations and Numerical Methods. Int. J. Comp. Vision **103**(2), 190–212 (2013)
21. Rebagliati, N., Rota Bulò, S., Pelillo, M.: Correlation clustering with stochastic labellings. In: Hancock, E., Pelillo, M. (eds.) SIMBAD 2013. LNCS, vol. 7953, pp. 120–133. Springer, Heidelberg (2013)
22. Shi, J., Malik, J.: Normalized cuts and image segmentation. IEEE Trans. Pattern Anal. Mach. Intell. **22**(8), 888–905 (2000)
23. von Luxburg, U.: A Tutorial on Spectral Clustering. Statistics and Computing **17**(4), 395–416 (2007)
24. von Luxburg, U.: Clustering Stability: An Overview. Found. Trends Mach. Learning **2**(3), 235–274 (2009)
25. Wainwright, M.J., Jordan, M.I.: Graphical models, exponential families, and variational inference. Foundations and Trends in Machine Learning **1**, 1–305 (2008)

Optimizing the Relevance-Redundancy Tradeoff for Efficient Semantic Segmentation

Caner Hazırbaş[✉], Julia Diebold, and Daniel Cremers

Technical University of Munich, Munich, Germany
{c.hazirbas,julia.diebold,cremers}@tum.de

Abstract. Semantic segmentation aims at jointly computing a segmentation and a semantic labeling of the image plane. The main ingredient is an efficient feature selection strategy. In this work we perform a systematic information-theoretic evaluation of existing features in order to address the question which and how many features are appropriate for an efficient semantic segmentation. To this end, we discuss the tradeoff between relevance and redundancy and present an information-theoretic feature evaluation strategy. Subsequently, we perform a systematic experimental validation which shows that the proposed feature selection strategy provides state-of-the-art semantic segmentations on five semantic segmentation datasets at significantly reduced runtimes. Moreover, it provides a systematic overview of which features are the most relevant for various benchmarks.

Keywords: Feature analysis · Feature selection · Image segmentation · Semantic scene understanding

1 Introduction

1.1 Semantic Segmentation and Feature Selection

Semantic segmentation – sometimes also referred to as class-specific segmentation – aims at jointly computing a partitioning of the image plane and a semantic labeling of the various regions in terms of previously learned object classes. Numerous works are focused on the development of sophisticated regularizers for this problem: co-occurrence priors [9,18] have been suggested to learn and penalize the joint occurrence of semantic labels within the same image. Proximity priors [1] have been proposed to penalize the co-occurrence of labels within a certain spatial neighborhood. Hierarchical priors [17,20] have been introduced to impose certain label hierarchies – for example that an office is composed of chairs and tables, whereas an outdoor scene is composed of water, grass, cows, etc. Proportion priors [11] have been proposed to learn and impose priors on the relative size of object parts. The quantitative performance in terms of segmentation accuracy of respective methods, however, is generally dominated by respective data terms. In this paper we therefore focus on the data term.

A multitude of data terms have been proposed over the last years to take texture, color, spatial location and even depth into account in the construction of appropriate observation likelihoods associated with each pixel. Not surprisingly, depending on the object class and image benchmark, some features are more relevant than others. While in principle taking more and more features into account should improve the segmentation accuracy, in the interest of computational efficiency, the redundancy among features should be minimized. How can we quantify relevance and redundancy of features? How can we devise a systematic feature selection strategy to identify a small set of optimal features for semantic image segmentation? And how can we automatically determine the number of features to use?

In this work we make use of information-theoretic quantities in order to characterize and optimize the relevance and redundancy tradeoff of respective features for semantic segmentation. An overview of the studied features is given in Section 2. For two continuous random variables X and Y, the *mutual information*

$$MI(X;Y) = \int_Y \int_X p(x,y) \log \frac{p(x,y)}{p(x)p(y)} dxdy, \qquad (1)$$

is a measure of the mutual dependency of X and Y, where p denotes their probability density function. A feature f_i is relevant for the class labeling c if the mutual information $MI(f_i; c)$ of the feature and the class label is large. Moreover, it is redundant with respect to another feature f_j if the mutual information $MI(f_i; f_j)$ is high. In the following we will show that an appropriate information-theoretic feature selection strategy will lead to semantic segmentation methods which provide state-of-the-art performance at substantially reduced computation

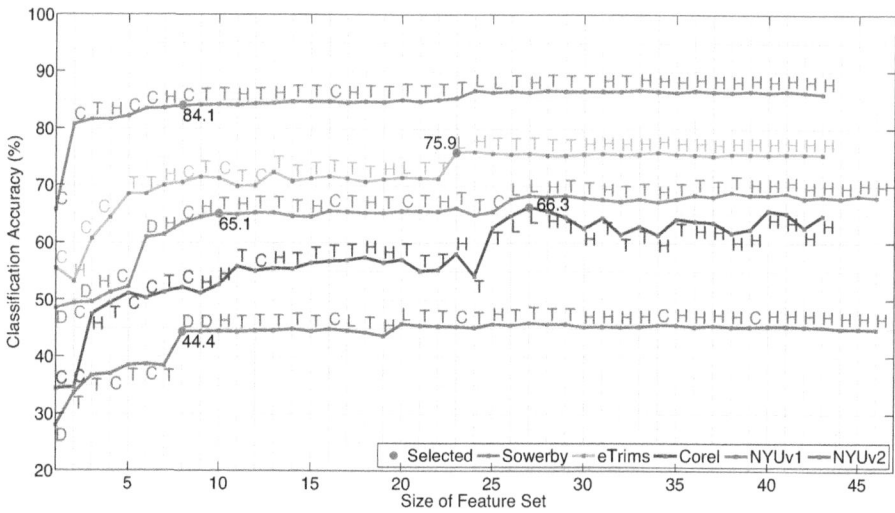

Fig. 1. Impact of features on the classification accuracy. The labels indicate the type of feature added to the feature set: Haar-like (H), color (C), texton (T), location (L) and depth (D). For each benchmark a green dot indicates the feature set which is selected by the proposed approach.

time. Figure 1 shows the improvement of classification accuracy on different benchmarks with increasing size of the feature set. The features are ordered based on their relevance and redundancy.

This paper is organized as follows: we introduce the studied features in Section 2. In Section 3 we propose an information-theoretic feature analysis method and in Section 4 we show the list of ranked and selected features for five different benchmarks. Finally, we compare our runtime as well as qualitative and quantitative results to state-of-the-art methods (Section 5).

1.2 Related Work

The literature on object detection can be roughly grouped into two complementary approaches. Conventional object detectors deal with the task of finding bounding boxes around each object [4,10,19]. In contrast, dense object detection approaches [7,13] focus on detecting objects at pixel level. We focus on the choice of the best visual object recognition features for dense object detection.

Shotton *et al.* [13] proposed texture-layout filters based on textons which jointly model patterns of texture and their spatial layout for dense object detection. As they use a large set of features in their computations, their method is not applicable in real-time. On the contrary, our method only chooses the most *significant* features. Thus, we are able to improve the detection performance at a highly reduced runtime.

In 2012, Fröhlich *et al.* [5] proposed an iterative approach for semantic segmentation of a facade dataset. This approach uses millions of features and refines the semantic segmentation by iteratively adding context features derived from coarser levels to a Random Forests classifier. As a result, this approach is fairly slow. In contrast, we determine the optimal set of features and are thus able to receive similar detection accuracies with a significantly smaller set of features at a reduced runtime.

Couprie *et al.* [3] introduced a multiscale convolutional network to segment indoor RGB-D images. They implicitly compute and select features by constructing complex and deep architectures. In contrast, our method is based on a transparent selection criterion.

Recently, Hermans *et al.* [7] discussed 2D semantic segmentation for RGB-D sensor data in order to reconstruct 3D scenes. They use a very basic set of features. However, this basic set of features is determined by experiments and no clear selection criterion is given. In general, none of the above approaches gives justification for their chosen set of features. We specifically address this problem and give detailed explanations on how to choose the best feature set for dense object detection.

1.3 Contributions

We present an information-theoretic feature analysis method which resolves the following challenges:

+ We answer the questions *which features are the most significant for object recognition* and *how many features are needed for a good tradeoff between accuracy and runtime*.
+ The proposed feature analysis method is easy to use and immediately applicable to different datasets. It runs fast in real-time even on large datasets with high-resolution images. All parameters are determined automatically from the information-theoretic formulation.[1]
+ We evaluate our method on five different datasets and compare our classification and segmentation results with the state-of-the-art methods by Shotton et al. [14], Fröhlich et al. [5], Couprie et al. [3] and Hermans et al. [7]. The proposed feature selection strategy provides state-of-the-art semantic classifications and segmentations at significantly reduced runtimes.

2 The Feature Set

We consider 17 shape and texture features composed of 6 Haar-like, 2 color, 4 texton, 2 location and 3 depth features. The features are computed in a patch surrounding the image pixels. Thereby, different patch sizes of the features are used. We convert the images from the RGB(-D) to the CIELab color space and compute the features on the channels: L, a, b (and D). Depth maps are normalized and converted to gray scale.

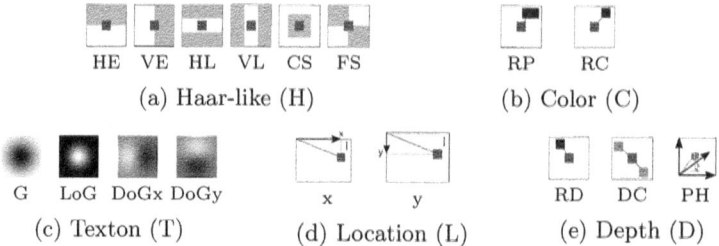

Fig. 2. The feature set. Illustration of the 17 shape and texture features which are studied in various patch sizes on different image channels. We analyze the significance of the features and explain which and how many of them to use.

Haar-like features We use six types of Haar-like features [19]: horizontal and vertical edge (HE/VE) and line (HL/VL), center surround (CS) and four square (FS) illustrated in Figure 2a.

Color features We use the average of the relative patch (RP) and the relative color (RC) feature shown in Figure 2b.

Texton features As texton features we use Gaussian filter (G), Laplacian of Gaussian (LoG) and the first order derivatives of Gaussian filter (DoG) in x and y direction with different bandwidths (see Figure 2c).

---

[1] Our code is publicly available at vision.in.tum.de/data/software

Location features We use normalized canonical location features (see Figure 2d) computed for each pixel p in the image I.

Depth features We use the relative depth (RD), the relative depth comparison (DC) and the height of a pixel (PH) [7], illustrated in Figure 2e.

3 Feature Ranking and Selection for Object Recognition

Among the discussed features, *which* are the most significant for object recognition? And *how many* are needed for a good tradeoff between accuracy and runtime? To this end, we first rank the features according to their significance, then we analyze them and propose an automatic selection criterion.

3.1 Feature Ranking

In the first step, a set of training images is used to compute a ranked set of features $\mathcal{F}_R$ of the full feature set $\mathcal{F}$ where the ranking is based on significance. As described in the introduction, features are significant if they are relevant for the classification performance but as little redundant as possible. Ideally, the optimal set of features $\{f_1, .., f_N\}$ is obtained by maximizing the expression

$$\max_{\{f_1,...,f_N\} \in \mathcal{F}} \sum_{f_i \in \mathcal{F}} MI(f_i; c) - \frac{1}{N} \sum_{f_i, f_j \in \mathcal{F}} MI(f_i; f_j), \qquad (2)$$

where the first term aims at maximizing the relevance of each feature in terms of the mutual information with respect to the target class c and the second term aims at minimizing the redundancy between pairs of features. We call a feature *significant* if it maximizes the relevance for the classification task while minimizing the redundancy with respect to the other features. First of all, the joint optimization over all features is computationally demanding. Secondly, it does not provide us with a ranking of features by significance.

To address these drawbacks, we revert to a greedy strategy for feature selection introduced by Peng *et al.* [12] in the context of biological feature analysis and handwritten digit recognition.

For a fixed target class c, let $\mathcal{F}_{m-1} = \{f_1, \ldots, f_{m-1}\}$ be the *best* feature set with $m-1$ features. To identify the *best additional* feature $f_m \in \mathcal{F} \setminus \mathcal{F}_{m-1}$, we simply optimize its relevance-redundancy tradeoff with respect to the existing features:

$$f_m = \arg\max_{f_i \in \mathcal{F} \setminus \mathcal{F}_{m-1}} \left[MI(f_i; c) - \frac{1}{m-1} \sum_{f_j \in \mathcal{F}_{m-1}} MI(f_i; f_j) \right]. \qquad (3)$$

This leads to a set of features $\mathcal{F}_R = \{f_1, \ldots, f_N\}$ which are ranked with respect to their significance for the target class c.

3.2 Automatic Feature Selection

Let the first n features in $\mathcal{F}_R$ be denoted by $\mathcal{F}_R(n) := \{f_1, \ldots, f_n\}$. In the following step, we determine $n^* \in \{1, \ldots, N\}$ such that $\mathcal{F}_R(n^*)$ consists of only the most significant features. Therefore, we initially apply an *incremental feature analysis* returning the classification accuracy $Acc(n)$ for each feature set $\mathcal{F}_R(n)$. Algorithm 1 sketches the steps we carried out to obtain $(Acc(1), \ldots, Acc(N))$.

To figure out *how many* features $n^* \in \{1, \ldots, N\}$ to choose, the following conditions have to be met: a) For optimizing the runtime a small n^* is preferred, while b) for the optimization of the accuracy a large n^* is desired. Hence, n^* should be small but still lead to a satisfying accuracy. We therefore propose the following optimization criterion:

$$n^* = \arg\max_{n \in \{1, \ldots, N\}} \left(Acc(n) \right)^\alpha (N + 1 - n)^{\frac{1}{\beta}}, \qquad (4)$$

where $\alpha, \beta \geq 1$ (we set $\alpha = 5$, $\beta = 2$). This function jointly maximizes the accuracy $Acc(n)$ and minimizes the number of features n. Taking $Acc(n)$ to the power of α emphasizes the jumps in the accuracy in which we are interested. Taking the βth root of $(N - n)$ prevents too strong influence of the size of $\mathcal{F}_R(n)$. By varying the values of α and β, the method can be adapted to the user's interest focusing on optimal runtime and/or accuracy.

This two-step approach leads to the feature set $\mathcal{F}_R(n^*)$ which consists of only the most significant features for the respective dataset. Compared to other approaches which mostly use arbitrary large feature sets, we are able to obtain competitive classification accuracies at a remarkably reduced runtime.

Related works such as [5, 7] mostly tune the parameters used for training the Random Forests. In contrast, we use default settings for all benchmarks. Our experimental results (Section 5) show that the choice of the right features is more important than the best parameter settings for Random Forests. Reduced redundancy in the feature set keeps the accuracy high while it decreases the runtime significantly.

3.3 Implementation

The algorithm runs fast in real-time even on large datasets with high-resolution images. The whole algorithm runs on a single CPU. We restricted the system to the minimal number of parameters. This makes the application independent from parameter tuning for different benchmarks. Except for the patch size of the features and the grid size Δ_{ss} all other parameters are fixed. Therefore, the proposed method is easy to use and immediately applicable for different datasets.

4 Which and How Many Features?

We apply the proposed feature ranking and selection method using the 17 shape and texture features introduced in Section 2 on five different benchmarks. In the

Algorithm 1. Incremental Feature Analysis

1: **procedure** ANALYZEFEATURES($\mathcal{D}, \mathcal{F}_R$) ▷ $\mathcal{D}$: Dataset, $\mathcal{F}_R$: Ranked Features
2:   $n = 0$, $Acc = \emptyset$ ▷ Acc: Classification Accuracy
3:   **while** $n < N$ **do**
4:     $n \leftarrow n + 1$
5:     Extract the features $\mathcal{F}_R(n)$ on the training set.
6:     Train K Random Trees $\{T_1(\cdot), \ldots, T_K(\cdot)\}$ on the training samples.
7:     For each class $c \in \{1, \ldots, C\}$ estimate the class probabilities $\widetilde{P}$
       at each pixel p on the validation set: ▷ C: #Classes

$$\widetilde{P}(c \mid p, \mathcal{F}_R(n)) = \frac{\sum_{k=1}^{K} [T_k(p, \mathcal{F}_R(n)) == c]}{K}. \qquad (5)$$

8:     Predict the class label $c^*(p)$ for each pixel p with:

$$c^*(p) = \arg\max_{c \in \{1,\ldots,C\}} \widetilde{P}(c \mid p, \mathcal{F}_R(n)).$$

9:     Compute $Acc(n)$ with the predicted class labels c^* on the validation set:

$$Acc(n) = \frac{\text{Number of correctly classified pixels}}{\text{Total number of labeled pixels}}.$$

10:   **end while**
11:   **return** Acc ▷ List of accuracies $(Acc(1), \ldots, Acc(N))$
12: **end procedure**

following we discuss the resulting significance of the different features. We made similar observations on all benchmarks.

The following benchmarks are studied: (i) the 8-class facade dataset eTrims [8], (ii) the 7-class Corel and (iii) Sowerby datasets [6] and (iv) the 12-class NYUv1 [7,15] as well as (v) the 13-class NYUv2 [3,16] RGB-D benchmark. For the eTrims dataset we follow Fröhlich et al. [5] and split the dataset by a ratio of 60/40 for training and testing. We split the Corel and Sowerby benchmark by a ratio of 60/40, the NYUv1 dataset by a ratio of 50/50 and the NYUv2 by 55/45 for training and testing, similar to [3]. For each benchmark 20% of the training set is used as validation set. On the Corel benchmark we follow Shotton et al. [14] and normalize the color and intensity of the images.

For the eTrims, Corel and Sowerby benchmarks we use 50 trees to train the Random Forests, each having at most a depth of 15. For the NYUv1 and NYUv2 benchmark we follow Hermans et al. [7] and use 8 trees, each having at most a depth of 10.

To reduce the computational cost during the training process, filter responses are computed on a $\Delta_{ss} \times \Delta_{ss}$ grid on the image [14]. We set $\Delta_{ss} = 3$ for the Corel and Sowerby benchmark and $\Delta_{ss} = 5$ for the eTrims, NYUv1 and NYUv2 benchmark.

4.1 Which Features

The ranked set of features $\mathcal{F}_R$, listed in Table 1, is computed for each dataset with the method proposed in Section 3.1. The following observations can be made on the relevance of the studied features:

Haar-like features *(orange)* In the literature Haar-like features are commonly evaluated on a gray-scale image or on the luminance channel. Table 1, however, shows that for all five benchmarks the top ranked Haar-like features are particularly those ones evaluated on the 'a' and 'b' color channel.

Color features *(turquoise)* Independently of the benchmark, almost all color features appear among the top ranked features. Hence, color features should definitely be used for training object classifiers.

Texton features *(gray)* Several texton features are ranked on a top position. Most of the higher ranked texton features (≤ 20) are computed on the 'L' channel. We conclude that texton features are more distinctive on the luminance channel.

Location features *(blue)* All location features are ranked in the lower half (≥ 17). However, for the eTrims and Corel benchmark, they significantly enhance the classification accuracy (cf. Figure 1).

Depth features *(purple)* are only available for the NYUv1 and NYUv2 benchmark (columns 4,5). All depth features are ranked among the top nine features and strongly boost the accuracy (cf. Figure 1).

We gained a valuable insight into the significance of various features for the task of pixel-wise object recognition. In summary, Haar-like features should particularly be evaluated on the color channels. Color features are important in general. Texton features should be considered especially on the 'L' channel. Location features can be essential and depth features are the most distinctive ones (when available).

4.2 How Many Features

In the following we answer the question on the best size of the feature set. For each benchmark, Figure 1 illustrates the classification accuracies $Acc(n)$ with increasing n. n indicates the size of the feature set $\mathcal{F}_R(n)$ which leads to $Acc(n)$ (cf. Algorithm 1). The green dots indicate the numbers n^* which are chosen by the proposed optimization criterion in Equation (4). The intention is to chose n^* small, but large enough to obtain an optimal tradeoff between accuracy and number of features.

For the eTrims benchmark, *e.g.*, the accuracy has a significant jump from $n = 22$ to $n = 23$. For values of n larger than 23, only very minor improvements can be achieved. Hence, one would prefer n^* to be equal to 23. As marked by the green dot in Figure 1, the proposed optimization criterion (4) selects $n^* = 23$.

The accuracy plot computed for the Corel benchmark has a peak at $n = 27$. Thus, the selected $n^* = 27$ gives the best tradeoff between the accuracy and the size of the feature set. The accuracy plot for the NYUv2 benchmark shows a jump from $n = 7$ to $n = 8$. All values $n \in [9, 46]$ only provide an insignificant increase of $Acc(8)$. Thus, $n^* = 8$ is the perfect value for n and selected by Equation (4).

Table 1. Ranked features $\mathcal{F}_R$ for the eTrims, Corel, Sowerby, NYUv1 and NYUv2 benchmark. Different colors are set for Haar-like (H), color (C), texton (T), location (L) and depth (D) features. The features are labeled as follows: {feature type}_{feature name}_{patch size}_{color channel}. For an interpretation see Section 4.1.

Rank	eTrims	Corel	Sowerby	NYUv1	NYUv2
1	C_RP_25_b	C_RP_11_a	C_RC_7_a	D_PH_25_D	D_PH_25_D
2	H_VL_25_a	C_RC_11_b	C_RP_7_L	C_RP_25_a	T_G_3_L
3	C_RC_25_L	H_CS_11_L	T_DoGy_13x5_L	D_DC_25_D	T_LoG_17_L
4	C_RP_25_a	T_DoGy_13x5_L	H_CS_7_a	H_FS_25_b	C_RP_25_a
5	T_LoG_3_L	C_RP_11_L	C_RC_7_b	C_RC_25_b	T_LoG_5_L
6	T_G_3_L	C_RC_11_a	C_RP_7_a	D_RD_25_D	C_RC_25_L
7	H_CS_25_L	T_DoGx_9x25_L	H_VL_7_b	H_FS_25_L	T_G_5_L
8	C_RC_25_b	C_RP_11_b	C_RC_7_L	C_RP_25_L	D_RD_25_D
9	T_DoGy_25x9_L	H_HE_11_a	T_DoGx_9x25_L	H_CS_25_a	D_DC_25_D
10	C_RP_25_L	H_CS_11_a	T_DoGy_25x9_L	T_LoG_17_L	H_FS_25_L
11	T_DoGy_13x5_L	T_G_9_b	H_HL_7_a	H_VE_25_b	T_DoGy_25x9_L
12	C_RC_25_a	C_RC_11_L	T_G_9_b	T_LoG_3_L	T_G_9_L
13	T_G_9_a	H_CS_11_b	H_CS_7_b	T_DoGx_9x25_L	T_LoG_9_L
14	T_G_5_L	T_DoGy_25x9_L	T_LoG_3_L	T_LoG_5_L	T_DoGx_5x13_L
15	T_LoG_5_L	T_LoG_3_L	T_LoG_5_L	H_CS_25_b	T_LoG_3_L
16	T_LoG_9_L	T_LoG_5_L	C_RP_7_b	C_RC_25_a	C_RP_25_b
17	T_DoGx_9x25_L	T_LoG_9_L	H_CS_7_L	T_LoG_9_L	L_y
18	T_G_9_L	H_FS_11_a	T_LoG_9_L	H_HL_25_L	T_DoGx_9x25_L
19	H_VL_25_b	H_VL_11_a	T_DoGx_5x13_L	T_DoGy_25x9_L	H_HE_25_a
20	L_y	T_DoGx_5x13_L	T_G_3_L	C_RP_25_b	L_x
21	T_DoGx_5x13_L	T_G_5_L	T_G_9_a	T_G_9_a	T_G_5_b
22	T_G_9_b	T_G_9_a	T_G_3_a	H_FS_25_a	T_G_3_b
23	L_x	H_VL_11_b	T_G_3_b	T_G_3_b	C_RP_25_L
24	H_HE_25_L	T_G_3_L	L_x	T_G_5_a	T_DoGy_13x5_L
25	T_G_5_b	T_G_3_a	L_y	C_RC_25_L	H_VL_25_L
26	T_G_5_a	L_x	T_G_9_L	L_x	T_G_5_a
27	T_G_3_b	L_y	H_VL_7_L	L_y	T_G_3_a
28	T_G_3_a	H_VE_11_a	T_G_5_b	H_VE_25_a	T_G_9_b
29	T_LoG_17_L	T_G_9_L	T_G_5_L	T_DoGy_13x5_L	T_G_9_a
30	H_FS_25_a	H_HL_11_a	T_G_5_a	T_DoGx_5x13_L	H_FS_25_a
31	H_VL_25_L	T_G_5_b	H_HE_7_a	H_HE_25_L	H_HL_25_L
32	H_FS_25_b	T_G_3_b	T_LoG_17_L	T_G_5_b	H_CS_25_a
33	H_HL_25_a	T_G_5_a	H_VL_7_a	T_G_9_b	H_FS_25_b
34	H_VE_25_a	H_HL_11_b	H_FS_7_b	H_VL_25_b	C_RC_25_a
35	H_HE_25_a	T_LoG_17_L	H_VE_7_a	T_G_3_a	H_VE_25_a
36	H_CS_25_b	H_FS_11_b	H_FS_7_a	T_G_9_L	H_CS_25_b
37	H_CS_25_a	H_HE_11_b	H_HE_7_b	T_G_5_L	H_HE_25_b
38	H_HE_25_b	H_VE_11_b	H_VE_7_b	T_G_3_L	H_VE_25_L
39	H_VE_25_b	H_FS_11_L	H_FS_7_L	H_VL_25_L	C_RC_25_b
40	H_HL_25_b	H_VL_11_L	H_HL_7_b	H_HE_25_a	H_VL_25_a
41	H_FS_25_L	H_VE_11_L	H_VE_7_L	H_HE_25_b	H_HL_25_a
42	H_VE_25_L	H_HE_11_L	H_HE_7_L	H_VL_25_a	H_VL_25_L
43	H_HL_25_L	H_HL_11_L	H_HL_7_L	H_HL_25_a	H_HL_25_b
44				H_HL_25_b	H_HE_25_L
45				H_VE_25_L	H_VE_25_L
46				H_CS_25_L	H_CS_25_L

The accuracy plots obtained for the Sowerby and the NYUv1 benchmark show a less significant jump than the plots of the other benchmarks. For the Sowerby benchmark, the proposed method selects $n^* = 8$. Still, this value can be seen as optimal. For smaller values of n, the accuracy is not good enough. For larger values of n, up to $n = 23$, the accuracy improves only very little, whereas the feature set grows much more. The small gain in accuracy would have to be paid for by a much larger runtime. The same holds for the NYUv1 benchmark.

5 Experimental Results

Our framework chooses the feature set small but still large enough to obtain a satisfying accuracy. The above observations already show an experimental proof of the proposed feature ranking and selection method. In the following, we compare our runtime, classification and segmentation accuracies as well as qualitative results with state-of-the-art methods.

5.1 Significantly Improved Runtime

We ran our experiments on an Intel® Core™ i7-3770 3.40GHz CPU equipped with 32 GB RAM which is similar to the hardware used by competing approaches. Table 2 compares the training and testing runtimes for the classification task. Our framework runs much faster than state-of-the-art methods. In particular for the Sowerby and NYUv2 benchmark, we reduce the training time by a factor of 600 and 900, respectively. Furthermore, our method accelerates the testing runtime on all benchmarks.

Table 2. Comparison of runtimes for object classification in seconds. The training time is given for the whole training set whereas the testing time is averaged over all test images. The proposed method significantly outperforms the other methods in terms of training and testing runtime.

	eTrims		Corel		Sowerby		NYUv1		NYUv2	
	Train	Test	Train	Test	Train	Test	Train	Test	Train	Test
Shotton et al. [14]	-	-	1800	1.10	1200	2.50	-	-	-	-
Fröhlich et al. [5]	-	17.0	-	-	-	-	-	-	-	-
Hermans et al. [7]	-	-	-	-	-	-	-	0.38	-	0.38
Couprie et al. [3]	-	-	-	-	-	-	-	-	172800	0.70
Proposed	143	6.6	20	0.27	2	0.07	133	0.32	183	0.26

5.2 Competitive Classification and Segmentation Results

In Table 3 we compare the classification and segmentation accuracies to Shotton et al. [14], Fröhlich et al. [5], Hermans et al. [7] and Couprie et al. [3]. To obtain a smooth segmentation result we minimize the following energy [2]:

$$E(\Omega_1, .., \Omega_C) = \sum_{c=1}^{C} \left(\text{Per}(\Omega_c) + \lambda \int_{\Omega_c} f_c(p) \, dp \right), \tag{6}$$

Table 3. Quantitative results compared in terms of accuracies. The accuracies are computed as the percentage of correctly labeled pixels on the test set. At significantly reduced runtime our method achieves competitive classification and segmentation accuracies with state-of-the-art methods.

	eTrims		Corel		Sowerby		NYUv1		NYUv2	
	Class.	Segm.	Class.	Segm.	Class.	Segm.	Class.	Segm.	Class.	Segm.
Shotton et al. [14]	-	-	68.4	74.6	85.6	88.6	-	-	-	-
Fröhlich et al. [5]	-	77.22	-	-	-	-	-	-	-	-
Hermans et al. [7]	-	-	-	-	-	-	65.0	71.5	-	54.2
Couprie et al. [3]	-	-	-	-	-	-	-	-	-	52.4
Proposed	**77.1**	**77.9**	**74.4**	**78.2**	**87.1**	**88.8**	**65.0**	66.5	**44.0**	45.0

where $\Omega_1, .., \Omega_C$ denote the partitions of the image plane, Per (Ω_c) the perimeter of each set Ω_c which is minimized to favor segments of shorter boundary and $f_c(p) = -\log \widetilde{P}(c \mid p, \mathcal{F}_R(n^*))$ the data term, where $\widetilde{P}$ are the class probabilities estimated with the proposed method. λ is a weighting parameter and optimized during the computation.

Table 3 indicates that our classification and segmentation accuracies are competitive with the state-of-the-art approaches. For each benchmark, our method achieves the best accuracies at a remarkably speeded up runtime (cf. Table 2).

Most importantly our scores are a) obtained at a significantly improved runtime and b) by using an automatically chosen feature set. We neither tuned the parameters nor the feature set manually to obtain better scores on the specific benchmarks. The proposed method is designed to autonomously compute accurate classifications/segmentations at a significantly reduced runtime for all benchmarks.

Figure 3 shows exemplary qualitative classification and segmentation results obtained with the proposed method. In column b), we additionally provide the classification results of the related methods.

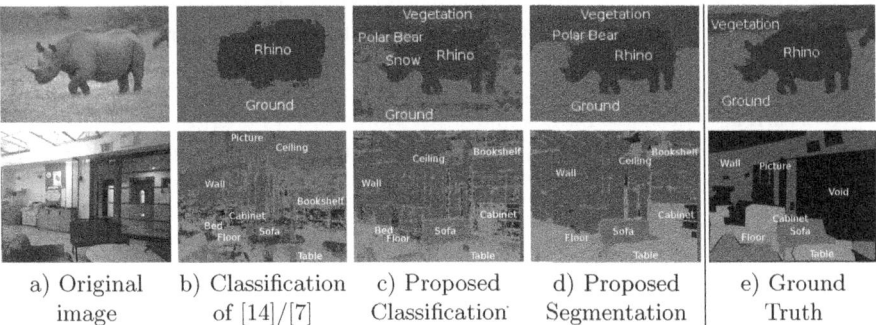

| a) Original image | b) Classification of [14]/[7] | c) Proposed Classification | d) Proposed Segmentation | e) Ground Truth |

Fig. 3. Accurate qualitative classification and segmentation results are achieved with the proposed framework. We compare our classification result to Shotton et al. [14] on the Corel benchmark (first row) and to Hermans et al. [7] on the NYUv1 benchmark (second row).

6 Conclusion

We introduced a framework for automatic feature selection for semantic image segmentation. Starting from a large set of popular features, we sequentially construct a ranked set of features by maximizing the relevance of each feature for the classification task while minimizing its redundancy with respect to the previously selected features. Subsequently, we define an automatic criterion to choose a small number of the most significant features. Integrated in a variational approach to multi-region segmentation, we obtain a fully automatic algorithm which provides state-of-the-art semantic classifications and segmentations on five popular benchmarks at drastically reduced computation time.

References

1. Bergbauer, J., Nieuwenhuis, C., Souiai, M., Cremers, D.: Proximity priors for variational semantic segmentation and recognition. In: ICCV Workshop (2013)
2. Chambolle, A., Cremers, D., Pock, T.: A convex approach to minimal partitions. SIAM Journal on Imaging Sciences 5(4), 1113–1158 (2012)
3. Couprie, C., Farabet, C., Najman, L., LeCun, Y.: Indoor semantic segmentation using depth information. In: Int. Conf. on Learning Representations (2013)
4. Dalal, N., Triggs, B.: Histograms of oriented gradients for human detection. In: Int. Conf. on Comp. Vision and Pattern Recog. (2005)
5. Fröhlich, B., Rodner, E., Denzler, J.: Semantic segmentation with millions of features: integrating multiple cues in a combined random forest approach. In: Lee, K.M., Matsushita, Y., Rehg, J.M., Hu, Z. (eds.) ACCV 2012, Part I. LNCS, vol. 7724, pp. 218–231. Springer, Heidelberg (2013)
6. He, X., Zemel, R.S., Carreira-Perpindn, M.A.: Multiscale conditional random fields for image labeling. In: Int. Conf. on Comp. Vision and Pattern Recog. (2004)
7. Hermans, A., Floros, G., Leibe, B.: Dense 3D semantic mapping of indoor scenes from RGB-D images. In: Int. Conf. on Robotics and Automation (2014)
8. Korč, F., Förstner, W.: eTRIMS Image Database for Interpreting Images of Man-Made Scenes. Technical report, Department of Photogrammetry, University of Bonn (2009)
9. Ladicky, L., Russell, C., Kohli, P., Torr, P.H.S.: Graph cut based inference with co-occurrence statistics. In: Daniilidis, K., Maragos, P., Paragios, N. (eds.) ECCV 2010, Part V. LNCS, vol. 6315, pp. 239–253. Springer, Heidelberg (2010)
10. Lowe, D.: Object recognition from local scale-invariant features. In: Int. Conf. on Comp. Vision (1999)
11. Nieuwenhuis, C., Strekalovskiy, E., Cremers, D.: Proportion priors for image sequence segmentation. In: Int. Conf. on Comp. Vision (2013)
12. Peng, H., Long, F., Ding, C.: Feature selection based on mutual information criteria of max-dependency, max-relevance, and min-redundancy. Trans. on Pattern Analysis and Machine Intelligence 27(8), 1226–1238 (2005)
13. Shotton, J., Winn, J.M., Rother, C., Criminisi, A.: *TextonBoost*: Joint Appearance, Shape and Context Modeling for Multi-class Object Recognition and Segmentation. In: Leonardis, A., Bischof, H., Pinz, A. (eds.) ECCV 2006, Part I. LNCS, vol. 3951, pp. 1–15. Springer, Heidelberg (2006)

14. Shotton, J., Winn, J., Rother, C., Criminisi, A.: TextonBoost for Image Understanding: Multi-Class Object Recognition and Segmentation by Jointly Modeling Texture, Layout, and Context. Int. Journal of Comp. Vision **81**(1), 2–23 (2009)
15. Silberman, N., Fergus, R.: Indoor Scene segmentation using a structured Light Sensor. In: ICCV Workshop on 3D Representation and Recognition (2011)
16. Silberman, N., Hoiem, D., Kohli, P., Fergus, R.: Indoor segmentation and support inference from RGBD images. In: Fitzgibbon, A., Lazebnik, S., Perona, P., Sato, Y., Schmid, C. (eds.) ECCV 2012, Part V. LNCS, vol. 7576, pp. 746–760. Springer, Heidelberg (2012)
17. Souiai, M., Nieuwenhuis, C., Strekalovskiy, E., Cremers, D.: Convex optimization for scene understanding. In: ICCV Workshop (2013)
18. Souiai, M., Strekalovskiy, E., Nieuwenhuis, C., Cremers, D.: A co-occurrence prior for continuous multi-label optimization. In: Int. Conf. on Energy Minimization Methods for Comp. Vision and Pattern Recog. (2013)
19. Viola, P., Jones, M.: Rapid object detection using a boosted cascade of simple features. In: Int. Conf. on Comp. Vision and Pattern Recog. (2001)
20. Yao, J., Fidler, S., Urtasun, R.: Describing the scene as a whole: joint object detection, scene classification and semantic segmentation. In: Int. Conf. on Comp. Vision and Pattern Recog. (2012)

Convex Color Image Segmentation with Optimal Transport Distances

Julien Rabin[1](✉) and Nicolas Papadakis[2]

[1] GREYC, CNRS UMR 6072, Université de Caen, Caen, France
julien.rabin@unicaen.fr
[2] CNRS, IMB, UMR 5251, Université de Bordeaux, Talence, France
nicolas.papadakis@math.u-bordeaux.fr

Abstract. This work is about the use of regularized optimal-transport distances for convex, histogram-based image segmentation. In the considered framework, fixed exemplar histograms define a prior on the statistical features of the two regions in competition. In this paper, we investigate the use of various transport-based cost functions as discrepancy measures and rely on a primal-dual algorithm to solve the obtained convex optimization problem.

Keywords: Optimal transport · Wasserstein distance · Sinkhorn distance · Convex optimization · Image segmentation

1 Introduction

Optimal Transport. Optimal transport theory has received a lot of attention during the last decade as it provides a powerful framework to address problems which embed statistical constraints. Its successful application in various image processing tasks has demonstrated its practical interest (see *e.g.* [5,7,8,11]). Some limitations have been also shown and partially addressed, such as time complexity, regularity and relaxation [1,4].

Segmentation. Statistical based image segmentation has been thoroughly studied in the literature, first using parametric models (such as the mean and variance), and then empirical distributions combined with adapted statistical distances, such as the Kullback-Leibler divergence. In this work, we are interested in the use of the optimal transport framework for Image segmentation. This has been first investigated in [7] for 1D features, then extended to multi-dimensional features using approximations of the optimal transport cost [5,9], and adapted to region-based active contour in [9], relying on a non-convex formulation. In [12], a convex formulation is proposed, making use of sub-iterations to compute the proximity operator of the Wasserstein distance, which use is restricted to low dimensions.

In this paper, we extend the convex formulation for two-phase image segmentation of [14] for non-regularized as well as regularized [1,2] optimal transport distances. This work shares some common features with the recent work of [3] in which the authors investigate the use of the Legendre-Fenchel transform of regularized transport cost for imaging problems.

2 Convex Histogram-Based Image Segmentation

2.1 Notation

We consider here vector spaces equipped with the scalar product $\langle .,.\rangle$ and the norm $\|.\| = \sqrt{\langle .,.\rangle}$. The conjugate operator of A is denoted by A^* and satisfies $\langle Ax, y\rangle = \langle x, A^*y\rangle$. We denote as $\mathbf{1}_n$ and $\mathbf{0}_n \in \mathbb{R}^n$ the n-dimensional vectors full of ones and zeros respectively, x^T the transpose of x, and ∇ the discrete gradient operator, while Id stands for the identity operator. The operator $\mathrm{diag}(x)$ defines a square matrix whose diagonal is x. Functions ι_S and $\mathbb{1}_S$ are respectively the characteristic and indicator functions of a set S. *Proj* and *Prox* stands respectively for the Euclidean projection and proximity operator. The set $\mathcal{S}_{k,n} := \{x \in \mathbb{R}^n_+, \langle x, \mathbf{1}_n\rangle = k\}$ is the simplex of histogram vectors ($\mathcal{S}_{1,n}$ being therefore the discrete probability simplex of $\mathbb{R}^n$).

2.2 General Formulation of Distribution-Based Image Segmentation

Let $I : x \in \Omega \mapsto I(x) \in \mathbb{R}^d$ be a color image, defined over the N-pixel domain Ω ($N = |\Omega|$), and $\mathcal{F}$ a feature-transform of n-dimensional descriptors $\mathcal{F}I(x) \in \mathbb{R}^n$. We would like to define a binary segmentation $u : \Omega \mapsto \{0,1\}$ of the whole image domain, using two fixed probability distributions of features a and b. Following the variational model introduced in [14], we consider the energy

$$J(u) = \rho TV(u) + D(a, h(u)) + D(b, h(\mathbf{1} - u)) \qquad (1)$$

where $\rho \geq 0$ is the regularization parameter,

- the fidelity terms are defined using $D(.,.)$, a dissimilarity measure between features;
- $h(u)$ is the empirical discrete probability distribution of features $\mathcal{F}I$ using the binary map u, which is written as a sum of Dirac masses

$$h(u) : y \in \mathbb{R}^n \mapsto \frac{1}{\sum_{x \in \Omega} u(x)} \sum_{x \in \Omega} u(x) \delta_{\mathcal{F}I(x)}(y) \,;$$

- $TV(u)$ is the total variation norm of the binary image u, which is related to the perimeter of the region $R_1(u) := \{x \in \Omega \,|\, u(x) = 1\}$ (co-area formula).

Observe that this energy is highly non-convex since h is a non linear operator, and that we would like to find a minimum over the non-convex set $\{0,1\}^N$.

2.3 Convex Relaxation of Histogram-Based Segmentation Energy

The authors of [14] propose some relaxations and a reformulation in order to handle the minimization of energy (1) using convex optimization tools.

Probability Map. The first relaxation consists in using a segmentation variable $u : \Omega \mapsto [0,1]$ which is a weight function (probability map). A threshold is therefore required to get a binary segmentation of the image into two regions $R_t(u) := \{x \in \Omega \,|\, u(x) \geq t\}$ and its complement $R_t(u)^c$.

Feature Histogram. The feature histogram of the probability map is denoted $H_{\mathcal{X}}(u)$ and defined as the **quantized, non-normalized, and weighted histogram** of the feature image $\mathcal{F}I$ using the relaxed variable $u : \Omega \mapsto [0,1]$ and a feature set $\mathcal{X} = \{X_i \in \mathbb{R}^n\}_{1 \leq i \leq M_{\mathcal{X}}}$ composed of $M_{\mathcal{X}}$ bins

$$(H_{\mathcal{X}}(u))_i = \sum_{x \in \Omega} u(x) \mathbb{1}_{\mathcal{C}_{\mathcal{X}}(i)}(\mathcal{F}I(x)), \quad \forall i \in \{1, \dots M_{\mathcal{X}}\}$$

where i a bin index, X_i is the centroid of the corresponding bin, and $\mathcal{C}_{\mathcal{X}}(i) \subset \mathbb{R}^n$ is the corresponding set of features (*e.g.* the Voronoï cell obtained from *hard assignment* method). Therefore, we can write $H_{\mathcal{X}}$ as a linear operator

$$H_{\mathcal{X}} : u \in \mathbb{R}^N \mapsto \mathbb{1}_{\mathcal{X}} \cdot u \in \mathbb{R}^{M_{\mathcal{X}}}, \quad \text{with } \mathbb{1}_{\mathcal{X}}(i,j) := 1 \text{ if } \mathcal{F}I(j) \in \mathcal{C}_{\mathcal{X}}(i), 0 \text{ otherwise.}$$

Note that $\mathbb{1}_{\mathcal{X}} \in \mathbb{R}^{M_{\mathcal{X}} \times N}$ is a fixed assignment matrix that indicates which pixels of $\mathcal{F}I$ contribute to each bin i of the histogram. As a consequence, $\langle H_{\mathcal{X}}(u), \mathbb{1}_{\mathcal{X}} \rangle = \sum_{x \in \Omega} u(x) = \langle u, \mathbb{1}_N \rangle$, so that $H_{\mathcal{X}}(u) \in \mathcal{S}_{M_{\mathcal{X}}, \langle u, \mathbb{1} \rangle}$.

Exemplar Histograms. The segmentation is driven from two fixed histograms $a \in \mathcal{S}_{M_a,1}$ and $b \in \mathcal{S}_{M_b,1}$, which are normalized (*i.e.* sum to 1), have respective dimension M_a and M_b, and are obtained using the respective sets of features $\mathcal{A}$ and $\mathcal{B}$. In order to measure the similarity between the non-normalized histogram $H_{\mathcal{A}}u$ and the normalized histogram a, while obtaining a convex formulation, we follow [14] and consider the fidelity term $D(a\langle u, \mathbb{1}_N \rangle, H_{\mathcal{A}}u)$, where the constant vector a has been scaled to $H_{\mathcal{A}}u \in \mathcal{S}_{M_a, \langle u, \mathbb{1} \rangle}$.

Segmentation Energy. Observe that the problem can now be written as finding the minimum of the following energy

$$\tilde{E}(u) = \rho TV(u) + \tfrac{1}{\gamma} D(a\langle u, \mathbb{1}_N \rangle, H_{\mathcal{A}}u) + \tfrac{1}{N-\gamma} D(b\langle \mathbb{1}_N - u, \mathbb{1}_N \rangle, H_{\mathcal{B}}(\mathbb{1}_N - u)).$$

The constant $\gamma \in (0, N)$ is meant to compensate for the fact that the binary regions $R_t(u)$ and $R_t(u)^c$ may have different size. More precisely, as we are interested in a discrete probability segmentation map, we consider the following constrained problem:

$$\min_{u \in [0,1]^N} \tilde{E}(u) = \min_{u \in \mathbb{R}^N} \left\{ E(u) := \tilde{E}(u) + \iota_{[0,1]^N}(u) \right\}.$$

Simplification. From now on, and without loss of generality, we will assume that all histograms are computed using the same set of features, *namely* $\mathcal{A} = \mathcal{B}$. We will also omit unnecessary subscripts in order to simplify notation. Moreover, we also omit the parameter γ since its value seems not to be critical in practice, as demonstrated in [14]. Finally, introducing linear operators

$$A := a\mathbf{1}_N^T \in \mathbb{R}^{M \cdot N} \quad \text{and} \quad B := b\mathbf{1}_N^T \in \mathbb{R}^{M \cdot N} \tag{2}$$

such that $Au = (a\mathbf{1}_N^T)u = a\langle u, \mathbf{1}_N\rangle$, we have the following minimization problem:

$$\min_u \rho\|\nabla u\| + D(Au, Hu) + D(B(1-u), H(1-u)) + \iota_{[0,1]^N}(u). \tag{3}$$

Notice that matrix $H \in \mathbb{R}^{M \cdot N}$ is sparse (with N non zero values) and A and B are of rank 1, so that storing or manipulating these matrices is not an issue.

In [14], the distance function D was defined as the L_1 norm. In the following sections, we investigate the use of similarity measure based on optimal transport, which is known to be more robust and appropriate for histogram comparison. The next paragraph details the optimization framework used in this work.

2.4 Optimization

In order to solve (3), we consider the following dualization of the problem using the Legendre-Fenchel transforms of the L^2 norm and the function D

$$\min_{u \in \mathbb{R}^N} \max_{\substack{p_A, q_A, p_B, q_B \in \mathbb{R}^M \\ p_C \in \mathbb{R}^{2N}}} \langle Hu, p_A\rangle + \langle Au, q_A\rangle + \langle H(1-u), p_B\rangle + \langle B(1-u), q_B\rangle + \langle \nabla u, p_C\rangle$$

$$+ \iota_{[0,1]^N}(u) - D^*(p_A, q_A) - D^*(p_B, q_B) - \iota_{\|.\| \leqslant \rho}(p_C), \tag{4}$$

where $\iota_{\|.\|\leqslant \rho}$ is the characteristic function of the convex ℓ_2 ball of radius ρ, while D^* is the dual of the function D. In order to accommodate the different models studied in this paper, we assume here that D^* is a sum of two convex functions $D^* = D_1^* + D_2^*$, where D_1^* is non-smooth and D_2^* is differentiable and has a Lipschitz continuous gradient.

We recover a general primal-dual problem of the form

$$\min_u \max_p \langle Ku, p\rangle + \iota_{[0,1]^N}(u) + H(u) - F^*(p) - G^*(p), \tag{5}$$

with primal variable $u \in \mathbb{R}^N$ and dual vector $p = [p_A^T, q_A^T, p_B^T, q_B^T, p_C^T]^T \in \mathbb{R}^{4M+2N}$, where

- $K = [H^T, A^T, -H^T, -B^T, \nabla^T]^T \in \mathbb{R}^{(4M+2N) \times N}$ is a sparse, linear operator;
- H is convex and smooth ($H(u) = 0$ in the setting of problem (5)) with Lipschitz continuous gradient ∇H with constant L_H;
- $\iota_{[0,1]^N}(u)$ is convex and non-smooth;
- $F^*(p) = D_1^*(p_A, q_A) + D_1^*(p_B, q_B) + \iota_{\|.\|\leqslant \rho}(p_C)$ is convex and non-smooth;
- $G^*(p) = D_2^*(p_A, q_A) + D_2^*(p_B, q_B) - \langle H\mathbf{1}_N, p_B\rangle - \langle B\mathbf{1}_N, q_B\rangle$ is convex and differentiable with Lipschitz constant L_{G^*}.

To solve this problem, we consider the preconditioned primal dual algorithm of [6]

$$\begin{cases} u^{k+1} = \text{Proj}_{[0,1]^N}\left(u^k - \tau(K^T p^k + \nabla H(u^k))\right) \\ p^{k+1} = \text{Prox}_{\sigma F^*}\left(p^k + \sigma(K(2u^{k+1} - u^k) - \nabla G^*(p^k))\right) \end{cases} \quad (6)$$

that converges to a saddle point of (5) as soon as (see for instance [6])

$$\left(\tfrac{1}{\tau} - L_H\right)\left(\tfrac{1}{\sigma} - L_{G^*}\right) \geqslant \|K\|^2. \quad (7)$$

3 Monge-Kantorovitch Distance for Image Segmentation

3.1 Wasserstein Distance and Optimal Transport Problem

Optimal Transport Problem. We consider in this work the discrete formulation of the Monge-Kantorovitch optimal mass transportation problem (see e.g. [13]) between a pair of histograms $a \in \mathcal{S}_{M_a,k}$ and $b \in \mathcal{S}_{M_b,k}$. Given a fixed assignment cost matrix $C_{\mathcal{A},\mathcal{B}} \in \mathbb{R}^{M_a \times M_b}$ between the corresponding histogram centroids $\mathcal{A} = \{A_i\}_{1 \leq i \leq M_a}$ and $\mathcal{B} = \{B_j\}_{1 \leq j \leq M_b}$, an optimal transport plan minimizes the global transport cost, defined as a weighted sum of assignments

$$\forall (a,b) \in \mathcal{S}, \quad \mathbf{MK}(a,b) := \min_{P \in \mathcal{P}(a,b)} \left\{ \langle P, C \rangle = \sum_{i=1}^{M_a} \sum_{j=1}^{M_b} P_{i,j} C_{i,j} \right\}. \quad (8)$$

The sets of admissible histogram and transport matrices are respectively

$$\mathcal{S} := \{a \in \mathbb{R}^{M_a}, b \in \mathbb{R}^{M_b} \mid a \geq 0, b \geq 0 \text{ and } \langle a, \mathbf{1}_{M_a}\rangle = \langle b, \mathbf{1}_{M_b}\rangle\}, \quad (9)$$

$$\mathcal{P}(a,b) := \{P \in \mathbb{R}_+^{M_a \times M_b}, P\mathbf{1}_{M_b} = a \text{ and } P^T \mathbf{1}_{M_a} = b\}. \quad (10)$$

Observe that the norm of histograms is not prescribed in $\mathcal{S}$, and that we only consider histograms with positive entries since null entries do not play any role.

Wasserstein Distance. When using $C_{i,j} = \|A_i - B_j\|^p$, then $\mathbf{W}_p(a,b) = \mathbf{MK}(a,b)^{1/p}$ is a metric between normalized histograms. In the general case where C does not verify such a condition, by a slight abuse of terminology we will refer to the **MK** transport cost function as the Monge-Kantorovich *distance*.

Monge-Kantorovitch Distance. In the following, due to the use of duality, it would be more convenient to introduce the following reformulation:

$$\forall a, b \quad \mathbf{MK}(a,b) = \min_{P \in \mathcal{P}(a,b)} \langle P, C \rangle + \iota_{\mathcal{S}}(a,b). \quad (11)$$

LP Formulation. We can rewrite the optimal transport problem as a linear program (LP) with vector variables. The primal and dual problems write

$$\mathbf{MK}(\alpha) = \min_{\substack{p \in \mathbb{R}^{M_a \cdot M_b} \\ \text{s.t. } p \geq 0, \, L^T p = \alpha}} \langle c, p \rangle + \iota_S(\alpha) = \max_{\substack{\beta \in \mathbb{R}^{M_a + M_b} \\ \text{s.t. } L\beta \leq c}} \langle \alpha, \beta \rangle. \quad (12)$$

where α is the concatenation of histograms: $\alpha^T = [a^T, b^T]$ and the unknown vector $p \in \mathbb{R}^{M_a \cdot M_b}$ corresponds to the bi-stochastic matrix P being read column-wise (i.e. $P_{i,j} = p_{i+(j-1) \cdot M_a}$). The $M_a + M_b$ linear marginal constraints on p are defined by the matrix $L^T \in \mathbb{R}^{(M_a + M_b) \times (M_a M_b)}$ through equation $L^T p = \alpha$, where

$$L^T = \begin{bmatrix} \mathbf{1}_{M_b} e_1^T & \mathbf{1}_{M_b} e_2^T & \cdots & \mathbf{1}_{M_b} e_{M_a}^T \\ \mathrm{Id}_{M_b} & \mathrm{Id}_{M_b} & \cdots & \mathrm{Id}_{M_b} \end{bmatrix} \quad \text{with} \quad e_i(j) = \delta_{i-j} \; \forall \, j \leq M_b.$$

Note that we have the following property: $(L\alpha)_{i,j} = \left(L \begin{bmatrix} a \\ b \end{bmatrix}\right)_{i,j} = a_i + b_j$.

The dual formulation shows that the function $\mathbf{MK}(\alpha)$ is not strictly convex in α. We draw the reader's attention to the fact that the indicator of set $\mathcal{S}$ is not required anymore with the dual formulation, which will later come in handy.

Dual Distance. From Eq. (12), we have that the Legendre–Fenchel conjugate of $\mathbf{MK}$ writes simply as the characteristic function of the set $\mathcal{L}_c := \{\beta \,|\, L\beta - c \leq 0\}$

$$\forall \beta \in \mathbb{R}^{M_a + M_b}, \quad \mathbf{MK}^*(\beta) = \iota_{L\beta \leqslant c}(\beta). \quad (13)$$

3.2 Integration in the Segmentation Framework

We propose to substitute in problem (3) the dissimilarity functions by the convex Monge-Kantorovich optimal transport cost (11).

In order to apply our minimization scheme described in (6), we should be able to compute the proximity operator of $\mathbf{MK}^*$, which is the projection onto the convex set $\mathcal{L}_c$. However, because the linear operator L is not invertible, we cannot compute this projector in a closed form and an optimization problem should be solved at each iteration of the process (6) as in [12].

Bidualization. To circumvent this problem, we resort to a bidualization to rewrite the $\mathbf{MK}$ distance as a primal-dual problem. First, we have that $\mathbf{MK}^*(\beta) = f^*(L\beta)$ with $f^*(r) = \iota_{r \leq c}(r)$, so that $f(r) = \langle r, c \rangle + \iota_{r \geq 0}(r)$. Then,

$$\mathbf{MK}^*(\beta) = f^*(L\beta) = \max_r \langle r, L\beta \rangle - f(r) = \max_r \langle r, L\beta - c \rangle - \iota_{\cdot \geq 0}(r)$$

$$\mathbf{MK}(\alpha) = \max_\beta \langle \alpha, \beta \rangle - f^*(L\beta) = \max_\beta \langle \alpha, \beta \rangle + \min_r \langle r, c - L\beta \rangle + \iota_{\cdot \geq 0}(r) \quad (14)$$

$$= \min_r \max_\beta \langle r, c \rangle + \iota_{\cdot \geq 0}(r) + \langle \alpha - L^T r, \beta \rangle.$$

Segmentation Problem. Plugging the previous expression into Eq. (4) enables us to solve it using algorithm (6). Indeed, introducing new primal variables

$r_A, r_B \in \mathbb{R}^{M^2}$ related to transport mapping, we recover the following primal dual problem

$$\min_{\substack{u \in \mathbb{R}^N \\ r_A, r_B \in \mathbb{R}^{M^2}}} \max_{\substack{p_A, q_A, p_B, q_B \in \mathbb{R}^M \\ p_C \in \mathbb{R}^{2N}}} \langle Hu, p_A \rangle + \langle Au, q_A \rangle + \langle H(\mathbf{1}-u), p_B \rangle + \langle B(\mathbf{1}-u), q_B \rangle$$
$$\langle r_A,\, c - L \begin{bmatrix} p_A \\ q_A \end{bmatrix} \rangle + \langle r_B,\, c - L \begin{bmatrix} p_B \\ q_B \end{bmatrix} \rangle + \langle \nabla u, p_C \rangle \quad (15)$$
$$+ \iota_{[0,1]^N}(u) + \iota_{\cdot \geq 0}(r_A) + \iota_{\cdot \geq 0}(r_B) - \iota_{\|\cdot\| \leqslant \rho}(p_C).$$

Observe that now we have a linear term $H(u, r_A, r_B) = \langle r_A + r_B, c \rangle$ whose gradient has a Lipschitz constant $L_H = 0$. We have also gained extra non smooth characteristic functions $\iota_{\cdot \geq 0}$, whose proximity operators are trivial (projection onto the positive quadrant $\mathbb{R}_+^{M^2}$: $\text{prox}_{\iota_{\cdot \geq 0}}(x) = \max\{\mathbf{0}, x\}$).

Advantages and Drawback. The main advantage of this new segmentation framework is that it makes use of optimal transport to compare histograms of features, without sub-iterative routines such as solving optimal transport problems to compute sub-gradients or proximity operators (see for instance [1,12]), or without making use of approximation (such as the Sliced-Wasserstein distance [9], generalized cumulative histograms [8] or entropy-based regularization [2]). Last, the proposed framework is not restricted to Wasserstein distances, since it enables the use of any cost matrix, and does not depend on features dimensionality.

However, a major drawback of this method is that it requires two additional primal variables r_A and r_B whose dimension is M^2 in our simplified setting, M being the dimension of histograms involved in the model. As soon as $M^2 \gg N$, the number of pixels, the proposed method could be significantly slower than when using L^1 as in [14] due to time complexity and memory limitation. This is more likely to happen when considering high dimensional features, such as patches or computer vision descriptors, as M increases with feature dimension n.

4 Regularized MK Distance for Image Segmentation

As already mentioned in the last section, the previous approach based on optimal transport may be very slow for large histograms. In such a case, we propose to use instead the entropy smoothing of optimal transport recently proposed and investigated in [1–3], that may offer increased robustness to outliers [1]. While it has been initially studied for probability simplex S_1, we here investigate its use for our framework with unnormalized histograms on S.

4.1 Sinkhorn Distances MK_λ

The entropy-regularized optimal transport problem (11) on set S (Eq. (9)) is

$$\mathbf{MK}_\lambda(a,b) := \min_{P \in \mathcal{P}(a,b)} \left\{ \langle P, C \rangle - \tfrac{1}{\lambda} h(P) \right\} + \iota_S(a,b), \quad (16)$$

where the entropy of the matrix P is defined as $h(P) := -\langle P, \log P\rangle$. Thanks to the negative entropy term which is strictly convex, the regularized optimal transport problem has a unique minimizer, denoted $P_\lambda^\star$, which can be recovered using a fixed point algorithm studied by Sinkhorn (see *e.g.* [1]). The regularized transport cost $\mathbf{MK}_\lambda(a, b)$ is thus referred to as the *Sinkhorn distance*.

Interpretation. Another way to express the negative entropic term is:

$$-h(p) : p \in \mathbb{R}_+^k \mapsto \mathbf{KL}(p\|\mathbf{1}_k) \in \mathbb{R}, \quad \text{with } k = M_a \cdot M_b$$

that is the Kullback-Leibler divergence between transport map p and the uniform mapping. This shows that, as λ decreases, the model encourages smooth, uniform transport so that the mass is spread everywhere. This also explains why this distance shows better robustness to outliers, as reported in [1]. To conclude, one thus would like to use in practice large values of λ to be close to the original Monge-Kantorovich distance, but low enough to deal with feature perturbation.

Structure of the Solution. First, the Sinkhorn distance (16) reads as

$$\mathbf{MK}_\lambda(\alpha) := \min_{\substack{p \in \mathbb{R}^{M_a \cdot M_b} \\ \text{s.t. } p \geq 0,\ L^T p = \alpha}} \langle p, c + \tfrac{1}{\lambda}\log p\rangle + \iota_S(\alpha). \qquad (17)$$

As demonstrated in [1], when writing the Lagrangian of this problem with a multiplier β to take into account the constraint $L^T p = \alpha$, we can show that the respective solutions $p_\lambda^\star$ and $P_\lambda^\star$ of problem (16) and (17) write

$$\log p_\lambda^\star = \lambda(L\beta - c) - \mathbf{1} \iff (\log P_\lambda^\star)_{i,j} = \lambda(u_i + v_i - C_{i,j}) - 1 \text{ with } \beta = \begin{bmatrix} u \\ v \end{bmatrix}.$$

Remark 1. The constant -1 is due to the fact that we use the unnormalized KL divergence $\mathbf{KL}(p\|\mathbf{1}_k)$, instead of $\mathbf{KL}(p\|\tfrac{1}{k}\mathbf{1}_k)$ for instance.

Sinkhorn Algorithm. Sinkhorn showed that the alternate normalization of rows and columns of any positive matrix M converges to a unique bistochastic matrix $P = \text{diag}(x) M \text{diag}(y)$. The following fixed-point iteration algorithm can thus be used to find the solution $P_\lambda^\star$: setting $M_\lambda = e^{-\lambda C}$, one has

$$P_\lambda^\star = \text{diag}(x^\infty) M_\lambda \text{diag}(y^\infty) \quad \text{where } x^{k+1} = \frac{a}{M_\lambda y^k} \text{ and } y^{k+1} = \frac{b}{M_\lambda^T x^k},$$

where a and b are the desired marginals of the matrix. This result enables us to design fast algorithms to compute the regularized optimal transport plan, and the the Sinkhorn distance or its derivative, as demonstrated in [1,2].

4.2 Legendre–Fenchel Transformation of Sinkhorn Distance MK_λ

Now, in order to use the Sinkhorn distance in algorithm (6), we need to compute its Legendre-Fenchel transform, which has been expressed in [2].

Proposition 1 (Cuturi-Doucet). *The convex conjugate of $MK_\lambda(\alpha)$ reads*

$$MK_\lambda^*(\beta) = \tfrac{1}{\lambda} \langle Q_\lambda(\beta), \mathbf{1} \rangle \quad \text{with } Q_\lambda(\beta) := e^{\lambda(L\beta - c) - 1}. \tag{18}$$

We obtain a simple expression of the Legendre–Fenchel transform which is C^∞, but unfortunately, its gradient is not Lipschitz continuous.

To overcome this problem, we propose two solutions in the next paragraphs: either we use a new normalized Sinkhorn distance (§ 4.3), whose gradient is Lipschitz continuous (§ 4.4), or we rely on the use of proximity operator (§ 4.6).

4.3 Normalized Sinkhorn Distance $MK_{\lambda, \leq N}$ on $\mathcal{S}_{\leq N}$

As the set $\mathcal{S}$ of admissible histograms does not prescribe the sum of histograms, we consider here a different setting in which the histograms' total mass are bounded above by N, the number of pixels of the image domain Ω

$$\mathcal{S}_{\leq N} := \left\{ a \in \mathbb{R}^{M_a}, b \in \mathbb{R}^{M_b} \,\middle|\, a > 0, b > 0, \langle a, \mathbf{1}_{M_a} \rangle = \langle b, \mathbf{1}_{M_b} \rangle \leq N \right\}. \tag{19}$$

Moreover, as the transport matrix $P_\lambda^\star$ is not normalized (*i.e.* $\langle P_\lambda^\star, \mathbf{1} \rangle \leq N$), we also propose to use a slightly normalized variant of the entropic regularization:

$$\tilde{h}(p) := Nh\left(\tfrac{p}{N}\right) = -N\,\mathbf{KL}\left(\tfrac{p}{N} \| \mathbf{1}\right) = -\langle p, \log p \rangle + \langle p, \mathbf{1} \rangle \log N. \tag{20}$$

Corollary 1. *The convex conjugate of the normalized Sinkhorn distance*

$$MK_{\lambda, \leq N}(\alpha) := \min_{\substack{p \in \mathbb{R}^{M_a \cdot M_b} \\ \text{s.t. } p \geq 0,\ L^T p = \alpha}} \left\{ \langle p, c + \tfrac{1}{\lambda} \log p - \tfrac{\log N}{\lambda} \mathbf{1} \rangle \right\} + \iota_{\mathcal{S}_{\leq N}}(\alpha) \tag{21}$$

reads, using the matrix-valued function $Q_\lambda(.) \mapsto e^{\lambda(L. - c) - 1}$ defined in (18)

$$MK_{\lambda, \leq N}^*(\beta) = \begin{cases} \tfrac{N}{\lambda} \langle Q_\lambda(\beta), \mathbf{1} \rangle & \text{if } \langle Q_\lambda(\beta), \mathbf{1} \rangle \leq 1 \\ \tfrac{N}{\lambda} \log \langle Q_\lambda(\beta), \mathbf{1} \rangle + \tfrac{N}{\lambda} & \text{if } \langle Q_\lambda(\beta), \mathbf{1} \rangle \geq 1 \end{cases} \tag{22}$$

Proof. The proof [10, A.1] is omitted here for the sake of shortness.

Observe that the dual function $MK_{\lambda, \leq N}^*(\beta)$ is continuous for $\langle Q_\lambda(\beta^\star), \mathbf{1} \rangle = 1$. Note also that the optimal matrix now is written $P_\lambda^\star = N Q_\lambda(\beta^\star)$ if $\langle Q_\lambda(\beta^\star), \mathbf{1} \rangle \leq 1$, and $P_\lambda^\star = N \frac{Q_\lambda(\beta^\star)}{\langle Q_\lambda(\beta^\star), \mathbf{1} \rangle}$ otherwise.

4.4 Gradient of $\mathbf{MK}^*_{\lambda,\leq N}$

From Corollary 1, we can express the gradient of $\mathbf{MK}^*_{\lambda,\leq N}$ which is continuous (writing Q in place of $Q_\lambda(\beta)$ to simplify expression)

$$\nabla \mathbf{MK}^*_{\lambda,\leq N}(\beta) = \begin{cases} N\left(Q\mathbf{1}_{M_b}, \mathbf{1}^T_{M_a} Q\right) & \text{if } \langle Q, \mathbf{1} \rangle \leq 1 \\ \frac{N}{\langle Q,\mathbf{1}\rangle}\left(Q\mathbf{1}_{M_b}, \mathbf{1}^T_{M_a} Q\right) & \text{if } \langle Q, \mathbf{1} \rangle \geq 1 \end{cases}. \quad (23)$$

We emphasis here that we retrieve a similar expression than the one originatively demonstrated in [3], where the authors consider the Sinkhorn distance on the probability simplex $\mathcal{S}_1$ (*i.e.* the special case where $N = 1$ and $\langle Q, \mathbf{1} \rangle = 1$).

Proposition 2. *The gradient* $\nabla \mathbf{MK}^*_{\lambda,\leq N}$ *is a Lipschitz continuous function of constant* L_{MK^*} *bounded by* $2\lambda N$.

Proof. The proof [10, A.2] is omitted here for the sake of shortness.

4.5 Optimization Using $\nabla \mathbf{MK}^*_{\lambda,\leq N}$

The general final problem we want to solve can be expressed as:

$$\min_u \rho TV(u) + \mathbf{MK}_{\lambda,\leq N}(H_a u, Au) + \mathbf{MK}_{\lambda,\leq N}(H_b(\mathbf{1}-u), B(\mathbf{1}-u)) + \iota_{[0,1]^N}(u). \quad (24)$$

Using the Legendre–Fenchel transform, the problem (24) can be reformulated as:

$$\min_u \max_{\substack{p_A, q_A \\ p_B, q_B, p_C}} \langle H_a u, p_A \rangle + \langle Au, q_A \rangle + \langle H_b(\mathbf{1}-u), p_B \rangle + \langle B(\mathbf{1}-u), q_B \rangle + \langle \nabla u, p_C \rangle$$
$$+ \iota_{[0,1]^N}(u) - \mathbf{MK}^*_{\lambda,\leq N}(p_A, q_A) - \mathbf{MK}^*_{\lambda,\leq N}(p_B, q_B) - \iota_{\|.\|\leq \rho}(p_C),$$

and can be optimized with the algorithm (6). Using proposition 2, ∇G^* is a Lipschitz continuous function with constant L_{G^*} checking $L_{G^*} = 2L_{MK^*} + \|H_b\| + \|B\| = 2\lambda N + \|H_b\| + \|B\|$, where N is the number of pixels. It will be large for high resolution images and huge for good approximations of the **MK** cost (*i.e.* $\lambda \gg 1$). Such a scheme may thus involve a very slow explicit gradient ascent in the dual update (6). In such a case, we can resort to the alternative scheme proposed in the next subsection.

4.6 Optimization Using Proximity Operator of $\mathbf{MK}^*_{\lambda^*}$

An alternative optimization of (24) consists in using the proximity operator of $\mathbf{MK}^*_\lambda$. Since we cannot compute the proximity operator of $\mathbf{MK}^*_\lambda$ in a closed form, we resort instead to a bidualization, as previously done in Section 3.2.

Considering now the normalized function $\mathbf{MK}_\lambda(\alpha)$ using entropy normalization (20) on set $\mathcal{S}$, we thus have $\mathbf{MK}^*_\lambda(\beta) = \frac{N}{\lambda}\langle Q_\lambda(\beta), \mathbf{1}\rangle = g^*_\lambda(L\beta)$.

Proposition 3. The proximity operators of $g_\lambda^*(q) = \frac{N}{\lambda}\langle e^{\lambda(q-c)-1}, \mathbb{1}\rangle$ is

$$\mathrm{prox}_{\tau g_\lambda^*}(p) = p - \frac{1}{\lambda}W\left(\lambda\tau N e^{\lambda(p-c)-1}\right). \quad (25)$$

where W is the Lambert function, such that $w = W(z)$ is solution of $we^w = z$. The solution is unique as $z = \lambda\tau N e^{\lambda(p-c)-1} \geq 0$.

Proof. The proof [10, A.3] is omitted here for the sake of shortness.

Remark 2. Note that the Lambert function can be evaluated very fast.

5 Experiments

Experimental Setting. In this experimental section, exemplar regions are defined by the user with scribbles (see Figures 1 to 5). These regions are only used to built prior histograms, so erroneous labeling is tolerated. Histograms a and b are built using hard-assignment on $M = 8^n$ clusters, which are obtained with the K-means algorithm. We use either RGB color ($\mathcal{F} = \mathrm{Id}$ and $n = d = 3$) or the gradient color norm ($\mathcal{F} = \|\nabla\cdot\|$ and again $n = d = 3$) features. The cost matrix is defined from the Euclidean metric $\|\cdot\|$ in $\mathbb{R}^n$ space, combined with the concave function $1 - e^{-\gamma\|\cdot\|}$, which is known to be more robust to outliers. Region $R_t(u)$ is obtained with threshold $t = \frac{1}{2}$, as illustrated in Figure 1. Approximately 1 minute is required to run 500 iterations and segment a 1 Megapixel color image.

Input $t = 0.9$ $t = 0.5$ $t = 0.1$

Fig. 1. Influence of the threshold on OT segmentation ($\lambda = \infty$)

Input L_1 OT ($\lambda = \infty$)

Fig. 2. Robustness of OT with respect to L_1: the blue colors that are not in the reference histograms are considered as background with OT distance and as foreground with the L_1 model, since no color transport is taken into account

| Input histograms | Segmentation 1 | Segmentation 2 | Segmentation 3 |

Fig. 3. Illustration of the interest of optimal transport for comparison of histograms. Prior histograms taken from image 1 are used to segment images 2 and 3.

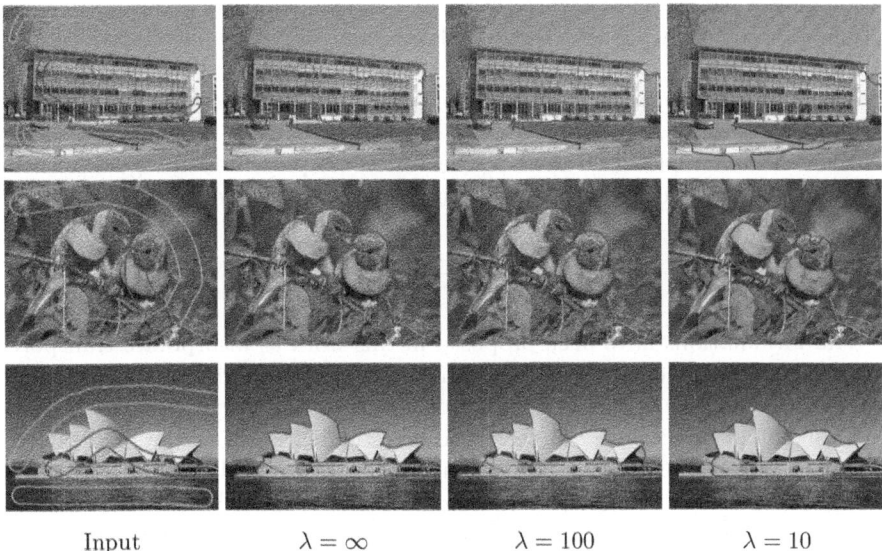

Input $\lambda = \infty$ $\lambda = 100$ $\lambda = 10$

Fig. 4. Comparison of segmentations obtained from the proposed models. The input areas are used to compute the reference color distributions a and b. The non-regularized model corresponds to $\lambda = +\infty$, increasing regularization effects are then shown.

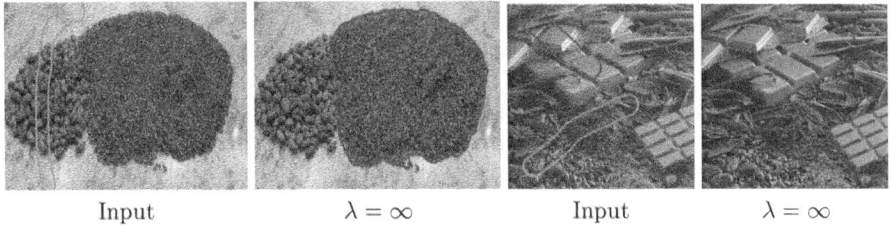

Input $\lambda = \infty$ Input $\lambda = \infty$

Fig. 5. Texture segmentation using histograms of gradient norms

Results. Figure 1 shows the influence of the threshold t used to get a binary segmentation. A small comparison with the model of [14] is then given in Figure 2. This underlines the robustness of optimal transport distance with respect to bin-to-bin L^1 distance. Contrary to optimal transport, when a color is not present in the reference histograms, the L^1 distance does not take into account the color distance between bins which can lead to incorrect segmentation. The robustness is further illustrated in Figure 3. It is indeed possible to use a prior histogram from a different image, even with a different clustering of the feature space. Note that it is not possible with a bin-to-bin metric, which requires the same clustering. Figure 4 shows comparisons between the non-regularized model, quite fast but high dimensional model, with the regularized model, using a low dimensional formulation. One can see that setting a large value of λ gives interesting results. On the other hand, using a very small value of λ always yields poor segmentation results. Some other results are proposed in the supplementary material (Section B).

Some last examples on texture segmentation are presented in Figure 5 where the proposed method is perfectly able to recover the textured areas.

6 Conclusion and Future Work

Several formulations have been proposed in this work to incorporate transport-based distances in convex variational model for image processing, using either regularization of the optimal-transport or not.

Different perspectives have yet to be investigated, such as the final thresholding operation, the use of capacity transport constraint relaxation [4], of other statistical features, of pre-conditionned optimization algorithms, and the extension to region-based segmentation and to multi-phase segmentation problem.

References

1. Cuturi, M.: Sinkhorn distances: Lightspeed computation of optimal transport. In: Neural Information Processing Systems (NIPS 2013), pp. 2292–2300 (2013)
2. Cuturi, M., Doucet, A.: Fast computation of wasserstein barycenters. In: International Conference on Machine Learning (ICML 2014), pp. 685–693 (2014)
3. Cuturi, M., Peyré, G., Rolet, A.: A smoothed dual approach for variational wasserstein problems. arXiv:1503.02533, March 2015 (preprint)
4. Ferradans, S., Papadakis, N., Peyré, G., Aujol, J.-F.: Regularized discrete optimal transport. SIAM J. Imaging Sciences **7**(1), 212–238 (2014)
5. Jung, M., Peyré, G., Cohen, L.D.: Texture segmentation via non-local non-parametric active contours. In: Boykov, Y., Kahl, F., Lempitsky, V., Schmidt, F.R. (eds.) EMMCVPR 2011. LNCS, vol. 6819, pp. 74–88. Springer, Heidelberg (2011)
6. Lorenz, D., Pock, T.: An inertial forward-backward algorithm for monotone inclusions. Journal of Mathematical Imaging and Vision **51**(2), 311–325 (2015)
7. Ni, K., Bresson, X., Chan, T., Esedoglu, S.: Local histogram based segmentation using the wasserstein distance. Int. J. of Computer Vision **84**(1), 97–111 (2009)

8. Papadakis, N., Provenzi, E., Caselles, V.: A variational model for histogram transfer of color images. IEEE Trans. on Image Processing **20**(6), 1682–1695 (2011)
9. Peyré, G., Fadili, J., Rabin, J.: Wasserstein active contours. In: IEEE International Conference on Image Processing, ICIP 2012 (2012)
10. Rabin, J., Papadakis, N.: Convex Color Image Segmentation with Optimal Transport Distances. ArXiv e-prints arXiv:1503.01986 (March 2015)
11. Rabin, J., Peyré, G.: Wasserstein regularization of imaging problem. In: IEEE International Conderence on Image Processing (ICIP 2011), pp. 1541–1544 (2011)
12. Swoboda, P., Schnörr, C.: Variational image segmentation and cosegmentation with the wasserstein distance. In: Heyden, A., Kahl, F., Olsson, C., Oskarsson, M., Tai, X.-C. (eds.) EMMCVPR 2013. LNCS, vol. 8081, pp. 321–334. Springer, Heidelberg (2013)
13. Villani, C.: Topics in Optimal Transportation. AMS (2003)
14. Yıldızoğlu, R., Aujol, J.-F., Papadakis, N.: A convex formulation for global histogram based binary segmentation. In: Heyden, A., Kahl, F., Olsson, C., Oskarsson, M., Tai, X.-C. (eds.) EMMCVPR 2013. LNCS, vol. 8081, pp. 335–349. Springer, Heidelberg (2013)

Piecewise Geodesics for Vessel Centerline Extraction and Boundary Delineation with Application to Retina Segmentation

Da Chen[✉] and Laurent D. Cohen

CEREMADE, UMR 7534, Université Paris Dauphine PSL,
75775 Paris Cedex 16, France
{chenda,cohen}@ceremade.dauphine.fr

Abstract. Geodesic methods have been widely applied to image analysis [17]. In this paper, we propose an automatic anisotropic fast marching based geodesic method to extract the centrelines of retinal vessel segments and their boundaries. Our method is related to the geodesic or minimal path technique which is particularly efficient to extract a tubular shape, such as a blood vessel. The proposed method consists of a set of pairs of points. Each pair of points provides the Initial point and Target point for one geodesic. For each pair of Initial point and Target point, we calculate a special Riemannian metric with an additional *Radius* dimension to constrain the fast marching propagation so that our method can get a nice path without any shortcut. The given pairs of points can be easily obtained from a pre-segmented skeletonized image by any vessel detection filter like Hessian or Oriented Flux method. Experimental results demonstrate that our method can extract vessel segments at a finer scale, with increased accuracy.

Keywords: Geodesic · Minimal path · Tubular structure extraction · Retinal vessel segmentation · Anisotropic fast marching

1 Introduction

Automatic segmentation and analysis of vascular structures has been deeply developed during the last two decades[10]. Tubular structure enhancement filters, like Hessian based method[9] and Oriented Flux[13] are widely used methods. The response of those filters, named *vesselness* can be thresholded directly to extract the vessel boundaries and then apply a sequential thinning filter[12] to the binary vessel segmentation to obtain the vessel centrelines which can be further processed. Those centrelines sometimes are not exactly located in the middle of the tubular shape. And it is a difficult task to compute the width of the tubular shape from those binary segmented images.

In this paper, we deal with the problem of automatically finding a set of vessel segments by piecewise geodesics consisting of centreline positions and radii. The minimal path model has been improved deeply since the seminal Cohen-Kimmel model[5], in which tubular structures, or object edges are extracted as the form of geodesics or minimal paths. This classic minimal path model can lead to finding the global minimum with respect to a geodesic energy potential $\mathcal{P}$ between two given endpoints. The geodesic potential or metric can be isotropic[6–8] ($\mathcal{P}$ only depends on the pixel position), or anisotropic in the sense that path length depends on the path orientation as well[2,3]. Once this potential is properly defined, Fast Marching methods[16,18] are the favored methods to estimate geodesic distances, from which minimal paths can be extracted. However, for the minimal path models mentioned above, it is difficult for them to extract the centreline of the tubular structure and the local width information or boundaries simultaneously. In order to solve this drawback, Li and Yezzi[14] proposed a variant minimal path technique, which defines the potential domain $\boldsymbol{\Omega} \subset \mathbb{R}^{n+1}$, connected open and bounded, as the product of spatial space $\Omega \subset \mathbb{R}^n$ with a parameter space $]R_{min}, R_{max}[$ representing vessel radius collection. Thus, each point in the extracted path by [14] contains spatial position and the last dimension represents the vessel thickness at this spatial point, i.e, one point coordinate consists of spatial dimensions and one radius dimension. And the extracted path is also located on the centreline of the tubular structure with appropriate potential.

Unfortunately, Li and Yezzi model suffers from a drawback that they did not take advantage of vessel orientation information which plays an important role in vessel detection. Benmansour and Cohen[2] proposed to use an anisotropic Riemannian metric to enhance the Li and Yezzi model. In [2], the authors construct a multi-resolution Riemannian metric guiding the Anisotropic Fast Marching propagation in the domain $\boldsymbol{\Omega}$. Both [2] and [14] require the user to give two or more endpoints as the prior knowledge to track the minimal paths. In order to reduce the user input, several papers[1,4,11,15] proposed to use keypoints searching method to detect recursively new start-points (keypoints) along the expected features by computing the curve length. But those methods require complicated stopping criteria.

The main purpose of this work is to introduce an automatic method to extract a complete tubular tree structure, such as the retinal vessel network, relying on the Benmansour-Cohen model[2] by using an Euclidean distance function to calculate the anisotropic metric for each initial vessel segment through thinning the thresholded vesselness image. The Euclidean distance function can constrain the anisotropic Fast Marching propagation and prevent shortcuts.

2 Background

In this paper, we only consider the 2D vessel segmentation so that one point $\mathbf{x} = (x, r) \in \boldsymbol{\Omega}$, where $x \in \Omega$ ($\Omega \subset \mathbb{R}^2$) denotes the point position in spatial dimensions and $r \in]R_{min}, R_{max}[$ denotes the position in radius dimension.

2.1 Minimal Path

Let $\Im$ denote the collection of Lipschitz paths $\gamma : [0, L] \to \boldsymbol{\Omega}$. The weighted length through a geodesic energy potential $\mathcal{P}$ can be formulated as follows:

$$l_{\mathcal{P}}(\gamma) := \int_0^L \mathcal{P}(\gamma(s), \gamma'(s))\, ds,\qquad(1)$$

where s is arc-length parameter and γ' denotes the tangent vector of path γ. The geodesic distance $\mathcal{U}_{\mathbf{s}}(\mathbf{x})$, or minimal action map, is the minimal energy of any path joining a point $\mathbf{x} \in \Omega$ to a given initial point $\mathbf{s}$:

$$\mathcal{U}_{\mathbf{s}}(\mathbf{x}) := \min\{l_{\mathcal{P}}(\gamma) | \gamma \in \Im,\ \gamma(1) = \mathbf{x},\ \gamma(0) = \mathbf{s}\}.\qquad(2)$$

The path $\mathcal{C}_{\mathbf{s},\mathbf{x}}$ is a *minimal path* if $l_{\mathcal{P}}(\mathcal{C}_{\mathbf{s},\mathbf{x}}) = \min_{\gamma}\{l_{\mathcal{P}}(\gamma),\ \gamma \in \Im\}$. There always exists at least one minimal path $\mathcal{C}_{\mathbf{s},\mathbf{x}}$.

2.2 Optimally Oriented Flux and Riemannian Metric Construction

The oriented flux[13] of an image $I: \Omega \to \mathbb{R}^2$, of dimension $d = 2$, is defined by the amount of the image gradient projected along the orientation $\mathbf{p}$ flowing out from a 2D circle at point x with radius r:

$$f(x; r, \mathbf{p}) = \int_{\partial \mathcal{C}_r} (\nabla(G_\sigma * I)(x + r\mathbf{p}) \cdot \mathbf{p})(\mathbf{p} \cdot \mathbf{n})\, ds,\qquad(3)$$

where G_σ is a Gaussian with variance σ and $\mathbf{n}$ is the outward unit normal vector along $\partial \mathcal{C}_r$. ds is the infinitesimal length on the boundary of $\mathcal{C}_r$. According to the divergence theory, one has $f(x; r, \mathbf{p}) = \mathbf{p}^T \cdot \mathbf{Q}(x, r) \cdot \mathbf{p}$ for some symmetric matrix $\mathbf{Q}(x, r)$ whose eigenvalues and eigenvectors we denote by λ_i and $\mathbf{v}_i$, $i = 1, 2$ (Suppose that $\lambda_1 \le \lambda_2$).

In this paper, as in Benmansour-Cohen model[2], the potential $\mathcal{P}(\gamma, \gamma')$ is set as a quadratic form with respect to a symmetric positive definite tensor $\mathcal{M}$ which is a 3×3 symmetric matrix:

$$\mathcal{P}(\gamma, \gamma') = \sqrt{\gamma'(.)^T \mathcal{M}(\gamma(.)) \gamma'(.)}\,.\qquad(4)$$

As described in [2], we consider only the orientations in the spatial dimensions. Thus $\mathcal{M}$ can be decomposed as follows:

$$\mathcal{M}(x, r) = \begin{pmatrix} \tilde{\mathcal{M}}(x, r) & \mathbf{0} \\ \mathbf{0} & \mathcal{P}_r(x, r) \end{pmatrix}.\qquad(5)$$

The anisotropic entry $\tilde{\mathcal{M}}(x, r)$, which is a 2×2 symmetric definite positive matrix, at point $\mathbf{x} = (x, r)$ can be constructed by the eigenvectors $\mathbf{v}_1$ and $\mathbf{v}_2$ as:

$$\tilde{\mathcal{M}}(\mathbf{x}) = e^{\alpha \cdot \lambda_2(\mathbf{x})} \mathbf{v}_1(\mathbf{x}) \mathbf{v}_1(\mathbf{x})^T + e^{\alpha \cdot \lambda_1(\mathbf{x})} \mathbf{v}_2(\mathbf{x}) \mathbf{v}_2(\mathbf{x})^T.\qquad(6)$$

The isotropic entry $\mathcal{P}_r(\mathbf{x})$ can be computed as:

$$\mathcal{P}_r(\mathbf{x}) = \beta \exp\left(\alpha \frac{\lambda_1(\mathbf{x}) + \lambda_2(\mathbf{x})}{2}\right),\qquad(7)$$

where α controls the spatial anisotropic ratio defined as

$$\mu = \max_{(x,r) \in \Omega} \sqrt{\exp\left(\alpha \cdot (\lambda_2(x, r) - \lambda_1(x, r))\right)}$$

while β controls the radius speed. For more details, we refer to [2].

2.3 Anisotropic Fast Marching Using Basis Reduction

Numerical methods for the minimal action map $\mathcal{U}_\mathbf{s}(\mathbf{x})$, see (2), introduce a discretization grid Z of Ω, and for each $\mathbf{x} \in Z$ a small mesh $S(\mathbf{x})$ of a neighborhood of $\mathbf{x}$ with vertices in Z (with the adequate modification if $\mathbf{x}$ is at or near the boundary). An approximation of $\mathcal{U}_\mathbf{s}$ is given by the solution of the following fixed point problem[16]: find $\mathcal{U}_\mathbf{s} : Z \to \mathbb{R}$ such that (i) $\mathcal{U}_\mathbf{s}(\mathbf{s}) = 0$ for the initial point $\mathbf{s}$, and (ii) for all $\mathbf{x} \in Z \setminus \mathbf{s}$

$$\mathcal{U}_\mathbf{s}(\mathbf{x}) = \min_{\mathbf{y} \in \partial S(\mathbf{x})} \mathcal{P}(\mathbf{x}, \mathbf{y} - \mathbf{x}) + \mathrm{I}_{S(\mathbf{x})} \mathcal{U}_\mathbf{s}(\mathbf{y}), \tag{8}$$

where $\mathrm{I}_{S(\mathbf{x})}$ denotes piecewise linear interpolation on a mesh $S(\mathbf{x})$. $\mathrm{I}_{S(\mathbf{x})}$ interpolates $\mathcal{U}_\mathbf{s}$ on $S(\mathbf{x})$ [2,16,20]. The expression (8) reflects the fact that the minimal path $\mathcal{C}_{\mathbf{s},\mathbf{x}}$, joining $\mathbf{x}$ to $\mathbf{s}$, needs to cross the stencil boundary $\partial S(\mathbf{x})$ at some point $\mathbf{y}$; hence it is the concatenation of a small path joining $\mathbf{x}$ to $\mathbf{y}$, of approximate length $\mathcal{P}(\mathbf{x}, \mathbf{y} - \mathbf{x})$, and of $\mathcal{C}_{\mathbf{y},\mathbf{x}}$, which energy is approximated by interpolation. A striking fact is that this N-dimensional fixed point system, with $N = \#(Z)$, can be solved in a single pass using the Fast Marching algorithm [20], provided the stencils $S(\mathbf{x})$ satisfy some geometric properties depending on the local geodesic potential $\mathcal{P}(\mathbf{x}, \cdot)$.

An adaptive construction of such stencils was introduced in [16], which led to breakthrough improvements in terms of computation time and accuracy for strongly anisotropic geodesic energy potentials, as in our application. It invokes Lattice Basis Reduction, a tool from discrete geometry which combines in an optimal way the geometric structure given by the Riemannian metric, and the arithmetic structure of the cartesian discretization grid.

2.4 Limitation of Classical Minimal Paths

Benmansour-Cohen model[2] can accurately extract the vessel boundaries and centrelines at the same time, and also very fast. Unfortunately, despite its numerous advantages, this model exhibits a disadvantage when applied to complete vessel network extraction such as retinal segmentation. It requires user provided endpoints at the end of each tubular structure end. This means expensive user intervention. For the keypoints method[1,4,11,15], which requires less user intervention, there may be some missing tubular segments. This is mainly because of the loops in the tubular structure network.

To solve those problems, we propose a new method based on Benmansour and Cohen model with pre-segmented vessel map to automatically extract the tubular structure segments. Our method can be divided as follows: presegmentation, endpoints correction and constrained Fast Marching propagation. We will give details of those steps in the next section and a summary in Section 3.4.

3 The Proposed Constrained Piecewise Geodesics

3.1 Pre-Processing

In this paper, we use a vessel detector to filter the image and obtain a vesselness map. Then a constant threshold is applied to this vesselness map to get the binary segmented vessel image. In order to find the endpoints for each vessel segment, we thin the binary image by a sequential morphological filters[12] and remove all the branch points and crossover points. The entire skeleton is broken up into a set of segments, in which each segment consists of two endpoints. The branch or crossover points are defined as any skeleton point having at least three neighbors in 8-neighborhood system. Any endpoint is discovered if it has only one neighbor and segment point has two neighbors. In Fig. 1(c), we show the skeletons after applying thinning filter and the labeled segments in different colours in Fig. 1(d).

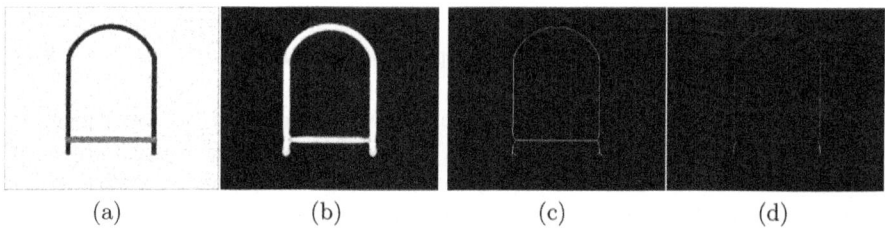

(a) (b) (c) (d)

Fig. 1. PreProcessing.(a) Original image. (b) Vesselness map computed by Hessian-based Filter[9]. (c) the Skeleton map of the image. (d) Label different segments with different colours after removing branch and crossover points.

In our work, we firstly scan the entire skeleton image to find all the vessel segments with two endpoints and then label them. Delete the segments whose length in pixels are smaller than a given threshold T_{len}, but retain the segments who connect two branch or crossover points. Those segments will be stored in the set $\mathcal{T}$.

3.2 Constrained Riemannian Metric and Anisotropic Fast Marching

In the previous section, we have all the segments and the corresponding endpoints stored in $\mathcal{T}$. Each segment consists of two endpoints and all the segment points connected to the endpoints. For each segment $\hbar$ with two endpoints p_s and p_e, it is easy to extract the centerline by Benmansour-Cohen model[2] by taking one of the two endpoints as initial point and track the path from another one. However, sometimes shortcuts will occur and some segments will be missed. In Fig. 2(a), the extracted geodesic follows the segment labeled as blue in Fig 1(d). But the result in Fig. 2(b) is a short cut path. In order to solve this problem,

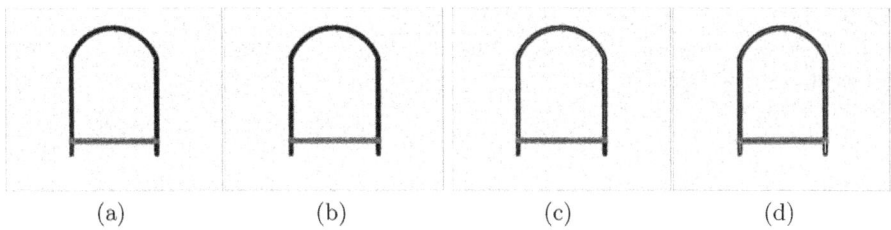

Fig. 2. Results from Benmansour and Cohen model.(a) and (b) Extracted centrelines corresponds to the vessel segments labeled as blue and red in Fig. 1(d), respectively. (c) is the result of our method. (d) is the result of our method with endpoint correction (see text).

we use the following function with respect to segment $\hbar \in \mathcal{T}$:

$$D_\hbar(x,r) = \begin{cases} 1, & \text{if } d_\hbar(x,r) \leq \ell; \\ +\infty, & \text{else}, \end{cases} \quad (9)$$

where ℓ is a given positive constant. And $d_\hbar(x,r)$ is a distance function:

$$d_\hbar(x,r) = \min_{x_\hbar \in \hbar} \|x - x_\hbar\|_2. \quad (10)$$

Note that (x,r) denotes a point in the domain $\mathbf{\Omega} = \Omega \times]R_{min}, R_{max}[$. Function $d_\hbar(x,r)$ represents the minimal Euclidean distance from spatial point $x \in \Omega$ to the segment $\hbar$. $D_\hbar$ in (9) gives a constraint volume computed by $d_\hbar$ and ℓ.

Based on (5), (9), and (10) we can construct the constrained Riemannian Metric for segment $\hbar \in \mathcal{T}$:

$$\mathcal{M}_\hbar = \begin{pmatrix} D_\hbar & 0 \\ 0 & D_\hbar \end{pmatrix} \begin{pmatrix} \tilde{\mathcal{M}} & 0 \\ 0 & \mathcal{P}_r \end{pmatrix} = \begin{pmatrix} (D_\hbar \cdot \tilde{\mathcal{M}}) & 0 \\ 0 & (D_\hbar \cdot \mathcal{P}_r) \end{pmatrix}. \quad (11)$$

In our method, in fact, distance $D_\hbar$ and $d_\hbar$ can be simply and fastly computed through applying the morphological dilation operation with radius ℓ to segment $\hbar$. Denote the dilated region as $\mathcal{R}_\hbar \subset \Omega$, $D_\hbar$ can be rewriten as:

$$D_\hbar(x,r) = \begin{cases} 1, & \text{if } x \in \mathcal{R}_\hbar; \\ +\infty, & \text{else}. \end{cases} \quad (12)$$

Combining the dilated region $\mathcal{R}_\hbar$ and $D_\hbar$, we use the Riemannian metric $\mathcal{M}$ in (5), instead of $\mathcal{M}_\hbar$ in (11). The detailed algorithm can be seen in Algorithm 1. In Algorithm 1, the input initial point $\mathbf{p}_s$ is defined in the domain $\Omega \times]R_{min}, R_{max}[$, i.e., $\mathbf{p}_s = (p_s, r_0)$ where $r_0 = 1$ which means one pixel length perimeter guess for $\mathbf{p}_s$. p_s and p_e are the two endpoints of segment $\hbar \in \mathcal{T}$.

In Algorithm 1 we give only a physical space endpoint p_e. Once the Fast Marching front meets one point $\mathbf{p} = (p_0, r)$ which follows $p_0 = p_e$, we consider $\mathbf{p} = (p_0, r)$ to be the endpoint. In Fig. 2(c), we demonstrate the result of our method. It can be seen that our method can overcome the shortcuts problem.

Algorithm 1. *ConstrainedAnisotropicFM*

Input: Metric $\mathcal{M}$, initial point $\mathbf{p}_s \in \Omega$, endpoint $p_e \in \Omega$, dilated region $\mathcal{R}_\hbar \subset \Omega$.
Output: Paths $\mathcal{C}_\hbar$.
Initialization:
  For each point $\mathbf{x} \in \Omega$, set $\mathcal{U}(\mathbf{x})=+\infty$ and $\mathcal{V}(\mathbf{x}) = $ *Trial*.
  Set $\mathcal{U}(\mathbf{p}_s)=0$.
Marching Loop:
1: Find $\mathbf{x}_{min} = (x_m, r)$, the *Trial* point which minimizes $\mathcal{U}$.
2: **if** $x_m \notin \mathcal{R}_\hbar$ **then**
3:   Set $\mathcal{U}(\mathbf{x}_{min}) = +\infty$ and $\mathcal{V}(\mathbf{x}_{min}) = $ *Accept*.
4:   Return to 1.
5: **end if**
6: **if** $x_m = p_e$ **then** ▷ Stop the propagation.
7:   Stop the Fast Marching Propagation and Track the minimal path $\mathcal{C}_\hbar$.
8:   Output the path $\mathcal{C}_\hbar$.
9: **end if**
10: Tag $\mathbf{x}$ as *Accepted*. ▷ "Standard" fast marching.
11: **for** All $\mathbf{y}$ such that $\mathbf{x}_{min} \in S(\mathbf{y})$ and $\mathcal{V}(\mathbf{x}_{min}) \neq $ *Accepted* **do**
12:   Compute $\mathcal{U}_{\text{new}}(\mathbf{y})$ using (8).
13:   **if** $\mathcal{U}_{\text{new}}(\mathbf{y}) < \mathcal{U}(\mathbf{y})$ **then**
14:     Set $\mathcal{U}(\mathbf{y}) \leftarrow \mathcal{U}_{\text{new}}(\mathbf{y})$
15:     Set $\mathcal{V}(\mathbf{y}) = $ *Trial*.
16:   **end if**
17: **end for**

3.3 Endpoints Correcting

Sometimes the endpoints of the segment $\hbar$ are not located at the exact center of the tubular structure. As an example, see the two endpoints of the segment in Fig. 1(d) labeled as red. This endpoint-bias will introduce inaccuracy to the extracted minimal paths around the initial point and endpoint (see the red path in Fig. 2(c)). In this section, we propose an endpoint correcting (EC) method to solve this problem before applying Algorithm 1. The proposed EC method relies on the Euclidean length $\mathcal{E}$ of the minimal path. We firstly introduce the Euclidean length calculation method during the Anisotropic Fast Marching propagation[4]: an approximation of $\mathcal{E}$ is the solution of the fixed point problem: find $\mathcal{E} : Z \to \mathbb{R}$ such that (i) for $\mathbf{p}_s \in \Omega$, $\mathcal{E}(\mathbf{p}_s) = 0$, and (ii) for all $\mathbf{x} = (x_0, r_0) \in Z \setminus \mathbf{p}_s$, let $\mathbf{y}_\mathbf{x} = (y, r)$ be the point at which the minimum eqrefeq:HopfLax is attained:

$$\mathcal{E}(\mathbf{x}) = \|y - x_0\|_2 + \mathbb{I}_{S(\mathbf{x})}\,\mathcal{E}(\mathbf{y}_\mathbf{x}), \tag{13}$$

Then a single pass solver is possible: whenever the Fast Marching updates $\mathcal{U}$, update $\mathcal{E}$ at the same time, by using the just computed minimizer $\mathbf{y}_\mathbf{x}$ from (8). In (13), the term $\|y - x_0\|_2$ is the Euclidean distance between y and x_0.

The EC method is described in Algorithm 2: for a given segment $\hbar \in \mathcal{T}$ and its two endpoints p_s, p_e we find its middle point $p_m \in \hbar$ and the dilated region $\mathcal{R}_\hbar$ with radius ℓ as input. Launch the Fast Marching from point $\mathbf{p}_m = (p_m, 1)$

Algorithm 2. *EndpointsCorrecting*

Input: Metric $\mathcal{M}$, endpoints p_s and p_e, initial point $\mathbf{p}_m$, dilated region $\mathcal{R}_{\hbar} \subset \Omega$.
Output: Paths $\mathcal{C}_{\hbar}$, new endpoints collection $\Phi_0 = \{\mathbf{p}_s, \mathbf{p}_e\}$.
Initialization:
  For each point $\mathbf{x} \in \Omega$, set $\mathcal{U}(\mathbf{x})=\mathcal{E}(\mathbf{x})=+\infty$ and $\mathcal{V}(\mathbf{x}) = $ *Trial*.
  Set $\mathcal{U}(\mathbf{p}_m)=\mathcal{E}(\mathbf{p}_m)=0$ and *RemainedEndpoints* $= 2$. Set point collection $\Phi = \varnothing$.
Marching Loop:
1: Find $\mathbf{x}_{min} = (x_m, r)$, the *Trial* point which minimizes $\mathcal{U}$.
2: **if** *RemainedEndpoints* $= 0$ **then**
3:   Track the minimal path $\mathcal{C}$ from each point of Φ_0 and set $\mathcal{C}_{\hbar} = \mathcal{C}_{\hbar} \cup \mathcal{C}$;
4:   Stop the algorithm completely.
5: **end if**
6: **if** $x_m \notin \mathcal{R}_{\hbar}$ **then**
7:   Set $\mathcal{U}(\mathbf{x}_{min}) = \mathcal{E}(\mathbf{x}_{min}) = +\infty$ and $\mathcal{V}(\mathbf{x}_{min}) =$*Accept*.
8:   Return to 1.
9: **end if**
10: **if** $x_m = p_e$ or $x_m = p_s$ **then**
11:   *RemainedEndpoints* $\leftarrow$ *RemainedEndpoints* $- 1$;
12:   **for** All $\mathbf{x} \in \mathcal{B}$ centred at $\mathbf{x}_{min}$ **do**   ▷ Endpoints searching criteria.
13:     **if** $\mathcal{E}(\mathbf{x}) \geq ([\mathcal{E}(\mathbf{x}_{min})] + 1)$ and $\mathcal{V}(\mathbf{x}) = $ *Accepted* **then**
14:       Set $\Phi \leftarrow \mathbf{x}$.
15:     **end if**
16:   **end for**
17:   **if** $\Phi \neq \varnothing$ **then**
18:     Set $\Phi_0 \leftarrow \arg\min_{\mathbf{x} \in \Phi} \mathcal{U}(\mathbf{x})$
19:   **else** Set $\Phi_0 \leftarrow \mathbf{x}_{min}$.
20:   **end if**
21: **end if**
22: Tag $\mathbf{x}$ as *Accepted* and update $\mathcal{E}(\mathbf{x})$ using (13).   ▷ "Standard" fast marching.
23: **for** All $\mathbf{y}$ such that $\mathbf{x}_{min} \in S(\mathbf{y})$ and $\mathcal{V}(\mathbf{x}_{min}) \neq $ *Accepted* **do**
24:   Compute $\mathcal{U}_{\text{new}}(\mathbf{y})$ using (8);
25:   **if** $\mathcal{U}_{\text{new}}(\mathbf{y}) < \mathcal{U}(\mathbf{y})$ **then**
26:     Set $\mathcal{U}(\mathbf{y}) \leftarrow \mathcal{U}_{\text{new}}(\mathbf{y})$, $\mathcal{V}(\mathbf{y})=$*Trial*.
27:   **end if**
28: **end for**

to propagate the weighted distance $\mathcal{U}$ and Euclidean distance $\mathcal{E}$ everywhere in Ω. Once either endpoint $\tilde{\mathbf{p}}_e = (p_e, r_e)$ is reached, search the desired point inside a set $\mathcal{B} : \{\mathbf{x} \in \Omega, \|\mathbf{x} - \tilde{\mathbf{p}}_e\|_2 \leq r_{\mathcal{B}}\}$ according to the criteria described in Algorithm 2: We find a collection of points $\Phi := \{\mathbf{x} \,|\, \mathcal{E}(\mathbf{x}) \geq [\mathcal{E}(\tilde{\mathbf{p}}_e)]+1, \mathbf{x} \in \mathcal{B}\}$ where $[n]$ means the largest integer which is smaller than $n \in \mathbb{R}$. Then the desired endpoint can be selected as $\mathbf{p}_e = \arg\min_{\mathbf{x} \in \Phi} \mathcal{U}(\mathbf{x})$. After another endpoint with the same criteria is corrected, stop the algorithm completely. The criteria are based on the fact that among all the points with the same curve length λ, any point which is located at the centreline of the tubular structure has a local minimum arrival time. In Fig. 2(d), we show the results with the boundaries delineation. We can see the endpoints of red, green and yellow lines have been placed at the better positions compared with Fig. 1(d).

3.4 Summary of Our Method

In this section, we summaries our method as follows:

1. For a given image $I : \Omega \subset \mathbb{R}^2$, obtain its skeletonized image by removing all the branch and crossover points. Label each segment of the skeletonized image and store them in $\mathcal{T}$.
2. For each segment $\hbar \in \mathcal{T}$, do *EndpointsCorrecting* as described in Algorithm 2 to get a new set of segments $\mathcal{T}_{new}$.
3. For each segment $\hbar_{new} \in \mathcal{T}_{new}$, do *ConstraintAnisotropicFM* described in Algorithm 1 to obtain a set of minimal paths, in which each minimal path $\mathcal{C}$ consists of the centrelines and the radius value representing the vessel width.

4 Experiments

In Fig. 3(b) we shown a complete results obtained by the proposed method. The green lines represent the boundaries while the red lines are the centrelines of the vessel segments. It can be seen that our method can capture almost all the vessel segments without shortcuts. In this experiment, we set the anisotropic ratio $\mu = 15$, $\beta = 2$, the radius for the dilated region $\mathcal{R}_\hbar$ as 3.

In Fig. 3(a) we show the results by Benmansour-Cohen model. Fig. 3(c), (d) and (e) illustrate the details indicated by arrows. We can see that some vessel segments are missed because of shortcuts. As comparison, we show the result details of our method in Fig. 3(f), (g) and (h). In Fig. 4, we show the improved results after endpoints correcting. Yellow lines are the paths without endpoints correcting. Compared to the red lines which are produced after endpoints correcting, we can see the endpoints are located at more precise positions.

For evaluation we apply our method on 20 retinal images got from the test set of the DRIVE dataset[19], acquired through a Canon CR5 non-mydriatic 3CCD camera with a 45 degree field of view (FOV). We show the comparison between Benmansour-Cohen model[2] and our method in Table 1 with evaluation measure Accuracy, which can be computed by the ratio of the summation of the statistical components: the true positive and the true negative to the total number of pixels in the FOV[10]. In this paper, we erode the FOV region by 11 pixels to remove the effect of the boundaries of the FOV to the vessel presegmentation. We evaluate our results only inside this eroded FOV region. In Table 2 we show the computational time (CPU) of our algorithm in endpoints correcting and constrained Fast Marching respectively. We also compare the CPU with Benmansour-Cohen model[2] with the same given segment set. Our method can achieve almost 2 times faster than [2]. In this experiment, we use the parameters as: anisotropic ratio $\mu = 15$, $\beta = 1$, the radius for the dilated region $\mathcal{R}_\hbar$ equals 3.

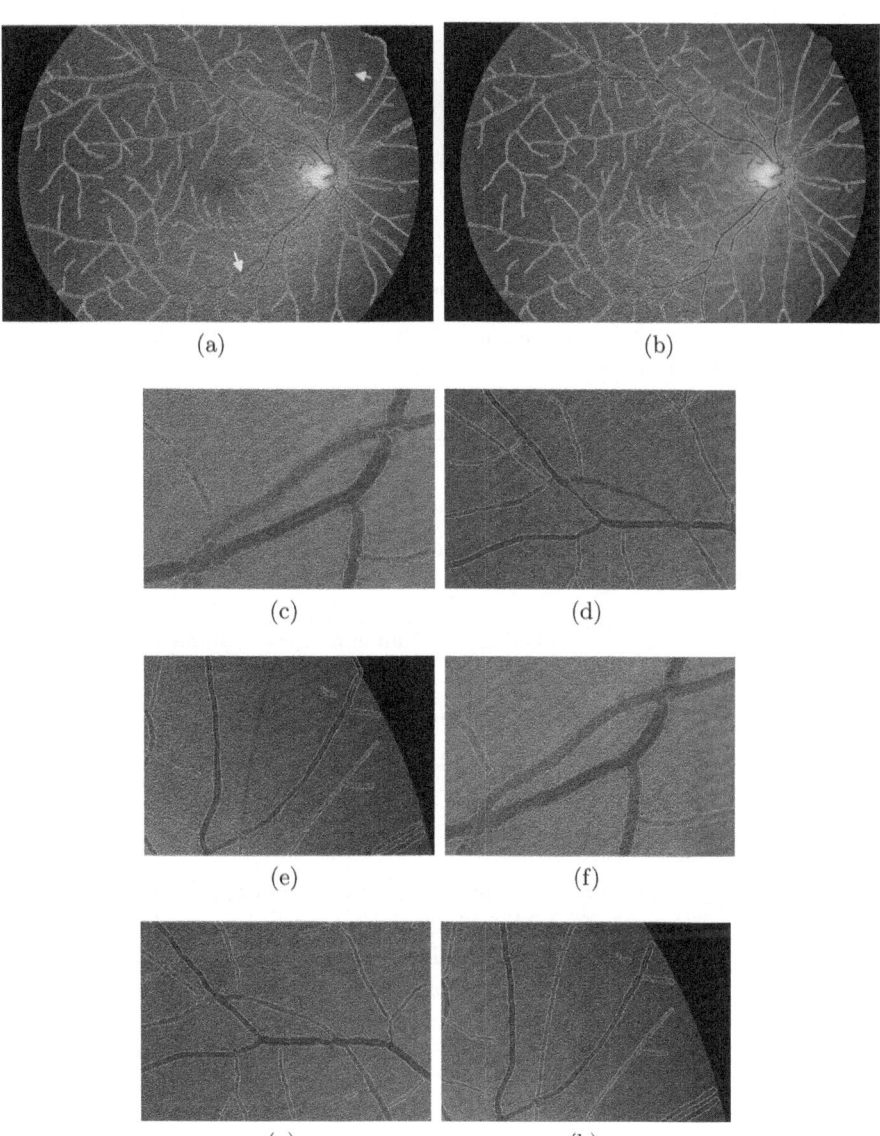

Fig. 3. Segmentation of a retinal image. (a) is the result by Benmansour and Cohen model and (b) is the result of our method (Green lines are the boundaries and red lines are the centrelines). (c-e) are the details of (a) indicated by arrows. (f-h) are the details shown in (b).

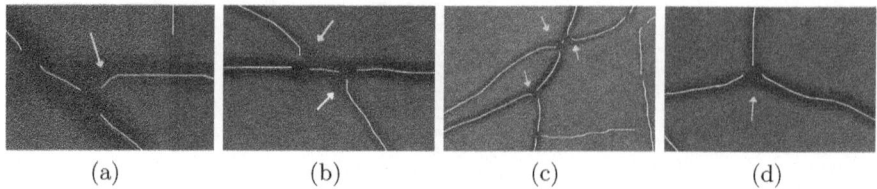

(a) (b) (c) (d)

Fig. 4. Improved results by Endpoints Correcting. Yellow lines are the paths without Endpoints Correcting while red lines are the paths after Endpoints Correcting.

Table 1. Comparison of our segmentations with the second manual segmentation on the test set of DRIVE database

Methods	Maximum	Minimum	Mean	Standard deviation
Benmansour-Cohen model[2]	0.947	0.9271	0.9372	0.0054
Proposed Method	0.949	0.9305	0.9397	0.0052

Table 2. Comparison of our segmentations CPU (in Seconds) with Benmansour-Cohen model[2] on 12 retinal images from DRIVE

	Maximum	Minimum	Mean	Standard deviation
Benmansour-Cohen model	22.6	9.16	13.17	3.2
Endpoints Correcting	5.1	4.0	4.39	0.27
Constrained Fast Marching	5.6	4.4	5.06	0.353

5 Conclusions

In this paper, we propose a new tubular structure extraction method based on the constraint anisotropic Fast Marching, and introduce a endpoints correcting method using Euclidean curve length. These ingredients allow our method to approximate piecewise minimal paths from complex tubular network, leading better extraction results compared to the classic Benmansour and Cohen model. Numerical experiments illustrate these improvements on several retinal images.

Acknowledgments. The authors thank Dr. Jean-Marie Mirebeau for helpful discussion about the Anisotropic Fast-Marching method. Also the authors would like to thank the suggestions and comments of anonymous reviewers.

References

1. Benmansour, F., Cohen, L.D.: Fast object segmentation by growing minimal paths from a single point on 2D or 3D images. Journal of Mathematical Imaging and Vision **33**(2), 209–221 (2009)
2. Benmansour, F., Cohen, L.D.: Tubular Structure Segmentation Based on Minimal Path Method and Anisotropic Enhancement. International Journal of Computer Vision **92**(2), 192–210 (2011)

3. Bougleux, S., Peyré, G., Cohen, L.: Anisotropic geodesics for perceptual grouping and domain meshing. In: Forsyth, D., Torr, P., Zisserman, A. (eds.) ECCV 2008, Part II. LNCS, vol. 5303, pp. 129–142. Springer, Heidelberg (2008)
4. Chen, D., Cohen, L., Mirebeau, J.M.: Vessel extraction using anisotropic minimal paths and path score. In Proc. ICIP, pp. 1570–1574 (2014)
5. Cohen, L.D., Kimmel, R.: Global minimum for active contour models: A minimal path approach. International Journal of Computer Vision 24(1), 57–78 (1997)
6. Cohen, L.D.: Multiple Contour Finding and Perceptual Grouping using Minimal Paths. Journal of Mathematical Imaging and Vision 14(3), 225–236 (2001)
7. Cohen, L.D., Deschamps, T.: Grouping connected components using minimal path techniques. Application to reconstruction of vessels in 2d and 3d images. In: Proc. IEEE CVPR (2001)
8. Deschamps, T., Cohen, L.D.: Fast extraction of minimal paths in 3D images and applications to virtual endoscopy. Medical Image Analysis 5(4), 281–299 (2001)
9. Frangi, A.F., Niessen, W.J., Vincken, K.L., Viergever, M.A.: Multiscale vessel enhancement filtering. In: Wells, W.M., Colchester, A.C.F., Delp, S.L. (eds.) MICCAI 1998. LNCS, vol. 1496, p. 130. Springer, Heidelberg (1998)
10. Fraz, M., Remagnino, P., Hoppe, A., Uyyanonvara, B., Rudnicka, A., Owen, C., Barman, S.: Blood vessel segmentation methodologies in retinal images - A survey. Computer Methods and Programs in Biomedicine 108(1), 130–137 (2012)
11. Kaul, V., Yezzi, A., Tsai, Y.: Detecting curves with unknown endpoints and arbitrary topology using minimal paths. IEEE Transactions on Pattern Analysis and Machine Intelligence 34(10), 1952–1965 (2012)
12. Lam, L., Lee, S.W., Suen, C.Y.: Thinning Methodologies - A Comprehensive Survey. IEEE Transactions on Pattern Analysis and Machine Intelligence 14(9), 869–885 (1992)
13. Law, M.W.K., Chung, A.C.S.: Three dimensional curvilinear structure detection using optimally oriented flux. In: Forsyth, D., Torr, P., Zisserman, A. (eds.) ECCV 2008, Part IV. LNCS, vol. 5305, pp. 368–382. Springer, Heidelberg (2008)
14. Li, H., Yezzi, A.: Vessels as 4-D curves: Global minimal 4-D paths to extract 3-D tubular surfaces and centrelines. IEEE Transactions on Medical Imaging 26(9), 1213–1223 (2007)
15. Li, H., Yezzi, A., Cohen, L.: 3D multi-branch tubular surface and centerline extraction with 4D iterative key points. In: Yang, G.-Z., Hawkes, D., Rueckert, D., Noble, A., Taylor, C. (eds.) MICCAI 2009, Part II. LNCS, vol. 5762, pp. 1042–1050. Springer, Heidelberg (2009)
16. Mirebeau, J.M.: Anisotropic Fast-Marching on cartesian grids using Lattice Basis Reduction. SIAM Journal on Numerical Analysis 52(4), 1573–1599 (2014)
17. Peyré, G., Péchaud, M., Keriven, R., Cohen, L.D.: Geodesic Methods in Computer Vision and Graphics. Foundations and Trends in Computer Graphics and Vision 5(3-4), 197–397 (2010)
18. Sethian, J.A.: Fast marching methods. SIAM Review 41(2), 199–235 (1999)
19. Staal, J., Abrámoff, M.D., Niemeijer, M., Viergever, M.A., Ginneken, B.V.: Ridge based vessel segmentation in color images of the retina. IEEE Transactions on Medical Imaging 23(4), 501–509 (2004)
20. Tsitsiklis, J.N.: Efficient algorithms for globally optimal trajectories. IEEE Transactions on Automatic Control 40(9), 1528–1538 (1995)

Unsupervised Learning Using the Tensor Voting Graph

Shay Deutsch$^{(\boxtimes)}$ and Gérard Medioni

Computer Science Department, Institute for Robotics and Intelligent Systems,
University of Southern California, Los Angeles, USA
{shaydeut,medioni}@usc.edu

Abstract. Tensor Voting is a local, non parametric method that provides an efficient way to learn the complex geometric manifold structure under a significant amount of outlier noise. The main limitation of the Tensor Voting framework is that it is strictly a local method, thus not efficient to infer the global properties of complex manifolds. We therefore suggest constructing a unique graph which we call the Tensor Voting Graph, in which the affinity is based on the contribution of neighboring points to a point local tangent space estimated by Tensor Voting. The Tensor Voting Graph compactly and effectively represents the global structure of the underlying manifold. We experimentally demonstrate that we can accurately estimate the geodesic distance on complex manifolds, and substantially outperform all state of the art competing approaches, especially when outliers are present. We also demonstrate our method's superior ability to segment manifolds, first on synthetic data, then on standard data sets for a motion segmentation, with graceful degradation in the presence of noise.

Keywords: Tensor voting · Manifold learning · Intersecting manifolds

1 Introduction

Given a set of points in a high dimensional space that lie on one or more smooth manifolds, possibly intersecting, a number of difficult and interesting problems need to be addressed: first, we may want to estimate the local structure at each data point, which includes estimation of dimensionality, and local normal and tangent spaces. Second, we may need to infer global properties, such as the geodesic distance between 2 points of the manifold. Also, given multiple manifolds, possibly intersecting, we need to define membership and distance to a new data point.

Additionally, although some significant progress has been made in manifold learning with noise-free data [13],[11], [1], handling noise is a critical and practical issue which significantly degrades the performance of state of the art methods.

These problems are ubiquitous in unsupervised manifold learning, and many applications, especially in computer vision would benefit from a principled approach to these problems.

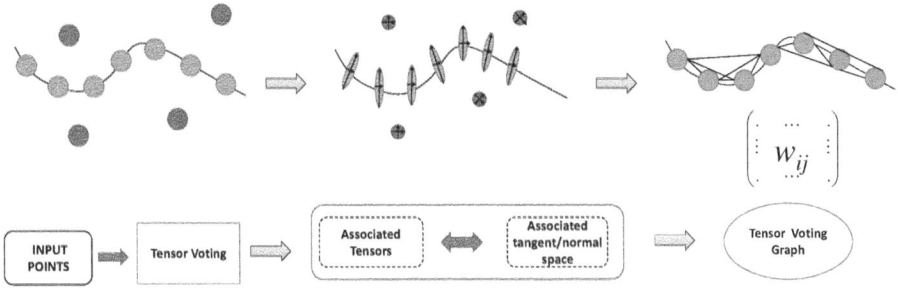

Fig. 1. Overview of the suggested Tensor Voting Graph Construction Method

A method that can reliably estimate the desired *local* properties mentioned above is Tensor Voting [7], a local, non parametric, perceptual organization framework that can infer the local geometric structure from sparse and noisy data using a local voting process. However, Tensor Voting does not provide a reliable and efficient way to learn the **global** structure of a complex manifold.

This paper aims at incorporating the powerful properties of Tensor Voting to infer the local manifold geometric structure into a unified framework that can infer the global structure of manifolds with complex topological structures.

To achieve this goal, we construct a graph in which the affinity between points is based on the contribution that was made at each point in the voting process from its neighbors. This graph provides an efficient tool to perform the desired global manifold learning tasks, augments the Tensor Voting framework, and is called the Tensor Voting Graph (TVG). This hybrid local-global approach can efficiently encode and represent the global properties of the manifolds and also serves to identify separate manifolds if appropriate.

As the TVG builds on the Tensor Voting framework, it leverages its algorithmic features that include robustness to a large amount of outliers, a reliable estimation of the tangent space, dimensionality and structure type, and the ability to handle the simultaneous presence of multiple structure types. We summarize our contributions:

Novel graph construction: Our Tensor Voting Graph encodes the contribution made to the tangent space estimation at each point by neighboring points.

A general framework for manifold learning: The new construction provides a general framework, which incorporates a rich geometric structure into a graph that can analyze a large class of manifolds, including those with intersections.

Global structure estimation: The TVG can be used to learn the manifold's global properties, using well known tools from graph theory. This includes efficient marching and geodesic distance estimation on manifolds using the Dijkstra algorithm, and clustering and classification using Spectral Clustering.

We have validated our approach on complex manifolds and Computer Vision application data. Experimental results demonstrate that our method significantly outperforms the state of the art methods on a set of manifolds with intricate manifold structure. In Computer Vision applications we demonstrate that our method achieves comparable results to the state of the art methods, with much more graceful degradation when contaminated with outliers.

The paper is organized as follows: Section 2 provides an overview of previous work. Section 3 details our approach for the Tensor Voting Graph construction. Section 4 evaluates the Tensor Voting Graph in estimating the geodesic distances on a single manifold. Section 5 illustrates the performance of our approach in clustering multiple manifolds, and Section 6 concludes the paper.

2 Related Work

We present an overview of related previous research in manifold learning, manifold clustering and Tensor Voting.

2.1 Manifold Learning

The central assumption in manifold learning is that the data lie on a low dimensional manifold that captures the dependencies between the observable parameters of the data. The main problem in manifold learning is to explore the geometry and the topology of the manifold. Most of the methods in manifold learning are inspired from PCA and multi-dimensional scaling (MDS), based on the assumption that nonlinear manifolds can be approximated by locally linear parts. Some of the most popular approaches in manifold learning are Isomap[13], LLE[11], Laplacian Eigenmaps [1], HLLE [4], LTSA [16] and Diffusion Maps [2], and more recently Vector Diffusion Maps[12] which generalize Diffusion Maps [2] using tangent space learning. Also related are manifold clustering methods that addresses the limitation of the k nearest neighbors and ε ball graph constructions. This includes Sparse Subsapce Clustering [5], Spectral Clustering on multiple Manifolds [15], and Robust Multiple Manifold Structure Learning [6]. The main limitation of these methods is that they are sensitive to a large amount of outliers.

2.2 Tensor Voting

We provide a brief introduction to Tensor Voting and refer to [8],[7] for a detailed treatment. Tensor Voting is a perceptual organization framework that can infer geometric structures from sparse and noisy data by a local voting process, and has been applied in many problems in Computer Vision. The Tensor Voting methodology consists of three important aspects [8]:

1. **Tensor for representation**: each point is encoded as a second order, positive semi definite symmetric tensor, which is equivalent to a $N \times N$ matrix, and an ellipsoid in N-D space. In the Tensor Voting framework, a tensor represents the structure of a manifold going through the point by encoding the normals to the

manifold as eigenvectors of the tensor that correspond to non-zero eigenvalues, and the tangents as eigenvectors that correspond to zero eigenvalues. The tensors can be formed by the summation of the direct products of the eigenvectors that span the normal space of the manifold. The tensor T at a point on a manifold of dimensionality d and with $\hat{n}_i$ corresponding to the unit vectors that span the normal space is expressed as $T = \sum_{i=1}^{d} \hat{n}_i \hat{n}_i^t$.

2. **Voting for communication**: The core of the Tensor Voting framework is the way information is propagated from point to point. The stick tensor voting is the fundamental voting element from which all other voting types and voting in higher dimensions can be derived. The following equation defines the stick tensor voting:

$$S_{vote} = DF(s, k, \sigma) \begin{bmatrix} -\sin(2\theta) \\ \cos(2\theta) \end{bmatrix} [-\sin(2\theta) \ \cos(2\theta)] \quad (1)$$

$$DF(s, k, \sigma) = e^{-\frac{s^2 + ck^2}{\sigma^2}}$$

$$\theta = \arcsin(\frac{v\hat{e}_1}{||v||}), s = \frac{\theta||v||}{||\sin\theta||}, \kappa = \frac{||2\sin\theta||}{||v||}$$

In the above equation, s is the length of the arc between the voter and receiver (OP), v is the vector connecting O and P, κ is its curvature which can be computed from the radius of the osculating circle, σ is the scale of voting, which controls the degree of decay with curvature, and c is a constant defined in [8]. The magnitude of the vote is a function of proximity and smooth continuation, and is called the saliency decay function.

3. **Voting analysis**: given an $N \times N$ second order, symmetric, non-negative definite matrix, the type of structure encoded in it can be inferred by examining its eigensystem. Any such tensor can be decomposed as in the following equation:

$$T = \sum \lambda_i \hat{e}_i \hat{e}_i^t = (\lambda_1 - \lambda_2)\hat{e}_1\hat{e}_1^t + \\ + (\lambda_2 - \lambda_3)(\hat{e}_1\hat{e}_1^t + \hat{e}_2\hat{e}_2^t) + \ldots \\ \lambda_N(\hat{e}_1\hat{e}_1^t + \hat{e}_2\hat{e}_2^t + \ldots \hat{e}_N\hat{e}_N^t)$$

where λ_i are the eigenvalues in descending order of magnitude and e_i are the corresponding eigenvectors. Based on the tensor spectral decomposition, the normal and tangent spaces, structure type, dimensionality and outliers are derived. The term $(\hat{e}_1\hat{e}_1^t + \hat{e}_2\hat{e}_2^t + \ldots \hat{e}_N\hat{e}_N^t)$ is called the ball component and is typically used to identify intersection areas, which correspond to peaks of the eigenvalue λ_N.

The main limitation of the Tensor Voting framework is that it is a strictly local method, and performing global operations such as estimating geodesic distances and clustering are not reliable. For example, to estimate geodesics distances on manifolds, previous methods using TV resort to an iterative, non-linear interpolation methods [8] that marches on the manifold by projecting the desired direction from the starting point, computing the tangent space of a new point and advancing in the desired direction until the destination is reached within ϵ. As pointed out in [8], this process is very slow and unreliable, and also diverges on figuration where points on the path are in deep concavities.

3 The Tensor Voting Graph

To perform global operations on complex manifolds, possibly with singularities, we suggest to construct a graph which encapsulates affinities between data points which is based on local tangent space distance. In the voting process that occurs in the Tensor Voting paradigm, points emit tensor votes to their neighbors to estimate the local tangent and normal space at each point. Here, we suggest constructing a graph using the reverse tensor votes: at each point, we estimate the contribution which was made to the local tangent space by the neighboring points that participated in the voting process. Thus, the affinity between points is not only a function of the local tangent space orientations; it is also highly correlated with the majority of the votes that contributed to each points local tangent space, which provides a measure of distance to these points on the local manifold. Figure 2 illustrates the Tensor Voting Graph construction: points which are close in Euclidean distance but far in manifold distance have zero affinity, since the affinity is defined using local tangent space distance similarity. Points that lie close on the same manifold part have small tangent space distance and hence high affinity value. Formally, given a set of unlabeled data points $X_1, ..X_n$, and the normal spaces of each point X_i, $O_i = \{(u_i)_1, .., (u_i)_d\}$. Let $\tilde{O}_{ij} = \{(\tilde{v}_{ij})_1, ..., (\tilde{v}_{ij})_d\}$ correspond to the subspace of the normal votes which were emitted from point X_j at X_i using Tensor Voting.

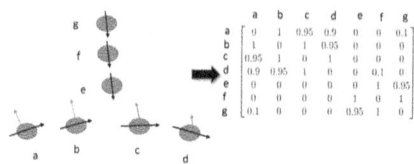

Fig. 2. Illustration of the TVG: points b and e that are close in Euclidean distance but far in manifold distance have zero affinity, whereas the points b and c are connected with high affinity corresponding to small distance on the manifold

Given these votes, the reverse tensor votes are encapsulated in the Graph $G = (X, W)$ with weights $w : E \to R$ where the affinity value is based on the principal angles between the normal spaces O_i and the subspace $\tilde{O}_{ij}$. Given two subspaces, $O_i, \tilde{O}_{ij}$, the maximal principal angle between the subspaces is defined as follows[10]:

$$f(O_i, \tilde{O}_{ij}) = \min_{u \in O_i} \max_{\tilde{v} \in \tilde{O}_{ij}} \langle u, \tilde{v} \rangle \qquad (2)$$

We use the affinity function in Equation 2, to define the affinity value w_{ij} in our TVG as

$$w_{ij} = \begin{cases} f(O_i, \tilde{O}_{ij}) & \text{if } X_j \in \text{kNN}(X_i) \text{ and} \\ & \arccos(f(O_i, O_{ij})) < 45°, \\ 0 & \text{else} \end{cases} \quad (3)$$

Where kNN(X_i) denotes the k nearest neighbors of X_i. The affinity matrix defines for each point its k nearest neighbors in terms of local tangent space proximity according to the largest affinities : $w_{i_{j_1}} \geq w_{i_{j_2}} ... \geq w_{i_{j_k}}$.

Algorithm 1. TVG (Tensor Voting Graph construction)

Input: The data set X (possibly with outliers), σ is the tensor voting scale, k for the number of k nearest neighbors on the local tangent space.

1: Perform Tensor Voting, $TV^{(i)}(X), i = 1$ (first iteration).
2: Remove outlier noise: points X_i, for which $\lambda_1 \ll \epsilon$, are removed.
3: 3For each X_i , normalize its Tensors eigenvalues $\lambda_l = \lambda_l / \sum_{i=1}^{N} \lambda_i$.
4: Refine tangent space estimation using second iteration $TV^{(i)}(X), i = 2$.
5: Compute the affinity matrix $W \in R^{N \times N}, (W)_{ij} = w_{ij}$, using Equation 3.
6: Fix the symmetry of the similarity matrix: $W = (W + W^T)/2$.
7: **Output:** Tensor Voting Graph $G = (X, W)$, and the local geometrical structure at each point $X_i : (O_i, O_i^\perp, \{\lambda_i\}_{i=1}^{N})$

Since the similarity graph is founded on the local tangent space, the strength of the affinity value between data points can be characterized into three categories: (I) Points which are close on the local tangent space have small geodesic distance and a large affinity value. (II) Points which are far away in geodesic distance but are close in terms of Euclidean distance, such as in the vicinity of intersections or high curvature, have small affinity values or zero. (III) Points which are far in Euclidean distance have zero affinity value. Thus the constructed Graph summarizes both local and global relationships within the whole data set.

Once the graph is built, we can estimate the geodesic distances efficiently and perform clustering and classification tasks using well known graph methods. Also note that the constructed graph is sparse by construction, which is a valuable property for classification purposes and also computationally efficient. To compute geodesic distances, first the TVG is constructed, which estimates for each point its k nearest neighbors on the local tangent space. Then, a new Euclidean distance graph is constructed, in which edges weights between pairs of points are connected and set to equal the Euclidean distance only between pairs which are k nearest neighbors on the Tensor Voting Graph. Then the algorithm of Dijkstra [3] is applied on the former constructed Graph to estimate the shortest distance paths. For clustering purpose, the value of an edge on the Graph is set directly to the affinity value on the TVG, and the unnormalized Spectral Clustering method is applied to the affinity matrix. The Tensor Voting Graph $G = (X, W)$ construction algorithm is described in the pseudo-code algorithm 1. Note that the complexity is O($Nn \log n$) for the Tensor Voting computation[8] and $O(n^2N^2d)$ for computing the affinity between the local tangent spaces, where n, N, and d correspond to the number of points, the ambient space and the normal space dimensionality, respectively.

4 Experimental Results

4.1 Geodesic Distance Comparison on Inliers

We evaluate the suggested Tensor Voting graph and compare it to some of state of the art algorithms in manifold learning: LLE, Isomap, Laplacian Eigenmaps, HLLE, and LTSA. All these methods use the kNN graph as the first stage prior to embedding. In all experiments, we perform a numerical evaluation of the geodesic distance error between all pair wise points on the manifold, where in our method we measure the geodesic distance between the points of each pair in the input space, and in the embedding space for all other methods. For the evaluation of the geodesic distance error we use the following measure (used also in [8]), the geodesic distance error is evaluated using:

$$err_{G_D} = \sum_{i,j} \frac{|d(i,j) - d_{est}(i,j)|}{d(i,j)}$$

where d_{ij} correspond to the ground truth estimated and $d_{est}(i,j)$ is the estimated distance for a given method. We tested a wide range of k for the number k nearest neighbors for all algorithms, and the results are reported for the best k only. For each embedding method (except Isomap), we computed a uniform scale to minimize the error between the computed distance and the true geodesic distances.

Table 1. Comparison with state of the art on geodesic distances: I corresponds to experiments with inliers noise, and I&O corresponds to data contaminated with outliers. The results reported are in terms of err_{G_D} percent.

Data/Method	ISOMAP		LLE		LE		HLLE		LTSA		TVG	
	I	I&O	I	I&O	I	I&O	I	I&O	I	I&O	I	I&O
Cylinder	0.2	4.8	8.5	7.8	15.3	17.2	8.5	-	7.1	8.5	0.25	**0.76**
Torus	12.0	12.28	11.7	12.3	19.4	17.8	15.8	-	11.6	11.7	**0.3**	**0.14**
Ennepers	13.4	28.3	21.4	26	29.4	65	25.5	-	22	22	**0.9**	**1.3**
Helicoid	8.4	14.8	23.4	38.8	23.8	38.8	20.6	-	24.8	19.0	**0.2**	**0.17**

Manifold data sets: The dataset used for the experiments is a cylinder section which spans 150° and consists of 2000 points, torus consists of 2000 points, Enneper's surface with 3000 points, Helicoid surface with 2500 points, and a torus curve with 800 points. The geodesic distance of the cylinder manifold can be computed analytically, and the other manifolds were sampled densely

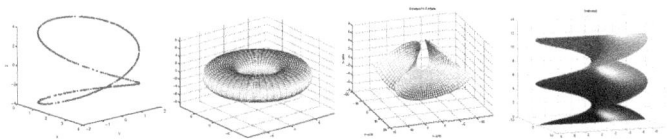

Fig. 3. Data set used for estimating the geodesic distances. From left to right: Viviani's curve, Torus, Ennepers and Helicoid surfaces

such that the shortest distance paths using Dijkstra on a kNN graph provides a good approximation for the true geodesic distances. The experimental results in Table 1 show that the compared methods produce significant distortion whereas the TVG performs well on these manifolds. Also note that the strictly local Tensor Voting method would fail to converge on most of the manifolds experimented in this paper, especially those with deep concavities such as the Helicoid, or Ennepers surface.

4.2 Comparison with Outliers

We apply our method in the presence of large amount of outliers. For the cylinder, torus, Enneper's, and Helicoid surfaces with the same number of inliers used in the previous section, we added 1000, 1500, 2000, and 1500 outliers, respectively. The outliers were generated according to a uniform distribution. Experimental results in Table 1 demonstrate that the Tensor Voting Graph can handle large amounts of outlier noise, with a very small effect on the accuracy of the estimated geodesic distance, while outlier noise degrades the competing methods, which obtained good results in the outlier free case. Note that in this section we have compared our method to Isomap in embedding space. In the next section our method will be contrasted with the k nearest neighbors in the Euclidean distance Graph, which is the first step in Isomap.

Table 2. Geodesic distances comparison on intersecting manifold

Data/Method	ISOMAP	TVG
	Err%	Err%
Curve of Viviani	34	**1.98**

4.3 Computing Geodesic Distances on Intersecting Manifolds

We can use the TVG to estimate geodesic distances on intersecting manifolds, which are also compared to the estimation of geodesic distance in the ambient space using Isomap. Both in TVG and Isomap, the shortest path distances are estimated using the Dijkstra algorithm. In our method, edges are connected with a distance which is equal to the Euclidean distance if and only if they are

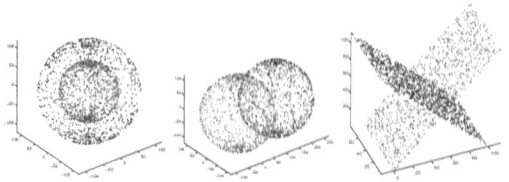

Fig. 4. Data set of the multiple manifolds used for the clustering experiments

connected on the TVG whereas, in Isomap, points are connected if they are k nearest neighbors on the Euclidean Graph. We test our method on Viviani's curve (Figure 3), which is the intersection of a sphere with a cylinder that is tangent to the sphere and passes through the center of the sphere. Table 2 shows a comparison of the two methods for Viviani's curve. The experimental results demonstrate that the TVG is also capable of efficiently traversing intersecting manifolds or manifolds with singularities.

5 Clustering Multiple Manifolds Using TVG

5.1 Clustering Synthetic Data

In this section we evaluate the effectiveness of the Tensor Voting graph in clustering multiple manifolds, and show quantitative comparisons. We compare our results to Spectral Clustering (SC [9]), Generalized PCA [14], Sparse Subspace Clustering (SSC, [5]), and Spectral Clustering on Multiple Manifolds (SMMC,[15]). Generalized PCA and SSC represent the state of the art for linear manifold clustering, and SMMC represents the state of the art in non-linear Manifold Clustering.

Data: The chosen dataset are three cases of multiple manifolds: one sphere inside another, two intersecting spheres, and two intersecting planes. In each experiment we used 2,000 randomly sampled points from two manifolds. The kernel bandwidth in spectral clustering was tested using 1, 5, 10, 15, 20, 50, 100. The sparse regularization parameter in the SSC algorithm was tested using 0.001, 0.002, 0.005, 0.01, 0.1. The best accuracy over 10 trials of the different methods is tabulated in Table 3. For the Tensor Voting graph we have computed the affinity matrix by using the suggested TVG as detailed in section (3). We then provide the affinity matrix to be used as an input for the unormalized Spectral Clustering algorithm. The output is the manifold cluster labels.

5.2 Experiment with Large Amount of Outliers

We also experiment with a large amount of outliers, adding 500 outliers to the intersecting spheres, and compare to Spectral Clustering on Multiple Manifolds. The Tensor Voting Graph method efficiently removes the outliers and achieves a clustering accuracy of 95% for the intersecting spheres data, which is significantly

Table 3. Clustering accuracy of clustering multiple manifolds

Data/Method	SC	GPCA	SSC	SMMC	TVG
Big-small spheres	100%	51%	56%	100%	100%
Two intersecting spheres	78%	50%	53%	96%	98%
Two intersecting planes	60%	85%	93%	99%	99%

better than the 60% obtained using the SMMC algorithm. [15]. The results clearly show the advantage of the TVG over competing methods, especially in the challenging cases of intersecting manifolds and in the presence of large amount of outliers.

5.3 Experiments with Real Data: Application to Motion Segmentation

For real data, we apply our method to the problem of motion segmentation. In this problem, we are given a set of feature points that are tracked through a sequence of video frames. We evaluate the TVG on the Hopkins155[1] motion database, where the goal is to segment a video sequence into multiple spatiotemporal regions corresponding to different rigid-body motions. The database includes 155 motion sequences of indoor and outdoor scenes containing two or three motions, which can be divided into three main categories: articulated, checkerboard, and traffic scenes. In this case, solving the motion segmentation problem is equivalent to a linear manifold clustering problem [14]. We first evaluate the TVG method on the 155 motion sequences without outliers, and compare it to the following methods: GPCA, SSC and SMMC. SSC and SMMC represent the state of the art methods for the 155 motion segmentation dataset. The comparison of our method in Table 4 shows that the TVG achieves similar results to SSC and SMMC, such that the results obtained by all three methods are within a close range to 100% on the entire dataset.

5.4 Clustering with Corrupted Trajectories

In realistic scenarios, the data points can often be corrupted due to the limitation of the tracker. For example, the tracker can lose track of the feature points, which leads to gross errors. We examine the robustness of our method in the presence of a large amount of corrupted trajectories and compare it to SSC. Among the state of the art methods, SSC is the only method that can handle corrupted trajectories, as it has demonstrated excellent results on both the outliers and outlier free cases. The evaluation is performed on a large amount of outliers,

---

[1] http://www.vision.jhu.edu/data/hopkins155/

Table 4. Clustering accuracy (%) of different methods on the Hopkins 155 motion segmentation database. The best are boldfaced

Method	Clustering Accuracy	Two Motions	Three Motions	All
GPCA	Mean	94.12%	77.30%	90.32%
	Median	98.84%	76.69%	96.89%
SSC	Mean	99.41%	**97.71%**	**99.03%**
	Median	**100%**	**100%**	**100%**
SMMC	Mean	**99.51%**	97.38%	**99.03%**
	Median	**100%**	99.39%	**100%**
TVG	Mean	98.60%	97.30%	98.3%
	Median	**100%**	98.48%	**100%**

as follows: for a tested sequence, we randomly select and corrupt 80% of a trajectory's entries, where the number of selected trajectories that were corrupted correspond to different percentages of the data: {20%, 25%, 30%, 35%, 40%}. For each sequence we perform ten trials. We also apply the SSC method algorithm which is designed for clustering corrupted data. The testing is performed on two sequences of two motions from the Hopkins155 dataset, 2R3RTC_g12 and cars10_g12. The comparison results are reported in Table 3. Figure 5 shows quantitative results for different levels of outlier noise for sequence cars10_g12. As can be seen, the Tensor Voting Graph consistently achieves very high clustering accuracy for different amount of outliers, such that the clustering errors degrade gracefully in their presence, and outperform SSC for all the tested noise levels.

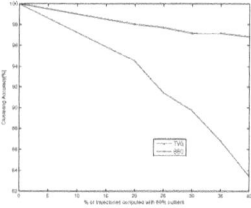

Fig. 5. Clustering accuracy comparison for the cars motion sequence with corrupted trajectories

6 Conclusion

We have presented a general method that allows operations to be performed on smooth manifolds regardless to their topology. By embedding the data into our novel TVG, we developed a hybrid local global framework which overcomes one of the main limitation of the Tensor Voting framework and is capable of efficiently learning the global features of the manifold. Qualitative results compared to the state of the art methods in manifold learning and clustering demonstrates that our method performs significantly better, especially for manifolds with complex topological structures and in the presence of outliers. Future work involves further validation on data and explicit handling of junctions and intersections.

Acknowledgments. This work was supported in part by grant DE-NA0001683 from the U.S. Department of Energy. We thank Tomer Levinboim, Dian Gong, and Xuemei Zhao for helpful discussions. We also thank the referees for their helpful suggestions.

References

1. Belkin, M., Niyogi, P.: Laplacian eigenmaps for dimensionality reduction and data representation. Neural Computation **15**(6), 1373–1396 (2003)
2. Coifman, R.R., Lafon, S., Lee, A.B., Maggioni, M., Warner, F., Zucker, S.: Geometric diffusions as a tool for harmonic analysis and structure definition of data: diffusion maps. In: Proceedings of the National Academy of Sciences, pp. 7426–7431 (2005)
3. Dijkstra, E.: Communication with an Automatic Computer. Ph.D thesis, University of Amsterdam (1959)
4. Donoho, D., Grimes, C.: Hessian eigenmaps: Locally linear embedding techniques for high dimensional data. Proceedings of the National Academy of Sciences of the United States of America **100**, 5591–5596 (2003)
5. Elhamifar, E., Vidal, R.: Sparse subspace clustering. In: CVPR, pp. 2790–2797 (2009)
6. Gong, D., Zhao, X., Medioni, G.: Robust multiple manifold structure learning. In: ICML (2012)
7. Mordohai, P., Medioni, G.: Tensor Voting: A Perceptual Organization Approach to Computer Vision and Machine Learning. Morgan & Claypool Publishers (2006)
8. Mordohai, P., Medioni, G.: Dimensionality estimation, manifold learning and function approximation using tensor voting. Journal of Machine Learning Research **11**, 411–450 (2010)
9. Ng, A., Jordan, M., Weiss, Y.: On spectral clustering: analysis and an algorithm. In: Advances in Neural Information Processing Systems, pp. 849–856 (2001)
10. Niyogi, P., Smale, S., Weinberger, S.: Finding the homology of submanifolds with high confidence from random samples. Discrete & Computational Geometry **39**(1), 419–441 (2008)
11. Roweis, S., Saul, L.: Nonlinear dimensionality reduction by locally linear embedding. SCIENCE **290**, 2323–2326 (2000)
12. Singer, A., Wu, H.: Vector diffusion maps and the connection laplacian. Communications on Pure and Applied Mathematics **65**(8), 1067–1144 (2012)
13. Tenenbaum, J., de Silva, V., Langford, J.: A Global Geometric Framework for Nonlinear Dimensionality Reduction. Science **290**(5500), 2319–2323 (2000)
14. Vidal, R., Ma, Y., Sastry, S.: Generalized principal component analysis (gpca) (2003)
15. Wang, Y., Jiang, Y., Wu, Y., Zhou, Z.: Spectral clustering on multiple manifolds. IEEE Transactions on Neural Networks **22**(7), 1149–1161 (2011)
16. Zhang, Z., Zha, H.: Principal manifolds and nonlinear dimensionality reduction via tangent space alignment. SIAM Journal on Scientific Computing **26**(1), 313–338 (2005)

Interactive Multi-label Segmentation of RGB-D Images

Julia Diebold[(✉)], Nikolaus Demmel, Caner Hazırbaş, Michael Moeller, and Daniel Cremers

Technical University of Munich, München, Germany
{julia.diebold,c.hazirbas,michael.moeller,cremers}@tum.de,
nikolaus@nikolaus-demmel.de

Abstract. We propose a novel interactive multi-label RGB-D image segmentation method by extending spatially varying color distributions [14] to additionally utilize depth information in two different ways. On the one hand, we consider the depth image as an additional data channel. On the other hand, we extend the idea of spatially varying color distributions in a plane to volumetrically varying color distributions in 3D. Furthermore, we improve the data fidelity term by locally adapting the influence of nearby scribbles around each pixel. Our approach is implemented for parallel hardware and evaluated on a novel interactive RGB-D image segmentation benchmark with pixel-accurate ground truth. We show that depth information leads to considerably more precise segmentation results. At the same time significantly less user scribbles are required for obtaining the same segmentation accuracy as without using depth clues.

Keywords: Multi-label segmentation · RGB-D images · Interactive segmentation · Spatially varying color distributions · Total variation

1 Introduction

A major challenge in computer vision is to compute accurate *image segmentations*, that is, the accurate partitioning of images into meaningful regions. Possible fields of application cover medical imaging, image editing software, object tracking and scene reconstructions. The definition of meaningful regions, however, highly depends on what application the segmentation is needed for. Thus, fully *automatic* image segmentation methods are usually tailored to very specific tasks and try to extract particular objects the methods have learned some prior knowledge about, *e.g.* indoor [5,7,23] or facade [8,26] segmentation.

One way to develop general purpose segmentation tools are *interactive* segmentation methods, where the user indicates the object to be segmented. In this work, we consider user inputs by so called *scribbles*, *i.e.* separate points the user indicated to belong to a certain object. Alternative interactive user input modalities not considered in this work include bounding boxes [12,20,27] or contours [1,3]. Due to their adaptability, interactive segmentation methods have recently attracted a lot of interest. Recent works focus on foreground/

a) Color image with scribbles   b) Depth image   c) RGB segmentation [14]   d) Proposed RGB-D segmentation

Fig. 1. **Depth information** significantly improves the segmentation result

background [3,11,12,27,28] as well as on multi-region segmentation [15,21,22], and mostly consider RGB images as input data.

Despite the segmentation constraints given by the user, accurate segmentation remains a challenging task. Extensive studies have led to significant improvements of segmentation quality in recent years [11,28]. Nevertheless, modern approaches often still fail for complex scenes, where objects with similar colors and difficult lightning conditions appear. Moreover, a good segmentation often requires a rather large number of scribbles.

Considering the recent increase and availability of depth-sensing cameras such as the Kinect, we investigate the segmentation of RGB-D images to overcome some of the aforementioned problems. We will mainly focus on the distinction of objects based on color and depth information. While some research has been done on extending interactive segmentation methods to medical imaging data (e.g. [4,13]), very little work has been done on the interactive segmentation of RGB-D images. The only other approach we found which explicitly addresses interactive multi-label RGB-D segmentation is the method by Shao et al. [22] on the semantic modeling of indoor scenes. Although this method is related to our approach in the sense that it also formulates the segmentation of RGB-D images as a variational approach, it is tailored towards the application of furniture segmentation. Therefore, the algorithm can use learned a-priori information about the objects to be segmented and the user interaction merely serves as a possible correction step for the first automatic segmentation step.

We investigate the application of interactive RGB-D multi-label segmentation and enhance the recently published work by Nieuwenhuis and Cremers [14] by including depth information. We propose to extend the spatially varying color distributions [14] to RGB-D images in two different ways: a) We consider the depth as an additional color channel. b) We enhance the spatially varying color distributions from varying in a plane to be volumetrically varying. Figure 1 d) shows an example of the improvements that can be obtained by taking the depth into account. In the above example, it is almost impossible to distinguish the radiator from the lamp (Figure 1 c), because both objects have a similar color and are close in the image plane. The proposed volumetrically varying color distributions (Figure 1 d) incorporate the depth information, which yields much more distinct color descriptions and thus better segmentation results.

2 Variational Interactive Segmentation of RGB Images

2.1 Multi-label Segmentation

Let $I: \Omega \to \mathbb{R}^d$ denote the input image, mapping the image domain $\Omega \subset \mathbb{R}^2$ to $\mathbb{R}^d$, with $d = 3$ for an RGB and $d = 4$ for an RGB-D image. Image segmentation denotes the task of partitioning the image plane into a set of n pairwise disjoint regions Ω_i: $\Omega = \bigcup_{i=1}^n \Omega_i$. The regions Ω_i can be computed by minimizing the following energy:

$$E(\Omega_1, \ldots, \Omega_n) = \frac{1}{2} \sum_{i=1}^n \operatorname{Per}_g(\Omega_i) + \lambda \sum_{i=1}^n \int_{\Omega_i} f_i(x)\, dx, \qquad (1)$$

where $\operatorname{Per}_g(\Omega_i)$ denotes the perimeter of each set Ω_i, which is minimized in order to favor segments of shorter boundaries. These boundaries are measured with either an Euclidean or an edge-dependent metric defined by the non-negative function $g: \Omega \to \mathbb{R}^+$. For example, $g(x) = \exp(-\gamma |\nabla I(x)|)$, favors the coincidence of object border and image edges. f_i denotes the appearance model and λ is a weighting parameter which regulates the influence of the second term.

2.2 Convex Relaxation

The usual strategy to address the nonconvex energy minimization problem arising from (1) is to use convex relaxation: One represents the disjoint regions Ω_i by indicator functions v_i, with $v_i(x) = 1$ if $x \in \Omega_i$ and $v_i(x) = 0$, else. Since the v_i are indicator functions, we can make use of the fact that the total variation (TV) of an indicator function is nothing but the perimeter of the set described by the functions. Hence, we can reformulate Equation (1) as

$$E(v_1, \ldots, v_n) = \frac{1}{2} \sum_{i=1}^n \int_\Omega g(x) |Dv_i(x)|\, dx + \lambda \sum_{i=1}^n \int_\Omega v_i(x) f_i(x)\, dx, \qquad (2)$$

where Dv_i is the distributional derivative of v_i. Determining the optimal segmentation can be stated as solving the minimization problem

$$(\tilde{v}_1, \ldots, \tilde{v}_n) = \arg\min_{v_i} E(v_1, \ldots, v_n) \text{ s.t. } v_i(x) \in \{0,1\},\ \sum_i v_i(x) = 1,\ \forall x. \qquad (3)$$

Since the nonconvexity of the above problem comes from the integer constraint $v_i(x) \in \{0,1\}$, a standard convex relaxation is to replace this constraint by $v_i(x) \in [0,1]$.

The key to obtain a good segmentation method based on (3) is to determine f_i that lead to a good data fidelity term guiding the segmentation. In the following, we recall the computation of the f_i motivated by maximum a-posteriori probability (MAP) estimates as suggested in [14].

2.3 Likelihood Estimation Based on User Scribbles

Let $I : \Omega \to \mathbb{R}^3$ and $u : \Omega \to \{1,..,n\}$ be a labeling, such that $\Omega_i = \{x \in \Omega \mid u(x) = i\}$. Motivated by a MAP estimate Nieuwenhuis and Cremers [14] proposed to compute the $f_i(x)$ as the negative log-likelihood of the estimated probability distribution:

$$f_i(x) = -\log \hat{\mathcal{P}}(I(x), x \mid u(x) = i). \tag{4}$$

The expression $\mathcal{P}(I(x), x \mid u(x) = i)$ denotes the joint probability density of observing a color value $I(x)$ at location x given that x is part of region Ω_i. Based on the ideas of kernel based probability estimates (cf. [25] for an overview), it can be estimated from the user scribbles by

$$\hat{\mathcal{P}}(I(x), x \mid u(x) = i) = \frac{1}{m_i} \sum_{j=1}^{m_i} k\left(\begin{array}{c} x - x_{ij} \\ I(x) - I(x_{ij}) \end{array}\right), \tag{5}$$

where $\{x_{ij}, j = 1,..,m_i\}$ is the set of user scribbles for region i, and k a suitable kernel function. The probability estimate in (5) only has to be computed for pixels $x \notin \{x_{ij}, j = 1,..,m_i\}$. For $x \in \{x_{ij}\}$ we keep the label given by the user scribble. We discuss the particular choice of k in more detail below.

3 From RGB to RGB-D Images

3.1 Pre-Processing the Depth Image

Prior to using the depth image, two pre-processing steps have to be conducted. One has to decide how to handle missing depth information and which range of the depth values to use.

Depth inpainting. Depth cameras such as the Kinect provide metric depth values in addition to color. However, depth information is usually not available for all pixels. We fill in the missing depths in a preprocessing step with an inpainting technique provided in the toolbox of Silberman et al. [24]. The implementation is a slight adaptation of the colorization proposed by Levin et al. [10]. For an example see Figure 2 b,c).

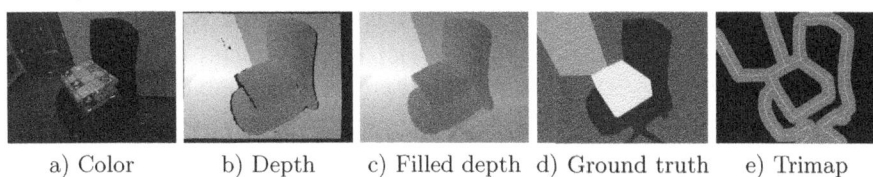

a) Color   b) Depth   c) Filled depth   d) Ground truth   e) Trimap

Fig. 2. Exemplary RGB-D input, scribbles, ground truth and trimap labeling. a) Color image with scribbles, b,c) (filled) normalized depth image, d) ground truth segmentation, e) trimap used for measuring the pixel labeling accuracy in a band surrounding the object boundaries [9]. The evaluation region is colored gray and was generated by taking a 25 pixel band surrounding the boundaries of the objects.

Normalization. For Kinect-like cameras the value range of the depth values $z(x)$ in meters is roughly $[0.5, 6]$. To be independent of physical units, for each image we normalize the actual depth range to $[0, 1]$. Similarly, to be independent of the image resolution, we normalize Ω to $[0, 1]^2$.

3.2 Depth as an Additional Color Channel

Following Nieuwenhuis and Cremers [14], we use Gaussian kernels with different bandwidths to model the joint probability distribution (5). Incorporating the depth image as an additional data channel leads to the following distribution for $\hat{\mathcal{P}}(I(x), D(x), x \mid u(x) = i)$:

$$\frac{1}{m_i} \sum_{j=1}^{m_i} \underbrace{k_{\rho_i(x)}(x - x_{ij})}_{\text{distance kernel}} \underbrace{k_\sigma(I(x) - I(x_{ij}))}_{\text{color kernel}} \underbrace{k_\tau(D(x) - D(x_{ij}))}_{\text{depth kernel}}, \qquad (6)$$

with the bandwidths ρ_i, σ and τ. Due to the comparability of their values, the color channels R, G and B are modeled by the same bandwidth σ. A separate fixed bandwidth τ is used for the depth channel. The bandwidth of the spatial kernel ρ_i on the other hand is chosen proportional to the distance to the closest scribble of label i [14]: $\rho_i(x) = \alpha \min_{j=1,\dots,m_i} |x - x_{ij}|$. Analogous ideas arise in generalized k-nearest neighbor probability density estimates (cf. [25]), where a similar dependence of the kernel variance on the distance to the nearest samples is considered. Note that although a single multivariate Gaussian could be used for modeling the probability density, this would require an estimation of the covariance matrix, e.g. on a training data set.

3.3 Active Scribbles

To overcome the fact that scribble positions are generally not distributed uniformly throughout the image, we furthermore introduce the idea of *active scribbles*. A general problem of (5) and (6) is, that the estimated distribution is heavily influenced by the total number m_i of scribbles in class i. This leads to the undesirable behavior that adding many scribbles in one particular region of the image actually reduces the likelihood of far-away-points belonging to the same class. To avoid this, we determine for each pixel x and each class i all scribbles x_{ij}, $j = 1, \dots, m_i$ that are within a radius of three times the distance to the closest scribble. We call these scribbles active. The distance is computed in 2D or 3D depending on the availability of depth. If less than 80% of the scribbles are active, we compute the probability density (6) of the active and inactive scribbles separately and combine the two by $0.8 \cdot \hat{\mathcal{P}}_a(I(x), D(x), x \mid u(x) = i) + 0.2 \cdot \hat{\mathcal{P}}_p(I(x), D(x), x \mid u(x) = i)$, where the subscripts a and p denote the estimates based on the active and passive (inactive) scribbles respectively. Otherwise we use all scribbles to compute (6).

3.4 Revised Pixel Distance by Depth Values

The main contribution of [14] was to introduce spatially varying color distributions, *i.e.* using a distance kernel in (6). The motivation for this kernel was that while an object often looks locally similar, its typical color distribution may change with the position that is considered. With the help of the distance kernel, scribbles that are close to the current position gain more influence than those that are far away. A limitation of this approach for RGB images is that the true 3D geometry cannot be represented: Due to the lack of depth information in RGB data, the method considered in [14] is a projection of a volumetrically varying color distribution onto the image plane.

The depth image allows us to compute color distributions that truly depend on the objects' position in space and thus lead to more distinct color descriptions. For illustration purposes Figure 3 a,b) considers a 2d color image. Pixels close in the image are not necessarily close in the 3-dimensional space as we can see in Figure 3 c,d). To better reflect the real object geometry, we therefore improve the computation of the distance kernel $k_{\rho_i(x)}(x - x_{ij})$ by using the depth information.

Back-Projection. To perform the distance computation in the 3-dimensional space, the 3-dimensional pixel position X has to be computed from the pixel coordinates x and the normalized depth value $D(x)$. While a physically correct back-projection would be perspective and therefore dependent on the intrinsic parameters of the camera, we found a planar back-projection that simply uses $D(x)$ as the third coordinate to be the better choice for two reasons: It not only compared favorable in our numerical experiments but also is easier to compute as it does not require the knowledge of camera parameters.

Thus, in Equation (6), instead of evaluating the distance kernel $k_{\rho_i(x)}(x - x_{ij})$ at $x \in [0,1]^2$ we incorporate the depth as a third dimension and evaluate the distance kernel at $X = (x, D(x))^\top$:

$$k_{\rho_i(X)}(X - X_{ij}) \quad \text{with} \quad \rho_i(X) = \alpha \min_{j=1,..,m_i} |X - X_{ij}|. \tag{7}$$

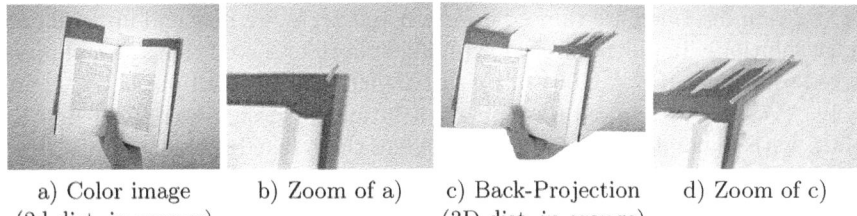

a) Color image   b) Zoom of a)   c) Back-Projection   d) Zoom of c)
(2d dist. in orange)   (3D dist. in orange)

Fig. 3. Recovering the scene geometry with depth information. Illustration of the distance in the 2-dimensional color image compared to the real distance in the 3-dimensional space. The incorporation of depth information in the computation of the distance kernel allows to capture the real object geometry.

3.5 The Novel Formulation

Combining the ideas of Sections 3.2 and 3.4 we propose the following appearance model for RGB-D images

$$f_i(x) = -\log \hat{\mathcal{P}}(I(x), D(x), x \mid u(x) = i), \qquad (8)$$

with

$$\hat{\mathcal{P}}(I(x), D(x), x \mid u(x) = i)$$
$$= \frac{1}{m_i} \sum_{j=1}^{m_i} \underbrace{k_{\rho_i(X)}(X - X_{ij})}_{\text{distance kernel}} \underbrace{k_\sigma(I(x) - I(x_{ij}))}_{\text{color kernel}} \underbrace{k_\tau(D(x) - D(x_{ij}))}_{\text{depth kernel}}. \qquad (9)$$

Here $\{x_{ij}, j = 1, ..., m_i\}$ denotes the set of user scribbles for region i, X the three-dimensional position $X = (x, D(x))^\top \in [0,1]^3$ and $\rho_i(X) = \alpha \min_j |X - X_{ij}|$, σ and τ denote the kernel bandwidths. The effect of both ways of incorporating depth information into the segmentation framework will be studied in detail in the experimental results (Section 5).

Finally, let us mention that the two ways the depth information is utilized in the above model is actually equivalent to using a single Gaussian kernel for the depth information. The single kernel would have a bandwidth that contains a spatially varying part as well as a constant part. Since the latter is rather difficult to interpret, we decided to motivate the proposed approach from two different perspectives. Thus, the depth information appears in our proposed model twice.

4 Implementation

To find the globally optimal solution to this relaxed convex optimization problem, we employ the primal-dual algorithm published in [6,16,17]. It consists of updating a primal and a dual variable in an alternating fashion. The update of each variable decouples for each pixel such that the approach can easily be parallelized and implemented on graphics hardware.

Since we are solving the relaxed problem, there may be pixels x at which $v_i(x)$ take on intermediate values between 0 and 1, i.e. we may end up with non-binary solutions. In our numerical experiments, we observed that the computed relaxed solutions $v_i(x) < 0.001$ or $v_i(x) > 0.999$ for 98% of all pixels $x \in \Omega$ and $i = 1, \ldots, n$. In order to obtain a binary solution, we assign each pixel x to the label L with maximum value after optimizing the relaxed problem.

5 Experimental Results

In this section we demonstrate the effectiveness of all proposed RGB-D image adaptions in several numerical experiments. The numerical study is divided into three parts: First, we discuss the data used for the numerical experiments.

Second, we compare RGB to RGB-D segmentation and demonstrate that the segmentation accuracy is improved by the additional depth information. Alternatively, less user scribbles are required by the RGB-D segmentation method to obtain the same accuracy as an RGB method. In a third part we demonstrate that not just one but all of our proposed extensions improve the segmentation results in the sense that the addition of each component individually yields an improvement in segmentation quality.

5.1 Experimental Data

As extensively discussed in [21], not every benchmark is suited for testing interactive segmentation. Typical interactive segmentation benchmarks (such as the iCoseg benchmark [2] for foreground/background segmentation or the IcgBench dataset [21] for multi-label segmentation) do not provide RGB-D data, and hence could not be used for our experiments. Popular RGB-D benchmarks such as the NYUv2 dataset [24] are not suitable for interactive segmentation since the scenes are typically composed of very many small objects.

Therefore, we chose the Object Segmentation Database (OSD) [18] as the starting point for numerical experiments. We, however, found that the images contained in the OSD were not challenging enough. They all have the same background and same colors. Furthermore, the objects are relatively small compared to the image size and the given depth. Hence, we decided to use 12 images from the OSD along with 16 images we captured ourselves using an RGB-D sensor. The new images were intentionally taken with challenging color and texture similarities between different objects. For all 28 images, we fixed the scribbles and manually created an accurate ground truth labeling.[1] An example is given in Figure 2.

5.2 Depth Information Is Crucial

We use the aforementioned image data set to compare our algorithm (using $\lambda = 10$, $\gamma = 5$, $\alpha = 1000$, $\sigma = 0.05$, $\tau = 0.2$ for all experiments) to the results obtained by Santner et al. [21] and Nieuwenhuis and Cremers [14]. Due to the similarity of our approach with the one in [14], we used the same parameters (without the additional depth information) for the implementation of [14]. For the framework in [21], we took the parameters that were mentioned to be the best general purpose choice.[2] Using exactly the same scribbles (see Fig. 4 a) for all three interactive segmentation methods, we obtain the results shown in Figure 4 c-e).

We have to mention that our comparison is unfair in the sense that the other methods do not make use of the depth information. However, as we could not

---

[1] Our framework as well as the RGB-D images, the scribbles and the ground truth labelings are publicly available on our website: vision.in.tum.de/data/software

[2] CIELab color space, LBP features with a patch size of 16 and a radius of 3, Random Forests with 200 trees, 750 iterations, $\lambda = 0.2$ and $\alpha = 15$.

find other suitable interactive RGB-D segmentation methods, we chose this comparison to illustrate the importance of depth information for image segmentation tasks.

For images with challenging color and lighting conditions, like *e.g.* in Figure 4 first row, an RGB based method can hardly find the correct segmentation of the scene. The depth channel, however, provides essential information regarding the spatial relation between the pixels in the image. Thus, the incorporation of the depth image results in significant improvements of the segmentation quality over the RGB based methods. For images in which the depth channel does not provide additional information, such as the image in the bottom row of Figure 4, the proposed method yields the same result as [14], as expected.

Another benefit which comes from the additional depth information is that less user scribbles are required compared to an RGB based segmentation method. Figure 5 exemplary illustrates this behavior: Running our method with the scribbles shown in Figure 5 d) we obtain the segmentation result in e). We incrementally

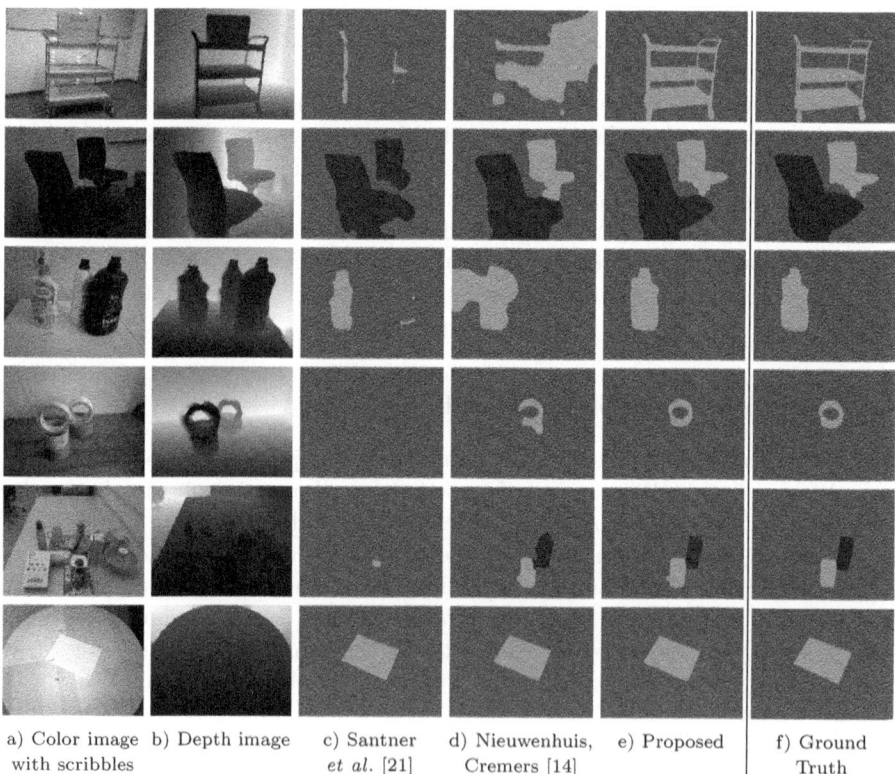

a) Color image with scribbles   b) Depth image   c) Santner *et al.* [21]   d) Nieuwenhuis, Cremers [14]   e) Proposed   f) Ground Truth

Fig. 4. Depth information improves the segmentation. The scribbled RGB-D input data is shown in the columns a,b). Columns c-e) compare the proposed RGB-D segmentation to the RGB segmentations of [14,21].

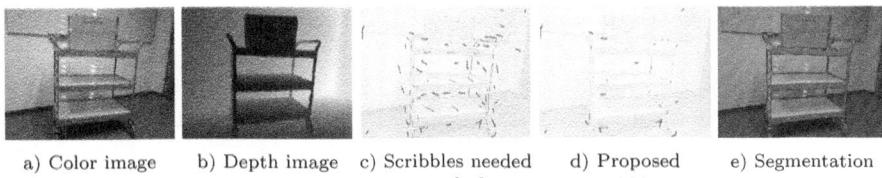

a) Color image   b) Depth image   c) Scribbles needed with [14]   d) Proposed scribbles   e) Segmentation result

Fig. 5. Depth yields less user input. The depth information provides valuable information which reduces the required user input. To retrieve a similar result as in e), the user needs to place more scribbles with [14] c) than with the proposed volumetrically varying color distributions d).

add scribbles in order to obtain a similar result with [14], see Figure 5 c). Due to the strong color similarity between foreground and background, the RGB based method requires significantly more user scribbles to obtain a similar result.

Finally, let us mention that the runtime of our method is – same as [14,21] – around one second on 640×480 images. The major computational time is needed for the optimization which is independent of our proposed components.

5.3 Impact of the Proposed Components

To quantify the results on our benchmark dataset, we compute the dice-scores suggested in [14,21] on the regular ground truth as well as on a trimap surrounding the object boundaries: Let S denote the labeling obtained for an image, GT the respective ground truth labeling. Then the dice-score is computed as

$$dice\,(S) = \frac{1}{n} \sum_{i=1}^{n} \frac{2\,|GT_i \cap S_i|}{|GT_i| + |S_i|}, \tag{10}$$

where the index i denotes the label i and $|\cdot|$ the area of a segment.

Table 1 shows the dice scores averaged over all images obtained by [21], [14], and a step by step addition of the proposed algorithm components. The scores not only give us the possibility of quantitatively evaluating the results obtained by the different methods, but also allow to study the effect of each of the proposed

Input	Segmentation method	Reg. GT	Trimap
RGB	Santner et al. [21]	72.56	67.69
RGB	Nieuwenhuis and Cremers [14] (Figure 6 b)	87.09	86.17
RGB	[14] with proposed AS (2D) (Figure 6 c)	87.79	88.40
RGB-D	[14] + AS (3D) + Depth for 3D distance (Figure 6 d)	91.51	93.63
RGB-D	[14] + AS (3D) + Depth as color channel (Figure 6 e)	92.93	93.07
RGB-D	Combination of all proposed components (Figure 6 f)	**93.70**	**94.84**

Table 1. The proposed method outperforms the previous ones. The dice scores are compared by means of the regular ground truth segmentations as well as the trimap width of 25 (compare Figure 2). The usage of active scribbles is abbreviated by 'AS'.

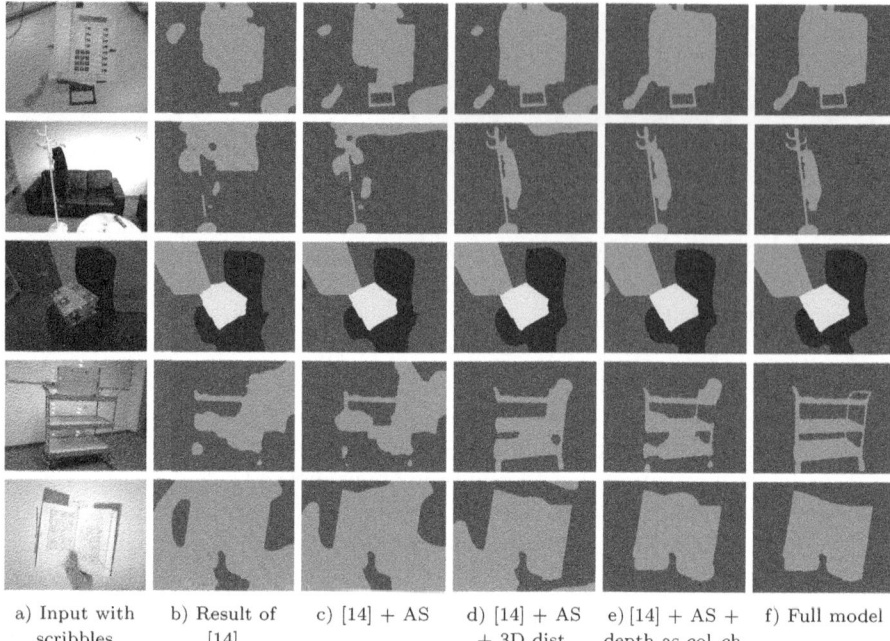

Fig. 6. Each of the proposed components improves the segmentation. We compare the segmentations obtained with different components of the proposed method. The usage of active scribbles is abbreviated by 'AS'. f) The combination of all components: Active scribbles, depth for 3D distance and depth as an additional color channel leads to the best result.

a) Input with scribbles   b) Result of [14]   c) [14] + AS   d) [14] + AS + 3D dist.   e) [14] + AS + depth as col. ch.   f) Full model

extensions of [14], namely using active scribbles, using depth as an additional data channel and using depth for the 3D distance.

It is interesting to see that the usage of active scribbles – which does not require any depth information – already improves the score on the regular ground truth by 0.7% and on the trimap by 2.2%. Additionally including the depth for either the 3D distance or as an additional color channel again improves the score. The best results are obtained when combining all three components as we can see in the last row of Table 1. To visualize the results from Table 1, Figure 6 shows a qualitative comparison of the different components. As we can see, in each column, from left to right the result improves.

6 Conclusion

We proposed a powerful extension of the spatially varying color distributions [14]. Our contributions include the idea of active scribbles to overcome the problem of non-uniformly distributed user scribbles. Furthermore, we improve the estimation of the data fidelity term by incorporating the depth as an additional color channel as well as using it to construct volumetrically varying color distributions in 3D. We have demonstrated that each of the proposed components contributes separately and improves the segmentation results. Due to the additional depth information, reliable segmentations are obtained with significantly less user input. For future work, one could also use a regularization that takes into account the geometry of the 3D surface as suggested in [19].

References

1. Arbelaez, P., Maire, M., Fowlkes, C.C., Malik, J.: From contours to regions: an empirical evaluation. In: CVPR (2009)
2. Batra, D., Kowdle, A., Parikh, D., Luo, J., Chen, T.: iCoseg: interactive co-segmentation with intelligent scribble guidance. In: CVPR (2010)
3. Blake, A., Rother, C., Brown, M., Perez, P., Torr, P.: Interactive image segmentation using an adaptive GMMRF model. In: Pajdla, T., Matas, J.G. (eds.) ECCV 2004. LNCS, vol. 3021, pp. 428–441. Springer, Heidelberg (2004)
4. Boykov, Y.Y., Jolly, M.-P.: Interactive graph cuts for optimal boundary & region segmentation of objects in ND images. In: ICCV (2001)
5. Couprie, C., Farabet, C., Najman, L., LeCun, Y.: Indoor semantic segmentation using depth information. In: ICLR (2013)
6. Esser, E., Zhang, X., Chan, T.F.: A general framework for a class of first order primal-dual algorithms for convex optimization in imaging science. SIIMS (2010)
7. Hermans, A., Floros, G., Leibe, B.: Dense 3D semantic mapping of indoor scenes from RGB-D images. In: ICRA (2014)
8. Hernandez, J. Marcotegui, B.: Morphological segmentation of building facade images. In: ICIP (2009)
9. Kohli, P., Ladicky, L., Torr, P.H.S.: Robust higher order potentials for enforcing label consistency. IJCV (2009)
10. Levin, A., Lischinski, D., Weiss, Y.: Colorization using optimization. In: TOG (2004)
11. Li, Y., Sun, J., Tang, C.-K., Shum, H.-Y.: Lazy snapping. TOG (2004)
12. Liu, D., Pulli, K., Shapiro, L.G., Xiong, Y.: Fast interactive image segmentation by discriminative clustering. In: MCMC (2010)
13. Lombaert, H., Sun, Y., Grady, L., Xu, C.: A multilevel banded graph cuts method for fast image segmentation. In: ICCV (2005)
14. Nieuwenhuis, C., Cremers, D.: Spatially varying color distributions for interactive multilabel segmentation. PAMI (2013)
15. Nieuwenhuis, C., Hawe, S., Kleinsteuber, M., Cremers, D.: Co-sparse textural similarity for interactive segmentation. In: Fleet, D., Pajdla, T., Schiele, B., Tuytelaars, T. (eds.) ECCV 2014, Part VI. LNCS, vol. 8694, pp. 285–301. Springer, Heidelberg (2014)
16. Pock, T., Chambolle, A.: Diagonal preconditioning for first order primal-dual algorithms in convex optimization. In: ICCV (2011)
17. Pock, T., Cremers, D., Bischof, H., Chambolle, A.: An algorithm for minimizing the mumford-shah functional. In: ICCV (2009)
18. Richtsfeld, A., Morwald, T., Prankl, J., Zillich, M., Vincze, M.: Segmentation of unknown objects in indoor environments. In: IROS (2012)

19. Rosman, G., Bronstein, A.M., Bronstein, M.M., Tai, X.-C., Kimmel, R.: Group-valued regularization for analysis of articulated motion. In: Fusiello, A., Murino, V., Cucchiara, R. (eds.) ECCV 2012 Ws/Demos, Part I. LNCS, vol. 7583, pp. 52–62. Springer, Heidelberg (2012)
20. Rother, C., Kolmogorov, V., Blake, A.: Grabcut: interactive foreground extraction using iterated graph cuts. In: TOG (2004)
21. Santner, J., Pock, T., Bischof, H.: Interactive multi-label segmentation. In: Kimmel, R., Klette, R., Sugimoto, A. (eds.) ACCV 2010, Part I. LNCS, vol. 6492, pp. 397–410. Springer, Heidelberg (2011)
22. Shao, T., Xu, W., Zhou, K., Wang, J., Li, D., Guo, B.: An interactive approach to semantic modeling of indoor scenes with an rgbd camera. TOG (2012)
23. Silberman, N., Fergus, R.: Indoor scene segmentation using a structured light sensor. In: ICCV (2011)
24. Silberman, N., Hoiem, D., Kohli, P., Fergus, R.: Indoor segmentation and support inference from RGBD images. In: Fitzgibbon, A., Lazebnik, S., Perona, P., Sato, Y., Schmid, C. (eds.) ECCV 2012, Part V. LNCS, vol. 7576, pp. 746–760. Springer, Heidelberg (2012)
25. Silverman, B.: Density estimation for statistics and data analysis. Chapman and Hall Ltd (1986)
26. Teboul, O., Simon, L., Koutsourakis, P., Paragios, N.: Segmentation of building facades using procedural shape priors. In: CVPR (2010)
27. Vicente, S., Kolmogorov, V., Rother, C.: Joint optimization of segmentation and appearance models. In: ICCV (2009)
28. Wang, J.: Discriminative gaussian mixtures for interactive image segmentation. In: ICASSP (2007)

Fast Minimization of Region-Based Active Contours Using the Shape Hessian of the Energy

Günay Doğan[✉]

Theiss Research, National Institute of Standards and Technology,
Gaithersburg, MD 20899-8990, USA
gunay.dogan@nist.gov

Abstract. We propose a novel shape optimization algorithm for region-based active contour models. Region-based active contours are preferred for many segmentation problems, because they incorporate more global information by aggregating cues or statistics over the distinct regions defined by the contour configuration. This makes them effective in a diverse array of segmentation scenarios, also more robust to contour initializations. Unfortunately they are also more expensive computationally, because a significant part of the optimization involves repeated integrations of the image features over the regions through the many iterations of the contour updates. Accordingly, we aim to decrease the overall computational cost of region-based active contours by reducing the cost of an individual iteration, and the total number of iterations. To this end, we first develop a Lagrangian curve representation that is spatially adaptive and economical in terms of the number of nodes used. Then we perform the shape sensitivity analysis of the general form of the region-based segmentation energy. In particular, we compute the second variation or the shape Hessian of the energy, and we use this to compute fast descent directions for the contours to significantly reduce the computational cost. Our implementation builds on a finite element discretization of the whole framework, including the contours. This results in efficient velocity computations in linear time with respect to the number of contour nodes.

1 Introduction

Image segmentation is the problem of partitioning a given image into distinct homogeneous regions with respect to image values or statistics. Thus, it is often formulated as the problem of finding the boundaries that define the best such partition: we would like each region to be as uniform as possible within itself, but as different as possible from its neighbors across the boundaries. For 2d images, this leads to a shape optimization problem, in which we try to compute the set of optimal curves minimizing a shape energy encoding this expectation of a good partition. Typically, one solves such problems by starting with a set of suboptimal initial curves (or guesses), and updating or deforming the curves until they reach an optimal configuration. In this paper, we propose to use efficient Lagrangian representations for the curves, and building on these representations, we develop a novel optimization algorithm that reaches the minima fast by exploiting the second order sensitivity (Hessian) of the shape energy.

Our target is region-based shape energies used for image segmentation. Note that the characteristics of each region in a segmentation formulation can be conveniently quantified by the statistics of the image features in the region [4]. The statistics computations can often be expressed as various integrals over the regions. This results in shape energies composed of such integrals. Often the integrands of these integrals vary spatially, but also depend on other integrals over these regions. An example is the following energy (1) proposed by Chan and Vese in [2]. It aims to find a partitioning of the image domain into a foreground region Ω_1 and a background region Ω_2 (inside and outside the boundary curve Γ respectively), each with distinct averages c_1, c_2 of the image intensity $I(x)$ respectively.

$$J(\Gamma) = \mu \int_\Gamma d\Gamma + \frac{1}{2} \sum_{i=1,2} \int_{\Omega_i} (I(x)-c_i)^2 dx, \quad \mu > 0, \quad c_i = \frac{1}{|\Omega_i|} \int_{\Omega_i} I(x) dx. \quad (1)$$

More general approaches to incorporating statistics into the shape optimization formulation are described in [4,10]. One can develop a more general statistical formulation, by considering a Bayesian interpretation of the estimation problem and trying to maximize the a posteriori probability $p(\{\Omega_1, \Omega_2\}|I)$, namely the likelihood of having a certain partitioning $\{\Omega_1, \Omega_2\}$ given the image I (multiple phases or regions $\{\Omega_i\}_{i=1}^m$ are possible, but not considered in this paper to simplify the presentation). We can write $p(\{\Omega_1, \Omega_2\}|I) \propto p(I|\{\Omega_1, \Omega_2\}) p(\{\Omega_1, \Omega_2\})$ and separate the a priori shape information $p(\{\Omega_1, \Omega_2\})$ from image-based cues encoded in $p(I|\{\Omega_1, \Omega_2\})$. A common example of the a priori shape term would be $p(\{\Omega_1, \Omega_2\}) \propto e^{-\mu|\Gamma|}$. Assuming no correlation between labelings of regions and parametric probability distributions with parameters θ_1, θ_2, one can simplify the conditional probability:
$p(I|\{\Omega_1, \Omega_2\}) = p(I|\Omega_1)p(I|\Omega_2) = p(I|\theta_1)p(I|\theta_2), \quad \theta_1 = \theta(\Omega_1), \theta_2 = \theta(\Omega_2).$
Maximizing the probability $p(\{\Omega_1, \Omega_2\}|I)$ is equivalent to minimizing its negative logarithm. Thus we end up with the following energy

$$J(\Gamma) = \mu \int_\Gamma d\Gamma - \int_{\Omega_1} \log p(I(x)|\theta_1) dx - \int_{\Omega_2} \log p(I(x)|\theta_2) dx. \quad (2)$$

The parameters θ_i depend on the form of the probability density function and often involve integrals over the regions Ω_i. For example, the Gaussian probability density function has the form $p_i(s) = p(s|\mu_i, \sigma_i) = \frac{1}{\sqrt{2\pi\sigma_i^2}} \exp\left(-\frac{(s-c_i)^2}{2\sigma_i^2}\right)$, where the parameters c_i, σ_i are computed by the integrals $c_i = \frac{1}{|\Omega_i|} \int_{\Omega_i} I(x) dx$, $\sigma_i^2 = \frac{1}{|\Omega_i|} \int_{\Omega_i} (I(x) - c_i)^2 dx$. It is not hard to see that we can concoct a diverse collection of statistical formulations where shape energies with region integrals play a central role. Thus, shape energies with integral parameters have significant use for image segmentation, and the prototype form for energies with integrals is

$$E(\Omega) = \int_\Omega g(x, \theta_w(\Omega)) dx, \quad \theta_w(\Omega) = \int_\Omega w(x) dx, \quad (3)$$

or one whose weight function g may depend on multiple such integrals

$$E(\Omega) = \int_\Omega g(x, \theta_{w_1}(\Omega), \ldots, \theta_{w_m}(\Omega))dx, \qquad \theta_{w_i}(\Omega) = \int_\Omega w_i(x)dx. \quad (4)$$

Combining (3), (4) for multiple regions leads to

$$J(\Gamma) = \mu \int_\Gamma d\Gamma + E(\Omega_1) + E(\Omega_2), \qquad \left(\text{or} \quad J(\Gamma) = \mu \int_\Gamma d\Gamma + \sum_{i=1}^{n_\Omega} E(\Omega_i)\right) \quad (5)$$

for background/foreground (or multi-region) segmentation energies. The building blocks (3), (4) and the resulting energy (5) will be the main focus of this paper. We will perform the shape sensitivity analysis for (3), (4), (5) and use it to develop a fast shape optimization algorithm to compute the optimal boundaries. Our first contribution in the shape sensitivity analysis is the computation of the shape Hessian of region energies (3), (4), (5) (the first shape derivative was computed in [1]). The explicit formula for the shape Hessian enables us to compute superior descent directions to perform the shape optimization effectively. Our second contribution is the efficient discretization of the velocity equations and descent process on a foundation of spatially adaptive Lagrangian curves using the finite element method. This results in linear time complexity with respect to the number of curve nodes, except for the region integrals, which require traversing the image pixels. We demonstrate the effectiveness of our algorithm using the Chan-Vese model (1) as a test case.

2 Differential Geometry and Shape Derivatives

We use the concept of shape derivatives to understand the change in the energy induced by a given velocity field V. Once we have the means to evaluate how any given velocity V affects the energy, we will be able to choose from the space of admissible velocities the particular velocity that decreases the energy for a given curve Γ. We define the *shape derivative* of an energy $J(\Gamma)$ at Γ with respect to velocity field V as the limit $dJ(\Gamma; V) = \lim_{t \to 0} \frac{1}{t}(J(\Gamma_t) - J(\Gamma))$, where $\Gamma_t = \{x(t, X) : X \in \Gamma\}$ is the deformation of Γ by V via the ordinary differential equation $\frac{dx}{dt} = V(x(t))$, $x(0) = X$. Shape derivative of energies $J(\Omega)$ depending on domains or regions Ω are defined similarly. We refer to the book [5] for more information on shape derivatives.

For a domain-dependent function $\varphi(\Omega)$, the *material derivative* $\dot\varphi(\Omega; V)$ and the *shape derivative* $\varphi'(\Omega; V)$ at Ω in direction V are defined as follows [11, Def.2.85,2.88]

$$\dot\varphi(\Omega; V) = \lim_{t\to 0} \tfrac{1}{t}\big(\varphi(x(t, \cdot), \Omega_t) - \varphi(\cdot, \Omega_0)\big), \qquad \varphi'(\Omega; V) = \dot\varphi(\Omega; V) - \nabla\varphi \cdot V.$$

Before we start deriving the shape derivatives of the energies (3), (4), (5), we need some definitions and concepts from differential geometry. We denote the outer unit normal, the scalar curvature and the curvature vector of a curve $\Gamma \in C^2$ by n, κ, $\boldsymbol{\kappa}(:= \kappa n)$ respectively. For a given function $f \in C^2(\mathcal{D})$ on

the image domain $\mathcal{D}$, we define tangential gradient $\nabla_\Gamma f$ and tangential Laplacian $\Delta_\Gamma f$:
$$\nabla_\Gamma f = (\nabla f - \partial_n f n)|_\Gamma, \quad \Delta_\Gamma f = \left(\Delta f - n \cdot D^2 f \cdot n - \kappa \partial_n f\right)\big|_\Gamma.$$
Now we can pursue the shape derivatives of the shape energies (1), (3), (4), (5).

Lemma 1 ([5]). *The shape derivative of curve length $J(\Gamma) = |\Gamma| = \int_\Gamma d\Gamma$ with respect to velocity field $\boldsymbol{V}$ is $dJ(\Gamma; \boldsymbol{V}) = \int_\Gamma \kappa V d\Gamma$, where $V = \boldsymbol{V} \cdot n$ is the normal component of the vector velocity.*

Theorem 1 ([11, Sect.2.31,2.33]). *Let $\phi = \phi(x, \Omega), \psi = \psi(x, \Gamma)$ be given so that the shape derivatives $\phi' = \phi'(\Omega; \boldsymbol{V}), \psi' = \psi'(\Gamma; \boldsymbol{V})$ exist. Then the shape energies $J_1(\Omega) = \int_\Omega \phi(x, \Omega) dx, J_2(\Gamma) = \int_\Gamma \psi(x, \Gamma) d\Gamma$ are shape differentiable and we have*
$$dJ_1(\Omega; \boldsymbol{V}) = \int_\Omega \phi' dx + \int_\Gamma \phi V d\Gamma, \quad dJ_2(\Gamma; \boldsymbol{V}) = \int_\Gamma (\psi' + (\psi\kappa + \partial_n \psi) V) d\Gamma. \quad (6)$$

As the shape derivative $dJ(\Gamma; \boldsymbol{V})$ depends only on $V = \boldsymbol{V} \cdot n$, the normal component of the velocity [5], we use V (to imply $\boldsymbol{V} = Vn$) in our derivations from now on and assume a normal extension, i.e. $\frac{\partial V}{\partial n} = 0$, if needed.

Now using scalar velocity fields V, W (recall $\boldsymbol{V} = Vn, \boldsymbol{W} = Wn$) to perturb Ω and we define the second shape derivative of $J(\Omega), \varphi(\Omega)$ as follows [5]
$$d^2 J(\Omega; V, W) = d\left(dJ(\Omega; V)\right)(\Omega; W), \quad \varphi''(\Omega; V, W) = (\varphi(\Omega; V))'(\Omega; W).$$

Lemma 2 ([5,8]). *The second shape derivative of curve length $J(\Gamma) = |\Gamma| = \int_\Gamma d\Gamma$ with respect to velocity fields V, W is $d^2 J(\Gamma; V, W) = \int_\Gamma \nabla_\Gamma V \cdot \nabla_\Gamma W d\Gamma$.*

Theorem 2. *Let $\phi = \phi(x, \Omega)$ be given so that the first and the second shape derivatives $\phi'_V = \phi'(\Omega; V), \phi'' = \phi''(\Omega; V, W)$ exist. Then the second shape derivative of the domain energy $J(\Omega) = \int_\Omega \phi(x, \Omega) dx$ with respect to velocities V, W is given by*
$$d^2 J(\Omega; V, W) = \int_\Omega \phi'' dx + \int_\Gamma (\phi'_W V + \phi'_V W) dS + \int_\Gamma (\partial_n \phi + \kappa \phi) VW d\Gamma. \quad (7)$$

Proof. For $J(\Omega) = \int_\Omega \phi(x, \Omega) dx$, the first shape derivative at Ω in direction V is
$$dJ(\Omega; V) = J_1(\Omega) + J_2(\Gamma) = \int_\Omega \phi'(\Omega; V) dx + \int_\Gamma \phi V d\Gamma, \text{ using Theorem 1.}$$
We can continue to compute
$$dJ_2(\Gamma; W) = \int_\Gamma \phi'(\Omega; W) V d\Gamma + \int_\Gamma (\partial_n \phi V + \phi V \kappa) W d\Gamma,$$
$$dJ_1(\Omega; W) = \int_\Omega \phi''(\Omega; V, W) dx + \int_\Gamma \phi'(\Omega; V) W d\Gamma.$$
which can be summed into $d^2 J(\Omega; V, W) = dJ_1(\Omega; W) + dJ_2(\Gamma; W)$.

Proposition 1. *The first shape derivative of the shape energy (3) at Ω with respect to velocity V is given by $dJ(\Omega; V) = \int_\Gamma (g(x, \theta_w(\Omega)) + \theta_{g_p}(\Omega) w(x)) V d\Gamma$ [1].*

The second shape derivative of (3) with respect to velocities V, W is given by

$$d^2 J(\Omega; V, W) = \int_\Gamma \left(\partial_n g + \theta_{g_p} \partial_n w + \kappa(g + \theta_{g_p} w) \right) VW d\Gamma$$

$$+ \int_\Gamma g_p V d\Gamma \int_\Gamma wW d\Gamma + \int_\Gamma wV d\Gamma \int_\Gamma g_p W d\Gamma + \theta_{g_{pp}} \int_\Gamma wV d\Gamma \int_\Gamma wW d\Gamma,$$

We use the short notation for the functions $g = g(x, \theta_w(\Omega))$, $w = w(x)$, and g_p, g_{pp} denote the derivatives of $g(x, \theta_w(\Omega))$ with respect to its second variable. $\theta_{g_p}, \theta_{g_{pp}}$ are the integrals of g_p, g_{pp} over the domain Ω.

Proof. Let $\phi(x, \Omega) = g(x, \theta_w(\Omega))$ in Theorem 1, and calculate $\phi'(\Omega; V)$.
$\phi'(\Omega; V) = g_p(x, \theta_w)\theta'_w = g_p(x, \theta_w) \int_\Gamma w(y) V d\Gamma(y)$.   (using Thm.1 on θ_w)
We substitute $\phi'(\Omega; V)$ in the form (6) for $dJ(\Omega; V)$
$dJ(\Omega; V) = \int_\Omega g_p(x, \theta_w) \left(\int_\Gamma w(y) V d\Gamma(y) \right) dx + \int_\Gamma g(x, \theta_w) V d\Gamma$.
Since $\theta_{g_p} = \int_\Omega g_p(x, \theta_w) dx$, we can exchange the order of integration and obtain
$dJ(\Omega; V) = \int_\Gamma \left(g(x, \theta_w) + \theta_{g_p} w(x) \right) V d\Gamma$.
For the second shape derivative, we use Theorem 2. Compute $\phi'' = \phi''(\Omega; V, W)$,
$\phi'' = (g_p)' \int_\Gamma w(y) V d\Gamma + g_p \left(\int_\Gamma w(y) V d\Gamma \right)'$ (we use Thm.1)
$\phi'' = g_{pp} \int_\Gamma w(z) V d\Gamma(z) \int_\Gamma w(y) W d\Gamma(y) + g_p \int_\Omega (\partial_n w(y) + \kappa w(y)) VW d\Gamma$.
We substitute in (7) and reorganize the various terms.

We do not derive the second shape derivative of the energy (4) because of limited space in this paper. It follows the same steps of the derivation of the energy (3). Its first derivative can be found in [1]. The first shape derivative of the Chan-Vese energy (1) is given by the following proposition ([2]).

Proposition 2. *The first shape derivative of the energy (1) at Γ with respect to V is*

$$dJ(\Gamma; V) = \int_\Gamma (\mu\kappa + f(\Gamma)) V d\Gamma = \int_\Gamma (\mu\kappa + (c_2 - c_1)(I(x) - \frac{1}{2}(c_1 + c_2))) V d\Gamma. \quad (8)$$

Proposition 3. *The second shape derivative of energy (1) at Γ with respect to V, W is*

$$d^2 J(\Gamma; V, W) = \mu \int_\Gamma \nabla_\Gamma V \cdot \nabla_\Gamma W d\Gamma + \int_\Gamma \beta(x, \Gamma) VW d\Gamma$$

$$- \sum_{i=1,2} \frac{1}{|\Omega_i|} \int_\Gamma (I(x) - c_i) V d\Gamma \int_\Gamma (I(x) - c_i) W d\Gamma,$$

where $\beta(x, \Gamma) = \frac{1}{2}(c_2 - c_1) \left((I - \frac{c_1 + c_2}{2})\kappa + \partial_n I \right)$. *Or more concisely:*

$$d^2 J(\Gamma; V, W) = \mu \langle \nabla_\Gamma V, \nabla_\Gamma W \rangle + \langle \beta V, W \rangle - S_1(V) S_1(W) - S_2(V) S_2(W), \quad (9)$$

where $\langle \cdot, \cdot \rangle$ denotes the L^2 scalar product $\langle f, g \rangle = \int_\Gamma f g d\Gamma$, and $S_i(V)$, is the boundary integral $S_i(V) = |\Omega_i|^{-1/2} \int_\Gamma (I(x) - c_i) V d\Gamma$, $i = 1, 2$.

Proof. The proof follows from Lemma 2 & Prop.1 with $g(x, p_1, p_2) = \frac{1}{2} \left(I(x) - \frac{p_1}{p_2} \right)^2$ substituted in $J(\Gamma) = \mu \int_\Gamma d\Gamma + \sum_{i=1,2} \int_{\Omega_i} g(x, \theta_I(\Omega_i), \theta_1(\Omega_i)) dx$.

3 The Minimization Algorithm

In this section, we use the shape derivatives to devise an iterative minimization algorithm for the energies (1), (5). The algorithm starts with a given initial curve Γ_0, computes a descent velocity V, deforms the curve with the descent velocity V, repeats this process until convergence, at which point the curve should be at a minimum of the energy, and a valid segmentation should be attained. Thus the energy minimization procedure involves updating the current curve Γ^k at each iteration to obtain the next curve Γ^{k+1} with the descent velocity $V (= Vn)$ by

$$X^{k+1} = X^k + \tau V, \quad \forall X^k \in \Gamma^k, \tag{10}$$

where $\tau > 0$ is a step size parameter (or time step for the curve evolution). Computing the descent velocity requires knowing the normal n and the curvature κ of the curve. Thus we use three additional identities $\boldsymbol{\kappa} = -\Delta_\Gamma X$, $\boldsymbol{\kappa} = \kappa \cdot n$, $V = Vn$, to relate the curve points X, the mean curvature κ, the vector curvature $\boldsymbol{\kappa}$, the scalar velocity V, finally the vector velocity V. Let us now state the outline of the minimization algorithm, which will consist of the following steps:

choose an initial curve Γ_0
repeat
    mark the pixels in the domains Ω_1, Ω_2
    compute integrals $\theta_I(\Omega_i) = \int_{\Omega_i} I$, $\theta_1(\Omega_i) = \int_{\Omega_i} 1$ and then the energy $J(\Gamma)$

    compute the descent velocity V
    compute step size τ ensuring energy decrease
    update Γ^k to obtain Γ^{k+1} using (10)
until stopping criterion is satisfied

The three critical components to effectiveness of this algorithm are: 1) the choice of the descent velocity, 2) the choice of step size, and 3) the stopping criterion. Some descent velocities, which we elaborate below, yield more stable evolutions and faster convergence. Moreover, for successful convergence, the step size should be matched to the velocity at each iteration (not set to a fixed value like many implementations in literature). Finally, the stopping criterion should be set appropriately depending on the image and the curves, in order to avoid early termination or unnecessary extra iterations that do not improve segmentation. We describe these components next.

Gradient Descent Velocities. The first shape derivative already gives us a gradient descent velocity, by setting the velocity equal to negative shape gradient: $V = -G = -(\mu\kappa + f(\Gamma))$, (because this implies $dJ(\Gamma; V) = -\int_\Gamma G^2 d\Gamma \leqslant 0$). The velocity $V = -G$ was used in the original paper [2] by Chan and Vese as part of a level set implementation.

A more general and flexible way to define a gradient descent velocity is to choose a scalar product $b(\cdot, \cdot)$ that induces a Hilbert space $B(\Gamma)$ on the curve Γ [3,12], and use the following equation to compute the associated gradient descent

velocity V:
$$b(V, W) = -dJ(\Gamma; W) = -\langle G, W \rangle, \qquad \forall W \in B(\Gamma). \tag{11}$$

The velocity V computed in this way is also a gradient descent velocity: $dJ(\Gamma; V) = -b(V, V) \leq 0$. Examples of possible scalar products are $b(\cdot, \cdot)$ the L^2 scalar product and the weighted H^1 scalar product

$$\langle V, W \rangle_{L^2} = \langle V, W \rangle = \int_\Gamma VW d\Gamma, \quad \langle V, W \rangle_{H^1} = \langle \alpha \nabla_\Gamma V, \nabla_\Gamma W \rangle + \langle \beta V, W \rangle, \tag{12}$$

where $\alpha = \alpha(x, \Gamma) > 0$ and $\beta = \beta(x, \Gamma) > 0$. The gradient descent velocity computed with the L^2 scalar product turns out to be $V = -G$ mentioned above, and is the most common choice in the literature for active contours problem.

In practice, the L^2 gradient velocity works reasonably, but it is not very efficient. The gradient descent method is known to converge slowly in the optimization literature [9]. The gradient depends on the scaling of the problem, and the choice of the right step size is not straight-forward. We propose to remedy this by normalizing the L^2 gradient velocity with its norm, and by using a standard line search algorithm for step size. This is explained in detail below. Another important problem with the velocity $V = -G$ is that the curvature term in $G = \mu\kappa + f$ makes the iterations unstable, and one has to take small steps to evolve the curve Γ in a stable manner. To address this, we use a semi-implicit time step discretization of the velocity and curve evolution, which is unconditionably stable. We should note that using an H^1 scalar product also stabilizes the velocity computation, and one can continue with the simpler and more efficient explicit stepping scheme for curve evolution.

Newton's Method for Minimization. Having the explicit formula for the second shape derivative or the shape Hessian (9) opens up opportunities to reduce the number of iterations or energy evaluations by pursuing a Newton-type optimization algorithm. One can compute a Newton velocity by setting $b(V, W) = d^2 J(\Gamma; V, W)$ in the velocity equation (11). This was proposed in the recent works [6–8]. Note that the expression (9) is symmetric and resembles an H^1 scalar product (12). However, it is not positive definite because of the arbitrary range of the coefficients $\beta(x, \Gamma)$ and the last two terms in (9), which are negative semi-definite. Therefore, using $b(V, W) = d^2 J(\Gamma; V, W)$ in (11) is not guaranteed to produce a descent direction. We would like to work with a positive definite Hessian and retain some structure of the second shape derivative $d^2 J(\Gamma; \cdot, \cdot)$ to help improve convergence. For this, we replace β in (9) with a thresholded version $\beta_+(x, \Gamma) = \max(\beta(x, \Gamma), \beta_M)$ ($\beta_M > 0$) and omit the last two terms. Then the sum of the first and second integrals in (9) is positive definite. The choice of β_M needs care. One is inclined to choose β_M as small as practically possible. But the corresponding discrete Hessian matrix gets more and more ill-conditioned as β_M gets smaller; therefore, in practice, we need to choose a value that is not very small as an acceptable trade-off. For energy (1), we set $\beta_M = 0.1|c_2 - c_1| \max |I|$, a threshold that is automatically adjusted to the image intensity and contrast between regions.

Explicit vs. Semi-implicit Stepping. At this point, we should take a closer look at the interaction of the descent velocity V and the step size τ. Although the crucial criterion of energy reduction for step size selection is encoded in the line search routine, described in the next subsection, the choice of velocity might impose more conditions on the step size. Given the curve points $\boldsymbol{X}$ of the curve, a natural sequence to compute the descent velocity and to update the curve is the following: 1) compute $f(\Gamma^k), n^k, \kappa^k$ from $\boldsymbol{X}$, 2) compute scalar velocity V^k using one of the methods described above, 3) compute $\boldsymbol{V}^k = Vn^k$, 4) update $\boldsymbol{X}^{k+1} = \boldsymbol{X}^k + \tau \boldsymbol{V}^k$. These steps constitute the explicit stepping scheme. This works well with H^1 gradient descent, Newton's method, and does not require any additional conditions on τ. If we use L^2 gradient descent, as mostly done for this problem, the iterations are not very stable and one needs to take small steps τ, consequently many more iterations.

An alternative stepping scheme in the case of L^2 gradient descent would be a semi-implicit stepping scheme [6]. In this approach, we take $\boldsymbol{X}^k, n^k$ as known quantities and $\kappa^{k+1}, \boldsymbol{\kappa}^{k+1}, V^{k+1}, \boldsymbol{V}^{k+1}$ as unknowns at each iteration. We write $\boldsymbol{\kappa}^{k+1} = -\Delta_\Gamma \boldsymbol{X}^{k+1} = -\Delta_\Gamma \boldsymbol{X}^k + \tau \Delta_\Gamma \boldsymbol{V}^{k+1}$, and obtain the following system of equations

$$\boldsymbol{\kappa}^{k+1} - \tau \Delta_\Gamma \boldsymbol{V}^{k+1} = -\Delta_\Gamma \boldsymbol{X}^k, \quad \kappa^{k+1} - \boldsymbol{\kappa}^k \cdot n^{k+1} = 0,$$
$$V^{k+1} + \mu \kappa^{k+1} = -f(\Gamma^k), \quad \boldsymbol{V}^{k+1} - V^{k+1} n^k = 0,$$

which we need to solve simultaneously for the unknowns. This semi-implicit scheme is unconditionally stable, i.e. it does not impose any conditions on the step size τ. Its disadvantage is that we now need to solve a system of equations, and handle a larger number of unknowns at each iteration. We use the semi-implicit stepping scheme only for L^2 gradient descent in our experiments, and the explicit scheme for Newton velocity.

Line Search for the Step Size. For many implementations of active contour models, the step size τ in the curve update (10) is fixed, and a preset number of iterations are taken with the fixed τ. This is not a very effective approach, as one might miss (overshoot) the minimum with a large τ or take too many iterations with a small τ. A better approach is to use a line search that chooses a step τ guaranteeing energy decrease from a range of τ values. For example, one can select τ that satisfies the Armijo criterion [9]

$$J(\Gamma^{k+1}) < J(\Gamma^k) + \alpha \tau dJ(\Gamma^k; V^k). \tag{13}$$

This criterion is mostly effective in ensuring energy decrease at each step and attaining convergence. But sometimes this monotone line search for the step size might fail; even the smallest τ may appear not to yield energy decrease. This is due to the inconsistency between the computed energy (obtained by summing up pixels) and the computed shape derivative (using the discretized curve and the interpolation of the image). To circumvent this, we pursued a nonmonotone line search strategy [13], which does not require strict energy decrease at each iteration, but rather decrease on average in the recent iterations. We used the following criterion

$$J(\Gamma^{k+1}) < C^k + \alpha \tau^k dJ(\Gamma^k; V^k), \tag{14}$$

where $C^k = (\eta Q^{k-1} C^{k-1} + J(\Gamma^k))/Q^k$, $C^0 = J(\Gamma^0)$, $Q^k = \eta Q^{k-1} + 1$, $Q^0 = 0$. We set $\alpha = 10^{-3}$, $\eta = 0.2$ in our experiments. Compared to the monotone strategy (13), the nonmonotone line search sometimes took more iterations to converge, but mostly resulted in fewer energy evaluations and curve updates, hence less computation. Moreover it converged with fewer line search failures.

The Stopping Criterion. The conventional approach to stop iterations in optimization literature is to track the norm of the gradient and to stop when it is small [9]. This is not as straightforward for a shape optimization implementation involving discretized geometries and real data. One needs to account for imperfections in the data, such as noise, lack of contrast, and limited resolution of the numerical model. Even the choice of the norm for the gradient requires care. Simply setting the stopping tolerance to a fixed value is not successful for this particular problem. Thus we tried to derive a robust stopping criterion starting from the following pointwise condition on the shape gradient $|G(x, \Gamma)| < \varepsilon \delta G(\Gamma)$, where $\varepsilon > 0$ is an absolute tolerance, $\delta G(\Gamma)$ is the difference between the max and min values of the shape gradient among distinct regions and provides a relative scaling. We chose to track the L^2 norm of the shape gradient, for which the threshold tolerance can be derived by integrating the pointwise condition over Γ

$$\|G\|_{L^2(\Gamma)} = \left(\int_\Gamma |G|^2 d\Gamma \right)^{\frac{1}{2}} < \varepsilon \delta G(\Gamma) |\Gamma|^{\frac{1}{2}}. \tag{15}$$

This criterion can be elaborated further for specific region-based energies. For example, for the Chan-Vese energy (1), we have $G(x, \Gamma) = (c_2 - c_1)(I(x) - \frac{1}{2}(c_1 + c_2))$, and we used $\delta G(\Gamma) \approx \frac{1}{2}|c_2 - c_1|^2$. Figure 2 shows the evolution of the shape gradient and stopping tolerance for a typical segmentation example. The norm of the shape gradient is small at the beginning, large in the middle, small at the end. If we used a small fixed tolerance, the iterations would stop immediately at the beginning of the minimization iterations. If we used a large fixed tolerance, the iterations would not stop for many more unnecessary iterations. Our tolerance (15) is dynamic; it stays small initially, then grows gradually through the iterations.

4 Geometry and Numerical Discretization

For efficiency, we build our numerical framework on a Lagrangian representation of the curves Γ. We find that this enables a faithful discretization of our shape optimization formulation, in particular, of the shape sensitivity relationships and the velocity (from Sections 2 and 3). Most calculations take place on the curves Γ, and we refer to the domains inside and outside Γ, only when we need to compute the region integrals for the shape energies (1), (5). We represent a curve as a list of elements $\{\Gamma_i\}_{i=1}^m$ such that $\Gamma = \bigcup_i \Gamma_i$. An element Γ_i is defined as the line segment connecting node $\boldsymbol{X}_i$ to node $\boldsymbol{X}_{i+1}$. *We do not use a parameterization of the curves.*

The curves can undergo large deformations between iterations, and this can cause the nodes to be scattered unevenly. Still it is crucial to maintain a *good* distribution of the nodes. We do not want the node distribution to be uniform, but rather to be spatially adaptive. We want fewer nodes for flat curves in flat image regions and more nodes in high curvature portions of the curves and in highly varying regions of the image (measured by comparing high and low order quadratures of the image intensity function on the curve elements). The adaptation of node distribution is done via refinement and coarsening procedures and ensures computational efficiency together with good resolution and accuracy. Moreover, to enable topological adaptivity of curves (like a level set model), we implemented intersection detection and curve surgery procedures for splitting and merging of curves. The implementation details of these adaptation procedures are beyond the scope of this paper, and will be elaborated in a separate report.

Discretizing Velocity Computations. We propose a finite element discretization of the continuous velocity equations from Section 3. For this, we introduce a set of piecewise linear basis functions $\{\phi_i\}_{i=1}^m$ satisfying $\phi_i(X_j) = \delta_{ij}$ (also vector version $\boldsymbol{\phi}_i = (\phi_i, \phi_i)^T$). We expand the variables, such as the velocity V and the geometric quantities $\boldsymbol{X}, \boldsymbol{\kappa}$, in terms of the basis functions:

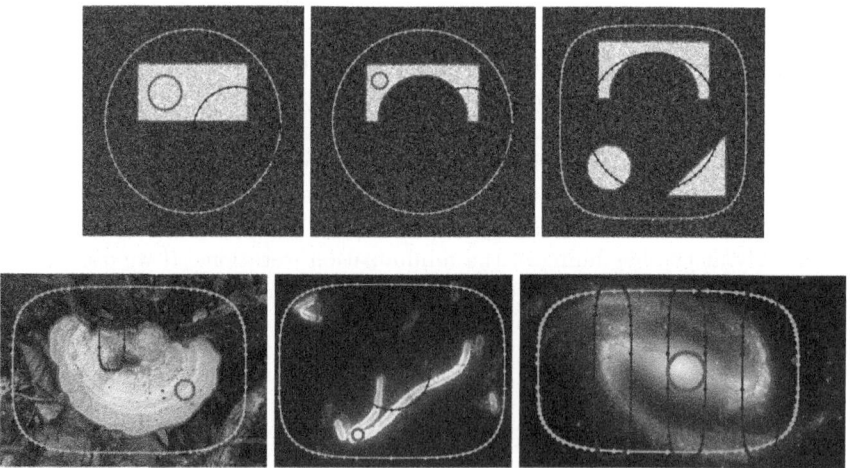

Fig. 1. Example images and initial curves used for testing. Top row: synthetic images (rectangle, concave, multiple). Bottom row: real images (fungus, bacteria, galaxy). Three different starting curves Γ_{in} (magenta), Γ_{out} (yellow), Γ_{part} (blue) used for each image.

$V = V_j \phi_j$ $(:= \Sigma_j V_j \phi_j)$, $\mathbf{X} = \mathbf{X}_j \phi_j$, $\kappa = \mathbf{K}_j \phi_j$, and we work with the corresponding coefficient vectors $\mathbf{X}, \mathbf{V}, \mathbf{K}$ respectively. This enables us to write the discretized versions of the key integral equations:

$$\langle \kappa, \phi \rangle = \langle \nabla_\Gamma \mathbf{X}, \nabla_\Gamma \phi \rangle, \quad \Rightarrow \kappa_j \langle \phi_j, \phi_i \rangle = \mathbf{X}_j \langle \nabla_\Gamma \phi_j, \nabla_\Gamma \phi_i \rangle, \quad \Rightarrow \mathbf{MK} = \mathbf{AX},$$
$$b(V, \phi) = -\langle G(\Gamma), \phi \rangle, \quad \Rightarrow V_j b(\phi_j, \phi_i) = -\langle G(\Gamma), \phi_i \rangle, \quad \Rightarrow B\mathbf{V} = -\mathbf{G},$$

where we have introduced the following matrices and vectors

$$A_{ij} := \langle \nabla_\Gamma \phi_i, \nabla_\Gamma \phi_j \rangle, \quad \mathbf{A}_{ij} := A_{ij} \mathbf{Id}, \quad M_{ij} := \langle \phi_i, \phi_j \rangle, \quad \mathbf{M}_{ij} := M_{ij} \mathbf{Id},$$
$$M_{\beta,ij} := \langle \beta \phi_i, \phi_j \rangle, \quad B_{ij} := b(\phi_i, \phi_j), \quad \mathbf{G}_i := \langle G(\Gamma), \phi_i \rangle.$$

We have $B = M$ for L^2 velocity, and $B = \mu A + M_\beta$ for Newton velocity. We emphasize that all the relevant operations with these matrices (matrix inversion, matrix-vector products) have linear time complexity. These matrices consist of circular tridiagonal blocks (corresponding to individual curves), and they can be inverted using the Thomas algorithm, e.g. for computing velocity $\mathbf{V} = -B^{-1}\mathbf{G}$ or curvature $\mathbf{K} = \mathbf{M}^{-1}\mathbf{AX}$.

5 Numerical Examples

In this section, we demonstrate that the Newton's method, which takes advantage of the shape Hessian, produces the segmentation in significantly less computation than the L^2 gradient descent. For this, we used a set of synthetic image examples (with increasing complexity of the regions), and a set of real images (see Figure 1). We set the length penalty in the energy (1) to $\mu = 10^{-3}$. Also to discourage curves extending beyond the image domain D, we added another weighted length term $\int_\Gamma (1 - \mathbb{1}_D) d\Gamma$, which has an effect only on the parts Γ outside D. We started the minimization iterations with different initial curve configurations: $\Gamma_{in}^0, \Gamma_{out}^0, \Gamma_{part}^0$, curves that were inside, outside or partially overlapping the regions of interest respectively. The results of these experiments are given in Table 1, where we report the number of energy evaluations and the number of iterations. As we used line search to determine the right step size

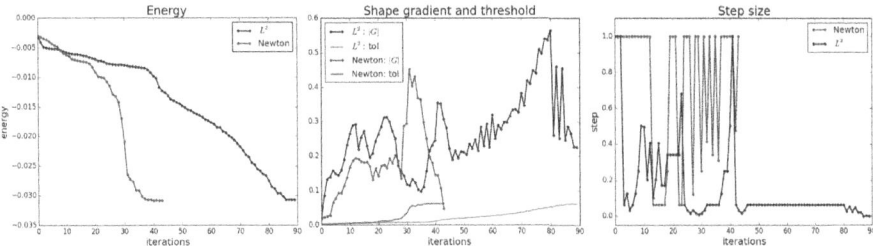

Fig. 2. The energy, shape gradient, scaled stopping tolerance and step size values for all the iterations of minimization (synthetic example with concave region)

Table 1. Performance of L^2 vs Newton velocity. The test images were segmented using both velocities with monotone (m) line search criterion (13) and nonmonotone (n) criterion (14). Some of these experiments terminated due to line search failures (rather than fulfilment of the stopping criterion (15)), albeit with successful segmentation (marked with !). A few terminated prematurely with line search failure (marked with !X). One did not finish in the maximum (100) number of iterations (marked with MAX). We report the number of energy evaluations for each experiment (and the iteration numbers in parantheses). The best results are highlighted in bold.

	rectangle			concave			multiple	
	Γ_{in}	Γ_{out}	Γ_{part}	Γ_{in}	Γ_{out}	Γ_{part}	Γ_{out}	Γ_{part}
L^2 (m)	35 (16)	47 (23!)	33 (19!)	35 (18)	99 (58)	40 (19)	54 (35)	54 (26!)
L^2 (n)	46 (20!)	46 (24)	40 (19)	51 (31)	83 (51!)	45 (20!)	59 (33!)	56 (27!)
Nwt (m)	26 (19!)	**23 (17)**	**23 (17)**	40 (19!)	38 (32)	**26 (17)**	43 (36)	32 (22)
Nwt (n)	**22 (20)**	25 (19)	28 (21)	**27 (19)**	**37 (34)**	27 (18)	**40 (33)**	**28 (22)**

	fungus			bacteria			galaxy		
	Γ_{in}	Γ_{out}	Γ_{part}	Γ_{in}	Γ_{out}	Γ_{part}	Γ_{in}	Γ_{out}	Γ_{part}
L^2 (m)	44 (21)	63 (34!X)	49 (24!)	74 (40)	117 (60!X)	86 (47)	46 (26)	33 (20!X)	60 (38)
L^2 (n)	52 (29!)	54 (31!X)	35 (21!)	64 (35)	MAX!	64 (35)	54 (29!)	83 (46!)	56 (36)
Nwt (m)	**17 (14)**	**22 (21)**	**30 (15!)**	**27 (25)**	**33 (28)**	**12 (11)**	**26 (18)**	32 (25!)	**26 (22)**
Nwt (n)	**17 (14)**	**22 (21)**	60 (58)	**27 (25)**	**33 (28)**	**12 (11)**	34 (26)	**29 (28)**	37 (34)

for an iteration in all methods, the number of energy evaluations was a better measure of computational cost than the number of iterations, because it also included steps or iterations that were tested by line search, but were not taken. We stopped the iterations when the L^2 norm of the shape gradient was less than the scaled tolerance (15) (with $\varepsilon = 0.5$) or when line search failed, namely, it returned the smallest step size, which did not give apparent energy decrease. In most of these cases, the segmentation was already complete when line search failure happened. We made the following observations:

- L^2 *velocity:* Normalizing the L^2 velocity (dividing by $\|V\|_2$) before line search improved its performance, especially in cases of poor contrast or low intensity when the L^2 velocity was slow (recall $V = -(c_2 - c_1)(I(x) - 0.5(c_1 + c_2))$).
- *Test step size:* We used $\tau = 1$ as an initial step size for line search in the Newton's method, whereas using twice the previous step size worked best for the L^2 gradient descent. The former takes full steps as much as it can all along, whereas the latter reduces τ when the curve is close to the minimum.
- *Monotone vs Nonmonotone:* The choice of nonmonotone line search using criterion (14) did not make a big difference for the L^2 gradient descent. For Newton's velocity, it reduced the number of energy evaluations on average and nearly eliminated line search failures. This is due to the fact the nonmonotone criterion does not impose strict energy decrease.
- *Newton velocity:* Required fewer energy evaluations than the L^2 velocity to reach the minimum. Especially, if some part of the curve is already on the region boundary, the Newton's method quickly pulls the rest of the curve to the region boundary.

Overall we observed that the Newton velocity consistently outperformed L^2 gradient descent. We should nonetheless add that, although our results were in favor of the Newton's method, one can concoct examples of images and initial curves, for which the performance difference is not as apparent.

Acknowledgments. This work was supported by the NIST grant 70NANB13H018.

References

1. Aubert, G., Barlaud, M., Faugeras, O., Jehan-Besson, S.: Image segmentation using active contours: calculus of variations or shape gradients? SIAM J. Appl. Math. **63**(6) (2003)
2. Chan, T.F., Vese, L.A.: Active contours without edges. IEEE Transactions on Image Processing **10**(2), 266–277 (2001)
3. Charpiat, G., Maurel, P., Pons, J.-P., Keriven, R., Faugeras, O.: Generalized gradients: Priors on minimization flows. International Journal of Computer Vision **73**, 325–344 (2007)
4. Cremers, D., Rousson, M., Deriche, R.: A review of statistical approaches to level set segmentation: Integrating color, texture, motion and shape. IJCV **72**, 195–215 (2007)
5. Delfour, M.C., Zolésio, J.-P.: Shapes and Geometries. Society for Industrial and Applied Mathematics (SIAM), Philadelphia, PA, Advances in Design and Control (2001)
6. Doğan, G., Morin, P., Nochetto, R.H.: A variational shape optimization approach for image segmentation with a Mumford-Shah functional. SIAM J. Sci. Comp. **30**(6) (2008)
7. Hintermüller, M., Ring, W.: A second order shape optimization approach for image segmentation. SIAM J. Appl. Math. **64**(2), 442–467 (2003/04)
8. Hintermüller, M., Ring, W.: An inexact Newton-CG-type active contour approach for the minimization of the Mumford-Shah functional. J. Math. Imaging Vision **20**(1–2) (2004)
9. Nocedal, J., Wright, S.J.: Numerical Optimization. Springer-Verlag, New York (1999)
10. Paragios, N., Deriche, R.: Geodesic active regions: A new framework to deal with frame partition problems in computer vision. J. Vis. Commun. Image Represent. **13**(1–2) (2002)
11. Sokołowski, J., Zolésio, J.-P.: Introduction to Shape Optimization, volume 16 of Springer Series in Computational Mathematics. Springer-Verlag, Berlin (1992)
12. Sundaramoorthi, G., Yezzi, A., Mennucci, A.: Sobolev active contours. International Journal of Computer Vision **73**, 345–366 (2007). doi:10.1007/s11263-006-0635-2
13. Zhang, H., Hager, W.W.: A nonmonotone line search technique and its application to unconstrained optimization. SIAM Journal on Optimization **14**(4), 1043–1056 (2004)

Flow, Motion and Registration

Sparse Aggregation Framework for Optical Flow Estimation

Denis Fortun[(✉)], Patrick Bouthemy, and Charles Kervrann

Centre de Rennes - Bretagne Atlantique, Inria, Rennes, France
denis.fortun@epfl.ch,
{patrick.bouthemy,charles.kervrann}@inria.fr

Abstract. We propose a sparse aggregation framework for optical flow estimation to overcome the limitations of variational methods introduced by coarse-to-fine strategies. The idea is to compute parametric motion candidates estimated in overlapping square windows of variable size taken in the semi-local neighborhood of a given point. In the second step, a sparse representation and an optimization procedure in the continuous setting are proposed to compute a motion vector close to motion candidates for each pixel. We demonstrate the feasibility and performance of our two-step approach on image pairs and compare its performances with competitive methods on the Middlebury benchmark.

Keywords: Motion estimation · Optical flow · Sparse representation · Optimization

1 Introduction

Optical flow estimation is based on a conservation assumption of image features able to capture the real motion (intensity image feature, gradient, feature descriptor ...). The so-called brightness constancy assumption is the mostly used one. It provides a single equation and is consequently insufficient to recover the two components of the motion vector. A usual way to overcome this underdetermination is to impose a spatial coherency constraint for the flow field. Existing methods can then be classified into two main approaches: *i/* the spatial coherency is ensured at pixel $x \in \Omega \subset \mathbb{R}^2$ (Ω is the image domain) by introducing parametric motion models in a neighborhood $V(x) \subset \Omega$ [17] ; *ii/* the flow field is assumed to be piecewise smooth and the strategy is to minimize a global energy that explicitly combines a potential $\rho_{data}(\cdot)$ which penalizes deviation from the brightness constancy equation with a regularization potential $\phi(\cdot)$ which penalizes high values of the norm of the gradient $\nabla \mathbf{w}$ of the velocity field $\mathbf{w} : \Omega \to \mathbb{R}^2$ [13]:

$$E_{global}(\mathbf{w}) = \int_{\Omega} \rho_{data}(x, I, \mathbf{w}) + \lambda \phi(\nabla \mathbf{w}(x)) \, dx \tag{1}$$

where $I : \Omega \times [0,T] \to \mathbb{R}$ is an image sequence and λ is a balance parameter.

The best state-of-the-art results are achieved by minimizing an energy of the form (1). An over-smoothing phenomenon was particularly visible in the seminal work of [13] which uses quadratic penalty function for the regularization potential. This shortcoming has been greatly reduced by the introduction of robust penalty functions [3,18], the adaptation of the regularization along image discontinuities [24] or non-local regularization strategies [26]. However, this family of methods is still limited by undesirable effects coming from the necessity to resort to coarse-to-fine schemes to handle large displacements. The motion of small objects is discarded at coarse scales, and the error is often propagated in the incremental updates at finer scales. As a result, motion details are often smoothed in the final estimated flow field.

We mention two non-variational approaches related to our method that have been investigated to reduce the over-smoothing effect of global variational methods: i/ parametric motion estimation based on motion field segmentation ; ii/ discrete optimization of the energy (1). In the first case, a parametric model of the flow field is estimated inside coherently moving regions. The estimation of the discontinuities is thus transferred to the segmentation step [23]. In the second case, discrete optimization of the energy (1) is able to find strong minima for non-convex functionals without coarse-to-fine schemes, but is limited by the quantization of the flow field range [4]. For more details about optical flow literature, see the recent survey [12].

In this paper, we present a method combining local parametric estimations and continuous optimization to preserve motion discontinuities and details while capturing large displacements, in a variational framework without coarse-to fine scheme. It is composed of two stages: first, local parametric estimations are performed on overlapping square windows (Section 2); second, the resulting local motion vectors are used as candidates for a global continuous optimization (Section 3). It is worth noting that this two-step approach has already been succesfully investigated in the discrete setting in [11]. We propose hereunder a sparse representation approach in the continuous setting which is faster and is able to produce competitive results (Section 4) on several sequences of the Middlebury database [1] when compared to [5,6,9,11].

2 Computation of Local Motion Candidates

To compute motion candidates, we follow the idea of [11] and perform local estimations in overlapping square patches of different sizes, so that each pixel is contained in several patches. This approach can be viewed as a alternative way to address the problem of the choice of the local neighborhood for parametric estimation. Rather than adapting the regions *a priori* or jointly with the motion field, we operate in two steps: 1) estimation of motion candidates on several supports at every pixel, 2) selection of the optimal candidate at each pixel within the aggregation step. In this section, we describe a combination of parametric estimation and patch correspondences for computing motion candidates. Nevertheless, the proposed framework allows for any types of local estimation.

2.1 Set of Overlapping Patches

The local supports for computing motion candidates are overlapping square patches of different sizes. Let us denote $\mathcal{P}(x) = \{P_{\nu,\tau} : x \in P_{\nu,\tau}\}$ the set of patches with patch size $\nu \in \{\nu_1, \cdots, \nu_{max}\}$, an overlapping ratio $\tau \in [0,1]$ indicating the proportion of surface shared by neighboring patches, and the set $P_{\nu,\tau}$ of patches covering Ω with sizes in ν and overlapping ratio τ. To capture different motion scales, the patch sizes must cover a large range of values. In all our experiments, we set $\nu \in \{15, 45, 115\}$. See [11] for a more detailed description of the set of patches. The motion vectors are estimated independently in each patch in two sub-steps including patch correspondences and affine motion estimations, as described in the following.

2.2 Patch Correspondences

Let us consider two successive images I_1 and I_2. For each patch $P_1 \in \mathcal{P}(x)$ in image I_1, we first determine the set $\mathcal{X}_N(P_1)$ of the N most similar patches to P_1 in I_2. In our experiments, we use a combination of the saturation and value channels of the HSV color space to cope with illumination changes [27]. We consider the Sum of Absolute Distances to compare patches and we impose a minimal distance between the correspondences of a given pixel to ensure the diversity of motion candidates. Multiple distances to compare patches could be jointly considered to enlarge the collection of candidates at each location. The final set of correspondences is denoted $\mathcal{X}_N(P_1)$. The correspondences are found with the PatchMatch algorithm [2]. Finally, for each established pair of corresponding patches (P_1, P_2) with $P_2 \in \mathcal{X}_N(P_1)$, we denote $\mathbf{d}_{1,2} \in \mathbb{Z}^2$ the translation vector shifting P_1 onto P_2.

2.3 Affine Motion Refinement

The displacements $\mathbf{d}_{1,2}$ estimated by patch correspondences are integer-pixel translational approximations. We refine the coarse translation computation with the estimation of a local affine motion model denoted $\delta \mathbf{w}_{1,2} : \Omega_{P_1} \to \mathbb{R}^2$ in every pair (P_1, P_2) where $\Omega_{P_1} \subset \Omega$ is the pixel domain of P_1. At pixel $x = (x_1, x_2)^\top$, we define:

$$\delta \mathbf{w}_{1,2}(x) = (a_1 + a_2 x_1 + a_3 x_2, \ a_4 + a_5 x_1 + a_6 x_2)^\top \quad (2)$$

and the parameter vector $\boldsymbol{\theta}_{1,2} = (a_1, a_2, a_3, a_4, a_5, a_6)^\top$ is estimated using the brightness constancy constraint:

$$\widehat{\boldsymbol{\theta}}_{1,2} = \arg\min_{\boldsymbol{\theta}_{1,2}} \int_{\Omega_{P_1}} \psi(P_2(x + \delta \mathbf{w}_{1,2}(x)) - P_1(x)) dx. \quad (3)$$

The penalty function $\psi(\cdot)$ is chosen as the robust Tukey's function. The problem (3) is solved with the publicly available Motion2D software[1] [21], which

---
[1] http://www.irisa.fr/vista/Motion2D/

implements a multi-resolution incremental minimization scheme involving an IRLS (Iteratively Reweighted Least Squares) technique for solving the successive linearizations of the penalty function in (3).

2.4 Definition of Motion Candidates

The above described two-step estimation is repeated for every patch of $\mathcal{P}(x)$ and generates a set of candidate motion vectors $\mathcal{C}(x)$ at each pixel $x \in \Omega$ defined as follows:

$$\mathcal{C}(x) = \{\mathbf{d}_{1,2} + \delta\mathbf{w}_{1,2}(x) : P_1 \in \mathcal{P}(x), P_2 \in \mathcal{X}_N(P_1)\}. \tag{4}$$

In what follows, we will denote $\boldsymbol{w_C}(x) = (\mathbf{w}_1(x), \cdots \mathbf{w}_M(x))^\top$ the vector of M motion candidates computed from the M overlapping patches in $\mathcal{P}(x)$ and $\mathcal{C}(x) = \{\mathbf{w}_1(x), \cdots, \mathbf{w}_M(x)\}$ the corresponding set of candidate motion vectors.

Combining a coarse motion estimation with a refinement step has already been investigated in [10,16,20] but essentially for global dense motion field estimation. This strategy is applied to semi-local neighborhoods and patches in our approach. Unlike [17], each pixel gets several motion vectors computed from overlapping patches. Finally, in contrast to several other methods based on feature matching [6,10,25], we select the $N > 1$ best correspondences. Note that the correspondence sub-step enables to capture large displacements even for small patch sizes and allows us to deal with small structures undergoing large displacements unlike coarse-to-fine schemes. Generally, local parametric motion estimation needs an appropriate selection of spatial neighborhoods [17]. In our framework, we consider square patches with several sizes to tackle adaptively motion of different amplitudes. The selection of patches/neighborhoods is postponed in the aggregation step.

3 Sparse Aggregation and Continuous Optimization

In this section, we present an aggregation strategy in a continuous setting which can be considered as an alternative to the discrete aggregation method described in [11]. The sparse aggregation we propose enables significantly lower computational time than [11], it is less dependent on the quality of candidates estimation, and it recovers more accurately smooth regions of the motion field. In a continuous setting, we minimize an energy of the form

$$E(\mathbf{w}) = \int_\Omega \rho(\mathbf{w}(x), \boldsymbol{w_C}(x)) + \lambda_1 \phi(\nabla \mathbf{w}(x)) dx, \tag{5}$$

where $\rho(\mathbf{w}(x), \boldsymbol{w_C}(x))$ is a fidelity term and the second term imposes smoothness of $\mathbf{w}$ while preserving motion discontinuities, balanced by the parameter λ_1. In the following, we consider a Total Variation regularization: $\phi(\nabla \mathbf{w}(x)) = \|\nabla \mathbf{w}(x)\|_1$. Unlike usual approaches for optical flow, the image intensities are

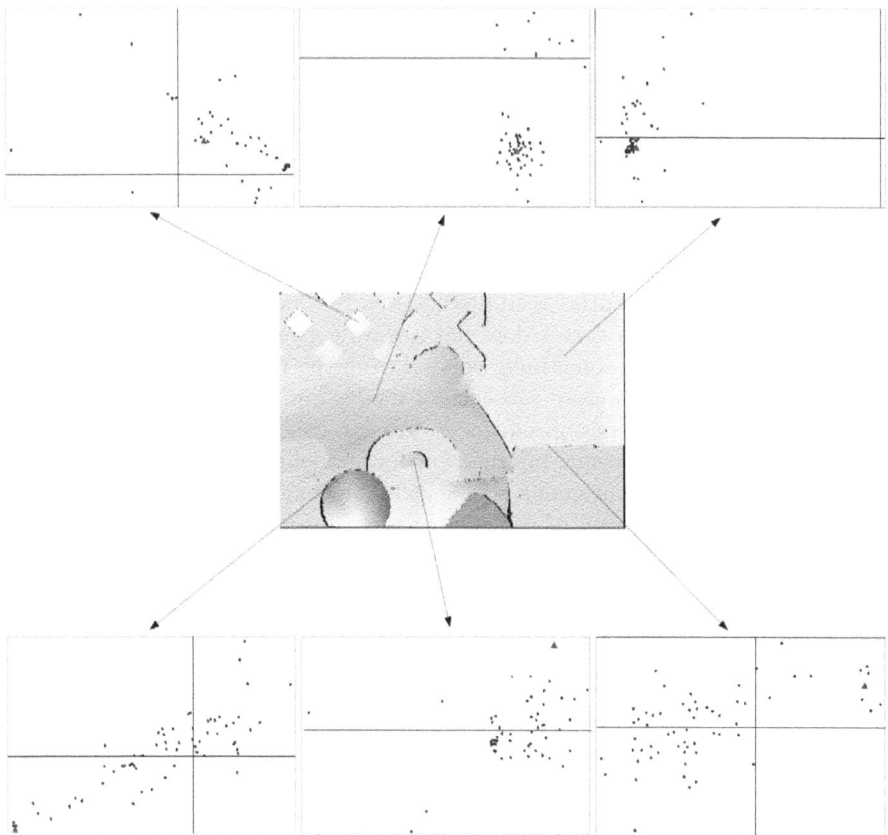

Fig. 1. Visualization of the distribution of the motion candidates at several locations in the image. The central image is the ground-truth motion field of the *RubberWhale* sequence of the Middlebury benchmark. The six plots represent the motion vector candidates and the motion vector ground-truth at each corresponding pixel. The horizontal and vertical axes are respectively the horizontal and vertical components of the motion vectors. Blue points are motion candidates and red triangles are ground-truth motion vectors.

not used as input of the data potential $\rho(\mathbf{w}(x), \boldsymbol{w}_\mathcal{C}(x))$, but are replaced by the motion candidate vector $\boldsymbol{w}_\mathcal{C}(x)$.

Minimizing in the continuous domain w.r.t. $\mathbf{w}$ implies that the estimated motion field is allowed to deviate from the motion candidate vectors whereas in [11], the fixed motion vectors are necessarily vectors selected among the motion candidates by the discrete optimization scheme. From a practical point of view, this deviation allows us to achieve good results even when the sets of candidates are less accurate. Thus, critical parameters for the computational cost of the method, such as the overlapping ratio α, could be adapted to speed up candidates computation.

3.1 Candidate Distribution

If the motion candidates set is considered as the input data for the aggregation stage, we have to study the distribution of the candidates. Figure 1 illustrates the 2D distribution of candidates at several locations in an image (blue points), while also plotting the ground truth motion vector among them (red triangle). We can first observe that it is not always possible to identify modes of the distribution of motion candidates. While in regions of constant or smoothly varying motion, most motion vectors are clustered around the same mode, the distribution at motion discontinuities is unpredictable. Secondly, when a mode exists, the ground truth motion vector does not always correspond to this mode. The best motion candidate is sometimes isolated from the rest of the candidates. As a matter of fact, the two cases (absence of modes and isolated best candidate) frequently occur in all types of sequences. We can conclude that the candidates distribution is not a relevant information for modeling the data term of the energy function in the continuous aggregation. Options like dense linear combination of candidates, fitting of a statistical distribution or clustering are then excluded.

3.2 Continuous Aggregation

We propose two versions for the data potential of (5). We define $\rho(\mathbf{w}(x), \boldsymbol{w}_\mathcal{C}(x))$ as a measure of proximity of $\mathbf{w}(x)$ to components of the motion candidate vector $\boldsymbol{w}_\mathcal{C}(x) = (\mathbf{w}_1(x), \cdots, \mathbf{w}_M(x))^\top$. However, the potential must not be a distance measure to a mode of $\mathcal{C}(x)$ or a weighted average of candidates, as pointed out in the previous section. We rather define it as the distance to a single appropriately selected candidate from $\mathcal{C}$. Therefore, differently from [11], we exploit the selected candidate as a constraint in the data potential.

Minimum Distance. A first natural idea is to define $\rho(\mathbf{w}(x), \boldsymbol{w}_\mathcal{C}(x))$ as the distance to the closest component of $\boldsymbol{w}_\mathcal{C}(x)$:

$$\rho(\mathbf{w}(x), \boldsymbol{w}_\mathcal{C}(x)) = \min_{m \in \{1, \cdots, M\}} \|\mathbf{w}(x) - \mathbf{w}_m(x)\|_1. \tag{6}$$

The min function naturally selects one candidate used for distance measure. The proximal operator of $\rho(\mathbf{w}(x), \boldsymbol{w}_\mathcal{C}(x))$ can be computed exactly and the resulting energy can then be minimized in a proximal splitting framework [9]. However, the problem of the potential (6) lies in high non convexity, leading inevitably to local minima. In practice, we experimentally observe a convergence of the algorithm, but it stays trapped in a local minimum very dependent on the initialization. In the next subsection, we introduce another model to relax the selection of a unique candidate and achieve more efficient minimization.

Sparse Constraint and Dictionaries. In what follows, we propose an alternative potential composed of two terms to select a linear combination of a few candidates:

$$\rho(\mathbf{w}(x), \mathbf{w}_\mathcal{C}(x), \boldsymbol{\alpha}(x)) = \|\mathbf{w}(x) - \boldsymbol{\alpha}(x)^\top \mathbf{w}_\mathcal{C}(x)\|_1 + \lambda_2 \|\boldsymbol{\alpha}(x)\|_1 \quad (7)$$

where $\boldsymbol{\alpha}(x) = (\alpha_1(x), .., \alpha_M(x))^\top$ is a sparse coefficient vector associated to the M candidates at pixel x and λ_2 balances the influence of the two terms. The first term is a a reconstruction term which approximates the unknown motion vector $\mathbf{w}(x)$ by a linear combination of motion candidates $\mathbf{w}_m(x)$ in the set $\mathcal{C}(x)$ viewed as a local motion dictionary. The second term imposes sparsity of the coefficients $\boldsymbol{\alpha}(x)$. A probabilistic interpretation could be given to alpha(x) as in [22] it was not considered in the proposed framework. If the balance coefficient λ_2 is high enough, a few components of $\boldsymbol{\alpha}(x)$ will be non null, which amounts to selecting almost one single candidate in (7). Besides, potential (7) is convex and minimization is more tractable compared to the optimization problem described in the previous subsection.

In an alternate optimization scheme, the tight coupling between $\mathbf{w}$ and $\boldsymbol{\alpha}$ could imply that in practice $\boldsymbol{\alpha}(x)$ stays trapped in the local minimum at the first iteration. We overcome this problem by replacing the pure sparsity constraint of (7) by a weighted sparsity constraint defined by:

$$\|\boldsymbol{\alpha}(x)\|_{1,\boldsymbol{\beta}(x)} = \sum_{m=1}^{M} \beta_m(x) |\alpha_m(x)| \quad (8)$$

where $\beta_m(x)$ is a confidence measure associated to $\mathbf{w}_m(x)$. Apart from [14,15], existing confidence measures are dedicated to specific motion estimation methods. For a variational approach, [7] uses the inverse of the global energy. For local approaches like [17], eigenvalues of the structure tensor are usually exploited [19]. For parametric estimations in general, the variance of the estimate is also a possible confidence measure. To keep the generality and simplicity of our method, we consider the following general weights:

$$\beta_m(x) = \exp-\left(\sigma^{-2} \int_\Omega g(x,y,I_1) \rho_0(\mathbf{w}_m(x), I_1(y), I_2(y)) dy\right) \quad (9)$$

where $g(x,y,I_1)$ are bilateral weights defined as:

$$g(x,y,I_1) = \exp-\left(\frac{\|x-y\|_2^2}{\sigma_s^2} + \frac{(I_1(x) - I_1(y))^2}{\sigma_r^2}\right) \quad (10)$$

and $\rho_0(\mathbf{w}_m(x), I_1(y), I_2(y)) = |I_2(y+\mathbf{w}_m(x)) - I_1(y)|$ is a classical data potential penalizing deviation from the brightness constancy equation. The weight $\beta_m(x)$ is then a measure of the local coherency of brightness constancy through bilateral filtering. The final energy is:

$$E(\mathbf{w}, \boldsymbol{\alpha}) = \int_\Omega \|\mathbf{w}(x) - \boldsymbol{\alpha}(x)^\top \mathbf{w}_\mathcal{C}(x)\|_1 + \lambda_2 \|\boldsymbol{\alpha}(x)\|_{1,\boldsymbol{\beta}(x)} + \lambda_1 \|\nabla \mathbf{w}(x)\|_1 dx. \quad (11)$$

We minimize $E(\mathbf{w}, \boldsymbol{\alpha})$ alternatively on $\mathbf{w}$ and $\boldsymbol{\alpha}$. Minimization w.r.t. $\mathbf{w}$ is performed by solving the Euler-Lagrange equations with fixed point iterations [5].

Fig. 2. Preservation of small motion details and discontinuities on the *Grove3* sequence of the Middlebury benchmark. Top row: first frame, ground truth motion field and motion field estimated with SAFlow. Bottom row: motion field estimated with [9], [6] and [11]. Zooms on regions of interest overlay the images.

To minimize w.r.t. $\boldsymbol{\alpha}$, we resort to a greedy algorithm. From an initial configuration of $\boldsymbol{\alpha}$, we search for possible configurations of $\boldsymbol{\alpha}$, and a configuration is kept if it leads to a decreasing of the energy. The search strategy consists in iteratively adding non null components ordered by decreasing value of the confidence measure.

4 Experimental Results

We have evaluated our method on sequences of the Middlebury benchmark [1]. We experimentally compare our method named SAFlow (Sparse Aggregation for optical Flow) to the AggregFlow method (but without occlusion handling and designated by AggregFlow-wo)) [11] and the variational methods described in [6,9]. Local improvements related to discontinuity preservation are illustrated visually. The candidates sets were obtained with parameters $\nu \in \{15, 45, 115\}$, $\alpha = 0.8$, $N = 2$. Other parameters are set as follows: $\sigma = 0.1$, $\sigma_s = 5$ and $\sigma_r = 20$.

Figure 2 illustrates the ability of SAFlow to capture motion discontinuities and small details. Motion fields are less sharp than with AggregFlow-wo but, they are significantly better than [6,9].

In Fig. 3, the displacement of the small ball is typically badly handled by variational methods using coarse-to-fine schemes, as [9]. In contrast, SAFlow satisfyingly recovers the displacement. The method of [6] integrating feature matching in a variational framework also captures the motion of the ball, but the shape of the ball is less preserved. It is also more impacted by the associated occlusion region.

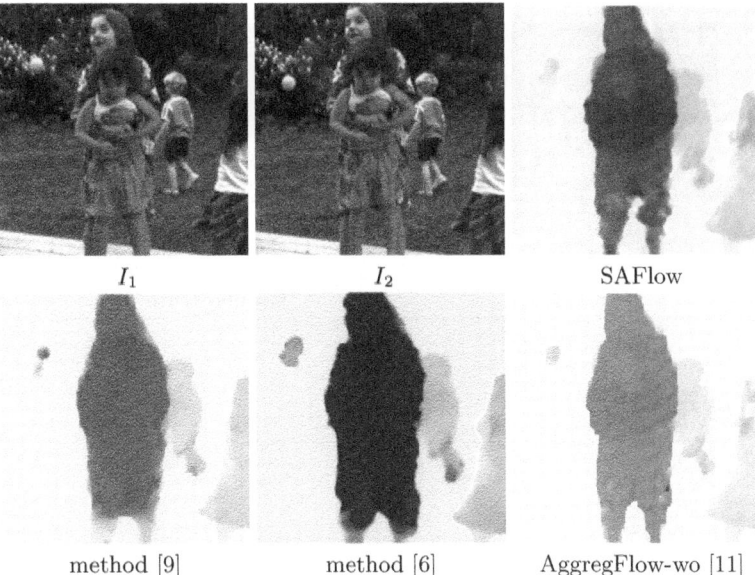

Fig. 3. Results on the *Backyard* sequence of the Middlebury benchmark. Top row: first and second frames (ground truth is not available for this sequence) and motion field estimated with SAFlow. Second row: motion field estimated with [9] , [6] and [11].

Figure 4 illustrates the ability of SAFlow to deal with less accurate motion candidates. In this experiment, we set the overlap ratio, i.e. the proportion of area shared by two neighbor patches, to $\alpha = 0.5$. This parameter is essential to deliver good candidates. In Fig. 4, typical artifacts of AggregFlow-wo can be observed. At motion discontinuities, the patches are not overlapping enough to produce accurate candidates, which implies block artifacts for AggregFlow-wo, due to the hard selection of one candidate. In contrast, SAFlow can deviate from the set of candidates to preserve clean discontinuities.

Discrete optimization in [11] tends to produce block artifacts for complex smooth deformations, as illustrated in Fig. 5. The variational optimization of SAFlow does not have this problem and estimate more accurately smooth flow fields. Finally, the computational time of SAFlow is around 5 minutes, mostly spent in the candidates computation step, while AggregFlow-wo requires 20 minutes.

Table 1 contains Angular Errors obtained with SAFlow, AggregFlow-wo [11] and the variational methods [6,9] for sequences of the Middlebury benchmark. The results of SAFlow are generally less accurate than those produced by AggregFlow-wo, especially sequences showing small motion details or sharp motion discontinuities. The performance of SAFlow can be affected by the confidence measures $\beta_m(x)$. Large errors of confidence measures can significantly decrease the accuracy of SAFlow. Nevertheless SAFlow yields better performance than the method [9] and is competitive with the method [6].

Fig. 4. Comparison of discrete and continuous aggregation for a small set of candidates on the *Grove2* sequence of the Middlebury benchmark. The candidates were computed with $\alpha = 0.5$. From left to right: first frame, ground truth, motion field estimated with AggregFlow-wo [11] and SAFlo w. Zooms on regions of interest overlay the images.

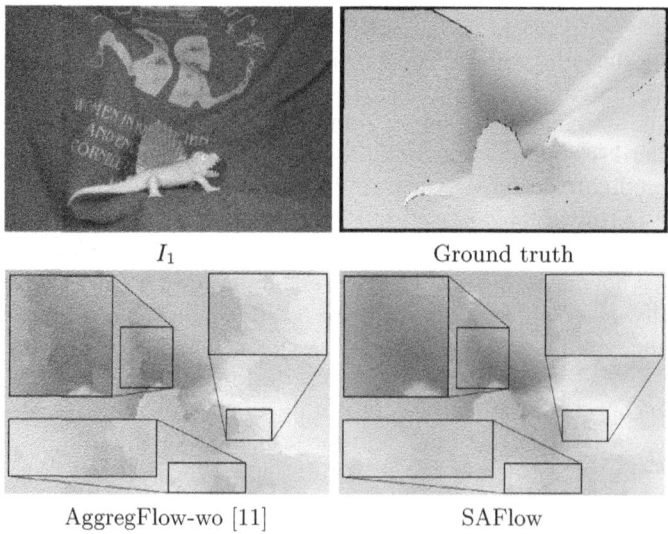

Fig. 5. Comparison of discrete and continuous aggregation for complex and smooth flow fields on the *Dimetrodon* sequence of the Middlebury benchmark. From left to right: first frame and ground truth motion field, motion field estimated.

Table 1. Angular errors obtained with SAFlow, AggregFlow-wo [11] and the methods [6] and [9] on sequences of the Middlebury benchmark

	Grove2	Grove3	Hydrangea	Urban2	Urban3
SAFlow	2.43	5.92	2.29	2.53	4.12
AggregFlow-wo	2.19	5.43	2.47	2.47	3.42
method [6]	2.38	5.97	2.10	2.50	3.91
method [9]	2.92	6.72	2.29	2.63	6.10

5 Conclusion

We have proposed a continuous aggregation strategy minimizing a global energy for optical flow computation as an alternative to the discrete aggregation presented in [11]. A first version uses the min function but is limited because of severe non-convexity of the energy. A more attractive convex formulation exploits a sparse dictionary model. Experiments show that the overall quantitative performance remains lower than with discrete aggregation. Additional experiments on the Sintel MPI database will be performed as in [8]. However results are still competitive with standard variational methods. Moreover, the ability to reconstruct motion vectors beyond the candidates set makes the continuous aggregation more robust to smaller and suboptimal candidate sets. It also better behaves in case of complex and smooth motion fields. The computational cost of continuous aggregation is significantly lower than for discrete aggregation.

Acknowledgments. This work was carried out as part of the Quaero program, funded by OSEO, French State agency for innovation. It was also partly supported by the France-BioImaging project (ANR-10-INBS-04-07, "Investments for the future"). We thank also Dr. O. Demetz, Dr. S. Setzer and Prof. J. Weickert for fruitfull discussions, and the reviewers for suggestions.

References

1. Baker, S., Scharstein, D., Lewis, J.P., Roth, S., Black, M.J., Szeliski, R.: A database and evaluation methodology for optical flow. IJCV **92**(1), 1–31 (2011)
2. Barnes, C., Shechtman, E., Goldman, D.B., Finkelstein, A.: The generalized patchmatch correspondence algorithm. In: Daniilidis, K., Maragos, P., Paragios, N. (eds.) ECCV 2010, Part III. LNCS, vol. 6313, pp. 29–43. Springer, Heidelberg (2010)
3. Black, M.J., Anandan, P.: The robust estimation of multiple motions: Parametric and piecewise-smooth flow fields. CVIU **63**(1), 75–104 (1996)
4. Boykov, Y., Veksler, O., Zabih, R.: Fast approximate energy minimization via graph cuts. PAMI **23**(11), 1222–1239 (2001)
5. Brox, T., Bruhn, A., Papenberg, N., Weickert, J.: High accuracy optical flow estimation based on a theory for warping. In: Pajdla, T., Matas, J.G. (eds.) ECCV 2004. LNCS, vol. 3024, pp. 25–36. Springer, Heidelberg (2004)
6. Brox, T., Malik, J.: Large displacement optical flow: descriptor matching in variational motion estimation. PAMI **33**(3), 500–513 (2011)
7. Bruhn, A., Weickert, W.: A confidence measure for variational optic flow methods. In: Geometric Properties for Incomplete Data, pp. 283–298 (2006)

8. Butler, D.J., Wulff, J., Stanley, G.B., Black, M.J.: A naturalistic open source movie for optical flow evaluation. In: Fitzgibbon, A., Lazebnik, S., Perona, P., Sato, Y., Schmid, C. (eds.) ECCV 2012, Part VI. LNCS, vol. 7577, pp. 611–625. Springer, Heidelberg (2012)
9. Chambolle, A., Pock, T.: A first-order primal-dual algorithm for convex problems with applications to imaging. Journal of Mathematical Imaging and Vision **40**(1), 120–145 (2011)
10. Chen, Z., Jin, H., Lin, Z., Cohen, S., Wu, Y.: Large displacement optical flow from nearest neighbor fields. In: CVPR, pp. 2443–2450 (2013)
11. Fortun, D., Bouthemy, P., Kervrann, C.: Aggregation of local parametric candidates with exemplar-based occlusion handling for optical flow. arXiv:1407.5759 (2014) (preprint)
12. Fortun, D., Bouthemy, P., Kervrann, C.: Optical flow modeling and computation: a survey. In: CVIU (2015)
13. Horn, B.K.P., Schunck, B.G.: Determining optical flow. Art. Intel. **17**(1–3), 185–203 (1981)
14. Kondermann, C., Mester, R., Garbe, C.S.: A statistical confidence measure for optical flows. In: Forsyth, D., Torr, P., Zisserman, A. (eds.) ECCV 2008, Part III. LNCS, vol. 5304, pp. 290–301. Springer, Heidelberg (2008)
15. Kybic, J., Nieuwenhuis, C.: Bootstrap optical flow confidence and uncertainty measure. CVIU **115**(10), 1449–1462 (2011)
16. Leordeanu, M., Zanfir, A., Sminchisescu, C.: Locally affine sparse-to-dense matching for motion and occlusion estimation. In: ICCV, Sydney, Australia, pp. 1221–1728 (2013)
17. Lucas, B.D., Kanade, T.: An iterative image registration technique with an application to stereo vision. Int. Joint Conf. Art. Intel., pp. 674–679 (1981)
18. Mémin, E., Pérez, P.: Dense estimation and object-based segmentation of the optical flow with robust techniques. TIP **7**(5), 703–719 (1998)
19. Mota, C., Stuke, L., Barth, E.: Analytic solutions for multiple motions. In: ICIP, Thessaloniki, Greece, pp. 917–920 (2001)
20. Mozerov, M.: Constrained optical flow estimation as a matching problem. TIP **22**(5), 2044–2055 (2013)
21. Odobez, J.M., Bouthemy, P.: Robust multiresolution estimation of parametric motion models. JVCIR **6**(4), 348–365 (1995)
22. Rose, K.: Deterministic annealing for clustering, compression, classification, regression, and related optimization problems. Proceedings of the IEEE **86**(11), 2210–2239 (1998)
23. Sun, D., Sudderth, E.B., Black, M.J.: Layered image motion with explicit occlusions, temporal consistency, and depth ordering. In: NIPS, Vancouver, Canada, pp. 2226–2234 (2010)
24. Wedel, A., Cremers, D., Pock, T., Bischof, H.: Structure-and motion-adaptive regularization for high accuracy optic flow. In: ICCV, Kyoto, Japan, pp. 1663–1668 (October 2009)
25. Weinzaepfel, P., Revaud, J., Harchaoui, Z., Schmid, C., et al.: Deepflow: large displacement optical flow with deep matching. In: ICCV, Sydney, Australia, pp. 1385–1392 (2013)
26. Werlberger, M., Pock, T., Bischof, H.: Motion estimation with non-local total variation regularization. In: CVPR, San-Fransisco, pp. 2464–2471 (2010)
27. Zimmer, H., Bruhn, A., Weickert, J.: Optic flow in harmony. IJCV **93**(3), 1–21 (2011)

An Image Registration Framework for Sliding Motion with Piecewise Smooth Deformations

Stefan Heldmann[1](✉), Thomas Polzin[2], Alexander Derksen[1], and Benjamin Berkels[3]

[1] Fraunhofer MEVIS Project Group Image Registration, Lübeck, Germany
stefan.heldmann@mevis.fraunhofer.de
[2] Institute of Mathematics and Image Computing, University of Lübeck, Lübeck, Germany
[3] Aachen Inst. for Advanced Study in Comp. Eng. Science, RWTH Aachen, Aachen, Germany

Abstract. We present a novel variational framework for image registration with explicit modeling of sliding motion, as it occurs, e.g., in the medical context at organ boundaries. The key of our method is a piecewise smooth deformation model that allows for discontinuities at the sliding interfaces while keeping the sliding domain in contact with its surrounding. The presented approach is generic and can be used with a large class of both image similarity measures and regularizers for the deformations. A useful byproduct of the proposed method is an automatic propagation of a given segmentation from one image to the other. We proof existence of minimizers under rather mild assumptions and present an efficient scheme for computing a numerical solution. The minimization is based on a splitting approach with alternating derivative based Gauss-Newton and fast first order convex optimization. Finally, we evaluate the proposed method on synthetic and real data.

Keywords: Image registration · Sliding motion · Deformation modeling · Convex optimization

1 Introduction

Image registration plays a crucial role in many fields, e.g., remote sensing, geophysics, robotics, computer vision and medical imaging [1]. Its goal is to establish correspondences between two or more given images that may differ due to different acquisition modalities, angles or time points. To this end, a typical approach is to look for a geometrical deformation that maps one image to the other in such a way that corresponding regions overlap. Here, the selected deformation type has a large impact on the solution and must be chosen carefully in a problem specific manner. In medical image registration, nonlinear deformation models are often a necessity as the assumptions of rigid or affine deformation of soft organ tissue usually do not hold. Nonlinear registration approaches have typically in common that they assume a continuous and smooth deformation on the whole image domain. While this assumption often holds, it is not fulfilled in certain registration cases. Using a deformation model based on the smoothness assumption in such a case leads to reduced registration accuracy. A well studied example is respiratory motion induced by the in- and deflation of the lungs, during which the lungs slide along the ribcage. The deformations occurring at the common sliding interface cannot be described in a continuous way. Comparable noncontinuous sliding behavior can be located at various organ interfaces in the human body, e.g. in joints with a socket during movement or along muscles during expansion and contraction. Recently, registration of sliding interfaces has gathered some attention and consequently numerous works have been published.

The following briefly highlights recent work concerned with registration of sliding interfaces in the context of lung CT images. A B-spline based registration allowing for direction and location dependent switching between smooth and discontinuous motion was proposed by Delmon et al. [2]. They used a level set segmentation to cope with local differences in motion properties. The computed transformation comprises of two continuous B-spline transformations that were computed independently. Schmidt-Richberg et al. [3] introduced a modified diffusive registration with direction dependent regularization. At the sliding interface, the deformation is split into tangential and normal motion and regularized direction-dependently, i.e. the displacement is smoothed in normal direction only. Pace et al. [4] used diffusion tensors to augment these ideas by the possibility to control the direction of regularization. Hence, their diffusion regularization is locally adaptive whereas the penalized energy is globally defined. In addition to a proper handling of sliding motion, Baluwala et al. [5] accounted for local rigidity of e.g. bones. They determined the external forces driving the registration process and split them into tangential and normal direction near the sliding boundary. Fluid regularization is incorporated for direction dependent regularization. Recently, the usage of individual biomechanical models allowing for sliding motion followed by a deformable registration was proposed by Han et al. [6]. The main volume change and motion is captured by physical modeling of pressures and applying them to a finite element model. A free-form registration is subsequently performed to handle inaccuracies. In [7], a constraint is introduced to the registration problem that explicitly models sliding of interfaces. The introduced constraint enforces contact between, e.g. lung and ribcage but allows for sliding of their interfaces. This approach is not tied to a specific distance measure or regularizer.

Like most approaches tackling the problem of sliding motion in thoracical CT images, the idea in this paper is to handle the apparent deformation independently inside and outside the lungs. Unlike most of the referenced work, we determine the location of the sliding interface not by explicitly computing the normals of the surface of a segmentation but constrain the two computed transformations at the boundary of the segmentation such that they are adhesive in a setwise manner. Therefore, we need a segmentation on one of the scans which is propagated to the other one. Conceptually our method relates to joint motion estimation and segmentation, cf. [8–10]. The proposed model does not incorporate physical properties like friction since sliding of lung and ribcage is commonly considered to be nearly frictionless [5]. Our approach is generic in the sense that it does not depend on a particular choice of distance measure and regularization in the registration. Note that, however, for proof of existence of a solution we restrain to data terms of the form $\int_{\mathcal{O}} \theta[T(y), R](x)\,\mathrm{d}x$, where pointwise a.e. convergence of the deformation has to imply pointwise a.e. convergence of the integrand, e.g. on Sum of Squared Differences [11] and a H^1-weakly lower semicontinuous regularizer that bounds the H^1-seminorm, e.g. diffusive regularization. Furthermore, thanks to a non-parametric segmentation representation based on the convexification of the Mumford-Shah model, the proposed model is easily usable for multiple objects with sliding behavior like the different organs in human bodies.

2 Method

2.1 Model

As sketched before, we assume that there is a sliding organ, represented by a subset of the computational domain and that sliding movement only happens at the boundary of the subset. This excludes sliding at "slashes", but still allows for multiple sliding organs, since the subset does not need to be connected.

Given two images $R, T \colon \mathbb{R}^d \to \mathbb{R}$ and an image domain $\Omega \subset \mathbb{R}^d$ the set of the sliding organ in R and T is denoted by $\mathcal{O} \subset \Omega$ and $\Sigma \subset \mathbb{R}^d$ respectively. We assume Σ to be known and are looking for two deformations, $y_{\mathrm{in}}, y_{\mathrm{out}} \colon \Omega \to \mathbb{R}^d$ such that $R \approx T \circ y_{\mathrm{in}}$ in $\mathcal{O}$ and $R \approx T \circ y_{\mathrm{out}}$ in $\Omega \setminus \mathcal{O}$. Furthermore, we require $y_{\mathrm{in}}(\partial \mathcal{O}) = \partial \Sigma = y_{\mathrm{out}}(\partial \mathcal{O})$. Note that this is just an equality of sets not a pointwise equality. Together, y_{in} and y_{out} describe a deformation of the whole domain $y \colon \Omega \to \mathbb{R}^d$, $y(x) = y_{\mathrm{in}}(x)$ for $x \in \mathcal{O}$, $y(x) = y_{\mathrm{out}}(x)$ otherwise, where the set constraint ensures that the deformation does not create a gap or an overlap between the sliding organ and its surrounding.

Instead of only looking at the boundary, it is easier to consider the whole sets. This leads to $y_{\mathrm{in}}(\mathcal{O}) = \Sigma$ and $y_{\mathrm{out}}(\mathcal{O}) = \Sigma$ or, in terms of characteristic functions, $\chi_{\mathcal{O}} = \chi_{\Sigma} \circ y_{\mathrm{in}}$ and $\chi_{\mathcal{O}} = \chi_{\Sigma} \circ y_{\mathrm{out}}$ in Ω. Here we implicitly assumed some smoothness of y_{in} and y_{out} in the sense that $y_{\mathrm{in}}(\Omega \setminus \mathcal{O}) \cap \Sigma = \emptyset$ and $y_{\mathrm{out}}(\Omega \setminus \mathcal{O}) \cap \Sigma = \emptyset$.

In practice, R, T and χ_{Σ} are given as nodal values on a regular grid that discretizes Ω. To obtain functions on Ω from the nodal values, we extend the values from the nodes to the whole domain Ω using piecewise multi-linear interpolation. Furthermore, T and χ_{Σ} are extended to $\mathbb{R}^d$ by assuming that they are zero on all nodes of the extensions of the regular grid that are outside of Ω. Thus, we can assume that R, T and χ_{Σ} are continuous functions. Since characteristic functions are not continuous, we denote the continuous function obtained by interpolating the nodal mask for Σ by $\tilde{\chi}_{\Sigma}$ instead of χ_{Σ} as above.

Using a soft penalty for the reformulated conditions with a penalty weight $\gamma > 0$, we get the objective functional

$$\mathcal{E}[y_{\text{in}}, y_{\text{out}}, \mathcal{O}] = \frac{1}{2} \int_\Omega \chi_\mathcal{O} (T(y_{\text{in}}) - R)^2 + (1 - \chi_\mathcal{O})(T(y_{\text{out}}) - R)^2 \, dx$$
$$+ \lambda (\mathcal{R}[y_{\text{in}}] + \mathcal{R}[y_{\text{out}}]) + \beta \operatorname{Per}(\mathcal{O})$$
$$+ \frac{\gamma}{2} \int_\Omega (\chi_\mathcal{O} - \tilde{\chi}_\Sigma(y_{\text{in}}))^2 + (\chi_\mathcal{O} - \tilde{\chi}_\Sigma(y_{\text{out}}))^2 \, dx$$

with $\mathcal{R}[y] = \frac{1}{2} \int_\Omega \|D(y(x) - x)\|_F^2 \, dx$. Here, D is the Jacobian matrix. Before we consider a minimization strategy, we prove existence of minimizers. This reveals in which spaces the deformations $y_{\text{in}}, y_{\text{out}}$ and the set $\mathcal{O}$ should be searched for. $\operatorname{Per}(\mathcal{O})$ makes it natural to use $\mathcal{B} = \{\mathcal{O} \subset \mathbb{R}^d : \mathcal{O} \text{ measurable}, \operatorname{Per}(\mathcal{O}) < \infty\}$, the sets of finite perimeter, as admissible set for $\mathcal{O}$. The diffusive regularization suggests Sobolev space $H^1(\Omega, \mathbb{R}^d)$ for the deformations. Since neither the similarity measure nor the soft penalty term put any restriction on the L^2-norm of the deformation, we constrain this by requiring the deformations to be in the set

$$M := \left\{ y \in H^{1,2}(\Omega, \mathbb{R}^d) : \big\| \|y - x\|_2 \big\|_{L^\infty} \le \operatorname{diam}(\Omega) \right\},$$

where x is the identity mapping on Ω, i.e. $y - x$ is the displacement component of the deformation. This is only a very weak assumption that typical numerical minimization strategies fulfill automatically: If the deformation shifts a point out of the image domain, this point should not be shifted further. In fact, M is even weaker, it just prevents any point from being shifted by more than the diameter of the image domain. This leads to the admissible set $\mathcal{A} = M \times M \times \mathcal{B}$.

Theorem 1. *Let $R \in C(\Omega)$ and $\tilde{\chi}_\Sigma, T \in C(\mathbb{R}^d)$. Then, the objective functional $\mathcal{E} : \mathcal{A} \to \mathbb{R}$ has a minimizer.*

Proof. The proof uses the direct method in the calculus of variations. Since $\mathcal{E}$ is bounded from below by 0, there exists a minimizing sequence $(y_n, z_n, \mathcal{O}_n) \subset \mathcal{A}$, i.e.

$$\lim_{n \to \infty} \mathcal{E}[y_n, z_n, \mathcal{O}_n] = \inf_{(y_{\text{in}}, y_{\text{out}}, \mathcal{O}) \in \mathcal{A}} \mathcal{E}[y_{\text{in}}, y_{\text{out}}, \mathcal{O}] =: \underline{\mathcal{E}}.$$

For $(y, z, \mathcal{O}) \in \mathcal{A}$ we have

$$\|Dy\|_{L^2}^2 \le \int_\Omega (\|Dy(x) - I_d\|_F + \|I_d\|_F)^2 \, dx$$
$$\le \int_\Omega 2\|Dy(x) - I_d\|_F^2 + 2\|I_d\|_F^2 \, dx \le \frac{4}{\lambda} \mathcal{E}[y, z, \mathcal{O}] + 2\|I_d\|_{L^2}^2.$$

Here, I_d denotes the identity matrix. Moreover, we have

$$\|y\|_{L^2} \le \|y - x\|_{L^2} + \|x\|_{L^2} = \big\| \|y - x\|_2 \big\|_{L^2} + \|x\|_{L^2}$$
$$\le \big\| \|y - x\|_2 \big\|_{L^\infty} \|1\|_{L^2} + \|x\|_{L^2} \le \operatorname{diam}(\Omega) \sqrt{|\Omega|} + \|x\|_{L^2}.$$

Combining the previous two estimates, we get

$$\|y\|_{H^{1,2}}^2 \le \left(\text{diam}(\Omega)\sqrt{|\Omega|} + \|x\|_{L^2}\right)^2 + \frac{4}{\lambda}\mathcal{E}[y, z, \mathcal{O}] + 2\|I_d\|_{L^2}^2.$$

Since $\mathcal{E}[y_n, z_n, \mathcal{O}_n]$ is bounded, the above shows that y_n and z_n are bounded in $H^{1,2}$. Furthermore, $\text{Per}(\mathcal{O}_n)$ is bounded and according to [12, 3.39] there exists a subsequence (again denoted by $\mathcal{O}_n$) and a set $\mathcal{O}$ with finite perimeter such that $|\Omega \cap (\mathcal{O}_n \Delta \mathcal{O})| \to 0$. Hence,

$$0 = \lim_{n\to\infty} \int_\Omega \chi_{\mathcal{O}_n \Delta \mathcal{O}}(x)\,\mathrm{d}x = \lim_{n\to\infty} \int_\Omega (\chi_{\mathcal{O}_n}(x) - \chi_{\mathcal{O}}(x))^2\,\mathrm{d}x.$$

Thus, $\chi_{\mathcal{O}_n}$ converges strongly to $\chi_{\mathcal{O}}$ in L^2, which allows us to select a subsequence (again denoted by $\mathcal{O}_n$) such that $\chi_{\mathcal{O}_n} \to \chi_{\mathcal{O}}$ pointwise a.e. and we can select a subsequence $(y_n, z_n, \mathcal{O}_n)$ with the same properties for $\mathcal{O}_n$. With the boundedness of y_n and z_n in $H^{1,2}$, we obtain a subsequence $(y_n, z_n, \mathcal{O}_n)$ (using the boundedness in H^1 and reflexivity of H^1 for weak convergence in H^1, Rellich's Theorem for strong convergence in L^2 and then measure theory for pointwise a.e. convergence) such that y_n and z_n converge strongly in L^2 and pointwise a.e. to y and $z \in H^1(\Omega, \mathbb{R}^d)$, respectively. From the pointwise convergence and the continuity of T and R we deduce the pointwise a.e. convergence of $\chi_{\mathcal{O}_n}(T(y_n)-R)^2 + (1-\chi_{\mathcal{O}_n})(T(z_n)-R)^2$ to $\chi_{\mathcal{O}}(T(y)-R)^2 + (1-\chi_{\mathcal{O}})(T(z)-R)^2$. Using Fatou's Lemma, we obtain the weak lower semicontinuity of the data term. The weak lower semicontinuity of the regularizers for the deformations follows from [13, page453], the weak lower semicontinuity of the perimeter from [12, 3.39]. Since $\tilde{\chi}_\Sigma$ is continuous the weak lower semicontinuity of the soft penalty follows analogously to the one of the data term und we get

$$\mathcal{E}[y, z, \mathcal{O}] \le \liminf_{n\to\infty} \mathcal{E}[y_n, z_n, \mathcal{O}_n] = \lim_{n\to\infty} \mathcal{E}[y_n, z_n, \mathcal{O}_n] = \underline{\mathcal{E}}.$$

Thus, $(y, z, \mathcal{O})$ is a minimizer.

Note, the existence proof is not limited to the diffusive regularizer. It works for any weakly lower semicontinuous $\mathcal{R}: H^{1,2}(\Omega, \mathbb{R}^d) \to \mathbb{R}$ that bounds the H^1 semi norm, i.e. there are constants $c_1, c_2, r > 0$ such that $\|Dy\|_{L^2} \le c_1(\mathcal{R}[y])^r + c_2$ for all $y \in H^{1,2}(\Omega, \mathbb{R}^d)$. Furthermore, it also applies to data terms of the form $\int_\Omega \theta[T(y), R](x)\,\mathrm{d}x$ as long as pointwise a.e. convergence of y_n implies pointwise a.e. convergence of the integrand $\theta[T(y_n), R]$.

2.2 Optimization Strategy

Since $\chi_{\mathcal{O}}(x) \in \{0,1\}$ ($\tilde{\chi}_\Sigma$ is not limited to $\{0,1\}$, but does not need to be for our argument), the following identity holds

$$(\chi_{\mathcal{O}}(x) - \tilde{\chi}_\Sigma(y(x)))^2 = \chi_{\mathcal{O}}(x)(1 - \tilde{\chi}_\Sigma(y(x)))^2 + (1 - \chi_{\mathcal{O}}(x))\tilde{\chi}_\Sigma(y(x))^2.$$

Hence, $\mathcal{E}$ can also expressed as follows

$$\mathcal{E}[y_{\text{in}}, y_{\text{out}}, \mathcal{O}] = \int_\Omega \chi_\mathcal{O} f[y_{\text{in}}, y_{\text{out}}] + (1 - \chi_\mathcal{O}) g[y_{\text{in}}, y_{\text{out}}]\, dx$$
$$+ \beta \operatorname{Per}(\mathcal{O}) + \lambda (\mathcal{R}[y_{\text{in}}] + \mathcal{R}[y_{\text{out}}]),$$

where

$$f[y_{\text{in}}, y_{\text{out}}] := \frac{1}{2}\left[(T(y_{\text{in}}) - R)^2 + \gamma\left((1 - \tilde{\chi}_\Sigma(y_{\text{in}}))^2 + (1 - \tilde{\chi}_\Sigma(y_{\text{out}}))^2\right)\right],$$

$$g[y_{\text{in}}, y_{\text{out}}] := \frac{1}{2}\left[(T(y_{\text{out}}) - R)^2 + \gamma\left(\tilde{\chi}_\Sigma(y_{\text{in}})^2 + \tilde{\chi}_\Sigma(y_{\text{out}})^2\right)\right].$$

This shows that (for fixed y_{in} and y_{out}) the minimization with respect to $\mathcal{O}$ is a classical binary Mumford–Shah segmentation problem. Thus, a global minimizer can be obtained by convexification and thresholding [14,15]. First, we note that $\mathcal{O}$ can be represented by its characteristic function $\chi_\mathcal{O}$. For $\mathcal{O} \in \mathcal{B}$, we know $\chi_\mathcal{O} \in BV(\Omega, \{0, 1\})$ and $\operatorname{Per}(\mathcal{O}) = \operatorname{TV}(\chi_\mathcal{O})$. Following [15], we consider the uniformly (without loss of generality, we can assume $f, g \geq c > 0$) convex functional

$$\mathcal{J}[y_{\text{in}}, y_{\text{out}}, u] = \int_\Omega u^2 f[y_{\text{in}}, y_{\text{out}}] + (1 - u)^2 g[y_{\text{in}}, y_{\text{out}}]\, dx$$
$$+ \beta \operatorname{TV}(u) + \lambda (\mathcal{R}[y_{\text{in}}] + \mathcal{R}[y_{\text{out}}]).$$

Obviously, $\mathcal{E}[y_{\text{in}}, y_{\text{out}}, \mathcal{O}] = \mathcal{J}[y_{\text{in}}, y_{\text{out}}, \chi_\mathcal{O}]$. Furthermore, a thresholding theorem holds. If u is a minimizer of $\mathcal{J}[y_{\text{in}}, y_{\text{out}}, \cdot]$ over $BV(\Omega)$, then the $\frac{1}{2}$-super-levelset $\{u > \frac{1}{2}\}$ is a minimizer of $\mathcal{E}[y_{\text{in}}, y_{\text{out}}, \cdot]$ over $\mathcal{B}$ (see [15]). This means that we can solve the non-convex minimization problem for $\mathcal{O}$ by solving an unconstrained uniformly convex minimization problem and simple thresholding. To better understand the structure of $\mathcal{J}$ with respect to $y_{\text{in}}, y_{\text{out}}$ and u, we define

$$\mathcal{D}[w, y] := \frac{1}{2}\int_\Omega w^2 (T(y) - R)^2\, dx \text{ and}$$
$$\mathcal{P}[w, y] := \frac{1}{2}\int_\Omega w^2\left(1 - \tilde{\chi}_\Sigma(y)\right)^2 + (1 - w)^2 \tilde{\chi}_\Sigma(y)^2\, dx$$

and obtain

$$\mathcal{J}[y_{\text{in}}, y_{\text{out}}, u] = \mathcal{D}[u, y_{\text{in}}] + \mathcal{D}[1 - u, y_{\text{out}}] + \gamma(\mathcal{P}[u, y_{\text{in}}] + \mathcal{P}[u, y_{\text{out}}])$$
$$+ \lambda(\mathcal{R}[y_{\text{in}}] + \mathcal{R}[y_{\text{out}}]) + \beta \operatorname{TV}[u].$$

The necessary condition for a minimizer is given by $0 \in \partial \mathcal{J}[y_{\text{in}}, y_{\text{out}}, u]$ with

$$\partial \mathcal{J}[y_{\text{in}}, y_{\text{out}}, u] = \begin{pmatrix} \partial_{y_{\text{in}}}\left(\mathcal{D}[u, y_{\text{in}}] + \lambda \mathcal{R}[y_{\text{in}}] + \gamma \mathcal{P}[u, y_{\text{in}}]\right) \\ \partial_{y_{\text{out}}}\left(\mathcal{D}[1 - u, y_{\text{out}}] + \lambda \mathcal{R}[y_{\text{out}}] + \gamma \mathcal{P}[u, y_{\text{out}}]\right) \\ \partial_u \left(\int_\Omega u^2 f[y_{\text{in}}, y_{\text{out}}] + (1 - u)^2 g[y_{\text{in}}, y_{\text{out}}]\, dx + \beta \operatorname{TV}(u)\right) \end{pmatrix}.$$

Note that $\partial_{y_{\text{in}}} \mathcal{J}$ is independent from y_{out} and vice versa. The deformations are only coupled by their dependency on u. This inspires us to propose a splitting scheme with alternating optimization on y_{in}, y_{out}, and u. Thus, for fixed u the optimization w.r.t. y_{in} and y_{out}, respectively, turns out as pure registration problems and optimization on u with fixed deformations y_{in}, y_{out} is convex. Our overall iteration ($k = 1, 2, ...$) is

$$\begin{cases} y_{\text{in}}^{k+1} \in \underset{y}{\operatorname{argmin}}\left\{\mathcal{D}[u^k, y] + \lambda \mathcal{R}[y] + \gamma \mathcal{P}[u^k, y]\right\} \\ y_{\text{out}}^{k+1} \in \underset{y}{\operatorname{argmin}}\left\{\mathcal{D}[1 - u^k, y] + \lambda \mathcal{R}[y] + \gamma \mathcal{P}[u^k, y]\right\} \\ u^{k+1} \in \underset{u}{\operatorname{argmin}}\left\{\int_\Omega u^2 f[y_{\text{in}}^{k+1}, y_{\text{out}}^{k+1}] + (1-u)^2 g[y_{\text{in}}^{k+1}, y_{\text{out}}^{k+1}]\, dx + \beta \text{TV}(u)\right\} \end{cases}.$$

For the numerical solution of the three subproblems, we use a discretize-then-optimize approach, i.e., we first discretize the objective functional and then compute a numerical solution by optimization of the discretized functional.

2.3 Discretization

For ease of presentation, we assume that Ω is a 2D rectangular domain. The discretization for higher dimensions is analogous. We use common mid-point rule for an approximation of integrals. Therefore, the image domain Ω is uniformly discretized with $N = n_1 \times n_2$ cell centered grid points (x_i, x_{i+N}) and grid size $h = h_1 h_2$. Deformations are also represented on a uniform nodal discretization of Ω (not necessarily identical with the cell centered one above) with $M = m_1 \times m_2$ nodal grid points and bilinear interpolation is used for the evaluation at arbitrary points. Furthermore, let $Q \in \mathbb{R}^{2N \times 2M}$ be an interpolation matrix, such that Qy ($y \in \mathbb{R}^{2M}$) are the values of the deformation at the N cell centered grid points (x_i, x_{i+N}). This leads to the discretized components of the objective function:

$$\mathcal{D}^h[w, y] = \frac{h}{2} w^{2\top}(T(Qy) - R)^2, \quad \mathcal{R}^h[y] = \frac{h}{2}(y - y_0)^\top A(y - y_0),$$

$$\mathcal{P}^h[w, y] = \frac{h}{2}\left(w^{2\top}(1 - \tilde{\chi}_\Sigma(Qy))^2 + (1-w)^{2\top} \tilde{\chi}_\Sigma(Qy)^2\right), \text{ and}$$

$$\text{TV}^h[u] = h \max_{v \in P} u^\top K v, \quad P := \{v \in \mathbb{R}^{2N} : \|(v_i, v_{i+N})\| \leq 1, i = 1, \ldots, N\}.$$

Here, squares are meant elementwise, $K \in \mathbb{R}^{N \times 2N}$ approximates the divergence (using forward finite differences and Neumann boundary conditions), $A \in \mathbb{R}^{2M \times 2M}$ a finite difference matrix for computing the regularizer, and $y_0 \in \mathbb{R}^{2M}$ is the identity deformation. Furthermore, R, $T(Qy)$, and $\tilde{\chi}_\Sigma(Qy)$ are considered as vectors of length N that contain the corresponding function values at the cell-centered grid points (x_i, x_{i+N}). Thus, our discretized iterative scheme reads

$$\begin{cases} y_{\text{in}}^{k+1} \in \underset{y \in \mathbb{R}^{2M}}{\operatorname{argmin}}\left\{\mathcal{D}^h[u^k, y] + \lambda \mathcal{R}^h[y] + \gamma \mathcal{P}^h[u^k, y]\right\} \\ y_{\text{out}}^{k+1} \in \underset{y \in \mathbb{R}^{2M}}{\operatorname{argmin}}\left\{\mathcal{D}^h[1 - u^k, y] + \lambda \mathcal{R}^h[y] + \gamma \mathcal{P}^h[u^k, y]\right\} \\ u^{k+1} \in \underset{u \in \mathbb{R}^N}{\operatorname{argmin}}\left\{h(u^{2\top} f^{k+1} + (1-u)^{2\top} g^{k+1}) + \beta \text{TV}^h[u]\right\} \end{cases}$$

where we set $g^{k+1} := \frac{1}{2}[(T(Qy_{\text{out}}^{k+1}) - R)^2 + \gamma(\tilde{\chi}_\Sigma(Qy_{\text{in}}^{k+1})^2 + \tilde{\chi}_\Sigma(Qy_{\text{out}}^{k+1})^2)]$ and $f^{k+1} := \frac{1}{2}[(T(Qy_{\text{in}}^{k+1}) - R)^2 + \gamma((1 - \tilde{\chi}_\Sigma(Qy_{\text{in}}^{k+1}))^2 + (1 - \tilde{\chi}_\Sigma(Qy_{\text{out}}^{k+1}))^2)]$. To solve for $y_{\text{in}}^{k+1}, y_{\text{out}}^{k+1} \in \mathbb{R}^{2M}$ in the first two steps, we propose standard Gauss-Newton optimization [11,16] . For computing $u^{k+1} \in \mathbb{R}^N$ we propose a first order primal-dual method [17]. Note that u^{k+1} is a saddle point of

$$\min_u \max_v \beta u^\top K v + G[u] - F^*[v]$$

with $G[u] = u^\top f^{k+1} + (1 - u)^\top g^{k+1}$ and projection $F^*[v] = 0$ if $v \in P$ and $F^*[v] = \infty$ else. Following the work from Chambolle and Pock [17], we iterate

$$\begin{cases} v^{n+1} = (I + \sigma \partial F^*)^{-1}(v^n + \sigma \beta K^* \bar{u}^n) \\ u^{n+1} = (I + \tau \partial G)^{-1}(u^n - \tau \beta K v^{n+1}) \\ \bar{u}^{n+1} = 2u^{n+1} - u^n \end{cases}$$

The resolvent operator for the primal variable is defined as $(I + \tau \partial G)^{-1}(\tilde{u}) = \operatorname{argmin}_u \{\|u - \tilde{u}\|^2/(2\tau) + G[u]\}$. Note that G is pointwise quadratic and direct computation shows

$$(I + \tau \partial G)^{-1}(\tilde{u}) = u \Leftrightarrow u_i = \frac{\tilde{u}_i + 2\tau g_i^{k+1}}{1 + 2\tau(f_i^{k+1} + g_i^{k+1})}.$$

Since F^* is an indicator function of a convex set P, its resolvent $(I + \tau \partial F^*)^{-1}(\tilde{v}) = \operatorname{argmin}_v \{\|v - \tilde{v}\|^2/(2\tau) + F^*[v]\}$ simply projects onto P (cf. [17]), i.e.,

$$(I + \tau \partial F^*)^{-1}(\tilde{v}) = v$$
$$\Leftrightarrow (v_i, v_{i+N}) = \left(\frac{\tilde{v}_i}{\max(1, \|(\tilde{v}_i, \tilde{v}_{i+N})\|)}, \frac{\tilde{v}_{i+N}}{\max(1, \|(\tilde{v}_i, \tilde{v}_{i+N})\|)} \right).$$

3 Numerical Experiments

In this section, we perform numerical experiments on synthetical data as well as on medical CT lung inhale-exhale data from publicly available 4D CT thorax scans [18]. To handle large deformations and speed up computations, optimization was performed in a coarse-to-fine manner on a four level Gaussian image pyramid. For all experiments the sliding set $\mathcal{O}$ was initialized with Σ, i.e., $u^0 := \chi_\Sigma$.

3.1 Synthetic Example: Moving Bar

Our first experiment is inspired by [5] and depicted in Fig. 1. It illustrates our model for sliding motion. The reference are two bars stacked on top of each other (Fig. 1(b)). In the template image, the lower bar is moved to the right (Fig. 1(a)). The challenge of the registration is to slide along the horizontal interface between the bars. Therefore, the sliding area Σ in Fig. 1(a) is defined along the horizontal

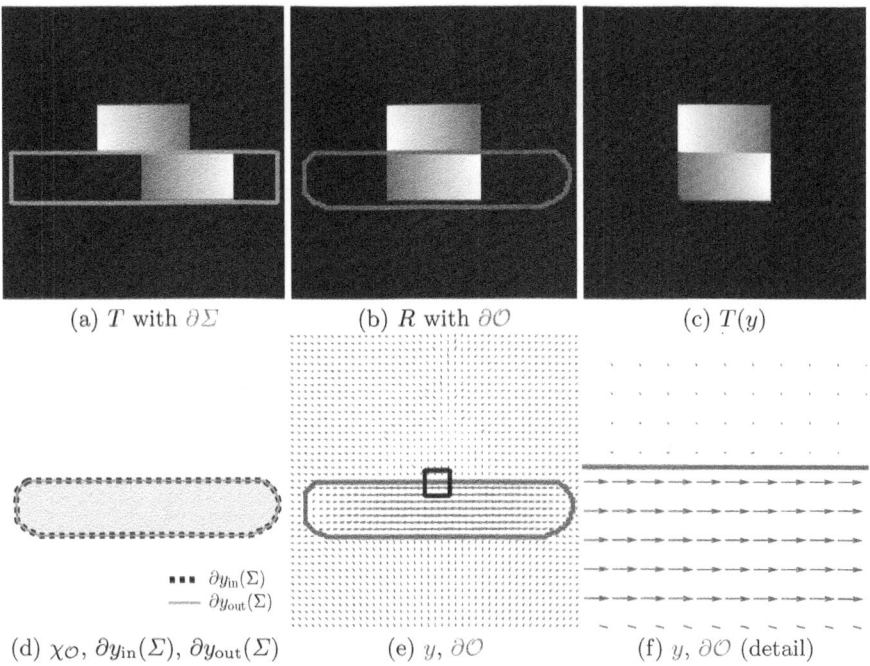

Fig. 1. Results of the "Moving Bar" synthetic example. (a) Template T with initial segmentation Σ (green), (b) reference R with propagated segmentation $\mathcal{O}$ (red), (c) registered template $T \circ y$, (d) $\mathcal{O}$ (gray) with deformed set $y_{\text{in}}(\Sigma)$ (dashed) and $y_{\text{out}}(\Sigma)$ (solid), (e) deformation y with computed set $\mathcal{O}$ and location of the detail given in (f).

border. Note that it has significant larger extent in x direction than the "moving" bar itself. This is due to our sliding model, since ideal registration will expand the area left from the moving bar and shrink the area on the right. Fig. 1(c)–(f) shows that the registration reasonably aligned the images by horizontal sliding in Σ. Furthermore, $\mathcal{O}$, $y_{\text{in}}(\Sigma)$, and $y_{\text{out}}(\Sigma)$ almost perfectly fulfill the sliding condition enforced by the penalty in our objective function. For the experiment, we chose parameters $\beta = 100$, $\lambda = 10^3$, $\gamma = 10^5$.

3.2 Synthetic Example: Rotating Square

Our second example is shown in Fig. 2 and illustrates sliding of two counter-rotated objects along their interface. Therefore a square is embedded into an ellipse, cf. the reference in Fig. 2(b). The template (Fig. 2(a)) is a deformed version of the reference, where we performed 40 degrees counterclockwise rotation of the square and 80 degrees clockwise rotation of the ellipse. Σ is choosen as the region occupied by the square in the template image. Furthermore, the ellipse and square have textures with different intensity gradients, such that registration should be generally able to recover the artificial deformation.

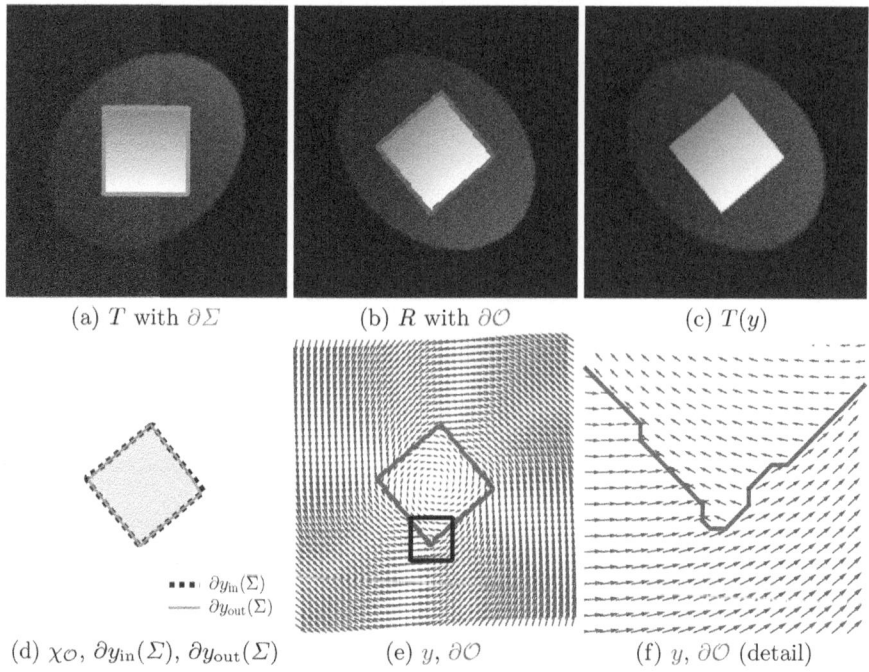

Fig. 2. Results of the "Rotating Square" synthetic example. (a) Template T with initial segmentation Σ (green), (b) reference R with propagated segmentation $\mathcal{O}$ (red), (c) registered template $T \circ y$, (d) $\mathcal{O}$ (gray) with deformed set $y_{\text{in}}(\Sigma)$ (dashed) and $y_{\text{out}}(\Sigma)$ (solid), (e) deformation y with computed set $\mathcal{O}$ and location of the detail given in (f).

This is clearly an extreme example and for this experiment we deviate little from above model. We aim to recover large rotations but the proposed diffusive regularization prevents deformations of such type. Note that the null space of the diffusive regularizer only contains global translations. To this end, here we used second order curvature regularization [11,19], i.e., we chose $\mathcal{R}(y) := \|\Delta y\|^2_{L^2(\Omega)}$ whose null space contains harmonic and in particular affine deformations.

However, the results obtained by this example are quite remarkable. We were able to almost perfectly recover the applied large counterrotations, cf. Fig. 2(c)–(f). In this experiment, we set $\lambda = 10$, $\beta = 1$ and $\gamma = 1000$.

3.3 Lung CT Data

This example is inspired by medical background and we aim for recovery of breathing motion in lungs. Therefore, we register 2D slices taken from 4D inhale (template T) and exhale (reference R) lung CT scans, see Fig. 3(a) and (b). Both are coronal slices taken from the publicly available DIR-Lab 4D-CT data set 4 [18] and Σ is a lung segmentation of the template image (cf. Fig. 3(a)). In this example,

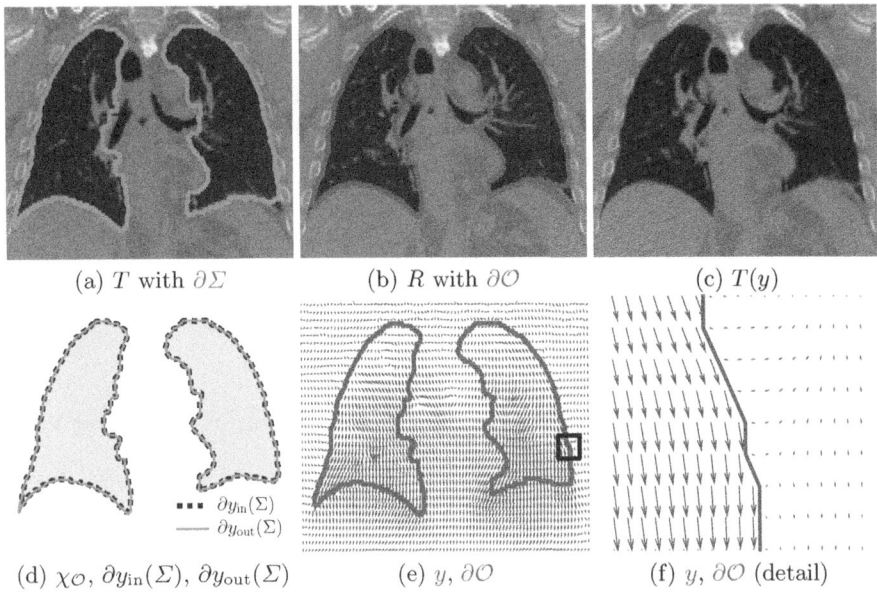

Fig. 3. Results of the "Lung CT data" medical example. (a) Template T with initial segmentation Σ (green), (b) reference R with propagated segmentation $\mathcal{O}$ (red), (c) registered template $T \circ y$, (d) $\mathcal{O}$ (gray) with deformed set $y_{\text{in}}(\Sigma)$ (dashed) and $y_{\text{out}}(\Sigma)$ (solid), (e) deformation y with computed set $\mathcal{O}$ and location of the detail given in (f).

a perfect pixel-wise alignment of the images is not possible although the coronal slices were chosen carefully but not all structures have corresponding ones in the other image. Note that Σ is not connected and consists of two subdomains. Nevertheless, both domains are linked via the interior deformation y_{in}. The parameters were chosen empirically as $\lambda = 10^6$, $\beta = 10^5$, $\gamma = 10^3$.

Figure 3(c)–(f) depicts the result. The given segmentation Σ on the template image is successfully propagated to the reference image by the computed $\mathcal{O}$, cf. Fig. 3(b) and (d). Fig. 3(e) reveals plausible motion patterns with small motion in upper regions and apart of the ribs and the detail presented in Fig. 3(f) shows sliding motion by opposite vectors left and right from the sliding interface.

4 Discussion

We introduced a novel registration approach capable of recovering sliding motion. A single segmentation of the sliding objects given in the template image is used during the registration process and propagated on the reference image. The basic idea is a decomposition of the total deformation into two spatially independent ones and mixing them based on the evolving segmentation. For segmentation a convexified Mumford-Shah problem [15] is solved with a primal-dual method proposed by Chambolle and Pock [17]. Registration is done independently on the whole domain with proper masking of the data for the Sum of Squared Differences distance measure and diffusive regularization favoring piecewise smooth deformations whilst allowing for discontinuities at the sliding interface. An existence proof of a minimizer of the stated joint functional is given. Because of the modular design other choices for the distance measure or regularizer are easily integrable. The implementation of the algorithm is done for 2D images but straightforward extendable to higher dimensional data. First results on synthetic data and thoracic CT scans are very promising. In future work, we plan to extend the methods to higher dimensions and elaborate on other choices for the distance measures like Cross Correlation or Normalized Gradient Fields [11].

References

1. Zitová, B., Flusser, J.: Image registration methods: a survey. Image and Vision Computing **21**, 977–1000 (2003)
2. Delmon, V., Rit, S., Pinho, R., Sarrut, D.: Direction dependent B-splines decomposition for the registration of sliding objects. In: Proceedings of the Fourth International Workshop on Pulmonary Image Analysis, pp. 45–55 (2011)
3. Schmidt-Richberg, A., Werner, R., Handels, H., Ehrhardt, J.: Estimation of slipping organ motion by registration with direction-dependent regularization. Medical Image Analysis **16**, 150–159 (2012)
4. Pace, D., Aylward, S., Niethammer, M.: A locally adaptive regularization based on anisotropic diffusion for deformable image registration of sliding organs. IEEE Transactions on Medical Imaging **32**, 2114–2126 (2013)
5. Baluwala, H.Y., Risser, L., Schnabel, J.A., Saddi, K.A.: Toward physiologically motivated registration of diagnostic CT and PET/CT of lung volumes. Medical Physics **40**(2), 021 903-1–021 903-13 (2013)
6. Han, L., Hawkes, D., Barratt, D.: A hybrid biomechanical model-based image registration method for sliding objects. In: SPIE Medical Imaging, pp. 90 340G-1-6 (2014)
7. Derksen, A., Heldmann, S., Polzin, T., Berkels, B.: Image registration with sliding motion constraints for 4D CT motion correction. In: Bildverarbeitung für die Medizin 2015 (2015)
8. Vemuri, B., Chen, Y.: Joint image registration and segmentation. In: Vemuri, B., Chen, Y. (eds.) Geometric Level Set Methods in Imaging, Vision, and Graphics, pp. 251–269. Springer, New York (2003)
9. Yezzi, A., Zöllei, L., Kapur, T.: A variational framework for integrating segmentation and registration through active contours. Medical Image Analysis **7**(2), 171–185 (2003)
10. Amiaz, T., Kiryati, N.: Piecewise-smooth dense optical flow via level sets. International Journal of Computer Vision **68**(2), 111–124 (2006)
11. Modersitzki, J.: FAIR: Flexible Algorithms for Image Registration. SIAM (2009)
12. Ambrosio, L., Fusco, N., Pallara, D.: Functions of bounded variation and free discontinuity problems, ser. The Clarendon Press, Oxford Mathematical Monographs, New York (2000)
13. Evans, L.C.: Partial Differential Equations. American Math. Soc. (1998)
14. Nikolova, M., Esedoḡlu, S., Chan, T.F.: Algorithms for finding global minimizers of image segmentation and denoising models. SIAM Journal on Applied Mathematics **66**(5), 1632–1648 (2006)

15. Berkels, B.: An unconstrained multiphase thresholding approach for image segmentation. In: Tai, X.-C., Mørken, K., Lysaker, M., Lie, K.-A. (eds.) SSVM 2009. LNCS, vol. 5567, pp. 26–37. Springer, Heidelberg (2009)
16. Nocedal, J., Wright, S.J.: Numerical Optimization. Springer, New York (2006)
17. Chambolle, A., Pock, T.: A first-order primal-dual algorithm for convex problems with applications to imaging. Journal of Mathematical Imaging and Vision **40**(1), 120–145 (2011)
18. Castillo, R., Castillo, E., Guerra, R., Johnson, V.E., McPhail, T., Garg, A.K., Guerrero, T.: A framework for evaluation of deformable image registration spatial accuracy using large landmark point sets. Physics in Medicine and Biology **54**, 1849–1870 (2009)
19. Fischer, B., Modersitzki, J.: Curvature based image registration. Journal of Mathematical Imaging and Vision **18**(1), 81–85 (2003)

Nonlocal Joint Segmentation Registration Model

Solène Ozeré and Carole Le Guyader[✉]

Laboratoire de Mathématiques, Normandie Université, INSA de Rouen,
685 avenue de l'Université, 76801 Saint-Etienne-du-Rouvray Cedex, France
{solene.ozere,carole.le-guyader}@insa-rouen.fr

Abstract. In this paper, we address the issue of designing a theoretically well-motivated joint segmentation-registration method capable of handling large deformations. The shapes to be matched are implicitly modeled by level set functions and are evolved in order to minimize a functional containing both a nonlinear-elasticity-based regularizer and a criterion that forces the evolving shape to match intermediate topology-preserving segmentation results. Theoretical results encompassing existence of minimizers, Γ-convergence result and existence of a weak viscosity solution of the related evolution problem are provided.

Keywords: Topology-preserving segmentation · Registration · Nonlinear elasticity · Saint Venant-Kirchhoff material · Quasiconvexity · Relaxed problem · Γ-convergence · Weak viscosity solutions

1 Introduction

While image segmentation aims to partition a given image into meaningful constituents or to find boundaries delineating such objects (see [1, Chapter4] for instance, for a relevant analysis of this problem), registration, given two images called Template and Reference, consists in determining a smooth deformation field φ such that the deformed Template is aligned with the Reference. According to the modalities of the involved images, the goal of registration might differ: for images of the same modality, the purpose of registration is to match the geometrical features, the shapes and the intensity level distribution of the Reference with those of the Template. When the images have been acquired through different mechanisms and have different modalities, registration aims to correlate both images in terms of shapes and salient components, while preserving the modality of the Template image. In a recent survey, Sotiras *et al.* ([21]) provide an extensive overview of existing registration methods and analyze the three components they consider to be part of a registration algorithm: a deformation model *(itself organized into three classes: geometric transformations derived from physical models – our model falls within this category –; geometric transformations derived from interpolation theory; knowledge-based geometric transformations)*, an objective function, i.e., a matching criterion *(geometric methods including landmarks; iconic methods; hybrid methods)* and an optimization method *(continuous methods; discrete methods; greedy approaches)*. In this paper, instead of considering these two tasks, segmentation and registration, as independent ones, we propose to jointly treat them: the segmentation result obtained at intermediate steps will serve as a target to reach in the registration process and will guide it. The scope of the proposed work is thus first to devise a theoretically well-motivated registration model in a variational formulation, authorizing large and smooth deformations. In particular, classical regularizers such as linear elasticity (see [6]) are not suitable for this kind of problems involving large deformations since assuming small strains and the validity of Hooke's law. In addition, to handle a large class of images, we propose defining a geometric dissimilarity measure based on shape comparisons thanks to successive segmentation results that will serve as inputs in our registration model. Thus the algorithm produces both a smooth mapping between the two shapes as well as a segmentation of the Reference image. Let us emphasize that the focus of the paper is on the mathematical presentation and well-posedness of a nonlinear elasticity-based registration model in the two dimensional case. Hence, the computational results are currently preliminary. Later work may go to higher dimensions. The idea of combining segmentation and registration is not new. Prior related works suggest to take advantage of both processes: in [24], a curve evolution approach is used and phrased in terms of level set functions. In [22], Vemuri et al. propose a coupled PDE model to perform both segmentation and registration. In the first PDE, the level sets of the source image are evolved along their normals with a speed defined as the difference between the target and the evolving source image. In [17], the model combines a matching criterion based on the active contours without edges ([9]) and a nonlinear-elasticity-based regularizer. In [18], Lord et al. propose a unified method that simultaneously treats segmentation and registration based on metric structure comparisons. In [14], Droske et al. aim to match the edges and the normals of the two images by applying a Mumford-Shah type free discontinuity problem. More recently, Ozeré et al. ([20]) have introduced a variational joint segmentation/registration model combining a measure of dissimilarity based on weighted total variation and a regularizer based on the stored energy function of a Saint Venant-Kirchhoff material.

2   Mathematical Modeling

Let Ω be a connected bounded open subset of $\mathbb{R}^2$ of class $\mathcal{C}^1$. Let us denote by $R : \bar{\Omega} \to \mathbb{R}$ the Reference image assumed to be sufficiently smooth, and by $\tilde{T} : \bar{\Omega} \to \mathbb{R}$ the Template image. The shape contained in the Template image is supposed to be modeled by a Lipschitz continuous function Φ_0 whose zero level line is the shape boundary. Denoting by $\mathcal{C}$ the zero level set of Φ_0 and by $w \subset \Omega$ the open set it delineates, Φ_0 is chosen such that $\mathcal{C} = \{x \in \Omega \,|\, \Phi_0(x) = 0\}$, $w = \{x \in \Omega \,|\, \Phi_0(x) > 0\}$ and $\Omega \setminus \bar{w} = \{x \in \Omega \,|\, \Phi_0(x) < 0\}$. For theoretical and numerical purposes, we may consider a linear extension operator (see [5, p.158]) $P : W^{1,\infty}(\Omega) \to W^{1,\infty}(\mathbb{R}^2)$ such that for all $\Phi \in W^{1,\infty}(\Omega)$, (i) $P\Phi_{|\Omega} = \Phi$, (ii) $\|P\Phi\|_{L^\infty(\mathbb{R}^2)} \leq C \|\Phi\|_{L^\infty(\Omega)}$ and (iii) $\|P\Phi\|_{W^{1,\infty}(\mathbb{R}^2)} \leq C \|\Phi\|_{W^{1,\infty}(\Omega)}$, with C

depending only on Ω. By this extension process, we consider then that $\Phi_0 \in W^{1,\infty}(\mathbb{R}^2)$ to ensure that $\Phi_0 \circ \varphi$ – with φ introduced later – is always defined. Let $\varphi : \bar{\Omega} \to \mathbb{R}^2$ be the sought deformation. A deformation is a smooth mapping that is orientation-preserving and injective, except possibly on $\partial \Omega$. We also denote by u the associated displacement such that $\varphi = Id + u$, Id denoting the identity mapping. The deformation gradient is $\nabla \varphi = I + \nabla u$, $\bar{\Omega} \to M_2(\mathbb{R})$, the set $M_2(\mathbb{R})$ being the set of all real square matrices of order 2 identified to $\mathbb{R}^4$. The idea is thus to find a smooth deformation field φ such that the zero level line of $\Phi_0 \circ \varphi$ gives a relevant partition of the Reference image R, relating then segmentation and registration. The model is phrased as a functional minimization problem with unknown φ; it combines a smoother on the deformation field and a distance measure criterion between $\Phi_0 \circ \varphi$ and an input resulting from the topology-preserving segmentation process of Le Guyader and Vese ([16]). In many applications, such as medical imaging, topology preservation is a desirable property: when the shape to be detected has a known topology (e.g. spherical topology for the brain), or when the resulting shape must be homeomorphic to the initial one. In other words, an initial contour should be deformed without change of topology as merging or breaking. We expect this property to be inherited by the registration process. This measure constitutes an alternative to classical intensity-based/information-theoretic-based matching measures, mutual information – suitable when dealing with images that have been acquired through different sensors –, measures based on the comparison of gradient vector fields of both images, metric structure comparisons, mass-preserving measures, etc. The proposed matching criterion is complemented by a nonlinear-elasticity-based regularizer on the deformation field φ. To allow large and nonlinear deformations, we propose to view the shapes to be warped as isotropic, homogeneous, hyperelastic materials and more precisely as Saint Venant-Kirchhoff materials (see [10] for further details and [7] for an alternative hyperelastic model). A motivation for this choice is that the stored energy function of such materials is the simplest one that agrees with the generic expression of the stored energy of an isotropic, homogeneous, hyperelastic material. To ensure that the distribution of the deformation Jacobian determinants does not exhibit shrinkages or growths, we propose complementing the model by a term controlling that the Jacobian determinant remains close to 1. At this stage, the considered regularizer would be, setting $F = \nabla \varphi$

$$W(F) = W_{SVK}(F) + \mu \left(\det F - 1 \right)^2,$$

with $W_{SVK}(F) = \dfrac{\lambda}{2} (\operatorname{tr} E)^2 + \mu \operatorname{tr} E^2$, the stored energy function of a Saint Venant-Kirchhoff material, λ and μ the Lamé coefficients, $E = \left(F^T F - I \right)/2$ the Green-Saint Venant stress tensor measuring the deviation between φ and a rigid deformation, and with the following notation $A : B = \operatorname{tr} A^T B$, the matrix inner product and $\|A\| = \sqrt{A : A}$ the related matrix norm (Frobenius norm).

Nevertheless, the stored energy function W written as is exhibits undesirable properties: it is not rank-1 convex (as the density W_{SVK}), and consequently neither quasiconvex, nor polyconvex, which raises a drawback of theoretical nature since we cannot obtain the weak lower semi-continuity of the introduced functional. The idea is thus to replace W by its quasiconvex envelope QW (see [12] for a deeper presentation of these notions). In general, deriving the explicit expression of this envelope is an hopeless task, but in this case, using Jensen's inequality and a decomposition result by Bousselsal ([4]), one can establish that

$$QW(F) = \begin{vmatrix} W(F) = \beta \left(\|F\|^2 - \alpha\right)^2 + \Psi(\det F) & \text{if } \|F\|^2 \geq \alpha, \\ \Psi(\det F) & \text{if } \|F\|^2 < \alpha, \end{vmatrix}$$

with $\alpha = 2\frac{\lambda+\mu}{\lambda+2\mu}$, $\beta = \frac{\lambda+2\mu}{8}$ and Ψ the convex mapping defined by $\Psi : t \mapsto -\frac{\mu}{2}t^2 + \mu(t-1)^2 + \frac{\mu(\lambda+\mu)}{2(\lambda+2\mu)}$.

Remark 1. In fact, we can prove a stronger result, namely, that the polyconvex envelope of W, PW, coincides with the quasiconvex envelope of W: $PW = QW$.

Ultimately, we propose to consider the following minimization problem, with $T > 0$ fixed

$$\inf \left\{ \bar{I}(\varphi) = \int_\Omega f(x, \varphi(x), \nabla\varphi(x)) \, dx \ : \ \varphi \in \text{Id} + W_0^{1,4}(\Omega, \mathbb{R}^2) \right\}, \quad (1)$$

with $f(x, \varphi, \xi) = \frac{\nu}{2} \|\Phi_0 \circ \varphi - \tilde{\Phi}(\cdot, T)\|^2_{L^2(\Omega)} + QW(\xi)$ and $\tilde{\Phi}$ a solution of the evolution equation stemming from the topology-preserving segmentation model by Le Guyader and Vese ([16])

$$\begin{cases} \frac{\partial \tilde{\Phi}}{\partial t} = |\nabla \tilde{\Phi}| \left[\text{div}\left(\tilde{g}(|\nabla R|)\frac{\nabla \tilde{\Phi}}{|\nabla \tilde{\Phi}|}\right) \right] + 4\frac{\mu'}{d^2}\bar{H}(\tilde{\Phi}(x)+l)\bar{H}(l-\tilde{\Phi}(x)) \\ \int_\Omega \left[\langle x-y, \nabla\tilde{\Phi}(y)\rangle \, e^{-\|x-y\|_2^2/d^2} \bar{H}(\tilde{\Phi}(y)+l)\bar{H}(l-\tilde{\Phi}(y)) \right] dy, \\ \tilde{\Phi}(x,0) = \Phi_0(x), \\ \frac{\partial \tilde{\Phi}}{\partial \nu} = 0, \quad \text{on } \partial\Omega. \end{cases} \quad (2)$$

Function $\tilde{g}$ is an edge-detector function satisfying $\tilde{g}(0) = 1$, $\tilde{g}$ strictly decreasing and $\lim_{r\to+\infty} \tilde{g}(r) = 0$. This evolution equation results from the minimization of functional $J(\tilde{\Phi}) + \mu'L(\tilde{\Phi})$ ($\mu' > 0$, tuning parameter), combination of $J(\tilde{\Phi}) = \int_\Omega \tilde{g}(|\nabla R|)|\nabla \bar{H}(\Phi)|$ coming from the classical geodesic active contour model ([8]) ($\bar{H}$ being the one-dimensional Heaviside function) and L, related to the topological constraint:

$$L(\tilde{\Phi}) = -\int_\Omega\int_\Omega \left[\exp\left(-\frac{\|x-y\|_2^2}{d^2}\right) \langle \nabla\tilde{\Phi}(x), \nabla\tilde{\Phi}(y)\rangle \, \bar{H}(\tilde{\Phi}(x)+l)\bar{H}(l-\tilde{\Phi}(x)) \right. \\ \left. \bar{H}(\tilde{\Phi}(y)+l)\bar{H}(l-\tilde{\Phi}(y)) \right] dx\, dy \quad (3)$$

The Euclidean scalar product in $\mathbb{R}^2$ is denoted by $\langle \cdot, \cdot \rangle$ and $\|\cdot\|_2$ is the associated norm. A geometrical observation motivates the introduction of L. Indeed, in the case when Φ is a signed-distance function, $|\nabla\Phi| = 1$ and the unit outward normal vector to the zero level line at point x is $-\nabla\Phi(x)$. Let us now consider two points $(x,y) \in \Omega \times \Omega$ belonging to the zero level line of Φ, close enough to each other, and let $-\nabla\Phi(x)$ and $-\nabla\Phi(y)$ be the two unit outward normal vectors to the contour at these points. When the contour is about to merge or split, that is, when the topology of the evolving contour is to change, then $\langle \nabla\Phi(x), \nabla\Phi(y)\rangle \simeq -1$. This remark justifies the construction of L. The registration process is then fed by the knowledge of the segmentation of the Reference image at time T. In practice, we may apply several times this step.

Also, $\varphi \in \mathrm{Id} + W_0^{1,4}(\Omega, \mathbb{R}^2)$ means that $\varphi = \mathrm{Id}$ —the identity mapping— on $\partial\Omega$ and $\varphi \in W^{1,4}(\Omega, \mathbb{R}^2)$. $W^{1,4}(\Omega, \mathbb{R}^2)$ denotes the Sobolev space of functions $\varphi \in L^4(\Omega, \mathbb{R}^2)$ with distributional derivatives up to order 1 which also belong to $L^4(\Omega)$. (The rewriting of $W(F)$ into $\beta\left(\|F\|^2 - \alpha\right)^2 + \Psi(\det F)$ allows to see that $W^{1,4}(\Omega, \mathbb{R}^2)$ is a suitable functional space for the considered minimization problem (1): from Hölder's inequality, if $\varphi \in W^{1,4}(\Omega, \mathbb{R}^2)$, then $\det \nabla\varphi \in L^2(\Omega)$).

In the next section, we prove that the infimum of problem (1) is attained and that if $\bar\varphi$ is a solution of (1), then there exists a minimizing sequence $\{\varphi_\nu\}$ of problem (P) defined by

$$\inf_{\varphi \in \mathrm{Id}+W_0^{1,4}(\Omega,\mathbb{R}^2)} I(\varphi) \text{ with } I(\varphi) = \frac{\nu}{2}\|\Phi_0 \circ \varphi - \tilde\Phi(\cdot,T)\|_{L^2(\Omega)}^2 + \int_\Omega W(\nabla\varphi)\,dx,$$

(i.e., the functional expressed in terms of the Saint Venant-Kirchhoff stored energy function) such that φ_ν weakly converges to $\bar\varphi$ and $I(\varphi_\nu) \to \bar I(\bar\varphi)$. The solutions of (1) are considered as generalized solutions of (P), in the sense of weak convergence. We also ensure that $\tilde\Phi(\cdot,T)$ is well-defined, using the viscosity solution theoretical framework.

3 Theoretical Results

3.1 Existence of Minimizers and Relaxation Theorem

We state the main theoretical result related to the existence of minimizers, following arguments similar to those used in [13].

Theorem 1. *The infimum of (1) is attained. Let then $\bar\varphi \in W^{1,4}(\Omega, \mathbb{R}^2)$ be a minimizer of the relaxed problem (1). Then there exists a sequence $\{\varphi_\nu\}_{\nu=1}^\infty \subset \bar\varphi + W_0^{1,4}(\Omega, \mathbb{R}^2)$ such that $\varphi_\nu \to \bar\varphi$ in $L^4(\Omega, \mathbb{R}^2)$ as $\nu \to \infty$ and $I(\varphi_\nu) \to \bar I(\bar\varphi)$ as $\nu \to \infty$. Moreover, the following holds: $\varphi_\nu \rightharpoonup \bar\varphi$ in $W^{1,4}(\Omega, \mathbb{R}^2)$ as $\nu \to \infty$. It means in particular that $\inf_{\varphi \in \mathrm{Id}+W_0^{1,4}(\Omega,\mathbb{R}^2)} I(\varphi) = \min_{\varphi \in \mathrm{Id}+W_0^{1,4}(\Omega,\mathbb{R}^2)} \bar I(\varphi)$, as $QW \leq W$. The solutions of (1) are considered as generalized solutions of problem (P).*

We now investigate the well-definedness of $\tilde\Phi(\cdot,T)$.

3.2 Well-Definedness of $\tilde{\Phi}$

Problem (2) is hard to handle from a theoretical point of view. A suitable setting would be the one of the viscosity solution theory ([11]) (owing to the nonlinearity induced by the modified mean curvature term), but the dependency of the nonlocal term on the gradient $\nabla \tilde{\Phi}(y)$ and the failure to fulfill the monotony property in $\tilde{\Phi}$ make it difficult. For this reason, for the theoretical part, we consider a slightly modified problem: we assume that the topological constraint is only applied to the zero level line. Assuming that $\tilde{\Phi}$ is a signed-distance function, the topological constraint L is then rephrased as

$$L(\tilde{\Phi}) = -\int_\Omega \int_\Omega \left[\exp\left(-\frac{\|x-y\|_2^2}{d^2}\right)\langle \nabla\tilde{\Phi}(x), \nabla\tilde{\Phi}(y)\rangle \delta(\tilde{\Phi}(x))\delta(\tilde{\Phi}(y))dx\,dy\right],$$

with δ the Dirac measure. Computing the Euler-Lagrange equation, then applying a gradient descent method and doing an integration by parts and a rescaling by replacing $\delta(\tilde{\Phi})$ by $|\nabla\tilde{\Phi}|$, yields to the evolution problem (defined on $\mathbb{R}^2$ for the space coordinates for the sake of simplicity)

$$\frac{\partial \tilde{\Phi}}{\partial t} = |\nabla\tilde{\Phi}|\left\{\operatorname{div}\left(\tilde{g}(|\nabla R|)\frac{\nabla\tilde{\Phi}}{|\nabla\tilde{\Phi}|}\right) + c_0 * \left[\tilde{\Phi}(\cdot,t)\right]\right\}, \qquad (4)$$

with $\left[\tilde{\Phi}(\cdot,t)\right]$ the characteristic function of the set $\left\{\tilde{\Phi}(\cdot,t) \geq 0\right\}$ and

$$c_0 : \begin{cases} \mathbb{R}^2 \to \mathbb{R} \\ x \mapsto \frac{4\mu}{d^2}\left(2 - \frac{2}{d^2}\|x\|_2^2\right)\exp\left(-\frac{\|x\|_2^2}{d^2}\right). \end{cases} \qquad (5)$$

Remark 2. A sample of experiments shows that this simplified model qualitatively performs in a similar way to [16] (see [15] in particular).

We now describe the general framework our equation falls within, recall the definition of weak solutions in this context, give the general existence theorem (in the unbounded case) introduced by Barles et al. ([2]) and check whether it applies to the considered problem (4). Note that the proposed result, which is a result of existence of weak solutions to problem (4)– with no restriction on time T – is different from the one obtained in [15], which is a short-time existence/uniqueness result in the classical sense.

General Framework

We follow the notations of [2]. Let us consider the class of nonlocal and nonlinear parabolic equations which can be rewritten as

$$\begin{cases} u_t = H[\mathbb{1}_{\{u\geq 0\}}](x,t,u,Du,D^2u) & \text{in } \mathbb{R}^N \times (0,T), \\ u(\cdot,0) = u_0 & \text{in } \mathbb{R}^N, \end{cases} \qquad (6)$$

where u_t, Du and D^2u stand respectively for the time derivative, gradient and Hessian matrix with respect to the space variable x of $u : \mathbb{R}^N \times [0,T] \to \mathbb{R}$ and where $\mathbb{1}_A$ denotes the indicator function of a set A. The initial datum u_0 is a bounded and Lipschitz continuous function on $\mathbb{R}^N$.

For any indicator function $\chi : \mathbb{R}^N \times [0,T] \to \mathbb{R}$, or more generally for any $\chi \in L^\infty(\mathbb{R}^N \times [0,T]; [0,1])$, $H[\chi]$ denotes a function of $(x,t,r,p,A) \in \mathbb{R}^N \times [0,T] \times \mathbb{R} \times \mathbb{R}^N \setminus \{0\} \times \mathcal{S}_N$ where $\mathcal{S}_N$ is the set of real, $N \times N$ symmetric matrices. For almost any $t \in [0,T]$, $(x,r,p,A) \mapsto H[\chi](x,t,r,p,A)$ is a continuous function on $\mathbb{R}^N \times \mathbb{R} \times \mathbb{R}^N \setminus \{0\} \times \mathcal{S}_N$ with a possible singularity at $p = 0$, while $t \mapsto H[\chi](x,t,r,p,A)$ is a bounded measurable function for all $(x,r,p,A) \in \mathbb{R}^N \times \mathbb{R} \times \mathbb{R}^N \setminus \{0\} \times \mathcal{S}_N$. The equation is said to be degenerate elliptic if, for any $\chi \in L^\infty(\mathbb{R}^N \times [0,T]; [0,1])$, for any $(x,r,p) \in \mathbb{R}^N \times \mathbb{R} \times \mathbb{R}^N \setminus \{0\}$, for almost every $t \in [0,T]$ and for all $A, B \in \mathcal{S}_N$, one has:

$$H[\chi](x,t,r,p,A) \leq H[\chi](x,t,r,p,B) \text{ if } A \leq B,$$

with $\leq$ the usual partial ordering for symmetric matrices.

The notion of viscosity solutions for equations with a measurable dependence in time (called L^1-viscosity solution) is needed to define weak solutions. For a complete presentation of the theory, the reader may refer to [3]. The following definition of weak solutions is introduced in [2].

Definition 1. *Taken from [2]*
Let $u : \mathbb{R}^N \times [0,T] \to \mathbb{R}$ be a continuous function. u is said to be a weak solution of (6) if there exists $\chi \in L^\infty(\mathbb{R}^N \times [0,T]; [0,1])$ such that:

i) u is a L^1-viscosity solution of

$$\begin{cases} u_t(x,t) = H[\chi](x,t,u,Du,D^2u) \text{ in } \mathbb{R}^N \times (0,T), \\ u(\cdot,0) = u_0 \text{ in } \mathbb{R}^N. \end{cases} \quad (7)$$

ii) For almost all $t \in [0,T]$,

$$\mathbb{1}_{\{u(\cdot,t)>0\}} \leq \chi(\cdot,t) \leq \mathbb{1}_{\{u(\cdot,t)\geq 0\}} \text{ a.e. in } \mathbb{R}^N. \quad (8)$$

Moreover, we say that u is a classical solution of (6) if in addition, for almost every $t \in [0,T]$,

$$\mathbb{1}_{\{u(\cdot,t)>0\}} = \mathbb{1}_{\{u(\cdot,t)\geq 0\}} \text{ a.e in } \mathbb{R}^N.$$

We now state some assumptions (still following [2]) that are needed to establish the result of existence of at least one weak solution to general problem (6).

[A1]
  i) For any $\chi \in X \subset L^\infty(\mathbb{R}^N \times [0,T]; [0,1])$, equation (7) has a bounded uniformly continuous L^1-viscosity solution u. Moreover, there exists a constant $L > 0$ independent of $\chi \in X$ such that $|u|_\infty \leq L$.
  ii) For any fixed $\chi \in X$, a comparison principle holds for equation (7): if u is a bounded, upper semi-continuous L^1-viscosity subsolution of (7) in $\mathbb{R}^N \times (0,T)$ and v is a bounded, lower semi-continuous L^1-viscosity supersolution of (7) in $\mathbb{R}^N \times (0,T)$ with $u(\cdot,0) \leq v(\cdot,0)$ in $\mathbb{R}^N$, then $u \leq v$ in $\mathbb{R}^N \times (0,T)$.

[A2]
i) For any compact subset $K \subset \mathbb{R}^N \times \mathbb{R} \times \mathbb{R}^N \setminus \{0\} \times \mathcal{S}^N$, there exists a (locally bounded) modulus of continuity $m_K : [0,T] \times \mathbb{R}^+ \to \mathbb{R}^+$ such that $m_K(\cdot, \varepsilon) \to 0$ in $L^1(0,T)$ as $\varepsilon \to 0$, and

$$|H[\chi](x_1, t, r_1, p_1, A_1) - H[\chi](x_2, t, r_2, p_2, A_2)| \le$$
$$m_K(t, |x_1 - x_2| + |r_1 - r_2| + |p_1 - p_2| + |A_1 - A_2|),$$

for any $\chi \in X$, for almost all $t \in [0,T]$ and all (x_1, r_1, p_1, A_1), $(x_2, r_2, p_2, A_2) \in K$.

ii) There exists a bounded function $h(x,t,r)$, which is continuous in x and r for almost every t and measurable in t, such that: for any neighborhood V of $(0,0)$ in $\mathbb{R}^N \setminus \{0\} \times \mathcal{S}^N$ and any compact subset $K \subset \mathbb{R}^N \times \mathbb{R}$, there exists a modulus of continuity $m_{K,V} : [0,T] \times \mathbb{R}^+ \to \mathbb{R}^+$ such that $m_{K,V}(\cdot, \varepsilon) \to 0$ in $L^1(0,T)$ as $\varepsilon \to 0$, and

$$|H[\chi](x, t, r, p, A) - h(x, t, r)| \le m_{K,V}(t, |p| + |A|),$$

for any $\chi \in X$, for almost all $t \in [0,T]$, all $(x,r) \in K$ and $(p, A) \in V$.

iii) If $\chi_n \rightharpoonup \chi$ weakly-$*$ in $L^\infty(\mathbb{R}^N \times [0,T]; [0,1])$ with $\chi_n, \chi \in X$ for all n, then for all $(x, t, r, p, A) \in \mathbb{R}^N \times [0,T] \times \mathbb{R} \times \mathbb{R}^N \setminus \{0\} \times \mathcal{S}^N$,

$$\int_0^1 H[\chi_n](x, s, r, p, A)\,ds \xrightarrow[n \to +\infty]{} \int_0^1 H[\chi](x, s, r, p, A)\,ds,$$

locally uniformly for $t \in [0,T]$

[A3] For any $\chi \in X$, for almost every $t \in [0,T]$, for all $(x, p, A) \in \mathbb{R}^N \times \mathbb{R}^N \setminus \{0\} \times \mathcal{S}^N$, and for any $r_1 \le r_2$,

$$H[\chi](x, t, r_1, p, A) \ge H[\chi](x, t, r_2, p, A).$$

The general existence theorem proposed by Barles et al. ([2]) is then:

Theorem 2. *General existence theorem by Barles et al. ([2])*
Assume that [A1], [A2] and [A3] hold. Then there exists at least a weak solution to (6).

Existence of Weak Solutions of the Considered Evolution Problem

Equipped with these theoretical elements, we now state the main theoretical result regarding the existence of at least one weak solution to problem (4).

Theorem 3. *Assuming that $g := \tilde{g}(|\nabla R|)$, $g^{\frac{1}{2}}$ and ∇g are bounded and Lipschitz continuous on $\mathbb{R}^2$, problem (4) admits at least one weak solution.*

Proof. First, one can easily check that setting $C(p) := (I - \frac{p \otimes p}{|p|^2})$,

$$H[\chi](x, t, p, A) = g(x)\mathrm{tr}\,(C(p)A) + \langle \nabla g(x), p \rangle + |p| \int_{\mathbb{R}^2} c_0(x - y)\chi(y, t)\,dy.$$

We give the sketch of the proof by mainly checking that the assumptions of Theorem 2 are fulfilled. Assumption [A1] is rather classical and due to page number limitation we cannot go into details. Assumption [A3] is obviously fulfilled, $H[\chi]$ being independent of r in the considered problem. Let us now focus on assumption [A2] i). $M > 0$ denotes a positive constant that may change line to line and that may depend on K, g, ∇g, $\|c_0\|_{L^1(\mathbb{R}^2)}$ or $\|\nabla c_0\|_{L^1(\mathbb{R}^2)}$. Recall that (x_i, p_i, A_i) belongs to the compact subset K. One then has

$$|\langle \nabla g(x_1), p_1 \rangle - \langle \nabla g(x_2), p_2 \rangle| = |\langle \nabla g(x_1) - \nabla g(x_2), p_1 \rangle + \langle \nabla g(x_2), p_1 - p_2 \rangle|$$
$$\leq M \left(|x_1 - x_2| + |p_1 - p_2| \right),$$

due to the properties of ∇g. Also,

$$\left| |p_1| \int_{\mathbb{R}^2} c_0(x_1 - y)\chi(y, t)\, dy - |p_2| \int_{\mathbb{R}^2} c_0(x_2 - y)\chi(y, t)\, dy \right|$$
$$\leq ||p_1| - |p_2|| \left| \int_{\mathbb{R}^2} c_0(x_1 - y)\chi(y, t)\, dy \right|$$
$$+ |p_2| \left| \int_{\mathbb{R}^2} (c_0(x_1 - y) - c_0(x_2 - y))\chi(y, t)\, dy \right|,$$
$$\leq |p_1 - p_2| \|c_0\|_{L^1(\mathbb{R}^2)} \|\chi\|_{L^\infty(\mathbb{R}^2 \times [0,T])}$$
$$+ |p_2| \left| \int_{\mathbb{R}^2} \left(\int_0^1 \langle \nabla c_0((x_2 - y) + s(x_1 - x_2)), x_1 - x_2 \rangle\, ds \right) \chi(y, t)\, dy \right|.$$

A change of variable in the integral allows to conclude that

$$\left| |p_1| \int_{\mathbb{R}^2} c_0(x_1 - y)\chi(y, t)\, dy - |p_2| \int_{\mathbb{R}^2} c_0(x_2 - y)\chi(y, t)\, dy \right|$$
$$\leq |p_1 - p_2| \|c_0\|_{L^1(\mathbb{R}^2)} \|\chi\|_{L^\infty(\mathbb{R}^2 \times [0,T])}$$
$$+ |p_2| |x_1 - x_2| \|\chi\|_{L^\infty(\mathbb{R}^2 \times [0,T])} \|\nabla c_0\|_{L^1(\mathbb{R}^2)},$$
$$\leq M \left(|p_1 - p_2| + |x_1 - x_2| \right).$$

It remains to estimate $|g(x_1)\text{tr}\,(C(p_1)A_1) - g(x_2)\text{tr}\,(C(p_2)A_2)|$. One has

$$|g(x_1)\text{tr}\,(C(p_1)A_1) - g(x_2)\text{tr}\,(C(p_2)A_2)| \leq |g(x_1) - g(x_2)|\,|\text{tr}\,(C(p_1)A_1)|$$
$$+ g(x_2)\,|\text{tr}\,(C(p_1)A_1) - \text{tr}\,(C(p_2)A_2)|,$$
$$\leq M\,|x_1 - x_2|\,\|C(p_1)\|_F \|A_1\|_F + g(x_2)\,|\text{tr}\,((C(p_1) - C(p_2))A_1)$$
$$+ \text{tr}\,(C(p_2)(A_1 - A_2))|,$$

$\|\cdot\|_F$ denoting the Frobenius norm. Remarking that $\|C(p_1)\|_F = 1$ and that one has $\|A_1\|_F \leq \sqrt{2}\|A_1\|_2 = \sqrt{2}|A_1|$, it yields to

$$|g(x_1)\text{tr}\,(C(p_1)A_1) - g(x_2)\text{tr}\,(C(p_2)A_2)| \leq M\left(|x_1 - x_2| + |A_1 - A_2|\right)$$
$$+ g(x_2)\,|\text{tr}\,((C(p_1) - C(p_2))A_1)|. \quad (9)$$

One can notice that $C(p) = \sigma(p)\sigma(p)^T$ with $\sigma(p) = \begin{pmatrix} \frac{p_{02}}{|p|} & 0 \\ -\frac{p_{01}}{|p|} & 0 \end{pmatrix}$ given $p = (p_{01}, p_{02})^T \neq 0$. Consequently,

$$g(x_2)\left|\operatorname{tr}\left((C(p_1) - C(p_2))A_1\right)\right| \leq$$
$$M\left|\operatorname{tr}\left((\sigma(p_1) - \sigma(p_2))\sigma(p_1)^T A_1\right) + \operatorname{tr}\left(\sigma(p_2)\left(\sigma(p_1)^T - \sigma(p_2)^T\right)A_1\right)\right|.$$

Focusing on the first term of the right part of the inequality, the result being similar for the second component, one obtains

$$\left|\operatorname{tr}\left((\sigma(p_1) - \sigma(p_2))\sigma(p_1)^T A_1\right)\right| \leq \|A_1\|_F \|\sigma(p_1) - \sigma(p_2)\|_F \|\sigma(p_1)^T\|_F,$$
$$\leq M \left|\frac{p_1}{|p_1|} - \frac{p_2}{|p_2|}\right| \leq \frac{|p_1 - p_2|}{\min(|p_1|, |p_2|)},$$

so

$$\left|\operatorname{tr}\left((\sigma(p_1) - \sigma(p_2))\sigma(p_1)^T A_1\right)\right| \leq M|p_1 - p_2|.$$

Including this result in equation (9) yields to the desired estimation.
The two remaining assumptions are checked using the same arguments as above and taking h the null function for assumption [A2] ii), and by definition of the L^∞-weak $*$ convergence for assumption [A2] iii).

4 Numerical Method of Resolution

In [19], Negrón Marrero describes and analyzes a numerical method that detects singular minimizers and avoids the Lavrentiev phenomenon for three dimensional problems in nonlinear elasticity. This method consists in decoupling the function φ from its gradient and in formulating a related decoupled problem under inequality constraint. In the same spirit, we introduce an auxiliary variable V simulating the Jacobian deformation field $\nabla\varphi$ (–the underlying idea being to remove the nonlinearity in the derivatives of the deformation–) and derive a functional minimization problem phrased in terms of the two variables φ and V. The decoupled problem is thus defined by means of the following functional:

$$\bar{I}_\gamma(\varphi, V) = \frac{\nu}{2}\|\Phi_0 \circ \varphi - \tilde{\Phi}(\cdot, T)\|^2_{L^2(\Omega)} + \int_\Omega QW(V)\,dx + \frac{\gamma}{2}\|V - \nabla\varphi\|^2_{L^2(\Omega, M_2)}. \tag{10}$$

Let us now denote by $\widehat{\mathcal{W}}$ the functional space defined by $\widehat{\mathcal{W}} = \operatorname{Id} + W_0^{1,2}(\Omega, \mathbb{R}^2)$ and by $\widehat{\chi}$, the functional space $\widehat{\chi} = \{V \in L^4(\Omega, M_2)\}$. The decoupled problem consists in minimizing (10) on $\widehat{\mathcal{W}} \times \widehat{\chi}$. Then the following theorem holds.

Theorem 4. *Let (γ_j) be an increasing sequence of positive real numbers such that $\lim_{j \to +\infty} \gamma_j = +\infty$. Let also $(\varphi_k(\gamma_j), V_k(\gamma_j))$ be a minimizing sequence of the decoupled problem with $\gamma = \gamma_j$. Then there exist a subsequence denoted by*

$\left(\varphi_{N(\gamma_{\Psi \circ \varsigma(j)})}(\gamma_{\Psi \circ \varsigma(j)}), V_{N(\gamma_{\Psi \circ \varsigma(j)})}(\gamma_{\Psi \circ \varsigma(j)}) \right)$ of $(\varphi_k(\gamma_j), V_k(\gamma_j))$ and a minimizer $\bar{\varphi}$ of $\bar{I}$ ($\bar{\varphi} \in Id + W_0^{1,4}(\Omega, \mathbb{R}^2)$) such that:

$$\lim_{j \to +\infty} \bar{I}_{\gamma_{\Psi \circ \varsigma(j)}} \left(\varphi_{N(\gamma_{\Psi \circ \varsigma(j)})}(\gamma_{\Psi \circ \varsigma(j)}), V_{N(\gamma_{\Psi \circ \varsigma(j)})}(\gamma_{\Psi \circ \varsigma(j)}) \right) = \bar{I}(\bar{\varphi}).$$

For the discretization of the evolution problem (2), an Additive Operator Splitting scheme is implemented (see [23] and [16]), requiring a linear computational cost at each step. The matrices involved in the sub-problems are monotone and their inverse matrices are such that the sum of the coefficients of each row is equal to 1. The scheme is thus unconditionally stable for the L^∞-norm. We conclude the paper by presenting a preliminary result dedicated to the mapping of mouse brain gene expression data.

5 Numerical Results

We now present some preliminary results. The method has been applied on medical images with the goal to map a 2D slice of mouse brain gene expression data (Template $\bar{T}$) to its corresponding 2D slice of mouse brain atlas. The data are provided by the Center for Computational Biology, UCLA.

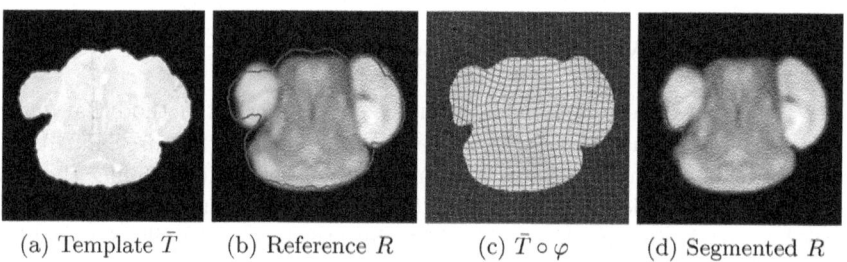

(a) Template $\bar{T}$ (b) Reference R (c) $\bar{T} \circ \varphi$ (d) Segmented R

Acknowledgments. The authors thank the Région Haute-Normandie and the GRR Logistique-Mobilité-Numérique (via M2NUM project) for supporting this work.

References

1. Aubert, G., Kornprobst, P.: Mathematical Problems in Image processing: Partial Differential Equations and the Calculus of Variations. Applied Mathematical Sciences., vol. 147. Springer, New York (2001)
2. Barles, G., Cardaliaguet, P., Ley, O., Monteillet, A.: Existence of weak solutions for general nonlocal and nonlinear second-order parabolic equations. Nonlinear Anal-Theor. **71**(7–8), 2801–2810 (2009)
3. Bourgoing, M.: Viscosity solutions of fully nonlinear second order parabolic equations with L^1-time dependence and Neumann boundary conditions. Discrete Contin. Dyn. S. **21**(3), 763–800 (2008)

4. Bousselsal, M.: Étude de Quelques Problèmes de Calcul des Variations Liés à la Mécanique. PhD Thesis, University of Metz, France (1993)
5. Brezis, H.: Analyse fonctionelle. Dunod, Théorie et Applications (2005)
6. Broit, C.: Registration of Deformed Images. PhD Thesis, University of Pennsylvania, USA (1981)
7. Burger, M., Modersitzki, J., Ruthotto, L.: A hyperelastic regularization energy for image registration. SIAM J. Sci. Comput. **35**(1), B132–B148 (2013)
8. Caselles, V., Kimmel, R., Sapiro, G.: Geodesic Active Contours. Int. J. Comput. Vis. **22**(1), 61–87 (1993)
9. Chan, T., Vese, L.: Active Contours Without Edges. IEEE T. Image Process. **10**(2), 266–277 (2001)
10. Ciarlet, P.G.: Elasticité Tridimensionnelle. Masson (1985)
11. Crandall, M.G., Ishii, H., Lions, P.-L.: User's guide to viscosity solutions of second order partial differential equations. Bull. Amer. Math. Soc. **27**, 1–67 (1992)
12. Dacorogna, B.: Direct Methods in the Calculus of Variations. Applied Mathematical Sciences, vol. 78, 2nd edn. Springer, New York (2008)
13. Derfoul, R., Le Guyader, C.: A relaxed problem of registration based on the Saint Venant-Kirchhoff material stored energy for the mapping of mouse brain gene expression data to a neuroanatomical mouse atlas. SIAM J. Imaging Sci. **7**(4), 2175–2195 (2014)
14. Droske, M., Rumpf, M.: Multiscale joint segmentation and registration of image morphology. IEEE T. Pattern Anal. **29**(12), 2181–2194 (2007)
15. Forcadel, N., Le Guyader, C.: A short time existence/uniqueness result for a nonlocal topology-preserving segmentation model. J. Differ. Equations. **253**(3), 977–995 (2012)
16. Le Guyader, C., Vese, L.: Self-repelling snakes for topology-preserving segmentation models. IEEE T. Image Process. **17**(5), 767–779 (2008)
17. Le Guyader, C., Vese, L.: A combined segmentation and registration framework with a nonlinear elasticity smoother. Comput. Vis. Image Und. **115**(12), 1689–1709 (2011)
18. Lord, N.A., Ho, J., Vemuri, B.C., Eisenschenk, S.: Simultaneous Registration and Parcellation of Bilateral Hippocampal Surface Pairs for Local Asymmetry Quantification. IEEE Trans. Med. Imaging. **26**(4), 471–478 (2007)
19. Marrero-Negrón, P.V.: A numerical method for detecting singular minimizers of multidimensional problems in nonlinear elasticity. Numer. Math. **58**, 135–144 (1990)
20. Ozeré, S., Gout, C., Le Guyader, C.: Joint segmentation/registration model by shape alignment via weighted total variation minimization and nonlinear elasticity. Under revision (2015)
21. Sotiras, A., Davatzikos, C., Paragios, N.: Deformable medical image registration: A survey. IEEE T. Med. Imaging. **32**, 1153–1190 (2013)
22. Vemuri, B., Ye, J., Chen, Y., Leonard, C.: Image Registration via level-set motion: Applications to atlas-based segmentation. Med. Image Anal. **7**(1), 1–20 (2003)
23. Weickert, J., Kühne, G.: Fast methods for implicit active contour models. In: Osher, S., Paragios, N. (eds.) Geometric Level Set Methods in Imaging, Vision, and Graphics, 43–57. Springer, New York (2003)
24. Yezzi, A., Zollei, L., Kapur, T.: A variational framework for joint segmentation and registration. In: IEEE Workshop on Mathematical Methods in Biomedical Image Analysis (MMBIA), pp. 44–51. IEEE (2001)

Deformable Image Registration with Automatic Non-correspondence Detection

Kanglin Chen[1], Alexander Derksen[1]($\boxtimes$), Stefan Heldmann[1],
Marc Hallmann[1], and Benjamin Berkels[2]

[1] Fraunhofer MEVIS Project Group Image Registration, Maria-Goeppert-Str. 3,
23562 Lübeck, Germany
{kanglin.chen,alexander.derksen,stefan.heldmann,
marc.hallmann}@mevis.fraunhofer.de
[2] AICES, RWTH Aachen University, Schinkelstr. 2, 52062 Aachen, Germany
berkels@aices.rwth-aachen.de

Abstract. Image registration aims at establishing pointwise correspondences between given images. However, in many practical applications, no correspondences can be established in certain parts of the images. A typical example is the tumor resection area in pre- and post-operative medical images. In this paper, we introduce a novel variational framework that combines registration with an automatic detection of non-correspondence regions. The formulation of the proposed approach is simple but efficient, and compatible with a large class of image registration similarity measures and regularizers. The resulting minimization problem is solved numerically with a non-alternating gradient flow scheme. Furthermore, the method is validated on synthetic data as well as axial slices of pre-, post- and intra-operative MR T1 head scans.

Keywords: Joint method · Image registration · Segmentation · Level set · Non-correspondence detection · Lesion · Resection

1 Introduction

Image registration is an important technique for many different fields of application, e.g. robotics, remote sensing or medical imaging. Consequently, image registration techniques of various kinds have been developed in the last two decades. In general, the goal of image registration is to align two or more given images so that corresponding structures in those images overlap. A very common assumption among those approaches is that pixel-wise/voxel-wise correspondence can be established between the given images. However, especially in medical image registration, this assumption is often not applicable, e.g. when registering pre- and post-operative brain tumor resection scans, no correspondences can be established in the resection area. Still, for tasks like therapy validation, accurate registration of remaining tissue with correspondences is a necessity.

In the last few years, publications that explicitly tackle the topic of registration with missing correspondences have captured some attention. These publications follow very different approaches and even use different terminology for very similar problem descriptions. Apart from our terminology of *missing correspondence*, the problem is also described as e.g. *registration with inconsistent image differences* [1], *registration with outliers* [2] or more application related as *registration with tumor detection* [3]. An early approach by Brett et al. [4] used a simple masking of the non-correspondence region to prevent this region from interfering with the registration problem. In the following years, multiple publications introduced statistical approaches [3,5,6], tumor models [7–10] and modified distance measures [1,2]. Recently, Ou et al. published the DRAMMS framework [11]. By incorporating a so-called mutual-saliency function, they enable their algorithm to register images with missing correspondences. Even though some promising results have been shown, all mentioned works have in common that they are either computationally and algorithmically challenging or require some kind of user interaction that goes beyond a simple choice of parameters.

In this paper, we introduce a novel approach that combines classical image registration with an automatic detection of non-correspondence regions using level set based segmentation. Note that the introduced non-correspondence segmentation does not depend on an image specific zero level set initialization. On the whole, the formulation of the proposed approach is simple, but leads to a robust and computationally efficient algorithm that does not rely on special user interaction.

2 Methods

In this section, we introduce our registration model with automatic non-correspondence detection.

2.1 Modeling

Let T and R be the input images, $\Omega \subset \mathbb{R}^d$ the image domain and assume $T, R \in L^\infty(\Omega)$. The region in R that has no correspondence in T is denoted by $\mathcal{O} \subset \Omega$ (cf. Figure 1). Furthermore, $y : \Omega \to \mathbb{R}^d$ denotes the deformation with $T \circ y \sim R$ in $\Omega \setminus \mathcal{O}$. To define $T \circ y$ for such deformations, T is extended to $L^\infty(\mathbb{R}^d)$ using zero extension, i.e. $T(x) := 0$ for $x \in \mathbb{R}^d \setminus \Omega$. Let $\mathcal{D}[T \circ y, R, \Omega \setminus \mathcal{O}]$ be a suitable similarity measure for $T \circ y$ and R on $\Omega \setminus \mathcal{O}$ and $\mathcal{S}[y]$ a suitable regularizer for y on the whole image domain Ω. Then, the combined registration and non-correspondence detection problem means finding a deformation y that minimizes $\mathcal{D}+\lambda\mathcal{S}$ while keeping the size of $\mathcal{O}$ as small as possible. This is modeled by the minimization problem

$$\min_{y,\mathcal{O}} \left(\mathcal{D}[T \circ y, R, \Omega \setminus \mathcal{O}] + \lambda \mathcal{S}[y] + \gamma \operatorname{Vol}[\mathcal{O}] + \beta \operatorname{Per}[\mathcal{O}] \right). \quad (1)$$

Here, $\operatorname{Per}[\mathcal{O}]$ denotes the perimeter of $\mathcal{O}$, i.e. the boundary length. Thus, the canonical admissible set for $\mathcal{O}$ is $\mathcal{B} = \{\mathcal{O} \subset \Omega : \mathcal{O} \text{ measurable}, \operatorname{Per}[\mathcal{O}] < \infty\}$, the sets of finite perimeter. The admissible set for y depends on the choice of $\mathcal{S}$.

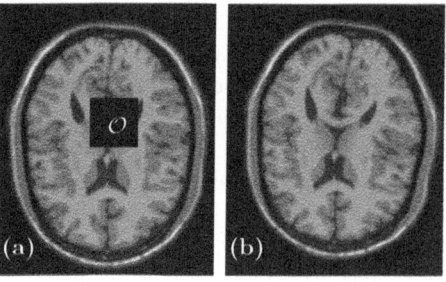

Fig. 1. Example for registration with missing correspondences. (a) Reference image R with an artificial tumor resection region $\mathcal{O}$ simulated by a black box. (b) Template image T. Up to $\mathcal{O}$ the template image can be exactly deformed to the reference image by a plausible deformation y.

For a fixed deformation y, we want the non-correspondence problem to be of binary Mumford–Shah type [12] since this allows us to tap into existing approaches for image segmentation. To this end, we have to assume that $\mathcal{D}$ can be expressed as integral as follows

$$\mathcal{D}[T \circ y, R, \Omega \setminus \mathcal{O}] = \int_{\Omega \setminus \mathcal{O}} f[T \circ y, R](x)\,\mathrm{d}x,$$

where f does not depend on $\mathcal{O}$ and can be evaluated in Ω. Thus, we consider the objective functional

$$J[y, \mathcal{O}] = \int_{\Omega \setminus \mathcal{O}} f[T \circ y, R](x)\,\mathrm{d}x + \gamma \operatorname{Vol}[\mathcal{O}] + \beta \operatorname{Per}[\mathcal{O}] + \lambda \mathcal{S}[y].$$

Considering the recent convexification models for the binary Mumford–Shah problem that allow to find global minimizers of the binary Mumford–Shah functional [13,14], one may be tempted to use such a model to handle the minimization with respect to $\mathcal{O}$. Here, one would fix y, solve a convex reformulation of the segmentation problem and threshold the solution of the convex problem to obtain the minimizing set. To apply the thresholding theorem, it is necessary to fully solve the convex problem, which would result into an alternating minimization strategy, where the $\mathcal{O}$-update step computes the actual minimizer with respect to $\mathcal{O}$ for a fixed y. Unfortunately, this strategy turned out to be infeasible for J in our experiments. The way y and $\mathcal{O}$ are intertwined caused the alternating minimization to get stuck in undesirable local minima. Hence, it is necessary to use a minimization strategy that jointly updates y and $\mathcal{O}$. For instance, this is possible with a level set representation of the segmentation.

The set $\mathcal{O}$ is represented by a level set function ϕ via $\mathcal{O} = \{x \in \Omega : \phi(x) < 0\}$. Using the Heaviside function $H(t) = 1$ if $t > 0$ and $H(t) = 0$ otherwise, we get the level set formulation of J:

$$E[y, \phi] = \int_{\Omega} H(\phi) f[T \circ y, R] + \gamma(1 - H(\phi))\,\mathrm{d}x + \beta\,|H(\phi)|_{BV(\Omega)} + \lambda \mathcal{S}[y]. \quad (2)$$

It is straightforward to verify that $J[y, \{\phi < 0\}] = E[y, \phi]$ holds.

Following Chan and Vese [15], we regularize E by replacing H with the continuous approximation $H_\delta(t) := \frac{1}{2} + \frac{1}{\pi}\arctan\left(\frac{t}{\delta}\right)$ and regularize the absolute value of the gradient for the total variation via $|z|_\varepsilon = \sqrt{z^2 + \varepsilon^2}$ for $z \in \mathbb{R}^d$. Here, δ and ε are small, positive parameters that control the strength of the regularization.

The simplest similarity measure that fulfills our mild assumptions is the sum of squared distances, i.e. $f[T \circ y, R](x) = ((T \circ y)(x) - R(x))^2$. Since our aim is to introduce a model for joint registration and segmentation, we confine to this well known similarity measure here.

The data term $\mathcal{D}$ provides information about y only on the set $\Omega \setminus \mathcal{O}$. Thus, the regularizer $\mathcal{S}$ is the only term that takes care of extending y form $\Omega \setminus \mathcal{O}$ to Ω. This extension is closely related to inpainting and comes with similar problems. It turned out that first order regularizers do not provide enough regularity for a proper extension. Hence, we turn to higher order regularization like the curvature regularizer. Let $d = 2$ and $y = [y^1; y^2]$. The curvature regularizer introduced in [16] is given by

$$\mathcal{S}[y] = \frac{1}{2}\int_\Omega (\Delta y^1)^2 + (\Delta y^2)^2 \, dx$$

and thus suggests to consider $H^2(\Omega, \mathbb{R}^d)$ as admissible set for the deformation.

2.2 Optimization

We discretize the image domain Ω using N grid-points $\{x_i\}_{i=1}^N$ with equidistant spacing in each coordinate direction. The vectors of the nodal values of ϕ, y and R are denoted by, respectively, $\boldsymbol{\phi} = \{\phi_i\}_{i=1}^N = \{\phi(x_i)\}_{i=1}^N$, $\mathbf{y} = \{y_i\}_{i=1}^N = \{y(x_i)\}_{i=1}^N$ and $\mathbf{R} = \{R_i\}_{i=1}^N = \{R(x_i)\}_{i=1}^N$. The discretization of (2) is

$$E^h := \frac{1}{N}\sum_{i=1}^N H_\delta(\phi_i)(T(y_i) - R_i)^2 + \gamma(1 - H_\delta(\phi_i)) + \beta|\nabla_h H_\delta(\phi_i)|_\varepsilon + \lambda \mathcal{S}^h(y_i). \quad (3)$$

Here, ∇_h denotes the discrete gradient. For the discretization of the curvature regularizer $\mathcal{S}^h$, we follow [17]. This gives a good trade-off between the accuracy of the non-linear registration and computational efficiency. To find a minimizer of (3), we employ a gradient flow approach along the lines of [18]. Let $\Phi := [\mathbf{y}; \boldsymbol{\phi}]$, then the gradient flow with explicit time discretization is

$$\Phi^{n+1} = \Phi^n - \tau A^{-1} J_E^h,$$

where A is the matrix representation of the scalar product used for the gradient flow and J_E^h denotes the Jacobian of E. We perform a backtracking line search [19] to determine the stepsize τ. Since A represents a scalar product, it can be any arbitrary symmetric positive definite matrix. A proper problem specific choice of A is known to accelerate the convergence. The Jacobian J_E^h is given by

$$J_E^h = \left[\frac{\partial E^h}{\partial \mathbf{y}}; \frac{\partial E^h}{\partial \boldsymbol{\phi}}\right].$$

If A is the Hessian of E and $\tau = 1$, the explicit gradient flow is equivalent to Newton's method applied to find a zero crossing of J_E^h. This motivates us to design A as an approximation of the Hessian of E^h:

$$A := \begin{pmatrix} \left(\dfrac{\partial E^h}{\partial \mathbf{y}}\right)^t \dfrac{\partial E^h}{\partial \mathbf{y}} & 0 \\ 0 & B \end{pmatrix}.$$

The matrix B is an approximated Hessian [17] related to the level set function and is constructed as follows

$$B = \mathrm{diag}(|H_\delta''(\phi)(T(\mathbf{y}) - \mathbf{R}))| + \gamma |H_\delta''(\phi)|)$$
$$+ \mathrm{diag}(H_\delta'(\phi))(\partial_x^h)^t \mathrm{diag}\left(\left\{\frac{1}{2|\nabla_h H_\delta(\phi_i)|_\varepsilon}\right\}_{i=1}^N\right)(\partial_x^h)\mathrm{diag}(H_\delta'(\phi))$$
$$+ \mathrm{diag}(H_\delta'(\phi))(\partial_y^h)^t \mathrm{diag}\left(\left\{\frac{1}{2|\nabla_h H_\delta(\phi_i)|_\varepsilon}\right\}_{i=1}^N\right)(\partial_y^h)\mathrm{diag}(H_\delta'(\phi)),$$

where ∂_x^t and ∂_y^t are sparse differential matrices approximating ∇_x and ∇_y. It is straightforward to show that A is symmetric positive semi-definite and we add a small positive number (in all experiments this number was 10^{-10}) onto its diagonal to ensure positive definiteness.

3 Experiments

To evaluate the proposed registration approach, a series of experiments on axial 2D slices of T1 MRI brain scans were conducted. The experiments include artificial deformations and artificially created non-correspondence regions as well as experiments on real world pre-, intra- and postoperative datasets. On each dataset, we compare results computed with non-correspondence detection (NCD) with results computed without NCD.

3.1 Choice of Parameters

As usual for variational approaches, there are some parameters that need to be chosen appropriately to achieve reasonable results. To make the choice of parameters more robust against intensity variations between reference and template image, we used the standard score as introduced in [20]. This keeps the image data in a comparable intensity range.

We fixed ε equal to 10^{-3} for all experiments and set δ equal to 10^{-3} for an almost binary segmentation or equal to 10^{-1} for a more loose segmentation. The regularization parameters $\gamma = s \times 10^{-5}$ for the volume and $\beta = s \times 10^{-3}$ for the perimeter were implemented in fixed relation to each other, i.e. $s > 0$ controls the volume and the perimeter of the non-correspondence region. This specific relation of γ and β prefers solutions with connected non-correspondence regions with smoother perimeter.

Another invisible parameter, which is often required and influences segmentation results in many active contours models [15,21], is the initial zero level set contour. In our approach, we use a constant initial level set function $\phi^0 = 10^{-2}$, i.e. we don't initialize ϕ^0 with a zero level set. Hence, we rely especially on the data term $\mathcal{D}$ to be the driving force for NCD. Therefore, there are two parameters we have to chose image-dependently: first, the deformation smoothness by λ and second, the segmentation behavior by s.

3.2 Artificial Dataset Registration

In order to validate the the proposed model, we designed an artificial dataset based on a 2D T1 brain scan from BrainWeb[1]. To construct the reference image R (cf. Figure 2(b)), we masked the original image from BrainWeb with a black box. The black box is regarded as lesion and hence as a non-correspondence region. The template image T (cf. Figure 2(a)) was constructed by a 2D spline transformation [17] of the original image. Hence, except for the masked region, pixel-wise correspondence can be established between R and T.

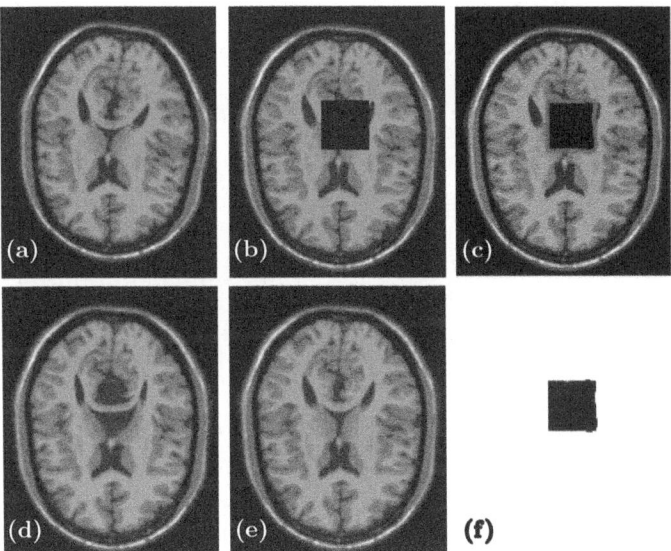

Fig. 2. (a) Template image. (b) Reference image with simulated lesion marked by a black box. (c) Reference image with contour-overlay of the zero level set estimated by the NCD approach. Enclosed in the contour is the detected non-correspondence area. (d) Deformed template without NCD. (e) Deformed template with NCD. (f) $H_\delta(\phi)$ estimated by the NCD approach. (colorcode: 0 ▬▬▬ 1 (f)).

---

[1] http://brainweb.bic.mni.mcgill.ca/brainweb/

We compare the proposed approach with an equal registration setup but without the level set term for NCD. In both cases, initialization of y^0 was done by an affine pre-alignment. Based on this pre-registration, we compute registrations with and without NCD. The benefit of the proposed algorithm is clearly shown by Figure 2. Without NCD, the registration warps brain structures of the template image unnaturally to fit the black box in the reference. By contrast, the result estimated by the proposed NCD approach looks almost identical to the original image. Observing the difference image showed in Figure 3, the residual of the registration is nearly zero up to the non-correspondence region. Registration without NCD results in undesirable foldings in the deformation field (cf. Figure 3(d)), which often lead to destruction of object geometries. However, registration with NCD successfully detects the square non-correspondence area and and extends the deformations smoothly to the non-correspondence region (cf. Figure 2(c),(f) and Figure 3(e)).

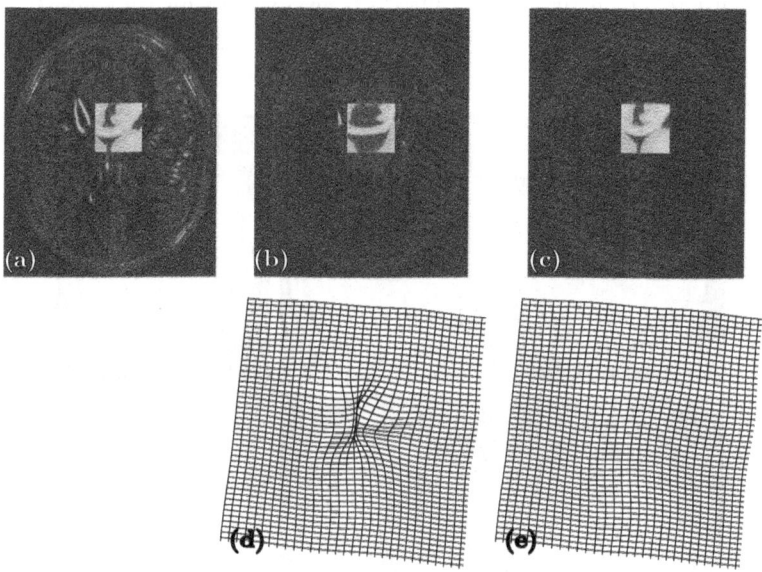

Fig. 3. $\delta = 10^{-3}, s = 10^{0.5}, \lambda = 10^{-2.5}$. (a) Initial image difference $|T - R|$. (b) Image difference after registration without NCD. (c) Image difference after registration with NCD. (d) Deformation field computed without NCD. (e) Deformation field computed with NCD. (colorcode: 0 ■■■ 3.86 (a-c)).

3.3 Pre- to Post-operative Dataset Registration

Alignment of pre-operative planing images and post-operative resection images is an important procedure to validate the outcome of a surgery. From a registration point of view, this is a difficult task due to lack of correspondence in the resected

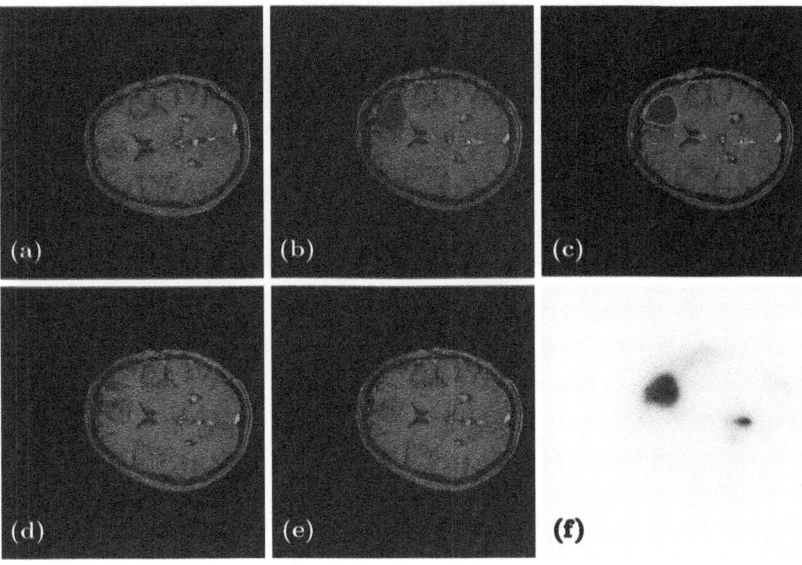

Fig. 4. (a) Template image. (b) Reference image with lesion. (c) Reference image with contour-overlay of the zero level set estimated by the NCD approach (enclosed is the detected non-correspondence area). (d) Deformed template without NCD. (e) Deformed template with NCD. (f) $H_\delta(\phi)$ estimated by NCD. (colorcode: 0 ▬▬ 1 (f)).

tumor area. In the following experiment, we tackle such a registration task with our proposed NCD approach.

For validation, we utilize the publicly available pre- and post-operative T1-weighted MR datasets introduced in [22]. We chose an axial slice from each of the pre- and post-operative scans, cf. Figure 4(a),(b). However, due to the slice selection process, the existence of a perfect voxel-wise correspondence in the non-resection areas can not be guaranteed. Again, we compare the NCD approach with registration without NCD. In Figure 4(d),(e) the deformed template images of both approaches are visualized. Registration without NCD leads to unnatural tissue deformations due to the resected tumor in the reference image. Such a phenomenon does not occur in the approach with NCD. In Figure 5, one can see that in the case of NCD registration the image difference in the tumor region is preserved. However, without NCD registration the image difference is implausibly reduced. Looking at the left (and bigger) zero level set contour (cf. Figure 4(c)), it is clear that the tumor region is well detected. By comparing the right (and smaller) contour with the corresponding region in template and reference image, it becomes clear that this indeed is region of non-correspondence.

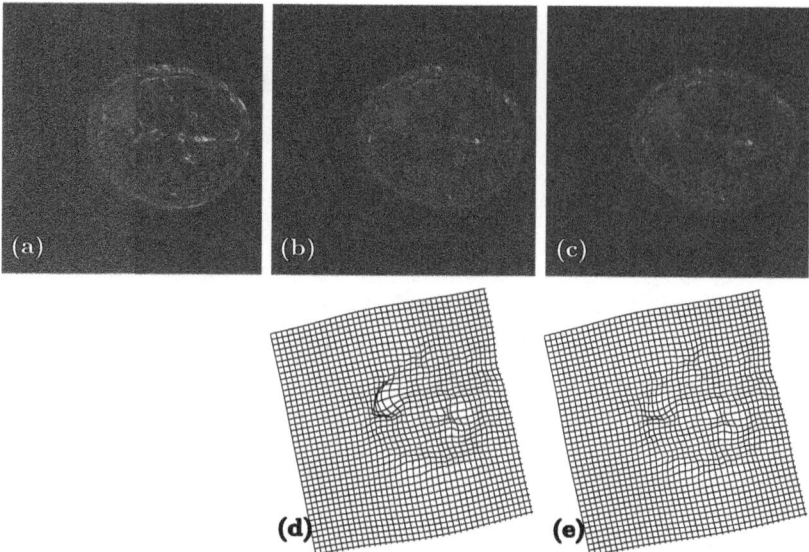

Fig. 5. $\delta = 10^{-3}, s = 10^{0.5}, \lambda = 10^{-2.5}$. (a) Initial image difference $|T - R|$. (b) Image difference after registration without NCD. (c) Image difference after registration with NCD. (d) Deformation field computed without NCD. (e) Deformation field computed with NCD. (colorcode: 0 ■■■ 8.60 (a-c)).

3.4 Pre- to Intra-operative Dataset Registration

A typical application of pre- to intra-operative registration is the evaluation of surgery success. However, during the operation skull and dura are opened and missing correspondences as well as brain shift are challenging issues. We register two example slices based on data provided by the International Neuroscience Institute[2] in Hannover, Germany to compare registrations with and without NCD.

The selected axial slices were taken from pre- and intra-operative MR T1 scans based on a tumor resection case (cf. Figure 6(a),(b)). Besides the missing correspondence in the tumor and skull regions, a large brain shift is recognized next to the resected tumor region by the NCD approach, cf. Figure 6(c),(e). Figure 6(d) shows the futile attempt of a registration without NCD to recreate the resection area and extreme bone deformations. As a result, skull and tumor are unnaturally deformed, which is confirmed by the corresponding deformation field in Figure 7(d). Also, registration without NCD incorrectly reduces the image difference in non-correspondence regions (cf. Figure 7(b)). In contrast, registration with the proposed approach did not reduce the error in the non-correspondence region (cf. Figure 7(c)). Still, the brain shift in the reference image could be restored in Figure 6(e). We notice that the corresponding

---

[2] http://www.ini-hannover.de/en/home.html

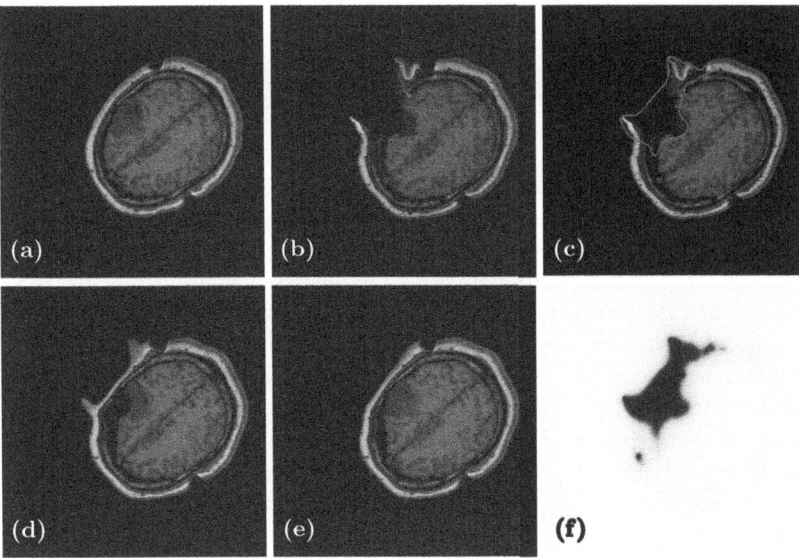

Fig. 6. (a) Template image. (b) Reference image (intra-operative). (c) Reference image with contour-overlay of the zero level set estimated by the NCD approach (detected non-correspondence area is enclosed). (d) Deformed template without NCD. (e) Deformed template with NCD. (f) $H_\delta(\phi)$ estimated by NCD. (colorcode: 0 ■■■ 1 (f)).

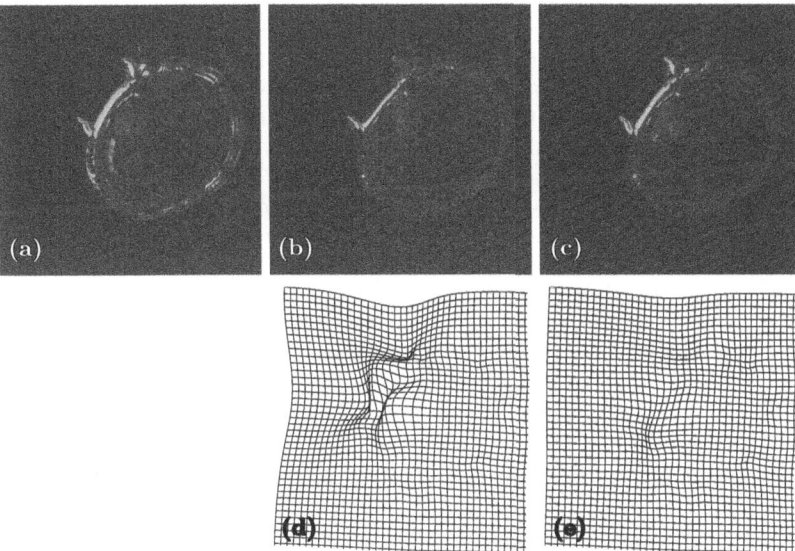

Fig. 7. $\delta = 10^{-3}, s = 10^{0.5}, \lambda = 10^{-2.5}$. (a) Initial image difference $|T - R|$. (b) Image difference after registration without NCD. (c) Image difference after registration with NCD. (d) Deformation field computed without NCD. (e) Deformation field computed with NCD. (colorcode: 0 ■■■ 7.16 (a-c)).

deformation field looks more natural and the uncertainty maps covers mainly the non-correspondence region.

4 Conclusion

In this paper, we introduce a new variational model for image registration with automatic non-correspondence detection. This model combines nonlinear registration and level set based segmentation. We use a gradient flow to efficiently solve the numerical problem. In contrast to many active contour models, the proposed approach does not rely on an image specific zero level set initialization, which mitigates the fact that the alternating minimization tied to convexification approaches due to the thresholding theorem made these approaches appear infeasible for our model. The proposed method was evaluated on registration of synthetic datasets, pre- and post-operative datasets as well as pre- and intra-operative datasets. Results were convincing in both simulated and real cases. The contributed approach is simple but efficient and allows a free choice of common similarity measures and regularizers for the registration.

References

1. Richard, F.J.: A new approach for the registration of images with inconsistent differences. In: 2004 Proceedings of the 17th International Conference on Pattern Recognition. ICPR 2004. vol. 4, pp. 649–652. IEEE (2004)
2. Kim, J., Fessler, J.A.: Intensity-based image registration using robust correlation coefficients. IEEE Transactions on Medical Imaging **23**(11), 1430–1444 (2004)
3. Lu, C., Chelikani, S., Duncan, J.S.: A unified framework for joint segmentation, nonrigid registration and tumor detection: application to MR-guided radiotherapy. In: Székely, G., Hahn, H.K. (eds.) IPMI 2011. LNCS, vol. 6801, pp. 525–537. Springer, Heidelberg (2011)
4. Brett, M., Leff, A.P., Rorden, C., Ashburner, J.: Spatial normalization of brain images with focal lesions using cost function masking. Neuroimage **14**(2), 486–500 (2001)
5. Hachama, M., Desolneux, A., Richard, F.J.: Bayesian technique for image classifying registration. IEEE Transactions on Image Processing **21**(9), 4080–4091 (2012)
6. Chitphakdithai, N., Duncan, J.S.: Non-rigid registration with missing correspondences in preoperative and postresection brain images. In: Jiang, T., Navab, N., Pluim, J.P.W., Viergever, M.A. (eds.) MICCAI 2010, Part I. LNCS, vol. 6361, pp. 367–374. Springer, Heidelberg (2010)
7. Zacharaki, E.I., Shen, D., Lee, S.-K., Davatzikos, C.: Orbit: a multiresolution framework for deformable registration of brain tumor images. IEEE Transactions on Medical Imaging **27**(8), 1003–1017 (2008)
8. Gooya, A., Pohl, K.M., Bilello, M., Biros, G., Davatzikos, C.: Joint segmentation and deformable registration of brain scans guided by a tumor growth model. In: Fichtinger, G., Martel, A., Peters, T. (eds.) MICCAI 2011, Part II. LNCS, vol. 6892, pp. 532–540. Springer, Heidelberg (2011)

9. Parisot, S., Duffau, H., Chemouny, S., Paragios, N.: Joint tumor segmentation and dense deformable registration of brain MR images. In: Ayache, N., Delingette, H., Golland, P., Mori, K. (eds.) MICCAI 2012, Part II. LNCS, vol. 7511, pp. 651–658. Springer, Heidelberg (2012)
10. Kwon, D., Niethammer, M., Akbari, H., Bilello, M., Davatzikos, C., Pohl, K.: Portr: Pre-operative and post-recurrence brain tumor registration. IEEE Transactions on Medical Imaging **33**(3), 651–667 (2014)
11. Ou, Y., Sotiras, A., Paragios, N., Davatzikos, C.: Dramms: Deformable registration via attribute matching and mutual-saliency weighting. Medical image analysis **15**(4), 622–639 (2011)
12. Mumford, D., Shah, J.: Optimal approximation by piecewise smooth functions and associated variational problems. Communications on Pure and Applied Mathematics **42**(5), 577–685 (1989)
13. Nikolova, M., Esedoḡlu, S., Chan, T.F.: Algorithms for finding global minimizers of image segmentation and denoising models. SIAM Journal on Applied Mathematics **66**(5), 1632–1648 (2006)
14. Berkels, B.: An Unconstrained Multiphase Thresholding Approach for Image Segmentation. In: Tai, X.-C., Mørken, K., Lysaker, M., Lie, K.-A. (eds.) SSVM 2009. LNCS, vol. 5567, pp. 26–37. Springer, Heidelberg (2009)
15. Chan, T.F., Vese, L.A.: Active contours without edges. IEEE Transactions on Image Processing **10**(2), 266–277 (2001)
16. Fischer, B., Modersitzki, J.: Curvature based image registration. Journal of Mathematical Imaging and Vision **18**(1), 81–85 (2003)
17. Modersitzki, J.: FAIR: flexible algorithms for image registration. SIAM, vol. 6 (2009)
18. Sundaramoorthi, G., Yezzi, A., Mennucci, A.: Sobolev active contours. International Journal of Computer Vision. **73**(3), 345–366 (2007)
19. Wright, S., Nocedal, J.: Numerical optimization, vol. 2. Springer, New York (1999)
20. Marx, M.L., Larsen, R.J.: Introduction to mathematical statistics and its applications. Pearson/Prentice Hall (2006)
21. Kass, M., Witkin, A., Terzopoulos, D.: Snakes: Active contour models. International journal of computer vision **1**(4), 321–331 (1988)
22. Mercier, L., Del Maestro, R.F., Petrecca, K., Araujo, D., Haegelen, C., Collins, D.L.: Online database of clinical mr and ultrasound images of brain tumors. Medical physics **39**(6), 3253–3261 (2012)

Bézier Curves in the Space of Images

Alexander Effland[1], Martin Rumpf[1], Stefan Simon[1]([✉]),
Kirsten Stahn[1], and Benedikt Wirth[2]

[1] Institute for Numerical Simulation, Universität Bonn, Bonn, Germany
{alexander.effland,martin.rumpf}@ins.uni-bonn.de,
{s6stsimo,s6kistah}@uni-bonn.de
[2] Institute for Computational and Applied Mathematics,
University of Muenster, Muenster, Germany
benedikt.wirth@uni-muenster.de

Abstract. Bézier curves are a widespread tool for the design of curves in Euclidian space. This paper generalizes the notion of Bézier curves to the infinite-dimensional space of images. To this end the space of images is equipped with a Riemannian metric which measures the cost of image transport and intensity variation in the sense of the metamorphosis model [MY01]. Bézier curves are then computed via the Riemannian version of de Casteljau's algorithm, which is based on a hierarchical scheme of convex combination along geodesic curves. Geodesics are approximated using a variational discretization of the Riemannian path energy. This leads to a generalized de Casteljau method to compute suitable discrete Bézier curves in image space. Selected test cases demonstrate qualitative properties of the approach. Furthermore, a Bézier approach for the modulation of face interpolation and shape animation via image sketches is presented.

Keywords: De Casteljau algorithm · Shape manifolds · Metamorphosis

1 Introduction

Bézier curves are a classical tool in computer aided geometric design. We generalize this tool to an infinite-dimensional manifold of images. To this end we consider images as control points and compute a curve in the space of images by a Riemannian version of de Casteljau's algorithm. Thus, our approach relies on the definition of a Riemannian structure and the resulting notion of geodesic curves on the space of images.

The study of the space of images from a Riemannian manifold perspective allows to transfer various tools from classical geometry and computer-aided design to this infinite-dimensional space. *E.g.*, geodesics as minimizers of the path length generalize the notion of straight lines from Euclidian space, the geodesic distance allows to measure dissimilarity of images in a rigorous way, the geometric exponential map allows to generate natural extrapolation paths starting from an infinitesimal variation of an image. During the past decade, this geometric approach triggered the development of new methods in computer

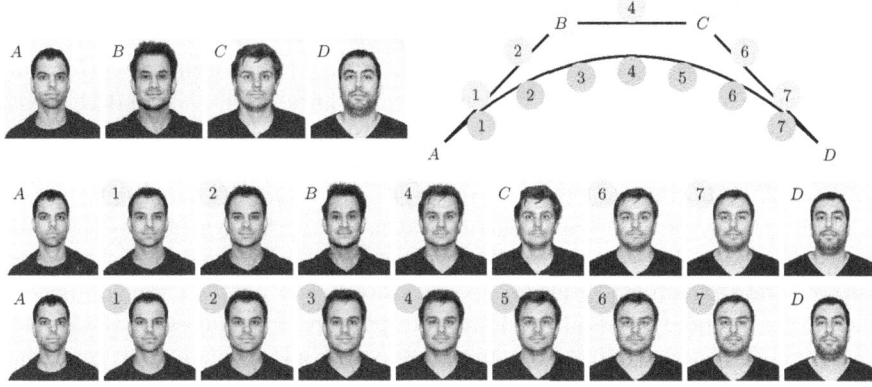

Fig. 1. Given 4 portrait images as control points (A–D) a discrete Bézier curves in the metamorphosis manifold (marked in blue) are compared with the geodesic interpolation (marked in green)

vision and imaging, ranging from shape statistics [FLPJ04] to computational anatomy [BMTY02].

Different image manifolds have been investigated. The concept of optimal transport was used to study the space of images, where image intensity functions are considered as probability measures [BB00,ZYHT07]. Following the classical paradigm by Arnold [Arn66,AK98], the temporal change of images can be studied based on the flow of diffeomorphism concept, where a family of diffeomorphisms $(\psi(t))_{t \in [0,1]} : \bar{D} \to \mathbb{R}^d$ on $\bar{D} \subset \mathbb{R}^d$ describes a flow transporting image intensities along particle paths. The metamorphosis approach was first proposed by Miller and Younes [MY01] as a generalization of the flow of diffeomorphism model and comprehensively analyzed by Trouvé and Younes [TY05b]. Besides pure transport it allows in addition for image intensity variations along motion paths.

On any Riemannian image manifold geodesics are not only minimizers of the length functional but also of the path energy, which is the time integral of the squared path velocity. In addition, minimizers of the path energy have constant speed parameterization. Hence, these geodesics are not only the obvious generalization of straight lines in Euclidian space, but also allow a simple procedure to compute convex combinations with convex coefficients t and $1-t$: one simply evaluates the path in image space at time $t\ell$, where ℓ is the total path length. Convex combination is the key ingredient of de Casteljau's algorithm. This is our starting point, and in this paper we will focus on the metamorphosis model and use the above insight to study Bézier curves in this space.

Already in 1995, Park and Ravani realized how de Casteljau's classical algorithm can be applied on Riemannian manifolds (just replacing straight lines by geodesics) to define smooth Bézier curves, and they applied this concept to generate smooth trajectories for moving objects on a manifold of kinematically admissible motions [PR95]. Such Bézier curve segments on manifolds can also be patched together to yield a spline interpolation of points on the manifold. To this end, Popiel and Noakes derived formulae for the endpoint velocities and (covariant) accelerations of Bézier curves in terms of the Bézier control points [PN07b], which can be employed to ensure smoothness of up to two derivatives. In [MCV08], a concept of geodesics from discrete differential geometry is used to apply de Casteljau's algorithm for the purpose of curve modeling on triangulated surfaces. C^1 smoothness of Bézier splines is here ensured by extrapolating the endpoint velocity of a Bézier patch via so-called straightest geodesics to obtain control points of the next patch. The authors also implement a classical control point refinement procedure to approximate Bézier curves via a subdivision scheme. Gousenbourger et al. compute interpolating C^1 splines on the sphere, $SO(3)$, and a shape manifold of closed curves [GSA14], where they generalize the idea of cubic Bézier splines with minimum acceleration to manifolds. Let us finally mention that there are also alternative generalizations of polynomial curves to manifolds based on variational definitions. In particular, generalized cubic curves can be defined as minimizers of the integrated squared second covariant derivative [CSC01, PN07a].

In this paper we discuss Bézier curves in the space of images considered as a Riemannian manifold using the metamorphosis approach. Figure 1 shows the comparison of piecewise geodesic interpolation and a discrete cubic Bézier curve for four different facial images as control points—from now on called control images. The Bézier curve is temporally smooth, comes close to the two intermediate images, and features of the control images globally pervade the curve.

2 Time Discrete Metamorphosis

In this section, we briefly review the metamorphosis model and introduce a suitable variational time discretization. With the notion of continuous and discrete path energy at hand we can define a continuous and discrete geodesic interpolation.

2.1 Continuous Model

The Riemannian metric in the metamorphosis model combines a measurement of friction caused by the flow of the image intensities and a measure of the variation of intensity values along motion paths. More explicitly, along a path $u : [0,1] \to L^2(D)$ in the manifold of images on a bounded Lipschitz domain D we consider the Riemannian metric

$$g_{u(t)}(\dot{u}(t), \dot{u}(t)) = \min_v \int_D L[v(t), v(t)] + \frac{1}{\delta}\left(\frac{D}{\partial t}u(t)\right)^2 \, \mathrm{d}x, \qquad (1)$$

where $\dot{u}(t)$ represents the velocity along the path (and is just the pointwise time derivative of the image $u(t)$). The first term describes the viscous dissipation in a multipolar fluid model (cf. [Nv91]). Here, we assume that velocities field vanish on ∂D and consider $L[v, v] := \frac{\lambda}{2}(\mathrm{tr}\,\varepsilon[v])^2 + \mu\mathrm{tr}(\varepsilon[v]^2) + \gamma|D^m v|^2$ as the classical viscous dissipation model for a Newtonian flow plus a simple multipolar dissipation model, where $\varepsilon[v] = \frac{1}{2}(\nabla v + \nabla v^T)$, $m > 1 + \frac{d}{2}$ (for d the space dimension) and $\lambda, \mu, \gamma > 0$. The second term with weight $\frac{1}{\delta} > 0$ measures the temporal variation of the intensity in terms of the material derivative $\frac{D}{\partial t}u = \dot{u} + \nabla u \cdot v$. Obviously, the same temporal change $\dot{u}(t)$ in the image intensity can be produced by different motion fields $v(t)$ and associated material derivatives $\frac{D}{\partial t}u$, which makes the minimization with respect to v in the definition of the metric necessary. The path energy is given by

$$\mathcal{E}[(u(t))_{t \in [0,1]}] = \int_0^1 g_{u(t)}(\dot{u}(t), \dot{u}(t)) \, dt . \qquad (2)$$

Dupuis et al. [DGM98] showed already for the pure transport model ($\delta = \infty$) that paths of finite energy are indeed one-parameter families of diffeomorphisms. A rigorous analytical treatment of the general model can be found in [TY05a] including the existence of minimizing paths connecting two images in $L^2(D)$. It relies on an appropriate notion of tangent vectors, which are equivalence classes of pairs (v, z), where v is a motion field with square integrable Jacobian, and z is a weak representation of the material derivative $\frac{D}{\partial t}u$. Let $(u(t))_{t \in [0,1]}$ denote a continuous geodesic curve in the space of images given as the minimizer of the path energy for given images $u(0) = u_A$ and $u(1) = u_B$, then we can define a convex combination of the images u_A and u_B with weight λ via an interpolation of the geodesic at time $t = \lambda$, i.e.

$$\mathcal{I}(u_A, u_B, \lambda) = u(\lambda) . \qquad (3)$$

Here, we in particular make use of the fact that the "speed" $\sqrt{g_{u(t)}(\dot{u}(t), \dot{u}(t))}$ is constant for a minimizer of the path energy.

2.2 Time Discrete Model

To robustly and efficiently approximate geodesic curves in the metamorphosis model we define a suitable time discrete version of the continuous path energy (2). To this end, we consider $(K+1)$-tuples $(u_0, \ldots, u_K)$ of images and define on them an energy

$$\mathbf{E}[(u_0, \ldots, u_K)] = K \sum_{k=1}^{K} \mathcal{W}[u_{k-1}, u_k] , \qquad (4)$$

where $\mathcal{W}[u_{k-1}, u_k]$ is a classical matching functional measuring the cost to match the image u_{k-1} with the image u_k. In detail,

$$\mathcal{W}[u, \tilde{u}] = \min_\phi \int_D W(D\phi) + \gamma |D^m \phi|^2 + \frac{1}{\delta} |\tilde{u} \circ \phi - u|^2 \, dx \qquad (5)$$

for an isotropic and rigid body motion invariant energy density W. A suitable choice in the case $d = 2$ is given in [BER14]. In our numerical computations we will use the simplified energy $W(D\phi) = |D\phi|^2$ and we will replace $\gamma|D^m\phi|^2$ by $\gamma|\triangle\phi|^2$ corresponding to the quadratic form $L[v(t), v(t)] = Dv : Dv + \gamma\triangle v \cdot \triangle v$. Minimization is performed over a set of admissible deformations with $\phi(x) = x$ on ∂D. A *discrete geodesic path* is defined as a minimizer of the discrete path energy $\mathbf{E}$ for $u_0 = u_A$ and $u_K = u_B$. In this discrete path energy, two opposing effects can be observed. The last term in (5) penalizes intensity variations along the discrete motion path $(x, \phi_1(x), (\phi_2 \circ \phi_1)(x), \ldots, (\phi_K \circ \ldots \circ \phi_1)(x))$, whereas the first two terms penalize deviations of the (discrete) flow along these discrete motion paths from rigid body motions. In fact, $K(u_k \circ \phi_k - u_{k-1})$ plays the role of a time discrete material derivative along the above discrete motion path. This ansatz ensures that the discrete energy $\mathbf{E}$ Γ–converges for $K \to \infty$ to the continuous energy $\mathcal{E}$. For the proof we refer to [BER14]. In particular, discrete geodesics converge to continuous geodesics for $K \to \infty$. An introduction to variational time discretization on shape manifolds can be found in [RW14]. Obviously, the energy scales quadratically in the deformation ϕ, which itself is expected to scale linearly in the time step $\tau = \frac{1}{K}$. This motivates the coefficient K in front of the discrete path energy. Now, assuming uniqueness of discrete geodesics a discrete geodesic interpolation in analogy to the continuous interpolation is defined as

$$\mathbf{I}^K(u_A, u_B, k) = u_k \qquad (6)$$

for the discrete geodesic path $(u_0, \ldots, u_K)$.

3 De Casteljau's Algorithm on the Manifold of Images

A Bézier curve is a polynomial curve of degree $n > 1$ in Euclidean space $\mathbb{R}^d$ that is defined by $n + 1$ control points $x_0, \ldots, x_n \in \mathbb{R}^d$. The curve emanates from the first and ends in the last control point, but does not interpolate the intermediate control points. However, it roughly follows those points and always remains within their convex hull. From another viewpoint, the choice of the $n+1$ control points is equivalent to specifying the first $\frac{n+1}{2}$ derivatives at the curve end points. The classical de Casteljau algorithm for evaluating points on a Bézier curve can be used to generalize those curves from $\mathbb{R}^n$ to Riemannian manifolds [PR95].

3.1 Continuous Bézier Curves

De Casteljau's algorithm constructs each point along a Bézier curve recursively via an iteration of weighted interpolations between point pairs, starting from weighted interpolations between all neighboring control points. Since weighted interpolation between points can also be performed on Riemannian manifolds, the algorithm can directly be applied to control points on a manifold, yielding a generalisation of Bézier curves. Note that on a Riemannian manifold, weighted interpolation between two points yields a point along the connecting geodesic as opposed to a point along the connecting straight line in Euclidean space.

In our case, the control points are images $u_0^0, \ldots, u_n^0 : D \to \mathbb{R}$, and the corresponding Bézier curve $t \mapsto \mathcal{B}(u_0^0, \ldots, u_n^0, t)$ at any time $t \in [0, 1]$ is recursively defined via de Casteljau's algorithm as

$$\mathcal{B}(u_i, \ldots, u_j, t) = \mathcal{I}(\mathcal{B}(u_i, \ldots, u_{j-1}, t), \mathcal{B}(u_{i+1}, \ldots, u_j, t), t).$$

Geodesics are not unique in general, hence the interpolations and the resulting Bézier curve for a given set of input images are in general non-unique as well. We obtain the following existence and continuity result.

Theorem 1 (Existence and stability of Bézier curves). *Let D be a Lipschitz domain and $n \geq 1$. For any $n + 1$ input images $u_0^0, \ldots, u_n^0 \in L^2(D)$ there exists a Bézier curve $\mathcal{B}(u_0^0, \ldots, u_n^0, \cdot) : [0, 1] \to L^2(D)$. Furthermore, if $(u_{0,k}^0, \ldots, u_{n,k}^0)_{k=1,2,\ldots}$ is a sequence of control points converging against $(u_0^0, \ldots, u_n^0)$ in $(L^2(D))^{n+1}$, then there exist Bézier curves $\mathcal{B}(u_{0,k}^0, \ldots, u_{n,k}^0, \cdot)$ of which a subsequence converges pointwise against a Bézier curve $\mathcal{B}(u_0^0, \ldots, u_n^0, \cdot)$.*

Remark 1. In the case that all involved geodesics and thus all Bézier curves are unique, we even have convergence of the full sequence.

Proof. The result automatically follows from the recursive definition of Bézier curves if we can show that for every $t \in [0, 1]$ the interpolation $(u_1, u_2) \mapsto \mathcal{I}(u_1, u_2, t)$ exists and is a well-defined, continuous map from $(L^2(D))^2$ to $L^2(D)$. To keep the exposition compact, we argue here formally and do not expand the arguments for the proper weak notion of the material derivative.

Trouvé and Younes [TY05a, Theorem 6] have shown the existence of a geodesic between any $u_1, u_2 \in L^2(D)$, so for the well-definedness of $\mathcal{I}(u_1, u_2, t)$ we only need to show the well-definedness of evaluating such a geodesic at any time $t \in [0, 1]$. From [TY05a] we know that any geodesic $u(t)_{t \in [0,1]}$ is associated with a family $\psi(t)_{t \in [0,1]}$ of diffeomorphisms and the generating motion field $v_\psi(t) = \dot{\psi}(t) \circ \psi(t)^{-1}$, and $u(t)_{t \in [0,1]}$ and $\psi(t)_{t \in [0,1]}$ minimize the energy

$$\tilde{\mathcal{E}}[\psi(t)_{t \in [0,1]}, u(t)_{t \in [0,1]}] = \int_0^1 \int_D L[v_\psi(t), v_\psi(t)] + \tfrac{1}{\delta}(\dot{u}(t) + \nabla u(t) \cdot v_\psi(t))^2 \, \mathrm{d}x \, \mathrm{d}t,$$

i.e., $\mathcal{E}[u(t)_{t \in [0,1]}] = \min_{\psi(t)_{t \in [0,1]}} \tilde{\mathcal{E}}[\psi(t)_{t \in [0,1]}, u(t)_{t \in [0,1]}]$. As in [BER14], for given $u(0)$, $u(1)$, and $\psi(t)_{t \in [0,1]}$, from [TY05a, Theorem 4] and [TY05a, Theorem 2] one obtains an explicit representation of the minimizer $u(t) = u_{\psi, u(0), u(1)}(t)$ of $\tilde{\mathcal{E}}[\psi(t)_{t \in [0,1]}, \cdot]$ with

$$u_{\psi, u(0), u(1)}(t) := \left[u(0) + (u(1) \circ \psi(1) - u(0)) \frac{\int_0^t (\det D\psi)^{-1}(s) \, \mathrm{d}s}{\int_0^1 (\det D\psi)^{-1}(s) \, \mathrm{d}s} \right] \circ \psi(t)^{-1}.$$

Thus, taking $u(0) = u_1$, $u(1) = u_2$, and ψ the diffeomorphism family associated with the geodesic, the evaluation of the geodesic at t is given by $u_{\psi, u_1, u_2}(t) \in L^2(D)$.

As for the continuity of $(u_1, u_2) \mapsto \mathcal{I}(u_1, u_2, t)$, consider a sequence $(u_{1,k}, u_{2,k})$ converging to (u_1, u_2) in $(L^2(D))^2$. Let us express the path energy in terms of the diffeomorphisms according to

$$\psi(t)_{t\in[0,1]} \mapsto \tilde{\mathcal{E}}^k[\psi(t)_{t\in[0,1]}] := \tilde{\mathcal{E}}[\psi(t)_{t\in[0,1]}, u_{\psi,u_{1,k},u_{2,k}}(t)_{t\in[0,1]}],$$
$$\psi(t)_{t\in[0,1]} \mapsto \tilde{\mathcal{E}}^\infty[\psi(t)_{t\in[0,1]}] := \tilde{\mathcal{E}}[\psi(t)_{t\in[0,1]}, u_{\psi,u_1,u_2}(t)_{t\in[0,1]}].$$

It is relatively straightforward to show that minimizers $(\psi_k(t))_{t\in[0,1]}$ of $\tilde{\mathcal{E}}^k$ converge against minimizers $(\psi_\infty(t))_{t\in[0,1]}$ of $\tilde{\mathcal{E}}^\infty$, arguing by Γ-convergence of $\tilde{\mathcal{E}}^k$ to $\tilde{\mathcal{E}}^\infty$ and equicoerciveness of the $\tilde{\mathcal{E}}^k$. Note that the paths $u_{\psi_k,u_{1,k},u_{2,k}}$ and u_{ψ_∞,u_1,u_2} of images are geodesics. As shown in [TY05a], the $\psi_k(t)_{t\in[0,1]}$ and their inverses are even uniformly bounded in $C^{0,\frac{1}{2}}([0,1], C^{1,\alpha}(\bar{D}))$ for every $\alpha < m - 1 - \frac{d}{2}$ and thus admit strongly convergent subsequences in $C^{0,\beta}([0,1], C^{1,\alpha}(\bar{D}))$ for every $0 < \beta < \frac{1}{2}$ and $\alpha < m - 1 - \frac{d}{2}$ (which we again index by k for simplicity). This strong convergence of the ψ_k and their inverses now implies the desired convergence $u_{\psi_k,u_{1,k},u_{2,k}}(t) \to u_{\psi_\infty,u_1,u_2}(t) = \mathcal{I}(u_1, u_2, t)$ in $L^2(D)$. Indeed, this follows from the definition of the $u_{\psi_k,u_{1,k},u_{2,k}}$ since for any $\tilde{u}_k \to \tilde{u}$ in $L^2(D)$ and $\phi_k \to \phi$, $\phi_k^{-1} \to \phi^{-1}$ in $C^{1,\alpha}(\bar{D})$ we have $\|\tilde{u}_k \circ \phi_k - \tilde{u} \circ \phi\|_{L^2} \leq \|\det D\phi_k^{-1}\|_{L^\infty} \|\tilde{u}_k - \tilde{u}\|_{L^2} + \|\tilde{u} \circ \phi_k - \tilde{u} \circ \phi\|_{L^2}$. The second integral converges to 0 because of the convergence of ϕ_k in $C^{0,\beta}((0,1), C^{1,\alpha}(\bar{D}))$. □

3.2 Discrete Bézier Curves

In analogy to discrete geodesics, we define a discrete Bézier curve

$$(\mathbf{B}^K(u_0^0, \ldots, u_n^0, k))_{k=0,\ldots,K}$$

by replacing the continuous operations in the defining algorithm by discrete ones. In explicit, a discrete K-Bézier curve of degree n is a discrete path of images $(u_0, \ldots, u_K)$ defined by $n+1$ control points $u_0^0, \ldots, u_n^0$. For the evaluation we replace the continuous geodesic interpolation $\mathcal{I}(u, \tilde{u}, t)$ by the discrete geodesic interpolation $\mathbf{I}^K(u, \tilde{u}, k)$ with $t = \frac{k}{K}$ and obtain the recursive relation

$$\mathbf{B}^K(u_i, \ldots, u_j, k) = \mathbf{I}^K(\mathbf{B}^K(u_i, \ldots, u_{j-1}, k), \mathbf{B}^K(u_{i+1}, \ldots, u_j, k), k).$$

For the actual computation we use the hierarchical algorithm (cf. Fig. 2).

If we restrict ourselves to the space of images in $L^2(D)$ which are continuous up to a null set, we also obtain in the discrete context an existence and continuity result.

Theorem 2 (Existence and stability of discrete Bézier curves). *Let D be a Lipschitz domain and $n, K \geq 1$. For any $n+1$ input images $u_0^0, \ldots, u_n^0 \in L^2(D)$ there exists a discrete Bézier curve $\mathbf{B}^K(u_0^0, \ldots, u_n^0, k) \in L^2(D)$, $k = 0, \ldots, K$. Furthermore, if $(u_{0,j}^0, \ldots, u_{n,j}^0)_{j=1,2,\ldots}$ is a sequence of control points converging against $(u_0^0, \ldots, u_n^0)$ in $(L^2(D))^{n+1}$, then there exist Bézier curves $\mathbf{B}^K(u_{0,j}^0, \ldots, u_{n,j}^0, \cdot)$ of which a subsequence converges pointwise against a Bézier curve $\mathbf{B}^K(u_0^0, \ldots, u_n^0, \cdot)$.*

```
for j = 1 to n
  for i = j to n
    u_i^j = I^K(u_{i-1}^{j-1}, u_i^{j-1}, k)
  end
end
B^K(u_0^0, ..., u_n^0, k) = u_n^n
```

Fig. 2. The Discrete de Casteljau algorithm with a schematic sketch for $n = 3$, $K = 7$, and $k = 4$ ($j = 1$ green, $j = 2$ orange, $j = 3$ blue)

Proof. The existence follows directly from the existence result [BER14, Theorem 3.4] for discrete geodesics. The proof of continuity follows the line of argumentation in the proof of Theorem 1, using compactness for the underlying family of deformations and the fact that for two images u_0, u_K and a discrete connecting geodesic with associated deformations $\phi_1, \ldots, \phi_K$, the images $u_k = \mathbf{I}^K(u_0, u_K, k)$ along the geodesic can be expressed as the unique solution of a block tridiagonal system of operator equations [BER14, Proposition 3.2] whose entries continuously depend on $\phi_1, \ldots, \phi_K$. □

Let us remark that the convergence of discrete Bézier curves for $K \to \infty$ to a continuous Bézier curve for the same set of input shapes is still open. In fact, in [BER14] Γ-convergence of discrete geodesics is proven in the $L^2((0,1) \times D)$ topology, which is too weak to control the convergence of the interpolated images in the de Casteljau algorithm pointwise with respect to time.

To compute discrete geodesics numerically we have to introduce a suitable space discretization. To this end, we use a finite element discretization both for the family of images and for the family of deformations. For details we refer to [BER14].

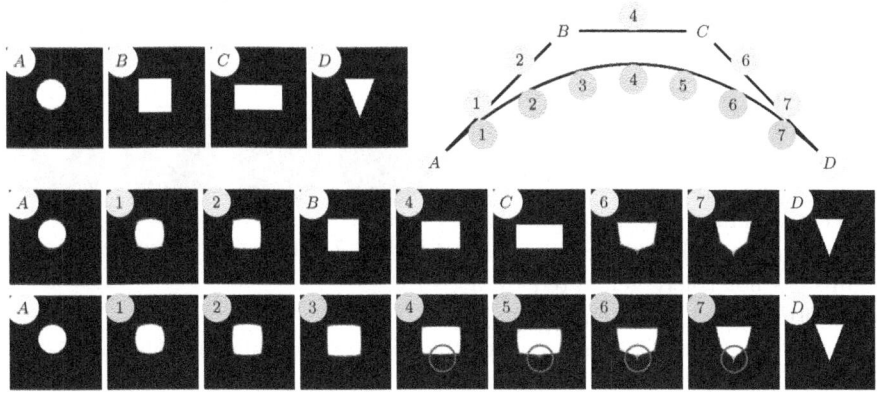

Fig. 3. Piecewise discrete geodesic (middle) and cubic Bézier curve (bottom). $K = 8$, $\delta = 5 \cdot 10^{-2}$, $\gamma = 10^{-3}$.

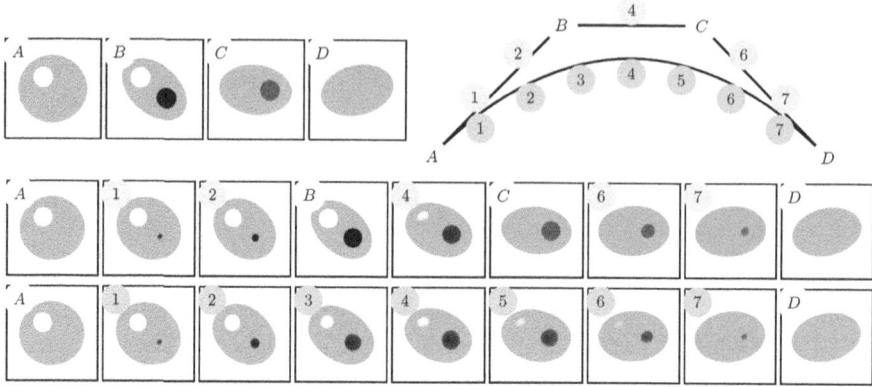

Fig. 4. Piecewise discrete geodesic (middle) and cubic Bézier curve (bottom). $K = 8$, $\delta = 5 \cdot 10^{-3}$, $\gamma = 10^{-3}$.

Fig. 3 and Fig. 4 show discrete Bézier curves for two different test cases to highlight some of the general characteristics of Bézier curves in the space of images equipped with the Riemannian structure of the metamorphosis approach. In both cases the initial image at $t = 0$ and the final image at $t = 1$ coincide with the corresponding control images, where as for the other control images the cubic Bézier curves approximately recovers them at times $t = \frac{1}{3}$ and $t = \frac{2}{3}$. The Bézier curve is smooth in time and structures in the images are smoothly blended and transported (cf. also the accompanying video sequence). The impact of the control images is global in time. Thus particular features of a single control image persist over the whole time interval $(0, 1)$. In Fig. 3 this can be best observed for the rectangular outline of the second and third control images and for the lower tip of the triangle. In Fig. 4 one obtains a simultaneous rotation of the emerging grey ellipsoid and a continuous fading in and out of the white and black circle, respectively.

Compared to this the piecewise geodesic interpolation is not smooth in time and local features of the input images spread just over two consecutive time intervals. Note that the metamorphosis Bézier curve in Figure 3 is not solely generated by a transport. Indeed, the generation of the lower tip of the triangle is not possible via a flow of diffeomorphisms. Hence, the triangle tip is generated via intensity modulation (cf. Fig. 5).

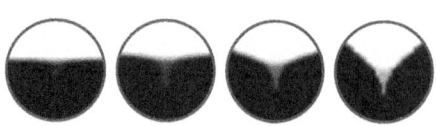

Fig. 5. Zoom into marked regions in Figure 3

4 Applications

In this section we present two applications of Bézier curves in the space of images. First, we use our approach for the modulation of human face interpolation. Then we compute discrete Bézier curves to reconstruct animations of shapes.

4.1 Modulation of Interpolation Path

Bézier curves can be used to modulate a (geodesic) interpolation path between two given images via prescribing additional control images, which are used to let additional image pattern appear and spread along a smooth and natural looking path connecting the two end images. Figures 6 and 1 display a quadratic and a cubic Bézier curve between different portraits. Furthermore the Bézier curves are compared with piecewise geodesic interpolations between the control images. The resulting path between the start and the end image ((A,C) and (A,D), respectively) consists of natural looking facial image for all times. The resulting path in image space is smooth in time. Features of the control images are clearly visible and significantly spread in time over the image sequence. $E.g.$ in Fig. 6 the hairstyle of face C is clearly visible in the images at time steps $2-7$ of the Bézier curve. Furthermore, the shape of the chin of face A carries over up to the time step $5-6$ and the moustache from face B spreads over the whole sequence from time step 1 to 7.

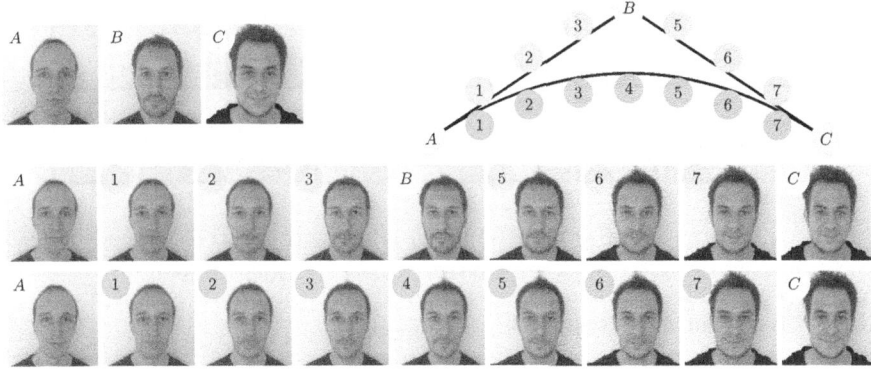

Fig. 6. Piecewise discrete geodesic (middle) and quadratic Bézier curve (bottom) between human faces. $K = 8$, $\delta = 7.5 \cdot 10^{-3}$, $\gamma = 10^{-3}$.

4.2 Image Sketches as Control Shapes for Animation

Discrete Bézier curves can also be used to design animation paths in the space of images based on very moderate user interaction. In fact, to animate an object in an image the user might cut the object into pieces and generate control images via translation, rotation or scaling of the different pieces. Then, de Casteljau's algorithm is used to generate from these sketches a smooth animation path in the space of images, which approximately recovers the poses described by the control images. As a proof of concept we consider in Fig. 8 four control images (A-D), which are generated from a very simple model of an arm (top left). While a geodesic curve between the first (A) and the last image (D) prefers to collapse the forearm (second row), the additional control points (B,C) give further guidance to reconstruct the bending of the arm along a discrete cubic Bézier curve (third row). Next, we consider in Fig. 7 a photograph of an elephant cut into three pieces (A), which are reconfigured into four control images (A-D). These control images are then taken into account to compute a discrete cubic Bézier curve (Figure 9). The resulting sequence represents the turning and stretching of the head and the raising of the forelegs.

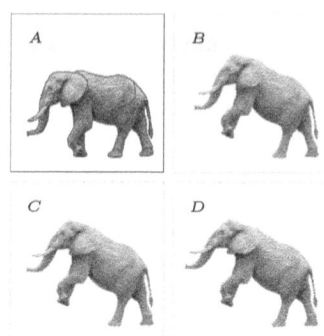

Fig. 7. Modeling of control images

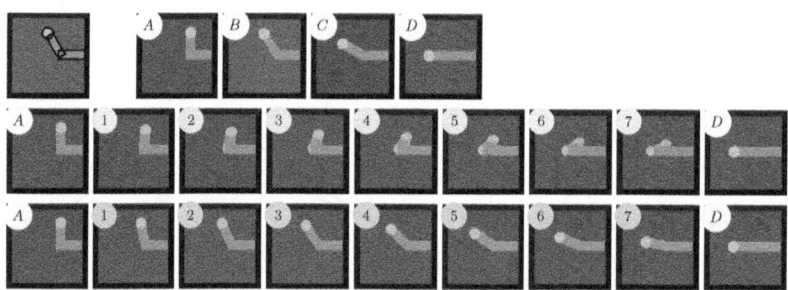

Fig. 8. A simple model of an arm (top left) is split up into three pieces, they are reconfigured into four control images (A-D). A geodesic interpolation of the images (A) and (D) (middle row) and a discrete cubic Bézier curve with $K = 8$, $\delta = 10^{-2}$, $\gamma = 10^{-3}$ is computed (bottom row).

5 Conclusions

We have defined Bézier curves on the image manifold equipped with the metamorphosis metric. Based on the notion of a discrete metamorphosis path energy and a corresponding discrete geodesic interpolation, de Casteljau's algorithm allows the robust and efficient computation of discrete Bézier curves in the space of images. Striking features of this approach are the smoothness in time and the global impact of features of the control images. This approach can be regarded as a conceptual study for curve modeling on shape spaces. Indeed, Bézier curves

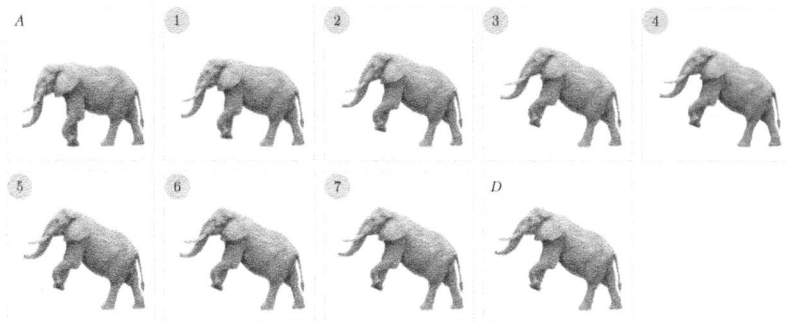

Fig. 9. An animation sequence based on the image of an elephant (www.fotolia.com ©eyetronic) via discrete cubic Bézier curve is shown for $K = 8$, $\delta = 4 \cdot 10^{-3}$, $\gamma = 10^{-3}$. The underlying control images are depicted in Fig. 7.

are just one prominent example for classes of curves constructed via hierarchical convex combination along straight lines. Perspective future generalizations include the Neville–Aitken scheme for general polynomials and B-Spline curves.

References

AK98. Arnold, V., Khesin, B.: Topological methods in hydrodynamics. Springer, New York (1998)

Arn66. Arnold, V.: Sur la géométrie différentielle des groupes de lie de dimension infinie et ses applications à l'hydrodynamique des fluides parfaits. Annales de l'institut Fourier **16**, 319–361 (1966)

BB00. Benamou, J.-D., Brenier, Y.: A computational fluid mechanics solution to the Monge-Kantorovich mass transfer problem. Numer. Math. **84**(3), 375–393 (2000)

BER14. Time discrete geodesic paths in the space of images (2014) (submitted)

BMTY02. Beg, M.F., Miller, M.I., Trouvé, A., Younes, L.: Computational anatomy: Computing metrics on anatomical shapes. In: Proceedings of 2002 IEEE ISBI, pp. 341–344 (2002)

CSC01. Camarinha, M., Silva Leite, F., Crouch, P.: On the geometry of Riemannian cubic polynomials. Differential Geom. Appl. **15**(2), 107–135 (2001)

DGM98. Dupuis, D., Grenander, U., Miller, M.I.: Variational problems on flows of diffeomorphisms for image matching. Quarterly of Applied Mathematics **56**, 587–600 (1998)

FLPJ04. Fletcher, P.T., Lu, C., Pizer, S.M., Joshi, S.: Principal geodesic analysis for the study of nonlinear statistics of shape. IEEE Transactions on Medical Imaging **23**(8), 995–1005 (2004)

GSA14. Gousenbourger, P.-Y., Samir, C., Absil, P.-A.: Piecewise-Bezier C^1 interpolation on Riemannian manifolds with application to 2D shape morphing. In: Proceedings of ICPR 2014 (2014)

MCV08. Morera, D.M., Carvalho, P.C., Velho, L.: Modeling on triangulations with geodesic curves. The Visual Computer **24**(12), 1025–1037 (2008)

MY01. Miller, M.I., Younes, L.: Group actions, homeomorphisms, and matching: a general framework. International Journal of Computer Vision **41**(1–2), 61–84 (2001)
Nv91. Nečas, J., Šilhavý, M.: Multipolar viscous fluids. Quarterly of Applied Mathematics **49**(2), 247–265 (1991)
PR95. Park, F.C., Ravani, B.: Bézier curves on Riemannian manifolds and Lie groups with kinematics applications. J. Mech. Des. **117**(1), 36–40 (1995)
PN07a. Popiel, T., Noakes, L.: Elastica in SO(3). J. Aust. Math. Soc. **83**(1), 105–124 (2007)
PN07b. Popiel, T., Noakes, L.: Bézier curves and C^2 interpolation in Riemannian manifolds. J. Approx. Theory **148**(2), 111–127 (2007)
RW14. Rumpf, M., Wirth, B.: Variational time discretization of geodesic calculus. IMA Journal of Numerical Analysis (2014) (to appear)
TY05a. Trouvé, A., Younes, L.: Local geometry of deformable templates. SIAM J. MATH. ANAL. **37**(2), 17–59 (2005)
TY05b. Trouvé, A., Younes, L.: Metamorphoses through Lie group action. Foundations of Computational Mathematics **5**(2), 173–198 (2005)
ZYHT07. Zhu, L., Yang, Y., Haker, S., Tannenbaum, A.: An image morphing technique based on optimal mass preserving mapping. IEEE Transactions on Image Processing **16**(6), 1481–1495 (2007)

Computation and Visualization of Local Deformation for Multiphase Metallic Materials by Infimal Convolution of TV-Type Functionals

Frank Balle[1], Dietmar Eifler[1], Jan Henrik Fitschen[2]([✉]),
Sebastian Schuff[1], and Gabriele Steidl[2]

[1] Department of Mechanical and Process Engineering, University of Kaiserslautern,
Kaiserslautern, Germany
{balle,eifler,schuff}@mv.uni-kl.de
[2] Department of Mathematics, University of Kaiserslautern, Kaiserslautern, Germany
{fitschen,steidl}@mathematik.uni-kl.de

Abstract. Estimating the local strain tensor from a sequence of microstructural images, realized during a tensile test of an engineering material, is a challenging problem. In this paper we propose to compute the strain tensor from image sequences acquired during tensile tests with increasing forces in horizontal direction by a variational optical flow model. To separate the global displacement during insitu tensile testing, which can be roughly approximated by a plane, from the local displacement we use an infimal convolution regularization consisting of first and second order terms. We apply a primal-dual method to find a minimizer of the energy function. This approach has the advantage that the strain tensor is directly computed within the algorithm and no additional derivative of the displacement must be computed. The algorithm is equipped with a coarse-to-fine strategy to cope with larger displacements and an adaptive parameter choice. Numerical examples with simulated and experimental data demonstrate the advantageous performance of our algorithm.

1 Introduction

The (Cauchy) strain tensor plays a fundamental role in mechanical engineering for deriving local mechanical properties of materials. Aluminum matrix composites (AMC) are highly suitable for lightweight applications in aerospace, defense and automotive industry due to their advantageous properties in contrast to monolithic materials, especially the strength and stiffness to density ratio. In this paper, we calculate local strains of silicon carbide particle reinforced AMCs from a sequence of scanning electron microscope (SEM) images acquired during tensile tests, where the micro-specimen is pulled in horizontal direction and elongates with increasing force. Fig. 1 illustrates the experimental setup and the resulting image sequence schematically. We are interested in the local deformation behavior of the composite material on a micro scale. Therefore it is necessary to perform SEM monitored tensile tests to study inhomogeneous deformation and

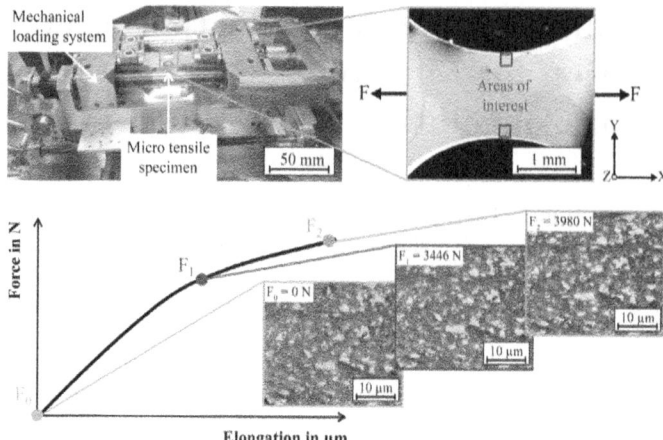

Fig. 1. Top: Experimental setup for the tensile test inside a scanning electron microscope. Bottom: Load-deformation diagram with three selected micrographs taken under increasing load.

crack initiation due to microstructural effects. For deformations of a continuum body the strain tensor ε is defined via the Jacobian of the displacement vector u, i.e.,

$$\varepsilon = \begin{pmatrix} \varepsilon_{xx} & \varepsilon_{xy} \\ \varepsilon_{yx} & \varepsilon_{yy} \end{pmatrix} := \frac{1}{2}(\nabla u^\mathrm{T} + \nabla u) = \begin{pmatrix} \partial_x u_1 & \frac{1}{2}(\partial_y u_1 + \partial_x u_2) \\ \frac{1}{2}(\partial_y u_1 + \partial_x u_2) & \partial_y u_2 \end{pmatrix}.$$

We will especially focus on ε_{xx} which describes the change in displacement u_1 for the horizontal direction x. A positive value indicates tension and a negative one compression.

Estimating strain tensors from an image sequence by variational methods has been rarely addressed in the literature. Most computer vision methods on motion apply optical flow models which compute the displacements between frames of image sequences by minimizing an energy functional

$$E(u) = E_\mathrm{Data}(u) + E_\mathrm{Reg}(u). \tag{1}$$

Our Contribution. We propose an optical flow model with a regularization term which fits to the uniaxial tensile test for estimating the strain tensor. Since the global displacement can be roughly approximated by a plane, we are interested in splitting the motion field into a non-smooth/local and a smooth/global part by applying the infimal convolution of a first and second order term and focus on the non-smooth part. We use a primal-dual method to minimize the functional. The advantage of this method is that the corresponding Lagrangian contains the derivative of the displacement, i.e., the strain tensor, so that the algorithm provides not only the non-smooth motion part but also directly the corresponding strain tensor.

Related Work. One of the few papers which address the (Lagrangian) strain tensor computation by a variational method is [11]. The authors propose a smooth fourth order optical flow model which directly computes the strain tensor from an image sequence obtained in a biaxial tensile test with an elastomer. In contrast to our paper they were interested in the macro scale behavior and compute the minimizer of their smooth energy function by solving the corresponding Euler-Lagrange equations; see Remark 2 for more details. The papers [1,9] aim at computing derivatives simultaneously to the optical flow field, but are not related to engineering applications. For engineering purposes there are some approaches and commercial software packages based on image correlation such as [4,15,18,20]. However, these methods are only suitable for computing strains on a macro scale. Variational methods for optical flow estimation go back to Horn and Schunck [12]. There is a vast number of refinements and extensions of their approach and we refer to [3] for a comprehensive overview. In particular higher order optical flow models were successfully used, e.g., in [1,19,21,22].

Organization of the Paper. In Section 2 we introduce our variational model for the strain tensor computation and motivate its choice in comparison to other models. Then, in Section 3, a primal dual algorithm is presented for finding the minimizer which also directly computes the strain tensor. This algorithm is applied in conjunction with a coarse-to-fine multiscale technique to cope with large displacements. Moreover, an adaptive parameter adjustment is used. Section 4 demonstrates the performance of our algorithm for image sequences obtained in the tensile test described in Fig. 1. Conclusions for future research are given in Section 5.

2 Model

In this paper we deal with gray-value images $f\colon \mathcal{G} \to \mathbb{R}$ defined on the grid $\mathcal{G} := \{1,\ldots,m\} \times \{1,\ldots,n\}$ and flow fields $u = (u_1, u_2)\colon \mathcal{G} \to \mathbb{R}^2$.

Remark 1. To have a convenient vector-matrix notion we reorder f and u_l, $l = 1,2$ columnwise into vectors vec f and vec u_l of length $N := mn$. If the meaning is clear from the context we keep the notation f instead of vec f. In particular we will have $u_l \in \mathbb{R}^N$ and $u = (u_1^\mathrm{T}, u_2^\mathrm{T})^\mathrm{T} \in \mathbb{R}^{2N}$.

In the task at hand we focus on two micrographs f_1 and f_2 from the tensile test belonging to different loads. The data term in (1) relies on an invariance requirement between these images. Here we focus on the brightness invariance assumption which reads in the continuous setting as

$$f_1(x,y) - f_2\big((x,y) + u(x,y)\big) \approx 0, \quad u = (u_1, u_2). \tag{2}$$

Using a first order Taylor expansion around an initial optical flow field $\bar{u} = (\bar{u}_1, \bar{u}_2)$ gives

$$f_2\big((x,y) + u\big) \approx f_2\big((x,y) + \bar{u}\big) + \begin{pmatrix} \partial_x f_2 \\ \partial_y f_2 \end{pmatrix}\big((x,y) + \bar{u}\big) \cdot \big(u(x,y) - \bar{u}(x,y)\big). \tag{3}$$

Later we will apply a coarse-to-fine scheme [2,7] and use the result from one scale as an initialization for the next scale. By (3) the requirement (2) becomes

$$0 \approx f_1(x,y) - f_2\big((x,y)+\bar{u}\big) - \begin{pmatrix}\partial_x f_2\\ \partial_y f_2\end{pmatrix}\big((x,y)+\bar{u}\big)\cdot\big(u(x,y)-\bar{u}(x,y)\big).$$

Note that $f_2((x,y)+\bar{u})$ is only well defined in the discrete setting if $(i,j)+\bar{u}$ is in $\mathcal{G}$. Here, bilinear interpolation is used to compute values between grid points. Other methods, e.g., bicubic or spline interpolation, have also been tested and give similar results. Using a non-negative increasing function $\varphi\colon \mathbb{R}\to\mathbb{R}_{\geq 0}$ and considering only grid points $(x,y)=(i,j)\in\mathcal{G}$, the data term becomes

$$\sum_{(i,j)\in\mathcal{G}} \varphi\left(-\begin{pmatrix}D_m f_2((i,j)+\bar{u})\\ f_2((i,j)+\bar{u})D_n^{\mathrm{T}}\end{pmatrix}\cdot\big(u(i,j)-\bar{u}(i,j)\big) - f_2\big((i,j)+\bar{u}\big) + f_1(i,j)\right),$$

where D_m denotes the discrete forward difference operator with mirror boundary. In this paper we will deal with $\varphi(t):=|t|$ to reduce the influence of outliers. Using the notation in Remark 1 our data term becomes

$$E_{\mathrm{Data}}(u) := \frac{1}{2}\|Au_1 + Bu_2 + c\|_1, \qquad (4)$$

where

$$A := \mathrm{diag}\Big(\mathrm{vec}\,\big(D_m f_2((i,j)+\bar{u})\big)\Big),\quad B := \mathrm{diag}\Big(\mathrm{vec}\,\big(f_2((i,j)+\bar{u})D_n^{\mathrm{T}}\big)\Big),$$

$$c := -\mathrm{vec}\left(\begin{pmatrix}D_m f_2((i,j)+\bar{u})\\ f_2((i,j)+\bar{u})D_n^{\mathrm{T}}\end{pmatrix}\cdot\bar{u}(i,j) - f_2\big((i,j)+\bar{u}\big) + f_1(i,j)\right).$$

The choice of the regularization term is of crucial importance for our model. We are interested in areas having high local strain so that cracks can initiate. The global displacement due to the uniaxial tension, which can be approximated by a plane, is of minor interest. In the following, we will motivate that the infimal convolution of first and second order TV-like terms is an appropriate choice for the regularization term. Let $\otimes$ be the Kronecker product operator. By

$$\nabla := \begin{pmatrix}D_x\\ D_y\end{pmatrix} \quad\text{with}\quad D_x := I_n\otimes D_m,\ D_y := D_n\otimes I_m$$

we denote the discrete gradient operator and by

$$\nabla^2 := \begin{pmatrix}D_{xx}\\ \frac{1}{2}(D_{xy}+D_{yx})\\ D_{yy}\end{pmatrix},\quad \tilde{\nabla} := \begin{pmatrix}D_x^{\mathrm{T}} & 0\\ \frac{1}{2}D_y^{\mathrm{T}} & \frac{1}{2}D_x^{\mathrm{T}}\\ 0 & D_y^{\mathrm{T}}\end{pmatrix}$$

a second order difference operator and the symmetrized discrete gradient of a vector field, resp., with

$$D_{xx} := I_n\otimes D_m^{\mathrm{T}}D_m, \qquad D_{yy} := D_n^{\mathrm{T}}D_n\otimes I_m,$$
$$D_{xy} := D_n^{\mathrm{T}}\otimes D_m, \qquad D_{yx} := D_n\otimes D_m^{\mathrm{T}}.$$

The application of second order terms seems natural for the task at hand since the linear motion field due to the tension will not be penalized by the corresponding regularizers. For a vector $x \in \mathbb{R}^{Nd}$ we define the grouped $\ell_2(\mathbb{R}^d) - \ell_1(\mathbb{R}^N)$ norm

$$\|x\|_{L_2(\mathbb{R}^d), L_1(\mathbb{R}^N)} = \|x\|_{2,1} := \sum_{i=1}^{N} \left(\sum_{j=0}^{d-1} x_{jN+i}^2 \right)^{\frac{1}{2}}. \tag{5}$$

Further, we will use $\boldsymbol{\nabla} u := (I_2 \otimes \nabla)u$, $\boldsymbol{\nabla}^2 u := (I_2 \otimes \nabla^2)u$ and $\tilde{\boldsymbol{\nabla}} u := (I_2 \otimes \tilde{\nabla})u$. Let us have a look at the following discrete regularization terms for $\lambda_1, \lambda_2 > 0$:

- H_1 related regularizer used, e.g., in the Horn-Schunck model [12],

$$E_{\text{Reg}}(u) := \lambda \|\boldsymbol{\nabla} u\|_2^2, \tag{H_1}$$

- TV regularizer proposed in [14],

$$E_{\text{Reg}}(u) := \lambda \|\boldsymbol{\nabla} u\|_{2,1}, \tag{TV}$$

where the norm is meant with $d = 4$ in (5),
- TV_2 regularizer with second order differences

$$E_{\text{Reg}}(u) := \lambda \|\boldsymbol{\nabla}^2 u\|_{2,1}, \tag{TV_2}$$

where the norm is used with $d = 6$ in (5),
- coupled TV-TV_2 regularizer

$$E_{\text{Reg}}(u) := \lambda_1 \|\boldsymbol{\nabla} u\|_{2,1} + \lambda_2 \|\boldsymbol{\nabla}^2 u\|_{2,1}, \tag{$TV-TV_2$}$$

- infimal convolution TV-TV_2-type regularizer with

$$E_{\text{Reg}}(u) = \inf_{v+w=u} \{\lambda_1 \|\boldsymbol{\nabla} v\|_{2,1} + \lambda_2 \|\boldsymbol{\nabla}^2 w\|_{2,1}\}.$$

Since the functions in the infimal convolution term are continuous, convex and even, the infimum is attained, see, e.g., [17]. For the kernels of the linear operators $\boldsymbol{\nabla}$ and $\boldsymbol{\nabla}^2$ we have

$$\ker(\boldsymbol{\nabla}^2) \supseteq \ker(\boldsymbol{\nabla}) = \{(c_1 \mathbf{1}_N^\mathsf{T}, c_2 \mathbf{1}_N^\mathsf{T})^\mathsf{T} : c_1, c_2 \in \mathbb{R}\}, \tag{6}$$

where $\mathbf{1}_N$ denotes the vector consisting of N entries one. To ensure the uniqueness of the minimizer in the infimal convolution term we add a small quadratic term and consider

$$E_{\text{Reg}}(u) := \min_{v+w=u} \{\lambda_1 \|\boldsymbol{\nabla} v\|_{2,1} + \lambda_2 \|\boldsymbol{\nabla}^2 w\|_{2,1} + \frac{\lambda_3}{2} \|w\|_2^2\}, \tag{IC}$$

where $0 < \lambda_3 \ll 1$. Setting $\lambda_3 = 0$ in the numerical examples gives up to a constant image very similar results. Indeed, we are not interested in u, but in its non-smooth part v or more precisely in the strain $\varepsilon = \varepsilon(v)$.

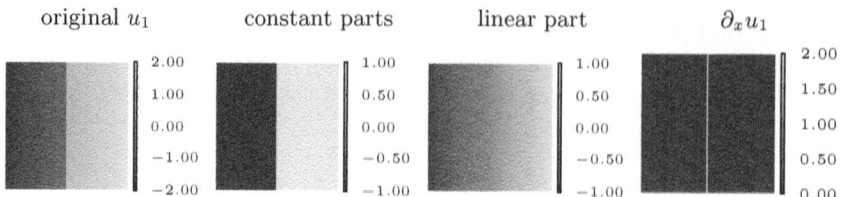

Fig. 2. Original flow field u_1 in pixels consisting of a piecewise constant and a linear part and $\partial_x u_1$

- TGV^2 regularizer [5,6], see also [16,17],

$$E_{\text{Reg}}(u) := \inf_a \alpha_1(\|\boldsymbol{\nabla} u - a\|_{2,1} + \alpha_2\|\tilde{\boldsymbol{\nabla}} a\|_{2,1}). \quad (7)$$

Setting $a := \tilde{\boldsymbol{\nabla}} w$ in (7) gives the infimal convolution regularization. Using TGV^2 instead of the infimal convolution for our problem leads to similar results which we do not include in this paper due to page constraints.

To explain the differences between various regularization terms, we use the following simplified example: a segment of 100×100 pixels of one exemplary micrograph is taken and the simulated flow field in Fig. 2 consisting of the sum of a piecewise constant and a linear part is applied to warp this image. Then the warped and the initial images are used as input to reconstruct the simulated flow field and its strain tensor via the variational models with the same data term (4) and the above regularization terms.

The minimizers u_1 of the various models together with the part $\partial_x u_1$ of the corresponding (discrete) strains are depicted in Fig. 3. First, we show a result using Ncorr [4] which is a software package for strain analysis based on digital image correlation. Whereas this approach gives competitive results in the smooth regions, the result around the discontinuity is much worse compared to all variational methods. The models with H_1 and TV_2 regularization terms cannot find a sharp motion field boundary, while the TV model introduces additional boundaries due to the staircasing effect. The TV-TV_2 regularized model is better, but is clearly worse than the (IC) method. We note that in this simple example $\partial_x u_1$ is visually nearly the same as $\partial_x v_1$ which is used in our experimental data in Section 4 where it performs better.

By the above arguments we restrict our attention to the variational model

$$\|Au_1 + Bu_2 + c\|_1 + \min_{v+w=u} \{\lambda_1\|\boldsymbol{\nabla} v\|_{2,1} + \lambda_2\|\boldsymbol{\nabla}^2 w\|_{2,1} + \frac{\lambda_3}{2}\|w\|_2^2\}. \quad (8)$$

Proposition 1. *Let* $\ker((A\ B)) \cap \ker(\boldsymbol{\nabla}) = \{\mathbf{0}\}$. *Then there exists a minimizer of* (8).

Proof. The existence of a minimizer follows by standard arguments. We show that the continuous, convex function E is coercive which implies the assertion.

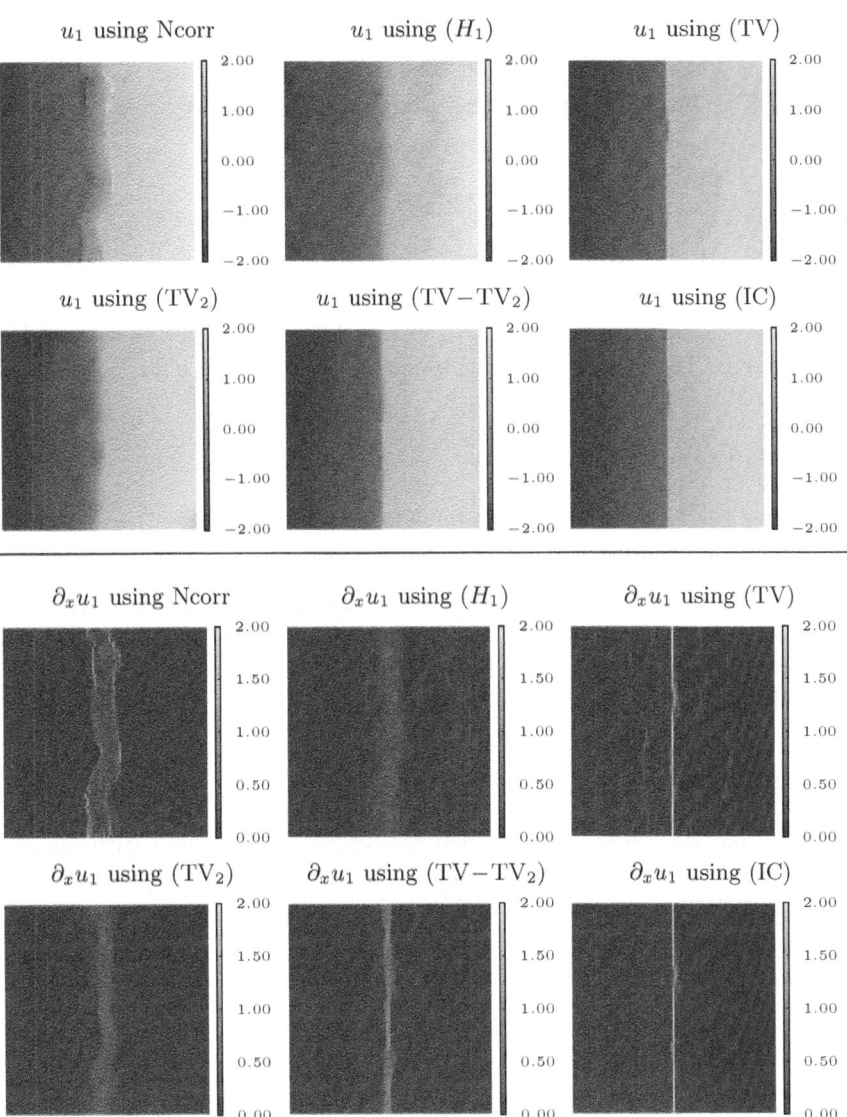

Fig. 3. Computation of the flow field and the strain tensor for the simulated example from Fig. 2. The first six images show the displacement component u_1 in pixels and the second ones its horizontal derivative $\partial_x u_1$ (strain). Note that $\partial_x u_1$ is hardly to distinguish from $\partial_x v_1$ in the (IC) model in this simple setting. While the Ncorr, H_1 and TV_2 models cannot find a sharp motion field boundary, the TV model introduces additional boundaries due to the staircasing effect. Combining first and second order differences leads to better results, where the (IC) regularized model performs even better than the $TV\text{-}TV_2$ regularized one.

Assume in contrast that there exists a sequence $(u^k)_{k\in\mathbb{N}}$ with $\|u^k\|_2 \to +\infty$ but $E(u^k) \not\to +\infty$ as $k \to +\infty$. Then there exists a subsequence $(u^{k_j})_{j\in\mathbb{N}}$ such that $E(u^{k_j}) \leq C$ for all $j \in \mathbb{N}$. We split $u^{k_j} = u_a^{k_j} + u_b^{k_j}$ with $u_a^{k_j} \in \ker(\boldsymbol{\nabla})$ and $u_b^{k_j} \in \ker(\boldsymbol{\nabla})^\perp$. Assume that $\|u_b^{k_j}\| \to +\infty$ as $k \to +\infty$. Since

$$\min_{v+w=u^{k_j}} \{\lambda_1\|\boldsymbol{\nabla}v\|_{2,1} + \lambda_2\|\boldsymbol{\nabla}^2 w\|_{2,1} + \frac{\lambda_3}{2}\|w\|_2^2\}$$

$$\geq \min_{v+w=u^{k_j}} \{\lambda_1\|\boldsymbol{\nabla}v\|_{2,1} + \frac{\lambda_3}{2}\|w\|_2^2\} = \min_w \{\lambda_1\|\boldsymbol{\nabla}(u_b^{k_j} - w)\|_{2,1} + \frac{\lambda_3}{2}\|w\|_2^2\},$$

we see that $E_{\text{Reg}}(u^{k_j}) \to +\infty$ as $k \to +\infty$ which is a contradiction. Assume that $\|u_b^{k_j}\|_2 \not\to +\infty$. Then there exists a subsequence $(u_b^{k_{j_l}})_{l\in\mathbb{N}}$ with $\|u_b^{k_{j_l}}\|_2 < \tilde{C}$ and it follows

$$\|(A\ B)u^{k_{j_l}} + c\|_1 \geq \|(A\ B)u_a^{k_{j_l}} + c\|_1 - \|(A\ B)u_b^{k_{j_l}}\|_1 \geq \|(A\ B)u_a^{k_{j_l}} + c\|_1 - \tilde{C}.$$

Since $u_a^{k_{j_l}} \notin \ker((A\ B))$ the right-hand side goes to $+\infty$ as $l \to +\infty$ which is a contradiction. This finishes the proof. □

By (6) the assumption is fulfilled except for the specific case that $A = \lambda B$, $\lambda \in \mathbb{R}$. By definition of A and B this case can only appear if the derivative of the image f_2 in horizontal direction is a multiple of its derivative in vertical direction which is most likely not the case for real images.

3 Algorithm

In this section we use the primal dual hybrid gradient method with modified dual variable (PDHGMp) [8,13] to compute a minimizer of (8). Our problem is equivalent to finding a minimizer (u^*, w^*) of

$$\arg\min_{(u,w)} \left\{ \|Au_1 + Bu_2 + c\|_1 + \lambda_1\|\boldsymbol{\nabla}(u-w)\|_{2,1} + \lambda_2\|\boldsymbol{\nabla}^2 w\|_{2,1} + \frac{\lambda_3}{2}\|w\|_2^2 \right\}.$$

This can be rewritten as

$$\min_{u,w,s,t} \left\{ \|Au_1 + Bu_2 + c\|_1 + \lambda_1\|s\|_{2,1} + \lambda_2\|t\|_{2,1} + \frac{\lambda_3}{2}\|w\|_2^2 \right\} \quad (9)$$

$$\text{such that } \begin{pmatrix} \boldsymbol{\nabla} & -\boldsymbol{\nabla} \\ 0 & \boldsymbol{\nabla}^2 \end{pmatrix} \begin{pmatrix} u \\ w \end{pmatrix} = \begin{pmatrix} s \\ t \end{pmatrix}.$$

The basic (without 1. and 2. below) PDHGMp algorithm for this problem is given in Algorithm 1. Due to the diagonal structure of A and B the proximal step to get u can be computed explicitly by a generalized form of the soft shrinkage. The update for w can be computed by setting the corresponding gradient to zero and s, t can be obtained by applying grouped soft shrinkage.

We have updated this algorithm as follows:

1. To cope with large displacements the algorithm uses a coarse-to-fine scheme, see, e.g., [2,7]. A detailed description is skipped here due to the page limit.
2. To handle the internal parameters σ and τ of the algorithm the adaptive parameter strategy from [10] was implemented.

Remark 2. (Computation of ε within the Primal Dual Algorithm)
The primal-dual method uses the Lagrangian of (9) which contains the summand $\langle \nabla(u-w) - s, b \rangle = \langle \nabla v - s, b \rangle$ with the dual variable b. Hence the algorithm computes $s = \nabla v$, i.e., the desired strain tensor directly within the iteration process and no subsequent computation of the derivative of the optical flow is required. A similar property was also emphasized in [11]. Using our notation the model in [11] consists of a smoothed L_1 data term together with a term to cope with illumination changes, which was not necessary for our image sequence. As a second order regularization term the authors propose the smooth function

$$\inf_a \alpha_1(\|\nabla u - a\|_2^2 + \alpha_2 \|(I_2 \otimes \nabla)a\|_2^2). \tag{10}$$

Variants of such a similarity term can also be found in [9]. We mention that a related non-smooth regularizer is the TGV^2 regularization term in (7). Since the biaxial tensile experiments in [11] resemble globally rather a fourth order polynomial than a linear one, the authors use finally a fourth order model based on a similar substitution idea as in (10).

Algorithm 1. PDHGMp for strain and optical flow computation.

Initialization: $u^{(0)} = u_0$, $w^{(0)} = w_0$, $b^{(0)} = 0$, $c^{(0)} = 0$, $\bar{b}^{(0)} = 0$, $\bar{c}^{(0)} = 0$, $\theta = 1$, $\tau = \frac{1}{8}$, $\sigma = \frac{1}{8}$.
Iteration: For $k = 0, 1, \ldots$ iterate

$$u^{(k+1)} = \arg\min_{u \in \mathbb{R}^{2N}} \left\{ \|(A\ B)u + c\|_1 + \frac{1}{2\tau} \|u - (u^{(k)} - \tau\sigma \nabla^T \bar{b}^{(k)})\|_2^2 \right\}$$

$$w^{(k+1)} = \arg\min_{w \in \mathbb{R}^{2N}} \left\{ \frac{\lambda_3}{2} \|w\|_2^2 + \frac{1}{2\tau} \left\|w - \left(w^{(k)} - \tau\sigma \begin{pmatrix} -\nabla \\ \nabla^2 \end{pmatrix}^T \begin{pmatrix} \bar{b}^{(k)} \\ \bar{c}^{(k)} \end{pmatrix} \right)\right\|_2^2 \right\}$$

$$s^{(k+1)} = \arg\min_{s \in \mathbb{R}^{4N}} \{\lambda_1 \|s\|_{2,1} + \frac{\sigma}{2} \|s - (b^{(k)} + \nabla(u^{(k+1)} - w^{(k+1)}))\|_2^2\}$$

$$t^{(k+1)} = \arg\min_{t \in \mathbb{R}^{6N}} \{\lambda_2 \|t\|_{2,1} + \frac{\sigma}{2} \|t - (c^{(k)} + \nabla^2 w^{(k+1)})\|_2^2\}$$

$$b^{(k+1)} = b^{(k)} + \nabla(u^{(k+1)} - w^{(k+1)}) - s^{(k+1)}$$

$$c^{(k+1)} = c^{(k)} + \nabla^2 w^{(k+1)} - t^{(k+1)}$$

$$\bar{b}^{(k+1)} = b^{(k+1)} + \theta(b^{(k+1)} - b^{(k)})$$

$$\bar{c}^{(k+1)} = c^{(k+1)} + \theta(c^{(k+1)} - c^{(k)})$$

Output: Strain s, optical flow u

4 Numerical Examples

In this section we present the results of our algorithm for the tensile test of an AMC micro-specimen described in the introduction. The algorithm was implemented in MATLAB2014b. Here we only show the values $\varepsilon_{xx} = \partial_x v_1$ which are of main interest.

In Fig. 4 the results based on the first and the last image from the tensile test together with their splitting into the non-smooth part v and the smooth part w are shown. As regularization parameters we have chosen $\lambda_1 = 0.2, \lambda_2 = 2000, \lambda_3 = 10^{-5}$. As expected high local strain values appear in the non-smooth, TV regularized part v, whereas the derivatives of the second order regularized part w are nearly constant which resembles the plane structure.

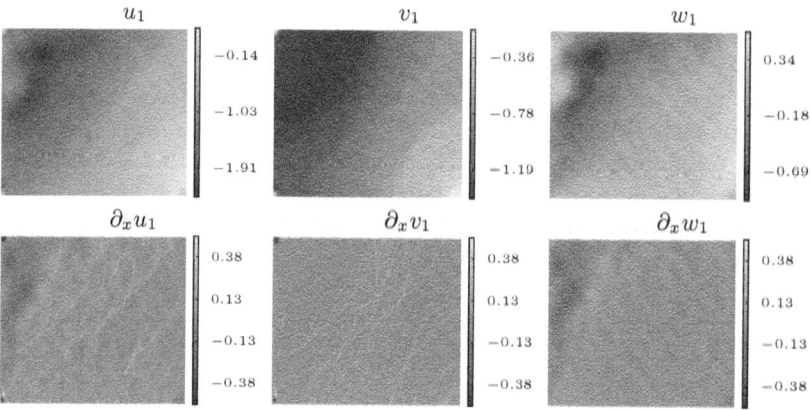

Fig. 4. Result of the (IC) model: first row: whole flow u_1 in μm and the two components $v_1 = u_1 - w_1, w_1$, second row: $\partial_x u_1, \partial_x v_1, \partial_x w_1$

Next we have applied our method to different images f_2 obtained during the tensile test at a low ($F_1 = 3446N$) and a high ($F_2 = 3980N$) load level. Fig. 5 shows magnified micrographs of two different regions where cracks were initiated. In both experiments the areas of computed high local strains correspond to crack areas in the material. It is remarkable that even under low load, when the cracks are not or hardly visible in the images, the strain tensor in the corresponding regions is high and seems to be a sensitive and useful tool to study crack initiation mechanisms of silicon carbide reinforced AMCs.

5 Conclusions

In this paper we have proposed a variational optical flow model for computing engineering strains on a micro scale for multiphase metallic materials. Motivated by the setting of the tensile test an infimal convolution of first and second order

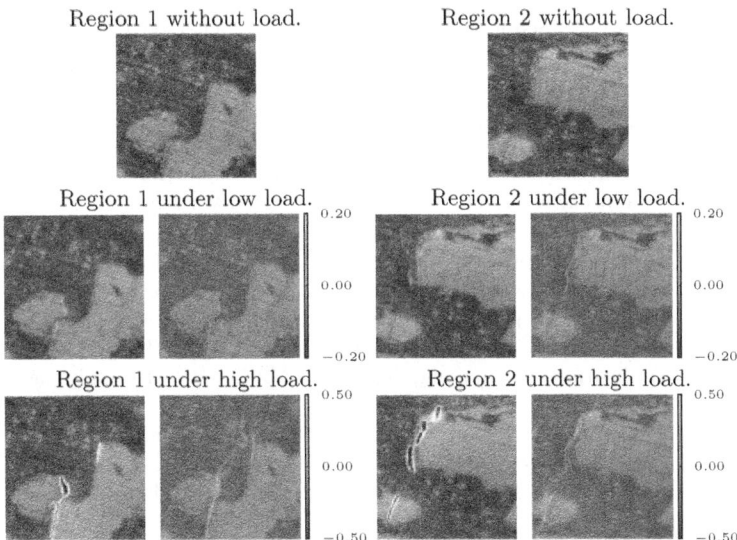

Fig. 5. Result of the (IC) model for images under low and high load. Zooms into different regions of size 100 × 100 pixels, i.e., $5\mu m \times 5\mu m$, within the whole image (1024×884 pixels). Top: The two initial image regions without load. Bottom: $\varepsilon_{xx} = \partial_x v_1$ for the two different regions under low and high load together with the image frame. The cracks in the high load images correspond to areas of high strain ε_{xx}. The high strain areas can also be detected from the low load images, where the cracks in the images themselves are (nearly) not visible.

terms was used for regularization. The primal-dual method for finding a minimum of the corresponding energy function is well-suited since it directly computes the strain tensor within the iteration process. For future work we plan to extend our approach to multiple frames. Further we want to apply our method in a more general framework for different materials as well as in other experiments such as monotonic compression and fatigue tests. Further, as suggested by one of the referees, techniques from an optimal control strategy should be considered.

Acknowledgments. Funding by the German Research Foundation (DFG) within the Research Training Group 1932 "Stochastic Models for Innovations in the Engineering Sciences", project area P3, is gratefully acknowledged.

References

1. Alvarez, L., Castaño, C., Garca, M., Krissian, K., Mazorra, L., Salgado, A., Sinchez, J.: Variational second order flow estimation for PIV sequences. Experiments in Fluids **44**(2), 291–304 (2008)
2. Anandan, P.: A computational framework and an algorithm for the measurement of visual motion. International Journal of Computer Vision **2**(3), 283–310 (1989)

3. Becker, F., Petra, S., Schnörr, C.: Optical flow. In: Scherzer, O. (ed.) Handbook of Mathematical Methods in Imaging, 2nd edition. Springer (2014)
4. Blaber, J., Adair, B., Antoniou, A.: Ncorr: Open-source 2D digital image correlation Matlab software. http://www.ncorr.com/ (2014)
5. Bredies, K., Holler, M.: Regularization of linear inverse problems with total generalized variation. Journal of Inverse and Ill-posed Problems **22**(6), 871–913 (2014)
6. Bredies, K., Kunisch, K., Pock, T.: Total generalized variation. SIAM Journal on Imaging Sciences **3**(3), 1–42 (2009)
7. Brox, T., Bruhn, A., Papenberg, N., Weickert, J.: High accuracy optical flow estimation based on a theory for warping. In: Pajdla, T., Matas, J.G. (eds.) ECCV 2004. LNCS, vol. 3024, pp. 25–36. Springer, Heidelberg (2004)
8. Chambolle, A., Pock, T.: A First-Order Primal-Dual Algorithm for Convex Problems with Applications to Imaging. Journal of Mathematical Imaging and Vision **40**(1), 120–145 (2011)
9. Corpetti, T., Memin, E., Perez, P.: Dense estimation of fluid flows. IEEE Transactions on Pattern Analysis and Machine Intelligence **24**(3), 365–380 (2002)
10. Goldstein, T., Esser, E., Baraniuk, R.: Adaptive primal-dual hybrid gradient methods for saddle-point problems. Preprint, ArXiv:1305.0546 (2013)
11. Hewer, A., Weickert, J., Seibert, H., Scheffer, T., Diebels, S.: Lagrangian strain tensor computation with higher order variational models. In: Proceedings of the British Machine Vision Conference. BMVA Press (2013)
12. Horn, B.K., Schunck, B.G.: Determining optical flow. Artificial Intelligence **17**(1–3), 185–203 (1981)
13. Pock, T., Chambolle, A., Cremers, D., Bischof, H.: A convex relaxation approach for computing minimal partitions. In: IEEE Conference on Computer Vision and Pattern Recognition, pp. 810–817 (2009)
14. Rudin, L.I., Osher, S., Fatemi, E.: Nonlinear total variation based noise removal algorithms. Physica D **60**(1), 259–268 (1992)
15. Scherer, S., Werth, P., Pinz, A.: The discriminatory power of ordinal measures - towards a new coefficient. In: IEEE Computer Society Conference on Computer Vision and Pattern Recognition vol. 1, pp. 76–81 (1999)
16. Setzer, S., Steidl, G.: Variational methods with higher order derivatives in image processing. Approximation XII: San Antonio 2007, 360–385 (2008)
17. Setzer, S., Steidl, G., Teuber, T.: Infimal convolution regularizations with discrete ℓ_1-type functionals. Communications in Mathematical Sciences **9**(3), 797–872 (2011)
18. Tatschl, A., Kolednik, O.: A new tool for the experimental characterization of micro-plasticity. Materials Science and Engineering: A **339**(1–2), 265–280 (2003)
19. Trobin, W., Pock, T., Cremers, D., Bischof, H.: An unbiased second-order prior for high-accuracy motion estimation. In: Rigoll, G. (ed.) DAGM 2008. LNCS, vol. 5096, pp. 396–405. Springer, Heidelberg (2008)
20. Werth, P., Scherer, S.: A novel bidirectional framework for control and refinement of area based correlation techniques. In: Proceedings of the 15th International Conference on Pattern Recognition, 2000, vol. 3, pp. 730–733 (2000)
21. Yuan, J., Schnörr, C., Mémin, E.: Discrete orthogonal decomposition and variational fluid flow estimation. Journal of Mathematical Imaging and Vision **28**, 67–80 (2007)
22. Yuan, J., Schnörr, C., Steidl, G.: Simultaneous higher order optical flow estimation and decomposition. SIAM Journal on Scientific Computing **29**(6), 2283–2304 (2007)

Second Order Minimum Energy Filtering on SE_3 with Nonlinear Measurement Equations

Johannes Berger[✉], Andreas Neufeld, Florian Becker,
Frank Lenzen, and Christoph Schnörr

IPA & HCI, University of Heidelberg, Heidelberg, Germany
{johannes.berger,frank.lenzen}@iwr.uni-heidelberg.de,
{neufeld,becker,schnoerr}@math.uni-heidelberg.de

Abstract. Accurate camera motion estimation is a fundamental building block for many Computer Vision algorithms. For improved robustness, temporal consistency of translational and rotational camera velocity is often assumed by propagating motion information forward using stochastic filters. Classical stochastic filters, however, use linear approximations for the non-linear observer model and for the non-linear structure of the underlying Lie Group SE_3 and have to approximate the unknown posteriori distribution. In this paper we employ a non-linear measurement model for the camera motion estimation problem that incorporates multiple observation equations. We solve the underlying filtering problem using a novel Minimum Energy Filter on SE_3 and give explicit expressions for the optimal state variables. Experiments on the challenging KITTI benchmark show that, although a simple motion model is only employed, our approach improves rotational velocity estimation and otherwise is on par with the state-of-the-art.

Keywords: Minimum energy filter · Lie groups · Optimal control · Visual odometry

1 Introduction

Camera motion estimation is an important task in autonomous driving for which the ego-motion of the camera is fully determined by images from cameras mounted on the car. Most approaches require only temporal correpondences [4] or additional depth information [8,12] e.g. obtained from stereo estimation. Given two frames and a depth map, the underlying motion of the camera can be determined uniquely. However, two-frame methods are sensitive to noise and thus past information needs to be propagated with filtering approaches. Stochastic filters require assumptions about the a posteriori distribution, which is often unknown and thus can not be modeled adequately. Furthermore, an adaption to Lie groups is unknown for almost all stochastic filters. Application of state-of-the-art particle filters is limited due to the high amount of required particles. Mortensen [16] derived a second order deterministic filter for the classical filtering problem on $\mathbb{R}^n$ based on classical control theory. This result has been generalized to Lie groups [17].

In this article we present a filtering model with state and observation equations for the camera motion estimation problem. We adapt the approach [17] to this model on SE_3 and generalize it to incorporate *multiple* measurement equations depending non-linearly on the camera motion. We also show how the abstract exponential functor [17] can be computed explicitly and finally derive a matrix representation of the inverse Hessian operator on $\mathfrak{se}_3$ using special Kronecker products. Numerical experiments show the fast convergence of the filter.

Related Work. The task of estimating the current state of a dynamical system only based on past observations of the system is known as *filtering*. In the last century numerous *stochastic filters* have been developed starting from the seminal work of Kalman [11]. See [3] for an overview and background. Since for non-linear dynamical systems with non-Gaussian noise processes this problem cannot be solved exactly, several approaches tried to cope with these non-linearities [6]. In general, as the a-posteriori distribution is unknown, most Gaussian filters are doomed to fail. State-of-the-art particle filters [7] alleviate the problem of not knowing the distribution. For large dimensions, however, generating enough particles becomes infeasible. Brigo et al. [5] use exponential families to model the a posteriori distribution, but the choice of an admissible sufficient statistic is critical and too restricted for our multiple measurement model.

For the considered filtering problems on Lie groups we have to take into account the non-linear geometry of the manifold to find an optimal filter. Markley [15] worked out a method for filtering problems on SO_3 whereas [14] investigates particle filters on SE_3. While the dimension of the embedding space is not excessively large (e.g, 16 for SE_3), the generation of samples *on* the respective Lie group is considerably more expensive. Mortensen [16] derived a *deterministic and recursive second order optimal filter* based on results of *control theory* and the *dynamic principle*. In the last years this approach was generalized to specific Lie groups [17,20]. In various scenarios it has been shown that minimum energy filters have an *exponential* convergence rate [13] and perform superior to extended Kalman filters [20].

Contributions

- Formulation of *filtering equations* for the camera motion estimation problem on rigid scenes with constant motion assumption;
- adaptation of the second order Minimum Energy Filter [17] such that it incorporates *multiple* and *non-linear* measurement equations;
- derivation of *explicit* ordinary differential equations of the optimal state and the inverse Hessian for which we derive a matrix representation;
- experiments that show the comparable performance in accuracy of the camera motion against a state-of the art-method [8] on the challenging real-life KITTI benchmark.

Preliminaries. We use the notation SE_3 to denote the special Euclidean group equipped with its tangent space $T_E SE_3$ and Lie algebra $\mathfrak{se}_3$. Tangent vectors $E\Gamma \in T_E SE_3$ are obtained as evaluations of left-invariant vector fields $\mathbf{D}L_E(I)[\Gamma]$ that one-to-one correspond to the tangent vector $\Gamma \in \mathfrak{se}_3$. Here, $L_E F = EF$ denotes left-translation and $\mathbf{D}L_E$ denotes the differential of L_E. SE_3 can be identified with a matrix Lie subgroup of $GL(4)$. We adopt the Riemannian metric $\langle X, Y \rangle_E := \langle E^{-1}X, E^{-1}Y \rangle, \forall X, Y \in T_E SE_3$, where $\langle A, B \rangle = \operatorname{tr}(A^\top B)$ denotes the canonical matrix inner product. The Riemannian gradient $\operatorname{grad} f$ of a differentiable function $f : SE_3 \to \mathbb{R}$ is defined through the directional derivative $\mathbf{D}f(E)[E\Omega] =: \langle \operatorname{grad} f(E), E\Omega \rangle_E$ for all $\Omega \in \mathfrak{se}_3$. The Riemannian Hessian $\operatorname{Hess} f(E)[\cdot] : T_E SE_3 \to T_E SE_3$ at $E \in SE_3$ is defined through the relation $\langle \operatorname{Hess} f(g)[E\Gamma], E\Omega \rangle := \mathbf{D}(\mathbf{D}f(E)[E\Omega])[E\Gamma] - \mathbf{D}f(E)[\nabla_{E\Gamma} E\Omega]$ for all $\Gamma, \Omega \in \mathfrak{se}_3$. Here, ∇ denotes the Riemannian (Levi-Civita) connection. The Lie algebra $\mathfrak{se}_3$ can be associated with a 6-dimensional vector space and we define the operation $\operatorname{vec}_{\mathfrak{se}} : \mathfrak{se}_3 \to \mathbb{R}^6$ given by

$$\operatorname{vec}_{\mathfrak{se}}\left(\begin{pmatrix} 0 & -\gamma_3 & \gamma_2 & \gamma_4 \\ \gamma_3 & 0 & -\gamma_1 & \gamma_5 \\ -\gamma_2 & \gamma_1 & 0 & \gamma_6 \\ 0 & 0 & 0 & 0 \end{pmatrix} \right) = (\gamma_1, \gamma_2, \gamma_3, \gamma_4, \gamma_5, \gamma_6)^\top. \quad (1)$$

We denote the inverse operation by $\operatorname{mat}_{\mathfrak{se}} : \mathbb{R}^6 \to \mathfrak{se}_3$ and the projection onto the Lie algebra by $\operatorname{Pr} : GL(4) \to \mathfrak{se}_3$. The standard basis of $\mathfrak{se}_3$ is given by $\{B_i = \operatorname{mat}_{\mathfrak{se}}(b_i)\}$, where $b_i, i = 1, \ldots, 6$ is the standard basis of $\mathbb{R}^6$.

2 Minimum Energy Filtering Approach

The classical filtering problem consists of a *state equation* that describes the dynamics of an *unknown* state $E(t)$ and *observation equations* connecting measurements to the state of the system. These *real-valued* equations are given by

$$\dot{E}(t) = f_t(E(t)) + \delta(t), \quad E(0) = E_0, \qquad \text{(state)} \qquad (2)$$
$$y(t) = h_t(E(t)) + \epsilon(t), \qquad \text{(observation)} \qquad (3)$$

where the functions f_t and h_t describe the state and observation dynamics, respectively, and $\delta(t), \epsilon(t)$ are noise processes. Stochastic filters usually understand these equations as stochastic differential equations and try to find for each t the maximum of the a posteriori distribution $P(E(t)|y(s), s \leq t)$. In contrast, Mortensen [16] investigated (2) and (3) from control theory point of view: He considered the equation (2) as a dynamical system, controlled by a control process $\delta(t)$ such that the residual $\|\epsilon(t)\| = \|y(t) - h_t(E(t))\|$ is minimized.

2.1 Measurement Model for Ego-Motions

Supported Models. In this section we derive an optical flow observer model with corresponding state equation on the Lie group SE_3. They support two models that incorporate two different kinds of given data, i.e.

- temporal optical flow and stereo matches (stereo approach),
- temporal optical flow and depth map (monocular approach).

Since the proposed filter supports both models and shares the same derivation, we only consider the *monocular* model in the following.

Optical Flow Induced by Egomotion. In this work we denote the time space by $T := \mathbb{R}_{\geq 0}$ and the image sequence recorded by a camera moving through a static scene by $f = \{f_t, t \in T\}$. Let $(R(t), v(t)) = E(t) \in \text{SE}_3$ be the incremental camera motion from frame f_t to f_{t+1}. W.l.o.g. at time t we set the coordinate system to be identical to the one of the camera recording f_t, i.e. the extrinsic camera parameters are $C_t = (I, 0)$ and $C_{t+1} = (R(t), v(t))$. Let $X \in \mathbb{R}^3$ be a scene point and we denote its perspective projection into camera C_t by $x^t = (x_1^t, x_2^t, 1)^\top = P_C(X)$ where $P_C((x_1, x_2, x_3)^\top) := x_3^{-1}(x_1, x_2, x_3)^\top$. Furthermore, we denote by $d(x^t) \in \mathbb{R}$ the depth of X in camera C_t such that the scene point can be reconstructed by $X = x^t d(x^t)$, see Fig. 1.

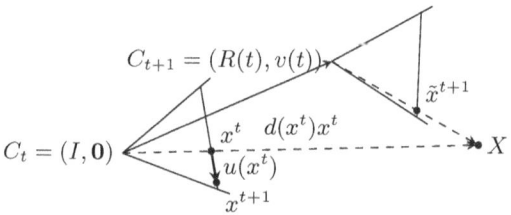

Fig. 1. Setup for temporal optical flow for either a given depth map or stereo matchings. Correspondences are given by $x^{t+1} = x^t + u(x^{t,l})$, and $\tilde{x}^{t+1} = v(t) + R(t)x^{t+1}$ denotes the perspective projection of X to the camera plane of C_{t+1}.

With this relation we obtain the optical flow induced by the camera motion $(R(t), v(t))$ and depth $d(x^t)$:

$$u(R(t), v(t), x^t, d(x^t)) + x^t = P_C\Big(R(t)^\top (x^t d(x^t) - v(t))\Big). \quad (4)$$

We introduce index k to distinguish multiple observations and reformulate the observer equations in terms of $E(t) = (R(t), v(t)) \in \text{SE}_3$ yielding

$$u(E(t), g_k(t)) + x_k^t = P_C(\hat{I} E(t)^{-1} g_k(t)), \quad \hat{I} := \begin{pmatrix} 1 & 0 & 0 & 0 \\ 0 & 1 & 0 & 0 \\ 0 & 0 & 1 & 0 \end{pmatrix} \quad (5)$$

where $g_k(t) = g(t; x_k^t, d(x_k^t)) := (d(x_k^t)(x_k^t)^\top, 1)^\top \in \mathbb{R}^4$ for a single measurement.

3 Minimum Energy Filter Derivation

State and Observation Equations. As we want to recover the camera motion from the image data, we cannot incorporate any prior knowledge of the cameras' kinematics such as data from external acceleration sensors. The only assumption we make is to demand a constant camera motion $E(t) \in SE_3$ that is influenced by a noise process $\delta(t) \in \mathfrak{se}_3$, which also models accelerations. This kinematic state equation on SE_3 without dynamics f_t (i.e. $f_t \equiv 0$) is given by

$$\dot{E}(t) = E(t)\delta(t) \in T_{E(t)} SE_3, \quad E(0) = E_0 \in SE_3 . \tag{6}$$

We incorporate multiple flow observations $y_k(t) := u_k(E(t), g_k(t), t) + x_k$ at different image points x_k for $k \in \{1, \ldots, n\}$ that depend on the ego-motion $E(t)$ and are corrupted by noise vectors $\epsilon_k(t) \in \mathbb{R}^3$. This gives

$$y_k(t) = h_k(E(t)) + \epsilon_k(t), \quad k \in \{1, \ldots, n\} . \tag{7}$$

Here we used the observation functions $h_k : SE_3 \times \mathbb{R}^4 \to \mathbb{R}^3, k \in \{1, \ldots, n\}$ that we define as is Eq. (5), i.e. $h_k(E(t)) = h_k(E(t), g_k(t)) := P_C(\hat{I}E(t)^{-1}g_k(t))$.

Energy Function. We want to find the camera motion that describes the observation process best up to a small error ϵ, i.e. we want to minimize the residual $\|\epsilon_k(t)\|_Q^2$ ($\|\cdot\|_Q^2 := \cdot^\top Q \cdot$) for all t such that the dynamical system on $E(t)$ (6) is also fulfilled. The latter means that also the error term $\|\text{vec}_{\mathfrak{se}}(\delta(t))\|_S^2$ is minimized. Here $S \in \mathbb{R}^{6 \times 6}$ and $Q \in \mathbb{R}^{3 \times 3}$ are symmetric and positive definite weighting matrices. We define the following energy function

$$\mathcal{J}(\epsilon, \delta, t_0, t) := m_0(E_0, t, t_0) + \int_{t_0}^{t} c(\delta, \epsilon, \tau, t) \, d\tau, \tag{8}$$

where $\epsilon := \{\epsilon_k, k = 1, \ldots, n\}$, $\delta := (\delta(\tau), \tau \leq t), t \in T, c : \mathfrak{se}_3 \times \mathbb{R}^{3n} \times T \times T \to \mathbb{R}$ is a quadratic penalty function for δ and ϵ given by

$$c(\delta, \epsilon, \tau, t) := \tfrac{1}{2} e^{-\alpha(t-\tau)} \left(\|\text{vec}_{\mathfrak{se}}(\delta(\tau))\|_S^2 + \sum_{k=1}^{n} \|\epsilon_k(\tau)\|_Q^2 \right) \tag{9}$$

and $m_0 : SE_3 \times T \times T \to \mathbb{R}_{\geq 0}, (E_0, t_0, t_1) \mapsto \tfrac{1}{2} e^{-\alpha(t-t_0)} \text{tr}((E_0 - \mathbb{1})^\top (E_0 - \mathbb{1}))$, with $\mathbb{1}$ being the identity matrix in $\mathbb{R}^{4 \times 4}$, is a penalty function for the initial condition. Here we also used the idea of a decay rate $\alpha \geq 0$ from [17] at which old information is forgotten. To incorporate the observations (7) we substitute the error term $\epsilon_k(t) = \epsilon_k(E(t), t)$ by $y_k(t) - h_k(E(t))$ in Eq. (9).

Optimal Control Problem. The optimal control theory allows us to determine the optimal control input δ that minimize the energy $\mathcal{J}(\epsilon(E(t), t), \delta, t_0, t)$ for each $t \in T$ subject to the state constraint (6). To be precise, we want to find $\delta|_{[t_0, t]}$ for all $t \in T$ and fixed $E \in SE_3$ defining the value function

$$\mathcal{V}(E(t), t) := \min_{\delta|_{[t_0, t]}} \mathcal{J}(\epsilon(E(t), t), \delta, t_0, t) \text{ s.t. } \dot{E}(t) = E(t)\delta(t), E(0) = E_0 . \tag{10}$$

The optimal trajectory is $E^*(t) := \arg\min_{E(t) \in SE_3} \mathcal{V}(E(t), t)$ for all $t \in T$ and $\mathcal{V}(E, t_0) = m_0(E_0, t_0, t_0)$. This problem is a classical optimal control problem, for which the classical Hamilton-Jacobi theory [2,10] gives the well known Hamilton-Jacobi-Bellman equation. Pontryagin [2] proved that the minimization of the Hamiltonian gives a solution of the corresponding optimal control problem (*Pontryagin's Minimum Principle*).

However, since SE_3 is a non-compact Riemannian manifold we cannot apply the classical Hamilton-Jacobi theory for real-valued problems (cf. [2]). Instead we follow the approach of Saccon et al. [17] which derive a *left-trivialized optimal Hamiltonian* based on control theory on Lie groups [10], which is given by $\tilde{\mathcal{H}}^-$: $SE_3 \times \mathfrak{se}_3 \times \mathfrak{se}_3 \times T \to \mathbb{R}$,

$$\tilde{\mathcal{H}}^-(E, \mu, \delta, t) = c(\delta, \epsilon(E, t), t_0, t) - \langle \mu, \delta \rangle. \tag{11}$$

The minimization of (11) w.r.t. the variable δ leads [17, Prop. 4.2] to the optimal Hamiltonian $\mathcal{H}^-(E, \mu, t) := \tilde{\mathcal{H}}^-(E, \mu, \delta^*, t)$, where $\text{vec}_{\mathfrak{se}}(\delta^*) = e^{\alpha(t-t_0)} S^{-1} \text{vec}_{\mathfrak{se}}(\mu)$. $\mathcal{H}^-$ is given by

$$\mathcal{H}^-(E, \mu, t) = \tfrac{1}{2} e^{-\alpha(t-t_0)} \sum_{k=1}^n \|y_k - h_k(E)\|_Q^2 - \tfrac{1}{2} e^{\alpha(t-t_0)} \langle \mu, \text{mat}_{\mathfrak{se}}(S^{-1} \text{vec}_{\mathfrak{se}}(\mu)) \rangle. \tag{12}$$

In the next section we compute explicit ordinary differential equations for the optimal state $E^*(t)$ for each $t \in T$ that consists of different derivatives of the left trivialized Hamilton function (12).

3.1 Recursive Filtering Principle of Mortensen

In order to find a recursive filter we compute the total time derivative of the optimality condition on the value function, which is

$$\text{grad}_1 \mathcal{V}(E^*, t) = 0, \tag{13}$$

for each $t \in T$. This equation must be fulfilled by an optimal solution of the filtering problem $E^* \in SE_3$. Unfortunately, because the filtering problem is in general infinite dimensional, this leads to an expression containing derivatives of every order. In practice (cf. [17,20]) derivatives of third order and higher are neglected, since they are complicated to compute. Omitting these leads to a second order approximation of the optimal filter.

Theorem 1. *The differential equations of the second order Minimum Energy Filter for our state* (6) *and nonlinear observer* (7) *model is given by*

$$\dot{E}^* = - E^* \text{mat}_{\mathfrak{se}}\left(P \text{vec}_{\mathfrak{se}}\left(\sum_k \Pr(A_k(E^*))\right)\right), \quad E^*(t_0) = E_0, \tag{14}$$

$$\dot{P} = - \alpha P + S^{-1} - P \sum_k \left(\tilde{\Gamma}_{\text{vec}_{\mathfrak{se}}(\Pr(A_k(E^*)))} + D_k(E^*)\right) P$$
$$- \tilde{\Gamma}^*_{\text{vec}_{\mathfrak{se}}(E^{*-1}\dot{E}^*)} P + P(\tilde{\Gamma}^*_{\text{vec}_{\mathfrak{se}}(E^{*-1}\dot{E}^*)})^\top, \quad P(t_0) = P_0, \tag{15}$$

where $A_k(E) = A_k(E, g_k) := \left(\kappa_k^{-1}\hat{I} - \kappa_k^{-2}\hat{I}E^{-1}e_3 g_k^\top \hat{I}\right)^\top Q(y_k - h_k(E)) g_k^\top E^{-\top}$, $\kappa_k := \kappa_k(E) := e_3^\top \hat{I} E^{-1} g_k$ and $\Pr(A) := \arg\min_{\Omega \in \mathfrak{se}_3} \langle \Omega, A \rangle$. $D_k(E)$ is derived in the appendix in Eq. (A.4) and the matrix valued functions $\tilde{\Gamma}_\cdot, \tilde{\Gamma}^*_\cdot : \mathbb{R}^6 \to \mathbb{R}^{6\times 6}$ come from the vectorization of the connection functions. Their components are given by $(\tilde{\Gamma}_z)_{ij} := \sum_{k=1}^6 \hat{\Gamma}^i_{jk} z^k$ and $(\tilde{\Gamma}^*_z)_{ik} := \sum_{j=1}^6 \hat{\Gamma}^i_{jk} z^j$ with $z \in \mathbb{R}^6$ and Christoffel-Symbols $\hat{\Gamma}^i_{jk} := \Gamma^i_{kj}$ from [21].

The initial $P_0 \in \mathbb{R}^{6 \times 6}$ is given by $P_0 \operatorname{vec}_{\mathfrak{se}}(\Omega) = \operatorname{vec}_{\mathfrak{se}}((E \operatorname{Hess} m_0(E_0)[E\Omega])^{-1})$, and E_0 is an initialization in SE_3.

The sketch of the proof is given at the end of this section. For the proof we need some lemmas listed below, the proofs of which can be found in the appendix.

We adapt the minimum energy filter for general Lie groups derived in [17] to our nonlinear measurement model on SE_3. Following [17, Eq.(37)] the estimate of the optimal state E^* is given by

$$\dot{E}^* = -E^* Z(E^*, t)^{-1}\bigl(\operatorname{grad}_1 \mathcal{H}^-(E^*, \mu, t)\bigr), \tag{16}$$

which contains the second order information matrix $Z(E^*, t) : \mathfrak{se}_3 \to \mathfrak{se}_3$ of the value function $\mathcal{V}$ (cf. (10)), defined by $Z(E^*, t)(\Omega) \mapsto E^{*-1} \operatorname{Hess}_1 \mathcal{V}(E^*, t)[E^*\Omega]$. The gradient of the Hamiltonian in (16) is given in the following lemma.

Lemma 1. *The Riemannian gradient on $T_E SE_3$ of the Hamiltonian $\mathcal{H}^-(E, \mu, t)$ with $A_k(E) = A_k(E, g_k)$ defined in Theorem 1 is given by*

$$\operatorname{grad}_1 \mathcal{H}^-(E, \mu, t) = e^{-\alpha(t-t_0)} \sum_k E \Pr(A_k(E)). \tag{17}$$

In order to derive a second order filter, we also need a recursive expression of the operator Z, that has been derived in [17, Eq.(51)] and is approximately

$$\frac{d}{dt} Z(E^*(t), t) \approx \omega^*_{E^{*-1}\dot{E}^*} \circ Z(E^*, t) + Z(E^*, t) \circ \omega_{E^{*-1}\dot{E}^*} \\ + Z(E^*, t) \circ \operatorname{Hess}_2 \mathcal{H}^-(E^*, 0, t) \circ Z(E^*, t) + E^{*-1} \operatorname{Hess}_1 \mathcal{H}^-(E^*, 0, t) \circ E^*, \tag{18}$$

where third order derivatives are neglected. For the computation of the Hessian we need implicitly the Riemannian connection ∇ with connection function $\omega_\Omega \Delta := E \nabla_\Omega \Delta$. The dual operator ω^*_Ω is given by $\langle \omega^*_\Omega \Delta, \Theta \rangle := \langle \Delta, \omega_\Omega \Theta \rangle$.

Next, we derive a matrix representation for all terms in Eq. (18) provided by the $\operatorname{vec}_{\mathfrak{se}}$–operation defined in section 1 and the following lemmas.

Lemma 2 (Matrix representation of Z). *Let $Z(E^*, t) : \mathfrak{se}_3 \to \mathfrak{se}_3$ be the operator in equation (16). Then there exists a matrix $K = K(t) \in \mathbb{R}^{6\times 6}$ such that we can vectorize $Z(E^*, t)(\Omega)$ for each $\Omega \in \mathfrak{se}_3$. Then it holds $\operatorname{vec}_{\mathfrak{se}}(Z(E^*, t)(\Omega)) = K(t) \operatorname{vec}_{\mathfrak{se}}(\Omega)$, and thus $\operatorname{vec}_{\mathfrak{se}}(d/dt Z(E^*, t)(\Omega)) = \dot{K}(t) \operatorname{vec}_{\mathfrak{se}}(\Omega)$, as well as*

1. $\operatorname{vec}_{\mathfrak{se}}(\omega^*_{E^{*-1}\dot{E}^*} Z(E^*, t) \circ \Omega) = (\tilde{\Gamma}^*_{\operatorname{vec}_{\mathfrak{se}}(E^{*-1}\dot{E}^*)})^\top K(t) \operatorname{vec}_{\mathfrak{se}}(\Omega)$
2. $\operatorname{vec}_{\mathfrak{se}}(Z(E^*, t) \circ \omega_{E^{*-1}\dot{E}^*} \Omega) = K(t) \tilde{\Gamma}^*_{\operatorname{vec}_{\mathfrak{se}}(E^{*-1}\dot{E}^*)} \operatorname{vec}_{\mathfrak{se}}(\Omega)$,

3. $\text{vec}_{\mathfrak{se}}(Z(E^*,t)(\text{Hess}_2\,\mathcal{H}^-(E^*,0,t)[Z(E^*,t)(\Omega)]))$
$= -e^{\alpha(t-t_0)}K(t)S^{-1}K(t)\,\text{vec}_{\mathfrak{se}}(\Omega)$,

with $\tilde{\Gamma}$ and $\tilde{\Gamma}^*$ from Thm. 1.

Finally we have to apply the $\text{vec}_{\mathfrak{se}}$–operation to the last remaining term in (18):

Lemma 3. *It holds*

$$\text{vec}_{\mathfrak{se}}(E^{*-1}\,\text{Hess}_1\,\mathcal{H}^-(E^*,0,t)[E^*\Omega])$$
$$= e^{-\alpha(t-t_0)}\sum_k (\tilde{\Gamma}_{\text{vec}_{\mathfrak{se}}(\text{Pr}(A_k(E^*)))} + D_k(E^*))\,\text{vec}_{\mathfrak{se}}(\Omega)$$

where $D_k(\cdot):\text{SE}_3\to\mathbb{R}^{6\times 6}$ and $\tilde{\Gamma}:\mathbb{R}^6\to\mathbb{R}^{6\times 6}$ are given in the appendix.

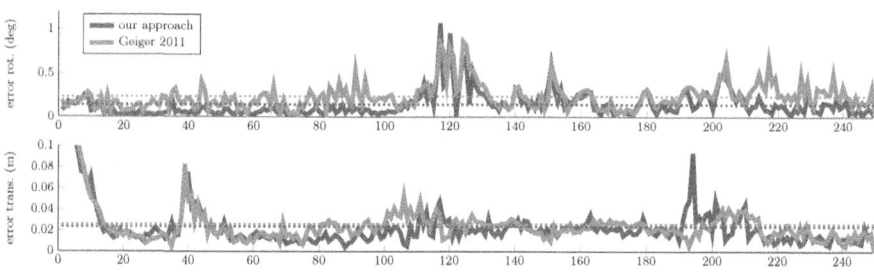

Fig. 2. Comparison of the rotational error (top, in degree) and the translational (bottom, in meters) of our approach and Geiger et al. [8] on the first 250 frames of sequence 0 of the Kitti odometry benchmark. We used the parameters ($\alpha = 2$, $S = \text{diag}((s_1,s_1,s_1,s_2,s_2,s_2))$, $s_1 = 10^{-3}$, $s_2 = 10^{-6}$, $Q = 0.02\mathbb{1}$). The dotted lines indicate the mean errors. In the translational part (bottom) both methods are competitive. In the rotational part (top) we outperform [8].

Sketch of proof of Thm. 1. Insertion of (17) into (16) and $\text{vec}_{\mathfrak{se}}(Z(E^*,t)(\Omega)) = K(t)\,\text{vec}_{\mathfrak{se}}(\Omega)$ (cf. Lem. 2) give

$$\dot{E}^* = -e^{-\alpha(t-t_0)}E^*\,\text{mat}_{\mathfrak{se}}\Big(K^{-1}\,\text{vec}_{\mathfrak{se}}(\sum_k E^*\,\text{Pr}(A_k(E^*)))\Big). \quad (19)$$

By evaluation of (18) at $\Omega \in \mathfrak{se}_3$ and application of the $\text{vec}_{\mathfrak{se}}$–operation to both sides of (18) we obtain with Lemmas 2 and 3 the following dynamics of K:

$$\dot{K}\,\text{vec}_{\mathfrak{se}}(\Omega) = \Big((\tilde{\Gamma}^*_{\text{vec}_{\mathfrak{se}}(E^{*-1}\dot{E}^*)})^\top K + K\tilde{\Gamma}^*_{\text{vec}_{\mathfrak{se}}(E^{*-1}\dot{E}^*)} - e^{\alpha(t-t_0)}KS^{-1}K$$
$$+ \Big(e^{-\alpha(t-t_0)}\sum_k(\tilde{\Gamma}_{\text{vec}_{\mathfrak{se}}(\text{Pr}(A_k(E^*)))} + D_k(E^*))\Big)\Big)\,\text{vec}_{\mathfrak{se}}(\Omega). \quad (20)$$

Since Ω was chosen arbitrarily we can neglect $\text{vec}_{\mathfrak{se}}(\Omega)$ on both sides of (20). A change of variables $P(t) := e^{-\alpha(t-t_0)}K(t)^{-1}$ in (19) and (20) gives the ODEs (14) and (15) in Theorem 1. For brevity we omit the computations here. □

Table 1. Comparison between our approach and Geiger et al. [8] on the first six sequences of the KITTI visual odometry benchmark. Our approach is usually better than [8] in the rotational part, since we model the Lie Group explicitly, but inferior in the translation since our input data from [18] is often not correct, (cf. seq.1,2).

sequence	0	1	2	3	4	5
Geiger [8] trans. err. (m)	0.023	0.050	0.027	0.017	0.017	0.017
ours trans. err. (m)	0.027	0.84	0.060	0.020	0.024	0.027
Geiger [8] rot. err. (deg)	0.27	**0.15**	**0.26**	0.25	**0.10**	**0.22**
ours rot. err. (deg)	**0.19**	0.17	0.28	**0.22**	**0.10**	**0.22**

3.2 Numerical Geometric Integration

In order to solve the differential equations (14) and (15) we use *Crouch-Grossman* methods [9]. We adapt the version for right invariant Lie groups from the standard literature by permuting the order of the factors, i.e.

$$E_{n+1} = E_n \operatorname{Exp}(\tfrac{h}{2} K_1^E) \operatorname{Exp}(\tfrac{h}{2} K_2^E), \tag{21}$$

with $K_1^E := \phi(E_n)$ and $K_2^E := \phi(E_n \operatorname{Exp}(h K_1^E))$ and step size h. We use the method (21) to integrate equation (14), where $E^{*-1}\phi(E^*)$ is defined by the right hand side of (14). For the integration of equation (15) we used a standard 2-stage Runge-Kutta schemes on $\mathbb{R}^{6\times 6}$, since P does not lie on a non-trivial manifold.

4 Experiments

Preprocessing. We computed the depth map from stereo images with [19] and the temporal optical flow between left images by the method [18]. Both methods are the top ranked on the Kitti Benchmark and the code is publicly available. To remove outliers in the flow / depth map we computed for each image on 50 points x the energy $E(x) := \|y(x) - h(x, E)\|$, and removed all points x with $E(x) < \lambda$, where we selected λ as 80% quantile the energy of all points.

Evaluation on KITTI Benchmark. We compare our approach with Geiger et al. [8] on the challenging KITTI benchmark. We evaluated the first six sequences of the KITTI benchmark. Both algorithms have as initialization the identity matrix, i.e. $E_0 = \mathbb{1}$ thus it takes some frames until the approaches converge. For this reason, we omitted the first 10 frames in the evaluations. The translational and rotational error of our approach and Geiger et al. [8] w.r.t. ground truth ego-motion in depicted in Tab. 1. Usually, in the rotational component our approach works better than [8], since we model rotations explicitly on a manifold, as depicted in Fig 2. However, our approach less exact in the translational component because the optical flow estimation by [18] fails on some frames of sequences 1 and 2 yielding a high energy and error.

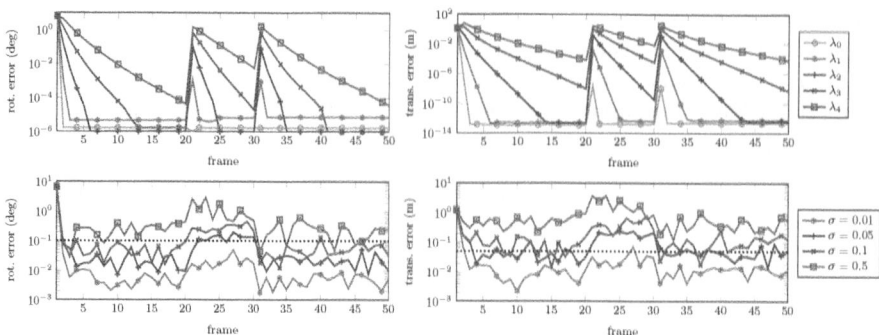

Fig. 3. Evaluation of our method on synthetic data. In the top row we observe the linear convergence in the logarithmic scale, which means exponential convergence behavior. In frames 21 and 31 there is an immediate change of direction which causes errors since the motion-constancy assumption is violated. However, our method adapts to the change in the subsequent steps. In the bottom row we consider multiplicative Gaussian noise with mean 1 and standard deviation σ to the input data (optical flow). For little noise rates ($\sigma \leq 0.01$) we obtain the accuracy required for practical applications (dotted lines): (0.1 degree, 0.05 meters).

Synthetic Data. We evaluated our method on synthetic data with known depth maps and optical flow. Fig. 3 (top) shows the convergence from a wrong initialization for different weights of the penalty term of δ, i.e. $S_i = \lambda_i \operatorname{diag}(s_1, s_1, s_1, s_2, s_2, s_2)$ with $s_1 = 10^{-3}$, $s_2 = 10^{-6}$ and $\lambda_i = 10^i$ for $i = 0, \ldots, 4$, $\alpha = 0$ and $Q = 0.1 \mathbb{1}$. In frames 21 and 51 constant motion assumption is violated, leading to a high error. However, for small weights of the penalty term of δ the filter converges almost immediately. Fig. 3 (bottom) shows the performance of the filter on data distorted by multiplicative Gaussian noise. For high noise rates ($\sigma > 0.1$) the filter fails while for small noise rates ($\sigma < 0.05$) filter results have an accuracy comparable to state-of-the-art filters on real data. On the other hand this means that the input data is allowed to be wrong up to 1% in order to reach state-of-the-art results. For our evaluations on Tab. 1 this was not always the case.

5 Conclusion

We presented a second order Minimum Energy Filter with non-linear observation equations for the ego-motion estimation problem and derived explicit differential equations for the optimal state. Our experiments showed that our approach is comparable with the state-of-the-art approaches [8]: In the translational component our method is inferior but it is superior in the rotational component. The experiments also confirm the exponential convergence rate and robustness against multiplicative noise.

In future work, we will generalize our model by allowing an acceleration of the camera. We expect this generalization to reduce the error in the translational part. Moreover, we plan to design a filter for monocular depth map estimation.

A Proofs of Lemmas 1–3

Proof (of Lem. 1). We begin with the directional derivative of h_k which is

$$\mathbf{D}h_k(E)[E\Omega] = -\kappa_k^{-1}\hat{I}\Omega E^{-1}g_k + \kappa_k^{-2}(e_3^\top \hat{I}\Omega E^{-1}g_k)\hat{I}E^{-1}g_k, \qquad (A.1)$$

where $\kappa_k = \kappa_k(E) := e_3^\top \hat{I} E^{-1} g_k$. Then the following holds:

$$\mathbf{D}_1 \mathcal{H}^-(E,\mu,t)[E\Omega] = -e^{-\alpha(t-t_0)} \sum_{k=1}^{n} \mathrm{tr}\big(\mathbf{D}h_k(E)[E\Omega](y_k - h_k(E))^\top Q\big)$$

$$= e^{-\alpha(t-t_0)} \sum_{k=1}^{n} \big\langle \big(\kappa_k^{-1}\hat{I} - \kappa_k^{-2}\hat{I}E^{-1}e_3 g_k^\top \hat{I}\big)^\top Q(y_k - h_k(E))g_k^\top E^{-\top}, \Omega \big\rangle. \qquad (A.2)$$

We obtain the Riemannian gradient on SE_3 by projecting (cf. [1, Sec. 3.6.1]) the left hand side of the Riemannian metric in (A.2) onto $T_E \, SE_3$, which is

$$\mathrm{grad}_1 \, \mathcal{H}^-(E,\mu,t) = e^{-\alpha(t-t_0)} \sum_{k} E \, \mathrm{Pr}\big(A_k(E)\big).$$

with $A_k(E) := \big(\kappa_k^{-1}\hat{I} - \kappa_k^{-2}\hat{I}E^{-1}e_3 g_k^\top \hat{I}\big)^\top Q(y_k - h_k(E))g_k^\top E^{-\top}$ and Pr is this mentioned projection. □

Proof (of Lem. 2). The existence of a matrix K such that $K \, \mathrm{vec}_{\mathfrak{se}}(\Omega) = Z(E^*,t)[\Omega]$ follows from considering the basis of $\mathfrak{se}_3$ (cf. Sec. 1) and also its inverse representation. The Hessian of the Hamiltonian w.r.t. the second argument evaluated at zero is $\mathrm{vec}_{\mathfrak{se}}(\mathrm{Hess}_2 \, \mathcal{H}^-(E^*,0,t)[\Omega]) = -e^{\alpha(t-t_0)} S^{-1} \, \mathrm{vec}_{\mathfrak{se}}(\Omega)$, thus

$$\mathrm{vec}_{\mathfrak{se}}(Z(E^*,t)(\mathrm{Hess}_2 \, \mathcal{H}^-(E^*,0,t)[Z(E^*,t)(\Omega)])) = -e^{\alpha(t-t_0)} K(t) S^{-1} K(t) \, \mathrm{vec}_{\mathfrak{se}}(\Omega).$$

For left-invariant Lie groups the vectorized representation of affine connection holds (cf. [1]), i.e.

$$\mathrm{vec}_{\mathfrak{se}}(\omega_\Omega \Delta) = \tilde{\Gamma}_{\mathrm{vec}_{\mathfrak{se}}(\Delta)} \, \mathrm{vec}_{\mathfrak{se}}(\Omega) + \mathrm{vec}_{\mathfrak{se}}(\mathbf{D}\Delta[\Omega]), \qquad (A.3)$$

where matrix $\tilde{\Gamma}_{\mathrm{vec}_{\mathfrak{se}}(\Delta)}$ has the components $(\tilde{\Gamma}_{\mathrm{vec}_{\mathfrak{se}}(\Delta)})_{ij} = \sum_{k=1}^{6} \hat{\Gamma}^i_{jk} \Delta^k$. Note that we yield the definition in [1] by exchanging i and j. In the case of a constant function Δ we have $\mathbf{D}\Delta[\Omega] = 0$. For the dual expression it holds for all $\Omega, \Delta \in \mathfrak{se}_3$: $\mathrm{vec}_{\mathfrak{se}}(\omega_\Omega^* \Delta) = \tilde{\Gamma}^*_{\mathrm{vec}_{\mathfrak{se}}(\Delta)} \, \mathrm{vec}_{\mathfrak{se}}(\Omega)$ with $(\tilde{\Gamma}^*_{\mathrm{vec}_{\mathfrak{se}}(\Delta)})_{ik} = \sum_{j=1}^{6} \hat{\Gamma}^i_{jk} \Delta^j$. □

Proof (of Lem. 3). For any matrices $A, B \in \mathbb{R}^{4\times 4}$ and $\Omega \in \mathfrak{se}_3$ let $\otimes_{\mathfrak{se}}, \otimes_{\mathfrak{se}}^\top$ denote the operators which extract the vector form of Ω and are defined as $\mathrm{vec}_{\mathfrak{se}}(A\Omega B) =: (A \otimes_{\mathfrak{se}} B) \, \mathrm{vec}_{\mathfrak{se}}(\Omega)$ and $\mathrm{vec}_{\mathfrak{se}}(A\Omega^\top B) =: (A \otimes_{\mathfrak{se}}^\top B) \, \mathrm{vec}_{\mathfrak{se}}(\Omega)$, respectively, for which explicit expressions exist. By definition of the Hessian, Lemma 1 and with Eq. (A.3) we obtain

$$\text{vec}_{\mathfrak{se}}(E^{*-1}\text{Hess}_1 \mathcal{H}^-(E^*,0,t)[E^*\Omega]) = \text{vec}_{\mathfrak{se}}(E^{*-1}\nabla_{E^*\Omega}\text{grad}_1 \mathcal{H}^-(E^*,0,t))$$
$$= e^{-\alpha(t-t_0)}\sum_k \left(\tilde{\Gamma}_{\text{vec}_{\mathfrak{se}}(\Pr(A_k(E^*)))}\text{vec}_{\mathfrak{se}}(\Omega) + \text{vec}_{\mathfrak{se}}(\mathbf{D}_{E^*}\Pr(A_k(E^*))[\Omega])\right).$$

It can be shown that we can omit the projection Pr, i.e. $\text{vec}_{\mathfrak{se}}(\mathbf{D}\Pr(A_k(E))[\Omega]) = \text{vec}_{\mathfrak{se}}(\mathbf{D}(A_k(E))[\Omega])$ for all $\Omega \in \mathfrak{se}_3$. After computing the directional derivative of $A_k(E)$ in direction Ω we apply the $\text{vec}_{\mathfrak{se}}$ − operation and extract with the $\otimes_{\mathfrak{se}}-, \otimes_{\mathfrak{se}}^\top-$ operations the direction Ω. This gives

$$\begin{aligned}\text{vec}_{\mathfrak{se}}(\mathbf{D}A_k(E)[\Omega]) &= \Big(\kappa_k^{-2}\hat{I}^\top Q(y_k - h_k(E))e_3^\top \hat{I}E^{-1} \otimes_{\mathfrak{se}} E^{-1}g_k g_k^\top E^{-\top}\\
&\quad - 2\kappa_k^{-3}\hat{I}^\top e_3 e_3^\top \hat{I}E^{-1} \otimes_{\mathfrak{se}} E^{-1}g_k g_k^\top E^{-\top}\hat{I}^\top Q(y_k-h_k(E))g_k^\top E^{-\top}\\
&\quad + \kappa_k^{-2}\hat{I}^\top e_3 g_k^\top E^{-\top} \otimes_{\mathfrak{se}}^\top E^{-\top}\hat{I}^\top Q(y_k-h_k(E))g_k^\top E^{-\top}\\
&\quad - (\kappa_k^{-1}\hat{I}^\top - \kappa_k^{-2}\hat{I}^\top e_3 g_k^\top E^{-\top}\hat{I}^\top)Q(y_k-h_k(E))g_k^\top E^{-\top} \otimes_{\mathfrak{se}}^\top E^{-\top}\\
&\quad - (\kappa_k^{-3}\hat{I}^\top - \kappa_k^{-4}\hat{I}^\top e_3 g_k^\top E^{-\top}\hat{I}^\top)\hat{I}E^{-1}g_k e_3^\top Q\hat{I}E^{-1} \otimes_{\mathfrak{se}} E^{-1}g_k g_k^\top E^{-\top}\\
&\quad + (\kappa_k^{-2}\hat{I}^\top - \kappa_k^{-3}\hat{I}^\top e_3 g_k^\top E^{-\top}\hat{I}^\top)Q\hat{I}E^{-1} \otimes_{\mathfrak{se}} E^{-1}g_k g_k^\top E^{-\top}\Big)\text{vec}_{\mathfrak{se}}(\Omega)\\
&=: D_k(E)\text{vec}_{\mathfrak{se}}(\Omega).\end{aligned}\tag{A.4}$$

References

1. Absil, P.-A., Mahony, R., Sepulchre, R.: Optimization Algorithms on Matrix Manifolds. Princeton University Press (2008)
2. Athans, M., Falb, P.: Optimal Control. An Introduction to the Theory and Its Applications. McGraw-Hill (1966)
3. Bain, A., Crisan, D.: Fundamentals of Stochastic Filtering. Springer (2009)
4. Becker, F., Lenzen, F., Kappes, J.H., Schnörr, C.: Variational Recursive Joint Estimation of Dense Scene Structure and Camera Motion from Monocular High Speed Traffic Sequences. IJCV **105**, 269–297 (2013)
5. Brigo, D., Hanzon, B., Le Gland, F.: Approximate Nonlinear Filtering by Projection on Exponential Manifolds of Densities. Bernoulli **5**(3), 495–534 (1999)
6. Daum, F.: Nonlinear Filters: Beyond the Kalman Filter. IEEE A&E Systems Magazin **20**(8, Part 2), 57–69 (2005)
7. Daum, F., Huang, J.: Curse of dimensionality and particle filters. In: Aerospace Conference (2003)
8. Geiger, A., Ziegler, J., Stiller, C.: Stereoscan: Dense 3D Reconstruction in Real-Time. In: Intelligent Vehicles Symposium (IV). IEEE (2011)
9. Hairer, E., Lubich, C., Wanner, G.: Geometric Numerical Integration: Structure-Preserving Algorithms for Ordinary Differential Equations. Springer (2006)
10. Jurdjevic, V.: Geometric control theory. Cambridge University Press (1997)
11. Kalman, R.E.: A New Approach to Linear Filtering and Prediction Problems. Journal of Fluids Engineering **82**(1), 35–45 (1960)

12. Kitt, B., Geiger, A., Lategahn, H.: Visual odometry based on stereo image sequences with RANSAC-based outlier rejection scheme. In: IV (2010)
13. Krener, A.J.: The convergence of the minimum energy estimator. In: Kang, W., Borges, C., Xiao, M. (eds.) New Trends in Nonlinear Dynamics and Control and their Applications. LNCIS, vol. 295, pp. 187–208. Springer, Heidelberg (2003)
14. Kwon, J., Choi, M., Park, F.C., Chun, C.: Particle Filtering on the Euclidean Group: Framework and Applications. Robotica **25**(6), 725–737 (2007)
15. Markley, F.L.: Attitude Error Representations for Kalman Filtering. Journal of guidance, control, and dynamics **26**(2), 311–317 (2003)
16. Mortensen, R.E.: Maximum-Likelihood Recursive Nonlinear Filtering. J. Opt. Theory Appl. **2**(6), 386–394 (1968)
17. Saccon, A., Trumpf, J., Mahony, R., Aguiar, A.P.: Second-order-optimal filters on lie groups. In: CDC (2013)
18. Sun, D., Roth, S., Black, M.J.: A Quantitative Analysis of Current Practices in Optical Flow Estimation and the Principles Behind them. IJCV **106**(2), 115–137 (2014)
19. Yamaguchi, K., McAllester, D., Urtasun, R.: Efficient joint segmentation, occlusion labeling, stereo and flow estimation. In: Fleet, D., Pajdla, T., Schiele, B., Tuytelaars, T. (eds.) ECCV 2014, Part V. LNCS, vol. 8693, pp. 756–771. Springer, Heidelberg (2014)
20. Zamani, M., Trumpf, J., Mahoney, M.: A second order minimum-energy filter on the special orthogonal group. In: Proc. ACC (2012)
21. Žefran, M., Kumar, V., Croke, C.: Metrics and Connections for Rigid-Body Kinematics. The International Journal of Robotics Research **18**(2), 242–1 (1999)

Photography, Texture and Color Processing

Luminance-Hue Specification in the RGB Space

Fabien Pierre[1,2](✉), Jean-François Aujol[1], Aurélie Bugeau[2], and Vinh-Thong Ta[3]

[1] University of Bordeaux, IMB, CNRS, UMR 5251,
33400 Talence, France
fabien.pierre@math.u-bordeaux.fr
[2] University of Bordeaux, LaBRI, CNRS, UMR 5800, PICTURA,
33400 Talence, France
[3] Bordeaux INP, LaBRI, CNRS, UMR 5800, PICTURA, 33400 Talence, France

Abstract. This paper is concerned with a problem arising when editing color images, namely the Luminance-Hue Specification. This problem often occurs when converting an edited image in a given color-space to RGB. Indeed, the colors often get out of the standard range of the RGB space which is commonly used by most of display hardwares. Simple truncations lead to inconsistency in the hue and luminance of the edited image. We formalize and describe this problem from a geometrical point of view. A fast algorithm to solve the considered problem is given. We next focus on its application to image colorization in the RGB color space while most of the methods use other ones. Using directly the three RGB channels, our model avoids artifact effects which appear with other color spaces. Finally a variational model that regularizes color images while dealing with Luminance Hue Specification problem is proposed.

Keywords: Color · Luminance hue specification · Color-spaces · Colorization · Total variation · Optimization

1 Introduction

Color images can be characterized by their luminance, hue and saturation. The hue represents the human perception of the pure color while the saturation represents how the color is mixed to the white color. Many editing operations can be performed on the colors. For instance one may want to modify the hue while keeping the luminance, or conversely, to modify the luminance while keeping the hue constant. These operations are not as trivial as they seem. They can be performed in a hue-saturation-value color-space (*e.g.*, HSV) or luminance-chrominance space (*e.g.*, YUV) in which it is easy to modify or specify one channel while keeping the two others constant. Unfortunately the conversion

---

This study has been carried out with financial support from the French State, managed by the French National Research Agency (ANR) in the frame of the Investments for the future Programme IdEx Bordeaux (ANR-10-IDEX-03-02). J.-F. Aujol is a member of Institut Universitaire de France.

Table 1. The original color is first transformed into the YUV color-space. The value of Y is then specified to 40 and the YUV values are turned back to RGB with standard linear transformation. When this transformation is out of range, the final results is obtained with truncations which leads to some inconsistent results.

Initial color	Initial Y	Initial hue	Specified Y	Final after truncation	Final Y	Final hue	Method of [13]	Hue of [13]	Our result
	90	28	40		47	10		6	
	180	84	40		58	120		62	

back to RGB does not ensure the computed values of the three channels H, S, or Y are maintained. In most of imaging problems, the final RGB color has to be maintained between 0 and 255 in order to be displayed onto the screen of a device. If the conversion of the HSY image does not remain in the RGB standard range, the channels are truncated in order to stay in this range. This truncation is done without paying attention neither to the hue or the luminance. Obviously this problem arises with any color spaces and in particular to luminance-chrominance spaces (*i.e.*, Lab, YUV or $l\alpha\beta$).

Table 1 proposes an example to observe the problem in the YUV color-space. We illustrate the specification of the same luminance for two different colors. Both colors are first converted into the YUV color-space. In this space, the channel Y is changed to the specified value. Finally, we transform back the color into the RGB color-space. Theoretically, the luminance, chrominances and even the hue should not be changed after this conversion. Nevertheless, the range of the RGB color-space was not respected. The final result is obtained by truncation of coordinates, leading to a change of the luminance and the hue. The change of the hue during conversions between color-spaces highlights an important and common problem. In particular, in the real world, a change of lighting of an object should not change its hue. The method of [13] performs an orthogonal projection onto the constraint of constant luminance, that provides a color with the required luminance. Nevertheless, the hue is not preserved. The method proposed in this paper tackles with this issue which can be summarized as follows.

Problem. Given an RGB color, can we compute another color with the same hue, a specified luminance and which lives in the standard range of the RGB color-space ? The answer to this question will turn out to be yes as shown in Section 2. We will refer to this problem as the *Luminance-Hue Specification* in the rest of the paper.

This problem has already been addressed for image enhancement in [6,12,20,21]. The objective is to specify the histogram of the intensity channel of a given image in order to enhance it. After specifying the intensity histogram, the final color image is computed by taking care of keeping the original hue. The algorithm proposed in [12] will be detailed in section 2.3 and compared to ours. Contrary to this previous approach, we will give a geometric point of view of the Luminance-Hue Specification problem and propose a fast algorithm to solve it.

In this paper, we also focus the application of the Luminance-Hue Specification to image colorization. Image colorization consists in turning a gray-scale image into a color one by adding some color information to each pixel. The gray-scale image is considered to be the luminance channel. In order to preserve the initial image content, colorization methods impose that the luminance channel remains constant and equals to the original one.

To add color information, there exist two types of approaches. The first category includes the manual methods. The user puts some colors (referred as *scribbles*) directly onto the gray-scale image [9,11,17]. The second category, called exemplar-based methods, replaces the manual intervention by providing a color image (also called *source*) as prior information. This color image is used to colorize the gray-scale image (also called *target*). [4,10,18] propose exemplar-based methods with regularized results.

To colorize images, most approaches keep the luminance constant and compute the chrominance channels of a luminance-chrominance space (*e.g.*, Lab, YUV or l$\alpha\beta$). As explained previously, the final transformation from this luminance-chrominance space into the RGB does not guarantee the consistency of the solution. Changes of the luminance or the hue may occur. A solution to avoid any range problems in the final result is to work directly in the RGB color-space. To our best knowledge, only three colorization methods work in the RGB color-space: [17], [9] and [15]. For instance [9] limits the choice of color for a given luminance to all colors having this luminance. This method is therefore very difficult to adapt to the exemplar-based colorization where the color extracted from the source image may have a different luminance. [15] proposes a variational model working in the RGB color-space. This method does not ensure the preservation of the luminance, leading to blur effects.

In this paper we propose to solve the Luminance-Hue Specification problem within the seminal work of [18]. More specifically we propose an exemplar-based colorization method which works directly in the RGB color-space. The best RGB vector for each pixel of the target image is chosen within the source image. We further apply our new Luminance-Hue Specification algorithm to obtain a coherent color. Since the proposed approach works in the RGB color-space, we do not convert the images into a luminance-chrominance space and the result naturally stays in the standard range to be displayed.

To go further with image colorization, this paper also presents in detail a new model for color image regularization. It is based on the Rudin Osher and Fatemi functional [16] with a luminance constraint. The final algorithm is inspired by a primal-dual scheme [5]. The proposed regularization method is able to couple the R, G and B channels which encourages clean contours in the final result. The control of the hue during the optimization process enables realistic regularized images.

Contributions and Outline. First, the Luminance-Hue Specification problem is formalized and described from a geometrical point of view. Next, a fast algorithm inspired from the Smit's algorithm for ray-tracing [19] is proposed to solve this problem. Its application to image colorization is later presented with a non-regularized exemplar-based colorization method. Color image regularization with a luminance constraint is finally addressed by designing an optimization scheme. To that end, the Luminance-Hue Specification algorithm is integrated into an iterative primal-dual algorithm.

2 The Luminance-Hue Specification Problem

In this section, we present the Luminance-Hue Specification problem from a geometrical point of view and we propose an efficient algorithm to solve it.

2.1 The HSI Color-Space

The RGB color-space is not adapted to the human perception and description of colors. To tackle with this issue, particular color-spaces have been created. For instance, the HSV color-space defines colors with three particular channels: the hue, the saturation and the value. In the same trend, other spaces exist, *e.g.*, HSI, HSL or HSY. In the following, we focus on the HSI color-space (presented in [8]) for its simplicity in terms of geometric interpretation. This point of view has been used recently for image enhancement by Nikolova *et al.* [12].

The hue represents the human perception of the pure color. The hue is not defined if $R = G = B$, *i.e.*, the color *gray* has no hue. Otherwise, the hue H is defined as

$$H = \begin{cases} \theta & \text{if } B \leq G \\ 360 - \theta & \text{otherwise,} \end{cases} \quad (1)$$

where θ is an angle in degrees, such as:

$$\theta = \arccos\left\{ \frac{\frac{1}{2}((R-G) + (R-B))}{\sqrt{(R-G)^2 + (R-B)(G-B)}} \right\}. \quad (2)$$

The saturation S represents how the color is mixed with the white color and is defined as:

$$S = 1 - \frac{3}{R+G+B}(\min(R,G,B)). \quad (3)$$

It is equal to 0 if the color is gray, and has its maximum value if the color is away from any gray color.

The value of the intensity I can be compared to the luminosity of an electric light. If the light is turned off, the intensity is low. If it is turned on, the value of intensity is high. I is defined as:

$$I = \frac{R+G+B}{3}. \quad (4)$$

The parametrization of $\mathbb{R}^3$ by the coordinates HSI describes all this space.

Another way to model the luminosity of a scene is the luminance defined by:

$$Y = 0.299R + 0.587G + 0.114B. \quad (5)$$

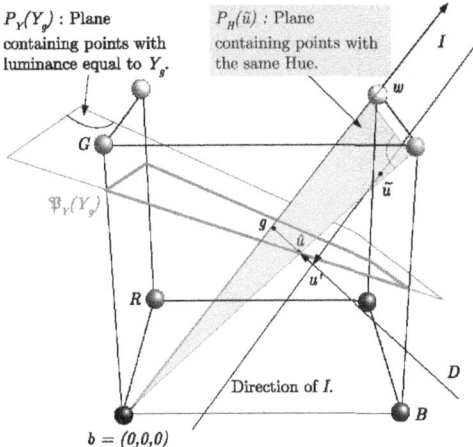

Fig. 1. The projection of $\tilde{u}$ on the convex set $\mathfrak{P}_Y(Y_g)$ is computed in two steps. First the oblique projection of $\tilde{u}$ on D in the direction of I (*i.e.*, the diagonal of the cube) is computed and denoted by u'. Secondly, the algorithm computes $\hat{u}$, the closest point of u' onto the convex set $D \cap [0, 255]^3$.

2.2 An Oblique Projection from a Geometrical Point of View

In this section an oblique projection $\tilde{P}_G$, maintaining the hue constant and specifying a luminance, is formalized. Fig. 1 shows elements described below.

Let us first introduce some notations and properties.

Proposition 1. *All the points in the RGB color-space which have the same hue as a given color $\tilde{u}$ live on the same open half-plane denoted by*

$$P_H(\tilde{u}) := \left\{ u' \in \mathbb{R}^3 \text{ such that } H(\tilde{u}) = H(u') \right\}. \tag{6}$$

Proof. See, *e.g.*, [7]. □

The half-plane $P_H(\tilde{u})$ (blue in Fig. 1) contains $\tilde{u}$ and is bounded by the line I passing through coordinates $(0, 0, 0)$ (black b) and $(255, 255, 255)$ (white w).

In order to specify a luminance, let us define the set of all colors for which the luminance is equal to a given scalar Y_g. According to equation (5), this set is a plane denoted by:

$$P_Y(Y_g) := \left\{ u \in \mathbb{R}^3 \text{ such that } Y(u) = Y_g \right\}. \tag{7}$$

Since the final result has to be displayed, it has to be in the standard range of the RGB space. Let us define the set of possible specified results:

$$\mathfrak{P}_Y(Y_g) := \left\{ u \in [0, 255]^3 \text{ such that } Y(u) = Y_g \right\}. \tag{8}$$

To solve the Luminance-Hue Specification problem, we define an oblique projection. Its result has the same hue as the original color (denoted by $\tilde{u}$) and its

Algorithm 1. Algorithm for oblique projection, inspired by ray-tracing.

1: (R, G, B) is the input. Y_g is the target luminance. $(\hat{R}, \hat{G}, \hat{B})$ is the output.
2: $Y \leftarrow 0.299R + 0.587G + 0.114B$
3: $(\hat{R}, \hat{G}, \hat{B}) \leftarrow (R, G, B) - (Y, Y, Y) + (Y_g, Y_g, Y_g)$
4: **if** $(\hat{R}, \hat{G}, \hat{B}) \in [0, 255]^3$ **then**
5: $\quad (\hat{R}, \hat{G}, \hat{B})$ is the result.
6: **else**
7: $\quad T \leftarrow \emptyset$
8: $\quad$ **for** $K \in \{\hat{R}, \hat{G}, \hat{B}\}$ **do**
9: $\quad\quad$ **if** $K > 255$ **then**
10: $\quad\quad\quad T \leftarrow T \cup \{\dfrac{255 - Y_g}{K - Y_g}\}$
11: $\quad\quad$ **end if**
12: $\quad\quad$ **if** $K < 0$ **then**
13: $\quad\quad\quad T \leftarrow T \cup \{\dfrac{-Y_g}{K - Y_g}\}$
14: $\quad\quad$ **end if**
15: $\quad$ **end for**
16: $\quad t_{min} \leftarrow \min T$
17: $\quad (\hat{R}, \hat{G}, \hat{B}) \leftarrow (1 - t_{min}).(Y_g, Y_g, Y_g) + t_{min}.(\hat{R}, \hat{G}, \hat{B})$
18: **end if**

luminance is equal to Y_g. Thus, the result belongs to the half-line $P_Y(Y_g) \cap P_H(\tilde{u})$ denoted by D. An oblique projection onto $P_Y(Y_g)$ in the direction of I can solve the problem. To compute it, we define γ such that $Y[\tilde{u} + \gamma(1, 1, 1)] = Y_g$, leading to $\gamma = Y_g - Y(\tilde{u})$, and the first result $u' = \tilde{u} + \gamma(1, 1, 1)$. After this first step there are two possibilities: u' is inside the cube $[0, 255]^3$ or it is not. If it is in the cube, no further processing is needed. Otherwise the Smit's algorithm for ray-tracing [19] is used to compute the contact point of the RGB cube $[0, 255]^3$ and D (See Algorithm 1 for details). This algorithm uses a parametrization of D for computing its intersection with the cube.

2.3 Equivalence with Nikolova et al [12]

In this section the oblique projection is compared to the additive algorithm of Nikolova et al [12] used for image enhancement. The problem is to compute a color with a given hue and intensity, and living in the standard range of the RGB color-space. The only difference with ours is that we specify luminance and not intensity. This algorithm is directly adaptable for our problem by replacing the constraint of intensity by the constraint of luminance.

Proposition 2. *Algorithm 1 and additive algorithm of [12] provide the same result.*

Proof. Let us denote the input (R, G, B). In the case when $(R, G, B) - (Y, Y, Y) + (Y_g, Y_g, Y_g)$ is in $[0, 255]^3$ it is straightforward, because the algebraic expression of the result is exactly the same for the two algorithms.

In the case when this point is out of the cube, the two algorithms process a point in one face of the cube. Remark that this point is only obtained by multiplying the vector (R, G, B) by a scalar and adding an equal value to each component. Next, the resulting point is onto the half-plane $\{u \in \mathbb{R}^3$ such that $H(u) = H(R, G, B)\}$. Moreover, the luminance of the final result is equal to Y_g in the two cases. Thus, the result lives on a half-line D that is the intersection of these two planes. D is not contained in one of the faces of the cube. Moreover, one of the coordinates of the result is equal to 0 or 255 for the two algorithms and the others are in the cube. Thus, the final result is at the intersection of a face of the cube $[0, 255]^3$ and the half-line D. This last intersection is unique, thus, the results are the same for the two algorithms. Let us remark that the two algorithms perform almost the same computations. In its formulation, Algorithm 1 is closer of the geometric interpretation than the additive algorithm of [12]. □

2.4 Application to Non-regularized Colorization

Welsh et al. [18] propose a patch-based method to colorize images. This method works in the $l\alpha\beta$ color-space. This method has been extended by Bugeau et al. [4] in the YUV color-space. In these two methods, the final result of the colorization process may not be in the standard range of RGB. By working directly in the RGB color-space, we avoid this problem. To colorize an image, we first compute a mapping between the target image and the gray-scale version of the source. We then extract the RGB vectors for each pixel and finally specify the luminance value with Algorithm 1.

Fig. 2 shows two colorization examples, each from a source image and a target one to be colorized. To obtain the results, we consider for each pixel of the target image, the patch around this pixel. We then search in the luminance channel of the source image the closest patch using the PatchMatch algorithm [1]. The final result is the RGB color of the source image at this closest patch central pixel. The comparison of patches is performed with the L^1 norm between standard-deviations (see, e.g., distance f_1 used in [4]). This result leads to blurring effects since it does not respect the Y channel. The specified image provides a more consistent result (column (d)). The specified luminance is directly the target image.

3 RGB Variational Model for Image Colorization

In order to improve colorization results, we now propose a variational model and an optimization scheme, holding the luminance specification constraint.

3.1 A Variational Approach

Assume that c is an image, totally or partially colored. We want to regularize or to inpaint the color image by minimization of the Total Variation (TV). Moreover, we want to constrain the final solution to have a specified luminance.

Fig. 2. (a) Source images. (b) Target images. (c) Exemplar-based colorization in the RGB space. (d) represents Image (c) with specified Y (Algorithm 1). Exemplar-based colorization by simple mapping with and without luminance specification. The Y grayscale image contains essential information.

A standard approach for this problem is the use of a variational model. We introduce a functional where $u = (R, G, B)$ stands for a RGB image:

$$\inf_u TV_{RGB}(u) + \lambda/2 \|M(u-c)\|_2^2 + \chi_{u \in [0,255]^3} + \chi_{Y(u)=Y_g}, \quad (9)$$

where

$$TV_{RGB}(u) = \int_\Omega \sqrt{\gamma \partial_x Y_g(\mathbf{x})^2 + \gamma \partial_y Y_g(\mathbf{x})^2 + \sum_{K=R,G,B} \partial_x K(\mathbf{x})^2 + \partial_y K(\mathbf{x})^2} \, d\mathbf{x}. \quad (10)$$

The term $\|M(u-c)\|_2^2$ is the data fidelity term. M is a mask whose value is equal to 0 if no color is defined at the current pixel, 1 otherwise. With this formulation, the data term may be not complete. TV_{RGB} is the regularization term. The parameter γ enforces the coupling of the Y channel with the RGB ones in order to preserve contours (see, e.g., [14] for the influence of γ). Y_g is the luminance to be specified. The parameter λ controls the trade-off between the regularization and the data fidelity term. The χ functions model the constraints. Its values are 0 if the constraint is respected and $+\infty$ otherwise. The constraint $Y(u) = Y_g$ means that the luminance of the final result is equal to the specification Y_g. This constraint preserves the initial image content. $\chi_{u \in [0,255]^3}$ ensures that the final result is in the standard range of RGB space.

3.2 Minimization of the RGB Model

To minimize problems related to the Total Variation, a primal-dual formulation is proposed and solved by Chambolle and Pock [5]. The FISTA algorithm of Beck

Fig. 3. (a) Original color image. (b) Luminance of (a) computed by (5). (c) Method of [13], equivalent to Algorithm 2. (d) Result obtained with Algorithm 3. The minimization of the model (9) (Algorithm 2) leads to some unrealistic colors different from the original ones. The control of the hue during the iterative process performs relevant results (Algorithm 3).

et al. [2] could also minimize this model. Our experiment has shown a faster convergence of the primal-dual algorithm for this problem. Applied to our model, the primal-dual algorithm reads as Algorithm 2. P_B represents the projection onto L^2 unit ball due to the dual formulation of TV [5]. P_G is the orthogonal projection onto $\mathfrak{P}_Y(Y_g)$ described in [13]. The discrete gradient ∇ and divergence div operators are defined as in [3]. Time-steps are fixed to $\sigma = 10^{-3}$ and $\tau = 20$.

Since the functional is convex, our algorithm computes a solution of the problem (9). At this point, the algorithm does not produce satisfying results. This problem is highlighted in Fig. 3 where we propose to regularize the data image but holding its luminance channel constant. We choose $\gamma = 25$, $\lambda = 1$ and $M = Id$, the identity operator. Algorithm 2 is applied with the orthogonal

---

Algorithm 2. Primal-dual algorithm minimizing the RGB model (9).

1: $p_0 \leftarrow 0$
2: **for** $n \geq 0$ **do**
3: $\quad p_{n+1} \leftarrow P_B(p_n + \sigma \nabla \bar{u}_n)$
4: $\quad u_{n+1} \leftarrow P_G \left(M \dfrac{u_n + \tau(\operatorname{div}(p_{n+1}) + \lambda c)}{1 + \tau \lambda} + (1 - M)(u_n + \tau \operatorname{div}(p_{n+1})) \right)$
5: $\quad \bar{u}_{n+1} \leftarrow 2u_{n+1} - u_n$
6: **end for**

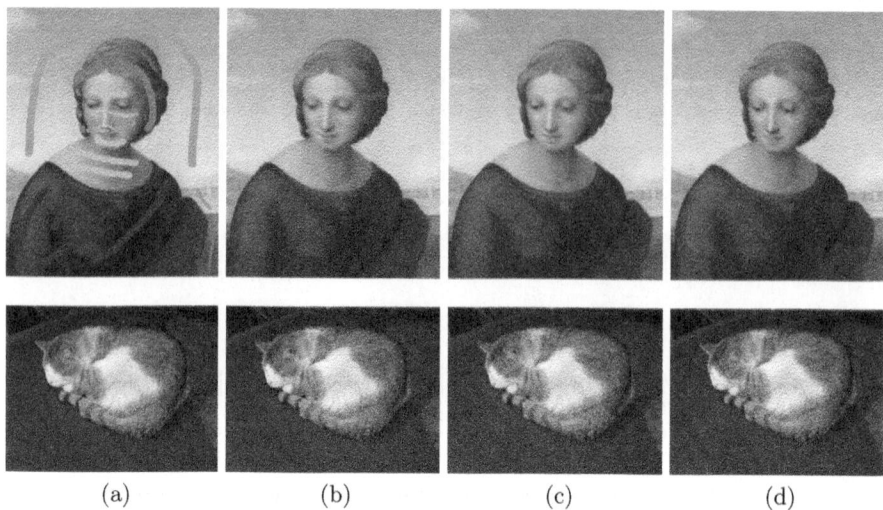

Fig. 4. (a) Scribbles. (b) TV on chrominances. (c) Result obtained with Algorithm 2. (d) Result obtained with Algorithm 3. Manual colorization with diffusion with TV. Neither the TV on the chrominance channels, nor the classical TV-L2 model (9) are able to perform realistic results. With a control of the hue during the iterative process, Algorithm 3 provides a relevant solution. Remark that scribbles on the cat are not easy to see because they are one pixel sized and sampled in a regular grid on 1% of the image.

projection (Fig. 3). The contours are well respected and the images are not drab, but they are now too shiny, containing irrelevant colors (green or violet) due to the orthogonal projection P_G that does not preserve the hue. To tackle this issue, we replace the projection P_G in Algorithm 2 by $\tilde{P}_G$, the Luminance-Hue Specification Algorithm 1, leading to Algorithm 3. With this new algorithm, the iterative process produces realistic images with natural colors. For example, the textures do not become green (see Fig. 3). This figure is an artificial experiment to illustrate the interest of Algorithm 3 compared to [13]. We also propose, in Fig. 4 to inpaint the colors of an image. Some colors are given by the user, then the algorithm diffuses them to recover a complete image. In this case the value of the mask M is equal to 1 where the user puts a color and 0 otherwise. From left

---

Algorithm 3. Primal-dual algorithm inspired from Algorithm 2.

1: $p_0 \leftarrow 0$
2: **for** $n \geq 0$ **do**
3: $\quad p_{n+1} \leftarrow P_B\left(p_n + \sigma \nabla \overline{u}_n\right)$
4: $\quad u_{n+1} \leftarrow \tilde{P}_G\left(M\dfrac{u_n + \tau\left(\operatorname{div}(p_{n+1}) + \lambda c\right)}{1+\tau\lambda} + (1-M)\left(u_n + \tau \operatorname{div}(p_{n+1})\right)\right)$
5: $\quad \overline{u}_{n+1} \leftarrow 2u_{n+1} - u_n$
6: **end for**

Table 2. Comparison of PSNR for techniques presented in Fig. 4 for the image of the cat. This quantitative comparison highlights the quality of the results provided by Algorithm 3

Method	TV on chrominances	Result of Algorithm 2	Result of Algorithm 3
PSNR	28.9	31.8	37.4

to right, one can see the original image with scribbles, the result obtained with an inpainting of chrominance channels, the minimization of model (9) (Algorithm 2) and the result of Algorithm 3. In the first case, the chrominance channels are diffused with the Total Variation without taking care of the initial luminance contours. Moreover the result is more drab for the cat. We choose $\gamma = 35$ and $\lambda = 10^{-5}$. In the case of the minimization of (9), we can see that the orthogonal projection does not respect the original palette to colorize the image. For example, the edge of the clothe of the *Madonna* is green, although there is no green color among scribbles at this location. Moreover, her face is violet, which does not correspond to any scribble, and it appears unnatural. By replacing the orthogonal projection by the Luminance-Hue Specification Algorithm 1, we solve the problem. The final result has respected contours and realistic colors. In the case of the cat, the original image is available. The scribbles are sub-sampled from it in a sparse regular grid. We compare the PSNR of the results obtained with the three different techniques. The values are summarized in Table 2. This measure confirms numerically the superiority of Algorithm 3.

Conclusion

In this paper, we propose an oblique projection, able to solve the Luminance-Hue Specification problem. We also show that a classical variational model fails for the regularization of images with the luminance specification. We finally see that the control of the hue during the iterative process for the minimization of the first variational model performs suitable results. This algorithm could be extended to correction of chromatic artefacts in the problem of dehazing or to the reduction of JPEG color artefacts.

References

1. Barnes, C., Shechtman, E., Finkelstein, A., Goldman, D.: Patchmatch: a randomized correspondence algorithm for structural image editing. ACM Transactions on Graphics **28**(3), 24 (2009)
2. Beck, A., Teboulle, M.: A fast iterative shrinkage-thresholding algorithm for linear inverse problems. SIAM Journal on Mathematical Analysis **2**(1), 183–202 (2009)
3. Bresson, X., Chan, T.F.: Fast dual minimization of the vectorial total variation norm and applications to color image processing. Inverse Problems and Imaging **2**(4), 455–484 (2008)
4. Bugeau, A., Ta, V.T., Papadakis, N.: Variational exemplar-based image colorization. IEEE Transactions on Image Processing **23**(1), 298–307 (2014)

5. Chambolle, A., Pock, T.: A first-order primal-dual algorithm for convex problems with applications to imaging. Journal of Mathematical Imaging and Vision **40**(1), 120–145 (2011)
6. Chien, C.L., Tseng, D.C.: Color image enhancement with exact hsi color model. international journal of innovative computing, information and control **7**(12), 6691–6710 (2011)
7. Fitschen, J.H., Nikolova, M., Pierre, F., Steidl, G.: A variational model for color assignment. In: SSVM, pp. 1–12 (to appear 2015)
8. Gonzales, R.C., Woods, R.E.: Digital image processing. Addison-Wesley Publishing Company (1993)
9. Horiuchi, T.: Colorization algorithm using probabilistic relaxation. Image and Vision Computing **22**(3), 197–202 (2004)
10. Irony, R., Cohen-Or, D., Lischinski, D.: Colorization by example. In: Eurographics Conference on Rendering Techniques, pp. 201–210. Eurographics Association (2005)
11. Levin, A., Lischinski, D., Weiss, Y.: Colorization using optimization. ACM Transactions on Graphics **23**(3), 689–694 (2004)
12. Nikolova, M., Steidl, G.: Fast hue and range preserving histogram specification: Theory and new algorithms for color image enhancement. IEEE Transactions on Image Processing **23**(9), 4087–4100 (2014)
13. Pierre, F., Aujol, J.F., Bugeau, A., Papadakis, N., Ta, V.T.: Exemplar-based colorization in RGB color space. IEEE International Conference on Image Processing (2014)
14. Pierre, F., Aujol, J.F., Bugeau, A., Papadakis, N., Ta, V.T.: Luminance-chrominance model for image colorization. SIAM Journal on Imaging Sciences (to appear). https://hal.archives-ouvertes.fr/hal-01051308
15. Quang, M.H., Kang, S.H., Le, T.M.: Image and video colorization using vector-valued reproducing kernel hilbert spaces. Journal of Mathematical Imaging and Vision **37**(1), 49–65 (2010)
16. Rudin, L.I., Osher, S., Fatemi, E.: Nonlinear total variation based noise removal algorithms. Physica D: Nonlinear Phenomena **60**(1), 259–268 (1992)
17. Takahama, T., Horiuchi, T., Kotera, H.: Improvement on colorization accuracy by partitioning algorithm in cielab color space. In: Aizawa, K., Nakamura, Y., Satoh, S. (eds.) PCM 2004. LNCS, vol. 3332, pp. 794–801. Springer, Heidelberg (2004)
18. Welsh, T., Ashikhmin, M., Mueller, K.: Transferring color to greyscale images. ACM Transactions on Graphics **21**(3), 277–280 (2002)
19. Williams, A., Barrus, S., Morley, R.K., Shirley, P.: An efficient and robust ray-box intersection algorithm. In: ACM SIGGRAPH 2005 Courses, p. 9 (2005)
20. Yoshinari, K., Hoshi, Y., Taguchi, A.: Color image enhancement in hsi color space without gamut problem. In: 6th International Symposium on Communications, Control and Signal Processing (ISCCSP), pp. 578–581. IEEE (2014)
21. Yoshinari, K., Murahira, K., Hoshi, Y., Taguchi, A.: Color image enhancement in improved hsi color space. In: International Symposium on Intelligent Signal Processing and Communications Systems (ISPACS), 2013, pp. 429–434. IEEE (2013)

Variational Exposure Fusion with Optimal Local Contrast

David Hafner[✉] and Joachim Weickert

Mathematical Image Analysis Group, Faculty of Mathematics and Computer Science,
Campus E1.7, Saarland University, 66041 Saarbrücken, Germany
{hafner,weickert}@mia.uni-saarland.de

Abstract. In this paper, we present a variational method for exposure fusion. In particular, we combine differently exposed images to a single composite that offers optimal exposedness, saturation, and local contrast. To this end, we formulate the output image as a convex combination of the input, and design an energy functional that implements important perceptually inspired concepts from contrast enhancement such as a local and nonlinear response. Several experiments demonstrate the quality of our technique and show improvements w.r.t. state-of-the-art methods.

Keywords: Exposure fusion · Variational method · Contrast enhancement

1 Introduction

Classical high dynamic range (HDR) methods combine several low dynamic range (LDR) images to one HDR image with the help of the exposure times and the camera response function [15,21]. However, displaying these HDR results on standard monitors or printing them requires to compress the high dynamic range again. This process is called *tone mapping* [28]. If the main focus lies on such a displayable, well-exposed LDR image and the HDR composite is just seen as a necessary byproduct, the so-called *exposure fusion* technique is an interesting alternative [23]. In contrast to the described two-step procedure, the task here is to directly fuse the differently exposed images to an overall well-exposed composite. Such an exposure fusion approach has several advantages: First, there is no need to know the exposure times or the camera response function. Second, this one-step approach allows a direct tuning of the final results without the need of an intermediate HDR reconstruction. Most existing exposure fusion methods pursue the following processing pipeline: Based on some defined well-exposedness measures, weighting maps are determined for each of the input images. With these weighting maps all images are fused to the final composite.

Our Contributions. In contrast to those methods, our main idea is not to select the best input image parts in a first step and to combine them to one image afterwards. Instead, we directly formulate an energy whose minimiser gives the optimal result. More specifically, we do not compute the weighting maps just by considering features of the input images. Rather, we determine them in a result-driven fashion, i.e. in such a way that the fused image shows the best quality in terms of our model assumptions. We base our model on fundamental findings in histogram modification and contrast enhancement with differential equations [7,24,29], and formulate it in a transparent variational framework. This results in a mathematically well-founded method that yields better quality than state-of-the-art approaches, e.g. in terms of perceived local contrast.

Outline. We start with a discussion of related work in Section 2. After that, we present our variational approach for exposure fusion in Section 3. Its minimisation (Section 4) gives the desired fused image. The experiments in Section 5 demonstrate the quality of our method. We conclude with a summary and outlook in Section 6.

2 Related Work

Most previous exposure fusion approaches have the following workflow: In a first step they determine, based on specific quality measures, for each pixel or region of the input images how much it should contribute to the final composite. Such quality measures are for instance the magnitude of the Laplacian [10,23], the textureness [27], the entropy [17,18], or the colour saturation [23,32,33]. In a second step, these pixels or regions are fused to the resulting overall well-exposed image. Here, the fusion strategies vary from region-based blending [17,35] and pixelwise weighted averaging [18,27,31–33] to gradient domain fusion [13,34] and pyramid-based techniques [10,12,23].

In contrast to all these approaches, we do not specify the quality of the input images first and then fuse them later on. Instead, we directly design the quality of the fusion result. In this regard, Raman and Chaudhuri [26] formulate an energy functional whose minimiser gives the fused composite. However, optimising the energy immediately for the image itself has several drawbacks: First, it restricts the possible model assumptions. Second and even more severely, it requires to impose a smoothness constraint on the resulting image. This is not intuitive and may lead to over-smoothed results. A more suitable idea of Kotwal and Chaudhuri [19] is to express the composite image as a weighted average of the input images and to optimise for these weights. This still allows to directly model assumptions on the fusion result, but additionally opens the possibility to impose a smoothness constraint on the weight maps and not on the image itself.

We follow this idea and incorporate perceptually inspired model assumptions that allow superior results. To formulate these assumptions by a suitable energy functional, we make use of important findings in variational histogram modification and contrast enhancement. Based on the seminal work of Sapiro and Caselles [29], Bertalmío et al. [7] introduce a variational approach to locally increase the contrast of an image. In this context, Palma-Amestoy et al. [24] investigate several perceptually inspired energy terms. In his recent study, Bertalmío [6] shows connections to visual neuroscience.

These contrast enhancement approaches have found first applications in an exposure fusion related context: In their two-stage tone mapping operator, Ferradans et al. [16] apply a variational contrast enhancement in the second stage. Moreover, Bertalmío et al. [8] propose an energy-based method to fuse two differently exposed images. The fused result includes the details of the short exposure, and the colours are intended to resemble them of the long exposure. Piella [25] incorporates a gradient domain term in the energy of [7]. This forces the similarity to a precomputed gradient field that combines the gradients from multiple images. The success of these approaches motivates us to also base our model on those perceptually inspired contrast enhancement concepts. Along this line, we present in this paper a variational exposure fusion technique that handles multiple input images and is tailored to static scenes.

3 Energy Formulation

Our goal is to fuse n differently exposed images $f_1, \ldots, f_n$ to a single composite that is well-exposed everywhere and shows a visually pleasant local contrast. Basically, we propose to compute the fused image u as a pixelwise weighted average:

$$u(\boldsymbol{x}) = \sum_{i=1}^{n} w_i(\boldsymbol{x}) \cdot f_i(\boldsymbol{x}), \qquad (1)$$

where $\boldsymbol{x} = (x_1, x_2)^\top$ denotes the position on the rectangular image domain $\Omega \in \mathbb{R}^2$ and w_i the weight of the input image i. We constrain these weights to be non-negative and to sum up to 1, i.e. $w_i(\boldsymbol{x}) \geq 0$ and $\sum_{i=1}^{n} w_i(\boldsymbol{x}) = 1$. This provides a close attachment to the input data that prevents undesirable effects such as colour shifts or halos.

Most previous research concentrates on defining the image weights $w_1, \ldots, w_n$ based on the quality of the *input*. In contrast, we compute optimal weight maps for fusing an *output* image that features important perceptual properties such as a high local contrast. More specifically, they are optimal in the sense that the resulting composite u is optimal for the following energy functional:

$$\begin{aligned} E(w_1, \ldots, w_n) = &\; \frac{1}{2} \int_\Omega \left((u(\boldsymbol{x}) - \mu)^2 + (u(\boldsymbol{x}) - \bar{f}(\boldsymbol{x}))^2 \right) d\boldsymbol{x} \\ &\; - \frac{\gamma}{2} \iint_{\Omega\Omega} g_\sigma(\boldsymbol{x}, \boldsymbol{y}) \cdot \Psi_\lambda(u(\boldsymbol{x}) - u(\boldsymbol{y})) \, d\boldsymbol{x} \, d\boldsymbol{y} \\ &\; + \frac{\alpha}{2} \int_\Omega \sum_{i=1}^{n} |\nabla w_i(\boldsymbol{x})|^2 \, d\boldsymbol{x} \end{aligned} \qquad (2)$$

subject to

$$w_i(\boldsymbol{x}) \geq 0 \quad \text{and} \quad \sum_{i=1}^{n} w_i(\boldsymbol{x}) = 1, \qquad (3)$$

where the dependency of $w_1, \ldots, w_n$ from u is given by (1).

Let us examine the components of the presented energy step by step:

Dispersion Term. Following Bertalmío et al. [7], we model a so-called dispersion term in the first line of (2): The first part of this dispersion term favours solutions with an average grey value close to μ, which is in general set to $1/2$ for grey values in the range of 0 and 1. This implements the grey world principle [11,24] and provides well-exposed images. The second part forces a similarity of u to the attachment image $\bar{f}$, which we determine by an average over all input images. As discussed in [24], this provides an attachment to the original data and accounts for the colour constancy assumption [20].

Contrast Term. The second term, the contrast term, counteracts this dispersion term, since it penalises uniform images much more than images with a high local contrast. Intuitively speaking, the energy favours solutions that differ a lot from pixel to pixel. Please note the minus sign in front of the contrast term. Here, the locality is introduced by the Gaussian weighting $g_\sigma(\boldsymbol{x}, \boldsymbol{y}) := \frac{1}{2\pi\sigma^2} \exp\left(\frac{-|\boldsymbol{x}-\boldsymbol{y}|^2}{2\sigma^2}\right)$. Furthermore, $\Psi_\lambda(s) := \sqrt{s^2 + \lambda^2}$ is a function with a sigmoid-shaped derivative that shows connections to the nonlinear response of the visual system [22,24]. The parameter λ allows to tune this nonlinear behaviour, and $\gamma \geq 0$ weights the influence of the contrast term.

Regularisation Term. The third term in our energy functional is a regularisation term that rewards smooth weight maps. It renders the assumption that neighbouring pixels in the fused composite should have similar weights. Here $\boldsymbol{\nabla} := (\partial_{x_1}, \partial_{x_2})^\top$ denotes the spatial gradient operator, and $\alpha \geq 0$ steers the amount of smoothness.

Simplex Constraint. Last but not least, the simplex constraint (3) restricts the fusion result to (pixelwise) convex combinations of the input images. Hence, it provides an additional natural attachment to the input data.

Adaptation to Colour Images. In the case of colour images, we compute joint weight maps for all channels. To this end, we transform the input images from the RGB to the YCbCr colour space and define u in (2) as the Y channel. Moreover, saturated colours make images to look vivid and expressive. Hence, we extend our energy (2) with the following *saturation term*:

$$-\frac{\beta}{2} \int_\Omega \left(\left(u_{Cb}(\boldsymbol{x}) - 1/2\right)^2 + \left(u_{Cr}(\boldsymbol{x}) - 1/2\right)^2 \right) \mathrm{d}\boldsymbol{x}, \qquad (4)$$

where u_{Cb} and u_{Cr} denote the Cb and Cr channels of u, respectively. This term favours values different from grey, and thus fused images with vivid colours. Here, the positive parameter β allows to control the amount of colour saturation. Once again, the minus sign should be noted.

Algorithm 1. Projection onto simplex [30]

Input: weights $w_1, \ldots, w_n$
Output: projected weights $\tilde{w}_1, \ldots, \tilde{w}_n$

1   $s = \text{sort}(w_1, \ldots, w_n)$ such that $s_1 \geq \ldots \geq s_n$
2   $m = \max \left\{ j \in \{1, \ldots, n\} \ \middle| \ s_j - \frac{1}{j} \left(\sum_{i=1}^{j} s_i - 1 \right) > 0 \right\}$
3   $\theta = \frac{1}{m} \left(\sum_{i=1}^{m} s_i - 1 \right)$
4   $\tilde{w}_i = \max \{w_i - \theta, 0\}$

4 Minimisation

To minimise energy (2) with the simplex constraint (3), we apply a projected gradient method; see e.g. Bertsekas [9]. Basically, each iteration consists of (i) a gradient descent step, followed by (ii) a projection onto the simplex.

Gradient Descent. With iteration index k and time step size τ, the gradient descent of the energy functional (2) with the saturation term (4) reads

$$
\begin{aligned}
w_i^{k+1}(\boldsymbol{x}) = w_i^k(\boldsymbol{x}) - \tau \cdot \Big(& f_{Y_i}(\boldsymbol{x}) \left(2u_Y^k(\boldsymbol{x}) - \mu - \bar{f}_Y(\boldsymbol{x}) \right) \\
& - \gamma \int_\Omega g_\sigma(\boldsymbol{x}, \boldsymbol{y}) \cdot \Psi'_\lambda(u_Y^k(\boldsymbol{x}) - u_Y^k(\boldsymbol{y})) \, \mathrm{d}\boldsymbol{y} \\
& - \beta \left(f_{Cb_i}(\boldsymbol{x}) \left(u_{Cb}^k - 1/2 \right) + f_{Cr_i}(\boldsymbol{x}) \left(u_{Cr}^k - 1/2 \right) \right) \\
& - \alpha \, \Delta w_i^k(\boldsymbol{x}) \Big),
\end{aligned}
\quad (5)
$$

for $i = 1, \ldots, n$ and $(u_Y^k, u_{Cb}^k, u_{Cr}^k)^\top = \sum_{i=1}^n w_i^k(\boldsymbol{x}) \cdot (f_{Y_i}, f_{Cb_i}, f_{Cr_i})^\top$. We discretise this equation with finite differences on a rectangular grid, and approximate the integral with the rectangle method.

Projection onto Simplex. After each gradient descent step, we account for the constraint (3) by projecting the computed weights onto the n-dimensional simplex; see Algorithm 1.

We assume the complete algorithm to be converged if the root mean square difference of two fusion results between 100 iterations is less than 10^{-4}.

5 Evaluation

Our evaluation consists of three main parts: First, we illustrate the general difference between a global and a local contrast term. Second, we show the influence of our main model parameters. Last but not least, we demonstrate the quality of our technique with several test image sets and compare to state-of-the-art approaches.

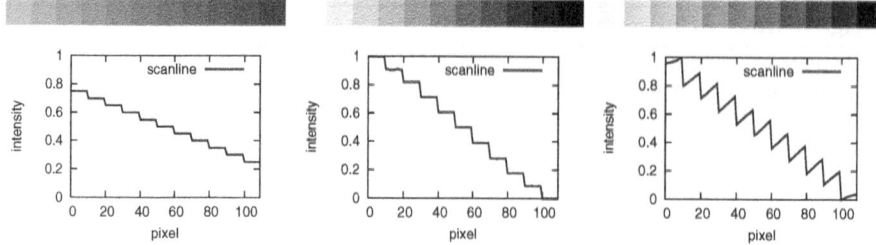

Fig. 1. Global vs. local contrast term for histogram equalisation. *From left to right*: Input, with global contrast term, with local contrast term. *Top*: Intensity images. *Bottom*: Corresponding scanlines.

5.1 Local Contrast Term

Inspired by Bertalmío et al. [7], let us consider a variational histogram equalisation in Figure 1. In our framework, this can be achieved by setting $\alpha = 0$ and replacing the simplex constraint (3) by $0 \leq w(\boldsymbol{x})f(\boldsymbol{x}) \leq 1$. Applying a global contrast term, i.e. degrading $g_\sigma(\boldsymbol{x},\boldsymbol{y})$ to the constant $1/|\Omega|$, yields a standard histogram equalisation (*middle*). On the other hand, a local contrast term allows to visually increase the contrast in the sense of a *Cornsweet illusion* [14] (*right*). This illustrates the general advantages of a local term compared to a global one.

Moreover, we want to point out the following: Our fusion approach is capable of computing weights that produce fusion results with the just discussed Cornsweet illusions. This is very hard to accomplish with standard fusion methods since they do not take into account the quality of the final output image when computing the weights in advance.

5.2 Parameters

With this section we illustrate the influence of our model parameters. To this end, we depict several fused images for varying parameter settings in Figure 2.

In the first column, we test the influence of the proposed saturation term. As expected, larger values of β yield more saturated colours. There is a trade-off between a vivid appearance and an unnaturally high amount of colour saturation. In all our experiments, setting β to 1 gives good results. In the second column, different values of μ are applied. Since the dispersion term favours solutions that are close to μ, it is obvious that larger values lead to brighter results. We propose to determine μ automatically as the average over all input images, i.e. the mean of the attachment image $\bar{f}$. The third column depicts the composite images for different contrast parameters γ. Choosing it too small yields an image with low contrast, and choosing it too large gives unrealistic appearing images. In general, setting it to $1/4$ provides good results. Similar observations apply to the scale parameter σ of the Gaussian in the local contrast term. We observe a larger local contrast with decreasing σ. Also here a trade-off exists: A too large local

Fig. 2. Influence of model parameters. *From left to right*: Varying β (0 and 2). Larger values of β lead to more saturated colours in the fused image. Varying μ (0.1 and 0.9). The larger μ, the brighter the fused image. Varying γ (0 and 0.5). The larger γ, the higher the contrast. Varying σ (1% and 100% of image diagonal). The smaller σ, the more local contrast. (Input image source: J. Joffre [3])

Table 1. Default parameter setting for all image sets

α	β	γ	λ	μ	σ
1	1	1/4	0.1	mean of $\bar{f}$	10% of image diagonal

contrast might be perceived as unnatural. As a rule of thumb, we propose to set σ to 10% of the image diagonal.

In all our experiments below, we apply the discussed procedure to determine μ and σ automatically. All other parameters are fixed (cf. Table 1). This allows an easy and straightforward use of our method, even for non-experts. Furthermore, we exploit the complete dynamic range by an affine rescaling of our fused result using the minimal and maximal value of the input stack.

5.3 Comparison

Let us now compare our results with competing state-of-the-art exposure fusion methods. In particular, we compare to the method of Kotwal and Chaudhuri [19] (result provided by the authors) and to the popular method of Mertens et al. [23] (code available, executed with recommended parameter setting).

Figure 3 depicts our computed weight maps for an example input image set with five images. Figure 4 (*right*) shows our corresponding fused composite. Especially in the zooms the higher local contrast of our approach compared to both other methods (*left* and *middle*) is obvious. Moreover, we also observe a colour cast with the method of Kotwal and Chaudhuri. They estimate three individual weights maps for each colour channel. In contrast, our coupled approach that computes joint maps for all channels prevents this colour cast. Additionally, our proposed saturation term provides a vivid colour impression.

Fig. 3. Input images (*first row*) and computed weight maps (*second row*) for an example image set [2]. The brighter the weight map, the larger the weight.

Fig. 4. *From left to right*: Fused images of Kotwal and Chaudhuri [19], Mertens et al. [23], and our result. *Top*: Full images. *Bottom*: Zooms. Particularly at the lamps, the better local contrast provided by our method is obvious.

To rate the quality of tone mapping operators, Aydin et al. [5] introduced a *Dynamic Range Independent Metric* (DRIM). Based on a model of the human visual system, it measures the distortions between a reference and a test image with different dynamic ranges. We apply this metric here to judge different exposure fusion results. To this end, we use publicly available HDR images [1] as reference, and compute for each HDR image five LDR images separated by one exposure value. These images serve as input for the exposure fusion techniques. Finally, we apply DRIM to compare the reference HDR image with the fused LDR results. DRIM uses the following colour code: Green indicates a loss of visible contrast, blue an amplification of invisible contrast, and red a reversal of visible contrast. In addition, the colour saturation is proportional to the amount of distortion. Figure 5 depicts the fused results and the corresponding DRIM distortion maps for two image sets using the method of Mertens et al. (*left*) and our approach (*right*). It is clearly visible that our results show much less distortions: Especially in the background of the image in the first row, our result contains details that are not visible in the result of Mertens et al. Also our fused composite of the second image set shows less distortions than the one of Mertens et al. Some of the errors in their result are caused by block-like artefacts

Fig. 5. Comparison to exposure fusion of Mertens et al. [23]. *From left to right*: Fused images and DRIM distortion maps of Mertens et al. Fused images and DRIM distortion maps of our method. The more colours, the more distortions.

Fig. 6. Fusion of flash and no-flash photographs. *From left to right*: Ambient image, flash image, and our fused result.

introduced by the pyramid-based fusion technique. Since we do not apply such a pyramid fusion, our result does not suffer from these distortions.

This evaluation shows that our model produces images with little visible distortions, and thus is well-suited for exposure fusion. To further demonstrate the general applicability of our technique, Figure 7 depicts our fused images for several test data sets. They feature a high amount of visible local contrast, both in dark and bright image regions.

Besides being independent of the knowledge of the exposure times and the camera response function, our method additionally allows to fuse flash and no-flash photographs. This is illustrated in Figure 6.

6 Conclusions and Future Work

We have presented a variational approach for the task of exposure fusion. Our transparent model assumptions implement important perceptually inspired con-

Fig. 7. The fusion results for several test image sets demonstrate the high local contrast provided by our method, both in dark and bright image regions. In each case, we show only three representative images of the input set. (Input image sources in reading order: [3], [4], J. Joffre [3], J. Joffre [3])

cepts from histogram modification and contrast enhancement. Moreover, all model parameters have an intuitive meaning and can be fixed or determined automatically in a straightforward way. The results of our fusion technique are of high quality and show desirable properties, such as a high local contrast. They compare favourably to state-of-the-art approaches. Moreover, in contrast to the two-stage procedure of HDR reconstruction and tone mapping, we do not require exposure times or the camera-specific response function. As an additional benefit of that, our approach also shows good results for the fusion of flash and no-flash photographs.

The main concepts of our model are not limited to the fusion of differently exposed images. It might also be applied for all kind of image fusion where features such as a high local contrast are of great importance. Hence, we plan to test and adapt the presented method for other fusion tasks. Moreover, a modification of our approach to unaligned input images is part of future work.

Acknowledgments. Our research has been partially funded by the Deutsche Forschungsgemeinschaft (DFG) through a Gottfried Wilhelm Leibniz Prize for Joachim Weickert. This is gratefully acknowledged.

References

1. www.resources.mpi-inf.mpg.de/hdr/gallery.html
2. www.cs.columbia.edu/CAVE/software/rascal/rrslrr.php
3. www.hdrsoft.com/examples2.html
4. www.pauldebevec.com/Research/HDR/
5. Aydin, T.O., Mantiuk, R., Myszkowski, K., Seidel, H.P.: Dynamic range independent image quality assessment. ACM Transactions on Graphics **27**(3), Article No. 69, August 2008
6. Bertalmío, M.: From image processing to computational neuroscience: A neural model based on histogram equalization. Frontiers in Neuroscience **8**, Article No. 71, June 2014
7. Bertalmío, M., Caselles, V., Provenzi, E., Rizzi, A.: Perceptual color correction through variational techniques. IEEE Transactions on Image Processing **16**(4), 1058–1072 (2007)
8. Bertalmío, M., Levine, S.: Variational approach for the fusion of exposure bracketed pairs. IEEE Transactions on Image Processing **22**(2), 712–723 (2013)
9. Bertsekas, D.: On the Goldstein-Levitin-Polyak gradient projection method. IEEE Transactions on Automatic Control **21**(2), 174–184 (1976)
10. Bogoni, L.: Extending dynamic range of monochrome and color images through fusion. In: Proc. International Conference on Pattern Recognition, Barcelona, Spain, vol. 3, pp. 7–12, September 2000
11. Buchsbaum, G.: A spatial processor model for object colour perception. Journal of the Franklin Institute **310**(1), 1–26 (1980)
12. Burt, P., Kolczynski, R.: Enhanced image capture through fusion. In: Proc. International Conference on Computer Vision, Berlin, Germany, pp. 173–182, May 1993
13. Cho, W.H., Hong, K.S.: Extending dynamic range of two color images under different exposures. In: Proc. International Conference on Pattern Recognition, Cambridge, UK, vol. 4, pp. 853–856, August 2004
14. Cornsweet, T.N.: Visual Perception. Harcourt College Publishers, Fort Worth (1970)
15. Debevec, P.E., Malik, J.: Recovering high dynamic range radiance maps from photographs. In: Proc. SIGGRAPH 1997, Los Angeles, CA, pp. 369–378, August 1997
16. Ferradans, S., Bertalmío, M., Provenzi, E., Caselles, V.: An analysis of visual adaptation and contrast perception for tone mapping. IEEE Transactions on Pattern Analysis and Machine Intelligence **33**(10), 2002–2012 (2011)
17. Goshtasby, A.A.: Fusion of multi-exposure images. Image and Vision Computing **23**(6), 611–618 (2005)
18. Herwig, J., Pauli, J.: An information-theoretic approach to multi-exposure fusion via statistical filtering using local entropy. In: Proc. International Conference on Signal Processing, Pattern Recognition and Applications, Innsbruck, Austria, pp. 50–57, February 2010

19. Kotwal, K., Chaudhuri, S.: An optimization-based approach to fusion of multi-exposure, low dynamic range images. In: Proc. International Conference on Information Fusion, Chicago, IL, pp. 1942–1948, July 2011
20. Land, E.H., McCann, J.J.: Lightness and retinex theory. Journal of the Optical Society of America **61**(1), 1–11 (1971)
21. Mann, S., Picard, R.W.: On being 'undigital' with digital cameras: extending dynamic range by combining differently exposed pictures. In: Proc. IS&T Annual Conference, Springfield, VA, pp. 442–448, May 1995
22. McCann, J.J.: The role of simple nonlinear operations in modeling human lightness and color sensations. In: Rogowitz, B.E. (ed.) Human Vision, Visual Processing, and Digital Display, Proc. SPIE, vol. 1077, pp. 355–363. SPIE Press, Bellingham (1989)
23. Mertens, T., Kautz, J., Van Reeth, F.: Exposure fusion: A simple and practical alternative to high dynamic range photography. Computer Graphics Forum **28**(1), 161–171 (2009). research.edm.uhasselt.be/~tmertens/
24. Palma-Amestoy, R., Provenzi, E., Bertalmío, M., Caselles, V.: A perceptually inspired variational framework for color enhancement. IEEE Transactions on Pattern Analysis and Machine Intelligence **31**(3), 458–474 (2009)
25. Piella, G.: Image fusion for enhanced visualization: A variational approach. International Journal of Computer Vision **83**(1), 1–11 (2009)
26. Raman, S., Chaudhuri, S.: A matte-less, variational approach to automatic scene compositing. In: Proc. International Conference on Computer Vision, Rio de Janeiro, Brazil, pp. 574–579, October 2007
27. Raman, S., Chaudhuri, S.: Bilateral filter based compositing for variable exposure photography. In: Proc. EUROGRAPHICS 2009 (Short Papers), Munich, Germany, pp. 369–378, March 2009
28. Reinhard, E., Heidrich, W., Debevec, P., Pattanaik, S., Ward, G., Myszkowski, K.: High Dynamic Range Imaging: Acquisition, Display, and Image-Based Lighting, 2nd edn. Elsevier, Oxford (2010)
29. Sapiro, G., Caselles, V.: Histogram modification via differential equations. Journal of Differential Equations **135**(2), 238–268 (1997)
30. Shalev-Shwartz, S., Singer, Y.: Efficient learning of label ranking by soft projections onto polyhedra. Journal of Machine Learning Research **7**, 1567–1599 (2006)
31. Shen, R., Cheng, I., Basu, A.: QoE-based multi-exposure fusion in hierarchical multivariate Gaussian CRF. IEEE Transactions on Image Processing **22**(6), 2469–2478 (2013)
32. Shen, R., Cheng, I., Shi, J., Basu, A.: Generalized random walks for fusion of multi-exposure images. IEEE Transactions on Image Processing **20**(12), 3634–3646 (2011)
33. Singh, H., Kumar, V., Bhooshan, S.: Weighted least squares based detail enhanced exposure fusion. ISNR Signal Processing **2014**, Article No. 498762, February 2014
34. Song, M., Tao, D., Chen, C., Bu, J., Luo, J., Zhang, C.: Probabilistic exposure fusion. IEEE Transactions on Image Processing **21**(1), 341–357 (2012)
35. Vavilin, A., Jo, K.H.: Recursive HDR image generation from differently exposed images based on local image properties. In: Proc. International Conference on Control, Automation and Systems, Seoul, Korea, pp. 2791–2796, October 2008

A Variational Model for Color Assignment

Jan Henrik Fitschen[1]([✉]), Mila Nikolova[2], Fabien Pierre[3],
and Gabriele Steidl[1]

[1] Department of Mathematics, University of Kaiserslautern, Kaiserslautern, Germany
{fitschen,steidl}@mathematik.uni-kl.de
[2] CMLA − CNRS, ENS Cachan, Cachan, France
nikolova@cmla.ens-cachan.fr
[3] University of Bordeaux, CNRS, IMB,
UMR 5251, LaBRI, UMR 5800, Talence, France
fabien.pierre@math.u-bordeaux1.fr

Abstract. Color image enhancement is a challenging task in digital imaging with many applications. This paper contributes to image enhancement methods. We propose a new variational model for color improvement in the RGB space based on a desired target intensity image. Our model improves the visual quality of the color image while it preserves the range and takes the hue of the original, badly exposed image into account without amplifying its color artifacts. To approximate the hue of the original image we use the fact that affine transforms are hue preserving. To cope with the noise in the color channels we design a particular coupled TV regularization term. Since the target intensity of the image is unaltered our model respects important image structures. Numerical results demonstrate the very good performance of our method.

1 Introduction

This paper contributes to the tremendous progress in digital color imaging. Since the inaugural paper [25] providing PDE-based and variational formulations for image histogram modifications, these methods were further expanded to color image enhancement, see, e.g., [2,19,20]. These approaches provide flexible tools to incorporate various knowledge on human visual perceptual phenomena, typically in relation with Retinex theory [11]. For restoration in the luminance-chrominance space, see [1,5].

In this paper we are interested in the enhancement of RGB images given a desired intensity image. Such target intensity image can be computed, depending on the task at hand, from the initial intensity image for example by histogram specification or by finding the image reflectance, e.g., within a retinex model. Given the desired intensity, color adjustment methods which preserve the hue of the original image tend to amplify erroneous color pixels. These artifacts were often not visible in the initial image due to low intensity values in the respective areas. Examples of hue preserving color adjustment methods are the frequently used technique to transform the RGB image into the HSI space, replace the intensity by the desired one and transform back or the methods in [14,16,18] which work directly in the RGB space. An illustration is given in Fig. 1. The same effect can also be observed in other color image enhancement methods as in the automatic color enhancement method [6,22] or in the perceptually inspired variational approach [2,19]. To cope with noisy pixels we suggest a variational

Fig. 1. Original image. Enhanced image by the multiplicative algorithm in [18] $((l,r) = (0.5, 10^{-4}))$, erroneous color pixels become visible due to their higher intensity. Enhanced image with our new model and the same target intensity. The errors are corrected while image edges are still sharp.

model which handles the hue in a more flexible manner. The basic ideas of the model are i) the utilization of affine transforms which preserve the hue, and ii) the incorporation of a specialized TV regularization term to allow a smoothing of the RGB channels. It is worth emphasizing that our method is different from L_p-TV-like denoising methods for RGB images. On the one hand, these methods cannot be directly applied to the original image, and, on the other hand, applied to a previously enhanced RGB image, they smooth much more than our method which takes the target intensity into account.

Organization of the Paper. In Section 2 we deal with hue preserving color assignments. We recall that the hue of two RGB pixels coincides if and only they are related by an affine map. Further, we review the multiplicative color assignment model proposed in [18] which was the starting point of this paper. Our new model is introduced in Section 3. We prove the existence and uniqueness of a minimizer and show the relation to the multiplicative model. Section 4 demonstrates the very good performance of our algorithm. The paper ends with conclusions for future work in Section 5.

2 Hue Preservation

There exist different definitions of the hue. In the HSI (hue-saturation-intensity) model the *hue* of a pixel $w := (r,g,b)$ is given by $H(w) := 0$ if $r = g = b$ and otherwise by

$$H(w) := \begin{cases} \theta & \text{if } b \leq g, \\ 360^\circ - \theta & \text{if } b > g, \end{cases}$$

where
$$\theta := \arccos \frac{\frac{1}{2}((r-g)+(r-b))}{((r-g)^2+(r-b)(g-b))^{\frac{1}{2}}}, \qquad (1)$$

see [8]. Note that the denominator of θ can be rewritten as $(\frac{1}{2}((r-g)^2+(r-b)^2+(g-b)^2))^{\frac{1}{2}}$ using the binomial formula.

Proposition 1. *The pixels (r_0, g_0, b_0) and (r, g, b) have the same hue if and only if there exist $a, y \in \mathbb{R}$ such that*

$$(r, g, b) = a(r_0, g_0, b_0) + y\mathbf{1}, \quad a, y \in \mathbb{R}, \qquad (2)$$

i.e., if they lie in the same half-plane trough the origin and $\mathbf{1} := (1,1,1)$.

From (1) it follows immediately that the hue of a pixel is preserved by an affine transform (2). Although the converse is also somehow known we could not find a proof in the literature and add it in the appendix.

In [16,18] the following hue and range preserving color adjustment model, called 'multiplicative model' has been applied successfully: for a given pixel $w_0 := (r_0, g_0, b_0) \in [0, L-1]^3$ with intensity $f_0 := \frac{1}{3}(r_0 + g_0 + b_0) > 0$ and $M_0 := \max\{r_0, g_0, b_0\}$, a new pixel $w := (r, g, b)$ of the form (2) with prescribed intensity

$$f = \frac{1}{3}(r+g+b) = \frac{1}{3}a(r_0+g_0+b_0) + y = af_0 + y$$

is obtained by the following **multiplicative model (MM)**:
Set $w := (f, f, f)$ if $f_0 = 0$ and otherwise

$$w := \begin{cases} \frac{f}{f_0}w_0 & \text{if } \frac{M_0}{f_0}f \leq L-1, \\ \frac{L-1-f}{M_0-f_0}(w_0 - f_0\mathbf{1}) + f\mathbf{1} & \text{if } \frac{M_0}{f_0}f > L-1. \end{cases} \qquad (3)$$

Indeed only the first formula is a pure multiplication with w_0, i.e., $y = 0$ in (2). By Proposition 1 it is clear that w_0 and w have the same hue. The consideration of two cases ensures that the range is preserved, i.e., $w \in [0, L-1]^3$ and that the full range $[0, L-1]^3$ is optimally exploited Note that the second formula (3) follows just by switching the first formula from RGB to CMY (Cyan $= L-1-$R, Magenta $= L-1-$G, Yellow $= L-1-$B) and subsequent back-transform, i.e., the second formula in (3) can be rewritten as

$$w = (L-1)\mathbf{1} - \frac{L-1-f}{L-1-f_0}((L-1)\mathbf{1} - w_0).$$

This idea also appears in [14]. The adjustment (3) works fine as long as the hue of the original image is noise-free and should be exactly preserved. However, as shown in the introduction this model amplifies hue errors which are hardly visible in the original image if they appear in low intensity regions. Up to now the model works pixelwise. Noise removal requires to take the spatial image information into account. This is done in the next section.

3 New Model for Color Adjustment

We consider RGB images of size $M \times N$ with columnwise reshaped RGB channels into vectors of length $n := MN$. For a given image $w_0 := (r_0, g_0, b_0) \in [0, L-1]^{n,3}$ with intensity $f_0 := \frac{1}{3}(r_0 + g_0 + b_0)$ we want to adjust a new image $w := (r, g, b) \in [0, L-1]^{n,3}$ with prescribed intensity $f := \frac{1}{3}(r + g + b) \in [0, L-1]^n$. If the meaning is clear from the context, we will use the notation w, r, g, b both for individual pixels and the whole image.

Inspired by the model (3) we are looking for $x_{RGB} := (x_R, x_G, x_B) \in \mathbb{R}^{n,3}$, $y \in \mathbb{R}^n$ with certain properties and then set $r := \frac{r_0}{f_0} x_R + y$, $g := \frac{g_0}{f_0} x_G + y$, $b := \frac{b_0}{f_0} x_B + y$, i.e.,

$$r := A_R x_R + y, \quad g := A_G x_G + y, \quad b := A_B x_B + y \quad (4)$$

with

$$A_R := \operatorname{diag} \frac{r_0}{f_0}, \quad A_G := \operatorname{diag} \frac{g_0}{f_0}, \quad A_B := \operatorname{diag} \frac{b_0}{f_0},$$

where we agree that

$$\frac{r_0(i)}{f_0(i)} = \frac{g_0(i)}{f_0(i)} = \frac{b_0(i)}{f_0(i)} := 1 \quad \text{if} \quad f_0(i) = 0, \; i \in \{1, \ldots, n\}.$$

Then the prescribed intensity is obtained if $f = \frac{1}{3}(A_R x_R + A_G x_G + A_B x_B) + y$, and the range is preserved if $A_\nu x_\nu + y \in [0, L-1]$, $\nu \in \{R, G, B\}$. We do not assume that the hue of w_0 is exactly preserved which by (2) would be the case if $x_R = x_G = x_B$, but relax the condition by demanding that the following value becomes small:

$$\|x_R - x_G\|_2^2 + \|x_R - x_B\|_2^2 + \|x_G - x_B\|_2^2 = \| x_{RGB} \underbrace{\begin{pmatrix} -1 & 1 & 0 \\ 0 & -1 & 1 \\ 1 & 0 & -1 \end{pmatrix}}_{D_{per}} \|_F^2,$$

where $\| \cdot \|_F$ denotes the *Frobenius norm*. Further we want to keep $\|y\|_p^p$, $p \geq 1$ small to enforce the model to approximate the first (multiplicative) formula in (3). To cope with noisy pixels we demand that the discrete total variation (TV) [23] of the new image is small. Using the discrete gradient-like operator $\nabla \colon \mathbb{R}^n \mapsto \mathbb{R}^{2n}$ below

$$\nabla := \begin{pmatrix} I_N \otimes D_M \\ D_N \otimes I_M \end{pmatrix}, \quad D_M := \begin{pmatrix} -1 & 1 & & \\ & \ddots & \ddots & \\ & & -1 & 1 \\ & & & 0 \end{pmatrix} \in \mathbb{R}^{M,M},$$

where $\otimes$ denotes the Kronecker product of matrices, and the notation

$$TV(x_{RGB}, y) := \sum_{i=1}^n \Big(\sum_{\nu \in \{R,G,B\}} (\nabla(A_\nu x_\nu + y))_i^2 + (\nabla(A_\nu x_\nu + y))_{i+n}^2 \Big)^{\frac{1}{2}},$$

related to [24] (see conclusions), we propose the following model:

$$\min_{x_{RGB}, y} \frac{1}{p}\|y\|_p^p + \frac{\mu}{2}\|x_{RGB}D_{per}\|_F^2 + \lambda TV(x_{RGB}, y) \quad (5)$$

$$\text{subject to } A_\nu x_\nu + y \in [0, L-1], \; \nu \in \{R, G, B\},$$

$$f = \frac{1}{3}(A_R x_R + A_G x_G + A_B x_B) + y,$$

where $\lambda, \mu \geq 0$ and $p \in [1, +\infty]$. Replacing y in the TV term by the equality constraint gives, e.g., in the first summand $\nu = R$ the expression $\left(\nabla(\frac{2}{3}A_R x_R - \frac{1}{3}A_G x_G - \frac{1}{3}A_B x_B) + \nabla f\right)_i^2$. Therefore the gradient of the target intensity image is prominent in our TV term.

Proposition 2. *For $\lambda = 0$ and $x_R = x_G = x_B$ (μ large enough) the minimizer (x_{RGB}, y) of (5) together with the setting (4) coincides with the model (3).*

Proof. We have that $\|x_{RGB}D_{per}\|_F^2 = 0$ if and only if $x_R = x_G = x_B = x$ which is the case for large μ. In this case (5) becomes

$$\min_x \frac{1}{p}\|f - x\|_p^p \quad \text{subject to} \quad A_\nu x - x + f \in [0, L-1], \; \nu \in \{R, G, B\} \quad (6)$$

and $y = f - x$. This problem can be treated pixelwise as follows: let $M_0 := \max\{r_0, g_0, b_0\}$ and $m_0 := \min\{r_0, g_0, b_0\}$. If $\frac{M_0}{f_0}f \leq L - 1$ then $x = f$ is the solution of (6) and we obtain with (4) the first formula in (3). If $M_0 = f_0 = m_0$ then $x = r = g = b = f$. Otherwise $M_0 > f_0$ and $m_0 < f_0$. If $\frac{M_0}{f_0}f > L - 1$, then

$$f > \frac{(L-1)f_0}{M_0} > \frac{f_0(L-1-f)}{M_0 - f_0} \quad (7)$$

and the right boundary condition in (6) becomes $x \leq \min\{\frac{(L-1-f)f_0}{M_0 - f_0}, \frac{ff_0}{f_0 - m_0}\} = \frac{(L-1-f)f_0}{M_0 - f_0}$. By (7) we see that (6) has its minimizer in $x = \frac{(L-1-f)f_0}{M_0 - f_0}$. Together with (4) this leads to the second formula in (3). □

Theorem 1. *For $\lambda, \mu \geq 0$ there exists a solution $(\hat{y}, \hat{x}_{RGB})$ of (5). If $p > 1$, then $\hat{y}$ is unique and if in addition $\mu > 0$, then $\hat{x}_{RGB}$ is unique as well.*

Proof. 1. The functional (equivalent to (5))

$$E(x_{RGB}, y) := \frac{1}{p}\|y\|_p^p + \frac{\mu}{2}\|x_{RGB}D_{per}\|_F^2 + \lambda TV(x_{RGB}, y) + \iota_{C_1 \cap C_2}(x_{RGB}, y)$$

with the indicator function ι_C of C and $C_1 := \{(x_{RGB}, y) : f = \frac{1}{3}(A_R x_R + A_G x_G + A_B x_B) + y\}$, $C_2 := \{(x_{RGB}, y) : A_\nu x_\nu + y \in [0, L-1], \; \nu \in \{R, G, B\}\}$ is lower semi-continuous and proper since $(x_{RGB}, y) = (0, f) \in \text{dom } E$.

First we consider the case $\mu > 0$. We will show that the functional is coercive. Let $(x_{RGB}^{(k)}, y^{(k)})_{k \in \mathbb{N}}$ be a sequence with $\|(x_{RGB}^{(k)}, y^{(k)})\| \to +\infty$. Assume that E is not coercive. Then there exists a constant $K \in \mathbb{R}$ and an infinite subsequence such that $E(x_{RGB}^{(k_j)}, y^{(k_j)}) \leq K$ for all $j \in \mathbb{N}$. This implies $\|y^{(k_j)}\|_p^p \leq K$. By definition of A_ν we have for each $i = 1, \ldots, n$ that $A_\nu(i,i) > 0$ for at least one $\nu \in \{R, G, B\}$. For such $\tilde{\nu}$ we obtain that $x_{\tilde{\nu}}(i)$ is bounded due to the constraints in C_2. Then, by $\|x_{RGB}^{(k_j)}(i) D_{per}\|_F^2 \leq K$ also $x_{RGB}^{(k_j)}(i)$ is bounded. This is a contradiction to $\|(x_{RGB}^{(k)}, y^{(k)})\| \to +\infty$.

Now we consider the case $\mu = 0$. Let $x_{\tilde{\nu}}$ be the vector containing all variables corresponding to non zero diagonal entries of A_ν, $\nu \in \{R, G, B\}$, i.e., $x_{\tilde{\nu}} := (x_\nu(i))_{\{(i,\nu): A_\nu(i,i) > 0\}}$. Only the values in $x_{\tilde{\nu}}$ and y have an influence on the value of E. Now the coercivity follows for $E(x_{\tilde{\nu}}, y)$ by considering the ℓ_p term for y and the constraints in C_2 as in the previous case. Thus, the minimization problem restricted to $(x_{\tilde{\nu}}, y)$ possesses a minimizer. Since we can choose $x_\nu(i)$ arbitrarily if $A_\nu(i,i) = 0$, there exists also a minimizer for the whole problem.

2. Assume that $\hat{z} = (\hat{x}_{RGB}, \hat{y})$ and $\tilde{z} = (\tilde{x}_{RGB}, \tilde{y})$ are two minimizers of (5). Then $\frac{1}{2}(\hat{z} + \tilde{z})$ is also a minimizer and we have in the three convex summands S_i, $i = 1, 2, 3$ of (5) that $S_i(\frac{1}{2}(\hat{z} + \tilde{z})) = \frac{1}{2} S_i(\hat{z}_i) + \frac{1}{2} S_i(\tilde{z}_i)$. Now $S_1(y, x_{RGB}) = \frac{1}{p}\|y\|_p^p$ is strictly convex for $p > 1$ so that $\hat{y} = \tilde{y}$. For $\mu > 0$, we obtain by the strict convexity of the squared Frobenius norm in S_2 that $\hat{x}_{RGB} D_{per} = \tilde{x}_{RGB} D_{per}$. Since the kernel of D_{per} consists of constant vectors this implies $\tilde{x}_{RGB} = \hat{x}_{RGB} + (1, 1, 1)^\mathrm{T} \otimes v$ with some $v \in \mathbb{R}^n$. Now the intensity constraint

$$f = \frac{1}{3}(A_R \tilde{x}_R + A_G \tilde{x}_G + A_B \tilde{x}_B) + \hat{y}$$
$$= \frac{1}{3}(A_R \hat{x}_R + A_G \hat{x}_G + A_B \hat{x}_B) + \hat{y} + \frac{1}{3}(A_R + A_G + A_B)v$$
$$= \frac{1}{3}(A_R \hat{x}_R + A_G \hat{x}_G + A_B \hat{x}_B) + \hat{y}$$

implies, since $A_R + A_G + A_B$ has positive diagonal elements, that v is the zero vector. Hence, $\hat{x}_{RGB} = \tilde{x}_{RGB}$ and we are done. □

The minimization problem in (5) can be solved by using, e.g., the primal dual hybrid gradient method [4, 21]. We apply the form given in [3, Alg. 8] with the substitution

$$\begin{pmatrix} (I_3 \otimes \nabla)A & \mathbf{1}_3 \otimes \nabla \\ S & I_n \\ A & \mathbf{1}_3 \otimes I_n \end{pmatrix} \begin{pmatrix} x \\ y \end{pmatrix} = \begin{pmatrix} s \\ t_1 \\ t_2 \end{pmatrix}$$

where $x := (x_R^\mathrm{T}, x_B^\mathrm{T}, x_G^\mathrm{T})^\mathrm{T}$, $\mathbf{1}_3 := (1, 1, 1)^\mathrm{T}$, and

$$A := \begin{pmatrix} A_R & 0 & 0 \\ 0 & A_G & 0 \\ 0 & 0 & A_B \end{pmatrix}, \quad S := \frac{1}{3}(A_R \,|\, A_G \,|\, A_B).$$

Further we use, in accordance with the definition of the coupled TV semi norm, the mixed $\ell_2(\mathbb{R}^d) - \ell_1(\mathbb{R}^n)$ norm defined for $s \in \mathbb{R}^{2nd}$ as

$$\|s\|_{2,1} := \sum_{i=1}^n \left(\sum_{j=0}^{d-1} s_{2jn+i}^2 + s_{(2j+1)n+i}^2 \right)^{\frac{1}{2}} = \sum_{i=1}^n \left(\sum_{j=0}^{2d-1} s_{jn+i}^2 \right)^{\frac{1}{2}}, \quad d = 3.$$

Algorithm 1. PDHGMp Algorithm for (5)

Initialization: $x^{(0)} = (f^T, f^T, f^T)^T$, $y^{(0)} = 0$,
$b^{(0)} = ((b_1^{(0)})^T, (b_2^{(0)})^T, (b_3^{(0)})^T)^T = 0$, $\bar{b}^{(0)} = 0$, $\theta = 1$, $\tau = \frac{1}{5}$, $\sigma = \frac{1}{20}$, $p \in \{1, 2\}$.

Iteration: For $k = 0, 1, \ldots$ iterate

$$x^{(k+1)} = \arg\min_{x \in \mathbb{R}^{3n}} \left\{ \frac{\mu}{2} \|(D_{per} \otimes I_n)x\|_2^2 + \frac{1}{2\tau} \|x - \left(x^{(k)}\right.\right.$$
$$\left.\left. - \tau\sigma(A(I_3 \otimes \nabla^T)\bar{b}_1^{(k)} + S^T\bar{b}_2^{(k)} + A\bar{b}_3^{(k)})\right)\|_2^2 \right\}$$

$$y^{(k+1)} = \arg\min_{y \in \mathbb{R}^n} \left\{ \frac{1}{p}\|y\|_p^p + \frac{1}{2\tau}\|y - \left(y^{(k)}\right.\right.$$
$$\left.\left. - \tau\sigma((1_3^T \otimes \nabla^T)\bar{b}_1^{(k)} + \bar{b}_2^{(k)} + (1_3^T \otimes I_n)\bar{b}_3^{(k)})\right)\|_2^2 \right\}$$

$$s^{(k+1)} = \arg\min_{s \in \mathbb{R}^{6n}} \{\lambda\|s\|_{2,1} + \frac{\sigma}{2}\|s - (b_1^{(k)} + ((I_3 \otimes \nabla)Ax^{(k+1)} + (I_3 \otimes \nabla)y^{(k+1)})\|_2^2\}$$

$$t_1^{(k+1)} = f$$

$$t_2^{(k+1)} = \arg\min_{t \in [0, L-1]^{3n}} \{\frac{\sigma}{2}\|t - (b_3^{(k)} + Ax^{(k+1)} + (1_3 \otimes I_n)y^{(k+1)})\|_2^2\}$$

$$b_1^{(k+1)} = b^{(k)} + (I_3 \otimes \nabla)Ax^{(k+1)} + (I_3 \otimes \nabla)y^{(k+1)} - s^{k+1}$$

$$b_2^{(k+1)} = b_2^{(k)} + Sx^{(k+1)} + y^{(k+1)} - t_1^{(k+1)}$$

$$b_3^{(k+1)} = b_3^{(k)} + Ax^{(k+1)} + (1_3 \otimes I_n)y^{(k+1)} - t_2^{(k+1)}$$

$$\bar{b}^{(k+1)} = b^{(k+1)} + \theta(b^{(k+1)} - b^{(k)})$$

4 Numerical Examples

In this section we demonstrate the very good performance of our method. Algorithm 1 was implemented in MATLAB2014b. In all examples we have $p = 2$ and $L = 256$. The desired intensity images f were computed from the given intensity f_0 in a preprocessing step as follows:

- For the enhancement examples in Fig. 2 - 4 the exact histogram specification method of [18] was applied with a Gaussian target histogram and specific parameters l, r. For exact histogram specification see also [15, 17]. A program package for automatic histogram specification is available at [10].
- For the illumination example in Fig. 5 we have used the retinex model with higher order TV in [12] (parameters: $\alpha = \beta = 0.1$, $\tau = 0.01$, $\nu = 0.005$). Here f_0 is considered as the approximate product of reflectance and luminance. The model in [12] computes the reflectance which serves as the desired target image f. Clearly, other reflectance-luminance models can be used as well.

The photo in Fig. 2 is too dark. The desired intensity is obtained as in [18] with $(l, r) = (0.9, 0.1)$. Using this target intensity we have applied the MM in (3) and our new algorithm with $(\lambda, \mu) = (200, \frac{20}{3})$. The improvement by our method is clearly visible. We have also added the result obtained by the ACE method [6] with default parameter $\alpha = 5$. As in the MM erroneous color pixels are visible.

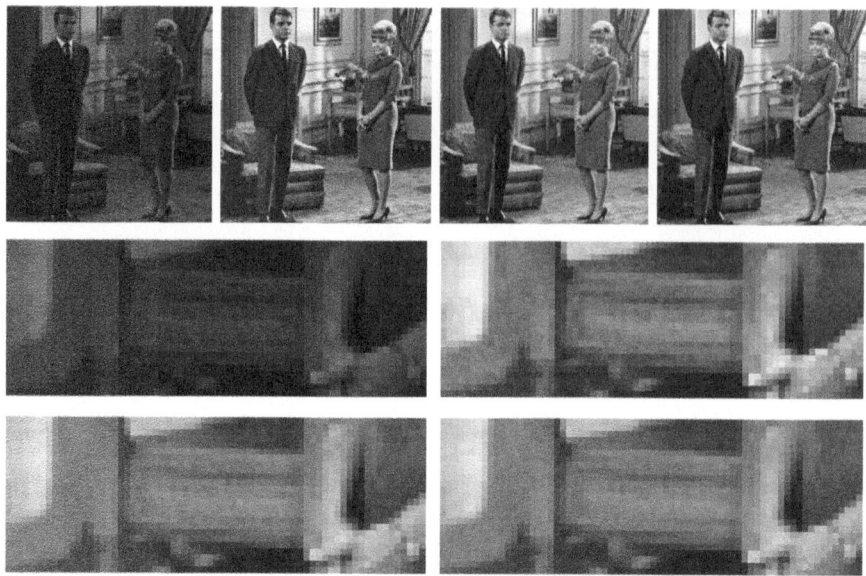

Fig. 2. Top: Original image, enhanced image by ACE, by the MM, and by the proposed model. Middle: Zoom into the original image and the ACE enhanced image. Bottom: Zoom into the MM enhanced image and the one by our proposed model.

The first image in Fig. 3 top was taken from [18]. It has a flashlight effect. We take the target intensity image from the same paper. The flashlight artifact can be removed by the MM as can be seen in the second image. However, zooming into the images we see color errors which were removed by our algorithm with parameters $(\lambda, \mu) = (100, 2)$. This zoom clearly shows that the color channels are denoised without visible smoothing of the whole image.

Fig. 4 shows another image enhancement example, where the target intensity histogram was obtained from the automatic specification package [10]. Our algorithm with parameters $(\lambda, \mu) = (160, 2)$ provides a smoother image without destroying important image details.

Finally, Fig. 5 shows an example where the illumination was corrected. The model in [12] was used to separate reflectance and luminance and the reflectance function was taken as target intensity image. For color images the authors in [12] propose to transfer the image from RGB to HSI, apply their model to the intensity, change the intensity by the computed reflectance and transform back (a gamut correction will be necessary). We have used the computed reflectance as target intensity for our new model with parameters $(\lambda, \mu) = (300, 10)$.

5 Conclusions

We have provided a new variational model for adapting colors of an image with prescribed intensity given its corrupted version. The model approximates the hue

Fig. 3. Top: Original image and enhanced images by the MM and the proposed model. Bottom: Zoom into the enhanced images.

Fig. 4. Top: Original image and enhanced images by the MM and the proposed method. Bottom: Zoom into the enhanced images.

of the original image, but is flexible enough to correct color artifacts so that it gives very good results. Indeed our initial model creates many interesting future research tasks. In particular, we want to discuss the choice of the parameter p (up to now we have concentrated on $p = 2$) and different couplings of the color

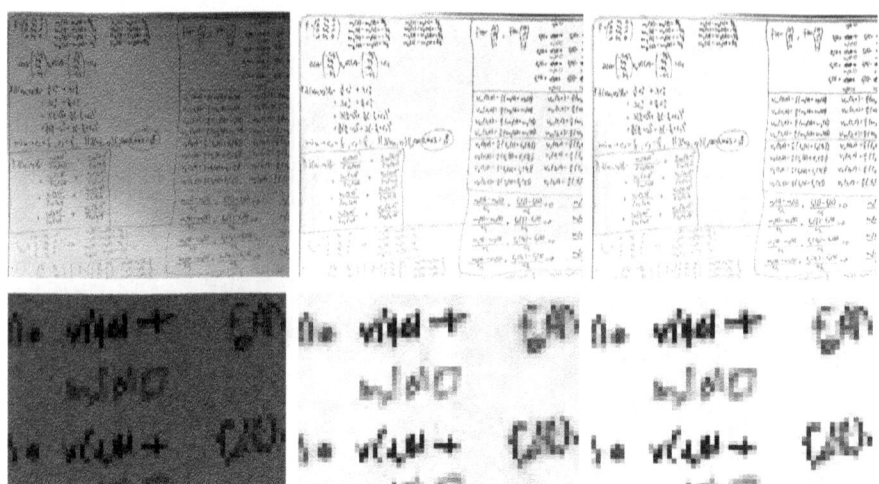

Fig. 5. Top: Original image and luminance corrected images by the model in [12] and our model. Bottom: Zoom into the images.

channel in the TV term, see [7,9,24]. Using the luma $0.299r + 0.587g + 0.114b$ instead of the intensity seems to be important in certain applications. Finally, incorporating the finding of an appropriate intensity function into the variational model instead of focusing on a given one is of great interest.

6 Appendix

Proof. (of Proposition 1) If (2) is fulfilled, (r, g, b) and (r_0, g_0, b_0) have the same hue by the definition of the hue in (1).

Conversely, assume that $b \leq g$ and the hue of (r, g, b) is constant, i.e.,

$$c = \frac{1/2\left((r-g) + (r-b)\right)}{\sqrt{(r-g)^2 + (r-b)(g-b)}}.$$

Clearly, we have $|c| \leq 1$. Then we obtain

$$r - \frac{g}{2} - \frac{b}{2} = c\sqrt{r^2 + g^2 + b^2 - rg - rb - bg},$$

$$r^2 + \frac{g^2}{4} + \frac{b^2}{4} - rg - rb + \frac{gb}{2} = c^2\left(r^2 + g^2 + b^2 - rg - rb - bg\right),$$

$$(1-c^2)\left(r^2 - r(g+b)\right) = c^2\left(g^2 + b^2 - bg\right) - \frac{g^2}{4} - \frac{b^2}{4} - \frac{bg}{2},$$

$$(1-c^2)\left[\left(r - \frac{g+b}{2}\right)^2 - \left(\frac{b+g}{2}\right)^2\right] = c^2\left(g^2 + b^2 - bg\right) - \frac{g^2}{4} - \frac{b^2}{4} - \frac{bg}{2},$$

$$(1-c^2)\left(r - \frac{b+g}{2}\right)^2 = 3c^2\left(\frac{g^2}{4} + \frac{b^2}{4} - \frac{bg}{2}\right) = 3c^2\left(\frac{b-g}{2}\right)^2.$$

By the first equality we see that c and $r - (g+b)/2$ have the same sign. Hence,

$$\sqrt{1-c^2}\left(r - \frac{b+g}{2}\right) = \sqrt{3}c\left(\frac{b-g}{2}\right).$$

Since $b \geq g$, this can finally be rewritten as the plane equation

$$\sqrt{1-c^2}\,r + \frac{\sqrt{3}c - \sqrt{1-c^2}}{2}g - \frac{\sqrt{3}c + \sqrt{1-c^2}}{2}b = 0.$$

The case $b < g$ can be treated similarly and we are done. □

Acknowledgments. This study has been carried out with financial support from the French State, managed by the French National Research Agency (ANR) in the frame of the Investments for the future Programme IdEx Bordeaux (ANR-10-IDEX-03-02). This study has been funded by "Mobilité junior LaBRI". Funding by the German Research Foundation (DFG) within the Research Training Group 1932 "Stochastic Models for Innovations in the Engineering Sciences" is gratefully acknowledged. The work of M. Nikolova was supported by the "FMJH Program Gaspard Monge in optimization and operation research", and by the support to this program from EDF.

References

1. Alleysson, D., Süsstrunk, S., Herault, J.: Linear demosaicing inspired by the human visual system. IEEE Transactions on Image Processing **14**(4), 439–449 (2005)
2. Bertalmío, M., Caselles, V., Provenzi, E., Rizzi, A.: Perceptual color correction through variational techniques. IEEE Transactions on Image Processing **16**(4), 1058–1072 (2007)
3. Burger, M., Sawatzky, A., Steidl, G.: First Order Algorithms in Variational Image Processing (2014). arXiv preprint arXiv:1412.4237
4. Chambolle, A., Pock, T.: A First-Order Primal-Dual Algorithm for Convex Problems with Applications to Imaging. Journal of Mathematical Imaging and Vision **40**(1), 120–145 (2011)
5. Condat, L.: A new color filter array with optimal properties for noiseless and noisy color image acquisition. IEEE Transactions on Image Processing **20**(8), 2200–2210 (2011)
6. Getreuer, P.: Automatic color enhancement (ACE) and its fast implementation. Image Processing On Line (2012). doi:10.5201/ipol.2012.g-ace
7. Goldluecke, B., Strekalovskiy, E., Cremers, D.: The natural total variation which arises from geometric measure theory. SIAM Journal on Imaging Sciences **5**(2), 537–563 (2012)
8. Gonzalez, R., Woods, R.: Digital Image Processing, 3rd edn. NJ, Prentice-Hall (2007)
9. Grimalt, J.D., Moeller, M., Sbert, C., Cremers, D.: A framework for nonlocal vectorial total variation based on $\ell^{p,q,r}$-norms. In: Tai, X.-C., Bae, E., Chan, T.F., Lysaker, M. (eds.) MMCVPR 2015. LNCS, vol. 8932, pp. 141–154. Springer International Publishing, Switzerland (2015)

10. Häuser, S., Nikolova, M., Steidl, G.: Hue and range preserving RGB image enhancement. In: Preparation (2015). http://www.mathematik.uni-kl.de/imagepro/software/rgb-hp-enhance/
11. Land, E.H.: The retinex theory of color vision. Scientific American **237**(6) (1977)
12. Liang, J., Zhang, X.: Retinex by higher order total variation L^1 decomposition. Journal of Mathematical Imaging and Vision (2015)
13. Limare, N., Petro, A.B., Sbert, C., Morel, J.M.: Retinex Poisson equation: a model for color perception. Image Processing On Line **1** (2011)
14. Naik, S.F., Murthy, C.A.: Hue-preserving color image enhancement without gamut problem. IEEE Transactions on Image Processing **12**(12), 1591–1598 (2003)
15. Nikolova, M., Wen, Y.-W., Chan, R.: Exact histogram specification for digital images using a variational approach. Journal of Mathematical Imaging and Vision **46**(3), 309–325 (2013)
16. Nikolova, M.: A fast algorithm for exact histogram specification. Simple extension to colour images. In: Pack, T. (ed.) SSVM 2013. LNCS, vol. 7893, pp. 174–185. Springer, Heidelberg (2013)
17. Nikolova, M., Steidl, G.: Fast sorting algorithm for exact histogram specification, Preprint hal-00870501 (2013)
18. Nikolova, M., Steidl, G.: Fast hue and range preserving histogram specification: theory and new algorithms for color image enhancement. IEEE Transactions on Image Processing **23**(9), 4087–4100 (2014)
19. Palma-Amestoy, R., Provenzi, E., Bertalmío, M., Caselles, V.: A perceptually inspired variational framework for color enhancement. IEEE Transactions on Pattern Analysis and and Machine Intelligence **31**(3), 458–474 (2009)
20. Papadakis, N., Provenzi, E., Caselles, V.: A variational model for histogram transfer of color images. IEEE Transactions on Image Processing **30**(6), 1682–1695 (2011)
21. Pock, T., Chambolle, A., Cremers, D., Bischof, H.: A convex relaxation approach for computing minimal partitions. In: IEEE Conference on Computer Vision and Pattern Recognition, pp. 810–817 (2009)
22. Rizzi, A., Gatta, C., Marini, D.: A new algorithm for unsupervised global and local color correction. Pattern Recognition Letters **124** (2003)
23. Rudin, L.I., Osher, S., Fatemi, E.: Nonlinear total variation based noise removal algorithms. Physica D **60**(1), 259–268 (1992)
24. Sapiro, G..: Vector-valued active contours. In: IEEE Conference on Computer Vision and Pattern Recognition, pp. 680–685 (1996)
25. Sapiro, G., Caselles, V.: Histogram Modification via Differential Equations. Journal of Differential Equations **135**(2), 238–268 (1997)

Duality Principle for Image Regularization and Perceptual Color Correction Models

Thomas Batard[✉] and Marcelo Bertalmío

Department of Information and Communication Technologies,
Universitat Pompeu Fabra, Barcelona, Spain
{thomas.batard,marcelo.bertalmio}@upf.edu

Abstract. In this paper, we show that the anisotropic nonlocal total variation involved in the image regularization model of Gilboa and Osher [15] as well as in the perceptual color correction model of Bertalmío et al. [4] possesses a dual formulation. We then obtain novel formulations of their solutions, which provide new insights on these models. In particular, we show that the model of Bertalmío et al. can be split into two steps: first, it performs global color constancy, then local contrast enhancement. We also extend these two channel-wise variational models in a vectorial way by extending the anisotropic nonlocal total variation to vector-valued functions.

Keywords: Nonlocal variational problem · Duality principle · Contrast enhancement · Regularization · Perception

1 Introduction

Regularizing an image and modifying its contrast are very useful tasks for correcting defects produced during the acquisition process of a real-world scene and its reproduction on a display, due to physical and technological limitations (see e.g. [3] for more details). These tasks are also useful as pre-processing stage in order to improve the results of higher level applications like pattern recognition.

Variational methods are a very powerful tool for performing regularization and contrast modification of an image, and have been extensively used over the last two decades. Regarding contrast modification, the pioneer variational approach is due to Sapiro and Caselles [23], who performed contrast enhancement for histogram equalization purpose. Since then, this variational formulation has been generalized and applied in different contexts: perceptual color correction [4],[20], tone mapping [14], and gamut mapping [25] to name a few. Connections have also been made between the variational formulation [4] and Retinex theory [5],[6]. Concerning regularization tasks, the Rudin-Osher-Fatemi (ROF) denoising model [22] based on minimizing the total variation of an image has influenced

---

This work was supported by the European Research Council, Starting Grant ref. 306337, by the Spanish government, grant ref. TIN2012-38112, and by the Icrea Academia Award.

many local variational approaches that use generalizations of the total variation (see e.g. [2],[7],[8],[16]). On the other hand, since the seminal nonlocal approaches of Buades et al. [9], and Awate et al. [1] for image denoising, several nonlocal variational formulations for image regularization have been proposed (see e.g. [15],[17],[18]). In particular, Gilboa and Osher [15] introduced the concept of nonlocal gradient operator from which they derive a nonlocal total variation.

Computing the solutions of the variational problems aforementioned is not straightforward, mainly due to their non differentiability that makes the solutions not reachable through standard gradient descent algorithms. The situation is even more tricky when dealing with the contrast modification variational models [4],[20] since they are not convex. The use of duality principle in convex optimization (see e.g. [21] for an introduction) has been a breakthrough for solving non differentiable variational convex problems in imaging. For instance, Chambolle [11] made use of the duality principle for solving the Rudin-Osher-Fatemi model [22]. This approach had two assets compared with the original approach of Rudin, Osher and Fatemi. First, it provides a better approximation of the solution since it does not require a regularization of the variational model. Secondly, it provides a better insight on the model by showing that this latter consists in removing oscillating patterns of the original image, which includes noise but also texture as showed by Meyer [19].

In [15], Gilboa and Osher proposed two nonlocal variational models for image regularization based on two nonlocal extensions of the total variation, called isotropic and anisotropic (nonlocal) total variation, and in this paper we point out that the anisotropic total variation corresponds to the contrast modification term in the perceptual color correction model of Bertalmío et al. [4]. Whereras Gilboa and Osher propose to solve the corresponding variational formulation with graph-cut techniques and Bertalmío et al. with a gradient descent associated to a regularized version of the variational model, none of them investigated whether the variational model possesses a dual formulation, and the main contribution of this paper is to show that both do possess a dual formulation. Other contributions are the reinterpretation of their solutions from the proposed dual formulations as well as the vectorial extension of these models by extending the anisotropic nonlocal total variation to vector-valued functions.

The outline of this work is as follows. We first show in section 2 that the anisotropic nonlocal total variation and its vectorial extension possess a dual formulation, from which we derive in section 3 dual formulations of both variational models and novel formulations of their solutions. Finally, we show in section 4 that the novel formulation of the solution of the perceptual color correction model provides a new insight on this model.

2 Dual Formulation of the Anisotropic Nonlocal Vectorial Total Variation

Definition 1 (Non local gradient). *Let Ω be a compact subset of $\mathbb{R}^2$ and $u \colon \Omega \longrightarrow \mathbb{R}^n$ be an n-channel image. We assume that $\mathbb{R}^n$ is equipped with a definite positive quadratic form h.*

A nonlocal gradient is an operator $\nabla_w^{NL}: C^\infty(\Omega; \mathbb{R}^n) \longmapsto C^\infty(\Omega \times \Omega; \mathbb{R}^n)$ *of the form*

$$\nabla_w^{NL} u: (x,y) \longmapsto w(x,y)(u(y) - u(x)) \quad (1)$$

and $w: \Omega \times \Omega \longrightarrow \mathbb{R}^{+*}$ *is a smooth symmetric function.*

Note that definition (1) is nothing but the vectorial extension of the nonlocal gradient introduced by Gilboa and Osher [15].

Standard choices for the weight function w are Euclidean distance, Gaussian kernel, and patch-based distances. We refer to Zosso et al. [26] for a weight function specific to color images determined by the hue difference between two colors. The choice of the definite positive quadratic form h greatly depends on the nature of the image to be processed. Dealing with color images, a suitable choice for h is the perceptual metric associated to the color space involved (e.g. the Euclidean metric associated to the CIE Lab color space).

Definition 2 (The space $W_{1,p}^{NL}(\Omega; \mathbb{R}^n)$). *The quadratic form h induces a scalar product* $\langle \, , \, \rangle$ *on* $C^\infty(\Omega \times \Omega; \mathbb{R}^n)$ *defined by*

$$\langle \eta_1, \eta_2 \rangle := \int_{\Omega \times \Omega} (\eta_1(x,y), \eta_2(x,y))_h \, dx \, dy.$$

where $(\, , \,)_h$ *denotes the scalar product with respect to h.*

The L^p norm on $C^\infty(\Omega \times \Omega; \mathbb{R}^n)$ *is defined by*

$$\|\eta\|_{L^p} := \left(\int_{\Omega \times \Omega} \|\eta(x,y)\|_h^p \, dx \, dy \right)^{1/p}$$

where $\|\,\|_h$ *denotes the norm associated to h. In particular, we have*

$$\|\nabla_w^{NL} u\|_{L^p} = \left(\int_{\Omega \times \Omega} \|w(x,y)(u(y) - u(x))\|_h^p \, dx \, dy \right)^{1/p}.$$

Finally, we define the space

$$W_{1,p}^{NL}(\Omega; \mathbb{R}^n) := \{ u \in L^p(\Omega; \mathbb{R}^n) : \nabla_w^{NL} u \in L^p(\Omega \times \Omega; \mathbb{R}^n) \}.$$

Assuming that the function u is scalar-valued, the norm $\|\nabla_w^{NL} u\|_{L^1}$ corresponds to the anisotropic nonlocal total variation introduced by Gilboa and Osher [15], as well as the contrast modification term in the perceptual color correction model proposed by Bertalmío et al. [4].

Definition 3 (Adjoint of a nonlocal gradient operator). *We define the adjoint of the operator* ∇_w^{NL} *as the operator* $\nabla_w^{NL*}: C^\infty(\Omega \times \Omega; \mathbb{R}^n) \longrightarrow C^\infty(\Omega; \mathbb{R}^n)$ *satisfying*

$$\langle \nabla_w^{NL} u, \eta \rangle = (u, \nabla_w^{NL*} \eta)$$

where $(\, , \,)$ *is the L^2 scalar product on* $C^\infty(\Omega; \mathbb{R}^n)$ *induced by h.*

As in the scalar case in [15], a straightforward computation yields

$$\nabla_w^{NL*}\eta : x \longmapsto \int_\Omega w(x,y)(\eta(y,x) - \eta(x,y))\, dy. \tag{2}$$

We derive from Definition 3 the definition of nonlocal vectorial total variation.

Definition 4 (Nonlocal vectorial total variation). *We define the nonlocal vectorial total variation VTV_w^{NL} of $u \in L^1(\Omega; \mathbb{R}^n)$ as the quantity*

$$\sup_{\xi \in \mathcal{K}_1} \left(\int_\Omega (u(x), \xi(x))_h\, dx \right) \tag{3}$$

where, for $a \in \mathbb{R}$,

$$\mathcal{K}_a := \left\{ \nabla_w^{NL*}\eta : \eta \in C^\infty(\Omega \times \Omega; \mathbb{R}^n), \|\eta(x,y)\|_h \leq a\ \forall x,y \in \Omega \right\}. \tag{4}$$

We denote by $BV_w^{NL}(\Omega, \mathbb{R}^n)$ the set of functions $u \in L^1(\Omega; \mathbb{R}^n)$ such that $VTV_w^{NL}(u) < +\infty$.

Proposition 1. *If $u \in W_{1,1}^{NL}(\Omega; \mathbb{R}^n)$ then,*

$$VTV_w^{NL}(u) = \|\nabla_w^{NL} u\|_{L^1}. \tag{5}$$

Proof. The proof is omitted for the sake of shortness.

Properties of VTV_w^{NL}:

Let us first notice that VTV_w^{NL} is a sup of linear forms

$$J_\eta : u \longmapsto \int_\Omega (u(x), \nabla_w^{NL*}\eta(x))_h\, dx$$

which are continuous with respect to the weak topology of $L^2(\Omega; \mathbb{R}^n)$ since they are bounded. Hence, for $u \in L^2(\Omega, \mathbb{R}^n)$ and $u_n \rightharpoonup u$, we have $J_\eta(u_n) \to J_\eta(u)$. We then deduce that VTV_w^{NL} is lower semi-continuous and convex.

3 Dual Principle of Two Nonlocal Image Processing Models

3.1 Color Image Regularization

In [15], Gilboa and Osher developed a nonlocal extension of the Rudin-Osher-Fatemi model [22] based on the anisotropic nonlocal total variation. More precisely, they proposed the following variational problem

$$\arg\min_u \frac{\lambda}{2} \|u - u_0\|_{L^2}^2 + \|\nabla_w^{NL} u\|_{L^1}, \tag{6}$$

and solved it numerically through a graph-cut technique.

The following proposition shows that we can express the solution of the model (6) assuming that it belongs to the space $L^2 \cap BV_w^{NL}(\Omega; \mathbb{R})$. We actually prove this result in the more general case of vector-valued functions.

Proposition 2. *The unique solution $\underline{u}$ of the variational problem*

$$\arg\min_{u \in L^2 \cap BV_w^{NL}(\Omega;\mathbb{R}^n)} E(u) := \frac{\lambda}{2}\|u - u_0\|_{L^2}^2 + VTV_w^{NL}(u) \quad (7)$$

is

$$\underline{u} = u_0 - P_{K_{\frac{1}{\lambda}}} u_0, \quad (8)$$

where P is the projection operator, and $K_{\frac{1}{\lambda}}$ is the closure in $L^2(\Omega;\mathbb{R}^n)$ of the set $K_{\frac{1}{\lambda}}$ defined in (4).

Proof. The proof is a straightforward generalization of the proof in the case of the Rudin-Osher-Fatemi model whose details can be found in [12], and we omit it for the sake of shortness.

In the discrete case, the set $K_{\frac{1}{\lambda}}$ is its own closure, and we have

$$P_{K_{\frac{1}{\lambda}}}(u_0) = \frac{1}{\lambda}\nabla_w^{NL*}\eta, \quad \text{where} \quad \eta = \arg\min_{\eta,\|\eta\|_h \leq 1} \|\lambda u_0 - \nabla_w^{NL*}\eta\|_{L^2}.$$

The Karush-Kuhn-Tucker conditions for the minimization problem

$$\arg\min_{\eta, \|\eta\|_h \leq 1} \|\lambda u_0 - \nabla_w^{NL*}\eta\|_{L^2} \quad (9)$$

are

$$\begin{cases} \nabla_w^{NL}(\nabla_w^{NL*}\eta - \lambda u_0)_{i,j} + \alpha_{i,j}\eta_{i,j} = 0 \\ \alpha_{i,j}(\|\eta_{i,j}\|_h - 1) = 0 \\ \alpha_{i,j} \geq 0 \end{cases} \quad (10)$$

$\forall (i,j) \in \Omega$, from which follows that the Lagrange multipliers $\alpha_{i,j}$ satisfy

$$\alpha_{i,j} = \|\nabla_w^{NL}(\nabla_w^{NL*}\eta - \lambda u_0)_{i,j}\|_h.$$

We can then adapt Chambolle's projection algorithm in [11] to the minimization problem (9) and straightforward computations show that, if we consider the semi-implicit gradient descent

$$\eta^{n+1} = \frac{\eta^n - dt\,\nabla_w^{NL}(\nabla_w^{NL*}\eta^n - \lambda u_0)}{1 + dt\,\|\nabla_w^{NL}(\nabla_w^{NL*}\eta^n - \lambda u_0)\|_h}, \quad (11)$$

then the sequence $\frac{1}{\lambda}\nabla_w^{NL*}\eta^n$ converges towards $P_{K_{1/\lambda}}u_0$, assuming that $dt \leq 1/\|\nabla_w^{NL*}\|^2$.

3.2 Perceptual Color Correction

In [4], Bertalmío et al. propose the following variational model for performing perceptual correction of a color image $u_0 = (u_0^1, u_0^2, u_0^3)$

$$\arg\min_{u^k} \frac{\lambda}{2}\|u^k - u_0^k\|_{L^2}^2 + \frac{\beta}{2}\|u^k - 1/2\|_{L^2}^2 - \|\nabla_w^{NL}u^k\|_{L^1}, \quad k = 1,2,3 \quad (12)$$

They showed that the problem (12) has a solution in the discrete case. In order to construct a solution, they considered a regularized version of the problem (12) by regularizing the anisotropic total variation $\|\nabla_w^{NL} u^k\|_{L^1}$ and performed a gradient descent until reaching a steady-state.

In the following proposition, we show that we can express the solutions of the model (12) in the discrete case by assuming that they belong to the discrete space $L^2 \cap BV_w^{NL}(\Omega; \mathbb{R})$. We actually prove this result in the more general case of vector-valued functions.

Proposition 3. *Let X be the discrete space $L^2 \cap BV_w^{NL}(\Omega; \mathbb{R}^n)$, and $u_0, v \in X$. The solutions of the variational problem*

$$\arg\min_{u \in X} \frac{\lambda}{2} \|u - u_0\|_{L^2}^2 + \frac{\beta}{2} \|u - v\|_{L^2}^2 - VTV_w^{NL}(u) \qquad (13)$$

are

$$\underline{u} = \frac{1}{\lambda + \beta}(\lambda u_0 + \beta v) - \arg\max_{u^* \in K_{\frac{1}{\lambda+\beta}}} \left\| \frac{1}{\lambda + \beta}(\lambda u_0 + \beta v) - u^* \right\|_{L^2}^2, \qquad (14)$$

where $K_{\frac{1}{\lambda+\beta}}$ is the discretization of the space $K_{\frac{1}{\lambda+\beta}}$ defined in (4).

Proof. Let us first observe that the problem (13) is equivalent to

$$\arg\min_{u \in X} \frac{\lambda + \beta}{2} \left\| u - \frac{1}{\lambda + \beta}(\lambda u_0 + \beta v) \right\|_{L^2}^2 - VTV_w^{NL}(u). \qquad (15)$$

The problem (15) is of the form

$$\inf_{u \in V} \{G(u) - F(u)\}, \qquad (16)$$

where F and G are two lower semi-continuous functionals on a reflexive Banach space V such that F is convex and G satisfies $G(u)/\|u\| \to \infty$ as $\|u\| \to \infty$. Then according to Theorem 2.7 in [24], if $\underline{u}^*$ is a solution of the dual problem

$$\inf_{u^* \in V^*} \{F^*(u^*) - G^*(u^*)\}, \qquad (17)$$

then there exists a solution $\underline{u}$ of the primal problem (16), and the solutions of both problems are connected by the formulas

$$F(\underline{u}) + F^*(\underline{u}^*) = (\underline{u}, \underline{u}^*) \qquad (18)$$

$$G(\underline{u}) + G^*(\underline{u}^*) = (\underline{u}, \underline{u}^*). \qquad (19)$$

Hence, the problem (13) can be solved through its dual problem (17).

The convex conjugate of the functional

$$G: u \longmapsto \frac{\lambda + \beta}{2} \left\| u - \frac{1}{\lambda + \beta}(\lambda u_0 + \beta v) \right\|_{L^2}^2$$

is
$$G^*: u^* \longmapsto \frac{1}{2(\lambda+\beta)}\left[\|u^*\|_{L^2}^2 + 2(u^*, \lambda u_0 + \beta v)\right]. \tag{20}$$

The functional $F := VTV_w^{NL}$ being one homogeneous, proper, lower semi-continuous and convex, its convex conjugate F^* is the indicator function $\chi_{\mathcal{K}_1}$ of the set $\mathcal{K}_1$, which is the discretization of the set $\mathcal{K}_1$ defined in (4). Then, the dual problem (17) reads

$$\underset{u^* \in X}{\arg\min} \ \chi_{\mathcal{K}_1}(u^*) - \frac{1}{2(\lambda+\beta)}\left[\|u^*\|_{L^2}^2 + 2(u^*, \lambda u_0 + \beta v)\right]. \tag{21}$$

The functional (21) is bounded from below and coercive since X is a subspace of the discrete space $L^2(\Omega; \mathbb{R}^n)$, and Theorem 2.9 in [24] guarantees then that the problem (21) has a solution $\underline{u}^*$. The dual problem can then be rewritten

$$\underline{u}^* = \underset{u^* \in \mathcal{K}_1}{\arg\max} \ \|u^*\|_{L^2}^2 + 2(u^*, \lambda u_0 + \beta v). \tag{22}$$

Modifying the coefficients of the terms $\|u_0\|$ and $\|v\|$ does not affect the problem (22), hence we can write

$$\underline{u}^* = \underset{u^* \in \mathcal{K}_1}{\arg\max} \ \|u^*\|_{L^2}^2 + 2(u^*, \lambda u_0 + \beta v) + \|\lambda u_0 + \beta v_0\|_{L^2}^2 \tag{23}$$

i.e.

$$\underline{u}^* = \underset{u^* \in \mathcal{K}_1}{\arg\max} \ \|\lambda u_0 + \beta v + u^*\|_{L^2}^2, \tag{24}$$

which is equivalent to

$$\underline{u}^* = -\underset{u^* \in \mathcal{K}_1}{\arg\max} \ \|\lambda u_0 + \beta v - u^*\|_{L^2}^2. \tag{25}$$

Finally, we deduce from (19) and (20) that the solutions $\underline{u}$ of the original problem (13) are

$$\underline{u} = \frac{1}{\lambda+\beta}\left[\lambda u_0 + \beta v + \underline{u}^*\right],$$

which is equivalent to the expression (14). □

We have

$$\underset{u^* \in \mathcal{K}_1}{\arg\max} \ \|\lambda u_0 + \beta v - u^*\|_{L^2}^2 = \nabla_w^{NL*}\underline{\eta}, \text{ where } \underline{\eta} = \underset{\eta, \|\eta\|_h \leq 1}{\arg\max} \ \|\lambda u_0 + \beta v - \nabla_w^{NL*}\eta\|_{L^2}. \tag{26}$$

The Karush-Kuhn-Tucker conditions for the maximization problem

$$\underset{\eta, \|\eta\|_h \leq 1}{\arg\max} \|\lambda u_0 + \beta v - \nabla_w^{NL*}\eta\|_{L^2} \tag{27}$$

are

$$\begin{cases} \nabla_w^{NL}(\nabla_w^{NL*}\eta - (\lambda u_0 + \beta v))_{i,j} - \alpha_{i,j}\eta_{i,j} = 0 \\ \alpha_{i,j}(\|\eta_{i,j}\|_h - 1) = 0 \\ \alpha_{i,j} \geq 0 \end{cases} \tag{28}$$

$\forall (i,j) \in \Omega$, from which follows that the Lagrange multipliers $\alpha_{i,j}$ satisfy

$$\alpha_{i,j} = \|\nabla_w^{NL}(\nabla_w^{NL*}\eta - (\lambda u_0 + \beta v))_{i,j}\|_h.$$

We deduce from the Karush-Kuhn-Tucker conditions (28) that we can adapt Chambolle's projection algorithm in [11] to the maximization problem (27): we consider the following semi-implicit gradient ascent

$$\eta^{n+1} = \frac{\eta^n + dt\,\nabla_w^{NL}(\nabla_w^{NL*}\eta^n - (\lambda u_0 + \beta v))}{1 + dt\,\|\nabla_w^{NL}(\nabla_w^{NL*}\eta^n - (\lambda u_0 + \beta v))\|_h}, \quad (29)$$

and a computation similar to the one done in the proof of Theorem 3.1.in [11] shows that the sequence $\|\lambda u_0 + \beta v - \nabla_w^{NL*}\eta^n\|$ is strictly increasing with n unless the sequence (29) reaches a fixed point η, which is either a local or global maximum. Indeed, we have

$$\eta^{n+1} = \eta^n \implies \nabla_w^{NL}(\nabla_w^{NL*}\eta - (\lambda u_0 + \beta v))_{i,j} - \alpha_{i,j}\eta_{i,j} = 0 \quad \forall (i,j) \in \Omega$$

and unlike minima, local maxima of convex functions are not necessarily global.

It can also be shown that any converging subsequence η^{n_k} of η^n converges towards a fixed point, i.e. a local maximum. Hence, the sequence η^n possesses local maxima as adherent points.

4 A New Insight on the Two Variational Problems

4.1 Duality Principle for a Reinterpretation of the Models

We showed in section 3.1 that the regularization model of Gilboa and Osher [15] based on the so-called **anisotropic nonlocal total variation** has also a dual formulation, that yields the following expression of its unique solution $\underline{u}_R$:

$$\underline{u}_R = u_0 - \arg\min_{u^* \in K_{1/\lambda}} \|u_0 - u^*\|_{L^2}^2, \quad (30)$$

where the functional space $K_{1/\lambda}$ is the closure of the space $\mathcal{K}_{1/\lambda}$ defined in (4). The spaces $\mathcal{K}_{1/\lambda}$, for $\lambda \in \mathbb{R}$, can be viewed as subspaces of the space

$$G_w^{NL} := \{\nabla_w^{NL*}\eta \colon \eta \in L^\infty(\Omega \times \Omega; \mathbb{R}^n)\}, \quad (31)$$

which has been introduced by Gilboa and Osher [15] in the scalar case, as a nonlocal extension of the Meyer's space of oscillating patterns [19]. They interpret the space G_w^{NL} as characterizing irregular and random (scalar-valued) patterns. Assuming that the conjecture is true, our dual formulation (30) provides a better understanding of the original model: it consists in removing the main irregular and random patterns of the image u_0, the measure of irregularity and randomness being given by both the scalar λ and the function w.

Note that this conclusion had already been provided by Gilboa and Osher when the anisotropic nonlocal total variation in the regularization model is replaced by the **isotropic nonlocal total variation**. We then deduce that the difference between the two regularization models holds in the measure of irregularity and randomness of the patterns.

We showed in section 3.2 that the discrete perceptual color correction model of Bertalmío et al. (12) possesses a dual formulation too, from which derive a novel expression of its solutions $\underline{u}_{CE} = (\underline{u}_{CE}^1, \underline{u}_{CE}^2, \underline{u}_{CE}^3)$, given, for $k = 1, 2, 3$, by

$$\underline{u}_{CE}^k = \frac{1}{\lambda+\beta}(\lambda u_0^k + \beta/2) - \arg\max_{u^\star \in K_{\frac{1}{\lambda+\beta}}} \left\| \frac{1}{\lambda+\beta}(\lambda u_0^k + \beta/2) - u^\star \right\|_{L^2}^2, \qquad (32)$$

where $K_{\frac{1}{\lambda+\beta}}$ denotes here the discretization of the space $\mathcal{K}_{\frac{1}{\lambda+\beta}}$ defined in (4).

We then deduce that the model (12) can be decomposed into two steps:

1. It first performs global color constancy of the original image $u_0 = (u_0^1, u_0^2, u_0^3)$ through the functions

$$\frac{1}{\lambda+\beta}(\lambda u_0^k + \beta/2), \qquad k = 1, 2, 3. \qquad (33)$$

Indeed, a straightforward computation shows that $(\lambda u_0^k + \beta/2)/(\lambda + \beta)$ is closer to $1/2$ than u_0^k, $\forall k \in \{1, 2, 3\}$, meaning that the color cast of u_0 has been reduced (see [20] for details).

2. It performs contrast enhancement of the color corrected image (33) by removing the most distant element in the space $K_{\frac{1}{\lambda+\beta}}$ of each of its channel, given by

$$\arg\max_{u^\star \in K_{\frac{1}{\lambda+\beta}}} \left\| \frac{1}{\lambda+\beta}(\lambda u_0^k + \beta/2) - u^\star \right\|_{L^2}^2, \qquad k = 1.2.3, \qquad (34)$$

where $K_{\frac{1}{\alpha+\beta}}$ has been interpreted above as a subspace of a nonlocal extension of the Meyer's space of oscillating patterns.

4.2 Applications

We apply on a color image (Fig. 1(a)) the proposed vectorial extensions of the regularization model of Gilboa and Osher [15], whose unique solution is given in (8), and the perceptual color correction model of Bertalmío et al. [4], whose solutions are given in (14). On this latter model, we have set the constant β to 0, i.e. we reduce the model to enhance the contrast of the original image. Then, taking the same values for the other parameters, both models only differ by the sign of the nonlocal total variation, and their solutions only differ by the element taken in the discrete set $K_{\frac{1}{\lambda}}$, whose continuous version is defined in (4).

In the experiment we perform, the parameter λ has been set to 0.05, and the definite positive quadratic form h is nothing but the Euclidean metric in the RGB color space. The symmetric positive function w has been chosen as

(a) Image u_0 (tone-mapped version of the high dynamic range image "507" in the database [13])

(b) Regularization $\underline{u}_R$ of u_0    (c) Contrast enhancement $\underline{u}_{CE}$ of u_0

(d) Negative component of $u_0 - \underline{u}_R$    (e) Negative component of $u_0 - \underline{u}_{CE}$

(f) Positive component of $u_0 - \underline{u}_R$    (g) Positive component of $u_0 - \underline{u}_{CE}$

Fig. 1. Comparison between the proposed vectorial extensions $\underline{u}_R$ of the regularization model of Gilboa and Osher [15] and $\underline{u}_{CE}$ of the second step (contrast enhancement) of the perceptual color correction model of Bertalmío et al. [4]. Intensity values of the figures (d),(e),(f),(g) have been multiplied by 10 in order to improve the visibility.

the 2D Gaussian kernel of variance 2000 that we have truncated by setting the values $w(x,y)$ to 0 if y is not in the 15×15 neighborhood of x, the aim of this procedure being to reduce the complexity of the algorithm. We use the same stopping criteria for both algorithms (11) and (29), which is

$$\|\eta^{n+1} - \eta^n\|_{L^2} < 0.001$$

Results are respectively shown on Fig. 1(b) and Fig. 1(c). We also show the differences between the results and the original image, which are elements of the discrete set $K_{\frac{1}{\lambda}}$. In both models, we observe that the negative part (Fig. 1(d,e)) tends to vanish where the positive part (Fig. 1(f,g)) does not vanish and vice versa. We also observe that the negative component in the regularization model behaves like the positive component in the contrast enhancement model and vice versa, which is coherent with the fact that the models only differ by the sign of the anisotropic nonlocal total variation. Note that by our choice of the parameter w, the regularization model is acting as a contrast reduction model, which is actually the vectorial extension of the model used by Zamir et al. [25] for color gamut reduction purpose.

Finally, we would like to point out that the contrast enhancement model can produce values out of the range $[0, 255]$ if the parameter λ is taken too small.

5 Conclusion

In this paper, we have constructed dual formulations of two existing image processing variational models, namely the image regularization model of Gilboa and Osher [15] and the perceptual color correction model of Bertalmío et al. [4]. Using these dual formulations, we have been able to reinterpret their solutions, providing a new insight on these models.

Further work will be devoted to investigate whether the nonlocal space (4) that came out from our dual formulations has a perceptual interpretation. Moreover, inspired by the local case with the work of Meyer [19] on the space of oscillating patterns, we expect that there exists a norm on the space (4) that would yield a better perceptual color correction than the L2 norm in (34).

References

1. Awate, S.P., Whitaker, R.T.: Unsupervised, information-theoretic, adaptive image filtering for image restoration. IEEE Trans. Pattern Anal. Mach. Intell. **28**(3), 364–376 (2006)
2. Batard, T., Bertalmío, M.: On covariant derivatives and their applications to image regularization. SIAM J. Imaging Sci. **7**(4), 2393–2422 (2014)
3. Bertalmío, M.: Image Processing for Cinema. Chapman & Hall/CRC (2014)
4. Bertalmío, M., Casselles, V., Provenzi, E., Rizzi, A.: Perceptual color correction through variational techniques. IEEE Trans. Im. Processing **16**(4), 1058–1072 (2007)

5. Bertalmío, M., Caselles, V., Provenzi, E.: Issues about Retinex theory and contrast enhancement. Int. J. Computer Vision **83**, 101–119 (2009)
6. Bertalmío, M., Cowan, J.D.: Implementing the Retinex algorithm with Wilson-Cowan equations. J. Physiology **103**, 69–72 (2009)
7. Bredies, K., Kunish, K., Pock, T.: Total generalized variation. SIAM J. Imaging Sci. **3**(3), 492–526 (2010)
8. Bresson, X., Chan, T.F.: Fast dual minimization of the vectorial total variation norm and applications to color image processing. Inverse Probl. Imaging **2**(4), 455–484 (2008)
9. Buades, A., Coll, B., Morel, J.-M.: A non-local algorithm for image denoising. Proceedings of CVPR **2**, 60–65 (2005)
10. Buchsbaum, G.: A spatial processor model for object color perception. J. Franklin Inst. **310**(1), 1–26 (1980)
11. Chambolle, A.: An algorithm for total variation minimization and applications. J. Math. Imaging Vision **20**, 89–97 (2004)
12. Chambolle, A., Caselles, V., Cremers, D., Novaga, M., Pock, T.: An introduction to total variation for image analysis. Theoretical Foundations and Numerical Methods for Sparse Recovery **9**, 263–340 (2010)
13. http://rit-mcsl.org/fairchild/HDR.html
14. Ferradans, S., Bertalmío, M., Provenzi, E., Caselles, V.: An analysis of visual adaptation and contrast perception for tone mapping. IEEE Trans. Pattern Anal. Mach. Intell. **33**(10), 2002–2012 (2011)
15. Gilboa, G., Osher, S.: Nonlocal operators with applications to image processing. Multiscale Model. Simul. **7**(3), 1005–1028 (2008)
16. Goldluecke, B., Strekalovskiy, E., Cremers, D.: The natural vectorial total variation which arises from geometric measure theory. SIAM J. Imaging Sci. **5**, 537–563 (2012)
17. Jin, Y., Jost, J., Wang, G.: A new nonlocal H^1 model for image denoising. J. Math. Imaging Vision **48**(1), 93–105 (2014)
18. Kindermann, S., Osher, S., Jones, P.W.: Deblurring and denoising of images by nonlocal functionals. Multiscale Model. Simul. 1091–1115 (2005)
19. Meyer, Y.: Oscillating Patterns in Image Processing and in some Nonlinear Evolution Equations. The Fifteenth Dean Jacqueline B, Lewis Memorial Lectures (2001)
20. Palma-Amestoy, R., Provenzi, E., Bertalmío, M., Caselles, V.: A perceptually inspired variational framework for color enhancement. IEEE Trans. Pattern Anal. Mach. Intell. **31**(3), 458–474 (2009)
21. Rockafellar, R.T.: Convex Analysis. Princeton University Press (1970)
22. Rudin, L.I., Osher, S., Fatemi, E.: Nonlinear total variation based noise removal algorithms. Physica D **60**, 259–268 (1992)
23. Sapiro, G., Caselles, V.: Histogram modification via differential equations. J. Differential Equations **135**, 238–268 (1997)
24. Toland, J.F.: A duality principle for non-convex optimisation and the calculus of variations. Archiv. Rational Mech. Analysis **71**(1), 41–61 (1979)
25. Zamir, S.W., Vazquez-Corral, J., Bertalmío, M.: Gamut mapping in cinematography through perceptually-based contrast modification. J. Sel. Topics Signal Processing **8**(3), 490–503 (2014)
26. Zosso, D., Tran, G., Osher, S.: Non-local Retinex- A unifying framework and beyond. SIAM J. Imaging Sci. (to appear)

PDE-Based Color Morphology Using Matrix Fields

Ali Sharifi Boroujerdi[1(✉)], Michael Breuß[1], Bernhard Burgeth[2], and Andreas Kleefeld[1]

[1] Faculty of Mathematics, Natural Sciences and Computer Science, Brandenburg Technical University Cottbus-Senftenberg, 03046 Cottbus, Germany
{boroujerdi,breuss,kleefeld}@tu-cottbus.de

[2] Department of Mathematics and Computer Science, Saarland University, 66123 Saarbrücken, Germany
burgeth@math.uni-sb.de

Abstract. In this work, we propose a novel way for performing operations of mathematical morphology on color images. To this end, we convert pixelwise the *rgb*-values into symmetric 2×2 matrices. The new color space can be interpreted geometrically as a biconal color space structure. Motivated by the formulation of the fundamental morphological operations dilation and erosion in terms of partial differential equations (PDEs), we show how to define finite difference schemes making use of the matrix field formulation. The computation of a pseudo supremum and a pseudo infimum of three color matrices is a crucial step for setting up advanced PDE-based methods. We show that this can be achieved for our goal by an algebraic technique. We investigate our approach by dedicated experiments and confirm useful properties of the new PDE-based color morphology operations.

Keywords: PDE-based morphology · Matrix fields · Color morphology · Finite difference schemes · FCT scheme · Pseudo supremum · Pseudo infimum

1 Introduction

In modern digital imagery color images are very common, as e.g. smartphones often feature a digital camera yielding color images. With abundant sources of available color information, it becomes increasingly important to consider this information in the construction of image processing tools.

A fundamental class of image analysis processes are the methods of mathematical morphology pioneered by Serra and Matheron [16,22]. Morphological processing is a nonlinear method consisting of operations on sets of pixels arranged in structuring elements. The building blocks of mathematical morphology for gray-scale images are the processes of *dilation* and *erosion*. Many other processes such as opening, closing, top hats, and other morphological operators such as derivatives can be derived from these two operations.

Considering the important underlying mathematical structure of these operations, it is required that one can define a total order of the values contributing in a structuring element. While for gray-scale images the corresponding lattice theory framework is satisfactory and adequate, the extension of this concept to work with colors is difficult because of the lack of a total order for vector-valued data such as *rgb* values. Therefore, performing even the simplest morphological operation on color images is not trivial.

There have been numerous attempts to establish a morphological framework for color images. Generally speaking, the use of ranking schemes and properly defined extremal operators as substitutes for maxima and minima are the main building blocks in these attempts, see e.g. [3,12,13,23]. For a conceptually different development, let us mention here the approach by Van de Gronde *et al.* [14] that relies on a partial order rather than a total order. However, one may conclude that the optimal way to define morphological operations on color images is still an open issue and that a proper solution might depend on the purpose of the filtering.

In this paper, we tackle the issue from a different point of view. To this end, we combine two existing approaches to mathematical morphology in order to formulate our novel strategy for color image morphology.

The first approach we consider is the formulation of dilation and erosion in terms of partial differential equations (PDEs), see [2,4,6,19,21]. Mimicking a special wave propagation process, the arising PDEs are hyperbolic Hamilton-Jacobi equations. Then, important numerical methods for discretizing the PDEs for dilation and erosion in the gray-value setting are the schemes of Rouy and Tourin [19], Osher and Sethian [18] and the flux-corrected transport (FCT) scheme of Breuß and Weickert [5]. Motivated by these developments and driven by an interest to filter data arising in diffusion tensor magnetic resonance imaging (DT-MRI), the PDE-based approach as well as the above mentioned schemes have been generalised to deal with specific matrix fields, see e.g. [7,8] and the references therein. The matrices defining the data for these PDE-based morphological methods are symmetric, positive semi-definite and of size three times three.

Secondly, we consider the developments in the recent work [11]. There, color images are embedded into matrix fields consisting of symmetric 2×2 matrices. For these, matrix-based operations are described that mimic dilation and erosion in the spirit of the classical, set-theoretic approach.

As indicated we combine in this work the above mentioned developments in defining PDE-based methods for mathematical morphology of color images. We employ the framework presented in [11] to transform *rgb* data into a biconeshaped color space that corresponds to symmetric 2×2 matrices. For such matrices we define finite difference schemes that describe in the discrete sense the PDEs of morphological dilation/erosion.

While on the technical side this translation of the schemes as described e.g. in [7] to the color matrix framework seems at a first glance to be relatively straightforward, let us comment on several issues. First, let us note that the matrices we deal with here are not positive semidefinite. Thus, taking over technical parts from methods developed in the aforementioned DT-MRI context may not lead to useful results. Secondly, and as a technical difference to the proceeding in [11], we do not employ here the procedures of addition and subtraction motivated by Einstein addition in Hilbert spaces. Furthermore, and again in the light of the many attempts in previous literature [3,12,13,23], let us stress that it is not at all self-evident that one obtains reasonable numerical results when constructing a method for the purpose of color morphology. However, for our approach we confirm experimentally that it does not give so-called false colors, cf. [23]. This means, that our PDE-based dilation and erosion processes may only lead to color modifications in the sense that they appear in higher and lower saturated versions of contributing colors, and not as a completely different color.

Paper Organisation. In accordance to the described paper contents, in Section 2 some background on the basic morphological operators is presented. In Section 3, the PDE concept behind our approach is introduced. Section 4 is devoted to recalling the transfer of *rgb* images to matrix fields. In Section 5, the solution of finding pseudo suprema and infima of three matrices is discussed which we need to define numerical schemes. Section 6 contains experimental results. We conclude the paper with some remarks in Section 7.

2 Morphological Operations and PDEs

Morphological Operations. We first give a brief account of the two operations that are at the basis of our developments, namely morphological dilation and erosion. As we seek to emphasize the underlying ideas here, we stick to a simple presentation.

A structuring element E is a mask that allows us to specify neighborhood structures in an image. Then one may use SEs to define morphological operators acting on them. For a given, initial image f we write the *dilation* and the *erosion* with such a structuring element E as

$$f \oplus E := \sup\{f(x - x', y - y') \,|\, (x', y') \in E\} \quad \text{and} \tag{1}$$
$$f \ominus E := \inf\{f(x - x', y - y') \,|\, (x', y') \in E\} \tag{2}$$

respectively. Making use of these building blocks, one can define e.g. morphological derivative operators. One which is useful in the context of this work is the so-called *morphological Laplacian* [23] which reads as

$$\Delta_E f := (f \oplus E) - 2f + (f \ominus E) \tag{3}$$

As it is evident, the morphological Laplacian is a morphological counterpart of the second derivative of a function. It allows to distinguish regions influenced by brightness minima and maxima in an image. This is useful for defining so-called *shock filters*, see e.g. [17]. In the gray-value setting, one step of shock filtering applied pixelwise at an image f may be described as

$$S_E f := \begin{cases} f \oplus E, & \Delta_E f < 0 \\ f, & \Delta_E f = 0 \\ f \ominus E, & \Delta_E f > 0 \end{cases} \tag{4}$$

As can be seen by considering (4), shock filtering amounts to applying dilation and erosion in order to enlarge brightness maxima and minima, respectively, while the transition line between these regions is managed by the morphological Laplacian. In a PDE-based setting as already described in [17], the dilation and erosion PDEs are solved iteratively in accordance to the process (4).

PDEs for Mathematical Morphology. Thinking of a gray-valued image as a discrete representation of a continuous-scale function, some of the geometric characteristics of continuous morphology are omitted in its discrete version. As an example, the definition of a disk-shaped structuring element is easy in the continuous plane but especially on a small scale this is difficult or even impossible to realize conveniently on a discrete grid.

To this end, it is necessary to specify continuous mathematical morphology from the angle of curve evolution. By this method, discrete mathematical morphology can be interpreted as the numerical implementation of a continuous-scale evolution.

According to [20] dilation can be performed at infinitesimal steps. This motion generates a set of velocity vectors, one for each point on the boundary of the disk-shaped (or more generally, convex) structuring element. For this purpose, let us parameterize these vectors by the angle θ running over all possible angles about a central point in the plane, so that $\theta \in [0, 2\pi]$. For a given initial image $f := f(x,y)$, where (x,y) denotes a point in the image domain Ω, let $u := u(x,y,t)$ be the image evolving under the process of interest in time t. Then we have

$$\partial_t u = \sup_{\theta} \{R(\theta) \cdot \nabla u\}, \qquad (5)$$

where $R(\theta)$ is a function representing the boundary of the convex structuring element. In this way, the following velocities are obtained for popular structuring elements S:

$$\sup_{\theta} \{R(\theta) \cdot \nabla u\} = \begin{cases} \|\nabla u\|_1, & S = \text{diamond} \\ \|\nabla u\|_2, & S = \text{disk} \\ \|\nabla u\|_\infty, & S = \text{square} \end{cases} \qquad (6)$$

Focusing again on the use of a disk-shaped structuring element and generalising the process to include erosion, we obtain the PDEs for gray-value dilation (+) and erosion (−) as

$$\partial_t u = \pm \|\nabla u\|_2 = \pm \sqrt{(\partial_x u)^2 + (\partial_y u)^2} \quad \text{on} \quad \Omega \times (0, \infty) \qquad (7)$$

which we supplement by Neumann boundary conditions

$$\partial_n u = 0 \quad \text{on} \quad \partial \Omega \times (0, \infty) \qquad (8)$$

and the initial condition defined by an input image f

$$u(x,y,0) := f(x,y) \quad \forall (x,y) \in \Omega \qquad (9)$$

While it is possible to describe already at this point a matrix-valued counterpart of the PDEs as in (7) as can be seen in [7,8], we refrain from this here for shortness of presentation.

3 Numerical Methods for the PDEs of Dilation and Erosion

In this part, we briefly survey the schemes mentioned in the introduction that we will also consider here for realizing our PDE-based approach. These are the first-order accurate *Rouy-Tourin (RT)* scheme which is proposed in [19], the second-order method of *Osher and Sethian (OS)* [18], and as a state-of-the-art approach we consider the *flux corrected transport (FCT)* algorithm [5].

Notice that we apply the symbol of $u_{i,j}^n$ as the gray-value of the evolving image u at the pixel located in the ith row and j^{th} column of the image at the nth time step during the morphological progress. We recall standard notations for backward and forward differences in x- and y-directions as follows:

$$D_-^x u_{i,j}^n = u_{i,j}^n - u_{i-1,j}^n, \quad D_+^x u_{i,j}^n = u_{i+1,j}^n - u_{i,j}^n,$$
$$D_-^y u_{i,j}^n = u_{i,j}^n - u_{i,j-1}^n, \quad D_+^y u_{i,j}^n = u_{i,j+1}^n - u_{i,j}^n \tag{10}$$

Let us now consider a uniform pixel width h in both spatial grid directions in an image and a numerical time step size τ for the evolution. Our aim is now to discretise the PDE (7), sticking thereby for the presentation here to the case of *dilation* with a disk-shaped structuring element.

Then, in the *RT scheme*, the dilation operation is expressed by

$$u_{i,j}^{n+1} = u_{i,j}^n + \frac{\tau}{h}\sqrt{(\max(0, D_+^x u_{i,j}^n, -D_-^x u_{i,j}^n))^2 + (\max(0, D_+^y u_{i,j}^n, -D_-^y u_{i,j}^n))^2} \tag{11}$$

while the second-order *OS method* is given by

$$u_{i,j}^{n+1} = \frac{u_{i,j}^n}{2} + \frac{u_{i,j}^{-n+1}}{2} + \frac{\tau}{2h} L\left(u^{-n+1}, i, j\right)) \tag{12}$$

where

$$u_{i,j}^{-n+1} = u_{i,j}^n + \frac{\tau}{h} L\left(u^n, i, j\right)) \tag{13}$$

and

$$L(u^n, i, j) = \Big[\left(\min\left\{D_-^x u_{i,j}^n + \tfrac{1}{2}\mathrm{mm}(D_-^x D_+^x u_{i,j}^n, D_-^x D_-^x u_{i,j}^n), 0\right\}\right)^2$$
$$+ \left(\max\left\{D_+^x u_{i,j}^n - \tfrac{1}{2}\mathrm{mm}(D_+^x D_+^x u_{i,j}^n, D_-^x D_+^x u_{i,j}^n), 0\right\}\right)^2 \tag{14}$$
$$+ \left(\min\left\{D_-^y u_{i,j}^n + \tfrac{1}{2}\mathrm{mm}(D_-^y D_+^y u_{i,j}^n, D_-^y D_-^y u_{i,j}^n), 0\right\}\right)^2$$
$$+ \left(\max\left\{D_+^y u_{i,j}^n - \tfrac{1}{2}\mathrm{mm}(D_+^y D_+^y u_{i,j}^n, D_-^y D_+^y u_{i,j}^n), 0\right\}\right)^2\Big]^{\frac{1}{2}}$$

The function $\mathrm{mm}(\cdot, \cdot)$ indicates the *minmod function* which is given as

$$\mathrm{mm}(\alpha, \beta) := \begin{cases} \max(\alpha, \beta), & \alpha < 0, \beta < 0 \\ \min(\alpha, \beta), & \alpha > 0, \beta > 0 \\ 0, & \text{otherwise} \end{cases} \tag{15}$$

Let us also give a brief account of the *FCT scheme*. The main concept in the FCT scheme is to use the RT scheme in a *predictor step* in a first phase. Then the unwanted blurring effects generated by the first-order upwind derivatives in the RT scheme are measured to reverse the associated quantity in a *corrector step* that performs stabilized inverse diffusion.

Let us now write the values obtained after the predictor step performed by the RT scheme in the format $u_{i,j}^p$ at pixel (i,j). With the definitions

$$g_{i+1/2,j} := \mathrm{mm}\left(D_-^x u_{i,j}^p, \frac{\tau}{2h} D_+^x u_{i,j}^p, D_+^x u_{i+1,j}^p\right), \tag{16}$$

$$g_{i,j+1/2} := \mathrm{mm}\left(D_-^y u_{i,j}^p, \frac{\tau}{2h} D_+^y u_{i,j}^p, D_+^y u_{i,j+1}^p\right), \tag{17}$$

where $\mathrm{mm}(\cdot,\cdot,\cdot)$ is a straightforward extension of (15) and

$$Q_h := \sqrt{\left(\frac{\tau}{2h}|u_{i+1,j}^p - u_{i-1,j}^p|\right)^2 + \left(\frac{\tau}{2h}|u_{i,j+1}^p - u_{i,j-1}^p|\right)^2}, \tag{18}$$

$$Q_l := \sqrt{(\delta u_i^p)^2 + (\delta u_j^p)^2}, \tag{19}$$

where the stabilized inverse diffusive fluxes are given by

$$u_i^p := \frac{\tau}{2h}|u_{i+1,j}^p - u_{i-1,j}^p| + g_{i+1/2,j} - g_{i-1/2,j}, \tag{20}$$

$$u_j^p := \frac{\tau}{2h}|u_{i,j+1}^p - u_{i,j-1}^p| + g_{i,j+1/2} - g_{i,j-1/2}, \tag{21}$$

we can write the subsequent *corrector step* of the FCT scheme as

$$u_{i,j}^{n+1} = u_{i,j}^p + Q_h - Q_l \tag{22}$$

To summarise, a subsequent application of scheme (11) for obtaining predicted data $u_{i,j}^p$ – instead of $u_{i,j}^{n+1}$ in (11) – and the corrector step (22) making use of the predicted values is equivalent to the FCT scheme.

Finite Difference Methods for Dilation/Erosion of Color Data. Finally, our aim is to work with fields of symmetric 2×2 matrices which represent color data instead of gray-values. For the definition of corresponding numerical schemes, we proceed in a straightforward fashion building upon (10)–(22). Instead of the evolving gray-values $u_{i,j}^n$ we will plug in the 2×2 matrices $U_{i,j}^n$, with $U_{i,j}^0 := f_{i,j}$ where f corresponds to a given color image. This implicitly defines underlying color-valued PDEs.

Obviously, in order to give a meaning to the formulae (10)–(22) in the latter setting, we must define suitable notions for maximum and minimum of up to three matrices, and we must give useful expressions for the square root and the absolute value of occuring matrices. This will be done in Section 5.

4 Color Images and Matrix Fields

In this section, we briefly recall the conversion of *rgb* values to matrices as in [11]. Given an *rgb* image we transform it in two steps into a matrix field of equal dimensions, i.e. we assign each pixel of the image a symmetric 2×2 matrix.

In the first step, we transform the *rgb* color values to the *hcl* color space, assuming that red, green and blue intensities are normalized to $[0, 1]$. For a pixel with such intensities r, g, b, we obtain its hue h, chroma c and luminance l via $M = \max\{r, g, b\}$, $m = \min\{r, g, b\}$, $c = M - m$, $l = \frac{1}{2}(M + m)$, and $h = \frac{1}{6}(g-b)/M$ modulo 1 if $M = r$, $h = \frac{1}{6}(b-r)/M + \frac{1}{3}$ if $M = g$, $h = \frac{1}{6}(r-g)/M + \frac{2}{3}$ if $M = b$, cf. [1].

Replacing then luminance l with $\tilde{l} := 2l - 1$, and interpreting c, $2\pi h$, and $\tilde{l}$ as radial, angular and axial coordinates of a cylindrical coordinate system, we have a bijection from the unit cube of triples (r, g, b) onto a solid bi-cone, see Figure 1.

The bi-cone is then transformed to the Cartesian coordinates via $x = c \cos(2\pi h)$, $y = c \sin(2\pi h)$, $z = \tilde{l}$. The second step takes the coordinates (x, y, z) and maps them to symmetric matrices $A \in \mathrm{Sym}(2)$ via

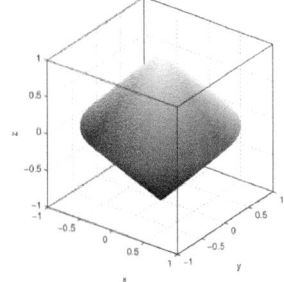

Fig. 1. Color bi-cone, figure adapted from [11]

$$A := \frac{\sqrt{2}}{2} \begin{pmatrix} z - y & x \\ x & z + y \end{pmatrix} \qquad (23)$$

Note that the mapping $\Psi : \mathbb{R}^3 \to \mathrm{Sym}(2)$ in (23) is bijective.

Denoting by $\mathcal{M} \subset \mathrm{Sym}(2)$ the set of all matrices A that correspond to points of the bi-cone, we have in fact by (23) a bijection between the *rgb* color space and the bi-cone $\mathcal{M}$. The inverse transform is obtained in a straightforward way, cf. [11].

5 Pseudo Supremum and Infimum and Functions of Matrices

As indicated at the end of Section 3, we need to give meaning to the maximum and minimum of up to three matrices of $\mathrm{Sym}(2)$, as well as to the square root and the absolute value of such matrices. Thereby we rely on corresponding notions as discussed e.g. in [7].

Let us recall that any matrix $A \in \mathrm{Sym}(2)$ can be decomposed into the format $A = V \mathrm{diag}(\lambda_1, \lambda_2) V^\top$ where $V := (v_1, v_2)$ accumulates the eigenvectors v_1, v_2 of A as column vectors and $\lambda_{1,2}$ denote the corresponding eigenvalues. Then one may define a function φ of a matrix A via

$$\varphi(A) := V \mathrm{diag}(\varphi(\lambda_1), \varphi(\lambda_2)) V^\top \qquad (24)$$

in terms of its standard scalar representation. With $\varphi(\cdot) = \sqrt{\cdot}$ and $\varphi(\cdot) = |\cdot|$ we thus obtain square root and absolute value of a symmetric matrix, respectively.

Regarding the formulae of numerical schemes in Section 3, we need to calculate the maximum and minimum of up to three symmetric matrices. It will turn out that instead of maximum and minimum we will seek a supremum and infimum, respectively, and it will suffice to elaborate in detail on the supremum.

Let us consider matrices $A, B, C \in \mathrm{Sym}(2)$. Determining the supremum of two such matrices can be done making use of (24) by

$$\sup(A, B) := \frac{A+B}{2} + \frac{|A-B|}{2} \qquad (25)$$

adopting a corresponding scalar relation. Obviously, we can proceed by

$$\begin{aligned} \sup_1 &:= \sup(A, \sup(B, C)), \\ \sup_2 &:= \sup(B, \sup(A, C)), \\ \sup_3 &:= \sup(C, \sup(A, B)) \end{aligned} \qquad (26)$$

But generally, for $A, B, C \in \mathrm{Sym}(2)$ we have

$$\sup_1 \neq \sup_2 \neq \sup_3 \neq \sup_1 \qquad (27)$$

Consequently, we approximate the supremum of $\{A, B, C\}$ by calculating the average of $\sup_1$, $\sup_2$ and $\sup_3$, as the $\sup_{avg}$ which is an upper bound of each initial matrix.

To improve this often very generous upper bound, we find the optimal value of $\eta \geq 0$ in such a way that

$$\sup_{avg} - \eta I \geq W, \qquad W \in \{A, B, C\}, \qquad (28)$$

where I is the 2×2 identity matrix. The optimal amount η_{opt} of η in (28) is the minimum eigenvalue of $(\sup_{avg} - A)$, $(\sup_{avg} - B)$, and $(\sup_{avg} - C)$. At the end of this process, we obtain a proper supremum of $\{A, B, C\}$ as

$$\sup_{opt}(A, B, C) := \sup_{avg} - \eta_{opt} I \qquad (29)$$

To obtain an infimum of three matrices, one may simply set

$$\inf_{opt}(A, B, C) := \sup_{opt}(-A, -B, -C) \qquad (30)$$

6 Experiments

As the first experiment we test if our color morphology operations retrieve grayscale morphology, since this may be considered a necessary condition to obtain a reasonable extension of the latter. To this end, we employ *rgb* values for black and white and use the new color-valued FCT scheme as described in Section 3. In Fig. 2 we exhibit the result of dilation and erosion on the *yin-yang* image of size 256×256.

Fig. 2. Centre. Input image yin-yang defined using *rgb* values for black and white. **Left.** Ten times dilation with color-valued FCT. **Right.** Ten times erosion with color-valued FCT.

Operations are performed ten times with time step size $\tau = 1/2$ and the disk-shaped stucturing element. As observed, outcomes are equivalent to gray-scale morphology.

In our second test we aim to observe dilation and erosion in color space with the RT scheme. The reasoning is here, that independently from its usefulness by its own the RT scheme serves as the basis of the FCT method and it is very similar to the first-order method that the OS scheme builds upon. Therefore, it is of fundamental importance for our PDE-based approach that the RT scheme yields reasonable results, as otherwise the more advanced OS and FCT schemes cannot be expected to do something valuable.

As observed in Fig. 3 we can confirm that the RT scheme performs as expected. Taking the classic *Lena* test image of resolution 128×128 as input image, we see that after six iterations of dilation and erosion with time step size $\tau = 1/2$ that bright and dark colors are enhanced, respectively. The blurring we observe here is the standard numerical artefacts resulting from the first-order upwind discretization. In an extension of these experiments, we compute the morphological Laplacian and show results of shock filtering based on our framework using also the RT scheme with $\tau = 1/2$. As observed, we obtain visually very plausible results for this process. Let us note that for the purpose of shock filtering the RT scheme is the optimal PDE-based method since the shock-filtering process is designed to give sharp edges.

Our next experiment serves two purposes. On the one hand we compare the quality of the numerical schemes RT, OS, and FCT in our new framework in order to see if the non-linear operations performed in the algorithms still give reasonable, interpretable results. On the other hand, we compare here with the method of Burgeth and Kleefeld (BK) [11] that is technically more similar to classic, lattice-based morphology than our PDE-based schemes. Let us emphasize in the latter context again, that the BK method employs the same color space yet with a different means of addition and subtraction of color matrices. Let us note that we employ in BK a cross-shaped structuring element here as the approximation of a disk on a 3×3 grid.

To this end, we employ a test image based on a micro biological scene, based on an oil painting of Carolyn K. Snyder. It is of resolution 128×128 and features diverse colors as well as round structures, see Fig. 4.

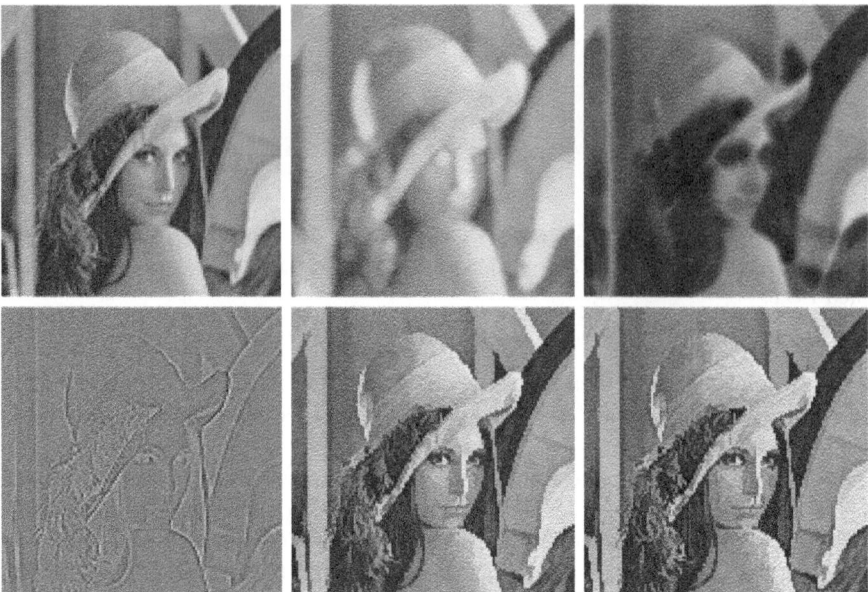

Fig. 3. Top row. Original *Lena* image, and results of dilation and erosion computed with the RT scheme. **Bottom row.** Morphological Laplacian and results of five and ten iterations of shock filtering with the RT scheme.

The results of our comparison are displayed in Fig. 5 where we show the images after several dilation steps. They show that all of the PDE-based methods give results of expected quality. The RT scheme yields a blurry dilated image and the FCT scheme very sharp edges while the OS method is somewhere in between those schemes. We also see no obvious color distortions, and round shapes evolve in a round way as by the underlying disk-shaped structuring element used for the PDE-based methods. In the result of the BK method for discrete morphology, we recognize the influence of the cross-shaped structuring

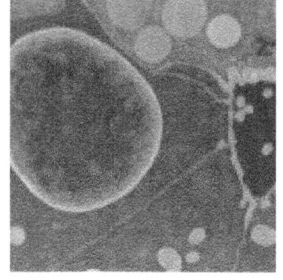

Fig. 4. Input image for comparison of numerical methods

element while we do not observe other color effects as in the results of the PDE-based schemes, although these employ different addition and subtraction rules. Note that the PDE-based FCT method gives visually as sharp edges as the BK method.

Our next and final experiment is dealing with the influence of the color space. Obviously, the value of the pseudo supremum resp. infimum of two colors in the dilation resp. erosion process is dependent on the location of those colors in the bi-conal color structure. Generally, the pseudo supremum of any color faced with

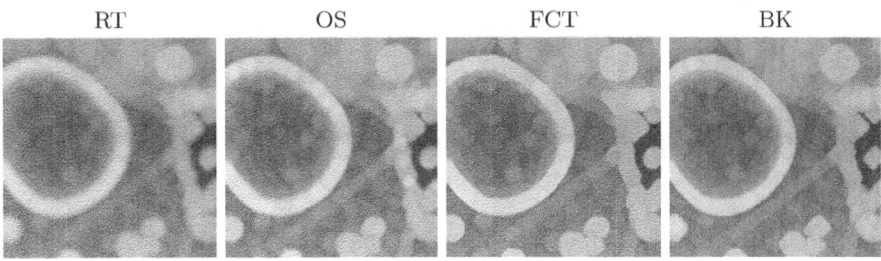

Fig. 5. Results of eight time steps dilation with $\tau = 1/2$ for indicated PDE-based schemes and in accordance four times erosion of BK method.

white is white and the pseudo infimum of any color faced with black is black. Thus we will not see any new appearing color at the edge to a black or white region.

Also in other cases, if one of the primary colors equals the pseudo supremum or infimum of them, then we do not have any color changes in the border of those colors during basic morphological operations. Some examples of this situation are indicated in Fig. 6 by yellow frames. But, if the pseudo supremum or infimum of the two colors equals another color, it appears as a modified color. Some situations like these are marked with black frames in Fig. 6. Note that the new colors are not false colors [23] but appear as more resp. less saturated versions of bordering colors.

Let us investigate this phenomenon at hand of an example dealing with the colors *light magenta (lm)*, *dark magenta (dm)* and *cyan (cy)*. Light magenta has the *rgb* values $(252, 58, 157)$, the numbers are $(217, 57, 153)$ for dark magenta,

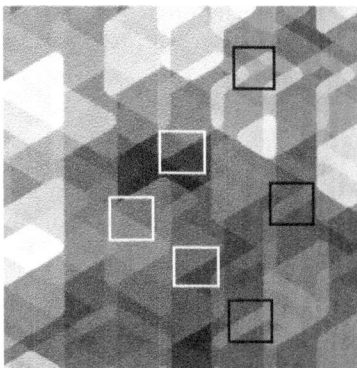

Fig. 6. Original image of size 256×256 (left) and result after five iterations of dilation using FCT with $\tau = 1/2$ and a disk-shaped structuring element. Black frames indicate new colors that appear by use of the supremum rule and the yellow ones mark color interaction without new colors.

and (62, 186, 212) for cyan. The equivalent matrices of these colors are as follows (entries rounded):

$$\text{lm} = \begin{bmatrix} 0.427 & 0.463 \\ 0.463 & -0.122 \end{bmatrix}, \quad \text{dm} = \begin{bmatrix} 0.314 & 0.359 \\ 0.359 & -0.208 \end{bmatrix}, \quad \text{cy} = \begin{bmatrix} 0.128 & -0.409 \\ -0.409 & -0.022 \end{bmatrix} \tag{31}$$

By computing corresponding pseudo suprema of two matrices, we obtain (rounded):

$$\sup(\text{lm},\text{dm}) = \begin{bmatrix} 0.429 & 0.461 \\ 0.461 & -0.119 \end{bmatrix}, \quad \sup(\text{dm},\text{cy}) = \begin{bmatrix} 0.616 & -0.025 \\ -0.025 & 0.280 \end{bmatrix} \tag{32}$$

The *rgb* amounts of the first pseudo supremum are (252, 59, 157), while in the second one we gain (200, 178, 239).

These observations show that during a dilation process, for the left inner edge as seen in Fig. 7, we have a color almost like light magenta which appears at the border as the extension of the light magenta color, while in the right inner border, a new color emerges as the supremum of the dark magenta and the cyan areas. However, observe also here that this is not a false color.

Fig. 7. Colors in the example

7 Conclusion

In this paper, we have proposed a new approach for implementing various morphological operators for color images using PDE-based methods. The numerical experiments done with Matlab show that we obtain qualitatively competitive results to a recent approach from the literature [11], while our approach offers the conceptual benefits of digital scalability and potential sub-pixel accuracy.

References

1. Agoston, M.K.: Computer Graphics and Geometric Modeling: Implementation and Algorithms. Springer, London (2005)
2. Alvarez, L., Guichard, F., Lions, P.-L., Morel, J.-M.: Axioms and fundamental equations in image processing. Archive for Rational Mechanics and Analysis **123**, 199–257 (1993)
3. Aptoula, E., Lefèvre, S.: A Comparative Study on Multivariate Mathematical Morphology. Pattern Recognition **40**(11), 2914–2929 (2007)
4. Arehart, A.B., Vincent, L., Kimia, B.B.: Mathematical morphology: The Hamilton-Jacobi connection. In: Proc. Fourth International Conference on Computer Vision pp. 215–219 (1993)
5. Breuß, M., Weickert, J.: A Shock-Capturing Algorithm for the Differential Equations of Dilation and Erosion. Journal of Mathematical Imaging and Vision **25**(2), 187–201 (2006)

6. Brockett, R.W., Maragos, P.: Evolution equations for continuous-scale morphology, In: Proc. IEEE International Conference on Acoustics, Speech and Signal Processing vol. 3, 125–128 (1992)
7. Burgeth, B., Breuß, M., Didas, S., Weickert, J.: PDE-based Morphology for Matrix Fields: Numerical Solution Schemes, Tensors in Image Processing and Computer Vision, pp. 125–150 (2009)
8. Burgeth, B., Bruhn, A., Didas, S., Weickert, J., Welk, M.: Morphology for tensor data: ordering versus PDE-based approach. Image and Vision Computing **25**(4), 496–511 (2007)
9. Burgeth, B., Kleefeld, A.: An approach to color-morphology based on Einstein addition and Loewner order. Pattern Recognition Letters **47**, 29–39 (2014)
10. Comer, M.L., Delp, E.J.: Morphological operations for color image processing. J. Electron. Imaging **8**(3), 279–289 (1999)
11. Goutsias, J., Heijmans, H.J.A.M., Sivakumar, K.: Morphological operators for image sequences. Computer Vision and Image Understanding **62**, 326–346 (1995)
12. van de Gronde, Jasper J., Roerdink, Jos B.T.M.: Group-invariant frames for colour morphology. In: Hendriks, Cris LLuengo, Borgefors, Gunilla, Strand, Robin (eds.) ISMM 2013. LNCS, vol. 7883, pp. 267–278. Springer, Heidelberg (2013)
13. Haralick, R.M., Sternberg, S.R., Zhuang, X.: Image analysis using mathematical morphology. IEEE Trans. Pattern Anal, Machine Intell **9**(4), 532–550 (1987)
14. Matheron, G.: Eléments Pour une Thorie des Milieux Poreux. Masson, Paris (1967)
15. Osher, S., Rudin, L.I.: Feature-oriented image enhancement using shock filters. SIAM Journal on Numerical Analysis **27**, 919–940 (1990)
16. Osher, S., Sethian, J.A.: Fronts propagating with curvature-dependent speed: algorithms based on Hamilton-Jacobi formulations. J. of Computational Physics **79**, 12–49 (1988)
17. Rouy, E., Tourin, A.: A viscosity solutions approach to shape-from-shading. SIAM Journal on Numerical Analysis **29**, 867–884 (1992)
18. G. Sapiro, Geometric Partial Differential Equations and Image Analysis, pp. 96–102. Cambridge University Press (2001)
19. Sapiro, G., Kimmel, R., Shaked, D., Kimia, B.B., Bruckstein, A.M.: Implementing continuous-scale morphology via curve evolution. Pattern Recognition **26**, 1363–1372 (1993)
20. Serra, J.: Échantillonnage et estimation des phénomènes de transition minier, Ph.D thesis, University of Nancy, France (1967)
21. Serra, Jean: The "False Colour" problem. In: Wilkinson, Michael H.F., Roerdink, Jos B.T.M. (eds.) ISMM 2009. LNCS, vol. 5720, pp. 13–23. Springer, Heidelberg (2009)
22. van den Boomgaard, R.: Mathematical Morphology: Extensions Towards Computer Vision, Ph.D thesis, University of Amsterdam, The Netherlands (1992)
23. van Vliet, L.J., Young, I.T., Beckers, A.L.D.: A nonlinear Laplace operator as edge detector in noisy images. Computer Vision, Graphics and Image Processing **45**(2), 167–195 (1989)

Conditional Gaussian Models for Texture Synthesis

Lara Raad[✉], Agnès Desolneux, and Jean-Michel Morel

CMLA, Ecole Normale Supérieure de Cachan, Cachan, France
lara.raad@cmal.ens-cachan.fr

Abstract. An ideal exemplar-based texture synthesis algorithm should create a new texture that is perceptually equivalent to its texture example. To this goal it should respect the statistics of the example and avoid proceeding to a "copy-paste" process, which is the main drawback of the non-parametric approaches. In a previous work we modeled textures as a locally Gaussian patch model. This model was estimated for each patch before stitching it to the preceding ones. In the present work, we extend this model to a local conditional Gaussian patch distribution. The condition is taken over the already computed values. Our experiments here show that the conditional model reproduces well periodic and pseudo-periodic textures without requiring the use of any stitching technique. The experiments put also in evidence the importance of the right choice for the patch size. We conclude by pointing out the remaining limitations of the approach and the necessity of a multiscale approach.

Keywords: Texture synthesis · Conditional locally gaussian · Patch size

1 Introduction

Exemplar based texture synthesis is the problem of synthesizing from an input sample a perceptually equivalent larger texture sample. This problem has applications in computer graphics, computer vision and image processing, for example for fast scene generation, inpainting, and texture restoration. From the mathematical viewpoint the problem can be posed as the retrieval of the stochastic process underlying the sample, followed by the generation of new samples by simulating the reconstructed stochastic process. Texture synthesis methods are generally divided into two categories, the parametric [5,7,14] and non-parametric [1,3,4,10–12,17]. Using the texture sample, the parametric methods estimate statistical parameters characterizing the stochastic process. Although these methods can reproduce faithfully some of the global statistics of the sample, they generally do not yield high quality visual results. The non-parametric methods give up any statistical modeling and proceed to a direct simulation by iterating a copy-paste process with texture patches extracted from the original sample. Even though these methods can yield satisfactory results, they lack flexibility and often turn into practising verbatim copies of large parts of the input sample. More recently methods such as the work of Tartavel et al. in [16] combine the parametric and non-parametric methods using a variational approach with the aim of overcoming the copy-paste effects. They propose to minimize an energy function that takes into account the use of a sparse, patch-based dictionary combined to constraints on the textures' spectrum.

Statistics-based methods were initiated by Julesz [9], who discovered that many texture pairs having the same second-order statistics would not be discerned by human preattentive vision. This hypothesis is referred to as the first Julesz axiom for texture perception. Its validity can been checked in [5] which proposes to emulate microtextures by maintaining the Fourier modulus of the sample image and randomizing its phase, thus maintaining the second order statistics of the sample. This random phase method correctly emulates certain textures, which turn out to be Gaussian stationary fields. Yet, the method also fails for more structured ones. Both effects can be experimented online in the executable paper [6].

Julesz' approach was extended by Heeger and Bergen in [7] using multiscale statistics. The texture sample is characterized by the histograms of its wavelet coefficients and a new texture is created by enforcing these statistics on a white noise image. Yet this method only measures marginal statistics of the sample and misses important correlations between pixels across scales and orientations. Again, the model gives convincing results on certain textures, but for example fails on oriented textures, as verifiable in the executable paper [8].

Heeger and Bergen's model was extended by Portilla and Simoncelli in [14] who proposed to estimate on the texture sample not less than 700 autocorrelations, cross-correlations and statistical moments of the wavelet coefficients. The synthesis results obtained with this method are strikingly good compared to the previous statistical attempts. Convincing results are observable on a very wide range of textures. Although this method represents the state of the art for psychophysically and statistically founded algorithms, it has too many parameters to learn, and the results often present blur and phantoms effects.

Neighbourhood-based methods were initialized by Efros and Leung [4]. This method extends to images Shannon's Markov random field model for the English language. The simulated texture is constructed pixelwise. For each new pixel, a patch centered at the pixel is compared to all patches with the same size in the input sample. The nearest matches help predict the pixel value in the reconstructed image. This method was significantly accelerated by Wei and Levoy in [17] who fixed the shape and size of the learning patch and also by Ashikmin in [1] who proposed to extend existing patches whenever possible instead of searching in the entire sample texture. These pixelwise algorithms are not quite satisfactory. They are known to produce "garbage" when the compared patches are too small, or may lead to verbatim copies of significant parts of the input sample for large ones. To resolve the "garbage" issue and accelerate the procedure the more recent methods stitch together entire patches instead of synthesizing pixel by pixel. The question then is how to blend a new patch in the existing texture. In [12] this is done by a smooth transition. Efros and Freeman [3] refined this process by stitching each new patch along a minimum cost path across its overlapping zone with the texture under construction. Kwatra et al. in [11] extended the stitching procedure of [3] by a graph cut approach where the edges of the patches are redefined and then quilted in the synthesis image. They also proposed in [10] to synthesize a texture by sequentially improving the quality of the synthesized image by minimizing a patch-based energy function. The patch-based approaches often present satisfactory visual results. Yet, there is still a risk of copying verbatim large parts of the input sample. Furthermore, a respect of the global statistics of the initial sample is not guaranteed.

In a previous work [15] we proposed an algorithm that introduces some degree of statistical modeling in the non-parametric approach, thus trying to blend both approaches. A texture is synthesized in a patch-based approach, but the copy-paste process is preceded by the estimation of a Gaussian texture model for each new patch. In [15] we completed this process by adding a blending step in the spirit of [3].

In this work, we present a refinement of the stochastic modeling introduced in [15]. Our motivation was to dispose of the patch stitching step by using a more robust local model for the texture. To that end, we condition the Gaussian distribution of a patch to the values of its overlapping region and simulate the patch as the most probable sample of that conditional distribution. We present two different models: a conditional locally Gaussian where the overlapping region is maintained as is, and a regularized version that slightly relaxes the conditioning on the overlap region. Using this refined model, we shall prove that it is possible to avoid the blending step for a wide class of periodic or pseudo-periodic textures. Yet our experiments also show that for macro-textures we still need a blending step.

We finally give an interpretation of this fact, that points to the necessity of a multiscale generalization of the conditional approach, to cope with complex multiscale textures.

The rest of this paper is structured as follows. In Section 2 we present two conditional Gaussian models for the patches: a conditional locally Gaussian (CLG) and a regularized conditional locally Gaussian (RCLG). In Section 3 we discuss the synthesis results obtained from the three models: the locally Gaussian ([15]) and the two conditional locally Gaussian. We also analyze the behavior of the RCLG model when varying the patch size and the neighbourhood size. Conclusions are presented in Section 4.

2 Patch Models

We modeled in [15] a texture as a Locally Gaussian (LG) distribution. Given an input texture I_0, an output image I_s is synthesized sequentially patch by patch in a raster-scan order (left to right, top to bottom). Each new patch added to I_s overlaps part of the previously synthesized patch as can be seen in Figure 1. Each patch is simulated following a multivariate Gaussian distribution of mean μ and covariance matrix Σ where

$$\mu = \frac{1}{N}\sum_{i=1}^{N} p_i \text{ and } \Sigma = \frac{1}{N}(P-\mu)(P-\mu)^t, \qquad (1)$$

P is a matrix whose columns are the patches p_i in vector form and N is the considered number of nearest neighbours.

To define the patches p_i, let us consider p as the patch being currently synthesized and taken as a column vector of size $w \times 1$. The patch p will overlap part of the previous synthesis. To synthesize p, we decompose it as

$$p = \begin{pmatrix} Sp \\ Mp \end{pmatrix}, \quad S : \mathbb{R}^w \to \mathbb{R}^{w-k}, \quad M : \mathbb{R}^w \to \mathbb{R}^k \qquad (2)$$

where S and M are projection operators such that Mp is a vector of size $k \times 1$ with the values of p on the overlap area and Sp is a vector of size $(w-k) \times 1$ with the other components of p.

The patches p_i used to learn the parameters of the multivariate Gaussian distribution (1) are the N nearest neighbours in I_0 to the current patch p, for the L^2 distance restricted to the overlap area, given by $\|Mp_i - Mp\|_2$. Once the patch p is synthesized from the Gaussian model (1), the values of Mp change.

Fig. 1. We show three different iterations of the synthesis process. At each iteration a patch is being synthesized. This patch is represented by the pink square in the three iterations shown.

We observed unwanted transition effects when new patches were added into I_s. To overcome this problem we used Efros and Freeman's stitching method [3]. Yet we found that this solution is not quite satisfactory, as the new patch is simulated without conditioning it to the overlap area. We therefore propose a new patch model that aims to model directly the transition effect between patches. Each new patch will be estimated as a Gaussian vector conditioned to the pixel values of the corresponding overlap region. In this way the simulated patch would naturally "agree" with I_s in the overlap area, thus avoiding a stitching procedure.

2.1 The Conditional Locally Gaussian Model

Let I_s denote the texture image that is being synthesized. At each step of the algorithm a new patch p is added to I_s overlapping the previously synthesized ones. We want p to match with the overlap area pixels, to avoid creating unwanted discontinuities. This can be done by a Conditional Locally Gaussian (CLG) model.

Each patch p is taken as a column vector of size $w \times 1$. Then p can be partitioned as in (2).

We assume throughout that the vector p follows a Gaussian distribution of mean μ and covariance matrix Σ (the LG model). Then these parameters can be partitioned as follows :

$$\mu = \begin{bmatrix} \mu_1 \\ \mu_2 \end{bmatrix} = \begin{bmatrix} S\mu \\ M\mu \end{bmatrix} \text{ and } \Sigma = \begin{bmatrix} \Sigma_{11} & \Sigma_{12} \\ \Sigma_{21} & \Sigma_{22} \end{bmatrix} = \begin{bmatrix} S\Sigma S^t & S\Sigma M^t \\ M\Sigma S^t & M\Sigma M^t \end{bmatrix}.$$

Our problem can be formulated as finding the "best sample" $\tilde{p} = (\tilde{x}_1, \tilde{x}_2)$ conditioned to the overlap values y_0 that are known, i.e. we have $\tilde{x}_2 = y_0$ and the value of $\tilde{x}_1$ is the most probable one conditioned to $\tilde{x}_2$. It is given by

$$\tilde{x}_1 = \arg\max_{x_1} \mathbb{P}_{\mu,\Sigma}(Sp = x_1 \mid Mp = y_0) \tag{3}$$

By classic results on conditional multivariate Gaussian distributions [13], the distribution of Sp conditioned to $Mp = y_0$ is a multivariate Gaussian distribution of parameters $\bar{\mu}$ and $\bar{\Sigma}$ where

$$\bar{\mu} = \mu_1 + (S\Sigma M^t)(M\Sigma M^t)^{-1}(y_0 - \mu_2)$$

and

$$\bar{\Sigma} = (S\Sigma S^t) - S\Sigma M^t(M\Sigma M^t)^{-1}M\Sigma S^t.$$

Since the most probable sample of a multivariate Gaussian distribution is its mean, the solution to ($\mathcal{P}_1$) is

$$\tilde{p} = \begin{pmatrix} \tilde{x}_1 \\ y_0 \end{pmatrix} = \begin{pmatrix} \mu_1 + (S\Sigma M^t)(M\Sigma M^t)^{-1}(y_0 - \mu_2) \\ y_0 \end{pmatrix}. \tag{4}$$

Feasibility. Yet equation (4) shows that this solution does not make sense if $(M\Sigma M^t)$ is not invertible. This unfortunately is frequent, as the number of neighbours N used to build the Gaussian distribution is often very small compared to the dimension of the vectors we aim to model. Therefore the learnt Gaussian models are strongly degenerated.

This does not necessarily imply that there is no solution to ($\mathcal{P}_1$). The fact that Σ is not invertible implies that the Gaussian vectors $p \sim \mathcal{N}(\mu, \Sigma)$ live in a subspace of $\mathbb{R}^w$. This leads to the following alternative:

1. The Gaussian vectors subspace intersects the set of Gaussian vectors $(x_1, y_0)^t$.
2. There is no intersection and in that case no solution to our problem.

To overcome the fact that we may have no solution one can modify the Gaussian distribution learnt for p as follows

$$p \sim \mathcal{N}(\mu, \Sigma + \sigma^2 I_w),$$

where σ^2 is a real positive number and I_w is the identity matrix of size $w \times w$. In that way the Gaussian vectors p live in $\mathbb{R}^w$, and this ensures the existence of a solution to problem $(\mathcal{P}_1)$. We denote $\Gamma = \Sigma + \sigma^2 I_w$. When $(\mathcal{P}_1)$ has a solution for $p \sim \mathcal{N}(\mu, \Sigma)$, the new distribution $\mathcal{N}(\mu, \Gamma)$ will slightly modify the solution in (4) for a small value of σ^2. It is thus enough to take a low value for this parameter and the solutions obtained in both cases (with and without the Gaussian noise) will be very close to each other.

2.2 Regularized Conditional Locally Gaussian

In the previous section we conditioned the patches' statistical model to the exact values of the synthesized pixels across the overlap area. This could be too restrictive and then create samples that are very unlikely to exist. Instead of forcing each patch p to take the exact same values on the previously synthesized part, it is therefore natural to allow the patch p to vary slightly on the overlap area. This variation is rendered necessary by the scarcity of patch samples in a small texture sample. Consider the same patch model $\mathcal{N}(\mu, \Sigma)$, but let us now allow the overlap components Mp to take values $x_2 = y_0 + n$ where $n \sim \mathcal{N}(0, \theta^2 I_k)$. Then the most probable sample

$$\tilde{p} = (\tilde{x}_1, \tilde{x}_2) = \arg\max_{(x_1, x_2)} \mathbb{P}_{\mu, \Sigma}(Sp = x_1 | Mp = x_2) \mathbb{P}_{0, \theta^2 I_k}(x_2 - y_0)$$

still is exactly the same as in the CLG model. Thus, to slightly relax the constraint on the overlap we propose to minimize the following energy function

$$E(x_1, x_2) = -\log \mathbb{P}_{\mu, \Sigma}(Sp = x_1, Mp = x_2) + \frac{1}{2\theta^2} \|x_2 - y_0\|_2^2, \quad (5)$$

where the first term is the fidelity term to the Gaussian distribution of p and the second term is a regularization term to impose that x_2 keeps close to y_0. The parameter θ^2 controls the distance between the values of x_2 and the synthesized part over the overlap area. We shall call this model Regularized Conditional Locally Gaussian (RCLG). The optimal sample $\tilde{p}$ is then

$$\tilde{p} = (\tilde{x}_1, \tilde{x}_2) = \arg\min_{(x_1, x_2)} E(x_1, x_2) = (\theta^2 \Sigma^{-1} + M^t M)^{-1} (M^t y_0 + \theta^2 \Sigma^{-1} \mu) \quad (6)$$

Once again the solution in (6) makes sense when the inverse of the matrices Σ and $\theta^2 \Sigma^{-1} + M^t M$ exists. To be sure that we always find a solution, we shall slightly modify the Gaussian distribution of p, as we did previously, and this guarantees that these matrices are invertible. Considering $p \sim \mathcal{N}(\mu, \Sigma + \sigma^2 I_w)$ the optimal simulated patch $\tilde{p}$ is as shown in (7).

$$\tilde{p} = (\theta^2 (\Sigma + \sigma^2 I_w)^{-1} + M^t M)^{-1} (M^t y_0 + \theta^2 (\Sigma + \sigma^2 I_w)^{-1} \mu). \quad (7)$$

3 Experiments

The proposed patch models were tested with several types of textures: synthetic periodic, real pseudo-periodic and macro-textures. A summary of the results is presented in this section. The first results are a comparison of the three patch models: LG, CLG and RCLG without using any blending technique. The second ones compare the LG model and RCLG with an addional blending step. The last experiments are focused on comparing the influence of the parameters w and N on the synthesis results where w is the patch size and N the neighbourhood size (number of nearest neighbours used to build the Gaussian model). We do not compare here the proposed synthesis methods to other classical texture synthesis algorithm because this was already done extensively in [15]. Our aim is rather to discuss the different local Gaussian models and their parameters.

3.1 Patch Models Comparison

For the examples shown in Figure 2 the pacth size w varies between 10×10 and 40×40 and the neighbourhood size N between 10 and 20. The comparisons were made without using a blending step when stitching the patches. This permitted to better evaluate the positive impact of considering a local Gaussian model conditioned to the overlap values.

For the first example in Figure 2 one can observe that the three models achieve very good results regardless of the overlap information. This was expected, as periodic synthetic textures present many reliable examples to learn the Gaussian distribution of a patch. No boundary effect is therefore observable. For the LG model minor transitions are visible due to the presence of "dégradé" in this particular example. In the examples 2 and 3 in Figure 2 the stitching effects start being noticeable. For the LG model the patch itself is correctly synthesized but a blending step is necessary to avoid losing the global structure. However, for both models CLG and RCLG we still obtain a reliable patch model and a good global coherence without any blending technique. In the three last examples we meet the case where there are not enough patch examples in the sample texture to build an acceptable Gaussian distribution for the patch. Thus, achieving a correct synthesis requires adding a blending step. Once again, the transitions between the patches are more conspicuous in the LG model compared to the conditioned models.

The RCLG clearly yielded better results then the CLG model. This is due to the fact that we slightly relaxed the condition on the overlap area, thus achieving a more flexible model for the patch itself. For the conditional model (CLG) it might have seemed attractive to impose that a patch keeps exactly the same values in the overlap area. Indeed, this might have generated a patch that is very unlikely to happen. Yet, one can observe in the last two examples how the quality of the synthesis declines by this strong imposition.

In Figure 3 two models were compared: LG and RCLG, with an additional blending step for both cases. We can see in a general way that for the pair of parameters chosen for each texture example the RCLG model conserves a better

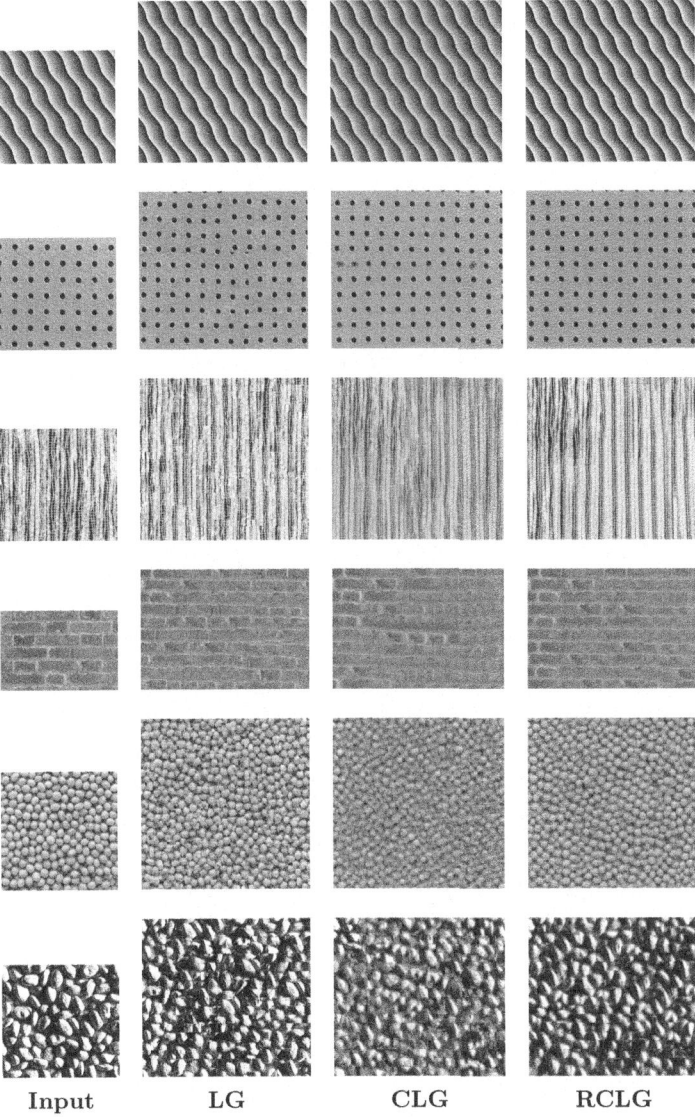

Fig. 2. Patch model comparison on several texture examples. From left to right: local Gaussian model, conditional local Gaussian model and regularized conditional local Gaussian model. The pair of parameters (w, N) used for each example from top to bottom are $(30, 20), (40, 10), (30, 10), (40, 10), (10, 10), (40, 20)$.

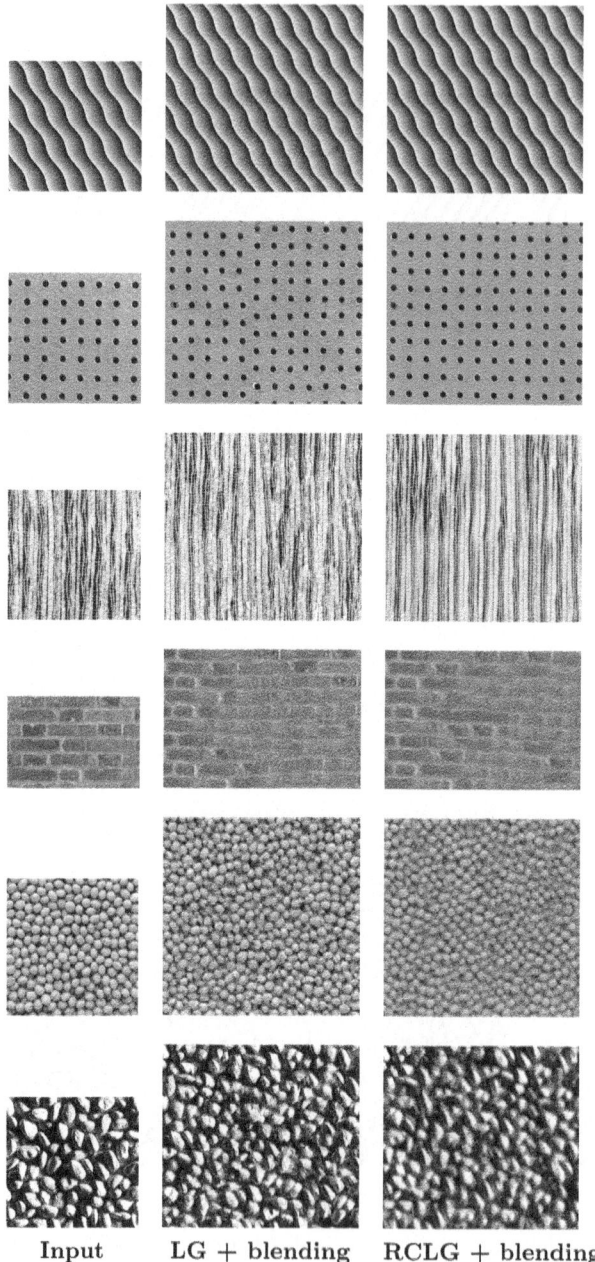

Fig. 3. Comparison of two patch models (LG an RCLG) combined with a blending step as in [3]. From left to right: input texture, local Gaussian model and regularized conditional local Gaussian model. The pair of parameters (w, N) used for each example from top to bottom are $(30, 20), (40, 10), (30, 10), (40, 10), (10, 10), (40, 20)$.

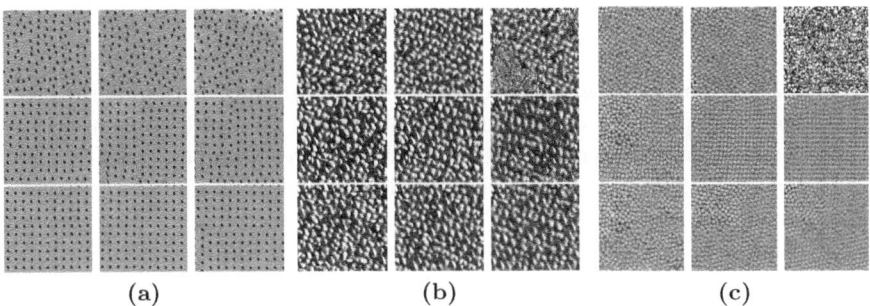

Fig. 4. Comparison of the patch size w and neighbourhood size N influence on three examples synthesis results using the RCLG model. For (a) and (b): from top to bottom, $w = 20, 30, 40$ and from left to right, $N = 10, 20, 50$. For (c): from top to bottom, $w = 10, 20, 30$ and from left to right, $N = 10, 20, 50$.

global coherence at the cost of losing finer details that the LG model manages to keep. These results are not surprising since all patches in the RCLG model were simulated minimizing (5) achieving a smoother result (it is the same as finding the most probable sample from the underlying probability distribution). A possible solution to overcome this effect could be to define the probability law of the RCLG model and sample a patch from it instead of taking the most probable one.

Finally, we noticed that on every synthesis example using any of the three patch models some details of the original texture can be lost (except for the periodic synthetic texture where there is no lack of examples). This brings us to the comparison of the next section, where we shall clearly see how varying the patch size permits on the one hand to capture the thinner details (using a smaller patch size) and on the other to capture the global structure of the texture (using a larger patch size).

3.2 Influence of Parameters

As mentioned above we will compare the influence of the patch size w and of the neighbourhood size N on the synthesis results. We can clearly conclude from the examples shown in Figure 4 that, by increasing the neighbourhood size for a fixed w, the RCLG patch model loses accuracy. Another important conclusion is that for different patch sizes the model is able to capture different details at different scales. In particular in the first example of Figure 4 for a patch of size 20×20 the salient structure is well simulated with the model, although the synthesis of the global arrangement of the black circles fails. Increasing the value of w permits to achieve a good global reconstruction, at the cost of sightly smoothing out the texture. The same observation can be made for the other displayed examples. We can conclude from these experiments that a unique patch size for the synthesis of macro-textures, i.e. containing information at different scales, is not enough to model at the same time the global structure and the finer details.

4 Conclusion

In this work, we have proposed a novel local texture sampling method in the patch space where each patch is conditioned to the values in the overlapping area.

The experiments in Section 3 show that both resulting models CLG and RCLG yield good synthesis results on periodic and quasi-periodic textures, without requiring the use of a stitching technique. For general macro-textures this need is reduced with CLG an RCLG with respect to the locally Gaussian model, that did not take into account the overlap values. Comparing both conditional models, CLG and RCLG, we observed that the results obtained for the regularized version are visually better. Indeed, imposing the simulated Gaussian patch to have exactly the same values over the overlap area was excessive. The experiments of Section 3.2 show the importance of fixing a correct patch size for a given texture example. They prove that a macro-texture cannot be correctly synthesized with a single patch size.

Hence, future work will focus on a multi-scale approach to catch both the global structure of the texture and its details, in the spirit of the recent work [16].

References

1. Ashikhmin, M.: Synthesizing natural textures. In: Proceedings of the 2001 symposium on Interactive 3D graphics, pp. 217–226. ACM (2001)
2. Desolneux, A., Moisan, L., Ronsin, S.: A compact representation of random phase and gaussian textures. In: 2012 IEEE International Conference on Acoustics, Speech and Signal Processing, ICASSP 2012, Kyoto, Japan, March 25–30, 2012, pp. 1381–1384 (2012)
3. Efros, A.A., Freeman, W.T.: Image quilting for texture synthesis and transfer. In: SIGGRAPH, pp. 341–346 (2001)
4. Efros, A.A., Leung, T.K.: Texture synthesis by non-parametric sampling. In: IEEE International Conference on Computer Vision, pp. 1033–1038 (1999)
5. Galerne, B., Gousseau, Y., Morel, J.-M.: Random phase textures: Theory and synthesis. IEEE Transactions in Image Processing (2010)
6. Galerne, B., Gousseau, Y., Morel, J.-M.: Micro-Texture Synthesis by Phase Randomization. Image Processing On Line (2011). http://dx.doi.org/10.5201/ipol.2011.ggm_rpn
7. Heeger, D.J., Bergen, J.R.: Pyramid-based texture analysis/synthesis. In: SIGGRAPH, New York, NY, USA, pp. 229–238 (1995)
8. Briand, T., Vacher, J., Galerne, B., Rabin, J.: The Heeger and Bergen Pyramid Based Texture Synthesis Algorithm. Image Processing On Line 4, 276–299 (2014). http://dx.doi.org/10.5201/ipol.2014.79
9. Julesz, B.: Visual pattern discrimination. IEEE Trans. Inf. Theory 8(2), 84–92 (1962)
10. Kwatra, V., Essa, I., Bobick, A., Kwatra, N.: Texture optimization for example-based synthesis. In ACM Transactions on Graphics (TOG), vol. 24, pp. 795–802. ACM (2005)
11. Kwatra, V., Schödl, A., Essa, I., Turk, G., Bobick, A.: Graphcut textures: image and video synthesis using graph cuts. In: ACM Transactions on Graphics (TOG), vol. 22, pp. 277–286. ACM (2003)

12. Liang, L., Liu, C., Xu, Y.-Q., Guo, B., Shum, H.-Y.: Real-time texture synthesis by patch-based sampling. ACM Transactions on Graphics (ToG) **20**(3), 127–150 (2001)
13. Morrison, D.F.: Multivariate statistical methods. 3. New York, NY. Mc (1990)
14. Portilla, J., Simoncelli, E.P.: A parametric texture model based on joint statistics of complex wavelet coefficients. International Journal of Computer Vision **40**(1), 49–70 (2000)
15. Raad, L., Desolneux, A., Morel, J.-M.: Locally gaussian exemplar-based texture synthesis. In: IEEE International Conference on Image Processing, ICIP 2014, Paris (2014)
16. Tartavel, G., Gousseau, Y., Peyré, G.: Variational texture synthesis with sparsity and spectrum constraints. Journal of Mathematical Imaging and Vision (2014)
17. Wei, L.-Y., Levoy, M.: Fast texture synthesis using tree-structured vector quantization. In: SIGGRAPH, pp. 479–488 (2000)

Multiscale Texture Orientation Analysis Using Spectral Total-Variation Decomposition

Dikla Horesh[✉] and Guy Gilboa

Department of Electrical Engineering, Technion - Israel Institute of Technology,
32000 Haifa, Israel
dikla@tx.technion.ac.il

Abstract. Multi-level texture separation can considerably improve texture analysis, a significant component in many computer vision tasks. This paper aims at obtaining precise local texture orientations of images in a multiscale manner, characterizing the main obvious ones as well as the very subtle ones. We use the total variation spectral framework to decompose the image into its different textural scales. Gabor filter banks are then employed to detect prominent orientations within the multiscale representation. A necessary condition for perfect texture separation is given, based on the spectral total-variation theory. We show that using this method we can detect and differentiate a mixture of overlapping textures and obtain with high fidelity a multi-valued orientation representation of the image.

Keywords: Total variation · Spectral total variation · Image decomposition · Image enhancement · Nonlinear eigenfunction analysis

1 Introduction

Texture analysis plays an important role in computer vision, image processing and pattern recognition. It is essential in many applications, among those medical imaging, shape analysis image segmentation, and content-based image retrieval. The general concept of structure-texture decomposition is that an image can be regarded as composed of a structural part, corresponding to the main large objects in the image, and a textural part, containing one scale details, usually with some periodicity and oscillatory nature. An image f can be decomposed as $f = u + v$, where u represents image cartoon or geometric (piecewise-smooth) component and v represents the oscillatory or textured component of f. The oscillatory part v should contain essentially the noise (if exists) and the texture. In this work we extend the common structure and texture decomposition to multi-scale texture separation in order to get all textures, the coarse and fine-scaled and even the hidden textures.

Tadmor, Nezzar and Vese [22] proposed a multiscale procedure using hierarchical representations of several layers of signals and textures to capture different features at the different scales. The idea is that whatever is interpreted as texture in a given scale consists of significant features on a finer scale. They use the conventional TV and therefore the outcome separation is not optimal. Gilles [14] combined Meyer's decomposition model [17] and a specifically chose Littlewood-Paley filter, to extract a certain class of textures in an image. While this works well for synthetic images, it is not ideal for some real world images.

1.1 Nonlinear Eigenfunctions

Classical linear eigenfunction analysis has shown to provide many state-of-the-art algorithms in signal processing, computer vision and machine-learning. Some examples are segmentation [21], clustering [18], subspace clustering [16] and dimensionality reduction [3]. Eigenfunctions of an operator can be viewed as the operator's inherent atoms with an intrinsic scale represented by the respective eigenvalue. Recent studies [5,13] indicate that a generalized theory can be developed for the convex nonlinear case.

Nonlinear eigenfunctions induced by a convex functional emerge by the following *nonlinear eigenvalue problem*:

$$\lambda u \in \partial J(u), \qquad (1)$$

where $J(u)$ is a convex functional and $\partial J(u)$ is its subgradient. A function u admitting Eq. (1) is referred to as an eigenfunction with a corresponding eigenvalue λ. We can briefly study the linear case, to get some intuition.

A linear example Let us examine the functional

$$J(u) = \frac{1}{2} \int_\Omega |\nabla u(x)|^2 dx,$$

where ∇ is the gradient. The convex functional induces an operator through its subgradient. Here the subgradient (in this case single valued) is $p(u) = -\Delta u$ (Δ denotes the Laplacian). The corresponding eigenvalue problem is

$$-\Delta u = \lambda u.$$

In the one-dimensional case, with appropriate boundary conditions, functions of the form $u = \sin(\omega x)$ are eigenfunctions with corresponding eigenvalues $\lambda = \omega^2$.

Thus Fourier frequencies naturally emerge as solving an eigenvalue problem related to a quadratic smoothing convex functional.

In [12,13] an image decomposition and filtering framework was suggested. It presents a notion of generalized nonlinear eigenfunctions which are used to define forward and inverse TV transforms. This can be used to decompose the image into well defined scales and allows a new variety of filtering methods.

We use the multi level texture separation in order to fully describe the orientation space of the image. After decomposing the image we fully map the orientation of each level, allowing the visual description of the orientation of the different image features. This is extremely useful when analyzing image with complex textures content and enables us to perform fine analysis and inner texture actions and synthesis.

One main contribution of this paper is introducing a method for separating well orthogonal signals. A necessary condition for perfect separation based on the spectral total-variation theory is stated in Proposition 1. Examples of decomposition of textures in images even for overlapping textures are shown. Finally, it is shown how by using a maximal response of a bank of Gabor filters one can characterize each texture separately and fully map the orientation of the different texture layers.

2 Methods

2.1 TV Transform

In [13] a non-conventional way of defining a transform through a partial-differential-equation (PDE) is suggested, based on the total-variation (TV) functional:

$$J(u) = \int_\Omega |Du|, \qquad (2)$$

where Du denotes the distributional gradient of u. The corresponding gradient descent of the functional, known as total-variation flow [1], is formally written as:

$$\begin{aligned} \frac{\partial u}{\partial t} &= \operatorname{div}\left(\frac{Du}{|Du|}\right), & \text{in } (0,\infty) \times \Omega \\ \frac{\partial u}{\partial n} &= 0, & \text{on } (0,\infty) \times \partial\Omega \\ u(0;x) &= f(x), & \text{in } x \in \Omega, \end{aligned} \qquad (3)$$

where Ω is the image domain (a bounded set in $\mathbb{R}^N$ with Lipschitz continuous boundary $\partial\Omega$). The TV transform is defined by:

$$\phi(t;x) = u_{tt}(t;x)t, \qquad (4)$$

where u_{tt} is the second time derivative of the solution $u(t;x)$ of (3). The inverse transform is:

$$f(x) = \int_0^\infty \phi(t;x)dt + \bar{f}, \qquad (5)$$

where $\bar{f} = \frac{1}{\Omega}\int_\Omega f(x)dx$ is the mean value of the initial condition. Filtering is performed using a transfer function $H(t) \in \mathbb{R}$:

$$f_H(x) := \int_0^\infty \phi(t;x)H(t)dt + \bar{f}. \qquad (6)$$

The spectrum $S^f(t)$ of the input signal $f(x)$ corresponds to the L^1 amplitude of each scale:

$$S^f(t) = \|\phi(t;x)\|_{L^1} = \int_\Omega |\phi(t;x)|dx. \qquad (7)$$

Two significant results were shown in [13] for this transform:

- **Atoms as eigenfunctions:** Let $f(x)$ be a function which admits the nonlinear eigenvalue problem (1), ($f = u$), for the TV functional. Then the transform yields a measure (single impulse), multiplied by $f(x)$, at time $t = 1/\lambda$ and is zero for all other t: $\phi(t;x) = \delta(t - 1/\lambda)f(x)$, where $\delta(\cdot)$ is the Dirac delta function.
- **Relations to TV-flow:** The TV flow solution $u(t)$ is given by:

$$u(t) = \int_0^\infty H^t(\tau)\phi(\tau;x)d\tau + \bar{f}; \quad H^t(\tau) = \begin{cases} 0, & 0 \leq \tau < t \\ \frac{\tau-t}{\tau}, & t \leq \tau < \infty \end{cases}. \quad (8)$$

The first result relates to nonlinear spectral theory, which has attracted increasing interest lately, see e.g. [5,11] and [7] in the segmentation and learning context.

The second result shows that the framework is a generalization of standard TV filters and that many other filters related to the functional can be designed.

The TV-transform decomposition can be seen as a generalization and extension of earlier studies concerning image decomposition methods, such as [17,19,2,23]. The TV-transform relies on the established theory of the TV flow proposed by Andreu et al in [1] and further developed in [4].

2.2 A Necessary Condition for Perfect Separability

In [8] an orthogonality relation between ϕ, Eq. (4), and u is established:

$$\langle u(t), \phi(t) \rangle = 0, \forall t \in (0, \infty), \quad (9)$$

where $\langle \cdot, \cdot \rangle$ denotes the L^2 inner product over the domain Ω. Using the above relation and the one given in (8) a necessary condition for perfect separability of eigenfunctions can be shown:

Proposition 1. *Let $f_1(x)$, $f_2(x)$ admit the eigenvalue problem (1), with J the TV functional (2), and λ_1, λ_2 the corresponding eigenvalues ($\lambda_1 > \lambda_2$). Then for $f = f_1 + f_2$ a necessary condition to have*

$$\phi(t) = \delta(t - \frac{1}{\lambda_1})f_1(x) + \delta(t - \frac{1}{\lambda_2})f_2(x), \quad (10)$$

is

$$\langle f_1, f_2 \rangle = 0.$$

Proof. Let us assume Eq. (10) holds and $\langle f_2(x), f_1(x) \rangle \neq 0$. We express $u(t_1)$ using (8), with $t_1 := \frac{1}{\lambda_1}$ (note that $H^{t_1}(t_1) = 0$):

$$u(t_1) = \int_{t_1}^\infty H^{t_1}(\tau)\phi(\tau;x)d\tau = H^{t_1}(t_2)f_2(x).$$

From Eq. (9) we have

$$\langle u(t_1), \phi(t_1) \rangle = 0,$$

and therefore

$$H^{t_1}(t_2)\delta(t=0)\langle f_2(x), f_1(x) \rangle = 0,$$

which contradicts our assumption. □

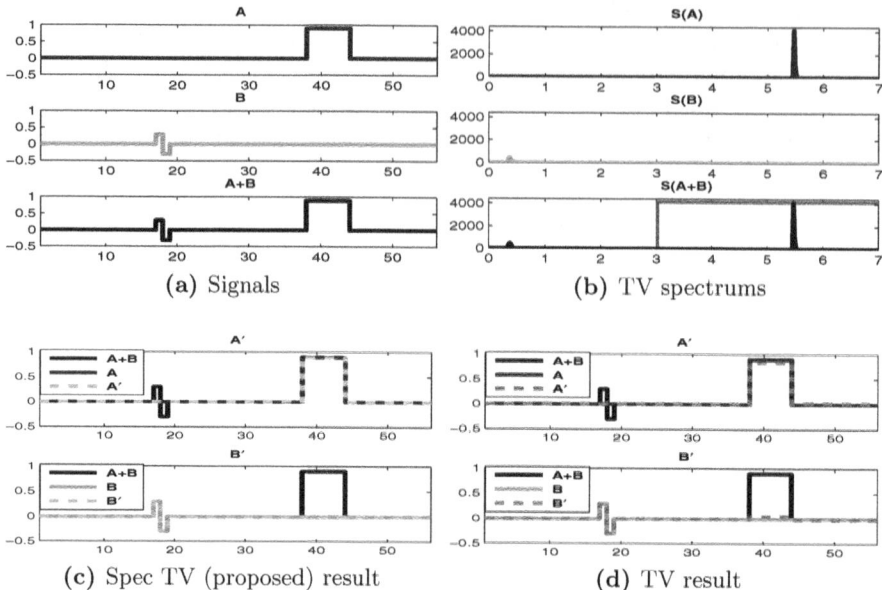

Fig. 1. Separating 1D orthogonal signals

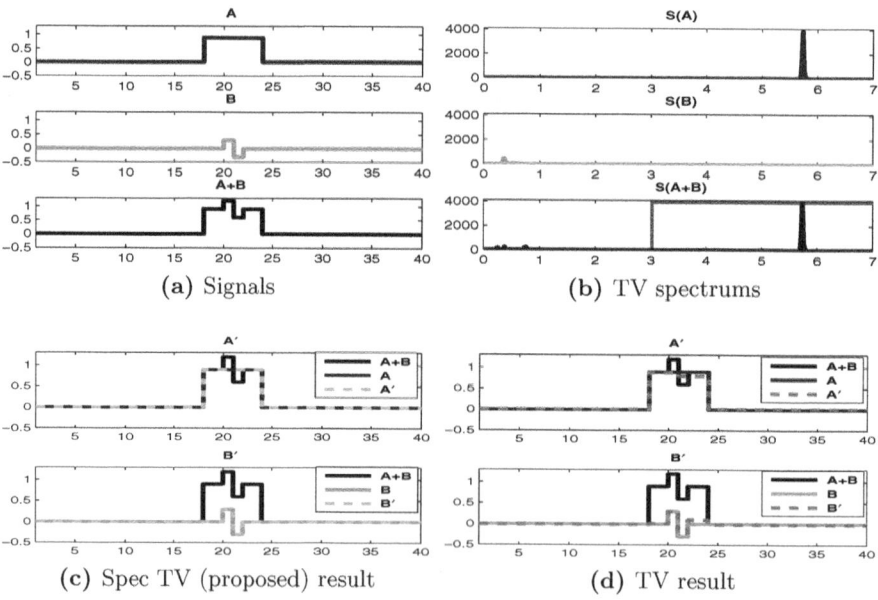

Fig. 2. Separating 1D overlapping orthogonal signals

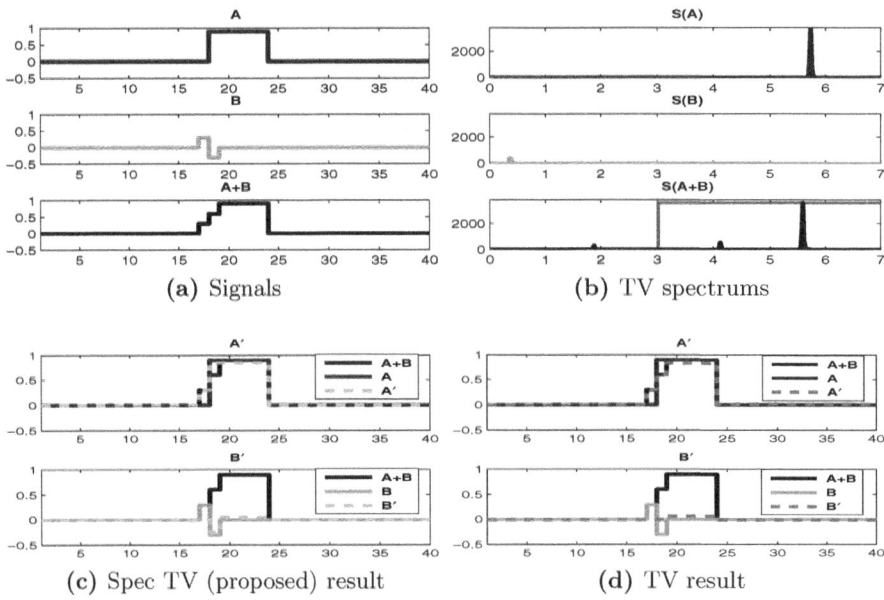

Fig. 3. Separating 1D overlapping correlated signals

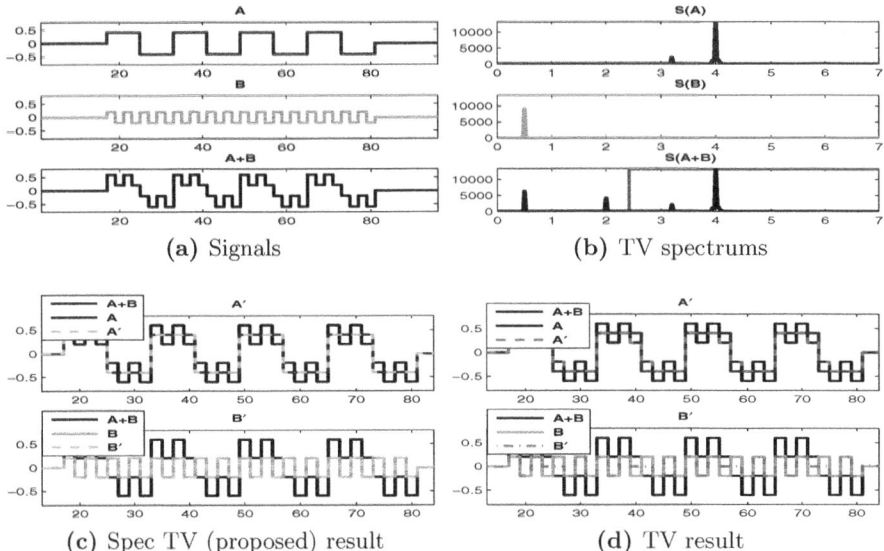

Fig. 4. Separating 1D oscillating uncorrelated signals

Note that in the case of perfect separability, Eq. (10), simple spectral filtering (6) with $H(t) = 1$ for $t < t_c$ and 0 otherwise, where $t_c \in (1/\lambda_1, 1/\lambda_2)$, can perfectly separate f_1 and f_2. Examples demonstrating the signals' separability in 1D are shown in Figs. 1-4. Separation of the larger scale signal is performed using (6) with $H(t)$ a step signal ($\{0, 1\}$ values) as superimposed in red on the combined spectrum plot (bottom of Figures 1-4 (b)). In Fig. 1 two well-separated orthogonal signals are shown, their spectrum, Eq. (7), has one peak for each signal, and the combined spectrum $S^{(A+B)}(t)$ is the sum $S^A(t) + S^B(t)$. Decomposition using spectral TV yields a perfect separation. In Fig. 2 a case of two overlapping orthogonal signals is shown, their combined spectrum is not the sum of the original spectra anymore but it remains separated so that a perfect separation is achieved. In Fig. 3 the signals are correlated, and their spectrum changes and mixes when added together, the decomposition is degraded. We can see also the optimal possible results of standard TV regularization for comparison in all these cases. Note that even in the first simplest case TV does not yield perfect separation and the decomposition mixes both signals.

In Fig. 4, two orthogonal oscillating signals are combined. Their combined spectrum slightly changes, compared to the original isolated signals, as a result of the overlap. However they can still be perfectly separated using spectral TV, while the standard TV has significant artifacts and the signals are not well separated. We use the projection algorithm of Chambolle [9] to implement the TV-flow time steps [13]. For more details, see http://guygilboa.eew.technion.ac.il/code/.

2.3 Finding Orientations with Gabor

A Gabor filter bank is a set of regularly spaced filters that roughly mimic the behavior of the human visual system (HVS) for texture detection. According to this model, the HVS perceives the image through a set of filtered images, so that each image contains some unique visual information over a narrow range of orientation channel. In that manner, Gabor filtering has been shown to be a good fitting to this model, providing optimal localization of image details in a joint spatial and frequency domain [15,10]. Gabor Filters are often used in texture analysis to extract local image features for texture classification and segmentation [6]. Several comparative studies were done on texture descriptors [20], showing a clear predominance in the use of descriptors based on Gabor filters. The Gabor wavelet definition is

$$g(x,y) = \frac{1}{2\pi\sigma_x\sigma_y} exp[-\frac{1}{2}(\frac{\tilde{x}^2}{\sigma_x^2} + \frac{\tilde{y}^2}{\sigma_y^2}) + 2\pi jW\tilde{x}] \quad (11)$$

$$\tilde{x} = x\cos(\frac{\mu\pi}{M}) + y\sin(\frac{\mu\pi}{M}), \tilde{y} = -x\sin(\frac{\mu\pi}{M}) + y\cos(\frac{\mu\pi}{M}) \quad (12)$$

μ controls the orientation of the filters, with M being the total number of different orientations and W scales the center of the filter in the frequency domain. The Gabor filter response was calculated in 30 orientations ($M = 30, \mu = 0, 1, ..., 30$), spanning 180° and 4 spatial frequencies for finer and coarser scales. In Fig. 5 presented a concentric circles image (left) and the colored orientation map of 8 (middle) and 30 (right) Gabor filters response. The use of 30 orientations was chosen in order to get improved resolution for better texture analysis despite the cost in calculation time. The input image was convolved with each of the 2D

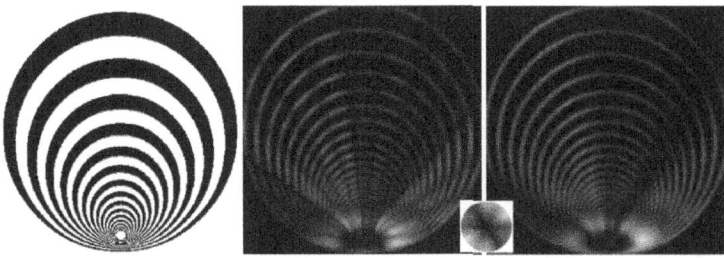

Fig. 5. Concentric circles image (left), orientation map of 8 Gabor filters response (middle) and orientation map of 30 Gabor filters response (right)

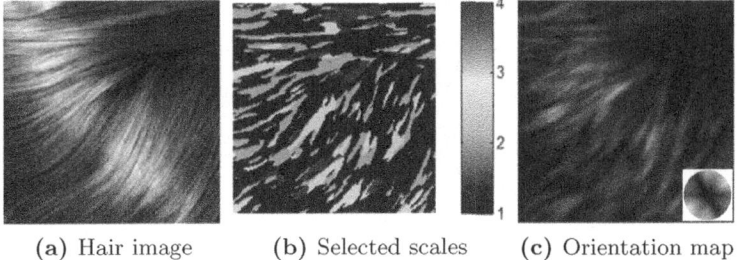

(a) Hair image   (b) Selected scales   (c) Orientation map

Fig. 6. Hair texture image (left), the selected scale from fine to coarse (middle) and the Gabor orientation map (right), in the small image - the color map

Gabor filters detailed above to get the 120 Gabor feature images. In each scale, the orientation giving the maximum response was taken, and the maximum of the 4 scales was taken to describe the orientation of each pixel. In this way we get the best orientation characterization for the image. This procedure was done for each of the texture images received in the spectral TV decomposition, for full orientation mapping of the input image textures. In Fig. 6 we can see a hair example, the scales selected for each pixel (middle) and the resulting orientation map of the image calculated of all 4 scales (right).

3 Results

Decomposition using spectral TV was applied to multi-textured images. The orientation map was calculated for the resulting texture images using the Gabor filters. Decomposition can be done to as many different layers as required, limited numerically only by the chosen time step (the theoretical formulation is

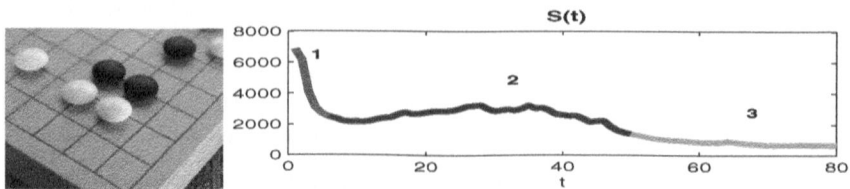

Fig. 7. Game board image (left) and TV spectrum of the image with separated textures marked in different colors (right)

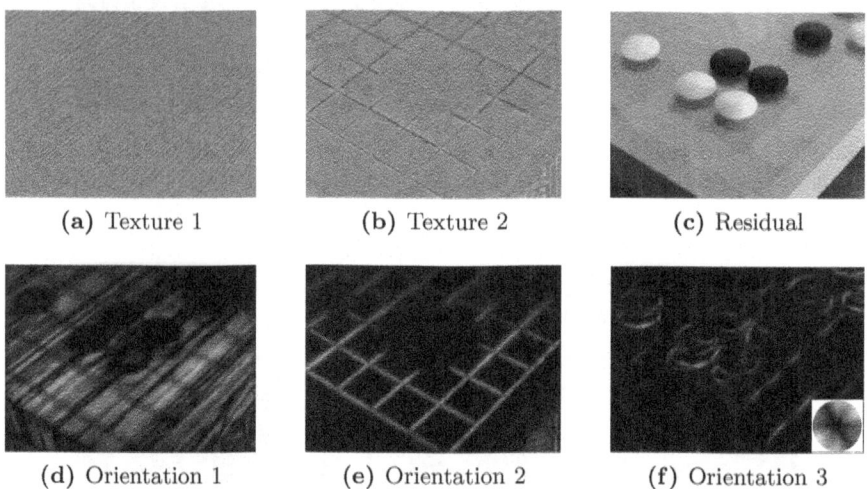

Fig. 8. Our decomposition of game board image (Fig. 7) to textures (top) and the corresponding orientation maps (bottom)

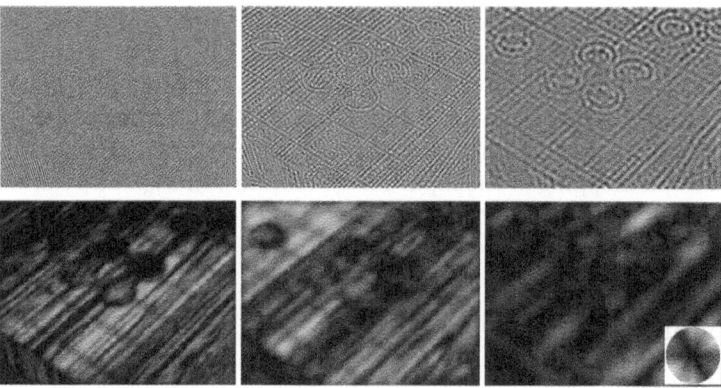

Fig. 9. Compared method [14] decomposition result for game board image to 3 textures (top) and Gabor orientation visualization (bottom)

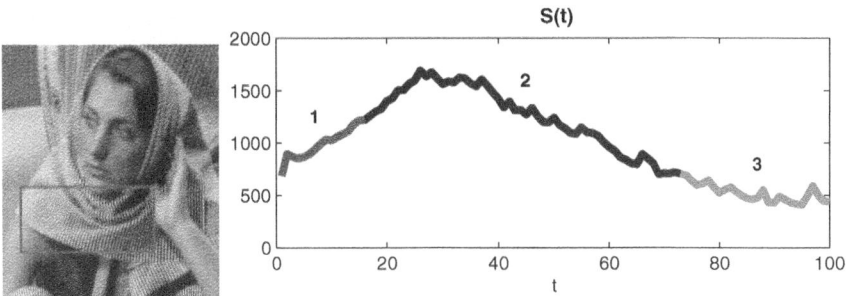

Fig. 10. Barbara image on the left and TV spectrum of the image with separated textures marked in different colors

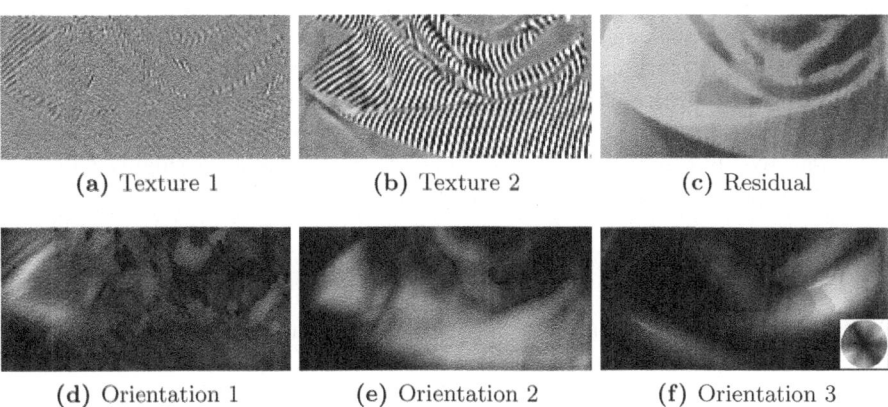

Fig. 11. Our decomposition of Barabara's image (Fig. 10) to textures (top): subtle textures (left), coarser textures (middle) and the residual image structure (right). Bottom: Corresponding orientation maps.

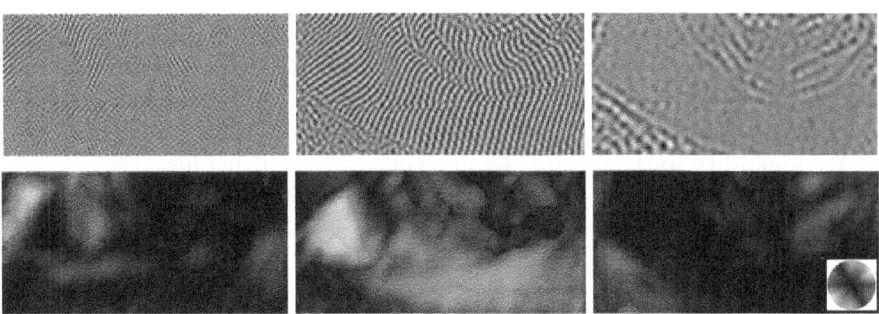

Fig. 12. Compared method [14] decomposition result for Barbara's image to 3 textures (top) and Gabor orientation visualization (bottom)

continuous in time). The separation points of the decomposition were manually chosen according to the image.In Fig. 7 a game board image is shown (left) and its spectrum (right) in different colors to demonstrate the separation points of the decomposition (or integration intervals of the ϕ's, using (6) with $H = 1$ in the desired interval and 0 otherwise) appearing respectively in Fig. 8: the wood pattern, the game board lines and the structure with the round game pieces. The contrast is enhanced for better visualization. We can observe the great separation of the different layers as seen in the colored orientation figures as processed from the Gabor filters response (Fig. 8, bottom). The orientation in each pixel is taken from the Gabor scale which gave the strongest response, usually corresponding to the texture coarseness. The result of Gilles decomposition [14] for this image are on Fig. 9, as can be seen, the textures nicely appear there in different scales but the different textures are not separated. Another example is the image of Barbara in Fig. 10 (only a part was taken for visualization reasons). In this example we can see the decomposition to textures (Fig. 11): the coarse one on the right showing the structure of the image, the middle one showing the stripes on her cloth and on the left we can uniquely see a previously hidden textures of the subtle pattern of the fabric, not seen in the original image. The decomposition result of [14] for this image (Fig. 12) is fair, some of the textures are separated, but as not distinct as ours. Also, we can see a ringing effect on the bottom left of the compared method result.

4 Conclusion

A novel method for multilayer texture decomposition was introduced. A necessary condition for perfect separation in this framework is given, in which orthogonality of the separated signals is required. Examples of different cases in 1D were shown to illustrate the different possible cases. The method was then applied for color images using the vectorial TV functional where the ϕ layers were integrated to decompose the image into its different textural components. In this work the time (scale) integration domains were selected manually, however, we intend to automate this by using a minimal correlation criterion between the textures as done in [2] for structure-texture decomposition. It was shown that the spectral total-variation framework suffices for well edge and contrast preserving decomposition. This is done without the need for minimization with an additional dual norm (such as the G-norm [17] or H^{-1} norm [19]). The method was compared favourably to state-of-the-art multiscale decomposition [14].

We would like to thank Prof. Jerome Gilles for supplying his code.

References

1. Andreu, F., Ballester, C., Caselles, V., Mazón, J.M.: Minimizing total variation flow. Differential and Integral Equations **14**(3), 321–360 (2001)
2. Aujol, J., Gilboa, G., Chan, T., Osher, S.: Structure-texture image decomposition - modeling, algorithms, and parameter selection. Int. J. Computer Vision **67**(1), 111–136 (2006)

3. Belkin, M., Niyogi, P.: Laplacian eigenmaps for dimensionality reduction and data representation. Neural Computation **15**(6), 1373–1396 (2003)
4. Bellettini, G., Caselles, V., Novaga, M.: The total variation flow in R^N. Journal of Differential Equations **184**(2), 475–525 (2002)
5. Benning, M., Burger, M.: Ground states and singular vectors of convex variational regularization methods. Methods and Apps. of Anal. **20**(4), 295–334 (2013)
6. Bianconi, F., Fernández, A.: Evaluation of the effects of gabor filter parameters on texture classification. Pattern Recognition **40**(12), 3325–3335 (2007)
7. Bresson, X., Tai, X.C., Chan, T., Szlam, A.: Multi-class transductive learning based on $\ell 1$ relaxations of cheeger cut and mumford-shah-potts model. Journal of Mathematical Imaging and Vision **49**(1), 191–201 (2014)
8. Burger, M., Eckardt, L., Gilboa, G., Moeller, M.: Spectral representations of one-homogeneous functionals. In: Proc. Scale Space and Variational Methods in Computer Vision, SSVM (2015)
9. Chambolle, A.: An algorithm for total variation minimization and applications. JMIV **20**, 89–97 (2004)
10. Daugman, J.G.: Two-dimensional spectral analysis of cortical receptive field profiles. Vision Research **20**(10), 847–856 (1980)
11. Giannakis, D., Majda, A.: Nonlinear laplacian spectral analysis for time series with intermittency and low-frequency variability. Proceedings of the National Academy of Sciences **109**(7), 2222–2227 (2012)
12. Gilboa, G.: A spectral approach to total variation. In: Kuijper, A., Bredies, K., Pock, T., Bischof, H. (eds.) SSVM 2013. LNCS, vol. 7893, pp. 36–47. Springer, Heidelberg (2013)
13. Gilboa, G.: A total variation spectral framework for scale and texture analysis. SIAM J. Imaging Sciences **7**(4), 1937–1961 (2014)
14. Gilles, J.: Multiscale texture separation. Multiscale Modeling & Simulation **10**(4), 1409–1427 (2012)
15. Jain, A.K., Farrokhnia, F.: Unsupervised texture segmentation using gabor filters. Pattern Recognition **24**(12), 1167–1186 (1991)
16. Liu, G., Lin, Z., Yan, S., Sun, J., Yu, Y., Ma, Y.: Robust recovery of subspace structures by low-rank representation. IEEE Transactions on Pattern Analysis and Machine Intelligence **35**(1), 171–184 (2013)
17. Meyer, Y.: Oscillating patterns in image processing and in some nonlinear evolution equations: The 15th Dean Jacquelines B. Lewis Memorial Lectures (March 2001)
18. Ng, A., Jordan, M., Weiss, Y.: On spectral clustering: Analysis and an algorithm. Advances in Neural Information Processing Systems **2**, 849–856 (2002)
19. Osher, S., Sole, A., Vese, L.: Image decomposition and restoration using total variation minimization and the H^{-1} norm. SIAM Multiscale Modeling and Simulation **1**(3), 349–370 (2003)
20. Penatti, O.A., Valle, E., Torres, R.D.S.: Comparative study of global color and texture descriptors for web image retrieval. Journal of Visual Communication and Image Representation **23**(2), 359–380 (2012)
21. Shi, J., Malik, J.: Normalized cuts and image segmentation. IEEE Transactions on Pattern Analysis and Machine Intelligence **22**(8), 888–905 (2000)
22. Tadmor, E., Nezzar, S., Vese, L.: A multiscale image representation using hierarchical (BV, L2) decompositions. SIAM Multiscale Modeling and Simulation **2**(4), 554–579 (2004)
23. Yang, Y., Han, S., Wang, T., Tao, W., Tai, X.C.: Multilayer graph cuts based unsupervised color-texture image segmentation using multivariate mixed student's t-distribution. Pattern Recognition **46**(4), 1101–1124 (2013)

A L^1-TV Algorithm for Robust Perspective Photometric Stereo with Spatially-Varying Lightings

Yvain Quéau[1]([✉]), François Lauze[2], and Jean-Denis Durou[1]

[1] IRIT, UMR CNRS 5505, Toulouse, France
yvain.queau@enseeiht.fr, durou@irit.fr
[2] Department of Computer Science, University of Copenhagen, Copenhagen, Denmark
francois@diku.dk

Abstract. We tackle the problem of perspective 3D-reconstruction of Lambertian surfaces through photometric stereo, in the presence of outliers to Lambert's law, depth discontinuities, and unknown spatially-varying lightings. To this purpose, we introduce a robust L^1-TV variational formulation of the recovery problem where the shape itself is the main unknown, which naturally enforces integrability and permits to avoid integrating the normal field.

Keywords: Uncalibrated photometric stereo · Spatially-varying lightings · Perspective projection · Total variation · Proximal methods

1 Introduction

Photometric stereo refers to the problem of inferring the shape of an object, given a set of m images of this object acquired under different known (*calibrated* photometric stereo) or unknown (*uncalibrated* photometric stereo) illuminations but from the same point of view, by inverting a generative image model accounting for the projection model (orthographic or perspective), the object reflectance (Lambert, Phong, etc.) and the lighting model (directional, punctual, etc.). Early photometric stereo considered orthographic projection, Lambertian reflectance and directional lightings [17], which is the simplest case. Extending photometric stereo to more general models has become an important research direction, along with the natural need for fast and robust solutions. For example, perspective projection can replace the orthographic projection in both calibrated [11] and uncalibrated [14] cases, the Lambertian assumption can be relaxed so as to take specular highlights into account [7] and robustness to outliers like shadows can be obtained through numerous techniques such as sparse regression [10]. However, extending photometric stereo to non-directional lightings remains an open and challenging problem. We focus on this aspect of the problem and propose a robust variational formulation of perspective photometric stereo with spatially-varying lightings, considered as additional unknowns so as not to impose a parametric lighting model. The different hypotheses our approach relies on are described hereafter.

1.1 Image Formation Model

Radiance Model. Lambert's law assumes that the surface $\mathcal{S}$ reflects light diffusively, the reflectance at $\mathbf{x} \in \mathcal{S}$ being characterised by the albedo $\rho(\mathbf{x}) \in [0,1]$. Given a parallel uniform light beam $\mathbf{s}_0 \in \mathbb{R}^3$, oriented towards the source, and the unit outward normal $\mathbf{n}(\mathbf{x}) \in \mathbb{R}^3$ to the surface at $\mathbf{x}$, the *emitted* Lambertian radiance $r_e(\mathbf{x})$ at $\mathbf{x}$ is proportional to the irradiance $\max\{0, \mathbf{s}_0 \cdot \mathbf{n}(\mathbf{x})\}$, where the max operator aims at modeling the self-shadows. Forgetting this operator (shadows will be dealt with by robust estimators), the Lambertian emitted radiance reads:

$$r_e(\mathbf{x}) = \frac{\rho(\mathbf{x})}{\pi} \mathbf{s}_0 \cdot \mathbf{n}(\mathbf{x}) \qquad (1)$$

In this work, we do not suppose that the lightings consist in parallel uniform beams. Even more, we do not use any explicit lighting model, allowing us to cope with, for instance, near point light sources, large sources, self- and cast-shadows and even secondary reflections. In the most general case, the irradiance at $\mathbf{x}$ is equal to the sum of elementary contributions coming from all the unit directions $\mathbf{v}(\theta, \phi)$ characterised by the spherical angles (θ, ϕ) defined with respect to $\mathbf{n}(\mathbf{x})$:

$$r_e(\mathbf{x}) = \frac{\rho(\mathbf{x})}{\pi} \iint_{\theta \in [0,\pi/2],\, \phi \in [0,2\pi]} r_i(\mathbf{x}, \theta, \phi) \mathbf{v}(\theta, \phi) \cdot \mathbf{n}(\mathbf{x}) \sin\theta \, d\theta \, d\phi \qquad (2)$$

where $r_i(\mathbf{x}, \theta, \phi)$ is the *incident* radiance at $\mathbf{x}$ in the direction $\mathbf{v}(\theta, \phi)$. Let $\mathbf{s}(\mathbf{x}) = \iint_{\theta,\phi} r_i(\mathbf{x}, \theta, \phi) \mathbf{v}(\theta, \phi) \sin\theta \, d\theta \, d\phi$. We call the vector field $\mathbf{s}$ the *light field*. Eq. (2) then provides a more general Lambertian emitted radiance model than (1):

$$r_e(\mathbf{x}) = \frac{\rho(\mathbf{x})}{\pi} \mathbf{s}(\mathbf{x}) \cdot \mathbf{n}(\mathbf{x}) \qquad (3)$$

In the photometric stereo framework, m different light fields $\mathbf{s}^i$, $i \in [1,m]$, successively illuminate the scene, providing m images I^i, $i \in [1,m]$, assumed to be graylevel images. The graylevel is assumed to be proportional to the emitted radiance $r_e(\mathbf{x})$ as expressed in (3). To our knowledge, this very general radiance model has not been used in the context of photometric stereo so far. In most applications, a single point light source at infinity is assumed, so that each lighting is represented by a constant vector in $\mathbb{R}^3$ [1,7,14,15,17]. Closer to this general expression is the important work of Basri et al. in [2], where a distribution of point light sources at infinity is assumed, allowing the authors to develop shape recovery algorithms based on low order spherical harmonic decompositions.

Camera Model. We assume the camera is a calibrated pinhole camera, represented by its focal length f and its principal point, considered as the origin of the image domain $\Omega \subset \mathbb{R}^2$. Each pixel $\mathbf{x}_p \in \Omega$ is then uniquely associated to a 3D point $\mathbf{x}(\mathbf{x}_p) = [x(\mathbf{x}_p), y(\mathbf{x}_p), z(\mathbf{x}_p)]^\top \in \mathbb{R}^3$, where $z > 0$ is called the *depth*, so that the surface of the object to be reconstructed can be represented as the set of 3D points $\mathcal{S} = \{\mathbf{x}(\mathbf{x}_p),\, \mathbf{x}_p \in \Omega\}$, with:

$$\mathbf{x}(\mathbf{x}_p) = \exp(u(\mathbf{x}_p)/f) \begin{bmatrix} \frac{1}{f} \mathbf{x}_p \\ 1 \end{bmatrix}, \quad u(\mathbf{x}_p) = f \log z(\mathbf{x}_p) \qquad (4)$$

It follows from (4) that the unit outward normal $\mathbf{n}(\mathbf{x})$ to the surface at $\mathbf{x}$ can be equivalently defined on the image domain Ω, through (see e.g. [11]):

$$\mathbf{n}_u(\mathbf{x}_p) = \frac{1}{\sqrt{\|\nabla u(\mathbf{x}_p)\|^2 + \left(1 + \frac{1}{f}\mathbf{x}_p \cdot \nabla u(\mathbf{x}_p)\right)^2}} \left[\begin{array}{c} -\nabla u(\mathbf{x}_p) \\ 1 + \frac{1}{f}\mathbf{x}_p \cdot \nabla u(\mathbf{x}_p) \end{array} \right] \quad (5)$$

In the radiance model (3), the albedo ρ and the light field $\mathbf{s}$ are defined on the surface $\mathcal{S}$, which is a subset of $\mathbb{R}^3$. Yet, since they are independent from the projection model, they can be equivalently defined onto the image domain Ω through the mapping (4). We will thus refer to their values as $\rho(\mathbf{x}_p)$ and $\mathbf{s}(\mathbf{x}_p)$. Forgetting the normalisation factor $\frac{1}{\pi}$, the image formation model finally reads:

$$I^i(\mathbf{x}_p) = \rho(\mathbf{x}_p)\, \mathbf{s}^i(\mathbf{x}_p) \cdot \mathbf{n}_u(\mathbf{x}_p), \qquad \mathbf{x}_p \in \Omega,\ i \in [1, m] \quad (6)$$

knowing that this equality is in fact a relation of proportionality.

1.2 Overview of Our Contributions

In most of literature on photometric stereo, the main unknown is the couple (albedo, normal field) which is estimated from the set of linear equations (6) without any prior on the camera model: knowledge of the camera parameters only has importance when *integrating* this estimated normal field into a depth map [6]. Yet, recent photometric approaches explicitely benefit from the perspective camera model: it is shown in [14] that the directional uncalibrated photometric stereo problem is better constrained under perspective projection, provided the normal field is considered integrable. Also, Mecca et al. show in [11] that the system of nonlinear PDEs in $z = \exp(u/f)$ resulting from (5) and (6) can be solved through a semi-Lagrangian scheme, avoiding the classical two-steps approach. The path we follow here combines the benefits from both these recent works, and improve their robustness through the introduction of a variational formalism.

To emphasise the advantages of our approach over prior work, let us state that: 1) it is the first variational approach to uncalibrated photometric stereo; 2) it enhances robustness through L^1-TV optimisation (only least-squares approaches were considered in the uncalibrated case so far [7,14,15]); 3) depth discontinuities can be recovered without the need for *a posteriori* robust normal field integration through e.g., techniques like those described in [6]; and 4) unknown, spatially-varying, lightings and albedo are considered (the one-step approach from [11] assumes calibrated directional lightings and known albedo).

The rest of this paper is organised as follows. Using a Bayesian rationale, we use the hypotheses above to derive in Section 2 a generic maximum a posteriori formulation of the recovery problem, and a variational formulation where regularisations use total variation semi-norms. Then, we propose in Section 3 a proximal algorithm for minimising the associated energy, before demonstrating in Section 4 the benefit of using spatially-varying lightings and the proposed robust recovery.

2 From Bayesian Inference to Variational Formulation

We derive in this section a variational approach for inverting the image formation model (6), via ideas from Bayesian inference for factoring the posterior probability, in the spirit of Mumford's work [12]. For the sake of compactness, we will denote the set of images $\mathbf{i} = [I^1, \ldots, I^m]^\top$ (vector field $\Omega \to \mathbb{R}^m$) and that of lightings $\mathbf{S} = [\mathbf{s}^1, \ldots, \mathbf{s}^m]$ (matrix field $\Omega \to \mathbb{R}^{3 \times m}$).

2.1 MAP Estimation

We first propose to recover $(u, \rho, \mathbf{S})$ as the maximum a posteriori (MAP) of the distribution

$$\mathcal{P}(u, \rho, \mathbf{S}|\mathbf{i}) = \frac{\mathcal{P}(\mathbf{i}|u, \rho, \mathbf{S})\,\mathcal{P}(u, \rho, \mathbf{S})}{\mathcal{P}(\mathbf{i})} \qquad (7)$$

where $\mathcal{P}(\mathbf{i})$ is the evidence, which can be discarded since it is constant and plays no role in MAP, $\mathcal{P}(\mathbf{i}|u, \rho, \mathbf{S})$ is the likelihood, and $\mathcal{P}(u, \rho, \mathbf{S})$ is the prior, which is factored as $\mathcal{P}(u, \rho, \mathbf{S}) = \mathcal{P}(\mathbf{S}|u, \rho)\mathcal{P}(u, \rho)$. In all photometric stereo works, u and ρ are expressed as independent functions on Ω, which is also the point of view used here, thus we factor $\mathcal{P}(u, \rho) = \mathcal{P}(u)\mathcal{P}(\rho)$.

For sake of simplicity, we assume that the lightings are independent from the surface and the albedo as well, so that the conditional prior simplifies: $\mathcal{P}(\mathbf{S}|u, \rho) = \mathcal{P}(\mathbf{S})$. Of course, this simplification is abusive in the presence of secondary reflections. Yet, such reflections are in general sufficiently sparse to be neglected almost everywhere, and their effect on depth recovery can be limited by an appropriate choice of regularisation, as the one proposed hereafter. Studying the benefit of using a joint conditional prior is left as a future research direction.

With these assumptions, we eventually obtain $\mathcal{P}(u, \rho, \mathbf{S}) = \mathcal{P}(u)\mathcal{P}(\rho)\mathcal{P}(\mathbf{S})$. Maximisation of the probability (7) is then equivalent to minimisation of the neg-log-posterior $\mathcal{E}(u, \rho, \mathbf{S}) = -\log \mathcal{P}(u, \rho, \mathbf{S}|\mathbf{i}) - \log \mathcal{P}(\mathbf{i})$ which is given by:

$$\mathcal{E}(u, \rho, \mathbf{S}) = -\log \mathcal{P}(\mathbf{i}|u, \rho, \mathbf{S}) - \log \mathcal{P}(u) - \log \mathcal{P}(\rho) - \log \mathcal{P}(\mathbf{S}) \qquad (8)$$

where the first term is a data term, and the others are regularisation measures.

2.2 Continuous Variational Energy

Data Term. Lambert's law (6) does generally not hold perfectly: noise in the measurements will prevent the equality. We assume that Lambert's law residuals are iid Laplacian, with some outliers that will account for the shadows (unexplained low graylevels), the highlights (unexplained high graylevels) and the depth discontinuities (∇u not defined). We thus use a L^1-norm based data term that accounts for the sparsity of such effects:

$$\mathcal{E}_D(u, \rho, \mathbf{S}) = \sum_{i=1}^m \int_\Omega |I^i(\mathbf{x}_p) - \rho(\mathbf{x}_p)\mathbf{s}^i(\mathbf{x}_p) \cdot \mathbf{n}_u(\mathbf{x}_p)| d\mathbf{x}_p = \sum_{i=1}^m \left\| I^i - \rho \mathbf{s}^i \cdot \mathbf{n}_u \right\|_{L^1(\Omega)} \qquad (9)$$

Regularisations. In the 3D-reconstruction framework, surfaces are usually assumed to be differentiable, but this hypothesis is rarely realistic because of the presence of edges and depth discontinuities. At a macroscopic scale, surfaces should, more reasonably, be supposed to be smooth almost everywhere, with continuous, non-differentiable edges and some depth discontinuities. A regulariser that naturally allows for the corresponding class of depth functions is the total variation (TV) semi-norm:

$$J(u) = \int_\Omega \|\nabla u(\mathbf{x}_p)\| \, \mathrm{d}\mathbf{x}_p = \|\nabla u\|_{L^1(\Omega)} \tag{10}$$

As suggested in literature [1,15], we restrict our study to the case of piecewise-smooth ("Arlequin-like") albedos, which can be enforced by a TV semi-norm as well:

$$J(\rho) = \int_\Omega \|\nabla \rho(\mathbf{x}_p)\| \mathrm{d}\mathbf{x}_p = \|\nabla \rho\|_{L^1(\Omega)} \tag{11}$$

In the directional orthographic case, the problem is inherently ill-posed, but it is shown in [15] that TV-regularisation of both the depth and the albedo reduces the ambiguities to a simple translational ambiguity. The perspective case is better constrained (u can be recovered up to a scale ambiguity on $\mathcal{S}$ without regularisation [14]), so these regularisations would essentially enforce smoothness. Well-posedness is less clear in perspective case with spatially-varying lightings. Yet, it seems rather intuitive that, by limiting the variations of the lightings, the problem gets closer to the directional one, at least piecewise. This general discussion is left as future work, but it invites us to introduce a regularisation measure for the lightings as well. Since the depth discontinuities of both u and $\mathbf{s}^i$ will, in general, coincide, it is reasonable to assume that $\mathbf{s}^i$ should have bounded variations too, and to introduce its TV-regularisation:

$$J(\mathbf{s}^i) = \int_\Omega \|\mathbf{J}(\mathbf{s}^i)(\mathbf{x}_p)\|_F \, \mathrm{d}\mathbf{x}_p = \|\mathbf{J}(\mathbf{s}^i)\|_{L^1(\Omega)}, \qquad i \in [1, m] \tag{12}$$

where $\mathbf{J}(\mathbf{s}^i)$ is the Jacobian matrix of $\mathbf{s}^i$ and $\|\cdot\|_F$ denotes the Frobenius norm. For the sake of compactness, we will denote $J(\mathbf{S}) = \sum_{i=1}^m J(\mathbf{s}^i)$. As stated earlier, the independence of $\mathbf{S}$ and u serves as a simplifying hypothesis, but it has no physical motivation: in future work, a joint regularisation of both these fields shall be introduced, using for instance a coupled L^1 semi-norm [8].

Energy. A continuous analogue of the MAP problem of minimising the neg-log posterior (8) can thus be written as the minimisation of $\mathcal{E}(u, \rho, \mathbf{S}) = \mathcal{E}_D(u, \rho, \mathbf{S}) + \alpha J(u) + \beta J(\rho) + \gamma J(\mathbf{S})$, with α, β, γ some positive weights. This functional is however not coercive in u, because of the scale ambiguity on $\mathcal{S}$ inherent to monocular perspective 3D-reconstruction. Coercivity can be forced by setting arbitrarily the depth in one point, or by adding a quadratic prior u_0:

$$\mathcal{E}(u, \rho, \mathbf{S}) = \sum_{i=1}^m \|I^i - \rho \mathbf{s}^i \cdot \mathbf{n}_u\|_{L^1} + \frac{\epsilon}{2} \|u - u_0\|_{L^2}^2 + \alpha J(u) + \beta J(\rho) + \gamma J(\mathbf{S}) \tag{13}$$

with $\epsilon > 0$ (u_0 can for instance be a prior on the mean camera-object distance).

3 Proximal Recovery Using Split-Bregman Iterations

We propose a proximal algorithm [5] for dealing with the TV semi-norms in (13), and introduce Split-Bregman iterations for decoupling the L^1 data term. Adopting the same notations as in [9] for the Bregman variables (d, b), whose components will be denoted (d^i, b^i), the augmented energy is then defined as:

$$\bar{\mathcal{E}}(u, \bar{u}, \rho, \bar{\rho}, \mathbf{S}, \bar{\mathbf{S}}, d, b) = \sum_{i=1}^{m} \left\| d^i \right\|_{L^1} + \frac{1}{2\theta_d} \sum_{i=1}^{m} \left\| d^i - (I^i - \bar{\rho}\,\bar{\mathbf{s}}^i \cdot \mathbf{n}_{\bar{u}}) - b^i \right\|_{L^2}^2 + \frac{\epsilon}{2} \left\| \bar{u} - u_0 \right\|_{L^2}^2$$

$$+ \frac{1}{2\theta_u} \left\| \bar{u} - u \right\|_{L^2}^2 + \alpha J(u) + \frac{1}{2\theta_\rho} \left\| \bar{\rho} - \rho \right\|_{L^2}^2 + \beta J(\rho) + \frac{1}{2\theta_{\mathbf{S}}} \left\| \bar{\mathbf{S}} - \mathbf{S} \right\|_{L^2}^2 + \gamma J(\mathbf{S}) \quad (22)$$

Algorithm 1 L^1-TV Perspective Photometric Stereo

Input: Images I^i, $i \in [1, m]$; camera parameters; initial light fields $\mathbf{s}^{i,0}$, $i \in [1, m]$; shape prior u_0; model parameters α, β, γ, ϵ; proximal parameters θ_d, θ_ρ, θ_u and $\theta_{\mathbf{S}}$; maximum number of iterations N.
Output: Point cloud $\mathbf{x}$, albedo ρ and updated light fields $\mathbf{s}^i$, $i \in [1, m]$.
Initialisation: Compute the normals and initialise the albedo ρ^0 by per-pixel classical photometric stereo; integrate the normals to initialise u^0; $\bar{\rho}^0 = \rho^0$, $\bar{u}^0 = u^0$; $d^{i,0} = b^{i,0} = 0$, $\bar{\mathbf{s}}^{i,0} = \mathbf{s}^{i,0}$, $i \in [1, m]$.
for $k = 1 \ldots N$ **do**

$$\bar{u}^{k+1} = \underset{\bar{u}}{\mathrm{argmin}}\,\frac{1}{2\theta_d}\sum_{i=1}^{m}\left\|d^{i,k}-\left(I^i-\bar{\rho}^k\bar{\mathbf{s}}^{i,k}\cdot\mathbf{n}_{\bar{u}}\right)-b^{i,k}\right\|_{L^2}^2 + \frac{\epsilon}{2}\|\bar{u}-u_0\|_{L^2}^2 + \frac{1}{2\theta_u}\|\bar{u}-u^k\|_{L^2}^2 \tag{14}$$

$$\bar{\rho}^{k+1} = \underset{\bar{\rho}}{\mathrm{argmin}}\,\frac{1}{2\theta_d}\sum_{i=1}^{m}\left\|d^{i,k}-\left(I^i-\bar{\rho}\,\bar{\mathbf{s}}^{i,k}\cdot\mathbf{n}_{\bar{u}^{k+1}}\right)-b^{i,k}\right\|_{L^2}^2 + \frac{1}{2\theta_\rho}\|\bar{\rho}-\rho^k\|_{L^2}^2 \tag{15}$$

$$\bar{\mathbf{s}}^{i,k+1} = \underset{\bar{\mathbf{s}}^i}{\mathrm{argmin}}\,\frac{1}{2\theta_d}\left\|d^{i,k}-\left(I^i-\bar{\rho}^{k+1}\bar{\mathbf{s}}^i\cdot\mathbf{n}_{\bar{u}^{k+1}}\right)-b^{i,k}\right\|_{L^2}^2 + \frac{1}{2\theta_{\mathbf{S}}}\|\bar{\mathbf{s}}^i-\mathbf{s}^{i,k}\|_{L^2}^2, i \in [1,m] \tag{16}$$

$$d^{i,k+1} = \underset{d^i}{\mathrm{argmin}}\,\|d^i\|_{L^1} + \frac{1}{2\theta_d}\left\|d^i-\left(I^i-\bar{\rho}^{k+1}\bar{\mathbf{s}}^{i,k+1}\cdot\mathbf{n}_{\bar{u}^{k+1}}\right)-b^{i,k}\right\|_{L^2}^2, i \in [1,m] \tag{17}$$

$$b^{i,k+1} = b^{i,k} + \left(I^i - \bar{\rho}^{k+1}\bar{\mathbf{s}}^{i,k+1}\cdot\mathbf{n}_{\bar{u}^{k+1}} - d^{i,k+1}\right), i \in [1,m] \tag{18}$$

$$u^{k+1} = \underset{u}{\mathrm{argmin}}\,\frac{1}{2\theta_u}\left\|\bar{u}^{k+1}-u\right\|_{L^2}^2 + \alpha J(u) \tag{19}$$

$$\rho^{k+1} = \underset{\rho}{\mathrm{argmin}}\,\frac{1}{2\theta_\rho}\left\|\bar{\rho}^{k+1}-\rho\right\|_{L^2}^2 + \beta J(\rho) \tag{20}$$

$$\mathbf{s}^{i,k+1} = \underset{\mathbf{s}^i}{\mathrm{argmin}}\,\frac{1}{2\theta_{\mathbf{S}}}\left\|\bar{\mathbf{s}}^{i,k+1}-\mathbf{s}^i\right\|_{L^2}^2 + \gamma J(\mathbf{s}^i), i \in [1,m] \tag{21}$$

end for
$\mathbf{x} = \exp(u/f)\,[\mathbf{x}_p^\top/f,\,1]^\top$

---

for some small positive $\theta_d, \theta_u, \theta_\rho, \theta_\mathbf{S}$. We minimise the augmented energy (22) iteratively w.r.t. each variable, according to Algorithm 1.

3.1 Solutions of Convex Subproblems in Algorithm 1

The update (17) in d is a basis pursuit problem, which is solvable explicitely by shrinkage:

$$d^{i,k+1} = \text{shrink}(I^i - \bar{\rho}^{k+1} \bar{\mathbf{s}}^{i,k+1} \cdot \mathbf{n}_{\bar{u}^{k+1}} + b^{i,k}, 1/\theta_d), \ i \in [1,m] \quad (23)$$

with $\text{shrink}(x, \gamma) = \text{sign}(x) \max\{|x| - \gamma, 0\}$. The update (18) in b is the Bregman update. Justification for this update can be found in [9]. It is the equivalent of "adding back the noise" in iterative image denoising methods [13].

Regarding the updates in u, ρ and $\mathbf{S}$ (Eqs (19), (20), and (21)), they are instances of the L^2-TV problem which we solve using Chambolle's dual projection algorithm [4], with the natural vectorial extension presented in [3] in the case of $\mathbf{S}$. We experimentally noticed that the convergence rate is better when only performing a few projection iterations (typically 5) at each global iteration k, rather than solving these problems to full convergence (the same behaviour is observed in [9]). As for the update (15) in $\bar{\rho}$, writing the normal equations leads to the explicit update:

$$\bar{\rho}^{k+1} = \frac{\theta_d \rho^k + \theta_\rho \sum_{i=1}^m (I^i - d^{i,k} + b^{i,k})(\bar{\mathbf{s}}^{i,k} \cdot \mathbf{n}_{\bar{u}^{k+1}})}{\theta_d + \theta_\rho \sum_{i=1}^m (\bar{\mathbf{s}}^{i,k} \cdot \mathbf{n}_{\bar{u}^{k+1}})^2} \quad (24)$$

In a similar way, from the vectorial normal equations derived from (16), one obtains the explicit solution in $\bar{\mathbf{s}}^i$, $i \in [1,m]$:

$$\bar{\mathbf{s}}^{i,k+1} = \left(\theta_d \mathbf{I}_3 + \theta_\mathbf{S} \left(\bar{\rho}^{k+1}\right)^2 \mathbf{n}_{\bar{u}^{k+1}} \mathbf{n}_{\bar{u}^{k+1}}^\top\right)^{-1} \left(\theta_d \mathbf{s}^{i,k} + \theta_\mathbf{S} \bar{\rho}^{k+1}(I^i - d^{i,k} + b^{i,k}) \mathbf{n}_{\bar{u}^{k+1}}\right) \quad (25)$$

which can be computed e.g., through Cholesky factorisation.

3.2 Solution in $\bar{u}$

We now describe the minimisation in $\bar{u}$ with greater care. Let us denote:

$$\mathcal{E}_{\bar{u}}^k(\bar{u}) = \frac{1}{2\theta_d} \sum_{i=1}^m \left\| d^{i,k} - (I^i - \bar{\rho}^k \bar{\mathbf{s}}^{i,k} \cdot \mathbf{n}_{\bar{u}}) - b^{i,k} \right\|_{L^2}^2 + \frac{\epsilon}{2} \left\| \bar{u} - u_0 \right\|_{L^2}^2 + \frac{1}{2\theta_u} \left\| \bar{u} - u^k \right\|_{L^2}^2 \quad (26)$$

Proposition 1. *The necessary optimality condition for $\bar{u}$ reads as the vanishing of the gradient of the energy* (26) *w.r.t. $\bar{u}$, which is given by:*

$$\nabla_{\bar{u}} \mathcal{E}_{\bar{u}}^k(\bar{u}) = \text{div}\left(\frac{f_{\bar{u}}^k}{\theta_d}(\nabla \bar{u} + (1 + \nabla \bar{u} \cdot \mathbf{u})\mathbf{u})\right) + \text{div}\left(\frac{1}{\theta_d} \pi_{1,2}(\mathbf{g}_{\bar{u}}^k)\right)$$

$$- \text{div}\left(\frac{\pi_3(\mathbf{g}_{\bar{u}}^k)}{\theta_d}\mathbf{u}\right) + \left(\epsilon + \frac{1}{\theta_u}\right)\bar{u} - \epsilon u_0 - \frac{1}{\theta_u}u^k \quad (27)$$

where $\pi_{1,2}$ and π_3 are the projections $\pi_{1,2}(a,b,c) = (a,b)$, $\pi_3(a,b,c) = c$, and

$$f_{\bar{u}}^k = \sum_{i=1}^m \frac{\tilde{I}^{i,k}\left(\tilde{I}^{i,k}+d^{i,k}-I^i-b^{i,k}\right)}{\|\nabla\bar{u}\|^2+(1+\nabla\bar{u}\cdot\mathbf{u})^2}, \quad \mathbf{g}_{\bar{u}}^k = \sum_{i=1}^m \frac{\bar{\rho}^k\left(\tilde{I}^{i,k}+d^{i,k}-I^i-b^{i,k}\right)}{\sqrt{\|\nabla\bar{u}\|^2+(1+\nabla\bar{u}\cdot\mathbf{u})^2}}\bar{\mathbf{s}}^{i,k}$$

$$\mathbf{u} = \mathbf{x}_p/f, \qquad \tilde{I}^{i,k} = \bar{\rho}^k\,\bar{\mathbf{s}}^{i,k}\cdot\mathbf{n}_{\bar{u}} \tag{28}$$

Proof. The directional derivative of $\mathbf{n}_{\bar{u}}$ at $\bar{u}$ in the direction w is given by:

$$d_w\mathbf{n}_{\bar{u}}(\bar{u}) = -\frac{\nabla w\cdot(\nabla\bar{u}+(1+\nabla\bar{u}\cdot\mathbf{u})\mathbf{u})}{\|\nabla\bar{u}\|^2+(1+\nabla\bar{u}\cdot\mathbf{u})^2}\mathbf{n}_{\bar{u}} - \frac{1}{\sqrt{\|\nabla\bar{u}\|^2+(1+\nabla\bar{u}\cdot\mathbf{u})^2}}\begin{bmatrix}\nabla w\\-\nabla w\cdot\mathbf{u}\end{bmatrix} \tag{29}$$

Let $D^i(\bar{u}) = \frac{1}{2\theta_d}\|d^{i,k}-(I^i-\bar{\rho}^k\,\bar{\mathbf{s}}^{i,k}\cdot\mathbf{n}_{\bar{u}})-b^{i,k}\|_{L^2}^2$. Using the chain rule, its first variation $L^i(w)$ is given by:

$$L^i(w) = -\frac{1}{\theta_d}\int_\Omega f_{\bar{u}}^{i,k}\nabla w\cdot(\nabla\bar{u}+(1+\nabla\bar{u}\cdot\mathbf{u})\mathbf{u}) - \frac{1}{\theta_d}\int_\Omega \mathbf{g}_{\bar{u}}^{i,k}\cdot\begin{bmatrix}\nabla w\\-\nabla w\cdot\mathbf{u}\end{bmatrix} \tag{30}$$

where $f_{\bar{u}}^{i,k}$ and $\mathbf{g}_{\bar{u}}^{i,k}$ represent the terms inside the sums in (28). The first variation of (26) is thus given by:

$$L(w) = -\frac{1}{\theta_d}\int_\Omega\left(\sum_{i=1}^m f_{\bar{u}}^{i,k}\right)(\nabla\bar{u}+(1+\nabla\bar{u}\cdot\mathbf{u})\mathbf{u})\cdot\nabla w + \int_\Omega\left(\left(\epsilon+\frac{1}{\theta_u}\right)\bar{u}-\epsilon u_0 - \frac{1}{\theta_u}u^k\right)w$$

$$-\frac{1}{\theta_d}\int_\Omega\left[\pi_{1,2}\left(\sum_{i=1}^m \mathbf{g}_{\bar{u}}^{i,k}\right)-\pi_3\left(\sum_{i=1}^m \mathbf{g}_{\bar{u}}^{i,k}\right)\mathbf{u}\right]\cdot\nabla w \tag{31}$$

Using Dirichlet boundary conditions on $\bar{u}$, application of the Green formula eventually provides the result announced in (27). □

This ressembles the steady state of a reaction-diffusion equation. The data term of (26) being nonlinear and non-convex in $\bar{u}$, there is no guarantee for the negativity of $f_{\bar{u}}^k$. For this reason, we choose a descent solver with a quasi-Newton step (BFGS) in the implementation. We now evaluate experimentally the benefit of using the proposed approach.

4 Experiments

Robustness to Noise and Outliers. We first evaluate the ability of the proposed proximal algorithm to enhance the results of classical photometric stereo. We create 20 images, of size 128×128, of a "Canadian tent" shape with a "pears" albedo, illuminated from $m = 20$ known lightings, and corrupt them simultaneously by an additive zero-mean Gaussian noise with standard deviation equal to $\sigma\%$ of the maximum graylevel, and a salt-and-pepper noise affecting $p\%$ of the pixels. We use the method from [10] to estimate the initial albedo ρ^0 and the normals which minimise the L^1 data term (9). Up to this point,

Fig. 1. Robustness to noise and outliers. First and second columns: 4 of the $m = 20$ images, with $\sigma = 20\%$ and $p = 10\%$; Third column: ground-truth depth map and albedo; Fourth column: results from [10], using a least squares integrator with homogeneous Dirichlet BC; Fifth column: results after L^1-TV refinement. State-of-the-art methods provide a rather noisy albedo, and the quality of the final depth map is widely dependent from the choice of a specific integrator. Rather than choosing a robust integrator, as advised e.g. in [6], we believe that it makes more sense to use the proposed scheme to directly refine the depth map and the albedo from the images, so as to avoid the propagation of any bias due to normal estimation. Indeed, rather than seeking a piecewise-smooth shape explaining a possibly biased normal field, it makes more sense to look for a piecewise-smooth shape explaining the images themselves.

in view of the piecewise smooth nature of the shape, robust integration should be considered to obtain a depth map [6]. To emphasise the ability of our scheme to recover such shapes as well, we integrate the normals using the DCT solver from [16] instead, with homogeneous Dirichlet BC, before iteratively refining the depth and the albedo through the proposed L^1-TV scheme (Figure 1): this allows recovering the depth discontinuities, while simultaneously denoising the albedo. We used $\theta_d = 0.1$, $\theta_u = 0.1\theta_d$, $\theta_\rho = 0.001\theta_u$, $\theta_{\mathbf{S}} = \theta_\rho$, $\epsilon = 10^{-8}$, $u_0 = 0$, $\alpha = 2/\theta_u$, $\beta = 5\alpha$, and $\gamma = \alpha$.

Influence of the Parameters. Since the proposed proximal algorithm involves numerous parameters, it is natural to question their influence. Let us first make a distinction between the model parameters α, β, γ and ϵ, and the optimisation parameters $\theta_\star$. Those latter will mainly affect the convergence rate (though, since we consider nonconvex optimisation, they may also affect the results), while the choice of the former corresponds to some *a priori* knowledge about the regularity of the unknowns. If we choose high values for α, β, γ, we will get oversmoothed results, while the 3D-reconstruction may not be robust to noise, or not well-conditioned, if we choose low values. The parameter ϵ only enforces coercivity, thus any low value should be satisfactory (we set $\epsilon = 10^{-8}$ in all the experiments). As for the optimisation parameters, setting high $\theta_\star$ values will result in slow convergence, while the optimisation may become unstable with low values. In our tests, we experimented no major difficulty in finding a set of these numerous parameters offering "reasonable" results. Tuning more precisely

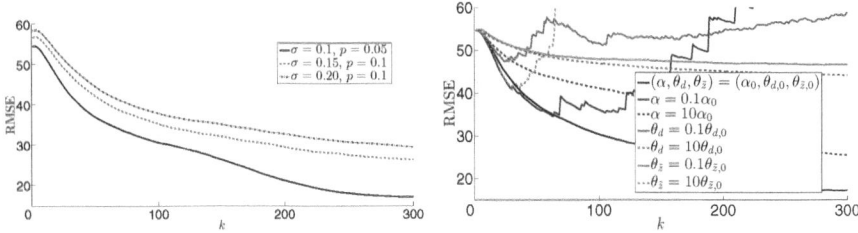

Fig. 2. Quantitative evaluation of the diffusion process. Left: RMSE in u as a function of the number k of iterations, for several levels of noise (σ, p), with the same reference values of the parameters as in the first test, denoted $(\alpha_0, \theta_{d,0}, \theta_{u,0})$ in the case of $(\alpha, \theta_d, \theta_u)$. Right: influence of the model parameter α and of the optimisation parameters θ_d and θ_u on the diffusion process. Convergence is stable but slow if α or θ_d is too high (oversmoothed depth map), or if θ_u is too high (small descent steps). On the contrary, the descent is too fast to be stable if we set a too low value for α or θ_d (no regularisation, inducing numerical difficulties), or if θ_u is too low (large descent steps).

one or the other parameter can be a little more tricky, as illustrated in Figure 2. We used the same data as in the previous test, with $\sigma = 0.1$ and $p = 0.05$, for studying the evolution of the RMSE in u (the scale ambiguity on $\mathcal{S}$ is a posteriori solved to minimise this RMSE) with respect to a specific choice of α, θ_d or θ_u (the

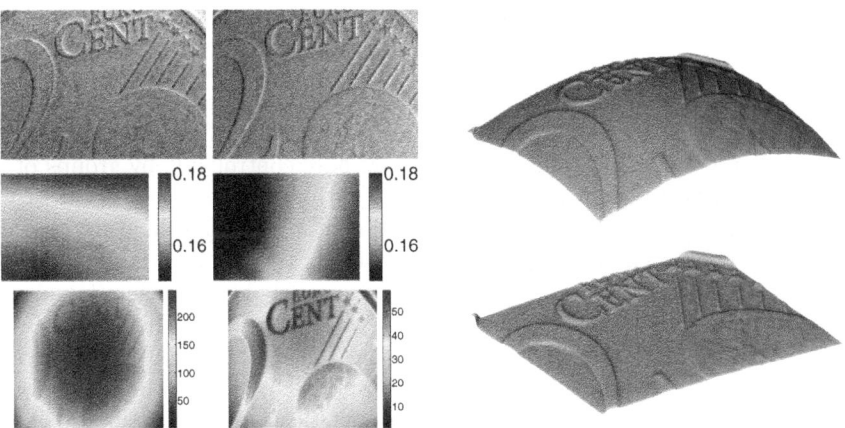

Fig. 3. Bias correction by using spatially-varying lightings. Left, from top to bottom: two of the $m = 15$ input images; associated calibrated lighting intensities; estimated log depth maps using least-squares photometric stereo with a directional model and with the calibrated spatially-varying lightings. Right: relighted views of the estimated sets of 3D-points, using directional (top) or spatially-varying lightings (bottom). Neglecting the spatial variations of the lightings creates a global drift in the reconstruction, which is drastically reduced by considering spatially-varying lightings. This 3D-reconstruction could then be further improved using the proposed L^1-TV scheme.

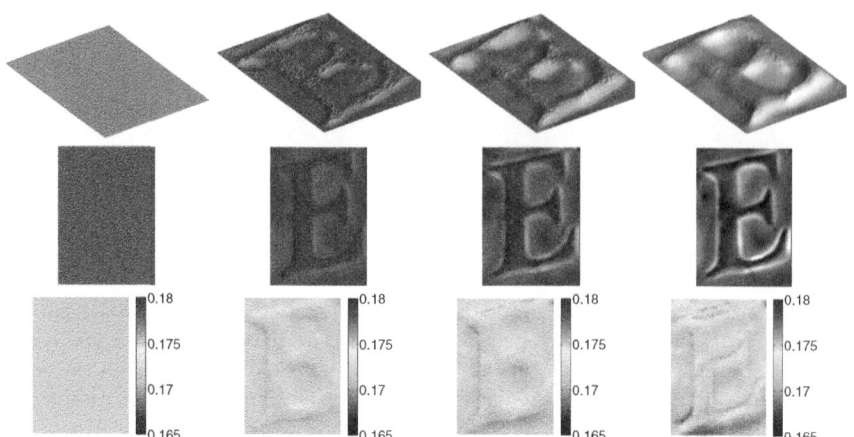

Fig. 4. L^1-TV optimisation with rough initialisation. We show the diffusion process of u (top), ρ (middle) and $\|\mathbf{s}^1\|$ (bottom), at $k = 0$, $k = 10$, $k = 20$ and $k = 40$. The sharp features are first captured by the L^1 data term, and then the TV proximal operators smooth out the residual noise. Realistic estimation can be provided, even with a very rough initialisation.

other parameters behave similarly). Finding heuristics for automatic selection of the parameters, based on these observations, is left as future work.

Experimental Setup and Lighting Initialisation. For tests on real-world data, we used a calibrated camera surrounded by twenty LEDs oriented towards a white-painted two cents coin. The LEDs are only controllable by groups of 5, providing 15 different lighting configurations with either 5, 10, 15 or 20 LEDs turned on together. Thanks to the proposed spatially-varying lightings, we do not need model-driven calibration of the lightings: to initialise the light fields, we used a planar calibration grid composed of regularly located white truncated pyramids, before interpolating them so as to obtain dense light fields.

We first evaluate the benefit of using spatially-varying lightings, by comparing the results of the classical two-steps approach, using either directional lightings or the calibrated spatially-varying ones (least-squares estimations are used). Results shown in Figure 3 prove that the widely-spread idea according to which photometric stereo can recover high-frequency details, but not low-frequency ones is wrong: it is only a matter of correctly estimating the lightings.

L^1-TV Refinement from Rough Initialisation. We now question the importance of the initialisation for the full (shape, reflectance and lightings) proximal recovery, regarding the non-convexity of the energy. Due to the computational cost required to perform one Cholesky factorisation per pixel at each iteration in the lightings estimation, we consider a small close-up on the "E" letter of the coin, with size 201 × 146 pixels. The evolution of the anisotropic diffusion process, starting from a flat shape with uniform albedo and directional lightings, is illustrated in Figure 4: it proves that the proposed proximal algorithm converges towards a realistic solution even if a rough initialisation is considered. We used $\theta_d = 0.05$, $\theta_u = 100\theta_d$, $\theta_\rho = \theta_{\tilde{d}}$, $\theta_\mathbf{S} = 0.1\theta_d$, $\epsilon = 10^{-8}$, $\alpha = 0.05/\theta_u$, $\beta = 0.05/\theta_\rho$, $u_0 = 0$ and $\gamma = 0.0001/\theta_S$.

5 Conclusion and Perspectives

We proposed a variational formulation for the joint recovery of shape, reflectance and spatially-varying lightings from observed images, derived from a formal MAP approach. Despite the apparent difficulty of tackling a non-convex problem, robust recovery of the depth can be obtained without integrating the normals. By considering the lightings as unknown vector fields, situations usually considered as "hard", like nearby or extended sources, are easily handled. In future work, we will explore joint regularisation of the lightings, the depth and the albedo and study with more care the well-posedness of the inverse problem, the robustness with respect to the numerous parameters, and more efficient numerics.

Acknowledgments. This work is part of a technological transfer between IRIT and the Pixience company, funded by Toulouse Tech Transfer.

References

1. Alldrin, N.G., Mallick, S.P., Kriegman, D.J.: Resolving the generalized bas-relief ambiguity by entropy minimization. In: CVPR (2007)
2. Basri, R., Jacobs, D., Kemelmacher, I.: Photometric stereo with general, unknown lighting. IJCV **72**(3), 239–257 (2007)
3. Bresson, X., Chan, T.: Fast dual minimization of the vectorial total variation norm and applications to color image processing. IPI **2**(4), 455–484 (2008)
4. Chambolle, A.: An algorithm for total variation minimization and applications. JMIV **20**(1–2), 89–97 (2004)
5. Chambolle, A., Pock, T.: A first-order primal-dual algorithm for convex problems with applications to imaging. JMIV **40**(1), 120–145 (2011)
6. Durou, J.-D., Aujol, J.-F., Courteille, F.: Integrating the normal field of a surface in the presence of discontinuities. In: Cremers, D., Boykov, Y., Blake, A., Schmidt, F.R. (eds.) EMMCVPR 2009. LNCS, vol. 5681, pp. 261–273. Springer, Heidelberg (2009)
7. Georghiades, A.: Incorporating the torrance and sparrow model of reflectance in uncalibrated photometric stereo. In: ICCV (2003)
8. Goldluecke, B., Strekalovskiy, E., Cremers, D.: The natural vectorial total variation which arises from geometric measure theory. SIIMS **5**(2), 537–563 (2012)
9. Goldstein, T., Osher, S.: The Split Bregman method for L1-regularized problems. SIIMS **2**(2), 323–343 (2009)
10. Ikehata, S., Wipf, D., Matsushita, Y., Aizawa, K.: Robust photometric stereo using sparse regression. In: CVPR (2012)

11. Mecca, R., Tankus, A., Wetzler, A., Bruckstein, A.M.: A direct differential approach to photometric stereo with perspective wiewing. SIIMS **7**(2), 579–612 (2014)
12. Mumford, D.: Bayesian rationale for the variational formulation. In: Geometry-Driven Diffusion in Computer Vision, pp. 135–146 (1994)
13. Osher, S., Burger, M., Goldfarb, D., Xu, J., Yin, W.: An iterative regularization method for total variation-based image restoration. MMS **4**(2), 460–489 (2005)
14. Papadhimitri, T., Favaro, P.: A new perspective on uncalibrated photometric stereo. In: CVPR (2013)
15. Quéau, Y., Lauze, F., Durou, J.D.: Solving uncalibrated photometric stereo using total variation. To appear in JMIV (2015)
16. Simchony, T., Chellappa, R., Shao, M.: Direct analytical methods for solving Poisson equations in computer vision problems. PAMI **12**(5), 435–446 (1990)
17. Woodham, R.J.: Photometric method for determining surface orientation from multiple images. Optical Engineering **19**(1), 139–144 (1980)

Shape, Surface and 3D Problems

Discrete Varifolds: A Unified Framework for Discrete Approximations of Surfaces and Mean Curvature

B. Buet[1(✉)], G.P. Leonardi[2], and S. Masnou[1]

[1] Institut Camille Jordan, Université Claude Bernard Lyon 1, Lyon, France
buet@math.univ-lyon1.fr
[2] Dipartimento di Scienze Fisiche, Informatiche e Matematiche,
Università degli studi di Modena e Reggio Emilia, Modena, Italia

Abstract. We propose a unified theory for the discretization of manifolds (triangulations, volumetric approximations, pixelization, point clouds etc.) which provides a common framework for describing discrete and continuous surfaces, allows a control of the weak regularity of the limit surface and provides a consistent notion of mean curvature. This is made possible by the theory of varifolds. Varifolds have been introduced more than 40 years ago as a generalized notion of k-surface, with a number of relevant applications (for example to the existence and regularity of soap bubble clusters and soap films). Our extension of the theory consists in a new discrete framework, including in particular a scale-dependent notion of mean curvature, by which one can approximate variational problems on (generalized) surfaces by minimizing suitable energies defined on discrete varifolds. As an example, we apply the theory of discrete varifolds to estimate the mean curvature of a point cloud and to approximate its evolution by mean curvature flow.

Keywords: Surface approximation · Discrete mean curvature · Varifolds · Point clouds

1 Introduction

Approximation is a central issue in computer graphics and image processing. In particular, given a point cloud, a triangulation, or a digital line/surface in a 2D/3D image, it is often very useful to characterize the geometry of the underlying continuous line/surface/volume, to estimate the accuracy of the discrete representation of both regular parts and singularities (corners, edges, cusps, darts, etc.), and to estimate in a robust and consistent way geometric informations as the tangent or the curvatures, and geometric energies as lengths, areas, volumes, or first and second-order energies. There is a huge literature regarding this issue in various fields like digital geometry, computational geometry, or image processing. The purpose of this paper is twofold:

1. introducing *discrete varifolds* as a general and flexible tool to represent in a common framework a large category of discrete representations of surfaces, e.g. point clouds, triangulated surfaces or pixel/voxel representations. A key property of varifolds is that they carry both spatial and tangential informations;
2. introducing a new notion of discrete mean curvature which has nice estimation and convergence properties.

It is well known that, unlike the classical mean curvature of a regular surface, there is no unique notion of discrete curvature but many of them, depending in particular of the choice of a discretization. When considering a polyhedral surface, the *cotangent formula* (see [2]) provides the curvature as the discrete gradient of the area. The link between mean curvature and first variation of the area is in fact the key of several approaches for giving a notion of discrete curvature in different settings, for instance the discrete curvature of digital shapes can be computed from the volumes of the intersection with local balls, with good convergence properties [3].

The approach we propose in this paper is based on geometric measure theory and more precisely on *varifolds theory*. Varifolds have been introduced by F. Almgren in 1965 to study the existence of critical points of the area functional. As we will explain, both regular and discrete objects can be provided with a varifold structure, allowing to study surfaces and their different discretizations in a consistent unified setting.

Other tools from geometric measure theory have been used in the literature for surface approximation and curvature estimation. For instance, *normal cycles* have been introduced in [5], first defined for surfaces and triangulations [4] and recently extended in [6] to more general discrete surfaces like point clouds. The accuracy of the approximation of the surface is measured in terms of Hausdorff distance while the error between the curvature measure of the surface and the curvature measure of the approximation is controlled in terms of the *Bounded Lipschitz distance* which is a distance close to Wasserstein distance. Another application of geometric measure theory arises in shape registration: Trouvé and Charon [8] provide triangulated surfaces with a varifold structure and define a distance between varifolds, both computable from a numerical point of view and adapted to surface comparison.

Before entering into more details, let us emphasize that the theoretical results contained in this paper will be stated without proof for obvious reasons of space. The interested reader may refer to [9,10,11].

2 Discrete Varifolds

2.1 Varifolds

We denote by $C_c^k(\Omega)$ the space of real continuous compactly supported functions of class C^k ($k \in \mathbb{N}$) in Ω. We recall here a few facts about varifolds, see [9,10] for more details and [1] for a complete introduction to varifolds.

Definition 1 (Varifold). *Let $\Omega \subset \mathbb{R}^n$ be an open set. A d–varifold in Ω is a positive Radon measure on $\Omega \times G_{d,n}$, where the Grassmannian $G_{d,n}$ is defined by $G_{d,n} = \{P \subset \mathbb{R}^n \,|\, P \text{ is a vector subspace of dimension } d\}$. The mass of a d–varifold V is the positive Radon measure $\|V\|(B) = V(\pi^{-1}(B))$ for every $B \subset \Omega$ Borel, with $\pi : (x,S) \in \Omega \times G_{d,n} \mapsto x \in \Omega$ the projection onto Ω.*

If $S \subset \mathbb{R}^3$ is a smooth surface, there is a natural varifold associated with S defined as the measure $\mathcal{H}^2_{|S} \otimes \delta_{T_x S}$ (see (1) below for the rigorous meaning of $\mathcal{H}^2_{|S} \otimes \delta_{T_x S}$ thanks to its action on $C^0_c(\Omega \times G_{d,n})$), where $\mathcal{H}^2_{|S}$ is the 2-dimensional Hausdorff measure restricted to S (i.e. the area measure restricted to S). In other words, varifolds carry two informations about a surface: spatial and tangential informations. Let us now introduce the notion of rectifiable varifold.

Definition 2 (Rectifiable d–varifold). *Given an open set $\Omega \subset \mathbb{R}^n$, let M be a countably d–rectifiable set and θ be a non negative function with $\theta > 0$ $\mathcal{H}^d$–almost everywhere in M. A rectifiable d–varifold $V = v(M, \theta)$ in Ω is a positive Radon measure on $\Omega \times G_{d,n}$ of the form $V = \theta \mathcal{H}^d_{|M} \otimes \delta_{T_x M}$ i.e., $\forall \varphi \in C^0_c(\Omega \times G_{d,n})$*

$$\int_{\Omega \times G_{d,n}} \varphi(x, T) \, dV(x, T) = \int_M \varphi(x, T_x M) \, \theta(x) \, d\mathcal{H}^d(x) \,, \tag{1}$$

where $T_x M$ is the approximative tangent space at x which exists $\mathcal{H}^d$–almost everywhere in M. The function θ is called the multiplicity *of the rectifiable varifold.*

2.2 Discrete Varifolds

The first general type of discrete varifolds are volumetric, i.e. they can naturally be associated with a pixel/voxel representation of an object.

Discrete Volumetric Varifolds. Let $\Omega \subset \mathbb{R}^n$ be an open set and let $(\mathcal{K}, \mathcal{E})$ be a mesh of Ω, where $\mathcal{K}$ is the set of cells and $\mathcal{E}$ is the set of faces, $(\mathcal{K}, \mathcal{E})$ will be often shortened in $\mathcal{K}$ in the following. Given a d–rectifiable set $M \subset \mathbb{R}^n$ (a curve, a surface...), we can define for any cell $K \in \mathcal{K}$, a mass $m_K = \mathcal{H}^d(M \cap K)$ (the length of the piece of curve in the cell, the area of the piece of surface in the cell...) and a mean tangent plane $P_K \in \arg\min_{S \in G_{d,n}} \int_{M \cap K} |T_x M - S| \, d\mathcal{H}^d(x)$. Similarly, given a rectifiable d–varifold V, defining $m_K = \|V\|(K)$ and $P_K \in \arg\min_{S \in G_{d,n}} \int_{K \times G_{d,n}} |P - S| \, dV(x, P)$ provides a volumetric approximation of V. This leads us to the following structure of *discrete volumetric varifolds*:

Definition 3. *Let $\Omega \subset \mathbb{R}^n$ be an open set. Consider $(\mathcal{K}, \mathcal{E})$ a mesh of Ω and a family $\{m_K, P_K\}_{K \in \mathcal{K}} \subset \mathbb{R}_+ \times G_{d,n}$. The associated* discrete volumetric varifold *is defined as $V_\mathcal{K} = \sum_{K \in \mathcal{K}} \frac{m_K}{|K|} \mathcal{L}^n_{|K} \otimes \delta_{P_K}$ with $|K| = \mathcal{L}^n(K)$.*

These d–varifolds are not rectifiable since their support is n–rectifiable but not d–rectifiable.

Point Clouds and Triangulated Varifolds

Definition 4 (Point cloud varifolds). *Consider a finite set of points $\{x_i\}_{i=1...N} \subset \mathbb{R}^n$, weighted by the masses $\{m_i\}_{i=1...N}$ and provided with directions $\{P_i\}_{i=1...N} \subset G_{d,n}$. The canonical d–varifold on $\mathbb{R}^n \times G_{d,n}$ associated with this point cloud is*

$$V = \sum_{i=1}^{N} m_i \, \delta_{x_i} \otimes \delta_{P_i} \, .$$

Remark 1. In practice, all directions P_i's are either provided by the capture system or computed by regression. As for the masses, they correspond to local densities of points. In the experiments presented here, all masses are taken unitary for the points are roughly uniformly distributed along the curves/surfaces. In more general situations however, a careful computation of densities is necessary because artificial variations (due for instance to directional inhomogeneities of the scanner) may result in artificial curvature. Addressing this issue is the purpose of current work.

Definition 5 (Triangulated varifold). *Consider a triangulated d-surface in $\mathbb{R}^n$ defined by a set of triangles $\{T_j\}_{j=1}^{N}$ canonically associated with the collection of tangent planes $\{P_j\}_{j=1}^{N}$. Then the measure $\sum_{j=1}^{N} \mathcal{H}^d_{|T_j} \otimes \delta_{P_j}$ defines a d–varifold associated with the triangulated surface.*

Remark 2. Point cloud or triangulated varifolds can be reformulated as volumetric varifolds: it suffices to define a mesh of the ambient space and to compute the contribution in each mesh cell of the point cloud or the triangulated varifold. For this reason, we focus on convergence properties of volumetric varifolds. More precisely, we address the following question: considering a sequence of meshes $(\mathcal{K}_i)_i$ whose size is tending to 0, **what class of varifolds is it possible to approximate by discrete volumetric varifolds $(V_i)_i$ associated with these prescribed successive meshes?**

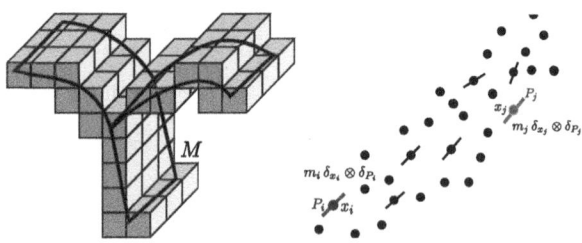

Fig. 1. Left: a discrete volumetric varifold; right: a point cloud varifold

2.3 Approximation by Discrete Varifolds

We state in the following result that discrete volumetric varifolds approximate well rectifiable varifolds in the sense of weak–∗ convergence. Under an additional regularity assumption of the tangent planes of the limit varifold (this assumption can be relaxed, see [10] for more details), one can even obtain a more accurate control involving the bounded Lipschitz distance and the size of the successive meshes. The bounded Lipschitz distance (or flat distance) is similar to a Wasserstein distance, except that it allows to compare measures even if they do not have the same finite mass:

Definition 6 (Bounded Lipschitz distance). *Let μ and ν be two Radon measures on a locally compact metric space (X, d). The quantity*

$$\Delta^{1,1}(\mu, \nu) = \sup\left\{ \left| \int_X \phi \, d\mu - \int_X \phi \, d\nu \right| \, : \, \phi \in Lip(X), \, \|\phi\|_\infty \leq 1 \text{ and } lip(\phi) \leq 1 \right\}$$

defines a distance in the space of Radon measure in X, called the bounded Lipschitz distance.

An example of application to image processing of such distance is provided in [7].

Theorem 1. *Let $\Omega \subset \mathbb{R}^n$ be an open set and let $(\mathcal{K}_i)_i$ be a family of meshes of Ω such that $\delta_i = \sup_{K \in \mathcal{K}_i} \operatorname{diam}(K) \xrightarrow[i \to +\infty]{} 0$. Let $V = v(M, \theta)$ be a rectifiable d–varifold in Ω and for all i, define the discrete volumetric varifold V_i by*

$$V_i = \sum_{K \in \mathcal{K}_i} \frac{m_K^i}{|K|} \mathcal{L}^n \otimes \delta_{P_K^i} \text{ with } P_K^i \in \arg\min_{P \in G_{d,n}} \int_{K \times G_{d,n}} \|P - S\| \, dV(x, S)$$

and $m_K^i = \|V\|(K)$. Then $V_i \xrightarrow[i \to \infty]{*} V$.
Assume in addition that there exist $0 < \beta \leq 1$ and $C > 0$ such that for $\|V\|$–almost $x, y \in \Omega$,

$$\|T_x M - T_y M\| \leq C|x - y|^\beta, \tag{2}$$

then $\Delta^{1,1}(V_i, V) \leq \left(\delta_i + 2C\delta_i^\beta \right) \|V\|(\Omega)$.

Conversely, the following theorem provides **a quantitative way of ensuring that a sequence of volumetric varifolds does indeed converge to a rectifiable varifold**. In image processing, this provides an asymptotic way to identify edges which are really associated with a well-defined geometric object, in contrast with edges which are due to strong but unstructured oscillations, for instance in some texture regions.

Theorem 2. *Let $\Omega \subset \mathbb{R}^n$ be an open set and $(V_i)_i$ a sequence of d–varifolds in Ω weakly–∗ converging to some d–varifold V of finite mass $\|V\|(\Omega) < +\infty$. Fix two decreasing and infinitesimal (tending to 0) sequences of positive numbers $(\alpha_i)_i$ and $(\beta_i)_i$ and assume that:*

(i) there exist $0 < C_1 < C_2$ such that for $\|V_i\|$–almost every $x \in \Omega$ and for every $\beta_i < r < d(x, \Omega^c)$, $C_1 r^d \leq \|V_i\|(B_r(x)) \leq C_2 r^d$,

(ii) $\sup_i \int_{\Omega \times G_{d,n}} E_{\alpha_i}(x, P, V_i) \, dV_i(x, P) < +\infty$, where

$$E_\alpha(x, P, W) = \int_\alpha^1 \frac{1}{r^d} \int_{y \in B_r(x) \cap \Omega} \left(\frac{d(y-x, P)}{r} \right)^2 d\|W\|(y) \frac{dr}{r}$$

denotes the α-approximate averaged height excess.

Then V is a rectifiable d-varifold.

The density assumption is a natural way to avoid mass dispersion. The α-approximate averaged height excess $E_\alpha(x, P, W)$ estimates how the measure $\|W\|$ is concentrated around the plane P at a point x and at the scale α (considering balls centered at x and of radius larger than α). The proofs of both results above are lengthy and fall out of the scope of the present paper. The interested reader may refer to [9].

3 Curvature of a Discrete Varifold

We are now interested in a consistent estimation of the mean curvature of discrete varifolds. Let us first explain why the classical notion of first variation for varifolds is not adapted even in the simple situation where discrete varifolds converge to a regular varifold.

3.1 First Variation of a Varifold

The set of d-varifolds is endowed with a notion of generalized curvature called *first variation* [1].

Definition 7. *The first variation of a d-varifold in $\Omega \subset \mathbb{R}^n$ is the linear functional*

$$\begin{aligned} \delta V : C_c^1(\Omega, \mathbb{R}^n) &\to \mathbb{R} \\ X &\mapsto \int_{\Omega \times G_{d,n}} \mathrm{div}_P X(x) \, dV(x, P) \end{aligned}$$

It is a distribution of order 1 but not necessarily a Radon measure.

For $P \in G_{d,n}$ and $X = (X_1, \ldots, X_n) \in C_c^1(\Omega, \mathbb{R}^n)$, the operator div_P in the previous definition is defined as

$$\mathrm{div}_P(x) = \sum_{j=1}^n \langle \nabla^P X_j(x), e_j \rangle = \sum_{j=1}^n \langle \Pi_P(\nabla X_j(x)), e_j \rangle, \quad (3)$$

with $(e_1, \ldots, e_n)$ the canonical basis of $\mathbb{R}^n$ and Π_P the orthogonal projector onto $P \in G_{d,n}$. When $V = \mathcal{H}_{|S}^2 \otimes \delta_{T_x S}$ is a 2-varifold associated with a regular surface S, then δV is a Radon measure and we simply have

$$\delta V = -H \mathcal{H}_{|S}^2 . \quad (4)$$

where H is the classical mean curvature of S. More generally, the *generalized mean curvature* H of a d-varifold with **bounded first variation** is (minus) the Radon-Nikodym derivative of δV with respect to the varifold's mass. This definition is, however, **not suitable for discrete varifolds**: it is very easy to construct discrete volumetric varifolds $(V_i)_i$ which approximate the varifold $V = \mathcal{H}^1_{|D} \otimes \delta_D$ associated with a straight line D but have no uniformly bounded first variation, more precisely

$$\delta V_i \xrightarrow[i \to \infty]{*} \delta V = 0 \text{ but } \|\delta V_i\| \xrightarrow[i \to \infty]{} +\infty. \tag{5}$$

We therefore introduce a regularized form of the first variation which appears to be more adapted to discrete varifolds.

3.2 Regularized First Variation and Mean Curvature

As the first variation can be seen as a distribution of order 1, it is possible to regularize it by convolution with a Lipschitz kernel. From now on, $\rho \in W^{1,\infty}(\mathbb{R}^n)$ is a symmetric positive function such that $\int \rho = 1$ and $\operatorname{supp} \rho \subset B_1(0)$, and we let $\rho_\epsilon = \frac{1}{\epsilon^n} \rho\left(\frac{x}{\epsilon}\right)$.

Definition 8 (ϵ-regularized first variation). *The ϵ-regularized first variation of a general varifold V is $\delta V * \rho_\epsilon \in L^1(\mathbb{R}^n)$ given for $\mathcal{L}^n$-almost any $x \in \mathbb{R}^n$ by*

$$\delta V * \rho_\epsilon(x) = \int_{B_\epsilon(x) \times G_{d,n}} \nabla^S \rho_\epsilon(y - x) \, dV(y, S) = \frac{1}{\epsilon^{n+1}} \int_{B_\epsilon(x) \times G_{d,n}} \nabla^S \rho\left(\frac{y - x}{\epsilon}\right) dV(y, S).$$

Mimicking the expression of the generalized mean curvature of a varifold, we define the ϵ-*approximate mean curvature* H_ϵ as:

$$H_\epsilon(x) = -\frac{\delta V * \rho_\epsilon(x)}{\|V\| * \rho_\epsilon(x)}. \tag{6}$$

It is however crucial to notice the key difference between the generalized mean curvature and the ϵ-approximate mean curvature. As already said, the former can be defined only for varifolds with bounded first variation whereas the latter can be defined for **any** varifold, in particular discrete varifolds.

Natural by-products of this general notion of mean curvature are the approximate p–Willmore energies associated with a kernel ρ:

Definition 9 (Approximate Willmore energies). *Let $p \geq 1$ and $\epsilon > 0$. Let $\Omega \subset \mathbb{R}^n$ be an open set. For any d-varifold V in Ω, we define*

$$W^p_\epsilon(V) = \int_{x \in \mathbb{R}^n} \left|\frac{\delta V * \rho_\epsilon(x)}{\|V\| * \rho_\epsilon(x)}\right|^p \|V\| * \rho_\epsilon(x) \, d\mathcal{L}^n(x). \tag{7}$$

Convergence properties of these ϵ-approximate geometric energies can be proved [10]:

Theorem 3. *Let $\Omega \subset \mathbb{R}^n$ be an open set and let $V = v(M, \theta)$ be a rectifiable d–varifold with bounded first variation $\delta V = -H \|V\| + \delta V_s$. Then,*

- $\delta V * \rho_\epsilon \xrightarrow[\epsilon \to 0]{*} \delta V$,
- *for any sequence of d–varifolds $(V_\epsilon)_\epsilon$ such that $V_\epsilon \xrightarrow[\epsilon \to 0]{*} V$*

$$\|\delta V\| \leq \liminf_{\epsilon \to 0} \mathcal{W}_\epsilon^1(V_\epsilon) \quad \text{and} \quad \mathcal{W}^p(V) \leq \liminf_{\epsilon \to 0} \mathcal{W}_\epsilon^p(V_\epsilon) \,.$$

- $\mathcal{W}_\epsilon^1(V) \xrightarrow[\epsilon \to 0]{} \|\delta V\|$ *and* $\mathcal{W}_\epsilon^p(V) \xrightarrow[\epsilon \to 0]{} \mathcal{W}^p(V)$.

In particular, the approximate Willmore energies $\mathcal{W}_\epsilon^p$ Γ–converge to the p–Willmore energy $\mathcal{W}^p$ if $1 < p < +\infty$ and to the total variation of the first variation $V \mapsto \|\delta V\|$ if $p = 1$.
If, moreover, the kernel ρ is radial, then for $\|V\|$–almost any $x \in \Omega$,

$$H_\epsilon(x) = -\frac{\delta V * \rho_\epsilon(x)}{\|V\| * \rho_\epsilon(x)} \xrightarrow[\epsilon \to 0]{} H(x) \,. \tag{8}$$

3.3 Regularized First Variation and Discrete Volumetric Varifolds

We now exhibit quantitative conditions linking the size of the successive meshes δ_i and the approximation scales ϵ_i, and ensuring that for a d–rectifiable varifold V (with the additional regularity assumption (2)) the approximate first variation, mean curvature and Willmore energies of the sequence of discrete volumetric varifolds $(V_i)_i$ given by Theorem 1 do converge, respectively, to the first variation, generalized mean curvature and Willmore energy of V [10].

Theorem 4. *Let $\Omega \subset \mathbb{R}^n$ be an open set and let $V = v(M, \theta)$ be a rectifiable d–varifold in Ω with finite mass $\|V\|(\Omega)$ and bounded first variation $\delta V = -H \|V\| + (\delta V)_s$, and satisfying (2) for some $\beta > 0$. Let $(\mathcal{K}_i)_i$ be a family of meshes of size $\delta_i = \sup_{K \in \mathcal{K}_i} \operatorname{diam}(K) \xrightarrow[i \to +\infty]{} 0$. Let $V_i \xrightarrow[i \to \infty]{*} V$ given by Theorem 1.*

Assume in addition that the kernel ρ is in $W^{2,\infty}$ and that moreover $\rho(x) = \zeta(|x|)$ is radial, with $\zeta \in W^{2,\infty}(\mathbb{R}_+)$ decreasing. If $\frac{\delta_i^\beta}{\epsilon_i^2} \xrightarrow[i \to \infty]{} 0$ then,

- $\delta V_i * \rho_{\epsilon_i} \xrightarrow[i \to \infty]{*} \delta V$,
- $\mathcal{W}_{\epsilon_i}^1(V_i) \to \|\delta V\|$,
- *for $\|V\|$–almost any $x \in \Omega$,* $-\dfrac{\delta V_i * \rho_{\epsilon_i}(x)}{\|V_i\| * \rho_{\epsilon_i}(x)} \xrightarrow[i \to \infty]{} H(x)$.

If $V = v(M, 1)$ is associated with a C^2 submanifold M, with constant multiplicity $\theta = 1$, the speed of convergence is controlled by a constant depending on the regularity of ρ times $\dfrac{\delta_i}{\epsilon_i^2}$. See [11] for more details.

4 Approximate Mean Curvature of a Point Cloud

Convenient choices for the kernel ρ in Definition 8 yield simple expressions of the approximate mean curvature which have natural and simple discrete counterparts. For instance, if ρ is the "tepee" kernel $T(z) = \frac{1}{\lambda_n}(1 - |z|)$ if $|z| \leq 1$, 0 otherwise, with $\lambda_n = \int_{|z|\leq 1}(1 - |z|)\,d\mathcal{L}^n(z)$, replacing ρ_ϵ in Definition 8 with $T_\epsilon(z) = \frac{1}{\epsilon^n}T\left(\frac{z}{\epsilon}\right)$ yields after easy calculations

$$\delta V * T_\epsilon(x) = -\frac{1}{\lambda_n \epsilon^{n+1}} \int_{B_\epsilon(x)} \frac{\Pi_P(y-x)}{|y-x|}\,d\|V\|(y)$$

and thus, if $V = \sum_{i=1}^{N} m_i \delta_{x_i} \otimes \delta_{P_i}$ is a point cloud with weight m_i at each point x_i, one has

$$H_\epsilon(x) = -\frac{\delta V * \rho_\epsilon(x)}{\|V\| * \rho_\epsilon(x)} = \frac{1}{\epsilon} \frac{\sum_{x_j \in B_\epsilon} m_j \Pi_{P_j} \frac{x_j-x}{|x_j-x|}}{\sum_{x_j \in B_\epsilon} m_j \left(1 - \frac{|x_j-x|}{\epsilon}\right)}.$$

Another possible kernel is the "reversed tepee" $\rho(x) = |x|$ if $|x| \leq 1$, 0 otherwise, which is not regular but seems to provide experimentally more stable estimations of the mean curvature. Combining with the "tepee" kernel, the associated ϵ-approximate mean curvature is

$$H_\epsilon(x) = \frac{\int_{B_\epsilon(x)} \frac{\Pi_P(y-x)}{|y-x|}\,d\|V\|(y)}{\int_{B_\epsilon(x)} |y-x|\,d\|V\|(y)}$$

whose discrete counterpart is

$$H_\epsilon^N(x) = \frac{\sum_{j=1}^{N} \mathbb{1}_{\{|x_j-x|<\epsilon\}} m_j \frac{\Pi_{P_j}(x_j-x)}{|x_j-x|}}{\sum_{j=1}^{N} \mathbb{1}_{\{|x_j-x|<\epsilon\}} m_j |x_j-x|} \qquad (9)$$

Both formulas are easy to implement, and we provide in the next section a few experiments made with them. We do not know yet what are the best kernels from the numerical viewpoint, it is the subject of ongoing work. Among the issues which must be addressed, the local stability is important. One of the weaknesses of the approximate curvatures given by the above formulas is their lack of robustness with respect to variations of the density of points within the point cloud. In the case of constant density of points, the formulas behave very well, but it is no more the case with varying densities. An alternative is to replace the projection onto the tangent plane by a projection onto the normal. For a point cloud varifold

$V_N = \sum_{j=1}^{N} m_j \delta_{x_j} \otimes \delta_{P_j}$, the ϵ-approximate mean curvature with the "reversed tepee" kernel and with projections onto the normals can be computed as

$$H_\epsilon^N(x) = -2 \frac{\sum_{j=1}^{N} \mathbb{1}_{\{|x_j - x| < \epsilon\}} m_j \frac{\Pi_{P_j^\perp}(x_j - x)}{|x_j - x|}}{\sum_{j=1}^{N} \mathbb{1}_{\{|x_j - x| < \epsilon\}} m_j |x_j - x|} . \tag{10}$$

This appears to yield a correct approximation for smooth curves in dimension 1, but we do not have yet general convergence results for this alternative. Nevertheless, our first numerical tests indicate that the formula may have good properties.

5 Experimental Results

5.1 A Parametric 2D Case

We first test formula (9) on a 2D point cloud given by uniformly distributed samples of a "flower" parametrized by $r(\theta) = 0.5(1 + 0.5\sin(6\theta + \frac{\pi}{2}))$. The point cloud varifold is constructed from the parametrization by computing the exact unit tangent vector $T(t)$, evaluating at the N points $\{0, h, 2h, \ldots, (N-1)h\}$ for $h = \frac{2\pi}{N}$, and setting

$$V_N = \sum_{j=1}^{N} m_j \delta_{(x(jh),y(jh))} \otimes \delta_{T(jh)} . \tag{11}$$

As this way of constructing point clouds is almost uniform, we consider that the weight m_j of each point is the same that is, for all j, $m_j = m$. In this case, there is no need to fix m since, after simplification, it disappears from (10). The curvature vector $H(t)$ can be computed explicitly and evaluated at all $t_j = jh$, $j = 0 \ldots N-1$. To test the accuracy of the approximation, we compute the following mean error on the curvature vector

$$E = \frac{1}{N} \sum_{j=1}^{N} |H_\epsilon^N(x_j) - H(t_j)| . \tag{12}$$

Computations were done with Matlab. Results are presented in Figure 2.

5.2 Approximate Mean Curvature of 3D Point Clouds

We now address $3D$ point clouds. We use formula (10) with projection onto the normal space. In order to be more general, we do not prescribe the normals like in the 2D parametric case, but we compute them. This can be simply done by constructing the covariance matrix of centered coordinates associated with

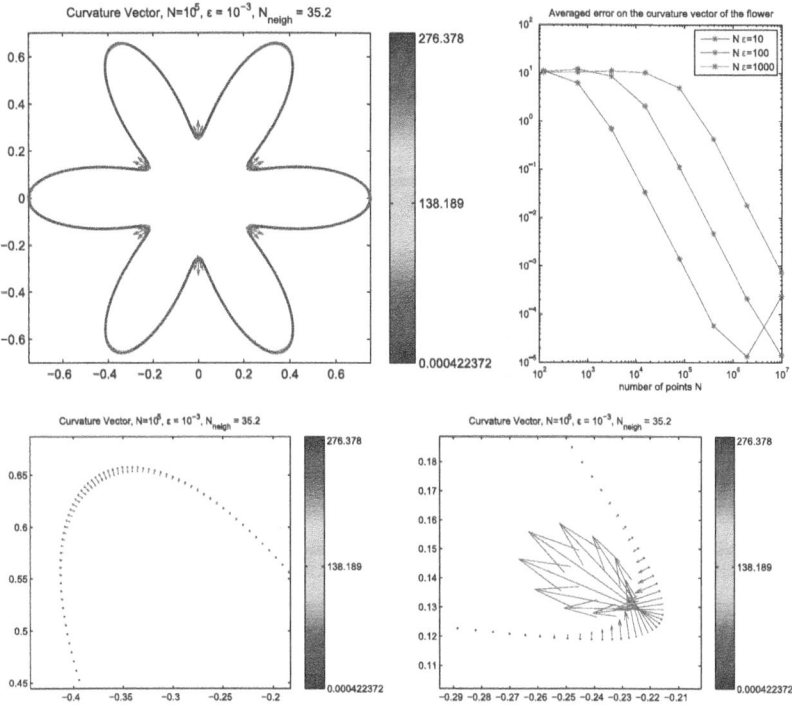

Fig. 2. Curvature approximation for a 2D parametric flower. In the top right figure, each curve corresponds to a constant number of points in a ball B_ϵ. The shape of the curves indicate that, given a number of points in a ball of radius ϵ, there is a resolution for which the computation of the discrete mean curvature is optimal, which is natural. The mean curvature vector at each point and the intensity of the mean curvature are represented in the top left figure, the two other figures are details of the tip of a petal (bottom left) and of the region between two petals (bottom right).

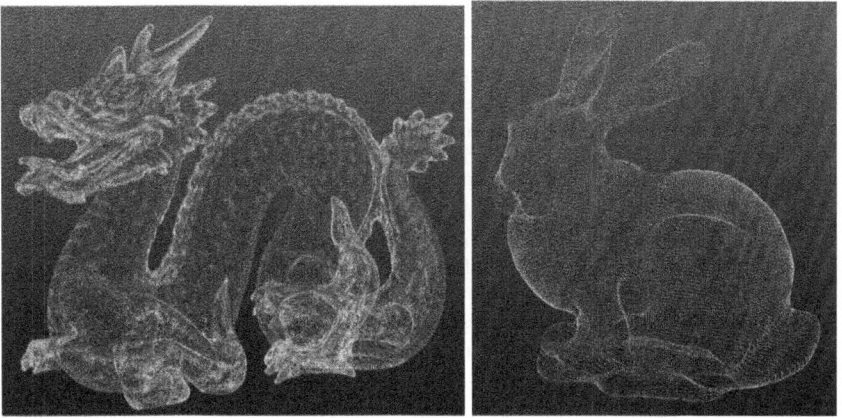

Fig. 3. Intensity of the mean curvature of a "dragon" (435000 points, $\epsilon = 0.02$, dragon's diameter=1) and of "Bunny" (34835 points, $\epsilon = 0.5$, Bunny's diameter$\simeq 7$).

the point cloud, and by choosing the eigenvector associated with the smallest eigenvalue (the computation is done in a ball of radius $\frac{\epsilon}{2}$).

To perform the tests, we wrote a C++ code and used the freely available *nanoflann* and *eigen* libraries. The visualization is made with *CloudCompare*.

The experiments presented in Figure 3 are point clouds with 435000 points for the "dragon" and 34835 points for "bunny". Each point is endowed with a color which indicates the norm of the mean curvature at this point. Our estimation method clearly discriminates between regular, singular or almost-singular zones.

6 Conclusion

We introduced a common formalism for discrete and continuous objects in the context of surface approximation. We discussed how this formalism is suitable for characterizing and quantifying the approximation. We also proposed a new definition of discrete mean curvature which has good convergence properties and is easy to implement. Many things remain to be understood: how to incorporate non homogeneous densities in order to keep guaranteeing good convergence properties, how to be insensitive to noise, how to design stable discrete mean curvature flow and Willmore flow. How to incorporate other curvature notions (principal curvatures, Gaussian curvature). This is the purpose of future work, and we strongly believe that discrete varifolds are the appropriate tools for this.

References

1. Simon, L.: Lectures on geometric measure theory. Australian National University Centre for Mathematical Analysis, Canberra (1983)
2. Pinkall, U., Polthier, K.: Computing discrete minimal surfaces and their conjugates. Experiment. Math. **2**, 15–36 (1993)
3. Coeurjolly, D., Lachaud, J.-O., Roussillon, T.: Multigrid convergence of discrete geometric estimators. In: Digital Geometry Algorithms. Lect. Notes Comput. Vis. Biomech., vol. 2. Springer, Dordrecht (2012)
4. Morvan, J.-M.: Generalized curvatures. Geometry and Computing, vol. 2. Springer-Verlag, Berlin (2008)
5. Cohen-Steiner, D., Morvan, J.-M.: Second fundamental measure of geometric sets and local approximation of curvatures. J. Differential Geom. **74**(3), 363–394 (2006)
6. Chazal, F., Cohen-Steiner, D., Lieutier, A., Thibert, B.: Stability of Curvature Measures. Computer Graphics Forum **28**(5) (2009)
7. Lellmann, J., Lorenz, D., Schönlieb, C.-B., Valkonen, T.: Imaging with Kantorovich-Rubinstein discrepancy. SIAM J. Imaging Sci. **7**(4), 2833–2859 (2014)
8. Charon, N., Trouvé, A.: The varifold representation of nonoriented shapes for diffeomorphic registration. SIAM J. Imaging Sci. **6**(4), 2547–2580 (2013)
9. Buet, B.: Quantitative conditions of rectifiability for varifolds. Annales de l'Institut Fourier (to appear, 2015)
10. Buet, B.: Approximation de surfaces par des varifolds discrets: représentation, courbure, rectifiabilité. Ph.D. thesis, Université Lyon 1 (2014)
11. Buet, B., Leonardi, G. P., Masnou, S.: Surface approximation, discrete varifolds, and regularized first variation (submitted 2015)
12. Leonardi, G.P., Masnou, S.: Locality of the mean curvature of rectifiable varifolds. Adv. Calc. Var. **2**(1), 17–42 (2009)

Robust Poisson Surface Reconstruction

Virginia Estellers[1](✉), Michael Scott[2], Kevin Tew[2], and Stefano Soatto[1]

[1] Univeristy of California, Los Angeles, USA
evstellers@math.ucla.edu
[2] Brigham Young University, Provo, USA

Abstract. We propose a method to reconstruct surfaces from oriented point clouds with non-uniform sampling and noise by formulating the problem as a convex minimization that reconstructs the indicator function of the surface's interior. Compared to previous models, our reconstruction is robust to noise and outliers because it substitutes the least-squares fidelity term by a robust Huber penalty; this allows to recover sharp corners and avoids the shrinking bias of least squares. We choose an implicit parametrization to reconstruct surfaces of unknown topology and close large gaps in the point cloud. For an efficient representation, we approximate the implicit function by a hierarchy of locally supported basis elements adapted to the geometry of the surface. Unlike ad-hoc bases over an octree, our hierarchical B-splines from isogeometric analysis locally adapt the mesh and degree of the splines during reconstruction. The hierarchical structure of the basis speeds-up the minimization and efficiently represents clustered data. We also advocate for convex optimization, instead isogeometric finite-element techniques, to efficiently solve the minimization and allow for non-differentiable functionals. Experiments show state-of-the-art performance within a more flexible framework.

1 Introduction

New challenges to surface reconstruction from measurements emerge as datasets grow in size but lose in accuracy. The reduction in accuracy appears as sensors evolve from short to long range, low-cost commodity scanners become widely available, and computer vision is increasingly used to infer 3D geometry from point sets. As a result, surface reconstruction methods must be robust to noise and outliers, and scale favorably in terms of computation and memory usage. This impacts the parametrization of the surface and the inference techniques.

We propose a robust but simple algorithm to reconstruct a water-tight surface from an oriented point cloud. We formulate the reconstruction as a convex optimization that recovers the indicator function of the interior of the surface. Our objective function penalizes deviations in the normal orientation with a Huber loss function to robustly recover the topology of the surface and allow for sharp corners; this makes our model more robust to noise and avoids the "shrinking bias" of least-squares models [1,2]. Our minimization exploits the convexity of the objective with an efficient first-order algorithm that is easy to parallelize and scales well with the size of the point cloud. This is our first contribution.

Our second contribution is to merge state of the art isogeometric analysis and surface reconstruction. Isogeometric analysis [3,4] is a generalization of finite element analysis which improves the link between geometric design and analysis. The isogeometric paradigm is simple: the smooth spline basis used to define the geometry is used as the basis for analysis. As a result, exact geometry is introduced into the analysis. The smooth basis can then be leveraged in analysis [5–7] and lead to innovative approaches to model design [8–10], analysis [11–14], optimization [15], and adaptivity [16–20].

The underlying implicit function is represented by an adaptive spline forest [18] developed in isogeometric analysis [3]. An isogeometric spline forest is a hierarchical spline representation capable of representing surfaces or volumes of arbitrarily complex geometry and topological genus. Spline forests can accommodate arbitrary degree and smoothness in the underlying hierarchical basis as well as non-uniform knot interval configurations. They accommodate efficient h, p, k-refinement and coarsening algorithms which we utilize in this work. In h-adaptivity the elements are subdivided or merged, in p-adaptivity the polynomial degree of the basis is changed, and in k-adaptivity the smoothness of the basis is changed. In all cases, the adaptive process remains local and preserves exact geometry at the coarsest level of the discretization. In the context of surface reconstruction, a hierarchical spline forest basis efficiently represents functions in three dimensions by their spline coefficients and provides analytic expressions for their derivatives. Our reconstruction exploits this local adaptivity to efficiently represent complex surfaces with sharp corners.

2 Related Methods and Choice of Representation

Surface reconstruction methods can be first classified by their surface representation: parametric or implicit. Parametric techniques represent the surface as a topological embedding of a 2D parameter domain into 3D space. Among them, approaches based on computational geometry partition the space into Voronoi cells from the input samples and exploit the intuitive idea that eliminating facets of Delaunay tetrahedra provides a triangulated parametrization of the surface [21–27]. The reconstructed surface thus interpolates most of the input samples and requires post-processing to smooth the surface and correct the topology. Parametric methods generally require clean data because they assume the topology of the surface to be known, while implicit methods are designed to reconstruct surfaces from noisy point clouds with unknown topology.

Implicit representations both reconstruct the surface and estimate its topology, but increase the dimension of the problem by representing the surface as the zero-level set of a volumetric function. Their accuracy is thus limited by the resolution of the grid, with efficient representations requiring non-uniform grids.

Implicit representations can be formulated as either global or local. Local methods consider subsets of nearby points one at a time and handle large datasets efficiently. Earlier methods [28,29] estimate tangent planes from the nearest neighbors of each sample and parametrize the surface by the signed distance to the tangent plane of the closest point in space. Moving least squares (MLS) techniques [30–33] reconstruct surfaces locally by solving an optimization that finds a local reference plane and fit a polynomial to the surface. The least-squares fit of MLS, however, is sensitive to outliers and smooths out small features; for this reason variants robust to outliers [34,35] and sharp features [36,37] appeared. [38] also constructs implicit functions locally but blends them together with partitions of unity. Common to these methods is their locality –partitioning into neighborhoods and merging local functions– that makes them highly scalable but sensitive to non-uniform sampling and point-cloud gaps.

Global methods define the implicit function as the sum of basis functions (RBFs[39], splines[1,2], wavelets [40]) and consider all the data at once without heuristic partitioning. Kazhdan et al. [1] solve a Poisson problem that aligns the gradient of the indicator function to the normals of the point cloud with a least-squares fit, not robust to outliers. Manson et al. [40] similarly approximate the indicator function with wavelets efficiently designed to compute basis coefficients with local sums over an octree. Calakli and Taubin [41] use instead a signed-distance function to represent the surface, but also rely on least squares to fit the normals and include screening and regularization terms. While the Hessian regularization introduces derivatives of higher order and limits the basis functions, the screening improves accuracy by fitting the input points to the zero-level set of the implicit function and has been lately adopted by [2]. For this reason, our model includes a screening term together with a robust Huber penalty to fit the normal field and allow for sharp edges. Existing methods account for sharp features by explicit representations [36,42,43] or anisotropic smoothing [44–46]; they are fast but depend on local operators that do not seek a global optimum.

Our reconstruction combines benefits of global and local schemes. It is global and does not involve heuristics on neighborhoods, while the basis functions are locally supported and adapt to the surface through the local refinement techniques of the spline forests [18]; this can be viewed as a generalization of well-known uniform splines [47–49]. Our minimization algorithm, however, departs from standard isogeometric finite element formulations and is instead inspired by [50].

3 Variational Model

The reconstruction of a surface S from oriented points can be cast as a minimization problem to estimate the indicator function χ of the interior of the surface. Let $\{x_k, n_k\}_{k=1}^N$ be the oriented point cloud, with $x_k \in \mathbb{R}^3$ the point location and $n_k \in \mathbb{S}^2$ its associated normal; we estimate $\chi \colon \mathbb{R}^3 \to \mathbb{R}$ such that $S = \{x \colon \chi(x) = 0\}$, $\chi < 0$ in the interior enclosed by S and $\chi > 0$ outside.

We reconstruct S by observing that each point in $\{x_k, n_k\}_{k=1}^N$ is a sample of the gradient of the indicator function, that is, $\nabla \chi(x_k) = n_k$. Given a continuous field n that approximately interpolates these samples[1], $n(x_k) = n_k$, we can reconstruct S by finding the scalar function whose gradient best matches this field. To account for noise in the data, we formulate the reconstruction as a minimization, instead of interpolation, problem:

$$\min_{\chi} \int_{\mathbb{R}^3} f(n - \nabla\chi) + \frac{\alpha}{2} \sum_{k=1}^{N} \chi(x_k)^2 \quad \text{with} \quad f(v) = \begin{cases} \frac{1}{2}|v|_2^2 & |v|_2 < \epsilon \\ \epsilon(|v|_2 - \frac{\epsilon}{2}) & |v|_2 \geq \epsilon \end{cases}, \quad (1)$$

where $\alpha > 0$ is a model parameter. The Huber loss function f is a convex and differentiable penalty that avoids two artifacts of least squares: shrinkage of thin structures and smoothing of sharp edges as the square norm over-penalizes outliers. It overcomes these limitations by using different penalties for small errors and outliers, but results in a minimization harder to solve than the Poisson problem of a least-squares fit. The second term in (1) sets the points as soft interpolation constraints for the zero-level set of χ and is a generalization of the screening term of [51], but defined over a sparse set of points rather than $\mathbb{R}^3$.

Since χ only contains surface information in its zero-level set, we approximate it with an adaptive spline forest basis defined over a non-uniform grid. Each basis function is a (smooth) piecewise polynomial inferred from the local knot structure of the underlying spline forest. For a complete description of spline forest basis functions we refer the reader to [18]. In one dimension, a spline forest is a hierarchical B-spline as illustrated in Figure 1, where the basis functions that span the hierarchical spline space are indicated by solid lines. The multi-level adaptive nature of the basis is evident. Similarly, in higher dimensions the first level of the hierarchy is as a NURBS or T-spline.

Our method is related to the Poisson reconstruction of [2], but our representation of the surface, model, and minimization technique are different. In terms of the model, we propose a robust Huber penalty on the normals to be resilient to outliers, instead of the least-squares penalty of [2]. We represent χ with spline forests from isogeometric analysis – instead of uniform splines over an octree not defining a basis – to use h- and p-refinement to adapt our representation to the complexity of the surface, not to the noisy point cloud. Finally, our minimization exploits the convexity of (1) to develop an efficient primal-dual algorithm, instead of finite-element methods that cannot handle the Huber loss function.

4 Minimization Algorithm

To exploit the convexity of the functional in the minimization, we discretize the integral in (1) with standard quadrature rules used with non-uniform splines:

$$\int_{\mathbb{R}^3} f(\nabla\chi - n) \approx \sum_{i=1}^{Q} w_i f(\nabla\chi(p_i) - n(p_i)), \quad (2)$$

---

[1] We approximate n with a standard ℓ_2 projection into a linear B-spline basis defined over the same grid as χ. We omit here the details to focus on reconstruction.

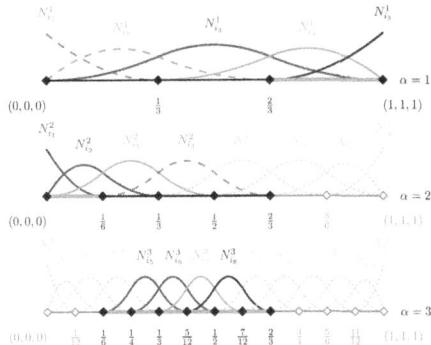

Fig. 1. Basis functions for a three-level quadratic hierarchical spline space, where N_i^l denotes the i-th spline function at level l. Basis functions are indicated by solid colored lines, functions that are linearly dependent on higher-level functions by dashed colored lines, and inactive functions by grey dotted lines. The finite elements correspond to the cells in green.

where $\{p_i, w_i\}_{i=1}^Q$ are the quadrature points and their weights. Finding the location and value of $\{p_i, w_i\}_{i=1}^Q$ that best approximates the integral is a classical problem with exact solution for polynomials. By restricting χ to the span of the hierarchical basis $\{N_A\}_{A=1}^n$, we confine the minimization to coefficients $c \in \mathbb{R}^n$:

$$\min_c \sum_{i=1}^Q w_i f(\sum_A c_A \nabla N_A(p_i) - \mathbf{n}(p_i)) + \frac{\alpha}{2} \sum_{k=1}^N [\sum_A c_A N_A(x_k)]^2. \quad (3)$$

We solve (3) efficiently with the primal-dual algorithm [52] by providing closed-form solutions for each proximal update. We choose a first-order method because the size of the problem makes second-order methods unfeasible. The convexity of each term in the objective allows us to re-formulate the minimization as a saddle-point problem that is separable and easy to solve in each variable.

Let $P \in \mathbb{R}^{3Q \times n}$ be the matrix with block components $P_{ij} = \nabla N_j(p_i)$ and

$$F(V) = \sum_{i=1}^Q w_i f(V_i - \mathbf{n}(p_i)), \quad G(c) = \frac{\alpha}{2} \sum_{k=1}^N [\sum_A c_A N_A(x_k)]^2,$$

we can write (3) as the constrained minimization

$$\min_{c,V} F(V) + G(c) \quad \text{s.t.} \quad V = Pc \quad (4)$$

and use convex analysis to find the equivalent saddle-point problem with dual variable $\lambda \in \mathbb{R}^{3Q}$, F^* the convex conjugate of F, and the inner product $\langle \cdot, \cdot \rangle$:

$$\max_\lambda \min_c -F^*(\lambda) + G(c) + \langle \lambda, Pc \rangle. \quad (5)$$

This formulation allows us to apply the primal-dual algorithm of Chambolle and Pock [52], which solves (5) by iteratively solving the following sub-problems:

$$\lambda^{n+1} \leftarrow \min_{\lambda} \sigma F^*(\lambda) + \frac{1}{2}\|\lambda - \lambda^n - \sigma P\bar{c}^n\|^2 \tag{6}$$

$$c^{n+1} \leftarrow \min_{c} \tau G(c) + \frac{1}{2}\|c - c^n + \tau P^* \lambda^{n+1}\|^2 \tag{7}$$

where $\bar{c}^{n+1} = c^{n+1} + \theta(c^{n+1} - c^n)$, P^* is the adjoint of P, and τ, σ, θ are algorithm parameters. As G is strongly convex, our algorithm can be further accelerated by updating parameters τ, σ, θ according to Alg. 2 in [52].

The efficiency of the proposed algorithm comes from the spatial separability of F^* and from the ability to find closed-form solutions for each of the minimization problems. The derivation of closed-form solutions is detailed next, and Algorithm 1 summarizes the resulting updates, which are easy to parallelize.

Initialize $c = 0$, $\boldsymbol{\lambda} = \mathbf{0}$, $\bar{c} = c$. Choose $\tau, \sigma > 0$, $\theta \in [0,1]$.
while $\|c^{n+1} - c^n\| > 1^{-4}$ **do**
$\quad \lambda_i^{n+1} = \epsilon w_i \dfrac{\hat{\lambda}_i^n - \sigma \boldsymbol{n}(p_i)}{\max(\;\epsilon(w_i + \sigma), |\hat{\lambda}_i^n - \sigma \boldsymbol{n}(p_i)|_2\;)}$ with $\hat{\lambda}_i^n = \lambda_i^n + \sigma \sum_A \bar{c}_A^n \nabla N_A(p_i)$
$\quad c^{n+1} = [I_n + \alpha \tau M]^{-1} \hat{c}$ with $\hat{c}_A = c_A^n - \tau \sum_{i=1}^{Q} \nabla N_A(p_i) \cdot \lambda^{n+1}$
$\quad \bar{c}^{n+1} = c^{n+1} + \theta(c^{n+1} - c^n)$
end

Algorithm 1. Primal-dual minimization algorithm.

Minimization in Dual Variable. Let $\hat{\lambda} = \lambda + \sigma P\bar{c}$, we solve the minimization in λ (6) through Moreau's identity [53]:

$$\lambda \leftarrow \min_{\lambda} \sigma F^*(\lambda) + \frac{1}{2}\|\lambda - \hat{\lambda}\|^2 \iff \lambda = \hat{\lambda} - \sigma V^*, \quad V^* \leftarrow \min_{V} F(V) + \frac{\sigma}{2}\left\|V - \frac{\hat{\lambda}}{\sigma}\right\|^2.$$

The minimization in V is decoupled spatially in each quadrature point as follows:

$$\min_{V} \sum_{i=1}^{Q} \underbrace{w_i f(V_i - \boldsymbol{n}(p_i)) + 0.5\sigma(V_i - \sigma^{-1}\hat{\lambda}_i)^2}_{h_i(V_i)} = \min_{V_1,\ldots,V_Q} \sum_{i=1}^{Q} h_i(V_i). \tag{8}$$

It is thus solved by independently minimizing $h_i(V_i)$ in each $V_i \in \mathbb{R}^3$. Due to the convexity and differentiability of the Huber norm, the optimality conditions are obtained by differentiating the objective function with respect to V_i; i.e.,

$$\epsilon w_i \frac{V_i^* - \boldsymbol{n}(p_i)}{\max(\epsilon, |V_i^* - \boldsymbol{n}(p_i)|_2)} + \sigma V_i^* - \hat{\lambda}_i = 0. \tag{9}$$

After some algebra, we obtain the closed-form update for the dual variable,

$$\lambda_i = \epsilon w_i \frac{\hat{\lambda}_i - \sigma \boldsymbol{n}(p_i)}{\max(\;\epsilon(w_i + \sigma), |\hat{\lambda}_i - \sigma \boldsymbol{n}(p_i)|_2\;)}. \tag{10}$$

Minimization in Primal Variable. Let $\hat{c} = c^n - \tau P^* \lambda^{n+1}$, the minimization in c (7) is the least-squares problem

$$\min_c \alpha\tau \sum_{k=1}^{N} [\sum_A c_A N_A(x_k)]^2 + \sum_A (c_A - \hat{c}_A)^2, \qquad (11)$$

whose optimality conditions lead to the sparse linear system: $c + \alpha\tau Mc = \hat{c}$. Indeed, differentiating with respect to c_B and equating to 0 gives

$$\alpha\tau \sum_A [\sum_{k=1}^{N} N_A(x_k) N_B(x_k)] c_A + c_B = \hat{c}_B \iff c_B + \alpha\tau \sum_A M_{AB} c_B = \hat{c}_B,$$

with coefficients $M_{AB} = \sum_k N_A(x_k) N_B(x_k)$, $\hat{c}_A = c_A^n - \tau \sum_{i=1}^{Q} \nabla N_A(p_i) \cdot \lambda^{n+1}$. As M is fixed, we only decompose it once for all the primal-dual iterations.

5 Refinement

We start our reconstruction with first-order splines over a coarse uniform grid and refine the basis in two stages: we first refine the resolution of the basis by partitioning cells with large values of the objective function or interpolation error, and we then increase the degree of basis elements over cells where first order splines have large objective values. Refinement is illustrated in Figure 3(d).

5.1 h-Refinement: Minimizing Point-Cloud and Surface Errors

For every cell Ω_i in our grid, we compute the error between the continuous approximation to the normal field and the input normal at the sampled points, $e(\Omega_i) = \sum_{x_k \in \Omega_i} |n(x_k) - n_k|^2$, and refine the cells whose error is larger than the average mean error over the grid. The size of the cells is thus determined by the input point cloud, not by the reconstructed surface, and is sensitive to noise. This first refinement assures an accurate approximation of the normal field n from the samples and is used to obtain a first approximate surface.

Given this first estimate of χ, we refine the mesh based on the error in the reconstructed surface. To be robust to outliers, we measure this error with the Huber penalty, that is, $e_s(\Omega_i) = \sum_{x_k \in \Omega_i} f(\nabla \chi(x_i) - n_i)$, and refine cells whose error is larger than the mean error over the grid. Compared to h-refinement based on the interpolation error, this new criterion is robust to noise in the point cloud and implicitly measures the complexity of the surface's geometry over each cell.

5.2 p-Refinement: Degree Elevation

Elevating the degree of the spline basis allows to better approximate smooth regions and represent higher-order geometric properties of the surface. Higher-order splines, however, lead to computationally more demanding models that smooth out corners; for this reason it is critical to only increase the degree of the spline basis over cells where the surface is smooth. We thus increase the degree of the spline basis over cells already refined, but with large residual objective.

6 Experimental Results

We perform experiments with two kinds of data: synthetic data with ground truth, and point clouds obtained from structured-light scanning with a Kinect camera [54]. Kinect data suffers from non-uniform noise, large scanning gaps and artifacts. We use the synthetic point clouds for quantitative evaluation and the noisy ones to test reconstruction with data with real noise and artifacts.

Our first experiment does not include refinement to focus on our first contribution, the use of a robust penalty for the normal field. Figure 2 compares our model to a least-squares fit equivalent to the Poisson reconstruction of [2] without the octree structure. Our model reconstructs a cube with sharp corners and avoids shrinkage artifacts in the horns and legs of the cow. In all our experiments, we hand-picked the best parameters for each model.

Our second experiment investigates the effects of refinement in the accuracy of the reconstruction, see Figure 3. We again compare our model to the least-squares model of [2] –where refinement is defined by point density through the octree– implemented with our spline forest to focus on the refinement strategies. For synthetic data both models perform similarly, showing how a correctly refined basis compensates for the use of a non-robust penalty. For noisy data, however, our method reconstructs more accurately the topology of the cleaning spray of Figure 4, while refinement based on point density replicates the artifacts in the noisy point cloud. The effects of p-refinement, which is only possible in our isogeometric framework, are analyzed in Figure 3(c). This kind of refinement allows us to obtain both smooth regions and sharp edges within a single surface.

A third set of experiments shows that model and implementation lead to reconstructions comparable to state-of-the-art techniques [1,2,41]. Table 1 presents a quantitative comparison of the methods with synthetic or high quality point clouds that have been perturbed, by sub-sampling or adding noise to the point locations, and evaluates the Haussdorf distance to the reconstructed surface. All the methods lead to reconstructions with similar mean Haussdorf distance, but the average reconstruction time of our algorithm – with a resolution comparable to the octree-based methods – is an order of magnitude larger than [1,2,41] with the current non-optimized code. Finally, Figure 5 shows a qualitative comparison with a noisy point cloud scanned with Kinect: our method is better at recovering shape and topology from noisy data, e.g., the holding hands of the statue.

Table 1. Average reconstruction time and Haussdorf distance $d_\mathcal{D}$ (10^{-2} distance units) between the point cloud and the reconstructed surface

$d_\mathcal{D}$	subsampled point cloud bunny cow horse cube	perturbed point-cloud bunny cow horse cube	time (s)
[1]	0.074 4.85 0.237 6.25	0.086 3.04 0.232 4.65	2.7
[41]	0.065 1.72 0.107 1.16	0.069 1.80 0.108 2.37	1.2
[2]	0.073 4.84 0.232 3.94	0.337 3.07 0.249 4.58	2.8
ours	0.0708 2.92 0.143 2.37	0.0768 3.38 0.137 3.05	476

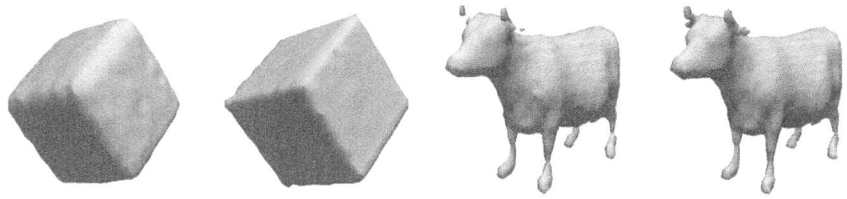

(a) Least-squares   (b) Our model   (c) Least-squares   (d) Our model

Fig. 2. Reconstruction in uniform grid: Poisson reconstruction rounds the cube's corners and shrinks the cows horns because least-squares fits overpenalize outliers, our robust model overcomes avoids this limitation with a Huber penalty.

(a) Least-squares   (b) Our model   (c) p-ref, ours   (d) Hierarchy

Fig. 3. Refinement: 3(a) h-refinement of least-squares model 2(c); 3(b) h-refinement of our model 2(d); 3(c) p-refinement of 3(b). The Hierarchical mesh 3(d) with first-level elements in blue, second level in gray, and third level in red.

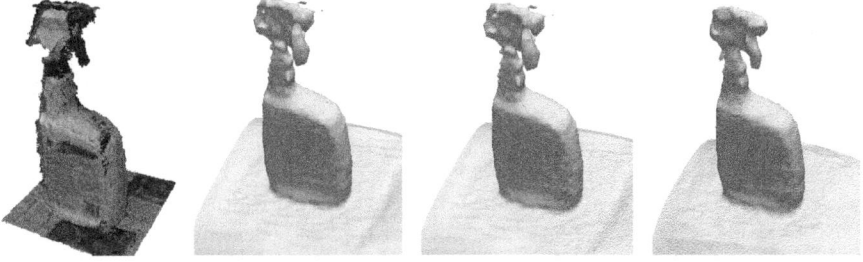

(a) Point cloud   (b) Point density   (c) Interpolation err.   (d) Reconstruct. err.

Fig. 4. Reconstruction with different refinement criteria: refinement based on point density, (4(b)) like [1,2,40,41], or on the interpolation error (4(c)) reconstruct the artifacts present in the point cloud, while refinement based on the reconstruction error recover the right shape in the cleaner's head. (4(d)).

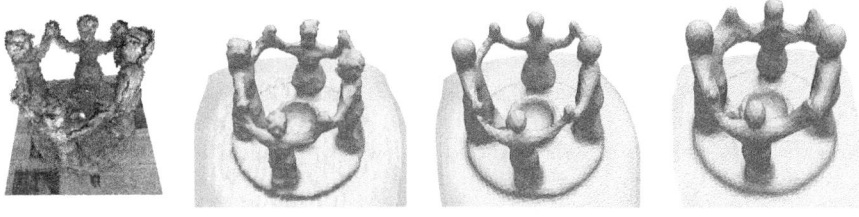

(a) Point cloud   (b) Ours   (c) Method [2]   (d) Method [41]

Fig. 5. Comparison of our model to state-of-the-art methods [2,41]. Our model better recovers the shape of the faces and hands of the statues: avoids disconnecting the joined hands ([2]) or their merging with the person's arms ([41]).

7 Conclusions and Future Work

We reconstruct surfaces from corrupted point clouds by formulating the problem as a convex minimization that is robust to outliers, avoids the shrinking bias of least squares, and is able to recover sharp corners as well as smooth regions. For an efficient parametrization, we approximate the implicit function with a hierarchical B-spline forest that locally adapts its resolution and smoothness to the surface. This allows us to dynamically refine the reconstruction guided by the surface, instead of the input point cloud, and be robust to noise and artifacts.

Hierarchical spline forests and isogeometric analysis are powerful tools for vision and imaging and open a new line of future work, from more efficient implementations that exploit the capabilities of GPU to new isogeometric models designed for the noisy data and unknown geometries common in computer vision.

Acknowledgments. This research is supported by the Swiss National Science Foundation grant P2ELP2_148890, Air Force Office of Scientific Research FA9550-14-1-0113, FA9550-12-1-0364:P00002 and N00014-11-1-0863:P00010.

References

1. Kazhdan, M., Bolitho, M., Hoppe, H.: Poisson surface reconstruction. In: Eurographics Symposium on Geometry Processing, pp. 61–70 (2006)
2. Kazhdan, M., Hoppe, H.: Screened poisson surface reconstruction. ACM Trans. Graph **32**(3), 1–13 (2013)
3. Hughes, T., Cottrell, J., Bazilevs, Y.: Isogeometric analysis: CAD, finite elements, NURBS, exact geometry and mesh refinement. Comput. Methods in Appl. Mech. Eng. **194**(39–41), 4135–4195 (2005)
4. Cottrell, J.A., Hughes, T.J.R., Bazilevs, Y.: Isogeometric analysis: Toward Integration of CAD and FEA. Wiley, Chichester (2009)
5. Evans, J.A., Bazilevs, Y., Babuška, I., Hughes, T.J.R.: n-widths, sup-infs, and optimality ratios for the k-version of the isogeometric finite element method. Comput. Methods in Appl. Mech. Eng. **198**(21–26), 1726–1741 (2009)
6. Hughes, T.J.R., Evans, J.A., Reali, A.: Finite element and NURBS approximations of eigenvalue, boundary-value, and initial-value problems. Comput. Methods in Appl. Mech. Eng. **272**, 290–320 (2014)
7. Cottrell, J.A., Hughes, T.J.R., Reali, A.: Studies of refinement and continuity in isogeometric analysis. Comput. Methods in Appl. Mech. Eng. **196**, 4160–4183 (2007)
8. Cohen, E., Martin, T., Kirby, R.M., Lyche, T., Riesenfeld, R.F.: Analysis-aware modeling: Understanding quality considerations in modeling for isogeometric analysis. Comput. Methods in Appl. Mech. Eng. **199**(5–8), 334–356 (2010)
9. Wang, W., Zhang, Y., Scott, M.A., Hughes, T.J.R.: Converting an unstructured quadrilateral mesh to a standard T-spline surface. Computational Mechanics **48**, 477–498 (2011)

10. Liu, L., Zhang, Y., Hughes, T.J.R., Scott, M.A., Sederberg, T.W.: Volumetric T-spline Construction Using Boolean Operations. In: Sarrate, J., Staten, M. (eds.) Proceedings of the 22nd International Meshing Roundtable. Non-series, vol. 144, pp. 405–424. Springer, Heidelberg (2014)
11. Schillinger, D., Dedè, L., Scott, M.A., Evans, J.A., Borden, M.J., Rank, E., Hughes, T.J.R.: An isogeometric design-through-analysis methodology based on adaptive hierarchical refinement of NURBS, immersed boundary methods, and T-spline CAD surfaces. Comput. Methods in Appl. Mech. Eng. **249–252**, 116–150 (2012)
12. Scott, M.A., Simpson, R.N., Evans, J.A., Lipton, S., Bordas, S.P.A., Hughes, T.J.R., Sederberg, T.W.: Isogeometric boundary element analysis using unstructured T-splines. Comput. Methods in Appl. Mech. Eng. **254**, 197–221 (2013)
13. Schmidt, R., Wüchner, R., Bletzinger, K.-U.: Isogeometric analysis of trimmed NURBS geometries. Comput. Methods in Appl. Mech. Eng. **241–244**, 93–111 (2012)
14. Benson, D.J., Bazilevs, Y., De Luycker, E., Hsu, M.C., Scott, M.A., Hughes, T.J.R., Belytschko, T.: A generalized finite element formulation for arbitrary basis functions: From isogeometric analysis to XFEM. International Journal for Numerical Methods in Engineering **83**, 765–785 (2010)
15. Wall, W.A., Frenzel, M.A., Cyron, C.: Isogeometric structural shape optimization. Comput. Methods in Appl. Mech. Eng. **197**, 2976–2988 (2008)
16. Bazilevs, Y., Calo, V.M., Cottrell, J.A., Evans, J.A., Hughes, T.J.R., Lipton, S., Scott, M.A., Sederberg, T.W.: Isogeometric analysis using T-splines. Comput. Methods in Appl. Mech. Eng. **199**(5–8), 229–263 (2010)
17. Dörfel, M., Jüttler, B., Simeon, B.: Adaptive isogeometric analysis by local h-refinement with T-splines. Comput. Methods in Appl. Mech. Eng. **199**(5–8), 264–275 (2009)
18. Scott, M.A., Thomas, D.C., Evans, E.J.: Isogeometric spline forests. Comput. Methods in Appl. Mech. Eng. **269**, 222–264 (2014)
19. Evans, E.J., Scott, M.A., Li, X., Thomas, D.C.: Hierarchical T-splines: Analysis-suitability, Bézier extraction, and application as an adaptive basis for isogeometric analysis. Comput. Methods in Appl. Mech. Eng. **284**, 1–20 (2015)
20. Thomas, D.C., Scott, M.A., Evans, J.A., Tew, K., Evans, E.J.: Bézier projection: a unified approach for local projection and quadrature-free refinement and coarsening of NURBS and T-splines with particular application to isogeometric design and analysis (2014) (submitted)
21. Amenta, N., Bern, M., Kamvysselis, M.: A New Voronoi-Based Surface Reconstruction Algorithm. ACM SIGGRAPH, pp. 415–421 (1998)
22. Dey, T., Goswami, S.: Tight cocone: a water-tight surface reconstructor. In: ACM Symposium on Solid Modeling and Applications, pp. 127–134 (2003)
23. Amenta, N., Choi, S., Kolluri, R.K.: The power crust. In: ACM Symposium on Solid Modeling and Applications, pp. 249–266 (2001)
24. Podolak, J., Rusinkiewicz, S.: Atomic Volumes for Mesh Completion. In: Symposium on Geometry Processing, pp. 33–41 (2005)
25. Boissonnat, J.-D., Oudot, S.: Provably good sampling and meshing of surfaces. Graphical Models **67**(5), 405–451 (2005)
26. Shewchuk, J.R., Brien, J.F.O.: Spectral Surface Reconstruction from Noisy Point Clouds. ACM SIGGRAPH **14**, 11–21 (2004)

27. Labatut, P., Pons, J.-P., Keriven, R.: Robust and efficient surface reconstruction from range data. Computer Graphics Forum **28**(8), 2275–2290 (2009)
28. Hoppe, H., DeRose, T., Duchamp, T., McDonald, J., Stuetzle, W.: Surface reconstruction from unorganized points. In: ACM SIGGRAPH, pp. 71–78 (1992)
29. Curless, B., Levoy, M.: A Volumetric Method for Building Complex Models from Range Images Volumetric integration. In: ACM SIGGRAPH, pp. 303–312 (1996)
30. Alexa, M., Behr, J., Cohen-or, D., Fleishman, S., Levin, D., Silva, C.T.: Computing and rendering point set surfaces. IEEE Transactions on Visualization and Computer Graphics **9**(1), 3–15 (2003)
31. Levin, D.: Mesh-Independent surface Interpolation. In: Geometric Modeling for Scientific Visualization, pp. 37–49 (2004)
32. Shen, C., O'Brien, J.F., Shewchuk, J.R.: Interpolating and approximating implicit surfaces from polygon soup. ACM SIGGRAPH **23**(3), 896–904 (2004)
33. Amenta, N., Kil, Y.J.: Defining point-set surfaces. ACM SIGGRAPH **23**(3), 264–270 (2004)
34. Öztireli, A.C., Guennebaud, G., Gross, M.: Feature Preserving Point Set Surfaces based on Non-Linear Kernel Regression. Computer Graphics Forum **28**(2), 493–501 (2009)
35. Fleishman, S., Cohen-or, D., Silva, C.T.: Robust moving least-squares fitting with sharp features. ACM SIGGRAPH **44**(3), 544–552 (2005)
36. Lipman, Y., Cohen-or, D., Levin, D.: Data-dependent MLS for faithful surface approximation. In: Eurographics Symposium on Geometry Processing, pp. 59–67 (2007)
37. Daniels II, J., Ha, L.K., Ochotta, T., Silva, C.T.: Robust Smooth Feature Extraction from Point Clouds. In: IEEE International Conference on Shape Modeling and Applications (SMI 2007), pp. 123–136 (2007)
38. Ohtake, Y., Belyaev, A., Alexa, M., Turk, G., Seidel, H.-P.: Multi-level partition of unity implicits. ACM Trans. Graph. **22**(3), 463 (2003)
39. Carr, J.C., Beatson, R.K., Evans, T.R.: Reconstruction and Representation of 3D Objects with Radial Basis Functions. In: ACM SIGGRAPH, pp. 67–76 (2001)
40. Manson, J., Petrova, G., Schaefer, S.: Streaming surface reconstruction using wavelets. Computer Graphics Forum **27**(5), 1411–1420 (2008)
41. Calakli, F., Taubin, G.: SSD: Smooth Signed Distance Surface Reconstruction. Computer Graphics Forum **30**(7), 1993–2002 (2011)
42. Adamson, A., Alexa, M.: Point-sampled cell complexes. ACM Trans. Graph. **1**(212), 671–680 (2006)
43. Guennebaud, G., Gross, M.: Algebraic Point Set Surfaces. ACM Trans. Graph. **26**(3), 1–10 (2007)
44. Clarenz, U., Diewald, U., Rumpf, M.: Anisotropic geometric diffusion in surface processing. In: Proceedings of the Conference on Visualization, pp. 397–405 (2000)
45. Tasdizen, T., Whitaker, R., Burchard, P., Osher, S.: Geometric surface smoothing via anisotropic diffusion of normals. In: Proceedings of IEEE Visualization (VIS 2002), pp. 125–132 (2002)
46. Chuang, M., Kazhdan, M.: Interactive and anisotropic geometry processing using the screened Poisson equation. ACM SIGGRAPH **30**(4), 57 (2011)
47. Unser, M.: Splines a Perfect Fit for Signal and Image Processing. IEEE Signal Processing Magazine 22–38 (November 1999)

48. Arigovindan, M., Sühling, M., Hunziker, P., Unser, M.: Variational Image Reconstruction from Arbitrarily Spaced Samples: a Fast Multiresolution Spline Solution. IEEE Trans. Image Process. **14**(4), 450–460 (2005)
49. Steidl, G., Didas, S., Neumann, J.: Splines in Higher Order TV Regularization. International Journal of Computer Vision **70**(3), 241–255 (2006)
50. Balzer, J., Morwald, T.: Isogeometric finite-elements methods and variational reconstruction tasks in vision–A perfect match. In: International Conference on Computer Vision and Pattern Recognition, pp. 1624–1631 (2012)
51. Nehab, D., Rusinkiewicz, S., Davis, J., Ramamoorthi, R.: Efficiently combining positions and normals for precise 3D geometry. ACM Trans. Graph. **24**(3), 536 (2005)
52. Chambolle, A., Pock, T.: A First-Order Primal-Dual Algorithm for Convex Problems with Applications to Imaging. Journal of Mathematical Imaging and Vision **40**(1), 120–145 (2010)
53. Rockafellar, R.T.: Convex analysis, no. 28. Princeton University Press (1997)
54. Balzer, J., Peters, M., Soatto, S.: Volumetric Reconstruction Applied to Perceptual Studies of Size and Weight. IEEE WACV **704** (November 2013)

Variational Perspective Shape from Shading

Yong Chul Ju[1,2](✉), Andrés Bruhn[1], and Michael Breuß[2]

[1] Computer Vision and Intelligent Systems Group,
Institute for Visualization and Interactive Systems, Universitätsstraße 38,
University of Stuttgart, 70569 Stuttgart, Germany
{ju,bruhn}@vis.uni-stuttgart.de
[2] Applied Mathematics and Computer Vision Group,
Institute for Applied Mathematics and Scientic Computing, Platz der Deutschen
Einheit 1, BTU Cottbus-Senftenberg, 03046 Cottbus, Germany
breuss@tu-cottbus.de

Abstract. Many recent methods for perspective shape from shading (SfS) are based on formulations in terms of partial differential equations (PDEs). However, while the quality of such methods steadily improves, their lacking robustness is still an open issue. In this context, variational methods seem to be a promising alternative, since they allow to incorporate smoothness assumptions that have proven to be useful for many other tasks in computer vision. Surprisingly, however, such methods have hardly been considered for perspective SfS so far. In our article we address this problem and develop a novel variational model for this task. By combining building blocks of recent PDE-based methods such as a Lambertian reflectance model and camera-centred illumination with a discontinuity-preserving second-order smoothness term, we obtain a variational method for perspective SfS that offers by construction an improved degree of robustness compared to existing PDE-based approaches. Our experiments confirm the success of our strategy. They show that embedding the assumptions of PDE-based approaches into a variational model with a suitable smoothness term can be very beneficial – in particular in scenarios with noise or partially missing information.

Keywords: Shape from shading · Variational methods · Perspective camera model

1 Introduction

Shape from Shading (SfS) is one of the classic tasks in computer vision. Given information on light reflectance and illumination in a photographed scene, the goal is to reconstruct the 3D surface of a depicted object from a single input image. Modern applications of SfS range from large scale problems such as terrain reconstruction [2] to small scale tasks such as medical endoscopy [21].

In his pioneering work [11], Horn investigated the problem systematically and coined the name *shape from shading*. He was the first one to formulate the SfS problem in terms of a partial differential equation (PDE). Moreover, he and

Ikeuchi were also the first ones to model the SfS problem using a variational framework [12]: Assuming a simple *orthographic* projection model, a light source at *infinity* as well as a *Lambertian* reflectance model, they proposed to compute the normals of the desired surface as minimiser of a suitable energy functional.

Those first approaches, however, had several drawbacks. The model assumptions were designed to be *very simple*. Moreover, the *depth was not estimated directly* such that the computation of the final surface from the estimated normals required additionally a numerical integration. Thereby, *inconsistent gradient fields* turned out to be a problem, such that extensions of the original model were required that tried to enforce this consistency [10]. Finally, in case of variational methods, the smoothness term was restricted to a simple quadratic regulariser which lead to *oversmoothed solutions* [13]. Only recently, a variational model has been proposed in [20] that made use of adaptive regularisation strategies. However, even in this case, the underlying modelling assumptions were still the same as the ones of Horn [11].

Perspective Shape from Shading. At the end of the 1990's research in SfS was considered dead, since results were not satisfactory [22]. Then the situation changed completely. Independently, Prados *et al.* [14,15] as well as two other research groups [7,18] proposed to consider a *perspective* camera model. Such a model is appropriate if the object is relatively close to the camera which is typically the case in optical quality assessment or medical endoscopy. Here, perspective effects become important and the classical orthographic projection causes significant systematic errors [19]. Moreover, Prados *et al.* proposed to set the light source to the camera position which may approximate a camera with photoflash. This was combined with a light attenuation term that simulates a quadratic fall-off. The use of these modelling ingredients largely resolved the notorious convex-concave ambiguity [3]. Summarising, by considering more realistic model assumptions, the quality of results improved dramatically.

However, while classical, orthographic SfS methods often made use of a variational approach [22], perspective SfS was formulated in terms of geometrically motivated, hyperbolic PDEs [15]. In contrast to a variational framework, these models do not allow to incorporate smoothness terms that regularise the solution by implicitly averaging local information. Although the original PDE formulation of the perspective SfS problem with quadratic fall-off term is well-posed in the sense of viscosity solutions [3,15], the use of such regularisers can be worthwhile, since they control the degree of smoothness and thus prevent to interpret image noise as shape variations. Moreover, such terms allow the filling-in of regions with missing information instead of leaving holes in the reconstruction. Given these advantages, it seems evidently desirable to combine the quality of PDE-based approaches with the robustness of variational methods.

While there are approaches in the literature that introduce some form of regularisation by formulating a PDE-based perspective SfS model in terms of a spline basis [8], there is only one work so far that tries to embed a perspective SfS model into a variational framework [1]. Although this approach allows the direct computation of the depth, however, it defines smoothness based on surface normals and thus needs an additional integrability constraint. Moreover the smoothness term is equipped with a simple quadratic penaliser that does not allow to preserve edges in the final result. Finally, also no experiments with noise and missing information are performed, in which a variational method could show its actual benefits compared to PDE-based methods.

Our Contributions. In our paper we address these problems and improve upon the literature in several ways: (i) We describe a novel variational method for perspective SfS. Therefore, we consider the recent PDE-based SfS model of Prados et al. [15] and complement it with a suitable second-order smoothness term. (ii) Thereby we propose a direct approach to depth computation, i.e. our method does not yield gradient fields that need to be integrated in a subsequent step, nor do we employ integrability constraints. (iii) We show the usefulness of our approach in the context of incomplete or noisy data. (iv) Conceptually related to [20], we study the effect of using a discontinuity-preserving smoothness term that allows to recover sharp edges in the reconstruction.

Organisation. In Section 2 we review the perspective SfS model of Prados et al. that serves as basis for our variational method. In Section 3 we the embed this model into an energy functional with homogeneous second-order smoothness term. How the proposed energy functional can be minimised is then discussed in Section 4. While Section 5 proposes model extensions such as a discontinuity-preserving smoothness term and a confidence function, Section 6 presents our experimental evaluation. The paper concludes with a summary in Section 7.

2 Perspective Shape from Shading

Let us start by recalling briefly the PDE-based model of Prados et al. [15] for perspective SfS that serves as basis for our variational method. It assumes that a point light source is located at the *optical centre* of a perspective camera and that the surface reflectance is *Lambertian* with uniform albedo.

In order to derive the relationship between the acquired 2D image and the original 3D surface, we follow [15] and parametrise the unknown surface $\mathcal{S}$ as

$$\mathcal{S} = \left\{ \frac{\mathbf{f}}{\sqrt{|\mathbf{x}|^2 + \mathbf{f}^2}} u(x_1, x_2) \begin{bmatrix} x_1 \\ x_2 \\ -\mathbf{f} \end{bmatrix} \middle| \mathbf{x} := (x_1, x_2)^\top \in \Omega \right\}, \quad \mathcal{S} : \Omega \to \mathbb{R}^3, \quad (1)$$

where $\mathbf{x} = (x_1, x_2)^\top \in \Omega$ is a pixel position in the image plane $\Omega \subset \mathbb{R}^2$, the parameter $\mathbf{f}$ is the focal length of the camera, and $u(\mathbf{x})$ is a multiple of the focal length that describes the radial distance (depth) of the surface from the camera centre.

Moreover, we consider the following brightness equation for the image I that combines Lambertian reflectance with the inverse square law for light attenuation [15]:

$$I = \frac{1}{r^2} \left(\frac{\mathbf{n}}{|\mathbf{n}|} \cdot \mathbf{L} \right). \quad (2)$$

Here, $r = \mathtt{f}\, u(\mathbf{x})$ represents the radial depth from the light source to the surface point, $\cdot$ denotes the usual scalar product, $\mathbf{L}$ is the normalised light direction, $\mathbf{n}$ stands for the surface normal vector, and $|\cdot|$ is the Euclidean norm. Note that the light vector $\mathbf{L} := \mathbf{L}(\mathbf{x})$ is spatially varying, since the light source is located at the optical centre.

In the described setting, the surface normal $\mathbf{n}$ and the light direction $\mathbf{L}$ that are required in (2) are given as

$$\mathbf{n}(\mathbf{x}) = \begin{bmatrix} \mathtt{f}\, u_{x_1} \\ \mathtt{f}\, u_{x_2} \\ x_1\, u_{x_1} + x_2\, u_{x_2} \end{bmatrix} - \frac{\mathtt{f}}{|\mathbf{x}|^2 + \mathtt{f}^2} \begin{bmatrix} x_1\, u_{x_1} \\ x_2\, u_{x_2} \\ -\mathtt{f}\, u \end{bmatrix}, \quad \mathbf{L}(\mathbf{x}) = \frac{1}{|\mathbf{x}|^2 + \mathtt{f}^2} \begin{bmatrix} -x_1 \\ -x_2 \\ \mathtt{f} \end{bmatrix}. \tag{3}$$

Plugging (3) into (2) one finally obtains the perspective SfS model

$$\frac{I(\mathbf{x})\, \mathtt{f}^2}{Q(\mathbf{x})} \sqrt{\mathtt{f}^2\, |\nabla v(\mathbf{x})|^2 + (\nabla v(\mathbf{x}) \cdot \mathbf{x})^2 + Q(\mathbf{x})^2} - e^{-2\, v(\mathbf{x})} = 0, \tag{4}$$

where $v(\mathbf{x}) = \ln u(\mathbf{x})$ and $Q(\mathbf{x}) = \mathtt{f}/\sqrt{|\mathbf{x}|^2 + \mathtt{f}^2}$.

The main properties of the model (4) are: (i) Equation (4) is a Hamilton-Jacobi equation (HJE). (ii) Well-posedness can be achieved in the viscosity sense, cf. [3,15]. (iii) In order to solve (4), proper numerical discretisations must be considered that take into account the hyperbolic character of the HJE.

3 Variational Model

After we have discussed the perspective SfS model, let us now turn towards its integration into a variational framework. To this end we rearrange the HJE in (4) and embed it into a variational set-up with smoothness term. Thus we obtain the following model for *variational perspective SfS*:

$$E\left(v(\mathbf{x})\right) = \int_\Omega \underbrace{\{D(\mathbf{x}, v(\mathbf{x}), \nabla v(\mathbf{x}))\}^2}_{\text{Data term}} + \alpha \underbrace{\{S(\mathrm{Hess}(v))\}^2}_{\text{Smoothness term}}\, d\mathbf{x} \tag{5}$$

where D denotes the data term

$$D\left(\mathbf{x}, v(\mathbf{x}), \nabla v(\mathbf{x})\right) = \mathtt{f}^2\, I(\mathbf{x})\, W(\mathbf{x}) - Q(\mathbf{x})\, e^{-2\, v(\mathbf{x})} \tag{6}$$

with

$$W(\mathbf{x}) = \sqrt{\mathtt{f}^2\, |\nabla v(\mathbf{x})|^2 + (\nabla v(\mathbf{x}) \cdot \mathbf{x})^2 + Q(\mathbf{x})^2} \tag{7}$$

and $\alpha \in \mathbb{R}^+$ is a regularisation parameter that allows to steer the degree of smoothness of the solution. As proposed in [20] in the context of orthographic shape from shading, we employ the Frobenius norm of the Hessian of v as smoothness term:

$$S\left(\mathrm{Hess}(v)\right) = \|\mathrm{Hess}(v)\|_F = \sqrt{(v_{x_1 x_1})^2 + 2\, (v_{x_1 x_2})^2 + (v_{x_2 x_2})^2} \tag{8}$$

Please note that a second-order smoothness term is required in our case, since the data term D already depends on the first derivatives of v, i.e. ∇v.

Our variational model (5) has the following distinctive features: (i) Since the data term (6) is inherited from (4), the perspective camera projection is already taken into account. (ii) The depth of the surface is *directly* computed since we minimise for the unknown depth v in (8). This is in contrast to most variational methods that estimate the depth in two steps, see for instance [4,10,12] where first the surface normals are computed by a variational model and then the depth is determined by integration. (iii) The minimiser of our model fulfils the *integrability constraint* per construction since we solve for v. This fact becomes explicit from using $v_{x_1 x_2} = v_{x_2 x_1}$ in (8).

4 Minimisation

Let us now turn towards the minimisation of the proposed energy. The calculus of variations [6] tells us that the minimiser $v(\mathbf{x})$ of our energy in (5) has to fulfil the following *Euler-Lagrange (EL)* equation:

$$0 = \left[D^2 + \alpha S^2\right]_v - \frac{\partial}{\partial x_1}\left[D^2 + \alpha S^2\right]_{v_{x_1}} - \frac{\partial}{\partial x_2}\left[D^2 + \alpha S^2\right]_{v_{x_2}} \quad (9)$$
$$+ \frac{\partial^2}{\partial x_1^2}\left[D^2 + \alpha S^2\right]_{v_{x_1 x_1}} + 2\frac{\partial^2}{\partial x_1 \partial x_2}\left[D^2 + \alpha S^2\right]_{v_{x_1 x_2}} + \frac{\partial^2}{\partial x_2^2}\left[D^2 + \alpha S^2\right]_{v_{x_2 x_2}}$$

Resolving the brackets and slightly rearranging the ordering of terms, we see that the right hand side of (9) is equal to

$$[D^2]_v - \frac{\partial}{\partial x_1}[D^2]_{v_{x_1}} - \frac{\partial}{\partial x_2}[D^2]_{v_{x_2}} + \overbrace{\frac{\partial^2}{\partial x_1^2}[D^2]_{v_{x_1 x_1}}}^{=0} + \overbrace{2\frac{\partial^2}{\partial x_1 \partial x_2}[D^2]_{v_{x_1 x_2}}}^{=0}$$
$$+ \underbrace{\frac{\partial^2}{\partial x_2^2}[D^2]_{v_{x_2 x_2}}}_{=0} + \underbrace{[\alpha S^2]_v}_{=0} - \underbrace{\frac{\partial}{\partial x_1}[\alpha S^2]_{v_{x_1}}}_{=0} - \underbrace{\frac{\partial}{\partial x_2}[\alpha S^2]_{v_{x_2}}}_{=0}$$
$$+ \frac{\partial^2}{\partial x_1^2}[\alpha S^2]_{v_{x_1 x_1}} + 2\frac{\partial^2}{\partial x_2 \partial x_1}[\alpha S^2]_{v_{x_1 x_2}} + \frac{\partial^2}{\partial x_2^2}[\alpha S^2]_{v_{x_2 x_2}} \quad (10)$$

$$= [D^2]_v - \frac{\partial}{\partial x_1}[D^2]_{v_{x_1}} - \frac{\partial}{\partial x_2}[D^2]_{v_{x_2}}$$
$$+ \frac{\partial^2}{\partial x_1^2}[\alpha S^2]_{v_{x_1 x_1}} + 2\frac{\partial^2}{\partial x_1 \partial x_2}[\alpha S^2]_{v_{x_1 x_2}} + \frac{\partial^2}{\partial x_2^2}[\alpha S^2]_{v_{x_2 x_2}} \quad (11)$$

where we exploited the fact that

$$\frac{\partial^2}{\partial x_1 \partial x_2}\left[D^2 + \alpha S^2\right]_{v_{x_1 x_2}} = \frac{\partial^2}{\partial x_2 \partial x_1}\left[D^2 + \alpha S^2\right]_{v_{x_1 x_2}}. \quad (12)$$

Please note that in contrast to many other models in computer vision, our data term D not only depends on v but also on ∇v which gives additional contributions in the EL equation, i.e. the terms $\frac{\partial}{\partial x_1}[D^2]_{v_{x_1}}$ and $\frac{\partial}{\partial x_2}[D^2]_{v_{x_2}}$.

Let us now consider all the individual terms that occur in (11). After some computations we obtain

$$[D^2]_v = 4\,Q\,D\,e^{-2v}\,,\tag{13}$$

$$\frac{\partial}{\partial x_1}\left[D^2\right]_{v_{x_1}} = 2\mathbf{f}^2\left(I_{x_1}\eta_1\frac{D}{W} + I\eta_1\left[\frac{D}{W}\right]_{x_1} + I\left[\eta_1\right]_{x_1}\frac{D}{W}\right),\tag{14}$$

$$\frac{\partial}{\partial x_1}\left[D^2\right]_{v_{x_2}} = 2\mathbf{f}^2\left(I_{x_2}\eta_2\frac{D}{W} + I\eta_2\left[\frac{D}{W}\right]_{x_2} + I\left[\eta_2\right]_{x_2}\frac{D}{W}\right),\tag{15}$$

with

$$\eta_1 := \mathbf{f}^2 v_{x_1} + (\nabla v \cdot \mathbf{x})\,x_1\,,\quad \eta_2 := \mathbf{f}^2 v_{x_2} + (\nabla v \cdot \mathbf{x})\,x_2\,,\tag{16}$$

as well as

$$\frac{\partial^2}{\partial x_1^2}\left[\alpha S^2\right]_{v_{x_1x_1}} = 2\,\alpha\,v_{x_1x_1x_1x_1}\,,\tag{17}$$

$$2\frac{\partial^2}{\partial x_1 \partial x_2}\left[\alpha S^2\right]_{v_{x_1x_2}} = 4\,\alpha\,v_{x_1x_1x_2x_2}\,,\tag{18}$$

$$\frac{\partial^2}{\partial x_2^2}\left[\alpha S^2\right]_{v_{x_2x_2}} = 2\,\alpha\,v_{x_2x_2x_2x_2}\,.\tag{19}$$

Plugging (17)-(19) into (11) allows to simplify at least the smoothness term such that we obtain our final equation

$$\underbrace{[D^2]_v - \frac{\partial}{\partial x_1}[D^2]_{v_{x_1}} - \frac{\partial}{\partial x_2}[D^2]_{v_{x_2}}}_{\text{Data term}} + \alpha\underbrace{\left(2\,\Delta^2\,v\right)}_{\text{Smoothness term}} = 0\,,\tag{20}$$

where

$$\Delta^2 v = \nabla^4 v = v_{x_1x_1x_1x_1} + 2\,v_{x_1x_1x_2x_2} + v_{x_2x_2x_2x_2}\tag{21}$$

is the biharmonic operator. The corresponding fourth-order diffusion term arises in the Euler-Lagrange equation as a result of the second-order smoothness term in (8). So far the smoothness term is homogeneous. In Section 5 we will show how to modify this term such that the underlying diffusion process becomes edge-preserving.

Numerical Solution. In order to discretise the data term in (20), we employ the upwind scheme from [16] in view of the hyperbolic nature of the HJE. In 1D, the upwind discretisation reads as

$$\widehat{v}_{x_1} = \max\left(D^-v, -D^+v, 0\right)\,,\tag{22}$$

with

$$D^-v = \frac{v_i - v_{i-1}}{h_{x_1}} > 0 \quad \text{and} \quad D^+v = \frac{v_{i+1} - v_i}{h_{x_1}} < 0\,,\tag{23}$$

where h_{x_1} denotes the grid size and with $\widehat{v}_{x_1} := D^+ v$ if the second argument in (22) is used. The scheme can be extended in a straightforward way to 2D. For discretising the smoothness term, a standard central difference scheme is used. Then, by applying the Euler forward time discretisation $v_t \approx \left(v^{n+1} - v^n\right)/\tau$ with τ being a time step size, we can reformulate the solution of (20) as the steady state of the corresponding evolution equation in artificial time. Thereby we obtain the explicit scheme

$$\frac{v^{n+1} - v^n}{\tau} + EL^n = 0 \quad \Leftrightarrow \quad v^{n+1} = v^n - \tau\, EL^n, \tag{24}$$

where EL^n is the discretisation of Euler-Lagrange equation (20) evaluated at time n. Although the eigenvalues of the biharmonic operator are known and would thus allow us to restrict the time step size τ to guarantee stability with respect to the contributions of the smoothness term, the rather complex contributions of the data term make it hard to derive an overall stability limit. Hence, in our experiments τ was chosen such that the overall energy was mainly decreasing and the results look visually pleasant.

5 Model Extensions

Edge-Preserving Smoothness Term. First, we extend our model by employing an edge-preserving smoothness term. Since the homogeneous second-order regulariser in (5) cannot preserve edges during the reconstruction, it typically leads to oversmoothed solutions. In order to deal with this problem, we propose to use a subquadratic penaliser function Ψ that reduces smoothness at locations of high curvature. Thus we obtain

$$E(v) = \int_\Omega \{D(\mathbf{x}, v, \nabla v)\}^2 + \alpha\, \Psi\left(\|\mathrm{Hess}(v)\|_F^2\right) d\mathbf{x}, \tag{25}$$

where we choose Ψ to be the Charbonnier regulariser [5] given by

$$\Psi(s^2) = 2\lambda^2 \sqrt{1 + \frac{s^2}{\lambda^2}} \tag{26}$$

with contrast parameter λ. Similar second-order smoothness terms have already been applied successfully in the context of orthographic SFS [20] and motion estimation [9].

The corresponding EL equation for this subquadratic model is given by

$$\begin{aligned}&\left[D^2\right]_v - \frac{\partial}{\partial x_1}\left[D^2\right]_{v_{x_1}} - \frac{\partial}{\partial x_2}\left[D^2\right]_{v_{x_2}} \\ &+ 2\frac{\partial^2}{\partial x_1^2}\left[\Psi'(\cdot)v_{x_1 x_1}\right] + 4\frac{\partial^2}{\partial x_1 \partial x_2}\left[\Psi'(\cdot)v_{x_1 x_2}\right] + 2\frac{\partial^2}{\partial x_2^2}\left[\Psi'(\cdot)v_{x_2 x_2}\right] = 0,\end{aligned} \tag{27}$$

where we omitted the argument $\|\mathrm{Hess}(v)\|_F^2$ of $\Psi'(\cdot)$ for the sake of brevity and where the derivative of the penaliser function $\Psi(s^2)$ reads

$$\Psi'(s^2) = \frac{\partial}{\partial s^2}\Psi(s^2) = 1/\sqrt{1 + \frac{s^2}{\lambda^2}}. \tag{28}$$

Evidently, $\Psi'(s^2)$ becomes small for large values of s^2. Thus we obtain the desired reduction of the smoothing at locations with high curvature, i.e. where $\|\text{Hess}(v)\|_F^2$ is large. Moreover, one can easily verify that for a quadratic penaliser $\Psi(s^2) = s^2$ the EL equation of the subquadratic model boils down to the EL equation of our original model in (20), since $\Psi'(s^2) = 1$. Although, in general, the new EL equation in (27) is somewhat more complicated than its original counterpart (20), the discretisation of its terms can be performed in accordance with our explanations from the previous section.

Confidence Function. Secondly, we extend the model in such a way that it is able to ignore image data at locations where information is not available or has been identified as unreliable in a suitable preprocessing step, e.g. by using an edge or texture detector. To this end, we introduce a binary confidence function $c : \mathbf{x} \in \Omega \subset \mathbb{R}^2 \to \{0, 1\}$. This can be understood as a pointwise equivalent of appropriate node selection strategies in the context of spline-based perspective SfS methods [8].

Since the computation of the EL equation is not feasible if c is not differentiable, we follow the literature on PDE-based image inpainting [17] and integrate the confidence function directly into the EL equation (20):

$$c\left([D^2]_v - \frac{\partial}{\partial x_1}[D^2]_{v_{x_1}} - \frac{\partial}{\partial x_2}[D^2]_{v_{x_2}}\right) + 2\alpha(1-c)\left(\Delta^2 v\right) = 0 \qquad (29)$$

As can be seen from the modified EL equation, the fourth-order diffusion process resulting from the smoothness term now takes over at locations with low confidence and fills-in information from the neighbourhood. This allows us to obtain dense reconstructions even in the case of partially missing data.

6 Experiments

Influence of Homogeneous and Edge-Preserving Regularisation. The first experiment shows the influence of the homogeneous smoothness term defined in (5) on the reconstruction. As input image we have used the classical vase test image (128 × 128) depicted in Fig. 1(a), however, in a perspective rendering. The corresponding results are depicted in Figs. 1(b) and 1(c) where the legend shows how colours are assigned to Cartesian depth values. As one can see the reconstruction of the vases are stronger connected with the background as the smoothness parameter α increases from 10^{-4} to 10^{-1}. Let us compare these results with those one can obtain by using the edge-preserving smoothness term (26). Since the regulariser in (8) is non-adaptive, one can notice that the edge between object boundary and background is not preserved sharply as can be observed in Fig 1(c). Fig. 1(d), however, demonstrates that one can retain the sharp edge with the help of an edge-preserving smoothness term (26). Let us note that the smoothness weight α is the same in the computations of Fig. 1(c). and Fig. 1(d).

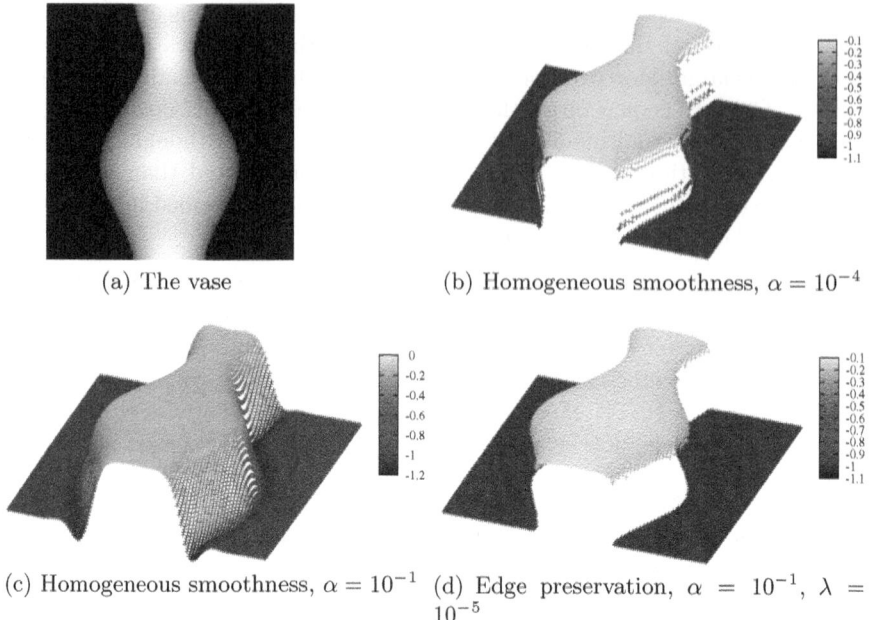

(a) The vase (b) Homogeneous smoothness, $\alpha = 10^{-4}$

(c) Homogeneous smoothness, $\alpha = 10^{-1}$ (d) Edge preservation, $\alpha = 10^{-1}$, $\lambda = 10^{-5}$

Fig. 1. Homogeneous vs. edge-preserving regularisation. Employed parameters are: Time step size $\tau = 10^{-1}$ with 2000 iterations.

(a) Input image (b) Confidence (c) $\alpha = 0.2$

Fig. 2. Impact of confidence function: Inpainting a reconstruction. Employed parameters are: Time step size $\tau = 10^{-1}$, 2500 iterations. The runtime is 890 seconds.

Reconstruction with Inpainting. The second experiment shows the capability of our extended model that employs the adaptive smoothness term. We take Fig. 2(a) as an input image (resolution is 690 × 590) which has some black degraded region which we call K. To reconstruct the surface, we make use of the binary confidence function shown in Fig. 2(b) defined as

$$c(\mathbf{x}) = \begin{cases} 1, \mathbf{x} \in (\Omega \setminus K) \\ 0, \mathbf{x} \in K \end{cases}, \tag{30}$$

where K is the black marked region to be inpainted in Fig. 2(b). Notice that we choose the region K in the confidence function larger than the degraded regions

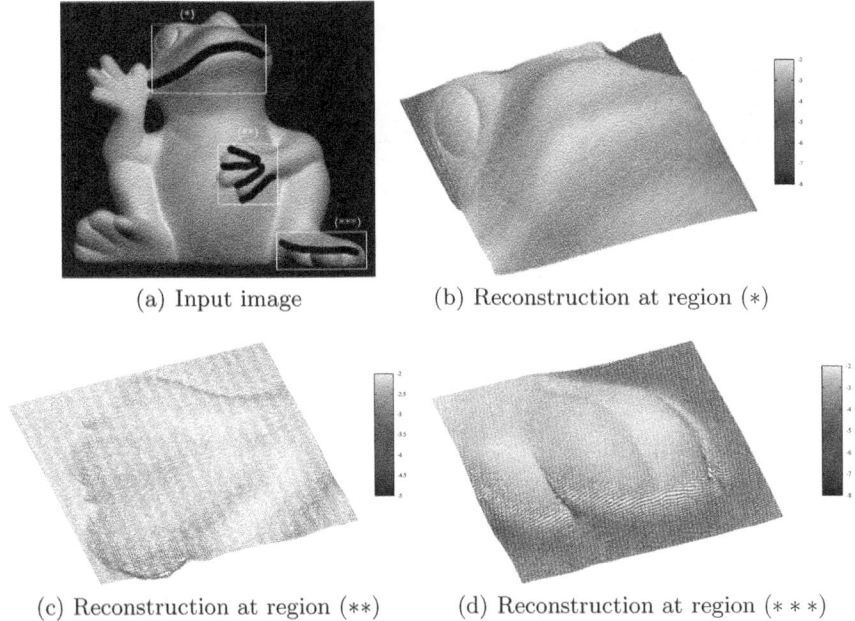

Fig. 3. Interpolation with edge-preserving smoothness term. Employed parameters are: Time step size $\tau = 10^{-1}$, 25000 iterations, $\alpha = 0.3$. The runtime is 9200 seconds for image size 690×590.

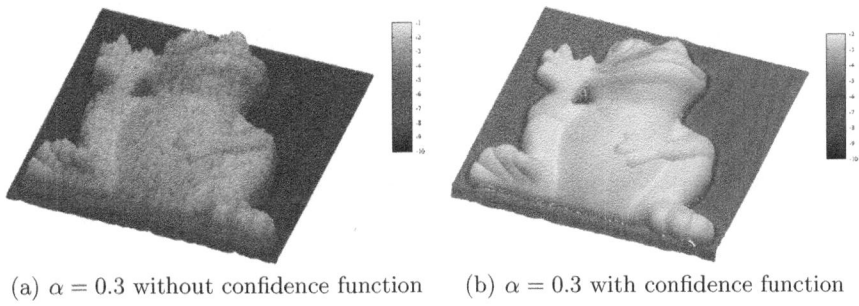

Fig. 4. Reconstruction of frog input image with 5% salt and pepper noise. Employed parameters are: Time step size $\tau = 10^{-1}$, 5000 iterations. Runtime: 1720 seconds.

as shown in Fig. 2(a) (via morphological erosion) in order to employ unspoiled data for inpainting.

Evidently, a reconstruction without smoothness term could not give a useful result in the region K. However, when we harness the smoothness term with the confidence function, as noticeable in Fig. 2(c) we can obtain a reasonable, smooth reconstruction: the smoothness term fills in the solution in the region K by acquiring information from neighbouring pixels. For the region $\Omega \setminus K$, the data term plays the major role.

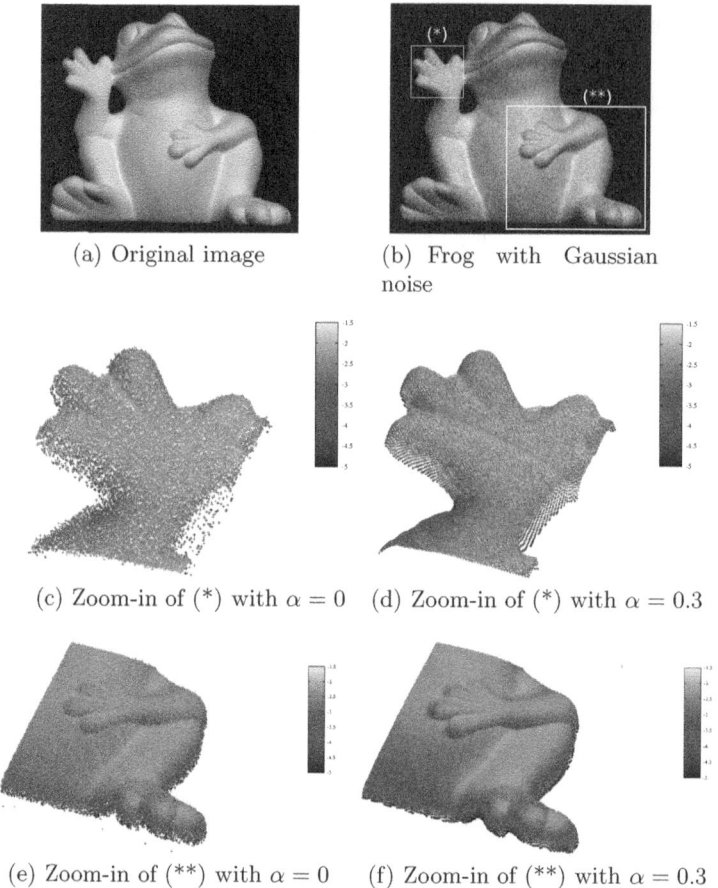

Fig. 5. Reconstructions of noisy image ($\tau = 10^{-1}$, 5000 iterations; runtime is 1830 seconds).

Reconstruction with Inpainting and Edge-Preserving Regulariser. Let us now investigate the capability of the edge-preserving regulariser to interpolate difficult features of the solution, see Fig. 3(a). By using a binary confidence function as in the previous experiment we have chosen here regions for inpainting that contain kinks and anisotropic structures. As shown in the computed solutions in Fig. 3, the reconstruction in such critical regions looks very convincing given the premise that important, semantic features have been erased in input data. In this context, it should be evident that inpainting can only give reasonable results if regions with missing information are of moderate size such that missing information can be recovered from the neighbourhood.

Robustness with Respect to Noise. Finally, in order to validate the applicability of our variational approach we applied it at input images *(i)* in the presence of 5% salt and pepper noise and *(ii)* Gaussian noise with standard deviation $\sigma = 20$. The original, unspoiled image is displayed in Fig. 5(a). As can be seen by Fig. 4, our method performs well in the case of salt and pepper noise since the confidence function allows to exclude noisy pixels and the smoothness term fills in missing information. For dealing with the salt and pepper noise we employed the confidence function to inpaint at noisy pixels during the reconstruction. With respect to Gaussian noise we take the noisy input image directly without making use of a filling-in strategy. As can be observed in Figs. 5(d) and 5(f) in our test with Gaussian noise, the use of a smoothness term also leads here to a useful representation of the 3D frog shape, whereas results obtained without regularisation show again a noisy behaviour, see Figs. 5(c) and 5(e).

Let us note that we used for these experiments the homogeneous regulariser. The edge-preserving regulariser does not have an experimental advantage in our denoising experiments and is therefore not addressed here.

7 Conclusion

In this paper, we demonstrated the usefulness of variational methods for perspective shape from shading. To this end, we embedded the Hamilton-Jacobi equation of a recent PDE-based approach as data term into a variational method and complemented it with a homogeneous second-order smoothness term. Moreover, we extended our approach by considering a spatially variant confidence function and a discontinuity-preserving smoothness term. Experiments clearly show the benefits of regularisation for perspective SfS: It does not only improve the performance under noise, it also allows the inpainting of information in the case of missing or unreliable image data. For future work, we plan to extend this approach to more sophisticated reflection models and to investigate suitable mechanisms to identify texture or other problematic locations.

Acknowledgments. This work has been partially funded by the Deutsche Forschungsgemeinschaft (DFG) as a joint project (BR 2245/3-1, BR 4372/1-1).

References

1. Abdelrahim, A.S., Abdelmunim, H., Graham, J., Farag, A.: Novel variational approach for the perspective shape from shading problem using calibrated images. In: Proc. International Conference on Image Processing, pp. 2563–2566 (2013)
2. Bors, A.G., Hancock, E.R., Wilson, R.C.: Terrain analysis using radar shape-from-shading. IEEE Trans. on Pattern Analysis and Machine Intelligence **25**, 974–992 (2003)
3. Breuß, M., Cristiani, E., Durou, J.-D., Falcone, M., Vogel, O.: Perspective Shape from Shading: Ambiguity Analysis and Numerical Approximations. SIAM Journal on Imaging Sciences **5**(1), 311–342 (2012)
4. Brooks, M.J., Horn, B.K.P.: Shape and source from shading. In: Proc. International Joint Conference in Artificial Intelligence, pp. 932–936 (1985)
5. Charbonnier, P., Blanc-Féraud, L., Aubert, G., Barlaud, M.: Deterministic Edge-Preserving Regularization in Computed Imaging. IEEE Trans. on Image Processing **6**(2), 298–311 (1997)

6. Courant, R., Hilbert, D.: Methods of Mathematical Physics. Interscience Publishers Inc., New York (1953)
7. Courteille, F., Crouzil, A., Durou, J.-D., Gurdjos, P.: Towards shape from shading under realistic photographic conditions. In: Int. Conference on Pattern Recognition, pp. 277–280 (2004)
8. Courteille, F., Crouzil, A., Durou, J.-D., Gurdjos, P.: 3D-spline reconstruction using shape from shading: spline from shading. Image and Vision Computing **26**(4), 466–479 (2008)
9. Demetz, O., Stoll, M., Volz, S., Weickert, J., Bruhn, A.: Learning Brightness Transfer Functions for the Joint Recovery of Illumination Changes and Optical Flow. In: Fleet, D., Pajdla, T., Schiele, B., Tuytelaars, T. (eds.) ECCV 2014, Part I. LNCS, vol. 8689, pp. 455–471. Springer, Heidelberg (2014)
10. Frankot, R.T., Chellappa, R.: A method for enforcing integrability in shape from shading algorithms. IEEE Trans. on Pattern Analysis and Machine Intelligence **10**(4), 439–451 (1988)
11. Horn, B.K.P.: Shape from Shading: A Method for Obtaining the Shape of a Smooth Opaque Object from One View. PhD thesis. MIT, Cambridge (1970)
12. Ikeuchi, K., Horn, B.K.P.: Numerical shape from shading and occluding boundaries. Artificial Intelligence **17**(1–3), 141–184 (1981)
13. Oliensis, J.: Shape from Shading as a Partially Well-Constrained Problem. Computer Vision, Graphics, and Image Processing: Image Understanding **54**(2), 163–183 (1991)
14. Prados, E., Faugeras, O.: "Perspective Shape from Shading" and Viscosity Solutions. In: Proc. International Conference Computer Vision, pp. 826–831 (2003)
15. Prados, E., Faugeras, O.: Shape from shading: A well-posed problem? In: Proc. Conference on Computer Vision and Pattern Recognition, pp. 870–877 (2005)
16. Rouy, E., Tourin, A.: A Viscosity Solution Approach to Shape-From-Shading. SIAM Journal on Numerical Analysis **29**(3), 867–884 (1992)
17. Schmaltz, C., Peter, P., Mainberger, M., Eberl, F., Weickert, J., Bruhn, A.: Understanding, optimising, and extending data compression with anisotropic diffusion. International Journal of Computer Vision **108**(3), 222–240 (2014)
18. Tankus, A., Sochen, N., Yeshurun, Y.: A New Perspective [on] Shape-from-Shading. In: Proc. Conference on Computer Vision and Pattern Recognition, pp. 862–869 (2003)
19. Tankus, A., Sochen, N., Yeshurun, Y.: Shape-from-Shading Under Perspective Projection. International Journal of Computer Vision **63**(1), 21–43 (2005)
20. Vogel, O., Bruhn, A., Weickert, J., Didas, S.: Direct Shape-from-Shading with Adaptive Higher Order Regularisation. In: Sgallari, F., Murli, A., Paragios, N. (eds.) SSVM 2007. LNCS, vol. 4485, pp. 871–882. Springer, Heidelberg (2007)
21. Wang, G.H., Han, J.Q., Zhang, X.M.: Three-dimensional reconstruction of endoscope images by a fast shape from shading method. Measurement Science and Technology 20 (2009)
22. Zhang, R., Tsai, P.-S., Cryer, J.E., Shah, M.: Shape from Shading: A Survey. IEEE Trans. on Pattern Analysis and Machine Intelligence **21**(8), 690–706 (1999)

Multiview Depth Parameterisation with Second Order Regularisation

Christopher Schroers[✉], David Hafner, and Joachim Weickert

Mathematical Image Analysis Group, Faculty of Mathematics and Computer Science,
Saarland University, Campus E1.7, 66041 Saarbrücken, Germany
{schroers,hafner,weickert}@mia.uni-saarland.de

Abstract. In this paper we consider the problem of estimating depth maps from multiple views within a variational framework. Previous work has demonstrated that multiple views improve the depth reconstruction, and that higher order regularisers model a good prior for typical real-world 3D scenes. We build on these findings and stress an important aspect that has not been considered in variational multiview depth estimation so far: We investigate several parameterisations of the unknown depth. This allows us to show, both analytically and experimentally, that directly working with depth values introduces an undesirable bias. As a remedy, we reveal that an inverse depth parameterisation is generally preferable. Our analysis clearly points out its benefits w.r.t. the data and the smoothness term. We verify these theoretical findings by means of experiments.

1 Introduction

The task of reconstructing 3D scenes from a number of images along with corresponding camera poses is commonly referred to as *multiview stereo*. It is important for a variety of applications, and thus has received a huge amount of attention over the last decades. One can approach the multiview stereo problem by dividing it into the following two steps: First, one computes depth maps for a number of input images. Second, these depth maps are merged with a volumetric approach, see e.g. [1–3]. In this way, the multiview stereo problem constitutes a common example, where one is interested in obtaining a depth map given multiple views. This is the problem we focus on in our paper.

Related Work. Ignoring the fact that multiple views are available, variational stereo algorithms that consider image pairs can be regarded as related work, see e.g. [4–9]. While these variational formulations compute disparities relying on a first order regularisation, higher order regularisation has proven to be a very successful strategy for many applications [10–12]. Often, coupled formulations are used instead of directly implementing a higher order regulariser. Popular variants for this are total generalised variation [13] or an approach as in [11]. Also infimal convolution is a much related alternative, where first ideas of this can be found in [14]. Recently, Ranftl et al. demonstrated the benefits of second order regularisation in the context of optic flow [12] and stereo [10].

However, considering only two of the multiple views discards a lot of the available information. Unfortunately, it is not convenient to extend the concept of computing disparities to a general multiview setting. Hence, there are a number of variational formulations that directly estimate depth from multiple views. Such methods have shown the benefits of using multiple images in the process of depth map estimation. To the best of our knowledge, the basic idea of considering multiple views to estimate a single depth map within a variational formulation is almost two decades old and goes back to Robert and Deriche [15]. They employed a quadratic data term along with a nonquadratic regulariser that is able to preserve depth discontinuities. More recently, Stühmer et al. [16] presented a similar formulation with a robust penaliser for the smoothness term as well as the data term. Instead of the brightness constancy, assumed by [15] and [16], Semerijan [17] uses a gradient constancy assumption and a finite element discretisation.

All of the aforementioned approaches are directly parameterised by the unknown depth. However, in related problems such as monocular SLAM, an inverse depth parameterisation of point features has been shown to be beneficial [18]. Also the dense tracking and mapping approach of Newcombe et al. uses inverse depth to compute cost values in a discrete cost volume [19] and the recently developed LSD-SLAM estimates probabilistic semi-dense inverse depth maps [20].

Contributions. While existing variational multiview formulations [15–17] directly compute the unknown depth from a number of arbitrarily placed cameras, we generalise them by introducing a depth parameterisation. This allows us to efficiently analyse advantages and drawbacks of different parameterisations such as a direct depth parameterisation and an inverse depth parameterisation. More specifically, we analyse two important aspects: On the one hand, the choice of parameterisation is important when considering the linearisation of the data term in a variational framework. Here, we show that for common camera setups, the inverse depth parameterisation is preferable. On the other hand, the choice of parameterisation is also important in the smoothness term, especially in the presence of second order regularisation. Here, we show that for an inverse depth parameterisation, piecewise affine functions correspond to piecewise planar surfaces. This is not the case for a direct depth parameterisation. We give deep insights into the introduced bias by analysing the shape operator of the corresponding 3D surface.

Paper Organisation. In Section 2, we present a variational formulation for the estimation of depth maps from multiple views with an arbitrary parameterisation. Subsequently, we analyse different parameterisations in detail (Section 3). In Section 4, we discuss the minimisation. Finally, we show experimental results (Section 5) before we conclude our work (Section 6).

2 Variational Multiview Depth Estimation

In this section, we describe a variational framework that allows the estimation of a depth map d from multiple views under an arbitrary parameterisation. To this end, we express d as the composition of an unknown $\rho : \Omega \to \mathbb{R}_+$ and a parameterisation $\phi : \mathbb{R}_+ \to \mathbb{R}_+$ such that $d = \phi \circ \rho$. Then our energy functional has the form

$$E(\rho, \boldsymbol{w}) = \int_\Omega \Big(D(\phi \circ \rho) + \alpha \, S(\rho, \boldsymbol{w}) \Big) \, \mathrm{d}\boldsymbol{x}, \tag{1}$$

with a data term $D(\phi \circ \rho)$, a smoothness term $S(\rho, \boldsymbol{w})$, and a positive smoothness weight α. Since we apply second order regularisation in terms of a coupling model, we require the additional coupling variable $\boldsymbol{w}$. In the following sections, we explain our model components in more detail.

Data Term. Let us assume we are given n colour images $\boldsymbol{f}_1, \ldots, \boldsymbol{f}_n$ and a reference image $\boldsymbol{f}_0$. The task of the data term $D(\phi \circ \rho)$ is to enforce photoconsistency between all available views. To this end, we first introduce a function $\boldsymbol{g}_i(\boldsymbol{x}, \phi \circ \rho)$ that maps a location $\boldsymbol{x} \in \Omega$ in the reference frame $\boldsymbol{f}_0$ with its depth $(\phi \circ \rho)(\boldsymbol{x})$ to the corresponding location in another image $\boldsymbol{f}_i$. This allows to model the assumption that corresponding points $\boldsymbol{x}$ and $\boldsymbol{g}_i(\boldsymbol{x}, \phi \circ \rho)$ have similar colour values as follows:

$$D(\phi \circ \rho) = \frac{1}{n} \sum_{i=1}^{n} \Psi \Big(\| \boldsymbol{f}_i(\boldsymbol{g}_i(\boldsymbol{x}, \phi \circ \rho)) - \boldsymbol{f}_0(\boldsymbol{x}) \|^2 \Big), \tag{2}$$

where $\| \cdot \|$ denotes the Euclidean norm and the function $\Psi : \mathbb{R}_+ \to \mathbb{R}_+$ provides a robust penalisation. A common choice is $\Psi(s^2) = \sqrt{s^2 + \epsilon^2}$, which approximates an L_1 data term for $\epsilon \to 0$.

Smoothness Term. Higher order regularisation has shown its potential in several applications. Essentially, there are two possibilities to design such regularisers: Either by a direct penalisation of higher order derivatives or by introducing a coupling variable. We opt for the second choice that results in the smoothness term

$$S(\rho, \boldsymbol{w}) = \Psi \big(\| \boldsymbol{\nabla} \rho - \boldsymbol{w} \|^2 \big) + \beta \, \Psi \big(\| \boldsymbol{\mathcal{J}} \boldsymbol{w} \|_F^2 \big), \tag{3}$$

where $\boldsymbol{\nabla}$ is the spatial gradient, $\boldsymbol{\mathcal{J}}$ the Jacobian, and $\| \cdot \|_F$ the Frobenius norm.

Since our main focus is the analysis of different parameterisations, we restrict ourselves to the discussed model assumptions. Once the parameterisations are well understood, they can be incorporated in more sophisticated methods that rank favourably in public benchmark systems.

3 Depth Parameterisations

Before analysing possible parameterisations ϕ in (1), we briefly explain the pinhole camera model as it builds the basis for our analysis. Subsequently, we consider the backprojection of constant and affine patches for each parameterisation.

This yields important insights on the effect of the regularisation on the resulting surface. Finally, we treat the effects of different paramterisations on the data term.

3.1 Pinhole Camera Model

With homogeneous coordinates, the projection by a pinhole camera model can be described by the linear map $P \in \mathbb{R}^{3\times 4}$:

$$P = K\,(R\,t),\qquad(4)$$

where $R \in SO(3)$ is a rotation matrix and $t \in \mathbb{R}^3$ is a translation, such that the blockmatrix $(R\,t)$ describes the extrinsic camera parameters. On the other hand, the matrix

$$K = \begin{pmatrix} k_x & 0 & u \\ 0 & k_y & v \\ 0 & 0 & 1 \end{pmatrix} \qquad(5)$$

contains the intrinsic camera parameters k_x and k_y, which specify the focal length, and the principal point $(u,v)^\top$. With this notation, we express the projection of a 3D point $X \in \mathbb{R}^3$ to a point $x \in \mathbb{R}^2$ in the image plane by

$$x = \pi(P\tilde{X}),\qquad(6)$$

where $\tilde{X} = (X^\top, 1)^\top$ is the homogeneous version of X. We use this notation to denote homogeneous coordinates throughout the whole paper. The function $\pi(a,b,c) = (a/c,\ b/c)^\top$ maps a homogeneous coordinate to its Euclidean counterpart.

3.2 Backprojection of Parameterised Depth Maps

The previous section showed how to project a 3D point to the image plane. Here we are interested in the other way around, i.e. the backprojection. We analyse the following parameterisations:

(i) direct depth: $\phi(r) = r$, (7)
(ii) inverse depth: $\phi(r) = 1/r$. (8)

In each case, there is a further design choice that we want to analyse, namely the choice of the distance, in which we measure. Basically, there are two meaningful possibilities to compute a backprojection:

(a) along the line of sight: $\ell(x, \phi \circ \rho) = \|K^{-1}\tilde{x}\|^{-1} K^{-1}\tilde{x} \cdot (\phi \circ \rho)(x)$, (9)
(b) along the optical axis: $s(x, \phi \circ \rho) = K^{-1}\tilde{x} \cdot (\phi \circ \rho)(x)$. (10)

Figure 1 shows the resulting surfaces when backprojecting a constant and an affine function along the line of sight. Note that both parameterisations (i) and

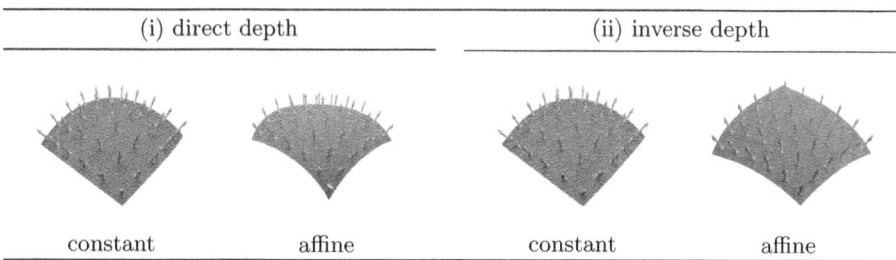

(i) direct depth		(ii) inverse depth	
constant	affine	constant	affine

Fig. 1. Resulting surfaces when backprojecting along the line of sight

(ii) map constant and affine functions to curved surfaces. This means that a first order regulariser would already introduce an unwanted bias because it favours a (piecewise) constant ρ and thus curved surfaces. Therefore, we will not further consider parameterisations along the line of sight in our context.

In contrast, Figure 2 shows that both parameterisations along the optical axis map constant depth functions to surfaces with constant depth, and thus seem to be reasonable choices when employing a first order regularisation. However, considering an affine function (with a nonzero slope), we see that the depth parameterisation does not create a planar surface whereas the inverse depth parameterisation does. In the following sections, we analyse this in detail to get a better understanding of both choices.

3.3 Analysis of Backprojected Depth Maps

Let us consider (10) as a mapping from some parameter space Ω to a surface M, i.e. $s : \Omega \subset \mathbb{R}^2 \to M \subset \mathbb{R}^3$. Generally, the tangent plane of a regular parameterised surface corresponding to a point $(x_0, y_0)^\top$ is spanned by the two tangent vectors

$$s_x = \frac{\partial s}{\partial x} \quad \text{and} \quad s_y = \frac{\partial s}{\partial y}, \tag{11}$$

evaluated at $(x_0, y_0)^\top$. The *first fundamental form* describes the inner product of two tangent vectors. It can be represented by the symmetric matrix

$$I = \begin{pmatrix} \langle s_x, s_x \rangle & \langle s_x, s_y \rangle \\ \langle s_y, s_x \rangle & \langle s_y, s_y \rangle \end{pmatrix}, \tag{12}$$

and allows the evaluation of metric properties such as the surface area. Similarly, the *second fundamental form* is important for describing curvatures. It can be represented by the symmetric matrix

$$II = \begin{pmatrix} \langle n, s_{xx} \rangle & \langle n, s_{xy} \rangle \\ \langle n, s_{yx} \rangle & \langle n, s_{yy} \rangle \end{pmatrix}, \tag{13}$$

where n is the unit surface normal

$$n = \frac{s_x \times s_y}{\|s_x \times s_y\|}. \tag{14}$$

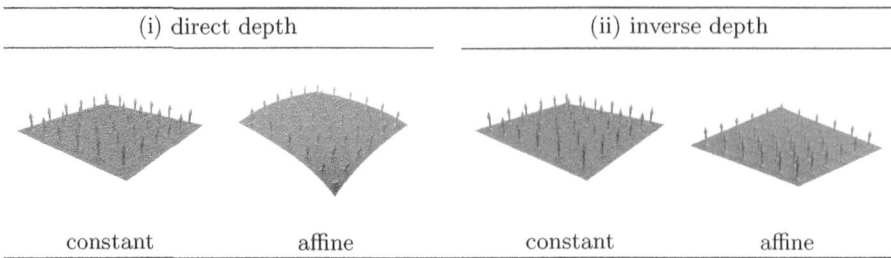

(i) direct depth		(ii) inverse depth	
constant	affine	constant	affine

Fig. 2. Resulting surfaces when backprojecting along the optical axis

The composition of the first and second fundamental form defines the *shape operator*

$$S = I^{-1} \, II. \quad (15)$$

It allows to evaluate the Gaussian curvature K and the mean curvature H, which are given by $\det(S)$ and $1/2 \cdot \mathrm{tr}(S)$, respectively.

Direct Depth. Let us first consider the direct depth parameterisation where the unknown ρ corresponds to the sought depth. With this, we analyse the resulting surface in the case that the *depth is affine*: $\rho(x) = \langle a, \tilde{x} \rangle$ with $a = (a,b,c)^\top$. This is a reasonable and interesting case because a second order regulariser favours (piecewise) affine functions. For this case we obtain the two tangent vectors

$$s_x = K^{-1} \begin{pmatrix} \langle a, \tilde{x} \rangle + ax \\ ay \\ a \end{pmatrix} \quad \text{and} \quad s_y = K^{-1} \begin{pmatrix} bx \\ \langle a, \tilde{x} \rangle + by \\ b \end{pmatrix}, \quad (16)$$

such that

$$\hat{n} = K^\top \begin{pmatrix} -a \\ -b \\ 2ax + 2by + c \end{pmatrix} \quad (17)$$

points along the surface normal (14), i.e. $\hat{n} = \|\hat{n}\| \cdot n$. Equation 17 shows that the normal direction depends on the location $x = (x,y)^\top$ when backprojecting an affine depth function. To get deeper insights on how the surface normals vary, let us consider the surface curvature by means of the shape operator. With (13), the second fundamental form for this example reads

$$II = -\frac{2}{\|\hat{n}\|} \begin{pmatrix} a^2 & ab \\ ab & b^2 \end{pmatrix}. \quad (18)$$

Since this matrix is singular, we can directly conclude that the determinant of the shape operator (15) and consequently the Gaussian curvature K is zero. This further implies that at least one of the principal curvatures is zero. To check if both principal curvatures are zero, let us additionally consider the mean curvature

$$H = \frac{1}{2} \mathrm{tr}(S) = -\frac{(ak_x)^2 + (bk_y)^2}{\det(K^{-1}) \|\hat{n}\|^3}. \quad (19)$$

This shows that the mean curvature is in general not equal to zero, i.e. the surface is bent in one direction. Only for constant functions, i.e. with a and b equal to zero, we also obtain a vanishing mean curvature and thus, a planar surface.

Inverse Depth. Let us now consider the alternative parameterisation $\phi(r) = 1/r$. Then the unknown ρ corresponds to the inverse depth. Again we assume that the unknown, in this case the *inverse depth*, is affine. Accordingly, we obtain the two tangent vectors

$$s_x = \frac{K^{-1}}{\langle a, \tilde{x} \rangle^2} \begin{pmatrix} by + c \\ -ay \\ -a \end{pmatrix} \quad \text{and} \quad s_y = \frac{K^{-1}}{\langle a, \tilde{x} \rangle^2} \begin{pmatrix} -bx \\ ax + c \\ -b \end{pmatrix}, \tag{20}$$

such that

$$\hat{n} = K^\top a \tag{21}$$

points along the surface normal (14). Thus the surface normal is constant in all considered cases for the inverse depth parameterisation. In other words, backprojecting an affine inverse depth always results in a planar surface. In the same way as before, one can verify that both the Gaussian and the mean curvature of the surface are zero.

Summary. Table 1 summarises the discussed findings for all four parameterisations. In conclusion, this shows that the inverse depth parameterisation along the optical axis is preferable when using a second order regularisation.

3.4 Linearity Analysis of the Data Term

Previously, we analysed the influence of parameterisations w.r.t. the smoothness term. Now we analyse its effects on the data term. Since the unknown ρ appears as argument of f_i, the presented energy (1) is non-convex. To cope with this, most minimisation strategies perform a linearisation. In this regard, we analyse how the different depth parameterisations affect this linearisation. In particular, we are interested in the deviation from linearity of g_i in ρ because this quantity depends on the chosen parameterisation. As introduced in Section 2, the function g_i maps a location $x \in \Omega$ in the reference frame f_0 with its depth $(\phi \circ \rho)(x)$ to the corresponding location in another image f_i. This mapping can be described as a composition of a backprojection (10) and a projection (6):

$$g_i(x, \phi \circ \rho) = \pi\big(P_i \cdot \tilde{s}_i(x, \phi \circ \rho)\big). \tag{22}$$

Since scaled homogeneous coordinates are equivalent, it is possible to multiply $\tilde{s}_i$ by $(\phi \circ \rho)(x)^{-1}$ and rewrite Equation 22 as

$$g_i(x, \phi \circ \rho) = \pi\big(K_i R_i K^{-1} \tilde{x} + K_i t_i \, (\phi \circ \rho)(x)^{-1}\big). \tag{23}$$

Table 1. Preservation of planarity

	(i) direct depth		(ii) inverse depth	
	(a) line of sight	(b) optical axis	(a) line of sight	(b) optical axis
constant	no	yes	no	yes
affine	no	no	no	yes

Direct Depth. For common setups, the camera offsets in z-direction are much smaller than the occurring depth values. This is because one typically walks around an object mainly with lateral motion while roughly keeping the distance with only small rotations between views. This causes converging camera setups that keep the object in the middle of the view. Hence, we assume in the following analysis that the z-component of t_i is zero. Please note the relation $t = -Rc_i$ between t_i and the camera centre c_i and that setting the z-component of t_i to zero does not restrict us to camera motions in the x-y-plane. This allows to simplify (23) to

$$r_3^{-1} \cdot \left(\begin{pmatrix} r_1 \\ r_2 \end{pmatrix} + \begin{pmatrix} z_1 \\ z_2 \end{pmatrix} (\phi \circ \rho)(x)^{-1} \right), \tag{24}$$

with the abbreviations $r = K_i R_i K^{-1} \tilde{x}$ and $z = K_i t_i$ that do not depend on $\rho(x)$. With the direct depth parameterisation $(\phi \circ \rho)(x)^{-1} = \rho(x)^{-1}$, we obtain a hyperbola and thus expect an additional linearisation error.

Inverse Depth. This is not the case for the inverse depth parameterisation with $(\phi \circ \rho)(x)^{-1} = \rho(x)$. In fact, Equation 24 reveals that g_i is linear in $\rho(x)$ in this case. Thus, no error is introduced when linearising g_i w.r.t. the inverse depth. To summarise, also the linearisation analysis shows that an inverse depth parameterisation turns out to be more appropriate for multiview depth estimation than the standard direct depth parameterisation.

4 Minimisation

To solve the energy (1), we perform a first order Taylor linearisation around ρ_0 in the data term (2):

$$f_i(g_i(x, \phi \circ \rho)) \approx f_i(g_i(x, \phi \circ \rho_0)) + (\rho - \rho_0) \cdot \partial_\rho f_i(g_i(x, \phi \circ \rho))|_{\rho=\rho_0}. \tag{25}$$

Applying the chain rule gives

$$\partial_\rho f_i(g_i(x, \phi \circ \rho)) = \mathcal{J} f_i(g_i(x, \phi \circ \rho)) \cdot \mathcal{J} g_i(x, \phi \circ \rho), \tag{26}$$

where the image derivatives $\mathcal{J} f_i$ are independent of the parameterisation. The second term in (26) is given by

$$\mathcal{J} g_i(x, \phi \circ \rho) = \mathcal{J} \pi \left(P_i \begin{pmatrix} K^{-1} \tilde{x} \\ (\phi \circ \rho)(x)^{-1} \end{pmatrix} \right) K_i t_i \, \partial_\rho (\phi \circ \rho)(x)^{-1}, \tag{27}$$

where for the direct depth parameterisation $\partial_\rho(\phi \circ \rho)(x)^{-1} = -\rho(x)^{-2}$, and for the inverse depth parameterisation $\partial_\rho(\phi \circ \rho)(x)^{-1} = 1$. With the abbreviations

$$m_i = \partial_\rho f_i(g_i(x, \phi \circ \rho))|_{\rho=\rho_0} \quad \text{and} \quad b_i = m_i \rho_0 + f_0(x) - f_i(g_i(x, \phi \circ \rho_0)) \quad (28)$$

the energy (1) with the linearised data term reads

$$E(\rho, w) = \int_\Omega \frac{1}{n} \sum_{i=1}^n \Psi\left(\|m_i \rho - b_i\|^2\right) + \alpha\left(\Psi(\|\nabla \rho - w\|^2) + \beta \Psi(\|\mathcal{J}w\|_F^2)\right) dx.$$

Euler-Lagrange Equations. The minimiser of the linearised energy functional fulfils the corresponding Euler-Lagrange equations w.r.t. ρ and w. With

$$\Psi'_{Di} = \Psi'(\|m_i \rho - b_i\|^2), \quad \Psi'_C = \Psi'(\|\nabla \rho - w\|^2), \quad \Psi'_S = \Psi'(\|\mathcal{J}w\|_F^2) \quad (29)$$

they are given by

$$\begin{aligned}
\frac{1}{n} \sum_{i=1}^n \Psi'_{Di} \cdot \langle m_i, m_i \rho + b_i \rangle - \alpha \ \mathrm{div}(\Psi'_C \cdot (\nabla \rho - w)) &= 0, \\
\Psi'_C \cdot (w_1 - \rho_x) - \beta \ \mathrm{div}(\Psi'_S \cdot \nabla w_1) &= 0, \\
\Psi'_C \cdot (w_2 - \rho_y) - \beta \ \mathrm{div}(\Psi'_S \cdot \nabla w_2) &= 0
\end{aligned} \quad (30)$$

with boundary conditions $(\nabla \rho - w)^\top n = 0$ and $\mathcal{J}w\, n = 0$, where n is the 2D outer normal here.

Implementation. We discretise (30) with finite differences on a regular grid. This results in a nonlinear system of equations, which we solve with two nested loops. While we update the nonlinear terms Ψ_D, Ψ_C, and Ψ_S (29) in the outer loop, we solve the linear system in the inner loop with the Fast-Jacobi algorithm [21]. Furthermore, we employ a coarse-to-fine approach to overcome linearisation errors.

5 Experiments

Our evaluation consists of two main parts. First, we underpin our theoretical findings from Section 3 by means of experiments with synthetic data. Figure 3(a) shows a 3D scene with a planar surface and three cameras, and Figure 3(b) depicts the images captured with the corresponding cameras. Figure 3 (c) and (d) show the computed reconstructions with a direct depth and an inverse depth parameterisation, respectively. We clearly see that performing second order regularisation on the *depth* introduces a bias towards curved surfaces as discussed in Section 3. In contrast, performing second order regularisation on the *inverse depth* does not introduce such as bias and thus yields a significantly better reconstruction. In Figure 3 (c) and (d), we apply the following colour code to visualise

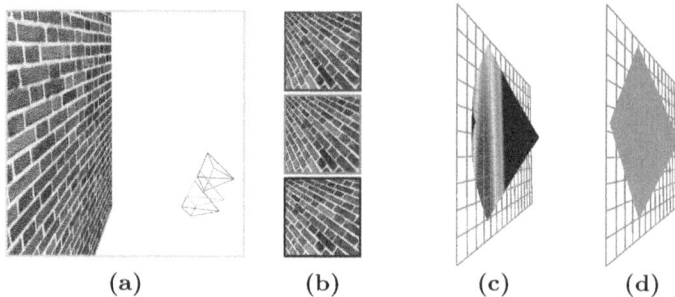

Fig. 3. *From left to right*: **(a)** Camera setup and geometry. **(b)** Corresponding input images. **(c)** Reconstruction with direct depth parameterisation. **(d)** Reconstruction with inverse depth parameterisation. See text for details

Table 2. Root mean square errors for six data sets from the Middlebury benchmark [22]

	direct depth	inverse depth
Barn 1	0.67	**0.25**
Barn 2	1.48	**0.51**
Bull	0.50	**0.23**
Poster	0.48	**0.22**
Sawtooth	1.09	**0.43**
Venus	0.58	**0.29**

the reconstruction errors: Green represents an error of zero, whereas red and blue correspond to behind and in front of the ground truth surface, respectively.

In the second part of our evaluation, we run tests on six publically available multiview data sets from the Middlebury benchmark [22] to obtain a quantitative comparison between both parameterisations. More specifically, we use five images for each 3D scene to compute the depth map. We have optimised the smoothness parameters α and β for each parameterisation, but kept them fixed over the individual scenes. Here, we measure for both parameterisation the reconstruction quality in terms of the root mean square error in depth. Table 2 shows that the inverse depth parameterisation provides a significantly better reconstruction quality than the direct depth parameterisation in all cases. These quantitative experiments confirm our findings from Section 3. The inverse depth parameterisation does not only have advantages in theory, but also practically achieves superior reconstructions. Besides the discussed benefits for the linearisation and second order regularisation, there is another advantage that we have not stressed so far: It is a natural choice to initialise the inverse depth with zero. This corresponds to a depth of infinity. Thus, an initialisation of the direct depth with a large constant seems desirable but turns out to be problematic.

6 Conclusions

In this work, we have analysed different depth parameterisations within the context of multiview depth estimation with higher order regularisation. Our first finding is that parameterisations along the line of sight are not suitable for such a scenario. In fact, we show that parameterisations along the optical axis are much more reasonable. For them, we present a detailed analysis of a direct depth and an inverse depth parameterisation. We point out several advantages of the inverse depth parameterisation: First, it is compatible with second order regularisation. Piecewise affine inverse depth leads to piecewise planar 3D surfaces. On the contrary, this is not the case for the direct depth parameterisation. It introduces a bias which we quantify both theoretically by means of the shape operator as well as by experiments. Second, we show that an inverse depth parameterisation is not only advantageous for the smoothness term. It is also preferable for the linearisation required in the data term compared to a direct depth parameterisation. Last but not least, the inverse depth approach additionally admits a more meaningful initialisation.

Based on our findings, we recommend the inverse depth parameterisation along the optical axis as the parameterisation of choice for variational multiview depth estimation. We believe that this insight can improve the performance of existing methods. In future work, we plan to extend our model with more sophisticated assumptions on the data term and regulariser.

Acknowledgments. Funding by the Cluster of Excellence *Multimodal Computing and Interaction* is gratefully acknowledged.

References

1. Curless, B., Levoy, M.: A volumetric method for building complex models from range images. In: Proc. SIGGRAPH 1996, vol. 3, New Orleans, LA, pp. 303–312, August 1996
2. Zach, C., Pock, T., Bischof, H.: A globally optimal algorithm for robust TV-L^1 range image integration. In: Proc. Ninth International Conference on Computer Vision, Rio de Janeiro, Brazil, pp. 1–8, October 2007
3. Zach, C.: Fast and high quality fusion of depth maps. In: Proc. Fourth International Symposium on 3D Data Processing, Visualization and Transmission, Atlanta, GA, pp. 1–8, June 2008
4. March, R.: Computation of stereo disparity using regularization. Pattern Recognition Letters **8**(3), 181–187 (1988)
5. Mansouri, A.R., Mitiche, A., Konrad, J.: Selective image diffusion: Application to disparity estimation. In: Proc. IEEE International Conference on Image Processing, Chicago, IL, pp. 284–288, October 1998
6. Scharstein, D., Szeliski, R.: Stereo matching with non-linear diffusion. International Journal of Computer Vision **28**, 155–174 (1998)
7. Slesareva, N., Bruhn, A., Weickert, J.: Optic Flow Goes Stereo: A Variational Method for Estimating Discontinuity-Preserving Dense Disparity Maps. In: Kropatsch, W.G., Sablatnig, R., Hanbury, A. (eds.) DAGM 2005. LNCS, vol. 3663, pp. 33–40. Springer, Heidelberg (2005)

8. Zimmer, H., Bruhn, A., Valgaerts, L., Breuß, M., Weickert, J., Rosenhahn, B., Seidel, H.P.: PDE-based anisotropic disparity-driven stereo vision. In: Proc. Vision, Modeling, and Visualization, Konstanz, Germany, Akademische Verlagsgesellschaft Aka, pp. 263–272, October 2008
9. Valgaerts, L., Bruhn, A., Weickert, J.: A Variational Model for the Joint Recovery of the Fundamental Matrix and the Optical Flow. In: Rigoll, G. (ed.) DAGM 2008. LNCS, vol. 5096, pp. 314–324. Springer, Heidelberg (2008)
10. Ranftl, R., Gehrig, S., Pock, T., Bischof, H.: Pushing the limits of stereo using variational stereo estimation. In: Proc. IEEE Intelligent Vehicles Symposium, Alcala de Henares, Spain, pp. 401–407 (2012)
11. Hewer, A., Weickert, J., Seibert, H., Scheffer, T., Diebels, S.: Lagrangian strain tensor computation with higher order variational models. In: Proc. British Machine Vision Conference. BMVA Press, Bristol (September 2013)
12. Ranftl, R., Bredies, K., Pock, T.: Non-local Total Generalized Variation for Optical Flow Estimation. In: Fleet, D., Pajdla, T., Schiele, B., Tuytelaars, T. (eds.) ECCV 2014, Part I. LNCS, vol. 8689, pp. 439–454. Springer, Heidelberg (2014)
13. Bredies, K., Kunisch, K., Pock, T.: Total generalized variation. SIAM Journal on Imaging Sciences **3**(3), 492–526 (2010)
14. Chambolle, A., Lions, P.L.: Image recovery via total variation minimization and related problems. Numerische Mathematik **76**(2), 167–188 (1997)
15. Robert, L., Deriche, R.: Dense depth map reconstruction: A minimization and regularization approach which preserves discontinuities. In: Buxton, B., Cipolla, R. (eds.) ECCV 1996. Lecture Notes in Computer Science, vol. 1064, pp. 439–451. Springer, Berlin (1996)
16. Stühmer, J., Gumhold, S., Cremers, D.: Real-Time Dense Geometry from a Handheld Camera. In: Goesele, M., Roth, S., Kuijper, A., Schiele, B., Schindler, K. (eds.) Pattern Recognition. LNCS, vol. 6376, pp. 11–20. Springer, Heidelberg (2010)
17. Semerjian, B.: A New Variational Framework for Multiview Surface Reconstruction. In: Fleet, D., Pajdla, T., Schiele, B., Tuytelaars, T. (eds.) ECCV 2014, Part VI. LNCS, vol. 8694, pp. 719–734. Springer, Heidelberg (2014)
18. Civera, J., Davison, A.J., Montiel, J.: Inverse depth parametrization for monocular SLAM. IEEE Transactions on Robotics **24**(5), 932–945 (2008)
19. Newcombe, R.A., Lovegrove, S.J., Davison, A.J.: DTAM: Dense tracking and mapping in real-time. In: Proc. IEEE International Conference on Computer Vision, Barcelona, Spain, pp. 2320–2327, November 2011
20. Engel, J., Schöps, T., Cremers, D.: LSD-SLAM: Large-Scale Direct Monocular SLAM. In: Fleet, D., Pajdla, T., Schiele, B., Tuytelaars, T. (eds.) ECCV 2014, Part II. LNCS, vol. 8690, pp. 834–849. Springer, Heidelberg (2014)
21. Grewenig, S., Weickert, J., Schroers, C., Bruhn, A.: Cyclic schemes for PDE-based image analysis. Technical Report 327, Saarland University, Saarbrücken, Germany (March 2013)
22. Scharstein, D., Szeliski, R.: A taxonomy and evaluation of dense two-frame stereo correspondence algorithms. International Journal of Computer Vision **47**, 7–42 (2002)

Invertible Orientation Scores of 3D Images

Michiel Janssen[1]($\boxtimes$), Remco Duits[1,2], and Marcel Breeuwer[2]

[1] Department of Mathematics and Computer Science,
Eindhoven University of Technology, Eindhoven, The Netherlands
{M.H.J.Janssen,R.Duits}@tue.nl
[2] Department of Biomedical Engineering,
Eindhoven University of Technology, Eindhoven, The Netherlands
M.Breeuwer@tue.nl

Abstract. The enhancement and detection of elongated structures in noisy image data is relevant for many biomedical applications. To handle complex crossing structures in 2D images, 2D orientation scores $U : \mathbb{R}^2 \times S^1 \to \mathbb{R}$ were introduced, which already showed their use in a variety of applications. Here we extend this work to 3D orientation scores $U : \mathbb{R}^3 \times S^2 \to \mathbb{R}$. First, we construct the orientation score from a given dataset, which is achieved by an invertible coherent state type of transform. For this transformation we introduce 3D versions of the 2D cake-wavelets, which are complex wavelets that can simultaneously detect oriented structures and oriented edges. For efficient implementation of the different steps in the wavelet creation we use a spherical harmonic transform. Finally, we show some first results of practical applications of 3D orientation scores.

Keywords: Orientation scores · Reproducing kernel spaces · 3D wavelet design · Scale spaces on SE(3) · Coherence enhancing Diffusion on SE(3)

1 Introduction

The enhancement and detection of elongated structures is important in many biomedical image analysis applications. These tasks become problematic when multiple elongated structures cross or touch each other in the data. In these cases it is useful to decompose an image in local orientations by constructing an orientation score. In the orientation score, we extend the domain of the data to include orientation in order to separate the crossing or touching structures (Fig. 1). From 3D data $f : \mathbb{R}^3 \to \mathbb{R}$ we construct a 3D orientation score $U : \mathbb{R}^3 \times S^2 \to \mathbb{R}$, in a similar way as is done for the more common case of 2D data $f : \mathbb{R}^2 \to \mathbb{R}$ and 2D orientation score $U : \mathbb{R}^2 \times S^1 \to \mathbb{R}$. Next, we consider operations on orientation scores, and process our data via orientation scores (Fig. 2). For such operations it is important that the orientation score transform is invertible, in a well-posed manner. In comparison to continuous wavelet transforms on the group of 3D rotations, translations and scalings, we use all scales simultaneously and exclude the scaling group from the wavelet transform and its adjoint, yielding a coherent state type of transform [1], see App.A. This makes it harder to design appropriate wavelets, but has the computational advantage of only needing a single scale transformation.

The 2D orientation scores have already showed their use in a variety of applications. In [11,17] the orientation scores were used to perform crossing-preserving coherence-enhancing diffusions. These diffusions greatly reduce the noise in the data, while preserving the elongated crossing structures. Next to these generic enhancement techniques, the orientation scores also showed their use in retinal vessel segmentation [3], where they were used to better handle crossing vessels in the segmentation procedure.

To perform detection and enhancement operations on the orientation score, we first need to transform a given greyscale image or 3D dataset to an orientation score in an invertible way. In previous works various wavelets were introduced to perform a 2D orientation score transform. Some of these wavelets did not allow for an invertible transformation (e.g. Gabor wavelets [15]). A wavelet that allows an invertible transformation was proposed by Kalitzin [14]. A generalization of these wavelets was found by Duits [8] who derived a unitarity result and expressed the wavelets in a basis of eigenfunctions of the harmonic oscillator. This type of wavelet was also extended to 3D. This wavelet however has some unwanted properties such as poor spatial localization (oscillations) and the fact that the maximum of the wavelet did not lie at its center [8, Fig.4.11]. In [8] a class of cake-wavelets were introduced, that have a cake-piece shaped form in the Fourier domain (Fig. 5). The cake-wavelets simultaneously detect oriented structures and oriented edges by constructing a complex orientation score $U : \mathbb{R}^2 \times S^1 \to \mathbb{C}$. Because the different cake-wavelets cover the full Fourier spectrum, invertibility is guaranteed.

In this paper we propose an extension of the 2D cake-wavelets to 3D. First, we discuss the theory of invertible orientation score transforms. Then we construct 3D cake-wavelets and give an efficient implementation using a spherical harmonic transform. Finally we mention two application areas for 3D orientation scores and show some preliminary results for both of them. In the first application, we present a practical proof of concept of a natural extension of the crossing preserving coherence enhancing diffusion on invertible orientation scores (CEDOS) [11] to the 3D setting. Compared to the original idea of coherence enhancing diffusion acting directly on image-data [4,5,18] we have the advantage of preserving crossings. Diffusions on SE(3) have been studied in previous SSVM-articles, see e.g. [6], but the full generalization of CEDOS to 3D was never established.

2 Invertible Orientation Scores

An invertible orientation score $\mathcal{W}_\psi[f] : \mathbb{R}^3 \times S^2 \to \mathbb{C}$ is constructed from a given ball-limited 3D dataset $f \in \mathbb{L}_2^\varrho(\mathbb{R}^3) = \{f \in \mathbb{L}_2(\mathbb{R}^3) | \mathrm{supp}(\mathcal{F}f) \subset B_{0,\varrho}\}$, with $\varrho > 0$ by correlation $\star$ with an anisotropic kernel

$$(\mathcal{W}_\psi[f])(\mathbf{x}, \mathbf{n}) = (\overline{\psi_\mathbf{n}} \star f)(\mathbf{x}) = \int_{\mathbb{R}^3} \overline{\psi_\mathbf{n}(\mathbf{x}' - \mathbf{x})} f(\mathbf{x}') \mathrm{d}\mathbf{x}', \tag{1}$$

where $\psi \in \mathbb{L}_2(\mathbb{R}^3) \cap \mathbb{L}_1(\mathbb{R}^3)$ is a wavelet aligned with and rotationally symmetric around the z-axis, and $\psi_{\mathbf{n}}(\mathbf{x}) = \psi(\mathbf{R}_{\mathbf{n}}^T \mathbf{x}) \in \mathbb{L}_2(\mathbb{R}^3)$ the rotated wavelet aligned with $\mathbf{n}$. Here $\mathbf{R}_{\mathbf{n}}$ is any rotation which rotates the z-axis onto $\mathbf{n}$ where the specific choice of rotation does not matter because of the rotational symmetry of ψ. The overline denotes a complex conjugate. The exact reconstruction formula for this transformation is

$$f(\mathbf{x}) = (\mathcal{W}_\psi^{-1}[\mathcal{W}_\psi[f]])(\mathbf{x}) \\ = \mathcal{F}_{\mathbb{R}^3}^{-1}\left[M_\psi^{-1} \mathcal{F}_{\mathbb{R}^3}\left[\tilde{\mathbf{x}} \mapsto \int_{S^2} (\check{\psi}_{\mathbf{n}} \star \mathcal{W}_\psi[f](\cdot, \mathbf{n}))(\tilde{\mathbf{x}}) d\sigma(\mathbf{n})\right]\right](\mathbf{x}), \quad (2)$$

with $\mathcal{F}_{\mathbb{R}^3}$ the Fourier transform on $\mathbb{R}^3$ given by $(\mathcal{F}f)(\boldsymbol{\omega}) = (2\pi)^{-\frac{3}{2}} \int_{\mathbb{R}^3} e^{-i\boldsymbol{\omega}\cdot\mathbf{x}} f(\mathbf{x}) \, d\mathbf{x}$ and $\check{\psi}_{\mathbf{n}}(\mathbf{x}) = \psi_{\mathbf{n}}(-\mathbf{x})$. In fact $\mathcal{W}_\psi$ is a unitary mapping on to a reproducing kernel space, see App. A. The function $M_\psi : \mathbb{R}^3 \to \mathbb{R}^+$ is given by

$$M_\psi(\boldsymbol{\omega}) = (2\pi)^{\frac{3}{2}} \int_{S^2} |\mathcal{F}_{\mathbb{R}^3}[\psi_{\mathbf{n}}](\boldsymbol{\omega})|^2 \, d\sigma(\mathbf{n}). \quad (3)$$

The function M_ψ quantifies the stability of the inverse transformation [8], since $M_\psi(\boldsymbol{\omega})$ specifies how well frequency component $\boldsymbol{\omega}$ is preserved by the cascade of construction and reconstruction when M_ψ^{-1} would not be included in Eq. (2). An exact reconstruction is possible as long as

$$\exists_{M>0,\delta>0} \quad 0 < \delta \leq M_\psi(\boldsymbol{\omega}) \leq M < \infty, \quad \text{for all } \boldsymbol{\omega} = B_{0,\varrho}. \quad (4)$$

In practice it is best to aim for $M_\psi(\boldsymbol{\omega}) \approx 1$, in view of the condition number of $\mathcal{W}_\psi : \mathbb{L}_2^\varrho(\mathbb{R}^3) \to \mathbb{L}_2^\varrho(\mathbb{R}^3 \times S^2)$ with $\mathcal{W}_\psi f = \mathcal{W}_\psi f$. Also, when $M_\psi(\boldsymbol{\omega}) = 1$ we have $\mathbb{L}_2$-norm preservation

$$\|f\|_{\mathbb{L}_2(\mathbb{R}^3)}^2 = \|\mathcal{W}_\psi f\|_{\mathbb{L}_2(\mathbb{R}^3 \times S^2)}^2, \quad \text{for all } f \in \mathbb{L}_2^\varrho(\mathbb{R}^3), \quad (5)$$

and Eq. (2) simplifies to $f(\mathbf{x}) = \int_{S^2} (\check{\psi}_{\mathbf{n}} \star \mathcal{W}_\psi[f](\cdot, \mathbf{n}))(\mathbf{x}) d\sigma(\mathbf{n})$. We can further simplify the reconstruction for wavelets for which $(2\pi)^{\frac{3}{2}} \int_{S^2} \mathcal{F}_{\mathbb{R}^3}[\psi_{\mathbf{n}}](\boldsymbol{\omega}) d\sigma(\mathbf{n}) \approx 1$, where the reconstruction formula simplifies to an integration over orientations

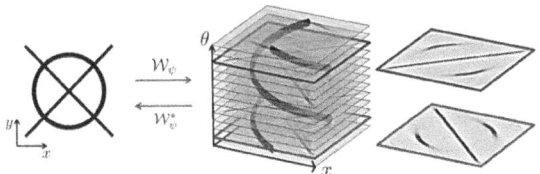
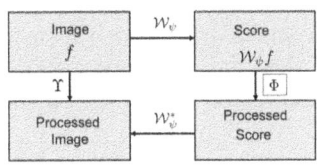

Fig. 1. 2D Orientation score for an exemplary image. In the orientation score crossing structures are disentangled because the different structures have a different orientation.

Fig. 2. A schematic view of image processing via invertible orientation scores

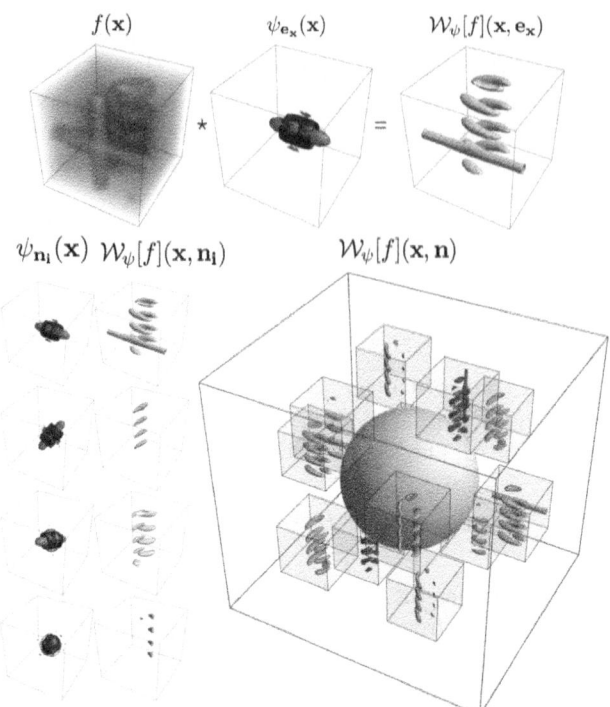

Fig. 3. Creating a 3D orientation score. Top: The data f is correlated with an oriented filter $\psi_{\mathbf{e}_x}$ to detect structures aligned with the filter orientation $\mathbf{e}_x$. Bottom left: This is repeated for a discrete set of filters with different orientations. Bottom right: The collection of 3D datasets constructed by correlation with the different filters is an orientation score and is visualized by placing a 3D dataset on a number of orientations.

$$f(\mathbf{x}) \approx \int_{S^2} U_f(\mathbf{x}, \mathbf{n}) \mathrm{d}\sigma(\mathbf{n}). \qquad (6)$$

2.1 Discrete Invertible Orientation Score Transformation

In the previous section, we considered a continuous orientation score transformation. In practice, we have only a finite number of orientations. To determine this discrete set of orientations we uniformly sample the sphere using platonic solids and/or refine this using tessellations of the platonic solids.

Assume we have a number N_o of orientations $\mathcal{V} = \{\mathbf{n}_1, \mathbf{n}_2, ..., \mathbf{n}_{N_o}\} \subset S^2$, and define the discrete invertible orientation score $\mathcal{W}_\psi^d[f] : \mathbb{R}^3 \times \mathcal{V} \to \mathbb{C}$ by

$$(\mathcal{W}_\psi^d[f])(\mathbf{x}, \mathbf{n}_i) = (\overline{\psi_{\mathbf{n}_i}} \star f)(\mathbf{x}). \qquad (7)$$

The exact reconstruction formula is in the discrete setting given by

$$f(\mathbf{x}) = ((\mathcal{W}_\psi^d)^{-1}[\mathcal{W}_\psi^d[f]])(\mathbf{x})$$
$$= \mathcal{F}_{\mathbb{R}^3}^{-1}\left[(M_\psi^d)^{-1}\mathcal{F}_{\mathbb{R}^3}\left[\tilde{\mathbf{x}} \to \sum_{i=1}^{N_o}(\check{\psi}_{\mathbf{n}_i} * \mathcal{W}_\psi^d[f](\cdot, \mathbf{n}_i))(\tilde{\mathbf{x}})d\sigma(\mathbf{n}_i)\right]\right](\mathbf{x}), \quad (8)$$

with $d\sigma(\mathbf{n}_i)$ the discrete spherical area measure which for reasonably uniform spherical sampling can be approximated by $d\sigma(\mathbf{n}_i) \approx \frac{4\pi}{N_o}$, and

$$M_\psi^d(\boldsymbol{\omega}) = (2\pi)^{\frac{3}{2}} \sum_{i=1}^{N_o} |\mathcal{F}_{\mathbb{R}^3}[\psi_{\mathbf{n}_i}](\boldsymbol{\omega})|^2 \, d\sigma(\mathbf{n}_i). \quad (9)$$

Again, an exact reconstruction is possible iff $0 < \delta \le M_\psi^d(\boldsymbol{\omega}) \le M < \infty$.

3 3D Cake-Wavelets

A class of 2D cake-wavelets, see [8], was successfully used for the 2D orientation score transformation. We now generalize these 2D cake-wavelets to 3D cake-wavelets. Our 3D transformation using the 3D cake-wavelets should fulfill a set of requirements, compare [11]:

1. The orientation score should be constructed for a finite number (N_o) of orientations.
2. The transformation should be invertible and all frequencies should be transferred equally to the orientation score domain ($M_\psi^d \approx 1$).
3. The kernel should be strongly directional.
4. The kernel should be polar separable in the Fourier domain, i.e., $(\mathcal{F}\psi)(\boldsymbol{\omega}) = g(\rho)h(\theta, \phi)$, with $\boldsymbol{\omega} = (\omega_x, \omega_y, \omega_z) = (\rho\sin\theta\cos\phi, \rho\sin\theta\sin\phi, \rho\cos\theta)$. Because by definition the wavelet ψ has rotational symmetry around the z-axis we have $h(\theta, \phi) = \mathfrak{h}(\phi)$.
5. The kernel should be localized in the spatial domain, since we want to pick up local oriented structures.
6. The real part of the kernel should detect oriented structures and the imaginary part should detect oriented edges. The constructed oriented score is therefore a complex orientation score.

3.1 Construction of Line and Edge Detectors

We now discuss the procedure used to make 3D cake-wavelets. According to requirement 4 we only consider polar separable wavelets in the Fourier domain, so that $(\mathcal{F}\psi)(\boldsymbol{\omega}) = g(\rho)\mathfrak{h}(\phi)$. For the radial function $g(\rho)$ we use, as in [11],

$$g(\rho) = \mathcal{M}_N(\rho^2 t^{-1}) = e^{-\frac{\rho^2}{t}} \sum_{k=0}^{N} \frac{(\rho^2 t^{-1})^k}{k!}, \quad (10)$$

which is a Gaussian function with scale parameter t multiplied by the Taylor approximation of its reciprocal to order N to ensure a slower decay. This function should go to 0 when ρ tends to the Nyquist frequency ρ_N. Therefore the inflection point of this function is fixed at $\gamma \rho_N$ with $0 \ll \gamma < 1$ by setting $t = \frac{2(\gamma \rho_N)^2}{1+2N}$. In practice we have $\varrho = \rho_N$, and because radial function g causes M_ψ^d to become really small when coming close to the Nyquist frequency, reconstruction Eq.(8) becomes unstable. We solve this by either using approximate reconstruction Eq.(6) or by replacing $M_\psi^d \to \max(M_\psi^d, \epsilon)$, with ϵ small. Both make the reconstruction stable at the cost of not completely reconstructing the highest frequencies which causes some additional blurring.

We now need to find an appropriate angular part $\mathfrak{h}$ for the cake-wavelets. First, we specify an orientation distribution $A : S^2 \to \mathbb{R}^+$, which determines what orientations the wavelet should measure. To satisfy requirement 3 this function should be a localized spherical window, for which we propose a B-spline $A(\theta, \phi) = B^k(\frac{\phi}{s_\phi})$, with $s_\phi > 0$ and B^k the kth order B-spline given by

$$B^k(x) = (B^{k-1} * B^0)(x), \quad B^0(x) = \begin{cases} 1 & \text{if } -\frac{1}{2} < x < \frac{1}{2} \\ 0 & \text{otherwise} \end{cases}. \quad (11)$$

The parameter s_ϕ determines the trade-off between requirements 2 and 3, where higher values give a more uniform M_ψ^d at the cost of less directionality.

First consider setting $h = A$ so that ψ has compact support within a convex cone in the Fourier domain. The real part of the corresponding wavelet would however be a plate detector and not a line detector (Fig. 4). The imaginary part is already an oriented edge detector, and so we set

$$\mathfrak{h}_{Im}(\phi) = A(\theta, \phi) - A(\theta, \pi - \phi) = B^k(\frac{\phi}{s_\phi}) - B^k(\frac{\pi - \phi}{s_\phi}), \quad (12)$$

where the real part of the earlier found wavelet vanishes by anti-symmetrization of the orientation distribution A while the imaginary part remains. As to the construction of h_{Re}, there is the general observation that we detect a structure that is perpendicular to the shape in the Fourier domain, so for line detection we should aim for a plane detector in the Fourier domain. To achieve this we apply the Funk transform to A, and we define

$$h_{Re}(\theta, \phi) = FA(\theta, \phi) = \int_{S_p(\mathbf{n}(\theta,\phi))} A(\mathbf{n}') \, ds(\mathbf{n}'), \quad (13)$$

where integration is performed over $S_p(\mathbf{n})$ denoting the great circle perpendicular to $\mathbf{n}(\theta, \phi) = (\sin\theta\cos\phi, \sin\theta\sin\phi, \cos\theta)$. This transformation preserves the symmetry of A, so we have $h_{Re}(\theta, \phi) = \mathfrak{h}_{Re}(\phi)$. Thus, we finally set

$$\mathfrak{h}(\phi) = \mathfrak{h}_{Re}(\phi) + \mathfrak{h}_{Im}(\phi). \quad (14)$$

For an overview of the transformations see Fig. 5.

3.2 Efficient Implementations Via Spherical Harmonics

In Subsection 3.1 we defined the real part and the imaginary part of the wavelets in terms of a given orientation distribution. In order to efficiently implement the various transformations (e.g. Funk transform), and to create the various rotated versions of the wavelet we express our orientation distribution A in a spherical harmonic basis $\{Y_l^m\}$ up to order L:

$$A(\theta,\phi) = \sum_{l=0}^{L}\sum_{m=-l}^{l} c_{l,m}Y_l^m(\theta,\phi), \quad L \in \mathbb{N}. \tag{15}$$

Because of the rotational symmetry around the z-axis, we only need the spherical harmonics with $m = 0$, i.e., $A(\theta,\phi) = \sum_{l=0}^{L} c_{l,0}Y_l^0(\theta,\phi)$. For determining the spherical harmonic coefficients we use the pseudo-inverse of the discretized inverse spherical harmonic transform (see [9, Section 7.1]), with discrete orientations given by an icosahedron of tesselation order 15.

Funk Transform. According to [7], the Funk transform of a spherical harmonic equals

$$FY_l^m(\theta,\phi) = \int_{S_p(\mathbf{n}(\theta,\phi))} Y_l^m(\mathbf{n'})\,\mathrm{d}s(\mathbf{n'}) = 2\pi P_l(0)Y_l^m(\theta,\phi), \tag{16}$$

with $P_l(0)$ the Legendre polynomial of degree l evaluated at 0. We can therefore apply the Funk transform to a function expressed in a spherical harmonic basis by a simple transformation of the coefficients $c_l^m \to 2\pi P_l(0)c_l^m$.

Anti-symmetrization. We have $Y_l^m(\theta, \pi - \phi) = (-1)^l Y_l^m(\theta,\phi)$. We therefore anti-symmetrize the orientation distribution Eq. (12) via $c_l^m \to (1 - (-1)^l)c_l^m$.

Making Rotated Wavelets. To make the rotated versions $\psi_\mathbf{n}$ of wavelet ψ we have to find $h_\mathbf{n}$ in $\Psi_\mathbf{n} = g(\rho)h_\mathbf{n}(\theta,\phi)$. To achieve this we use the steerability of the spherical harmonic basis. Spherical harmonics rotate according to the irreducible representations of the SO(3) group $D_{m,m'}^l(\alpha,\beta,\gamma)$ (Wigner-D functions)

$$\mathcal{R}_{\mathbf{R}_{\alpha,\beta,\gamma}}Y_l^m(\theta,\phi) = \sum_{m'=l}^{l} D_{m,m'}^l(\alpha,\beta,\gamma)Y_l^{m'}(\theta,\phi). \tag{17}$$

Here α, β and γ denote the Euler angles with counterclockwise rotations, i.e., $\mathbf{R} = \mathbf{R}_{\mathbf{e}_z,\alpha}\mathbf{R}_{\mathbf{e}_y,\beta}\mathbf{R}_{\mathbf{e}_z,\gamma}$. This gives

$$h_\mathbf{n}(\theta,\phi) = \mathcal{R}_{\mathbf{R}_{\alpha,\beta,\gamma}}h(\theta,\phi) = \sum_{l=0}^{L}\sum_{m=-l}^{l}\sum_{m'=-l}^{l} a_{l,m}D_{m,m'}^l(\alpha,\beta,\gamma)Y_l^{m'}(\theta,\phi). \tag{18}$$

Because both anti-symmetrization and Funk transform preserve the rotational symmetry of A, we have $h(\theta,\phi) = \sum_{l=0}^{L} a_{l,0}Y_l^0(\theta,\phi)$, and Eq. (18) reduces to

$$h_\mathbf{n}(\theta,\phi) = \sum_{l=0}^{L}\sum_{m'=-l}^{l} a_{l,0}D_{0,m'}^l(0,\beta,\gamma)Y_l^{m'}(\theta,\phi). \tag{19}$$

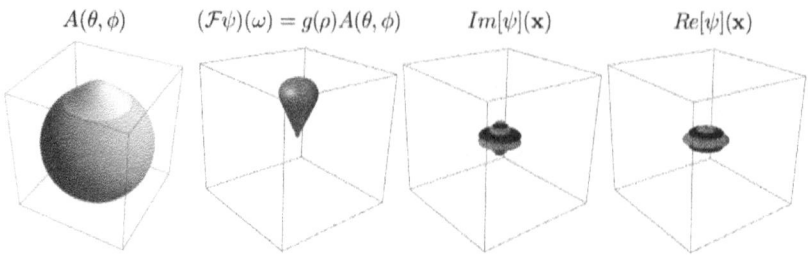

Fig. 4. When directly setting orientation distribution A as angular part of the wavelet h we construct plate detectors. From left to right: Orientation distribution A, wavelet in the Fourier domain, the plate detector (real part) and the edge detector (imaginary part). Orange: Positive iso-contour. Blue: Negative iso-contour. Parameters used: $L = 16, s_\theta = 0.6, k = 2, N = 20, \gamma = 0.8$ and evaluated on a grid of 51x51x51 pixels.

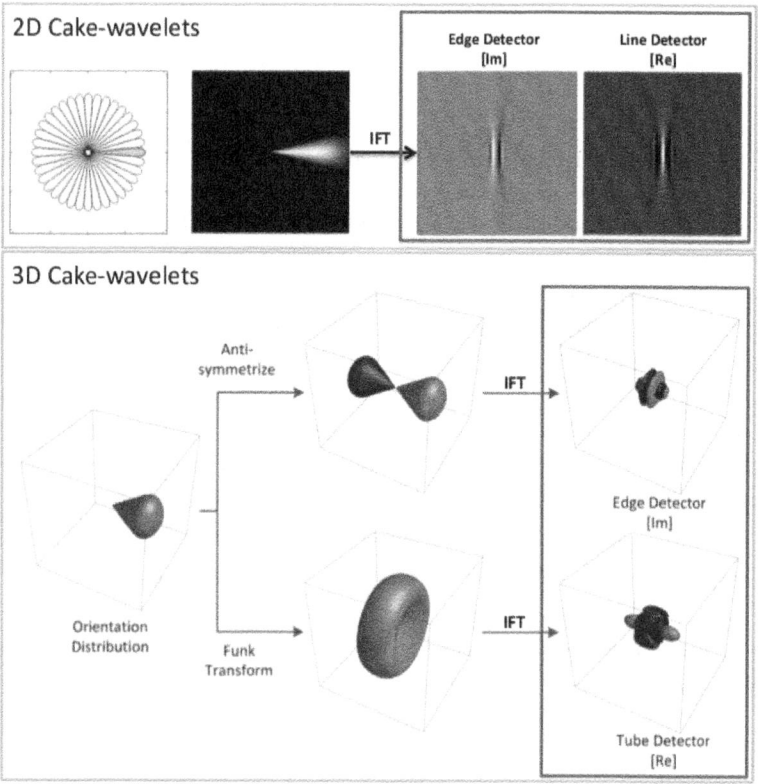

Fig. 5. Cake-Wavelets. Top: 2D cake-wavelets. From left to right: Illustration of the Fourier domain coverage, the wavelet in the Fourier domain and the real and imaginary part of the wavelet in the spatial domain. [3]. Bottom: 3D cake-wavelets. Overview of the transformations used to construct the wavelets from a given orientation distribution. Upper part: The wavelet according to Eq. (12). Lower part: The wavelet according to Eq. (13). IFT: Inverse Fourier Transform. Parameters used: $L = 16, s_\theta = 1.05, k = 2, N = 20, \gamma = 0.8$ and evaluated on a grid of 31x31x31 pixels.

4 Applications

4.1 Adaptive Crossing Preserving Flows

We now use the invertible orientation score transformation to perform data-enhancement according to Fig. 2. Because $\mathbb{R}^3 \times S^2$ is not a Lie group, it is common practice to embed the space of positions and orientations in the Lie group of positions and rotations SE(3) by setting

$$\tilde{U}(\mathbf{x}, \mathbf{R}) = U(\mathbf{x}, \mathbf{R} \cdot \mathbf{e}_z), \quad U(\mathbf{x}, \mathbf{n}) = \tilde{U}(\mathbf{x}, \mathbf{R}_\mathbf{n}), \tag{20}$$

with $\mathbf{R}_\mathbf{n}$ any rotation for which $\mathbf{R}_\mathbf{n} \cdot \mathbf{e}_z = \mathbf{n}$. The operations Φ which we consider are scale spaces on SE(3) (diffusions), and are given by $\Phi = \Phi_t$ with

$$\Phi_t(U)(\mathbf{y}, \mathbf{n}) = \tilde{W}(y, \mathbf{R}_\mathbf{n}, t). \tag{21}$$

Here $\tilde{W}$ is the solution of

$$\frac{\partial \tilde{W}}{\partial t}(g, t) = \sum_{i,j=1}^{6} \mathcal{A}_i|_g D_{ij} \mathcal{A}_j|_g \tilde{W}(g, t), \quad \tilde{W}|_{t=0} = \widetilde{\mathcal{W}_\psi[f]}, \tag{22}$$

where in coherence enhancing diffusion on orientation scores (CEDOS) D_{ij} is adapted locally to data $\widetilde{\mathcal{W}_\psi[f]}$ based on exponential curve fits (see [10]), and with $\mathcal{A}_i|_{g=(\mathbf{x},\mathbf{R})} = (L_g)_* \mathcal{A}_i|_e$ the left-invariant vector fields on SE(3), for motivation and details see [9]. Furthermore D_{ij} is chosen such that equivalence relation Eq. (20) is maintained for $\tilde{W}$. These operations are already used without adaptivity in the field of diffusion weighted MRI, where similar data ($\mathbb{R}^3 \times S^2 \to \mathbb{R}^+$) is enhanced [9]. We then obtain Euclidean invariant image processing via

$$\Upsilon f = \mathcal{W}_\psi^{*,ext} \circ \Phi \circ \mathcal{W}_\psi f = \mathcal{W}_\psi^* \circ \mathbb{P}_\psi \Phi \circ \mathcal{W}_\psi f \tag{23}$$

which includes inherent projection $\mathbb{P}_\psi$ of orientation scores, even if $\Phi = \Phi_t$ maps outside of the space of orientation scores in the embedding space (see App. A). Below we show some preliminary results of these flows that enhance the elongated structures while preserving the crossing, Fig. 6 and Fig. 7.

4.2 3D Vessel Tracking in Magnetic Resonance Angiography (MRA) Data

We use the 3D orientation scores to extend the earlier work on 2D vessel segmentation via invertible orientation scores [3] to 3D vessel segmentation in MRA-data. Even though true crossing structures hardly appear in 3D data, we do encounter vessels touching other vessels/structures. The orientation scores also allow us to better handle complex structures, such as bifurcations. In Fig. 8 we show some first results of the vessel segmentation algorithm.

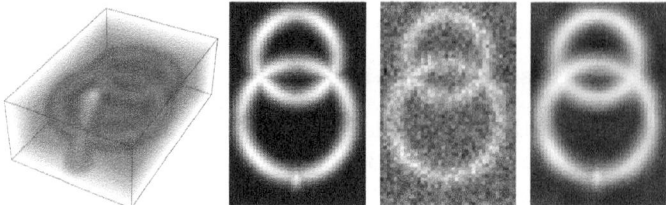

Fig. 6. Adaptive Crossing Preserving Flows. From left to right 3D visualization of artificial data, slice of data, slice of (data + Gaussian noise), slice of enhanced data. For the orientation score transformation we use: $N_0 = 42, s_\phi = 0.7, k = 2, N = 20, \gamma = 0.85, L = 16$ evaluated on a grid of 21x21x21 pixels. We use approximate reconstruction Eq.(8), and for diffusion we set $t = 10$. For the choice of D_{ij} in CEDOS, see [10].

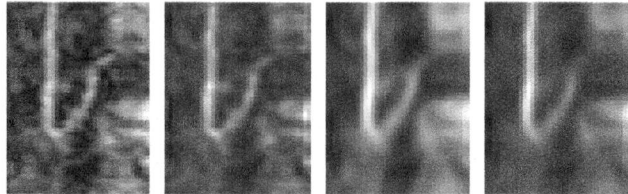

Fig. 7. Adaptive Crossing Preserving Flows combined with soft thresholding $\Phi(U)(\mathbf{x}, \mathbf{n}) = |U(\mathbf{x}, \mathbf{n})|^{1.5} \text{sgn}(U(\mathbf{x}, \mathbf{n}))$ on data containing the Adam Kiewitzc vessel. From left to right: Slice of data, data after soft thresholding, data after CEDOS, data after CEDOS followed by soft thresholding. For parameters see Fig.6, but now $t = 5$.

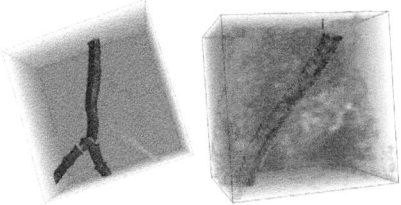

Fig. 8. MRA vessel segmentation via invertible orientation scores

5 Conclusion

We have extended 2D cake-wavelets to 3D cake-wavelets, which can be used for a 3D invertible orientation score transformation. Efficient implementation for calculating the wavelets via spherical harmonics were introduced. The developed transformation allows us to consider all kinds of enhancement operations via orientation scores such as the adaptive crossing preserving flows which we are currently working on. Next to data-enhancement we also showed some first results of 3D vessel segmentation using 3D orientation scores.

Acknowledgments. We thank Dr. A.J.E.M. Janssen for advice on the presentation of this paper. The research leading to these results has received funding from the European Research Council under the European Community's Seventh Framework Programme (FP7/2007-2013) / ERC grant *Lie Analysis*, agr. nr. 335555.

A Invertible Orientation Scores of 3D-Images and Continuous Wavelet Theory

The continuous wavelet transform constructed by unitary irreducible representations of locally compact groups was first formulated by Grossman et al. [13]. Given a Hilbert space H and a unitary irreducible representation $g \mapsto \mathcal{U}_g$ of any locally compact group G in H, a non-zero vector $\psi \in H$ is called admissible if

$$C_\psi := \int_G \frac{|(\mathcal{U}_g \psi, \psi)|^2}{(\psi, \psi)_H} d\mu_G(g) < \infty, \tag{24}$$

where μ_G denotes the left-invariant Haar measure. Given an admissible vector ψ and a unitary representation of a locally compact group G in H, the Coherent State (CS) transform $W_\psi : H \to \mathbb{L}_2(G)$ is given by $(W_\psi[f])(g) = (\mathcal{U}_g \psi, f)_H$. W_ψ is an isometric transform onto a unique closed reproducing kernel space $\mathbb{C}_{K_\psi}^G$ with $K_\psi(g, g') = \frac{1}{C_\psi}(\mathcal{U}_g \psi, \mathcal{U}_{g'} \psi)_H$ as an $\mathbb{L}_2$-subspace [1].

We distinguish between the isometric wavelet transform $W_\psi : \mathbb{L}_2^\varrho(\mathbb{R}^3) \to \mathbb{L}_2(G)$ and the unitary wavelet transform $\mathcal{W}_\psi : \mathbb{L}_2^\varrho(\mathbb{R}^3) \to \mathbb{C}_K^G$. We drop the formal requirement of $\mathcal{U}$ being square-integrable and ψ being admissible in the sense of (24), and replace the requirement by (4), as it is not strictly needed in many cases. This includes our case of interest $G = SE(3)$ and its left-regular action on $\mathbb{L}_2(\mathbb{R}^3)$ where $\mathcal{W}_\psi$ gives rise to an orientation score $\mathcal{W}_\psi f : \mathbb{R}^3 \rtimes S^2 \to \mathbb{C}$

$$\mathcal{W}_\psi f(\boldsymbol{x}, \boldsymbol{n}) = \widetilde{W_\psi f}(\boldsymbol{x}, R_{\boldsymbol{n}}), \tag{25}$$

with $R_{\boldsymbol{n}}$ any rotation mapping $\boldsymbol{e}_z$ onto $\boldsymbol{n}$ and ψ symmetric around the z-axis. Here the domain is the coupled space of positions and orientations: $\mathbb{R}^3 \rtimes S^2 := SE(3)/(\{\mathbf{0}\} \times SO(2))$, cf. [9].

From the general theory of reproducing kernel spaces [8, Thm 18],[2] (where one does not even rely on the group structure), it follows that $\mathcal{W}_\psi : \mathbb{L}_2^\varrho(\mathbb{R}^3) \to \mathbb{C}_K^{\mathbb{R}^3 \rtimes S^2}$ is unitary, where $\mathbb{C}_K^{\mathbb{R}^3 \rtimes S^2}$ denotes the abstract complex reproducing kernel space consisting of functions on $\mathbb{R}^3 \rtimes S^2$ with reproducing kernel

$$K_{(\mathbf{y},\mathbf{n})}(\mathbf{y}', \mathbf{n}') = (\mathcal{U}_{(\mathbf{y}, R_{\mathbf{n}})} \psi, \mathcal{U}_{(\mathbf{y}', R_{\mathbf{n}'})} \psi)_{\mathbb{L}_2(\mathbb{R}^3)}, \tag{26}$$

with left-regular representation $(\mathbf{y}, R) \mapsto \mathcal{U}_{(\mathbf{y},R)} \psi$ given by $(\mathcal{U}_{(\mathbf{y},R)} \psi)(\mathbf{x}) = \psi(R^T(\mathbf{x} - \mathbf{y}))$. Now, as the characterization of the inner product on $\mathbb{C}_K^{\mathbb{R}^3 \rtimes S^2}$ is awkward [16], we provide a basic characterization next via the so-called M_ψ inner product. This is in line with the admissibility conditions in [12].

Theorem 1. *Let ψ be such that (4) holds. Then $\mathcal{W}_\psi : \mathbb{L}_2^\varrho(\mathbb{R}^3) \to \mathbb{C}_K^{\mathbb{R}^3 \rtimes S^2}$ is unitary, and we have*

$$(f, g)_{\mathbb{L}_2(\mathbb{R}^3)} = (\mathcal{W}_\psi f, \mathcal{W}_\psi g)_{M_\psi}, \tag{27}$$

where $(\mathcal{W}_\psi f, \mathcal{W}_\psi g)_{M_\psi} = (\mathcal{T}_{M_\psi}[\mathcal{W}_\psi f], \mathcal{T}_{M_\psi}[\mathcal{W}_\psi g])_{\mathbb{L}_2(\mathbb{R}^3 \rtimes S^2))}$, *with* $[\mathcal{T}_{M_\psi}[U]](\mathbf{y}, \mathbf{n})$
$:= \mathcal{F}^{-1}\left[\boldsymbol{\omega} \mapsto (2\pi)^{-3/4} M_\psi^{-1/2}(\boldsymbol{\omega}) \mathcal{F}[U(\cdot, \mathbf{n})](\boldsymbol{\omega})\right](\mathbf{y})$.

Proof. We rely on [17, Thm 1], where we set $H = \mathbb{L}_2(\mathbb{R}^3)$. The rest follows by well posed restriction to the quotient $\mathbb{R}^3 \rtimes S^2$.

Corollary 1. *Let $M_\psi > 0$ on $\mathbb{R}^3$. The space $\mathbb{C}_K^{\mathbb{R}^3 \rtimes S^2}$ is a closed subspace of Hilbert space $\mathbb{H}_\psi \otimes \mathbb{L}_2(S^2)$, where $\mathbb{H}_\psi = \{f \in \mathbb{L}_2(\mathbb{R}^3)|\ M_\psi^{-\frac{1}{2}} \mathcal{F}[f] \in \mathbb{L}_2(\mathbb{R}^3)\}$, and projection of embedding space onto the space of orientation scores is given by $(\mathbb{P}_\psi(U))(\mathbf{y},\mathbf{n}) = (K_{(\mathbf{n},\mathbf{y})}, U)_{M_\psi} = (\mathcal{W}_\psi \mathcal{W}_\psi^{*,ext}(U))(\mathbf{y},\mathbf{n})$, where $\mathcal{W}_\psi^{*,ext}$ is the natural extension of the adjoint to the embedding space.*

References

1. Ali, S.T.: A general theorem on square-integrability: Vector coherent states. J. Math. Phys. **39**(8), 3954 (1998)
2. Ali, ST., Antoine, J.-P., Gazeau, J.-P.: Coherent states, wavelets, and their generalizations. Springer (2014)
3. Bekkers, E., Duits, R.: A multi-orientation analysis approach to retinal vessel tracking. JMIV (2014)
4. Burgeth, B., Didas, S., Weickert, J.: A general structure tensor concept and coherence-enhancing diffusion filtering for matrix fields. In: Visualization and Processing of Tensor Fields, pp. 305–324. Springer, Berlin (2009)
5. Burgeth, B., Pizarro, L., Didas, S., Weickert, J.: 3D-Coherence-enhancing diffusion filtering for matrix fields. In: Mathematical Methods for Signal and Image Analysis and Representation, pp. 49–63. Springer, London (2012)
6. Creusen, E.J., Duits, R., Dela Haije, T.C.J.: Numerical Schemes for Linear and Non-linear Enhancement of DW-MRI. In: Bruckstein, A.M., ter Haar Romeny, B.M., Bronstein, A.M., Bronstein, M.M. (eds.) SSVM 2011. LNCS, vol. 6667, pp. 14–25. Springer, Heidelberg (2012)
7. Descoteaux, M., Angelino, E., Fitzgibbons, S., Deriche, R.: Regularized, fast, and robust analytical Q-ball imaging. MRM **58**(3), 497–510 (2007)
8. Duits, R.: Perceptual organization in image analysis. PhD thesis, Technische Universiteit Eindhoven (2005)
9. Duits, R., Franken, E.M.: Left-invariant diffusions on the space of positions and orientations and their application to crossing-preserving smoothing of HARDI images. IJCV **92**(3), 231–264 (2010)
10. Duits, R., Janssen, M.H.J., Hannink, J., Sanguinetti, G.R.: Locally Adaptive Frames in the Roto-Translation Group and their Applications in Medical Imaging. arXiv preprint: http://arxiv.org/abs/1502.0800arXiv:1502.08002
11. Franken, E.M., Duits, R.: Crossing-preserving coherence-enhancing diffusion on invertible orientation scores. IJCV **85**(3), 253–278 (2009)
12. Führ, F.: Abstract harmonic analysis of continuous wavelet transforms. Lecture Notes in Mathematics 1863 (2005)
13. Grossmann, A., Morlet, J., Paul, T.: Transforms associated to square integrable group representations. I. General results. J. Math. Phys. **26**(10), 2473 (1985)
14. Kalitzin, S.N., ter Haar Romeny, B.M., Viergever, M.A.: Invertible apertured orientation filters in image analysis. IJCV 31, 145–158 (1999)
15. Lee, T.S.: Image representation using 2D Gabor wavelets. IEEE TPAMI **18**(10) (1996)

16. Martens, F.J.L.: Spaces of analytical functions on inductive/projective limits of Hilbert spaces. PhD thesis, Technische Universiteit Eindhoven (1988)
17. Sharma, U., Duits, R.: Left-invariant evolutions of wavelet transforms on the similitude group (accepted for publication ACHA). doi:10.1016/j.acha.2014.09.001
18. Weickert, J.: Coherence-enhancing diffusion filtering. IJCV **31**, 111–127 (1999)

Edge-Preserving Integration of a Normal Field: Weighted Least-Squares, TV and L^1 Approaches

Yvain Quéau[✉] and Jean-Denis Durou

IRIT, UMR CNRS 5505, Université de Toulouse, Toulouse, France
yvain.queau@enseeiht.fr, durou@irit.fr

Abstract. We introduce several new functionals, inspired from variational image denoising models, for recovering a piecewise-smooth surface from a dense estimation of its normal field (Sample codes for testing the proposed methods can be found on http://ubee.enseeiht.fr/photometricstereo/). In the weighted least-squares approach, the non-differentiable elements of the surface are *a priori* detected so as to weight the least-squares model. To avoid this detection step, we introduce reweighted least-squares for minimising an isotropic TV-like functional, and split-Bregman iterations for L^1 minimisation.

Keywords: Integration · Shape-from-gradient · Photometric stereo

1 Introduction

Problem Statement. The normal field **n** of a surface can be estimated by 3D-reconstruction techniques such as photometric stereo [17]. To obtain a set of 3D points located on the surface, the estimated normal field must then be *integrated* into a depth map z, over a subset Ω of the image domain. This second step is crucial in the 3D-reconstruction process, since the accuracy of the recovered surface widely depends on the robustness of integration to noise and outliers.

Let us first recall the equations describing this integration problem, which are similar under both orthographic and perspective projections. In the orthographic case, z is related to the normal field **n**, for every $(x,y) \in \Omega$, through [6]:

$$\mathbf{n}(x,y) = \frac{1}{\sqrt{\|\nabla z(x,y)\|_2^2 + 1}} \begin{bmatrix} -\nabla z(x,y) \\ 1 \end{bmatrix} \quad (1)$$

where $\nabla z = [\partial_x z, \partial_y z]^\top$ is the gradient of z. Denoting:

$$p_\mathcal{O}(x,y) = -\frac{n_1(x,y)}{n_3(x,y)}, \quad q_\mathcal{O}(x,y) = -\frac{n_2(x,y)}{n_3(x,y)}, \quad \mathbf{g}_\mathcal{O}(x,y) = [p_\mathcal{O}(x,y), q_\mathcal{O}(x,y)]^\top \quad (2)$$

where n_i, $i \in [1,3]$, is the i-th component of **n**, we obtain from (1) and (2):

$$\nabla z(x,y) = \mathbf{g}_\mathcal{O}(x,y) \quad (3)$$

In the case of perspective projection, we need to know the focal length f of the camera, and to set the origin of image coordinates to the principal point. Introducing the change of variable $\tilde{z} = \log z$, we obtain [6]:

$$\mathbf{n}(x,y) = \frac{1}{\sqrt{\|\nabla \tilde{z}(x,y)\|_2^2 + \left(1 + \nabla \tilde{z}(x,y) \cdot \frac{1}{f}[x,y]^\top\right)^2}} \begin{bmatrix} -\nabla \tilde{z}(x,y) \\ 1 + \nabla \tilde{z}(x,y) \cdot \frac{1}{f}[x,y]^\top \end{bmatrix} \quad (4)$$

By setting $d(x,y) = x n_1(x,y) + y n_2(x,y) + f n_3(x,y)$, and:

$$p_\mathcal{P}(x,y) = -\frac{n_1(x,y)}{d(x,y)}, \; q_\mathcal{P}(x,y) = -\frac{n_2(x,y)}{d(x,y)}, \; \mathbf{g}_\mathcal{P}(x,y) = [p_\mathcal{P}(x,y), q_\mathcal{P}(x,y)]^\top \quad (5)$$

we get from (4) and (5), after some algebra:

$$\nabla \tilde{z}(x,y) = \mathbf{g}_\mathcal{P}(x,y) \quad (6)$$

Thus, for both these projection models, one has to solve, in every $(x,y) \in \Omega$, the same equation:

$$\nabla u(x,y) = \mathbf{g}(x,y) \quad (7)$$

where $(u, \mathbf{g}) = (z, \mathbf{g}_\mathcal{O})$ in the orthographic case, and $(u, \mathbf{g}) = (\tilde{z}, \mathbf{g}_\mathcal{P})$ in the perspective one.

Integrating the normal field refers to the process of recovering the unknown u, which will be abusively referred to as "depth map" in the following, from an estimation $\mathbf{g} = [p,q]^\top$ of its gradient field over Ω. This problem, which has a long history since it dates back to the Dirichlet problem, has given rise to numerous studies in the area of mathematics for imaging, using many different approaches such as Fourier analysis [7,16], fast marching [8] or Sylvester equations [10, 11]. In this paper, as in many recent works [1,2,4,5,14], we choose the energy minimisation way, which offers a natural framework for controlling the influence of noise and outliers.

Summary of our Contributions. We focus on the case where solving Eq. (7) makes sense only *almost everywhere*, which happens as soon as the surface to be reconstructed contains edges and depth discontinuities: the gradient ∇u of u cannot be defined on the neighborhood of such non-differentiable elements. In this case, classical least-squares solvers fail (Figure 1) and more robust estimation must be considered. Completing the study proposed in [5], we introduce three new functionals inspired by image denoising models, whose minimisation is shown to provide piecewise-smooth surfaces on an arbitrary connected domain Ω. They are based, respectively, on weighted least-squares (WLS), isotropic total variation (TV), and L^1 optimisation.

The rest of this paper is organized as follows. After reviewing in Section 2 the main energy minimisation methods for surface reconstruction from a gradient field, we detail in Section 3 the proposed edge-preserving approaches, which are eventually evaluated on both synthetic and real-world datasets in Section 4.

Fig. 1. Least-squares normal integration. First row, from left to right: ground truth $\mathcal{C}^\infty$ depth map u, analytical derivatives p and q corrupted by an additive zero-mean Gaussian noise with standard deviation $\sigma = 5\%$ of $\|\mathbf{g}\|_\infty$, and least-squares reconstruction [10]. Second row: same, for piecewise-$\mathcal{C}^\infty$ surface. Noise in the data is successfully handled by least-squares (first row), but discontinuities are smoothed (second row).

2 Related Work

2.1 Integrability of a Gradient Field

In the ideal case, $\mathbf{g} = [p, q]^\top$ is the true gradient of a $\mathcal{C}^2$ function u holding: $\partial_{yx} u = \partial_{xy} u$ (Schwarz' theorem). The distance from a gradient field $\mathbf{g}$ to an ideal (integrable) field holding $\partial_y p = \partial_x q$ can thus be measured by the *integrability* term [7]:

$$\mathcal{I}(x, y) = |\partial_y p(x, y) - \partial_x q(x, y)| \tag{8}$$

which is never null in real-world scenarios, because of noise and of depth discontinuities. In such cases, it makes sense to estimate an approximate solution u of Eq. (7) whose gradient ∇u is integrable, rather than to solve Eq. (7) exactly.

This can be performed efficiently through energy minimisation, by seeking u as the solution of an optimisation problem, lying in an appropriate function space. For instance, if u is sought in $L^2(\Omega)$, integrability of its gradient is implicitely granted (in the presence of discontinuities, the space of functions with bounded variations $BV(\Omega)$ should be preferred, so as to allow piecewise-smooth functions). We provide hereafter a brief overview of the main normal integration methods relying on energy minimisation.

2.2 Continuous Least-Squares Formulation

The most natural energy minimisation approach to solve (7) consists in estimating u in a least-squares sense [6,7,10,16], by introducing the functional:

$$\mathcal{F}_{LS}(u) = \iint_\Omega \|\nabla u(x, y) - \mathbf{g}(x, y)\|_2^2 \, dx \, dy \tag{9}$$

According to the calculus of variations, minimising this functional is equivalent to solving the associated Euler-Lagrange equation on the interior part $\overset{\circ}{\Omega}$ of Ω:

$$\Delta u = \nabla \cdot \mathbf{g} \tag{10}$$

which is a Poisson equation ($\nabla\cdot$ is the divergence operator, which is the adjoint of the gradient, and $\Delta = \nabla \cdot \nabla$ is the Laplacian operator), along with the natural boundary condition (BC), which is of the Neumann type:

$$(\nabla u - \mathbf{g}) \cdot \mu = 0 \qquad (11)$$

on the boundary $\partial \Omega$ of Ω, μ being normal to $\partial \Omega$.

Discretising Eqs (10) and (11) provides a linear system of equations which can be solved in linear time through Fast Fourier Transform (FFT), if Ω is rectangular. Indeed, replacing the natural BC (11) by a periodic one, Frankot and Chellappa's well-known algorithm [7] recovers the Fourier transform of the depth map analytically, and inverse FFT eventually provides a solution u of (10). This algorithm was extended by Simchony et al. in [16] to the natural BC, through the use of Discrete Cosine Transform (DCT).

2.3 Discretising the Functional, or the Optimality Conditions?

Instead of discretising the optimality conditions (10) and (11), the functional (9) itself can be discretised. This is the approach followed in [6], where it is shown that doing so, no explicit BC is needed (yet, the natural BC is *implicitely* satisfied). After proper discretisation, a new linear system is obtained, which is solved using Jacobi iterations. Alternatively, Harker and O'Leary show in [10] that the discrete least-squares functional can be minimised by solving a Sylvester equation, provided Ω is rectangular (this hypothesis is neither required in [6], nor in the present paper).

Examples of results obtained using the least-squares solver from [10] are shown in the last column of Figure 1. These experiments illustrate the robustness of least-squares against additive Gaussian noise, but also the edge smoothing which occurs using quadratic regularisation. As we shall see later, quadratic regularisation can be improved by introducing weights, or by replacing the squared L^2 norm by a non-differentiable regularisation.

Since the functional (9) is convex, discretising the functional or the associated optimality condition should be strictly equivalent, provided the natural BC is enforced. Yet, as noted by Harker and O'Leary in [11], Poisson-based integration relying on DCT suffers from a bias, due to inconsistent numerical approximations of the gradient ∇u in the discretisation of the natural BC (11). The choice of such inconsistent derivatives, as well as a rectangular domain Ω, are actually necessary for obtaining a matrix of the block-Toeplitz type, and thus allowing fast recovery by DCT. Choosing consistent numerical derivatives, or a non-rectangular domain Ω, the structure of this matrix is lost, and the system resulting from the discretisation of the continuous optimality condition must be solved using standard sparse solvers.

In this paper, as in [6,10], we choose to consider discrete functionals so as to avoid dealing with boundary conditions. Rather than relying on special matrix structures [10], we use standard solvers for the numerics, allowing us to deal with non-rectangular domains, as in [6].

2.4 Non-quadratic Regularisations

In [11], Harker and O'Leary extend the method from [10] to the case of spectral and Sobolev regularisations, improving the robustness of their method to Gaussian noise. Yet, such regularisations are not adapted to depth discontinuities, since they remain quadratic. In [1], Agrawal *et al.* study several functionals having the following general form:

$$\mathcal{F}_\Psi(u) = \iint_\Omega \Psi\left(\|\nabla u(x,y) - \mathbf{g}(x,y)\|_2\right)\,\mathrm{d}x\,\mathrm{d}y \tag{12}$$

where Ψ is chosen so as to reduce the influence of outliers. A numerical study of the discrete versions of several such functionals is presented in [5], where the Jacobi iterations used in [6] are extended to the minimisation of non-convex functionals through semi-implicit schemes. The use of sparse regularisations derived from the L^1 norm has also become an important research direction [4,14]: we will show how to accelerate such schemes using split-Bregman iterations. Extension to L^p minimisation, $p < 1$, is also presented in [2]. The results are indeed impressive in the presence of very noisy data, but involve setting numerous parameters, which is hardly tractable in real-world applications.

Furthermore, since photometric stereo is a technique which is mostly performed inside laboratories, the presence of a huge amount of Gaussian noise in the measurements is very unlikely, and thus greater care is given in this paper to *outliers* such as discontinuities, which cannot be avoided since they describe the surface itself and not the acquisition procedure. We introduce in the next section several new functionals related to this issue.

3 New functionals

3.1 Quadratic Prior

The functional (12) is not coercive, because of the ambiguity $u \mapsto u + k$, k constant, in the initial equation (7). In the literature, this ambiguity is usually solved *a posteriori*, for instance by manually setting the mean value of u. In this work, we proceed this way to first compute an approximate solution u_0 through DCT [16] (if Ω is not rectangular, $\mathbf{g}$ has to be completed with null values, which obviously creates a bias), before introducing u_0 as a quadratic prior to force coercivity.

This prior being biased in the presence of discontinuities and non-rectangular domains, it can be seen as an initial depth map that we want to denoise using an edge-preserving regularisation Φ which shall ensure diffusion along $\mathbf{g}$:

$$\mathcal{F}_\Phi(u) = \iint_\Omega \Phi\left(\nabla u(x,y) - \mathbf{g}(x,y)\right) + \frac{\lambda}{2}\left(u(x,y) - u_0(x,y)\right)^2\,\mathrm{d}x\,\mathrm{d}y \tag{13}$$

with $\lambda > 0$ chosen according to the quality of the approximate solution u_0. In this paper, we consider three types of regularisation: $\Phi = w\|.\|_2^2$ (weighted least-squares), $\Phi = \|.\|_2$ (isotropic TV-like), and $\Phi = \|.\|_1$ (L^1).

3.2 Weighted Least-Squares Functional

In a first approach, we assume that it is possible to *a priori* detect outliers through the evaluation of the integrability term (8). This *a priori* detection is used to weight the influence of discontinuities. Setting $\Phi(.) = w\|.\|_2^2$, where w is a weighting function depending only on the integrability term (8), and not on u, we obtain the weighted least-squares functional:

$$\mathcal{F}_{WLS}(u) = \iint_\Omega w(x,y) \|\nabla u(x,y) - \mathbf{g}(x,y)\|_2^2 + \frac{\lambda}{2}(u(x,y) - u_0(x,y))^2 \, dx \, dy \quad (14)$$

Since we know that the integrability (8) is an indicator of the presence of discontinuities (though having null integrability does not imply being smooth: think of a piecewise flat shape), it seems natural to choose for w an integrability-based weighting function, which should be a decreasing function of $\mathcal{I}$. To choose effectively the weights, let us use the continuous optimality condition associated with $\mathcal{F}_{WLS}$. Assuming $w > 0$, and remarking that $\frac{\nabla w}{w} = \nabla(\log w)$, we obtain:

$$\Delta u + \nabla(\log w) \cdot (\nabla u - \mathbf{g}) - \lambda(u - u_0) = \nabla \cdot \mathbf{g} \quad (15)$$

Because of the presence of the logarithm, we consider:

$$w(x,y) = \exp(-\gamma \mathcal{I}(x,y)^2) \quad (16)$$

where $\gamma \geq 0$ is a parameter for controlling the weights ($\gamma = 0$ corresponds to the standard least-squares formulation).

We now discretise u uniformly over a grid (which does not need to be rectangular, unlike in [7,10,11,16]), with spacing 1, also denoted Ω for convenience. Extending the rationale in [6] for least-squares functionals, a consistent second-order accurate discretisation of (14) is obtained by first-order forward differences in u, and computation of the forward means of the components p and q of $\mathbf{g}$:

$$F_{WLS}(u) = \sum_{(i,j) \in \Omega^{x+}} w^{i,j} \left(\partial_x^+ u^{i,j} - \bar{p}^{i,j}\right)^2 + \sum_{(i,j) \in \Omega^{y+}} w^{i,j} \left(\partial_y^+ u^{i,j} - \bar{q}^{i,j}\right)^2 + \frac{\lambda}{2} \sum_{(i,j) \in \Omega} \left(u^{i,j} - u_0^{i,j}\right)^2 \quad (17)$$

where we denote $u^{i,j}$ the value of u at discrete point (i,j), $\bar{p}^{i,j} = \frac{p^{i+1,j} + p^{i,j}}{2}$, $\bar{q}^{i,j} = \frac{q^{i,j+1} + q^{i,j}}{2}$, $\partial_x^+ u^{i,j} = u^{i+1,j} - u^{i,j}$, $\partial_y^+ u^{i,j} = u^{i,j+1} - u^{i,j}$, $\Omega^{x+} = \{(i,j) \in \Omega \text{ s.t. } (i+1,j) \in \Omega\}$ and $\Omega^{y+} = \{(i,j) \in \Omega \text{ s.t. } (i,j+1) \in \Omega\}$. The optimality condition in $u^{i,j} \in \Omega$ reads:

$$\chi^{i+1,j} w^{i,j}\left(u^{i+1,j} - u^{i,j}\right) + \chi^{i,j+1} w^{i,j}\left(u^{i,j+1} - u^{i,j}\right) + \chi^{i-1,j} w^{i-1,j}\left(u^{i-1,j} - u^{i,j}\right)$$
$$+ \chi^{i,j-1} w^{i,j-1}\left(u^{i,j-1} - u^{i,j}\right) - \frac{\lambda}{2} u^{i,j} = \chi^{i+1,j} w^{i,j} \bar{p}^{i,j} + \chi^{i,j+1} w^{i,j} \bar{q}^{i,j} \quad (18)$$
$$- \chi^{i-1,j} w^{i-1,j} \bar{p}^{i-1,j} - \chi^{i,j-1} w^{i,j-1} \bar{q}^{i,j-1} - \frac{\lambda}{2} u_0^{i,j}$$

where χ is the characteristic function of Ω. If w is constant and $\lambda = 0$, it is easily verified that (18) is a discrete approximation of both the Poisson equation (10) and the natural BC (11).

Stacking the $u^{i,j}$ column-wise in a vector $\mathbf{u}$ of size $n \times 1$, where n is the cardinal of Ω, the optimality condition (18) reads as a linear system $\mathbf{Au} = \mathbf{b}$, where $\mathbf{A}$ is a block-pentadiagonal $n \times n$ full-rank matrix with strictly dominant diagonal. We experimentally found that, for relatively small grids (up to 512×512), direct sparse solvers provide a fast solution to this system: since $\mathbf{A}$ has a small bandwidth (equal to the number of rows in Ω), computation of the sparse product $\mathbf{A}^\top \mathbf{A}$ is very fast, and the normal equation $\mathbf{A}^\top \mathbf{Au} = \mathbf{A}^\top \mathbf{b}$ can be solved through sparse Cholesky factorisation, though it artificially increases the order of points involved in the finite differences, leading to a small additional smoothing (see the numerical results on the peaks dataset in Section 4). Studying more efficient solvers for this problem, as for instance Krylov subspace methods applied to the initial $\mathbf{Au} = \mathbf{b}$ problem, will be the subject of a future research.

3.3 Isotropic TV Functional

The previous approach relies on *a priori* detection of the discontinuities, so that the corresponding points are "manually" discarded from the equality (7). Yet, *a priori* setting the weights might sometimes be tedious. The weights can also be automatically chosen as a function of $\|\nabla u - \mathbf{g}\|_2$ [1,5], but the problem cannot be solved directly anymore, and requires an iterative minimisation. We show how to use this idea to minimise a functional resembling the L^2-TV model [15].

It is well known in the image processing community that the isotropic total variation (TV) measure $TV(u) = \int_\Omega \|\nabla u(x,y)\|_2 \, dxdy$ has interesting edge-preserving properties, and tends to favor piecewise-smooth solutions. Considering the discontinuities as the equivalent of edges in image denoising, one would expect the residual $\nabla u - \mathbf{g}$ to be piecewise-smooth as well, with jumps located in discontinuities. This remark invites us to adapt the ROF model [15] to our problem: choosing $\Phi(.) = \|.\|_2$, we obtain from (13) the following functional:

$$\mathcal{F}_{TV}(u) = \iint_\Omega \|\nabla u(x,y) - \mathbf{g}(x,y)\|_2 + \frac{\lambda}{2}(u(x,y) - u_0(x,y))^2 \, dx\, dy \quad (19)$$

Remarking that $\|.\|_2 = \frac{\|.\|_2^2}{\|.\|_2}\|.\|_2^2$, this functional can be minimised through iteratively reweighted least-squares:

$$\begin{cases} w^k(x,y) = \dfrac{\|\nabla u^k(x,y) - \mathbf{g}(x,y)\|_2}{\|\nabla u^k(x,y) - \mathbf{g}(x,y) + \theta\|_2^2}, \quad \forall (x,y) \in \Omega \\ u^{k+1} = \underset{u}{\operatorname{argmin}} \int_\Omega w^k(x,y) \|\nabla u(x,y) - \mathbf{g}(x,y)\|_2^2 + \dfrac{\lambda}{2}(u(x,y) - u_0(x,y))^2 dxdy \end{cases} \quad (20)$$

with $u^0 = u_0$, $w^0 = 1$, and $\theta > 0$, small. The update in u, using Cholesky factorisation, has already been described in Section 3.2. Proceeding so, the normal equations are solved at each iteration, as in [1]. As a consequence, few iterations are needed, though this might become memory-hungry for large grids. Iterative Jacobi approximations, in the manner of what is proposed in [5], would probably offer a less memory-hungry solution. Alternatively, split-Bregman iterations can be considered: we show in the following paragraph how to use such iterations for minimising the anisotropic TV (L^1) model.

3.4 L^1 Functional

The discontinuities being sparsely distributed in essence, it seems natural to rely on the sparsity enhancing properties of the L^1 norm [4,14]. Considering the choice $\Phi(.) = \|.\|_1$, we get from (13):

$$\mathcal{F}_{L^1}(u) = \iint_\Omega \|\nabla u(x,y) - \mathbf{g}(x,y)\|_1 + \frac{\lambda}{2}(u(x,y) - u_0(x,y))^2 \, dx\, dy \quad (21)$$

This new functional is still convex, but cannot be minimised through differentiable optimisation. Split-Bregman iterations [9] can be considered:

$$u^{k+1} = \operatorname*{argmin}_u \frac{\alpha}{2}\|\mathbf{d}^k - (\nabla u - \mathbf{g}) - \mathbf{b}^k\|_2^2 + \frac{\lambda}{2}\|u - u_0\|_2^2 \quad (22)$$

$$\mathbf{d}^{k+1} = \operatorname*{argmin}_\mathbf{d} \|\mathbf{d}\|_1 + \frac{\alpha}{2}\|\mathbf{d} - (\nabla u^{k+1} - \mathbf{g}) - \mathbf{b}^k\|_2^2 \quad (23)$$

$$\mathbf{b}^{k+1} = \mathbf{b}^k + (\nabla u^{k+1} - \mathbf{g}) - \mathbf{d}^{k+1} \quad (24)$$

where $(\mathbf{d}^k, \mathbf{b}^k) = ([d_1^k, d_2^k]^\top, [b_1^k, b_2^k]^\top)$ are auxiliary variables related to the Bregman distance at iteration k. We solve the discrete version of (22) using the same kind of discretisation as in Section 3.2. Yet, unlike in Section 3.2 and 3.3, it is preferable not to solve the problem exactly [9], so as to improve convergence properties of the split-Bregman iterations: as advised in the literature, we perform only a few (typically 5) Gauss-Seidel updates at each iteration k. Regarding the basis pursuit problem (23), solution is obtained by shrinkage:

$$\begin{cases} d_1^{k+1} = \dfrac{\partial_x u^{k+1} - p + b_1^k}{|\partial_x u^{k+1} - p + b_1^k|} \max\left\{|\partial_x u^{k+1} - p + b_1^k|, 0\right\} \\ d_2^{k+1} = \dfrac{\partial_y u^{k+1} - q + b_2^k}{|\partial_y u^{k+1} - q + b_2^k|} \max\left\{|\partial_y u^{k+1} - q + b_2^k|, 0\right\} \end{cases} \quad (25)$$

where $|.|$ is the absolute value.

We now experimentally compare the proposed schemes on synthetic data, and show results of the L^1 approach on real-world datasets.

4 Results

4.1 Synthetic Data

We first evaluate the performances of the proposed algorithms on synthetic datasets (Figure 2 and Table 1). In each test, a small Gaussian noise with zero-mean and standard deviation $\sigma = 0.5\%$ of $\|\mathbf{g}\|_\infty$ was added to the gradient field, before it was integrated using, respectively, least-squares [10,16], spectral regularisation [11], weighted least-squares ($\lambda = 10^{-5}, \gamma = 10$), isotropic TV ($\lambda = 10^{-5}, \theta = 10^{-3}$) and L^1 ($\lambda = 10^{-4}, \alpha = 0.1$). The convergence criterion for the iterative methods was set to a 5.10^{-4} relative residual between u^k and u^{k+1}. For fair comparison, the integration constant was changed *a posteriori* so as to minimise the RMSE between the estimated depth map and the ground truth. The performances of each algorithm are evaluated by Matlab codes running on a I7 laptop at 2.9 Ghz.

Fig. 2. Results on synthetic data. We show the ground truth surface (first row), the results using spectral regularisation [11] (second row), and those using the weighted least-squares (third row), TV (fourth row) and L^1 (fifth row) functionals. L^1 minimisation qualitatively offers the sharper edges, though a staircase effect appears. Weighted least squares provide accurate results for the "Canadian Tent", because the discontinuities correspond to very high integrability values, but it does not perform as well on the "Synthetic Vase", since a part of the discontinuity has null integrability.

Table 1. RMSE (in pixels) between the ground truth depth maps and those recovered using three state-of-the-art algorithms and our three new ones. The "Peaks" depth map being $\mathcal{C}^\infty$, all methods succeed at recovering accurate results for this dataset. Since we solve the normal equation (by means of Cholesky factorisation) in the WLS and TV approaches, additional smoothing is introduced, and thus these methods perform a little better than L^1 in this test.

	Peaks (512×512)	Canadian Tent (256×256)	Synthetic Vase (320×320)
Least-squares (DCT) [16]	0.30 (0.05 s)	10.76 (0.02 s)	4.55 (0.03 s)
Least-squares (Sylvester) [10]	0.14 (0.84 s)	10.76 (0.32 s)	4.56 (0.46 s)
Spectral regularisation [11]	**0.13** (0.22 s)	10.76 (0.12 s)	4.56 (0.15 s)
WLS (Cholesky)	0.16 (2.06 s)	**0.42** (0.55 s)	6.81 (0.93 s)
TV (reweighted least-squares)	0.15 (2.27 s)	4.91 (3.77 s)	3.15 (6.70 s)
L^1 (split-Bregman)	0.31 (1.82 s)	5.07 (12.85 s)	**2.89** (21.09 s)

4.2 Applications on Real Data

Photometric Stereo. The proposed split-Bregman scheme (Section 3.4) was applied to real-world gradient fields (the other proposed schemes provide comparable results), obtained by applying the photometric stereo technique [17] to the "Scholar"[1] and to the "Beethoven"[2] datasets (Figure 3). To emphasize the discontinuity-preserving properties of the scheme, as well as the staircasing effect appearing on large flat areas, we applied the method on the whole rectangular domain, rather than manually segmenting Ω.

It should be noted that a staircasing effect occurs on the background. This effect is well known and studied in the context of image denoising: adapting the total generalised variations schemes (TGV) [3], we could probably get rid of it.

Yet, staircasing seems to affect only the background, and should thus not be considered as a really damaging effect, since our method is able to deal with non-trivial integration domains (which is not the case in many algorithms [7,10,11,16]): staircase-free 3D-reconstructions can be obtained by manually segmenting the reconstruction domain (Figure 4).

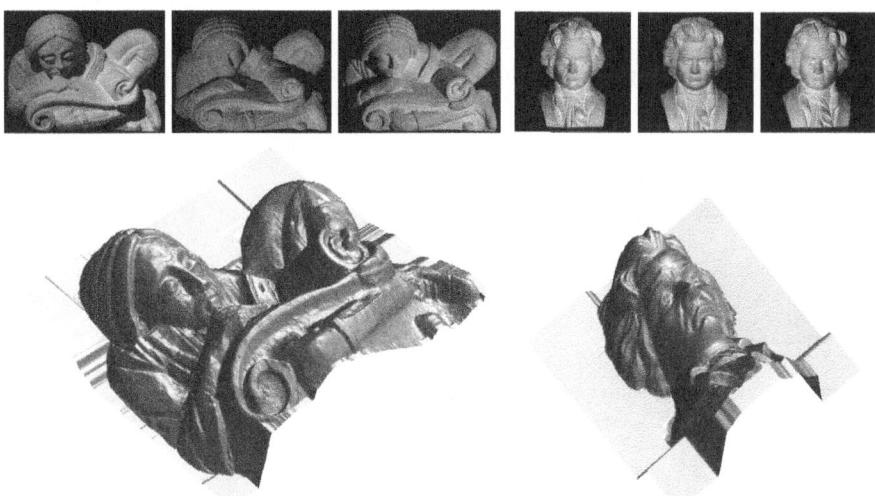

Fig. 3. Photometric stereo. A scene is captured from the same point of view, but under different lightings (top row), so that the normal field can be revealed using photometric stereo. By integrating this normal field (split-Bregman iterations), we obtain the surfaces on the bottom row. The staircase effect is clearly visible in these examples, though it only affects the background.

---

[1] http://vision.seas.harvard.edu/qsfs/Data.html
[2] http://www.ece.ncsu.edu/imaging/Archives/ImageDataBase/Industrial/

Surface Edition. In order to further illustrate the iterative normal integration through split-Bregman iterations, we consider a surface edition problem, consisting in inserting m small objects, whose gradient fields $\mathbf{g}^i$, $i = 1\dots m$, are known over $\Omega^i \subset \Omega$, into a larger object represented by its gradient field $\mathbf{g}^0$ over Ω and the corresponding least-squares depth map u_0, while preserving thin details. Setting $\Omega^0 = \Omega \setminus \left(\cup_{i=1}^{m} \Omega^i\right)$, this reads as the minimisation of:

$$\mathcal{G}(u) = \sum_{i=0}^{m} \iint_{\Omega^i} \|\nabla u(x,y) - \mathbf{g}^i(x,y)\|_1 \, dx \, dy + \frac{\lambda}{2} \iint_{\Omega} (u(x,y) - u_0(x,y))^2 \, dx \, dy \tag{26}$$

which is an extension of the Poisson image editing problem [13]. Functionals (21) and (26) are the same, provided that $\mathbf{g} = \sum_{i=0}^{m} \chi_{\Omega^i} \mathbf{g}^i$, where χ_{Ω^i} is the characteristic function of Ω^i.

Now, we merge both the gradient fields $\mathbf{g}^0$ of the "Scholar" dataset (the reconstruction domain Ω is set to the non-rectangular domain of this dataset), and $\mathbf{g}^1$ of the "Beethoven" dataset, so as to replace a small area $\Omega^1 \subset \Omega$ of the reconstructed "Scholar" surface, by Beethoven's bust. In addition, we would like to remove some details inside another domain $\Omega^2 \subset \Omega$ (Figure 4). To this purpose, we choose $\mathbf{g}^2 = \mathbf{0}$: this will perform TV-"inpainting" inside Ω^2. Denoting $\Omega^0 = \Omega \setminus \left(\Omega^1 \cup \Omega^2\right)$, we form the gradient field $\mathbf{g} = \sum_{i=0}^{2} \chi_{\Omega^i} \mathbf{g}^i$, and apply the proposed split-Bregman scheme. As shown in Figure 4, a detail-preserving blending of the statues is obtained, while removing the details inside Ω^2.

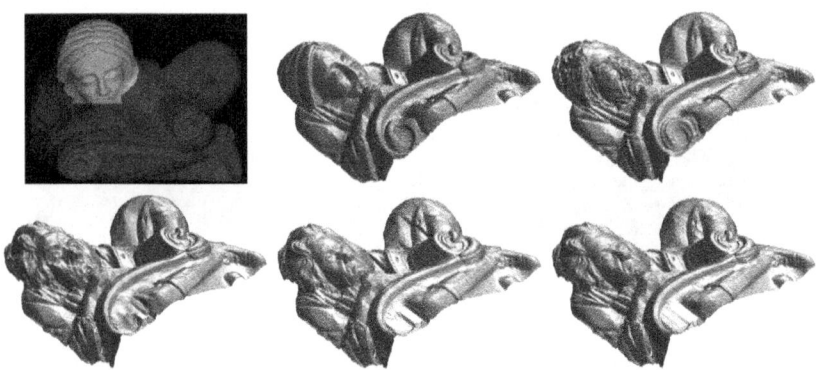

Fig. 4. Surface edition. In the top-left figure, the colored part is Ω, the red part is Ω^0 ("Scholar" gradient field), the yellow one is Ω^1 ("Beethoven" gradient field), and the purple one is Ω^2 (inpainting area). We show the diffusion process at iterations 0, 10 (fine details begin to appear in the "hair"), 50 (the details inside the inpainted area disappear), 200 and 1000 (stable). Apart from the initialisation u_0 using the DCT solver [16], which required to add the background to Ω with null values of the gradient, the background was removed from the reconstruction domain: this considerably improves the boundaries of the surface, proving the importance of considering integration schemes able to deal with non trivial domains.

5 Conclusion and Perspectives

We studied weighted least-squares, TV and L^1 functionals in the context of normal field integration, and provided efficient numerics for minimising these functionals, through sparse Cholesky factorisation, reweighted least-squares and split-Bregman iterations, respectively. We experimentally showed that these functionals provide sharp depth maps, and demonstrated how to use them in the context of photometric stereo and surface edition. In future work, we plan to accelerate the iterative schemes by multigrid techniques [12], so as to allow real-time surface reconstruction and edition, and to more deeply study the staircase effect appearing with L^1 minimisation. We believe that introducing higher order regularisation terms, in the spirit of the total generalised variation regularisation (TGV) [3], will annihilate this effect, while providing a higher order of accuracy.

References

1. Agrawal, A., Raskar, R., Chellappa, R.: What Is the Range of Surface Reconstructions from a Gradient Field? In: Leonardis, A., Bischof, H., Pinz, A. (eds.) ECCV 2006, Part I. LNCS, vol. 3951, pp. 578–591. Springer, Heidelberg (2006)
2. Badri, H., Yahia, H., Aboutajdine, D.: Robust surface reconstruction via triple sparsity. In: CVPR (2014)
3. Bredies, K., Kunisch, K., Pock, T.: Total generalized variation. SIIMS **3**(3), 492–526 (2010)
4. Du, Z., Robles-Kelly, A., Lu, F.: Robust surface reconstruction from gradient field using the L1 norm. In: DICTA (2007)
5. Durou, J.-D., Aujol, J.-F., Courteille, F.: Integrating the Normal Field of a Surface in the Presence of Discontinuities. In: Cremers, D., Boykov, Y., Blake, A., Schmidt, F.R. (eds.) EMMCVPR 2009. LNCS, vol. 5681, pp. 261–273. Springer, Heidelberg (2009)
6. Durou, J.D., Courteille, F.: Integration of a Normal Field without Boundary Condition. In: PACV (ICCV Workshops) (2007)
7. Frankot, R.T., Chellappa, R.: A Method for enforcing integrability in shape from shading algorithms. PAMI **10**(4), 439–451 (1988)
8. Galliani, S., Breuß, M., Ju, Y.C.: Fast and robust surface normal integration by a discrete eikonal equation. In: BMVC (2012)
9. Goldstein, T., Osher, S.: The Split Bregman method for L1-regularized problems. SIIMS **2**(2), 323–343 (2009)
10. Harker, M., O'Leary, P.: Least squares surface reconstruction from measured gradient fields. In: CVPR (2008)
11. Harker, M., O'Leary, P.: Regularized reconstruction of a surface from its measured gradient field. JMIV **51**(1), 46–70 (2015)
12. Kimmel, R., Yavneh, I.: An algebraic multigrid approach for image analysis. SISC **24**(4), 1218–1231 (2003)
13. Pérez, P., Gangnet, M., Blake, A.: Poisson image editing. In: SIGGRAPH (2003)

14. Reddy, D., Agrawal, A., Chellappa, R.: Enforcing integrability by error correction using L1-minimization. In: CVPR (2009)
15. Rudin, L.I., Osher, S., Fatemi, E.: Nonlinear total variation based noise removal algorithms. Physica D: Nonlinear Phenomena **60**(1), 259–268 (1992)
16. Simchony, T., Chellappa, R., Shao, M.: Direct analytical methods for solving Poisson equations in computer vision problems. PAMI **12**(5), 435–446 (1990)
17. Woodham, R.J.: Photometric method for determining surface orientation from multiple images. Optical Engineering **19**(1), 139–144 (1980)

Reconstruction of Surfaces from Point Clouds Using a Lagrangian Surface Evolution Model

Patrik Daniel, Matej Medl'a, Karol Mikula, and Mariana Remešíková[✉]

Department of Mathematics, Faculty of Civil Engineering,
Slovak University of Technology, Radlinského 11, 81005 Bratislava, Slovakia
patrik.daniel1@gmail.com, {medla,mikula,remesikova}@math.sk

Abstract. We present a method for reconstruction of surfaces in R^3 from point clouds. Given a set of points, we construct a triangular mesh approximation of a surface that they represent. The triangulation is obtained by a Lagrangian surface evolution model consisting of an advection and a curvature term. To construct them, we compute the distance function d to the given point cloud. Then the advection evolution is driven by ∇d and the curvature term depends on d and the mean curvature of the evolving surface. In order to control the quality of the mesh during the evolution, we perform tangential redistribution of mesh points as the surface evolves.

Keywords: Point cloud · Surface evolution · Lagrangian methods · Tangential redistribution

1 Introduction

One of the main tasks of modern computer graphics and computer vision is to obtain digital representation of real world objects. A common way of obtaining a representation of a 3D object is scanning a set of points lying on the object's surface. However, such a basic representation is not sufficient for most applications. Therefore, a lot of effort has been put in designing algorithms for obtaining a surface representation of an object given a representative point cloud [1].

We present a method that constructs a triangular mesh representation of an object's surface. As an input, we need the corresponding point cloud and a triangulated surface – an approximation of the desired surface. After, we apply an appropriately designed Lagrangian surface evolution model to obtain the representation we are looking for. The driving force of the evolution is the distance function d to the point cloud – the model consists of an advection term with the velocity proportional to ∇d and a curvature term with the evolution speed proportional do d. Moreover, the model is enriched with a specifically designed tangential movement term that moves the points around the evolving surface. This term is added to overcome one of the main difficulties arising in Lagrangian manifold evolution – the possible deterioration of the mesh quality during the evolution process.

The method that we propose is that it provides a straightforward way to obtain a good quality triangular representation of an object's surface. The initial condition for the evolution process is usually a simple surface (e.g. a sphere or an ellipsoid) that can be easily triangulated. Assuming that the initial condition is topologically equivalent to the desired surface, the topology of the triangulation remains intact during the evolution. The orientation of normals is also preserved; having oriented normals is important for determining the interior and exterior of the surface, resolving visibility, shading etc. However, a practically applicable method should also be robust enough to manage difficulties caused by various data imperfections. The scanned point clouds often suffer from defects such as non-uniform point distribution, noise, outlying points or missing parts (Figure 1). As we demonstrate in the last section, our method is well able to deal with such problematic situations due to the properties of the model that we use.

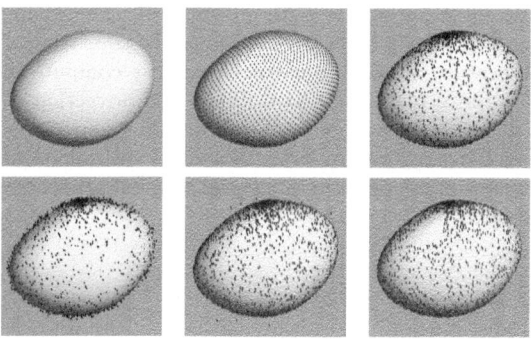

Fig. 1. A surface and its various point cloud representations – an ideal uniform point cloud, a non-uniform point cloud, a point cloud with 5% noise, a point cloud with several outlying points and a point cloud with a missing part.

The reason why we use a Lagrangian method is that obtaining a triangular representation of an object is more simple than in the case of, e.g., level set methods. Also, though not shown here, Lagrangian methods can be more easily applied to surfaces with boundaries. To our knowledge, Lagrangian evolution methods were so far only rarely applied to the point cloud problem and the existing works do not consider any mesh adjustment [7]. The strategy that we use in this paper is based on some of our previous works concerning surface evolution problems [5,6]. This paper extends the ideas to the point cloud problem that has not appeared in the cited works. Also, we suggest a new tangential redistribution technique based on the curvature of the evolving surface.

2 Mathematical Model

Let $\Omega \subseteq \mathbb{R}^3$ and let $C \subset \Omega$ be a set of n_p points with elements denoted by P_i, $i = 1 \ldots n_p$. Our goal is to find a closed surface approximating C.

Let $d_0 \colon \Omega \to \mathbb{R}$ represent the distance function to C. Starting at any point of Ω, we can approach C following the direction of ∇d_0. The basic idea of our mathematical model is to take a smooth closed surface surrounding C and let it evolve based on ∇d_0. Since d_0 is not everywhere differentiable, instead we will consider $d = G_\sigma * d_0$, where G_σ is a Gauss kernel.

Now, let X be a two-dimensional Riemannian manifold equipped with the metric g_X. Let $F\colon X \times \langle 0, t_s\rangle \to \Omega$ denote a time-dependent embedding of X in Ω and let g_F represent the corresponding induced metric. The image of $F^t = F(\cdot, t)$ will be denoted by S^t. The embedding F is the solution of the evolution equation

$$\partial_t F = w_a \left(\nabla d \cdot N\right) N + w_c d \Delta_{g_F} F + v_T, \tag{1}$$

where N is a unit normal to S. The symbol $\Delta_{g_F} F$ is the Laplace-Beltrami operator with respect to g_F that is equal to the mean curvature vector h of F. The parameters w_a and w_c are non-negative reals. The last term v_T represents the velocity of the tangential movement. This model, besides the tangential movement, is a Lagrangian analogue of the level set model used by Zhao [9].

To understand the mechanism of action of this model, let us take a closer look at the three terms on the right hand side. As written above, the first term represents the driving force that makes S^t approach C. The projection to the surface normal eliminates tangential movement that does not affect S^t and it also makes the movement of a point dependent on its neighborhood – the surface is moving as a whole rather than a set of independent points. If ∇d points in a tangential direction, the advective evolution stops and thus a surface patch is formed in the empty space between the points of C. The second term represents evolution by mean curvature that speeds up the evolution in the regions distant to C and it regularizes the surface during the evolution. It also causes forming of straight patches between the points of the point cloud. Moreover, as we will see later, it helps to deal with artifacts like noise or outlying points. The third term is used to control the induced metric g_F; in the discrete setting it means we can distribute mesh points around the surface according to our needs.

In our previous work [6], we suggest a method for constructing the tangential velocity based on the evolution of the induced metric, particularly the area density $G\colon X \times \langle 0, t_s\rangle \to \mathbb{R}$ defined as $G = \frac{\partial \mu_F}{\partial \mu_X}$, where μ_F and μ_X are the measures induced on X by g_F and g_X. This quantity expresses how much the embedding F locally shrinks or expands areas. It is easy to see this considering G constant over a domain $U \subset X$; then $\mu_F(U) = G\mu_X(U)$. From the discrete point of view it means that push-forwarding a discretization of X along F, the increase of the density of discretization points will be higher in regions with lower values of G. The evolution of G is given by [3]

$$\partial_t G = \left(-v_N \cdot h + \mathrm{div}_{g_F} w_T\right) G, \tag{2}$$

where h is the mean curvature vector, $v_N = w_a \left(\nabla d \cdot N\right) N + w_c d \Delta_{g_F} F$ and w_T is a vector field on X constructed as the pull-back of v_T along F. The area of X measured by μ_F (the area of S) evolves as

$$\partial_t G = \int_X \left(-v_N \cdot h\right) G \, \mathrm{d}\mu_F. \tag{3}$$

An embedding F with constant G can be called *area-uniform* with respect to g_X. Let us use the notation $A_X = \mu_X(X)$, $A = \mu_F(X)$. Since

$$\int_X G \, d\mu_X = A, \tag{4}$$

then for a constant G we must have $G = \frac{A}{A_X}$.

An embedding with this property provides a straightforward way to construct a discretization mesh with uniformly sized 2D mesh elements. This type of mesh has several practical advantages – it prevents mesh degeneration, it provides a reasonable discrete representation of a surface and it is likely to capture important information coming from the external vector field that drives the evolution. Thus, it has sense to require $G \to \frac{A}{A_X}$ as $t \to \infty$. The corresponding dimensionless condition is

$$\frac{G}{A} \xrightarrow[t \to \infty]{} \frac{1}{A_X}.$$

This can be guaranteed, if

$$\partial_t \left(\frac{G}{A}\right) = \omega \left(\frac{1}{A_X} - \frac{G}{A}\right), \tag{5}$$

where $\omega: \langle 0, t_s \rangle \times \mathbb{R}_+$. This equality combined with (2) and (3) yields a condition for the divergence of w_T,

$$\mathrm{div}_{g_F} w_T = v_N \cdot h - \frac{1}{A} \int_X v_N \cdot h \, d\mu_F + \omega \left(\frac{A}{A_X G} - 1\right). \tag{6}$$

To obtain a unique w_T, we can suppose, for example, that $w_T = \nabla_{g_F} \psi$, $\psi: X \times \langle 0, t_s \rangle \to \mathbb{R}$. Then we have

$$\Delta_{g_F} \psi = v_N \cdot h - \frac{1}{A} \int_X v_N \cdot h \, d\mu_F + \omega \left(\frac{A}{A_X G} - 1\right). \tag{7}$$

If we prescribe the value of ψ in one point of X, (7) has a unique solution.

An area-uniform mesh might not always be the best representation of a surface. In some applications, it makes sense, for example, to concentrate the mesh points in the regions of higher curvature. If we consider, for example, the mean curvature H, this can be achieved if we require a constant value of $Gf(H)$, where f is a positive increasing function. Similarly as in the previous case, (4) must hold and thus we get the condition

$$\frac{G}{A} \xrightarrow[t \to \infty]{} \frac{\frac{1}{f(H)}}{\int_X \frac{1}{f(H)} d\mu_X}.$$

This leads to the condition for ψ,

$$\Delta_{g_F} \psi = v_N \cdot h - \frac{1}{A} \int_X v_N \cdot h \, d\mu_F + \omega \left(\frac{A}{G} \frac{\frac{1}{f(H)}}{\int_X \frac{1}{f(H)} d\mu_X} - 1\right). \tag{8}$$

3 Discretization of the Mathematical Model

Since the problem of point cloud reconstruction is in principle analogous to the 3D image segmentation problem, we refer to our previous works concerning this topic [5,6] and we only provide a brief explanation of the numerical method.

Before we can apply our model, we need to compute the distance function d. For this purpose, we consider Ω to be a box and we discretize it by constructing a voxel mesh where each voxel is a cube of side length h. Then we approximate the value of d in each voxel. This approach is necessary since a brute-force computation of the distance function is practically inapplicable in most cases. Having an approximation of d, we approximate ∇d simply by central differences. To identify the voxel corresponding to a point $F(P,t)$, $P \in X$, we round its coordinates divided by h.

We consider a uniform discretization of the time interval and we use the notation $F^n = F^{t_n}$ and $S^n = S^{t_n}$. The time discretization of (1) is semi-implicit,

$$\frac{F^n - F^{n-1}}{\tau} = w_a \left(\nabla d \cdot N^{n-1}\right) N^{n-1} + w_c d \Delta_{g_{F^{n-1}}} F^n + v_T^{n-1}. \tag{9}$$

Now, we consider a triangular structure on X consisting of vertices X_i, $i = 1 \ldots n_v$, edges e_j, $j = 1 \ldots n_e$, and triangles $\mathcal{T}_k$, $k = 1 \ldots n_t$. We construct a piecewise linear approximation of F^n denoted by $\bar{F}^n$ – we set $\bar{F}^n(X_i) = F^n(X_i)$ and then, for any triangle $\mathcal{T}_p$ with vertices X_i, X_{i_p}, $X_{i_{p+1}}$, we set $\bar{F}^n(\lambda_1 X_i + \lambda_2 X_{i_p} + \lambda_3 X_{i_{p+1}}) = \lambda_1 F^n(X_i) + \lambda_2 F^n(X_{i_p}) + \lambda_3 F^n(X_{i_{p+1}})$. The embedding $\bar{F}^n$ induces a metric g^n on X which induces a measure μ^n on X. The approximation of the unit normal to $S^n = \bar{F}^n(X)$ at F_i^n is denoted by N_i^n. The numerical scheme that we apply uses the angles of $\mathcal{T}_p$ adjacent to X_{i_p} and $X_{i_{p+1}}$ measured in the metric g^n. We denote them by $\theta_{p,1}^n$ and $\theta_{p,2}^n$.

The space discretization of (9) is done by the finite volume approach. The control volume mesh is constructed by barycentric subdivision of the triangles $\mathcal{T}_k$ (Figure 2). We will denote by $\nu_{p,1}^n$, $\nu_{p,2}^n$ the outward unit normals to the control volume edges $\bar{F}^n(\sigma_{p,1})$ and $\bar{F}^n(\sigma_{p,2})$ in the plane of $\bar{\mathcal{T}}_p^n$. The principle of the method is to integrate (9) over a control volume V_i,

$$\int_{V_i} \frac{F^n - F^{n-1}}{\tau} d\mu_{F^{n-1}} = \int_{V_i} w_a \left(\nabla d \cdot N^{n-1}\right) N^{n-1} d\mu_{F^{n-1}}$$
$$+ \int_{V_i} w_c d \Delta_{g_{F^{n-1}}} F^n d\mu_{F^{n-1}} + \int_{V_i} v_T^{n-1} d\mu_{F^{n-1}}, \tag{10}$$

and then to approximate the integrals that we obtain.

For the first term of the right hand side, we need to approximate the surface normal at F_i^n. We take the arithmetic mean of the normals to all triangles containing F_i^n. For the second term, we use the cotangent scheme [4],

$$\int_{V_i} w_c d \Delta_{g_{F^{n-1}}} F^n d\mu_{F^{n-1}} \approx w_c d_i \frac{1}{2} \sum_{p=1}^{m} \left(\cot \theta_{i,p-1,1}^{n-1} + \cot \theta_{i,p,2}^{n-1}\right) \left(F_i^n - F_{i_p}^n\right),$$
$$\tag{11}$$

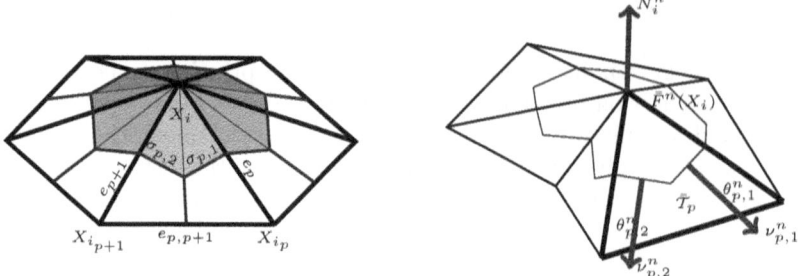

Fig. 2. The surface discretization mesh. Left, the triangulation of the abstract surface X. Right, the corresponding approximation of the embedded surface $F^n(X)$.

where m is the number of vertices connected to X_i by an edge and d_i is the value of d in the voxel corresponding to F_i^n. Dividing the right hand side by $\mu^{n-1}(V_i)$, we obtain an approximation of h^{n-1}.

To discretize the integral of the tangential velocity, we recall that w_T^n is a gradient field and we apply the following version of the Stokes theorem [2]

$$\int_{V_i} v_T^{n-1} \, d\mu_{F^{n-1}} = \int_{\partial V_i} \psi^{n-1} \nu_i^{n-1} \, dH_{\mu_{F^{n-1}}} - \int_{V_i} \psi^{n-1} h^{n-1} \, d\mu_{F^{n-1}}.$$

This gives

$$\int_{V_i} v_T^{n-1} \, d\mu_{F^{n-1}} \approx \sum_{p=1}^{m} \left(\|\sigma_{i,p,1}\|_{n-1} \psi_{i,p,1}^{n-1} \nu_{i,p,1}^{n-1} + \|\sigma_{i,p,2}\|_{n-1} \psi_{i,p,2}^{n-1} \nu_{i,p,2}^{n-1} \right) \qquad (12)$$
$$- \mu^{n-1}(V_i) \psi_i^{n-1} h_i^{n-1}$$

where $\|\cdot\|_{n-1}$ denotes the length computed by the metric g^{n-1} and $\psi_{i,p,1}^{n-1}$, $\psi_{i,p,2}^{n-1}$ are the values of ψ^{n-1} in the midpoints of $\sigma_{i,p,1}$ and $\sigma_{i,p,2}$. We obtain these values by linear interpolation.

The function ψ is computed from (7) where, again, we use the cotangent scheme to discretize the Laplace-Beltrami operator of ψ^{n-1}. The volume density is approximated by

$$G_i^{n-1} = \mu^{n-1}(V_i) \frac{n_v}{A_X}. \qquad (13)$$

4 Experiments and Results

In the first phase of testing, we used the surface and the uniform point cloud shown in Figure 1. The cloud contains 2562 points. The initial condition was a triangulated sphere with 2562 vertices. The distance function was computed in a box volume of $200 \times 200 \times 200$ voxels. In all experiments presented in this paper, it was approximated by the fast sweeping method [8]. The parameters of the model were set to $\tau = 0.002$, $w_a = 300.0$, $w_c = 100.0$. We used the area-uniform redistribution with the redistribution speed $\omega = 100.0$. The evolution was stopped after 400 time steps. Since d is a distance function smoothed by a heat kernel, it is nowhere zero and thus there is no stopping time implied by the model. However, we can stop the evolution if the difference between S^{n-1} and S^n is lower than some threshold. Figure 3 shows the initial condition as well as a few stages of the evolution. Since a point cloud is usually a rough approximation of an object, the resulting representative surface might benefit from some additional smoothing after the evolution stops. In our case, this can be done by using the same algorithm; we only need to set $d=1$ in all voxels and we obtain a mean curvature flow model. The last two pictures in Figure 3 show the result of such smoothing. Here, we set $w_c = 300.$, $\omega = 2000$, $\tau = 0.0005$ and we performed only 20 time steps to prevent excessive shrinking of our surface.

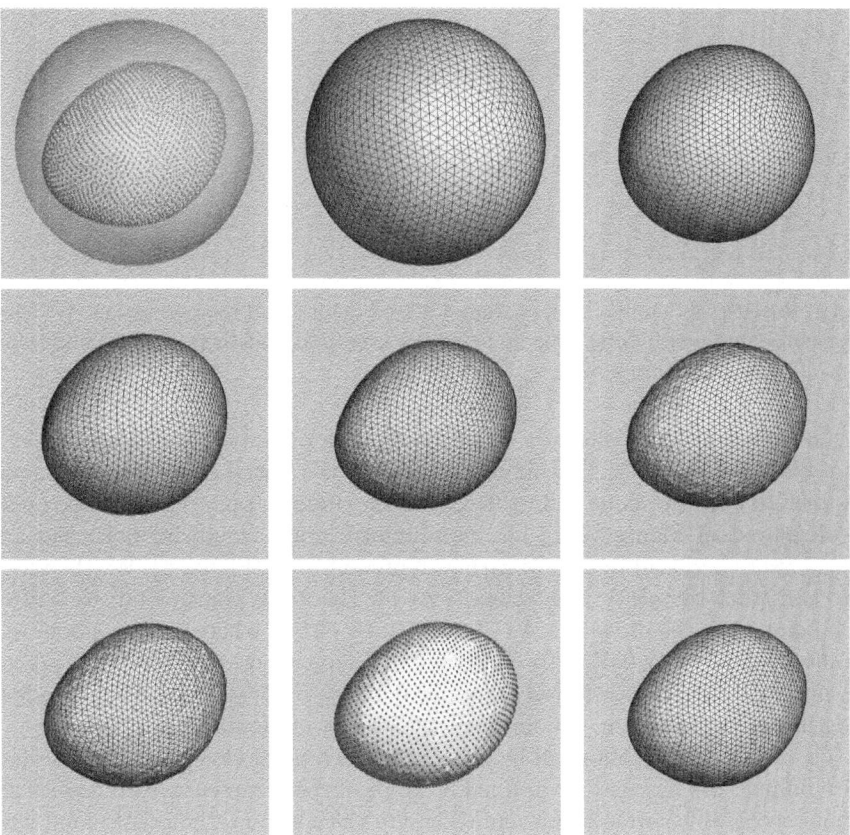

Fig. 3. Reconstruction of a surface from a uniform point cloud representation. We can see the initial surface together with the point cloud and the triangulation of this surface. What follows is the evolved surface after 100, 150, 200 and 250 time steps, the surface at the end of the evolution displayed with its triangulation and with the point cloud. Finally, we show the smoothed surface after applying 20 steps of mean curvature flow.

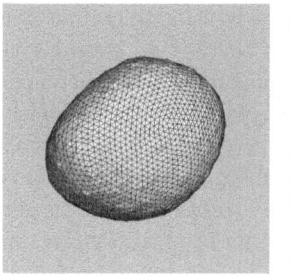
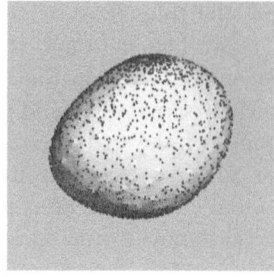

Fig. 4. Reconstruction of a surface from a non-uniform point cloud representation. We show the results obtained by 400 time steps of the evolution.

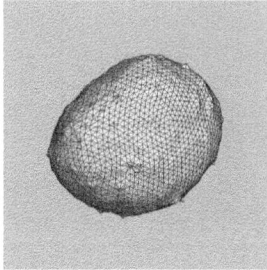
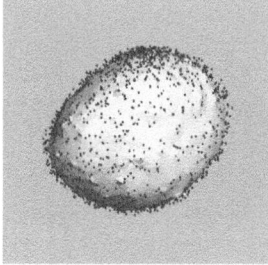
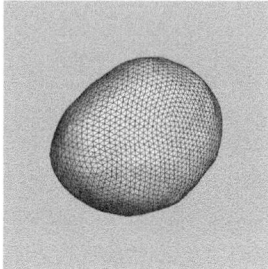

Fig. 5. Reconstruction of a surface from a noised point cloud representation. We show the results obtained by 400 time steps of the evolution and then after 30 additional steps of mean curvature flow.

The following experiments test our method on potentially more problematic point clouds (Figure 1). The number of points, the initial condition and model parameters were the same as in the case of the uniform point cloud. The results are displayed in Figures 4–7. The non-uniform point cloud did not yield any special issues and lead to a good surface representation (Figure 4). We then used it to construct the other point clouds. As for the noisy point cloud, we shifted each point P_i in the direction of $P_i - (0,0,0)$ by $r\|P_i\|$, where r is a random real number from $\langle -0.05, 0.05 \rangle$. To construct the point cloud with outlying points, we shifted 10 randomly selected points by $0.3\|P_i\|$. Finally, by deleting all points lying in a selected region, we obtained the last point cloud for our tests.

The result that we obtained by using the noised point cloud was, as expected, quite bumpy. In this case, we applied 30 steps of the mean curvature flow to get a more acceptable surface representation. On the contrary, the point cloud with several outlying points did not cause any major problems. Using the regularized distance function allows the evolving surface to run through an isolated point due to the non-vanishing curvature term. As we can see in Figure 6, the outliers are noticed by the evolving surface but afterwards, they are overcome. Finally, the ability of our method to patch empty regions has been already explained in Section 2. If some reasonably large part of the data is missing, the model will create a planar patch as a representation of this region (Figure 7).

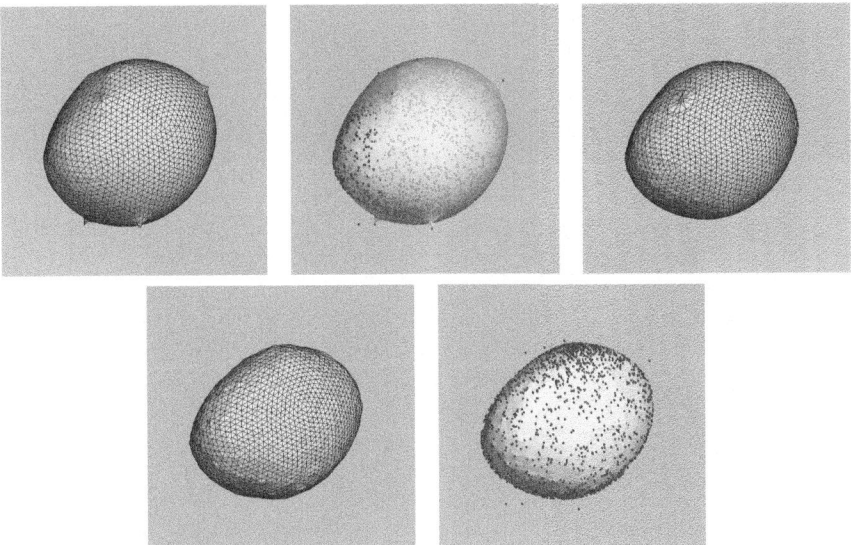

Fig. 6. Reconstruction of a surface from a point cloud representation with outlying points. We show the evolved surface after 180 time steps (first its triangulation and then displayed together with the corresponding point cloud), after 220 and 400 time steps of the evolution.

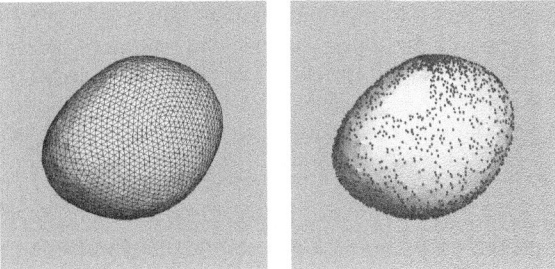

Fig. 7. Reconstruction of a surface from a point cloud representation with a missing part. We show the results obtained by 400 time steps of the evolution.

In the next example, we took a point cloud representing a much more complicated object (Figure 8). In this case, we computed the distance function on a finer grid of $300 \times 300 \times 300$ voxels. The initial surface was also more finely discretized, it was a sphere with 16386 vertices. The values of the model parameters were $\tau = 0.002$, $w_a = 300.$, $w_c = 30.$, $\omega = 100.$. We show the result obtained after 900 time steps and then after a slight smoothing by 5 steps of the mean curvature flow with parameter values mentioned above.

Finally, we present an experiment illustrating the effect of the curvature driven tangential redistribution. We use the uniform point cloud shown in Figure 3. The curvature driven redistribution was not used during the whole evolution

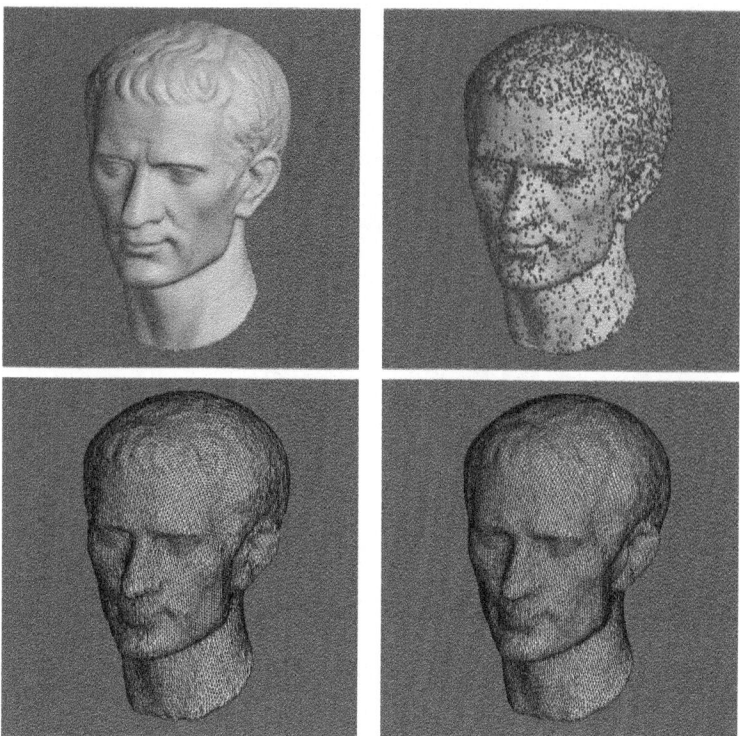

Fig. 8. Reconstruction of a more complicated surface (surface taken from http://segeval.cs.princeton.edu/) . We show the original surface and the point cloud representing it. In the second row, we can see our reconstruction obtained after 900 time steps of evolution and the surface smoothed by 5 additional steps of mean curvature flow.

process, but we rather used the area-uniform redistribution to optimally capture the external vector field. After 400 time steps and additional 20 steps of smoothing, we obtained the surface representation shown in the last two pictures of Figure 3. This was the starting point for the curvature driven redistribution. We kept evolving the surface by mean curvature flow but it was now by orders of magnitude slower; we set $w_c = 1.0$. The redistribution speed changed to $\omega = 200.0$ and we performed 15 steps of the evolution. The function f used to redistribute the points was $f(H) = e^{20H}$.

The result is shown in Figure 9. As we can see, the points are more densely distributed in the regions with higher mean curvature (compare to the resulting mesh shown in Figure 3). To provide an evaluation of the redistribution other than a visual inspection of the resulting mesh, we add two graphs. Here, we consider the ratio $r_{A,i} = \frac{\mu^n(V_i)}{A_V}$, where A_V is the average control volume area, $A_V = A/n_v$. The graphs show the dependence of $r_{A,i}$ on H – each point of the plot represents one pair $(H_i, r_{A,i})$. We can see that before the curvature driven

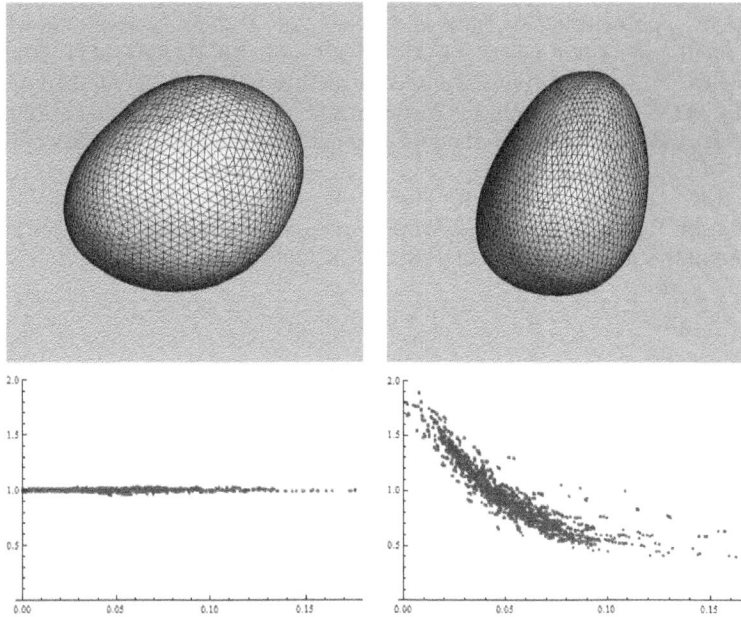

Fig. 9. A test example of a representation obtained with the help of curvature driven tangential redistribution. We show the resulting surface representation obtained after 15 time steps of the redistribution in two different views. Note that the density of discretization points is higher in the regions with higher mean curvature. The graphs show the dependence of $r_{A,i}$ on H before and after the curvature driven redistribution.

redistribution, $r_{A,i}$ is close to 1 in all vertices. After 15 steps of the redistribution, we can observe that $r_{A,i}$ is clearly decreasing with increasing H_i.

Acknowledgments. This work was supported by the grants APVV-0072-11 and APVV-0161-12.

References

1. Berger, M., Tagliasacchi, A., Seversky, L. M.: State of the Art in Surface Reconstruction from Point Clouds. In: Eurographics 2014 - State of the Art Reports, pp. 161–185. The Eurographics Association (2014)
2. Dziuk, G., Elliott, C.M.: Finite elements on evolving surfaces. IMA J. Numer. Anal. **27**, 262–292 (2007)
3. Mantegazza, C.: Lecture Notes on Mean Curvature Flow. Springer (2011)
4. Meyer, M., Desbrun, M., Schroeder, P., Barr, A.H.: Discrete differential geometry operators for triangulated 2manifolds. Visualization and Mathematics III, 35–57 (2003)
5. Mikula, K., Remešíková, M.: 3D Lagrangian Segmentation with Simultaneous Mesh Adjustment. In: Finite Volumes for Complex Applications VII. Springer Proceedings in Mathematics and Statistics, vol. 77, pp. 685–694 (2014)

6. Mikula, K., Remešíková, M., Sarkoci, P., Ševčovič, D.: Surface evolution with tangential redistribution of points. SIAM J. Sci. Comp. **36**(4), 1384–1414 (2014)
7. Surynková, P.: Curve and Surface Reconstruction Based on the Method of Evolution. In: WDS 2010 Proceedings, Part I, MATFYZPRESS, pp. 139–144 (2010)
8. Zhao, H.: A Fast Sweeping Method for Eikonal Equations. Mathematics of Computation **74**(250), 603–627 (2004)
9. Zhao, H.K., Osher, S., Fedkiw, R.: Fast Surface Reconstruction Using the Level Set Method. In: Proceedings of IEEE Workshop on Variational and Level Set Methods in Computer Vision 2001, pp. 194–201. IEEE (2001)

Solving Minimal Surface Problems on Surfaces and Point Clouds

Daniel Tenbrinck[1](✉), François Lozes[2], and Abderrahim Elmoataz[2]

[1] Institute for Computational and Applied Mathematics, Westfälische Wilhelms-Universität Münster, Einsteinstr. 62, 48149 Münster, Germany
daniel.tenbrinck@uni-muenster.de
[2] UMR6072 GREYC, ENSICAEN, Caen, France

Abstract. Minimal surface problems play an important role not only in physics or biology but also in mathematical signal and image processing. Although the computation of respective solutions is well-investigated in the setting of discrete images, only little attention has been payed to more complicated data, e.g., surfaces represented as meshes or point clouds. In this work we introduce a novel family of discrete total variation seminorms for weighted graphs based on the upwind gradient and incorporate them into an efficient minimization algorithm to perform total variation denoising on graphs. Furthermore, we demonstrate how to utilize the latter algorithm to uniquely solve minimal surface problems on graphs. To show the universal applicability of this approach, we illustrate results from filtering and segmentation of 3D point cloud data.

Keywords: Minimal surface problem · Discrete total variation · Upwind differences · Graphs · Segmentation · Denoising · Point cloud data

1 Introduction

Variational models and partial differential equation-based (PDE) methods are a fundamental tool in mathematical image processing and computer vision. The respective mathematical theory is well-understood and allows for important conclusions, e.g., existence and uniqueness of solutions. Traditionally, algorithms from this field are investigated and applied in the domain of Euclidean spaces. However, in many physical and biological contexts there exist problems involving PDEs on more complex and irregular domains. In particular, due to the technical advances in producing affordable 3D sensors in the past few years more and more applications are related to data defined on polygonal surfaces and point clouds. In general, the study of variational methods and PDEs needs significantly more effort in these cases. Moreover, in the case of point clouds the data is directly sampled from the underlying surface. Since there is a-priori no connectivity of these points provided this leads to additional problems in processing these data.

Today, variational problems and PDEs on surfaces can be tackled by one of the following techniques. First, there are methods which approximate surfaces by polygonal meshes and locally parametrize them by suitable functions, e.g., finite element methods [10]. Another possibility is to implicitly represent surfaces as level sets of a Lipschitz continuous function on Euclidean domains and use level set methods to solve PDEs [2]. Another example is the closest point method proposed in [16], which replaces surface differentials with Cartesian differentials of its closest point extension. Recently, discrete differential geometry on surfaces [3,13] gained increased attention, especially in computer graphics. While most of these methods do not immediately extend to arbitrary point cloud data, they could generally be used if these data were reconstructed into suitable surface representations - a process that can be very complex and cost-intensive in terms of computational effort. For a discussion of these different techniques with their advantages and disadvantages, see e.g., [13,14].

In this work we focus on the well-known minimal surface problem, see e.g., [9,18] and references therein. Deviating from the techniques discussed above, we perform discrete calculus on surfaces using graph-based representations [1,11,12,14]. Based on our previous work in [14] we represent the given data as a graph and use the proposed framework in [11] to transfer differential operators to graphs. We are able to solve minimal surface problems for meshes and arbitrary point clouds in a unified manner using this relatively simple approach.

1.1 Motivation

The minimal surface problem [5,8] consists of finding a subset Σ of an open, bounded domain $\Omega \subset \mathbb{R}^n$, which partitions Ω according to some external energy $g \colon \Omega \to \mathbb{R}$ while having a minimal surface $\Gamma \subset \Omega$ with respect to an adequate measure. Denoting this measure of the surface of Σ in Ω by $\mathrm{Per}(\Sigma; \Omega)$ one can formulate the minimal surface problem as follows:

For a fixed $\lambda > 0$ and $z \in \mathbb{R}$ find a minimizing set $\Sigma \subset \Omega$ of the energy

$$E(\Sigma) = \mathrm{Per}(\Sigma; \Omega) + \lambda \int_{\Sigma} z - g(x)\, \mathrm{d}x \ . \tag{1}$$

Here, λ is a regularization parameter controlling the smoothness of Γ. Solutions of the problem (1) are not unique as the problem is non-convex [8].

There exist various tasks in signal processing which can be associated to the minimal surface problem. To the best of our knowledge a unified manner for computing local and nonlocal minimal surface solutions on graphs has not been investigated so far. To motivate our work we discuss three examples from the literature. First, given an image $f \colon \Omega \to \mathbb{R}$ and setting the external energy to $g(x) = f(x)$, then solving (1) will perform a segmentation of f according to a threshold induced by $z \in \mathbb{R}$. Decreasing the parameter λ enforces regularity of the segmentation surface and thus makes the segmentation more robust to noise and outliers, e.g., see [18]. A second example is given by the popular Chan-Vese segmentation method in [8]. Based on an initial guess of a partition $\Sigma \subset \Omega$, the authors compute two mean values $c_1, c_2 \in \mathbb{R}$ of the image regions of f induced by Σ. Subsequently, the Chan-Vese method performs the actual segmentation step by setting $z = 0$ and $g(x) = (f(x)-c_1)^2 - (f(x)-c_2)^2$ and solving (1). In fact, this clusters the image values according to the estimated cluster centers c_1 and c_2. Another problem is the computation of the mean curvature flow. As the authors in [5] discuss, given an initial surface Γ of Σ and setting $z = 0$ and $g(x) = d_\Gamma(x)$ as the signed Euclidean distance of a point x to Γ, one approximates the mean curvature flow of Γ by computing a sequence of solutions to (1). This is especially interesting for modeling surface evolution in physics or biology.

1.2 Contributions

Our aim in this paper is to establish a unified method to solve various important tasks from image and data processing which can be formulated as minimal surface problems on data with arbitrary topology, such as point clouds. First, based on the notion of discrete total variation on graphs we introduce a new family of total variation seminorms based on the upwind gradient operator. We give two important relationships, namely the discrete coarea formula for graphs and a link between minimal surface problems and the popular ROF denoising model. Finally, we give an efficient iterative scheme to uniquely solve minimal surface problems on graphs. The advantage of this approach is that it is universally applicable for various tasks, such as total variation denoising, segmentation, data clustering, or computation of the mean curvature flow.

2 Methods

We start with the basic notation and mathematical basics of finite weighted graphs and give the definition of weighted finite differences for the latter. Subsequently, we formulate the notion of the discrete total variation of a function defined on graph vertices in Section 2.1 and introduce a novel family of discrete total variation seminorms based on the upwind gradient operator. For certain special cases of these seminorms we are able to prove a proposition in Section 2.2 which corresponds to the coarea formula in the continuous setting. Based on this, we give an important relationship on weighted graphs between total variation denoising problems and the minimal surface problem.

Let $\mathcal{G} = (\mathcal{V}, \mathcal{E}, w)$ be a weighted graph without loops and self-referencing, for which $w: \mathcal{V} \times \mathcal{V} \to \mathbb{R}^+$ is a weighting function depending on the interactions of the vertices in the finite set $\mathcal{V} = \{x_1, \ldots, x_N\}$ given by the edge set $\mathcal{E} \subset \mathcal{V} \times \mathcal{V}$. In the following we assume that the weighting function w is symmetric and hence $\mathcal{G}$ is an undirected graph. We denote by $\mathcal{H}(\mathcal{V})$ the Hilbert space of real-valued functions on the vertices of the graph and by $\mathcal{H}(\mathcal{E})$ the Hilbert space of real-valued functions on the graph edges. For $f \in \mathcal{H}(\mathcal{V})$ we define the p-norm as:

$$\|f\|_p = \left(\sum_{x_i \in \mathcal{V}} |f(x_i)|^p\right)^{1/p}, \ 1 \leq p < \infty \quad \text{and} \quad \|f\|_\infty = \max_{x_i \in \mathcal{V}} |f(x_i)|. \quad (2)$$

Following [11], we introduce weighted finite differences $d_w: \mathcal{H}(\mathcal{V}) \to \mathcal{H}(\mathcal{E})$ by:

$$(d_w f)(x_i, x_j) = \sqrt{w(x_i, x_j)}(f(x_j) - f(x_i)), \tag{3}$$

and for $H \in \mathcal{H}(\mathcal{E})$ one is able to give the adjoint operator $d_w^*: \mathcal{H}(\mathcal{E}) \to \mathcal{H}(\mathcal{V})$, as,

$$(d_w^* H)(x_i) = \sum_{x_j \sim x_i} \sqrt{w(x_i, x_j)}(H(x_j, x_i) - H(x_i, x_j)). \tag{4}$$

We define a weighted gradient operator ∇_w of a function $f \in \mathcal{H}(\mathcal{V})$ as:

$$(\nabla_w f)(x_i) = ((d_w f)(x_i, x_j))^T_{x_j \in \mathcal{V}}, \tag{5}$$

Based on the difference operator in (3) one can additionally get weighted upwind differences similar to upwind discretization schemes, e.g., see [14], by:

$$\begin{aligned}(d_w^+ f)(x_i, x_j) &= \max(0, (d_w f)(x_i, x_j)), \\ (d_w^- f)(x_i, x_j) &= \min(0, (d_w f)(x_i, x_j)) = -\max(0, (d_w f)(x_j, x_i)). \end{aligned} \tag{6}$$

Based on these weighted upwind difference one gets the discrete upwind weighted gradient operators ∇_w^+ and ∇_w^- analogously to (5).

2.1 Discrete Total Variation for Graphs

Based on the gradient operator of a function $f \in \mathcal{H}(\mathcal{V})$ introduced in (5) one can introduce a measure of the discrete total variation (TV) of f on a weighted graph $\mathcal{G}$. For this we define a family of discrete total variation seminorms as:

$$\begin{aligned}\|f\|_{TV,p} &= \sum_{x_i \in \mathcal{V}} \|(\nabla_w f)(x_i)\|_p = \sum_{x_i \in \mathcal{V}} \left(\sum_{x_j \sim x_i} |(d_w f)(x_i, x_j)|^p \right)^{1/p}, \quad 1 \le p < \infty, \\ \|f\|_{TV,\infty} &= \sum_{x_i \in \mathcal{V}} \|(\nabla_w f)(x_i)\|_\infty = \sum_{x_i \in \mathcal{V}} \max_{x_j \sim x_i} |(d_w f)(x_i, x_j)|, \qquad p = \infty.\end{aligned} \tag{7}$$

Inspired by the definition of a discrete upwind total variation seminorm by the authors in [6], we introduce a novel family of TV seminorms on graphs based on the weighted upwind differences in (6),

$$\begin{aligned}\|f\|^+_{TV,p} &= \sum_{x_i \in \mathcal{V}} \|(\nabla_w^+ f)(x_i)\|_p = \sum_{x_i \in \mathcal{V}} \left(\sum_{x_j \sim x_i} |(d_w^+ f)(x_i, x_j)|^p \right)^{1/p} \\ &= \sum_{x_i \in \mathcal{V}} \left(\sum_{x_j \sim x_i} (w(x_i, x_j))^{p/2} |\max(0, f(x_j) - f(x_i))|^p \right)^{1/p}, \quad 1 \le p < \infty, \\ \|f\|^+_{TV,\infty} &= \sum_{x_i \in \mathcal{V}} \|(\nabla_w^+ f)(x_i)\|_\infty = \sum_{x_i \in \mathcal{V}} \max_{x_j \sim x_i} |(d_w^+ f)(x_i, x_j)| \\ &= \sum_{x_i \in \mathcal{V}} \max_{x_j \sim x_i} \left(\sqrt{w(x_i, x_j)} |\max(0, f(x_j) - f(x_i))| \right), \qquad p = \infty.\end{aligned} \tag{8}$$

Using the definition of the weighted upwind differences d_w^- in (6), we introduce analogously a novel family of TV seminorms $\|\cdot\|_{TV,p}^-$ and $\|\cdot\|_{TV,\infty}^-$. Finally, we are also interested in a discrete total variation seminorm of the form:

$$\|f\|_{TV,\infty}^{\pm} = \frac{1}{2}\sum_{x_i\in\mathcal{V}} \|(\nabla_w^+ f)(x_i)\|_\infty + \|(\nabla_w^- f)(x_i)\|_\infty. \tag{9}$$

Given a subset of vertices $\mathcal{A}\subset\mathcal{V}$ of a weighted graph $\mathcal{G}$, we define a family of perimeters of $\mathcal{A}$ as the total variation (see Section 2.1) of its respective indicator function $\chi_\mathcal{A}$ for $1\leq p<\infty$:

$$\begin{aligned}\mathrm{Per}_p(\mathcal{A};\mathcal{V}) &= \frac{1}{p}\|\chi_\mathcal{A}\|_{TV,p} = \frac{1}{p}\sum_{x_i\in\mathcal{V}}\|(\nabla_w\chi_\mathcal{A})(x_i)\|_p, 1\leq p<\infty,\\ \mathrm{Per}_\infty(\mathcal{A};\mathcal{V}) &= \|\chi_\mathcal{A}\|_{TV,\infty} = \sum_{x_i\in\mathcal{V}}\|(\nabla_w\chi_\mathcal{A})(x_i)\|_\infty, \quad p=\infty.\end{aligned} \tag{10}$$

For the novel family of total variation seminorms on graphs in (8) we can analogously introduce families of perimeters as: $\mathrm{Per}_\infty^+(\mathcal{A};\mathcal{V}) = \frac{1}{2p}\|\chi_\mathcal{A}\|_{TV,\infty}^+$, $\mathrm{Per}_\infty^-(\mathcal{A};\mathcal{V}) = \frac{1}{2p}\|\chi_\mathcal{A}\|_{TV,\infty}^-$, and for (9) we obtain $\mathrm{Per}_\infty^\pm(\mathcal{A};\mathcal{V}) = \|\chi_\mathcal{A}\|_{TV,\infty}^\pm$.

2.2 The Coarea Formula and Total Variation Denoising

Based on the introduced families of perimeters of subsets of vertices above we can formulate the minimal surface problem (1) for a weighted graph $\mathcal{G}$ as follows:

For a fixed $\lambda>0$ and $z\in\mathbb{R}$ find a minimizing set of vertices $\mathcal{A}\subset\mathcal{V}$ of

$$E(\mathcal{A}) = \mathrm{Per}(\mathcal{A};\mathcal{V}) + \lambda \sum_{x_i\in\mathcal{A}} z - g(x_i), \tag{11}$$

for which $\mathrm{Per}(\mathcal{A};\mathcal{V})$ is one of the perimeters introduced in Section 2.1. Equivalently, the minimization problem (11) can be reformulated in terms of the characteristic function $\chi_\mathcal{A}$ of the subset $\mathcal{A}$ as:

For a fixed $\lambda>0$ and $z\in\mathbb{R}$ find an optimal function $\chi_\mathcal{A}\in\mathcal{I}(\mathcal{V})$ of

$$E(\chi_\mathcal{A}) = \|\chi_\mathcal{A}\|_{TV} + \lambda \sum_{x_i\in\mathcal{V}} \chi_\mathcal{A}(x_i)(z-g(x_i)), \tag{12}$$

for which $\|\cdot\|_{TV}$ is one of the total variation seminorms on graphs introduced in Section 2.1 and $\mathcal{I}(\mathcal{V})\subset\mathcal{H}(\mathcal{V})$ is the subset of indicator functions, which only take the values 0 and 1. As gets clear, the minimization problem (12) (and thus also (11)) is nonconvex, as the admissible set of functions in $\mathcal{I}(\mathcal{V})$ is nonconvex [8]. There exist different approaches to solve the discrete minimal surface problem. One popular approach is known as exact convex relaxation and performs optimization on a subset of functions which are bounded by the interval $[0,1]$ and subsequently perform thresholding, see [8] for details.

However, we refrain from using this approach for two reasons. First, we want to compute minimal surface solutions on graphs which can be used for different important image processing tasks, such as filtering and segmentation. Thus, we need a framework which covers these applications in a unified manner, which is not possible with the exact convex relaxation approach discussed above. Second, the latter method gives no conclusions about uniqueness of solutions, which is a desirable property in image and data processing.

In the case of images the approach in [4] exploits a useful relationship between minimal surface problems and the well-known Rudin-Osher-Fatemi (ROF) total variation denoising problem in [17]. This relationship is based on the coarea formula. Thus, we formulate the discrete coarea formula on graphs for certain families of the discrete TV seminorms introduced in Section 2.1. Note that these relationships can also be found in [1].

Proposition 1 (Coarea formula for graphs)
Let $u \in \mathcal{H}(\mathcal{V})$ be a vertex function of a weighted graph $\mathcal{G}$. Then in cases of the discrete TV seminorms given by $p = 1$ and $* \in \{\,, +, -\}$ as in (9) the coarea formula for graphs holds:

$$||u||^*_{TV,1} = \int_{-\infty}^{\infty} ||\chi_{\{u>t\}}||^*_{TV,1} \, dt = \int_{-\infty}^{\infty} \text{Per}_1^* (\{x_i \in \mathcal{V} : u(x_i) > t\}; \mathcal{V}) \, dt \ . \quad (13)$$

Proof. The proof is based on the definition of the discrete TV seminorms in Section 2.1 and the two identities $a - b = \int_{-\infty}^{\infty} \chi_{\{b>t\}} - \chi_{\{a>t\}} \, dt$ and $\max(0, u(x_j) - u(x_i)) = -\min(0, u(x_i) - u(x_j))$ as given in (6) for vertices $x_i, x_j \in \mathcal{V}$.

Remark 1. In the case of unweighted graphs, i.e., $w \equiv c \in \mathbb{R}$, the coarea formula (13) holds true for the discrete TV seminorm $||\cdot||_{TV,\infty}$, and also for the total variation seminorm $||\cdot||^{\pm}_{TV,\infty}$ in (9). This is of particular interest in the special case of traditional image processing with the weighting function $w \equiv \frac{1}{h^2}$.

Following [4, Prop.2.7] one can derive a useful relationship between the discrete minimal surface problem on graphs (12) and the ROF denoising problem.

Proposition 2 (Solving minimal surface problems by TV denoising)
Let $\mathcal{G}$ be a graph, $\lambda > 0$ a fixed parameter, $g \in \mathcal{H}(\mathcal{V})$, and $\hat{u} \in \mathcal{H}(\mathcal{V})$ the unique solution of the discrete ROF total variation denoising functional,

$$\min_{u \in \mathcal{H}(\mathcal{V})} \frac{\lambda}{2} ||u - g||_2^2 + ||u||_{TV} \ , \quad (14)$$

for which $||\cdot||_{TV}$ is one of the introduced discrete TV seminorms in Section 2.1 that fulfill the coarea formula in Proposition 1.

Then, for almost every $z \in \mathbb{R}$, the indicator function $\hat{\chi} \in \mathcal{H}(\mathcal{V})$ with

$$\hat{\chi}(x) = \begin{cases} 1, & \text{if } \hat{u}(x) > z \ , \\ 0, & \text{else} \ , \end{cases} \quad (15)$$

is a solution of the discrete minimal surface problem (12). In particular, for all z but a countable set, the solution is even unique.

Proof. The proof of this proposition is based on the coarea formula in Proposition 1 and follows directly the proof in [4, Prop.2.7]. □

In summary Proposition 2 states that one can obtain a unique solution of the discrete minimal surface problem by solving an associated strictly convex TV denoising problem and perform a single thresholding step afterwards. Hence, this basically reduces the solution of the minimization problem (12) (and thus also of (11)) to solving the ROF model (14) on graphs. Note that by this one can solve various important problems in image and data processing not only in a unified manner, but also very efficiently. We discuss this in the following section.

3 Algorithm

As discussed in Section 2 we can uniquely solve many important problems from data and image processing in a unified manner. For this we simply have to efficiently minimize an associated TV denoising energy on graphs. As the ROF problem in (14) is well-studied in the literature there exist various ways how to solve it. In this work we use the Chambolle-Pock (CP) primal-dual method proposed in [7] to minimize (14) since it connects different efficient minimization algorithms from the literature. Let U, V be finite-dimensional real vector spaces equipped with an inner product $\langle \cdot, \cdot \rangle$ and norm $|| \cdot || = \langle \cdot, \cdot \rangle^{1/2}$. The CP method is designed to minimize convex problems of the form:

$$\min_{u \in U} D(u) + R(Ku) , \qquad (16)$$

where in this setting $K: U \to V$ is a linear operator and D, R are convex, lower-semicon-tinuous functions. The problem in (16) is associated with a saddle-point problem given by:

$$\min_{u \in U} \max_{v \in V} \langle Ku, v \rangle + D(u) - R^*(v) , \qquad (17)$$

where R^* is the conjugate of R. To solve the saddle-point problem (17) the authors propose the following general iterative minimization scheme:

$$v^{n+1} = \text{prox}_{\sigma R^*}(v^n + \sigma K \bar{u}^n) \qquad (18a)$$

$$u^{n+1} = \text{prox}_{\tau D}(u^n - \tau K^* v^{n+1}) \qquad (18b)$$

$$\bar{u}^{n+1} = u^{n+1} + \theta(u^{n+1} - u^n) \qquad (18c)$$

In this context K^* denotes the adjoint operator of K, prox is the proximal operator with:

$$\text{prox}_f(x) = \text{argmin}_{y \in X} ||y - x||_X^2 + f(y)$$

and $\sigma, \tau, \theta > 0$ are step size parameters. The convergence of the CP algorithm in (18) is guaranteed for $\theta = 1$ and $\sigma\tau ||K||^2 < 1$. Since the ROF problem is strictly convex, using a modified version of the CP algorithm in [7] yields a convergence rate of $\mathcal{O}(1/N^2)$.

One is able to use the primal-dual CP algorithm on graphs in the setting of the minimization problem (14) if one chooses: $K = \nabla$, $D = \lambda ||. - f||_2^2$, and $R = ||.||_1$. In this setting it is reasonable to use the dual formulation of the discrete TV seminorms introduced in Section 2.1:

$$||u||_{TV} = \max_{\substack{v \in \mathcal{D}(\mathcal{V}) \\ ||v||_\infty \leq 1}} \sum_{x_i \in \mathcal{V}} \nabla_w u(x_i) v(x_i) = \max_{\substack{v \in \mathcal{D}(\mathcal{V}) \\ ||v||_\infty \leq 1}} -\sum_{x_i \in \mathcal{V}} u(x_i) \operatorname{div}_w v(x_i) , \quad (19)$$

for which $\mathcal{D}(\mathcal{E})$ is the Hilbert space of vertex functions $v \colon \mathcal{V} \to \mathbb{R}^N$ and div_w is the divergence operator given by the negative adjoint operator $-d_w^*$ in (4). Note that the condition $||v||_\infty = \max_{x_i \in \mathcal{V}} ||v(x_i)||_q \leq 1$ is based on the dual norm of the inner norm $||.||_p$ in (2) which fulfills the Hölder conjugate condition, i.e., $\frac{1}{p} + \frac{1}{q} = 1, 1 < p, q < \infty$ for which $q = \infty$ is the Hölder conjugate of $p = 1$ and vice versa. Following [7], one is able to show that the conjugate of a norm can be represented as the indicator function of its dual norm unit ball, i.e., $||.||^* = \chi_{||.||_* \leq 1}$. Furthermore, the proximal operator of a indicator function of a convex set is the respective projection onto this set, i.e., $\operatorname{prox}_{\chi_C}(x) = \operatorname{proj}_C(x)$.

In case of the discrete total variation seminorms in (7) and vertex functions $u, \bar{u} \in \mathcal{H}(\mathcal{V})$ and $v \in \mathcal{D}(\mathcal{V})$ the application of the CP primal-dual algorithm for the problem (14) thus leads to the following minimization scheme on graphs:

$$v^{n+1} = \frac{v^n + \sigma \nabla_w \bar{u}^n}{\max(1, ||v^n + \sigma \nabla_w \bar{u}^n||_q)} \quad (20a)$$

$$u^{n+1} = \frac{u^n + \tau(\operatorname{div}_w v^{n+1} + \lambda f)}{\lambda \tau + 1} \quad (20b)$$

$$\bar{u}^{n+1} = u^{n+1} + \theta(u^{n+1} - u^n) \quad (20c)$$

with the initialization $u^0 = \bar{u}^0 = f$ and $v^0 \equiv 0$.

In case of the novel discrete upwind total variation seminorms in (8) the CP algorithm is not directly applicable, since the upwind gradient operators ∇_w^+ and ∇_w^- are not linear. Following [6], one can deal with this problem by adding an additional constraint to the dual formulation of the discrete upwind total variation seminorms as follows:

$$||u||_{TV}^+ = \max_{\substack{v \in \mathcal{D}(\mathcal{V}) \\ ||v||_\infty \leq 1}} \sum_{x_i \in \mathcal{V}} \nabla_w^+ u(x_i) v(x_i) = \max_{\substack{v \in \mathcal{D}(\mathcal{V}) \\ ||v||_\infty \leq 1 \\ v_i \geq 0}} -\sum_{x_i \in \mathcal{V}} u(x_i) \operatorname{div}_w v(x_i) , \quad (21)$$

and analogously the condition $v_i \leq 0$ for the discrete upwind TV seminorm $||\cdot||_{TV}^-$. By this the convex set of possible minimizers of the dual minimization step gets restricted by an additional constraint and thus we have to adapt the projection step in (20a) of the deduced minimization scheme:

$$v^{n+1} = \frac{\max(0, v^n + \sigma \nabla_w \bar{u}^n)}{\max(1, ||\max(0, v^n + \sigma \nabla_w \bar{u}^n)||_q)} ,$$

for the case of the discrete upwind TV seminorm $||\cdot||_{TV}^+$ and for the case of $||\cdot||_{TV}^-$ one derives:

$$v^{n+1} = \frac{\min(0, v^n + \sigma \nabla_w \overline{u}^n)}{\max(1, ||\min(0, v^n + \sigma \nabla_w \overline{u}^n)||_q)}.$$

Finally, in the case of the discrete total variation seminorm $||.||_{TV,\infty}^{\pm}$ in (9) one has the following projection step:

$$v^{n+1} = \frac{\max(0, v^n + \sigma \nabla_w \overline{u}^n) + \min(0, v^n + \sigma \nabla_w \overline{u}^n)}{\max(2, ||\max(0, v^n + \sigma \nabla_w \overline{u}^n)||_1 + ||\min(0, v^n + \sigma \nabla_w \overline{u}^n)||_1)}.$$

The alternating minimization scheme (20a) is terminated after the relative change of the primal variable u falls under a certain accuracy, e.g., $\epsilon < 10^{-5}$. To finally obtain a solution of the minimal surface problem (12) one simply computes the indicator function $\chi_A = 1$ for $\hat{u}(x_i) > z$ for all $x_i \in \mathcal{V}$ and 0 else. Note that the computed solution $\hat{u}$ in fact gives a whole family of solutions of (12) since its respective level sets are minimal surface solutions for the respective value of z [5]. This is in particular intersting, as it allows to adapt the computed solution in real time, e.g., by changing the threshold value with a slider [18].

4 Results

In the following we demonstrate the universal applicability of our approach by illustrating applications from filtering and segmentation of arbitrary point cloud data. It gets clear that the proposed algorithm in Section 3 is applicable for any weighted graph and hence for a huge range of possible data, e.g., for images and meshes [11,14]. For the sake of brevity we discuss only the most complex case of arbitrary 3D point cloud data, which we took from [15]. We connect the neighborhoods of vertices using a symmetric k-nearest-neighbour (kNN) approach as described in [14]. Subsequently, we estimate the normal of the induced surface (if it is not given) in each vertex. We utilize this normal to determine an unique orientation of a patch within the tangent plane. By this we are able to average the signal values of the respective vertices which are projected into the patch cells. We compute the weight function of our graph based on the patch distance.

4.1 Filtering

For color filtering 3D point cloud data we simply solve the ROF denoising problem (14) for each color channel and thus filter the colors of the 3D points. In Figure 1 we projected a synthetic texture showing a strip pattern onto a 3D scanned vase. Subsequently, we added for each color channel Gaussian noise with mean $\mu = 0$ and standard deviation $\sigma = 40$ as shown in Figure 1a. We keep the regularization parameter fixed as $\lambda = \frac{1}{60}$ and use the isotropic ($p = 2$) discrete TV seminorm (7) to filter each color channel of the data. In this experiment we illustrate the impact of the graph construction by building a local graph

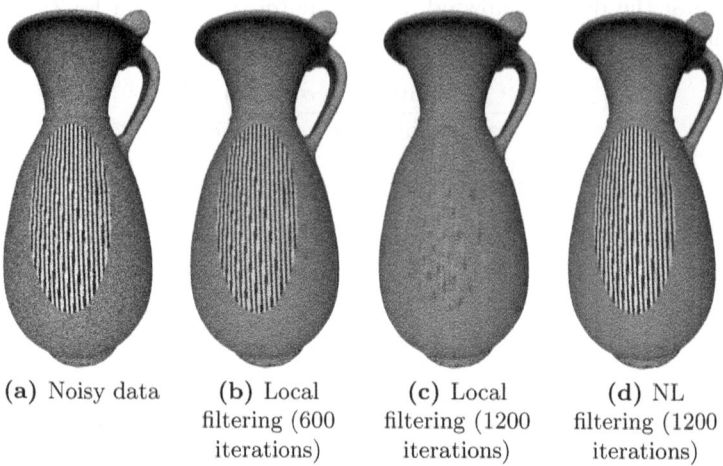

(a) Noisy data   (b) Local filtering (600 iterations)   (c) Local filtering (1200 iterations)   (d) NL filtering (1200 iterations)

Fig. 1. Results of local and nonlocal (NL) color filtering on a 3D point cloud

with a constant weight function and a nonlocal graph with a high value of k and a weight function based on the patch distance as described in [14]. Figures 1b and 1c show the result of local filtering the point cloud data for 600 and 1200 iterations, respectively. Clearly, it is unavoidable to blur the texture in order to suppress the impact of noise on the whole data. However, constructing a nonlocal graph enables us to remove the noise from the background while preserving the texture. The second application of the proposed algorithm is geometric filtering of 3D point cloud data. Figure 2a shows a scanned human face with lots of misplaced points, which can be interpreted as geometric noise. We use the same parameters as above but instead of the color information of each vertex we filter their geometric coordinates as described in [14]. We compare the results of TV denoising using the normal and the newly proposed family of discrete TV seminorms based on the upwind gradient in (8) in Figures 2b and 2c, respectively. Although the effect is only small, one can see that the upwind gradient gives smoother surfaces without loosing too much details of the face.

4.2 Segmentation

Finally, we perform segmentation of 3D point cloud data based on different features by using the Chan-Vese segmentation approach in [8] as discussed in Section 1.1. On the first data set of a scanned vase in Figure 3a we add several elliptic forms with a strip texture. We use the local standard deviation within the estimated patches as a scalar descriptor to perform binary segmentation of the surface. By using the grayscale values of the vertices directly we would not get the wanted segmentation result, as the background intensity lies between the grayscale values of the texture. In Figure 3b we show results for a mug surface with an color image of flowers after binary segmentation of the red color channel.

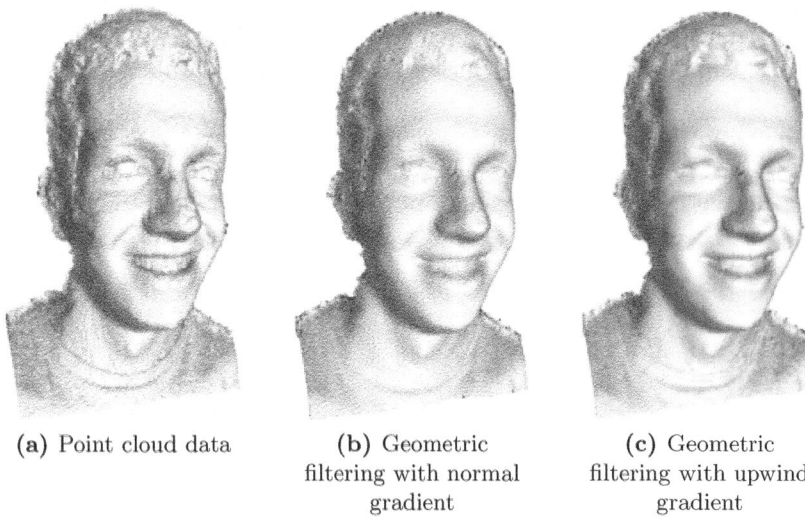

(a) Point cloud data (b) Geometric filtering with normal gradient (c) Geometric filtering with upwind gradient

Fig. 2. Geometric filtering on 3D point cloud data

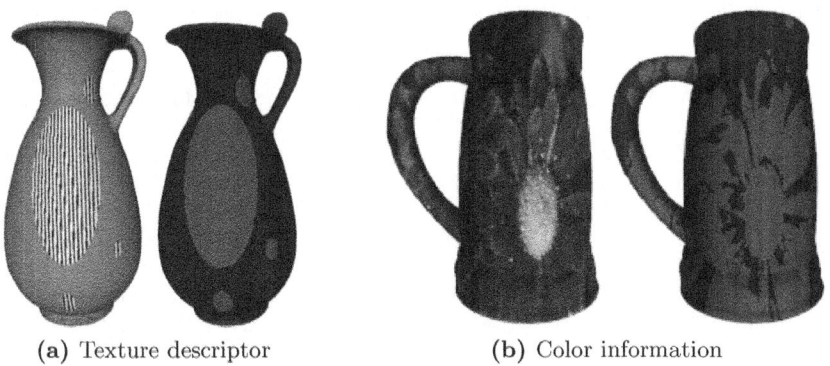

(a) Texture descriptor (b) Color information

Fig. 3. Segmentation of two 3D point clouds using different features

5 Discussion

In this work we investigated an approach of solving minimal surface problems for arbitrary surfaces such as meshes and point cloud data via an relatively simple approach using graph-based representations. By approximating differential operators by weighted finite differences we were able to formulate the minimal surface problem on graphs. Furthermore, we introduced a novel family of discrete total variation seminorms based on the upwind gradient in this context. To uniquely solve minimal surface problems on graphs we transferred the Chambolle-Pock minimization algorithm to this domain. The importance and universal applicability of this approach is illustrated by applications from filtering and segmentation of point cloud data. In future work we would like to extend the range of applications to data clustering and mean curvature flow on graphs.

Acknowledgments. DT has been supported by ERC via Grant EU FP 7 - ERC Consolidator Grant 615216 LifeInverse. This work is part of the OLOCYG project funded by the regional council of Lower-Normandy and the EU.

References

1. van Gennip, Y., Guillen, N., Osting, B., Bertozzi, A.L.: Mean Curvature, Threshold Dynamics, and Phase Field Theory on Finite Graphs. Milan Journal of Mathematics **82**(1), 3–65 (2014)
2. Bertalmio, M., Chen, L., Osher, S., Sapiro, G.: Variational Problems and Partial Differential Equations on Implicit Surfaces. J. Comput. Phys. **174**(2), 759–780 (2001)
3. Bobenko, A.I., Suris, Y.B.: Discrete Differential Geometry. AMS (2009)
4. Chambolle, A.: An Algorithm for Mean Curvature Motion. Interfaces and Free Boundaries **6**, 195–218 (2004)
5. Chambolle, A., Darbon, J.: On Total Variation Minimization and Surface Evolution Using Parametric Maximum Flows. IJCV **84**, 288–307 (2009)
6. Chambolle, A., Levine, S.E., Lucier, B.J.: An Upwind Finite-Difference Method for Total Variation-Based Image Smoothing. SIAM J. Imaging Sciences **4**(1), 277–299 (2011)
7. Chambolle, A., Pock, T.: A First-Order Primal-Dual Algorithm for Convex Problems with Applications to Imaging. JMIV **40**(1), 120–145 (2011)
8. Chan, T.F., Esedoglu, S., Nikolova, M.: Algorithms for Finding Global Minimizers of Image Segmentation and Denoising Models. SIAM J. Appl. Math. **66**(5), 1632–1648 (2006)
9. Dierkes, U., Hildebrandt, S., Kuester, A., Wohlrab, O.: Minimal Surfaces. Springer (1992)
10. Dhatt, G., Touzot, G., Lefrançois, E.: Finite Element Method. Wiley (2012)
11. Elmoataz, A., Lezoray, O., Bougleux, S.: Nonlocal Discrete Regularization on Weighted Graphs: A Framework for Image and Manifold Processing. IEEE TIP **17**(7), 1047–1060 (2008)
12. Grady, L., Polimeni, J.: Discrete Calculus: Applied Analysis on Graphs for Computational Science. Springer (2010)
13. Lai, R., Chan, T.F.: A Framework for Intrinsic Image Processing on Surfaces. Comput. Vis. Image Und. **115**(12), 1647–1661 (2011)
14. Lozes, F., Elmoataz, A., Lezoray, O.: Partial Difference Operators on Weighted Graphs for Image Processing on Surfaces and Point Clouds. IEEE TIP **23**(9), 3896–3909 (2014)
15. Lozes, F.: Public Point Cloud Data Sets. https://lozes.users.greyc.fr/ (2014)
16. März, T., Macdonald, C.B.: Calculus on Surfaces with General Closest Point Functions. SIAM J. Numer. Anal. **50**(6), 3303–3328 (2012)
17. Rudin, L.I., Osher, S., Fatemi, E.: Nonlinear Total Variation Based Noise Removal Algorithms. Physica D: Nonlinear Phenomena **60**, 259–268 (1992)
18. Tenbrinck, D., Jiang, X.: Image Segmentation with Arbitrary Noise Models by Solving Minimal Surface Problems. Pattern Recognition (in press 2015). doi:10.1016/j.patcog.2015.01.006

Data-Driven Sub-Riemannian Geodesics in SE(2)

E.J. Bekkers[2], R. Duits[1,2](✉), A. Mashtakov[2], and G.R. Sanguinetti[1](✉)

[1] Department of Mathematics and Computer Science,
Eindhoven University of Technology, Eindhoven, The Netherlands
G.R.Sanguinetti@tue.nl
[2] Department of Biomedical Engineering,
Eindhoven University of Technology, Eindhoven, The Netherlands
{E.J.Bekkers,R.Duits,A.Mashtakov,G.R.Sanguinetti}@tue.nl

Abstract. We present a new flexible wavefront propagation algorithm for the boundary value problem for sub-Riemannian (SR) geodesics in the roto-translation group $SE(2) = \mathbb{R}^2 \rtimes S^1$ with a metric tensor depending on a smooth external cost $\mathcal{C} : SE(2) \to [\delta, 1]$, $\delta > 0$, computed from image data. The method consists of a first step where geodesically equidistant surfaces are computed as a viscosity solution of a Hamilton-Jacobi-Bellman (HJB) system derived via Pontryagin's Maximum Principle (PMP). Subsequent backward integration, again relying on PMP, gives the SR-geodesics. We show that our method produces geodesically equidistant surfaces. For $\mathcal{C} = 1$ we show that our method produces the global minimizers, and comparison with exact solutions shows a remarkable accuracy of the SR-spheres/geodesics. Finally, trackings in synthetic and retinal images show the potential of including the SR-geometry.

Keywords: Roto-translation group · Hamilton-Jacobi equations · Vessel tracking · Sub-riemannian geometry · Morphological scale spaces

1 Introduction

In computer vision, a strategy to address the problem of salient curve extraction is the notion of geodesics or minimal paths where some cost function is considered over the image domain such that it has a low value on locations with high curve saliency. The minimizing geodesic is defined as the curve that minimizes the length of the curve weighted by the cost function. To compute data-adaptive geodesics many authors use a two step approach in which firstly a geodesic distance map to a source is computed and then steepest descent on the map

---

E.J. Bekkers, R. Duits, A. Mashtakov and G.R. Sanguinetti— Joint main Authors. The research leading to the results of this article has received funding from the European Research Council under the ECs 7th Framework Programme (FP7/2007 2014)/ERC grant agreement No. 335555 and from (FP7-PEOPLE-2013-ITN)/EU Marie-Curie ag. no. 607643.

gives the geodesics. In a PDE framework, the geodesic map can be obtained via wavefront propagation as the viscosity solution of a Hamilton-Jacobi equation. For a review of this approach and applications see [22,26,28].

Another set of geodesic methods, partially inspired by the psychology of vision was developed in [11,25]. Here, the roto-translation group $SE(2) = \mathbb{R}^2 \rtimes S^1$ endowed with a sub-Riemannian (SR) metric models the functional architecture of the primary visual cortex and geodesics are used for completion of occluded contours. A stable wavelet-like approach to lift 2D-images to functions on $SE(2)$ was proposed in [12]. Within the $SE(2)$ framework, images and curves are lifted to the 3D space $\mathbb{R}^2 \rtimes S^1$ of coupled positions and orientations in which intersecting curves are disentangled. The SR-structure applies a restriction to so-called horizontal curves which are the curves naturally lifted from the plane (see Fig. 1A). For explicit formulas of SR-geodesics and optimal synthesis see [27]. SR-geodesics in $SE(2)$ were also studied in [6,7,14,18,20]. Here, we propose a

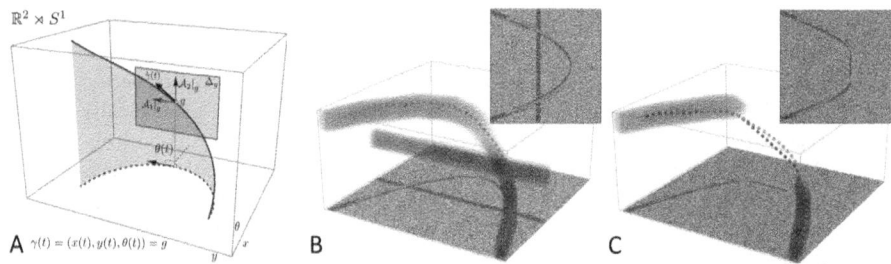

Fig. 1. A: Every point in the planar curve $\gamma_{2D}(t) = (x(t), y(t))$ is lifted to a point $g = \gamma(t) = (x(t), y(t), \theta(t)) \in SE(2)$ on an horizontal curve (solid line) by considering the direction of the tangent vector $\dot{\gamma}_{2D}(t)$ of the planar curve as the third coordinate. Then, tangent vectors $\dot{\gamma}(t) \in \text{span}\{\mathcal{A}_1|_{\gamma(t)}, \mathcal{A}_2|_{\gamma(t)}\} = \Delta|_{\gamma(t)}$, Eq. (1). **B**: In the lifted domain $SE(2)$ crossing structures are disentangled. **C**: The SR-geodesic (green) better follows the curvilinear structure along the gap than the Riemannian geodesic (red).

new wavefront propagation-based method for finding SR-geodesics within $SE(2)$ with a metric tensor depending on a smooth external cost $\mathcal{C} : SE(2) \to [\delta, 1]$, $\delta > 0$ fixed. Our solution is based on a Hamilton-Jacobi-Bellman (HJB) equation in $SE(2)$ with a SR metric including the cost. Using Pontryagin's Maximum Principle (PMP), we derive the HJB-system with an Eikonal equation providing the propagation of geodesically equidistant surfaces departing from the origin. We prove this in Thm. 1, and we show that SR-geodesics are computed by backtracking via PMP. In Thm. 2, we consider the case $\mathcal{C} = 1$ and we show that the surfaces coincide with the SR-spheres, i.e. the surfaces from which every tracked curve is globally optimal. We find a remarkable accuracy compared to exact solutions, 1st Maxwell sets, and to the cusp surface [7,14]. Potential towards applications of the method with non-uniform cost is demonstrated by performing vessel tracking in retinal images. Here the cost function is computed by lifting the images via oriented wavelets, as is explained in Section 3.1. Similar ideas of computing geodesics via wavefront propagation in the extended image domain of positions and orientations, and/or scales, have been proposed in [5,17,23]. In addition to these interesting works we propose to rely on a SR geometry. Let us illustrate some key features of our method. In Fig. 1B one can see how disentanglement of intersecting structures, due to their difference in orientations, allows to automatically deal with crossings (a similar result can be obtained with the algorithm in [23]). The extra benefit of using a SR geometry is shown in Fig. 1C where the SR-geodesic better follows the curvilinear structure along the gap.

2 Problem Formulation

The roto-translation group $SE(2)$ is equipped with the group product:
$gg' = (\mathbf{x}, R_\theta)(\mathbf{x}', R_{\theta'}) = (R_\theta \mathbf{x}' + \mathbf{x}, R_{\theta+\theta'})$, where R_θ is a counter-clockwise planar rotation over angle θ. This group can be naturally identified with the coupled space of positions and orientations $\mathbb{R}^2 \times S^1$, by identifying $R_\theta \leftrightarrow \theta$ while imposing 2π-periodicity on θ. Then for each $g \in SE(2)$ we have the left multiplication $L_g h = gh$. Via the push-forward $(L_g)_*$ of the left-multiplication we get the left-invariant vector fields $\{\mathcal{A}_1, \mathcal{A}_2, \mathcal{A}_3\}$ from the Lie-algebra basis $\{A_1, A_2, A_3\} = \{\partial_x|_e, \partial_\theta|_e, \partial_y|_e\}$ at the unity $e = (0,0,0)$:

$$\begin{aligned} \mathcal{A}_1|_g &= \cos\theta \, \partial_x|_g + \sin\theta \, \partial_y|_g = (L_g)_* \, \partial_x|_e, \\ \mathcal{A}_2|_g &= \partial_\theta|_g = (L_g)_* \, \partial_\theta|_e, \\ \mathcal{A}_3|_g &= -\sin\theta \, \partial_x|_g + \cos\theta \, \partial_y|_g = (L_g)_* \, \partial_y|_e. \end{aligned} \quad (1)$$

So all tangents $\dot\gamma(t) \in T_{\gamma(t)}(SE(2))$ along smooth curves $t \mapsto \gamma(t) \in SE(2)$ can be expanded as $\dot\gamma(t) = \sum_{k=1}^{3} u^k(t) \, \mathcal{A}_k|_{\gamma(t)}$, where the contravariant components $u^k(t)$ of the tangents (velocities) can be considered as the control variables. Not all curves $t \mapsto \gamma(t) = (x(t), y(t), \theta(t))$ in $SE(2)$ are naturally lifted from the plane in the sense that $\theta(t) = \arg(\dot x(t) + i\dot y(t))$. This only holds for so-called *horizontal curves* which have $u^3 = 0$ and thus $\dot\gamma(t) = \sum_{k=1}^{2} u^k(t) \, \mathcal{A}_k|_{\gamma(t)}$. The allowed (horizontal) directions in tangent bundle $T(SE(2))$ form a so-called distribution $\Delta := \mathrm{span}\{\mathcal{A}_1, \mathcal{A}_2\}$, see Fig. 1A.

Therefore we consider SR-manifold [21] $(SE(2), \Delta, G^\mathcal{C})$, with $G^\mathcal{C} : SE(2) \times \Delta \times \Delta \to \mathbb{R}$ denoting the inner product given by

$$G^\mathcal{C}|_{\gamma(t)}(\dot\gamma(t), \dot\gamma(t)) = \mathcal{C}^2(\gamma(t)) \left(\beta^2 |\dot x(t) \cos\theta(t) + \dot y(t) \sin\theta(t)|^2 + |\dot\theta(t)|^2 \right), \quad (2)$$

with $\gamma : \mathbb{R} \to SE(2)$ a smooth curve on $\mathbb{R}^2 \rtimes S^1$, $\beta > 0$ constant, $\mathcal{C} : SE(2) \to [\delta, 1]$ the *given external smooth cost which is bounded from below by* $\delta > 0$.

Remark 1. Define $\mathcal{L}_g \phi(h) = \phi(g^{-1}h)$ then we have:

$$G^\mathcal{C}|_\gamma(\dot\gamma, \dot\gamma) = G^{\mathcal{L}_g \mathcal{C}}|_{g\gamma} \left((L_g)_* \dot\gamma, (L_g)_* \dot\gamma \right).$$

Thus, $G^\mathcal{C}$ is not left-invariant, but if shifting the cost as well, we can, for the computation of SR-geodesics, restrict ourselves to $\gamma(0) = e$.

We study the problem of finding SR minimizers, i.e. for given boundary conditions $\gamma(0) = e, \gamma(T) = g$, we aim to find a horizontal curve $\gamma(t)$ (having $\dot\gamma \in \Delta$) that minimizes the total SR length

$$l = \int_0^T \sqrt{G^{\mathcal{C}}|_{\gamma(t)} (\dot\gamma(t), \dot\gamma(t))} dt. \tag{3}$$

If t is the SR arclength parameter, which will be our default parameter here, then $\sqrt{G^{\mathcal{C}}|_{\gamma(t)} (\dot\gamma(t), \dot\gamma(t))} = 1$ and $l = T$. Then, SR minimizers are solutions to the optimal control problem (with free $T > 0$):

$$\begin{aligned}
\dot\gamma &= u^1 \, \mathcal{A}_1|_\gamma + u^2 \, \mathcal{A}_2|_\gamma, \\
\gamma(0) &= e, \quad \gamma(T) = g, \\
l(\gamma(\cdot)) &= \int_0^T \mathcal{C}(\gamma(t)) \sqrt{\beta^2 |u^1(t)|^2 + |u^2(t)|^2} \, dt \to \min, \\
\gamma(t) &\in \mathrm{SE}(2), \quad (u^1(t), u^2(t)) \in \mathbb{R}^2, \quad \beta > 0.
\end{aligned} \tag{4}$$

Stationary curves of this problem are found via PMP [1].

Remark 2. The Cauchy-Schwarz inequality implies that the minimization problem for the SR length functional l is equivalent (see e.g. [21]) to the minimization problem for the action functional with fixed T:

$$J(\gamma) = \frac{1}{2} \int_0^T \mathcal{C}^2(\gamma(t))(\beta^2 |u^1(t)|^2 + |u^2(t)|^2) \, dt. \tag{5}$$

3 Solutions via Data-Driven Wavefront Propagation

The following theorem summarizes our method for the computation of data-adaptive sub-Riemannian geodesics in $SE(2)$, and is illustrated in Fig. 2.

Theorem 1. *Let $W^\infty(g)$ be a solution of the boundary value problem (BVP) with Eikonal-equation*

$$\begin{cases} 1 - \sqrt{(\mathcal{C}(g))^{-2} \left(\beta^{-2} |\mathcal{A}_1 W^\infty(g)|^2 + |\mathcal{A}_2 W^\infty(g)|^2\right)} = 0, & \text{for } g \neq e, \\ W^\infty(e) = 0. \end{cases} \tag{6}$$

Then the iso-contours

$$\mathcal{S}_t = \{g \in SE(2) \mid W^\infty(g) = t\} \tag{7}$$

are geodesically equidistant with speed $\frac{dt}{dt} = \mathcal{C}(\gamma(t)) \sqrt{\beta^2 |u^1(t)|^2 + |u^2(t)|^2} = 1$ and they provide a specific part of the SR-wavefronts departing from $e = (0,0,0)$. A SR-geodesic departing from $g \in SE(2)$ is found by backward integration

$$\dot\gamma_b(t) = -\frac{\mathcal{A}_1 W^\infty|_{\gamma_b(t)}}{(\beta \mathcal{C}(\gamma_b(t)))^2} \mathcal{A}_1|_{\gamma_b(t)} - \frac{\mathcal{A}_2 W^\infty|_{\gamma_b(t)}}{(\mathcal{C}(\gamma_b(t)))^2} \mathcal{A}_2|_{\gamma_b(t)}, \quad \gamma_b(0) = g. \tag{8}$$

As the proof of Thm. 1 is lengthy, we do not include its details in this conference paper. For the proof see [4]. In fact, the results on geodesically equidistant surfaces follow from connecting the Fenchel transform on Δ, to the Fenchel transform on $\mathbb{R}^2$ (Lemma 1 in [4, App. C]). Then, we derive the HJB-equation for the homogeneous Lagrangian as a limit from the HJB-equation for the squared Lagrangian (Lemma 2 in [4, App. C.1]). The back-tracking result follows from applying PMP to (5), (see [4, App. C.1]). Akin to the $\mathbb{R}^d$-case [8], characteristics are found by PMP. □

To obtain an iterative implementation to solve BVP Eq. (6), relying on viscosity solutions of initial value problems (IVP), we resort to subsequent auxiliary IVP's on $SE(2)$ for each $r \in [r_0, r_0 + \epsilon]$, with $r_0 = n\epsilon$ at step $n \in \mathbb{N} \cup \{0\}$, $\epsilon > 0$ fixed:

$$\begin{cases} \frac{\partial W^\epsilon}{\partial r}(g, r) = 1 - \sqrt{(\mathcal{C}(g))^{-2}\left(\beta^{-2}|\mathcal{A}_1 W^\epsilon(g,r)|^2 + |\mathcal{A}_2 W^\epsilon(g,r)|^2\right)}, \\ W^\epsilon(g, r_0) = W^\epsilon_{r_0}(g). \end{cases} \quad (9)$$

Here $W^\epsilon_{r_0=0} = \delta^M_e$ is the morphological delta (i.e. $\delta^M_e(g) = 0$ if $g = e$, and $\delta^M_e(g) = \infty$ if $g \neq e$). After each iteration at time-step $r = r_0$, we update $W^\epsilon(e, r_0) = W^\epsilon_{r_0}(e) = 0$. For $g \neq e$ and $n \geq 1$ we set $W^\epsilon_{r_0}(g) = W^\epsilon_{r_0-\epsilon}(g, r_0)$ (i.e. we use, only for $g \neq e$, the end condition at step n for the initial condition at step $n+1$). Then we obtain

$$W^\infty(g) = \lim_{\epsilon \to 0} \lim_{n \to \infty} W^\epsilon(g, (n+1)\epsilon). \quad (10)$$

Here we stress that, by general semigroup theory [2], *one cannot impose both the initial condition and a boundary condition $W^\epsilon(e, r) = 0$ at the same time*, which forced us to update the initial condition (at $g = e$) in our implementation scheme. It is important for optimality results below, that the solution $W^\epsilon(g, r)$ obtained from $W^\epsilon(g, r_0) = W^\epsilon_{r_0}(g)$ is the unique *viscosity* solution of (9).

The next theorem provides our main theoretical result. Recall that Maxwell points are $SE(2)$ points where two distinct geodesics with the same length meet.

Theorem 2. *Let $\mathcal{C} = 1$. Let $W^\infty(g)$ be given by (10), based on viscosity solutions of (9), solving (6). Then $\mathcal{S}_t$ equals the SR-sphere of radius t. Backward integration via (8) provides globally optimal geodesics reaching e at $t = d(g, e) :=$*

$$\min_{\substack{\gamma \in C^\infty(\mathbb{R}^+, SE(2)), T \geq 0, \\ \dot{\gamma} \in \Delta, \gamma(0) = e, \gamma(T) = g}} \int_0^T \sqrt{|\dot{\theta}(t)|^2 + \beta^2|\dot{x}(t)\cos\theta(t) + \dot{y}(t)\sin\theta(t)|^2} \, dt,$$

and $\gamma_b(t) = \gamma^{min}(d(g,e) - t)$. The SR-spheres $\mathcal{S}_t = \{g \in SE(2) \mid d(g,e) = t\}$ are non-smooth at the 1st Maxwell set $\mathcal{M}$, cf. [27],

$$\mathcal{M} \subset \left\{(x, y, \theta) \in SE(2) \mid x\cos\tfrac{\theta}{2} + y\sin\tfrac{\theta}{2} = 0 \vee \theta = \pi\right\}, \quad (11)$$

and the back-tracking (8) does not pass the 1st Maxwell set.

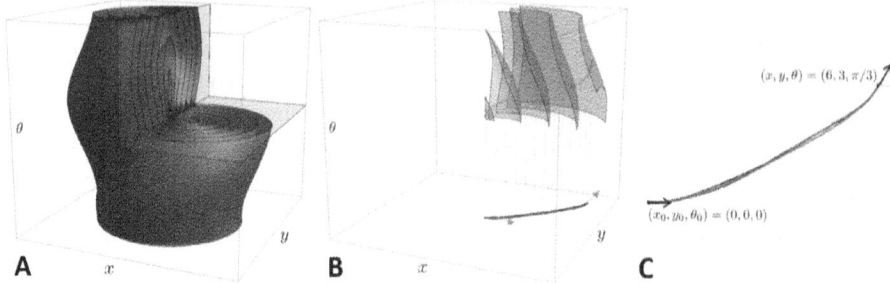

Fig. 2. A-B: Our method provides both geodesically equidistant surfaces $\mathcal{S}_t$ (7) and SR-geodesics. Geodesic equidistance holds with unit speed for all SR-geodesics passing through the surface, see Thm 1. Via Thm. 2 we have that $W^\infty(g) = d(g,e)$ and $\{\mathcal{S}_t\}_{t\geq 0}$ is the family of SR-spheres with radius t depicted in this figure. They are non-smooth at the 1st Maxwell set $\mathcal{M}$. **C**: SR-geodesic example (for $\mathcal{C} = 1$) shows our PDE-discretizations (with 12 and 64 sampled orientations in red and green resp.) are accurate in comparison to analytic approaches (black) in [14, 27].

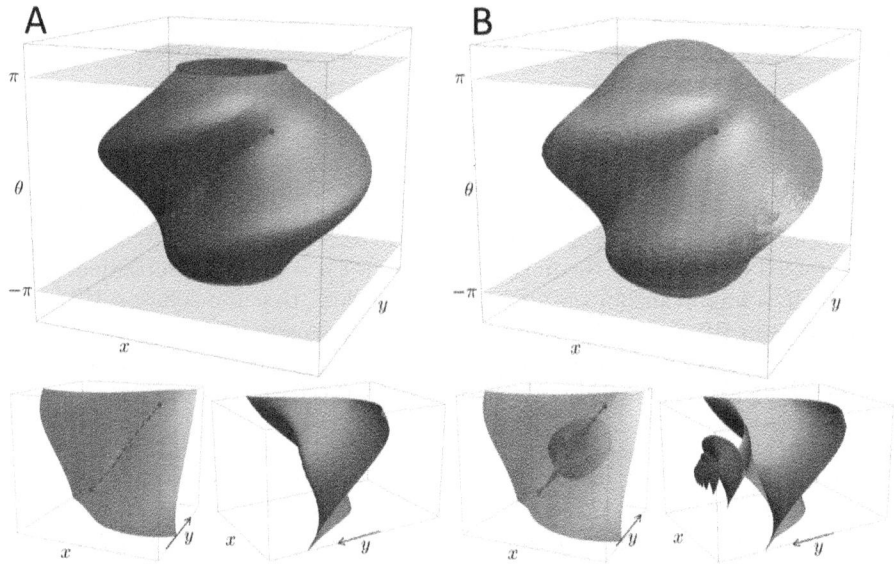

Fig. 3. A: SR-sphere $\mathcal{S}_t$ for $t = 4$ obtained by the method in Thm. 1 using $\mathcal{C} = 1$ and δ_e^M as initial condition via viscosity solutions of the HJB-equation (9) implemented according to Section 4. **B**: The full SR-wavefront departing from e via the method of characteristics giving rise to interior folds (corresponding to multiple valued non-viscosity solutions of the HJB-equation). The Maxwell set $\mathcal{M}$ consists precisely of the dashed line on $x\cos\frac{\theta}{2} + y\sin\frac{\theta}{2} = 0$ and the red circles at $|\theta| = \pi$. The dots are 2 (of the 4) conjugate points on $\mathcal{S}_t$ which are limits of 1st Maxwell points (but not Maxwell points themselves). In **B** we see the astroidal structure of the conjugate locus [10, 20]. In **A** we see that the *unique* viscosity solutions stop at the 1st Maxwell set. Comparison of **A** and **B** shows the global optimality and accuracy of our method at **A**.

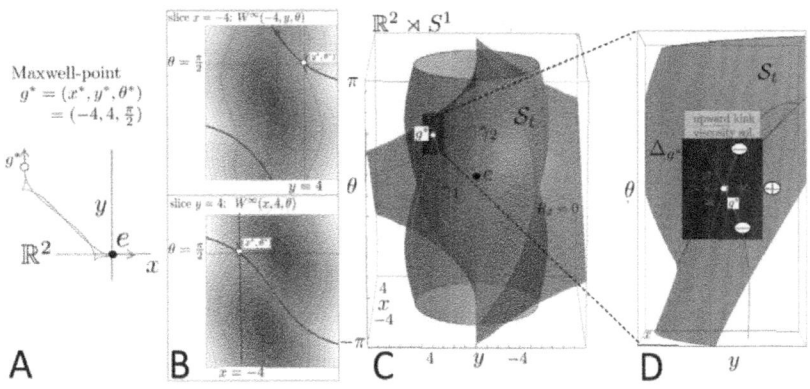

Fig. 4. Maxwell point $g^* = (-4, 4, \pi/2)$ (in white) on SR-sphere $\mathcal{S}_t$ (in orange) for $\mathcal{C} = 1$. At g^* two SR-geodesics $\gamma_1 \not\equiv \gamma_2$ with equal SR-length t meet $(\gamma_1(t) = \gamma_2(t))$. From left to right: **A**: projection of γ_1 and γ_2 on the plane (x, y), **B**: 2D-slices ($x = x^*$, $y = y^*$) of level sets of $W^\infty(g)$ with distinguished value $W^\infty(g) = t$ (again in orange). On top we plotted, the Maxwell point, the intersection of surface $x \cos \frac{\theta}{2} + y \sin \frac{\theta}{2} = 0$ (in purple, this set contains a part of the 1st Maxwell set) with the 2D-slices. **C**: The SR-sphere $\mathcal{S}_t$ in $SE(2)$, **D**: section around g^* revealing the upward kink due to the viscosity solution. From this kink we see that the tracking (8) does not cross a 1st Maxwell point as indicated in red, yielding global optimality in Thm. 2.

Proof of Thm. 2 can be found in [4, App. C.2]. The global optimality and the non-passing of the 1st Maxwell set can be observed in Fig. 3. The geometrical idea of the proof is illustrated in Fig. 4.

Remark 3. The stationary solutions of (9) satisfy the SR-Eikonal equation (6). The Hamiltonian H^{fixed} for the equivalent fixed time problem (5) equals $H^{fixed}(g, p) = (\mathcal{C}(g))^{-2} \left(\beta^{-2} h_1^2 + h_2^2 \right) = 1/2$, with momentum covector $p = h_1 \omega^1 + h_2 \omega^2 + h_3 \omega^3$ expressed in dual basis $\{\omega^i\}_{i=1}^3$ given by $\langle \omega^i, \mathcal{A}_j \rangle = \delta^i_j$. The Hamiltonian H^{free} for the free time problem (4) minimizing l equals $H^{free}(g, p) = \sqrt{2H^{fixed}(g, p)} - 1 = 0$. For details see [4, App. A and C]. Eq. (6) can be written as $H^{free}(g, p) = 0$ with momentum covector equal to $p = \sum_{i=1}^{2} (\mathcal{A}_i W^\infty) \omega^i$.

Remark 4. SR geodesics loose their optimality either at a Maxwell point or at a conjugate point (where the integrator of the canonical ODE's, mapping initial momentum p_0 and time $t > 0$ to end-point $\gamma(t)$, is degenerate [1]). Some conjugate points are limits of Maxwell points, see Fig. 4, where the 1st astroidal shaped conjugate locus coincides with the void regions (cf. [3, fig.1]) after 1st Maxwell set $\mathcal{M}$. When setting a Maxwell point as initial condition, initial gradient $dW|_{\gamma_b(0)}$ is not defined. Here there are 2 horizontal directions with minimal slope, taking these directions our algorithm produces the result in Fig. 6B.

Remark 5. The choice of our initial condition comes from the relation between linear and morphological scale spaces [2,9]. Here, for linear $SE(2)$-convolutions over the $(\cdot, +)$-algebra one has $\delta_e *_{SE(2)} U = U$. For morphological $SE(2)$-convolutions over the $(\min, +)$-algebra [14] one has a similar property:

$$(\delta_e^M \ominus U)(g) := \inf_{q \in SE(2)} \{\delta_e^M(q^{-1}g) + U(q)\} = U(g), \quad (12)$$

This is important for representing viscosity solutions of left-invariant HJB-equations on $SE(2)$ by Lax-Oleinik [15] type of formulas (akin to the $SE(3)$-case [13]).

3.1 Construction of the Non-uniform Cost

The cost should have low values on locations with high curve saliency, and high values otherwise. Based on image f we define the cost-function $\delta \leq C \leq 1$ via

$$C(\mathbf{x}, \theta) = \delta + (1-\delta)e^{-\lambda \mathcal{V}(\mathbf{x}, \theta)}, \quad \lambda > 0, \quad (13)$$

with $\mathcal{V}(\mathbf{x}, \theta) = \left|\frac{\mathcal{W}_\psi f(\mathbf{x}, \theta)}{\|\mathcal{W}_\psi f\|_\infty}\right|^p$, $p > 1$, a differentiable function in which the lines are enhanced, and where the lifting is done using anisotropic wavelets ψ:

$$(\mathcal{W}_\psi f)(\mathbf{x}, \theta) = \int_{\mathbb{R}^2} \overline{\psi(R_\theta^{-1}(\mathbf{y} - \mathbf{x}))} f(\mathbf{y}) d\mathbf{y}. \quad (14)$$

Here we take the modulus of the image lifted by (quadrature) wavelets ψ as a basic technique for the detection of curvi-linear structure. The power with exponent p after a max-normalization to $[0, 1]$ is used to sharpen the data. In this work we use so-called cake wavelets [12] to do the lifting. These wavelets have the property that they allow stable reconstruction and do not tamper data evidence before processing takes place in the $SE(2)$ domain. Other type of 2D wavelets could be used as well. In related work by Péchaud et al. [23] the cost C was obtained via normalized cross correlation with a set of templates. In Eq. (13) two parameters, δ and λ, are introduced. Parameter δ is used as a lower bound on the cost function, and may be used to increase the contrast in the cost function. E.g., by choosing $\delta = 1$ one creates a uniform cost function and by choosing $\delta < 1$ one adds more contrast. Parameter λ is used as a soft-thresholding parameter.

4 Implementation

To compute the SR geodesics with given boundary conditions we first construct the value function W^∞ in Eq. (6), implementing the iterations at Eq. (9), after which we obtain our geodesic γ via a gradient descent on W^∞ from g back to e, recall Thm. 1 (and Thm. 2). We use an iterative upwind scheme to obtain the viscosity solution W^ϵ at iteration Eq. (9). Here we initialize $W^\epsilon(\cdot, 0) = \delta_e^{MD}(\cdot)$, with the discrete morphological delta, given by $\delta^{MD}(g) = 0$ if $g = e$ and 1 if $g \neq e$, and iterate

$$\begin{cases} W^\epsilon(g, r + \Delta r) = W^\epsilon(g, r) - \Delta r \, H_D^{free}(g, dW^\epsilon(g, r)) & \text{for } g \neq e \\ W^\epsilon(e, r + \Delta r) = 0, \end{cases}$$
(15)

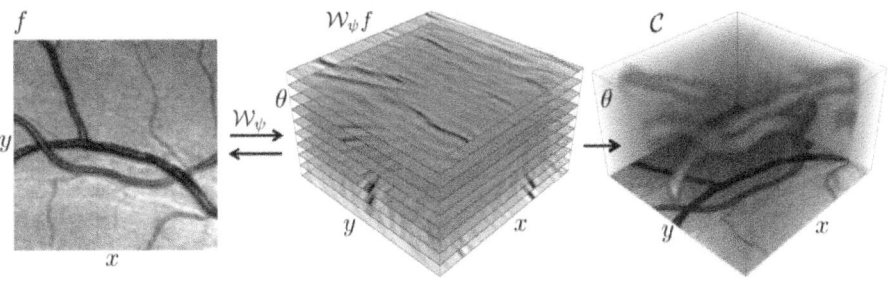

Fig. 5. Left: retinal image f and corresponding function $\mathcal{W}_\psi f$ ('invertible orientation score') using a cake-wavelet ψ [12]. The cost $\mathcal{C}$, constructed via the modulus of the score cf. (13) with $p = 3$, $\delta = 0.3$, $\lambda = 30$, yields a differentiable function.

with $H_D^{free}(g, dW^\epsilon(g,r)) = \left(\frac{1}{\mathcal{C}(g)}\sqrt{\beta^{-2}(\mathcal{A}_1 W^\epsilon(g,r))^2 + (\mathcal{A}_2 W^\epsilon(g,r))^2} - 1\right)$ until convergence. We set $\Delta r = \epsilon$ in Eq. (9). In the numerical upwind scheme we set $(\mathcal{A}_i W^\epsilon(g,r))^2 = \left(\max\left\{\mathcal{A}_i^- W^\epsilon(g,r), -\mathcal{A}_i^+ W^\epsilon(g,r), 0\right\}\right)^2$, where $\mathcal{A}_i^+$ and $\mathcal{A}_i^-$ denote respectively the forward and backward finite difference approximations of $\mathcal{A}_i$. Here finite differences applied in the moving frame, using B-spline interpolation, are favorable over finite differences in the fixed coordinate grid $\{x, y, \theta\}$. For details on left-invariant finite differences and comparisons see [16]. In our implementation the origin e is treated separately as our initial condition is not differentiable. We apply the update $W^\epsilon(e, r) = 0$ for all $r \in \epsilon \mathbb{N}$. We set step size $\epsilon = 0.1 \min(s_{xy}\beta, s_\theta)$ with s_{xy} and s_θ step sizes in respectively the x-y-directions and θ-direction.

5 Experiments and Results

5.1 Comparison and Validation $\mathcal{C} = 1$ Case

Throughout the paper we have illustrated the theory with figures obtained via our new wavefront propagation technique. In this section we go through the figures that support the accuracy of our method. As the problem (4) for $\mathcal{C} = 1$ was solved [14,27], we use this as a basis for comparison. Unless indicated otherwise, we used the implementation details as described in Section 4, and worked with a $\{x, y, \theta\}$-$121 \times 121 \times 64$ grid.

Let us consider Fig. 2C. Here an arbitrary SR-geodesic between the $SE(2)$ points $\gamma(0) = e$ and $\gamma(T) = (6, 3, \pi/3)$ is found via the initial value problem in [27] with end-time $T = 7.11$ and initial momentum $p_0 = h_1(0)\mathrm{d}x + h_2(0)\mathrm{d}y + h_3(0)\mathrm{d}\theta$, with $h_1(0) = \sqrt{1 - |h_2(0)|^2}$, $h_2(0) = 0.430$ and $h_3(0) = -0.428$, is used for reference (black curve in Fig 2C). Using the semi-analytic approach in [14] an almost identical result is obtained. The curves computed with our method with angular step-sizes of $2\pi/12$ and $2\pi/64$ are shown in Fig 2C in red and green respectively. Already at low resolution we observe accurate results.

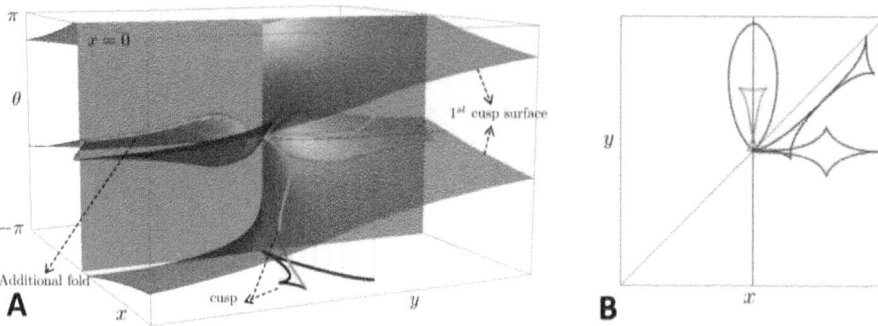

Fig. 6. A: The blue surface represents the cusp surface numerically computed via the proposed HJB-system (with $C = 1$) and subsequent calculation of the zero-crossings of $\mathcal{A}_1 W^\infty(x, y, \theta)$. Indeed if a SR-geodesic (in green) passes this surface, it passes in θ-direction (with infinite curvature [7,14]), yielding a cusp on the spatial ground plane. The same blue surface is computed in [14, Fig. 11]. We even see the additional fold (top left passing the grey-plane) as some globally optimal SR-geodesics even exhibit 2 cusps. **B**: Different configurations of projected SR-geodesics ending in Maxwell points, computed with our method.

In Fig. 3 we compare one SR-sphere for $T = 4$ (Fig. 3A) found via our method with the full SR-wavefront departing from e (Fig. 3B) computed by the method of characteristics [27]. We observe that our solution is non-smooth at the 1st Maxwell set $\mathcal{M}$ (11) and that the unique viscosity solution stops precisely there. Finally, the blue surface in Fig. 6A represents the cusp surface, i.e. the surface consisting of all cusp points. Cusps are singularities that can occur on geodesics when they are projected into the image plane (see Fig. 6A). This happens at points g_c where the geodesic is tangent to the vector $\partial_\theta|_{g_c} = \mathcal{A}_2|_{g_c}$ and this implies that the control u_1 vanishes. Then, the cusp surface is easily computed as the zero-crossing of $\mathcal{A}_1 W^\infty(x, y, \theta)$. The obtained surface is in agreement with the exact cusp surface given in [14, Fig. 11].

5.2 Feasibility Study for Application in Retinal Imaging

As a feasibility study for the application of our method in retinal images we tested the method on three image patches exhibiting both crossings and bifurcations (Fig. 7). For each patch two seed points were selected manually, one for an artery (red) and one for a vein (blue). For each seed point the value function W was calculated according to the implementation details in Section 4, after which multiple end-points were traced back to the seed point. The image dimensions were respectively 200×200, 125×125 and 125×125. For the construction of the cost function we set $p = 3$, $\delta = 0.3$, $\beta = 0.1$, $\lambda = 30$ (see e.g. Fig. 5), and the lifting was done using cake wavelets with angular resolution $2\pi/32$.

In Fig. 7 we see that all selected end-points were traced back correctly, and that the tracks smoothly follow the actual vessels. We note here that our

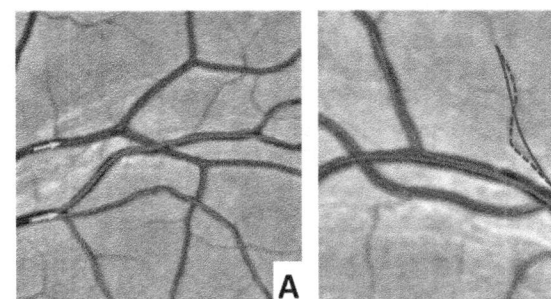
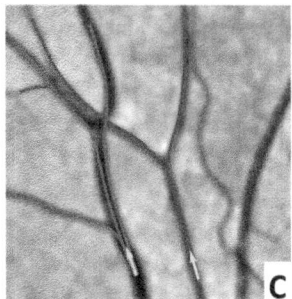

Fig. 7. Data-adaptive sub-Riemannian geodesics obtained via our proposed tracking method (Thm. 2), with external cost (13), with $p = 3$, $\delta = 0.3$, $\beta = 0.1$, $\lambda = 30$. The dashed, dark-red, curve indicates results obtained with $\beta = .5$.

sub-Riemannian approach enforces smoothness, and that flexibility is controlled via parameter β. This is a convenient property as it increases robustness to noise, missing data and complex crossing structures. However, it might not be wise to set the β parameter globally, as we did in these experiments, since smaller vessels are typically more tortuous and therefore require more flexibility. To demonstrate the effect of a larger value for β we retraced the small and low-contrast blood vessel in Fig. 7B (see dashed dark-red curve) with $\beta = .5$ and see that it now more accurately follows the true vessel curve. In this study, we do not focus on the precise centerline extraction, this could however be achieved by considering the vessel width as an extra feature (as in [5, 17, 23]).

6 Conclusion

In this paper we propose a novel, flexible and accurate numerical method for computing solutions to the optimal control problem (4), i.e. finding SR-geodesics in $SE(2)$ with non-uniform cost. The method consists of a wavefront propagation of geodesically equidistant surfaces computed via the viscosity solution of a HJB-system in $(SE(2), \Delta, G^{\mathcal{C}})$, and subsequent backwards integration, which gives the optimal tracks. We used PMP to derive both the HJB-equation and the backtracking. We have shown global optimality for the uniform case ($\mathcal{C} = 1$) and that our method generates geodesically equidistant surfaces. Compared to previous works regarding SR-geodesics in $(SE(2), \Delta, G^1)$ [14, 18, 27], we solve the boundary value problem without shooting techniques, using a computational method that always provides the optimal solution. Compared with wavefront propagation methods on the extended domain of positions and orientations in image analysis [23, 24], we consider a sub-Riemannian metric instead of a Riemannian metric. Results in retinal vessel tracking are promising.

Fast, efficient implementation using ordered upwind schemes (such as the anisotropic Fast Marching method presented in [19]) is planned as future work as well as adaptation to other Lie groups such as $SE(3)$ and $SO(3)$. Of particular interest in neuroimaging is application to high angular resolution diffusion imaging (HARDI) by considering the extension to $SE(3)$ [13,24].

References

1. Agrachev, A.A., Sachkov, Y.L.: Control Theory from the Geometric Viewpoint. Springer, Heidelberg (2004)
2. Akian, M., Quadrat, J.P., Viot, M.: Bellman processes. In: 11th Int. Conf. on Analysis and Opt. Systems. LNCIS. Springer-Verlag (1994)
3. Bayen, A.M., Tomlin, C.J.: A construction procedure using characteristics for viscosity solutions of the Hamilton-Jacobi equation. In: 40th IEEE Conf. on Decision and Control, pp. 1657–1662 (2001)
4. Bekkers, E., Duits, R., Mashtakov, A., Sanguinetti, G.: A PDE approach to Data-Driven Sub-Riemannian Geodesics. Preprint on arxiv (2015)
5. Benmansour, F., Cohen, L.D.: Tubular Structure Segmentation Based on Minimal Path Method and Anisotropic Enhancement. IJCV **92**(2), 192–210 (2011)
6. Ben-Yosef, G., Ben-Shahar, O.: A tangent bundle theory for visual curve completion. PAMI **34**(7), 1263–1280 (2012)
7. Boscain, U., Duits, R., Rossi, F., Sachkov, Y.: Curve Cuspless reconstruction via sub-Riemannian geometry. ESAIM: COCV 20, pp. 748–770 (2014)
8. Bressan, A.: Viscosity Solutions of Hamilton-Jacobi Equations and Optimal Control Problems. Pennsylvania State University, Lecture Notes Dep. of Math. (2011)
9. Burgeth, B., Weickert, J.: An Explanation for the Logarithmic Connection between Linear and Morpholgical System Theory. IJCV **64**(2–3), 157–169 (2005)
10. Chakir, H., Gauthier, J.P., Kupka, I.: Small Subriemannian Balls on $\mathbb{R}^3$. JDCS **2**(3), 359–421 (1996)
11. Citti, G., Sarti, A.: A Cortical Based Model of Perceptual Completion in the Roto-Translation Space. JMIV **24**(3), 307–326 (2006)
12. Duits, R., Felsberg, M., Granlund, G., Romeny, B.H.: Image Analysis and Reconstruction using a Wavelet Transform Constructed from a Reducible Representation of the Euclidean Motion Group. IJCV **72**(1), 79–102 (2007)
13. Duits, R., Haije, T.D., Creusen, E., Ghosh, A.: Morphological and Linear Scale Spaces for Fiber Enhancement in DW-MRI. JMIV **46**(3), 326–368 (2013)
14. Duits, R., Boscain, U., Rossi, F., Sachkov, Y.: Association Fields via Cuspless Sub-Riemannian Geodesics in SE(2). JMIV **49**(2), 384–417 (2014)
15. Evans, L.C.: Partial Differential Equations. Graduate Studies in Mathematics, vol. 19. AMS, Providence (USA) (1998)
16. Franken, E., Duits, R.: Crossing-Preserving Coherence-Enhancing Diffusion on Invertible Orientation Scores. IJCV **85**(3), 253–278 (2009)
17. Li, H., Yezzi, A.: Vessels as 4-d curves: Global minimal 4-d paths to extract 3-d tubular surfaces and centerlines. IEEE TMI **26**, 1213–1223 (2007)
18. Mashtakov, A.P., Ardentov, A.A., Sachkov, Y.L.: Parallel algorithm and software for image inpainting via sub-Riemannian minimizers on the group of rototranslations. Numer. Methods, Theory Appl. **6**(1), 95115 (2013)
19. Mirebeau, J.-M.: Anisotropic Fast-Marching on cartesian grids using Lattice Basis Reduction. SIAM J. Num. Anal. **52**(4), 1573 (2014)

20. Moiseev, I., Sachkov, Y.L.: Maxwell strata in sub-Riemannian problem on the group of motions of a plane. ESAIM: COCV 16, no. 2, pp. 380–399 (2010)
21. Montgomery, R.: A Tour of Subriemannian Geometries. American Mathematical Society, Their Geodesics and Applications (2002)
22. Osher, S., Fedkiw, R.P.: Level set methods and dynamic implicit surfaces. Applied mathematical science. Springer, New York (2003)
23. Péchaud, M., Peyré, G., Keriven, R.: Extraction of Tubular Structures over an Orientation Domain. In: Proc. IEEE Conf. CVPR, pp. 336–343 (2009)
24. Péchaud, M., Descoteaux, M., Keriven, R.: Brain connectivity using geodesics in HARDI. In: Yang, G.Z., Hawkes, D., Rueckert, D., Noble, A., Taylor, C. (eds.) Medical Image Computing and Computer-Assisted Intervention - MICCAI 2009. LNCS, vol. 5762, pp. 482–489. Springer, Heidelberg (2009)
25. Petitot, J.: The neurogeometry of pinwheels as a sub-Riemannian contact structure. J. Physiol., Paris 97, 265–309 (2003)
26. Peyré, G., Péchaud, M., Keriven, R., Cohen, L.D.: Geodesic methods in computer vision and graphics. Found Trends Comp in Computer Graphics and Vision **5**(34), 197–397 (2010)
27. Sachkov, Y.L.: Conjugate and cut time in the sub-Riemannian problem on the group of motions of a plane. ESAIM: COCV **16**(4), 1018–1039 (2009)
28. Sethian, J.A.: Level Set Methods and Fast Marching Methods. Cambridge University Press (1999)

Optimization Theory and Methods in Imaging

A Sparse Algorithm for Dense Optimal Transport

Bernhard Schmitzer(✉)

CEREMADE, Université Paris-Dauphine, Paris, France
schmitzer@ceremade.dauphine.fr

Abstract. Discrete optimal transport solvers do not scale well on dense large problems since they do not explicitly exploit the geometric structure of the cost function. In analogy to continuous optimal transport we provide a framework to verify global optimality of a discrete transport plan locally. This allows construction of a new sparse algorithm to solve large dense problems by considering a sequence of sparse problems instead. Any existing discrete solver can be used as internal black-box. The case of noisy squared Euclidean distance is explicitly detailed. We observe a significant reduction of run-time and memory requirements.

1 Introduction and Related Work

Optimal transport is a powerful and popular tool in image analysis, computer vision and statistics (e.g. [13,14,17]). However it is computationally more involved as 'simple' similarity measures such as L^p-distances or the Kullback-Leibler divergence. Consequently there is a necessity for efficient solvers.

Broadly speaking there are two classes of solvers: There are discrete combinatorial algorithms such as the Hungarian method [11], the auction algorithm [4], the network simplex [2] and more (e.g. [9]). They work for (almost) arbitrary cost functions, and are typically numerically robust w.r.t. input data regularity. They do not scale well for large, dense problems however, because the geometric structure of the cost function is not used. Alternatively, there are continuous solvers, based on the elegant theory of the 2-Wasserstein space on $\mathbb{R}^n$ [6,10]. These need not handle the full product space, but work directly with a transport map and so can solve large problems more efficiently. But they only apply to a restricted family of cost functions (most prominently squared Euclidean distance) and they are numerically more subtle (e.g. involving the Jacobian of the transport map), thus requiring some data regularity. The celebrated fluid-dynamics formulation [3] is more flexible but at the cost of introducing a time dimension. Moreover, there is a wide range of approximate methods: cost function thresholding [13], tangent space approximation [17] and entropy smoothing [7] among others.

In [12] and [15] computation time is reduced via multi-scale schemes: first solve a coarse approximate problem and then go to increasingly finer resolutions. However, [12] is limited strictly to the case of squared Euclidean distance and [15] only uses the cost function structure implicitly by keeping the problem sparse by hierarchical consistency checks, requiring low-level adaptions of the algorithm.

So there still is a need for efficient discrete exact solvers, that are more flexible than the W_2-scenario (both in terms of cost function and measure regularity), but which are still able to exploit geometric structure of the cost function.

An important feature of continuous solvers is that under suitable conditions optimality of the transport can be verified by a local criterion: the transport map is the gradient of a convex function. Whereas discrete solvers must check optimality globally (e.g. all dual constraints must be verified).

Contribution and Organization. We briefly recall discrete optimal transport in Sect. 2. Then a framework for the discrete setting is designed to mimic the continuum feature of locally verifying global optimality. Locally here means that we only need to look at a sparse subset of the full product space (Sect. 3). Based on this we propose a new algorithm that globally solves the dense problem via a sequence of sparse problems (Sect. 4). We show explicitly how the algorithm can be applied to the (noisy) squared Euclidean distance on $\mathbb{R}^n$ (Sect. 5).

Key features of the proposed algorithm are: (a) It works with any discrete OT solver as internal solver. (b) Due to sparsity the iterations are fast. (c) It can benefit from smart initialization: when the initial coupling is already close to being optimal, only few iterations are needed. (d) Consequently it can be used in a multi-scale scheme, where we obtain good initial guesses for fine scales from solutions on coarse scales. (e) This yields a significant decrease in run-time and memory requirements compared to naïve solving of dense problem.

Numerical examples are given in Sect. 6. We report a speed-up of one order of magnitude on state-of-the-art solver software, when simply used as black box and two orders of magnitude for the Hungarian method with smart re-initialization. This was observed both on smooth as well as locally concentrated measures, thus indicating a wide range of practical applicability. Hence, the algorithm can be used when the noisy cost function or irregular marginals cannot be handled by continuous solvers but when naïve combinatorial algorithms are too slow.

2 Background on Optimal Transport

Notation. For a discrete finite set A we write $|A|$ for its cardinality. Denote by $\mathcal{M}(A)$ the space of non-negative measures over A. For a measure $\mu \in \mathcal{M}(A)$ its support is defined by $\operatorname{spt} \mu = \{a \in A \colon \mu(a) > 0\}$. The space of real functions over A is identified with $\mathbb{R}^{|A|}$ where we index the components by elements of A. For a map $f \colon A \to B$ and a measure $\mu \in \mathcal{M}(A)$ we denote by $f_\sharp \mu \in \mathcal{M}(B)$ the *push-forward* of μ given by $f_\sharp \mu(\sigma) = \mu(f^{-1}(\sigma))$ for $\sigma \subset B$.

Discrete Optimal Transport. For two discrete finite sets X, Y and two non-negative measures $\mu \in \mathcal{M}(X)$, $\nu \in \mathcal{M}(Y)$ with equal total mass $\mu(X) = \nu(Y)$ the set of couplings is given by

$$\Pi(\mu,\nu) = \{\pi \in \mathcal{M}(X \times Y) \colon \pi(\{x\} \times Y) = \mu(x),\ \pi(X \times \{y\}) = \nu(y)\ \forall\, x, y\} \quad (2.1)$$

For a cost function $c: X \times Y \to \mathbb{R} \cup \{\infty\}$ the optimal transport problem consists of finding the coupling with minimal total transport cost:

$$\min_{\pi \in \Pi(\mu,\nu)} C(\pi) \quad \text{with} \quad C(\pi) = \sum_{(x,y) \in X \times Y} c(x,y)\, \pi(x,y) \qquad (2.2)$$

The problem is called feasible if its optimal value is finite. We call (2.2) the *dense* or *full problem*. For some $N \subset X \times Y$ we also consider problem (2.2) subject to the additional constraint $\operatorname{spt} \pi \subset N$, which we call the problem *restricted to N*. We call N a *neighbourhood*. And we will call π a local optimizer w.r.t. N if it solves the corresponding restricted problem.

The dual problem to (2.2) is given by

$$\max_{(\alpha,\beta) \in (\mathbb{R}^{|X|}, \mathbb{R}^{|Y|})} \sum_{x \in X} \alpha(x)\,\mu(x) + \sum_{y \in Y} \beta(y)\,\nu(y) \qquad (2.3a)$$

subject to $\quad \alpha(x) + \beta(y) \leq c(x,y) \quad \text{for all} \quad (x,y) \in X \times Y.$ (2.3b)

The relation between any primal and dual optimizers π and (α, β) of the same transport problem is

$$\pi(x,y) > 0 \quad \Rightarrow \quad \alpha(x) + \beta(y) = c(x,y). \qquad (2.4)$$

Restricting the primal problem to N corresponds to only enforcing the dual constraints (2.3b) on N. Analogously we speak of local dual optimizers (α, β) w.r.t N. If $(\pi, (\alpha, \beta))$ are local primal and dual optimizers and (α, β) satisfy (2.3b) on $X \times Y$, then one has found optimizers for the full problem.

One goal of this paper is to find suitable small subsets N such that the local optimizers $(\pi, (\alpha, \beta))$ w.r.t. N are also optimal for the full problem.

3 Optimal Transport and Short-Cuts

An Example for Intuition. Let μ, ν be absolutely continuous measures on $\mathbb{R}^n$ with compact convex support, let $c(x,y) = \|x - y\|^2$. Then we know that there is an optimal transport map which is the gradient of a convex function [16]. Let T be any transport map, $T_\sharp \mu = \nu$, with induced coupling $\pi = (\operatorname{id}, T)_\sharp \mu$. For simplicity let T be a homeomorphism. We want to verify optimality of T.

Let $\{U_i\}_i$ be an open covering of $\operatorname{spt} \mu$, then $\{V_i\}_i$ with $V_i = T(U_i)$ is an open covering of $\operatorname{spt} \nu$. Let $\mu|_{U_i}, \nu|_{V_i}$ be the restrictions of the measure μ to U_i and ν to V_i. Then T is a transport map between $\mu|_{U_i}$ and $\nu|_{V_i}$ for all i. If T is optimal for each restricted problem on $U_i \times V_i$ then optimality for the whole problem follows: when we know that T is the gradient of a convex function on each U_i, by convexity of $\operatorname{spt} \mu$ it follows that T is the gradient of a convex function on $\operatorname{spt} \mu$ and thus is the optimal transport map. Since the patches U_i can be made arbitrarily small, optimality of a coupling π can be verified on an arbitrary small open environment of $\operatorname{spt} \pi$ on $(\mathbb{R}^n)^2$. This is illustrated in Fig. 1 (left).

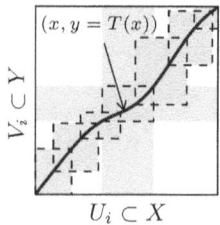 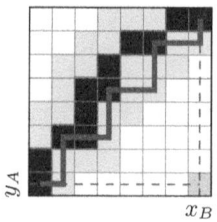

Fig. 1. *Left:* In the continuous case it suffices to check whether T is optimal on each of the sets $U_i \times V_i$. Global optimality then follows. *Right:* As a discrete analogy we introduce the concept of *short-cuts*. The dual constraint at (x_B, y_A) is implied by a sequence (solid red line) of points in spt π (blue) such that the 'jumps' lie in N (green).

The *Monge property* [5] is a simple discrete analogy in one dimension. In this paper we strive to find a discrete equivalent for higher-dimensional problems. We will return to this discussion for a brief comparison in Sect. 5. Now we introduce short-cuts, a tool to temporarily remove constraints from the dual problem.

Definition 1 (Short-Cut). *For a neighbourhood $N \subset X \times Y$ and a coupling π with spt $\pi \subset N$ let $((x_1, y_1), \ldots, (x_n, y_n))$ be an ordered tuple of pairs in spt π. We say $((x_1, y_1), \ldots, (x_n, y_n))$ is a short-cut between $(x_B, y_A) \in (X \times Y) \setminus N$ if $x_B = x_n$, $y_A = y_1$, $(x_{i+1}, y_i) \in N$ for $i = 1, \ldots, n-1$ and*

$$c(x_B, y_A) = c(x_n, y_1) \geq c(x_2, y_1) + \sum_{i=2}^{n-1} [c(x_{i+1}, y_i) - c(x_i, y_i)] . \quad (3.1)$$

Proposition 1. *For a set $N \subset X \times Y$ let $(\pi, (\alpha, \beta))$ be a pair of local primal and dual optimizers. Assume for a pair $(x_B, y_A) \notin N$ there exists a short-cut within N. Then the dual constraint (2.3b) corresponding to (x_B, y_A) is satisfied.*

Proof. Let $((x_1, y_1), \ldots, (x_n, y_n))$ be a short-cut. From (2.4) and (2.3b) restricted to N we find $\alpha(x_{i+1}) - \alpha(x_i) \leq c(x_{i+1}, y_i) - c(x_i, y_i)$ for $i = 1, \ldots, n-1$ and by summing up over i we obtain

$$\alpha(x_B) + \beta(y_A) = \alpha(x_n) + \beta(y_1) \leq c(x_2, y_1) + \sum_{i=2}^{n-1} [c(x_{i+1}, y_i) - c(x_i, y_i)] .$$

Validity of the dual constraint corresponding to (x_B, y_A) follows from (3.1). □

The concept of short-cuts is illustrated in Fig. 1 (right). Dual constraints for which a short-cut exists need no longer be checked. So is there a clever way to choose a small set N such that there is a short-cut for every $(x_B, y_A) \notin N$? But explicitly checking existence of short-cuts for each pair is far too expensive. We now introduce a simple sufficient condition for existence.

Definition 2 (Shielding Condition). *For a coupling π let $y_A \in Y$, $(x,y) \in$ spt π and $x_B \in X$. We say (x,y) shields y_A from x_B when*

$$c(x_B, y_A) - c(x_B, y) > c(x, y_A) - c(x, y). \tag{3.2}$$

The shielding condition states that $\{(x, y_A), (x_B, y)\}$ is ('strictly') c-cyclically monotone [16]. It implies that suitable n-tuples in spt π are in fact short-cuts.

Proposition 2. *For a given coupling π let $((x_1, y_1), \ldots, (x_n, y_n))$ be an ordered tuple in spt π. If $(x_{i+1}, y_i) \in N$ for $i = 1, \ldots, n-1$ and (x_{i+1}, y_{i+1}) shields y_i from x_n for $i = 1, \ldots, n-2$ then the tuple is a short-cut for (x_n, y_1).*

Proof. We need to show that (3.1) holds. For $i = 1, \ldots, n-2$ we have from (3.2)

$$c(x_n, y_i) - c(x_n, y_{i+1}) > c(x_{i+1}, y_i) - c(x_{i+1}, y_{i+1}).$$

Summing up yields $c(x_n, y_1) > \sum_{i=2}^{n-1} [c(x_i, y_{i-1}) - c(x_i, y_i)] + c(x_n, y_{n-1})$. □

We now introduce a sufficient condition for a set N such that short-cuts exist for all $(x_B, y_A) \notin N$ and an algorithm for construction.

Definition 3 (Shielding Neighbourhood). *For a given coupling π we say that a neighbourhood $N \subset X \times Y$, $N \supset$ spt π is shielding if for every $y_A \in Y$ and any $x_B \in X$ at least one of the following is true:*

(i) $(x_B, y_A) \in N$.
(ii) *There exists some $(x, y) \in$ spt π with $(x, y_A) \in N$ such that (x, y) shields y_A from x_B.*

Algorithm 1. *For a neighbourhood N let $(\pi, (\alpha, \beta))$ be the corresponding local optimizers. Assume N is shielding for π. We will construct a short-cut for a given pair $(x_B, y_A) \notin N$. Set $n \leftarrow 1$, $y_1 \leftarrow y_A$ and choose some x_1 such that $(x_1, y_1) \in$ spt π. Then iterate:*
  while $(x_B, y_n) \notin N$:
    find $(x_{n+1}, y_{n+1}) \in$ spt π with $(x_{n+1}, y_n) \in N$ such that
    (x_{n+1}, y_{n+1}) shields y_n from x_B; $n \leftarrow n+1$
  end while
  $x_{n+1} \leftarrow x_B$; pick some y_{n+1} such that $(x_{n+1}, y_{n+1}) \in$ spt π; $n \leftarrow n+1$

Proposition 3 (Existence of Short-Cuts). *Under the stated requirements Algorithm 1 terminates and produces a valid short-cut for any pair $(x_B, y_A) \notin N$.*

Proof. By virtue of Definition 3 one always finds either $(x_B, y_n) \in N$ or there exists a suitable shielding (x_{n+1}, y_{n+1}). Since the number of elements in spt π is finite, either the iteration must eventually terminate, or a cycle occurs. The existence of cycles along which the shielding condition holds is ruled out by (2.3b) and (2.4). Consequently the algorithm terminates. Then Proposition 2 provides that $((x_1, y_1), \ldots, (x_n, y_n))$ is a short-cut for (x_B, y_A). □

Remark 1. Note that the strict inequality in (3.2) is merely required to guarantee termination of Algorithm 1. Proposition 2 already follows from $\geq$ in (3.2).

Running Algorithm 1 is immensely more expensive than checking the corresponding dual constraint. We rely on Proposition 3 which directly implies existence of short-cuts and thus validity of constraints outside of N. We summarize:

Corollary 1 (Global Optimality from Local Optimality). *Let $(\pi, (\alpha, \beta))$ be local optimizers w.r.t. a neighbourhood N and let N be shielding for π. Then $(\pi, (\alpha, \beta))$ are optimizers of the dense problem.*

Remark 2. A primal local optimizer π w.r.t. N suffices for Corollary 1 to hold as shielding of N only depends on π. Results hold for any matching local dual optimizers (α, β). Explicitly knowing dual variables allows for verifying local optimality by checking the dual constraints.

4 A Sparse Algorithm

Corollary 1 can be used to construct an efficient sparse algorithm for large OT problems. The main ingredients of the algorithm are two maps:

(i) $F : N \mapsto \pi$ such that $F(N)$ is locally optimal w.r.t. N. When N is sparse, any discrete OT solver can quickly provide an answer. Given Remark 2 we see that also purely primal solvers suffice.

(ii) $G : \pi \mapsto N$ such that $G(\pi)$ is shielding for π. It is important for efficiency that $G(\pi)$ is sparse. To design such a map one must use the geometric structure of the cost function. In Sect. 5 we discuss the squared Euclidean distance.

Corollary 1 entails a 'chicken and egg'-problem: For a given N_1 let $\pi_1 = F(N_1)$. But if π_1 is not globally optimal, then N_1 cannot be shielding w.r.t. π_1. Conversely, for some π_1 let $N_2 = G(\pi_1)$, but π_1 will only be locally optimal w.r.t. N_2 iff it is globally optimal. To find a configuration (N, π) such that both criteria are satisfied simultaneously, one can iterate both maps.

Algorithm 2. *For an initial N_1 set $k = 1$ and run:*
```
do:
    π_{k+1} ← F(N_k);  N_{k+1} ← G(π_{k+1});  k ← k+1
until C(π_k) = C(π_{k-1})
```

Proposition 4. *For a feasible initial N_1 Algorithm 2 terminates after a finite number of steps with a globally optimal π_k.*

Proof. For $k > 1$ have $N_k = G(\pi_k)$ and $\pi_{k+1} = F(N_k)$. So $\mathrm{spt}\,\pi_k \subset N_k$ and therefore π_k is feasible when computing the optimal π_{k+1}, restricted to N_k. It follows $C(\pi_{k+1}) \leq C(\pi_k)$. One can see that after a finite number of iterations one must find $C(\pi_k) = C(\pi_{k+1})$. Then π_k is optimal w.r.t. N_k and by construction N_k is a shielding w.r.t. π_k. Therefore π_k and π_{k+1} are globally optimal.

The usefulness of this algorithm will be demonstrated numerically in Sect. 6. Important advantageous properties are:

(i) The solver F must only be applied to sparse problems, thus calling F will be quite fast, if a suitable function G is known.
(ii) In fact we will demonstrate in next section how G can be designed for squared Euclidean distance and extensions thereof, to quickly provide sparse sets N.
(iii) When a good initial coupling π_1 is known, the algorithm will only need few iterations. This is ideal for working in a multi-scale scheme, where an initial guess for π_1 or N_1 can be generated from a coarser version of the problem.

5 Squared Euclidean Distance

The Shielding Condition on $\mathbb{R}^n$. So far everything has been formulated for general cost functions. To run Algorithm 2 we need a function G that quickly generates a sparse shielding neighbourhood N for a given coupling π. For this we must exploit the particular geometric structure of the cost function. We now explicitly show how to do this for the squared Euclidean distance and noise.

For now assume $X, Y \subset \mathbb{R}^n$ and $c(x,y) = \|x - y\|^2$. Then the shielding condition (3.2) for some triple $y_A \in Y$, $(x,y) \in \operatorname{spt}\pi$, $x_B \in X$ is equivalent to

$$\langle x_B - x, y - y_A \rangle > 0. \tag{5.1}$$

This equation has a simple geometric interpretation: consider the hyperplane through x, normal to $y - y_A$. Then x_B must lie on the side facing in direction $y - y_A$. So (x,y) shields y_A from all potential x_B beyond this hyperplane. This provides us with a recipe for constructing shielding neighbourhoods:

$N \leftarrow \operatorname{spt}\pi$
for every $y_A \in Y$:
    find a set $\{(x_i, y_i)\}_i \subset \operatorname{spt}\pi$ such that the hyperplanes with
    normals $y_i - y_A$ through x_i form a small polytope $P \subset \mathbb{R}^n$.
    add the pairs (x_i, y_A) to N for all i // *(step-i)*
    for all $x' \in X \cap P$: add (x', y_1) to N. // *(step-ii)*

After (step-i) y_A is shielded from all x' outside of P by at least one (x_i, y_i), after (step-ii) from all $x' \in X \cap P$. Now we discuss finding suitable polytopes P.

Regular Grids on $\mathbb{R}^2$. Assume X and Y are regular orthogonal grids. For simplicity assume $n = 2$, higher dimensions work analogously. From a coupling π one can extract a map $T_\pi : Y \to X$ with $x = T_\pi(y) \Rightarrow \pi(x,y) > 0$.

For any $y_A \in Y$ let $\{y_1, y_2, y_3, y_4\}$ be the 4-neighbourhood of y_A on the grid Y and let $x_i = T_\pi(y_i)$ for $i = 1, \ldots, 4$. The normals of the faces of the resulting polytope P are therefore $\{(1,0), (0,1), (-1,0), (0,-1)\}$ and P is a bounded rectangle, aligned with the grid. So during (step-i) of the construction of N for each $y_A \in Y$ we add four elements (x_i, y_A), $i = 1, \ldots, 4$ to N. During (step-ii) we add

(x', y_A) for all $x' \in X \cap P$. Both the 4-neighbourhood of y_A and elements of the interior of P can be accessed in $\mathcal{O}(1)$ by using the grid structure on X and Y.

Provided some auxiliary data structures the scheme can be extended to more general point clouds, this is however beyond the scope of this paper.

Complexity. The critical components for the complexity of Algorithm 2 are: complexity characteristics of the internal solver F, sizes of neighbourhoods $\{N_k\}_k$ and the number of outer iterations. The latter two depend on the initial choice of N_1. A rigorous analysis of this dependency is beyond the scope of this paper. But beyond the empirically observed speed-up (Sect. 6) we can provide some intuition on the algorithm's behaviour: Given a spatially regular π (nearby x assign mass to nearby y), the points x_i are close and therefore P will have a small area (in particular $\mathcal{O}(1)$ w.r.t. $|X|$ and $|Y|$) and only few elements are added during (step-ii). So the resulting N will indeed be sparse, $|N| = \mathcal{O}(|Y|)$. This scaling will be confirmed numerically for the multi-scale initialization scheme that we chose (Sect. 6). We will even find $\sum_k |N_k| = \mathcal{O}(|X|)$, i.e. the sum of the neighbourhood-sizes over all iterations of Algorithm 2, still scales better than for the dense problem where $N = X \times Y$. Since the internal solver complexity is super-linear in $|N_k|$, this already implies a gain in performance.

Beyond Squared Euclidean Distance. Now consider a more general cost function:

$$c(x,y) = \|x - y\|^2 + \hat{c}(x,y) \quad \text{where we assume} \quad 0 \leq \hat{c}(x,y) \leq \delta \quad (5.2)$$

Such a cost function can describe a matching problem where we do not only consider geometric proximity of points x and y, but also additional descriptors attached to x and y (e.g. SIFT descriptors), whose comparison cost is given by $\hat{c}(x,y)$. Albeit useful from a modelling perspective, adding a term $\hat{c}$ to the cost function destroys the 2-Wasserstein space structure of the problem and thus solvers based on the polar factorization theorem can no longer be applied.

It is possible however to extended our method to this scenario. Consider (3.2) for this cost function. We find it is equivalent to

$$\langle x_B - x, y - y_A \rangle > \frac{1}{2} \left(\hat{c}(x, y_A) - \hat{c}(x, y) - \hat{c}(x_B, y_A) + \hat{c}(x_B, y) \right). \quad (5.3)$$

By using (5.2) we find the simpler sufficient condition $\langle x_B - x, y - y_A \rangle > \delta$. So to construct a shielding neighbourhood for such a cost function we can still apply the recipe outlined above, but all faces of P must be shifted outwards by δ to account for the fluctuations in $\hat{c}$. For each x_B within this enlarged polytope we can test via (5.3) whether (x_B, y_A) must be included into N.

Application to the Continuous Problem. We now return to the discussion in Sect. 3 and relate our new results to the continuous formulation. Given a transport map T, locally optimal on all the patches $U_i \times V_i$, let the tuple points $(x_1 = x_A, \ldots, x_n = x_B)$, $x_i \in \operatorname{spt} \mu$, be taken from a straight line between x_A and x_B in monotone order and picked fine enough such that every two successive points x_i, x_{i+1} lie in the same patch U_i. Let $y_i = T(x_i)$. It then follows that (x_{i+1}, y_{i+1}) is shielding y_i from x_n for $i = 1, \ldots, n-2$ (see (5.1) and Remark 1) and consequently the tuple $((x_1, y_1), \ldots, (x_n, y_n))$ is a short-cut for $(x_B, y_A = y_1)$. Therefore the transport map T is globally optimal.

We see that the shielding condition follows from local optimality along straight lines, which explains why local optimality is still sufficient in 1-d discrete problems. In discrete higher-dimensional problems we cannot always jump along straight lines between grid points and even small deviations may break the shielding condition. Thus we must explicitly keep track of π in Sect. 3.

6 Numerical Experiments

Algorithms and Adaptive Initialization. We test our algorithm on four discrete solvers: Our own implementation of the Hungarian method [11], the network simplex [2] implementation of CPLEX [1] and the network simplex and cost scaling [9] implementations of the LEMON library [8]. In the following we refer to these four algorithms by the short-hands HU, CPLEX, LEMON-NS and LEMON-CS.

While we expect CPLEX and LEMON-* to be faster than HU, they can only be used as black boxes, whereas we can manipulate our own implementation in more detail. In particular we can choose the initialization. This can be exploited by Algorithm 2: instead of solving each sparse problem $(\pi_{k+1}, (\alpha_{k+1}, \beta_{k+1})) \leftarrow F(N_k)$ from scratch, we initialize the algorithm using the previous optimizers $(\pi_k, (\alpha_k, \beta_k))$ as follows: We start with $\beta_{k+1,\text{init}} = \beta_k$ and $\alpha_{k+1,\text{init}}(x) = \alpha_k$ and then reduce all $\alpha_{k+1,\text{init}}$ entries where dual constraints on N_k are violated. We set $\pi_{k+1,\text{init}} = \pi_k$ and set all X-rows to zero where $\alpha_{k+1,\text{init}}$ has been reduced. When only few constraints were violated, we start with an 'almost feasible' coupling.

Test Data. As test data we used measures on regular grids in $\mathbb{R}^2$ with full support. Assuming full support is common for continuum solvers (e.g. [10]) and can be ensured by adding a small constant measure. With the exception of LEMON-CS we observed that the discrete solvers could handle very small constants and thus distortion of the problem was negligible. We test grid sizes between 30×30 and 90×90, so the cardinalities of X and Y range between 900 and 8100 and the dimensions of the full coupling-spaces between $8.1 \cdot 10^5$ and $6.6 \cdot 10^7$. The tested measures contained smoothly varying densities, strong Dirac-like local concentrations and sharp discontinuities, thus posing challenging problems (see Fig. 4 (right)) and representing a wide range of potential applications.

Multi-scale Solving. The purpose of Algorithm 2 is to accelerate solving large problems by obtaining a smart initial guess for the optimal coupling and then quickly solving a sequence of sparse problems, instead of trying to solve the dense problem directly. Similar to [12,15] we approximate the original problem by a sequence of successively coarser problems. We use a hierarchical quad-tree clustering over the grids X and Y. At any scale μ and ν are approximated by the masses of the clusters and c by the distance between the cluster centers. Then solve the problem from coarse to fine: each time we use the support of the optimal coupling as initialization for N_1 at the subsequent finer scale.

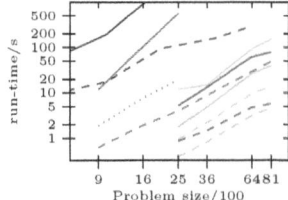 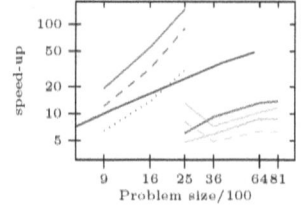 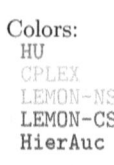

Fig. 2. Run-times and speed-up. Problem size refers to $|X| = |Y|$. Left: Run-times of naïve dense algorithms (solid lines) and Algorithm 2 with a multi-scale scheme (dashed lines). For HU: HU-STD dotted, HU-INIT dashed. Right: Relative speed-up for each algorithm. HU-STD dotted, HU-INIT solid. Dashed lines: results with noisy cost function (Sect. 5) for HU and CPLEX. We observe a huge speed-up for HU, which is even larger with adaptive initialization. But also the high-performance external solvers can be accelerated by about one order of magnitude for large problems. The speed-up tends to increase with problem size. HierAuc gives the run-times and speed-up reported in [15] for the scenario grid. The auction algorithm does not seem to perform well on this problem class and both the run-time and speed-up obtained by HU-INIT are better.

Run-times. We compare the run-times of the naïve algorithms with using them as internal solvers in Algorithm 2 combined with the multi-scale scheme. For the multi-scale timing we sum the times it takes to solve all levels, from coarse to fine. The observed run-times and the speed-up are illustrated in Fig. 2. Reported run-times were obtained on a single core of an Intel Core i5 processor at 3.2 GHz.

All solvers are sped up significantly, the ratio increasing with problem size. As expected HU is much slower than the other algorithms. But it allows to demonstrate the benefit of adaptive re-initialization over solving from scratch. Currently adaptive re-initialization for the external implementations is not available. But even by using them as black boxes one gains about one order of magnitude.

Sparsity and Number of Iterations. The demonstrated speed-up relies on the sparsity of N_k which also reduces the memory requirements of the algorithms. Our numerical findings are presented in Fig. 3. The ratio $|N_k|/|X \times Y|$ is consistently decreasing for all applied solvers and we observe $|N_k| = \mathcal{O}(|X| = |Y|)$, i.e. the number of neighbours per element in X or Y, $|N_k|/|X|$, is constant w.r.t. problem size. Even the sum of all $|N_k|$ over the iterations of Algorithm 2 is $\mathcal{O}(|Y|)$. On the test data the median number of iterations per scale with the multi-scale scheme was 4, the 95% quantile was 7 iterations, thus numerically confirming the complexity discussion in Sect. 5 and point (iii) in Sect. 4.

Fig. 4 gives an impression of the structure of N_k during the execution of Algorithm 2. We see that N_k locally adapts to the regularity of the assignment: in regular areas only very few elements in N_k are needed per element of $y \in Y$. In irregular regions the size of the neighbourhood increases, but this is only a local effect. The regular regions are not affected by this.

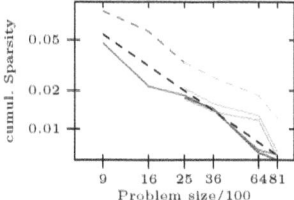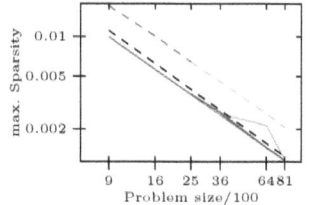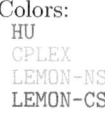

Fig. 3. Solid lines: squared Euclidean distance, dashed lines: noisy cost function. *Left:* Cumulative sparsity. The sum of all $|N_k|/(|X|\cdot|Y|)$ over iterations of Algorithm 2. *Right:* The maximum of $|N_k|/(|X|\cdot|Y|)$ during iterations. The plots illustrate that the neighbourhood construction (Sect. 5) works as intended. Comparison with $\mathcal{O}(|X|^{-1})$ (black dashed line) shows that the number of neighbours per element is $\mathcal{O}(1)$.

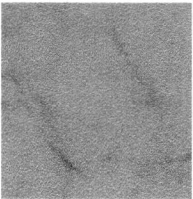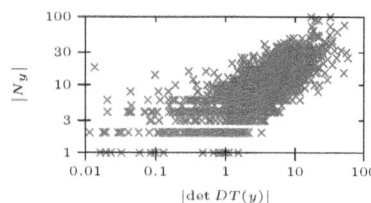

Fig. 4. Let $N_y = N_k \cap (X \times \{y\})$. *Left:* heat-map of $|N_y|$ over Y after one iteration of Algorithm 2 ($k = 2$). Green indicates $|N_y| = 1$, plain red $|N_y|/|X| \geq 1\%$. *Right:* Scatter-plot of $|N_y|$ vs. the Jacobian determinant of the average assignment map $T : Y \to X$ ($T(y)$ is averaged over X w.r.t. $\pi(y,\cdot)$). $|\det DT(y)|$ varies over 4 orders of magnitude, including both strong compression and expansion. We see that the sparsity adapts locally to the spatial regularity of the assignment. In non-expanding regions only few neighbours per element are necessary.

Noise. We also briefly studied the application of Algorithm 2 to 'noisy' Euclidean cost functions (Sect. 5). Uniform noise sampled from $[0, 5]$ was added to the clean cost function (the distance of neighbouring grid points is 1). This naturally increased the cardinality of the neighbourhoods and consequently reduced the speed-up by about a factor 0.6 (see Fig. 2). We still observe $N_k = \mathcal{O}(|X|)$ however (Fig. 3) and consequently observe better speed-up ratios at larger grid sizes.

Comparison with [15]. Fig. 2 compares the speed of the hierarchical auction algorithm (HierAuc) and our new method. HierAuc is more flexible in terms of cost functions. However, in Algorithm 2 validity of constraints outside of N is directly implied, without the need for hierarchical consistency checks. Therefore it is not restricted to the auction algorithm as internal solver and no adaptions need to be made within the solver. So it can be used with modern high-performance software, to obtain lower run-times. Also, HU-INIT yields better speed-up ratios.

7 Conclusion

Dense optimal transport problems are omnipresent. But there is a lack of efficient discrete solvers, exploiting the structure of the cost function.

Our paper provides a means of verifying global optimality of a coupling by only looking at a sparse subset of the full product space. This can be seen as discrete equivalent for well-known continuum results. We showed how to efficiently construct such sets for the squared Euclidean distance and noise. Based thereon we proposed an algorithm that solves dense problems via a sequence of sparse problems. This algorithm can be combined with coarse-to-fine multi-scale solution approaches. We demonstrated numerically the efficiency of the scheme in terms of run-time and sparsity and gave some intuition for the complexity behaviour. Our scheme thus allows the application of discrete solvers to larger problems, where continuum solvers may not be applicable either, due to noisy costs or irregular marginals with strongly fluctuating densities.

Future work will comprise a more detailed complexity analysis, adaptive re-initialization for other algorithms and studying of the shielding condition for other types of cost functions and manifolds.

Acknowledgments. The author gratefully acknowledges support by the German Science Foundation (DFG), grant GRK 1653 and a public grant overseen by the French National Research Agency (ANR) as part of the 'Investissements d'avenir', program-reference ANR-10-LABX-0098.

References

1. CPLEX. http://www.ilog.com
2. Ahuja, R.K., Magnanti, T.L., Orlin, J.B.: Network Flows: Theory, Algorithms, and Applications. Prentice-Hall Inc (1993)
3. Benamou, J.-D., Brenier, Y.: A computational fluid mechanics solution to the Monge-Kantorovich mass transfer problem. Numerische Mathematik **84**(3), 375–393 (2000)
4. Bertsekas, D.P.: A distributed algorithm for the assignment problem. Technical report, Lab. for Information and Decision Systems Report. MIT, May 1979
5. Burkhard, R.E., Klinz, B., Rudolf, R.: Perspectives of Monge properties in optimization. Discr. Appl. Math. **70**(2), 95–161 (1996)
6. Carlier, G., Galichon, A., Santambrogio, F.: From Knothe's transport to Brenier's map and a continuation method for optimal transport. SIAM J. Math. Anal. **41**, 2554–2576 (2010)
7. Cuturi, M.: Sinkhorn distances: lightspeed computation of optimal transportation distances. In: Advances in Neural Information Processing Systems 26 (NIPS), pp. 2292–2300 (2013). http://arxiv.org/abs/1306.0895
8. Dezsőa, B., Jüttnerb, A., Kovácsa, P.: LEMON – an open source C++ graph template library. In: Workshop on Generative Technologies (WGT) 2010, volume 264 of Electronic Notes in Theoretical Computer Science, pp. 23–45 (2011)
9. Goldberg, A.V., Tarjan, R.E.: Finding minimum-cost circulations by successive approximation. Math. Oper. Res. **15**(3), 430–466 (1990)

10. Haker, S., Zhu, L., Tannenbaum, A., Angenent, S.: Optimal mass transport for registration and warping. Int. J. Comp. Vision **60**, 225–240 (2004)
11. Kuhn, H.W.: The Hungarian method for the assignment problem. Naval Research Logistics **2**, 83–97 (1955)
12. Mérigot, Q.: A multiscale approach to optimal transport. Computer Graphics Forum **30**(5), 1583–1592 (2011)
13. Pele, O., Werman, W.: Fast and robust Earth Mover's Distances. In: International Conference on Computer Vision (ICCV 2009) (2009)
14. Rubner, Y., Tomasi, C., Guibas, L.J.: The earth mover's distance as a metric for image retrieval. Int. J. Comp. Vision **40**(2), 99–121 (2000)
15. Schmitzer, B., Schnörr, C.: A hierarchical approach to optimal transport. In Scale Space and Variational Methods (SSVM 2013), pp. 452–464 (2013)
16. Villani, C.: Optimal Transport: Old and New, volume 338 of Grundlehren der mathematischen Wissenschaften. Springer, Heidelberg (2009)
17. Wang, W., Slepčev, D., Basu, S., Ozolek, J.A., Rohde, G.K.: A linear optimal transportation framework for quantifying and visualizing variations in sets of images. Int. J. Comp. Vision **101**, 254–269 (2012)

Activity Identification and Local Linear Convergence of Douglas–Rachford/ADMM under Partial Smoothness

Jingwei Liang[1]([✉]), Jalal Fadili[1], Gabriel Peyré[2], and Russell Luke[3]

[1] GREYC, CNRS, ENSICAEN, Université de Caen, Caen, France
{Jingwei.Liang,Jalal.Fadili}@ensicaen.fr
[2] CNRS, Ceremade, Université Paris-Dauphine, Paris, France
Gabriel.Peyre@ceremade.dauphine.fr
[3] Institut für Numerische und Angewandte Mathematik, Universität Göttingen, Göttingen, Germany
r.luke@math.uni-goettingen.de

Abstract. Convex optimization has become ubiquitous in most quantitative disciplines of science, including variational image processing. Proximal splitting algorithms are becoming popular to solve such structured convex optimization problems. Within this class of algorithms, Douglas–Rachford (DR) and ADMM are designed to minimize the sum of two proper lower semi-continuous convex functions whose proximity operators are easy to compute. The goal of this work is to understand the local convergence behaviour of DR (resp. ADMM) when the involved functions (resp. their Legendre-Fenchel conjugates) are moreover partly smooth. More precisely, when both of the two functions (resp. their conjugates) are partly smooth relative to their respective manifolds, we show that DR (resp. ADMM) identifies these manifolds in finite time. Moreover, when these manifolds are affine or linear, we prove that DR/ADMM is locally linearly convergent with a rate in terms of the cosine of the Friedrichs angle between the tangent spaces of the identified manifolds. This is illustrated by several concrete examples and supported by numerical experiments.

Keywords: Douglas–Rachford splitting · ADMM · Partial smoothness · Finite activity identification · Local linear convergence

1 Introduction

1.1 Problem Formulation

In this work, we consider the problem of solving

$$\min_{x \in \mathbb{R}^n} J(x) + G(x), \qquad (1)$$

This work has been partly supported by the European Research Council (ERC project SIGMA-Vision). JF was partly supported by Institut Universitaire de France.

where both J and G are in $\Gamma_0(\mathbb{R}^n)$, the class of proper, lower semi-continuous (lsc) and convex functions. We assume that $\text{ri}(\text{dom}(J)) \cap \text{ri}(\text{dom}(G)) \neq \emptyset$, where $\text{ri}(C)$ is the relative interior of the nonempty convex set C, and $\text{dom}(F)$ is the domain of the function F. We also assume that the set of minimizers is non-empty, and that these two functions are simple, meaning that their respective proximity operators, $\text{prox}_{\gamma J}$ and $\text{prox}_{\gamma G}$, $\gamma > 0$, are easy to compute, either exactly or to a very good approximation. Problem (1) covers a large number of problems including those appearing in variational image processing (see Section 6).

An efficient and provably convergent algorithm to solve this class of problems is the Douglas–Rachford splitting method [16], which reads, in its relaxed form,

$$\begin{cases} v^{k+1} = \text{prox}_{\gamma G}(2x^k - z^k), \\ z^{k+1} = (1 - \lambda_k)z^k + \lambda_k(z^k + v^{k+1} - x^k), \\ x^{k+1} = \text{prox}_{\gamma J} z^{k+1}, \end{cases} \quad (2)$$

for $\gamma > 0$, $\lambda_k \in]0, 2]$ with $\sum_{k \in \mathbb{N}} \lambda_k(2 - \lambda_k) = +\infty$. The fixed-point operator B_{DR} with respect to z^k takes the form

$$B_{\text{DR}} \stackrel{\text{def.}}{=} \frac{1}{2}(\text{rprox}_{\gamma G} \circ \text{rprox}_{\gamma J} + \text{Id}),$$

$$\text{rprox}_{\gamma J} \stackrel{\text{def.}}{=} 2\text{prox}_{\gamma J} - \text{Id}, \quad \text{rprox}_{\gamma G} \stackrel{\text{def.}}{=} 2\text{prox}_{\gamma G} - \text{Id}.$$

The proximity operator of a proper lsc convex function is defined, for $\gamma > 0$, as

$$\text{prox}_{\gamma J}(z) = \text{argmin}_{x \in \mathbb{R}^n} \frac{1}{2} \|x - z\|^2 + \gamma J(x).$$

Since the set of minimizers of (1) is assumed to be non-empty, so is the $\text{Fix}(B_{\text{DR}})$ since the former is nothing but $\text{prox}_{\gamma J}(\text{Fix}(B_{\text{DR}}))$. See [3] for a more detailed account on DR in real Hilbert spaces.

Remark 1. *The DR algorithm is not symmetric w.r.t. the order of the functions J and G. Nevertheless, the convergence claims above hold true of course when this order is reversed in (2). In turn, all of our statements throughout also extend to this case with minor adaptations. Note also that the standard DR only accounts for the sum of 2 functions. But extension to more than 2 functions is straightforward through a product space trick, see Section 5 for details.*

1.2 Contributions

Based on the assumption that both J and G are partly smooth relative to smooth manifolds, we show that DR identifies in finite time these manifolds. In plain words, this means that after a finite number of iterations, the iterates (x^k, v^k) lie respectively in the partial smoothness manifolds associated to J and G respectively. When these manifolds are affine/linear, we establish local linear convergence of the fixed-point iterates z^k of DR. We show that the optimal convergence radius is given in terms of the cosine of the Friedrichs angle between the tangent spaces of the manifolds. We generalize these claims to the minimization of the sum of more than two functions. We finally exemplify our results with several experiments on variational signal and image processing.

It is important to note that our results readily apply to the alternating direction method of multipliers (ADMM), since it is well-known that ADMM is the DR method applied to the Fenchel dual problem of (1). More precisely, we only need to assume that the conjugates J^* and G^* are partly smooth. Therefore, to avoid unnecessary lengthy repetitions, we only focus in detail on the primal DR splitting method.

1.3 Relation to Prior Work

There are problem instances in the literature where DR was proved to converge locally linearly. For instance, in [16, Proposition 4], it was assumed that the "internal" function is strongly convex with a Lipschitz continuous gradient. This local linear convergence result was further investigated in [22,24] under smoothness and strong convexity assumptions. On the other hand, for the Basis Pursuit (BP) problem, i.e. ℓ_1 minimization with an affine constraint, is considered in [9] and an eventual local linear convergence is shown in the absence of strong convexity. The author in [23] analyzes the local convergence behaviour of ADMM for quadratic or linear programs, and shows local linear convergence if the optimal solution is unique and the strict complementarity holds. This turns out to be a special case of our framework. For the case of two subspaces, linear convergence of DR with the optimal rate being the cosine of the Friedrichs angle between the subspaces is proved in [2]. Our results generalize those of [2,9,23] to a much larger class of problems. For the non-convex case, [4] considered DR method for a feasibility problem of a sphere intersecting a line or more generally a proper affine subset. Such feasibility problems with an affine subspace and a super-regular set (in the sense of [14]) with strongly regular intersection was considered in [11], and was generalized later to two (ε, δ)-regular sets with linearly regular intersection [25], see also [18] for an even more general setting. However, even in the convex case, the rate provided in [18] is nowhere near the optimal rate given by the Friedrichs angle.

1.4 Notations

For a nonempty convex set $C \subset \mathbb{R}^n$, aff(C) is its affine hull, par(C) is the subspace parallel to it. Denote P_C the orthogonal projector onto C and N_C its normal cone. For $J \in \Gamma_0(\mathbb{R}^n)$, denote ∂J its subdifferential and prox$_J$ its proximity operator. Define the model subspace

$$T_x \stackrel{\text{def.}}{=} \mathrm{par}\bigl(\partial J(x)\bigr)^{\perp}.$$

It is obvious that $\mathrm{P}_{T_x}\bigl(\partial J(x)\bigr)$ is a singleton, and therefore defined as

$$e_x \stackrel{\text{def.}}{=} \mathrm{P}_{T_x}\bigl(\partial J(x)\bigr) = \mathrm{P}_{\mathrm{aff}(\partial J(x))}(0).$$

Suppose $\mathcal{M} \subset \mathbb{R}^n$ is a C^2-manifold around x, denote $\mathcal{T}_\mathcal{M}(x)$ the tangent space of $\mathcal{M}$ at $x \in \mathbb{R}^n$.

2 Partly Smooth Functions

2.1 Definition and Main Properties

Partial smoothness of functions was originally defined in [13], our definition hereafter specializes it to the case of proper lsc convex functions.

Definition 1. *(Partly smooth function) Let $J \in \Gamma_0(\mathbb{R}^n)$, and $x \in \mathbb{R}^n$ such that $\partial J(x) \neq \emptyset$. J is partly smooth at x relative to a set $\mathcal{M}$ containing x if*

(1) *(Smoothness) $\mathcal{M}$ is a C^2-manifold around x, $J|_\mathcal{M}$ is C^2 near x;*
(2) *(Sharpness) The tangent space $\mathcal{T}_\mathcal{M}(x)$ is T_x;*
(3) *(Continuity) The set-valued mapping ∂J is continuous at x relative to $\mathcal{M}$.*

The class of partly smooth functions at x relative to $\mathcal{M}$ is denoted as $\mathrm{PS}_x(\mathcal{M})$. When $\mathcal{M}$ is an affine manifold, then $\mathcal{M} = x + T_x$, and we denote this subclass as $\mathrm{PSA}_x(x + T_x)$. When $\mathcal{M}$ is a linear manifold, then $\mathcal{M} = T_x$, and we denote this subclass as $\mathrm{PSL}_x(T_x)$.

Capitalizing on the results of [13], it can be shown that, under mild transversality conditions, the set of lsc convex and partly smooth functions is closed under addition and pre-composition by a linear operator. Moreover, absolutely permutation-invariant convex and partly smooth functions of the singular values of a real matrix, i.e. spectral functions, are convex and partly smooth spectral functions of the matrix [7].

Examples of partly smooth functions that have become very popular recently in the signal processing, optimization, statistics and machine learning literature are ℓ_1, $\ell_{1,2}$, ℓ_∞, total variation (TV) and nuclear norm regularizations. In fact, the nuclear norm is partly smooth at a matrix x relative to the manifold $\mathcal{M} = \{x' : \mathrm{rank}(x') = \mathrm{rank}(x)\}$. The first four regularizers are all part of the class $\mathrm{PSL}_x(T_x)$.

We now define a subclass of partly smooth functions where the manifold is affine or linear and the vector e_x is locally constant.

Definition 2. *J belongs to the class $\mathrm{PSS}_x(x + T_x)$ (resp. $\mathrm{PSS}_x(T_x)$) if and only if $J \in \mathrm{PSA}_x(x + T_x)$ (resp. $J \in \mathrm{PSL}_x(T_x)$) and e_x is constant near x, i.e. there exists a neighbourhood U of x such that $\forall x' \in (x + T_x) \cap U$ (resp. $x' \in T_x \cap U$)*

$$e_{x'} = e_x.$$

The class of functions that conform with this definition is that of locally polyhedral functions [21, Section 6.5], which includes for instance the ℓ_1, ℓ_∞ norms and the anisotropic TV semi-norm that are widely used in signal and image processing, computer vision, machine learning and statistics. The indicator function of a polyhedral set is also in $\mathrm{PSS}_x(x+T_x)$ at each x in the relative interior of one of its faces relative to the affine hull of that face, i.e. $x + T_x = \mathrm{aff}(\text{Face of } x)$. Observe that for polyhedral functions, in fact, the subdifferential itself is constant along the partial smoothness subspace.

2.2 Proximity Operator

This part shows that the proximity operator of a partly smooth function can be given in an implicit form.

Proposition 1. *Let $p \stackrel{\text{def.}}{=} \mathrm{prox}_{\gamma J}(x) \in \mathcal{M}$. Assume that $J \in \mathrm{PS}_p(\mathcal{M})$. Then for any point x near p, we have*

$$p = \mathrm{P}_\mathcal{M}(x) - \gamma e_p + o(\|x - p\|).$$

In particular, if $J \in \mathrm{PSA}_p(p + T_p)$ (resp. $J \in \mathrm{PSL}_p(T_p)$), then for any $x \in \mathbb{R}^n$, we have

$$p = \mathrm{P}_{p+T_p}(x) - \gamma e_p \quad (\text{resp. } p = \mathrm{P}_{T_p}(x) - \gamma e_p).$$

Proof. We start with the following lemma whose proof can be found in [15].

Lemma 1. *Suppose that $J \in \mathrm{PS}_p(\mathcal{M})$. Then any point x near p has a unique projection $\mathrm{P}_\mathcal{M}(x)$, $\mathrm{P}_\mathcal{M}$ is C^1 around p, and thus*

$$\mathrm{P}_\mathcal{M}(x) - p = \mathrm{P}_{T_p}(x - p) + o(\|x - p\|).$$

Let's now turn to the proof of our proposition. We have the equivalent characterization

$$p = \mathrm{prox}_{\gamma J}(x) \iff x - p \in \gamma \partial J(p). \tag{3}$$

Projecting (3) on T_p and using Lemma 1, we get

$$\mathrm{P}_{T_p}(x - p) = \mathrm{P}_\mathcal{M}(x) - p + o(\|x - p\|) = \gamma e_p,$$

which is the desired result.

When $J \in \mathrm{PSA}_p(p + T_p)$, observe that $\mathrm{P}_{p+T_p}(x) = p + \mathrm{P}_{T_p}(x - p)$ for any $x \in \mathbb{R}^n$. Thus projecting again the monotone inclusion (3) on T_p, we get

$$\mathrm{P}_{T_p}(x - p) = \mathrm{P}_{p+T_p}(x) - p = \gamma e_p,$$

whence the claim follows. The linear case is immediate.

3 Activity Identification with Douglas–Rachford

In this section, we present the finite time activity identification of the DR method.

Theorem 1 (Finite activity identification). *Suppose that the DR scheme (2) is used to create a sequence (z^k, x^k, v^k). Then (z^k, x^k, v^k) converges to $(z^\star, x^\star, v^\star)$, where $z^\star \in \mathrm{Fix}(B_{\mathrm{DR}})$ and $x^\star$ is a global minimizer of (1). Assume that $J \in \mathrm{PS}_{x^\star}(\mathcal{M}^J)$ and $G \in \mathrm{PS}_{x^\star}(\mathcal{M}^G)$, and*

$$z^\star \in x^\star + \gamma\bigl(\mathrm{ri}(\partial J(x^\star)) \cap \mathrm{ri}(-\partial G(x^\star))\bigr). \tag{4}$$

Then,

(1) *The DR scheme has the finite activity identification property, i.e. for all k sufficiently large, $(x^k, v^k) \in \mathcal{M}^J \times \mathcal{M}^G$.*

(2) *If $G \in \mathrm{PSA}_{x^\star}(x^\star + T_{x^\star}^G)$ (resp. $G \in \mathrm{PSL}_{x^\star}(T_{x^\star}^G)$), then $v^k \in x^\star + T_{x^\star}^G$ (resp. $v^k \in T_{x^\star}^G$). In both cases $T_{v^k}^G = T_{x^\star}^G$ for all k sufficiently large.*

(3) *If $J \in \mathrm{PSA}_{x^\star}(x^\star + T_{x^\star}^J)$ (resp. $J \in \mathrm{PSL}_{x^\star}(T_{x^\star}^J)$), then $x^k \in x^\star + T_{x^\star}^J$ (resp. $x^k \in T_{x^\star}^J$). In both cases $T_{x^k}^J = T_{x^\star}^J$ for all k sufficiently large.*

Proof. Standard arguments using that B_{DR} is firmly non-expansive allow to show that the iterates z^k converge globally to a fixed point $z^\star \in \mathrm{Fix}(B_{\mathrm{DR}})$, by interpreting DR as a relaxed Krasnosel'skiĭ-Mann iteration. Moreover, the shadow point $x^\star \stackrel{\text{def.}}{=} \mathrm{prox}_{\gamma J}(z^\star)$ is a solution of (1), see e.g. [3]. In turn, using non-expansiveness of $\mathrm{prox}_{\gamma J}$, and as we are in finite dimension, we conclude also that the sequence x^k converges to $x^\star$. This entails that v^k converges to $x^\star$ (by non-expansiveness of $\mathrm{prox}_{\gamma G}$).

Now (4) is equivalent to

$$\tfrac{z^\star - x^\star}{\gamma} \in \mathrm{ri}(\partial J(x^\star)) \quad \text{and} \quad \tfrac{x^\star - z^\star}{\gamma} \in \mathrm{ri}(\partial G(x^\star)). \tag{5}$$

(1) The update of x^{k+1} and v^{k+1} in (2) is equivalent to the monotone inclusions

$$\tfrac{z^{k+1} - x^{k+1}}{\gamma} \in \partial J(x^{k+1}) \quad \text{and} \quad \tfrac{2x^k - z^k - v^{k+1}}{\gamma} \in \partial G(v^{k+1}).$$

It then follows that

$$\mathrm{dist}\big(\tfrac{z^\star - x^\star}{\gamma}, \partial J(x^{k+1})\big) \leqslant \tfrac{1}{\gamma}\big(\|z^{k+1} - z^\star\| + \|x^{k+1} - x^\star\|\big) \to 0$$

and

$$\mathrm{dist}\big(\tfrac{x^\star - z^\star}{\gamma}, \partial G(v^{k+1})\big) \leqslant \tfrac{1}{\gamma}\big(\|z^k - z^\star\| + 2\|x^k - x^\star\| + \|v^{k+1} - x^\star\|\big) \to 0.$$

By assumption, $J \in \Gamma_0(\mathbb{R}^n)$ and $G \in \Gamma_0(\mathbb{R}^n)$, and thus are sub-differentially continuous at every point in their respective domains [20, Example 13.30], and in particular at $x^\star$. It then follows that $J(x^k) \to J(x^\star)$ and $G(v^k) \to G(x^\star)$. Altogether, this shows that the conditions of [10, Theorem 5.3] are fulfilled for J and G, and the finite identification claim follows.

(2) In this case, we have either $v^k \in x^\star + T_{x^\star}^G$ (resp. $v^k \in T_{x^\star}^G$). Since $G(v)$ is partly smooth at $x^\star$ relative to $x^\star + T_{x^\star}^G$ (resp. $T_{x^\star}^G$), the sharpness property holds at all nearby points in $x^\star + T_{x^\star}^G$ (resp. $T_{x^\star}^G$) [13, Proposition 2.10]. Thus for k large enough, i.e. v^k sufficiently close to $x^\star$, we have indeed $\mathcal{T}_{x^\star + T_{x^\star}^G}(v^k) = T_{x^\star}^G = T_{v^k}^G$ as claimed.

(3) Similar to (2). □

Remark 2.

1. *Condition (4) can be interpreted as a non-degeneracy assumption. It can be viewed as a geometric generalization of the strict complementarity of non-linear programming. Such a condition is almost necessary for the finite identification of the partial smoothness active manifolds [8].*

2. *When the minimizer is unique, using the fixed-point set characterization of DR, it can be shown that condition (4) is also equivalent to $z^\star \in \mathrm{ri}(\mathrm{Fix}(B_{\mathrm{DR}}))$.*

4 Local Linear Convergence of Douglas–Rachford

Let us first recall the principal angles and the Friedrichs angle between two subspaces A and B, which are crucial for our quantitative analysis of the convergence rates. Without loss of generality, let $1 \leq p \stackrel{\text{def.}}{=} \dim(A) \leq q \stackrel{\text{def.}}{=} \dim(B) \leq n - 1$.

Definition 3 (Principal angles). *The principal angles $\theta_k \in [0, \frac{\pi}{2}]$, $k = 1, \ldots, p$ between A and B are defined by, with $u_0 = v_0 \stackrel{\text{def.}}{=} 0$*

$$\cos \theta_k \stackrel{\text{def.}}{=} \langle u_k, v_k \rangle = \max \langle u, v \rangle \quad s.t. \quad u \in A, v \in B, \|u\| = 1, \|v\| = 1,$$
$$\langle u, v_i \rangle = \langle u_i, v \rangle = 0, \quad i = 0, \ldots, k - 1.$$

The principal angles θ_k are unique with $0 \leq \theta_1 \leq \theta_2 \leq \ldots \leq \theta_p \leq \pi/2$.

Definition 4 (Friedrichs angle). *The Friedrichs angle $\theta_F \in]0, \frac{\pi}{2}]$ between A and B is*

$$\cos \theta_F(A, B) \stackrel{\text{def.}}{=} \max \langle u, v \rangle \quad s.t. \quad u \in A \cap (A \cap B)^\perp, \|u\| = 1, v \in B \cap (A \cap B)^\perp, \|v\| = 1.$$

The following relation between the Friedrichs and principal angles is of paramount importance to our analysis, whose proof can be found in [1, Proposition 3.3].

Lemma 2 (Principal angles and Friedrichs angle). *The Friedrichs angle is exactly θ_{d+1} where $d \stackrel{\text{def.}}{=} \dim(A \cap B)$. Moreover, $\theta_F(A, B) > 0$.*

Remark 3. *One approach to obtain the principal angles is through the singular value decomposition (SVD). For instance, let $X \in \mathbb{R}^{n \times p}$ and $Y \in \mathbb{R}^{n \times q}$ form the orthonormal bases for the subspaces A and B respectively. Let $U \Sigma V^T$ be the SVD of $X^T Y \in \mathbb{R}^{p \times q}$, then $\cos \theta_k = \sigma_k$, $k = 1, 2, \ldots, p$ and σ_k corresponds to the k'th largest singular value in Σ.*

We now turn to local linear convergence properties of DR. Let's denote $S_{x^\star}^J = \left(T_{x^\star}^J\right)^\perp$ and similarly for $S_{x^\star}^G$.

Theorem 2 (Local linear convergence). *Suppose that the DR scheme (2) is used with $\lambda_k \equiv \lambda \in]0, 2[$ to create a sequence (z^k, x^k, v^k) which converges to a pair $(z^\star, x^\star, x^\star)$ such that $J \in \text{PSS}_{x^\star}(T_{x^\star}^J)$ and $G \in \text{PSS}_{x^\star}(T_{x^\star}^G)$, and (4) holds. Then, there exists $K > 0$ such that for all $k \geq K$,*

$$\|z^k - z^\star\| \leq \rho^{k-K} \|z^K - z^\star\|, \tag{6}$$

with the optimal rate $\rho = \sqrt{(1-\lambda)^2 + \lambda(2-\lambda) \cos^2 \theta_F(T_{x^\star}^J, T_{x^\star}^G)} \in [0, 1[$.

This result is only valid for the class PSS. Extending this to general partly smooth functions will be left to a future work.

Remark 4. It can be observed that the best rate is obtained for $\lambda = 1$. This has been also pointed out in [9] for basis-pursuit. This assertion is however only on the local convergence behaviour and does not mean that the DR will globally converge faster for $\lambda_k \equiv 1$. Note also that the above result can be straightforwardly generalized to the case of varying λ_k.

Proof. We give the proof for the affine case, the linear one is similar. Combining Theorem 1(2)-(3), Proposition 1 and the definition of the class $\mathrm{PSS}_x(T_x)$, we get

$$x^k = \mathrm{P}_{T^J_{x^\star}} z^k - \gamma e^J_{x^\star} + \mathrm{P}_{S^J_{x^\star}} x^\star,$$

$$v^{k+1} = 2\mathrm{P}_{T^G_{x^\star}} x^k - \mathrm{P}_{T^G_{x^\star}} z^k - \gamma e^G_{x^\star} + \mathrm{P}_{S^G_{x^\star}} x^\star$$

$$= 2\mathrm{P}_{T^G_{x^\star}} \mathrm{P}_{T^J_{x^\star}} z^k - \mathrm{P}_{T^G_{x^\star}} z^k - \gamma e^G_{x^\star} - 2\gamma \mathrm{P}_{T^G_{x^\star}} e^J_{x^\star} + 2\mathrm{P}_{T^G_{x^\star}} \mathrm{P}_{S^J_{x^\star}} x^\star + \mathrm{P}_{S^G_{x^\star}} x^\star.$$

Similarly, we have

$$x^\star = \mathrm{P}_{T^J_{x^\star}} z^\star - \gamma e^J_{x^\star} + \mathrm{P}_{S^J_{x^\star}} x^\star,$$

$$x^\star = 2\mathrm{P}_{T^G_{x^\star}} \mathrm{P}_{T^J_{x^\star}} z^\star - \mathrm{P}_{T^G_{x^\star}} z^\star - \gamma e^G_{x^\star} - 2\gamma \mathrm{P}_{T^G_{x^\star}} e^J_{x^\star} + 2\mathrm{P}_{T^G_{x^\star}} \mathrm{P}_{S^J_{x^\star}} x^\star + \mathrm{P}_{S^G_{x^\star}} x^\star.$$

Cobining and rearranging the terms, we get

$$(z^k + v^{k+1} - x^k) - z^\star$$

$$= (z^k + v^{k+1} - x^k) - (z^\star + x^\star - x^\star) = \left(\mathrm{Id} - \mathrm{P}_{T^J_{x^\star}} + 2\mathrm{P}_{T^G_{x^\star}} \mathrm{P}_{T^J_{x^\star}} - \mathrm{P}_{T^G_{x^\star}}\right)(z^k - z^\star)$$

$$= (\mathrm{P}_{S^J_{x^\star}} - 2\mathrm{P}_{T^G_{x^\star}} \mathrm{P}_{S^J_{x^\star}} + \mathrm{P}_{T^G_{x^\star}})(z^k - z^\star) = (\mathrm{P}_{S^G_{x^\star}} \mathrm{P}_{S^J_{x^\star}} + \mathrm{P}_{T^G_{x^\star}} \mathrm{P}_{T^J_{x^\star}})(z^k - z^\star),$$

whence we obtain

$$z^{k+1} - z^\star = M(z^k - z^\star) = M^{k+1-K}(z^K - z^\star),$$

where

$$M = (1 - \lambda)\mathrm{Id} + \lambda(\mathrm{P}_{S^G_{x^\star}} \mathrm{P}_{S^J_{x^\star}} + \mathrm{P}_{T^G_{x^\star}} \mathrm{P}_{T^J_{x^\star}}).$$

It is immediate to check that M is normal and convergent for $\lambda \in [0, 2[$, and according to [1, Theorem 3.10] and Lemma 2, the optimal rate ρ is in terms of the Friedrichs angle as given by the theorem.

5 Sum of More than Two Functions

We now want to tackle the problem of solving

$$\min_{x \in \mathbb{R}^n} \sum_{i=1}^m J_i(x), \qquad (7)$$

where each $J_i \in \Gamma_0(\mathbb{R}^n)$. We assume that all the relative interiors of their domains have a non-empty intersection, that the set of minimizers is non-empty, and that these functions are simple.

In fact, problem (7) can be equivalently reformulated as (1) in a product space, see e.g. [6,19]. Let $\mathcal{H} = \underbrace{\mathbb{R}^n \times \cdots \times \mathbb{R}^n}_{m \text{ times}}$ endowed with the scalar inner-product and norm

$$\forall x, y \in \mathcal{H}, \ \langle x, y \rangle = \sum_{i=1}^{m} \langle x_i, y_i \rangle, \ \|x\| = \sqrt{\sum_{i=1}^{m} \|x_i\|^2}.$$

Let $\mathcal{S} = \{x = (x_i)_i \in \mathcal{H} : x_1 = \cdots = x_m\}$ and its orthogonal complement $\mathcal{S}^\perp = \{x = (x_i)_i \in \mathcal{H} : \sum_{i=1}^{m} x_i = 0\}$. Now define the canonical isometry,

$$C : \mathbb{R}^n \to \mathcal{S}, \ x \mapsto (x, \cdots, x),$$

then we have $P_{\mathcal{S}}(z) = C\big(\frac{1}{m} \sum_{i=1}^{m} z_i\big)$.

Problem (7) is now equivalent to

$$\min_{x \in \mathcal{H}} J(x) + G(x), \ \text{where} \ J(x) = \sum_{i=1}^{m} J_i(x_i) \ \text{and} \ G(x) = \iota_{\mathcal{S}}(x). \quad (8)$$

Obviously, J is separable and therefore,

$$\text{prox}_{\gamma J}(x) = \big(\text{prox}_{\gamma J_i}(x_i)\big)_i.$$

We have the following result.

Corollary 1. *Suppose that the DR scheme is used to solve (8) and creates a sequence (z^k, x^k, v^k). Then (z^k, x^k, v^k) converges to $(z^\star, x^\star, x^\star)$, where $x^\star = C(x^\star)$, and $x^\star$ is a minimizer of (7). Suppose that $J_i \in \text{PS}_{x^\star}(\mathcal{M}^{J_i})$ and*

$$z^\star \in x^\star + \gamma \text{ri}\big(\partial J(x^\star)\big) \cap \mathcal{S}^\perp. \quad (9)$$

Then,

(1) *the DR scheme has the finite activity identification property, i.e. for all k sufficiently large, $x^k \in \times_i \mathcal{M}^{J_i}$.*
(2) *Assume that $J_i \in \text{PSS}_{x^\star}(x^\star + T_{x^\star}^{J_i})$ (or $J_i \in \text{PSS}_{x^\star}(T_{x^\star}^{J_i})$) and DR is run with $\lambda_k \equiv \lambda \in]0, 2[$. Then, there exists $K > 0$ such that for all $k \geq K$,*

$$\|z^k - z^\star\| \leq \rho^{k-K} \|z^K - z^\star\|,$$

with the optimal rate $\rho = \sqrt{(1-\lambda)^2 + \lambda(2-\lambda)\cos^2 \theta_F\big(\times_i T_{x^\star}^{J_i}, \mathcal{S}\big)} \in [0, 1[.$

Proof. (1) By the separability rule, $J \in \text{PS}_{x^\star}(\times_i \mathcal{M}_{x^\star}^{J_i})$, see [13, Proposition 4.5]. We also have $\partial G(x^\star) = N_{\mathcal{S}}(x^\star) = \mathcal{S}^\perp$. Thus $G \in \text{PS}_{x^\star}(\mathcal{S})$, i.e. $T_{x^\star}^G = \mathcal{S}$. Then (9) is simply a specialization of condition (4) to problem (8). The claim then follows from Theorem 1.
(2) This is a direct consequence of Theorem 2.

6 Numerical Experiments

Here, we illustrate our theoretical results on several concrete examples. This section is by no means exhaustive, and we only focus on the problems that we consider as representative in variational signal/image processing.

Affinely-constrained Polyhedral Minimization Let us now consider the affine-constrained minimization problem

$$\min_{x \in \mathbb{R}^n} J(x) \quad \text{subject to} \quad y = Ax, \tag{10}$$

where $A \in \mathbb{R}^{m \times n}$, and J is finite-valued polyhedral. We assume that the problem is feasible, i.e. the observation $y \in \text{Im}(A)$. By identifying G with the indicator function of the affine constraint, it is immediate to see that $G = \iota_{\text{Ker}(A)}(\cdot)$, which is polyhedral, hence belongs to PSS, and is simple.

Problem (10) is of important interest in various areas, including signal and image processing to find regularized solutions to linear equations. Typically, J is a regularization term intended to promote solutions conforming to some notion of simplicity/low-dimensional structure. One can think of instance of the active area of compressed sensing (CS) and sparse recovery.

We here solve (10) with J being either ℓ_1, ℓ_∞, and anisotropic TV regularizers. For all these cases, $J \in \Gamma_0(\mathbb{R}^n)$, is simple and $J \in \text{PSS}_{x^*}(T_{x^*})$, where T_{x^*} can be easily computed, see e.g. [21]. In these experiments, A is drawn randomly from the standard Gaussian ensemble, i.e. CS scenario, detailed settings are

(a) ℓ_1-norm: $m = 32$ and $n = 128$, x_0 is 8-sparse;
(b) ℓ_∞-norm: $m = 120$ and $n = 128$, x_0 has 10 saturating entries;
(c) TV semi-norm: $m = 32$ and $n = 128$, (∇x_0) is 8-sparse;

Figure 1(a)-(c) displays the global profile of $\|z^k - z^*\|$ as a function of k, and the starting point of the solid line is the iteration number at which the partial smooth manifolds (here subspaces) are identified. One can easily see the linear convergence behaviour and that our rate estimate is indeed optimal.

TV based Image Inpainting In this image processing example, we observe $y = Ax_0$, where A is a binary mask operator. We aim at inpainting the missing regions from the observations y. This can be achieved by solving (10) with J the 2D anisotropic TV. The corresponding convergence profile is depicted in Figure 1(d).

Uniform Noise Removal For this problem, we assume that we observe $y = x_0 + \varepsilon$, where x_0 is a piecewise-smooth vector, and ε is a realization of a random vector whose entries are iid $\sim \mathcal{U}([-a, a])$, $a > 0$. It is then natural to solve the problem

$$\min_{x \in \mathbb{R}^n} \|x\|_{\text{TV}} \quad \text{subject to} \quad \|y - x\|_\infty \leq a. \tag{11}$$

G is now identified with the indicator function of the ℓ_∞-ball constraint, which is polyhedral and simple. The local convergence profile is shown in Figure 1(e) where we set $a = 1$ and $n = 100$. Again, the rate estimate is extremely tight.

Outliers Removal Consider solving

$$\min_{x \in \mathbb{R}^n} \|y - x\|_1 + \lambda \|x\|_{\text{TV}}, \tag{12}$$

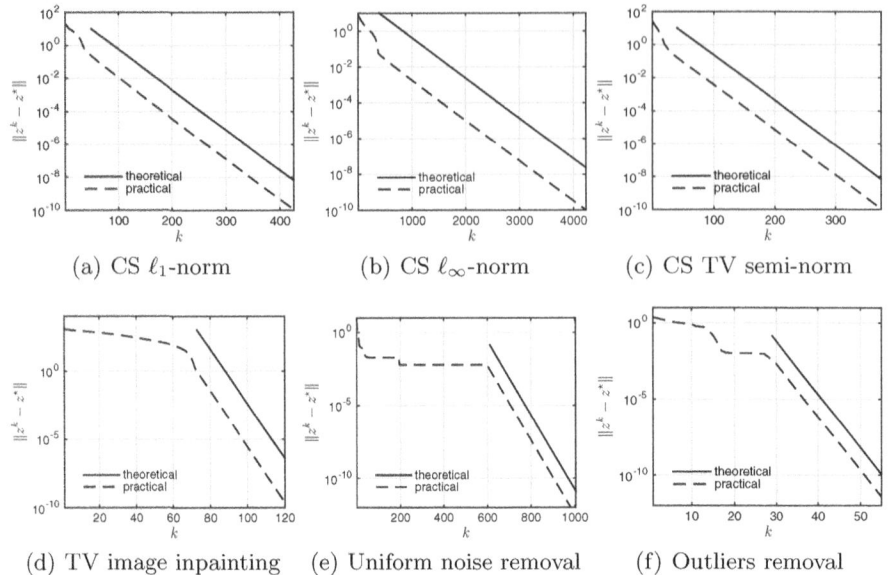

Fig. 1. Observed (dashed) and predicted (solid) convergence profiles of DR (2) in terms of $\|z^k - z^*\|$. (a) CS with ℓ_1. (b) CS with ℓ_∞. (c) CS with TV. (d) TV image inpainting. (e) Uniform noise removal by solving (11). (f) Outliers removal by solving (12). The starting point of the solid line is the iteration at which the manifolds are identified.

where $\lambda > 0$ is the tradeoff parameter. This problem has been proposed by [17] for outliers removal. We take $J = \lambda \|\cdot\|_{\mathrm{TV}}$ and $G = \|y - \cdot\|_1$, which is again simple and polyhedral. For this example we have $n = 100$, and $y - x$ is 10-sparse, the corresponding local convergence profile is depicted in Figure 1(f).

7 Conclusion

In this paper, we first showed that the DR splitting has the finite manifold identification under partial smoothness. When the involved manifolds are affine/linear and the generalized signs are locally constant, we proved local linear convergence of DR and provided a very tight rate estimate as illustrated by several numerical experiments. Our future work will focus on extending the linear convergence result to more general partly smooth functions.

References

1. Bauschke, H.H., Bello Cruz, J.Y., Nghia, T.A., Phan, H.M., Wang, X.: Optimal rates of convergence of matrices with applications. arxiv:1407.0671 (2014)
2. Bauschke, H.H., Bello Cruz, J.Y., Nghia, T.A., Phan, H.M., Wang, X.: The rate of linear convergence of the Douglas-Rachford algorithm for subspaces is the cosine of the friedrichs angle. J. of Approx. Theo. **185**, 63–79 (2014)

3. Bauschke, H.H., Combettes, P.L.: Convex analysis and monotone operator theory in Hilbert spaces. Springer, New York (2011)
4. Borwein, J.M., Sims, B.: The Douglas-Rachford algorithm in the absence of convexity (2010)
5. Chambolle, A., Pock, T.: A first-order primal-dual algorithm for convex problems with applications to imaging. J. of Math. Imag. and Vis. **40**(1), 120–145 (2011)
6. Combettes, P.L., Pesquet, J.C.: A proximal decomposition method for solving convex variational inverse problems. Inv. Prob. **24**(6), 065014 (2008)
7. Daniilidis, A., Drusvyatskiy, D., Lewis, A.L.: Orthogonal invariance and identifiability. SIAM Mat. Anal. Appl. (2014)
8. Hare, W.L., Lewis, A.L.: Identifying active manifolds. Alg. Op. Res **2**(2), 75–82 (2007)
9. Demanet, L., Zhang, X.: Eventual linear convergence of the Douglas-Rachford iteration for basis pursuit. Math. Prog. (2013)
10. Hare, W.L., Lewis, A.S.: Identifying active constraints via partial smoothness and prox-regularity. J. of Conv. Ana. **11**(2), 251–266 (2004)
11. Hesse, H., Luke, D.R., Neumann, P.: Alternating Projections and Douglas-Rachford for Sparse Affine Feasibility. IEEE Trans. on Sig. Proc. **62**(18), 4868–4881 (2014)
12. Hesse, H., Luke, D.R.: Nonconvex notions of regularity and convergence of fundamental algorithms for feasibility problems. SIAM J. Opt. **23**(4), 2397–2419 (2013)
13. Lewis, A.S.: Active sets, nonsmoothness, and sensitivity. SIAM J. Opt. **13**(3), 702–725 (2003)
14. Lewis, A.S., Luke, D.R., Malick, J.: Local linear convergence for alternating and averaged nonconvex projections. Found. Comput. Math. **9**(4), 485–513 (2009)
15. Liang, J., Fadili, M.J., Peyré, G.: Local linear convergence of Forward-Backward under partial smoothness. NIPS, 1970–1978 (2014)
16. Lions, P.L., Mercier, B.: Splitting algorithms for the sum of two nonlinear operators. SIAM J. on Num. Ana. **16**(6), 964–979 (1979)
17. Nikolova, M.: A variational approach to remove outliers and impulse noise. J. of Math. Imag. and Vis. **20**(1–2), 99–120 (2004)
18. Phan, H.M.: Linear convergence of the Douglas-Rachford method for two closed sets (2014). arXiv:1401.6509v1
19. Raguet, H., Fadili, J.M., Peyré, G.: Generalized Forward-Backward splitting. SIAM Im. Sciences **6**(3), 1199–1226 (2013)
20. Rockafellar, R.T., Wets, R.: Variational analysis, vol. 317. Springer Verlag, Heidelberg (1998)
21. Vaiter, S., Golbabaee, M., Fadili, M.J., Peyré, G.: Model selection with low complexity priors. Preprint Hal (2013)
22. Davis, D., Yin, W.: Convergence rates of relaxed Peaceman-Rachford and ADMM under regularity assumptions (2014). arXiv preprint arXiv:1407.5210
23. Boley, D.: Local linear convergence of the alternating direction method of multipliers on quadratic or linear programs. SIAM Journal on Optimization **23**(4), 2183–2207 (2013)
24. Giselsson, P., Boyd, S.: Metric selection in Douglas-Rachford splitting and ADMM (2014). arXiv preprint arXiv:1410.8479
25. Hesse, R., Luke, D.R.: Nonconvex notions of regularity and convergence of fundamental algorithms for feasibility problems. SIAM Journal on Optimization **23**(4), 2397–2419 (2013)

Bilevel Optimization with Nonsmooth Lower Level Problems

Peter Ochs[1]([✉]), René Ranftl[2], Thomas Brox[1], and Thomas Pock[2,3]

[1] Computer Vision Group, University of Freiburg, Freiburg, Germany
{ochs,brox}@cs.uni-freiburg.de
[2] Institute for Computer Graphics and Vision,
Graz University of Technology, Graz, Austria
{ranftl,pock}@icg.tugraz.at
[3] Digital Safety and Security Department, AIT Austrian Institute of Technology GmbH, 1220 Vienna, Austria

Abstract. We consider a bilevel optimization approach for parameter learning in nonsmooth variational models. Existing approaches solve this problem by applying implicit differentiation to a sufficiently smooth approximation of the nondifferentiable lower level problem. We propose an alternative method based on differentiating the iterations of a nonlinear primal–dual algorithm. Our method computes exact (sub)gradients and can be applied also in the nonsmooth setting. We show preliminary results for the case of multi-label image segmentation.

1 Introduction

Many problems in imaging applications and computer vision are approached by variational methods. The solutions are modeled as a state of minimal energy of a function(al). Deviations from multiple model assumptions are penalized by a higher energy. This immediately comes with an important question, namely, the relative importance of the individual assumptions. As it is traditionally hard to manually select the weights, we consider an automatic approach cast as a bilevel optimization problem—an optimization problem that consists of an upper and a lower level. The upper level tries to minimize a certain loss function with respect to the sought set of hyper-parameters. The quantification of the quality of a set of hyper-parameters is only given via the output of the lower level problem. The lower level problem models a specific computer vision task, given a set of hyper-parameters.

Present optimization algorithms for bilevel learning require the lower level problem to be twice differentiable. This limits the flexibility of the approach. For example, in computer vision only a smoothed version of the total variation can be used, whereby favorable properties are lost. Figure 1 plots the energy of a bilevel learning problem and shows the effect of smoothing the lower problem.

In some sense the requirement of regularized models in the lower level problem is a step back in time. In the last decades, people have put a lot of effort

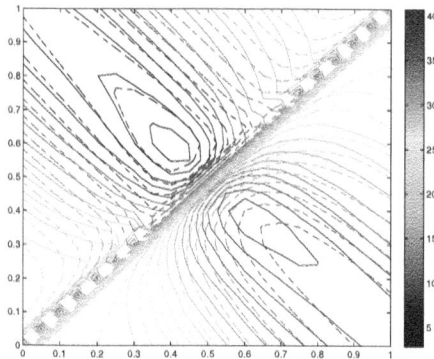

Fig. 1. Contour plot of the energy of a bilevel learning problem with two parameters. The dashed contours correspond to the same learning problem as the solid contours but with a smoothed lower level energy. Usually, gradient descent like schemes are used to find the optimal parameters. We propose a way to compute gradient directions directly on the original problem (solid lines), instead of the smoothed problem (dashed lines) where gradient directions can be completely wrong.

to efficiently solve also nonsmooth problems. The main driving force was that nonsmooth energies provide better solutions for many practical problems.

Why not to make use of these powerful optimization tools for bilevel learning? In this paper, we fill the gap between variational bilevel learning and the use of nonsmooth variational models in the lower level problem. The applicability of the developed technique is shown exemplarily for multi-label segmentation, which poses a difficult nonsmooth optimization problem.

2 Related Work

We consider a bilevel optimization problem for parameter learning of the form as considered in [1,2]. This model for parameter learning is motivated from [3,4]. The authors argue that the bilevel optimization approach has several advantages compared to classical probabilistic learning methods. In fact, their approach circumvents the problem of computing the partition function of the probability distribution, which is usually not tractable. Earlier, influential approaches are the tree-based bounds of Wainwright et al. [5], Hinton's contrastive divergence method [6] and discriminative learning of graphical models [7,8].

A generic approach for hyper-parameter optimization is to sample the upper level loss function and regress its shape using Gaussian processes [9] or Random Forests [10]. Since optimization is not based on gradients, it does not require any smoothness of the lower level problem. It rather makes assumptions about the shape of the loss function. This approach is currently limited to the optimization of a moderate number of parameters. Sampling the loss function becomes increasingly demanding if a large number of parameters have to be optimized.

Eggensperger [11], for example, reports problem sizes of a few hundred parameters which can be tackled using the generic approach, whereas the bilevel approach that we consider in this work was successfully applied to problems with up to 30000 parameters [12].

Bilevel optimization was considered for task specific sparse analysis prior learning [13] and applied to signal restoration. In [14,15] a bilevel approach was used to learn a model of natural image statistics, which was then applied to various image restoration tasks. Recently, it was used for the end-to-end training of a Convolutional Neural Network (CNN) and a graphical model for binary image segmentation [12].

So far all bilevel approaches required the lower level problem to be differentiable; Nonsmooth problems have to be handled using smooth approximations. In [3,4] differentiability is used in combination with implicit differentiation to analytically differentiate the (upper level) loss function with respect to the parameters. In [1] an efficient semi-smooth Newton method is proposed. In contrast to these approaches the method that we propose can solve bilevel learning problems with a nonsmooth lower level problem.

The procedure of our method is similar to that in [16]. The idea is to directly differentiate the update step of an algorithm that solves the lower level problem with respect to the parameters. Domke [17] applied algorithmic differentiation to derive gradients of truncated gradient based optimization schemes. In contrast to our method, this approach requires to store every intermediate result of the optimization algorithm, which results in a huge memory demand. In [16] the lower level problem is approximated with quadratic majorizers and thus is differentiable by construction. A similar approach was proposed earlier in [18].

Recently, the primal–dual (PD) algorithm from Chambolle and Pock [19] was extended to incorporate Bregman proximity functions [20]. The Bregman proximity function is key in this paper. It allows us to solve a nonsmooth lower level problem with a PD algorithm having differentiable update rules. In [21], in the setting of unbiased risk estimation and parameter selection, iterative (weak) differentiation of Euclidean proximal splitting algorithms is studied.

3 The Bilevel Learning Problem

The bilevel learning problem considered in this paper is the following:

$$\min_{\vartheta} \ \mathcal{L}(x(\vartheta)) \\ s.t. \ x(\vartheta) \in \arg\min_{x \in \mathbb{R}^N} E(x, \vartheta) \tag{1}$$

The continuously differentiable function $\mathcal{L} \colon \mathbb{R}^N \to \mathbb{R}_+$ is a loss function describing the discrepancy between a solution $x^*(\vartheta) \in \mathbb{R}^N$ of the lower level problem for a specific set of parameters $\vartheta \in \mathbb{R}^P$ and the training data. The goal is to learn optimal parameters for the lower level problem, given by the proper lower semi-continuous energy $E \colon \mathbb{R}^N \times \mathbb{R}^P \to \mathbb{R}_+$.

If the lower problem can be explicitly solved for $x^*(\vartheta)$, then the bilevel problem reduces to a single level problem. However, this construction is not always possible. In that case, implicit differentiation can be used to find a descent direction of $\mathcal{L}(x(\vartheta))$ with respect to ϑ. This is essential for a gradient based optimization method, like it is used in [3], however, twice continuous differentiability of the lower problem is required. We briefly recap the well-known idea before we propose a way to waive this requirement.

3.1 Bilevel Optimization via Implicit Differentiation

The optimality condition of the lower level problem is $\frac{\partial}{\partial x}E(x,\vartheta) = 0$, which under some conditions implicitly defines a function $x^*(\vartheta)$. Let us define $F(x,\vartheta) = \frac{\partial}{\partial x}E(x,\vartheta)$. As we assume that the problem $\min_x E(x,\vartheta)$ has a solution, there is (x^*, ϑ') such that $F(x^*, \vartheta') = 0$. Then the implicit function theorem says that, if F is continuously differentiable and the matrix $\frac{\partial}{\partial x}F(x^*, \vartheta')$ is invertible, there exists an explicit function $X: \vartheta \mapsto x(\vartheta)$ in a neighborhood of (x^*, ϑ'). Moreover, the function X is continuously differentiable and

$$\frac{\partial X}{\partial \vartheta}(\vartheta) = \left(-\frac{\partial F}{\partial x}(X(\vartheta),\vartheta)\right)^{-1}\frac{\partial F}{\partial \vartheta}(X(\vartheta),\vartheta).$$

Back-substituting $F = \frac{\partial}{\partial x}E$ and using the Hessian $H_E(X(\vartheta),\vartheta) = \frac{\partial^2 E}{\partial x^2}$ yields

$$\frac{\partial X}{\partial \vartheta}(\vartheta) = -(H_E(X(\vartheta),\vartheta))^{-1}\frac{\partial^2 E}{\partial \vartheta \partial x}(X(\vartheta),\vartheta). \qquad (2)$$

The requirement for using (2) from the implicit function theorem is the continuous differentiability of $\frac{\partial}{\partial x}E$ and the invertibility of H_E. Applying the chain rule for differentiation the derivative of the loss function $\mathcal{L}$ of (1) w.r.t. ϑ is

$$\frac{\partial}{\partial \vartheta}\mathcal{L}(x(\vartheta)) = -\frac{\partial \mathcal{L}}{\partial x}(x(\vartheta))\Big(H_E(X(\vartheta),\vartheta)\Big)^{-1}\frac{\partial^2 E}{\partial \vartheta \partial x}(X(\vartheta),\vartheta). \qquad (3)$$

A clever way of setting parentheses avoids explicit inversion of the Hessian matrix [22]. For large problems iterative solvers are required, however.

4 Bilevel Optimization with Nonsmooth Functions

In this section, we resolve the requirement of twice continuous differentiability of the lower level problem. The coarse idea is quite simple: even if the lower level problem is nondifferentiable, there can be algorithms with a differentiable update rule. Let $\mathcal{A}$ and $\mathcal{A}^{(n)}: \mathbb{R}^N \times \mathbb{R}^P \to \mathbb{R}^N$ describe one or n iterations, respectively, of algorithm $\mathcal{A}$ for minimizing E in (1). For a fixed $n \in \mathbb{N}$, we replace (1) by

$$\min_{\vartheta} \ \mathcal{L}(x(\vartheta))$$
$$\text{s.t.} \ x(\vartheta) = \mathcal{A}^{(n)}(x^0, \vartheta), \qquad (4)$$

where x^0 is some initialization of the algorithm. As the algorithm $\mathcal{A}$ is chosen to solve the (original) lower level problem in (1), we expect it to yield, for each ϑ, a solution $x^{(n)}(\vartheta) \to x^*(\vartheta)$ with $E(\mathcal{A}^{(n)}(x^0, \vartheta), \vartheta) \to \min_x E(x, \vartheta)$ for $n \to \infty$.

An interesting aspect of this approach is that, for a fixed n, the differentiation of $\mathcal{L}$ w.r.t. ϑ is exact; No additional approximation is required. In this way, the algorithm for solving the lower level problem learns parameters that yield an optimal solution after exactly n iterations.

Depending on the problem structure of $\min_x E(x, \vartheta)$ different algorithms can be chosen. We use the flexible PD algorithm from [20], which extends [19] to proximal terms involving Bregman distances. Using this technique, iterations can be made differentiable without requiring differentiability of the energy.

4.1 A Primal–Dual Algorithm with Bregman Distances

We consider the convex–concave saddle-point problem

$$\min_x \max_y \langle Kx, y \rangle + f(x) + g(x) - h^*(y),$$

which is derived from $\min_x f(x) + g(x) + h(Kx)$. One iteration of the PD algorithm [20] reads $(\hat{x}, \hat{y}) = \mathcal{PD}_{\tau,\sigma}(\bar{x}, \bar{y}, \tilde{x}, \tilde{y})$ or

$$\begin{aligned}
\hat{x} = \mathcal{PD}^x_\tau &:= \arg\min_x f(\bar{x}) + \langle \nabla f(\bar{x}), x - \bar{x} \rangle + g(x) + \langle Kx, \tilde{y} \rangle + \tfrac{1}{\tau} D_x(x, \bar{x}) \\
\hat{y} = \mathcal{PD}^y_\sigma &:= \arg\min_y h^*(y) - \langle K\tilde{x}, y \rangle + \tfrac{1}{\sigma} D_y(y, \bar{y}),
\end{aligned} \quad (5)$$

where $\mathcal{PD}^x_\tau = \mathcal{PD}^x_\tau(\bar{x}, \bar{y}, \tilde{x}, \tilde{y})$ (the same for $\mathcal{PD}^y_\sigma$) with step size parameter σ and τ. The step size parameter must be chosen according to $(\tau^{-1} - L_f)\sigma^{-1} \geq L^2$ where $L = \|K\|$ is the operator norm of K and L_f is the Lipschitz constant of ∇f. The Bregman function $D_x(x, \bar{x}) = \psi_x(x) - \psi_x(\bar{x}) - \langle \nabla \psi_x(\bar{x}), x - \bar{x} \rangle$ is generated by a 1-convex function ψ_x satisfying the requirements and properties in [20] (the same for D_y).

4.2 Primal–Dual Algorithm for Bilevel Learning

Although we assume $\mathcal{A} := \mathcal{PD}_{\tau,\sigma}$ to be differentiable, we do not require it for the lower energy in (4). This allows us to differentiate $\mathcal{A}$ with respect to the parameters. Using the chain rule iterations can be processed successively. A single PD step reads $\frac{\partial}{\partial \vartheta}(\hat{x}(\vartheta), \hat{y}(\vartheta)) = \frac{\partial}{\partial \vartheta} \mathcal{PD}_{\tau,\sigma}(\bar{x}(\vartheta), \bar{y}(\vartheta), \tilde{x}(\vartheta), \tilde{y}(\vartheta))$ where

$$\frac{\partial \mathcal{PD}^x_\tau}{\partial \vartheta} = \frac{\partial \mathcal{PD}^x_\tau}{\partial \bar{x}} \frac{\partial \bar{x}}{\partial \vartheta}(\vartheta) + \frac{\partial \mathcal{PD}^x_\tau}{\partial \bar{y}} \frac{\partial \bar{y}}{\partial \vartheta}(\vartheta) + \frac{\partial \mathcal{PD}^x_\tau}{\partial \tilde{x}} \frac{\partial \tilde{x}}{\partial \vartheta}(\vartheta) + \frac{\partial \mathcal{PD}^x_\tau}{\partial \tilde{y}} \frac{\partial \tilde{y}}{\partial \vartheta}(\vartheta), \quad (6)$$

and we dropped the dependency of $\mathcal{PD}^x_\tau$ on $(\bar{x}(\vartheta), \bar{y}(\vartheta), \tilde{x}(\vartheta), \tilde{y}(\vartheta))$ for clarity. The analogous expression holds for $\mathcal{PD}^y_\sigma$. As the functions $\bar{x}(\vartheta)$, $\bar{y}(\vartheta)$, $\tilde{x}(\vartheta)$ and $\tilde{y}(\vartheta)$ are simple combinations (products with scalars and sums) of the output of the previous PD iteration, the generalization to n iterations is straightforward.

5 Application to Multi-Label Segmentation

In this section, we show how the developed abstract idea is applied in practice. Before the actual bilevel learning problem is presented, we introduce the multi-label segmentation model. Then, the standard (nondifferentiable) PD approach to this problem, our (differentiable) formulation, and the PD algorithm for the smoothed energy (required by the implicit differentiation framework) are shown.

5.1 Model and Discretization

Given a cost tensor $\mathfrak{c} \in X^{N_l}$, where $X = \mathbb{R}^{N_x N_y}$, that assigns to each pixel (i,j) and each label k, $i = 1, \ldots, N_x$, $j = 1, \ldots, N_y$, $k = 1, \ldots, N_l$, a cost $\mathfrak{c}_{i,j}^k$ for the pixel taking label k. We often identify $\mathbb{R}^{N_x \times N_y}$ with $\mathbb{R}^{N_x N_y}$ by $(i,j) \mapsto i + (j-1)N_x$ to simplify the notation. The sought segmentation $u \in X_{[0,1]}^{N_l}$, where $X_{[0,1]} = [0,1]^{N_x N_y} \subset X$, is represented by a binary vector for each label. As a regularizer for a segment's plausibility we measure the boundary length using the total variation (TV). The discrete derivative operator $\nabla \colon X \to Y$, where we use the shorthand $Y := X \times X$ (elements from Y are considered as column vectors), is defined as (let the pixel dimension be 1×1):

$$(\nabla u^k)_{i,j} := \begin{pmatrix} (\nabla u^k)_{i,j}^x \\ (\nabla u^k)_{i,j}^y \end{pmatrix} \in Y (= \mathbb{R}^{2N_x N_y}), \quad Du := (\nabla u^1, \ldots, \nabla u^{N_l})$$

$$(\nabla u^k)_{i,j}^x := \begin{cases} u_{i+1,j}^k - u_{i,j}^k, & \text{if } 1 \leq i < N_x, 1 \leq j \leq N_y \\ 0, & \text{if } i = N_x, 1 \leq j \leq N_y \end{cases}$$

$(\nabla u^k)_{i,j}^y$ is defined analogously. From now on, we work with the image as a vector indexed by $\mathbf{i} = 1, \ldots, N_x N_y$. Let elements in Y be indexed with $\mathbf{j} = 1, \ldots, 2N_x N_y$. Let the inner product in X and Y be given, for $u^k, v^k \in X$ and $p^k, q^k \in Y$, as: $\langle u^k, v^k \rangle_X := \sum_{\mathbf{i}=1}^{N_x N_y} u_\mathbf{i}^k v_\mathbf{i}^k$ and $\langle p^k, q^k \rangle_Y := \sum_{\mathbf{j}=1}^{2N_x N_y} p_\mathbf{j}^k q_\mathbf{j}^k$, $\langle u, v \rangle_{X^{N_l}} := \sum_{k=1}^{N_l} \langle u^k, v^k \rangle_X$ and $\langle p, q \rangle_{Y^{N_l}} := \sum_{k=1}^{N_l} \langle p^k, q^k \rangle_Y$. The (discrete, anisotropic) TV norm is given by $\|Du\|_1 := \sum_{k=1}^{N_l} \sum_{\mathbf{j}=1}^{2N_x N_y} |(\nabla u^k)_\mathbf{j}|$, where $|\cdot|$ is the absolute value. In the following, the iteration variables $\mathbf{i} = 1, \ldots, N_x N_y$ and $\mathbf{j} = 1, \ldots, 2N_x N_y$ always run over these index sets, thus we drop the specification; the same for $k = 1, \ldots, N_l$. We define the pixel-wise nonnegative unit simplex

$$\Delta^{N_l} := \{u \in X^{N_l} \mid \forall (\mathbf{i}, k) \colon 0 \leq u_\mathbf{i}^k \leq 1 \text{ and } \forall \mathbf{i} \colon \sum_k u_\mathbf{i}^k = 1\}, \tag{7}$$

and the pixel-wise (closed) ℓ_∞-unit ball around the origin

$$B_1^{\ell_\infty}(0) := \{p \in Y^{N_l} \mid \forall (\mathbf{j}, k) \colon |p_\mathbf{j}^k| \leq 1\}.$$

Finally, the segmentation model reads

$$\min_{u \in X^{N_l}} \langle \mathfrak{c}, u \rangle_{X^{N_l}} + \|Du\|_1, \quad \text{s.t. } u \in \Delta^{N_l}. \tag{8}$$

This model and the following reformulation as a saddle-point problem are well known (see e.g. [19])

$$\min_{u \in X^{N_l}} \max_{p \in Y^{N_l}} \langle Du, p \rangle_{Y^{N_l}} + \langle u, \mathfrak{c} \rangle_{X^{N_l}}, \quad s.t.\ u \in \Delta^{N_l},\ p \in B_1^{\ell^\infty}(0). \quad (9)$$

5.2 Parameter Learning Setting

We consider (8) where the cost is given for each label k by $\mathfrak{c}_i^k = \lambda(\mathfrak{I}_i - \vartheta^k)^2$, where $\mathfrak{I} \in X$ is the image to be segmented and λ is a positive balancing parameter. ϑ^k can be interpreted as the mean value of the region with label k.

The training set consists of N_T images $\mathfrak{I}^1, \ldots, \mathfrak{I}^{N_T} \in X$ and corresponding ground truth segmentations $>^1, \ldots, >^{N_T}$. The ground truths are generated by solving (8) with $(\mathfrak{c}^t)_i^k = \lambda(\mathfrak{I}_i^t - \hat{\vartheta}^k)^2$ for each $t \in \{1, \ldots, N_T\}$ and predefined parameters $\hat{\vartheta}^1, \ldots, \hat{\vartheta}^{N_l}$.

We consider an instance of the general bilevel optimization problem (1):

$$\min_{\vartheta \in \mathbb{R}^{N_l}} \frac{1}{2} \sum_{t=1}^{N_T} \|u(\vartheta, \mathfrak{I}^t) - \mathfrak{g}^t\|_2^2 \quad (10)$$
$$s.t.\ u(\vartheta, \mathfrak{I}^t) = \arg\min_{u \in X^{N_l}} E(u, \mathfrak{c}^t), \quad (\mathfrak{c}^t)_i^k = \lambda(\mathfrak{I}_i^t - \vartheta^k)^2.$$

The goal is to learn the parameters (the mean values) ϑ^k and try to recover $\hat{\vartheta}^k$. The energy E in the lower level problem is (8).

5.3 The Standard Primal–Dual Algorithm

Problem (8) can be solved using the PD algorithm from (5). The standard way to apply it is by setting $x = u$, $y = p$, $f \equiv 0$, $g(u) = \langle u, \mathfrak{c} \rangle_{X^{N_l}} + \delta_{\Delta^{N_l}}(u)$, and $h^*(p) = \sum_k \sum_j \delta_{[-1,1]}(p_j^k)$, where δ_C is the indicator function of the convex set C. Furthermore, the Bregman functions are the squared Euclidean distance (for primal and dual update) and the constraints of the primal variable are incorporated in the proximal step. It reads

$$\hat{u} = \Pi_{\Delta^{N_l}} (\bar{u} - \tau D^\top \tilde{p} - \tau \mathfrak{c})$$
$$\hat{p} = \Pi_{B_1^{\ell^\infty}(0)} (\bar{p} + \sigma Du), \quad (11)$$

where Π_C denotes the orthogonal projection operator onto the set C. As these projections are nonsmooth functions, they are not suited for our framework.

5.4 A Primal–Dual Algorithm with Bregman Proximity Function

A differentiable PD iteration can be derived using the Bregman function

$$D_x(u, \bar{u}) = \frac{1}{2} \sum_k \sum_i u_i^k (\log(u_i^k) - \log(\bar{u}_i^k)) - u_i^k + \bar{u}_i^k,$$

which is generated by $\psi_x(u) = \frac{1}{2}\sum_{k,i} u_i^k \log(u_i^k)$. The key idea for choosing this Bregman function is that it takes finite values only for nonnegative coordinates. As a consequence the nonnegativity constraint in the primal update step can be dropped and the projection is given by a simple analytic expression:

$$\forall (k, \mathbf{i}): \quad \hat{u}_\mathbf{i}^k = \frac{\exp(-2\tau(\nabla^\top \tilde{p}^k)_\mathbf{i} - 2\tau c_\mathbf{i}^k) \bar{u}_\mathbf{i}^k}{\sum_{k'=1}^{N_l} \exp(-2\tau(\nabla^\top \tilde{p}^{k'})_\mathbf{i} - 2\tau c_\mathbf{i}^{k'}) \bar{u}_\mathbf{i}^{k'}}. \quad (12)$$

For the dual update step we use the Bregman proximity function

$$D_y(p,\bar{p}) = \frac{1}{2}\sum_k \sum_\mathbf{j} (1-p_\mathbf{j}^k)(\log(1-p_\mathbf{j}^k) - \log(1-\bar{p}_\mathbf{j}^k)) - p_\mathbf{j}^k + \bar{p}_\mathbf{j}^k$$
$$+ (1+p_\mathbf{j}^k)(\log(1+p_\mathbf{j}^k) - \log(1+\bar{p}_\mathbf{j}^k)) - p_\mathbf{j}^k + \bar{p}_\mathbf{j}^k,$$

which is generated by $\psi_y(p) = \frac{1}{2}\sum_k \sum_\mathbf{j}(1+p_\mathbf{j}^k)\log(1+p_\mathbf{j}^k) + (1-p_\mathbf{j}^k)\log(1-p_\mathbf{j}^k)$. It takes finite values only within the feasible set $[-1,1]$ for each coordinate.

$$\forall (k, \mathbf{j}): \quad \hat{p}_\mathbf{j}^k = \frac{\exp(2\sigma(\nabla \tilde{u}^k)_\mathbf{j}) - \frac{1-\bar{p}_\mathbf{j}^k}{1+\bar{p}_\mathbf{j}^k}}{\exp(2\sigma(\nabla \tilde{u}^k)_\mathbf{j}) + \frac{1-\bar{p}_\mathbf{j}^k}{1+\bar{p}_\mathbf{j}^k}} \quad (13)$$

emerges as the resulting update step. (12) and (13) define the update function $(\hat{u}, \hat{p}) = \mathcal{PD}_{\tau,\sigma}(\bar{u}, \bar{p}, \tilde{u}, \tilde{p})$ for the PD algorithm, which is differentiable.

5.5 A Smoothed Parameter Learning Problem

The method of implicit differentiation requires the lower level problem of (10) to be twice differentiable. As in [12] for binary segmentation, the domain constraint $u_i^k \in [0,1]$ is incorporated via a log barrier $\mu \sum_{k,i}(\log(u_i^k) + \log(1-u_i^k))$ with $\mu < 0$ and instead of the TV for each label function the smooth Charbonnier function $\|Du\|_\varepsilon := \sum_k \sum_\mathbf{j}((\nabla u^k)_\mathbf{j}^2 + \varepsilon^2)^{\frac{1}{2}}$ with $\varepsilon > 0$ is used. The simplex constraint (7) is incorporated using a Lagrange multiplier $\rho \in X$, such that the smoothed Lagrangian reads

$$E_\varepsilon(u,\rho) := \langle \mathbf{c}, u\rangle_{X^{N_l}} + \|Du\|_\varepsilon + \langle \rho, \sum_k u^k - \mathbf{1}\rangle_X + \mu \sum_{k,i}(\log(u_i^k) + \log(1-u_i^k)),$$

where $(1,\ldots,1)^\top =: \mathbf{1} \in X$. As the Hessian matrix of E_ε with respect to (u,ρ) needs to be computed at the optimum of $\min_u \max_\rho E_\varepsilon(u,\rho)$, we seek for its efficient optimization. We use the PD algorithm [20] (see (5)) with Euclidean proximity functions by setting $f(u) = \|Du\|_\varepsilon$, $g(u) = \langle \mathbf{c}, u\rangle_{X^{N_l}} + \mu \sum_{k,i}(\log(u_i^k) + \log(1-u_i^k))$, $h^*(\rho) = \langle \rho, \mathbf{1}\rangle_X$, and K such that $Ku := \sum_k u^k$. The Lipschitz constant of ∇f is $L_f = 8/\varepsilon$, the operator norm is $L = \|K\| = N_l$, and the strong convexity modulus of g is -8μ. These properties allow us to use the accelerated PD algorithm. Sadly, the proximal map of g requires to solve (coordinate-wise) for the unique root of a cubic polynomial in $[0,1]$, which is expensive.

Discussion of the smoothed model. Opposed to our approach, smoothing the energy has several disadvantages: (1) It is only an approximation to the actual energy; (2) additional terms for dealing with constraints are required; (3) the extra variable ρ increases the size of the Hessian matrix of E_ε by $N_x N_y$ to $N_x N_y (N_l + 1)$; (4) the proximal map is costly to solve; and (5) the Lipschitz constant, hence the step size, is directly affected by ε, i.e. by the approximation quality. (5) can be resolved by another approximation. If we set $f = 0$ and dualize the Charbonnier function, the step size becomes independent of ε. However, the proximal map for the Charbonnier function—the same holds for its dual function—is not simple, a numerical solver is required for its minimization.

5.6 Experiment for Parameter Learning

We consider the bilevel optimization problem in (10) with ground truth parameters $(\hat{\vartheta}^1, \hat{\vartheta}^2) = (0.4, 0.6)$. The balancing parameter was set to $\lambda = 20$. The dataset consists of 50 images from the Weizmann horse dataset [23]. Each image was converted to gray scale and downsampled by factor 10. For each image, we generated a segmentation by running 2000 iterations of (11) with the ground truth mean value parameters. Note that this is a numerical toy problem, where we are interested in retrieving the parameters that lead to these segmentations. We are *not* interested in segmentations that correspond to horses.

Figure 1 shows the upper level energy (solid lines) obtained using segmentations for parameters $(\vartheta^1, \vartheta^2)$ sampled on a regular grid. The dashed lines correspond to the smoothed lower level problem with $\varepsilon = 0.1$, $\mu = 10^{-4}$. The energies differ a lot, although this is a simple problem. Reducing ε yields better approximations but also makes the lower level problem harder to solve.

We solve the learning problem with a simple gradient descent method with backtracking initialized at $(0.13, 0.56)$ with a maximum of 50 iterations. Figure 2 compares the convergence of our method with the implicit differentiation approach (implDiff) for different numbers of inner iterations. Our approach reaches the optimum already for 200 iterations. It clearly requires fewer inner iterations than the implDiff method. The segmentations are shown in Figure 3.

As Figure 2 shows, the gradient directions computed with our framework align with the geometric gradient—this is the reason for optimizing with gradient descent—, which is orthogonal to the level lines. The gradients computed with the implDiff framework often point to a different direction. For a small number of inner iterations, the energy computed with the smoothed segmentation model deviates even more from the original energy than in Figure 1. Inverting the poorly conditioned Hessian matrix (by solving a system of equations) amplifies inaccuracies of the lower level solution significantly.

As the original and the smoothed energies have similar minimizers in this two-dimensional example, also the implDiff framework approaches the optimum with more inner iterations. Due to inappropriate step sizes determined by the simple backtracking that we use, our method fails to find the optimum when using 800 inner iterations. With iPiano [24] we found the exact optimum; see also Figure 3. Another option to iPiano is L-BFGS [25].

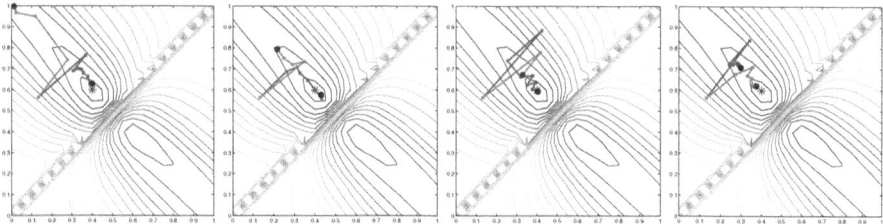

Fig. 2. Convergence of our approach (red line) vs. the implDiff approach (green line) visualized on a contour plot of the two-parameter problem. From left to right: The learning problem is solved with 20, 100, 400, and 800 inner iteration. The gradients computed with our method are orthogonal to the level lines even for few inner iterations.

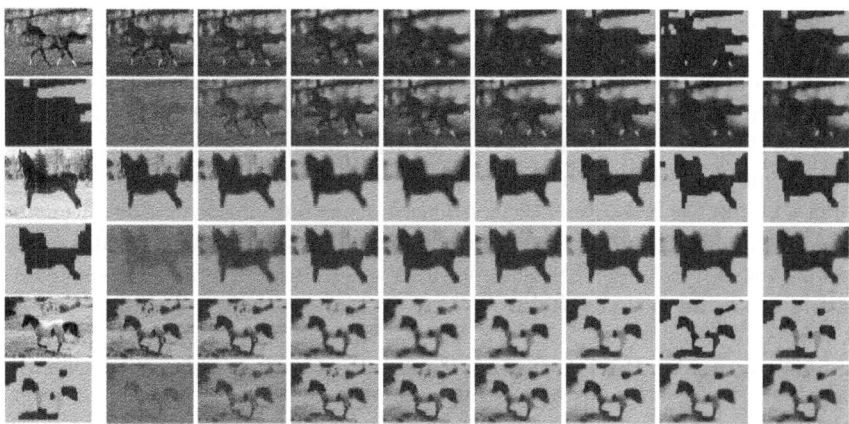

Fig. 3. Row-wise alternating: left column: input sample, ground truth segmentation; right block: our method, implDiff; and from left to right: numbers of inner iterations: 5, 20, 50, 100, 200, 400, 800, and 800 (iPiano) for the two-parameter problem.

Since the parameter learning problem is nonconvex, initialization matters. The initialization that we used was selected among 3 randomly generated proposals, to show a good performance of both approaches. In general our gradient based optimization could be a good complement to zero-order search methods. This will be subject to future work.

We simulate such a scenario by initializing the following 4-label segmentation experiment close to the optimum. We perturb the ground truth parameters $(0.17, 0.37, 0.42, 0.98)$ randomly with numbers drawn uniformly in $[-0.1, 0.1]$. λ is set to 120, and 400 inner iterations are performed on the single training example in Figure 4. The final Euclidean distance, the error, between our solution parameters and the ground truth parameters is about $0.4 \cdot 10^{-2}$, and for implDiff it is $4.75 \cdot 10^{-2}$. Corresponding segmentations are shown in Figure 4.

  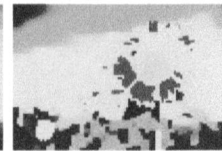

Fig. 4. Parameter learning problem and results for sunflowers (102×68). From left to right: input image, ground truth segmentation with mean values $(0.17, 0.37, 0.42, 0.98)$, segmentation obtained with implDiff, and our method, both with 400 inner iterations.

6 Conclusion

We considered a bilevel optimization problem for parameter learning and proposed a way to overcome one of its main drawbacks. Solving the problem with gradient based methods requires to compute the gradient with respect to the parameters and thus also requires (twice) differentiability of the lower level problem. With our approach the lower level problem can be nondifferentiable; Only a differentiable mapping from the parameters to a solution of the lower level problem is needed. We propose to use the iteration mapping of a recently proposed primal–dual algorithm with Bregman proximity functions as such a mapping. Fixing a number of iterations, the computation of gradients w.r.t. the parameters is exact. Our algorithm learns to yield optimal parameters when using exactly this number of iterations. The abstract idea was exemplified on the (nonsmooth) multi-label segmentation problem.

Acknowledgments. Peter Ochs and Thomas Brox acknowledge support by DFG grant BR 3815/8-1 in the SPP 1527 Autonomous Learning. René Ranftl and Thomas Pock acknowledge support from the Austrian science fund under the ANR-FWF project "Efficient algorithms for nonsmooth optimization in imaging", No. I1148 and the FWF-START project "Bilevel optimization for Computer Vision", No. Y729.

References

1. Kunisch, K., Pock, T.: A bilevel optimization approach for parameter learning in variational models. SIAM Journal on Imaging Sciences **6**(2), 938–983 (2013)
2. Reyes, J.C.D.L., Schönlieb, C.B.: Image denoising: Learning noise distribution via pde-constrained optimisation. Inverse Problems and Imaging **7**, 1183–1214 (2013)
3. Samuel, K., Tappen, M.: Learning optimized MAP estimates in continuously-valued MRF models. In: International Conference on Computer Vision and Pattern Recognition (CVPR), 477–484 (2009)
4. Tappen, M., Samuel, K., Dean, C., Lyle, D.: The logistic random field-a convenient graphical model for learning parameters for MRF-based labeling. In: International Conference on Computer Vision and Pattern Recognition (CVPR), pp. 1–8 (2008)
5. Wainwright, M., Jaakkola, T., Willsky, A.: MAP estimation via agreement on (hyper)trees: Message-passing and linear programming approaches. IEEE Transactions on Information Theory **51**, 3697–3717 (2002)
6. Hinton, G.: Training products of experts by minimizing contrastive divergence. Neural Computation **14**(8), 1771–1800 (2002)

7. Taskar, B., Chatalbashev, V., Koller, D., Guestrin, C.: Learning structured prediction models: a large margin approach. In: International Conference on Machine Learning (ICML), pp. 896–903 (2005)
8. LeCun, Y., Huang, F.: Loss functions for discriminative training of energy-based models. In: International Workshop on Artificial Intelligence and Statistics (2005)
9. Snoek, J., Larochelle, H., Adams, R.P.: Practical Bayesian optimization of machine learning algorithms. In: Advances in Neural Information Processing Systems (NIPS), pp. 2951–2959 (2012)
10. Hutter, F., Hoos, H.H., Leyton-Brown, K.: Sequential model-based optimization for general algorithm configuration. In: Coello, C.A.C. (ed.) LION 2011. LNCS, vol. 6683, pp. 507–523. Springer, Heidelberg (2011)
11. Eggensperger, K., Feurer, M., Hutter, F., Bergstra, J., Snoek, J., Hoos, H., Leyton-Brown, K.: Towards an empirical foundation for assessing Bayesian optimization of hyperparameters. In: NIPS Workshop (2013)
12. Ranftl, R., Pock, T.: A deep variational model for image segmentation. In: Jiang, X., Hornegger, J., Koch, R. (eds.) GCPR 2014. LNCS, vol. 8753, pp. 104–115. Springer, Heidelberg (2014)
13. Peyré, G., Fadili, J.: Learning analysis sparsity priors. In: Proceedings of Sampta (2011)
14. Chen, Y., Pock, T., Ranftl, R., Bischof, H.: Revisiting loss-specific training of filter-based MRFs for image restoration. In: Weickert, J., Hein, M., Schiele, B. (eds.) GCPR 2013. LNCS, vol. 8142, pp. 271–281. Springer, Heidelberg (2013)
15. Chen, Y., Ranftl, R., Pock, T.: Insights into analysis operator learning: From patch-based sparse models to higher order MRFs. IEEE Transactions on Image Processing **23**(3), 1060–1072 (2014)
16. Tappen, M.: Utilizing variational optimization to learn MRFs. In: International Conference on Computer Vision and Pattern Recognition (CVPR), pp. 1–8 (2007)
17. Domke, J.: Generic methods for optimization-based modeling. In: International Workshop on Artificial Intelligence and Statistics, pp. 318–326 (2012)
18. Geman, D., Reynolds, G.: Constrained restoration and the recovery of discontinuities. IEEE Transactions on Pattern Analysis and Machine Intelligence **14**, 367–383 (1992)
19. Chambolle, A., Pock, T.: A first-order primal-dual algorithm for convex problems with applications to imaging. Journal of Mathematical Imaging and Vision **40**(1), 120–145 (2011)
20. Chambolle, A., Pock, T.: On the ergodic convergence rates of a first-order primal-dual algorithm. Technical report (2014) (to appear)
21. Deledalle, C.A., Vaiter, S., Fadili, J., Peyré, G.: Stein Unbiased GrAdient estimator of the Risk (SUGAR) for multiple parameter selection. SIAM Journal on Imaging Sciences **7**(4), 2448–2487 (2014)
22. Foo, C.S., Do, C., Ng, A.: Efficient multiple hyperparameter learning for log-linear models. In: Advances in Neural Information Processing Systems (NIPS), pp. 377–384. Curran Associates, Inc. (2008)
23. Borenstein, E., Sharon, E., Ullman, S.: Combining top-down and bottom-up segmentation. In: International Conference on Computer Vision and Pattern Recognition Workshop (CVPR) (2004)
24. Ochs, P., Chen, Y., Brox, T., Pock, T.: ipiano: Inertial proximal algorithm for non-convex optimization. SIAM Journal on Imaging Sciences **7**(2), 1388–1419 (2014)
25. Liu, D.C., Nocedal, J.: On the limited memory BFGS method for large scale optimization. Mathematical Programming **45**(1), 503–528 (1989)

Convex Image Denoising via Non-Convex Regularization

Alessandro Lanza, Serena Morigi(✉), and Fiorella Sgallari

Department of Mathematics, University of Bologna, Bologna, Italy
{alessandro.lanza2,serena.morigi,fiorella.sgallari}@unibo.it

Abstract. Natural image statistics motivate the use of non-convex over convex regularizations for restoring images. However, they are rarely used in practice due to the challenge to find a good minimizer. We propose a Convex Non-Convex (CNC) denoising variational model and an efficient minimization algorithm based on the Alternating Directions Methods of Multipliers (ADMM) approach. We provide theoretical convexity conditions for both the CNC model and the optimization sub-problems arising in the ADMM-based procedure, such that convergence to a unique global minimizer is guaranteed. Numerical examples show that the proposed approach is particularly effective and well suited for images characterized by sparse-gradient distributions.

Keywords: Non-convex non-smooth regularization · Image denoising · Alternating directions method of multipliers

1 Introduction

This work is concerned with the computation of approximate solutions of the image denoising problem by the following variational model

$$\min_{u \in \mathbb{R}^n} \left\{ \mathcal{J}(u) = \frac{1}{2}\|u - b\|_2^2 + \mu \sum_{i=1}^n \phi(\|(\nabla u)_i\|_2) \right\}, \quad (1)$$

where $b, u \in \mathbb{R}^n$ are the available noisy image and the unknown uncorrupted image to be estimated, respectively, represented in vectorized form, $\mu > 0$ is the so-called regularization parameter, $\phi : \mathbb{R} \to \mathbb{R}$ is the regularization (or penalty) function, and $(\nabla x)_i \in \mathbb{R}^2$ denotes the discretization of the gradient of image u at pixel i, so that: $\|(\nabla u)_i\|_2 = \sqrt{(D_h u)_i^2 + (D_v u)_i^2}$, with the linear operators $D_h, D_v \in \mathbb{R}^{n \times n}$ representing finite difference approximations of first-order horizontal and vertical partial derivatives, respectively.

The regularization term in (1) encodes a prior on the image gradients magnitude, and the function ϕ is intended so as to strongly promote sparsity and consequently to better fit gradient distributions of real images.

A very popular choice for ϕ is the Tikhonov regularization, which involves a smooth, convex regularization term: e.g. ℓ_2 norm, $\phi(t) = t^2$. Although many efficient image restoration methods have been proposed [2],[3], Tikhonov regularization does not preserve edges well in the restoration process. Non-smooth, convex regularization terms, e.g. Total Variation (TV) regularization [11], ℓ_1 norm, $\phi(t) = |t|$, allow for discontinuities in the restored image, making them an acceptable penalty function for images. Convex formulations benefit from convex optimization theory which leads to robust algorithms with guaranteed convergence. On the other hand, non-smooth, non-convex regularization has remarkable advantages over convex regularization for restoring images, in particular to restore high-quality piecewise constant images with neat edges [6],[9],[7]. However, it may lead to challenging computation problems since it requires non-convex non-smooth minimization which, involving many minima, can often get stuck in shallow local minima. The non-smooth non-convex and non-Lipschitz regularization term, ℓ_p quasi-norm, $\phi(t) = |t|^p$, with $0 < p < 1$, has recently been proposed in image processing and compressed sensing since it promotes gradient-sparser solutions or sparser solutions, substantially improving upon the ℓ_1 norm results [1],[14].

This paper investigates the use of non-convex penalty functions ϕ, under the constraint that the total cost function J in (1) is convex and therefore reliably minimized. This approach has been successfully followed by [12][5] and [13], where convexity conditions for the functional are provided. However, in [12][5] the non-convex penalty depends only on $\|u\|_2$ and not on $\|\nabla u\|_2$, while in [13] only the 1D denoising case is considered.

Towards this aim, we employ penalty functions parameterized by variables a, i.e., $\phi(t) = \phi(t;a)$, wherein the parameters a are selected so as to ensure convexity of the total cost function J. Consequently, the minimizer is unique and can be computed by using efficient convex optimization algorithms.

In Section 2 we briefly illustrate the penalty functions considered in the proposed model, and in Section 3 we provide theoretical convexity conditions for the minimized functional. An efficient ADMM-based minimization algorithm is presented in Section 4, where we also provide suitable conditions on the parameter a for $\phi(t;a)$ to guarantee convexity of ADMM sub-problems. Numerical experiments are presented in Section 5, where the proposed convex model with non-convex non-smooth regularization is compared with a convex regularized convex model and a non-convex regularized non-convex model.

2 Non-Convex Penalty Functions

Different non-convex non-smooth penalty functions have been recently considered in the context of restoration for images with neat edges [7],[8].

We will consider penalty functions ϕ in (1) under the assumptions that they are continuous, symmetric, twice differentiable, increasing, and concave on $\mathbb{R}_* = \mathbb{R}_+ \cup 0$. In particular, we will consider the ϕ penalty functions proposed in [12],[5] and used in [13] for 1-D total variation denoising, which satisfy the above assumptions and are parameterized by a scalar parameter $a > 0$:

$$\phi(t;a) = \frac{1}{a}\log(1+a|t|), \qquad (2)$$

$$\phi(t;a) = \frac{2}{a\sqrt{3}}\left(\tan^{-1}\left(\frac{1+2a|t|}{\sqrt{3}}\right) - \frac{\pi}{6}\right), \qquad (3)$$

$$\phi(t;a) = \frac{|t|}{1+a|t|/2}. \qquad (4)$$

In the following we will consider model (1) with ϕ given by the penalty functions (2), (3), or (4) and we will refer to it as Convex Non-Convex (CNC) model. The choice of concave penalty functions ϕ in (1) is to enforce gradient sparsity more strongly than any convex regularizer [7].

We finally notice that the penalty functions (2), (3), and (4) all exhibit the following properties:

$$\phi'(0) = 1, \qquad \inf_{t\geq 0} \phi''(t;a) = \phi''(0) = -a, \qquad (5)$$

and $\phi(t;a) \longrightarrow |t|$ for a tending to zero, that is the TV regularization.

3 Convexity Conditions

We aim to find conditions on the regularization parameter μ and on the shape parameter a of the non-convex penalty functions $\phi(t;a)$ in (2), (3), (4) such that the cost function $\mathcal{J}$ in (1) is strictly convex.

Towards this aim, we rewrite the function $\mathcal{J}$ in (1) as follows:

$$\mathcal{J}(u) = \frac{1}{2}\sum_{(i,j)\in\Omega}(u_{i,j}-b_{i,j})^2 + \mu\sum_{(i,j)\in\Omega}\phi\left(\sqrt{(u_{i+1,j}-u_{i,j})^2 + (u_{i,j+1}-u_{i,j})^2}\right), \qquad (6)$$

where Ω represents the image lattice defined as

$$\Omega = \left\{(i,j)\in\mathbb{Z}^2 : i=1,\ldots,\sqrt{n},\ j=1,\ldots,\sqrt{n}\right\}. \qquad (7)$$

To the purpose of splitting the function $\mathcal{J}$ in (6) into the sum of easier functions, we define the sets of odd and even integers

$$\mathrm{O} := \{i\in\mathbb{Z}: i \text{ is odd}\} \quad \text{and} \quad \mathrm{E} := \{i\in\mathbb{Z}: i \text{ is even}\}, \qquad (8)$$

and we introduce the following partition of Ω, illustrated in Figure 1(left):

$$\begin{aligned}\mathrm{OO} &:= \{(i,j)\in\Omega: i\in\mathrm{O},\ j\in\mathrm{O}\} & \mathrm{EE} &:= \{(i,j)\in\Omega: i\in\mathrm{E},\ j\in\mathrm{E}\}\\ \mathrm{OE} &:= \{(i,j)\in\Omega: i\in\mathrm{O},\ j\in\mathrm{E}\} & \mathrm{EO} &:= \{(i,j)\in\Omega: i\in\mathrm{E},\ j\in\mathrm{O}\}\end{aligned}. \qquad (9)$$

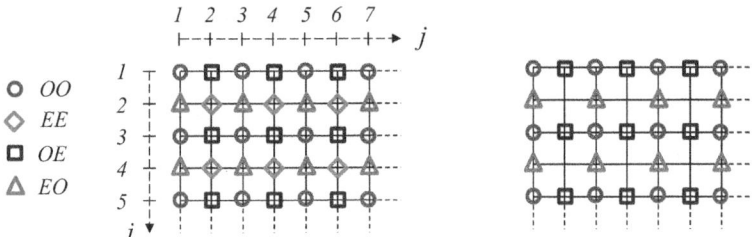

Fig. 1. Partition of the image lattice Ω in (7) into the four subsets OO, EE, OE and EO defined in (9) (left); image stencil involved by function $\mathcal{J}_{OO}$ in (11) (right)

It can be shown that the function $\mathcal{J}$ can be split as follows:
$$\mathcal{J}(x) = \mathcal{J}_{OO}(u) + \mathcal{J}_{EE}(u) + \mathcal{J}_{OE}(u) + \mathcal{J}_{EO}(u). \tag{10}$$
Since the four functions $\mathcal{J}_A$, A = OO, EE, OE, EO, have the same structure, convexity of $\mathcal{J}$ can be studied by just considering the function $\mathcal{J}_{OO}$. We rewrite $\mathcal{J}_{OO}$ as follows:

$$\mathcal{J}_{OO}(u) = \sum_{(i,j)\in OO} \left[\frac{1}{6}(u_{i,j} - b_{i,j})^2 + \frac{1}{6}(u_{i+1,j} - b_{i+1,j})^2 + \frac{1}{6}(u_{i,j+1} - b_{i,j+1})^2 + \right.$$
$$\left. + \mu\,\phi\left(\sqrt{(u_{i+1,j} - u_{i,j})^2 + (u_{i,j+1} - u_{i,j})^2}\right) \right] \tag{11}$$

In Figure 1(right) we illustrate the subset of the image lattice Ω involved by function $\mathcal{J}_{OO}$ in (11). Let us define the function $f : \mathbb{R}^3 \to \mathbb{R}$ as
$$f(x_1, x_2, x_3) = \frac{1}{6}(x_1^2 + x_2^2 + x_3^2) + \mu\,\phi\left(\sqrt{(x_2 - x_1)^2 + (x_3 - x_1)^2}\right). \tag{12}$$
Then, (11) can be rewritten as follows
$$\mathcal{J}_{OO}(u) = \sum_{(i,j)\in OO} \left[f(u_{i,j}, u_{i+1,j}, u_{i,j+1}) + L(u_{i,j}, u_{i+1,j}, u_{i,j+1}) \right], \tag{13}$$
where L is a linear function which, hence, does not affect convexity.

To study convexity of functional $\mathcal{J}$ in (1), we give three propositions which allow to reduce convexity investigation from the original functional $\mathcal{J}$ of n variables to easier functions f, g and h of three, two and one variables, respectively.

Proposition 1. *The function $\mathcal{J} : \mathbb{R}^n \to \mathbb{R}$ defined in (1) is convex if the function $f : \mathbb{R}^3 \to \mathbb{R}$ defined in (12) is convex.*

The proof is straightforward given (10) and (13).

Proposition 2. *The function $f : \mathbb{R}^3 \to \mathbb{R}$ defined in (12) is convex if and only if the function $g : \mathbb{R}^2 \to \mathbb{R}$ is convex, with*
$$g(y_1, y_2) = \frac{1}{6}(y_1^2 + y_2^2) + \mu\,\phi\left(\sqrt{y_1^2 + y_2^2}\right). \tag{14}$$

Proposition 3. Let $\phi : \mathbb{R}_* \to \mathbb{R}$ be a twice differentiable function. Then, the function $g : \mathbb{R}^2 \to \mathbb{R}$ defined in (14) is convex if and only if the function $h : \mathbb{R}_* \to \mathbb{R}$ defined as

$$h(t) = \frac{1}{6}t^2 + \mu\,\phi(t) \tag{15}$$

is monotonically increasing and convex.

Theorem 1. Let $\mu > 0$ and $\phi : \mathbb{R}_* \to \mathbb{R}$ be a function satisfying assumptions in Section 2. Then, the function $\mathcal{J} : \mathbb{R}^n \to \mathbb{R}$ in (1) is convex if the following condition holds:

$$\inf_{t \geq 0} \left[\phi''(t)\right] > -\frac{1}{3\mu}. \tag{16}$$

Proof. Based on Propositions 1–3, the function $\mathcal{J}$ in (1) is convex if the twice differentiable function h defined in (15) is monotonically increasing and convex everywhere in its domain $\mathbb{R}_*$, that is if the following two conditions hold:

$$\begin{cases} h'(t) = \dfrac{1}{3}t + \mu\,\phi'(t) > 0 \\ h''(t) = \dfrac{1}{3} + \mu\,\phi''(t) > 0 \end{cases} \equiv \begin{cases} \phi'(t) > -\dfrac{t}{3\mu} \\ \phi''(t) > -\dfrac{1}{3\mu} \end{cases} \forall t \geq 0. \tag{17}$$

Since by hypothesis $\mu > 0$ and the function ϕ is monotonically increasing in $\mathbb{R}_*$, i.e. $\phi'(t) > 0$ for every $t \geq 0$, the first condition in (17) is always satisfied. The second condition in (17) can be equivalently rewritten as in (16). □

For the proposed CNC model, where ϕ satisfies (5), condition (16) reduces to

$$\mu\,a < \frac{1}{3}. \tag{18}$$

4 Applying ADMM to the Proposed CNC Model

In this section, we illustrate the ADMM-based iterative approach used to solve the unconstrained minimization problem in (1). Towards this aim, we first introduce an auxiliary variables $t \in \mathbb{R}^{2n}$ to reformulate (1) into the following linearly constrained equivalent form:

$$\{u^*, t^*\} \leftarrow \arg\min_{u,t} \left\{ \frac{1}{2}\|u - b\|_2^2 + \mu \sum_{i=1}^{n} \phi(\|t_i\|_2) \right\} \quad \text{s.t.} \quad t = Du, \tag{19}$$

where $D = (D_h; D_v) \in \mathbb{R}^{2n \times n}$ and $t_i = \bigl((D_h u)_i, (D_v u)_i\bigr) \in \mathbb{R}^2$. The auxiliary variable t is introduced to transfer the discrete gradient operator $(\nabla u)_i$ in (1) out of the possibly non-differentiable and non-convex regularization term $\phi(\|\cdot\|_2)$.

To solve (19), we define the augmented Lagrangian functional

$$\mathcal{L}(u, t; \lambda) = \frac{1}{2}\|u - b\|_2^2 + \mu \sum_{i=1}^{n} \phi(\|t_i\|_2) - \langle \lambda, t - Du \rangle + \frac{\beta}{2}\|t - Du\|_2^2, \tag{20}$$

where $\beta > 0$ is a scalar penalty parameter and $\lambda \in \mathbb{R}^{2n}$ is the vector of Lagrange multipliers associated with the linear constraint $t = Dx$. Solving (19) is thus equivalent to search for the solutions of the following saddle point problem:

Find $(u^*, t^*; \lambda^*) \in V \times Q^2$

s.t. $\mathcal{L}(u^*, t^*; \lambda) \leq \mathcal{L}(u^*, t^*; \lambda^*) \leq \mathcal{L}(u, t; \lambda^*) \quad \forall (u, t; \lambda) \in V \times Q^2$, (21)

with $\mathcal{L}$ defined in (20), $V := \mathbb{R}^n$, $Q := \mathbb{R}^{2n}$.

Starting at $u = u^k$, $\lambda = \lambda^k$, the ADMM iterative scheme applied to the solution of (19) or, equivalently, of the saddle point problem (20)-(21), reads as:

$$t^{k+1} \leftarrow \arg\min_{t \in Q} \mathcal{L}(u^k, t; \lambda^k) \qquad (22)$$

$$u^{k+1} \leftarrow \arg\min_{u \in V} \mathcal{L}(u, t^{k+1}; \lambda^k) \qquad (23)$$

$$\lambda^{k+1} \leftarrow \lambda^k - \gamma\beta\left(t^{k+1} - Du^{k+1}\right) \qquad (24)$$

where γ is a relaxation parameter chosen in the interval $(0, (\sqrt{5}+1)/2)$, as analyzed in [4]. In the following we show in detail how to solve the two minimization sub-problems (22) and (23) for the variables t and u, respectively, then we present the overall iterative ADMM-based minimization algorithm.

Solving the Sub-Problem for u. Given λ^k and t^{k+1}, and recalling the definition of the augmented Lagrangian functional in (20), the minimization subproblem for u in (23) can be rewritten as follows:

$$u^{k+1} \leftarrow \arg\min_{u \in V} \left\{ \frac{1}{2}\|u - b\|_2^2 + \langle \lambda^k, Du \rangle + \frac{\beta}{2}\|t^{k+1} - Du\|_2^2 \right\}, \qquad (25)$$

where constant terms have been omitted. The quadratic minimization problem (25) has first-order optimality conditions which lead to the following linear system:

$$\left(\beta D^T D + I\right) u = b - D^T \lambda^k + \beta D^T t^{k+1}. \qquad (26)$$

The coefficient matrix of the linear system (26) is symmetric positive definite and does not change with iterations provided that the penalty parameter β is kept fixed. Moreover, since under periodic boundary conditions for u the matrix $D^T D$ is block circulant with circulant blocks, the coefficient matrix can be diagonalized once for all by the 2D discrete Fourier transform (FFT implementation). Therefore, at each iteration the linear system (26) can be solved by one forward FFT and one inverse FFT, each at a cost of $O(n \log \sqrt{n})$.

Solving the Sub-Problem for t. Given λ^k and u^k, and recalling definition (20), the minimization sub-problem for t in (22) can be written as follows:

$$t^{k+1} \leftarrow \arg\min_{t \in Q} \left\{ \mu \sum_{i=1}^{n} \phi(\|t_i\|_2) - \langle \lambda_t, t - Du^k \rangle + \frac{\beta}{2} \|t - Du^k\|_2^2 \right\}$$

$$\leftarrow \arg\min_{t \in Q} \left\{ \mu \sum_{i=1}^{n} \phi(\|t_i\|_2) + \frac{\beta}{2} \left\| t - \left(Du^k + \frac{1}{\beta}\lambda^k\right) \right\|_2^2 \right\}$$

$$\leftarrow \arg\min_{t \in Q} \sum_{i=1}^{n} \left\{ \mu \phi(\|t_i\|_2) + \frac{\beta}{2} \left\| t_i - \left((Du^k)_i + \frac{1}{\beta}\lambda_i^k\right) \right\|_2^2 \right\}. \quad (27)$$

Note that in (27) the minimized functional is written in explicit component-wise form, with $(Du^k)_i, \lambda_i^k \in \mathbb{R}^2$ denoting the discrete gradient and the Lagrange multipliers at pixel i, respectively. The minimization problem in (27) is thus equivalent to the following n independent 2-dimensional problems:

$$t_i^{k+1} \leftarrow \arg\min_{t_i \in \mathbb{R}^2} \left\{ \phi(\|t_i\|_2) + \frac{(\beta/\mu)}{2} \|t_i - q_i^k\|_2^2 \right\}, \quad i = 1, \ldots, n, \quad (28)$$

with the constant vectors $q_i^k \in \mathbb{R}^2$ defined as

$$q_i^k := (Du^k)_i + \frac{1}{\beta} \lambda_i^k, \quad i = 1, \ldots, n. \quad (29)$$

Since we have imposed convexity of the functional J minimized in (1), we want to avoid that (28) is a non-convex problem. In the first part of Proposition 4 below, we give necessary and sufficient conditions for convexity of the functions minimized in sub-problems (28).

Proposition 4. *Let $\alpha > 0$ and $q \in \mathbb{R}^2$ be given constants, and let $\phi : \mathbb{R}_* \to \mathbb{R}$ be a function satisfying assumptions in Section 2. Then, the function*

$$\theta(x) = \phi(\|x\|_2) + \frac{\alpha}{2} \|x - q\|_2^2, \quad x \in \mathbb{R}^2, \quad (30)$$

is convex if and only if the following condition holds:

$$\alpha > -\inf_{t \geq 0} [\phi''(t)]. \quad (31)$$

Moreover, in case that (31) holds, the convex minimization problem

$$\arg\min_{x \in \mathbb{R}^2} \theta(x) \quad (32)$$

admits the unique solution x^* given by the following shrinkage operator:

$$x^* = \xi^* q, \quad \text{with } \xi^* \in [0, 1[\quad (33)$$

equal to

a) $\xi^* = 0$ if $\|q\|_2 \leq \dfrac{1}{\alpha}\phi'(0)$

b) ξ^* in $]0,1[$ unique solution of :   (34)

$\phi'(\|q\|_2\,\xi) + \alpha\|q\|_2(\xi - 1) = 0$ otherwise

In particular, based on (30)-(31) in Proposition 4 and recalling the second property in (5) of the penalty functions used in our CNC model, we can state that sub-problems in (28) are convex if and only if the following condition holds:

$$\beta > \mu a. \tag{35}$$

In case that (35) is satisfied, the unique solution of the convex sub-problems in (28) can be obtained as reported in the second part of Proposition 4, that is:

$$t_i^{k+1} = \xi_i^{k+1}\, q_i^k, \quad i = 1,\ldots, n, \tag{36}$$

where the shrinkage coefficients $\xi_i^{k+1} \in [0,1[$ are computed according to (34). In particular, recalling the first property in (5), coefficients are computed as follows:

$$\xi_i^{k+1} = \begin{cases} 0 & \text{if } \|q_i^k\|_2 \leq \mu/\beta \\ \xi^* \in]0,1[\text{ s.t. } \phi'(\|q_i^k\|_2\xi^*) + \tfrac{\beta}{\mu}\|q_i^k\|_2(\xi^* - 1) = 0 & \text{otherwise} \end{cases} \tag{37}$$

The nonlinear equation in (37) is solved by very few steps of the iterative Newton-Raphson method. In particular, it can be demonstrated that by choosing $\xi^* = 1$ as the initial guess, the algorithm is guaranteed to converge (with quadratic rate) to the unique root of the nonlinear equation. Finally, we notice that the overall computational cost of this sub-problem is linear with the number of pixels n.

Algorithm 1. ADMM-based iterative scheme for the solution of problem (1)

Input: degraded image b, regularization parameter $\mu > 0$
Output: approximate solution u^* of (1)

1. *Initialize:* $u^0 = b$, $\lambda^0 = 0$
2. **For** $k = 0, 1, 2, \ldots$ *until convergence:*
        a) given u^k, λ^k,   compute t^{k+1} by (29), (36) and (37)
        b) given t^{k+1}, λ^k,   compute u^{k+1} by solving (26)
        c) given $u^{k+1}, t^{k+1}, \lambda^k$,   compute λ^{k+1} by (24)
   End For

ADMM-Based Minimization Algorithm. To summarize previous results, in Algorithm 1 we report the main steps of the proposed ADMM-based iterative scheme used to solve the minimization problem in (1).

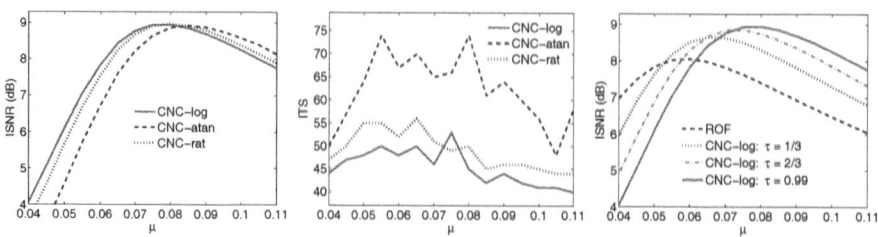

Fig. 2. Example 1: ISNR values (left); number of performed iterations (middle); ISNR values of CNC-log model vs. ROF (right)

5 Numerical Examples

In this section, we evaluate the performance of the proposed denoising algorithm when applied to three 256 × 256 test images cameraman, satellite and checkboard synthetically corrupted by additive zero-mean white Gaussian noise. More precisely, we aim at investigating the advantages of using convex models with non-convex instead of convex penalty functions, particularly for images characterized by sparse gradients. In Example 2 below, we compare the proposed CNC model with the well-known convex Rudin-Osher-Fatemi (ROF) model [11], based on the minimization of the so-called TV-ℓ_2 functional, and with the non-convex TV$_p$ model [1]. Especially for sparse-gradient images, among the denoising models of type (1) with convex regularizers, the ROF model [11] is known to be one of the best performing, while among the non-convex regularizers, the ℓ_p quasi-norm ($p < 1$) is known to provide very good results [1].

For minimizing the proposed CNC model we used the ADMM-based procedure reported in Algorithm 1, which requires the relaxation parameter γ in (24) and the penalty parameter β in (20) to be set. We used $\gamma = 1$ (no relaxation), which is a pretty standard choice, while we set $\beta = \max\{\mu a, 2\}$ so as to satisfy condition (35) for convexity of the ADMM sub-problems and, at the same time, guarantee fast convergence. Since the ROF and TV$_p$ models are particular instances of model (1) where $\phi(t) = |t|$ and $\phi(t) = |t|^p$, respectively, we used the same ADMM-based scheme as in Algorithm 1 with suitably chosen shrinkage coefficients as described in [4],[1], and we set the values $\gamma = 1$ and $\beta = 2$. Finally, for all the algorithms we stopped iterations as soon as the relative change between two successive iterates satisfies $\|u^k - u^{k-1}\|_2 / \|u^{k-1}\|_2 < 10^{-4}$. All these choices allow for a fair comparison of the three approaches.

The accuracy of the methods is evaluated by the Signal-to-Noise Ratio (SNR) defined as $\mathrm{SNR}(u^*, \bar{u}) := 10\log_{10}\left(\|\bar{u} - E(\bar{u})\|_2^2 / \|u^* - \bar{u}\|_2^2\right)$, where $u^* \in \mathbb{R}^n$ is the computed estimate of the uncorrupted image $\bar{u} \in \mathbb{R}^n$ and $E(\bar{u})$ denotes the mean gray level of $\bar{u}$. More precisely, the Improved Signal-to-Noise Ratio (ISNR), defined as $\mathrm{ISNR}(u^*, \bar{u}, b) := \mathrm{SNR}(u^*, \bar{u}) - \mathrm{SNR}(b, \bar{u})$ provides a quantitative measure of the improvement in the quality of the denoised image: a high ISNR value indicates that u^* is an accurate approximation of $\bar{u}$.

Table 1. Example 2: ISNR values and corresponding regularization parameters μ

		cameraman			satellite			checkboard		
	σ	5	10	20	5	10	20	5	10	20
	SNR$_0$	22.72	16.70	10.68	22.97	16.95	10.93	25.99	19.97	13.95
ISNR	ROF	2.33	4.00	6.19	6.13	6.82	8.06	7.73	7.99	8.26
	TVp	2.60	4.27	6.40	7.92	8.18	8.80	**20.24**	**20.53**	**20.20**
	CNC	**2.65**	**4.31**	**6.54**	**8.45**	**8.50**	**8.95**	16.63	15.29	13.72
μ	ROF	0.010	0.024	0.055	0.013	0.027	0.059	0.018	0.035	0.069
	TVp	0.005	0.014	0.042	0.006	0.011	0.033	0.006	0.024	0.088
	CNC	0.019	0.036	0.076	0.022	0.041	0.077	0.045	0.072	0.120
TVp	p	0.7	0.8	0.9	0.4	0.4	0.6	0.1	0.1	0.1

Example 1. In this example we analyze the performance of the proposed CNC model, investigating the behavior of the three different penalty functions introduced in Section 2. The CNC model is applied to the test image `satellite` corrupted by zero-mean additive white Gaussian noise with standard deviation $\sigma = 20$. In Figure 3(a) the perturbed image is shown.

The performance in terms of achieved ISNR values and in terms of number of performed iterations are illustrated in Figures 2(left) and 2(center), respectively. In particular, the value of the regularization parameter μ is set to vary in a suitable range so as to include all the best ISNR results. We notice that from the accuracy point of view there is no meaningful difference among the three considered non-convex penalties. However, the logarithmic penalty (2) provides the best performance in terms of number of required iterations.

In Figure 2(right) we show the different behaviors of the CNC method using the logarithmic penalty function with varying the parameter a according to:

$$a = \tau \frac{1}{3\mu} \qquad (38)$$

where, with respect to (18), we added the parameter $\tau, 0 < \tau \leq 1$, which allows to tune the convexity of the minimized functional. Assuming $\tau = 1/3, 2/3, 0.99$, the best performance are achieved for τ approaching to the upper bound value, while for τ approaching zero we get the ROF model.

Example 2. In this example we carry out a broader evaluation of the proposed CNC model by considering the three test images `cameraman`, `satellite` and `checkboard` corrupted by additive white Gaussian noise with different standard deviations $\sigma = 5, 10, 20$. In particular, based on the results commented in the previous example, we use the CNC-log model with shape parameter a given by (38) with $\tau = 0.99$. We compare our model with the convex ROF [11] and the non-convex TV$_p$ [1] models. In all the experiments, the regularization parameter μ is tuned so as to get the highest ISNR value of the denoised image.

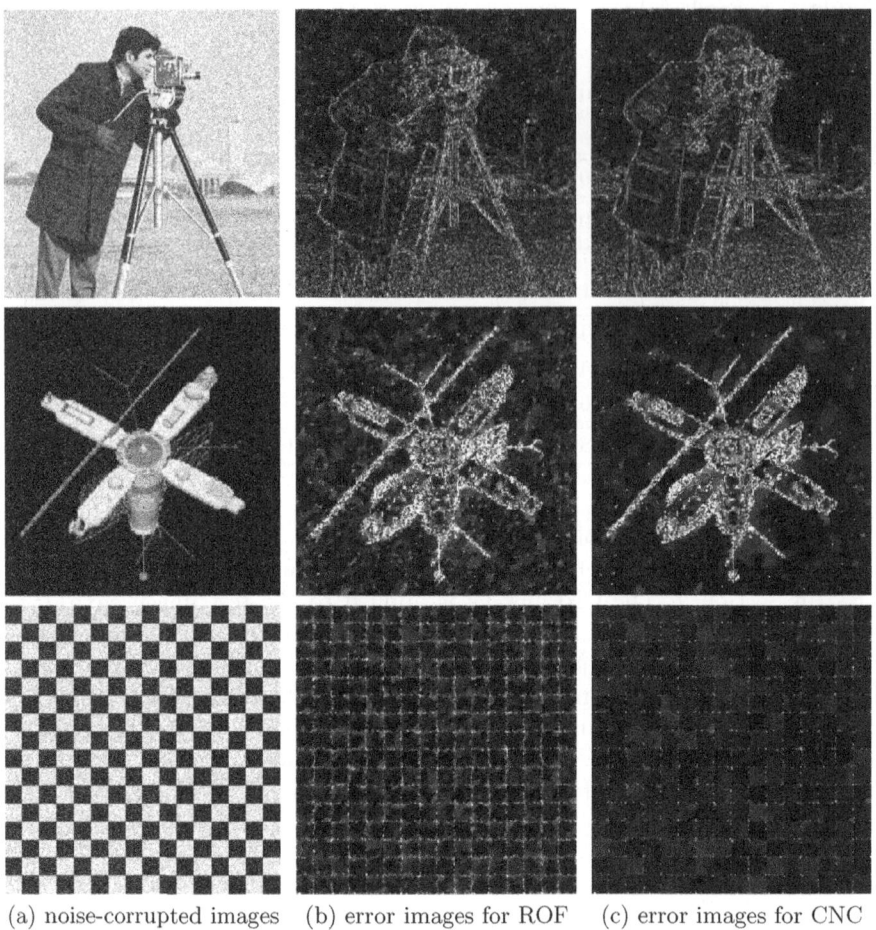

(a) noise-corrupted images   (b) error images for ROF   (c) error images for CNC

Fig. 3. Example 2: Denoising results for images `cameraman` (top), `satellite` (center), `checkboard` (bottom) corrupted by white Gaussian noise of standard deviation $\sigma = 20$

In Figures 3(b) and 3(c) the error images given by $|\bar{u} - u^*|$ are illustrated, as the result of applying ROF model and CNC-log model (with $\tau = 0.99$) to the noisy images shown in Figure 3(a). In Table 1 we report the results of the comparison, with SNR_0 denoting the SNR of the noise-corrupted image and with the highest ISNR values marked in boldface.

We notice that CNC outperforms ROF in all the examples. In particular, the ISNR improvements obtained by CNC with respect to ROF are greater for `satellite` and `checkboard` images. This is not surprising, since these two images are characterized by very sparse gradients and it is well-known that non-convex regularizers hold the potential to induce sparsity more effectively than convex regularizers. In fact, for the gradient-sparsest image `checkboard` the results in Table 1 show that the TV_p model with $p = 0.1$ obtains the best results. However, the choice of the parameter p remains a challenging problem.

6 Conclusions

We presented a variational model for image denoising, which includes a non-convex non-smooth regularization term, together with an efficient ADMM-based minimization algorithm. Theoretical convexity conditions guarantee convergence of the algorithm to a unique global minimizer. The proposed model thus holds the potential for efficient and stable computation due to its convexity and for high-quality denoising due to non-convex regularization. Preliminary numerical results on sparse-gradient images show that the proposed approach outperforms classical convex models with non-smooth but convex regularizers, such as ROF.

Acknowledgments. This work has been supported by INDAM-GNCS 2015 project grant and by the University of Bologna "Funds for selected research topics."

References

1. Lanza, A., Morigi, S., Sgallari, F.: Constrained TVp$-L_2$ model for Image Restoration. http://people.ciram.unibo.it/sgallari/Publications
2. Calvetti, D., Reichel, L.: Tikhonov regularization of large linear problems. BIT Numer. Math. **43**, 263–283 (2003)
3. Calvetti, D., Morigi, S., Reichel, L., Sgallari, F.: Tikhonov regularization and the L-curve for large discrete ill-posed problems. J. Comp. Appl. Math. **123**, 423–446 (2000)
4. Chan, R.H., Tao, M., Yuan, X.M.: Constrained Total Variational Deblurring Models and Fast Algorithms Based on Alternating Direction Method of Multipliers. SIAM J. Imag. Sci. **6**, 680–697 (2013)
5. Chen, P.Y., Selesnick, I.W.: Group-Sparse Signal Denoising: Non-Convex Regularization, Convex Optimization. IEEE Trans. on Sign. Proc. **62**, 3464–3478 (2014)
6. Lu, C.W.: Image restoration and decomposition using non-convex nonsmooth regularisation and negative Hilbert-Sobolev norm. IET Image Proc. **6**, 706–716 (2012)
7. Nikolova, M., Ng, M., Tam, C.P.: On ℓ_1 Data Fitting and Concave Regularization for Image Recovery. SIAM J. on Scientific Computing **35**(1), A397–A430 (2013)
8. Nikolova, M.: Minimizers of Cost-Functions Involving Nonsmooth Data-Fidelity Terms. Application to the Processing of Outliers. SIAM J. on Numerical Analysis **40**(3), 965–994 (2002)
9. Nikolova, M., Ng, M.K., Tam, C.P.: Fast Non-convex Non-smooth Minimization Methods for Image Restoration and Reconstruction. IEEE Trans. Image Proc. **19**(12), 3073–3088 (2010)
10. Rodríguez, P., Wohlberg, B.: Efficient minimization method for a generalized total variation functional. IEEE Trans. Image Proc. **18**, 322–332 (2009)
11. Rudin, L.I., Osher, S., Fatemi, E.: Nonlinear total variation based noise removal algorithms. Physics D **60**(1–4), 259–268 (1992)
12. Selesnick, I.W., Bayram, I.: Sparse Signal Estimation by Maximally Sparse Convex Optimization. IEEE Trans. on Signal Proc. **62**(5), 1078–1092 (2014)
13. Selesnick, I.W., Parekh, A., Bayram, I.: Convex 1-D total variation denoising with non-convex regularization. IEEE Signal Proc. Letters **22**(2), 141–144 (2015)
14. Sidky, E.Y., Chartrand, R., Boone, J.M., Pan, X.: Constrained TpV-Minimization for Enhanced Exploitation of Gradient Sparsity: Application to CT Image Reconstruction. IEEE Trans. Eng. in Health and Medicine **2**, 1–18 (2014)

Infinite Dimensional Optimization Models and PDEs for Dejittering

Guozhi Dong[1], Aniello Raffaele Patrone[1]([✉]), Otmar Scherzer[1,2], and Ozan Öktem[3]

[1] Computational Science Center, University of Vienna,
Oskar-Morgenstern-Platz 1, 1090 Wien, Austria
{guozhi.dong,aniello.patrone,otmar.scherzer}@univie.ac.at
[2] Johann Radon Institute for Computational and Applied Mathematics (RICAM),
Austrian Academy of Sciences, Altenberger Strasse 69, A-4040 Linz, Austria
[3] Department of Mathematics, KTH - Royal Institute of Technology,
Lindstedtsvägen 25, SE-10044 Stockholm, Sweden
ozan@kth.se

Abstract. In this paper we do a systematic investigation of continuous methods for pixel, line pixel and line dejittering. The basis for these investigations are the discrete line dejittering algorithm of Nikolova and the partial differential equation of Lenzen et al for pixel dejittering. To put these two different worlds in perspective we find infinite dimensional optimization algorithms linking to the finite dimensional optimization problems and formal flows associated with the infinite dimensional optimization problems. Two different kinds of optimization problems will be considered: Dejittering algorithms for determining the displacement and displacement error correction formulations, which correct the jittered image, without estimating the jitter. As a by-product we find novel variational methods for displacement error regularization and unify them into one family. The second novelty is a comprehensive comparison of the different models for different types of jitter, in terms of efficiency of reconstruction and numerical complexity.

Keywords: Dejittering · Variational methods · Nonlinear evolution PDEs

1 Introduction

A frequent task in image processing is *dejittering*, which is the process of assigning pixel positions to image data recorded with pixel displacements. Jitter is a type of distortions which arises frequently in signal processing, when the distance (time) between sampling points vary rendering signal errors. A specific form of jitter is line jitter that consists of horizontal shifts of each row (line) of an image. The shift is the same for the entire row. This may typically happen when digitizing analog noisy video frames and there are line registration problems due to bad synchronization pulses. The effect is that the image lines are (randomly) shifted with respect to their original location, so vertical lines become jagged resulting in a disturbing visual effect since all shapes become jagged. One may also have line pixel jitter where pixels in a row are shifted differently. Finally there is pixel jitter where one also experiences vertical shifts.

The main goal of this paper is to establish relations between discrete and continuous models for dejittering. In particular we consider line, line pixel, and pixel jitter. In the literature these problems have been considered in an infinite dimensional continuous and in a finite dimensional discrete setting, resulting in different problem formulations and analysis. To link these approaches and put the theory on solid grounds (based on an infinite dimensional - discretization free - theory) we require to link the approaches.

Presently there exists two kind of algorithms for dejittering which we catalog as follows:

- *Dejittering algorithms* find the displacements by an optimization routine first and then restore the image by composing the jittered image with the displacement.
- *Displacement correction algorithms* compute the image directly without calculating the displacement function first.

The algorithms will be implemented for different purposes: For dejittering we assume a deterministic jitter, while in the later we assume a random perturbation.

Starting point of this paper are publications in different worlds, which deal with dejittering: The discrete optimization formulation of Nikolova [13,14] and Lenzen et al [8,9], which deals with displacement correction. We are generalizing Nikolova's algorithm to the infinite dimensional setting and then establish a relation to displacement correction and systems of partial differential equations.

As a consequence we can discuss advantages and shortcuts of the different methods and discretization dependence.

The outline of this paper is as follows: In Section 2 we make the basic problem formulation for three types of jittering. Then we explain line dejittering and recall the standard formulation in the field from Nikolova [14] in Section 3. After deriving a continuous variant, we put this algorithm in perspective with displacement error regularization [3,8,9,15,16]. We explain the different philosophies but show the close relation of these areas in the general setting of line pixel dejittering; cf. Section 4. Moreover, we review continuous algorithms for pixel dejittering in Section 5. In Section 6 we formulate partial differential equations, which constitute the flows according to the continuous optimization energies. Finally we present numerical results in Section 7. The paper ends with a conclusion, where we outline the novelties of this work.

2 Basic Notation and Problem Formulation

In this paper we use the following notations:
- u can either denote a discrete (digital) gray valued image, in which case it is represented as a matrix $u \in \mathbb{R}^{m \times n}$, where m is number of columns, and n is number of rows, or

- u denotes a function $u : \Omega \to \mathbb{R}$ on the unit-square $\Omega = [0,1]^2$. For a continuous image $u : \Omega \to \mathbb{R}$, one way to have the digitized image pixels is

$$u_{ij} = \frac{1}{h_x h_y} \int_{(i-1)/m}^{i/m} \int_{(j-1)/n}^{j/n} u(x,y)\, d(x,y) .$$

Here, the pixel size is $h_x \times h_y$, with $h_x = \frac{1}{m}$ and $h_y = \frac{1}{n}$.
- η_{ij} and $\eta : \Omega \to \mathbb{R}$ denote noise. In the discrete setting the lines are horizontally numbered from bottom to top.

Let u^δ denote either a discrete, jittered image - then it is a matrix in $\mathbb{R}^{m \times n}$, or a continuous, jittered image, then it is function $u^\delta : \Omega \to \mathbb{R}$. Assuming that u denotes the original image without jittering, we consider the following discrete and continuous problem formulations:

Line jitter:

$$u^\delta(i,j) = u(i + \mathsf{d}_j, j) + \eta_{ij}, \quad u^\delta(x,y) = u(x + \mathsf{d}(y), y) + \eta(x,y), \quad (1)$$

respectively, where $\mathsf{d}_j \in \mathbb{Z}$ denotes the discrete jitter of the j-th line, and $\mathsf{d} : [0,1] \to \mathbb{R}$ denotes the jitter function of the y-th component.

Line pixel jitter:

$$u^\delta(i,j) = u(i + \mathsf{d}_{i,j}, j) + \eta_{ij}, \quad u^\delta(x,y) = u((x + \mathsf{d}(x,y)), y) + \eta(x,y), \quad (2)$$

respectively, where $\mathsf{d}_{i,j} \in \mathbb{Z}$ denotes the discrete jitter of the $i-th$ pixel in the j-th line, and $\mathsf{d} : \Omega \to \mathbb{R}$ denotes the jitter function of the point (x,y) in x-direction.

Pixel jitter:

$$u^\delta(i,j) = u((i,j) + \mathsf{d}_{i,j}) + \eta_{ij}, \quad u^\delta(x,y) = u((x,y) + \mathsf{d}(x,y)) + \eta(x,y), \quad (3)$$

respectively, where $\mathsf{d}_{i,j} \in \mathbb{Z}^2$ denotes the discrete jitter of the $(i,j)-th$ pixel, and $\mathsf{d} : \Omega \to \mathbb{R}^2$ denotes the jitter vector field at the point (x,y).

For those jittered pixels which run out of the domain of the original image u, we define their intensity values as 0.

In the literature, many dejittering algorithms are particularly designed for line jittering, referring to (1), see for instance [6,7,13,14,18]. In these algorithms, the jittering error is considered deterministic, and a probably noisy input image has to be smoothed in an additional step, either before or after dejittering. The problems of line pixel jitter (2) and pixel jitter (3) have been discussed for instance in [8,9], where a displacement error correction model has been considered. In this context, it is commonly assumed that noise is significant and jitter is stochastic, and the methods are supposed to dejitter and denoise simultaneously.

3 Line Dejittering

In this section we investigate algorithms for line dejittering. After reviewing algorithms from the literature, we will formulate line pixel and pixel dejittering below.

As we have mentioned in the introduction, there are two different kinds of algorithms for dejittering in the literature. The prime example of the first type approach is Nikolova's algorithm [13,14], which is outlined below. A-priori Nikolova's approach is formulated in a discrete setting. We provide a continuous formulation below, which allows us to put it in perspective with the second approach, and thus in turn to partial differential equation models in the spirit of [8,9].

3.1 Nikolova's Algorithm for Discrete Line Dejittering

Nikolova [13,14] proposed an efficient algorithm for discrete line dejittering. This algorithm is based on energy minimization and determines in an iterative way, from bottom to top, for each horizontal image line discrete integer values $\mathsf{d}_j, j \in \{1, 2, \cdots, n\}$, which indicate the horizontal displacement of the j-th line, respectively.

The algorithm involves setting values of an exponential parameter p, which Nikolova chooses as $p = 1$ or $p = 0.5$, $p = 0.5$ is better suited for discontinuous images, while $p = 1$ is better suited for smooth images. Moreover, it is assumed that the jitter is bounded, such that there is a parameter σ constraining the maximal line jitter (a typical values is $\sigma = 6$ pixels):

$$|\mathsf{d}_j| \leq \sigma, \qquad \forall j = 2, \ldots, n.$$

1. The algorithms is initialized by setting $j := 2$, $\mathsf{d}_1 := 0$, $\hat{u}(i,1) := u^\delta(i,1)$ and selecting the parameter $\sigma^* \geq \sigma$. The minimizer $\hat{\mathsf{d}}_2$ of the functional

$$\mathcal{J}_2(\mathsf{d}_2) := \sum_{i=\sigma^*+1}^{m-\sigma^*} \left|u^\delta(i - \mathsf{d}_2, 2) - u^\delta(i,1)\right|^p \tag{4}$$

is used to define $\hat{u}(i,2) := u^\delta(i - \hat{\mathsf{d}}_2, 2)$.

2. For $j = 3, \ldots, n$ determine $\hat{\mathsf{d}}_j$ as the minimizer of the functional

$$\mathcal{J}_j(\mathsf{d}_j) := \sum_{i=\sigma^*+1}^{m-\sigma^*} \left|u^\delta(i - \mathsf{d}_j, j) - 2\hat{u}(i, j-1) + \hat{u}(i, j-2)\right|^p, \tag{5}$$

and define $\hat{u}(i,j) = u^\delta(i - \hat{\mathsf{d}}_j, j)$.

3.2 A Continuous Optimization Problem for Line Dejittering

We here formulate a continuous variant of Nikolova's algorithm, which also establishes the relation to existing variational methods and partial differential equations for dejittering. Let $u^\delta : \Omega \to \mathbb{R}$ be the line jittered variant of u, so u^δ

satisfies (1). In order to recover u and $\mathbf{d}$, we minimize (6) for each $\hat{y} \in [0,1]$ separately, where $\hat{y}$ indicates the continuum position of the line in the image,

$$\mathcal{J}_c(\mathbf{d})(\hat{y}) := \lim_{\tau \to 0^+} \frac{1}{2\tau} \int_{\max\{\hat{y}-\tau,0\}}^{\min\{\hat{y}+\tau,1\}} \int_{\sigma_*}^{1-\sigma_*} |\partial_y^k u^\delta(x - \mathbf{d}(y), y)|^p \, d(x,y), \quad (6)$$

subject to

$$\|\mathbf{d}\|_{L^\infty([0,1])} \leq \sigma. \quad (7)$$

The parameter σ_* is chosen to satisfy $\sigma \leq \sigma_*$. With this choice the integrand in the integral $\int_{\sigma_*}^{1-\sigma_*} |\partial_y^k u^\delta(x - \mathbf{d}(y), y)|^p \, dx$ is evaluated only for arguments of u^δ in the interior of the image domain $[0,1] \times [0,1]$. This correspond to the discrete sum $\sum_{i=\sigma_*+1}^{m-\sigma_*}$ in the Nikolova algorithm. The term $\partial_y^k u^\delta$ denotes the k-th derivative of u^δ with respect to the second component. Since

$$\frac{u^\delta(i-\mathbf{d}_j, j) - 2\hat{u}(i, j-1) + \hat{u}(i, j-2)}{h_y^2} \approx \partial_y^2 u^\delta(ih_x - \mathbf{d}((j-1)h_y), (j-1)h_y),$$

we propose the following simplified variant of (6) and (7), namely to minimize

$$\mathcal{J}^{(k)}(\mathbf{d}) := \frac{1}{p} \int_\Omega |\partial_y^k u^\delta(x - \mathbf{d}(y), y)|^p \, d(x,y) \quad (8)$$

subject to

$$\|\mathbf{d}\|_{L^2([0,1])} \leq \hat{\sigma}. \quad (9)$$

The main difference to minimizing $\mathcal{J}_c$ is that we consider integration over all of Ω. To make this well-defined, we propose to extend u^δ symmetric across left and right, and top and bottom images boundaries, respectively. Another difference is that we consider an *a joint* approach, which optimizes globally over all pixels, instead of separately for each line. Moreover, from a modelling point of view taking the second derivative ($k = 2$) of u^δ in the functional $\mathcal{J}_c$ is not mandatory, for instance, we may take as well the derivative ($k = 1$) or another integer order. In practice, minimizing the functional with second order derivatives performs better than using first order derivatives in a noise free environment. For the other parameter p in (8), in the discrete setting, Nikolova has suggested to use either 0.5 or 1, however, we would propose to choose either $p = 1$ or $p = 2$, in order to keep the convexity of the functional in our continuous model, where $p = 1$ works better with the discontinuities.

4 Line Pixel Dejittering

In this section we review line pixel dejittering and displacement regularization: We find that within the continuous setting, formally, the optimization approach for line dejittering from last section can be similarly generalized to the case of line pixel dejittering. However, the formal difference is that for line pixel dejittering

$\mathsf{d}: \Omega \to \mathbb{R}$ is a bounded random field over the whole two dimensional domain Ω, while for line jitter $\mathsf{d}: [0,1] \to \mathbb{R}$. Thus, we propose to optimize the functional which is only slightly changed from (8)

$$\mathcal{J}_2^{(k)}(\mathsf{d}) := \frac{1}{p} \int_\Omega |\partial_y^k u^\delta(x - \mathsf{d}(x,y), y)|^p \, d(x,y) \tag{10}$$

subject to $\|\mathsf{d}\|_{L^2(\Omega)} \leq \hat{\sigma}$.

Because we assume small displacements d, we also consider approximating the term $\partial_y^k u^\delta(x - \mathsf{d}(x,y), y)$ by its linearisation:

$$\partial_y^k u^\delta(x - \mathsf{d}(x,y), y) \approx \partial_y^k u^\delta(x,y) - \mathsf{d}(x,y) \partial_x \partial_y^k u^\delta(x,y) \, .$$

Replacing the nonlinear term by its linearization, we arrive at the constrained optimization problem, which is to minimize

$$\mathcal{J}_2^{(k)}(\mathsf{d}) := \frac{1}{p} \int_\Omega |\partial_y^k u^\delta(x,y) - \mathsf{d}(x,y) \partial_x \partial_y^k u^\delta(x,y)|^p \, d(x,y), \quad k = 1,2 \tag{11}$$

subject to (9).

For $1 < p \leq 2$, $\mathcal{J}_2^{(k)}$ is strictly convex, and for three-times continuously differentiable u^δ also weakly lower semi-continuous. Then, the constrained optimization problem is equivalent to the method of Tikhonov-regularization with parameter choice by Morozov's discrepancy principle, consisting in calculation of

$$\mathsf{d}(\alpha) := \arg\min_{\mathsf{d}} \left\{ \mathcal{J}_2^{(k)}(\mathsf{d}) + \frac{\alpha}{2} \|\mathsf{d}\|_{L^2(\Omega)}^2 \right\}, \tag{12}$$

where α is chosen to satisfy $\|\mathsf{d}(\alpha)\|_{L^2(\Omega)} = \hat{\sigma}$. For further background on the relation between Tikhonov regularization and constrained optimization problems see for instance [1,4,5,10,11,17,19,20]. For $p \leq 1$ the relation is not obvious, but we ignore this difficulty.

We stress the fact that the minimizer of (12) with $p = 2$ can be explicitly calculated: We have

$$\mathsf{d}(\alpha) = \frac{\partial_y^k u^\delta \partial_x \partial_y^k u^\delta}{\alpha + (\partial_x \partial_y^k u^\delta)^2} \, . \tag{13}$$

This explicit linearised method provides insufficient results (cf. Figure 1).

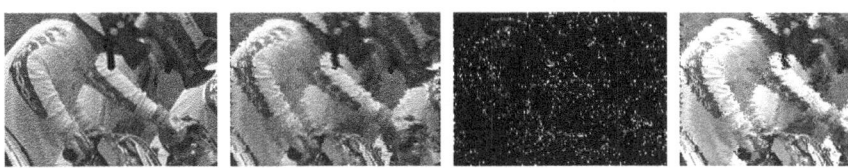

Fig. 1. Left to right: ground truth, line jittered image, displacement, recovered image

4.1 Displacement Error Correction for Line Pixel Dejittering

In the following we outline an approach for dejittering, which does not recover the jitter but the dejittered image directly. We use a first order approximation of the data by assuming that the jitter is only a small disturbance:

$$u^\delta(x,y) \approx u(x + \mathsf{d}(x,y), y) \approx u(x,y) + \partial_x u(x,y)\mathsf{d}(x,y). \tag{14}$$

Considering the approximation as an identity we find that

$$\mathsf{d}(x,y) = \frac{u^\delta(x,y) - u(x,y)}{\partial_x u(x,y)}. \tag{15}$$

Now, instead of minimizing $\mathcal{J}_2^{(k)}$ with respect to d, we replace in $\mathcal{J}^{(k)}$ the u^δ by $u(x + \mathsf{d}(x,y))$ and use the identity (15), and minimize with respect to u. Thus the optimization problem for line pixel dejittering consists in the minimization of the functional:

$$\mathcal{N}(u) := \alpha\frac{1}{2}\int_\Omega \left|\frac{u^\delta(x,y) - u(x,y)}{\partial_x u(x,y)}\right|^2 d(x,y) + \underbrace{\frac{1}{p}\int_\Omega |\partial_y^k u(x,y)|^p \, d(x,y)}_{\mathcal{R}}. \tag{16}$$

Remark 1. hen we use this approach to correct for line jitter, we have to respect the fact that each line has the same shift, which leads to

$$0 = \partial_x \mathsf{d}(y) \approx \partial_x\left(\frac{u^\delta(x,y) - u(x,y)}{\partial_x u(x,y)}\right).$$

Thus line jitter correction can be rephrased as an unconstrained minimization of the functional

$$\mathcal{N}(u) + \beta\int_\Omega \left(\partial_x\left(\frac{u^\delta(x,y) - u(x,y)}{\partial_x u(x,y)}\right)\right)^2 d(x,y), \tag{17}$$

where β is a penalty parameter.

5 Pixel Dejittering

The problem of pixel jitter correction can be formulated again as a constraint optimization problem, consisting in minimization of

$$\mathcal{J}_3^{(k)}(\mathsf{d}) := \frac{1}{p}\int_\Omega |\partial_y^k u^\delta((x,y) - \mathsf{d}(x,y))|^p \, d(x,y) \tag{18}$$

subject to $\|\mathsf{d}\|_{(L^2(\Omega))^2} \leq \hat{\sigma}$. Note the fundamental difference that $\mathsf{d}: \Omega \to \mathbb{R}^2$, while for line pixel jitter $\mathsf{d}: \Omega \to \mathbb{R}$, and for line jitter $\mathsf{d}: [0,1] \to \mathbb{R}$.

Displacement error regularization for correcting pixel jitter has been considered in [8,9]. It is again based on Taylor expansion

$$u^\delta(x,y) - u(x,y) \approx \mathsf{d} \cdot \nabla u,$$

which implies that we can choose as a solution $\mathbf{d} \approx (\nabla u)^\dagger (u^\delta - u)$, where $(\nabla u)^\dagger$ denotes the Moore-Penrose pseudo-inverse of ∇u. This choice of an inverse of ∇u considers displacement errors which are orthogonal to level lines of u.

Here, we define

$$\hat{S}(u) := \frac{1}{2} \left\| (\nabla u)^\dagger (u^\delta - u) \right\|_{L^2(\Omega)}^2 .$$

Assuming that u is of finite total variation we ended up with the following regularization functional [8,9]:

$$\hat{\mathcal{N}}(u) := \alpha \hat{S}(u) + \int_\Omega |\nabla u(x,y)| \, d(x,y) . \tag{19}$$

Note that in comparison with (16), $\int_\Omega |\partial_y^k u(x,y)|^p \, d(x,y)$ has been replaced by the TV-semi norm $\int_\Omega |\nabla u(x,y)| \, d(x,y)$.

6   PDE Models as Formal Energy Flows

Considering $\mathcal{S}$ as a metric, the minimization of functional $\mathcal{N}$ defined in (16), can be formally solved as metric flows of $\mathcal{S}$ with energy $\mathcal{R}$. In [9], a PDE according to (19) has been derived by considering $\hat{\mathcal{N}}(\alpha, \cdot)$ as an implicit time-step of the associated flow, following that, we state the flows according to (16) and (19).

- The flow associated with (16), for $k = 1, 2$ and $p = 1, 2$ is:

$$\begin{cases} \partial_t u = |\partial_x u|^2 \, \partial_y^k \left(\dfrac{\partial_y^k u}{|\partial_y^k u|^{2-p}} \right) ; \\ u = u^\delta , \quad \text{in } \Omega \times \{0\} ; \\ \partial_y^{2l-1} u = 0 , \quad \text{on } \{0,1\} \times [0,1] , \quad \forall l = 1, .., k . \end{cases} \tag{20}$$

- We emphasize that the flow associated to (19) is

$$\begin{cases} \partial_t u = |\nabla u|^2 \, \nabla \cdot \left(\dfrac{\nabla u}{|\nabla u|} \right) ; \\ u = u^\delta , \quad \text{in } \Omega \times \{0\} ; \\ \partial_n u = 0 , \quad \text{on } \partial \Omega . \end{cases} \tag{21}$$

7   Numerical Results

In this section we show the numerical results of our newly developed model (20) for different choices of k and p, making comparisons with the approach from [9], that consists in solving (21), and with Nikolova's algorithm [14]. In the implementation, for $p = 2$ in (20), we use standard finite differences discretization

Table 1. Comparison of noisy and noise free data affected by different jitter types

Measure	Test data	k=1,p=2	k=2,p=2	k=1,p=1	k=2,p=1	cf.[9]	cf.[14]
		Line Jitter Data without Adding Noise					
PSNR	17.814	19.886	20.031	20.109	20.461	19.807	24.818
MSE	1075.7	667.407	645.584	634.035	584.668	679.740	214.408
SSIM	0.622	0.704	0.714	0.709	0.729	0.691	0.998
		Line Pixel Jitter Data without Adding Noise					
PSNR	16.608	17.913	17.956	18.193	18.356	19.213	13.999
MSE	1420.0	1051.4	1040.9	985.634	949.517	779.525	2589
SSIM	0.484	0.552	0.558	0.566	0.571	0.618	0.308
		Pixel Jitter Data with Adding Noise					
PSNR	15.367	17.460	17.563	17.688	17.891	19.064	-
MSE	1889.8	1167.1	1139.6	1137	1056.6	806.614	-
SSIM	0.316	0.433	0.461	0.457	0.487	0.585	-

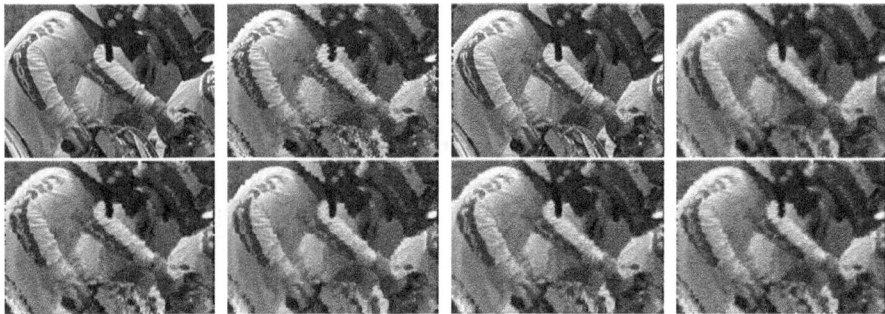

Fig. 2. Line Dejittering. Top row: The ground truth, the noisy free line jittered image, dejittered with [14], dejittered with (20) $k = 1$, $p = 2$. Bottom row: dejittered with (20) $k = 2$, $p = 2$, (20) $k = 1$, $p = 1$, (20) $k = 2$, $p = 1$, approach from [9].

with semi-implicit iteration, but for the case of $p = 1$, the solution of (20) is obtained by solving the convex optimization problem (22) iteratively, where we generalised the TV denoising algorithm from [2] to approximate the solution.

$$\begin{cases} u^{m+1} := \arg\min_u \left\{ \frac{\alpha}{2} \int_\Omega \frac{|u^m(x,y) - u(x,y)|^2}{|\partial_x u^m(x,y)|^2 + \epsilon} + \left|\partial_y^k u(x,y)\right| \, d(x,y) \right\}, \\ u^0 = u^\delta. \end{cases}$$

(22)

Here α corresponds to the time-stepping and $u^m \approx u(m\alpha)$. In all the experiments, we use as stopping criteria some threshold of $\|u^m - u^{m+1}\|_{L^2}$. The test data are generated by adding jitter to clean test images. In addition noisy test data are generated by composing the test image with Gaussian noise of mean 0 and standard deviation 10. In order to evaluate the results quantitatively, we consider the *mean square error* (MSE) computed by averaging the intensity difference between the analyzed pixel $\hat{u}(i,j)$ and the reference pixel $u(i,j)$, and the

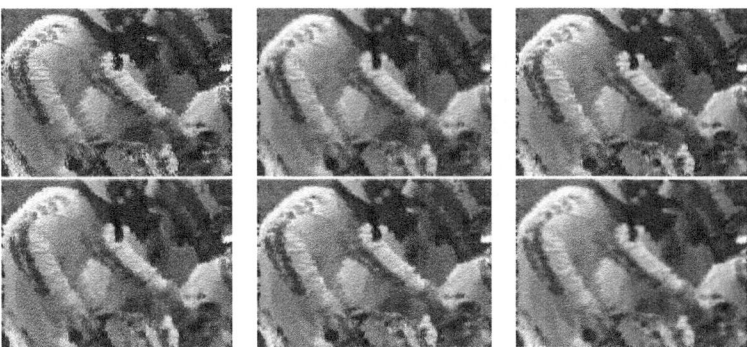

Fig. 3. Line Pixel Dejittering. Top row: The noisy line pixel jittered image, dejittered with (20) $k = 1$, $p = 2$, (20) $k = 2$, $p = 2$. Bottom row: (20) $k = 1$, $p = 1$, (20) $k = 2$, $p = 1$, approach from [9].

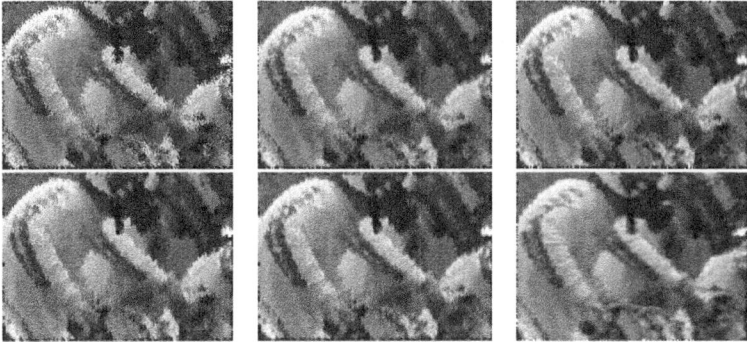

Fig. 4. Pixel Dejittering. Top row: The noisy line pixel jittered image, dejittered with (20) $k = 1$, $p = 2$, (20) $k = 2$, $p = 2$. Bottom row: (20) $k = 1$, $p = 1$, (20) $k = 2$, $p = 1$, approach from [9].

related quantity of *peak signal to noise ration* (PSNR)

$$MSE = \frac{1}{N} \sum_{i=1}^{m} \sum_{j=1}^{n} (\hat{u}(i,j) - u(i,j))^2 \quad \text{and} \quad PSNR = 10 \log_{10} \frac{L^2}{MSE},$$

where L is the dynamic range of allowable pixel intensities, e.g. for an 8-bit per pixel image $L = 2^8 - 1 = 255$. These quantity are appealing but not well matched to perceived visual quality as reported in [12] and [21]. For that reason we consider also the *structural similarity* (SSIM) index [21] defined as:

$$SSIM(\hat{u}, u) = f(l(\hat{u}, u), c(\hat{u}, u), s(\hat{u}, u)),$$

where the three independent components $l(\hat{u}, u), c(\hat{u}, u), s(\hat{u}, u)$ are the similarity functions of the luminance, the contrast and the structure, respectively, between the reconstructed and test image, and f is a combination function.

Quantitatively, the higher *PSNR* value the better similarity between the test data and the original clean image. Moreover, a small value of *MSE* points out a good intensity approximation of the original data, and a larger value of *SSIM* claims that the structure of the original image is better preserved.

Table 1 gives a comprehensive evaluation of different methods for image dejittering, which are the algorithm for solving (20) presented in this paper, and the algorithms from [9] and from [14], respectively. For the test images used for line dejittering and line pixel dejittering, we have not superimposed the data with additive noise. The test data used for pixel dejittered was considered with additive noise. For line dejittering, Nikolova's algorithm [14] gives the most superior results. Evaluating the two different PDE models, we notice that (20) performs better than [9] for line dejittering. [14] is not able to handle line pixel dejittering, in contrast with the PDE models. In this case the method in [9] achieves slightly better grades than (20); see Table 1. However visually, one may find that (20) (e.g.with parameter $k = 2, p = 1$) has less blurring of the reconstructed image and keeps more clear details; see Fig 3. The highlight of the approach [9] happens in the pixel dejittering task, where it outperforms the others both quantitatively and qualitatively. Over all the tests, it is not hard to find that, for the model (20), the choice of parameter $k = 2, p = 1$ gives the most competitive results in compare with the other parameter choices.

8 Conclusion

The novelties of this paper are that we have shown the formal connection of Nikolova's method with variational displacement error correction and PDE methods. To do this, we have unified a family of variational methods for displacement error regularization, which apply for different dejittering applications. The second novelty is a comparison of the different models for different types of jitter. An analysis of the proposed algorithms for minimizing models (16) is lacking and this might be a future research topic. Another aspect will be to investigate problems in tomography, which involve reconstruction of objects that show small (unknown) displacements while being imaged.

Acknowledgments. The work of GD and OS has been supported by the Austrian Science Fund (FWF) within the project *Variational Methods for Imaging on Manifolds* within the NFN Geometry and Simulation, project S11704. AP and OS are supported by the project *Modeling Visual Attention as a Key Factor in Visual Recognition and Quality of Experience* funded by the Wiener Wissenschafts und Technologie Funds - WWTF. The authors thank the reviewers for their comments to improve the presentation of the paper.

References

1. Engl, H.W., Hanke, M., Neubauer, A.: Regularization of inverse problems. Mathematics and its Applications, vol. 375. Kluwer Academic Publishers Group, Dordrecht (1996)

2. Figueiredo, M.A.T., Dias, J.B., Oliveira, J.P., et al.: On total variation denoising: A new majorization-minimization algorithm and an experimental comparison with wavalet denoising. In: IEEE International Conference on Image Processing, pp. 2633–2636. IEEE (2006)
3. Grasmair, M., Lenzen, F., Obereder, A., Scherzer, O., Fuchs, M.: A non-convex PDE scale space. In: Kimmel, R., Sochen, N.A., Weickert, J. (eds.) Scale-Space 2005. LNCS, vol. 3459, pp. 303–315. Springer, Heidelberg (2005)
4. Groetsch, C.W.: The Theory of Tikhonov Regularization for Fredholm Equations of the First Kind. Pitman, Boston (1984)
5. Groetsch, C.W.: Inverse Problems. Mathematical Association of America, Washington, DC (1999). Activities for undergraduates
6. Kang, S.H., Shen, J.: Video dejittering by bake and shake. Image Vision Comput. **24**(2), 143–152 (2006)
7. Kang, S.H., Shen, J.: Image dejittering based on slicing moments. In: Tai, X.C., Lie, K.A., Chan, T.F., Osher, S. (eds.) Image Processing Based on Partial Differential Equations. Mathematics and Visualization. Springer, New York (2007)
8. Lenzen, F., Scherzer, O.: A geometric pde for interpolation of m-channel data. In: Tai, X.C., Knut, M., Marius, L., Knut-Andreas, L. (eds.) SSVM 2009. LNCS, vol. 5567, pp. 413–425. Springer-Verlag, Heidelberg (2009)
9. Lenzen, F., Scherzer, O.: Partial differential equations for zooming, deinterlacing and dejittering. Int. J. Comput. Vision **92**(2), 162–176 (2011)
10. Morozov, V.A.: Methods for Solving Incorrectly Posed Problems. Springer Verlag, New York (1984)
11. Morozov, V.A.: Regularization Methods for Ill-Posed Problems. CRC Press, Boca Raton (1993)
12. Ndajah, P., Kikuchi, H., Yukawa, M., Watanabe, H., et al.: An investigation on the quality of denoised images. Int. J. Circ. Syst. Sign. Proc. **5**, 423–434 (2011)
13. Nikolova, M.: Fast dejittering for digital video frames. In: Tai, X.C., Knut, M., Marius, L., Knut-Andreas, L. (eds.) SSVM 2009. LNCS, pp. 439–451. Springer, Heidelberg (2009)
14. Nikolova, M.: One-iteration dejittering of digital video images. J. Vis. Commun. Image Represent. **20**, 254–274 (2009)
15. Scherzer, O.: Explicit versus implicit relative error regularization on the space of functions of bounded variation. In: Nashed, M.Z., Scherzer, O. (eds.) Inverse Problems, Image Analysis, and Medical Imaging. Contemporary Mathematics, vol. 313, pp. 171–198. AMC, Providence (2002)
16. Scherzer, O.: Scale space methods for denoising and inverse problem. Adv. Imaging Electron Phys. **128**, 445–530 (2003)
17. Scherzer, O., Grasmair, M., Grossauer, H., Haltmeier, M., Lenzen, F.: Variational methods in imaging. Applied Mathematical Sciences, vol. 167. Springer, New York (2009)
18. Shen, J.: Bayesian video dejittering by bv image model. SIAM J. Appl. Math. **64**(5), 1691–1708 (2004)
19. Tikhonov, A.N., Arsenin, V.Y.: Solutions of Ill-Posed Problems. John Wiley & Sons, Washington, D.C. (1977)
20. Tikhonov, A.N., Goncharsky, A., Stepanov, V., Yagola, A.: Numerical Methods for the Solution of Ill-Posed Problems. Kluwer, Dordrecht (1995)
21. Wang, Z., Bovik, A.C., Sheikh, H.R., Simoncelli, E.P.: Image quality assessment: from error visibility to structural similarity. IEEE Trans. Image Process. **13**(4), 600–612 (2004)

Alternating Direction Method of Multiplier for Euler's Elastica-Based Denoising

Maryam Yashtini[✉] and Sung Ha Kang

School of Mathematics, Georgia Institute of Technology,
686 Cherry Street NW, Atlanta, GA 30332, USA
{myashtini3,kang}@people.math.gatech.edu

Abstract. Inspired by recent numerical developments, we propose a new version of alternating direction method of multiplier (ADMM) for Euler's Elastica-based denoising model. The main contribution is to design a simple and fast method, which it is also easy to choose its parameters values. regularizer for instance the so called staircasing effect. The solution of each subproblem is given in a closed form using a discrete Fourier transform, a soft shrinkage operator, and a coupled Fourier transform. Compared to other methods, this algorithm has less parameters and we provide some insight on their values. provide some insights on how their values need to be determined. Numerical experiments on image denoising application demonstrate the effectiveness of the proposed scheme.

Keywords: Euler's Elastica · Curvature · Alternating direction method of multiplier · ADMM · Nonlinear nonsmooth optimization · Denoising

1 Introduction

We consider the Euler's Elastica-base denoising model such as:

$$E(\mathbf{u}) = \int_\Omega (\alpha + \beta \kappa^2) |\nabla \mathbf{u}| \, d\mathbf{x} + \frac{\lambda}{2} \int_\Omega (\mathbf{u} - \mathbf{f})^2 d\mathbf{x}. \tag{1}$$

Here $\alpha > 0$, $\beta \geq 0$, and $\lambda > 0$ are parameters, $\kappa = \nabla \cdot \frac{\nabla \mathbf{u}}{|\nabla \mathbf{u}|}$ is the curvature of a level curve in the image, and $\Omega \subset \mathbb{R}^2$ is the image domain. This Euler's Elastica (EE) model (1) has a benefit over Total Variation (TV) minimizing regularizer ($\beta = 0$) [17] in enforcing better curvature information and reducing the staircase effect; hence, it has received considerable attention. For instance, image inpainting and segmentation with depth show clear benefits of using curvature based model, and there are many related work such as [1,2,6,9,15,16]. While the Euler's Elastica is an effective regularization for many imaging applications, its associated Euler-Lagrange equation is fourth order and minimization of energy functionals becomes very complex. Therefore, alternative models for imporved TV model have been studied, e.g. [4,5].

In this paper, we focus on the numerical aspect of the EE model and propose a fast algorithm. This work is inspired by a number of recent works on fast computation of optimization problems involving Euler's Elastica regularization such as [8,18,20], which showed the alternating minimization techniques can be successfully used as an efficient computation. Tai, Hanh, and Chung in their pioneering work [18] developed a fast algorithm, called the ALM algorithm, for solving the Euler's Elastica image denoising and inpainting model. The algorithm is based on operator splitting techniques, augmented Lagrangian method, and relaxation approach to handle some singularity and unboundedness. Each iteration of this algorithm, involves five subproblems, with three model parameters and four Lagrange multipliers, i.e. this model has 7 parameters. Since the energy functional is nonconvex finding these parameters becomes challenging. However, with a good choice of parameters, it shows a fast convergence. Some related works include [8,14,21]. In [21], the mean curvature regularization was compared with TV and Euler's Elastica for image denoising problem.

In this paper, we focus on image denoising problem and propose a new algorithm based on the well known *alternating direction method of multiplier* (ADMM), originally proposed by Glowinski and Marrocco [11] and Gabay and Mercier [10]. We apply a discrete Fourier transform, a soft shrinkage operator [7,12,13,19], and a coupled discrete Fourier transform to solve the subproblems. This new algorithm has only two penalty parameters which can be found with some provided strategies. In the numerical section, we compare the performance of the proposed algorithm for solving the TV and the Euler's Elastica models. Then, we compare the efficiency of our proposed algorithm to the ALM algorithm[18].

This paper is organized as follow. In Section 2, we propose the ADMM algorithm for solving the Euler's Elastica-based denoising model. Section 3 provides the discretization of this algorithm. In Section 4, we give some discussion on the parameter selection. Numerical results are presented in Section 5.

2 ADMM for Euler's Elastica Image Denoising Model

In the energy functional (1), $|\nabla u|$ and κ are the terms contributing to the complexity of the problem, that we introduce two new variables $\mathbf{w} = \nabla \mathbf{u}$ and $\mathbf{n} = \mathbf{w}/|\mathbf{w}|_\epsilon$ to to split the optimization problem

$$\min_{\mathbf{u},\mathbf{w},\mathbf{n}} \int_\Omega (\alpha + \beta(\operatorname{div} \mathbf{n})^2)|\mathbf{w}| + \frac{\lambda}{2}\int_\Omega (\mathbf{u} - \mathbf{f})^2 \, d\mathbf{x}, \quad \text{s.t. } \mathbf{w} = \nabla \mathbf{u}, \; \mathbf{n} = \frac{\mathbf{w}}{|\mathbf{w}|_\epsilon}. \quad (2)$$

We note that the problems (1) and (2) share the same solution set. We use $|\nabla u|_\epsilon = \sqrt{|\nabla u|^2 + \epsilon^2}$ with small $\epsilon > 0$ to avoid the singularity. Then, the augmented Lagrangian associated with (2) is given by

$$\mathcal{L}^{\rho_1,\rho_2}(\mathbf{u},\mathbf{w},\mathbf{n};\mathbf{b},\mathbf{c}) = \int_\Omega \Big[(\alpha + \beta(\operatorname{div}\mathbf{n})^2)|\mathbf{w}| + \frac{\lambda}{2}(\mathbf{u}-\mathbf{f})^2 \quad (3)$$
$$+ \langle \mathbf{b}, \nabla\mathbf{u} - \mathbf{w}\rangle + \frac{\rho_1}{2}(\nabla\mathbf{u} - \mathbf{w})^2 + \langle \mathbf{c}, \tfrac{\mathbf{w}}{|\mathbf{w}|_\epsilon} - \mathbf{n}\rangle + \frac{\rho_2}{2}\Big(\tfrac{\mathbf{w}}{|\mathbf{w}|_\epsilon} - \mathbf{n}\Big)^2 \Big] d\mathbf{x},$$

where $\rho_1 > 0$ and $\rho_2 > 0$ are penalty parameters, $\mathbf{b}$ and $\mathbf{c}$ are Lagrange multipliers associated with the constraints $\mathbf{w} = \nabla \mathbf{u}$ and $\mathbf{n} = \mathbf{w}/|\mathbf{w}|_\epsilon$ respectively. Let $\mathbf{b}^k$ and $\mathbf{c}^k$ be the current approximation to the multipliers, then we have

$$\begin{cases} (\mathbf{u}^{k+1}, \mathbf{w}^{k+1}, \mathbf{n}^{k+1}) = \arg\min_{\mathbf{u},\mathbf{w},\mathbf{n}} \mathcal{L}^{\rho_1,\rho_2}(\mathbf{u},\mathbf{w},\mathbf{n}; \mathbf{b}^k, \mathbf{c}^k), \\ \mathbf{b}^{k+1} = \mathbf{b}^k + \rho_1(\nabla \mathbf{u}^{k+1} - \mathbf{w}^{k+1}), \\ \mathbf{c}^{k+1} = \mathbf{c}^k + \rho_2(\frac{\mathbf{w}^{k+1}}{|\mathbf{w}^{k+1}|_\epsilon} - \mathbf{n}^{k+1}). \end{cases}$$

Hence, at each iteration, the augmented Lagrangian is minimized jointly with respect to the primal variables $\mathbf{u}$, $\mathbf{w}$, and $\mathbf{n}$, then the multipliers $\mathbf{b}$ and $\mathbf{c}$ are updated. In ADMM, $\mathbf{u}$, $\mathbf{w}$, and $\mathbf{n}$ are updated by the alternating minimization over $\mathbf{u}$ with $\mathbf{w}$ and $\mathbf{n}$ fixed, over $\mathbf{w}$ with $\mathbf{u}$ and $\mathbf{n}$ fixed, and over $\mathbf{n}$ with $\mathbf{u}$ and $\mathbf{w}$ fixed. This consists of the following iterations:

$$\begin{cases} \mathbf{u}^{k+1} = \arg\min_{\mathbf{u}} \int_\Omega \left[\frac{\lambda}{2}(\mathbf{u}-\mathbf{f})^2 + \frac{\rho_1}{2}(\nabla \mathbf{u} - \mathbf{w}^k + \rho_1^{-1}\mathbf{b}^k)^2\right] d\mathbf{x}, \\ \mathbf{w}^{k+1} = \arg\min_{\mathbf{w}} \int_\Omega \left[(\alpha + \beta(\operatorname{div} \mathbf{n}^k)^2)|\mathbf{w}| + \frac{\rho_1}{2}(\mathbf{w} - \nabla \mathbf{u}^{k+1} - \rho_1^{-1}\mathbf{b}^k)^2 \right. \\ \qquad\qquad\qquad \left. + \frac{\rho_2}{2}\left(\frac{\mathbf{w}}{|\mathbf{w}|_\epsilon} - \mathbf{n}^k + \rho_2^{-1}\mathbf{c}^k\right)^2\right] d\mathbf{x}, \\ \mathbf{n}^{k+1} = \arg\min_{\mathbf{n}} \int_\Omega \left[\beta|\mathbf{w}^{k+1}|(\operatorname{div}\mathbf{n})^2 + \frac{\rho_2}{2}\left(\mathbf{n} - \frac{\mathbf{w}^{k+1}}{|\mathbf{w}^{k+1}|_\epsilon} - \rho_2^{-1}\mathbf{c}^k\right)^2\right] d\mathbf{x}, \\ \mathbf{b}^{k+1} = \mathbf{b}^k + \rho_1(\nabla \mathbf{u}^{k+1} - \mathbf{w}^{k+1}), \\ \mathbf{c}^{k+1} = \mathbf{c}^k + \rho_2(\frac{\mathbf{w}^{k+1}}{|\mathbf{w}^{k+1}|_\epsilon} - \mathbf{n}^{k+1}). \end{cases} \quad (4)$$

This algorithm updates the image $\mathbf{u}$, its gradient $\mathbf{w} = \nabla \mathbf{u}$, and the term $\mathbf{n} = \nabla \mathbf{u}/|\nabla \mathbf{u}|$ in each separate subproblem which are easier than solving (1) directly.

3 Numerical Discretization

We present the discretization of the functionals in (4) and express the solution to each subproblem explicitly. We assume that images are two dimensional matrices of size $M \times N$. We denote by X the Euclidean space $\mathbb{R}^{M \times N}$ and by $\|\cdot\|$ the Euclidean norm (ℓ_2-norm). We let $\mathbf{u}_{i,j}$ denotes the intensity of image $\mathbf{u} \in X$ at (i,j) pixel where $i = 1, \ldots, M$ and $j = 1, \ldots, N$. We use the forward ($+$) difference operator $\nabla^+ \mathbf{u}_{i,j} = (\mathbf{u}_{i+1,j} - \mathbf{u}_{i,j}, \mathbf{u}_{i,j+1} - \mathbf{u}_{i,j}) := (\nabla_+^x \mathbf{u}_{i,j}, \nabla_+^y \mathbf{u}_{i,j})$. We impose periodic boundary conditions on the image: $\mathbf{u}_{0,j} = \mathbf{u}_{M,j}, \mathbf{u}_{M+1,j} = \mathbf{u}_{1,j}$, for all $j = 1, \ldots, N$ and $\mathbf{u}_{i,0} = \mathbf{u}_{i,N}, \mathbf{u}_{i,N+1} = \mathbf{u}_{i,1}$, for all $i = 1, \ldots, M$. For for $\mathbf{p} = (\mathbf{p}^1, \mathbf{p}^2) \in Y := X \times X$, we define the discrete divergence operator as $\operatorname{div}^- \mathbf{p}_{i,j} = (\mathbf{p}_{i,j}^1 - \mathbf{p}_{i-1,j}^1) + (\mathbf{p}_{i,j}^2 - \mathbf{p}_{i,j-1}^2) := \nabla_-^x \mathbf{p}_{i,j}^1 + \nabla_-^y \mathbf{p}_{i,j}^2$.

To use the discrete Fourier transform, let the shifting operators be $\mathcal{S}_\pm^x \mathbf{u}_{i,j} = \mathbf{u}_{i\pm 1,j}$, $\mathcal{S}_\pm^y \mathbf{u}_{i,j} = \mathbf{u}_{i,j\pm 1}$ and $\mathcal{I}\mathbf{u}_{i,j} = \mathbf{u}_{i,j}$. Since the shifting operators are discrete convolutions, their discrete Fourier transform are the componentwise multiplication in the frequency domain. Let i and j denotes the discrete frequencies where $1 \leq i \leq M$ and $1 \leq j \leq N$, then for any j and i, we have

$$\mathcal{FS}^x_\pm \mathbf{u}_{i,j} = e^{\pm\sqrt{-1}\theta_i}\mathcal{F}\mathbf{u}_{i,j}, \quad \text{where } \theta_i = \frac{2\pi}{M}i, \quad i = 1, \ldots, M$$

$$\mathcal{FS}^y_\pm \mathbf{u}_{i,j} = e^{\pm\sqrt{-1}\theta_j}\mathcal{F}\mathbf{u}_{i,j}, \quad \text{where } \theta_j = \frac{2\pi}{N}j, \quad j = 1, \ldots, N.$$

In the following, we present the details of each subproblem.

3.1 u-subproblem

The energy function corresponding to $\mathbf{u}$ subproblem in (4) is quadratic, hence the minimizing solution $\mathbf{u}^{k+1}$ satisfies the first order optimality condition

$$(\lambda - \rho_1 \text{div}^-\nabla^+)\mathbf{u}^{k+1}_{i,j} = \mathbf{g}^k_{i,j}, \quad \mathbf{g}^k_{i,j} := \lambda \mathbf{f}_{i,j} + \text{div}^-(\mathbf{b}^k_{i,j} - \rho_1 \mathbf{w}^k_{i,j}). \quad (5)$$

Since the image satisfies the periodic boundary conditions, then the Laplacian matrix $\text{div}^-\nabla^+$ becomes block circulant. Hence, the linear equation (5) can be solve efficiently by the discrete Fourier transform $\mathcal{F}$. We first employ the shifting operators to rewrite (5) as

$$\begin{cases} \left(\lambda \mathcal{I} - \rho_1(\mathcal{S}^x_- + \mathcal{S}^x_+ - 4\mathcal{I} + \mathcal{S}^y_- + \mathcal{S}^y_+)\right)\mathbf{u}^{k+1}_{i,j} = \mathbf{g}^k_{i,j}, \\ \mathbf{g}^k = \lambda \mathbf{f} + (\mathcal{I} - \mathcal{S}^x_-)(\mathbf{b}^1 - \rho_1\mathbf{w}^1)^k + (\mathcal{I} - \mathcal{S}^y_-)(\mathbf{b}^2 - \rho_1\mathbf{w}^2)^k. \end{cases}$$

Then using the discrete Fourier transforms and the Euler's formula $e^{\pm\sqrt{-1}\theta} = \cos\theta \pm \sqrt{-1}\sin\theta$, we obtain the following algebraic equation:

$$\left(\lambda - 2\rho_1(\cos\theta_i + \cos\theta_j - 2)\right)\mathcal{F}\mathbf{u}_{i,j} = \mathcal{F}\mathbf{g}^k_{i,j} \quad i = 1, \ldots, M, \ j = 1, \ldots, N.$$

Solving this equations for $\mathbf{u}_{i,j}$ gives

$$\mathbf{u}_{i,j} = \mathcal{F}^{-1}\left(\frac{\mathcal{F}\mathbf{g}^k_{i,j}}{\lambda - 2\rho_1(\cos\theta_i + \cos\theta_j - 2)}\right), \quad i = 1, \ldots, M, \ j = 1, \ldots, N. \quad (6)$$

3.2 w-subproblem

To solve this subproblem, we need to find $\mathbf{w}^{k+1}$ such that $\mathbf{w}^{k+1}_{i,j} = (\mathbf{w}^1_{i,j}, \mathbf{w}^2_{i,j})^{k+1} \in \mathbb{R}^2$ minimizes the nonsmooth energy functional

$$\left(\alpha + \beta(\text{div } \mathbf{n}^k_{i,j})^2\right)\|\mathbf{w}_{i,j}\| + \frac{\rho_1}{2}\|\mathbf{w}_{i,j} - \nabla \mathbf{u}^{k+1}_{i,j} - \frac{1}{\rho_1}\mathbf{b}^k_{i,j}\|^2 + \frac{\rho_2}{2}\left\|\frac{\mathbf{w}_{i,j}}{\|\mathbf{w}_{i,j}\|_\epsilon} - \mathbf{n}^k_{i,j} + \frac{1}{\rho_2}\mathbf{c}^k_{i,j}\right\|^2.$$

Notice this subproblem is typically where the difficulties come from and careful considerations are needed. In this paper, we propose one relaxation which allows us to use a simple soft shrinkage operator for this step. We substitute $\|\mathbf{w}_{i,j}\|_\epsilon$ in the denominator with $\|\nabla \mathbf{u}^{k+1}_{i,j}\|_\epsilon$. By defintion $\mathbf{w} = \nabla \mathbf{u}$, hence we replaces $\mathbf{w}^{k+1}_{i,j}$. This relaxation helps us to find $\mathbf{w}^{k+1}_{i,j}$ explicitly using the following theorem.

Theorem 1. *For given* $\mathbf{m}_1$ *and* $\mathbf{m}_2 \in \mathbb{R}^2$ *and positive numbers* a, a_1 *and* $a_2 > 0$, *the solution to the minimization problem*

$$\min_{\mathbf{s}\in\mathbb{R}^2}\left\{a\|\mathbf{s}\| + \frac{a_1}{2}\|\mathbf{s}-\mathbf{m}_1\|^2 + \frac{a_2}{2}\|\mathbf{s}-\mathbf{m}_2\|^2\right\} \tag{7}$$

is given by the shrinkage of a weighted sum of $\mathbf{m}_1$ *and* $\mathbf{m}_2$:

$$\mathcal{S}_2(\mathbf{m}_1,\mathbf{m}_2;a,a_1,a_2) := \mathrm{shrink}_2\left(\frac{a_1\mathbf{m}_1+a_2\mathbf{m}_2}{a_1+a_2},\frac{a}{a_1+a_2}\right),$$

where shrink_2 *is the 2-dimensional soft shrinkage operator [19] defined by*

$$\mathrm{shrink}_2(\mathbf{m},\mu) := \max\{\|\mathbf{m}\|-\mu,0\}\frac{\mathbf{m}}{\|\mathbf{m}\|}.$$

Proof. e complete the squares in the minimization problem (7) to obtain

$$\min_{\mathbf{s}\in\mathbb{R}^2}\left\{a\|\mathbf{s}\| + \left(\frac{a_1+a_2}{2}\right)\left\|\mathbf{s}-\frac{a_1\mathbf{m}_1+a_2\mathbf{m}_2}{a_1+a_2}\right\|^2\right\}.$$

This minimization has a solver shrink_2 and hence the conclusion follows. □

With the relaxation to $\|\nabla \mathbf{u}_{i,j}^{k+1}\|_\epsilon$, the $\mathbf{w}$-subproblem becomes the same form as in Theorem 1 with

$$\begin{cases}\mathbf{m}_{i,j}^{k+1} := \nabla^+\mathbf{u}_{i,j}^{k+1} + \frac{1}{\rho_1}\mathbf{b}_{i,j}^k, & \hat{\mathbf{m}}_{i,j}^{k+1} := \|\nabla^+\mathbf{u}_{i,j}^{k+1}\|_\epsilon(\mathbf{n}_{i,j}^k - \frac{1}{\rho_2}\mathbf{c}_{i,j}^k), \\ \mathbf{x}_{i,j}^{k+1} = \alpha + \beta(\mathrm{div}\,\mathbf{n}_{i,j}^k)^2, & \mathbf{q}_{i,j}^{k+1} := \frac{\rho_2}{\|\nabla^+\mathbf{u}_{i,j}^{k+1}\|_\epsilon^2}.\end{cases}$$

Then the solution $\mathbf{w}_{i,j}^{k+1}$ can be obtained as

$$\mathbf{w}_{i,j}^{k+1} = \mathcal{S}_2\left(\mathbf{m}_{i,j}^{k+1},\hat{\mathbf{m}}_{i,j}^{k+1};\mathbf{x}_{i,j}^{k+1},\rho_1,\mathbf{q}_{i,j}^{k+1}\right). \tag{8}$$

3.3 n-subproblem

The energy function corresponding to $\mathbf{n}$-subproblem is quadratic; hence, the minimizing solution $\mathbf{n}^{k+1}$ satisfies in the first order optimality condition

$$\left(\mathbf{I} - \frac{\beta}{\rho_2}\|\mathbf{w}_{i,j}^{k+1}\|\nabla^+\mathrm{div}^-\right)\mathbf{n}_{i,j}^{k+1} = \frac{\mathbf{w}_{i,j}^{k+1}}{\|\mathbf{w}_{i,j}^{k+1}\|_\epsilon} + \rho_2^{-1}\mathbf{c}_{i,j}^k,$$

where $\mathbf{I} = (1,1)^T$, and $\nabla^+\mathrm{div}^- = \left(\nabla_+^x\nabla_-^x + \nabla_+^x\nabla_-^y, \nabla_+^y\nabla_-^x + \nabla_+^y\nabla_-^y\right)^T$. Let

$$s_{i,j}^{k+1} = \frac{\beta}{\rho_2}\|\mathbf{w}_{i,j}^{k+1}\|, \quad \mathbf{r}_{i,j}^1 = \frac{\mathbf{w}_{i,j}^1}{\|\mathbf{w}_{i,j}\|_\epsilon} + \rho_2^{-1}\mathbf{c}_{i,j}^1, \quad \mathbf{r}_{i,j}^2 = \frac{\mathbf{w}_{i,j}^2}{\|\mathbf{w}_{i,j}\|_\epsilon} + \rho_2^{-1}\mathbf{c}_{i,j}^2.$$

Then, $\mathbf{n}_{i,j}^{k+1} = (\mathbf{n}_{i,j}^1, \mathbf{n}_{i,j}^2)^{k+1}$ can be found by solving the following system

$$\begin{bmatrix} 1 - s_{i,j}^{k+1}\nabla_+^x\nabla_-^x & -s_{i,j}^{k+1}\nabla_+^x\nabla_-^y \\ -s_{i,j}^{k+1}\nabla_+^y\nabla_-^x & 1 - s_{i,j}^{k+1}\nabla_+^y\nabla_-^y \end{bmatrix} \begin{bmatrix} (\mathbf{n}_{i,j}^1)^{k+1} \\ (\mathbf{n}_{i,j}^2)^{k+1} \end{bmatrix} = \begin{bmatrix} (\mathbf{r}_{i,j}^1)^{k+1} \\ (\mathbf{r}_{i,j}^2)^{k+1} \end{bmatrix}. \quad (9)$$

We use the shifting operators, then we take the discrete transform $\mathcal{F}$ to get

$$\begin{bmatrix} \mathbf{a}_{i,j}^{k+1} & \hat{\mathbf{a}}_{i,j}^{k+1} \\ \bar{\mathbf{a}}_{i,j}^{k+1} & \tilde{\mathbf{a}}_{i,j}^{k+1} \end{bmatrix} \begin{bmatrix} \mathcal{F}(\mathbf{n}_{i,j}^1)^{k+1} \\ \mathcal{F}(\mathbf{n}_{i,j}^2)^{k+1} \end{bmatrix} = \begin{bmatrix} \mathcal{F}(\mathbf{r}_{i,j}^1)^{k+1} \\ \mathcal{F}(\mathbf{r}_{i,j}^2)^{k+1} \end{bmatrix},$$

where $\mathbf{a}_{i,j}^{k+1}$, $\hat{\mathbf{a}}_{i,j}^{k+1}$, $\bar{\mathbf{a}}_{i,j}^{k+1}$, and $\tilde{\mathbf{a}}_{i,j}^{k+1}$ are real-values obtained by

$$\begin{cases} \mathbf{a}_{i,j}^{k+1} = 1 - 2s_{i,j}^{k+1}(\cos\theta_i - 1), \\ \hat{\mathbf{a}}_{i,j}^{k+1} = -s_{i,j}^{k+1}\Big(1 - \cos\theta_j + \sqrt{-1}\sin\theta_j\Big)\Big(-1 + \cos\theta_i + \sqrt{-1}\sin\theta_i\Big), \\ \bar{\mathbf{a}}_{i,j}^{k+1} = -s_{i,j}^{k+1}\Big(1 - \cos\theta_i + \sqrt{-1}\sin\theta_i\Big)\Big(-1 + \cos\theta_j + \sqrt{-1}\sin\theta_j\Big), \\ \tilde{\mathbf{a}}_{i,j}^{k+1} = 1 - 2s_{i,j}^{k+1}(\cos\theta_j - 1). \end{cases}$$

Therefore, as long as $\mathbf{a}_{i,j}^{k+1}\tilde{\mathbf{a}}_{i,j}^{k+1} - \hat{\mathbf{a}}_{i,j}^{k+1}\bar{\mathbf{a}}_{i,j}^{k+1} \neq 0$, the solution of the system (9) can be explicitly obtained by

$$(\mathbf{n}_{i,j}^1)^{k+1} = \mathcal{F}^{-1}\Big(\frac{\tilde{\mathbf{a}}_{i,j}^{k+1}\mathcal{F}(\mathbf{r}_{i,j}^1)^{k+1} - \hat{\mathbf{a}}_{i,j}^{k+1}\mathcal{F}(\mathbf{r}_{i,j}^2)^{k+1}}{\mathbf{a}_{i,j}^{k+1}\tilde{\mathbf{a}}_{i,j}^{k+1} - \hat{\mathbf{a}}_{i,j}^{k+1}\bar{\mathbf{a}}_{i,j}^{k+1}}\Big), \quad (10)$$

$$(\mathbf{n}_{i,j}^2)^{k+1} = \mathcal{F}^{-1}\Big(\frac{-\bar{\mathbf{a}}_{i,j}^{k+1}\mathcal{F}(\mathbf{r}_{i,j}^1)^{k+1} + \mathbf{a}_{i,j}^{k+1}\mathcal{F}(\mathbf{r}_{i,j}^2)^{k+1}}{\mathbf{a}_{i,j}^{k+1}\tilde{\mathbf{a}}_{i,j}^{k+1} - \hat{\mathbf{a}}_{i,j}^{k+1}\bar{\mathbf{a}}_{i,j}^{k+1}}\Big).$$

3.4 Multiplier Updates

The multipliers $\mathbf{b}^k = (\mathbf{b}^1, \mathbf{b}^2)^k$ and $\mathbf{c}^k = (\mathbf{c}^1, \mathbf{c}^2)^k$ update linearly as follows

$$\begin{cases} (\mathbf{b}_{i,j}^1)^{k+1} = (\mathbf{b}_{i,j}^1)^k + \rho_1\big(\nabla_+^x \mathbf{u}_{i,j}^{k+1} - (\mathbf{w}_{i,j}^1)^{k+1}\big), \\ (\mathbf{b}_{i,j}^2)^{k+1} = (\mathbf{b}_{i,j}^2)^k + \rho_1\big(\nabla_+^y \mathbf{u}_{i,j}^{k+1} - (\mathbf{w}_{i,j}^2)^{k+1}\big), \\ (\mathbf{c}_{i,j}^1)^{k+1} = (\mathbf{c}_{i,j}^1)^k + \rho_2\Big(\frac{(\mathbf{w}_{i,j}^1)^{k+1}}{\|\mathbf{w}_{i,j}^{k+1}\|_\epsilon} - (\mathbf{n}_{i,j}^1)^{k+1}\Big), \\ (\mathbf{c}_{i,j}^2)^{k+1} = (\mathbf{c}_{i,j}^2)^k + \rho_2\Big(\frac{(\mathbf{w}_{i,j}^2)^{k+1}}{\|\mathbf{w}_{i,j}^{k+1}\|_\epsilon} - (\mathbf{n}_{i,j}^2)^{k+1}\Big). \end{cases} \quad (11)$$

3.5 ADMM-EE

The alternating direction method of multiplier algorithm (ADMM) for solving the Euler's Elastica-based denoising model can be summarized in the following Table. In summary, the ADMM-EE algorithm employs a Fourier transform in Step 1, a shrinkage operator in Step 2, a coupled Fourier transform in Step 3, and it linearly updates the two Lagrange multipliers in Step 4.

THE ADMM-EE ALGORITHM
Given: $\alpha > 0, \beta \geq 0, \lambda > 0, \rho_1 > 0, \rho_2 > 0$.
Starting guess: $\mathbf{w}^0 \in Y$, $\mathbf{n}^0 \in Y, \mathbf{b}^0 \in Y$, $\mathbf{c}^0 \in Y$.
For $k = 0, 1, 2, \ldots$ until converges
Step 1. Update $\mathbf{u}^{k+1}$ by (6).
Step 2. Update $\mathbf{w}^{k+1}$ by (8).
Step 3. Update $\mathbf{n}^{k+1}$ by (10).
Step 4. Update $\mathbf{b}^{k+1}$ and $\mathbf{c}^{k+1}$ by (11).

4 Parameters Discussion

We have five parameters in the ADMM-EE algorithm (4). The parameters α, β, and λ are the model parameters (2), while ρ_1 and ρ_2 are the penalty parameters in the augmented Lagrangian (3). The parameter α is the weight of the total variation regularization term while the parameter β influences the amount of curvature along the edges, and the parameter λ controls the treadoff between the regularization term and the fidelity term.

Notice that in (1) each term has a parameter, so we can fix one parameter and work with others. For instance, based on the amount of noise in the image we take λ fixed, then we can determine α and β which will give the smallest image relative error, defined by RelErr $= \frac{\|\mathbf{u}-\mathbf{u}^*\|_F}{\sqrt{M \times N} \|\mathbf{u}^*\|_F}$, where $\mathbf{u}^*$ is the clean image, and $\|\cdot\|_F$ is the Frobenius norm. Figure 1 (b) displays the RelErr of the Moon image (a) versus both values of α and β with $\lambda = 12$. The minimum error is achieved by taking $\alpha = 0.4$ and $\beta = 0.1$. Figure 1 (c) further shows the relative error versus β with $\alpha = 0.4$ and $\lambda = 12$ fixed, and versus α with fixed value for $\beta = 0.1$ and $\lambda = 12$. For the Shapes and Barbara images displayed in Figures 1 (d) and (e), we observed that the value of $\beta = 0.1$ is optimal; however, the optimal α for Shapes was 0.8 and for the Barbara was 0.5. Hence, in our experiments in Section 5 we take $\alpha = 0.6$ for all experiments.

The penalty parameters ρ_1 and ρ_2 have impact on the convergence speed of algorithm. In particular, the large values of ρ_1 and ρ_2 place a large penalty on violations of primal feasibility hence tend to produce small primal residual $R_1^{k+1} = \nabla \mathbf{u}^{k+1} - \mathbf{w}^{k+1}$ and $R_2^{k+1} = \mathbf{n}^{k+1} - \frac{\mathbf{w}^{k+1}}{\|\mathbf{w}^{k+1}\|_\epsilon}$ and vice versa. Moreover, the energy functional of $\mathbf{u}$-subproblem in (4) is convex if $\lambda - \rho_1 \Delta$, the hessian of the energy function, is positive definite. Here, Δ is the Laplacian operator. To find the minimizer, we choose $\rho_1 \leq \lambda/\rho(\Delta^\mathsf{T} \Delta)$, where $\rho(.)$ denotes the spectral radius. Since roughly $\rho(\Delta^\mathsf{T} \Delta) < 8$, we choose ρ_1 to be $\rho_1 < \lambda/8$.

For $\mathbf{n}$-subproblem, the energy functional is also quadratic, and its corresponding hessian matrix is given by $\mathbf{I} - \frac{\beta}{\rho_2} \|\mathbf{w}^{k+1}\| \nabla \text{div}$, involving β/ρ_2 and $\|\mathbf{w}^{k+1}\|$. Thus, it is almost impossible to say what values of ρ_2 makes the Hessian positive definite. However, experimentally we observed that for very small values of ρ_2 the algorithm lose stability, while the large values leads to a slow convergence.

Numerically, we consider different values for ρ_1 within $0 < \rho_1 < \lambda/8 = 12/8 = 1.5$, and compare the energy values ($\log_{10}$) obtained within the hundred iterations of ADMM-EE. Based on the results shown in Table 1 (top), we used

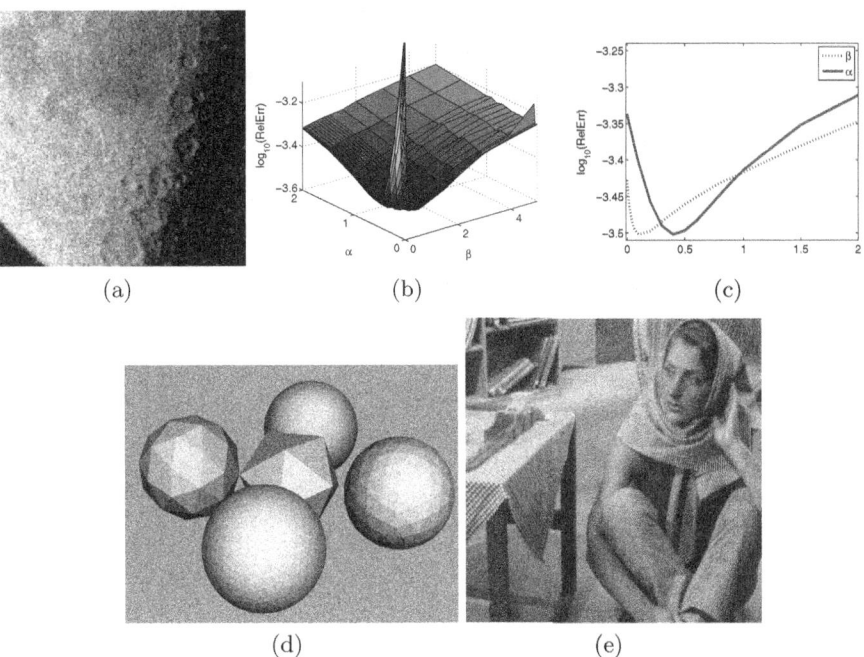

Fig. 1. (a) "Moon" image (151×151) with additive Gaussian noise of zero mean and standard deviation $\sigma = 15$, SNR: 20.56. (b) Image relative error (RelErr) versus α and β. The minimum error achieved at $\alpha = 0.4$ and $\beta = 0.1$. (c) RelErr versus β, with $\alpha = 0.4$ fixed and versus α, with $\beta = 0.1$ fixed. (d) "Shape" image (481×640), SNR: 10.51. (e) "Barbara" image (512×512), SNR: 16.40. For both images $\beta = 0.1$ is optimal, while the optimal α for Shapes is 0.8 and for the Barbara is 0.5.

$\rho_1 = 0.8$. Next, we consider different values for ρ_2 where $0.5 < \rho_2 < 3.5$, and compare the objective values. The results given in Table 1 (bottom) show that $\rho_1 = 2.5$ gives the smallest objective value for all test images.

Table 1. Top: energy value (1) versus ρ_1 ($\rho_2 = 0.8$ fixed). Bottom: energy value versus ρ_2 ($\rho_1 = 0.8$ fixed).

Objective value	ρ_1						
	0.2	0.4	0.6	0.8	1	1.2	1.4
Moon	2.8640	**2.8582**	2.8591	2.8583	2.86035	2.8646	2.8675
Shapes	3.9956	3.9852	3.9820	3.9808	**3.9807**	3.9813	3.9824
Barbara	4.0844	4.0770	4.0743	**4.0734**	4.0740	4.0757	4.0786

Objective value	ρ_2						
	0.5	1	1.5	2	2.5	3	3.5
Moon	2.8895	2.8569	2.8562	2.8559	**2.8558**	2.8558	2.8558
Shapes	3.9782	3.9775	3.9773	3.9773	**3.9773**	3.9774	3.9776
Barbara	4.0709	4.0699	4.0696	4.0694	**4.0694**	4.0694	4.0695

(a) (b) (c)

Fig. 2. Original images are in Figure 1. Resulted denoised test images obtained by the ADMM-EE algorithm. (a) SNR= 43.00 db. (b) SNR= 39.16 db. (c) SNR= 29.78 db.

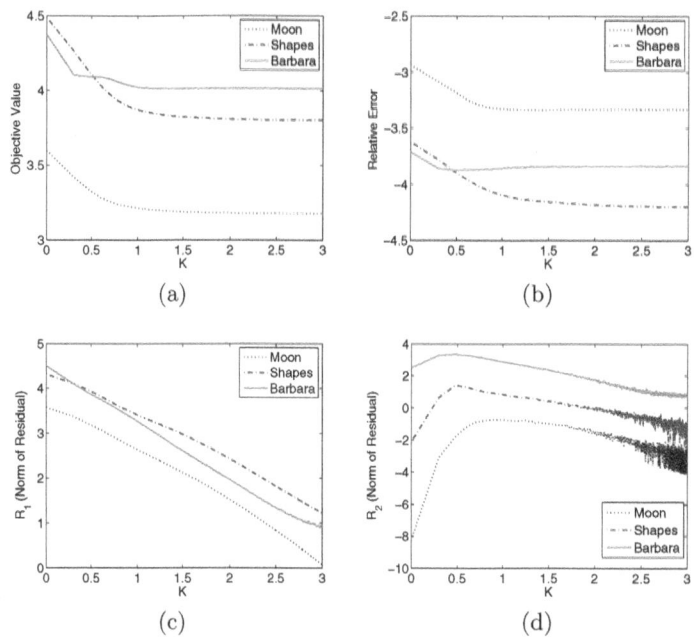

(a) (b)

(c) (d)

Fig. 3. The behavior of (a) energy value, (b) the relative error, (c) the primal residuals $R_1 = \|\nabla \mathbf{u} - \mathbf{w}\|_F$, and (d) $R_2 = \|\mathbf{n} - \frac{\mathbf{w}}{\|\mathbf{w}\|_\epsilon}\|_F$ versus thousand iteration numbers. Results are in $\log_{10}$ scale. The ADMM-EE algorithm converged in hundred iterations.

5 Numerical Comparisons

In this section, we demonstrate the effectiveness of the proposed ADMM-EE algorithm. We compare the performance of our algorithm for solving Total Variation and the Euler's Elastica models. Then, we give a comparison between the

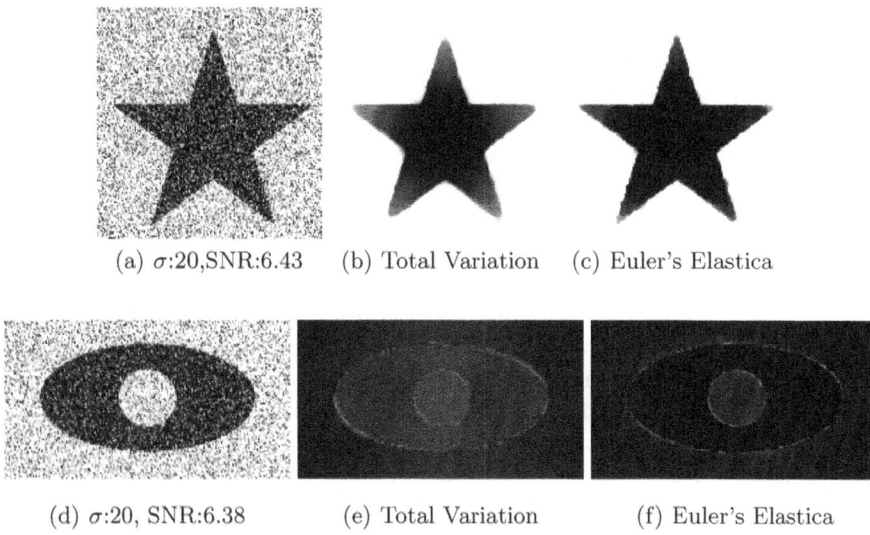

(a) σ:20,SNR:6.43   (b) Total Variation   (c) Euler's Elastica

(d) σ:20, SNR:6.38   (e) Total Variation   (f) Euler's Elastica

Fig. 4. The comparison of TV and the Euler's Elastica models. Top row: (a) noisy "Star" image, (b) restored by TV, (c) restored by the Euler's Elastica. Second row: (d) noisy "Donut" image, (a) absolute error of the clean image and the restored image by the TV model, (f) by the Euler's Elastica model. Euler's Elastica keeps the edges as well as image contrast much better than the total variation model. TV parameters: $\alpha = 1.2$, $\lambda = 0.7$, $\rho_1 = 0.1$, $\beta = 0$. Euler's Elastica parameters: $\alpha = 0.6, \beta = 0.4$, $\lambda = 0.7$, $\rho_1 = 0.1$, $\rho_2 = 2.5$.

ADMM-EE algorithm and the ALM method [18]. Numerical results were coded in MATLAB, version 2011b, and run on a MacbookPro version 10.9.4 with a 2.5 GHz Intel i5 processor.

ADMM-EE results: We apply the ADMM-EE algorithm with the parameter values $\alpha = 0.6$, $\beta = 0.1$, $\lambda = 12$, $\rho_1 = 0.8$, and $\rho_2 = 2.5$ to denoise the test images shown in Figure 1 (a), (d), and (f). Figure 2 displays the denoised results.

Figure 3 demonstrates the behavior of the relative error, energy value, the primal residual $R_1 = \|\nabla \mathbf{u} - \mathbf{w}\|_F$ and $R_2 = \|\mathbf{n} - \frac{\mathbf{w}}{\|\mathbf{w}\|_e}\|_F$ versus iteration numbers. Results are in $\log_{10}$ scale.

As we observe from Figure 3 (a) and (b) the objective value and relative error corresponding to three images do not change after 100 iterations which emphasis the convergence of our algorithm. Figure 3 (c) and (d) demonstrate the speed of ADMM-EE algorithm in reduction of primal residuals to zero.

Model Comparison to Total Variation: We consider the image displayed in Figure 4 (a) and (d), contaminated with Gaussian noise of zero mean and standard deviation $\sigma = 20$. Figure 4 (b) and (c) demonstrate the restored images by the Total Variation versus the Euler's Elastica model on the "star" test image. Figure 4 (e) and (f) display the absolute error of the clean image and the restored images corresponding to the "donut" image. The result using Euler's Elastica keeps more information closer to the clean image, including better boundary reconstruction and the intensity recovery.

Algorithm Comparison: ADMM-EE versus ALM: We compared the performance of the proposed ADMM-EE algorithm with the ALM algorithm on the three noisy test images, shown in Figure 1. The ALM algorithm has many parameters to choose and these parameters are very sensitive to the test images. For comparison, we took the penalty parameters: $r_1 = 1$, $r_2 = 50$, $r_3 = 0$, $r_4 = 50$ according to Figure 4.6 of [18]. For comparison, we ran the ALM for 100 cputime and we found the minimum relative error (see Figure 4.4 of [18]. There are osciation in the relative error, we took the minimum value). Then based on these values for each image, we choose the stopping criteria RelErr $< \epsilon_{\text{relerr}}$ to be $\epsilon_{\text{relerr}} = 3.3042 \times 10^{-4}$ for Moon, $\epsilon_{\text{relerr}} = 6.3 \times 10^{-5}$ for Shapes, and $\epsilon_{\text{relerr}} = 1.4998 \times 10^{-4}$ for Barbara test image. We compare the energy value (Obj), relative error (RelErr), CPU time (s), and the number of iterations after stopping criteria satisfied. These results are shown in Table 2, showing the fast convergence of the ADMM-EE algorithm.

Table 2. Comparison of ALM [18] versus ADMM-EE, based on the objective value (Obj), relative error (RelErr), CPU time (s), and the number of iterations after stopping criteria satisfied. ADMM-EE parameters: $\alpha = 0.6$, $\beta = 0.1$, $\lambda = 12$, $\rho_1 = 0.8$, $\rho_2 = 2.5$. ALM parameters: $\alpha = 0.6$, $\beta = 0.1$, $\eta = 12$, $r_1 = 1$, $r_2 = 50$, $r_3 = 0$, and $r_4 = 50$.

Test images	Moon		Shapes		Barbara	
	ADMM-EE	ALM	ADMM-EE	ALM	ADMM-EE	ALM
Obj	**2.9423**	2.9934	**4.0392**	4.0456	**4.2734**	4.3374
RelErr ($\times 10^{-4}$)	**3.2862**	3.3041	**0.62601**	0.62658	**1.4785**	1.4998
CPU(s)	**0.19**	0.45	**3.67**	11.44	**0.79**	1.27
Iteration	**5**	7	**9**	14	3	2

6 Concluding Remarks

An alternating direction method of multiplier (ADMM-EE) method was proposed to solve the Euler's Elastica-based denoising model. The algorithm apply a discrete Fourier transform, a shrinkage operator, and a coupled FFT to update the curvature of the image. According to Figure 3, the ADMM-EE algorithm converges to a point in which first order optimality conditions are satisfied. ADMM-EE also compared to ALM for image denoising, which showed fast convergence. ADMM has only two penalty parameters, and we gave some insights on how to choose their values.

References

1. Ambrosio, L., Masnou, S.: A direct variational approach to a problem arising in image reconstruction. Interfaces and Free Boundaries **5**(1), 63–82 (2003)

2. Ballester, C., Bertalmio, M., Caselles, V., Sapiro, G., Verdera, J.: Filling-in by joint interpolation of vector fields and gray levels. IEEE Trans. Image Proc. **10**, 1200–1211 (2002)
3. Boyd, S., Parikh, N., Chu, E., Peleato, B., Eckstein, J.: Distributed Optimization and Statistical Learning via the Alternating Direction Method of Multipliers. Foundations and Trends in Machine Learning **3**, 1–122 (2010)
4. Bredies, K., Kunisch, K., Pock, T.: Total Generalized Variation. SIAM J. Imaging Sci. **3**, 492–526 (2010)
5. Bredies, K., Pock, T., Wirth, B.: Convex relaxation of a class of vertex penalizing functionals. J. Math. Imaging Vision **47**, 278–302 (2013)
6. Chan, T., Kang, S.H., Shen, J.: Euler's Elastica and Curvature Based Inpaintings. SIAM J. Appl. Math. **63**, 564–592 (2002)
7. Chen, Y., Hager, W., Yashtini, M., Ye, X., Zhang, H.: Bregman Operator Splitting with Variable Stepsize for Total Variation Image Reconstruction. Comput. Optim. Appl. **54**, 317–342 (2013)
8. Duan, Y., Wang, Y., Tai, X.C., Hahn, J.: A Fast Augmented Lagrangian Method for Eulers Elastica Models. Numer. Math. Theor. Meth. Appli. **6**, 47–71 (2013)
9. Esedoglu, S., March, R.: Segmentation with depth but without detecting junctions. J. Math. Imaging Vision **18**, 7–15 (2003)
10. Gabay, D., Mercier, B.: A dual algorithm for the solution of nonlinear variational problems via finite element approximations. Computers and Mathematics with Applications **2**, 17–40 (1976)
11. Glowinski, R., Marrocco, A.: Sur l'approximation, par éléments finis d'ordre un, et la résolution, par pénalisation-dualité, dune classe de problèms de Dirichlet non linéares. Revue Fran caise dAutomatique, Informatique, et Recherche Operationelle **9**, 41–76 (1975)
12. Hager, W., Ngo, C., Yashtini, M., Zhang, H.: Alternating direction approximate Newton method for partially parallel imaging (2013, submitted)
13. Hager, W., Yashtini, M., Zhang, H.: Convergence rate of Bregman operator splitting with variable stepsize. SIAM J. Numer. Anal. (2013, submitted)
14. Hahn, J., Chung, G.J., Wang, Y., Tai, X.-C.: Fast algorithms for p-elastica energy with the application to image inpainting and curve reconstruction. In: Bruckstein, A.M., ter Haar Romeny, B.M., Bronstein, A.M., Bronstein, M.M. (eds.) SSVM 2011. LNCS, vol. 6667, pp. 169–182. Springer, Heidelberg (2012)
15. Masnou, S., Morel, J. M.: Level lines based disocclusion. In: IEEE Int. Conference Image Processing, pp. 259–263 (1998)
16. Nitzberg, M., Mumford, D., Shiota, T.: Filtering, segmentation and depth. Lecture Notes Computer Science. Springer-Verlag, Heidelberg (1993)
17. Rudin, L., Osher, S., Fatemi, E.: Non-linear Total Variation Noise Removal Algorithm. Physica D **60**, 259–268 (1992)
18. Tai, X., Hahn, J., Chung, G.: A Fast Algorithm For Euler's Elastica Model Using Augmented Lagrangian Method. SIAM J. Imaging Sci. **4**, 313–344 (2011)
19. Wang, Y., Yang, J., Yin, W., Zhang, Y.: A new alternating minimization algorithm for total variation image reconstruction. SIAM J. Imaging Sci. **1**, 248–272 (2008)
20. Zhu, W., Tai, X.C., Chan, T.: Image segmentation using Euler's elastica as the regularization. J. Sci. Comput. **57**, 414–438 (2013)
21. Zhu, W., Tai, X.-C., Chan, T.: Augmented Lagrangian Method for A Mean Curvature Based Image Denoising Model. Inverse Problems and Imaging **7**, 1409–1432 (2013)

Asymptotic Behaviour of Total Generalised Variation

Konstantinos Papafitsoros[✉] and Tuomo Valkonen

Department of Applied Mathematics and Theoretical Physics,
University of Cambridge, Cambridge, UK
kp366@cam.ac.uk

Abstract. The recently introduced second order total generalised variation functional $\mathrm{TGV}^2_{\beta,\alpha}$ has been a successful regulariser for image processing purposes. Its definition involves two positive parameters α and β whose values determine the amount and the quality of the regularisation. In this paper we report on the behaviour of $\mathrm{TGV}^2_{\beta,\alpha}$ in the cases where the parameters α, β as well as their ratio β/α becomes very large or very small. Among others, we prove that for sufficiently symmetric two dimensional data and large ratio β/α, $\mathrm{TGV}^2_{\beta,\alpha}$ regularisation coincides with total variation (TV) regularisation.

Keywords: Total variation · Total generalised variation · Regularisation parameters · Asymptotic behaviour of regularisers

1 Introduction

Parameterisation of variational image processing models has not yet been solved to full satisfaction. Towards the better understanding of such models, we study the behaviour of their solutions as the parameters change. Within the constraints of these proceedings, we concentrate in particular on the asymptotic behaviour of total generalised variation [2].

In the variational image reconstruction approach, one typically tries to recover an improved version u of a corrupted image f as a solution of a minimisation problem of the type

$$\min_u \; \Phi(f, Tu) + \Psi(u), \tag{1.1}$$

where T is a linear operator that models the type of corruption. Here the term $\Phi(f, Tu)$ ensures the fidelity of the reconstruction to the initial data. The term $\Psi(u)$, the *regulariser*, imposes extra regularity on u and it is responsible for the overall quality of the reconstruction. The two terms are balanced by one or more parameters within Ψ. A typical example is $\Psi(u) = \alpha \mathrm{TV}(u)$, i.e., the total variation of u weighted by a positive parameter α [5,11]. While total variation regularisation leads to image reconstructions with sharp edges, it also promotes piecewise constant structures leading to the *staircasing effect*. The second order total generalised variation $\mathrm{TGV}^2_{\beta,\alpha}$ [2] resolves that issue by optimally balancing

first and second order information in the image data. The $\mathrm{TGV}^2_{\beta,\alpha}$ functional reads
$$\mathrm{TGV}^2_{\beta,\alpha}(u) = \min_{w\in\mathrm{BD}(\Omega)} \alpha\|Du-w\|_\mathcal{M} + \beta\|\mathcal{E}w\|_\mathcal{M},$$
where $\|\cdot\|_\mathcal{M}$ is the Radon norm, $\mathrm{BD}(\Omega)$ is the space of functions of bounded deformation in the domain Ω, $\mathcal{E}$ is the symmetrised gradient and $\alpha,\beta>0$.

Since the values of α and β determine the amount and the quality of the reconstruction, it is important to understand their role in the regularisation process. In this paper we study the asymptotic behaviour of $\mathrm{TGV}^2_{\beta,\alpha}$ regularised solutions for the extremal cases, i.e., for large and small values of α, β and their ratio β/α. For simplicity we focus on the case where $\Phi(f,Tu) = \|f-u\|^2_{L^2(\Omega)}$ but in most cases, our results can be extended to more general fidelities.

Summary of our results: In Section 3.1 we show that as long as at least one of the parameters α,β is going to zero then the $\mathrm{TGV}^2_{\beta,\alpha}$ solutions converges to the data f. In one dimension we obtain a stronger result, showing in addition that for small values of β the solutions are continuous. In Section 3.2 we focus on the case when the ratio β/α is large, proving that in this regime $\mathrm{TGV}^2_{\beta,\alpha}$ is equivalent to TV modulo "an affine correction". In Section 3.3 we show that by setting the values of α and β large enough we obtain the linear regression of the data as a solution. In Section 3.4, we exploit the result of Section 3.2 and we show that for sufficiently symmetric data and large β/α, $\mathrm{TGV}^2_{\beta,\alpha}$ is equal to $\alpha\mathrm{TV}$. Our paper is furnished with some numerical experiments in Section 3.5, which verify our analytical results.

2 Preliminaries and Notation

In this section we briefly review the basic theory of functions of bounded variation, properties of TV and $\mathrm{TGV}^2_{\beta,\alpha}$ and we also fix our notation.

Let Ω be an open, bounded domain in $\mathbb{R}^d$. A function $u \in L^1(\Omega)$ is a *function of bounded variation* ($u \in \mathrm{BV}(\Omega)$) if its distributional derivative Du is represented by an $\mathbb{R}^d$–valued finite Radon measure. The total variation of u is defined as $\mathrm{TV}(u) = \|Du\|_\mathcal{M}$, where $\|\mathcal{T}\|_\mathcal{M}$ denotes the *Radon norm* of an $\mathbb{R}^\ell$–valued distribution $\mathcal{T}$ in Ω:

$$\|\mathcal{T}\|_\mathcal{M} := \sup\left\{\langle \mathcal{T},v\rangle : v \in C^\infty_c(\Omega;\mathbb{R}^\ell),\ \|v\|_\infty \le 1\right\}, \tag{2.1}$$

and it is equal to the total variation $|Du|(\Omega)$ of the measure Du when $u \in \mathrm{BV}(\Omega)$. The measure Du can be decomposed into the absolutely continuous and singular part with respect to the Lebesgue measure $\mathcal{L}^d$, $Du = D^a u + D^s u = \nabla u \mathcal{L}^d + D^s u$, where ∇u is the Radon-Nikodým derivative $D^a u/\mathcal{L}^d$. The space $\mathrm{BV}(\Omega)$ is a Banach space endowed with the norm $\|u\|_{\mathrm{BV}(\Omega)} = \|u\|_{L^1(\Omega)} + \|Du\|_\mathcal{M}$. We refer the reader to [1] for a complete account on the functions of bounded variation.

Analogously we define the space of *functions of bounded deformation* $\mathrm{BD}(\Omega)$ as the set of all the $L^1(\Omega;\mathbb{R}^d)$ functions whose symmetrised distributional derivative $\mathcal{E}u$ is represented by an $\mathbb{R}^{d\times d}$–valued finite Radon measure [12]. Notationwise one can readily check that $\|\mathcal{E}u\|_\mathcal{M} = |\mathcal{E}u|(\Omega)$. The space $\mathrm{BV}(\Omega)$ is strictly contained in $BD(\Omega)$ for $d > 1$ while $BD(\Omega) = BV(\Omega)$ for one dimensional domains Ω. We are not going to need much of the theory of BD functions apart from the so-called *Sobolev–Korn inequality*. The latter says that if Ω has a Lipschitz boundary then there exists a constant $C_{BD} > 0$ that depends only on Ω such that for every $w \in BD(\Omega)$ there exists an element $r_w \in \text{Ker}\mathcal{E}$ such that

$$\|w - r_w\|_{L^1(\Omega)} \leq C_{BD}\|\mathcal{E}w\|_{\mathcal{M}}. \tag{2.2}$$

Here the kernel of $\mathcal{E}$ consists of all the functions of the form $r(x) = Ax + b$, where $b \in \mathbb{R}^d$ and $A \in \mathbb{R}^{d \times d}$ is a skew symmetric matrix.

The *second order total generalised variation* $\text{TGV}^2_{\beta,\alpha}(u)$ of a function $u \in L^1(\Omega)$ is defined as [2–4]

$$\text{TGV}^2_{\beta,\alpha}(u) = \min_{w \in BD(\Omega)} \alpha\|Du - w\|_{\mathcal{M}} + \beta\|\mathcal{E}w\|_{\mathcal{M}}, \tag{2.3}$$

for $\alpha, \beta > 0$. The above definition is usually referred to as the *differentiation cascade* definition of $\text{TGV}^2_{\beta,\alpha}$, see [2] for the original formulation. It can be shown that $\text{TGV}^2_{\beta,\alpha}$ is a seminorm and together with $\|\cdot\|_{L^1(\Omega)}$ form a norm equivalent to $\|\cdot\|_{BV(\Omega)}$ [4], i.e., there exist constants $0 < c < C$ that depend only on Ω such that for every u with $\text{TGV}^2_{\beta,\alpha}(u) < \infty$

$$c\|u\|_{BV(\Omega)} \leq \|u\|_{L^1(\Omega)} + \text{TGV}^2_{\beta,\alpha}(u) \leq C\|u\|_{BV(\Omega)}. \tag{2.4}$$

Notice that the optimal w in (2.3) is not unique in general. In fact w is a solution of an L^1–$\|\mathcal{E}\|_{\mathcal{M}}$ problem (not strictly convex). Indeed since $\|Du\|_{\mathcal{M}} = \|D^a u\|_{\mathcal{M}} + \|D^s u\|_{\mathcal{M}}$, we have:

$$w \in \underset{w \in BD(\Omega)}{\operatorname{argmin}} \alpha\|Du - w\|_{\mathcal{M}} + \beta\|\mathcal{E}w\|_{\mathcal{M}} \iff$$

$$w \in \underset{w \in BD(\Omega)}{\operatorname{argmin}} \int_\Omega |\nabla u - w|\, dx + \frac{\beta}{\alpha}\|\mathcal{E}u\|_{\mathcal{M}}. \tag{2.5}$$

In the following sections, we will take specific advantage of the fact that w solves (2.5), a problem which can be seen as an analogous one to L^1–TV minimisation.

Let us finally mention that properties of $\text{TGV}^2_{\beta,\alpha}$ regularisation have been studied in the one dimensional case and when $\Phi(f, Tu) = \frac{1}{p}\|f - u\|^p_{L^p(\Omega)}$ for $p = 1$ or 2, in [3, 9, 10].

3 Asymptotic Behaviour

3.1 $\beta \to 0$ While α Is Fixed and $\alpha \to 0$ While β Is Fixed

In this section we study the limiting behaviour of $\text{TGV}^2_{\beta,\alpha}$ regularisation for small values of α, β. We first prove that by fixing α or β and sending β or α to zero respectively, then the regularised $\text{TGV}^2_{\beta,\alpha}$ solution converges to the data f. For simplicity we work on the L^2–$\text{TGV}^2_{\beta,\alpha}$ denoising problem, i.e., $T = Id$, but the next result can be extended in the more general case e.g. when the fidelity term reads $\frac{1}{p}\|f - Tu\|^p$, with $p \geq 1$ and T being a bounded, linear operator $T: L^p(\Omega) \to L^p(\Omega)$. For convenience we set

$$(u_{\beta,\alpha}, w_{\beta,\alpha}) = \operatorname*{argmin}_{\substack{u \in BV(\Omega) \\ w \in BD(\Omega)}} \frac{1}{2}\|f - u\|_{L^2(\Omega)}^2 + \alpha\|Du - w\|_{\mathcal{M}} + \beta\|\mathcal{E}w\|_{\mathcal{M}}. \quad (3.1)$$

Proposition 1. *Let $\Omega \subseteq \mathbb{R}^d$, open and bounded and $f \in L^2(\Omega) \cap BV(\Omega)$. Then*

(i) *Fixing $\alpha > 0$ we have that $\|f - u_{\beta,\alpha}\|_{L^2(\Omega)}^2 \to 0$ as $\beta \to 0$.*
(ii) *Fixing $\beta > 0$ we have that $\|f - u_{\beta,\alpha}\|_{L^2(\Omega)}^2 \to 0$ as $\alpha \to 0$.*

Proof. (i) Let $\epsilon > 0$ and $\{\rho_\delta\}_{\delta > 0}$ be a standard family of mollifiers, i.e., $\rho_\delta(x) = \delta^{-d}\rho(x/\delta)$, where $\rho \in \mathcal{C}_c^\infty(\mathbb{R}^d)$, and set $f_\delta := \rho_\delta * f$. Because $(u_{\beta,\alpha}, w_{\beta,\alpha})$ is an optimal pair in (3.1) by setting $u = f_\delta$ and $w = \nabla f_\delta$ we have the following estimates, for some constant $C > 0$

$$\frac{1}{2}\|f - u_{\beta,\alpha}\|_{L^2(\Omega)}^2 \leq \frac{1}{2}\|f - u_{\beta,\alpha}\|_{L^2(\Omega)}^2 + \alpha\|Du_{\beta,\alpha} - w_{\beta,\alpha}\|_{\mathcal{M}} + \beta\|\mathcal{E}w_{\beta,\alpha}\|_{\mathcal{M}}$$

$$\leq \frac{1}{2}\|f - f_\delta\|_{L^2(\Omega)}^2 + \beta\|\mathcal{E}(\nabla f_\delta)\|_{\mathcal{M}}$$

$$\leq \frac{1}{2}\|f - f_\delta\|_{L^2(\Omega)}^2 + \beta\|\mathcal{E}\rho_\delta * Df\|_{\mathcal{M}}$$

$$\leq \frac{1}{2}\|f - f_\delta\|_{L^2(\Omega)}^2 + \beta\frac{1}{\delta}\|Df\|_{\mathcal{M}}.$$

We set δ small enough such that $\|f - f_\delta\|_{L^2(\Omega)}^2 \leq \epsilon/2$. By choosing $\beta < \delta\epsilon/2\|Df\|_{\mathcal{M}}$, the result follows.
(ii) The proof is very similar to the (i) case, by setting $u = f_\delta$ and $w = 0$, instead. □

Remark: Of course in both (i)–(ii) cases of Proposition 1, we also get $\|Du_{\beta,\alpha} - w_{\beta,\alpha}\|_{\mathcal{M}} \to 0$ as well as $\|\mathcal{E}w_{\beta,\alpha}\|_{\mathcal{M}} \to 0$ as $\beta \to 0$ or $\alpha \to 0$.

Another interesting behaviour occurs when $\beta \to 0$. In [13], it is proved that for an arbitrary dimension and a fixed $\alpha > 0$ we have

$$\|D^s u_{\beta,\alpha}\|_{\mathcal{M}} \to 0, \quad \text{as } \beta \to 0.$$

However it turns out that in dimension one we are able to prove something stronger, provided the data are bounded:

Proposition 2. *Let $\Omega = (a,b) \subseteq \mathbb{R}$, $f \in L^\infty(\Omega) \cap BV(\Omega)$ and $\alpha > 0$. Then there exists a threshold $\beta^* > 0$ such that for every $\beta < \beta^*$ we have that*

$$\|D^s u_{\beta,\alpha}\|_{\mathcal{M}} = 0 \quad \text{and} \quad w_{\beta,\alpha} = \nabla u_{\beta,\alpha}.$$

In particular this means that for $\beta < \beta^*$

$$u_{\beta,\alpha} = \operatorname*{argmin}_{u \in BV(\Omega)} \frac{1}{2}\|f - u\|_{L^2(\Omega)}^2 + \beta\|D^2 u\|_{\mathcal{M}}. \quad (3.2)$$

Proof. From the optimality conditions derived in [9], we have that $(u_{\beta,\alpha}, w_{\beta,\alpha})$ solve (3.1) if and only if there exists a dual variable $v \in H_0^2(\Omega)$ such that

$$v'' = f - u_{\beta,\alpha} \ (C_f), \quad -v' \in \alpha \operatorname{Sgn}(Du_{\beta,\alpha} - w_{\beta,\alpha}) \ (C_\alpha), \quad v \in \beta \operatorname{Sgn}(Dw_{\beta,\alpha}) \ (C_\beta),$$

where for a finite Radon measure μ we define

$$\operatorname{Sgn}(\mu) := \left\{ v \in L^\infty(\Omega) \cap L^\infty(\Omega, |\mu|) : \|v\|_\infty \le 1, \ v = \frac{\mu}{|\mu|}, \ |\mu| - \text{a.e.} \right\}.$$

Note also that there exists a constant C depending only on Ω such that the following interpolation inequality holds [8, Section 5.10, ex.9]

$$\|Dv\|_{L^2(\Omega)} \le C \|v\|_{L^2(\Omega)}^{1/2} \|D^2 v\|_{L^2(\Omega)}^{1/2}, \quad \text{for all } v \in H_0^2(\Omega). \tag{3.3}$$

Observe first that (denoting this dual function v by $v_{\beta,\alpha}$)

$$\|Dv_{\beta,\alpha}\|_{L^2(\Omega)} \to 0 \quad \text{as } \beta \to 0. \tag{3.4}$$

Indeed, from Proposition 1 and condition (C_f) we have that $\|D^2 v_{\beta,\alpha}\|_{L^2(\Omega)} \to 0$ while from condition (C_β) we have that $\|v_{\beta,\alpha}\|_\infty \to 0$ and thus $\|v_{\beta,\alpha}\|_{L^2(\Omega)} \to 0$ as $\beta \to 0$. Then we just apply the estimate (3.3).

From the fact that we are in dimension one and from (2.4) we have for a generic constant C

$$\|u_{\beta,\alpha}\|_{L^\infty(\Omega)} \le C \|u_{\beta,\alpha}\|_{BV(\Omega)} \le C(\|u_{\beta,\alpha}\|_{L^2(\Omega)} + \operatorname{TGV}_{\beta,\alpha}^2(u_{\beta,\alpha}))$$
$$\le C(\|f - u_{\beta,\alpha}\|_{L^2(\Omega)} + \|f\|_{L^2(\Omega)} + \operatorname{TGV}_{\beta,\alpha}^2(u_{\beta,\alpha}))$$
$$\le C(\|f\|_{L^2(\Omega)}, \operatorname{TGV}_{\beta,\alpha}^2(f)) := M,$$

which in combination with (C_f) and the fact that $f \in L^\infty(\Omega)$ implies that $\|D^2 v_{\beta,\alpha}\|_\infty \le M$. Thus from the Arzelà-Ascoli theorem we get the existence of a sequence $\beta_n \to 0$ and a continuous function $\tilde{v}$ such that $v_{\beta_n,\alpha} \to \tilde{v}$ uniformly. We immediately deduce using (3.4) that $v_{\beta,\alpha} \to 0$ uniformly as $\beta \to 0$. But then condition (C_α) implies that there must exist a β_0 such that for every $\beta < \beta_0$ we have $Du_{\beta,\alpha} = w_{\beta,\alpha}$, as measures, i.e., $D^s u_{\beta,\alpha} = 0$ and $w_{\beta,\alpha} = \nabla u_{\beta,\alpha}$ since otherwise there would exist a point $x_{\beta_n,\alpha} \in (a,b)$ with $Dv_{\beta_n,\alpha}(x_{\beta_n,\alpha}) = \alpha$ for a sequence $(\beta_n)_{n \in \mathbb{N}}$ converging to 0, a contradiction. □

Remark: We believe that the above proof sets the basis for an analogue proof in higher dimensions even though admittedly this is a hard task. That would require an interpolation inequality for v, $\operatorname{div} v$ and $\operatorname{div}^2 v$ analogous to (3.3), as well as a proof that the $\operatorname{TGV}_{\beta,\alpha}^2$ regularised solution remains bounded, for bounded data f.

3.2 Large Ratio β/α

Recall from (2.5) that the optimal w is a solution to a L^1-$\|\mathcal{E}\|_\mathcal{M}$ type of problem. This motivates us to study some particular properties of the general form of such a problem:

$$\min_{w \in BD(\Omega)} \|g - w\|_{L^1(\Omega; \mathbb{R}^d)} + \lambda \|\mathcal{E} w\|_\mathcal{M}, \quad g \in L^1(\Omega; \mathbb{R}^d), \ \lambda > 0. \tag{3.5}$$

The next theorem states that if the parameter λ is larger than a certain threshold (depending only on Ω) then a solution w of (3.5) will belong to $\operatorname{Ker}\mathcal{E}$. This is analogous to the L^1–TV problem [6,7], where there for large enough value of the parameter λ, the solution is constant, i.e., belongs to the kernel of TV.

Proposition 3. *Let $\Omega \subseteq \mathbb{R}^d$ be an open, bounded set with Lipschitz boundary, $g \in L^1(\Omega; \mathbb{R}^d)$ and C_{BD} the constant that appears in the Sobolev–Korn inequality (2.2). Then if $\lambda > C_{\mathrm{BD}}$ and w_λ is a solution of (3.5) with parameter λ, then*

$$w_\lambda = m_{\mathcal{E}}(g) := \operatorname*{argmin}_{w \in \operatorname{Ker}\mathcal{E}} \|g - w\|_{L^1(\Omega;\mathbb{R}^d)}. \tag{3.6}$$

Proof. Since w_λ is a solution of (3.5), it is easy to check that if r_{w_λ} is the element of $\operatorname{Ker}\mathcal{E}$ that corresponds to w_λ in the Sobolev-Korn inequality then, $W_\lambda := w_\lambda - r_{w_\lambda}$ solves the following problem:

$$\min_{w \in \operatorname{BD}(\Omega)} \|(g - w_\lambda) - w\|_{L^1(\Omega;\mathbb{R}^d)} + \lambda \|\mathcal{E}w\|_{\mathcal{M}}. \tag{3.7}$$

Indeed, we have for an arbitrary $w \in \operatorname{BD}(\Omega)$

$$\|(g - r_{w_\lambda}) - W_\lambda\|_{L^1(\Omega;\mathbb{R}^d)} + \lambda\|\mathcal{E}W_\lambda\|_{\mathcal{M}} \le \|(g - r_{w_\lambda}) - w\|_{L^1(\Omega;\mathbb{R}^d)} + \lambda\|\mathcal{E}w\|_{\mathcal{M}},$$

$$\Longleftrightarrow$$

$$\|g - w_\lambda\|_{L^1(\Omega;\mathbb{R}^d)} + \lambda\|\mathcal{E}W_\lambda\|_{\mathcal{M}} \le \|g - (w + r_{w_\lambda})\|_{L^1(\Omega;\mathbb{R}^d)} + \lambda\|\mathcal{E}(w + r_{w_\lambda})\|_{\mathcal{M}},$$

with the latter being true since

$$\|g - w_\lambda\|_{L^1(\Omega;\mathbb{R}^d)} + \lambda\|\mathcal{E}w_\lambda\|_{\mathcal{M}} \le \|g - w\|_{L^1(\Omega;\mathbb{R}^d)} + \lambda\|\mathcal{E}w\|_{\mathcal{M}}, \quad \forall w \in \operatorname{BD}(\Omega).$$

Since W_λ solves (3.7), setting $G_\lambda := g - w_\lambda$ we have that

$$\|G_\lambda - W_\lambda\|_{L^1(\Omega;\mathbb{R}^d)} + \lambda\|\mathcal{E}W_\lambda\|_{\mathcal{M}} \le \|G_\lambda\|_{L^1(\Omega;\mathbb{R}^d)},$$

and using the Sobolev–Korn inequality $\|W_\lambda\|_{L^1(\Omega;\mathbb{R}^d)} \le C_{\mathrm{BD}}\|\mathcal{E}W_\lambda\|_{\mathcal{M}}$ we have

$$\|G_\lambda - W_\lambda\|_{L^1(\Omega;\mathbb{R}^d)} + \frac{\lambda}{C_{\mathrm{BD}}}\|W_\lambda\|_{L^1(\Omega;\mathbb{R}^d)} \le \|G_\lambda\|_{L^1(\Omega;\mathbb{R}^d)}. \tag{3.8}$$

A simple application of the triangle inequality in (3.8) yields that if $\lambda > C_{\mathrm{BD}}$, then we must have $W_\lambda = 0$, i.e., $w_\lambda = r_{w_\lambda}$ from which (3.6) straightforwardly follows. $\square$

The notation $m_{\mathcal{E}}(g)$ can be interpreted as the median of g with respect to $\operatorname{Ker}\mathcal{E}$. If $d = 1$, then this is nothing else than the usual median since in that case $\operatorname{Ker}\mathcal{E}$ consists of all the constant functions. The following corollary follows immediately from (2.5) and Proposition (3). It says that for large β/α, $\operatorname{TGV}^2_{\beta,\alpha}$ is almost equivalent to TV up to an "affine correction".

Corollary 4. *Let $\Omega \subseteq \mathbb{R}^d$ be an open, bounded set with Lipschitz boundary and let $\alpha, \beta > 0$ such that $\beta/\alpha > C_{\mathrm{BD}}$. Then for every $u \in \operatorname{BV}(\Omega)$*

$$\operatorname{TGV}^2_{\beta,\alpha}(u) = \alpha\|Du - m_{\mathcal{E}}(\nabla u)\|_{\mathcal{M}}.$$

3.3 Thresholds for Regression

In this section we show that there exist some thresholds for α and β above which the solution to the L^2-$\mathrm{TGV}^2_{\beta,\alpha}$ regularisation problem is the L^2-linear regression of the data f, denoted by $f^\star$:

$$f^\star := \operatorname*{argmin}_{\phi \text{ affine}} \|f - \phi\|^2_{L^2(\Omega)}.$$

We are going to need the following proposition proved in [4]:

Proposition 5 ([4, Proposition 4.1]). *Let $\Omega \subseteq \mathbb{R}^d$ be a bounded, open set with Lipschitz boundary. Then for every $1 \le p \le d/(d-1)$, there exists a constant $C_{\mathrm{BGV}}(\beta/\alpha) > 0$, that depends only on Ω, p and the ratio β/α such that*

$$\|u - u^\star\|_{L^p(\Omega)} \le C_{\mathrm{BGV}}(\beta/\alpha)\mathrm{TGV}^2_{\beta/\alpha,1}(u). \tag{3.9}$$

In the next proposition we show the existence of these regression thresholds for $d = 2$ and also for $d > 2$ under the extra assumption that the L^p norm of the data f controls the L^p norm of the solution for some $p \in [d, \infty]$.

Proposition 6. *Let $\Omega \subseteq \mathbb{R}^d$ be a bounded, open set with Lipschitz boundary. Suppose that either*
  (i) *$d = 2$ and $f \in \mathrm{BV}(\Omega)$ or*
  (ii) *$d > 2$, $f \in L^\infty(\Omega) \cap \mathrm{BV}(\Omega)$ and there exists a constant $C > 0$ depending only on the domain and $p \in [d, \infty]$ such that $\|u\|_{L^p(\Omega)} \le C\|f\|_{L^p(\Omega)}$ for u solution to (3.1),*

then there exist $\alpha^\star, \beta^\star > 0$ such that whenever $\alpha > \alpha^\star$, $\beta > \beta^\star$ then the solution to the L^2-$\mathrm{TGV}^2_{\beta,\alpha}$ regularisation problem is equal to $f^\star$.

Proof. Suppose initially that $d = 2$ and $f \in \mathrm{BV}(\Omega)$. Then using the Hölder inequality along with (3.9) and the fact that any function $u \in \mathrm{BV}(\Omega)$ that solves the L^2-$\mathrm{TGV}^2_{\beta,\alpha}$ problem has a L^2 norm bounded by a constant C depending only on f and not on α, β

$$\frac{1}{2}\|f - f^\star\|^2_{L^2(\Omega)} = \min_{\phi \text{ affine}} \frac{1}{2}\|f - \phi\|^2_{L^2(\Omega)} \le \frac{1}{2}\|f - u^\star\|^2_{L^2(\Omega)}$$

$$= \frac{1}{2}\|f - u\|^2_{L^2(\Omega)} + \frac{1}{2}\|u - u^\star\|^2_{L^2(\Omega)} + \int_\Omega (f - u)(u - u^\star)dx$$

$$\le \frac{1}{2}\|f - u\|^2_{L^2(\Omega)} + C(f)\|u - u^\star\|_{L^2(\Omega)} \tag{3.10}$$

$$\le \frac{1}{2}\|f - u\|^2_{L^2(\Omega)} + C(f)C_{\mathrm{BGV}}(\beta/\alpha)\mathrm{TGV}^2_{\beta/\alpha,1}(u).$$

Setting $\alpha^\star = C(f)C_{\mathrm{BGV}}(1)$ and $\beta^\star = \alpha^\star$ we have that if $\alpha > \alpha^\star$ and $\beta > \beta^\star$ we can further estimate

$$\frac{1}{2}\|f-f^\star\|_{L^2(\Omega)}^2 \le \frac{1}{2}\|f-u\|_{L^2(\Omega)}^2 + C(f)C_{\mathrm{BGV}}(1)\mathrm{TGV}^2_{\beta^*/\alpha^*,1}(u)$$

$$\le \frac{1}{2}\|f-u\|_{L^2(\Omega)}^2 + \alpha^\star \mathrm{TGV}^2_{\beta^*/\alpha^*,1}(u)$$

$$\le \frac{1}{2}\|f-u\|_{L^2(\Omega)}^2 + \mathrm{TGV}^2_{\beta^*,\alpha^*}(u)$$

$$\le \frac{1}{2}\|f-u\|_{L^2(\Omega)}^2 + \mathrm{TGV}^2_{\beta,\alpha}(u).$$

The proof goes through for the case (ii) as well, where the only difference is that Hölder inequality in (3.10) gives two terms $\|u-u^\star\|_{L^p(\Omega)}\|u-u^\star\|_{L^{p^*}(\Omega)}$ and $\|f-u\|_{L^p(\Omega)}\|u-u^\star\|_{L^{p^*}(\Omega)}$, where $p^* = p/(p-1)$ and $\infty^* := 1$. These terms can be further bounded using inequality (3.9) (note that $p^* \le d/(d-1)$) and the fact that $\|u\|_{L^p(\Omega)} \le C\|f\|_{L^p(\Omega)}$. $\square$

More explicit regression thresholds have been given in [9] both for general and specific one dimensional data f. Let us point out that the condition $\|u\|_{L^p(\Omega)} \le C\|f\|_{L^p(\Omega)}$ and in particular $\|u\|_\infty \le C\|f\|_\infty$ (which can be derived easily for TV regularisation with $C=1$), as natural as it may seems, it cannot be shown easily. However, if proved, it will also have positive implications as far as the inclusion of the jump set of the solution to the jump set of the data is concerned, see [13].

3.4 Equivalence to TV for Large Ratio β/α and Sufficiently Symmetric Data

In Corollary 4 we obtained a more precise characterisation of $\mathrm{TGV}^2_{\beta,\alpha}$ for large values of the ratio β/α. In this section we show that at least for symmetric enough data f, $\mathrm{TGV}^2_{\beta,\alpha}$ regularisation is actually equivalent to $\alpha\mathrm{TV}$ regularisation. For the sake of the simplicity of the analysis we assume here that Ω is a two dimensional domain, i.e., $\Omega \subseteq \mathbb{R}^2$. We will also need some symmetry for Ω, for the time being let Ω be a square centered at the origin. We shall prove the following theorem.

Theorem 7. *Suppose that $\Omega \subseteq \mathbb{R}^2$ is a bounded, open square, centred at the origin and let $f \in \mathrm{BV}(\Omega)$ satisfy the following symmetry properties:*

(i) f is symmetric with respect to both axes, i.e.,

$$f(x_1,x_2) = f(-x_1,x_2), \quad f(x_1,x_2) = f(x_1,-x_2), \quad \text{for a.e. } (x_1,x_2) \in \Omega.$$

(ii) f is invariant under $\pi/2$ rotations, i.e., $f(O_{\pi/2}x) = f(x)$, where $O_{\pi/2}$ denotes counterclockwise rotation by $\pi/2$ degrees.

Then if $\beta/\alpha > C_{\mathrm{BD}}$, the problems

$$\min_{u\in\mathrm{BV}(\Omega)} \frac{1}{p}\int_\Omega |f-u|^p dx + \mathrm{TGV}^2_{\beta,\alpha}(u) \quad \text{and} \quad \min_{u\in\mathrm{BV}(\Omega)} \frac{1}{p}\int_\Omega |f-u|^p dx + \alpha\mathrm{TV}(u)$$

for $p \ge 1$ are equivalent.

Remark 8. The proof of Theorem 7 is essentially based on the fact that the symmetry of the data f is inherited to the solution u and thus to ∇u. In that case we can show that $m_{\mathcal{E}}(\nabla u) = 0$ something that shows the equivalence of $\mathrm{TGV}^2_{\beta,\alpha}$ and $\alpha \mathrm{TV}$. Other symmetric domains, e.g. circles, rectangles, together with appropriate symmetry conditions for f can also guarantee that ∇u has the desired symmetry properties as well. The same holds for any fidelities $\Phi(f, Tu)$ that ensure that the symmetry of f is passed to u.

Let us also mention that abusing the notation a bit, by $m_{\mathcal{E}}(\nabla u) = 0$ we mean that zero is a solution of the problem (3.6) with $g = \nabla u$.

Proof (of Theorem 7). Since $\beta/\alpha > C_{\mathrm{BD}}$, from Corollary 4 we have that the $\mathrm{TGV}^2_{\beta,\alpha}$ regularisation problem is equivalent to

$$\min_{u \in \mathrm{BV}(\Omega)} \frac{1}{p} \int_\Omega |f - u|^p dx + \alpha \|Du - m_{\mathcal{E}}(\nabla u)\|_{\mathcal{M}}. \qquad (3.11)$$

Thus it suffices to show that $m_{\mathcal{E}}(\nabla u) = 0$. Since f satisfies the symmetry properties (i)–(ii), from the rotational invariance of $\mathrm{TGV}^2_{\beta,\alpha}$ [2] we have that the same conditions hold for the $\mathrm{TGV}^2_{\beta,\alpha}$ regularised solution u. This also means that $\nabla u = (\nabla_1 u, \nabla_2 u)$ has the following properties for almost all $x = (x_1, x_2) \in \Omega$:

$$\nabla_1 u(x_1, x_2) = \nabla_1 u(x_1, -x_2), \qquad \nabla_2 u(x_1, x_2) = \nabla_2 u(-x_1, x_2), \qquad (3.12)$$
$$\nabla u(x) = -\nabla u(-x), \qquad \nabla_1 u(O_{\pi/2} x) = \nabla_2 u(x). \qquad (3.13)$$

Recalling that

$$m_{\mathcal{E}}(\nabla u) = \underset{w \in \mathrm{Ker}\mathcal{E}}{\mathrm{argmin}} \, \|\nabla u - w\|_{L^1(\Omega; \mathbb{R}^d)},$$

and that $m_{\mathcal{E}}(\nabla u)$ has the form $Ax + b$ it is easy to check, see the following lemma, that $m_{\mathcal{E}}(\nabla u) = 0$. □

Lemma 9. *Let Ω be a square centred at the origin and suppose that $g = (g_1, g_2) \in L^1(\Omega; \mathbb{R}^2)$ satisfies the symmetry properties*

$$g(x) = -g(-x), \quad g_1(x_1, x_2) = g(x_1, -x_2), \quad g_2(x_1, x_2) = g_2(-x_1, x_2), \qquad (3.14)$$
$$g_1(O_{\pi/2} x) = g_2(x), \qquad (3.15)$$

for almost every $x = (x_1, x_2) \in \Omega$. Then the minimisation problem

$$\min_{w \in \mathrm{Ker}\mathcal{E}} \|g - w\|_{L^1(\Omega; \mathbb{R}^2)}, \qquad (3.16)$$

admits $w = 0$ as a solution.

Proof. Recalling that $\mathrm{Ker}\mathcal{E}$ consists of all the functions of the form $r(x) = Ax + b$ with A being a skew symmetric function, we have that the minimisation (3.16) is equivalent to

$$\min_{A,b} \int_\Omega |g(x) - Ax - b| dx, \qquad (3.17)$$

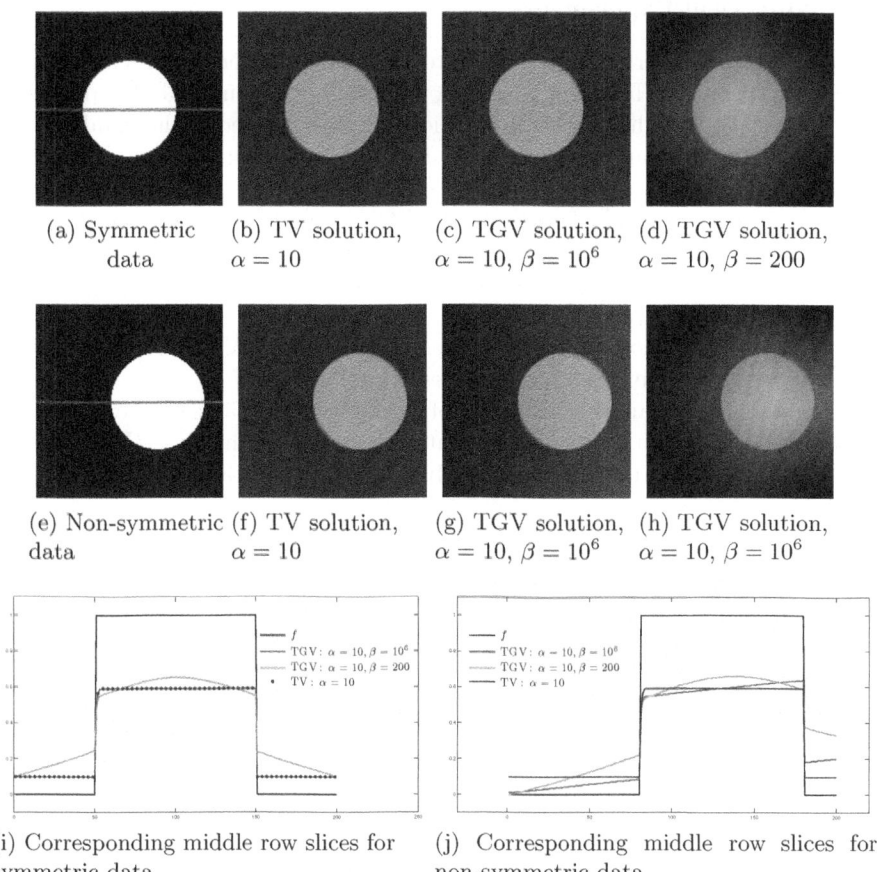

Fig. 1. Illustration of the two dimensional αTV and TGV$^2_{\beta,\alpha}$ equivalence for symmetric data when β/α is large enough. Notice that the equivalence does not hold once the symmetry is broken.

with corresponding optimality conditions

$$\int_\Omega \left\langle \frac{g(x) - AO_{\pi/2}x - b}{|g(x) - AO_{\pi/2}x - b|}, O_{\pi/2}x \right\rangle dx = 0, \quad \text{with } O_{\pi/2} = \begin{pmatrix} 0 & -1 \\ 1 & 0 \end{pmatrix}.$$

Using the equalities $g_2(x_1, x_2) = g_1(-x_2, x_1)$ and $g_1(-x_2, x_1) = g_1(-x_2, -x_1) = -g_1(x_1, x_2)$ we have that $A = 0$, $b = 0$ solve (3.17) if

$$\int_\Omega \left\langle \frac{O_{\pi/2}g(x)}{|O_{\pi/2}g(x)|}, x \right\rangle dx = 0 \iff \int \frac{x_2 g_1(x_1, x_2) - x_1 g_2(x_1, x_2)}{|g(x)|} dx = 0 \iff$$

$$\int_\Omega \frac{x_2 g_1(x_1, x_2) - x_1 g_1(-x_2, x_1)}{\sqrt{g_1(x_1, x_2)^2 + g_1(-x_2, x_1)^2}} dx = 0 \iff \int_\Omega (x_1 + x_2) \frac{g_1(x_1, x_2)}{|g_1(x_1, x_2)|} dx = 0,$$

with last equality being true since $-g(-x) = g(x)$. □

3.5 Numerical Experiments

In this section we verify some of our results using numerical experiments. In Figure 1 we confirm Theorem 7. There, we apply αTV and $\text{TGV}^2_{\beta,\alpha}$ denoising with L^2 fidelity, to a characteristic function of a disk centred at the middle of the domain, Figure 1(a) and away from it, Figure 1(e). Notice that the symmetry properties of Theorem 7 are satisfied for the first case. There, we observe that by choosing the ratio β/α large enough, $\text{TGV}^2_{\beta,\alpha}$ and αTV solutions coincide, Figures 1(b) and 1(c). However, they do not coincide for small ratio β/α, Figure 1(d), see also the middle row slices in Figure 1(i). In this case $\text{TGV}^2_{\beta,\alpha}$ produces a piecewise smooth result in comparison to the piecewise constant one of αTV. Note that when the symmetry is broken, αTV and $\text{TGV}^2_{\beta,\alpha}$ solutions do not coincide even for large ratio β/α, Figures 1(g), 1(h) and 1(j).

Figure 2 depicts another example of an image that satisfies the symmetry properties of Theorem 7. The αTV solution coincides with the $\text{TGV}^2_{\beta,\alpha}$ one for large ratio β/α, Figures 2(b) and 2(c), but not for small ratio, Figure 2(d).

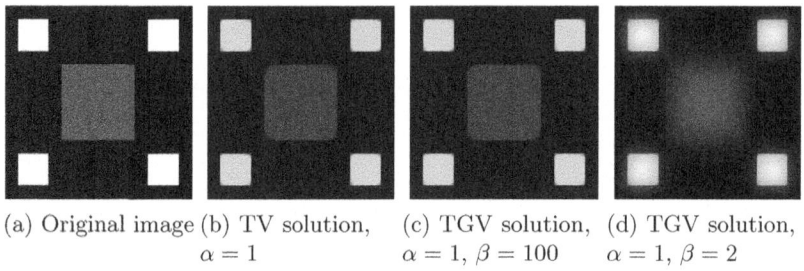

(a) Original image (b) TV solution, $\alpha = 1$ (c) TGV solution, $\alpha = 1$, $\beta = 100$ (d) TGV solution, $\alpha = 1$, $\beta = 2$

Fig. 2. Illustration of the two dimensional αTV and $\text{TGV}^2_{\beta,\alpha}$ equivalence for symmetric data when β/α is large enough

Finally in Figure 3, we solve the L^2–$\text{TGV}^2_{\beta,\alpha}$ regularisation problem in a noisy image. We observe that for very small values of β or α, essentially we have no regularisation at all, see Figures 3(c) and 3(d) respectively, verifying Proposition 1. In Figure 3(e), we choose a large ratio β/α, obtaining a TV–like result which is nevertheless quite different than the αTV result, Figure 3(f), having staircasing only inside the ellipse. This is due to the "affine" correction predicted by Corollary 4, see also the corresponding diagonal slices in Figure 3(i). Figure 3(g) depicts a typical TGV solution with no staircasing while in Figure 3(h) we set α and β large enough and we obtain the linear regression of the data, as expected from Proposition 6.

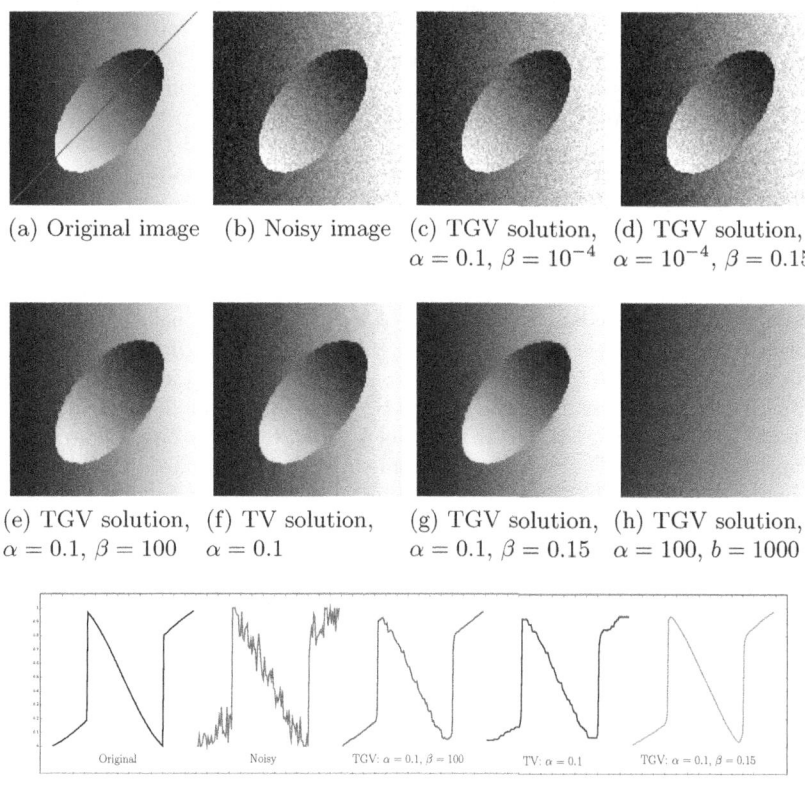

(a) Original image (b) Noisy image (c) TGV solution, $\alpha = 0.1$, $\beta = 10^{-4}$ (d) TGV solution, $\alpha = 10^{-4}$, $\beta = 0.15$

(e) TGV solution, $\alpha = 0.1$, $\beta = 100$ (f) TV solution, $\alpha = 0.1$ (g) TGV solution, $\alpha = 0.1$, $\beta = 0.15$ (h) TGV solution, $\alpha = 100$, $b = 1000$

(i) Corresponding diagonal slices

Fig. 3. L^2–$\mathrm{TGV}^2_{\beta,\alpha}$ denoising for extremal values of α and β

Acknowledgments. This work is supported by the King Abdullah University for Science and Technology (KAUST) Award No. KUK-I1-007-43. The first author acknowledges further support by the Cambridge Centre for Analysis (CCA) and the Engineering and Physical Sciences Research Council (EPSRC). The second author acknowledges further support from EPSRC grant EP/M00483X/1 "Efficient computational tools for inverse imaging problems".

References

1. Ambrosio, L., Fusco, N., Pallara, D.: Functions of bounded variation and free discontinuity problems. Oxford University Press, USA (2000)
2. Bredies, K., Kunisch, K., Pock, T.: Total generalized variation. SIAM Journal on Imaging Sciences **3**(3), 492–526 (2010)
3. Bredies, K., Kunisch, K., Valkonen, T.: Properties of L^1-TGV^2 : The one-dimensional case. Journal of Mathematical Analysis and Applications **398**(1), 438–454 (2013)

4. Bredies, K., Valkonen, T.: Inverse problems with second-order total generalized variation constraints. In: Proceedings of SampTA 2011–9th International Conference on Sampling Theory and Applications, Singapore (2011)
5. Chambolle, A., Lions, P.: Image recovery via total variation minimization and related problems. Numerische Mathematik **76**, 167–188
6. Chan, T., Esedoglu, S.: Aspects of total variation regularized L^1 function approximation. SIAM Journal on Applied Mathematics, pp. 1817–1837 (2005)
7. Duval, V., Aujol, J., Gousseau, Y.: The TVL1 model: a geometric point of view. SIAM Journal on Multiscale Modeling and Simulation **8**(1), 154–189
8. Evans, L.: Partial Differential Equations, volume 19 of Graduate Studies in Mathematics, Second Edition. American Mathematical Society (2010)
9. Papafitsoros, K., Bredies, K.: A study of the one dimensional total generalised variation regularisation problem. Inverse Problems and Imaging **9**(2) (2015)
10. Pöschl, C., Scherzer, O.: Exact solutions of one-dimensional total generalized variation. Communications in Mathematical Sciences **13**(1), 171–202 (2015)
11. Rudin, L., Osher, S., Fatemi, E.: Nonlinear total variation based noise removal algorithms. Physica D: Nonlinear Phenomena **60**(1–4), 259–268
12. Temam, R., Strang, G.: Functions of bounded deformation. Archive for Rational Mechanics and Analysis **75**(1), 7–21 (1980)
13. Valkonen, T.: The jump set under geometric regularisation. Part 2: Higher-order approaches. arXiv preprint 1407.2334

Author Index

Abergel, Rémy 178
Angulo, Jesús 78
Aujol, Jean-François 66, 413

Balle, Frank 385
Batard, Thomas 449
Becker, Florian 397
Bekkers, E.J. 613
Berger, Johannes 203, 397
Berkels, Benjamin 335, 360
Bertalmío, Marcelo 449
Boroujerdi, Ali Sharifi 461
Bouthemy, Patrick 323
Brauer, Christoph 142
Bredies, Kristian 216
Breeuwer, Marcel 563
Breuß, Michael 461, 538
Brinkmann, Eva-Maria 191
Brox, Thomas 654
Bruhn, Andrés 538
Buet, B. 513
Bugeau, Aurélie 413
Burger, Martin 16, 191
Burgeth, Bernhard 461

Cárdenas, Giovanno Marcelo 103
Chen, Da 270
Chen, Kanglin 360
Cohen, Laurent D. 270
Cremers, Daniel 243, 294

Daniel, Patrik 589
Deledalle, Charles-Alban 129
Demmel, Nikolaus 294
Derksen, Alexander 335, 360
Desolneux, Agnès 474
Deutsch, Shay 282
Diebold, Julia 243, 294
Doğan, Günay 307
Dong, Guozhi 678
Duits, Remco 40, 563, 613
Durou, Jean-Denis 498, 576

Eckardt, Lina 16
Effland, Alexander 372
Eifler, Dietmar 385
Elmoataz, Abderrahim 601
Estellers, Virginia 525

Fadili, Jalal 642
Fehrenbach, Jérôme 117
Fitschen, Jan Henrik 385, 437
Fortun, Denis 323
Friberg, Anders 3

Galiano, Gonzalo 166
Gilboa, Guy 16, 66, 486
Grah, Joana 191

Hafner, David 425, 551
Hallmann, Marc 360
Hazan, Tamir 231
Hazırbaş, Caner 243, 294
Heldmann, Stefan 335, 360
Holler, Martin 216
Horesh, Dikla 486

Janssen, Michiel 563
Ju, Yong Chul 538

Kang, Sung Ha 690
Kappes, Jörg Hendrik 231
Kervrann, Charles 323
Kleefeld, Andreas 461

Lanza, Alessandro 666
Lauze, François 498
Le Guyader, Carole 348
Lenzen, Frank 203, 397
Leonardi, G.P. 513
Liang, Jingwei 642
Lindeberg, Tony 3, 90
Lorenz, Dirk 142
Louchet, Cécile 178
Lozes, François 601
Luke, Russell 642

Author Index

Mashtakov, A. 613
Masnou, S. 513
Medioni, Gérard 282
Medl'a, Matej 589
Meesters, Stephan 40
Mikula, Karol 589
Moeller, Michael 16, 294
Moisan, Lionel 178
Morel, Jean-Michel 474
Morigi, Serena 666

Neufeld, Andreas 397
Nikolova, Mila 117, 437

Ochs, Peter 654
Öktem, Ozan 678
Ozeré, Solène 348

Papadakis, Nicolas 66, 129, 256
Papafitsoros, Konstantinos 702
Patrone, Aniello Raffaele 678
Peter, Pascal 154
Peyré, Gabriel 642
Pierre, Fabien 413, 437
Pock, Thomas 654
Polzin, Thomas 335
Portegies, Jorg 40

Quéau, Yvain 498, 576

Raad, Lara 474
Rabin, Julien 256
Ranftl, René 654
Remešíková, Mariana 589
Rumpf, Martin 372

Salmon, Joseph 129
Sanguinetti, Gonzalo 40, 613
Savchynskyy, Bogdan 231
Schäffer, Sarah 103
Scherzer, Otmar 678
Schmidt, Martin 28
Schmitzer, Bernhard 629
Schnörr, Christoph 231, 397
Schroers, Christopher 551
Schuff, Sebastian 385
Scott, Michael 525
Sgallari, Fiorella 666
Simon, Stefan 372
Soatto, Stefano 525
Stahn, Kirsten 372
Steidl, Gabriele 117, 385, 437
Swoboda, Paul 231

Ta, Vinh-Thong 413
Tenbrinck, Daniel 601
Tew, Kevin 525

Valkonen, Tuomo 702
Velasco, Julián 166

Weickert, Joachim 28, 103, 154, 425, 551
Weiss, Pierre 117
Welk, Martin 53
Wirth, Benedikt 372

Yashtini, Maryam 690

Zeng, Tieyong 178

The manufacturer's authorised representative in the EU is Springer Nature Customer Service Centre GmbH, Europaplatz 3, 69115 Heidelberg, Germany. If you have any concerns regarding our products, please contact ProductSafety@springernature.com

Printed and bound by CPI Group (UK) Ltd, Croydon, CR0 4YY

23/03/2026

02076662-0020